Yearbook
of
International Environmental Law

Volume 5

1994

Yearbook of International Environmental Law

Volume 5
1994

Günther Handl
Editor-in-Chief

Lothar Gündling
Linda A. Malone   Philippe Sands
Craig M. Scott
Associate Editors

Susan Casey-Lefkowitz   Suzanna Moran
Assistant Editors

Scott A. Hajost   Johan G. Lammers
Documents

Dinah L. Shelton
Literature Review

CLARENDON PRESS . OXFORD
1995

Oxford University Press, Walton Street, Oxford OX2 6DP
Oxford New York
Athens Auckland Bangkok Bombay
Calcutta Cape Town Dar es Salaam Delhi
Florence Hong Kong Istanbul Karachi
Kuala Lumpur Madras Madrid Melbourne
Mexico City Nairobi Paris Singapore
Taipei Tokyo Toronto
and associated companies in
Berlin Ibadan

Oxford is a trade mark of Oxford University Press

Published in the United States
by Oxford University Press Inc., New York

British Library Cataloguing in Publication Data
Data available

Library of Congress Cataloging in Publication Data
Data available
ISBN 0–19–825913–1

1 3 5 7 9 10 8 6 4 2

Typeset by Hope Services (Abingdon) Ltd.
Printed in Great Britain
on acid-free paper by
Biddles Ltd.,
Guildford & King's Lynn

Editors

Contents

Part 3: Literature Review

Part 4: Documents

List of Abbreviations

AJCL	American Journal of Comparative Law
AJIL	American Journal of International Law
AJPIL	Austrian Journal of Public International Law
AlbertLR	Alberta Law Review
ALI	American Law Institute
AmUJILP	American University Journal of International Law and Policy
ArizLR	Arizona Law Review
Aussenwirt	Aussenwirtschaft
AVR	Archiv des Völkerrechts
Benelux	Belgium, The Netherlands and Luxembourg
Bestuursw	Tijdschrift vorr Bestuurswetenschappen en Publiekrecht
BIMA	Bulletin d'Information du Ministère de l'Agriculture
BMONC	Bulletin Mensuel de l'Office National de la Chasse
BNA	Bureau of National Affairs (Washington, D.C.)
BNAITR	BNA International Trade Reporter
BostCEALR	Boston College Environmental Affairs Law Review
BostCICLR	Boston College International and Comparative Law Review
BuffELJ	Buffalo Environmental Law Journal
BuffLR	Buffalo Law Review
BusLawyer	The Business Lawyer
CanPA	Canadian Public Administration
CaseWRJIL	Case Western Reserve Journal of International Law (Cleveland, Ohio)
CaWILJ	California Western International Law Journal
C+C	Cooperation & Conflict
CE	Council of Europe
CEPA	Canadian Environmental Protection Act
CFCs	chlorofluorocarbons
ChiKLR	Chicago-Kent Law Review
CITES	Convention on International Trade in Endangered Species of Wild Fauna and Flora
Clunet	Journal du Droit International
CMLR	Common Market Law Reports
CMLRev	Common Market Law Review

CoastMgt	Coastal Management: An International Journal of Marine Environment, Resources, Law and Society
CoJIELP	Colorado Journal of International Environmental Law and Policy
CoLR	University of Colorado Law Review
ColumbJEL	Columbia Journal of Environmental Law
ColumbJTransL	Columbia Journal of Transnational Law
ColumbLR	Columbia Law Review
CRAMRA	Convention on the Regulation of Antarctic Mineral Resource Activities
DenvJILP	Denver Journal of International Law and Policy
DetMercy	University of Detroit Mercy Law Review
DickJELP	Dickenson Journal of Environmental Law and Policy
DickJIL	Dickinson Journal of International Law
DISP	Dokumente und Informationen zur schweizerischen Orts-, Regional- und Landesplanung
DÖV	Die öffentliche Verwaltung
DukeEL&P	Duke Environmental Law & Policy Forum
DukeLJ	Duke Law Journal
DukeJCIL	Duke Journal of Comparative and International Law
DVBl	Deutsches Verwaltungsblatt
EC	European Community
ECE	United Nations Economic Commission for Europe
ECLAC	United Nations Economic Commission for Latin America and the Caribbean
ELQ	Ecology Law Quarterly
EM	Environnement Magazine
EmoryILR	Emory International Law Review
EnvAffLR	Environmental Affairs Law Review
EnvC	Environmental Conservation
EnvIAR	Environmental Impact Assessment Review
Envist	The Environmentalist
EnvL	Environmental Law
EnvLNI	Environmental Law Network International
EnvLR	Environmental Law Review
EnvLRep	Environmental Law Reporter (Environmental Law Institute)
EnvM	Environmental Management
EnvP	Environmental Pollution
Envt	Environment (Washington D.C.)
EnvV	Environmental Values
EPA	Environmental Protection Agency (USA)
EPL	Environmental Policy and Law

EnvPlanLJ	Environmental and Planning Law Journal (Australia)
ET	Environment & Technology
ESCAP	United Nations Economic and Social Commission on Asia and the Pacific
EthIA	Ethics & International Affairs
ETS	European Treaties Series
EU	European Union
EuJIL	European Journal of International Law
EuELR	European Environmental Law Review
EuEnv	European Environment
EuLR	European Law Review
FE	Forêt-Entreprise
FAO	United Nations Food and Agriculture Organization
FletchF	The Fletcher Forum of World Affairs
FordELR	Fordham Environmental Law Review
GATT	General Agreement on Tariffs and Trade
GEMS	Global Environmental Monitoring Service
GeoIELR	Georgetown International Environmental Law Review
GeoLJ	Georgetown Law Journal
GMOs	Genetically Modified Organisms
GTZ	Gesellschaft für Technische Zusammenarbeit
HA	Habitat Australia
HamJPLP	Hamline Journal of Public Law & Policy
Harvard ELR	Harvard Environmental Law Review
Harvard HRJ	Harvard Human Rights Journal
Harvard ILJ	Harvard International Law Journal
HastICLR	Hastings International and Comparative Law Review
HousJIL	Houston Journal of International Law
IAEA	International Atomic Energy Agency
ICCOPS	International Centre for Coastal and Ocean Policy Studies (Genoa, Italy)
ICJ	International Court of Justice
ICLQ	International and Comparative Law Quarterly
Id.LR	Idaho Law Review
IEA	International Environmental Affairs (Dartmouth College)
IER	International Environment Reporter (BNA, Washington, D.C.)
IGO	intergovernmental organization
IIASA	International Institute for Applied Systems Analysis
IJECL	International Journal of Estuarine and Coastal Law
IJMCL	International Journal of Marine & Coastal Law
IJMC&L	International Journal of Maritime Commerce and Law

ILA	International Law Association
ILC	International Law Commission
ILM	International Legal Materials
ILO	International Labor Organization
ILQ	International Law Quarterly
ILR	International Law Report
IMO	International Maritime Organization
Ind.J.Global Leg.Stud.	Indiana Journal of Global Legal Studies
Indian JIL	Indian Journal of International Law
INTELSAT	International Telecommunications Satellite Consortium
Int'l Quart	International Quarterly
IO	International Organization
IRPTC	International Register of Potentially Toxic Chemicals
IUCN	International Union for the Conservation of Nature and Natural Resources
JCMS	Journal of Common Market Studies
JEnvDev	Journal of Environment and Development
JEnvL	Journal of Environmental Law (Oxford)
JEnvLLit	Journal of Environmental Law and Litigation
JEnvLPrac	Journal of Environmental Law and Practice (Calgary)
JEnvPLLAC	Journal of Environmental Policy & Law in Latin America & The Caribbean
JEuL	Journal of European Law
JDI	Journal du Droit International
JENR	Journal of Energy and Natural Resources
JIA	Journal of International AffairsJJLST Jurimetrics Journal of Law, Science and Technology
JLandUEL	Journal of Land Use and Environmental Law (Florida State University College of Law)
JMLC	Journal of Maritime Law & Commerce
JPL	Journal of Policy and Law
JusVerk	Justitiele Verkenningen (The Netherlands)
JWT	Journal of World Trade
LBMP	land-based marine pollution
LlLR	Lloyd's Law Reports
LlMarCommLQ	Lloyd's Maritime and Commercial Law Quarterly
LandMELR	Land Management and Environmental Law Report (Sussex UK)
LoyLAICLJ	Loyola of Los Angeles International and Comparative Law Journal
LoyLALR	Loyola of Los Angeles Law Review
LUP	Landscape and Urban Planning

LWLR	Land and Water Law Review
McGLJ	McGill Law Journal
MdJContemp LIssues	Maryland Journal of Contemporary Legal Issues
MdJILT	Maryland Journal of International Law and Trade
MediaLP	Media Law & Practice
MichJIL	Michigan Journal of International Law
MinnJGT	Minnesota Journal of Global Trade
MP	Marine Policy
N+R	Natur und Recht (Germany)
NBEnvLC	News Brief of the Environmental Law Centre
NCJILCR	North Carolina Journal of International law and Commercial Regulation
NEA	Nuclear Energy Agency (OECD)
NEPA	National Environmental Policy Act (USA)
NGO	non-governmental organization
NethILR	The Netherlands International Law Review
NethYBIL	Netherlands Yearbook of International Law
NIULR	Northern Illinois University Law Review
NJB	Nederlands Juristenblad
NJCM-Bull	Nederlands Juristen Comite voor de Mensenrechten-Bulletin
NJW	Neue Juristische Wochenschrift
NResEnv	Natural Resources & the Environment
NRJ	Natural Resources Journal
NucLBull	Nuclear Law Bulletin
NVwz	Neue Zeitschrift für Verwaltungsrecht (Germany)
NZV	
O&SM	Ocean and Shoreline Management
OAS	Organization of American States
OAU	Organization of African Unity
OCLJ	Ocean & Coastal Law Journal
OCM	Ocean & Coastal Management
ODIL	Ocean Development and International Law
ODILJ	Ocean Development and International Law Journal
OECD	Organisation for Economic Co-operation and Development
PacBLJ	UCLA Pacific Basin Law Journal
PaceELR	Pace Environmental Law Review (USA)
PAdminDev	Public Administration & Development
PEnvL	Planning & Environmental Law
P.L.	Public Law
PPP	polluter pays principle

QLJ	Queen's Law Journal
RdC	Recueil des Cours (Hague Academy of International Law)
RECIEL	Review of European Community and International Environmental Law
Revff	Revue forestière française
RevDA	Revista de Derecho Ambiental
RevIDC	Revue Internationale de Droit Comparé
Revue belge DI	Revue belge de droit international
RevTDE	Revue Trimestrielle de Droit Européen
RGDIP	Revue General de Droit International Public
RivDirInt	Rivista di Diritto Internazionale
RIW/AWD	Recht und Internationale Wirtschaft
RG Ambiente	Rivista Giuridica dell'Ambiente
RJE	Revue Juridique de l'Environnement
SC	Security Council
SDR	special drawing right
SoIlULJ	Southern Illinois University Law Journal
StMaryLJ	Saint Mary's Law Journal
StanELJ	Stanford Environmental Law Journal
SwRevWA	Swiss Review of World Affairs
TMA	Tijdschrift voor Milieu Aansprakelijkheid
TexILJ	Texas International Law Journal
TIAS	Treaties and Other International Acts Series (USA)
TICLJ	Temple International & Comparative Law Journal
TransL	Transnational Lawyer
TMA	Tijdschift voor milieu-aansprakelijkheid
TMil&R	Tijdschift voor Milieu & Recht
TulaneELJ	Tulane Environmental Law Journal
UChiLF	University of Chicago Legal Forum
UCLALR	University of California Los Angeles Law Review
UL	The Urban Lawyer
UN	United Nations
UNGA	United Nations General Assembly
UNCED	United Nations Conference on Environment and Development
UNCITRAL	United Nations Commission on Trade and Development
UNCLOS	United Nations Conference on the Law of the Sea
UNCOPUOS	United Nations Committee on Peaceful Uses of Outer Space
UNCTAD	United Nations Conference on Trade and Development
UNDP	United Nations Development Program

UNEP	United Nations Environment Programme
UNESCO	United Nations Educational, Scientific, and Cultural Organization
UNITAR	United Nations Institute for Training and Research
UNRIAA	United Nations Reports of International Arbitral Awards
UNTS	United Nations Treaty Series
UmweltPrax	Umweltrecht in der Praxis
UP	Umwelt und Planungsrecht
US-MexLJ	United States-Mexico Law Journal
VanderbJTL	Vanderbilt Journal of Transnational Law
VaELJ	Virginia Environmental Law Review
VillELJ	Villanova Environmental Law Journal
WashULQ	Washington University Law Quarterly
WHO	World Health Organization
WMO	World Meteorlogical Organization
WRI	World Resources Institute
YaleJIL	Yale Journal of International Law
YaleLJ	Yale Law Journal
ZaöRV	Zeitschrift für ausländisches öffentliches Recht und Völkerrecht
ZUPUR	Zeitschrift für Umweltpolitik & Umweltrecht

List of Contributors

Frederick M. Abbott
Associate Professor, and Norman and Edna Freehling Scholar, Chicago-Kent College of Law, Illinois Institute of Technology, Chicago.

Mahmood Y. Abdulraheem
Secretary General, Environment Protection Council, Kuwait City.

Eduardo Astorga J.
Coordinador, Programma Juridico, CODEFF, Santiago, Chile.

Bryan Bachner
Lecturer, Faculty of Law, City University of Hong Kong.

Inge Lorange Backer
Director-General, Legislation Department, Ministry of Justice, Oslo, Norway.

Rodrigo Barahona Israel
President, Centro de Derecho Ambiental y de los Recursos Naturales (CEDARENA), San José, Costa Rica.

Alicia Bárcena
Executive Director, Earth Council, San José, Costa Rica.

Anna Barreira López
Consultant and Lecturer on Environmental Law, Madrid.

Mohammed A. Bekhechi
Counsel, Environmental Affairs, Legal Department, The World Bank, Washington, D.C.

Nathalie F. Bernard
Environmental Lawyer and Associate, de Romilly & de Romilly, Halifax, Nova Scotia.

Alberto Blanco-Uribe Quintero
President, Fundación Jurídica para la Defensa de la Calidad de Vida, Caracas.

Ben Boer
Coors Chambers Westgarth Professor of Environmental Law and Director, Australian Centre for Environmental Law, Faculty of Law, University of Sydney.

John A. Boyd
Senior Counsel, Office of the General Counsel, Asian Development Bank, Manila.

Susan H. Bragdon
Legal Adviser, Secretariat of the Convention on Biological Diversity, Geneva.

Jutta Brunnée
Professor, McGill University, Faculty of Law, Montreal.

Françoise Burhenne-Guilmin
Member, Editorial Advisory Board.

Jorge Caillaux Zazzali
President, Sociedad Peruana de Derecho Ambiental, Lima.

Lynette Cardoch
Restoration Center, National Oceanographic & Atmospheric Administration, Silver Spring, Maryland.

Trevor A. Carmichael
Barrister-at-Law, Chancery Chambers, Bridgetown, Barbados.

Susan Casey-Lefkowitz
Assistant Editor.

Steve Charnovitz
Policy Director, Competitiveness Council, Washington, D.C.

Bakhytjan Chenguelbaev
Post-graduate Fellow, Al-Farabi Kazakh State University, Law Department, Almaty.

Maria Teresa Cirelli
Assistant Legal Officer, Development Law Service, United Nations Food and Agriculture Organization, Rome.

Marcelo J. Cousillas
Attorney at Law, Olivera & Peirano, Montevideo.

Martin David
Solicitor, Lovell White Durrant, Hong Kong, and Secretary, Hong Kong Environmental Law Association.

Cyrille de Klemm
Founder-member, International Council of Environmental Law, Paris.

Louise de La Fayette
Department of Foreign Affairs and International Trade, Ottawa.

Lalanath de Silva
Executive Director, Environmental Foundation Ltd., Colombo, Sri Lanka.

Charles E. Di Leva
Counsel, Environmental Affairs, Legal Department, The World Bank, Washington, D.C.

Hilal Zilelioglu Elver
Holder of UNEP Chair, Mediterranean Academy of Diplomatic Studies, University of Malta, Valletta.

Mohiuddin Farooque
Secretary General, Bangladesh Environmental Lawyers Association, Dhaka.

Paul Fauteux
Deputy Director, Legal Operations Division, Department of Foreign Affairs and International Trade, Ottawa.

David S. Favre
Dean and Professor of Law, Detroit College of Law, Detroit, Michigan.

Francesco Francioni
Professor, University of Siena, Faculty of Law, Siena, Italy.

Jan I. Glazewski
Director, Environmental Law Unit, University of Cape Town, Republic of South Africa.

Lyle Glowka
Projects Officer for Biological Diversity, IUCN Environmental Law Centre, Bonn.

Gretta Goldenman
Of Counsel, Oppenheimer, Wolff & Donnelly, Brussels.

Lothar Gündling
Associate Editor.

Achim A. Halpaap
Programme Officer, United Nations Institute for Training and Research, Geneva.

Samir M. Hamza
Attorney at Law, Helmy & Hamza, Cairo.

Syeda Rizwana Hasan
Bangladesh Environmental Lawyers Association, Dhaka.

Margaret F. Hayes
Assistant General Counsel for Fisheries, Office of General Counsel for Fisheries, Department of Commerce, National Oceanic and Atmospheric Administration, Silver Spring, Maryland.

Grant Hewison
Senior Lecturer, School of Integrated Business Studies, Auckland Institute of Technology, Auckland, New Zealand.

Ellen Hey
Lecturer in Public International Law, Faculty of Law, Erasmus University, Rotterdam.

Frank Horn
Director, Northern Institute for Environmental and Minority Law, University of Lapland, Rovaniemi, Finland.

Eric S. Howard
Associate, Benchmark Environmental Consulting, Portland, Maine.

Evelyn M. Hurwich
Director, Circumpolar Conservation Union, Washington, D.C.

David Hunter
Senior Attorney, Center for Internatinal Environmental Law (CIEL), Washington, D.C.

Lindy S. Johnson
Attorney Advisor, General Counsel's Office of International Environmental Law, National Oceanic and Atmospheric Administration, Washington D.C.

José Juste Ruiz
Professor of Public International Law and International Relations, Faculty of Law, University of Valencia, Valencia, Spain.

Willem J. Kakebeeke
Assistant Director General for International Cooperation, Ministry of Housing, Spatial Planning and the Environment, The Hague; and Professor, Wageningen Agricultural University.

Fouad Kanbour
Senior Environmental Affairs Officer, United Nations Environment Programme, Regional Office for West Asia, Bahrain.

Ruth Khalastchi
Lawyer, Foundation for International Environmental Law and Development (FIELD), London.

Paul Stanton Kibel
Staff Attorney, Pacific Environment and Resources Center, Sausalito, California.

Lee A. Kimball
Legal Consultant in International Institutions, Oceans and Antarctica, Washington, D.C.

Benedict Kingsbury
Professor, Duke University School of Law, Durham, North Carolina.

Jeffrey D. Kovar
Office of Legal Adviser, United States Department of State, Washington, D.C.

Pascale Kromarek-Voitellier
Legal Counsel, Direction Environnement, Elf Aquitaine, Paris.

Katharina Kummer
Programme Officer, International Affairs Division, Federal Office of Environment, Forests and Landscape,Berne, Switzerland.

Lal Kurukulasuriya
Chief, Environmental Law Training, Education & Information, Environmental Law & Institutions/Programme Activity Centre, United Nations Environment Programme, Nairobi.

Winfried Lang
President of 1985 (Vienna) and 1987 (Montreal) Conferences on Ozone Layer; Ambassador of Austria in Geneva; Professor of International Law and International Relations, University of Vienna.

Richard Laster
Attorney at Law, Laster & Gouldman, Jerusalem.

Peter Lawrence
Environmental Law Unit, Legal Office, Department of Foreign Affairs and Trade, Canberra, ACT.

Jae-Gon Lee
Professor, College of Law, Chungnam National University, Taejon, Republic of Korea.

Gerhard Loibl
Universitätsassistent, Institute of Public International Law, University of Vienna.

Alastair R. Lucas
Professor, Faculty of Law, The University of Calgary.

Ruth Mackenzie
Staff Lawyer, Foundation for International Environmental Law and Development (FIELD), London.

Patricia Madrigal Cordero
Environmental Law Consultant, San José, Costa Rica.

Peter Malanczuk
Professor of Law, University of Amsterdam.

Linda A. Malone
Associate Editor.

Howard Mann
Lawyer and Consultant, specializing in International and Environmental Law and Policy, Aylmen, Quebec.

Patricia Mariaca Zárate
Attorney specializing in Environmental Law, Mexico City.

Maria Marotta
Council of the European Union, General Secretariat, Brussels.

Dana V. Martin
Legal Department, Inter-American Development Bank, Washington, D.C.

Stephen C. McCaffrey
Professor of Law, McGeorge School of Law, Graduate and International Studies, University of the Pacific, Sacramento, California.

Winston McCalla
Attorney-at-Law, Kingston, Jamaica.

Amy McCrae
Legal Assistant, Center for Internatinal Environmental Law (CIEL), Washington, D.C.

Mohamed Ali Mekouar
Legal Officer, Food and Agriculture Organization of the United Nations, Rome.

Susan D. Mohan
Environmental Scientist, Bridgetown, Barbados.

T. Mohan
Indian Visiting Environmental Law Fellow, 1994-95, Pacific Environment and Resources Center, Sausalito, California.

Patricia F. Moore
IUCN Environmental Law Centre, Bonn.

Jennifer Morgan
Climate Action Network, Washington, D.C.

Terri Mottershead
Lecturer, Faculty of Law, University of Hong Kong.

Kalemani Mulongoy
Biotechnologist, Secretariat of the Convention on Biological Diversity, Geneva.

Shinya Murase
Professor of Law, Faculty of Law, Sophia University, Tokyo.

G.L. Anandalal Nanayakkara
Senior Law Officer, Environmental Foundation Ltd., Colombo, Sri Lanka.

Reggy Nelson
Lawyer, Member of the Board of Directors of Conservation International Suriname, Panamaribo, Surinam.

Nandan Nelivigi
Indian Visiting Environmental Law Fellow, 1994-95, Pacific Environment and Resources Center, Sausalito, California.

Alberto Ninio
Counsel, Environmental Affairs, Legal Department, The World Bank, Washington, D.C.

Gil Nolet
Legal Specialist, Environment Division, Inter-American Development Bank, Washington, D.C.

André Nollkaemper
Senior Research Fellow, Faculty of Law, Erasmus University Rotterdam.

Dan Bondi Ogolla
Legal Officer, Environmental Law & Institutons Programme Activity Centre, United Nations Environment Programme, Nairobi.

Marc Pallemaerts
Legal Adviser to the Flemish Minister of Environment and Housing, and Lecturer, Faculty of Law, Vrije Universiteit, Brussels.

Norbert Pelzer
Honorary President and Member of the Board of Administration, International Nuclear Law Association; Institute for Public International Law, University of Göttingen, Germany.

Efraín Pérez
Attorney at Law, Rusia y Los Shyris, Quito, Equador.

Zdenka Piskulich
Centro de Derecho Ambiental y de los Recursos Naturales (CEDARENA), San José, Costa Rica.

Mauro Politi
Legal Adviser, Permanent Mission of Italy to the United Nations, New York, and Professor of International Law, University of Trento, Italy.

Fiona Pompey
Attorney, Guyana Agency for Health Sciences Education, Environment and Food Policy, Greater Georgetown, Guyana.

Diana L. Ponce-Nava
Special Legal Adviser to the Minister of the Environment, Natural Resources and Fisheries, Mexico City.

Mohan Prabhu
Senior Counsel, Justice Canada, Ottawa.

Daniel C. Préfontaine
Director, International Centre for Criminal Law Reform and Criminal Justice Policy, Vancouver, British Columbia.

Manuel Pulgar-Vidal
Director of Environmental Policy, and General Coordinator, Sociedad Peruana de Derecho Ambiental, Lima.

Margaret Raymond
Program Consultant, Mekong River Law Center, Bangkok.

Bruce Rich
Chairman, International Program, Environmental Defense Fund, Washington, D.C.

Volker Röben
Referent, Max-Planck-Institut für ausländisches öffentliches Recht und Völkerrecht, Heidelberg.

George H. de Berdt Romilly
Senior Partner, de Romilly & de Romilly, Halifax, Nova Scotia; former Legal Advisor to the Department of Environment, Republic of Seychelles.

Gregory Rose
Head, Environmental Law Unit, International Organizations and Legal Affairs Office, Department of Foreign Affairs and Trade, Canberra, Australia.

Armin Rosencranz
President, Pacific Environment and Resources Center, Sausalito, California.

Iwona Rummel-Bulska
Coordinator, Basel Secretariat on Transboundary Movement of Hazardous Wastes and Their Disposal, United Nations Environment Programme, Geneva.

Shiraz Rustomjee
Indian Visiting Environmental Law Fellow, 1994-95, Pacific Environment and Resources Center, Sausalito, California.

Claudia Saladin
Staff Attorney, Center for International Environmental Law, Washington, D.C.

Philippe Sands
Associate Editor.

Germán Sarmiento Palacio
President, Fundacion para la Defensa del Interes Publico, Bogotá, Colombia.

Wiek Schrage
Environment and Human Settlements Division, United Nations Economic Commission for Europe, Geneva.

Tullio Scovazzi
Professor of International Law, University of Milan, Milan.

Maja Seršić
Assistant Professor, Faculty of Law, University of Zagreb, Croatia.

Dinah L. Shelton
Literature Review Editor.

Jyoti Shankar Singh
Director, Technical and Evaluation Division, United Nations Population Fund, New York.

Peter Skoberne
Directorate for Nature Conservation, Ministry of Environment, Ljubljana, Slovenia.

Paul Smith
Partner, Eversheds, Hepworth & Chadwick, Leeds.

Nikolai Storozhev
Corresponding Member of the Belarus Academy of Sciences, and Professor, Minsk.

Lilly Sucharipa-Behrmann
Senior Fellow, Center of International Studies, New York University, New York.

Daniel O. Suman
Professor, Division of Marine Affairs, Rosenstiel School of Marine and Atmospheric Science, University of Miami, Florida.

George C. Summerfield
Associate, Pennie & Edmonds, Washington, D.C.

Seiko Takahashi
Acting Executive Secretary, United Nations Economic and Social Commission for Asia, Bangkok.

Tang Chengyuan
Secretary General, Asian-African Legal Consultative Committee, New Delhi.

Pedro Tarak
Executive Director, Fundación Ambiente y Recursos Naturales, Buenos Aires.

Richard G. Tarasofsky
Legal Officer, Environmental Law Centre, IUCN-The World Conservation Union, Bonn.

Brendan Tobin
Advisor on International Environmental Law, Sociedad Peruana de Derecho Ambiental, Lima.

Amado S. Tolentino, Jr.
Vice-Chairman, IUCN Commission on Environmental Law; Attorney, and Resource Management Laws Adviser, Natural Resources Management and Development Project, Quezon City, Philippines.

Stephen J. Toope
Dean, McGill University, Faculty of Law, Montreal.

Anne Trebilcock
Principal Legal Officer, Office of the Legal Adviser, International Labour Office, Geneva.

Geir Ulfstein
Senior Lecturer, Institutt for Offentlig Rett, Department of Public and International Law, University of Oslo.

Sergei V. Vinogradov
Senior Research Fellow, Institute of State and Law, Russian Academy of Sciences, Moscow.

Budislav Vukas
Professor, Faculty of Law, University of Zagreb, Croatia.

Stanislaw Wajda
Legal Adviser, EC PHARE Programme, Ministry of Environmental Protection, Natural Resources and Forestry, Environment Coordination and Management Unit, Warsaw.

Wang Xi
Associate Professor of Law, Wuhan University Research Institute of Environmental Law.

Friedl Weiss
Professor, Faculty of Law, Europa Instituut, University of Amsterdam.

Amanda Wells
Lawyer, specializing in Environmental Law, London.

Jacob Werksman
Staff Lawyer, Co-Director, Climate Change and Energy Programme, Foundation for International Environmental Law and Development (FIELD), London.

Rona Westgate
Solicitor, Lovell White Durrant, Hong Kong, and Chairperson, Hong Kong Environmental Law Association.

Mary Pat Williams Silveira
Senior Officer, Human Development, Institutions and Technology Branch, Division of Sustainable Development, United Nations Department for Policy Coordination and Sustainable Development, New York.

Roger Wilson
Managing Director, Foundation for International Environmental Law and Development (FIELD), London.

Farhana Yamin
Staff Lawyer, Co-Director, Climate Change and Energy Programme,

Foundation for International Environmental Law and Development (FIELD), London.

Vincent Cheng Yang

Associate, International Centre for Criminal Law Reform and Criminal Justice Policy, Vancouver, British Columbia.

Jiunn-rong Yeh

Professor of Law, Department of Law, National Taiwan University, Taipei.

Tatiana Zaharchenko

Formerly, Professor, Ecological Law Department, Ukranian Law Academcy; LL.M. Candidate, George Washington National Law Center, Washington, D.C.

Victor M. Zarkov

Senior Researcher, Institute of Philosophy and Law, Belarus Academy of Sciences.

PART 1

ARTICLES

The Tuna–Dolphin Controversy, The World Trade Organization, and the Liberal Project to Reconceptualize International Law

Benedict Kingsbury[1]

I. INTRODUCTION

In the 1991 *Tuna-Dolphin I* case, a three-member dispute settlement panel of the General Agreement on Tariffs and Trade (GATT) reported that the United States had violated GATT by embargoing imports of tuna from Mexico—an embargo imposed because the Mexican tuna fleet did not meet US standards for reduced incidental dolphin mortality.[2] In 1994, another panel ruled in the *Tuna-Dolphin II* case that the United States had violated GATT by imposing 'intermediary nations' embargoes on imports of tuna from states and dependencies of the European Union (EU) that themselves imported tuna from nations subject to the primary embargo.[3] Neither panel report has been adopted by the GATT Council, so neither has direct legal effect within the GATT/World Trade Organization (WTO) system. The reasoning in the reports has nevertheless reinforced the position of WTO member states hostile to such sanctions, and has altered the negotiating environment with respect to trade sanctions in the WTO and in international environmental agreements. Concern about the implications of the 1991 panel report brought forth a torrent of environmentally oriented criticism and proposals for reinterpretation or reform of GATT and its procedures. The difficulty and divisiveness of the trade– environment issues made it impossible to reach useful agreement on most of them in the Uruguay Round package. A raft of unresolved trade–environment issues was left to the new WTO, and are under discussion in the WTO Trade and

[1] Portions of this article draw (with permission) on material in Benedict Kingsbury, *Environment and Trade: The GATT/WTO Regime in the International Legal System*, *in* ENVIRONMENTAL REGULATION AND ECONOMIC GROWTH 189–231 (Alan Boyle ed., 1994), although the theme of this article is different from the earlier work. The author is grateful for the comments of colleagues Robert Schapiro and Amy Chua, and the research assistance of Jonathan Gluck and Jeanne Capodano.

[2] United States Restrictions on Imports of Tuna (Mexico v. United States) (GATT Doc. DS 21/R), 30 ILM 1598 (1991).

[3] United States Restrictions on Imports of Tuna (European Economic Community & the Netherlands v. United States), 33 ILM 839 (1994).

Environment Committee as well as in several other intergovernmental organizations.[4]

The specific focus of the debate on the *Tuna-Dolphin* and other trade–environment controversies is the interpretation of GATT/WTO instruments in the context of the sudden need to connect environment and trade, two spheres of policy and institutional activity that have evolved largely in isolation from one another.[5] This article does not deal with much-discussed issues concerning the interpretation of specific provisions in GATT and other WTO instruments,[6] but focuses on some of the fundamental prob-

[4] The Organisation for Economic Cooperation and Development (OECD) Trade and Environment Committees have convened a series of Joint Sessions of Trade and Environment Experts. *See, e.g.*, OECD, THE ENVIRONMENTAL EFFECTS OF TRADE (1994). The United Nations Environment Program has published a series of papers on Trade and Environment. On the Organization of American States (OAS), see the report of a symposium sponsored by the OAS Committee on the Environment of the Permanent Secretariat: DIFFICULT LIAISON: TRADE AND THE ENVIRONMENT IN THE AMERICAS (Heraldo Muñoz & Robin Rosenberg eds., 1993). An important World Bank symposium was published: INTERNATIONAL TRADE AND THE ENVIRONMENT (Patrick Low ed., 1992). The UN Conference on Trade and Development has also been active in this area.

[5] The use of trade restrictions to achieve environmental objectives, and the use of environmental arguments to justify protectionist measures, were common during the early years of the development of international institutions, from about the 1870s. For example, the problem of occupational disease arising in the production of white phosphorus matches was addressed by a treaty in 1906 banning the production and importation of such matches, in order to level the playing field for manufacturers to switch to producing more costly matches that posed less risk to workers. (Level playing field issues, including concern that industries would migrate to sources of cheap labour in Asia, were frequently raised as arguments against proposals for international minimum wage or working hours and conditions standards. Another principal objection was that intergovernmental discussion of such issues intruded upon national sovereignty.) On national measures prohibiting import of white phosphorus after this treaty, *see* Steve Charnovitz, *Green Roots, Bad Pruning: GATT Rules and Their Application to Environmental Trade Measures*, 7 TULANE ELJ 299, 340 (1994). Conservation of fur seals was promoted by a treaty banning pelagic sealing (a wasteful method that reduced the proportion of females), together with a commitment not to import furs taken contrary to the treaty. *See* M.J. Peterson, *International Fisheries Management*, *in* INSTITUTIONS FOR THE EARTH: SOURCES OF EFFECTIVE INTERNATIONAL PROTECTION 249–305 (Peter Haas et al. eds., 1993). Unilateral measures were also taken against imports with a view to securing environmental objectives, including US and British legislation prohibiting the importation of plumes and feathers of certain wild birds threatened by the demands of milliners. Steve Charnovitz, *Exploring the Environmental Exceptions in GATT Article XX*, 25 JWT 37, 40 (1991), cites the US Underwood Tariff 1913, 38 Stat. 114, as an example. Historical material was canvassed quite extensively in the arguments of the European Community (EC), the Netherlands, and the United States in the *Tuna-Dolphin II* case, but the panel did not find the pre-1947 material to have much explicit bearing on interpretation of GATT—*see* paras. 5.20 and 5.33.

[6] A sample of works published shortly after the first *Tuna-Dolphin* case includes: James Cameron & Jonathan Robinson, *The Use of Trade Provisions in International Environmental Agreements and Their Compatibility with the GATT*, 2 YBIEL 3 (1992); Robert Housman & Durwood Zaelke, *Trade, Environment, and Sustainable Development: A Primer*, 15 HASTINGSICLR 535 (1992); John Jackson, *World Trade Rules and Environmental Policies: Congruence or Conflict?*, 49 WASH&LEELR 1227 (1992); Jan Klabbers, *Jurisprudence in International Trade Law: Article XX of GATT*, 26 JWT 63 (1992); Peter L. Lallas et al., *Environmental Protection and International Trade: Toward Mutually Supportive Rules and Policies*, 16 HARVARDELR 275 (1992); Thomas J. Schoenbaum, *Free International Trade and*

lems of international law that underlie debates on these issues. These problems have to do with the nature, contributions, and limitations of the international legal system as traditionally conceived, and raise the question whether some of the positions taken in the trade–environment debates depend on re-evaluation of the nature and roles of states and inter-state institutions, and on the articulation of a different conceptual framework for international law. These issues are vast, but the aim of this short article can only be extremely modest: to note problems with some of the principles espoused by the WTO in the trade–environment debates, and to broach the possibility that current proposals for a liberal reconceptualization of the framework of international law might meet some of the objections to existing WTO principles.

II. CONCEPTIONS OF THE INTERNATIONAL LEGAL SYSTEM IN ENVIRONMENTAL DISCOURSE

Deep ambivalence about the nature of the international political and legal system is manifest within the highly variegated environmentalist discourse.[7] It is not uncommon to find commitments to a group of core propositions which imply unreconciled—and perhaps unreconcilable—views of the international system and of the nature and roles of states and non-state forces. A sample might include the following propositions:[8] Environmental decision-making must be decentralized—preferably local—and loci of decision-making authority must be secure from interventions of external actors;[9] States are deeply entrenched, are expressive of local concerns and protective of important local interests, and provide powerful structures for effective environmental policy-making;[10] Territorial states are an artificial and

Protection of the Environment: Irreconcilable Conflict?, 86 AJIL 700 (1992). Some of the many other relevant recent works are referred to in later footnotes. A rare treatment of the issue in a much earlier period is Frederic Kirgis, *Effective Pollution Control in Industrialized Countries: International Economic Disincentives, Policy Responses, and the GATT*, 70 MICHIGAN LAW REVIEW 859 (1972). *See also* Frederic Kirgis, *Environment and Trade Measures after the Tuna/Dolphin Decision*, 49 WASH&LEELR 1221 (1992).

7 The examples that follow are taken mainly from Northern environmental discourse, as the liberal project to reconceptualize international law derives its impetus from the North. Different perspectives are alluded to in the Conclusion. See also the discussion of liberal commitments in relation to indigenous peoples in Benedict Kingsbury, *Whose International Law? Sovereignty and Non-State Groups*, 86 PROCEEDINGS OF THE AMERICAN SOCIETY OF INTERNATIONAL LAW 1 (1994).

8 Many of these tensions are exemplified and explored—if not resolved—in THE STATE AND SOCIAL POWER IN GLOBAL ENVIRONMENTAL POLITICS (Ronnie Lipschutz & Ken Conca eds., 1993).

9 *E.g.*, JOHN DRYZEK, RATIONAL ECOLOGY (1987).

10 'NGOs, by politicizing the biophysical and linking the local and the global, are tugging and pulling at states. Although some of what they do is entirely separate from state behaviour, much has the effect of setting the conditions under which states will act or, maybe more precisely, react.' Thomas Princen et al., *Translational Linkages*, *in* ENVIRONMENTAL NGOS IN

irrational imposition on the structure of ecosystems, and the division of the world into self-regarding states is a serious obstacle to global environmental policy-making and requires urgent reform;[11] The globalized economy is beyond the control of states or any other authority structure, and is wreaking environmental destruction;[12] A global environmental movement has been formed—as was manifest at the 1992 non-governmental organization (NGO) forum in Rio de Janeiro—empowering local groups, networking between them, and pursuing a global agenda.[13]

Such propositions are utilized by environmentalists in explaining present environmental trajectories and in developing policy prescriptions for improvement. The difficulties in resolving the tensions between them have inhibited the development among environmentalists of a common framework for understanding and explaining the international system.

The polar positions in trade–environment debates are so far apart as not really to join issue on the nature of the international legal system. At one pole are radical ecological views holding that insofar as the liberal trade system promotes economic growth, specialization, and integration of local economies into global markets, it runs counter to the ecologically preferred objectives of autarky and decentralization.[14] Such positions often overlap with more general opposition to the set of phenomena described loosely as 'globalization,' encompassing the different patterns of interconnectedness and homogenization in markets, capital, culture, information, and much else.[15] From such perspectives, tinkering with liberal trade rules will at best

World Politics: Linking the Local and the Global 217, 225 (Thomas Princen & Matthias Finger eds., 1994). *See also* Paul Ekins, A New World Order: Grassroots Movements for Global Change 208 (1992). For a useful discussion of the issue, see Andrew Hurrell, *A Crisis of Ecological Viability? Global Environmental Change and the Nation State*, 42 Political Studies 146 (1994).

[11] *E.g.*, William Ophuls, Ecology and the Politics of Scarcity Revisited (1992). *See also* Princen et al., *supra* note 10, at 223: 'States are either too large to meet local environmental needs (whether at home or in their foreign aid policies) or too small to address global issues. They operate to promote and to maintain the integrity of the state, for which the pursuit of industrial development is a necessary condition.'

[12] *E.g.*, Joseph Camilleri & Jim Falk, The End of Sovereignty? (1992).

[13] *E.g.*, Atiq Rahman & Annie Roncerel, *A View From the Ground Up*, *in* Negotiating Climate Change: The Inside Story of the Rio Convention 239 (Irving Mintzer & Amber Leonard eds., 1994). Of course, divergences and contestation within the NGO movement are widely recognized—*see e.g.*, Matthias Finger, *Environmental NGOs in the UNCED Process*, *in* Environmental NGOs in World Politics: Linking the Local and the Global, *supra* note 10, at 186; and Ann Hawkins, *Contested Ground: International Environmentalism and Global Climate Change*, *in* The State and Social Power in Global Environmental Politics 221 (Ronnie Lipschutz & Ken Conca eds., 1993).

[14] *Cf.* Dryzek, *supra* note 9.

[15] For criticism see, *e.g.*, Jeremy Brecher & Tim Costello, Global Village or Global Pillage: Economic Reconstruction from the Bottom Up (1994). 'Globalization' may have many different meanings, including: the existence of a global infrastructure; global harmonization or convergence of some important characteristic feature; borderlessness; global diffusion of some initially localized phenomenon; geographical dispersion of core competences.

effect mild improvements, but will fail to reach any of the fundamental ecological issues.[16]

At the opposite pole is the unreconstructed free-trade view that trade promotes economic growth and specialization and is either causally unrelated to environmental quality or is instrumental in environmental improvement through a positive correlation between prosperity and environmental protection.[17] 'Environmental protection' is thus another problem of protectionism or subsidy. In its major 1992 report on *Trade and the Environment*, the GATT Secretariat argued that sustainable development is not intrinsically linked to international trade, and that trade is simply a magnifier, enabling countries with adequate sustainable development policies to pursue these better.

Jeffrey A. Hart, *Comments on 'Changing Sovereignty Games and International Migration,'* 2 INDIANA JOURNAL OF GLOBAL LEGAL STUDIES 171 (1994). *See also* C. FRED BERGSTEN & EDWARD M. GRAHAM, THE GLOBALIZATION OF INDUSTRY AND NATIONAL GOVERNMENTS (1995). The utility of the concept of 'globalization' as cause or even as helpful description depends on answers to several essential questions: to what extent has 'global' interpenetration and interdependence occurred? (in many major economies international trade is less than 10 percent of gross domestic product, and much international trade and investment is only between a few prosperous countries); to what extent are the phenomena of globalization qualitatively new? (some suggest, for instance, that levels of trade interdependence in 1913 were comparable to present levels, and significant foreign investment interdependence also existed then); what exactly are its implications for state actions and policies?

[16] *See, e.g.*, COLIN HINES, THE NEW PROTECTIONISM (1993). The utter conflict between this view and that of state trade representatives is illustrated by the artful preamble of the 1994 Agreement Establishing the World Trade Organization, in which the parties recognize that:

> their relations in the field of trade and economic endeavour should be conducted with a view to raising standards of living, ensuring full employment and a large and steadily growing volume of real income and effective demand, and expanding the production and trade in goods and services, while allowing for the optimal use of the world's resources in accordance with the objective of sustainable development, seeking both to protect and preserve the environment and enhance the means for doing so in a manner consistent with their respective needs and concerns at different levels of development.

[17] The argument that the demand for environmental protection, and eventually the standard of national environmental protection in any particular country, rises with income, is often presented as a truism, with little discussion of the evidence as to conditions under which it does or does not apply. *See, e.g.*, Geza Feketekuty, *The Link Between Trade and Environmental Policy*, 2 MINNESOTA JOURNAL OF GLOBAL TRADE 171, 179 (1993). The rapidly growing number of research papers on the subject, of which the most discussed is Gene M. Grossman & Alan B. Krueger, *Environmental Impacts of a North American Free Trade Agreement* (Princeton, N.J.: Working Paper, 1991), in the main deal only with particular types of environmental degradation in particular settings. While the effective demand for, or at least delivery of, certain forms of environmental protection is highest in the richest countries, the process of attaining such levels of prosperity may have massive environmental effects. The essential problem of sustainable development is how to attain and maintain acceptable levels of prosperity world-wide without disastrous environmental degradation. As Jagdish Bhagwati points out, growth is not tightly linked to either the improvement of the environment or its degradation. Jagdish Bhagwati, *Trade and the Environment: The False Conflict?*, *in* TRADE AND THE ENVIRONMENT: LAW, ECONOMICS, AND POLICY 159, 163 (Durwood Zaelke et al. eds., 1993). *See also* Duane Chapman et al., INDUSTRIAL AND RESOURCE LOCATION, TRADE, AND POLLUTION (mimeo, Department of Agricultural, Resource, and Managerial Economics, Cornell University, April 1994).

> [I]f such policies are lacking, the country's international trade may contribute to a skewing of the country's development in an environmentally damaging direction, but then so will most of the other economic activities in the country. Clearly the correct action in such cases is to work for the adoption of an appropriate overall domestic environment policy, rather than focusing attention on problems that are allegedly trade-related.

Likewise, 'unilateral restrictions on trade would never be the most efficient instrument for dealing with an environmental problem.'[18]

Although these polar positions are influential, the trade–environment debates have gravitated toward more centrist positions. Many environmentalists do not adopt the radical ecological antipathy to the pursuit of economic growth and global market integration, but are nevertheless critical of the absence of real linkage between the trade regime and such values as sustainable development, elimination of environmental externalities, environmentally-conscious pricing, and recognition of the interests of future generations.[19] Environmental critics of the GATT Secretariat's *Trade and the Environment* report criticize the promotion of freer trade without concomitant measures to promote full internalization of environmental costs, and emphasize that trade liberalization without internalization of environmental and resource costs exacerbates adverse environmental impacts and to that extent is not intrinsically desirable.[20] A more fundamental critique of neoclassical economics by Herman Daly argues that growth models have depended upon constantly increasing throughput, but that this cannot be sustained in a 'full world' where natural capital is limited and is not fully substitutable by human capital.[21] While trade can increase resource efficiency through specialization,

> trade does postpone the day when countries must face up to the discipline of living within natural regenerative and absorptive capacities, and by doing that probably serves on balance to increase throughput growth and environmental degradation.

[18] GATT Secretariat, TRADE AND THE ENVIRONMENT, GATT Doc. (advance copy 1992) at 3–4. Seeking to hold the purist line, the Secretariat blithely avoided the stark real-world problem of what is to be done where a government shows no interest in improving its environmental policy, or where more efficient instruments for dealing with environmental problems are not available. For criticism of the Secretariat's position on unilateralism, see Steve Charnovitz, *GATT and the Environment: Examining the Issues*, 4 IEAFF 203, 206–08 (1992).

[19] *See, e.g.*, WORLD BANK, WORLD DEVELOPMENT REPORT 1992: DEVELOPMENT AND THE ENVIRONMENT (1992); and a critical review by Lance Taylor, *The World Bank and the Environment: The World Development Report 1992*, 21 WORLD DEVELOPMENT 868 (1993).

[20] CHARLES ARDEN-CLARKE, THE GENERAL AGREEMENT ON TARIFFS AND TRADE, ENVIRONMENTAL PROTECTION AND SUSTAINABLE DEVELOPMENT 10–11 (1991). *See also* the papers collected in the Special Issue on Trade and the Environment, 9 ECOLOGICAL ECONOMICS 1–92 (1994); and Lallas et al., *supra* note 6, at 318–23.

[21] *See* Herman Daly's contribution to ENVIRONMENTALLY SUSTAINABLE DEVELOPMENT: BUILDING ON BRUNDTLAND (Robert Goodland et al. eds., 1992).

Free trade also introduces greater spatial separation between the production benefits and the environmental costs of throughput growth, making it more difficult for the latter to temper the growth of the former.[22]

Where issue is joined in the middle ground of the trade–environment debates, frameworks for understanding the international legal system, and behaviour and outcomes within it, are of considerable practical importance. Amongst the most systematic efforts to build such a framework of understanding are those undertaken by academic theorists of international relations. For present purposes the three most influential theoretical approaches are political realism, international cooperation theory (regime theory), and liberal theory.[23] Each of these three approaches is more or less committed to providing a parsimonious and empirically testable set of hypotheses. The dominant theoretical paradigm remains political realism, which assumes states to be essentially similar ('unit homogeneity'), contends that explanation of state behavior proceeds from recognition that in a system without central government each state must be concerned primarily for its own survival and security, and views states as constrained in pursuit of power and interest only by their capacities and those of others.[24] Theories of international cooperation share some realist commitments, but focus on explaining and analysing the large number of cases of cooperation (or non-cooperation), which realism treats largely as epiphenomenal.[25] Liberal theories of international relations begin with the interests of individuals and groups (whether in national or transnational society) which influence the preferences and interactions of states. State preferences reflect the interests of some individuals and groups within the

[22] Herman Daly, *Problems With Free Trade: Neoclassical and Steady-State Perspectives, in* TRADE AND THE ENVIRONMENT, *supra* note 17, at 147, 156.

[23] Theories of international relations drawing on post-modernist thought presently command significant followings. *See* in particular Alex Wendt's proposed constructivist pre-theory, which accepts that states are the principal units of analysis but argues (against realists) that key structures in the states system are intersubjective rather than material, and (against rationalists) that state identities and interests are in some way constructed by these intersubjective structures, and are thus in some significant respects endogenous rather than exogenous. Alex Wendt, *Collective Identity Formation and the International State*, 88 AMERICAN POLITICAL SCIENCE REVIEW 384 (1994). Marxist theories have also been influential—*see, e.g.*, IMMANUEL WALLERSTEIN, THE CAPITALIST WORLD-ECONOMY (1979). Marxist and post-modernist theories of international relations have both stimulated environmental literature.

[24] The most influential contemporary statement of this view is KENNETH WALTZ, THEORY OF INTERNATIONAL POLITICS (1979). There are many varieties of realism, and some self-defined realists depart appreciably from Waltz's approach.

[25] *See, e.g.*, INTERNATIONAL REGIMES (Stephen Krasner ed., 1983); and ROBERT KEOHANE, INTERNATIONAL INSTITUTIONS AND STATE POWER (1989).

[26] This account is based on Andrew Moravcsik, *Liberalism and International Relations Theory, Harvard University Center for International Affairs*, Harvard University Center for International Affairs, Working Paper No. 92–6 (revised April 1993). *See also* Robert Keohane, *International Liberalism Reconsidered, in* THE ECONOMIC LIMITS OF MODERN POLITICS 165 (John Dunn ed., 1990); and Michael Doyle, *Liberalism and World Politics Revisited, in*

state, but not all of them. State regulation and other action affects wider sets of individuals and groups, however, shaping their interests and preferences.[26]

Realist frameworks, and even more so international cooperation frameworks, have been employed frequently in analysis of international environmental issues. Each has also had some indirect impact on literature concerning problems of international environmental law.[27] The liberal framework has not been used so frequently in systematic analysis of environmental issues. Moreover, efforts to use this liberal theory of international relations to ground an account of the international legal system are not yet fully developed.[28] None the less, the emerging liberal theory of international law has much in common with positions espoused in many debates about environment, development, and trade. The proposed liberal theory concept of international law offers an attractive framework for many widely-held views of international environmental law, and has particular salience in evaluating contemporary trade–environment controversies.

The practical exigencies of the *Tuna-Dolphin* cases and other trade-environment controversies have forced GATT/WTO panels, state representatives, NGOs, and commentators to take positions that do not always mesh with standard conceptions of the international legal system. These trade–environment debates are revealing in the views they embody about the extent to which the international legal system requires reform or reconceptualization. The panels in the *Tuna-Dolphin* cases relied explicitly or implicitly on several fundamental WTO principles associated with the traditional international legal order, but in the special trade–environment context each proves to have serious drawbacks. Five sets of fundamental problems concerning the international legal system raised by the *Tuna-Dolphin* cases command particular attention.

First are the increasing concerns about democratic participation in the international law-making and dispute-settlement process, especially in international institutions. The organizing assumption that the civil society of each state is sufficiently represented internationally by the executive branch of government has persisted in many institutions. There has long

Controversies in International Relations Theory 83 (Charles Kegley ed., 1994) (this is an updated version of Michael Doyle, *Liberalism and World Politics*, 80 American Political Science Review 1151 (1986).)

[27] *See, e.g.*, Ronald Mitchell, Intentional Oil Pollution at Sea (1994); Institutions for the Earth (Peter Haas et al. eds., 1993); *Developments in the Law—International Environmental Law*, 104 Harvard Law Review 1484 (1991).

[28] There are, however, significant points of overlap between the contemporary liberal project and the highly developed theoretical frameworks of writers in the New Haven School of international law. *See, e.g.*, Richard Falk, This Endangered Planet (1971); and Myres McDougal, *Legal Bases for Securing the Integrity of the Earth-Space Environment*, 184 Annals of the New York Academy of Sciences 375 (1971), and under the same title, 8 Journal of Natural Resources & Environmental Law 177 (1992–93).

been pressure for democratization in the sense of more equitable representation of different groups of states; more recently the topic of due process in international institutions has also become prominent. But the limited accountability of state representatives, their isolation from important elements of civil society, and their episodic inability to deliver on obligations undertaken in the names of their states, point to the inadequacy of the standard international legal analysis of states as functionally-equivalent unitary actors.

Second, relations between international and national action are of central importance, since many pressing issues, including environmental protection, can not be addressed effectively by individual states on their own, or by the action of international institutions alone, but depend on both. International cooperation entails making rules. These rules will be effective only if states are deterred from cheating or defecting, which usually means there must be demonstrable gains from cooperation, assurances that others are themselves complying, and dispute settlement mechanisms capable of addressing allegations, making authoritative findings, and promoting solutions. Yet international institutions are not always strong enough even to make adequate rules, and they are seldom strong enough to enforce these on their own. There thus remains a crucial need for national action: national monitoring, national enforcement (against both the forum state and other states), and sometimes even national rule-assertion to promote international rulemaking. Internationalist criticism of 'unilateralism,' like nationalist criticism of the 'invasion of national sovereignty by international technocrats,' often sets up a simplistic dichotomy between 'national' and 'international' that misses much of what is important in the interactions between them. These relations include interactions between national courts and foreign state executives,[29] between national legislatures and international institutions,[30] and indeed among the full range of state organs and other bodies with public functions.

Third, inter-state institutions are caught in the dual role of being created by and answerable to states while at the same time seeking to regulate state behavior and curtail state freedom of action. Specialist inter-state bodies such as the WTO secure the power to regulate certain trade practices of states by protecting the sovereignty of states in other areas. As more and more governance regimes are established, this kind of trade-off becomes

[29] *Cf. Japan Whaling Ass'n v. American Cetacean Soc'y*, 478 U.S. 221 (1986); *Greenpeace USA v. Stone*, 748 F. Supp. 749 (D. Hawaii 1990). David Wirth treats these cases as demonstrating 'the disruptive effect international agreements can have on domestic legislative regimes.' David Wirth, *A Matchmaker's Challenge: Marrying International Law and American Environmental Law*, 32 VAJIL 377, 414 (1992).

[30] *E.g.*, amendments to the *US Marine Mammal Protection Act* in response to the *1992 Agreements* reached in the Inter-American Tropical Tuna Commission.

harder to maintain. An emerging transnational civil society presses to curtail sovereign freedom in common areas such as the high seas. Standard international law analysis based on the consent of states is increasingly challenged by the enmeshment of states in a wider civil society and governance structure.

Fourth, the functional limits on competences of international institutions, imposed by their constitutive instruments and decision-making organs, are in tension with the continuous demand for modification (usually expansion) in the reach of governance regimes. These tensions are addressed by various doctrines, including those concerning implied powers, ambulatory interpretation, and *kompetenz-kompetenz*. Some environmentalist demands in trade–environment debates exceed the capacity of these doctrines. The WTO, a relatively effective body of limited competence, is pushed to become involved in governance problems vastly different from those specifically envisaged in its institutional mandate. On the other hand, effective implementation of the traditional trade mandate becomes a form of governance by omission in the absence of strong environmental institutions or resolution of overlaps with environmental regimes.

Fifth, the traditional horizontal analysis of international rules and institutions constructed by sovereign states, as minor consensual intrusions erecting small vertical edifices in the vast plane of sovereign freedom, makes it perfectly possible for international standards to conflict, and in extreme cases for a state to owe incompatible obligations to different groups of other states. This is already evident in the apparent conflict between some environmental treaties and WTO rules. Under standard international law analysis, any third-party choice between the conflicting rules involves doing violence either to the fundamental principle of consent or to important community values. A theory of international law is needed in which problems arising from this tension between contractual and legislative models of law are rendered soluble, if not simple.

These problems suggest that the traditional conception of international law as an inter-state consent-based system premised on the freedom and juridical equality of mono-voiced territorial states is overly beneficent toward states, and unpromising as a comprehensive framework within which to explain and systematize everything that happens already, let alone as a basis to deal with further evolution.

One response is to argue that it is time to reconceptualize international law, to move away from the state-centric paradigm toward a broader view of international law as the liberal law of an emerging transnational civil society. Such a society is said to be founded on shared values and transnational interactions among non-state entities: corporations, bar associations, environmental networks, feminist groups, political movements, internet usergroups, migrant workers, religious institutions, and thousands of other structures. States are important actors shaping such a society, but they are not the only actors. This is an attractive view to many environmentalists who see state sovereignty as an obstacle to rational management of global environmental resources and the web of interdependent ecosystems. On the other hand, national sovereignty and politically-accountable national management also has its attractions—for many people in developing countries as well as some of the US environmentalists who opposed the WTO agreements. Some liberals favor the strengthening of international organization to rein in states. Others fear that tendencies of state bureaucracies to dampen or channel the market-liberated energies of non-state actors are replicated and magnified in international institutions. Liberal views diverge, but the core features of the proposed liberal framework merit exploration. The final section of the article will use this case study to consider the possible contributions of the liberal project to reconceive international law.

III. THE TUNA-DOLPHIN CASES

The *Tuna-Dolphin* controversy provides an interesting case study with which to explore some of the implications of globalization and liberalism for evolving conceptions of the international legal system. The WTO is a trade body, established to give effect to a unified and well-ordered body of global trade rules, with very modest environmental expertise. Its core set of rules for trade in goods are those contained in the 1947 GATT (re-adopted by the Uruguay Round agreements), and these make no reference whatever to environmental protection as an explicit justification for departure from trade rules. The trade–environment debates forced it to confront a set of issues with which it was ill-equipped to deal. Ideally it might have looked to a body of coordinate competence specializing in environmental matters, but international environmental rules are still only fragmentary, and there is no comparable environmental body capable of settling a range of trade–environment disputes.

In the Eastern Tropical Pacific (ETP) herds of dolphin swim above schools of tuna and are often trapped by purse-seine nets used to catch tuna—indeed, as dolphin are visible from the surface, they have since the 1960s been used as a guide in setting nets. US initiatives to protect dolphins were formalized in 1972 in the Marine Mammal Protection Act (MMPA), which contained extensive provisions designed to reduce incidental dolphin mortality arising from tuna-fishing. The problem was also taken up in several international institutions, most notably the Inter-American Tropical Tuna Commission, which began to address the issue in 1976. Other states also adopted national dolphin conservation rules and policies. It is estimated that some 133,000 dolphins were killed in the ETP in 1986, but by 1991 the number had fallen to 27,500, and by 1993 it was believed to be under 3,700.[31] An Agreement for Reduction of Dolphin Mortality in the Eastern Pacific Ocean was concluded in June 1992 among the states fishing in the ETP.[32]

In addition to controlling dolphin mortality caused by US tunaboats, the MMPA required the US government to ban imports of tuna from other states fishing in the ETP unless these states met a series of requirements, including showings that they had comparable dolphin-protecting programs to the United States, and that for a given period the average incidental taking rate for their vessels did not exceed 1.25 times that recorded for US vessels during the same period. With the threat of sanctions as an inducement, the US executive branch tried—with some success—to persuade primary producers and intermediary nations to fall into line with US standards. The actual imposition of sanctions followed court orders obtained by environmental groups against the executive branch.

The *Tuna-Dolphin* cases (1991 and 1994) arose from these sanctions. The situation is unusual in that the United States unilaterally closed its markets to one product, yellowfin tuna, in order to promote direct protection of stocks of a different species, dolphins, found in the high seas and the fisheries zones of other countries. In the 1991 case, Mexico challenged the embargo imposed on tuna from Mexico and other primary-producing states whose performance with respect to incidental dolphin mortality was regarded by the United States as falling short of the standard set for foreign nations by the MMPA. The 1994 case was a challenge by the EC and the Netherlands to the US embargo on imports of tuna from 'intermediary' nations that had within the previous six months imported tuna from

[31] These figures are taken from the *United States Restrictions on Imports of Tuna*, (1994), *supra* note 3, at para. 5.1. Pressed by the MMPA and consumer concern, the US fleet progressively reduced its dolphin kills to some 12,643 in 1989, and 115 in the ETP in 1993: this was achieved partly by better practices and regulatory enforcement, partly by reflagging, and partly by relocating operations outside the ETP.

[32] Reproduced in 33 ILM 936 (1994). The parties to this agreement (done at La Jolla) are Colombia, Costa Rica, Ecuador, Mexico, Nicaragua, Panama, Spain, the United States, Vanuatu, and Venezuela—these are reported to be the only states whose fishing fleets are active in the ETP tuna fishery. An agreement along similar lines had been reached in April 1992 in the Inter-American Tropical Tuna Commission (IATTC). Membership of the IATTC is Costa Rica, France, Japan, Nicaragua, Panama, the United States, Vanuatu, and Venezuela. Mexico withdrew from the IATTC in 1978, but signed the June 1992 agreement, along with three other non-members of the IATTC: Colombia, Ecuador, and Spain. The June 1992 Agreement envisaged a fall in mortality from 19,500 in 1993 to less than 5,000 in 1999, and the actual rate of decline in mortality is reported to have been much more rapid, leading to subsequent IATTC resolutions on more rapid reduction in dolphin mortality limits. Several states fishing in the ETP have argued that these international agreements and their own national measures of dolphin conservation are the primary reasons for falls in non-US dolphin mortality. *See e.g.*, the statement by Venezuela in the GATT Council meeting of 4 Oct. 1994, GATT Doc. C/M/275 (24 Oct. 1994) at 5: 'In the light of the extraordinary success of the IATTC dolphin protection programme, it was obvious that the US embargo did not in fact meet any environmental objective. Furthermore, this embargo . . . had been counter-productive in that it had weakened the IATTC dolphin protection programme.'

primary-producing nations subject to the US embargo. The United States used the intermediary nation embargoes to pressure the EU and other GATT parties to take trade measures against tuna from nations subject to the US primary embargo, when the primary embargo had already been found in the unadopted 1991 report to be in breach of GATT, and the most obvious measure open to the EU to avoid the intermediary embargo was to join the United States in imposing just such a GATT-infringing primary embargo.

Defending itself in the GATT proceedings, the United States argued that the embargoes were simply the application to imports of rules comparable to those applied internally to tuna caught by US vessels. The panels found, however, that the US rules did not regulate tuna as a product so much as process and production methods (PPMs) for the product, and GATT has not hitherto countenanced regulation of foreign PPMs in most cases. The US measures were *prima facie* a quantitative restriction on imports contrary to GATT. The question was whether they were permitted under exceptions to GATT (contained in Art. XX) allowing certain measures necessary to protect animal life or health, or measures aimed at the conservation of exhaustible natural resources.

The 1994 panel determined that the Art. XX exceptions did not allow one state to take trade measures that can work only by forcing other states to change policies pursued within their own jurisdictions. Given that the US embargoes were *prima facie* contrary to GATT, to uphold them under the exceptions would be (as the 1991 panel had found) to change the balance of rights and obligations under GATT, and in particular to weaken the right of access to markets. In taking a circumscribed view of the relevant exceptions, the panels undoubtedly reflected the preferences of the vast majority of member states, and both panel reports were warmly welcomed.

IV. FIVE WTO PRINCIPLES CONCERNING THE NATURE OF THE INTERNATIONAL LEGAL SYSTEM

Amongst the myriad legal issues raised by the *Tuna-Dolphin* cases and related trade–environment debates, five principles bearing on the nature of the international legal system were adopted or implicitly relied on by the *Tuna-Dolphin* panels. The problems in maintaining each of these principles raise in a very practical way the question whether the present framework for international law is adequate for present and future needs. The five principles will be discussed in turn.

A. State 'Representatives' Define Interests, Make the Rules, and Settle Disputes

The WTO is a structure predicated on sovereign statehood and the centrality of states as makers and enforcers of trade rules and trade policy, arbiters of disputes, and negotiators of compromises. The WTO continues to regard international trade as the business of state representatives, even while most trading is by non-state bodies, and much of the pressure for and against trade rules and policies comes from sources not necessarily represented by the state 'representatives.' Consumer preferences, consumer boycotts, NGO eco-labelling schemes, industry-wide practice codes, and unofficial standards all have impacts on trade relations but are not necessarily within the control of states. Footloose capital, the rise of global sourcing and other forms of interdependence, and the decline of state traders have all affected the position of states. Yet states continue to use the WTO to reinforce their managerial roles in trade. The state representatives gathered at the WTO in Geneva cannot in practice represent the entire range of interests affected by trade rules. Nevertheless, the WTO remains largely closed to all but accredited state representatives. This has been particularly shocking to US and other environmental groups accustomed to considerable access to government. Very recently the GATT/WTO system has gingerly begun consultations with environmental groups, but a US proposal to invite such groups to participate in an open meeting of the GATT Council to discuss the *Tuna-Dolphin* case was drowned in a chorus of rejection in 1994.[33]

The WTO faces the essential difficulty that, as an organization created by and resting on the will of states and state representatives, it remains within their power to insulate the organization from national and transnational civil society. Yet such insulation threatens both the quality of the WTO's product and, more seriously, its legitimacy in an international system no longer monopolized by states. Unsurprisingly, this dilemma is evident in problems of rule-making and dispute settlement.

States are represented in WTO rule-making and dispute settlement by their executive branches, usually government agencies responsible for international trade or foreign policy. Particular positions taken by state representatives may reflect a range of interests projected from domestic politics,

[33] GATT Doc. C/M/274 (24 Aug. 1994) at 10–12. The representative of India is reported as asserting that 'the contracting parties would do a great disservice to themselves if they believed that what might be appropriate approaches at the city, state or village level would also be appropriate in an intergovernmental body such as the Council.' *Id.* at 11. Others speaking against the proposal included Argentina, Australia, Brazil, Brunei Darussalam, Canada, the EC, Mexico, New Zealand, the Nordic countries, and Venezuela. A similar discussion took place in response to a comparable US proposal in the Sub-Committee on Trade and Environment of the WTO Preparatory Committee, WTO Doc. PC/SCTE/M/3/Rev.1 (12 Oct. 1994) paras. 173–97. Many delegations favoured 'transparency,' and greater consultation with NGOs (and with national environmental officials) in the domestic political arena, but few were willing to support the US proposal to allow NGO observers at meetings of the (Sub-) Committee. Several delegations objected that opening the GATT/WTO system to NGOs would allow a flood of lobby groups (steel, agriculture, consumers), and that it would be impossible to determine which NGOs were 'environmental,' legitimate, and representative of geographic and other interests. Others expressed more deep-seated reservations. India, for example, feared 'politicization of the GATT/WTO' and emphasised that it was 'a legal contract between governments with rights and obligations and an advanced dispute settlement procedure' (*Id.* at para. 185).

with bureaucratic politics also playing a role. In channeling interests, articulating norms, and adding reasons for compliance, international institutions often support or legitimize particular positions taken by some political actors within states, and increase the price of adopting approaches pressed by other actors. In the case of the United States, the executive branch continues to enjoy considerable freedom in deciding how to argue a case before a GATT/WTO panel, and whether to acquiesce in the adoption of a panel report or to try to prevent adoption through diplomatic pressure and negotiation. The executive has on occasion welcomed—and perhaps even encouraged—adverse GATT rulings as a means to overcome opposing pressures in domestic politics. In 1986, the Reagan administration successfully used an adverse GATT Panel ruling, adopted by the GATT Council with US acquiescence, to discourage Congress from reenacting an 1891 law that protected the US printing industry by prohibiting import of various printed works written by US residents.[34] It has been speculated that Mexico may in 1991 have formed the impression that parts of the US executive branch would not be sorry if the *Tuna-Dolphin* case were raised before a panel: but there is no evidence of intentional US signalling to this effect.[35]

The complexities of representation were well illustrated by the 1993–94 maneuverings about US Environmental Protection Agency (EPA) rules on levels of pollutants in reformulated gasoline.[36] The new rules, designed to reduce city smog, posed particular problems for Venezuela, as Venezuelan gasoline is high in olefins, although not high in several other pollutants. Venezuela, which has a substantial share of the gas market in the US Northeast through its Citgo chain, faced very high costs of refinery modifications to comply. The rules were strongly supported by Citgo's main competitor, Sun Oil, and by some members of Congress. Venezuela was supported by the State Department, concerned to promote Venezuela's economic growth and not to undermine friendly relations. Venezuela also had some support in Congress. In February 1994 Venezuela raised the issue in GATT. This gave Venezuela considerable leverage, as there was an arguable case that the EPA rules discriminated against foreign producers in

[34] *United States: Manufacturing Clause in US Copyright Legislation,* BISD 31 Supp., 74 (1985). Attention is drawn to this example by ROBERT KEOHANE, CONTESTED COMMITMENTS IN US FOREIGN POLICY (1994) (unpublished manuscript). Also of interest is the US legislative ban on export of unprocessed lumber from federal and some state public lands, which includes a provision permitting (but not obliging) the President to terminate the ban in the event of an adverse ruling by a GATT or other trade agreement panel, even if the panel report has not been formally adopted. 16 USC §620c (Supp. 1992). This provision is discussed in Charnovitz, *Green Roots, Bad Pruning*, *supra* note 5, at 345–6.

[35] *See* George Mitchell & Patrick Adcock, *Between Compliance and Defiance: Executive Disposition of 'Unwanted' Environmental Legislation*, 3 JOURNAL OF ENVIRONMENT & DEVELOPMENT (1994).

[36] Regulation of Fuels and Fuel Additives: Standards for Reformulated and Conventional Gasoline, 59 Fed. Reg. 7716 (1994).

the way in which refinery baseline pollutant levels were measured. Rather than use up political capital blocking the GATT process, or take the risk of an adverse panel report, the United States Trade Representative (USTR) negotiated on behalf of the United States a settlement under which EPA would revisit the question. Supporters of the original EPA rules alleged that the USTR had caved in to Venezuela's supporters and given away US rights unnecessarily, and blocked EPA's revised rule. Venezuela thereupon raised the matter in GATT again.

The logic of a legal system based on the consent of state representatives leads to a rule-making system based on inter-state bargaining and reciprocity.[37] Instrumentally rational interest-maximizing states may rank their interests in environmental protection lower than other interests, and may bargain them away in reciprocal if not necessarily equal negotiations, where community norms do not prevent this.[38] Even where states rank their own environmental interests highest among their interests, unilateral pursuit of these individual interests through self-help will not necessarily achieve the best aggregate environmental results. If the interests of states become operational only where they suffer injury or lose a benefit, distortion may occur through focus on transboundary impacts rather than domestic impacts in other states. Useful lessons may be drawn from the area of human rights, where the limited and partisan interests of third states in violations by any particular state tend to diverge from the interests of the individuals and groups suffering violations. International human rights regimes were created using the standard forms of state–state obligations in multilateral treaties, but reciprocity has been gradually (although not completely) displaced by the answerability of each state to more-or-less independent international institutions.[39] If such institutions create greater space for transnational civil society actors, the concern that states are often incapable of bargaining to high levels of environmental protection may be alleviated; such actors are adept at using soft law and other devices to push standards

[37] A useful study of the trade regime is CAROLYN RHODES, RECIPROCITY, US TRADE POLICY, AND THE GATT REGIME (1993).

[38] The bargaining process may see environmental interests pursued in tandem with, or to reinforce, other interests, producing results supported by environmentalists even where environmental interests were not primary. For example, Ontario in 1992 sharply increased an environmental levy on beer cans (used mainly by US beer producers) in order to encourage use of refillable bottles (used mainly by local producers). The high rate of recycling of cans meant the differences in environmental impact between cans and bottles were modest or negligible. The backdrop was a long history of protectionist actions concerning interprovincial and international trade in beer. After retaliation and counter-retaliation outside GATT, the settlement negotiated in 1993 allowed continuation of the beer levy, recognizing not that the environmental case overwhelmed trade law considerations but that both the United States and Canada were vulnerable to challenge for numerous entrenched measures of beer protectionism, and that each state had a greater interest in establishing a political climate conducive to gradual dismantling of these measures.

[39] *See, e.g., Belilos v. Switzerland*, 132 EUROPEAN COURT OF HUMAN RIGHTS (Series A) (1988).

above what states are able formally to agree.

The system of rule-making and dispute settlement by narrowly-based state representatives—who may have more in common with each other than with many of the societal interests they 'represent'—is increasingly controversial. Many Northern environmental NGOs believe the WTO would reach more environment-friendly decisions with a different representative structure. The insufficient involvement of interest groups, civic organizations, legislatures, and other elements outside the executive branch—the 'democratic deficit'—has been a difficult problem for most international organizations. The EU has responded by strengthening the directly-elected European Parliament; the International Labour Organization has long had direct representation of employers and unions as well as governments; and some UN bodies have devised formulae for the limited inclusion of NGOs. These and other international institutions have begun to recognize the direct contributions of national and transnational civil society organizations to agenda-setting, information gathering, scientific knowledge, compliance monitoring, technical assistance, and other functions, although a surfeit of enthusiasm for NGOs has given way to more sober assessments of their capacities, representativity, and accountability. Much of the WTO dispute-settlement process remains closed to non-state involvement and secretive in hearings and documentation—law suits have recently been filed in national courts (in the United States) in an effort to force the government to disclose dispute settlement materials treated by the WTO as confidential. In extreme cases, failure to resolve these and other problems of representation and accountability in rule-making and dispute settlement may lead in the long run to the marginalization of international institutions.

B. Enforcement Should Be By Collectively-Approved Action, Not Unilateral Action

The *Tuna-Dolphin* panels manifest the belief that, except where authorized under GATT/WTO rules, trade rights protected by these rules ought not to be interfered with by unilateral action by other states.

The criticisms of unilateral trade measures are well-known. Unilateralism in this context is not subject to effective international supervision, and the risk of mixed motives or the appearance of self-serving behavior is high. In the 1991 *Tuna-Dolphin* case, Mexico pointed out that the US tuna boat industry had largely left the region where incidental catches of dolphins posed problems, and noted that Mexico had been subject to earlier US tuna embargoes imposed for quite different (protectionist or fisheries access-coercing) reasons.[40] There is also a likelihood of subjectivity in cases where

[40] *United States Restrictions on Imports of Tuna (1991)*, *supra* note 2, para. 3.58. Indonesia commented that this was the 23d time the United States had embargoed imports of tuna since 1975. (*Supra* note 2, para. 4.15).

the unilateral action is not taken to give effect to an international standard. People in the United States had formed a great affection for dolphins, whether endangered species or not, and the United States set about pushing Mexico and other states to respect this affection even in the absence of any international agreement on the point. Unless an international agreement on environmental standards is a prerequisite to trade action, it is difficult to see any basis for accepting US GATT-illegal enforcement of its dolphin policy short of accepting that any state might determine and enforce its own 'wildlife' or even 'environmental' policies. But other states endeavoring to enforce environmental standards against the United States are liable to find the price very high—the EU ban on beef fed with growth hormones has been met with substantial US trade retaliation against the EU. Less powerful states do not have as many options for environmental unilateralism, a point illustrated by Austria's 1992 law requiring eco-labelling of all tropical timber (but not softwoods, which Austria exported), which was repealed in 1993 under pressure from Austrian exporters threatened with trade retaliation by Malaysia and other tropical timber states. In the GATT Council debates on the 1994 *Tuna-Dolphin* report every representative to speak (apart from the United States)—a range including Australia, Canada, the EU, India, Japan, Mexico, the Nordic countries, the Philippines, and several others—was against the US measures, and many emphasized their deep-seated opposition to interventionism and unilateralism.[41] (Of course, this does not mean that none of these has taken unilateral trade measures!) This view of the overwhelming majority of states is reflected in the Declaration adopted by states at the 1992 UN Conference on Environment and Development (UNCED) in Rio de Janeiro: 'Unilateral actions to deal with environmental challenges outside the jurisdiction of the importing country should be avoided.'[42]

The problem is that unilateral measures, although repugnant to the overwhelming majority, have on occasion been effective in securing compliance with existing rules or speedy adoption of new and stronger rules.[43] The United States has the most explicit policies in this regard, raising familiar debates about US exceptionalism. It is possible that well-chosen measures by one state (particularly a hegemon) will not plunge the system into chaos, while widespread reciprocity in such measures might well do so. The WTO presumption of sovereign equality allows no space for such possibilities. Likewise, standard international legal theory has little to say about the weakness, in the present state of international trade politics, of a system

[41] GATT Doc. C/M/274 (24 Aug. 1994) at 6–10.

[42] *See also* Agenda 21, para. 2.22(i) (United Nations, 1992); and Kriangsak Kittichaisaree, *Using Trade Sanctions and Subsidies to Achieve Environmental Objectives in the Pacific Rim*, 4 ColoJIELP 296 (1993).

[43] *See, e.g.*, Steve Charnovitz, *Environmental Trade Measures: Multilateral or Unilateral?*, 23 EPL 154 (1993).

relying purely on collective or collectively-approved action. Enforcement of existing international trade standards involves a complex interaction of GATT/WTO institutional pressure, extra-institutional bilateral or multilateral negotiation, unilateral retaliatory trade action, and domestic political structures. Unilateral enforcement of trade standards under domestic legal procedures has become prevalent, and is likely to remain important. One aim of the Uruguay Round was to tie national trade enforcement action to the use of the WTO process. The long-term success of this ambitious reform will depend on highly effective operation of the WTO dispute-settlement process combined with a major shift in member practices; the likelihood is that some independent enforcement of trade rules will continue. The GATT/WTO system has had great difficulty dealing with challenges to trade embargos imposed for reasons of high politics rather than trade policy.[44] The more tightly rule-governed dispute settlement system of the WTO is likely also to be sorely tested by such confrontations.[45]

In the trade–environment area, the United States shows no sign of backing away from unilateral measures. In the Tuna-Dolphin controversy, the United States claimed that the threat and implementation of MMPA sanctions prompted the Inter-American Tropical Tuna Commission to adopt multilateral agreements on rapid reductions in incidental dolphin mortality. The target states replied that US sanctions have impoverished their tuna fishing industries, outraged national political sensibilities, and thus made their dolphin conservation efforts more difficult. The Clinton administration began in 1994 to deal with one of the multitude of objections to US conduct, that of unpredictability and arbitrariness in trade sanctions,

[44] No useful decision was reached in European Community, Canada and Australia: Trade Restrictions Applied for Non-Economic Reasons (Argentina v. EC, Canada and Australia), BISD 29 Supp., 23 (a complaint concerning the Falklands/Malvinas war embargo imposed by these states was never referred to a Panel); United States: Suspension of Most-Favoured Nation Treatment (Poland v. United States), Complaint of 1 Nov. 1982 concerning US suspension of Poland's MFN status following suppression of Solidarity movement was never referred to a Panel, GATT Doc. C/W/401; and United States: Trade Measures Affecting Nicaragua (Nicaragua v. United States), GATT Doc. L/6053 (13 Oct. 1986) (complaint by Nicaragua against US embargo was referred to a Panel but with terms of reference which proved too limited to reach a material result). In United States: Imports of Sugar from Nicaragua (Nicaragua v. United States), BISD 31 Supp., 67, a Panel ruled that the US reduction of Nicaragua's sugar quota violated GATT Art. XIII, and the ruling was adopted by the GATT Council, but the United States took the position that GATT had no role in such a dispute and ignored the ruling until sanctions were lifted in 1990. In EEC: Trade Measures Taken for Non-Economic Reasons, GATT Docs. L/6945, DS27/2, and C/M/254 at 35 (1991-92) Yugoslavia raised in the GATT Council the issue of the sanctions regime applied to it by the EC, and requested the establishment of a panel, but nothing concrete resulted.

[45] In considering initial responses to the seizure by Canada in March 1995 of a Spanish vessel fishing outside the Canadian 200-mile zone, the EU and its member states paid considerable attention to the constraints imposed by WTO disciplines. On Canadian interest in developing an international legal regime to limit depletion of fish stocks (including turbot) resulting from high seas fishing, see Paul Fauteux, *The Canadian Legal Initiative on High Seas Fishing*, 4 YBIEL 51 (1994).

by enunciating four situations in which trade sanctions would be considered: when required by an international treaty of the United States; when the environmental impact extended to the United States, such as a polluted river flowing into the United States; when a species anywhere is endangered or threatened; and when the effectiveness of a scientifically based international environmental or conservation standard is being diminished. The actual imposition of sanctions is thereafter to depend on further factors, including the existence of other options.[46]

C. The WTO Protects States, Within their Zones of Jurisdiction, from Impingement by Other States

The 1994 *Tuna-Dolphin* panel concluded that policies of one state that are effective only through affecting the conduct of other states within areas of their own jurisdictional competence are not within the GATT Art. XX exceptions.[47] Thus, if such policies are implemented through measures which *prima facie* infringe GATT rights, the measures will not be saved by the Art. XX exceptions to GATT covering measures aimed at such objectives as protection of life and conservation of natural resources. The GATT Secretariat has put the matter more broadly, treating territory (and perhaps nationality) as the essential basis for jurisdiction regardless of the transboundary or extra-jurisdictional dimension of many environmental and economic interests. A central distinction is drawn between actions taken by a state to protect its own domestic environment from domestic production

[46] Statement by State Department Counsellor Tim Wirth to the Subcommittee on Foreign Commerce and Tourism of the Senate Commerce, Science, and Transportation Committee, 3 Feb. 1994. INTERNATIONAL TRADE REPORTER (BNA) 11:6 at 221 (1994).

[47] The 1991 *Tuna-Dolphin* panel expressed a similar rationale, rejecting interpretations of GATT exceptions that, if adopted, would have the effect that 'each contracting party could unilaterally determine the . . . policies from which other contracting parties could not deviate without jeopardizing their rights under the General Agreement.' (*Supra* note 2, paras. 5.27, 5.32.) The 1991 Panel rejected what it described as 'extrajurisdictional' applications of these exceptions in GATT, suggesting that the exceptions apply only to protection of animal or plant life or health within the (territorial) jurisdiction of the state, and to conservation of natural resources within the jurisdiction of the state. (*Id.* at paras. 5.25 to 5.27, 5.31 to 5.32.) The 1994 panel recognized that this was an excessively narrow view, and accepted that these exceptions could apply no matter where the plants, animals or resources were located. (*Id.* at paras. 5.14 to 5.17, 5.30 to 5.33.) One factor supporting this view is that international law permits states to exercise jurisdiction over their own nationals and vessels wherever located. The implication of the 1991 report that the US measures involved 'extrajurisdictional' protection of dolphins was prudently avoided in the 1994 report, which shifted the focus away from the misconceived question of what was 'extrajurisdictional' for the United States to what was within the jurisdiction of other states. (For criticism of the approach taken in the 1991 report, see, *e.g.*, Steve Charnovitz, *The Environment vs. Trade Rules: Defogging the Debate*, 23 ENVL 475, 497 (1993); and Kingsbury, *supra* note 1, at 209–10.) This shift in analytical focus is an important improvement, but the conclusion ultimately reached was the same. For a more extensive treatment of the 1994 report, see Steve Charnovitz, *Dolphins and Tuna: An Analysis of the Second GATT Panel Report*, 24 ENVIRONMENTAL LAW REPORTER 10567 (Environmental Law Institute 1994).

or the consumption of domestically produced or imported products, which are broadly permitted under GATT/WTO rules, and trade actions intended to shape the environmental policies of other countries, which in many cases are not permitted.

The dilemma for the WTO is that protection of each state's competence in this sphere is a quid pro quo to states for agreeing to the intrusive substantive trade standards established and superintended by the WTO system. The WTO presses states to observe these trade standards within their territories, and a certain amount of enforcement by other states is countenanced. But the WTO's trade disciplines also function as a shield for states from other forms of intrusion.[48]

The WTO model is of state environmental autonomy (from trade measures) within territorially-defined spheres of jurisdiction. This is not a natural starting point for rational ecological management. Ecosystems and environmental damage both run across state borders. One of the core problems of global environmental policy is achieving the necessary cooperation among over 190 different states: further buttressing of national autonomy is not necessarily a step forward.

The problem is particularly acute in relation to global commons such as the high seas or the stratospheric ozone layer. The ideal of the inter-state system is that commons regimes are agreed by all nations, and enforced by all states against their own nationals and throughout their own jurisdictional zones. In reality, free-riding by some states, and failures of state will or capacity, are not infrequent. Many of the international commons agreements have not set high enough standards to achieve real protection. National standard-setting and enforcement are frequently necessary to effective commons management, even where the harm suffered by each state through commons degradation is too diffuse to establish a legal interest sounding in damages. Environmentalists are concerned that effective management will be impeded if WTO rules prevent states from taking even 'necessary' actions to apply policies in ways affecting the freedoms of other states in their own areas of jurisdictional competence. For example, in the latter part of the 1980s the small South Pacific nations expressed concern to Japan, South Korea, and Taiwan about damage their high seas driftnets were doing to fisheries in the region. The initial response was unreceptive,

[48] The matter was put succinctly by the representative of Sweden (speaking for the Nordic countries) in the GATT Council in 1991:

> In the GATT, contracting parties had voluntarily accepted some limits on their sovereignty. However, the GATT did not explicitly allow action to influence conditions within another contracting party's territory, or its policies outside the trade field. Indeed, the GATT's strong emphasis on non-discrimination underlined the opposite position. Contracting parties, therefore, retained a basic right to remain free from such pressures, which in many cases could effectively be brought to bear through trade measures.

GATT Doc. C/M/250 (28 June 1991) at 13.

yet by the end of 1992 all three had virtually abandoned South Pacific drift-netting. Adoption of multilateral standards played a part in this reversal,[49] but US political pressure combined with the US threat of trade sanctions was a significant element.[50]

A more straightforward problem with the non-impingement principle arises where transborder environmental problems have a direct effect on a neighboring state. Here trade measures intended to coerce the offending state may occasionally be the only politically viable strategy, despite the strictures of the WTO. For example, if a factory just across the international border increases the salinity of a common aquifer, but the host state fails to regulate it, trade sanctions against the factory's products may seem politically imperative, even if such sanctions are economically less efficient than a direct tax on the polluter. Such sanctions may be an acceptable second-best alternative if scientifically supportable, imposed for legitimate environmental reasons, and the least trade-disruptive of the available options.[51]

A significant moral and political dimension, not addressed by the *Tuna-Dolphin* panels, arises where a state imposes trade measures to prevent its own complicity in repugnant conduct. For example, US market demand for yellowfin tuna may well spur tuna fishing; even if the United States does not fish in the Eastern Tropical Pacific area where the tuna-dolphin problem mainly arises, the United States may nevertheless cast an 'ecological shadow' over dolphins in the ETP, implicating the United States and creating pressure to prevent US involvement.

D. The WTO Is Not Authorized to Interfere in 'Domestic' Environmental Policy

The WTO regime at present has few substantive standards concerning environmental policy.[52] Provided there is no discrimination or other breach of WTO trade disciplines, 'domestic' environmental policy is treated as an internal matter. The standard GATT/WTO line is that WTO rules 'place essentially no constraints on a country's right to protect its own environment,' and, except perhaps where there are physical spillovers to other nations, that national environmental policies 'are properly regarded as

[49] Especially the *Convention for the Prohibition of Fishing with Long Driftnets in the South Pacific (the Wellington Convention) of 1989*, and the series of UN General Assembly resolutions 44/225 (1989), 45/197 (1990), 46/215 (1991), 47/443 (1992), and 48/445 (1993).

[50] Grant Hewison, *Multilateral Efforts to Protect the Environment and International Trade: The Case of Driftnet Fishing, in* TRADE AND THE ENVIRONMENT (GATT Doc. TE009, (28 July 1994)) at 67–81.

[51] Bhagwati, *supra* note 17, at 159.

[52] Important provisions bearing on the interplay of national and international standards were adopted in the Uruguay Round: Agreement on Technical Barriers to Trade (the Standards Code), and the Agreement on the Application of Sanitary and Phyto-Sanitary Measures.

domestic choices reflecting, among other factors, the domestic trade-offs between income and environment.'[53]

The WTO thus subscribes to a rough counterpart to the doctrine in the United Nations Charter according to which the UN will not intervene in matters essentially within the domestic jurisdiction of member states. In the UN, the domain of domestic jurisdiction has been gradually diminished by the encroachment of substantive international law standards covering many matters of 'domestic' policy, including human rights. Similarly, the WTO observes no rule of abstinence with regard to domestic policies where these affect certain trade matters: the formal *raison d'être* of the WTO is to set rules protecting liberal trade, and to hold states internationally accountable for any trade-damaging non-compliance with these rules. The domain reserved to states has shrunk in this area too: WTO rules now reach well beyond tariffs to address non-tariff barriers to trade (including product standards), subsidies, trade in services, intellectual property, trade policy, and a host of other matters.

Going beyond the abstinence inherent in a principle of non-interference, the WTO confers a certain legitimacy on national decisions about environmental policy by treating them as entitled to respect. The WTO practice of treating national environmental and other policies as comparative advantages enjoyed by different states is seen by some environmentalists as conferring a benediction on benighted environmental policies, particularly when combined with the protection accorded by the WTO from certain forms of trade pressure exerted by other states. In effect the WTO assumes that political processes within each state will determine the best combination of environmental and other policies for that state, although the WTO is well aware that this is often not true in reality. Thus far the WTO has taken little interest in the nature of political decision-making systems within states: nor does it matter whether the environmental and developmental policies chosen are defensible or grotesque. The need to engage in some evaluation of the compatibility of particular policies with GATT/WTO rules, and of conformity of trade measures with both national policies and GATT/WTO rules, is unavoidable, however, and is increasingly a focus of Art. XX jurisprudence.[54]

[53] TRADE AND THE ENVIRONMENT, *supra* note 18, at 8 and 19–20.

[54] *See* in particular the United States: Taxes on Automobiles case, 33 ILM 1399 (1994) (not yet adopted), in which a GATT panel found that the system of foreign fleet accounting in the US Corporate Average Fuel Economy rules simply did not further the objective of conservation of gasoline and could therefore not be justified under Art. XX(g) (para. 5.60). In Canada: Restrictions on Export of Unprocessed Herring and Salmon, BISD 35 Supp., 98 (1988), a GATT Panel indicated that a GATT-infringing measure could be defended under Art. XX(g) only if it had conservation as a 'primary aim,' and if the measure is primarily intended to render effective restrictions on domestic production or consumption. The panel in *Tuna-Dolphin II*, *supra* note 3, paras. 5.21 to 5.27, followed this approach, and concluded that these tests could not be satisfied by measures taken 'to force other countries to change their policies, and

The operation of the GATT/WTO principle of non-interference in domestic environmental policy choices is illustrated by the 1994 Panel report in the *US Auto Taxes (CAFE)* case.[55] The European Union challenged three US measures concerning autos on the ground that they violated GATT's requirements that national laws and other measures not discriminate between like imported and domestic products. These were the luxury tax on autos retailing above $30,000, the gas-guzzler tax on autos getting less than 22.5 miles per gallon (mpg), and the Corporate Average Fuel Economy (CAFE) rules imposing civil penalties if the range of autos produced by a single manufacturer and used in the United States did not average at least 27.5mpg. All three measures had a much greater impact on such European producers as Mercedes and BMW than on US manufacturers—indeed over 99 percent of CAFE penalties were paid by foreign producers—and the EU suspected protectionism in the design of these taxes. The GATT Panel held that despite physical and market similarities, a foreign auto retailing above $30,000 need not be regarded as 'like' a US auto retailing at just under $30,000, so the luxury tax did not violate any GATT rule. The gas-guzzler tax was upheld on similar grounds. The key point was that these taxes did not have the aim or inherent effect of protecting US autos against imports. In these respects the Panel effectively acknowledged that taxes set with particular thresholds were increasingly important policy instruments and were not necessarily GATT-incompatible

that were effective only if such changes occurred' (para. 5.27). The *Tuna-Dolphin II* panel likewise concluded that such measures could not meet the requirement in Art. XX(b) that measures be 'necessary' to protect human, animal or plant life or health (para. 5.39). GATT/WTO Panels are apparently unwilling to second-guess states on the question of what level of protection is required (*see e.g.*, *Tuna-Dolphin I*, *supra* note 2, para. 5.27), but panels are willing to consider whether the particular measure was necessary to attain the level of protection sought by the state (*e.g.*, United States—Section 337 of the Tariff Act 1930 (*Akzo*), BISD 36 Supp., 345 at 392 (1989).) They have indicated that the necessity requirement precludes infringement of GATT obligations where a non-infringing means of attaining the same object would also have been available. This has been extended to holdings that Art. XX permits adoption only of the least GATT-infringing measure where a choice of GATT-infringing means of attaining the objective was open (*e.g.*, *Akzo*, *supra*; Thailand: Restrictions on Importation of and Internal Taxes on Cigarettes (United States v. Thailand), BISD 37 Supp., 200 (1990).) Very little guidance has yet been offered as to how to compare, *e.g.*, a violation of Art. XI with a violation of Art. III, and the EU has argued strongly that the 'least trade-restrictive' principle ought to operate in these Art. XX cases. Some have also advocated introduction of a 'proportionality' principle. A short note by the GATT Secretariat on the place of these principles in GATT law is in GATT Doc. TRE/W/16/Rev.1 (14 Oct. 1993).

[55] *Supra* note 54. The point is also illustrated by the Superfund case, United States: Taxes on Petroleum and Certain Imported Substances (Mexico, Canada and EC v. United States), BISD 34 Supp., 136 (adopted 17 June 1987). In the Superfund case, a Panel held that the reasons for imposing a border tax adjustment were irrelevant: any such tax on products was acceptable provided it was equivalent to that imposed on domestic products and did not otherwise infringe GATT. The EC argument that the US tax on US products was to make the polluter pay and that foreign products caused no or less pollution in the United States was held to be irrelevant.

even where their principal practical effect was on imports. The Panel acknowledged that the gas-guzzler tax may be a less efficient means to conserve fuel than *e.g.*, a direct tax on gas, but did not regard this as limiting the freedom of the United States to choose the less efficient measure. The Panel intimated that the CAFE rules might also be upheld in the future if the United States were to eliminate the one feature of them that was found to violate GATT.[56] This was the provision requiring manufacturers or importers to divide their vehicles used in the United States into two fleets, domestically-produced and foreign-produced vehicles, and to achieve the statutory fuel economy for each fleet. The practical result was that American producers of big cars could not bring in imported small cars to push their averages up, and Mercedes and BMW could not use American-made small cars to compensate for the low fuel economy of their big cars. Nor could Mercedes and BMW get credit for their smaller vehicles used outside the United States. The discrimination between foreign and domestic fleets, and between foreign and domestic producers, could not be justified under GATT as it was not aimed primarily at supporting the legitimate US aim of fuel conservation. US Trade Representative Mickey Kantor welcomed the GATT Panel decision, the loss on one 'technical issue' notwithstanding, and announced that no changes would be made to the CAFE rules as 'no trade damage results' from the GATT-illegal discrimination.[57] Although overly sanguine about the pressures for modification of the discriminatory aspects of the CAFE scheme,[58] this response does highlight the considerable latitude allowed to states by the Panel in the application of internal environmental taxes and penalties.

The difficulty for the WTO is that its decisions on 'trade' matters have implications for the environmental policies of many different states, and the distinction between 'international' and 'domestic' has become so uncertain as to sometimes appear untenable. The matrix of bright lines the WTO sees between 'domestic' and 'non-domestic,' and between 'trade' and 'environment,' is interpreted quite differently by others, including state policy-makers. Thus an environmental critic entirely endorsed the view that the WTO 'is not competent to weigh dolphin lives against shark lives, or to

[56] *Supra* note 54, para. 5.66.

[57] 11 INTERNATIONAL TRADE REPORTER 1532 (BNA 1994).

[58] *See* the Understanding Regarding Notification, Consultation, Dispute Settlement and Surveillance of 28 Nov. 1979 (BISD, 26 Supp., 210), Annex, para. 5, establishing a strong rebuttable presumption of nullification or impairment of GATT benefits, that arises where a *prima facie* violation of GATT is established. This was applied, for instance, in EEC: Import Regime for Bananas (Colombia, Costa Rica, Guatemala, Nicaragua and Venezuela v. EEC) (*Bananas II*), GATT Doc. 38/R (18 Jan. 1994) (not yet adopted), para. 167. In the *Superfund* case, *supra* note 55, at para. 5.1.9 (dealing with a violation of Art. III:2, whereas the *CAFE* case involved a violation of Art. III:4), this presumption was treated as virtually irrebuttable. In any event, some evidence of trade effects of the GATT-infringing aspect of the CAFE rules may well be procurable.

weigh dolphin lives against the commercial costs to the Mexican or EU tuna industries. GATT panels should not question the environmental goals of countries or the values that underlie these goals.'[59] But this argument is used to buttress the view that GATT should not have gotten involved in passing judgment on the US primary embargo on tuna, as GATT is the wrong forum and its 'consideration of environmental disputes is bound to be unbalanced.'[60]

Trade regimes have followed one of three basic patterns when required to address the problem of conflicts between trade objectives and environmental concerns. One pattern is for the trade body itself to 'go green,' setting its own environmental standards, pursuing active environmental programs, and resolving conflicts in accordance with substantive provisions setting priorities between trade and environmental rules. This is the strategy of the European Union, which has adopted numerous substantive environmental directives and regulations, a series of environmental Action Plans, and amendments to its constitutive Treaty placing environmental and trade goals on comparable footing and providing guidance in the event of conflict among them. After much wrangling, the EU finally established its own Environmental Agency in Copenhagen, although with nothing like the powers of the US Environmental Protection Agency. A second pattern is represented by the 1992 North American Free Trade Agreement (NAFTA) and the 1993 North American Agreement on Environmental Cooperation (the environmental side agreement). The initial unwillingness of the parties to include provisions on environmental protection was overborne by a political outcry in the United States. NAFTA and the side agreement do not themselves establish many substantive environmental standards, but they provide normative and institutional means to address several of the most contentious environment–trade problems. The 1993 Agreement established a North American Commission for Environmental Cooperation (based in Montreal) with some powers to supervise enforcement of national environmental laws and to initiate and promote environmental cooperation.[61] The WTO represents a third pattern. Its treaties

[59] Charnovitz, *Dolphins and Tuna*, *supra* note 47, at 10586.

[60] *Id.* at 10584.

[61] *See generally* Steve Charnovitz, *The NAFTA Environmental Side Agreement: Implications for Environmental Cooperation, Trade Policy, and American Treatymaking*, 8 TEMICLJ 257 (1994). For the purposes of provisions requiring states parties to enforce effectively their environmental law, the 1993 North American Agreement on Environmental Cooperation (Art. 45) stipulates:

> '[E]nvironmental law' means any statute or regulation of a Party, or provision thereof, the primary purpose of which is the protection of the environment, or the prevention of a danger to human life or health, through
>
> (i) the prevention, abatement or control of the release, discharge, or emission of pollutants or environmental contaminants,
>
> (ii) the control of environmentally hazardous or toxic chemicals, substances, materials and wastes, and the dissemination of information related thereto, or

establish a body of trade rules, and address environmental measures by channeling them through a set of exceptions and limitations, most of which are not expressly 'environmental'. The WTO regime has no authoritative source of substantive environmental standards to weigh alongside trade standards, only a politically limited and arduous process for making new rules, a modest set of exception clauses not wholly suited to environmental objectives, and a system of dispute settlement and supervision that has not hitherto been environment-oriented or as open as many environmentalists wish. Whereas the EU now has 15 members, and NAFTA at present has three, the WTO has over 120 members, with widely divergent interests in standards affecting trade and environmental policies. In such a heterogeneous body dealing with all manner of considerations bearing on global trade, a pluralist system of modest ambition is the inevitable starting point.

The *Tuna-Dolphin* and other trade–environment cases have forced the WTO—an institution established under international law to manage one regime, that of international trade—to confront measures affecting a historically quite distinct but increasingly important issue area, that of environmental protection. Pressure to move toward either the EU or the NAFTA model may also be understood as pressure to move from a system of governance—rules defining social practices, assigning roles, and guiding interactions to facilitate cooperation and overcome collective action problems—to government (material entities or organizations to administer rules). But, as Oran Young points out, experience of interagency and inter-regime problems within national systems indicates that 'the creation of a government offers no assurance that these linkage problems will be resolved efficiently, much less equitably.'[62] As a practical matter, there is no institution with the breath and effectiveness to resolve most trade–environment problems at the global level. In a more advanced legal system there might be a body of overarching competence to resolve such problems, but the only general judicial body, the International Court of Justice, is not likely to deal with such cases very often, and political bodies such as the UN Commission on Sustainable Development are not effective enough to resolve many sharply focused disputes.[63] Nor is there an environmental institution comparable to the WTO with which the WTO might enter into

(iii) the protection of wild flora or fauna, including endangered species, their habitat, and specially protected natural areas in the Party's territory.

(Provisions directly related to worker safety or health, and certain provisions concerning natural resources, are expressly excluded.)

[62] ORAN R. YOUNG, INTERNATIONAL GOVERNANCE: PROTECTING THE ENVIRONMENT IN A STATELESS SOCIETY 26 (1994). On governance and government, see *id.* at 15–16. On the theme of 'global governance,' which has entered the wider political realm, see, *e.g.*, COMMISSION ON GLOBAL GOVERNANCE, OUR GLOBAL NEIGHBOURHOOD (1995).

[63] *See*, however, Jeffrey Dunoff, *Institutional Misfits: The GATT, the ICJ & Trade–Environment Disputes*, 15 MICHJIL 1043 (1994), arguing that a negotiating body is of more value in complex polycentric disputes than is a body employing an adjudicative structure.

negotiations and accommodations. Struck by this imbalance, some environmentalists have argued for institutional emulation. The trade-environment debate has spawned post-UNCED proposals for a new Global (or International) Environmental Organization to match the GATT/WTO system, ranging from a powerful decision-making and implementation body incorporating many existing organizations[64] to a less grandiose institution modelled on the International Labour Organization with its distinctive tripartite structure of government, employer, and employee representatives.[65] While an environmental organization might well have been established had the idea been current in the period of institution building after World War II, the sentiment of states has turned against enlargement of costly international bureaucracy. Many such proposals were mooted before the 1992 UNCED,[66] but the outcome was more modest: creation of the intergovernmental UN Commission on Sustainable Development with limited resources, without superseding any existing bodies.[67] Even energetic advocates of a powerful new global environmental organization acknowledge that the creation of such a body is most unlikely in the near term.[68] The WTO provides the only global dispute settlement forum in which many trade–environment problems are likely to be resolved. Given the limited ambit of the WTO regime, trade–environment problems raise the need for what Young terms 'governance systems', wider than the regime but falling well short of 'government'. The system of public international law is the juridical expression of such a governance system.

E. The WTO Should Apply Only WTO Principles

The separation of trade and environment, and the absence of substantive environmental principles within the WTO system, amounts to an assertion of the autonomy of the trade sphere vis-à-vis environmental policy. In the 1991 *Tuna-Dolphin* case the panel stated that in accordance with its terms of reference, 'its task was limited to the examination of this matter "*in the light of the relevant GATT provisions*", and therefore did not call for a

[64] *E.g.*, Daniel Esty, *GATTing the Greens*, 72:5 FOREIGN AFFAIRS 32 (1993). *See also* DANIEL ESTY, GREENING THE GATT: TRADE, ENVIRONMENT, AND THE FUTURE (1994); and C. FORD RUNGE, FREER TRADE, PROTECTED ENVIRONMENT: BALANCING TRADE LIBERALIZATION AND ENVIRONMENTAL INTERESTS 101–5 (1994).

[65] Charnovitz, *The Environment vs. Trade Rules: Defogging the Debate*, *supra* note 47, at 513. See also Hilary French, *Strengthening Global Environmental Governance*, *in* STATE OF THE WORLD 1992, 155 (Lester R. Brown ed., 1992).

[66] *See, e.g.*, THE INTERNATIONAL POLITICS OF THE ENVIRONMENT 33–5 (Andrew Hurrell & Benedict Kingsbury eds., 1992); LEE KIMBALL, FORGING INTERNATIONAL AGREEMENTS: STRENGTHENING INTER-GOVERNMENTAL INSTITUTIONS FOR ENVIRONMENT AND DEVELOPMENT (1992).

[67] *See generally* Patricia Birnie, *The UN and the Environment*, *in* UNITED NATIONS, DIVIDED WORLD 327–83 (Adam Roberts & Benedict Kingsbury eds., 2nd ed. 1993).

[68] ESTY, GREENING THE GATT, *supra* note 64, at 98; Steve Charnovitz, *The World Trade Organization and Social Issues*, 28 JWT 17, 29 (1994).

finding on the appropriateness of the United States' and Mexico's conservation policies as such.'[69] The WTO's trade-oriented principles are thus hierarchically superior for WTO dispute settlement purposes to the environmental principles found in other parts of international law. The panel saw itself as applying GATT but not general international law; yet the GATT/WTO system is constituted and operated within the international legal system. Failure to make reference to applicable rules of international law because they are not WTO rules manifests the common voluntarist view in international law that parties can—within important limits—choose the applicable rules to be applied by a dispute-settlement body.

The most problematic implications for the WTO dispute settlement system of this principle of applying only WTO rules involve conflicts between WTO rules and state actions taken pursuant to explicit trade-restrictive provisions in a widely accepted multilateral environmental agreement.[70] Such trade restrictions are contemplated in treaties concerning endangered species, certain potentially harmful wastes, and products from certain drift-net fishing nations.[71] The clearest case is the 1987 Montreal Protocol on Protection of the Ozone Layer, which contemplates obligatory and discretionary trade sanctions against non-parties to prevent free-riding states from staying outside the regime and gaining a competitive advantage while undermining its effectiveness. The threat of sanctions seems to have influenced South Korea's belated 1992 decision to become a party to the Protocol—a decision that entailed considerable costs for the semiconductor industry and other users of chlorofluorocarbons. The question of the rights of a WTO member subjected to sanctions for refusing to subscribe to the

[69] *United States Restrictions on Imports of Tuna (1991)*, *supra* note 2, at para. 6.1. The 1994 report of the *Bananas II* panel, *supra* note 58, at para. 168, acknowledged a similar issue, stating that it was

> well aware of the economic and social effects of the EEC measures on ACP [a group of 69 African, Caribbean, and Pacific states parties to the Lomé Convention with the EC] and Latin American banana exporting countries. However, it had to take into account that its terms of reference were to examine the EEC measures at issue exclusively in terms of their legal consistency with the General Agreement . . . The purpose of these [dispute-settlement] procedures is not to modify the rights and obligations under the existing provisions in light of social and economic considerations.

This panel pointed to means (including waivers) that the GATT contracting parties could use to give effect to such considerations.

[70] For a useful 12-fold taxonomy distinguishing different degrees of unilateralism and different degrees of external reach in trade measures, see Steve Charnovitz, *A Taxonomy of Environmental Trade Measures*, 6 GeoIELR 1 (1993). In particular, he distinguishes measures required by, authorized by, supporting without explicit authorization, and unrelated to plurilateral agreements or other international standards.

[71] For discussion of the issues *see, e.g.*, GATT, Group on Environmental Measures and International Trade: Report of the Meeting Held on 5–7 July 1993, GATT Doc. TRE/12 (30 July 1993) at 13–20; Report of the Meeting Held on 5–6 October 1993, GATT Doc. TRE/13 (21 Oct. 1993); Submission by New Zealand, GATT Doc. TRE/W/8 (10 Mar. 1993); Submission by Austria, GATT Doc. TRE/W/19 (1 Oct. 1993); Preparatory Committee for the WTO, Sub-Committee on Trade and Environment, Report of the Meeting Held on 26–27 October 1994, GATT Doc. PC/SCTE/M/4 (14 Nov. 1994).

Montreal Protocol is a difficult one. In this case the coordinate treaties of a horizontal and decentralized legal system establish conflicting rights.

Article 30 of the 1969 Vienna Convention on the Law of Treaties focuses on consent as the basis of treaty obligation (leaving aside the complexities of *jus cogens*), so that in the absence of a contrary intention a treaty to which States A and B are parties continues to govern their relations notwithstanding subsequent conclusion of a contradictory treaty between States B and C.[72] This doctrine suggests that a GATT party ought to be able to insist upon compliance with GATT notwithstanding a widely accepted environmental treaty to which it is not party. There may be doctrinal reasons why this is not correct in a particular case, for example if an objective regime is created, if a state acquiesces in loss of its GATT rights, or if the environmental treaty can be construed as relevant as evidence of a separate rule of customary international law, as subsequent interpretive practice, or even as an authoritative interpretation of a treaty binding on all relevant parties. Despite broad participation, it seems unlikely that states intend GATT/WTO rules to have a hierarchical superiority to other widely accepted multilateral treaties, and practice does not support such an approach.[73] In this area, as in many others in international law, there is fundamental tension between consent-based approaches and the interests of the international community in effective regulation.[74] Several commentators on the problem of conflict of treaty obligations have pointed to the need to take account both of consent and of 'the interests of the international community'.[75] It is not easy (although not impossible) to imagine a

[72] The 1916 decision of the Central American Court of Justice in Costa Rica v. Nicaragua, 11 AJIL 181 (1917), suggests that in an extreme case a state may by one treaty render itself incompetent to conclude another inconsistent treaty with a different state. In general, however, the competence of a state is treated as not being so diminished, and the validity of the later treaty is accepted, leaving open the possibility of liability for breach. *See, e.g.*, OPPENHEIM'S INTERNATIONAL LAW 9th ed., vol. 1, ss. 590–1 (Robert Jennings & Arthur Watts eds., 1992); ARNOLD MCNAIR, THE LAW OF TREATIES 22–3 (1961); CHRISTINE CHINKIN, THIRD PARTIES IN INTERNATIONAL LAW 73–80 (Oxford, 1993).

[73] *See, e.g.*, Henry Zheng, *Defining Relationships and Resolving Conflicts between Interrelated Multinational Trade Agreements: The Experience of the MFA and the GATT*, 25 STANJIL 45 (1988); and Ted McDorman, *The 1991 U.S.–Mexico GATT Panel Report on Tuna and Dolphin: Implications for Trade and Environmental Conflicts*, 17 NORTH CAROLINA JOURNAL OF INTERNATIONAL LAW & COMMERCIAL REGULATION 461 (1992).

[74] *See, e.g.*, Christian Tomuschat, *Obligations Arising for States Without or Against their Will*, 241 RDC 195 (1993); Alain Pellet, *The Normative Dilemma: Will and Consent in International Lawmaking*, 12 AUSTRALIAN YEARBOOK OF INTERNATIONAL LAW 22 (1992); Jonathan Charney, *Universal International Law*, 87 AJIL 529 (1993).

[75] IAN SHEARER, STARKE'S INTERNATIONAL LAW 427–8 (11th ed. 1994); Geraldo Nascimento e Silva, *Le facteur temps et les traités*, 154 RDC 244 (1977); C. Wilfred Jenks, *The Conflict of Law-Making Treaties*, 30 BRITISH YEARBOOK OF INTERNATIONAL LAW 401 (1953). Charles Rousseau found problems with all of the maxims or other generalized solutions, CHARLES ROUSSEAU, DROIT INTERNATIONAL PUBLIC, tome 1, 151-63 (1970). Ian Sinclair concluded his analysis by remarking that it 'will be apparent . . . that Article 30 of the Vienna Convention is in many respects not entirely satisfactory,' and that 'it may possibly have been premature

panel starkly finding that WTO rights prevail over a widely supported multilateral environmental agreement,[76] or even over a clear rule of customary international law. Various rationales for declining to uphold WTO rights are possible, but in practice an element of community policy and non-consensual law-making is likely to be involved. The WTO thus faces the familiar international law conundrum of how to govern states while simultaneously respecting the will of states. On one view the existing structure of international legal argument makes this conundrum unresolvable: international law arguments are destined to move ceaselessly between mere apologias for state wishes and utopian attempts to control states, with each position vulnerable to criticism from the other standpoint.[77]

Most of the solutions presently under discussion in the WTO duck the conundrum by employing state consent.[78] The neatest such solution is a waiver of WTO rules, in favor of the Montreal Protocol and similar treaties: such a waiver may be granted by the vote of two-thirds of WTO members, and effectively binds the entire membership. The voting requirements provide at least a limited check on use of minilateral agreements to evade WTO disciplines for dubious reasons—but the reality of the GATT/WTO system is that votes on waivers would be heavily influenced by extraneous political considerations. If waivers are used, it may be desirable to adopt a code of practice on such waivers, or to base them on the advice of a more technocratic body. Waivers granted in the past, however, have not been to accommodate inconsistent multilateral treaties,[79] and the Uruguay Round Understanding on waivers gives no indication that broad multilateral waivers are contemplated.[80] Several of the major actors, including the United States and the EU, have expressed doubts about the

to establish fixed guidelines.' IAN SINCLAIR, THE VIENNA CONVENTION ON THE LAW OF TREATIES 98 (2nd ed. 1984).

[76] The issue of a possible conflict of obligations for the EEC between GATT and Protocol No. 5 of the Lomé IV Convention was raised by the EEC in EEC: Member States' Import Regimes for Bananas (*Bananas I*), GATT Doc. DS32/R (3 June 1993) (not yet adopted), para. 223, but was not regarded by the Panel as a significant issue.

[77] MARTTI KOSKENNIEMI, FROM APOLOGY TO UTOPIA (1989).

[78] NAFTA deals with the issue by providing (Art. 104) that in the event of a conflict between NAFTA and the specific trade obligations set out in the Convention on the International Trade in Endangered Species, the Basel Convention, the Montreal Protocol, and certain bilateral instruments, the obligations in the separate instrument 'shall prevail to the extent of the inconsistency, provided that where a Party has a choice among equally effective and reasonably available means of complying with such obligations, the Party chooses the alternative that is the least inconsistent with the other provisions of [NAFTA].'

[79] A brief note by the GATT Secretariat reviewing GATT practice concerning waivers is in GATT Doc. TRE/W/18 (1 Oct. 1993).

[80] The Uruguay Round Understanding in Respect of Waivers of Obligations under the General Agreement on Tariffs and Trade 1994 requires that any request 'shall describe the measures which the Member proposes to take, the specific policy objectives which the Member seeks to pursue and the reasons which prevent the Member from achieving its policy objectives by measures consistent with its obligations under the GATT 1994.'

adequacy and appropriateness of using waivers for such a fundamental long-term purpose, and the WTO does not yet have any agreed solution.

Whether the systemic purity of the WTO in applying only WTO principles will continue to be pursued in the future must be doubted. The standard terms of reference for panels have been broadened somewhat by the Uruguay Round, and panels may increasingly come to recognize the wider public function of the WTO and their place within a rule of law system.[81] Autonomy is no longer claimed for WTO trade principles vis-à-vis intellectual property, and it may be wondered whether the WTO will long hold the line on environmental issues. The WTO Trade and Environment Committee has already begun to discuss the relevance to the WTO of principles of environmental policy.[82] From an economic perspective, Robert Repetto argues, 'neither trade liberalization nor environmental protection are inherently or inevitably more important. The measurable efficiency gains from trade liberalization have usually been estimated to be in the range of 1 to 2 percent of GDP. Similarly, the costs of environmental controls and the residual economic losses from environmental damages are both typically 1 to 2 percent of GDP in countries with strong environmental policies, and 3 to 5 percent in countries with weaker policies. Therefore, there is no strong economic case that trade policy should take precedence over environmental policy, or vice versa.'[83]

V. THE LIBERAL THEORY OF INTERNATIONAL LAW

Proponents of a new liberal paradigm for international law envisage an expanding world of liberal states, spreading out from the Western heartland by diffusion or contagion. Such a world is characterized by tendencies toward: the declining use of large-scale military force in inter-state wars;

[81] In discussions in the GATT Council on the *Tuna-Dolphin I* report, several states commented that while the report dealt with a bilateral dispute, it had a wider importance as a statement of principles for the GATT system as a whole, and that this was an important general reason for speedy adoption of the report. On this ground, Mexico and the United States were criticised for not presenting the report for adoption. *See* GATT Docs. C/M/255 (10 Apr. 1992) at 7, and especially C/M/256 (29 May 1992) at 17–18. On the tension between the functions of maintaining law and settling disputes in the work of international arbitral and adjudicative bodies generally, see Christine Gray & Benedict Kingsbury, *Developments in Dispute Settlement: Inter-State Arbitration Since 1945*, 63 BRITISH YEARBOOK OF INTERNATIONAL LAW 97, 114–9 (1992).

[82] For an extensive list, ranging from the polluter pays and the precautionary principle to intergenerational equity and life cycle management, see OECD, Environmental Principles and Concepts, OECD Doc. COM/ENV/TD(93)117/REV2 (3 Oct. 1994). *See also* OECD, Trade Principles and Concepts, OECD Doc. COM/ENV/TD(93)91/REV2 (3 Oct. 1994). Both papers were prepared for the OECD Joint Meeting of Trade and Environment Experts, 10–12 Oct. 1994.

[83] *See* Robert Repetto, *Complementarities between Trade and Environment Policies*, *in* TRADE AND THE ENVIRONMENT, *supra* note 18, at 237.

states becoming representative liberal democracies with independent judiciaries and flourishing domestic and trans-border civil societies; free, if regulated, market economies fueling social interaction and demands for legal norms and institutions; increasingly dense patterns of transnational interactions among all organs exercising governmental authority, ranging from judiciaries to securities regulators and sub-national legislatures; and the erosion of significant distinctions between the international (including foreign policy) and the domestic. The international legal system should no longer be modelled as the law made by states to regulate their mutual relations. Rather it should be seen to comprise: norms of interaction for individuals and groups in transnational civil society, many of which are chosen voluntarily by contract even if they often rely on state power for enforcement; rules and decisions promulgated by state institutions in transnational dialogue with other relevant institutions; and the law controlling state action, which will be a mixture of international agreements and national law, and will generally be subject to enforcement in national courts and in supranational courts of which the EU's European Court of Justice is a prototype.[84]

This account seems to have much to offer. It captures the process of transnational legal interaction much better than do mainstream rule-oriented accounts. It acknowledges the impact of the market for legal rules and institutions, which has been well documented in such fields as international commercial arbitration. It incorporates the large bodies of legal practice which take place with little or no reference to state legal institutions, such as the establishment of standards (enforced by peer pressure) by transnational industry groups. It takes note of the ways in which political processes and transnational pressures condition state lawmaking and implementation. It gives some account of the patterns of convergence and harmonization among national laws, and through the analytical device of dialogue offers at least a possible view of ways to ameliorate conflicts among legal systems. It unifies public and private, domestic and international. It caters to a limited degree to the impulses of cosmopolitanism, but without implausible displacement of states or the even more implausible postulate that behavior will be based on a universalist ethic of equal duties to all human beings. It takes account of context and of values—at least process values, and probably liberal market values too.

Positing such a liberal conception of international law as a substitute for

[84] *See* in particular Anne-Marie Slaughter Burley, *International Law and International Relations Theory: A Dual Agenda*, 87 AJIL 205 (1993); Anne-Marie Slaughter, *International Law in a World of Liberal States*, EUROPEAN JOURNAL OF INTERNATIONAL LAW (forthcoming 1995). The account of international law as the liberal law of a transnational civil society discussed in the present article is an amalgam of various current ideas, not necessarily shared by any particular author—the comments relate to the hybrid account, not to the positions of individual authors.

the standard inter-state conception, does it cast any more illumination on the problems surrounding the five WTO principles discussed above?

First, the problem of the democratic deficit might be met by opening the WTO to wider participation. Systems of NGO participation and direct elections may be more richly described by the liberal account—while they are understood within the existing inter-state framework, they fit uneasily. The more fundamental problems of representation in international trade are, first, that national political processes attach much greater weight to the domestic interests represented there, and second, that both national and international political processes tend to attach more importance to the concretized interests of likely winners and losers than to the diffuse interests of larger groups whose losses or gains may in aggregate be much greater but more distant and less explicit.[85] One function of international institutions such as the WTO is to counter distortions introduced by these defects in representation. The liberal theory would suggest adopting a system in which interests, *e.g.*, of exporters in other states are directly represented in the national political process, and in which diffuse interests are concretized through specifically empowered representatives. There have already been modest developments in these directions, evident in limited representation of foreign and diffuse interests in US politics and in representational devices in the EU. The liberal scheme explains these developments much better than does the traditional framework with its assumption that foreign interests are represented through foreign states.

Second, the difficulty of unilateralism is that while almost all states are against it—and there would be dire consequences for the international system if most states regularly attempted unilateral enforcement—in the decentralized legal system unilateral trade measures can seem to bring results, not only for the state using them, but on occasion for the international community more generally. One influential theory holds that over and above unilateral attempts by states to enforce existing international rules, certain violations of WTO rules by unilateral enforcement of self-promulgated liberal trade standards above WTO levels make a positive contribution in forcing the evolution of WTO standards.[86] The perception of a degree of success for the United States with threats of trade sanctions in market access and intellectual property disputes, under Section 301 and related legislation, reinforces this view.[87] In states accustomed to commit-

[85] *See, e.g.*, Robert Hudec, *'Circumventing' Democracy: The Political Morality of Trade Negotiations*, 25 NYUJILP 311 (1993), drawing lessons from the circumstances (especially logrolling) in which US democracy produced the 1930 Smoot-Hawley tariff, which exacerbated the world-wide economic depression.

[86] Robert Hudec, *Thinking About the New Section 301: Beyond Good and Evil*, *in* AGGRESSIVE UNILATERALISM 113 (Jagdish Bhagwati & Hugh Patrick eds., 1990).

[87] Section 301 of the Trade and Tariff Act of 1974, reenacted and modified to become sections 301–310 of the Omnibus Trade and Competitiveness Act of 1988, and the Super 301 and

ting such forcing violations, it is a short step for domestic groups interested in environmental protection to advocate violations of trade rules to promote acceptance of these goals.

The dilemmas of unilateralism might theoretically be avoided by a radical shift to either a federal-type system with some central standard-setting and enforcement, or a supranational system with central standard-setting and local enforcement monitored from the center. At the international level such a vision applies at most to the EU—and unilateralism has not been eliminated there. The liberal framework does not resolve the problem, but posits the containment of unilateralism through the embedding of state power in a network of shared values and overlapping interests. Some liberals advocate unilateral enforcement as a substitute for collective action in rare cases where it is vitally needed to uphold a widely-supported norm and the arguments for it outweigh its very high costs. This argument for circumscribed unilateralism harmonizes with the liberal disinclination to maintain the equality of states as a central tenet. This is a highly controversial prescription, as the *Tuna-Dolphin* debates amply demonstrate, but the liberal framework does at least provide a structure within which to explain and make some sense of current US practice.

Third, the mismatch between ecosystems and the territorial structure of sovereign states creates grave problems of environmental management. The WTO principle of non-impingement may exacerbate some of these problems. The liberal conception of international law proposes several devices to address these problems: integrating local, national, and international decision-making and rule enforcement to promote optimal commons management; creating valuable interests in commons to overcome the market failures analyzed as tragedies of the commons, including some of the inequities resented by developing countries; and assuring adequate representation within national decision-making systems of interests of those living in other states. All of these devices are intelligible within the present inter-state system, but the liberal conception may well be richer in describing them and explaining their operation. When it comes to the hard issue of the use of trade sanctions as a technique for influencing environmental choices of other states, the liberal theory has fewer clear implications. Environmentalists often favor sanctions through market closure or selective incentives through market access, in order to expedite standard-setting, raise standards, and induce compliance. Yet sanctions have grave problems. As the *Tuna-Dolphin* cases graphically demonstrated, states are often

Special 301 procedures. For an extensive review of practice, see Thomas O. Bayard & Kimberly Ann Elliot, RECIPROCITY AND RETALIATION IN U.S. TRADE POLICY (1994). They argue that the expanded scope of WTO coverage and the reform of WTO dispute settlement machinery, achieved through the Uruguay Round agreements, will raise the cost of aggressive unilateralism, and should lead US practice to focus more on aggressive multilateralism (through WTO procedures).

bitterly hostile to sanctions as a means of pursuing environmental objectives even where they themselves endorse and pursue similar environmental policies. Sanctions may lead to domestic distortions, conflicts of externally-imposed conditions (*e.g.*, between International Monetary Fund government spending reductions, and monitoring and enforcement obligations under endangered species treaties), and half-hearted commitments, especially where internationally agreed standards do not exist or are not widely observed. Precise standards enforced by sanctions, and the timing of sanctions, are controlled by the sanctioning nations, and tend to coincide with the circumstances of their own industries and with the balance of domestic political interests. Developing countries often complain that they are willing to adopt new standards but that they are kept off balance by pressure to do this impossibly quickly, at the pace dictated by technological innovation, political change, and economic advantage in the rich countries. In some cases ineffectiveness of commons regimes is partly attributable to refusal of rich countries to compensate poor countries for lost opportunities or higher costs in complying with a new regime, an inequity generating compounded resentment where rich countries have in the past profited from depletion of the same commons. The liberal theory suggests that the damage sanctions cause to the people affected, and the inequities associated with sanctions, ought to weigh more heavily than the existing framework proposes: here, however, the liberal account may be more prescriptive than descriptive.

Fourth, the discordance arising from separate institutional competences, where trade bodies address 'trade' matters and environmental bodies address 'environmental' matters, is addressed in liberal theory through integration of these distinct but overlapping spheres into wider systems of governance. In a transnational civil society with sufficient density of interaction and mechanisms of participation, governance regimes of overarching competence will eventually emerge. While functional specialization and differentiation of formal institutions will remain, specialist regimes will be embedded within a wider structure allocating competences and via jurisdictional rules on the basis of more rational analysis of needs. The principle of respect for local decisions, expressed for example through the doctrine of subsidiarity, would apply, but with qualifications: for instance, that local decisions do not command respect if not reached authentically through procedural due process in a representative system. It is quite possible, however, that adherence to the WTO regime would be weakened if sovereign competence were routinely displaced in the environmental area. The permeability of transformed institutional competences envisaged in the liberal theory would thus have to follow from the existence of a flourishing transnational civil society, rather than leading it.

Fifth, the liberal theory holds out the possibility of transcending the conundrum created by the need of the inter-state legal system to both respect the will of states (which gives it authority) and restrain the exercise of that will (through international regulation and enforcement). The liberal theory proposes that states not be understood as autonomous sovereigns subject to nothing but themselves and the rules they have agreed to. It makes the plausible point that states and inter-state institutions do not and need not occupy the whole field. Rather states should be seen simply as important loci of power and authority within a transnational civil society which permeates through their borders. That society finds voice and political expression through states but not only through states—the interests of individuals and groups are also expressed in many other ways. International law can be seen as the law of such a transnational society, regulating states but not dependent entirely on states for its existence, content, or implementation. In more ambitious versions of this theory, state sovereignty is in some respects constituted by the law of the transnational civil society, escaping the tendency within the traditional framework for international law to take sovereignty as a pre-legal social fact. While the law of the transnational civil society is weak and overwhelmingly dominated by states, the basic conditions of the Hobbesian anarchy (the metaphoric war of all against all) and the security dilemma (the need of each state to achieve security, which inevitably threatens the security of others) may persist: but the possibility of their transcendence becomes a visible glimmer.

VI. CONCLUSION

The *Tuna-Dolphin* cases and the WTO trade–environment debates raise difficult issues for the international legal order. All five of the WTO principles discussed here are intelligible within the traditional framework of international law. The problems with them point to discordance between the traditional model of the inter-state legal system and contemporary needs. The liberal theory of international law as the law of an emerging transnational civil society has important attractions in responding to globalization and in proposing a theory of states in a legal system rather than a legal system of states. When applied to a set of specific problems, it exhibits useful explanatory power, but on some of the hard issues seems to be more a vision of future worlds than an operational problem-solving system for the present one. While the European Union, beloved archetype of liberal theorists, has departed in interesting ways from all five principles adhered to by the WTO, the EU remains an institution for the maintenance of states and sovereignty rather than their eclipse. As the expansive vision of European Union is being called into question even in Europe, its value as a model for the future of global organization must remain very doubtful.

The liberal framework of international law is helpful, but its proponents are often animated by a vision of a transformed world, and tend to use the theory to prescribe for the whole world rather than simply to explain parts. This triumphalist tendency sees the West as the only viable model, beckoning or coercing those in the outer zones of turmoil to transplant and internalize the Western liberal package.[88]

If the future world envisaged by proponents of the liberal framework were ever to evolve, would it be as rosy as the most optimistic depictions suggest? Probably not. The weakening of the juridical equality of states would probably magnify existing disparities of power, and license the increased use of that power. New layers of privilege among states and polities would emerge, probably rewarding particular types of democratic polities and particular thriving economic models. Some states would decline, but successful states could well maintain their positions and profit from the decline of others. Essential new principles about optimal levels of government and the management of regulatory competition at different levels would not easily be agreed. If a transnational civil society can be said to exist and to be important, the power relations within it are not necessarily more equitable than those in the interstate system, and it may contribute no more to solving fundamental problems of poverty, environmental degradation, and sustainable development besetting much of humanity than does the inter-state system as traditionally conceived. The emergence of necessary social patterns and structures within such a society would be a slow and conflictual process. The UN is already struggling with the problem of determining which NGOs legitimately represent which interest, and systems of accountability of civil society organizations are rudimentary at best. Such a society is bound to be associated by many with increasing globalization and cultural homogenization or dominance, and may well be viewed with suspicion by those people, including members of some indigenous and nationalist groups, who already oppose the WTO, NAFTA, and similar arrangements. Although it addresses problems with principles animating the WTO, the liberal vision of a future world is diametrically opposed to the foes of 'GATTzilla,' for whom neither transformative globalization nor the cosmopolitan liberal displacement of national sovereignty seem remotely desirable.

In the case of the WTO, major trade–environment issues clearly remain to be addressed, and the problems with the principles hitherto espoused by the WTO are manifest. Nevertheless, these principles serve important purposes for WTO constituencies. Many developing countries perceive in proposals for liberal modification of WTO principles the risks of inhibited economic development of the South, and legitimation of further Northern

[88] *Cf.* Daniel Deudney & John Ikenberry, *The Logic of the West*, 10 World Policy Journal 17 (1993–94).

involvement in matters of Southern sovereignty. The practical experience of many developing countries has included actual or threatened reductions of trade gains because of environmental trade measures taken by developed countries. Developing countries have strong environmental interests, and in some cases wish themselves to take environmental measures affecting trade. Many have benefitted from improved environmental technology or other advances made in the North. Nevertheless, they rightly perceive the current proposals to alter trade rules to have been raised and structured primarily in Organisation for Economic Cooperation and Development countries and to express particular Northern environmental concerns. Sorsa articulates a view widely held in developing countries:

> GATT rules can protect them from new forms of protectionism under the guise of environmental policy, reinforce the respect of sovereignty in trade relations and shift emphasis from the use of trade sanctions to negotiations and creation of incentives in promoting the adoption of environmental policies worldwide. The rule-based multilateral system protects the interests of small countries against power-based unilateral policing by large countries.[89]

The historical pattern is that developing countries, and NGOs from such countries, are able to secure hortatory provisions and rhetorical recognition of their positions, but that the substantive outcomes are heavily influenced by the North. This might suggest that the liberal agenda is likely to advance. The WTO trade–environment debate has a different dynamic, however, as the developing countries collectively have some commonality of interest and in many cases take positions close to the status quo, whereas the liberal revisionist agenda is constrained by the complex interplay of interests within Northern states and among policies those states pursue in the international legal system.

As a practical matter, the range of environmental-trade measures likely to be impeded by GATT 1994 is not vast.[90] Given the deep embeddedness of basic WTO values,[91] and the prevailing climate of pragmatism in and

[89] Piritta Sorsa, *GATT and Environment: Basic Issues and Developing Country Concerns*, *in* INTERNATIONAL TRADE AND THE ENVIRONMENT 325, 326 (Patrick Low ed., 1992). For the illustrative views of a Thai government official, see Kittichaisaree, *Using Trade Sanctions and Subsidies*, *supra* note 42. *See also* the views expressed in the May 1991 'Structured Debate' on Trade and Environment, held by the GATT Council, GATT Doc. C/M/250 (28 June 1991) at 2–21, and the comments in the GATT Council on the reports of the *Tuna-Dolphin* panels, in particular GATT Docs. C/M/254 (10 Mar. 1992) at 21–35, C/M/255 (10 Apr. 1992) at 3–14, and C/M/274 (24 Aug. 1994) at 6–10.

[90] *E.g.*, Charnovitz, *Green Roots, Bad Pruning*, *supra* note 5, at 347–52. Some commentators understate the significance of remaining problematic issues—*see*, *e.g.*, David Palmeter, *Environment and Trade: Much Ado About Little?*, 27 JWT 55 (1993).

[91] John Gerard Ruggie, *International Regimes, Transactions, and Change: Embedded Liberalism in the Postwar Economic Order*, 36 INTERNATIONAL ORGINIZATIONS 195 (1982); and Ruggie, *Embedded Liberalism Revisited: Institutions and Progress in International Economic Relations*, *in* PROGRESS IN POSTWAR INTERNATIONAL RELATIONS 201 (Emanuel Adler & Beverley Crawford eds., 1991).

around the WTO, it seems likely that there will be incremental developments in many of the directions addressed by the liberal project. Radical transformation of the existing framework, if it happens at all, is surely not imminent. Although the existing framework will evolve somewhat, the WTO cannot be expected to model itself on an economic integration organization such as the EU. A pragmatic five-fold strategy for the WTO seems possible: deferring to specific environmental rules adumbrated in widely accepted international treaties or (perhaps) in soft-law instruments; recognizing broad principles of environmental management developed in other international fora; accommodating certain trade measures taken in pursuit of mutually recognized domestic environmental policies meeting certain international standards; continuing to try to rein in tendencies toward unilateralism; and harmonizing WTO rules and procedures with international environmental principles, rules and institutions, including some accommodation of pressures for transparency, openness, participation, and consultation.

Environmental Security and Freshwater Resources: A Case for International Ecosystem Law[1]

Jutta Brunnée and Stephen J. Toope

I. INTRODUCTION

Water sustains life. Water is also fundamental for human society and its sustainable development. Therefore, its availability and quality are increasingly viewed not only as environmental, but also as security concerns. Various factors including population growth, unsustainable use, inefficient systems of distribution, the erosion of indigenous systems of water management, pollution, and ecological degradation suggest that pressure on freshwater supplies will increase substantially in the future. Environmental and security concerns related to freshwater resources will therefore become ever more urgent.

Historically, security analysts paid little attention to environmental issues. In recent years, however, the role of environmental degradation as a generator of local and international conflict has been widely recognized. Environmental factors generally, and competition over scarce resources in particular, have been observed in empirical research as exogenous factors prompting even violent conflict. In this limited sense, 'environmental security' has emerged as a broadly accepted concept. But the impact on security of environmental degradation is broader than the traditional strategic and military conceptions would allow. It arguably encompasses the need to foster a secure environment *per se* and to ensure that healthy ecosystems can continue to sustain human development.

Threats to environmental security are also fed by the lack of generally agreed-upon legal regimes to help shape debate and suggest the outlines of the bargaining endowment of parties to a potential conflict. Even more importantly, the current legal framework focuses almost exclusively on ter-

[1] This article was prepared with the financial assistance of the Cooperative Security Programme of the Department of Foreign Affairs and International Trade of the Government of Canada. We would like to thank the participants in a Workshop on Environmental Security and Freshwater Resources, held at the Faculty of Law, McGill University, Montreal, 11–12 November 1994, many of whom are quoted in the text. In work on our Freshwater Resources Project, we have been ably assisted by Elobaid Ahmed Elobaid, José Vicente Zapata Lugo, Martin Pammer, Greg Firnau, Andreas Sautter, Hiroko Sawai, and Jay Sinha. We are particularly grateful to José Vicente Zapata Lugo for his help in the final preparation of this paper.

ritorial interests of states and competing uses of resources. As a result, existing legal regimes fail to ensure environmental security because they promote neither cooperative behaviour nor effective environmental protection. These failures can only be addressed through the adoption of a more ecosystem-oriented approach to international environmental law.

The goals of this paper are threefold. First, the paper will explore briefly the parameters of environmental security. Second, it will identify factors that may pose threats to environmental security in the context of shared freshwater resources. These factors are relevant not simply to reveal possible sources of conflict, but also to indicate issues that must be addressed in the elaboration of appropriate legal principles, and ultimately regimes. And third, in light of the limitations of current normative frameworks, the paper will evaluate various options that might encourage a stronger ecosystem orientation in international environmental law. In pursuing these objectives, it will be concerned primarily with the elaboration of conceptual frameworks.

II. THE EMERGENCE OF 'ENVIRONMENTAL SECURITY' AS A CONCEPTUAL FRAMEWORK

Since at least the mid-1980s, a chorus of voices has been raised in support of the proposition that the concept of 'security' must be broadened to include recognition of increasing non-military threats to domestic and international peace. Chief amongst these non-military threats is said to be environmental degradation and often attendant resource scarcity.[2] The political science literature contains many references to environmental security as a new element in any sophisticated overall security assessment. Although some voices have cautioned against the invocation of environmental secu-

[2] In fact, at least two prescient observers argued as early as 1965 that ecological factors should be seen as relevant to a sophisticated foreign policy. *See* H. SPROUT & M. SPROUT, THE ECOLOGICAL PERSPECTIVE ON HUMAN AFFAIRS WITH SPECIAL REFERENCE TO INTERNATIONAL POLITICS (1965). This viewpoint became more common in the 1980s, and has been espoused notably by Ullman, *Redefining Security*, 8 INTERNATIONAL SECURITY 129 (1983); Brown, *An Untraditional View of National Security, in* AMERICAN DEFENSE POLICY, (J. Reichart & S. Sturm, eds., 5th ed. 1984); Westing, *The Environmental Component of Comprehensive Security,* 20 BULLETIN OF PEACE PROPOSALS 129 (1989); Mathews, *Redefining Security*, 68 FOREIGN AFFAIRS 162 (1989); Myers, *Environment and Security*, 74 FOREIGN POLICY 41 (1989); Timoshenko, *Ecological Security: Global Change Paradigm,* 1 CoJIELP 127 (1990); Handl, *Environmental Security and Global Change: The Challenge to International Law,* 1 YBIEL 3 (1990); Vinogradov, *International Environmental Security: The Concept and its Implementation, in* PERESTROIKA AND INTERNATIONAL LAW 196 (A. Carter and G. Danilenko, eds., 1990); Gleick, *Environment and Security: Clear Connections*, 47 BULLETIN OF ATOMIC SCIENTISTS 17 (1991); Frédérick, *La sécurité environnementale [:] éléments de définition*, 24 ETUDES INTERNATIONALES 753 (1993); and Gleick, *Water and Conflict: Fresh Water Resources and International Security*, 18 INTERNATIONAL SECURITY 79 (1993).

rity in policy discourse,[3] the term has been appropriated in recent legal literature as well.[4] Despite its currency, the concept of environmental security remains imprecisely defined. Indeed, that imprecision is one of the sources of discomfort noted by some opponents of the concept. Nonetheless, environmental security has become a stubborn fact in the rhetoric of international (and even domestic) security discourse;[5] and it is a useful heuristic device if sensitively defined and somewhat constrained in meaning. Therefore, rather than deny the emergence of the concept, it is more helpful to provide guidance as to its purpose, ambit, and potential influence.

In essence, the debate concerning the existence of a concept of environmental security is but a manifestation of the realist versus international institutionalist debate that has defined much contemporary international relations theory.[6] In explaining international behaviour, should one focus principally, or even entirely, on the self-identified interests of states or are there other sources of normativity affecting international political decision-making? The traditional military and political definitions of security tended to be built on realist assumptions. Attempts to move outside that context and to broaden the notion of security have been greeted with scepticism because some theorists doubt explanations of state behaviour not rooted in a model of patent self-interest.[7] Alternative sources of normativity have been identified, however, including formal or informal institutions, regimes and so-called 'epistemic communities'.

There is at least one approach to environmental security that would not in fact require rejection of the realist posture. Environmental security could

[3] *See, e.g.*, Deudney, *Environment and Security: Muddled Thinking* 47 BULLETIN OF ATOMIC SCIENTISTS 22 (1991); and Bilder, *Remarks During a Workshop on Environmental Security and Freshwater Resources*, held at the Faculty of Law, McGill University, Montreal, 11–12 November 1994 (minutes on file with authors).

[4] *See, e.g.*, Handl *supra* note 2; and Vinogradov, *supra* note 2.

[5] Indeed, the concept is increasingly widely used, and invoked at the highest levels of state policy apparatus. *See, e.g.*, the recent foreign policy statement of the Government of Canada:

> The Government Agrees on the need to adopt a broader concept of security. In addition to taking into account traditional military threats, security policy must include recognition of threats to stability, democracy and sustainable development as well as the threats posed by such factors as environmental degradation, overpopulation, involuntary population movements and organized international crime.

CANADA, GOVERNMENT RESPONSE TO THE RECOMMENDATIONS OF THE SPECIAL JOINT COMMITTEE REVIEWING CANADIAN FOREIGN POLICY 8 (1995).

The linkage between environmental issues and security is even being posited by the state security service in Canada. *See* Rodal, *The Environment and Changing Concepts of Security*, 47 COMMENTARY 1 (A Canadian Security Intelligence Service Publication, 1994).

[6] For a realist perspective in the current context, *see* Deudney, *supra* note 3. For an international institutionalist perspective, *see* O.R. YOUNG, INTERNATIONAL COOPERATION: BUILDING REGIMES FOR NATURAL RESOURCES AND THE ENVIRONMENT (1989); Haas, *Do Regimes Matter? Epistemic Communities and Mediterranean Pollution Control Mediterranean Action Plan (Med Plan)*, 43 INTERNATIONAL ORGANIZATIONS 377 (1989); and Haas *Introduction: Epistemic Communities and International Policy Coordination*, 46 INTERNATIONAL ORGANIZATIONS 1 (1992).

[7] *See, e.g.*, Sorensen, *Rethinking National Security*, 69 FOREIGN AFFAIRS 1 (1990).

be read simply as a signal to pay attention to environmental issues as a factor that may prompt sub-national conflict, and ultimately international conflict. Environmental factors pointing to potential conflict could therefore be treated as independent variables affecting the analysis of traditional *national* security.[8] Even such ground-breaking research as Homer-Dixon's, which focuses on the potential for conflict arising out of 'environmental scarcities',[9] could be assimilated within a standard national security model of international relations.[10]

Analyses rooted in national security preoccupations retain an emphasis on 'conflict' arising from a wide variety of sources. Within this framework, paying attention to environmental security merely calls upon one to analyze those conflicts that result, at least in part, from environmental scarcity, as a central exogenous source of conflict within and ultimately between states. Environmental scarcity encompasses issues of environmental change, population growth, and unequal social distribution of resources.[11] Although resource scarcity may initially lead to local or regional instability this instability, 'may escalate to the international level and may become violent.'[12] Such escalation is more likely if other preexisting social, political, military, or economic tensions are present.[13] The traditional national security focus, which may none the less invoke the rhetoric of environmental security, is also apparent in discussions that treat water as a source of 'strategic rivalry'.[14] Debates over water as an instrument of war are even

[8] Frédérick, *supra* note 2, at 759. *See* also Deudney, *The Case Against Linking Environmental Degradation and National Security*, 19 MILLENNIUM: JOURNAL OF INTERNATIONAL STUDIES 461 (1990).

[9] [E]nvironmental scarcity causes violent conflict. This conflict tends to be persistent, diffuse and sub-national. Its frequency will probably jump sharply in the next decades as scarcities rapidly worsen in many parts of the world. Of immediate concern are scarcities of cropland, water, forests and fish. . . . Countries experiencing chronic internal conflict because of environmental stress will probably either fragment or become more authoritarian. Either outcome could seriously disturb international relations.

Homer-Dixon, *Environmental Scarcities and Violent Conflict: Evidence from Cases*, 19 INTERNATIONAL SECURITY 5, 40 (1994).

[10] *See, e.g.*, Homer-Dixon, *On the Threshold: Environmental Changes as Causes of State Conflict*, 16 INTERNATIONAL SECURITY 76 (1991); Homer-Dixon, *Environmental Change and Violent International Conflict*, 268 SCIENTIFIC AMERICAN 38 (1993); and Homer-Dixon, *supra* note 9.

[11] *Id.*

[12] Like Homer-Dixon, Gleick argues that the security aspect of environmental scarcity is rooted in competition between states. Gleick, 1993, *supra* note 2, at 79. *See also* Mathews, *supra* note 2; Anderson, *Water: The Next Strategic Resource*, *in* THE POLITICS OF SCARCITY: WATER IN THE MIDDLE EAST 2, 19 (J. Starr & D. Stoll, eds., 1988); and Carter, *Remarks During a Workshop on Environmental Security and Freshwater Resources*, held at the Faculty of Law, McGill University, Montreal, 11-12 November 1994 (minutes on file with authors).

[13] *See, e.g.*, Gleick *supra* note 2, at 84; and Frédérick, *supra* note 2, at 760.

[14] *See, e.g.*, Anderson, *supra* note 12; Gleick, *Reducing the Risks of Conflict Over Fresh Water Resources in the Middle East*, *in* WATER AND PEACE IN THE MIDDLE EAST 41 (Isaac & Shuval, eds., 1994).

more firmly rooted in the national security paradigm, whatever the terminology used.[15]

An emphasis on conflict arising from environmental scarcity could, however, push the environmental security analysis in a different and far less traditional direction. Scarcity may result in part from unequal distribution of resources within societies. One way of analyzing inequality as a generator of conflict is through the lens of economic and social rights.[16] On this reading, the security concern would not relate so much to states as to people within states; environmental security would therefore be closely linked to human rights, and not merely to the so-called third-generation right to a healthy environment, but to the more broadly accepted economic and social rights, or even to the most basic right to life.[17]

Although this human rights approach to environmental security is morally attractive, it is unlikely to be politically persuasive. Bending the concept of security to encompass equality rights vis-à-vis resources is unlikely to attract the allegiance of state policymakers who are seeking some conceptual clarity. If every issue comes to be treated as a question of human rights, then no hard rules are likely to evolve; the restrictions on state action will prove to be too great. Moreover, governments of developed states will almost certainly resist a rights analysis of environmental security so as to avoid parallel political and legal arguments about equal distribution of resources between the North and the South.[18] Finally, speaking of rights to water, for example, may not make sense in contexts where demand exceeds supply.[19]

By rejecting the conceptual linkage between equal rights and environmental security, one need not, however, fall back into an exclusive preoccupation with state interests and national security. A middle road exists that can accommodate the legitimate environmental interests of individual human beings and sub-national communities within an analysis that makes sense in terms of security as historically understood. Thus, a more challenging version of environmental security may be articulated, one that emphasizes the maintenance (or re-establishment) of ecological balance, at

[15] *See, e.g.*, Dyer, *Environment and Security [:] Environmental Warfare in the Gulf*, 2 Ecodecision 21 (1991).

[16] International Covenant on Economic, Social and Cultural Rights, reprinted in 993 UNTS 3 (1966), Arts. 3, 11, and 12.

[17] *See, e.g.*, Kiss, *Remarks During a Workshop on Environmental Security and Freshwater Resources*, held at the Faculty of Law, McGill University, Montreal, 11–12 November 1994 (minutes on file with authors).

[18] *See, e.g.*, Gleick, *Environment, Resources, and International Security and Politics, in* Science and International Security: Responding to a Changing World 501, 514 (E. Arnett, ed., 1990).

[19] Davis, *Remarks During a Workshop on Environmental Security and Freshwater Resources*, held at the Faculty of Law, McGill University, Montreal, 11–12 November 1994 (minutes on file with authors).

least to the extent necessary to sustain resource supplies and life-support systems. The security dimension would thus become regional or global, not purely national, in orientation. Energy would be redirected to the protection of the security of the environment itself, rather than merely being concerned with the security of state structures.

As will be argued more fully below, it is not necessary to adopt an entirely ecocentric stance in order to claim that security of the environment *per se* should occupy a more prominent place in legal and policy debates. As a matter of *human* concern, and at an admittedly instrumental level, the security of the environment has become an increasingly important preoccupation: '"[S]ecurity" in a broad sense entails the strength of the economic, environmental, and ecological foundations that underpin our material and social welfare.'[20] An impaired environment, therefore, is relevant to security not only because of the violent subnational and international conflict that it may engender, but because security relates also to our quality of life and standard of living. Degraded ecosystems threaten to destroy 'goods' worth preserving even before violent conflict occurs; even if conflict is suppressed for various reasons, the people's security has been damaged when their way of life has been harmed, even destroyed.

In this extended sense, environmental security is best viewed as an aspect of sustainable development.[21] Security for the environment would suggest that in our desire to meet current needs we pay attention to the environmental consequences of our actions and inactions, both imminent and longer term.[22] Therefore, the term environmental security should be understood as two-dimensional. The expansive sense of the concept calls on us to consider the environment *per se*, even if from a homocentric and instrumentalist position, in assessing the consequences of policy decisions. The security referred to is the maintenance or re-establishment of ecological balance. On the other hand, in emphasizing the dimension of security in the traditional sense of state integrity, the term refers to the prevention or management of conflict over scarce or degraded resources.[23] In this paper, both senses of environmental security are relevant, although it will become obvious that the expansive understanding will shape many of our assessments of appropriate normative evolution. Though a focus on traditional national security and international conflict remains important, the needed changes

[20] Gleick, *supra* note 18, at 506. *See also* Mathews, *supra* note 2, at 166.

[21] *See infra* note 133 and accompanying text.

[22] *See* Timoshenko, *Remarks During a Workshop on Environmental Security and Freshwater Resources*, held at the Faculty of Law, McGill University, Montreal, 11–12 November 1994 (minutes on file with authors), and Kiss, *supra* note 17.

[23] It should not be overlooked that some developing states may perceive the very idea of 'environmental security' to be yet another device through which the developed world seeks to gain influence or control over sovereign resources. *See* Saad, *For Whose Benefit? Redefining Security*, 2 ECODECISION 59 (1991).

in the legal regimes related to freshwater resources will only become possible if the newer and more creative understanding of environmental security is effectively promoted. Indeed, it could be argued that security, even as traditionally understood, can only be assured in the future if appropriate attention is paid to ecological imperatives.

III. SOURCES OF ENVIRONMENTAL INSECURITY

Most of the analysis of factors relevant to the security dimension of shared freshwater resources adopts a traditional national security perspective. Hence, the focus is on potential sources of conflict. The conflict may originate within states, but it is treated as a distinct 'security' threat when the potential for conflict spills across international boundaries. Typically, categorizations of potential sources of conflict over international rivers emphasize: access and control over water flow; uses of the river system itself that negatively affect other present or future uses; and activities beyond the river system *per se*, but that adversely affect it.[24] While the first category is concerned primarily with issues of water quantity, the latter two are focused on water quality.

Although this dominant approach to freshwater resource conflict remains relevant, it is not adequate to address the broader conception of environmental security argued for in this paper. For example, the very distinction between water quantity and water quality that underlies much of the existing conflict analysis is of limited relevance to a model of environmental security aimed at protecting ecological balance and allowing for sustainable human development. Arguably, even under the traditional conflict framework, the explanatory power of the distinction is not compelling. Conflicts caused by water quantity problems and those caused by water quality degradation may not actually result in differing patterns of state behaviour, for, in both cases, access to usable water ultimately becomes constrained. To establish the factual underpinnings for the emerging normative frameworks, it is, therefore, important to clearly identify the factors that may prompt environmental insecurity in the context of freshwater resources. Some of these factors point directly to the necessity for ecologically centred legal principles; others are more directly related to the elaboration of specific treaty regimes.

[24] J. TROLLDALEN, INTERNATIONAL ENVIRONMENTAL CONFLICT RESOLUTION: THE ROLE OF THE UNITED NATIONS 63 (1992).

A. *Factors That Promote Environmental Insecurity*

(i) Population Growth and Migration

Population growth, especially if uncontrolled, is a principal contributor to conflict over shared freshwater resources, in part because it tends to exacerbate other conflict-inducing factors.[25] It is equally relevant to a security analysis focused on ecological balance and sustainable development. The population factor is very useful in revealing the impossibility of separating out issues of water quantity and water quality. Population growth leads to increased consumption and sometimes to demands for the damming and diversion of rivers. It also results in increased waste and pollution, which may adversely affect water quality.[26] Unsustainable population growth can also lead to social pressures, a breakdown of order, and to the erosion of traditional systems of water management, particularly in rural communities.[27] Although, as with many of the potential sources of environmental insecurity, the tension of population growth is likely to be felt first locally, the pressures will soon be felt by national governments.[28] Moreover, local population growth can lead to internal migration, shifting the pressure on water supply to new districts. Ultimately, if the national supply of water becomes insufficient or degraded, the migration may become international in scope, thereby providing a related but independently identifiable source of potential conflict.[29]

(ii) Unsustainable Agricultural Practices and Irrigation

Unsustainable agricultural practices, often linked to massive irrigation projects, can adversely affect both water quantity and water quality. A host of interrelated issues are involved. In many countries, irrigation consumes an

[25] *See, e.g.*, Utton, *The Development of International Groundwater Law*, in INTERNATIONAL GROUNDWATER LAW 1 (L. Teclaff & A. Utton, eds., 1981); J. Starr & D. Stoll, U.S. FOREIGN POLICY ON WATER RESOURCES IN THE MIDDLE EAST 11 (1987); Allen, *Review of Evolving Water Demands and National Development Options*, *in* THE NILE: RESOURCE EVALUATION, RESOURCE MANAGEMENT, HYDROPOLITICS AND LEGAL ISSUES 184, 185 (P. Howell & J. Allen, eds., 1990); Ohlsson, *Water—An Elusive and Ultimate Constraint for Development*, *in* REGIONAL CASE STUDIES OF WATER CONFLICTS 2, 11 (L. Ohlsson, ed., 1992); and Mathews, *supra* note 2, at 163.

[26] Starr, *Water Wars*, 82 FOREIGN POLICY 17, 19 (1991).

[27] A. SHEPHERD & A. EL NEIMA, POPULAR PARTICIPATION IN DECENTRALISED WATER SUPPLY PLANNING: A CASE STUDY IN THE WESTERN DISTRICT OF NORTHERN KORDOFAN PROVINCE OF SUDAN 7 (1983).

[28] Widstrand, *Conflicts over Water*, *in* WATER CONFLICTS AND RESEARCH PRIORITIES 121, 139 (C. Widstrand, ed., 1978).

[29] N. BESHORNER, WATER AND INSTABILITY IN THE MIDDLE EAST 6 (1992); and Mathews, *supra* note 2, at 168.

enormous percentage of water supplies.[30] Not only are the irrigation systems often inefficient, with massive wastage,[31] but the very goal being pursued—frequently 'food security'—may be misconceived. The internal production of food for the national population may be achieved at the expense of the water equally necessary to sustain life.[32] Most important for present puposes, irrigation, especially if inefficient systems are employed, may result in massive downstream pollution caused by the transmission of fertilizers and pesticides in surplus irrigation water.[33]

(iii) Conflicting Development Strategies and Objectives

Conflicting development goals often give rise to environmental insecurity, especially in relation to water.[34] Water availability is also one of the key constraints on development,[35] hence the emergence of the 'water barrier' as an analytical tool.[36] Governments are therefore aware that competition over water may have decisive consequences for their development strategies. If water is crucial, it is not only worth negotiating for, it is worth pressuring for. It may even, in admittedly circumscribed situations, be worth fighting for.

Water as a constraint to development is another issue where water quantity and water quality are closely interrelated. It is not enough to provide for equitable utilization of the resource, measured by volume, as between upstream and downstream states. The quality of the water is also a central concern, so environmental issues are relevant to any appropriate normative

[30] Beshorner, *supra* note 29, at 4, estimates that 70 percent of water supply in the Middle East is devoted to irrigation. *See also* Postel, *Saving Water for Agriculture*, in STATE OF THE WORLD 1990: A WORLDWATCH INSTITUTE REPORT ON PROGRESS TOWARDS A SUSTAINABLE SOCIETY 39 (L. Brown et al., 1990).

[31] *See, e.g,* T. NAFF & R. MATSON, WATER IN THE MIDDLE EAST: CONFLICT OR COOPERATION? 6 (1984); Postel, *supra* note 31, at 39; and W. ADAMS, WASTING THE RAIN: RIVERS, PEOPLE AND PLANNING IN AFRICA 14 (1992).

[32] Beshorner, *supra* note 29, at 12; and Lindhom, *Water and the Arab-Israeli Conflict: An Imperative for Regional Cooperation?, in* REGIONAL CASE STUDIES OF WATER CONFLICTS 47, 52 (L. Ohlsson, ed., 1992).

[33] UNITED NATIONS, TECHNICAL COOPERATION FOR DEVELOPMENT, WATER RESOURCES PLANNING TO MEET LONG-TERM DEMAND: GUIDELINES FOR DEVELOPING COUNTRIES 52 (1988).

[34] The most obvious example of insecurity caused by conflicting development strategies is the decision of an upstream state to build a major dam for irrigation or hydroelectric production on a river that is a main source of water for a downstream state. The downstream state may have its own development objectives dependent on the water supply available from that river. A case in point is the conflict among Turkey, Syria, and Iraq over Turkey's huge Southeast Anatolian water infrastructure programme. *See* Starr & Stoll, *supra* note 25, at 9; Schultz, *Turkey, Syria and Iraq: A Hydropolitical Security Complex*, in REGIONAL CASE STUDIES OF WATER CONFLICTS 86, 97 (L. Ohlsson, ed., 1992).

[35] Ohlsson, *supra* note 25, at 2; and R. CLARKE, WATER: THE INTERNATIONAL CRISIS 101 (1991).

[36] The notion of the water barrier appears to have originated with Falkenmark, *Fresh Water—Time for a Modified Approach*, 15 AMBIO 194 (1986).

regime.[37] For example, industrial pollution will significantly affect the availability of water for 'clean' uses.

(iv) Political and Attitudinal Factors

Human activity has significant environmental impact, not only in the obvious sense of use and abuse, but through political choices that indirectly lead to environmental decline and conflict. Domestic political considerations, for example, may prompt international conflict over shared freshwater resources: rather than addressing disputes as internal matters of resource allocation, governments may be inclined to turn the focus outward, and to blame the disputes on a lack of supply.[38] Ill-considered domestic strategies chosen to address restrictions on the water supply may also lead to unmanageable political conflict, which is then externalized.[39]

Issues of use and access to water cannot be entirely separated from other domestic political tensions, such as conflict over race, religion, and language. Conversely, a crisis over water may fan the flames of underlying social conflict, rooted, for example, in unfair systems of land tenure.[40]

The same sorts of social and cultural tensions that feed environmental insecurity domestically can do so internationally as well. It has been suggested that water conflicts are unlikely to lead to war unless set in a context of otherwise heightened tension.[41] Although this assessment may be somewhat optimistic,[42] there can be no doubt that water disputes may be used as a pretext for conflict that is otherwise desired.[43]

Viewing water as a traditionally conceived strategic 'security issue' may itself increase the chances of serious conflict by setting water problems in a context where military action has been seen as a form of 'solution'.[44] This dimension is particularly troubling because conflicts over water are more likely to take place in a regional, rather than global, context—precisely the setting in which disputes in the post-Cold War era prove most difficult to

[37] Bourne, *International Law on Shared Fresh Water Resources, in Proceedings—International Law: Critical Choices for Canada 1985–2000*, QUEEN'S LAW JOURNAL 342, 352 (1986); and McCaffrey, *The International Law Commission and its Efforts to Codify the International Law of Waterways*, 47 ANN. SUISSE DR. INTERNATIONAL 32, 48 (1990).

[38] Naff & Matson, *supra* note 31, at 54.

[39] Widstrand, *supra* note 38, at 140. A good example is water pricing. If user charges are imposed, or water is priced highly to reduce consumption across the board or in a specific sector, instability may result. Similarly, if restricted access to supplies is imposed, tensions may rise.

[40] Gleick, 1993, *supra* note 2, at 81; and Mathews, *supra* note 2, at 166.

[41] Homer-Dixon, *supra* note 9, at 11; and Beshorner, *supra* note 29, at 70.

[42] Starr, *supra* note 26, at 17.

[43] Naff & Matson, *supra* note 31; and Schultz, *supra* note 34, at 87–8.

[44] Anderson, *supra* note 12, at 19; Boyle, *Remarks During a Workshop on Environmental Security and Freshwater Resources*, held at the Faculty of Law, McGill University, Montreal, 11–12 November 1994 (minutes on file with authors); and Bilder, *supra* note 3.

contain. One answer to this concern is the recasting of environmental security as argued for above, moving it away from its historic focus on political and military concerns toward an emphasis on environmental protection *per se* and attention to sustainable human development.

Attitudes as well as interests shape politics. But attitudes are also independent of politics—they can often be deeper and culturally rooted. At times, attitudes may be suppressed for strategic political reasons, but unless modified, attitudes can reemerge and destroy fragile political consensus. Attitudinal factors are therefore directly relevant to environmental security as broadly conceived.

In traditional agricultural areas of many developing countries, attitudes toward water may be particularly difficult to alter: water may be viewed as a divine gift, and not as a commodity.[45] From an environmental perspective, the refusal to treat water as a commodity has distinct advantages, possibly fostering attitudes favouring ecosystem protection. State attempts to control water use could be hampered, however, with environmentally and economically damaging effects. Where the perception of water as sacred extends beyond agricultural communities, it can promote arguments concerning 'historic use' which limit possibilities for the reallocation of water resources.[46] At the international level, the same attitude can also breed environmental insecurity: water may be viewed as a symbol of national sovereignty, and as an emblem for governmental legitimacy.[47] It is for this reason that much of the data employed in debates concerning freshwater resources is politically charged.[48] Arguments may be based on incorrect assumptions or self-serving 'statistics'. The absence of shared technical data and neutral analysis breeds a lack of confidence.[49]

The fear that water supplies may be insufficient, or could even run out, is another important attitudinal issue. Fear, or a sense of vulnerability, may prompt irrational actions or responses.[50] This perception may also cause states to reject any notion of equality in access to water: if one's own population is vulnerable, it may not be seen as particularly relevant that it is consuming an 'unfair portion' of a shared water resource.

[45] Beshorner, *supra* note 28, at 5.

[46] Caelleigh, *Middle East Water: Vital Resource, Conflict, and Cooperation*, *in* A SHARED DESTINY: NEAR EAST REGIONAL DEVELOPMENT AND DEVELOPMENT COOPERATION 122, 126 (J. Starr, ed.).

[47] Naff & Matson, *supra* note 31, at 184–9.

[48] Beshorner, *supra* note 29, at 7.

[49] Starr, *supra* note 26, at 29. *See also infra* note 62 and accompanying text.

[50] It has been suggested, for example, that Egyptian policy concerning the Nile is deeply affected by a realization of vulnerability: J. WATERBURY, HYDROPOLITICS OF THE NILE VALLEY 63 (1979). It is probably for this reason that a number of high-ranking Egyptian officials have speculated over the last 20 years that Egypt is more likely to go to war over access to Nile waters than over any other issue: Gleick, *supra* note 2, at 86.

(v) 'Environmental' Factors

Water systems may also be damaged by environmental factors that do not seem directly linked to the system. For example, even entirely normal variations of climate may exacerbate actual and latent insecurities related to freshwater resources.[51] Longer-term climate changes such as an extended drought will obviously produce greater tensions. If the predictions of permanent climate change are accurate, water supplies may become even more uncertain and salient to international conflict and environmental insecurity generally.[52]

Deforestation is another environmental issue that can affect freshwater supplies. Erosion can result in the leaching of chemicals into the water system, in increased salinity, and in siltation. Similarly, airborne pollutants that fall as acidic rain can seriously damage a water system.[53]

B. Rethinking Sources of Environmental Insecurity

Because of the historical focus on national security, and a relatively narrow conflict analysis, the environmental dimension of insecurity has usually been treated as incidental, not central. From the preceding discussion, two broad categories of factors promoting conflict can be distinguished. The first relates to human activity and competition over use. Within this category, environmental decline, such as pollution, tends to be treated as merely a byproduct of factors that alone are seen to promote conflict. A second group of factors includes a limited number of environmental issues, such as climate change and deforestation, treated as separate causes of conflict. But problems encompassed within the category of 'environmental factors' are in many cases the result of a failure to deal adequately with sources of conflict generated by human activity. Conflict prevention or resolution strategies that focus on making competing uses compatible merely postpone the conflict caused by a degraded environment. Therefore, the environmental dimension of insecurity must be addressed initially, and not merely once environmental decline has reached crisis proportions. Normative frameworks must be reoriented toward an explicit integration of environmental concerns in regimes coordinating use. Any such reorientation will require a focus on ecosystem protection as a fundamental normative value.

[51] A low rainfall in one year is but one example. Neff & Matson, *supra* note 31, at 227.

[52] Gleick, *supra* note 2, at 97; and Mathews, *supra* note 2, at 169.

[53] On the interactions between aquatic, terrestrial, and atmospheric processes *see* Covich, *Water and Ecosystems*, *in* WATER IN CRISIS: A GUIDE TO THE WORLD'S FRESH WATER RESOURCES (P.H. Gleick, ed., 1993).

III. INTERNATIONAL ENVIRONMENTAL LAW

International environmental law is not effective in promoting environmental security as broadly conceived. Because the law is focused principally on the territorial interests of states, it does not sufficiently accommodate the widening range of ecological interests and needs.

A. Territorial Sovereignty and Environmental Protection

The notion of state sovereignty is the device through which international law has traditionally conceptualized environmental harm. The principle that a state's sovereign right to use its natural resources is limited by the obligation not to cause significant harm to the environment of other states, is one of the cornerstones of international environmental law.[54] The rule has found application in the context of transboundary freshwater pollution. It is central to the codification efforts of the International Law Association (ILA) and the International Law Commission (ILC) respectively,[55] and has found expression in a series of multilateral freshwater agreements.[56] But because the rule was molded by the need to balance conflicting sovereign rights, it is focused on the protection of territorial interests. Environmental harm is not legally relevant as such, but only to the extent that it coincides with a violation of territorial integrity.[57] As a result, the water resource at issue is not considered as a unified whole, but is partitioned into jurisdictional segments.

A second cornerstone of international environmental law is the obligation of riparian nations to share equitably the beneficial uses of transboundary freshwater resources.[58] This rule goes somewhat further than the transboundary harm rule in recognizing the interdependence of states that geographically share resources. Having evolved from early case law that

[54] It can be traced back to the *Trail Smelter* arbitration, 3 R. Int'l Arb. Awards 1095 (1941), and has since been endorsed by a multitude of international declarations and agreements. These include Principle 21 of the (Stockholm) Declaration on the Human Environment, reprinted in 11 ILM 1416 (1972) [hereinafter Stockholm Declaration], and Principle 2 of the (Rio) Declaration on Environment and Development, reprinted in 31 ILM 876 (1992) [hereinafter Rio Declaration].

[55] For the work of the ILA *see* Art. X of the Helsinki Rules on the Uses of Waters of International Rivers, Report of the Fifty-Second Conference 484, 496–7 (1966) [hereinafter Helsinki Rules], and Art. 1 of the Montreal Rules on Water Pollution in an International Drainage Basin, Report of the Sixtieth Conference 531, 535 (1982) [hereinafter Montreal Rules]. For the work of the ILC *see* Arts. 7 and 21(2) of the Draft Articles on the Non-Navigational Uses of International Watercourses, Report of the International Law Commission of Its Forty-Ninth Session 195, 236–89 (1994) [hereinafter ILC 1994 Report].

[56] *See* P.W. Birnie & A.E. Boyle, International Law and the Environment 230–32 (1992).

[57] *Id.* at 226.

[58] *See* Arts. IV, V of the ILA Helsinki Rules, *supra* note 55, at 486; Arts. 5, 6 of the ILC 1994 Report, *supra* note 55, at 218, 231.

recognized the existence of a 'community of interest' of riparian nations,[59] the rule better reflects the fact that natural resources transcend national boundaries.[60] It also recognizes that effects below the threshold of 'significant transboundary harm' may interfere with the interests of riparian states.[61] Yet the focus of the equitable use principle is on the balancing of different use interests in the resource and not on the protection of ecological interests. Furthermore, despite the tentative recognition of resource unity in the interest of continued resource use, rights and obligations under the equitable use rule also remain anchored in the territorial sovereignty of riparian states over the shared resource.

Closely connected to the two core rules of existing international environmental law are a series of procedural rights and obligations. Thus, with a view to ensuring equitable use and prevention of transboundary harm, states are subject to rules governing prior notification, information, consultation, and negotiation.[62] These rules are crucial to buttress the underlying substantive obligations as well as to the prevent and manage resource-related disputes. At least as rules of customary law, however, the procedural rules share the shortcomings of the previously mentioned substantive principles.

Therefore, the cornerstones of customary international environmental law do not effectively address the environmental security concerns discussed earlier. First, given their focus on territorial and use interests rather than environmental needs, the rules cannot ensure ecological balance. Second, they are ultimately incapable of preventing conflict over degraded resources. Third, because of the division of water resources into territorial segments and the focus on competing state interests, customary law is inherently confrontational and does little to promote cooperation in the common environmental interest of states. This is particularly true in view of the fact that the principles become operational only where there is scientific certainty as to the causal link between adverse effects in one country and activities in another. The countries involved thus tend to focus on gathering evidence and information supporting their respective positions and interests, rather than information suggesting there may be common interests.[63] Finally, as a result of their focus on territorial and contempo-

[59] Case Relating to the Territorial Jurisdiction of the International Commission of the River Oder, 1929 P.C.I.J (ser. A) No. 23, 26–7. *See also* the *Lac Lanoux Arbitration* (France v. Spain), 12 R. Int'l Arb. Awards 281 (1957).

[60] *See* H. Hohmann, Präventive Rechtspflichten und—prinzipien des modernen Umweltvölkerrechts 75 (1992).

[61] *See* Riphagen, *The International Concern for the Environment, as Expressed in the Concepts of 'Common Heritage of Mankind' and of 'Shared Natural Resources,' in* Trends in Environmental Policy and Law 343, 345 (M. Bothe, ed., 1980).

[62] *See* Birnie & Boyle, *supra* note 56, at 234.

[63] *But see* O.R. Young, International Governance: Protecting the Environment in a Stateless Society 95–8 (1994); and L.E. Susskind, Environmental Diplomacy:

rary use interests, neither the transboundary harm nor the equitable share rule consider the intertemporal dimension of resource use and long-term environmental interests.

B. Emerging International Ecosystem Law

In light of the issues outlined above, a rethinking of various aspects of international environmental law is urgently required. Environmental security in both its traditional and more expansive dimensions can be ensured only by the elaboration of legal concepts, and ultimately regimes, that reach beyond the specific water resource at issue and encompass all relevant components of an ecosystem. At the same time, normative frameworks must be shaped according to ecological criteria to better reflect both the short and long-term needs of ecosystems.[64] Although the creation of such broad-based rules and regimes may seem unlikely today, their development is imperative given the need to accommodate a growing web of interrelated environmental pressures and a broadening circle of interested parties, both present and future. The central hypothesis of this paper is that efforts to promote and ensure environmental security require that international environmental law shift emphasis from its territorial focus to a more ecosystem-oriented approach. This shift is imperative given the non-territorial scope of many of the previously noted factors threatening environmental security.

Simply put, an 'ecosystem approach' requires consideration of whole systems rather than individual components.[65] Living species and their physical environments must be recognized as interconnected, and the focus must be on the interaction between different sub-systems and their responses to stresses resulting from human activity.[66] Not only does interconnectedness imply management approaches that are broad-based in a spatial sense; it requires as well that human interaction with and use of the environment respect the need for maintaining 'ecosystem integrity', in other words, the system's capacity for self-organization.[67] More recently, these ideas have

NEGOTIATING MORE EFFECTIVE GLOBAL REGIMES 62–6 (1994), who appear to discount this factor.

[64] *See also* McCaffrey, *The Management of Water Resources*, *in* THE ENVIRONMENT AFTER RIO: INTERNATIONAL LAW AND ECONOMICS 149, 156–7 (L. Campiglio et al., eds., 1994).

[65] *See* Bocking, *Visions of Nature and Society: A History of the Ecosystem Approach*, 20 ALTERNATIVES 12 (1994).

[66] *See* Keith, *The Ecosystem Approach: Implications for the North*, 22 NORTHERN PERSPECTIVES 3 (1994).

[67] An ecosystem's capacity to 'self-organize' allows it to regenerate or to adapt to stresses, that is, to maintain or regain integrity. *See* Kay & Schneider, *Embracing Complexity: The Challenge of the Ecosystem Approach*, 20 ALTERNATIVES 32, 36–8 (1994). One of the first international agreements to reflect the concept of ecosystem integrity is the *Great Lakes Water Quality Agreement*, reprinted in Can.T.S. No. 20 (1978). According to Art. II, its purpose is '. . . to restore and maintain the chemical, physical, and biological integrity of the waters of the Great Lakes Basin Ecosystem.'

also been expressed through the concept of 'ecosystem health' as an ordering principle for water management efforts.[68] Finally, given the complexity of ecosystems and their interactions, ecosystem-oriented regimes and management systems must account for the limited human ability to predict ecosystem responses to stress.[69]

A full-fledged ecosystem approach would, according to some commentators, require subordination of human to environmental needs.[70] Not surprisingly, this type of ecocentric perspective does not enjoy broad support even among proponents of ecosystem orientation.[71] The more anthropocentric perspective, however, focusing on humanity's dependence on ecological 'life-support systems', is increasingly accepted.[72] It has begun to be reflected in efforts to reorient international environmental law accordingly.[73] Beyond promoting vital ecological interests, such a shift would also facilitate an emphasis on common rather than competing interests and thereby contribute to conflict prevention. Arguably, where common interests in long-term ecological stability are sufficiently articulated, they can facilitate the structuring of regimes with a view to merging competing interests. This is essential particularly in the context of increasing scarcity of resources. Without timely development of appropriate frameworks, it will become progressively more difficult to break out of the competitive paradigm and to prevent or even manage conflict.

There are four broad approaches to promoting ecosystem orientation. But today's sovereignty-based international legal order is, in a sense, antithetical to ecosystem orientation, and it will not readily accommodate reconceptualization from an ecosystem perspective. The present review will begin, therefore, with a discussion of two approaches that challenge state sovereignty to a lesser degree. It will then present two emerging approaches

[68] *See, e.g., Workgroup on Ecosystem Health, in* GREAT LAKES SCIENCE ADVISORY BOARD, 1993 REPORT TO THE INTERNATIONAL JOINT COMMISSION 33–9 (October 1993); and GREAT LAKES—GREAT LEGACY? 15–30 (T. Colborn et al., eds., 1990).

[69] *See* Kay & Schneider, *supra* note 67.

[70] For a discussion, *see, e.g.*, Sessions, *Deep Ecology and Global Ecosystem Protection, in* ENVIRONMENTAL PHILOSOPHY: FROM ANIMAL RIGHTS TO RADICAL ECOLOGY 233 (M. Zimmerman et al., eds., 1993).

[71] For a discussion *see* Bell, *Non-Human Nature and the Ecosystem Approach: The Limits of Anthropocentrism in Great Lakes Management*, 20 ALTERNATIVES 20, 21 (1994).

[72] *See id.*; E. ODUM, ECOLOGY AND OUR ENDANGERED LIFE-SUPPORT SYSTEMS (1989); and P. EHRLICH & A. EHRLICH, HEALING THE PLANET 4 (1991).

[73] *See, e.g.*, Art. 3 and commentary in Experts Group on Environmental Law of the World Commission on Environment and Development, *Environmental Protection and Sustainable Development—Legal Principles and Recommendations* 45-54 (1986) [hereinafter WCED Experts Group]. At the international environmental policy level, the approach was endorsed in Ch. 18 of Agenda 21, UN Doc. A/CONF.151/26 (Vol. I) 167. According to para. 18.2., the 'general objective' is '. . . to make certain that adequate supplies of water of good quality are maintained for the entire population of this planet, while preserving the hydrological, biological and chemical functions of the ecosystems, adapting human activities within the capacity limits of nature. . . .'

that entail more fundamental conceptual change and argue that, ultimately, it is in this direction that international environmental law must continue to evolve.

(i) Emphasizing Procedure

The least sovereignty-invasive approach consists in an emphasis on 'procedure' over 'substance'. As meaningful substantive principles are notoriously difficult to elaborate, a more effective means of promoting ecosystem-oriented cooperation may be the development of procedural rules and regimes. Thereby, one might argue, the ecosystem context of interstate relations will be addressed in practice, while allowing states to avoid the spectre of 'breach and sanction' raised by substantive norms.[74]

Existing freshwater regimes accord a central role to rules and mechanisms for information exchange, warning, scientific and technical cooperation or, although to a much lesser extent, dispute settlement.[75] Similarly, in international environmental law more generally, a trend emphasizing procedure and process has emerged.[76] For example, international agreements are now typically negotiated as frameworks setting out detailed procedural rules and establishing a process for the subsequent development of substantive obligations, rather than seeking to elaborate an immediate set of specific substantive rules.[77]

Because successful process depends on political consensus, however, procedure alone cannot ensure environmental security in the longer term.[78] Where such consensus must be achieved in a context of competing sovereign interests, a balancing of the latter must occur. As confirmed by state and treaty practice, procedure and process are more appropriately seen as catalysts for the development of substantive rules. The exchange and cooperative practice they generate can contribute significantly to the convergence of positions, thus allowing gradual agreement on substantive obligations and standards. At the same time, cooperative practice serves important trust-building and conflict-prevention functions.[79] Yet the question of substance is ultimately unavoidable.[80] In fact, where substantive

[74] *See* Koskenniemi, *Peaceful Settlement of Environmental Disputes*, 61 NORDIC JOURNAL OF INTERNATIONAL LAW 73 (1991).

[75] *See* Birnie & Boyle, *supra* note 56, at 234–48.

[76] *See* Brunnée, *Toward Effective International Environmental Law: Trends and Developments*, *in* LAW AND PROCESS IN ENVIRONMENTAL MANAGEMENT 217 (S.A. Kennett, ed., 1993).

[77] *Id.* at 223–6.

[78] Koskenniemi, *supra* note 74, at 74.

[79] Allin, *Written Comments in preparation for a Workshop on Environmental Security and Freshwater Resources*, held at the Faculty of Law, McGill University, Montreal, 11–12 November 1994 (on file with authors). Allin cites efforts to agree on solutions to water and environmental problems in the Middle East as key examples of the crucial role of confidence building measures.

[80] Koskenniemi, *supra* note 74, at 74–6, 84.

standards exist, the contours of the procedural framework will likely be better defined and any process more goal-oriented.

(ii) Improving the Existing Framework of Substantive Norms

The approach to improving substantive rules that appears to enjoy the most broadly based support is, not surprisingly, also the most cautious one. It seeks to reinforce existing rules and to improve them gradually from an ecosystem perspective. Perhaps the best example for this approach is the Draft Articles on the Non-Navigational Uses of International Watercourses which the ILC, after two decades of contentious debate, finally adopted and submitted to the UN General Assembly's Sixth Committee in 1994. Given the Commission's particular role in the UN system, the reality of international practice perforce served as frame of reference for its codification and may have constrained progressive development efforts. The Draft Articles are, at least in part, the product of an effort to avoid semantic battles over progressive concepts, and to focus instead on more subtle ways in which comparable results could be achieved. Four examples particularly relevant to environmental protection will be discussed by way of illustration.

First and foremost, in making the international watercourse the geographical reference point for the Draft Articles,[81] the ILC settled on a concept that is less explicitly ecosystem-oriented than the concepts of shared natural resource or international drainage basin it had considered during earlier stages of the drafting process.[82]

The concept of a 'shared natural resource' enjoyed prominence particularly in the 1970s when efforts were made to clarify its scope and legal implications.[83] While a definition of the concept was never agreed upon, it is generally assumed that it applies to resources shared by states in a

[81] The ILC was to some extent constrained by the terminology used in the UN General Assembly's recommendation in GA Resolution 2669 (XXV), UN GAOR, 25th Sess., Supp. No. 28, UN Doc. A/8028 (1970), 127, that the ILC 'take up the study of the law of the non-navigational uses of international watercourses with a view to its progressive development and codification.'

[82] *See* discussion of the conceptual evolution in McCaffrey, *International Organizations and the Holistic Approach to Water Problems*, 31 NRJ 139, 151–8 (1991). *See also* Wescoat, *Beyond the River System: The Changing Geography of International Water Problems and International Watercourse Law*, 3 CoJIELP 301 (1992); and, for a critical view, Okidi, *'Preservation and Protection' Under the 1991 ILC Draft Articles on the Law of International Watercourses*, 3 CoJIELP 143, 173 (1992).

[83] *See* United Nations Environment Programme (UNEP), *Principles of Conduct in the Field of the Environment for the Guidance of States in the Conservation and Harmonious Utilization of Natural Resources Shared by Two or more States,* reprinted in 17 ILM 1097 (1978) [hereinafter UNEP Principles]. For a detailed discussion, see A. Reinicke, DIE ANGEMESSENE NUTZUNG GEMEINSAMER NATURGÜTER (1991).

geographical sense.[84] In such a setting, it serves to anchor a range of cooperative duties of the sharing states and to require equitable use of the resource.[85] It has been suggested that, as a result, states do not have exclusive control over their portions of a shared resource.[86] Thus, although shared natural resources do not represent 'common property' of the sharing states,[87] they are internationalized to a certain degree.[88] This explains why, despite the fact that transboundary freshwater is the paradigmatic example of a shared natural resource, as emphasized by McCaffrey,[89] the ILC was ultimately unable to agree on the use of the concept in the Draft Articles. It also indicates why the international drainage basin concept met a similar fate. The term had been defined previously as encompassing 'a geographical area extending over two or more States determined by the watershed limits of the system of waters, including surface and underground waters.'[90] Both the shared natural resource and drainage basin concepts therefore met with resistance, due to the fear of states that they would progressively limit sovereignty not only over the water resources at issue, but also over surrounding land areas.[91]

[84] *See* Birnie & Boyle, *supra* note 56, at 115. And *see* the following comment in the Report of the Intergovernmental Working Group of Experts, which drafted the UNEP Principles, *supra* note 83, at 1097, No. 16: 'The term "shared natural resource" means an element of the natural environment used by man, which constitutes a biophysical unity and is located in the territory of two or more States.' Note, however, that this definition never became part of the UNEP Principles themselves.

[85] *See* UNEP Principles, *supra* note 83. And *see* Caponera, *Patterns of Cooperation in International Water Law: Principles and Institutions*, *in* TRANSBOUNDARY RESOURCES LAW 1, 4–10 (A.E. Utton & L.A. Teclaff, eds., 1987); Kiss, *The International Protection of the Environment*, *in* THE STRUCTURE AND PROCESS OF INTERNATIONAL LAW: ESSAYS IN LEGAL PHILOSOPHY, DOCTRINE AND THEORY 1069, 1080-83 (R.St.J. Macdonald & D.M. Johnston, eds., 1983).

[86] *See* Birnie & Boyle, *supra* note 56, at 114–15.

[87] *Id.*

[88] Handl, *The Principle of 'Equitable Use' as Applied to Internationally Shared Natural Resources: Its Role in Resolving Potential International Disputes over Transfrontier Pollution*, 14 REV.B.D.I. 40, 64 (1978/79) speaks of 'internationalizing the [resource-sharing] state's decision-making process' in respect of certain activities.

[89] *See, e.g.*, McCaffrey, former ILC Special Rapporteur on the watercourse project, in *The Work of the International Law Commission Relating to the Environment*, 11 ENVIRONMENTAL LAW QUARTERLY 189, 196 (1983):

> The principle . . . that an international watercourse system is a shared natural resource (SNR) seems self evident; yet it does not enjoy the unanimous support of the Commission. The questions . . . seem to stem from the fact that the legal implications of treating an international watercourse system as an SNR have not yet been fully defined. It is uncertain whether this . . . entails new obligations for upper riparian states.

[90] *See* Art. II of the Helsinki Rules, *supra* note 55, at 484–5.

[91] The colourful debate on this point during the early stages of the Commission's work is instructive. Opponents of more broadly conceived concepts maintained, for example, that the use of the purely territorial basin concept would lead to the unacceptable submission of substantial parts of many countries to 'a kind of dual or multiple sovereignty'. *See* the comments of Sette-Camara in [1976] I YBILC 270. *See also* the remnants of this debate in ILC, Report of the International Law Commission of Its Forty-third Session 152, 157 (1991) [hereinafter ILC 1991 Report].

The ILC initially attempted to retain the concepts while tempering their impact by stipulating that shared water resources were of only 'relative' international character, that is only to the extent a given use affected the interests of another system state.[92] But the idea of relativity was eventually rejected as both unnecessary and unworkable.[93] The Commission returned to the concept of 'international watercourse' but defined it somewhat more broadly as 'a system of surface and underground waters constituting by virtue of their physical relationship a unitary whole and normally flowing into a common terminus.'[94] With this definition, the ILC may be said to have brought much of the basin approach into the Draft Articles, while avoiding overt use of the controversial terminology. Yet, the question of ecosystem orientation is addressed at best implicitly, through the reach of other rules such as those prohibiting harm to other watercourse states and their environment,[95] rather than explicitly through the provision on scope. From an environmental protection and security perspective, the absence of any explicit reference to the interaction between water and other environmental components of the drainage basin is regrettable. Similarly, the Draft's only reference to ecosystem concerns is limited to the watercourse itself.[96]

A second example of the ILC's 'subtle' approach to the reorientation of the law on transboundary freshwater is its somewhat meandering and ultimately unsuccessful effort gently to push the normative horizons of accepted core rules. In contrast to the widely used notions of 'serious

[92] In then Special Rapporteur Evensen's *First Report on the Law of the Non-Navigational Uses of International Waterways*, [1983] II/1 YbILC 167, para. 67, Draft Art. 1 defined the notion of an 'international watercourse system' and provided in its para. 2:

> To the extent that a part or parts of a watercourse system situated in system State are not affected by or do not affect uses of the watercourse system in another system State, such parts shall not be treated as part of the international watercourse system for the purposes of these articles.

At pages 169–70, para. 81, in the same report, Draft Art. 6 sought to anchor the rights and obligations of states as follows:

> To the extent that the use of an international watercourse system and its waters in the territory of one system State affects the use of a watercourse system or its waters in the territory of another system State or other system States, the watercourse system and its waters are, for the purposes of this convention, a shared natural resource. Each system State is entitled to a reasonable and equitable participation (within its territory) in this shared resource.

[93] *See* ILC 1991 Report, *supra* note 91, at 158–9. The notion was considered to be unnecessary because, regardless of the approach to scope, the freedom of states to utilize a shared water resource would be limited only in cases of impact on legitimate uses by other states. While relativity would thus add nothing to the regime, it would introduce uncertainty as to whether or not the regime would even apply in a given case. *See also* McCaffrey, *supra* note 82, at 155–6.

[94] *See* ILC 1994 Report, *supra* note 55, at 199.

[95] *See* Draft Arts. 7, 20, and 21, *in* ILC 1991 Report, *supra* note 91, at 236, 280, 289.

[96] See *infra* note 128 and accompanying text.

damage,' 'significant damage,' or 'substantial injury'[97] the Commission initially opted for the term 'appreciable harm' to define the threshold for unlawful transboundary impact.[98] According to the commentary on the relevant provision, the intention was to introduce a factual standard and to lower the threshold to something that is 'not insignificant or barely detectable, but is not necessarily "serious"'.[99] In a parallel effort, the ILC originally sought to lower the relevant threshold even further to 'appreciable adverse effects' when defining the trigger for the notification duties of watercourse states.[100]

However well intentioned, neither terminology is contained in the Draft adopted in 1994. The ILC returned to the use of more widely accepted terminology with significant harm (Arts. 7 and 21(2)) and possible significant harm (Art. 12) being the relevant triggers. The threshold issue provides an example where the Commission chose to engage in a protracted debate over semantic detail only to have to retreat to the starting point in the end. Given that it is doubtful that there is any practical difference between the notions of appreciable and significant harm, the ILC might have devoted its energy more effectively to other issues.[101]

The Commission was more successful in resolving the long-standing debate as to the relationship between the transboundary harm and equitable share rules. A strong body of opinion, perhaps best represented by the relevant work of the ILA,[102] holds that in the context of shared water resources, the equitable use principle should take precedence. It is argued that according a priority to the transboundary harm rule would amount to

[97] For a detailed review of the threshold question *see* A. NOLLKAEMPER, THE LEGAL REGIME FOR TRANSBOUNDARY WATER POLLUTION: BETWEEN DISCRETION AND CONSTRAINT 35–9 (1993). Sachariev, *The Definition of Thresholds of Tolerance for Transboundary Environmental Injury Under International Law: Development and Present Status* XXXVII NETHERLANDS INTERNATIONAL LAW REVIEW 193 (1990) points to a trend of progressive lowering of the threshold.

[98] This terminology was still used in Art. 7 as contained in the ILC 1991 Report, *supra* note 91, at 164.

[99] *See* commentary to then-Draft Art. 8 in Report of the Commission to the General Assembly on the Work of its Fortieth Session, [1988] II YBILC 36 (Part 2) [hereinafter 1988 Report]. And *see* Sachariev, *supra* note 97, at 201, who places this threshold debate in the context of a larger trend.

[100] *See* Draft Art. 12 and commentary, 1988 Report, *supra* note 99, at 46, where it is explained that the standard had to be lower than in (then) Art. 8 because a state providing notification would otherwise '. . . be put in the position of admitting that the measures it was planning might cause appreciable harm to other watercourse States in violation of article 8.'

[101] Before becoming the Commission's Special Rapporteur, McCaffrey made this point quite forcefully in McCaffrey, *supra* note 89, at 202: 'It is therefore questionable whether the "appreciable harm" standard of the ILC draft and the "substantial injury" criterion of the Helsinki Rules are different tests, notwithstanding the semantically correct statement that "appreciable" means less in quantity than. . . "substantial".'

[102] See Art. X of the Helsinki Rules, *supra* note 55, at 496–7, and Art. 1 of the Montreal Rules, *supra* note 55, at 535.

an endorsement of a system of 'prior appropriation'.[103] New uses of a shared water resource would be preempted where they result in significant harm to another riparian state or their water use.[104] This could lead to potentially inequitable results for upper riparians and in particular for developing countries.[105] The transboundary harm rule, therefore, is criticized as too inflexible, whereas with equitable use as the dominant principle, factors such economic and technological abilities could be considered.[106]

The opposing view holds that causation of significant harm should be considered as a violation of the equitable use rule.[107] The strongest arguments in favour of according priority to the transboundary harm rule are built on environmental concerns.[108] Equitable considerations, it is suggested, should not serve to justify significant environmental damage. Handl argues that such harm should be at least a *prima facie* violation of the equitable use rule;[109] others seem to conclude that activities resulting in significant transboundary harm, by definition, exceed a nation's equitable share.[110] For the purposes of environmental protection, it is further argued, the equitable use rule is unsuitable also because its very flexibility does not permit the determination of predictable and enforceable thresholds.[111] Finally, the resulting difficulties in the delineation of rights and obligations

[103] *See* Bourne, *The International Law Commission's Draft Articles on the Law of International Watercourses: Principles and Planned Measures*, 3 CoJIELP 65, 92.

[104] *See* discussion in McCaffrey, *The Law of International Watercourses: Some Recent Developments and Unanswered Questions*, 17 DEN. JOURNAL OF INTERNATIONAL LAW & POLICY 505, 509 (1989).

[105] *See* Bourne, *supra* note 37, at 356. And *see* the discussion in McCaffrey, *supra* note 37, at 50–51.

[106] *See* Wouters, *Allocation of the Non-Navigational Uses of International Watercourses: Efforts at Codification and the Experience of Canada and the United States*, 30 CANADIAN YEARBOOK OF INTERNATIONAL LAW 43, 84 (1992), who argues that in U.S.–Canadian practice, the flexibility of the equitable utilization rule has prevailed, particularly in cases involving pollution harm.

[107] *See, e.g.*, McCaffrey, *supra* note 104, at 509–10.

[108] Many sources distinguish between water-use conflicts and cases involving environmental concerns. It is suggested that whereas in the former the principle of equitable utilization should predominate, the transboundary harm rule should be the governing principle in the latter. For a discussion *see* Lammers, *Commentary on Papers Presented by Charles Bourne and Alberto Székely*, 3 CoJIELP 103, 107–8 (1992); and Handl, *The International Law Commission's Draft Articles on the Law of International Watercourses (General Principles and Planned Measures): Progressive or Retrogressive Development of International Law?*, 3 CoJIELP 123, 131–2 (1992), who considers the ILC's decision to make the transboundary harm rule predominant in both situations 'unpersuasive from a policy perspective'.

[109] *See* discussion in Handl, *National Uses of Transboundary Air Resources: The International Entitlement Issue Reconsidered*, 26 NRJ 405, at 417–20 (1986).

[110] *See* Birnie & Boyle, *supra* note 56, at 228; and McCaffrey, *supra* note 37, at 52.

[111] *See* McCaffrey, *supra* note 37, at 51; but *see* Wouters, *supra* note 106, at 83, who argues that the criterion for a breach of the transboundary harm rule is similarly imprecise.

are said to limit the rule's usefulness in the prevention and resolution of resource conflicts.[112]

It has been rightly pointed out that the dichotomy may be more apparent than real.[113] While, from an environmental protection and security perspective, giving priority to the transboundary harm rule is preferable, the cooperative aspect inherent in the equitable use principle brings an equally important element of balance to environmental relations amongst states.[114] Yet, perhaps more importantly, it should not be overlooked that the transboundary harm rule is not as inflexible as it may appear at first glance. It does not prohibit significant transboundary harm in absolute terms. Rather, it imposes a due diligence obligation to prevent such harm.[115] From this vantage point it may be said that transboundary harm that results from a failure to exercise due diligence will in all likelihood also amount to a failure to use the resource equitably.[116]

Seen in this light, the ILC's approach to the issue, after swinging from one extreme to the other, eventually achieved an acceptable balance.[117] The Commission's early work was marked by its preference for a priority of the equitable use rule.[118] Subsequent drafts, emphasizing particular environmental concerns, made the transboundary harm rule the overriding principle.[119] The Draft Articles adopted in 1994, while leaning toward the latter

[112] *See* Biswas, *Shared Natural Resources: Future Conflicts or Peaceful Development?*, *in* THE SETTLEMENT OF DISPUTES ON THE NEW NATURAL RESOURCES 197, 213 (R.J. Dupuy, ed., 1983).

[113] Boyle, Remarks, *supra* note 44; and Boyle, *Written Comments in Preparation for the Workshop*, Oct. 4, 1994 (on file with authors).

[114] *See* Handl, *supra* note 108, at 132.

[115] *See, e.g.*, WCED Experts Group, *supra* note 73, at 79 (Comment on Art. 10).

[116] For a critical view on this argument *see* Handl, *supra* note 108, at 131, who states that the 'parameters bearing on "reasonableness" under each rule are significantly different.'

[117] For a comprehensive discussion of this evolution see Bourne, *supra* note 103, at 73–82. However, at 92, Bourne comes to the conclusion that a system of priority for the transboundary harm rule would constitute 'retrogressive, not progressive development of the law of international watercourses'.

[118] *See, e.g.*, the Third Report of then Special Rapporteur S.M. Schwebel, in [1982] II YBILC 103, para. 156, (Part 1), Draft Art. 8(1) of which read as follows: 'The right of a system State to use the water resources of an international watercourse system is limited by the duty not to cause appreciable harm to the interests of another system State, except as may be allowable under a determination for equitable participation for the watercourse system involved.'

[119] *See, e.g.*, the ILC 1988 Report, *supra* note 99, at 35–6. Then-Draft Art. 8 simply provided: 'Watercourse States shall utilize an international watercourse [system] in such a way as not to cause appreciable harm to other watercourse States.' The Commission's commentary explained that: 'A watercourse State's right to utilize an international watercourse [system] in an equitable and reasonable manner has its limit in the duty of that State not to cause appreciable harm to other watercourse States.' Yet, the ILC's struggle with this issue is evident in a subsequent passage where the commentary suggests that the attainment of equitable results may, in individual cases, require specific agreements providing for the toleration of harm.

solution, ultimately make due diligence the decisive criterion.[120] Thus, significant harm resulting from a failure to exercise due diligence violates both the transboundary harm and equitable use principles.[121] By contrast, where significant harm is caused despite the exercise of due diligence, it will be *prima facie* inequitable. Yet states are free to conclude agreements stipulating otherwise and, absent such an agreement, a state causing transboundary harm may enter into consultations with a view to demonstrating that its use of the watercourse was equitable and reasonable.[122] This general framework is applicable also to pollution and governs the states' duties to 'prevent, reduce and control pollution of an international watercourse that may cause significant harm to other watercourse States or to their environment.'[123]

A final example of the ILC's cautious normative development effort is the way in which it introduces the ecosystem concept to international watercourse law.[124] Draft Art. 20 requires watercourse states to 'protect and preserve the ecosystems of international watercourses', and Draft Art. 23 demands that watercourse states take 'all measures with respect to an international watercourse that are necessary to protect and preserve the marine environment.'[125] Perhaps the most noteworthy feature of these two environmental protection obligations is their independence from harm affecting another watercourse state. States are required to protect the ecology of the watercourse within their own territory and must take marine environmental protection into account. Necessary cooperative action is to

[120] *See* ILC 1994 Report, *supra* note 55, at 236. Draft Art. 7 provides as follows:

Obligation not to cause significant harm

1. Watercourse States shall exercise due diligence to utilize an international watercourse in such a way as not to cause significant harm to other watercourse States.

2. Where, despite the exercise of due diligence, significant harm is caused to another watercourse State, the State who causes the harm shall, in the absence of agreement to such use, consult with the State suffering such harm over:

(a) the extent to which such use is equitable and reasonable taking into account the factors listed in article 6;

(b) the question of ad hoc adjustments to its utilization, designed to eliminate or mitigate any such harm caused and, where appropriate, the question of compensation.

[121] Draft Art. 7(1). *See also* commentary, in ILC 1994 Report, *supra* note 55, at 236–40.

[122] Draft Art. 7(2). *See also* commentary in ILC 1994 Report, *supra* note 55, at 240–44. Some governments, including Canada's, have criticized an emphasis on due diligence in determining the relationship between Arts. 5 and 7. It is argued that by emphasizing due diligence, one is effectively weakening environmental protection obligations. See Allin, *Remarks During a Workshop on Environmental Security and Freshwater Resources*, held at the Faculty of Law, McGill University, Montreal, 11–12 November 1994 (minutes on file with authors).

[123] *See* ILC Draft Art. 21(2) and commentary, *supra* note 55, at 289–96.

[124] For a detailed discussion of the *Draft's* approach and relevant precedent, *see* Okidi, *supra* note 82.

[125] ILC 1994 Report, supra note 55, at 280, 298. The commentary to Art. 20 explains that 'ecosystem' was chosen over 'environment' as the more precise term. It is defined as 'an ecological unit consisting of living and non-living components that are interdependent and function as a community.'

be taken on an equitable basis, as the ILC perceives ecosystem protection as inherent in the idea of equitable use.[126] It may be concluded that both Draft Arts. 20 and 23 are an expression of certain common interests of states in environmental protection. The Commission has shied away, however, from formulating rights that would mirror these tentative ecosystem obligations.[127] The Draft Articles adhere to the traditional approach pursuant to which environmental harm triggers enforceable rights only where it affects another watercourse state as envisaged in Arts. 7 and 21(2).[128] Furthermore, the wording of Draft Art. 20, in referring to the 'ecosystem of the watercourse,' seems to have stopped short of acknowledging the interaction between water and its ecological context.[129]

(iii) Ecosystem-Orientation in Content

More onerous from the perspective of state sovereignty than an incremental evolution of the traditional approach would be the adoption of a more explicit ecosystem orientation within the existing normative framework.[130] As suggested in the preceding discussion, state sovereignty over resources and resource use currently finds its limits largely in the territorial rights of other states. Rules imposing limits according to purely ecological criteria, independent from transboundary impact, would be a significant departure from this traditional approach. In the context of specific regimes, an ecosystem orientation could be achieved by establishing limit values or emission standards pursuant to ecological, rather than human or economic, factors.[131] But the development of such technical criteria by scientists and

[126] *See id.* at 282, where the commentary suggests that the 'obligation to "protect" the ecosystems of international watercourses is a specific application of the requirement contained in article 5 that watercourse States are to use and develop an international watercourse in a manner that is consistent with adequate protection thereof.'

[127] *See* Okidi, *supra* note 82, at 153.

[128] Although it was suggested in the ILC's deliberations that, under (now) Draft Arts. 20 and 23, any watercourse state could be considered 'injured' even if not directly harmed, the Special Rapporteur cautioned that an *erga omnes* effect had not been intended. *See* ILC 1988 Report, *supra* note 99, at 31. On the question of 'standing' in the common environmental interest of states *see also infra* note 166 and accompanying text.

[129] *See* Okidi, *supra* note 82, at 173. But this criticism might be countered in part by pointing to the definition of 'international watercourse' and its implicit links to the surrounding environment through Draft Arts. 7 and 21(2).

[130] 'Ecosystem orientation in content' is used here to describe ecologically based thresholds, triggers, and goals for rights and obligations.

[131] It is important to recognize that the ultimate fine-tuning of an ecosystem approach is not a legal, but a scientific, task. The involvement of experts and their epistemic communities is also thought to contribute to the merging of conflicting positions and the formation of effective regimes. *See, e.g.,* Osherenko & Young, *The Formation of International Regimes: Hypotheses and Cases*, *in* POLAR POLITICS: CREATING INTERNATIONAL ENVIRONMENTAL REGIMES 1, 19–20 (G. Osherenko & O.R. Young, eds., 1993). Others have suggested that a 'downgrading' of the ecosystem approach from the legal to the scientific level might make it more viable in the current international climate: Timoshenko, *supra* note 22.

other specialists can occur only in the context of a conceptual framework that promotes ecosystem values rather than primarily territorial interests of states.[132] A number of emerging principles suggest that international environmental law may have begun to circumscribe environmentally appropriate conduct with a view to the carrying capacity of the environment.

First, the concept of sustainable development acknowledges the need for development, but suggests that it must meet the needs of present generations without compromising the ability of future generations to meet their needs.[133] Since its endorsement by the World Commission on Environment and Development in 1987, the concept has become woven firmly into the fabric of international environmental law and policy.[134] The 1992 Rio Conference on Environment and Development and the creation of a UN Commission on Sustainable Development are testimony to the emergence of sustainable development as an overarching formula for the balancing of environmental and developmental concerns.[135]

The concept has been criticized as overly broad.[136] But this very feature may explain its popularity and it may be argued that the notion need not develop into a binding principle with clear normative content to guide international environmental protection efforts effectively.[137] In fact, one may more appropriately conclude that sustainable development is an umbrella notion encompassing a range of more specific principles that give it effect.[138] Be that as it may, the notion that sustainable development is essential to ensure continued availability of the resource base on which con-

[132] *See, e.g.*, Osherenko & Young, *supra* note 131, at 20; and Susskind, *supra* note 63, at 47–8.

[133] World Commission on Environment and Development, OUR COMMON FUTURE 43 (1987) [hereinafter WCED].

[134] Note that the underlying idea goes back to the Stockholm Declaration, *supra* note 54, where it found expression in Principles 3 and 13.

[135] For an overview on recent activities within the Commission on Sustainable Development, *see Review of Sectoral Clusters: Freshwater Resources*, REPORT TO THE SECRETARY-GENERAL, UN Doc. E/CN.17/1994 [hereinafter CSD]; or *CSD Holds Second Session*, 24 EPL 212 (1994). On the use of the concept of sustainable development *see* Rio Declaration, *supra* note 54, at 874, which, while not defining the notion, explicitly relies on it in 12 of its 27 principles. The Convention on Biological Diversity, reprinted in 31 ILM 818 (1992), is premised on the notion of 'sustainable use', defined in its Art. 2. The Framework Convention on Climate Change, reprinted in 31 ILM 849 (1992), refers to sustainable development in its Art. 3(4). The notion is central to the Statement of Principles for a Global Consensus on the Management, Conservation and Sustainable Development of All Types of Forests, reprinted in 31 ILM 881 (1992). Finally, Agenda 21, *supra* note 73, devotes its Ch. 7 to the promotion of sustainable development and endorses the concept in the specific context of freshwater resources. For an overview *see* the note *Agenda 21* in 22 EPL 208 (1992).

[136] *See, e.g.,* Parson, *Assessing UNCED and the State of Sustainable Development*, *in* PROCEEDINGS OF THE 87TH ANNUAL MEETING 508, 513 (American Society of International Law 1993).

[137] *See* Handl, *supra* note 2, at 27.

[138] Some have attempted to distinguish between the notion's objective, normative and procedural components. *See* Sanwal, *Sustainable Development, the Rio Declaration and Multilateral Cooperation*, 4 CoJIELP 45, 48 (1993).

tinued development depends has obvious persuasive power.[139] Its explicit emphasis on present development interests, in line with the concerns of most developing countries, holds additional appeal. In limiting development only where it would undermine the environmental basis of future development, the concept is not primarily concerned with environmental protection.[140] Rather, ecological criteria are used in a utilitarian fashion to facilitate trade-offs between human priorities, and not to ensure environmental health *per se*. Ironically, this approach may be precisely what makes the introduction of ecological concerns into development decisions viable. To allow for effective ecosystem orientation, however, the ecological context of human development should be made more explicit than is currently the case.[141] This could be achieved, for example, by speaking of 'ecologically sustainable development' rather than simply 'sustainable development'.

The notion of sustainable development must become anchored in international watercourse law.[142] The ILC has rightly been criticized for neglecting much of the conceptual development that international environmental law has undergone recently.[143] Particularly given the Draft Articles' focus on 'uses' of freshwater, a requirement of ecologically sustainable use should have been explicitly incorporated into the provision governing equitable use.[144] A link between equitable use and sustainability would promote common environmental interests of states in several respects. First, the linkage emphasizes the need to consider the environmental context when balancing competing use interests. Below the threshold of transboundary harm, and even where there may be no current interference with the equitable share of another state, a sustainability criterion would articulate long-term environmental limits to water use.[145] Second, the notion of sustainable development ties a state's resource use into a broader international context. Because the concept applies both in the 'micro' and 'macro' context of environmental management, a state's performance will be measured against local, regional, and even global sustainability criteria. The concept thus

139 *See* Birnie & Boyle, *supra* note 56, at 123. *And see* Handl, *supra* note 2, at 25–6.

140 *See* Handl, *supra* note 2, at 24–5.

141 *See, e.g.*, Davis, *supra* note 19.

142 *See, e.g.*, Boyle, *supra* note 44.

143 During its Forty-Fourth Session, under Special Rapporteur Robert Rosenstock, the ILC considered the view that the *Draft* should be reconsidered and updated to reflect developments such as the emergence of sustainable development and 'holistic' approaches to the protection of the environment. *See Non-Navigational Uses of International Watercourses*, 23 EPL 241, 242 (1993).

144 *See, e.g.*, Allin, *supra* note 122. The relevant commentary of the ILC seems to suggest that this requirement is implicit in the notion of 'optimal utilization . . . consistent with the adequate protection of the watercourse' contained in Draft Art. 5(1): 'It should also be mentioned that, in line with the principle of sustainability, "Water resources development and management should be planned in an integrated manner, taking into account long-term planning needs and those with narrower horizons".' *See* ILC 1994 Report, *supra* note 55, at 219.

145 *See, e.g.*, Kiss, *supra* note 17.

acknowledges the commonality of environmental concerns and the indivisibility of ecosystems.

The crucial intertemporal dimension introduced by the principle of ecologically sustainable development is reinforced by a second emerging principle, intergenerational equity, first posited by Brown Weiss.[146] This principle requires today's decision-makers to go beyond the balancing of contemporary interests and to include future interests. The normative content of intergenerational equity flows from its goal to sustain the well-being of all generations of humanity.[147] The concept thus implies the obligation of each generation to ensure that the natural and cultural resources of the Earth are passed on to the next generation in no worse condition than they were received.[148] The concept of intergenerational equity implies limitations on state sovereignty over natural resources by requiring regard for certain overriding interests of present and future generations.[149] Therefore, states have been reticent to endorse the concept as an independent source of potential obligation.[150] The growing recognition of the inter-temporal dimension of current environmental concerns has found expression primarily in tandem with the notion of sustainable development.[151] Arguably, this approach serves to mitigate the impact of intergenerational equity requirements by giving more weight to current development interests.[152]

Finally, any successful effort to achieve sustainability and intergenerational equity must be based as well on the precautionary principle.[153] The principle is the single most important underpinning of any regime intended to promote ecological balance and ecosystem integrity.[154] The principle's

[146] *See* E. Brown Weiss, In Fairness to Future Generations: International Law, Common Patrimony and Intergenerational Equity (1989).

[147] *Id.* at 116.

[148] *Id.* at 37–8.

[149] *See* Handl, *supra* note 2, at 27, 31.

[150] On its own, the concept has typically found expression in preambular statements. *See, e.g.*, the preamble to the Convention on International Trade in Endangered Species of Wild Fauna and Flora, reprinted in 12 ILM 1085 (1973); the preamble to the (Barcelona) Convention for the Protection of the Mediterranean Sea Against Pollution, reprinted in 15 ILM 290 (1976); the preamble to the Biodiversity Convention, *supra* note 135; and the preamble to the Climate Change Convention, *supra* note 135. Noteworthy is the inclusion of the concept in a list of water management principles provided in Art. 2(5) of the (ECE) Convention on the Protection and Use of Transboundary Watercourses and International Lakes, reprinted in 31 ILM 1312 (1992) [hereinafter (ECE) Convention on Transboundary Watercourses].

[151] For example, Principle 2(b) of the Forest Principles, *supra* note 135, reads: 'Forest resources and forest lands should be sustainably managed to meet the . . . human needs of present and future generations.' *See also* Art. 1 of the Biodiversity Convention, *supra* note 135.

[152] See Principle 3 of the Rio Declaration, *supra* note 54, which goes even further and states: 'The right to development must be fulfilled to equitably meet developmental and environmental needs of present and future generations.'

[153] This link found clear expression in Art. 7 of the Bergen Ministerial Declaration on Sustainable Development in the ECE Region of May 16, 1990, UN Doc. A/CONF/151.PC10, Annex I, reprinted in 1 YbIEL 429 (1990) [hereinafter Bergen Declaration], which states: 'In order to achieve sustainable development, policies must be based on the precautionary principle.'

[154] *See supra* notes 66–69 and accompanying text; and Keith, *supra* note 66, at 5.

thrust is to require action or inaction in the face of uncertainty as to the causal links between certain activities and potential adverse environmental effects.[155] In the context of shared freshwater resources, as in general, the principle's importance rests in its ability to improve the existing normative framework by tempering the requirement of 'scientific certainty' that so often hinders timely environmental protection.[156] This effect extends beyond the substantive into the procedural realm, as the precautionary principle has given rise to assertions of complementary requirements such as environmental impact assessment or the use of 'best available technology'.[157]

In terms of legal acceptance, it remains unclear how great the risk of future harm and how serious potential damage must be to trigger any precautionary obligation.[158] More recent formulations of the principle suggest that 'threats of serious or irreversible damage' are the relevant threshold.[159] Yet it also seems that any resulting obligation has become watered down to taking 'cost-effective' preventive measures according to each state's capability.[160] The cost-effectiveness criterion may well be the exception that swallows the rule. Given the importance of the precautionary principle to effective ecosystem orientation, it is to be hoped that cost-effectiveness will not establish itself as a component of the principle.[161] Cost-effectiveness should not become a normative back door for 'business as usual'.[162]

[155] *See, e.g.*, Principle 15 of the Rio Declaration, *supra* note 54. And *see* Cameron & Abouchar, *The Precautionary Principle: A Fundamental Principle of Law and Policy for the Protection of the Global Environment*, 14 BostCICLR 1, 2–4 (1991).

[156] The ILC Draft Articles do not explicitly require a precautionary approach to fresh-water management. The commentary to Draft Art. 20 claims, however, that 'the principle of precautionary action [is] reflected in article 20.' *See* ILC 1994 Report, *supra* note 55, at 287. Unfortunately, even Agenda 21, *supra* note 73, para. 18.40(b)(v) merely recommends the 'introduction of the precautionary approach in water quality management' 'where appropriate'.

[157] *See* Birnie & Boyle, *supra* note 56, at 97.

[158] *See* Bodansky, *New Developments in International Environmental Law* in Proceedings of the 85th Annual Meeting 401 (ASIL 1991).

[159] *See, e.g.,* the preamble to the Biodiversity Convention, *supra* note 135; Art. 3(3) of the Climate Change Convention, *supra* note 135; and Principle 15 of the Rio Declaration, *supra* note 54.

[160] *See* Principle 15 of the Rio Declaration, *supra* note 54 and Art. 3(3) of the Climate Change Convention, *supra* note 135. Note also that Principle 15 merely requires states to 'prevent environmental degradation' whereas Art. 7 of the Bergen Declaration, *supra* note 153—the furthest reaching formulation of the precautionary principle—required states to 'anticipate, prevent and attack the causes of environmental degradation.' Article 3(3) of the Climate Change Convention steers a middle course by requiring 'precautionary measures that anticipate, prevent or minimize the causes of climate change.'

[161] It is encouraging that Art. 2.5(a) of the (ECE) Convention on Transboundary Watercourses, *supra* note 150, defines the principle as one 'by virtue of which action to avoid the potential transboundary impact of the release of hazardous substances shall not be postponed on the ground that scientific research has not fully proved a causal link.'

[162] But some economists suggest that the criterion is crucial to economically efficient operation of the principle. *See, e.g.*, Susskind, *supra* note 63, at 78–80.

Rather, pursuant to the idea of equitable participation, common interest in environmental security should translate into burden sharing among states.[163] In this context, the distribution of costs and benefits of a given measure could be taken into account as one among many relevant factors.[164]

Taken together, the three principles discussed above represent tentative yet important steps toward a conceptual framework regulating human activity from the perspective of its ecological context. Clearly, the notion of sustainable development, like that of intergenerational equity, remains anthropocentric and utilitarian in outlook. None the less, particularly in conjunction with a balanced version of the precautionary principle, an ecological dimension is introduced at least to the extent that human development must, irrespective of transboundary impact, respect limits defined by what the environment can sustain. Although perhaps these principles are ultimately not far-reaching enough, they represent a first step that is consistent with the anthropocentric interpretation of the ecosystem approach discussed earlier in this paper.[165]

In reaching beyond present-day state interests, all three principles reflect the actual impact of human activity more accurately than traditional watercourse law and should find explicit expression in the relevant normative framework. The broader perspective they introduce is essential to any strategy designed to safeguard long-term environmental security. In light of increasingly rapid and dramatic environmental change, an effective freshwater security regime must direct its attention to the future and seek to anticipate problems, while providing frameworks to address them.

(iv) Ecosystem Orientation in Scope

One of the issues left unaddressed by an ecosystem orientation in norm content is that of standing to demand adherence to the emerging rules. The

[163] This idea is reflected in Arts. 20 and 21 of the ILC Draft Articles and the requirement of joint environmental protection and preservation by watercourse states. The commentary to Draft Art. 20 states that this is

> to be understood as meaning that joint, co-operative action is to be taken where appropriate, and that such action is to be taken on an equitable basis. . . . What constitutes action on an equitable basis will, of course, vary with the circumstances. Among the factors to be taken into account in this connection are the extent to which the watercourse States concerned have contributed to the problem and the extent to which they will benefit from its solution.

See ILC 1994 Report, *supra* note 54, at 282–83. Note that this approach is in line with the notion of 'common but differentiated responsibilities' that has recently emerged as central to global environmental protection. *See, e.g.,* Art. 4 of the Climate Change Convention, *supra* note 134; and Principle 7 of the Rio Declaration, *supra* note 53.

[164] *See* ILC 1994 Report, *supra* note 54.

[165] *See supra* notes 19 and 88 and accompanying text.

interests of other states in the observance of ecological criteria are not necessarily reflected in these principles.[166] Ecosystem orientation in content must go hand in hand with an effort to render the conceptual framework of international environmental law more ecosystem-oriented in scope, and thus more reflective of ecosystem, rather than state boundaries.

From the perspective of state sovereignty, this proposition is also the most invasive of the four approaches surveyed in this paper. As was discussed earlier, past attempts to make ecological interdependence the yardstick of conceptual reach have been perceived as venturing too far into the sovereign domains of states.[167] Certainly, the web of environmental obligations of states has grown and brought about increasing limitations on sovereignty. At the same time, states have repeatedly affirmed sovereignty over natural resources as the ground rule upon which international environmental law builds.[168]

The experience of the ILC demonstrates that the 'internationalization' of a resource would meet with the resistance of states. But the very assumption that concepts shaped according to the boundaries of a shared resource entail a broad regime of shared sovereignty may exaggerate the actual legal implications of a shared resource setting. Such a setting does not give rise to 'internationalization', but rather to certain additional limitations on the freedom of each state to exploit its resources, flowing from the requirement of equitable use.[169] For states that do not physically share the resource, rights are correlative to the extent that their interests are affected. Necessarily, the rights and obligations of riparian states will differ from those of non-riparians. The former include rights to use the shared resource, whereas the latter relate to the environmental consequences of each state's activities.

To allow for a more coherent anchoring of the most likely range of interests, including those of some non-riparians, the conceptual basis of the law of shared freshwater resources must be more explicitly ecosystem-oriented.[170] Notwithstanding the concerns that led the ILC to abandon the concept, the building block of a freshwater regime should be the drainage basin.[171] It articulates more clearly the interaction between freshwater and the surrounding environment and better explains resulting limitations on

[166] *See supra* note 127 and accompanying text, on Art. 20 of the 1994 Draft, which introduces the ecosystem concept but gives no matching enforcement right to other states.

[167] *See supra* note 91 and accompanying text.

[168] *See e.g.* Principle 2 of the Rio Declaration, *supra* note 54. *See also* Resolution on Permanent Sovereignty over Natural Resources, UNGA Res. 1803 (XVII), UN GAOR, 17th Sess., Supp. No. 17, UN Doc. A/S 217 (1962), 17; and Diaz, *Permanent Sovereignty over Natural Resources*, 24 EPL 157 (1994).

[169] *See supra* note 85 and accompanying text.

[170] *See* Timoshenko, *supra* note 22.

[171] *See* Kiss, *supra* note 17.

the uses each state may make of its resources. The drainage basin provides the conceptual basis for a significant number of the more recent transboundary freshwater regimes.[172] Furthermore, recent policy initiatives pertaining to freshwater management all stress the need for broad-based and integrated approaches.[173]

From the perspective of ecosystem management, however, even the drainage basin approach may be too narrow.[174] True ecosystem orientation would focus not on water management in light of the broader ecosystem of which it is part, but on the ecosystem itself, with water being but one component.[175] Given that this type of management approach is the exception even at the national level,[176] the time may not be ripe for its international implementation.[177] Arguably, the approach would implicate an ever broader

[172] *See, e.g.*, Arts. 2(1), 3(2) of the Convention on the Protection of the Rhine Against Chemical Pollution, reprinted in 16 ILM 242 (1977). The (ECE) Convention on Transboundary Watercourses, *supra* note 150, uses the term 'transboundary waters' in Art. 1. However, it also provides for a definition of 'transboundary impact' that includes: 'effects on human health and safety, flora, fauna, soil, air water, climate, landscape.' Article I of the Great Lakes Water Quality Agreement, *supra* note 67, defines its area of application, the Great Lakes Basin Ecosystem, as 'the interacting components of air, land, water and living organisms, including humans, within the drainage basin.' The Agreement on the Action Plan for the Environmentally Sound Management of the Common Zambezi River System, reprinted in 27 ILM 1109 (1988), is particularly noteworthy in its basin-wide approach to integrated management and in the way in which, at para. 13, it acknowledges the link between broad-based management and environmental security: 'it is possible and highly desirable to deal with the water resources and environmental management problems of the river system in a co-ordinated manner to avoid possible future conflicts.'

[173] *See* Report of the United Nations Water Conference Mar del Plata 14–25 March 1977, UN Doc. E/CONF.70/29; the Dublin Statement on Water and Sustainable Development, reprinted in 22 EPL 54 (1992); Agenda 21, *supra* note 73; the deliberations during the 1994 Session of the CSD, *supra* note 135, at 6–29 (pts. 11–75). Recall also the endorsement of the concept by the ILA in its Helsinki Rules, *supra* note 55, and its Montreal Rules, *supra* note 55. And note that, similarly, the Institut de Droit International endorsed the basin concept in its Salzburg Resolution, 49-II ANNUAIRE DE L'INSTITUT DE DROIT INTERNATIONAL 381 (1961), and in its Athens Resolution, 58-I ANNUAIRE DE L'INSTITUT DE DROIT INTERNATIONAL 197 (1980).

[174] *See, e.g.*, Teclaff, *The River Basin Concept and Global Climate Change*, 8 PACEELR 355, 370 (1991). *See also* Shiklomanov, *World Fresh Water Resources*, *in* P.H. Gleick, *supra* note 53, at 13; and Slyfield, *Remarks During a Workshop on Environmental Security and Freshwater Resources*, held at the Faculty of Law, McGill University, Montreal, 11–12 November 1994 (minutes on file with authors).

[175] *See* Teclaff, *supra* note 173; and Francis, *Ecosystem Management*, 33 NRJ 316, 328 (1993). *See also* the ILA Draft Articles on the Relationship Between Water, Other Natural Resources and the Environment, Report of the Fifty-Ninth Conference 374 (1980).

[176] A noteworthy example is the Canadian Mackenzie River Basin Transboundary Waters Master Agreement. Relying in part on international legal principles, the agreement incorporates a series of more detailed principles which promote the maintenance of ecological integrity of the aquatic ecosystem. *See* D. DAVIS, CANADIAN EXPERIENCE IN INTERJURISDICTIONAL WATER RESOURCES MANAGEMENT 15–16 (1993) (unpublished manual on file with authors). *See also* the discussion in CSD, *supra* note 135, at 29–35 (pts. 76–95).

[177] *See, e.g.*, Agenda 21, *supra* note 73, para. 18.4, which, despite the endorsement of an integrated ecosystem approach, focuses narrowly on the interests of riparian states in their transboundary water resources. *But see* Art. I of the Great Lakes Water Quality Agreement, *supra* note 172.

range of non-riparians in freshwater management. Such non-riparian interests in ecological preservation could be related to the protection of the marine environment,[178] or to the role of the watercourse in broader ecosystem integrity, in the preservation of biodiversity or in the maintenance of regional climate.[179]

While the acceptability of rights and obligations extending beyond a drainage basin may seem unlikely today, the idea is not as untested as it may seem. Strictly speaking, it is but an extension of the reasoning underlying limitations resulting from the traditional transboundary harm rule. Just as that rule developed slowly and in reaction to the recognition of transboundary environmental interdependence, there now is evidence of further normative development driven by the recognition of broader ecological interdependence. Qualitatively, these new limitations do not differ much from the traditional normative framework. The only significant difference between the 'old' and 'new' limitations is that the latter are not triggered by interferences with territorial interests of states, but with ecological interests that may not be rooted in territorial integrity.

One example of new sovereignty limitations is the concept of 'common concern of humankind', which is emerging in the context of global environmental problems. Common concerns are typically triggered by those environmental problems that pose threats to the international community as a whole and thus, by definition, to each of its members. Therefore, common concerns may be argued to create rights and obligations *erga omnes*, owed to and enforceable by all states.[180] To date, the concept has found application mostly in the context of environmental threats related to resources beyond the jurisdiction of states.[181] But the concept also applies to situations where the object of the common concern is located within the jurisdiction of a given state.[182] Given the concerns over undue 'internationalization' of national resources, it is crucial that the concept of common concern, unlike the related notion of common heritage, does not purport to render the resource itself 'common.'[183] Rather the goal is to limit the jurisdiction of states over their resources only to the extent that their

[178] For a recent review *see* Platt, *Dying Seas* 8 WORLDWATCH 10 (1995).

[179] *See supra* note 51–3 and accompanying text.

[180] *See* Kirgis, *Standing to Challenge Human Endeavours That Could Change the Climate*, 84 AJIL 525 (1990).

[181] For example, the preamble to the Climate Change Convention, *supra* note 135, acknowledges that 'change in the Earth's climate and the adverse effects of rapid climate change are a common concern of humankind.'

[182] Thus the preamble to the Biodiversity Convention, *supra* note 135, states that 'the conservation of biological diversity is a common concern of humankind.'

[183] *See* Boyle, *The Convention on Biological Diversity in* Campiglio et al., *supra* note 64, at 111, 117.

activities affect ecological interests of third states.[184] Put differently, in giving rights to third states, the concept does not affect the 'ownership' dimension of a state's sovereignty over its resources, but the 'use' dimension.

The concept of common concern is not directly relevant to transboundary freshwater and we do not mean to suggest that an ecosystem orientation in international environmental law would require global involvement in national water management. Rather, the point is that the idea underlying the concept of global common concern is transferable to the regional setting. In light of the growing web of interrelated environmental pressures and the broadening circle of interested parties, certain environmental security concerns may warrant the participation of non-riparian nations in a watercourse regime. At the same time, as suggested above, this participation will have to be different in quality from that of riparians, limited to that necessary to address the common concern. Therefore, the idea of a regional common concern may be a suitable conceptual vehicle for the inclusion of non-riparian interests.

An encouraging example, pointing to the feasibility of such a differentiated approach, is the (ECE) Convention on the Protection and Use of Transboundary Watercourses and International Lakes of 1992.[185] Although relying on a relatively narrow definition of 'transboundary waters', the Convention achieves an ecosystem-oriented scope through a broad definition of 'transboundary impact' which links water to the surrounding environment.[186] Significantly, the Convention distinguishes between 'parties' and 'riparian parties',[187] and between provisions relating to all parties and those relating to riparian parties. The former provisions contain mostly common environmental protection and ecosystem management obligations,[188] whereas the latter focus on cooperation among riparian states and joint management of the water resource.[189]

The injection of a broader perspective will ultimately promote environmental security for riparians and non-riparians alike. Riparians are more likely to focus on the use of their freshwater resources whereas non-riparians are more likely to promote longer-term environmental inter-

[184] *See* Handl, *supra* note 2, at 31–2. For an example, *see* the Biodiversity Convention, *supra* note 135, which does not declare biological resources *per se*, but the conservation of biological diversity, a common concern.

[185] *Supra* note 150.

[186] *Id.*, according to Art. 1.1. '"Transboundary waters" means any surface or ground waters which mark, cross or are located between two or more States'. According to Art. 1.2.:

> 'Transboundary impact' means any significant adverse effect on the environment resulting from a change in the conditions of transboundary waters caused by a human activity, the physical origin of which is situated wholly or in part within an area under the jurisdiction of a Party. . . . Such effects on the environment include effects on human health and safety, flora, fauna, soil, air, water, climate, landscape and historical monuments or other physical structures or the interaction among these factors.

[187] *Id.*, Arts. 1.3. and 1.4.

[188] *Id.*, Arts. 2–8.

[189] *Id.*, Arts. 9–16.

ests.[190] The inclusion of non-riparian interests can thus make an important contribution to the articulation of the common ecological interests of all involved. This could, in turn, serve to counter-balance at least in part the impact of competing use interests of riparians on regime formation.[191]

IV. CONCLUSION

The preceding discussion suggests a number of strategies that may be pursued to reorient international environmental law so as to address environmental security concerns more effectively in the context of freshwater resources. Each strategy is premised on the relatively broad conception of environmental security adopted in this paper.

First, environmental security in both its traditional and expansive formulations can be ensured only by legal concepts, and ultimately by the elaboration of regimes, that extend beyond the water resource to encompass the entire ecosystem. Accordingly, the scope of rights and obligations must be defined, at least in part, by the ambit and needs of the ecosystem. Any appropriate regime should encompass all states whose activities can affect or be affected by the water resource.

Second, the focus of any emerging norms or regimes should be on the common interest of all relevant actors in the protection and preservation of the resource, rather than solely on competing state interests. The latter, traditional, approach emphasizes confrontation, and not the cooperation necessary for the achievement of true environmental security.

Third, in light of the reluctance of states to subject sovereignty over resources to international interests, any limitations on the 'ownership' dimension of sovereignty must be avoided. Norms should not aim at the 'internationalization' of the resource itself. Rather, any regulation should be limited to conduct adversely affecting the interests of concerned states.

Fourth, although it is important to develop the scope or physical ambit of legal principles according to ecosystem criteria, evolution of the substantive content of principles is equally important. The development of normative principles providing concrete guidelines for ecologically sound conduct must be promoted.

Fifth, to promote environmental security effectively, emerging normative frameworks must address future interests and provide a structure sufficiently flexible to accommodate new concerns and interests as they emerge. None the less, applicable norms and criteria to determine shares in a resource must be concrete enough to avoid conflict generated by incom-

[190] *See* Boyle, *supra* note 113; Kiss, *supra* note 17; and Davis, *supra* note 19.

[191] The structure of the (ECE) Convention on Transboundary Watercourses, *supra* note 150, would seem to confirm this assumption. It remains to be seen whether it will be borne out by the practice under this agreement.

patible activities pursued by states, each claiming adherence to ambiguous standards.

Finally, despite experience illustrating the benefits of a process-oriented approach and a procedural focus for international environmental cooperation, substantive principles have an important role to play in shaping individual regimes and in answering some basic questions that need not be renegotiated in each case. Perhaps even more important, principles developed outside a concrete regional setting are more likely to articulate common environmental, rather than competing use, interests. When transferred to a specific context, principles can inject a cooperative perspective and, in identifying common goals, may promote the reshaping of previously competing interests into, if not shared objectives, at least commensurate positions.

Fair Play, Fair Pay: Preserving Traditional Knowledge and Biological Resources

Dinah Shelton[1]

Indigenous people and their communities and other local communities have a vital role in environmental management and development because of their knowledge and traditional practices. States should recognize and duly support their identity, culture and interests and enable their effective participation in the achievement of sustainable development.

Principle 22, Rio Declaration on Environment and Development (1992)

I. INTRODUCTION

Rural communities, especially indigenous[2] peoples and forest dwellers, have sustainably used and developed their surrounding biological resources for many centuries. These groups have developed important technologies and arts, mastering crop varieties and irrigation methods, maintaining delicate ecosystems, and using flora and fauna. Through trial and error, they have applied their ecosystems' plants and animals to improving human health and well-being. Today, 80 percent of the world's population depends on traditional health care based on medicinal plants.[3]

[1] Professor of Law, Santa Clara University. This article was prepared as a report for the Biodiversity Policy Unit of the Worldwide Fund for Nature, with the assistance of John Lavorato, Edward Daniels, and Ellen Hey. The author is grateful for the review of earlier drafts by Günther Handl, Alexandre Kiss, Michel Pimbert, Darrell Posey, Renée Vellve and Farhana Yamin.

[2] Anthropologists originally used the term 'indigenous' interchangeably with 'folk,' linked to 'local' or 'non-formal' cultures. It could include people belonging to the majority ethnic group within a country, especially rural populations. In recent decades, the term 'indigenous' has been applied more narrowly to non- or pre-European ethnic groups, in place of the term 'native' or 'aboriginal.' Used in the latter sense, international instruments provide that self-identification is the fundamental criterion for determining indigenous status. *See* ILO Convention No. 169 concerning Indigenous and Tribal Peoples in Independent Countries, adopted 27 June 1989, Art. 1(2), 28 ILM 1382 (1989) [hereinafter ILO Convention on Indigenous Peoples]. In the present study, 'indigenous' is used in its narrower sense, and protection of indigenous communities is included as part of the general problem of protecting local livelihood systems.

[3] C. Joyce, *Western Medicine Men Return to the Field*, 42 BIOSCIENCE 399 (1992). *See also* N.R. Farnsworth et al., *Medicinal Plants in Therapy*, 63 BULLETIN OF THE WORLD HEALTH ORGANIZATION 965 (1985).

Local communities' knowledge and resources are rapidly disappearing, transforming rural communities. Many indigenous populations face pressures that threaten their lands and cultures and can lead to their disappearance as distinct groups. By one estimate, 85 Brazilian Indian groups became extinct in the first half of the twentieth century,[4] and an average of one indigenous group a year has gone extinct in the Amazon region since 1900.[5] More than two-thirds of the remaining tribes have fewer than 1,000 members.[6] These facts raise serious human rights concerns, and mean that the undocumented and increasingly valuable knowledge of nearly 15,000 existing cultures is disappearing before the cultures can transmit their knowledge to new generations.[7]

Biological diversity is also rapidly decreasing. Of approximately 1.4 million organisms that have scientific names, an estimated one plant or animal species becomes extinct every day, with the number likely to reach one species every hour by the year 2000.[8] Western scientists have studied only about 1,100 of the earth's plant species, yet as many as 40,000 may have undiscovered medicinal or nutritional value for humans.[9]

The loss of biological and cultural diversity has considerable economic implications. Local communities' knowledge and resources are increasing in global importance and economic value. Biological products and processes account for 40 percent of the world's market economy.[10] According to a 1990 experts meeting, pharmacologists draw 7,000 medical compounds—from aspirin to birth control pills—from plants.[11] The estimated annual world market value for these medicines is between $35 and $47 billion.[12] Biodiversity is clearly a 'common concern of mankind', a global resource of intrinsic value.[13]

[4] D. Ribeiro, De Indios e a Civilizacao (1965). Between 1987 and 1990 alone, more than one-sixth of the Yanomami tribe died, primarily due to an Amazonian gold rush: *Aid for an Ancient Tribe*, Newsweek, Apr. 9, 1990, at 34.

[5] E. Linden, *Lost Tribes, Lost Knowledge*, Time, Sept. 23, 1991, at 46.

[6] *Id.*

[7] J.W. Clay, *Indigenous Peoples and Tropical Forests: Models of Land Use and Management from Latin America*, Cultural Survival, 1988.

[8] J.R. Axt & M.L. Corn, Biotechnology, Indigenous Peoples, and Intellectual Property Rights 3 (CRS Report for Congress 1993).

[9] Linden, *supra* note 5, at 52. In early December 1994, a team of scientists from the United States and Malaysia, sponsored by the National Cancer Institute, reported tests on a species of Malaysian tree that showed promise in combatting HIV. P. Shenon, *In the Borneo Rain Forest, a Plant Might Just Fight the AIDS Virus*, The San Diego Union-Tribune, Dec. 7, 1994, E-5.

[10] Intellectual Property Rights—Global Consensus, Global Conflict? (R.M. Gadbow & T. J. Richards, eds., 1990).

[11] K.E. Mshigeni, *Foreword, in* Proceedings of the International Conference of Experts from Developing Countries on Traditional Medicinal Plants (K.E. Mshigeni, ed., 1991).

[12] United Nations Environment Program, Saving our Planet: Challenges and Hopes (1992). *See also* D. Posey, Basic Research into the Topics and Issues of Intellectual Property Rights and Just Compensation for Native Peoples (1990); J.H. Balick & R. Mendelsohn, *Assessing the Economic Value of Traditional Medicines from Tropical Rainforests*, 6 Conservation Biology 128 (1992).

[13] United Nations Convention on Biological Diversity, *adopted* June 5, 1992, Preamble,

Conservation of traditional knowledge and resources can produce widespread long-term benefits. It can help to ensure the survival of local communities and enhance biodiversity and environmental protection where these groups are located. It may also lead to the discovery of valuable new natural products.[14] To these ends, local communities should be able to control access to and use of their traditional resources and knowledge, and receive just and equitable compensation when outsiders use them.

Numerous interests must be balanced in order to meet the twin goals of protecting biological resources and preserving local communities fairly and equitably. These interests include those of the local communities, the states in which the knowledge and resources are located, researchers and collectors, companies that use the knowledge, and consumers of the products thereby developed.

This article analyzes legal avenues and techniques, including international environmental law, international human rights law, the regulation of transnational corporations and individuals, compensation through local rights and remedies, and principles of intellectual property, that may help conserve biological resources and protect local communities and their resources and traditional knowledge.[15]

A/CONF.151/26, 31 ILM 818 (1992) [Hereinafter Biodiversity Convention]. The Convention was opened for signature at the United Nations Conference on Environment and Development (UNCED).

[14] Indigenous knowledge led to current plant-based treatments based on alkaloids. N. TAYLOR, PLANT DRUGS THAT CHANGED THE WORLD 1–3 (1965).

[15] For other studies on this subject, see O. AKERELE ET AL., CONSERVATION OF MEDICINAL PLANTS (1991); R.C. Allen, *Collective Invention*, 4 JOURNAL OF ECONOMIC BEHAVIOR AND ORGANIZATIONS 1 (1983); J. H. Barton & E. Christensen, *Diversity Compensation Systems: Ways to Compensate Developing Nations for Providing Genetic Materials*, *in* SEED AND SOVEREIGNTY (J.R. Kloppenburg, ed., 1988); B.M. Boom, *Giving Native People a Share of the Profits*, 14 GARDEN 28 (1990); D. BROKENSHAW ET AL., INDIGENOUS KNOWLEDGE SYSTEMS AND DEVELOPMENT (1980); S. Brush, *A Farmer-Based Approach to Conserving Crop Germplasm*, 45 ECONOMIC BOTANY 153 (1991); S. Brush, *Farmers' Rights and Genetic Conservation in Traditional Farming Systems*, 21 WORLD DEVELOPMENT 1617 (1992); M. Chapin, *How the Kuna Keep the Scientists in Line*, 15 CULTURAL SURVIVAL QUARTERLY 17 (1991); A. CUNNINGHAM, ETHICS, BROKERS AND BIODIVERSITY (1993); A. Cunningham, *Indigenous Knowledge and Biodiversity: Global Commons or Regional Heritage* 15 CULTURAL SURVIVAL QUARTERLY 1 (1991); Q. CRONK & J. FULLER, PLANT INVADERS: THE THREAT TO NATURAL ECOSYSTEMS WORLDWIDE (1994); T. Eisner, *Prospecting for Nature's Riches*, 1 CHEMOECOLOGY 38 (1990); C. FOWLER & P. MOONEY, SHATTERING: FOOD, POLITICS AND THE LOSS OF GENETIC DIVERSITY (1990); C. Joyce, *Prospectors for Tropical Medicines*, 19 NEW SCIENTIST 32 (1991); SEEDS AND SOVEREIGNTY (J.R. Kloppenberg, ed., 1988); J. Kloppenburg & D.L. Kleinman, *The Plant Germplasm Controversy*, 37 BIOSCIENCE 190 (1987); W. LESSER, EQUITABLE PATENT PROTECTION IN THE DEVELOPING WORLD: ISSUES AND APPROACHES (1991); G. MARTIN, ETHNOBOTANY AND PLANT CONSERVATION (1994); R.J. McNeil & M.J. McNeil, *Ownership of Traditional Information: Moral and Legal Obligations to Compensate for Taking*, NORTHEAST INDIAN QUARTERLY 30 (1989); D.A. Posey, *Intellectual Property Rights and Just Compensation for Indigenous Knowledge,* 6 ANTHROPOLOGY TODAY 13 (1990); R. Stone, *The Biodiversity Treaty: Pandora's Box or Fair Deal?* 256 SCIENCE 1624 (1992); BIODIVERSITY (E.O. Wilson, ed., 1988).

II. INTERNATIONAL ENVIRONMENTAL LAW

A. Introduction

Environmental instruments reflect a consensus that preserving indigenous peoples' environments, including conserving and sustainably using biological resources, is in humanity's interest. Indigenous peoples' and local communities' knowledge is vital to attaining this goal, as well as to achieving more sustainable agriculture and conserving and sustainably using forests.

The relevant documents call for benefit sharing, both at the international and the national level. Concrete procedures for effecting such benefit sharing remain to be developed. From the perspective of international environmental obligations, benefit sharing with local communities is the responsibility of the states within whose territory the communities live. It is up to the states concerned to adopt the necessary legislation or take other measures to ensure that benefits are secured when others obtain traditional knowledge from local communities for commercial use.

Implementing the environmental rights to public participation and information and establishing an informed-consent requirement could greatly assist in this effort. Pressure from indigenous and environmental non-governmental organizations, interested states, and inter-governmental organizations can help to bring about the establishment of a system that compensates indigenous people for their traditional knowledge and resources.

B. The Importance of Indigenous Peoples to Environmental Protection

Local communities' knowledge is essential to protecting local ecosystems, conserving biodiversity,[16] and sustainably using biological resources,[17] including genetic resources.[18] International instruments thus stress access to and sharing of local information, technology, and resources. The Biodiversity Convention refers to biodiversity's importance for evolution and for maintaining the biosphere's life-sustaining systems.[19] It maintains that access to and sharing of both genetic resources and technologies are essential for these purposes.[20]

[16] The Biodiversity Convention defines biological diversity as 'the variability among living organisms from all sources including *inter alia*, terrestrial, marine and other aquatic ecosystems and the ecological complexes of which they are part; this includes diversity within species, between species and of ecosystems.' Biodiversity Convention, *supra* note 13, Art. 2.

[17] 'Biological resources' 'includes genetic resources, organisms or parts thereof, populations, or any other biotic component of ecosystems with actual or potential use or value for humanity'. *Id.*

[18] 'Genetic resources' is defined as 'genetic material of actual or potential value'. *Id.*

[19] *Id.*, preamble para. 2.

[20] *Id.* para. 20. Agenda 21 expresses the same idea, noting that 'essential goods and services depend on the variety and variability of genes, species, populations and ecosystems. Biological

Biological resources are also essential to biotechnology research which, according to Chapter 16 of Agenda 21, promises to make significant contributions to providing health care, food security, potable water, efficient industrial development processes for transforming raw materials, sustainable forestry, and detoxification of hazardous wastes.[21]

The instruments adopted at the United Nations Conference on Environment and Development (UNCED) recognize indigenous peoples' special role in developing traditional practices that are essential for conserving and sustainably using the environment in general and biodiversity and biological resources in particular.[22] The Biodiversity Convention, for example, calls on its parties to encourage customary use of biological resources, exchange traditional and indigenous knowledge, and develop methods of cooperation for the development and use of indigenous and traditional technologies. It makes no reference, however, to the consent or participation of local and indigenous groups in this process.[23]

Agenda 21 also emphasizes the importance of traditional knowledge and practices. With regard to forest and vegetation protection, it requires governments to research indigenous people's traditional uses of forest resources,[24] to collect and record indigenous farming knowledge, and facilitate the transfer of environmentally sound technologies.[25]

Chapter 15 of Agenda 21 provides an overview, calling on governments to '[r]ecognize and foster the traditional methods and the knowledge of indigenous people and their communities, emphasizing the role of women, relevant to the conservation of biological diversity and the sustainable use of biological resources.'[26] It also calls on governments to provide incentives for conserving biodiversity through traditional methods of agriculture, agroforestry, forestry, and range and wildlife management.[27]

The emphasis on state efforts to collect and disseminate traditional knowledge highlights the need to determine issues of local control and compensation. The Biodiversity Convention contains the most direct reference to compensation for knowledge and resource use. It recognizes, although

resources feed and clothe us and provide housing, medicines and spiritual nourishment.' Agenda 21, the program of action adopted at UNCED, Rio de Janeiro, June 1992, Ch. 15.

[21] Agenda 21, *supra* note 20, para. 16.1.

[22] *See* Rio Declaration on Environment and Development, *adopted* June 14, 1992, UN Doc. A/CONF.151/26 (vol. 1), principle 22, 31 ILM 874 (1992); *see also* Biodiversity Convention, *supra* note 13, Art. 10; Agenda 21, *supra* note 20, Chs. 11, 14, 15, 26; and Non-legally Binding Authoritative Statement of Principles for a Global Consensus on the Management, Conservation and Sustainable Development of all Types of Forests, *adopted* June 14, 1992, A/CONF.151/26 (vol. 1), 31 ILM 874 (1992) [hereinafter Forest Principles] (explicitly affirming the role of indigenous communities with respect to agriculture, biodiversity, biological resources, and the conservation of forests).

[23] Biodiversity Convention, *supra* note 13, Arts. 10, 17, 18.

[24] Agenda 21, *supra* note 20, para. 11.4.(g).

[25] *Id.* paras. 14.26(b), 14.28(b).

[26] *Id.* para. 15.4(g).

[27] *Id.* para. 15.5.(d).

only in its Preamble, 'the close and traditional dependence of many indigenous and local communities embodying traditional lifestyles on biological resources, and [the] desirability of sharing equitably benefits arising from the use of traditional knowledge, innovations and practices relevant to the conservation of biological diversity and the sustainable use of its components.'[28]

In the body of the Biodiversity Convention, Art. 8 on *in-situ* conservation[29] requires each state to preserve indigenous and local communities' practices and to promote wider application of traditional knowledge 'with the approval and involvement of the holders of such knowledge, innovations, and practices'. Access to the resources themselves is subject to the prior informed consent of the state providing such resources, unless the state itself determines otherwise.[30]

Other texts concerning public participation echo the Biodiversity Convention's reference to local consent and involvement. Agenda 21 provides that the local community should be involved developing and transferring indigenous ecological knowledge and farm practices[31] with a view to promoting environmentally sound and sustainable development. Agenda 21 also states that international organizations should provide technical and financial assistance for capacity-building programs and strengthen research and education programs to incorporate indigenous peoples' and local communities' 'values, views and knowledge including the unique contribution of indigenous women, in resource management and other policies and programs that may effect them.'[32]

The Non-legally Binding Authoritative Statement of Principles for a Global Consensus on the Management, Conservation and Sustainable Development of all Types of Forests (Forest Principles) also emphasizes indigenous knowledge's usefulness for conserving and sustainably developing forests, as well as the importance of involving local communities in these efforts.

On the regional level, the Declaration of San Francisco de Quito (Amazon Declaration) establishes an Amazonian Special Commission on Indigenous Affairs to ensure that indigenous populations' knowledge is

[28] Biodiversity Convention, *supra* note 13, preamble.

[29] *Id.* Art. 8. The Biodiversity Convention emphasizes that: 'the fundamental requirement for the conservation of biological diversity is the *in-situ* conservation of ecosystems and natural habitats and the maintenance and recovery of viable populations of species and their natural surroundings.' *Id.* preamble. *Ex-situ* conservation measures are to be taken 'predominantly for the purpose of complementing *in-situ* measures.' The explicit preference for *in-situ* conservation of biological diversity adds to the value of the knowledge and traditional practices of indigenous peoples. *Id.* Art. 9.

[30] *Id.* Art. 15(5).

[31] Agenda 21, *supra* note 20, paras. 14.22.(a), 26.3.(iii).

[32] Agenda 21, *supra* note 20, para. 26.5.

incorporated into regional development programs.[33] But it says nothing about compensation for acquiring this knowledge. Rather, it states that it respects Amazonian indigenous populations' right to have all measures adopted that aim at maintaining and preserving the integrity of these groups, their culture, and their ecological habitats, but only 'subject to the exercise of that right which is inherent in the sovereignty of each State'.[34]

These texts illustrate that the international community recognizes the vital importance of and the need to preserve indigenous peoples' knowledge and traditional practices for sustainable agriculture, environmental protection, and conservation of biological resources. The texts place emphasis on local participation in these efforts.

C. Benefit Sharing

UNCED texts recognize that the benefits of attaining sustainable development should be shared with those, including indigenous peoples, who invest in conservation or provide resources. Implementation at the international level is to be achieved through interstate benefit sharing. In general, based on traditional notions of state sovereignty, UNCED texts allow states to determine and allocate any share of benefits for local communities.

The Biodiversity Convention, Chs. 14 and 15 of Agenda 21, and the Forest Principles explicitly recognize, if often in conditional terms, that the benefits obtained from using traditional knowledge should be shared with local groups. The Biodiversity Convention provides that each contracting party shall 'encourage' the equitable sharing of the benefits arising from the use of traditional knowledge.[35] It does not explicitly recognize any right to compensation.

Agenda 21 contains stronger language in favor of benefit sharing. It calls on states to 'take appropriate measures for the fair and equitable sharing of benefits and results of research and development in plant breeding between the sources and users of plant genetic resources.'[36] Benefits derived from biological and genetic resources also are to be shared, and states are to take measures to ensure that local communities participate in the benefits derived from the use of their knowledge and technologies.[37]

The Forest Principles also refer to equitable sharing.[38] Paragraph 8(g) reinforces the sovereign rights of countries where forests are located to control access to biological resources, including genetic material. When access is granted, the technology and profits from products derived from these resources shall be shared on mutually agreed terms.[39] Benefits that arise

[33] Amazon Declaration, *adopted* May 6, 1989, UN Doc. A/44/275, E/1989/79, Annex of May 15, 1989, 28 ILM 1303 (1989).

[34] *Id.* at para. 3.

[35] *Id.* preamble.

[36] *Id.* para. 1.57(d).

[37] *Id.* para. 15.4(d).

[38] Forest Principles, *supra* note 22.

[39] *Id.* para 8(g).

from the use of indigenous knowledge should be equitably shared with such people.[40]

These provisions indicate a general commitment to promote benefit sharing with local communities that transmit their traditional knowledge to others. They also demonstrate agreement that it is primarily the responsibility of the states within whose jurisdiction the communities live to attain this objective—no provisions require adoption of international instruments to further this end. But there are no barriers preventing states from cooperating. In fact, the many general provisions requiring states to cooperate toward the attainment of expressed goals support the view that international cooperation is required if goals can not be reached solely through national instruments.

D. Participation in Decision-making

Various international instruments recognize the right of individuals and groups to participate in environmental decisions.[41] Information and citizen participation in safeguarding the environment are fundamental principles of environmental protection. According to the World Charter for Nature, '[a]ll persons, in accordance with their national legislation, shall have the opportunity to participate, individually or with others, in the formulation of decisions of direct concern to their environment, and shall have access to means of redress when their environment has suffered damage or degradation.'[42] The 1985 Association of Southeast Asian Nations Agreement on the Conservation of Natural Resources also contains this principle.[43] The Organisation for Economic Cooperation and Development recommends that its member states encourage public participation when preparing decisions with significant environmental consequences.

The documents adopted at UNCED recognize the need to involve local communities in conserving natural resources. The Rio Declaration supports a general right to participation and information in environmental matters.[44]

[40] *Id.* para 12(d).

[41] *See, e.g.*, African Charter of Human and Peoples Rights (June 20, 1981), Art. 24, OAU Doc. CAB/LEG/67/3/Rev. 5, 21 ILM 58 (1982); Additional Protocol to the American Convention on Human Rights in the Area of Economic, Social and Cultural Rights (Nov. 18, 1988), Art. 11, OASTS 69; 28 ILM 698 (1989); PERU CONSTITUTION (1979) Art. 123.

[42] World Charter for Nature, *adopted* Oct. 28, 1982, G.A. Res. 37/7, UN Doc. A/37/51 (1982) Principle 23, 27 UNGAOR Supp. (No. 51) at 17.

[43] Association of Southeast Asian Nations Agreement on the Conservation of Natural Resources, *adopted* July 9, 1985, 15 EPL 64 (1985).

[44] Rio Declaration, *supra* note 22. It states that:

> environmental issues are best handled with the participation of all concerned citizens, at the relevant level. At the national level, each individual shall have appropriate access to information concerning the environment that is held by public authorities, including information on hazardous materials and activities in their communities, and the opportunity to participate in decision-making processes. States shall facilitate and encourage public awareness and participation by making information widely available. Effective access to judicial and administrative proceedings, including redress and remedy, shall be provided.

Id. principle 10.

In addition, Principle 22 provides that '[s]tates should recognize and duly support the identity, culture and interests [of indigenous peoples and local communities] and enable their effective participation in the achievement of sustainable development.' This sentence emphasizes the importance of achieving a form of participation for indigenous peoples that respects and protects their identity, although the use of 'should' rather than 'shall' limits the sense of obligation.

As mentioned above, Art. 8(j) of the Biodiversity Convention provides that each contracting party is to promote the wider application of indigenous and local communities' knowledge 'with the approval and involvement of the holders of such knowledge, innovations and practices. . . .'[45] The Convention does not indicate how parties are to implement this provision.

Chapter 15 of Agenda 21 repeatedly calls for the participation of indigenous and local communities.[46] Paragraph 15.3 recognizes that 'the participation and support of local communities are elements essential' to conserving biological and genetic resources. Governments should take action 'with the support of indigenous people and their communities',[47] and promote mechanisms to involve indigenous and local communities in ecosystem conservation and management.

Chapter 26 indicates some of the means that might be used to secure the involvement of indigenous peoples, including developing and strengthening national dispute resolution arrangements; capacity-building; arrangements to strengthen active participation in national formulation of policies, laws, and programs; and involving indigenous people and their communities in national and local resource management and conservation strategies. In some instances, states may provide for self-management of resources, participation in development decisions, participation in the establishment or management of protected areas, and development or strengthening of national consultation arrangements.[48] The chapter places emphasis on securing national and local involvement.

At the international level, Chapter 26 mentions various actions to secure local communities' interests. The text recommends developing procedures within and between international organizations to help governments ensure that indigenous peoples' views are incorporated in policy and program design and implementation. It also calls for regional cooperation between governments to address common indigenous issues.[49]

[45] Biodiversity Convention, *supra* note 13, Art. 8(j).

[46] Chapters 11 and 14 of Agenda 21 contain provisions similar to those contained in Ch. 15. Agenda 21, *supra* note 20. Some refer specifically to indigenous peoples, while others refer more generally to local communities, rural farmers, and other groups. Relevant paragraphs include 11.2., 11.4(b), 11.14(i), 14.7., 14.22.(b), 14.23., and 14.45(b). *Id.*

[47] *Id.* para. 15.5.

[48] *Id.* para. 26.6.(a).

[49] *Id.* para. 26.6.(b).

E. Using International Environmental Law to Protect Indigenous Peoples and Their Environments

These international environmental texts may be of some use in preserving traditional knowledge and achieving equitable benefit sharing. The primary focus of the texts is obviously on conserving natural resources; preserving traditional knowledge is treated as a means to that end. The instruments adopted at UNCED strongly assert state sovereignty over natural resources. In turn, benefit sharing is largely seen as an interstate issue. The documents make little reference to local control over resources.

International legal recognition of permanent state sovereignty over natural resources is long-standing. The UNCED texts reaffirm this norm and draw out some of its implications in regard to state control over access to and benefits derived from biological resources. Moreover, the documents evidence a strong bias toward state-controlled commercial exploitation of traditional knowledge and technologies, with states encouraged to collect, research, and exchange indigenous knowledge and develop methods for use of indigenous technologies.

The fact that any role is included for non-state actors in regard to biological resources is a significant development and probably due to the active participation at UNCED of numerous non-governmental organizations. It is thus important that all the texts recognize and call on states to protect the special role of indigenous peoples in maintaining traditional practices that conserve and sustainably use biological resources. But nearly all the provisions in the UNCED texts concerning indigenous peoples are legally weak. They are drafted in terms of 'should' rather than 'shall', and qualified by phrases such as 'as far as possible and appropriate'. In some cases, key provisions appear only in the preamble to a legal instrument. Moreover, the most lengthy discussion of the role of indigenous peoples in contained in the non-binding Agenda 21.

In spite of the weakness of most provisions, overall there is a clear and new indication that states should take action to protect indigenous knowledge and traditional practices, and provide equitable benefit sharing. It is equally clear that national implementing measures will be necessary before indigenous groups can derive legal protection from the international texts. Few, if any, of the provisions are drafted in language that would make them immediately enforceable in the domestic law of any country. Thus, the first goal of local communities should be to push for and participate in the process of adopting implementing legislation.

International environmental instruments do include some provisions that can empower local communities and may enhance equitable benefit sharing. Rights of public participation in environmental decisions are particularly important in this regard and are found in numerous international instruments. The trend toward ensuring public participation is partly based on broad developments in democratic governance not directly tied to environmental protection. Participatory rights also seem to derive from an assumption that those closest to and dependent on a particular locale will be most protective of its sustainability and productivity. This assumption appears particularly strong where indigenous groups, especially forest dwellers, are concerned. Some may question whether this assumption accurately predicts decisions that will be made when the choice is between short-term gain and long-term sustainable practices. The evidence seems mixed.

The most important contribution of international environmental law to this issue may be to preserve biological resources from indigenous peoples and local communities, as well as from abusive state practices. The legal texts emphasize knowledge and traditional practices that are key to environmental management and development and those innovations and practices relevant to conservation of biodiversity. Although the international instruments and many scholars seem to assume that indigenous peoples and local communities are invariably in harmony with nature, using sustainable practices that conserve biological resources, this assumption may not always be borne out in practice. Some traditional practices may not be beneficial. Even those that are highly protective may give way to new uses of lands and resources that are commercially more profitable.

The objectives stated in Art. 1 of the Biodiversity Convention are all directed at protecting resources over the long term: conservation of biodiversity, sustainable use of its components, and fair and equitable sharing of the benefits arising out of the use of genetic resources. Indigenous groups with traditional practices consistent with these aims may derive benefit from the treaty, having gained some substantive and procedural protection, but the primary goal of international environmental law is to protect the resources. Indigenous and local communities are both the means to achieve this goal and the ultimate beneficiaries of it.

III. INTERNATIONAL HUMAN RIGHTS LAW

International human rights law offers an alternative basis to international environmental law for ensuring equitable treatment of local communities and preserving their biological resources. It seeks to conserve local communities' environments to ensure their cultural and physical survival, rather than using the local communities to further environmental protection. International human rights law is based on recognition of the inherent dignity and equal and inalienable rights of all members of the human family. It reflects global concern for the treatment of individuals and groups, demanding that this treatment meet internationally agreed minimum standards. Human rights obligations derive from the United Nations

Charter,[50] customary international law,[51] and the provisions of nearly 100 global and regional human rights treaties.

The loss of traditional knowledge and resources may implicate numerous internationally guaranteed human rights, including life, health, culture, religion, standard of living, development, well-being, property, information, participation, democracy, remedies, rights of future generations, self-determination, privacy, and the right to the product of one's labor and intellectual achievement. In addition, international human rights law involves the link between human rights and the environment, which has produced growing recognition of a human right to a safe, healthy, and sustainable environment.

A. The Relationship between Human Rights and the Environment

The 1972 Stockholm Declaration on the Human Environment (Stockholm Declaration) affirmed a connection between human rights and environmental protection, stating that 'man has the fundamental right to freedom, equality and adequate conditions of life, in an environment of a quality that permits a life of dignity and well-being.'[52] It implies that all persons have the right to a secure, healthy, and ecologically sound environment. This includes the right to be free from discrimination; pollution; environmental degradation; and activities that adversely affect the environment or threaten life, health, livelihood, well-being, or sustainable development. In particular, the Stockholm Declaration recognizes a right to land tenure and safe food and water. Principle 14 states that indigenous peoples have the right to control their lands and natural resources and to maintain their traditional ways of life. This includes 'the right to security in the enjoyment of their means of subsistence' and the right to protection against any action or course of conduct that may result in the destruction or degradation of their territories.[53]

Procedural rights include rights to environmental information, freedom of expression and opinions, environmental and human rights education,

[50] Among the purposes of the United Nations is 'to cooperate . . . in promoting respect for human rights and fundamental freedoms for all'. UN CHARTER Art. 1. Articles 55 and 56 contain obligations for the organization and member states to promote 'universal respect for, and observance of, human rights and fundamental freedoms for all without distinction as to race, sex, language or religion'. *Id.*

[51] Some provisions of the Universal Declaration of Human Rights contain customary international law. Universal Declaration of Human Rights, GA Res. 217 A(III), UNGA, at 71, UN Doc. A/810 (Dec. 10, 1948) [hereinafter UDHR]. *See Filartiga* v. *Pena-Irala*, 630 F.2d 876 (2d Cir. 1980). *See also* RESTATEMENT (THIRD) OF THE FOREIGN RELATIONS LAW OF THE UNITED STATES §702 (American Law Institute 1987).

[52] Stockholm Declaration on the Human Environment, *adopted* June 16, 1972, UN Doc. A/CONF.48/141 Rev. 1 at 3 (1973), principle 1, 11 ILM 1416 (1972) [hereinafter Stockholm Declaration].

[53] *Id.* at principle 14.

and 'active, free and meaningful participation in planning and decision-making activities and processes that may have an impact on the environment and development.'[54] This includes prior impact assessment of proposed governmental actions. Finally, the Stockholm Declaration restates the right of association and the right to effective remedies and redress for environmental harm or the threat of such harm.

A few United Nations treaties touch on the impact of environmental harm on human rights. The 1989 Convention on the Rights of the Child includes in its article on the right to health the obligation of states parties to take appropriate measures to combat disease and malnutrition, including providing nutritious foods and clean drinking water, 'taking into consideration the dangers and risks of environmental pollution'.[55] The 1989 Convention of the International Labor Organization concerning Indigenous and Tribal Peoples in Independent Countries also contains provisions related to environmental protection.[56]

United Nations organs responsible for human rights issues are paying increasing attention to environmental problems. The United Nations (UN) Sub-Commission on the Prevention of Discrimination and Protection of Minorities (Sub-Commission) began a study of the relationship between human rights and the environment in 1990, and has issued annual reports since then. The reports note that human rights violations often lead to environmental degradation and, conversely, that environmental deterioration can result in or itself be a human rights violation.[57] The 1994 Sub-Commission report includes a Declaration of Principles that affirms the interdependence and indivisibility of human rights, an ecologically sound environment, sustainable development and peace.[58]

At the regional level the African and Inter-American regional human rights systems include a general right to a safe and healthy environment among their treaty guarantees.[59] Many national constitutions also mention a right to environment.[60] In light of this body of law, actions that threaten

[54] *Id.*

[55] UN Convention on the Rights of the Child, *concluded* Nov. 20, 1989, GA Res. 44/25, 44 UNGAOR Supp. (No. 49), UN Doc. A/44/49 at 166 (1989), Art. 24, 30 ILM 1448 (1989).

[56] ILO Convention on Indigenous Peoples, *supra* note 2.

[57] Fatma Zohra Ksentini, Special Rapporteur, HUMAN RIGHTS AND THE ENVIRONMENT: FINAL REPORT, E/CN.4/Sub. 2/1994/9 and corr. 1, Annex.

[58] *Id.*

[59] The African [Banjul] Charter on Human and Peoples' Rights *adopted* June 27, 1981, Art. 24, 21 ILM 58 (1982), recognizes the right of all peoples to 'a generally satisfactory environment favorable to their development'. The Additional Protocol to the American Convention on Human Rights in the Area of Economic, Social and Cultural Rights, Nov. 22, 1969, Additional Protocol Art. 11, OAS Treaty Series No. 36, at 1, provides that everyone shall have the right to live in a healthy environment. The Protocol is not yet in force.

[60] For example, in *Minors Oposa* v. *Secretary of the Dep't of Env't and Natural Resources*, (Phil. 1993) 33 ILM 173 (1994), the Supreme Court of the Philippines held that the plaintiffs could sue to prevent the misappropriation or impairment of the Philippine rainforests due to

local communities' environments, such as taking or destroying local resources, could raise human rights concerns even though the right to a healthy environment is not included in United Nations human rights treaties. Of course, a right to a healthy environment would apply primarily to protect tangible community resources. Other human rights norms must be invoked to claim compensation for the use of traditional knowledge.

B. Internationally Guaranteed Human Rights

Among the human rights guaranteed by various international texts, those discussed below are most relevant to protecting the traditional knowledge and resources of local communities. They indicate the range of potential human rights claims that could be raised, which are discussed in part C below.

(i) The Right to Own Property

Property has long been characterized as the third absolute right, after life and liberty, and defined as including 'the free use, enjoyment and disposal of all . . . acquisitions, without any control or diminution, save only by the laws of the land.'[61] Both the Universal Declaration of Human Rights and the International Convention on the Elimination of all Forms of Racial Discrimination (Racial Convention) contain a right to property.[62] The Racial Convention states that everyone, without discrimination, shall have the right to own property alone as well as in association with others. The Racial Convention leaves defining property to national, customary, or traditional law. It does, however, recognize and protect collective ownership.

The American Convention on Human Rights provides that no one shall be deprived of his property except on payment of just compensation, for reasons of public utility or social interests, and in the cases and according to the forms established by law.[63] It also explicitly prohibits usury 'and any other form of exploitation of man by man'.

The UN Food and Agriculture Organization (FAO) resolution 5/89

logging, based on the constitutional right to a balanced and healthy ecology in accord with the rhythm and harmony of nature. Applicable national and international provisions containing similar language might be invoked to prevent resource destruction in appropriate cases in other parts of the world.

[61] 2 W. Blackstone, Commentaries 2.

[62] UDHR, *supra* note 49, Art. 17. International Convention on the Elimination of all Forms of Racial Discrimination, *entered into force* Jan. 4, 1969, Art. 5, 660 UNTS 195 [hereinafter Racial Convention].

[63] American Convention on Human Rights, *supra* note 62, Art. 21. *See also* American Declaration of the Rights and Duties of Man, *adopted* 1948, Art. XXIII, 6 Actas y Documentos 297–302 (1953) [hereinafter ADHR].

(Farmers' Rights) emphasizes the importance and rights of plant breeders,[64] although it recognizes that plant genetic resources are a 'heritage of mankind' that should be available without restriction. The Farmers' Rights resolution asks states to 'allow farmers, their communities, and countries in all regions, to participate fully in the benefits derived . . . from the improved use of plant genetic resources, through plant breeding and other scientific methods.'[65]

(ii) The Right to Culture and Recognition of Interests in Scientific Production

Human rights instruments contain various expressions of a right to culture and establish that minorities have the right to maintain and enjoy their own culture.[66] Article 22 of the Universal Declaration on Human Rights (Universal Declaration) states that everyone has the right to the economic, social, and cultural rights 'indispensable for his dignity and the free development of his personality'.[67] Article 27(1) provides that 'everyone has the right to freely participate in the cultural life of the community and to share in scientific advancement and its benefits'.[68] The Covenant on Economic, Social and Cultural Rights contains similar language.[69]

Various international instruments also specifically recognize intellectual property rights.[70] The Universal Declaration of Human Rights provides that '[e]veryone has the right to the protection of the moral and material interests resulting from any scientific, literary or artistic production of which he is the author', evidencing a policy in favor of protecting the rights of discovery.[71] The language of the other instruments is virtually identical. The provision seems to protect individual scientific achievement, which could preclude incremental, collective achievements over many generations. The singular 'he' in Art. 27(2) cannot be taken literally, however, or it would exclude all production by women. Legal instruments often use 'he' as an inclusive pronoun, thus, 'he' could mean 'he, she, or it' (the group) in this context.

In 1985, the United Nations Educational, Scientific, and Cultural Organization (UNESCO) and the World Intellectual Property Organization

[64] UN Food and Agriculture Organization (FAO) Res. 5/89 (Farmers' Rights), FAO Report of the Commission on Plant Genetic Resources (1989) 13.

[65] *Id.*

[66] International Covenant on Civil and Political Rights, Dec. 16, 1966, Art. 27, 999 UNTS 171 [hereinafter CCPR].

[67] UDHR, *supra* note 51, Art. 22.

[68] *Id.* Art. 27.

[69] International Covenant on Economic, Social and Cultural Rights, Dec. 16, 1966, Art. 15, 993 UNTS 3 [hereinafter CESCR].

[70] UDHR, *supra* note 51, Art. 27(2), CESCR, *supra* note 69, Art. 15(1)(c), ADHR, *supra* note 63, Art. XIII.

[71] UDHR, *supra* note 51, Art. 27(2).

drafted Model Provisions for National Laws on the Protection of Expressions of Folklore against Illicit Exploitation and Other Prejudicial Actions.[72] These rules recognize that folklore is a manifestation of intellectual creativity and deserves protection similar to that which intellectual property laws provide.

(iii) The Right to Health

The Constitution of the World Health Organization and international human rights treaties recognize the right to the 'highest attainable standard' of health. Read broadly, the right may be viewed to include 'protective environmental services, prevention and health promotion and therapeutic services as well as related actions in sanitation, environmental engineering, housing and social welfare.'[73]

States are not required to implement the right immediately, but to 'achieve progressively the full realization of the right'.[74] The required actions are listed in Art. 12 of the Covenant on Economic, Social and Cultural Rights.[75] These include reduction of stillbirth and infant mortality rates, measures for healthy child development, improvement of environmental hygiene, and disease control. The environment is particularly important to health, as shown by the 1985 case involving the Yanomami Indians in Brazil, discussed below.

(iv) Rights to Information and Participation

The right to information encompasses the right of individuals to seek, receive, and impart information, as well as the right to free expression.[76] In general, it includes the right of the public to be properly informed of issues affecting it.[77] Linked to this is the right to political participation. The Civil and Political Covenant provides that every citizen shall have the right and opportunity to take part in public affairs, directly or through freely chosen

[72] WIPO/UNESCO Model Provisions for National Laws on the Protection of Expressions of Folklore Against Illicit Exploitation and Other Prejudicial Actions, UNESCO/WIPO/WG.II/Folk/4 (Mar. 31, 1981).

[73] R. Roemer, *The Right to Health Care*, *in* THE RIGHT TO HEALTH IN THE AMERICAS 17 (H.L. Fuenzalida-Puelma & S. Scholle, eds., 1989).

[74] CESCR, *supra* note 69, Art. 12(1). *See also* UDHR, *supra* note 51, Art. 25; Convention on the Rights of the Child, US *supra* note 55, Art. 24(1); African Charter on Human and Peoples Rights, *supra* note 41, Art. 16; Racial Convention, *supra* note 62, Art. 5(e); Convention on the Elimination of All Forms of Discrimination Against Women, *entered into force* Sept. 3, 1981, Art. 11(1), UN GAOR Supp. (No. 46) at 193; ACHR (Protocol), *supra* note 41, Art. 10; ADHR, *supra* note 63, Art. XI.

[75] *Id.*

[76] UDHR, *supra* note 51, Art. 19; CCPR, *supra* note 66, Art 19; ACHR, *supra* note 63, Arts. 13, 23; ADHR, *supra* note 62, Art. 20; [European] Convention for the Protection of Human Rights and Fundamental Freedoms, Nov. 4, 1950, Art. 10, 213 UNTS 222.

[77] *Sunday Times* v. *United Kingdom*, 30 European Court of Human Rights (1979).

representatives.[78] Rights of information and participation have become particularly important in international environmental law. Through their implementation, decisions are taken only with the informed consent and participation of those likely to be affected by a proposed action. In the human rights context, participation and information are essential to the achievement of democracy.

(v) The Right of Peoples to Dispose of Their Natural Wealth and Resources

The right of peoples to dispose of their natural wealth and resources is part of the right of self-determination. As such it will not apply to many local communities within states. However, many indigenous groups claim recognition as peoples entitled to self-determination. If states afford them this recognition, control over natural wealth and resources includes endemic flora and fauna,[79] as well as any processes and uses of them known only in the community. The formulation in international texts provides that all peoples 'may, for their own ends, freely dispose of their natural wealth and resources';[80] thus they may conserve or preserve these resources and dispose of them in a sustainable or commercial manner. The provisions cited conclude by stating that 'in no case may a people be deprived of its own means of subsistence.'[81] This could be invoked to prevent the loss of habitat, ecosystems, or rare flora and fauna essential to the survival of local indigenous peoples.[82]

(vi) Rights Specific to Indigenous Populations

The only international human rights treaty specifically concerned with indigenous peoples is the International Labor Organization Convention Concerning Indigenous and Tribal Peoples in Independent Countries (Indigenous Peoples Convention).[83] Its purpose is to provide for indigenous peoples to enjoy the benefits of development while ensuring that their diversity is respected and protected. Article 2 generally requires governments to protect the rights of indigenous peoples and to guarantee respect for their integrity. Article 4 requires governments to adopt special measures as

[78] *See also Popular Participation in its Various Forms as an Important Factor in the Development and in the Realization of Human Rights*, GA Res. 1983/31, UNGAOR, 38th Sess., Agenda Item 85(c), at 5–15.

[79] However, texts of international environmental and international economic law provide that States have permanent sovereignty over natural resources, wealth, and economic activities.

[80] *See* Common Art. 1(2) to the Covenant on Civil and Political Rights, *supra* note 66, and the Covenant on Economic, Social, and Cultural Rights, *supra* note 69.

[81] *Id.*

[82] *See* CESCR, *supra* note 69, Art. 1; CCPR, *supra* note 66, Art. 1.

[83] ILO Convention on Indigenous Peoples, *supra* note 2.

appropriate for safeguarding the persons, institutions, property, labor, cultures, and environment of the peoples concerned. Article 7 guarantees participation in decision-making processes. It provides that indigenous peoples have the right to decide development priorities affecting their lives and lands. They are entitled to control their own economic, social, and cultural development and participate in plans for national and regional development that may affect them directly.

The Indigenous Peoples Convention evidences concern over environmental protection, and thus requires governments to ensure that studies are carried out to assess the social, spiritual, cultural, and environmental impact of planned development activities on indigenous peoples. The results of these studies shall be considered fundamental criteria for the implementation of these activities.[84] Governments also must take measures, in cooperation with indigenous peoples, to protect and preserve their environments and territories.[85] Finally, Art. 8 protects the customs and institutions of indigenous populations, and Art. 13 provides that governments shall respect the special importance of indigenous peoples' relationship with their lands, particularly the collective aspects of this relationship. Other United Nations human rights treaties do not specifically mention indigenous populations. However, during the past 20 years, the UN has actively discussed the topic.[86]

The Sub-Commission has adopted several resolutions on indigenous rights that refer to traditional knowledge and resources. Resolution 1990/27 of 31 August 1990 recommended that any convention adopted at UNCED 'provide explicitly for the role of indigenous peoples as resource users and managers, and for the protection of indigenous peoples' right to control of their own traditional knowledge of ecosystems.'[87] Resolution 1991/31, adopted 29 August, 1991, requested the World Intellectual Property Organization to assist the Working Group on Indigenous Populations in formulating recommendations for protecting indigenous peoples' intellectual property, and called for a report of the Secretary-General[88] and a

[84] *Id.* Art. 7(3).

[85] *Id.* Art. 7(4).

[86] In 1984, the Sub-Commission completed a comprehensive study on discrimination against indigenous populations. It concluded by calling for the protection of indigenous populations' right to preserve their cultures and institutions by transmitting them to future generations: J.R. Martinez Cobo, *Study of the Problem of Discrimination against Indigenous Populations*, Vol. V, E/CN.4/Sub.2/1986/7/Add.4, para 13. The UN Sub-Commission on Prevention of Discrimination and Protection of Minorities consists of 26 persons serving in their individual capacities as experts on human rights.

[87] Report of the UN Subcommission on Prevention of Discrimination and Protection of Minorities, Resolution 1990/27 of 31 August 1990.

[88] The Secretary General reported to the Sub-Commission on July 6, 1992 on the extent to which indigenous peoples can utilize existing international standards and mechanisms for the protection of their intellectual property. UN Doc. E/CN.4/Sub.2/1992/30 (1992).

technical meeting.[89] Resolution 1991/32 called for study of the rights of indigenous peoples to cultural property.[90]

In 1994, the Sub-Commission adopted the Draft Declaration on the Rights of Indigenous Peoples.[91] The Declaration's provisions support indigenous peoples' right to their resources and traditional knowledge. In particular, Art. 10 provides that indigenous peoples have both collective and individual rights to prevention and redress of any dispossession of resources. The right to redress is extended in Art. 12, where the right to maintain indigenous culture includes the right to restitution of cultural, religious, and spiritual property taken without free and informed consent or in violation of indigenous laws.

The Draft Declaration also guarantees land rights[92] and the right to protection and rehabilitation of the environment.[93] Article 29 further provides that indigenous peoples have the right to have their traditional cultural manifestations, such as literature, designs, visual and performing arts, seeds, genetic resources, medicine, and knowledge treated as intellectual property.[94] Article 30 supplements this provision by establishing guidelines for relations between indigenous peoples and both states and corporations. It requires consultation and free and informed consent before commencement of any large-scale natural resource development projects. It further states that compensation shall be provided for adverse consequences of any such activity.

The Declaration provides that indigenous peoples have the right to maintain and not be deprived of their traditional means of subsistence, and are entitled to compensation in case of deprivation.[95] Article 24 recognizes the

[89] The United Nations Technical Conference on Indigenous Peoples and the Environment took place in 1992. It adopted Conclusions and Recommendations on Indigenous Peoples and the Environment that recognize that the survival and well-being of indigenous peoples and the sustainability of the ecological systems on which they depend cannot be achieved without rights to land and other resources and the right to use and develop those resources. The Conference recommended prior environmental and socio-economic impact studies of national development projects that affect indigenous peoples, with the participation of indigenous peoples. It also recommended that the United Nations system take measures to protect indigenous property rights, including intellectual property, with regard to their cultural property, genetic resources, biotechnology, and biodiversity. The Conference emphasized participation and prior consent. UN Sub-Commission on Prevention of Discrimination and Protection of Minorities, *Economic and Social Relations between Indigenous Peoples and States*, Res. 1991/31, E/CN.4/Sub. 2/1991/65, at 69, *adopted* 29 August 1991.

[90] UN Subcommission on Prevention of Discrimination and Protection of Minorities, *Ownership and Control of the Cultural Property of Indigenous Peoples*, Res. 1991/32, E/CN.4/Sub. 2/1991/65, at 69, *adopted* 29 August 1991.

[91] Report of the UN Sub-Commission on Prevention of Discrimination and Protection of Minorities, Draft Declaration on the Rights of Indigenous Peoples, UN Doc. E/CN.4/Sub.2/1992/33, Annex I, at 105 (26 Aug. 1994).

[92] The collective and individual right to own, control, and use lands includes the right to management of resources and to restitution or compensation for lands and territories used or damaged without their free and informed consent: *id.* paras. 16–17.

[93] *Id.* Art. 28, operative para. 18.

[94] *Id.* Art. 29.

[95] *Id.* Art. 21.

right to protection of vital medicinal plants, animals, and minerals. Finally, several articles guarantee indigenous peoples a right to participate in decision-making on issues of concern to them.[96]

Because of the broad attention the UN has given indigenous peoples in recent years, international law generally now recognizes indigenous peoples' right to the territories they possess, the resources of the land, and the natural cultural heritage that the land contains. At the national level, indigenous lands are usually protected by law and title is often vested in the community or group. But many countries allow intervention on indigenous lands, including unilateral changes in the boundaries or rights of access. Illegal alienation is also a frequent problem.

C. Using International Human Rights to Protect Indigenous Peoples and Their Environments

Local communities may claim protection for their traditional knowledge and resources on the basis of human rights law.[97] Human rights protections include the right to information, consultation, and participation in decision-making on proposals that affect local communities.[98] Local communities can also seek to develop community economies and mechanisms to establish fair prices for forest products and the local knowledge about them.[99] In these ways, human rights law can be useful in establishing local control over resources and knowledge.

The right to property is one of the strongest human rights claims for protection of indigenous peoples and their environments. State-sanctioned taking of resources or knowledge without compensation could violate property rights. The success of such a claim would depend on a showing that the resources or knowledge constitute property under national or local community law. Property has no inherent attributes that would preclude such a showing. 'Property' is a legal label attached to those tangible and intangible interests deemed capable of individual or collective ownership. Today,

[96] *Id.* Arts. 19, 20, 23, 30.

[97] For example, the right to privacy (UDHR, *supra* note 51, Art. 12; CCPR, *supra* note 66; ACHR, *supra* note 63, Art. 11) may be implicated when the State licenses or permits exploitation or improper activities by researchers. Some individuals intrude into the privacy and seclusion of local communities. Those who study traditional cultures through working in a position of trust with indigenous herbalists or medical specialists may obtain confidential information. Control over the access to powerful medicines is widespread in Africa, as a means of maintaining survival of traditional leadership. Medicinal knowledge is hidden through ritual and taboo. Cunningham, *Ethics, Brokers and Biodiversity, supra* note 15, at 11. Researchers may obtain knowledge linked to initiation rites, taboos, and religious ceremonies private to the community, after establishing their credibility and good faith. In response to such practices, the Organization of African Unity urges secrecy in herbal medicine practices to prevent multinational companies from developing new drugs and selling them back to developing countries at high prices. J. Hanlon, *When the Scientist Meets the Medicine Men*, 279 NATURE 284 (1979).

[98] *See* Charter of the Indigenous Tribal Peoples of the Tropical Forests, Art. 23 (1992).

[99] *Id.* Art. 33.

property includes not only land and objects, but goodwill, animals, and airspace. Nearly all legal systems treat some human discoveries or creations as property and grant monopoly rights over them. Some legal systems are now debating whether human organs and tissues should be considered property.[100]

Under this framework, local resources and even traditional knowledge may constitute property under national or local law. Plants and animals, as tangible resources capable of exclusive appropriation and use, are frequently designated property. When they have been developed within the community or are located on private or tribal lands, they could constitute part of the land rights of the community or be individually owned. Resources on public lands, however, even if traditionally used, are often viewed as state property.[101]

In addition to plant and animal specimens, plant varieties, life forms, and plant-based pharmaceutical products may be subject to state-approved monopoly ownership.[102] Western scientific discoveries in this field are generally protected as intellectual property, which grants a limited monopoly to the inventor or originator. Protecting scientific discoveries as property is deemed to serve the public interest by stimulating research,[103] even though the attributes of property are difficult to apply to ideas or intellectual creations. Because of consumer demand and diminishing biodiversity, products that have been developed through genetic research and engineering for agriculture and pharmacology, with vast research and development costs,[104] are increasingly designated as property.

Local communities could similarly claim property protection for

[100] *See Moore* v. *Regents of University of California*, 793 P. 2d 479 (1990), where the California Supreme Court refused to recognize property rights in human blood cells and body parts. The case is discussed more fully below.

[101] National laws increasingly treat plants and animals as they treat mineral resources and archeological sites. Costa Rica's Law for the Conservation of Nature (1990) identifies genetic resources as a national patrimony, in the public domain. It reserves to the State the exclusive right to commercialize them.

[102] Louis Pasteur received a United States patent in 1873 for 'yeast, free from organic germs of disease, as an article of manufacture'. I. Cooper, Biotechnology and the Law, vol. 1, 2–5 (1982). In 1930, the United States adopted a Plant Variety Protection Act to stimulate research and assist in the development of news breeds: 7 USC §§2321–2582 (1988).

[103] For arguments that intellectual property laws may not serve the public interest, *see* Brush, *Indigenous Knowledge of Biological Resources and Intellectual Property Rights: The Role of Anthropology*, 95 American Anthropologist at 5 (Sept. 1993).

[104] Between 1962 and 1973, the estimated cost of developing a new drug in the United States rose from \$534,000 to \$11.5 million: D. Schwartzman, Innovation in the Pharmaceutical Industry 65–70 (1976). At the same time, return on research and development investment fell from 12 percent to 3.3 percent: *id.* at 160. Cost to later entrants who can benefit from the initial research is extremely small. Without the protection of intellectual property laws, it is claimed that few, if any, private companies would engage in research and development.

resources they develop or cultivate. Communities use traditional knowledge to conserve biodiversity and identify useful compounds and apply technology to the use and evolution of living things. Their knowledge holds the key to active ingredients of commercial value and the proper processing and use of plant resources. Existing studies show that selective breeding in local communities over the centuries has developed many important strains of plants. It is in the public interest to protect this knowledge like Western laboratory products.

Knowledge itself would not have to be considered intellectual property as currently defined—although it could be—but could constitute cultural property or simply be an intangible asset of the local community, under customary community or state law. There is no clear line between protecting biological resources and protecting knowledge about them.

Critics raise various objections to extending property rights to the traditional knowledge of local communities. First, they argue that biological knowledge is too valuable to be commoditized for individual gain, but rather that its benefits should be freely shared as a common heritage of mankind, even where the knowledge is not widespread.[105] Others also note that traditional knowledge, particularly about agricultural practices, is often freely exchanged with no expectation of payment or concept of exclusivity. Moreover, communities have acquired this knowledge incrementally over the centuries. Most of those who have contributed are dead, and it could be inequitable to compensate those who remain. Further, establishing a system of intellectual property rights in pre-capitalist societies may hasten the destruction that compensation is intended to prevent. Subsistence groups could be further marginalized or their territories transformed to produce the most 'useful' resources.[106] Finally, local communities may be unaware of important uses for plants they identify. For example, a plant may help combat a disease which is not endemic to the area where the plant grows and is used. When the discoveries are made in laboratories to which researchers take the plants for study, issues of compensation become more complex.

Most of these objections concern the fairness of restricting access and use of local resources and traditional knowledge in particular cases. But if property rights are generally appropriate to protect people and resources, and are also in the public interest, then the definition of property can exclude those cases in which protection is unwarranted.

Identification of the owners of local resources and traditional knowledge may be difficult. Claims could be made by the state, by persons who developed or possess the resources or knowledge, by the community that collec-

[105] *See* Brush, *supra* note 103, at 653 n. 3.

[106] *See* S. Corry, *'Harvest Moonshine' Taking You for a Ride*, SURVIVAL INTERNATIONAL (1993).

tively has used them, by those on whose land the resources are located, or by the company that acquires and screens the plants, then extracts or synthesizes the active ingredient for commercial use. One solution is to recognize national ownership of biodiversity. However, state ownership will likely result in channeling the value of biodiversity into urban centers and away from those who have made the most significant, often the only, contribution to it.[107]

The inability to identify the persons whose knowledge and resources are entitled to protection and to whom compensation should be paid may also make compensating local communities difficult in many cases. Knowledge may be endemic in a region that includes both tribal indigenous and non-tribal rural persons. Knowledge also may cross boundaries between cultural groups or between states. For example, the drug resperine, produced from a root and generally accepted to have originated in indigenous knowledge, is grown in Burma, India, Java, Malaysia, Sumatra, Thailand, and Vietnam.[108] People throughout South and Southeast Asia have long recognized the root's medicinal properties, and no particular 'owners' can be identified. Even in the case of resperine, however, western companies profiting from the knowledge could share the benefits throughout the region through appropriate development projects. The interests served by preserving resources and knowledge justify including the knowledge of non-indigenous communities and even 'folk healing' among rural inhabitants of industrialized countries among those to be compensated.[109]

The international right of indigenous peoples to the territories they posses is also a strong claim. But ownership of land resources is often contested. Many legal systems vest ownership of natural resources in the state, so that the granting of licenses for resource use is controlled by government authorities. In such cases, indigenous communities should be compensated for the resources taken and for damage caused to their environment.[110] In addition, they are entitled to consult and participate in licensing processes,

[107] *See* D. Posey, *Ways and Means of Strengthening Sustainable and Environmentally Sound Self-Development of Indigenous Peoples*, *in* REPORT OF THE UNITED NATIONS TECHNICAL CONFERENCE ON PRACTICAL EXPERIENCE IN THE REALIZATION OF SUSTAINABLE AND ENVIRONMENTALLY SOUND SELF-DEVELOPMENT OF INDIGENOUS PEOPLE at 54, paras. 6–7, UN Doc. E/CN.4/Sub.2/1992/31/Add.1 (May 25, 1992).

[108] Brush, *supra* note 103.

[109] *Contra* Tom Greaves, who argues that protection should not be extended to traditional knowledge in industrial societies. He recognizes the difficulties of defining the indigenous societies to whom compensation should be extended. He would include 'village peoples'—farmers inhabiting rural areas of most Third World countries—although he views this as potentially 'politically fatal'. T. Greaves, IPR, A Current Survey, *Address Before the 91st Annual Meeting of the American Anthropological Association*, (Dec. 1992).

[110] See J.R. Martinez Cobo, *Study of the Problem of Discrimination against Indigenous Populations* 18 (Vol. V: Conclusions and Recommendations), UN Doc. E/CN.4/Sub.2/1986/7/Add.4.

and should be permitted to examine the potential consequences of resource use so they may prohibit or exclude projects that would significantly threaten or destroy their environments. Finally, 'sacred land or land of historical and spiritual significance for indigenous peoples must in all cases be excluded from licenses or concessions and protected from intrusions of all kinds.'[111]

A strong argument has been presented by Survival International that protecting indigenous land rights and self-determination is the only way to ensure environmental protection, as well as survival of indigenous peoples.[112] The organization opposes harvesting and marketing of rainforest products as a destructive extension of northern over-consumption and profit-taking at the expense of the indigenous and their territories. The organization notes that the rainforest's value for the subsistence of forest dwellers receives little attention when companies or governments propose market-based resource harvesting. In addition, the organization notes that only certain rainforest products are likely to be economically important, causing increased cultivation or exploitation of those resources to the detriment of the forest as a whole—rubber and ivory being cases in point. Finally, it notes that the principal threat to tropical rainforests is colonization and settlement, which are likely to increase with the market value of rainforest products.

Several human rights instruments provide procedures for individual complaints about human rights violations. The Inter-American system has been most widely used to raise issues regarding local communities and environmental harm. As early as 1971, the Inter-American Commission adopted a resolution instructing the Secretariat to compile a list of all claims concerning violation of indigenous populations' human rights and to ask states about their national legislation.[113]

In 1989, the Inter-American Commission decided that the government of Brazil violated the rights of the Yanomami Indians by allowing development projects in their traditional lands. The Commission found that resource deprivation and environmental degradation resulted in violations of the right to health. The decision recognizes the broad range of human rights that may be affected by harm to environmental resources. The Inter-American Human Rights Commission stated that indigenous peoples have land rights in the territory as a whole and the right to the natural resources of their territory. It concluded that environmental degradation can violate the right to life and that the government's failure to take timely and effec-

[111] *Id.*

[112] *See* Corry, *supra* note 106.

[113] Inter-American Commission on Human Rights (IACHR), Annual Report to the General Assembly, OAS Doc. No. OEA/Ser.P/-AG/doc.305/73/Rev.1 (1973).

tive measures led to loss of life, cultural identity, and property.[114] The Commission noted that international law presently 'recognizes the right of ethnic groups to special protection of their use of their own language, for the practice of their own religion, and in general, for all those characteristics necessary for the preservation of their cultural identity.'[115]

Because international procedures are limited, states may be uncooperative, and international law does not provide a direct mechanism for pressing demands or complaints against companies or researchers, other approaches to protecting the rights of indigenous peoples are necessary.

IV. REGULATION OF TRANSNATIONAL CORPORATIONS AND INDIVIDUALS

Some international instruments and national laws regulate transnational companies and individuals. Recent amendments to the Charter of the Organization of American States added Art. 35, which provides, 'Transnational enterprises and foreign private investment shall be subject to the legislation of the host countries and to the jurisdiction of their competent courts and to the international treaties and agreements to which said countries are parties, and should conform to the development policies of the recipient countries.'[116] Article 35 is one of the few international treaty provisions directly addressed to multinational companies and investors. The United Nations Center on Transnational Corporations has also reported on transnational investments and operations on the lands of indigenous peoples.[117]

States could adopt national legislation, based on international human rights, environmental law, or development law, to regulate access to and use of traditional knowledge and resources. Costa Rica, for example, requires biologists to obtain permits and demands that they deliver samples

[114] IACHR Case 7615, OEA/Ser.L/V/11.66, doc. 10 rev. 1 (1985) [hereinafter Yanomami Case]. The case could be brought against the government because it sponsored the development causing the displacement. Another case has been brought against Ecuador on behalf of the Huaorani claiming that oil exploration and related development will have negative impacts on native lands. *See* M. Schwartz, *International Legal Protection for Victims of Environmental Abuse*, 18 YALE JIL 355, 363 (1993); W.A. Shutkin, *International Human Rights Law and the Earth: The Protection of Indigenous Peoples and the Environment*, 31 VA. JIL 479, 489–90 (1991).

[115] Yanomami Case, *supra* note 114, at 31.

[116] Charter of the Organization of American States, *signed* 1948, 119 UNTS 48, Art. 35, *amended* by the Protocol of Buenos Aires of 1967, 21 UST 607, and by the Protocol of Cartagena de Indias of 1985.

[117] UN Centre on Transnational Corporations Report to the Sub-Commission in pursuant to E/CN.4/Sub.2/1991/49 in *Transnational Investments and Operations on the Lands of Indigenous Peoples* (July 17, 1991).

of everything they collect to the National Biodiversity Institute, founded in 1989. Profits must be shared with Costa Rica.[118]

Indonesia has developed its own traditional medicine industry, with over 300 facilities to process medicinal plants. Its exports from this industry amounted to $20 million in 1990. In 1975, it established the Directorate for Traditional Drug Administration to encourage industrial production of traditional medicine, and it recently created the National Working Group for Indonesian Medicinal Plants to help improve and standardize quality control. Similarly, Madagascar's Center for National Pharmaceutical Research inventoried 2,274 species, 902 of which are endemic, with therapeutic uses.

In addition to national legislative control, codes of conduct and other professional guidelines could help regulate access to and use of traditional knowledge. In 1990, the Botanical Society of America and the Society for Economic Botany established ethics committees to develop professional codes for plant collecting organizations.[119] The FAO produced a draft code for plant collection.[120] A 1992 Manila Declaration on the ethical use of Asian Biological Resources similarly creates a code for foreign collectors of biological samples, and includes minimum contract guidelines.[121] Finally, companies themselves sometimes establish ethical standards.[122] It would be useful for these initiatives to be compiled, then supplemented by agreed-on procedures for informed consent and participation in or control of contractual arrangements.

[118] In a contract with the government, Merck Pharmaceutical paid the Institute $1 million in 1991 to screen collected samples. Merck obtains patent rights, with the Costa Rican Institute obtaining an undisclosed royalty if marketable products are discovered. Ten percent of the $1 million and 50 percent of any royalties are invested in conservation projects in Costa Rica, through a special fund. Local persons having knowledge are used as 'parataxonomists'; it is not known how, if at all, they are compensated. *See* S.A. Laird, *Contracts for Biodiversity Prospecting*, *in* BIODIVERSITY PROSPECTING: USING GENETIC RESOURCES FOR SUSTAINABLE DEVELOPMENT 99–130 (W.V. Reid, ed., 1993). *See also* D. Gershon, *If Biological Diversity has a Price, Who Sets it and Who Should Benefit?* 359 NATURE 565 (1992).

[119] The American Society of Pharmacognosy issued the Williamsburg Declaration in 1992: C. Padock & B. Boom, *Draft Code of Ethics* (unpublished). Another set of guidelines is contained in the Bukittinggi Declaration of the UNESCO seminar on the Chemistry of Rainforest Plants. *See* Society of Economic Botany (1991); T. Eisner & J. Meinwald, *The Goteburg Resolution*, 1 CHEMOECOLOGY 38 (1990).

[120] FAO COMMISSION ON PLANT GENETIC RESOURCES, DRAFT INTERNATIONAL CODE OF CONDUCT FOR PLANT GERMPLASM COLLECTING AND TRANSFER (1991).

[121] L.J. CRUZ ET. AL., SEVENTH ASIAN SYMPOSIUM ON MEDICINAL PLANTS, SPICES AND OTHER NATURAL PRODUCTS (APO Production Unit, Manila, 1992).

[122] *See, e.g.*, GLAXO GROUP RESEARCH LTD., POLICY FOR THE ACQUISITION OF PLANT MATERIALS (1992).

V. ATTAINING COMPENSATION FOR INDIGENOUS KNOWLEDGE THROUGH LOCAL RIGHTS AND REMEDIES

Several national constitutions protect indigenous or tribal rights. The 1988 Constitution of Brazil has a separate chapter on Indian rights, while the new Colombian and Nicaraguan Constitutions include provisions on the rights of indigenous peoples.[123] Recent amendments to the Mexican constitution added similar protections. Other constitutions have incorporated provisions on environmental rights. Indigenous people may use both sets of rights as a basis for obtaining compensation for use of their traditional knowledge and resources.

They may also invoke private international law, or conflicts of law, for the protection of indigenous knowledge and resources. Indigenous populations in most countries continue to observe traditional or tribal law, and in many states traditional law is a recognized legal system. Some countries recognize the personal jurisdiction of indigenous law over community members. In such countries, conflicts of law principles determine whether indigenous or national law applies in matters concerning the relations of non-indigenous persons with the indigenous. Other countries recognize the territorial applicability of indigenous norms. Thus, whether the acquisition of knowledge and the collection of plants is legal could be subject to traditional law under choice of law principles, with local jurisdiction to enforce the law.

Those seeking access to traditional knowledge could enter into agreements, based on national or traditional law, with those who hold the resources.[124] Such contracts would have to comply with laws prohibiting fraudulent or coercive agreements, and establish jurisdiction to enforce the contract. For example, participants in a Workshop on Drug Development, Biological Diversity and Economic Growth, held in March 1991 in the United States, proposed that in return for reliable access to natural products, pharmaceutical companies could help develop drugs for tropical diseases most relevant to developing countries.[125]

[123] BRAZ. CONST. (1988), Arts. 231–232, III Blaustein & Franz CONSTITUTIONS OF THE WORLD (1993); COLOM. CONST. (1991) Arts. 246, 329–330, IV Blaustein & Franz CONSTITUTIONS OF THE WORLD (1991); NICAR. CONST. (1987), Arts. 89–91, XIII Blaustein & Franz CONSTITUTIONS OF THE WORLD.

[124] *See* B. CARNEY ET AL., DRAFT AGREEMENT BETWEEN PHARMACEUTICAL COMPANY AND BIOLOGICAL SAMPLE COLLECTOR (Rainforest Alliance).

[125] *See* J. Schweitzer et al., *Summary of the Workshop on Drug Development, Biological Diversity and Economic Growth*, 83 JOURNAL OF THE NATIONAL CANCER INSTITUTE 1295 (1991). For example, Merck Sharp and Dohme states it has provided to certain West African nations, without charge, a drug to combat river blindness. Biotics Limited, a British biotechnology consulting firm, obtains plant sources and supplies plant samples and extracts for evaluation. It negotiates contracting agreements between plant-source countries and screening organizations that it says guarantee that income from sales of new products is distributed equitably to all participants.

Several factors make it difficult to determine the appropriate terms of such contracts. There may be uncertainty about both finding marketable products and the value of any products that are developed—the return from natural products is small. In 25 years, one company reported only five compounds from natural sources that became marketable drugs.[126] This may argue in favor of imposing initial collection fees rather than delayed royalty payments and requiring in-country screening and testing to afford local employment and research opportunities.

Even in the absence of a contractual agreement, other legal principles could permit claims for compensation for takings. If traditional knowledge constitutes property that is intended to be kept within the group, local communities could institute legal action for conversion to recover the value of the property taken. They could also bring trespass actions. In some countries, persons or groups are by law denied access to indigenous areas. Other laws may declare null and void actions and provisions that would affect the fauna and flora of indigenous areas. Costa Rica and Mexico, for example, both have provisions for the protection of indigenous lands. Malaysia's Aboriginal Peoples Ordinance allows the Minister to exclude anyone from aboriginal areas and provides that the state may assess a $1,000 fine against anyone caught in such areas in violation of a ministerial order, as well as arrest violators without a warrant. While these provisions do not directly affect compensation, they do provide legal grounds for conditioning entry or punishing conduct that threatens the rights of local communities.

Indigenous peoples could also rely on the requirement of informed consent in trust relationships to justify compensation. In a recent US case, *Moore* v. *Regents of the University of California*,[127] the California Supreme Court faced the unprecedented question of whether a cause of action existed against doctors who used an individual's cells without his knowledge in lucrative medical research. The Court held that a cause of action might exist for a breach of a duty of disclosure, but not for conversion of property, noting that only property can be converted. The Court determined the doctors had a fiduciary duty to disclose facts material to the patient's consent or, alternatively, a duty not to perform medical procedures without obtaining informed consent. Local communities could draw parallels to this case with regard to the taking of traditional knowledge without full disclosure, even when the knowledge does not constitute property.

[126] *Id.* [127] 793 P.2d 479 (Cal. 1990).

VI. INTELLECTUAL PROPERTY RIGHTS

A. Types of Intellectual Property

Intellectual property law identifies who has the right to exploit particular creations. Intellectual property consists of industrial property (inventions, trademarks, and industrial designs) and copyrights (primarily literary, musical, artistic, photographic, and audiovisual works). Patents, inventors' certificates, utility models, and industrial designs all protect inventions. The protection of utility models generally covers inventions in the mechanical field. Industrial designs coverage protects new ornamental or aesthetic aspects of a useful article, such as the shape, pattern, or color.

A patent, available in most countries, confers the right to protection on an inventor or her employer. The patent holder has the exclusive right to use the invention for a term, usually 15 to 20 years. Some governments issue inventor's certificates instead of patents, in which case the inventor receives remuneration and the government takes title to the invention. Some states require compulsory licensing of patented inventions.

Patents are a compromise between the public interest and the inventor. The inventor or discoverer discloses the invention or discovery in return for a short-term monopoly over its commercial use. Food, health, and energy endeavors usually cannot be patented, nor can processes vital to national security. Laws vary widely regarding compulsory licensing and the length of time for patents, making them flexible development tools. Many countries have withheld patenting in certain sectors to permit domestic industries to grow.[128] The European Patent Convention continues to prohibit patenting plant and animal varieties.[129] When Japan allowed pharmaceutical patents, it ranked second in world production of drugs and controlled 80 percent of its home market.[130] In India, patentability of inventions relating to substances intended for use as food, drugs, or medicines is limited to the manufacturing methods or processes; patents containing claims for the substances themselves are not permitted.[131]

Trademarks are signs used on or in connection with the marketing of goods, and may consist of one or more distinctive words, symbols, or devices to identify the product and distinguish it from others in the same commercial field. Service marks are trademarks for services, like McDonald's Corporation's golden arches. Association marks are for members of a group (labor union labels) or for a certification of origin or

[128] For example, France (1958), Germany (1968), Switzerland (1977), and Japan (1976) only recently allowed pharmaceuticals' patenting.

[129] Convention on the Grant of European Patents, *adopted* Oct. 5, 1973, UN Doc. 16207.

[130] Sistema Economico Latinoamericano, *Capitulos de SELA*, SELA, (October/December 1988).

[131] Indian Patents Act, 1970.

characteristic (roquefort). Trade names are commercial signs used to identify businesses. Finally, appellations of origin denote geographical origin and product characteristics (chianti).

Copyright protects literary and artistic works, including words, music, pictures, three-dimensional objects, and combinations of them. The author or her employer is protected for the author's life plus a specified number of years after her death. Copyrighted words may be used only with the copyright owner's authorization or for some personal and education purposes.

B. The Law of Intellectual Property

Each country extends intellectual property protection, and it normally is valid only within the boundaries of the granting state. But international protection may be obtained from the Organization Africaine de la Propriété Intellectuelle,[132] the European Patent Office[133] or the Benelux Trademarks Office.[134]

The German branch of the International Law Association has proposed Principles on Freedom of Transfer of Knowledge and International Protection of Intellectual Property.[135] It states that both parts of its title presuppose a fair balance between the legitimate interests of holders, suppliers, and recipients of intellectual property. Article 3 provides that new or original intellectual creations contribute to the international and national common good and wealth. Article 4 reiterates that international human rights law guarantees the right for any creator of intellectual property to benefit from the protection of the interests resulting from his intellectual production. This requires acceptance of the standards of the Paris Convention for the Protection of Industrial Property,[136] the Berne Convention for the Protection Literary and Artistic Works,[137] and the Universal Copyright Convention.[138] Article 5 of the Universal Copyright Convention requires states to protect the their citizens' intellectual property against violations by other states and individuals.[139]

[132] The Organization Africaine de la Propriété Intellectuelle (OAPI) is the official office for 12 francophone African States. A single patent, trademark or industrial designed granted by OAPI has effect in all the member countries.

[133] A patent granted by the EPO, based in Munich, is valid in eleven European states.

[134] Trademarks are valid in Belgium, the Netherlands, and Luxembourg.

[135] Principles on Freedom of Transfer of Knowledge and International Protection of Intellectual Property.

[136] Paris Convention for the Protection of Industrial Property, USTS 379 (Mar. 20, 1883). The Paris Convention has been revised several times, most recently in Stockholm, 828 UNTS 305 (1967).

[137] Berne Convention for the Protection of Literary and Artistic Works (Sept. 9, 1886) 168 Paris TS 185. The Berne Convention was revised by the Stockholm (1967) and Paris (1971) Acts, 828 UNTS 221.

[138] Universal Copyright Convention (Sept. 6, 1952) 216 UNTS 133.

[139] *Id.* at Art. 5.

The International Convention for the Protection of New Varieties of Plants[140] may be useful to protect breeders of new plant varieties or their successors in title. The Convention requires authorization for commercial marketing, and grants the breeder's rights regarding a new plant variety for a limited period, usually not less than 15 years. Local communities may be able to register locally developed and cultivated plants as new varieties.

Article 40 of the Charter of the Indigenous Tribal Peoples of the Tropical Forests (1992)[141] states that programs related to biodiversity must respect the collective right of such peoples to cultural and intellectual property, genetic resources, gene banks, biotechnology, and knowledge of biodiversity. This includes participation in the management of any project on indigenous territories and control of benefits that derive from them. Article 44 demands guaranteed rights to intellectual property and control over the development and manipulation of traditional technologies.

C. Using Intellectual Property Rights to Protect Indigenous Peoples and Biodiversity

Local communities and indigenous groups have begun to claim intellectual property protection for traditional knowledge. Such claims have had little success because intellectual property laws cannot easily be applied to protect the communal and intergenerational knowledge and technologies of local communities. Intellectual property laws are based on western concepts of property and intellectual activities, designed to protect readily identifiable, differentiated contributions to existing knowledge. A principal feature of patentability is that the product or process should be new and described in a way that makes it capable of reproduction. But traditional knowledge is generally collective, incrementally acquired over decades or centuries. Such attributes usually preclude the protection of intellectual property laws. Yet these laws protect the discoveries of modern research laboratories, although they often involve the work of large teams of people, each of whom contributes to the achievements of the laboratory.

Intellectual property laws should be extended to traditional, collective knowledge, or the utility and benefits of the entire system of intellectual property could be questioned. Today, most intellectual property protection is afforded to companies, not to the individual creator or discoverer. It is common practice for enterprises to require employees to sign waivers of rights to any discovery or new idea developed during the course of employment. Intellectual property laws also monopolize technological advances in industrial societies, although in many cases the raw materials and knowledge are derived from developing countries.

[140] International Convention for the Protection of New Varieties of Plants (Dec. 2, 1961) 815 UNTS 89.

[141] Charter of the Indigenous Tribal Peoples of the Tropical Forests, Art. 40 (1992).

In the GATT Uruguay Round of trade negotiations, industrialized countries sought trade-related intellectual property rights in order to extend patents in all fields of technology. This will enable companies using biotechnology to patent genetically altered seeds, plants, and products. At the same time, naturally occurring and previously developed organisms are classified as 'common heritage'. Under this regime, industrialized countries processing traditional knowledge will receive primary protection, without any benefits to those supplying the resources and traditional knowledge. Recent efforts to patent all genetically engineered cotton and soybean species indicate the enormity of the issue.[142] The problem is that the collective knowledge of a small group is confused with the public domain.

Traditional knowledge about plants is the most needful of this protection. The three primary means of protecting intellectual property relating to plants are patents (utility and plant patents), plant variety protection certificates, and copyrights. Applying any of these mechanisms to traditional knowledge or medicines presents problems. However, trade secrets laws and contractual mechanisms may provide protection or compensation to the originating state or group.

If traditional knowledge is defined as intellectual property it will be necessary to ensure that the rights are vested in the individuals or local communities and not in the governments, because of permanent sovereignty over natural resources. The 1989 FAO decisions on the concept of Farmers' Rights recognized the contribution of traditional farms to the breeding and selection process of genetic material. But UNCED texts establish a 'right' for governments to receive assistance in the maintenance of genetic resources.

An effective multinational component also will be necessary, because the property to be protected normally will be transferred beyond the borders of any one state. Discussions on the present methods for the protection of intellectual property illustrate that lack of multinational component often makes these methods ineffective.[143] International human rights and environmental texts generally refer to intellectual property rights as a national legal technique. However, this does not preclude international measures. Nothing prevents states from cooperating to protect traditional knowledge, especially when effective implementation cannot be attained through national action.

Traditional knowledge about ecosystems and their plants may also constitute proprietary 'know-how' or 'trade secrets'. The processing or use of

[142] The crop value of cotton exceeds $20 billion a year, while the soybean market is $27 billion. THE CRUCIBLE GROUP, PEOPLE, PLANTS AND PATENTS 10 (1994).

[143] *See* K.W. Dam, *The Growing Importance of International Protection of Intellectual Property*, 21 INTERNATIONAL LAWYER 627–38 (1987); J.M. Dettman, *GATT: An Opportunity for an Intellectual Property Rights Solution*, 4 TRANSNATIONAL LAWYER 347–76 (1991).

a plant may not be known outside a local community or an indigenous group and it could thus contractually be protected. But the existence of legal protection must be made known to local communities who then can withhold their knowledge until they negotiate satisfactory agreements on protection and remuneration. This might be coupled with imposing a duty on researchers and collectors to obtain informed consent.

Invocation of intellectual property rights could be a means to implement the benefit sharing provisions of human rights and environmental agreements. It could also assist in the internalization of environmental costs and the use of economic instruments to further environmental protection.[144] It would also support those arguing for the conservation of the environment in environmental impact assessment procedures.[145] Finally, it could provide an additional incentive for local communities to conserve their knowledge for future generations and to share their knowledge with others.

Uniform patent standards may not be appropriate to all circumstances. Clearly local communities make intellectual contribution to new natural products' development. But the type of intellectual property rights to be granted may depend on the level of technological and industrial development in different developing countries.[146] Some developing countries have developed local technology to prepare extracts and investigate the composition of local plants, without strong intellectual property protection. Some industrialized countries have limited recognition for pharmaceuticals, encouraging low-cost imitations.

Applying intellectual property concepts to indigenous knowledge raises other problematic questions. Is it new, is it innovative? What happens when those that acquire plants traditionally used by indigenous groups find that they have a different, previously unknown property?[147] Who should benefit—the individual or the group? Which group? Should money be paid or other, more culturally appropriate forms of compensation be used? Could biological conservation be considered the best form of compensation? Will intellectual property rights serve the twin goals of protecting indigenous cultures and biodiversity? The difficulties implied by these questions suggest that intellectual property law may have only a limited role in protecting the traditional knowledge and resources of local communities.

[144] Rio Declaration, *supra* note 22, principle 16.

[145] *Id.* principle 21.

[146] W. LESSER, EQUITABLE PATENT PROTECTION IN THE DEVELOPING WORLD: ISSUES AND APPROACHES (1991).

[147] For example, the rosy periwinkle is now valued for its anti-leukemia properties, making it one of the most important anti-cancer plants in the West. It does not appear to have ever been used as such by indigenous populations. J.A. Duke, *Folk Anticancer Plants Containing Antitumor Compounds*, *in* PLANTS IN INDIGENOUS MEDICINE AND DIET: BIOBEHAVIOURAL APPROACHES (N.L. Etkin, ed., 1985).

VII. CONCLUSIONS AND RECOMMENDATIONS

Effective regulation is needed at international, regional, and national levels to control the collection and export of biological material and traditional knowledge. Model legislation should be drafted drawing on international environmental and human rights principles, establishing a national policy for the conservation and sustainable use of biological diversity. Professional codes of conduct should be drafted to require informed consent and participation by local communities, respect for confidentiality, and fair compensation for assistance, knowledge, and plant identification.

Impact statements and licensing arrangements should be included in legal instruments. Impact assessment should include both environmental and cultural impacts of proposed projects for inventories, studies, collection, or use of plant species within traditional areas or the acquisition of traditional knowledge. Licensing fees should be explored as a technique of compensation, with a mandatory percentage returned to indigenous communities for projects to maintain their ecosystems and cultures. Collection and export of samples should be regulated, with access to traditional lands or communities subject to the prior informed consent of the population. Regulations should include sanctions for failure to abide by conditions of entry or refusal of entry, as well as for resort to deceit or bribery to obtain information.

Governments should review intellectual property laws to determine the scope of protection to be afforded for discoveries concerning living organisms. They should explore how such protection might provide for recognition of traditional knowledge and ensure adequate compensation for indigenous populations that choose to share their traditional knowledge.

Traditional knowledge and self-sufficiency should be promoted by developing renewable plant-based products and by establishing a national pharmaceutical industry to develop phytotherapeutic products derived from endemic flora.

Lawyers should draft flexible contract agreements protecting indigenous populations. Compensation for traditional knowledge need not always be in the form of cash, although financial compensation is important. Other forms of compensation could include technology transfer, training, resource maintenance, and institutional development.

Multinational corporations, anthropologists, botanists, and others involved in the use of natural products and traditional knowledge need to recognize their responsibility to provide reasonable compensation as an integral part of their business or research and development activities. Intermediate compensation mechanisms and incentives need to be developed to bridge the 10 to 15 year gap between identification of a potentially useful species and the production of a marketable and profitable drug from that species. In this regard, ethnobotanists and local communities need to study and record the use of plant resources, promote sustainable methods of harvesting plants, and ensure that local communities benefit from the conservation and use of plant resources.

PART 2

1994: THE YEAR IN REVIEW

Table of Reports
"1994: The Year in Review"

I. GENERAL DEVELOPMENTS

II. AIR AND ATMOSPHERE

III. FRESH WATER

IV. OCEANS

V. ENERGY

VI. INTERNATIONAL HAZARD MANAGEMENT OTHER THAN NUCLEAR

VII. INTERNATIONAL COMMONS/AREAS BEYOND NATIONAL JURISDICTION

VIII. NATURAL RESOURCE MANAGEMENT AND CONSERVATION

IX. INTERNATIONAL ECONOMY AND THE ENVIRONMENT

X. COUNTRY/REGION REPORTS

XI. REPORT FROM INTERNATIONAL COURTS AND TRIBUNALS

XII. REPORTS FROM ORGANIZATIONS

XIII. SPECIAL REPORTS

I. GENERAL DEVELOPMENTS

1. INSTITUTIONAL DEVELOPMENTS

(1) Introduction

As self-interest in sustainable development increasingly permeates national and international objectives, failures in implementation remain. These failures may be attributed to the need for better tools and methods for analyzing complex problems, improved assessment and documentation of available solutions, and wider dispersion of the skills required and of lessons learned. International institutions have a critical role to play in promoting and disseminating these means of implementation, drawing on the specialized skills and comparative advantages of numerous governmental and non-governmental actors. How they will fashion new relationships at global and regional levels to support national actions is a key challenge.

This report canvasses changes taking place in the operation of intergovernmental organizations as they undertake their three primary functions: data collection and analysis, policy development, and technical and financial assistance or "operational activities for development." It covers initiatives to re-shape international decision-making, to integrate environment and development while delineating more carefully the roles and responsibilities of different agencies, the UN Commission on Sustainable Development (CSD) and its substantial support from "privatized" undertakings, efforts to improve technical and financial assistance, the information base for sustainable development; international secretariats, and relationships with non-governmental actors.

(2) Decision-Making and Advisory Functions

(a) The United Nations

On economic and social issues, the Secretary-General, in reporting on his "Agenda for Development" to the General Assembly, proposed that the UN Economic and Social Council (ECOSOC) serve as an international review committee for donors and recipients to assess policies for international development assistance and UN operational activities. He also proposed that an expanded ECOSOC bureau meet inter-sessionally. Earlier, the President of ECOSOC, with reference to developments in Rwanda, had stated his intention to establish a flexible, high-level, inter-sessional mechanism to respond in a timely manner to situations in the economic and social area that constitute threats to international peace and security. He referred to the Secretary-General's earlier suggestion that ECOSOC be invited to provide the Security Council with reports on such situations. These proposals built on a series of events following the May circulation of the Agenda, including precedent-setting world hearings convened at the United Nations for five days in June for government representatives to hear and question 31 expert witnesses.

The 1994 United Nations Development Programme (UNDP) "Human Development Report" also made recommendations for institutional change. It circulated the idea of an Economic Security Council for dealing with critical emerging issues as they arise, rather than dealing with these issues through global conferences and summits that foster neither quiet compromise nor institutional continuity.

As a result of the 1994 International Conference on Population and Development (ICPD), the General Assembly decided that ECOSOC's Population Commission should meet annually starting in 1996, that ECOSOC should reconsider its composition in 1995 and revise its terms of reference to be consistent with the ICPD Programme of Action, and that the Commission should be renamed Population and Development.

With respect to operational activities, the General Assembly at the end of 1993 (RES 48/162) transformed the governing bodies of the UNDP, the UN Population Fund (UNFPA), the UN Children's Fund (UNICEF), and the World Food Programme (WFP) into 36-member executive boards. A single board was established for UNDP and UNFPA, pending the outcome of the ICPD, a second for UNICEF, and, once approved by both sponsoring agencies (United Nations and the UN Food and Agriculture Organization), a third for the WFP. At the policy level, the approaches of these four agencies and the International Fund for Agricultural Development are meant to be coordinated by the Joint Consultative Group on Policy. Following the ICPD, the General Assembly has requested the 1995 ECOSOC session to consider establishing a separate executive board for UNFPA. The boards report annually to ECOSOC.

The high-level Advisory Board on Sustainable Development, established by the Secretary-General in 1993 (*see* 4 *YbIEL* 104 (1993)) met twice in 1994. Its report was considered by the CSD.

(b) Global Environment Facility

The 32-member Council of the restructured Global Environment Facility (GEF) represents a unique departure from traditional international governance. It combines constituency representation with a double-weighted majority (if formal votes are required). The restructured GEF was accepted in March by 73 countries and approved formally by the governing bodies of the three implementing agencies (UNDP, the United Nations Environment Programme (UNEP), and the World Bank.) The Council will meet at least twice annually, the plenary Assembly every three years. The Council met in July and November.

(c) Intergovernmental Forum on Chemical Safety

The decision to establish the Intergovernmental Forum on Chemical Safety (Stockholm, April) as a "non-institutional arrangement" appears to be a cost-effective wedge for promoting institutional change. The Forum will provide clear and consistent advice and recommendations to governments, international bodies, and non-governmental organizations (NGOs) on chemical risk assessment and environmentally sound management of chemicals. It is also intended to improve delineation and mutual understanding of roles within and among governments and international agencies responsible for chemical safety. Its secretariat is located within, but functionally distinct from, the secretariat of the International Programme on Chemical Safety (jointly sponsored by the World Health Organization (WHO), UNEP, and the International Labour Organisation), and funded by voluntary contributions to a trust fund established under the auspices of WHO. All governments may participate in the forum, as well as observers from inter-governmental and non-governmental organizations. It will be guided by an inter-sessional group consisting of officers elected by the Forum and no more than 26 government representatives.

(3) Integrating Environment and Development

The UN effort to revitalize and restructure its economic and social sectors in 1994 highlights the need for further clarification of the roles of UN bodies—at global and regional levels. The process of analyzing comparative advantages in policy-setting and analysis versus operational activities, determining how to ensure the necessary cross-fertilization between them, and decentralizing some functions to the regional level is beginning to bear fruit.

To further this process, the Secretary-General resumed meetings with senior officials in the economic and social fields to: monitor progress on restructuring; harmonize information systems; and coordinate activities in relation to conferences, policies, and mobilizing resources for development. In relation to regional activities, he re-instituted periodic meetings of the executive secretaries of the regional commissions, together with the heads of UN organs. The regional commissions reported to the CSD on relevant programs in 1994 (efforts to integrate environment and development at the national level are considered *infra,* Section 5). Following the July ECOSOC meeting, the Secretary-General requested that the Administrator of UNDP assist him in ensuring policy coherence and coordination within the UN at headquarters and with the regional commissions and other UN agencies and programs. In addition, he asked the Administrator to assume responsibility for improving coordination regarding operational activities for development, including the resident coordinator system. Important aspects include access by the resident coordinators, which are responsible for field level operations, to the full range of data, research, and analytic capabilities within the UN system, and improving the quality of the coordinator's annual report so that field results can inform system-wide policy-setting and analytic functions and highlight opportunities for improved coordination.

The UN Department of Economic and Social Information and Policy Analysis reports that it is improving synergies between data collection and policy analysis, while UNDP reports a new initiative to improve feedback between program performance audits and strategic policy and planning decisions. In a related development, the UN Administrative Committee on Coordination (ACC) in 1994 reconstituted a Consultative Committee on Programme and Operational Questions to improve the interface between policies and operations. This supplements the ACC's establishment of the Inter-Agency Committee on Sustainable Development (IACSD) (*see* 4 *YbIEL* 98 (1993)) to enhance coordinated programming and reporting among UN agencies on follow-up to the Rio Conference. The IACSD met three times during 1994. The significance of the ACC role in UNCED follow-up is that the integrated environment and development theme has been taken up by the highest-level inter-agency coordinating mechanism within the UN system. In contrast to the institutional follow-up to the Stockholm Conference, UNCED continues to benefit from and contribute to a more fundamental restructuring effort within the UN system.

(4) UN Commission on Sustainable Development (CSD)

The CSD's second session took place 16–27 May. Reports were submitted from the inter-sessional working groups on finance and technology transfer and from the high-level Advisory Board on Sustainable Development. Additional reports addressed the cross-sectoral and sectoral themes of Agenda 21 up for review this year.

The effectiveness of the CSD as an institutional mechanism came under some fire. Several governments sought improvements in its working methods and stressed the need for technical, inter-sessional work to help support the deliberations and results of the annual meeting. Others called for the CSD to enhance its political profile as the engine of sustainable development and urged it to concentrate on reviewing national implementation of Agenda 21. There was widespread support for the Commission to continue to expand its close cooperation with NGOs and with the business community.

The CSD decided to retain its open-ended inter-sessional working group on finance and establish a second group to assist in preparing the sectoral issues before the 1995 meeting: land management; desertification; forests; and biodiversity. The working group on technology transfer was discontinued in favor of considering these issues in each of the 1995 groups, as relevant. To improve on the working arrangements, panel discussions were to be used in 1995 to focus the reports of the inter-sessional groups, followed by structured presentations from each regional group on national and local experiences with implementing Agenda 21. In addition, the chair of the CSD convened two days of informal consultations in November to inform and involve representatives from governments, inter-governmental organizations, and NGOs regarding inter-sessional activities. A bimonthly update on CSD-related developments, launched by the CSD secretariat following the 1994 session of the Commission, serves a similar purpose.

Modeled after the Rio Conference preparations, there has been a proliferation of government offers to sponsor and organize mission-oriented intergovernmental and expert fora in support of the CSD, sometimes in collaboration with NGOs. Although too numerous to identify in this report, there is a schedule available from the secretariat and published in numerous NGO newsletters. Like the new forum on chemical safety, this assumption of responsibility on the part of governments complements secretariat activities and offers greater flexibility. If approached systematically to advance discussions and decisions in a timely manner, these meetings may focus and expedite results.

(5) Technical and Financial Support

The watchword in funding for development (sustainable or otherwise) during 1994 was "donor fatigue." Against this backdrop, three trends are discernible among international assistance agencies: efforts to improve coherence and coordination; efforts to monitor and evaluate effectiveness from the perspective of sustainable development; and "winners and losers." The CSD continues to monitor resource flows for sustainable development.

(a) Operational Coherence and Coordination

Operational coherence and coordination plays out both within the UN system and among UN agencies and the banks and funds outside the UN. As governments urge the international agencies to avoid duplicative efforts that operate at cross purposes, it is hoped that bilateral assistance will be increasingly harnessed by the same objective. The most promising basis for achieving this result remains the formulation of a coherent, regularly updated national approach to sustainable development. A clear definition of national objectives and priorities defines the context for outside assistance. The CSD and several NGOs help track progress on national sustainable development plans and strategies and the national institutional structures responsible for them. Twenty-five national councils were reported to have been established by the end of the year.

International agencies and international policy processes have been instrumental in promoting national plans and strategies, often based on sectoral themes. The UN system launched a concerted effort in 1994 to examine how to avoid duplication and inconsistencies in the requirements placed on national governments. Results are expected to be reported to the CSD in 1996. The OECD's Development Assistance Committee (DAC), which serves as a forum for consultation among bilateral donors and is attended by observers from multilateral donors and NGOs, is undertaking a complementary effort to improve methodologies for national planning frameworks to assist both donors and recipients.

At the field level, the UN sought to strengthen and upgrade the role of the resident coordinator (normally UNDP's resident representative) in each recipient country, as the filter for UN activities. "Country strategy notes" are becoming useful vehicles to promote consistent and coordinated programming among the UN agencies and to help direct their initiatives toward national priorities and capacity-building. At the UN inter-agency level, the IACSD has urged more joint programming exercises to make the best use of available resources. Governments have also raised questions about integrating the many small, dedicated trust funds into coherent programming arrangements. Some of these serve international treaty objectives, while others exist in the UN specialized agencies or the international financial institutions for such purposes as "sustainable forestry" or "integrated coastal zone management."

The use of consultative meetings is also expanding as a means to cohere donor programming. The idea is to invite multilateral, bilateral, and private donor agencies to discuss larger-scale proposed programs and to explore and promote donor commitments. In addition to country-based consultative meetings, these meetings have also focused on sub-regional and regional programs. As a follow-up to ECOSOC's 1994 coordination segment on science and technology for development, the Department of Policy Coordination and Sustainable Development (DPCSD), in close cooperation with the UN Conference on Trade and Development (UNCTAD) and UNDP, hopes to hold a consultative meeting on this theme.

The Committee on International Development Institutions on the Environment (CIDIE), established in 1980 to integrate environmental practices into the development agencies' operations (with UNEP as secretariat), met in September to debate its post-UNCED role. Poor attendance from the seventeen member institutions hindered the discussion. An issues paper was circulated among member institutions for comment. If sufficient support exists for the continuation of CIDIE, the Executive Director of UNEP will convene another meeting in early 1995 to refine a future work program.

The challenge is to define a distinct role for CIDIE vis-a-vis the mandates of the IACSD, the CSD, and the technical/methodological analysis carried out in the newly-established environmental subgroup of the multilateral financial institutions' co-financing working group.

From a different perspective, the technical guidance produced by international development agencies and international treaties is fast becoming a major influence on sustainable development. Objectives and parameters defined by international agreements and rules for national implementation set conditions for national action that must be respected in projects assisted by international agencies. The respective roles of treaty processes and development agencies in shaping criteria for treaty implementation is being honed, not only under more recent international conventions like Climate Change and Biodiversity, but also as donor agencies support projects that affect the implementation of the regional seas agreements or various protected area and species conventions.

Although the need for a common technical framework will grow, flexibility in determining how to achieve objectives in varying conditions is vital. The recent emphasis in both development agencies and international treaty processes on best technologies/best practices offers an important mechanism for achieving both the common framework and flexibility. It has been used in such varied contexts as the World Bank's Best Practice on Social Assessment (1994) and the prevention and control of marine pollution from specific land-based sources/sectors (*e.g.*, agriculture) under the Northeast Atlantic and Baltic Conventions. The OECD/DAC's working party on the environment promotes agreement on guidelines and good practices among the national development agencies. Guidelines on marine pollution and wetlands management were to be completed in early 1995.

(b) Monitoring and Evaluation

Independent review of financial agencies is joining internal review as an accepted procedure, a development substantially influenced by the World Bank's independent review of the Narmada Dam project and its internal Wapenhans report (*see* 3 *YbIEL* 346 (1992)). The World Bank's establishment of an independent inspection panel in 1993 (*see* 4 *YbIEL* 586 (1993)) followed on the heels of the GEF decision to initiate an independent evaluation of its pilot phase. After its 1994 consideration of the evaluation and its recommendations, the GEF Council requested that the secretariat report regularly on implementation of the recommendations, with a more analytical report to be presented in July 1995. The GEF continued during 1994 to refine guidelines for monitoring and evaluating its activities and to consider the organizational framework for implementing them. In a related development, the first Conference of Parties (CoP) of the Biodiversity Convention (November/December) adopted interim guidelines for monitoring and evaluating the GEF's utilization of financial resources, and it is expected that the first CoP of the Climate Change Convention will address this issue in 1995. Within the UN system, progress on monitoring and evaluation procedures is more sluggish.

(c) Winners and Losers

The struggle among development agencies for donor attention continues. As UN organs strove to improve performance and accountability, and to consolidate their operations, UNDP in 1994 was forced to reduce its planning figures for individual countries to 70 percent of the original estimates. The General Assembly established a working group on funding in June 1994, charged with producing concrete results to improve the present system by June 1995. In summing up high-level ECOSOC discussions of the "Agenda for Development," the Australian ambassador identified the UN's ability to build consensus for globally relevant political decisions as its central comparative advantage. Recognizing that the UN disposes of only a fraction of resources relevant to development, he stated that:

> If that advantage is exercised on the basis of an accurate analysis of relevant data, it should assist those who dispose of very significant resources to commit them in ways compatible with the priorities identified by the UN and thus join with the UN in the crucial enterprise of development.

GEF funds were replenished with pledges amounting to over US$2 billion for the 1994–1997 period. The Biodiversity CoP agreed that the restructured GEF would continue to serve as the interim structure to operate the treaty's financial mechanism. The first CoP of the Climate Change Convention was to address this issue in 1995. GEF programs in international waters and land degradation will be considered following approval in 1995 of the respective scoping papers and operational strategies. In this context, there were discussions of a GEF role in the implementation of the Action Programme of the small island developing states (April 1994), the (→) Convention to Combat Desertification (June 1994), and the outcomes of the UN Conference on Fisheries (March–April and July–August 1995) and the Intergovernmental Meeting on the Protection of the Marine Environment from Land-Based Activities (November–December 1995). The possibility of an explicit GEF link with the comprehensive UN Convention on the Law of the Sea and associated international agreements affecting sustainable development also arose.

The UN agencies and the regional development banks have not yet worked out satisfactory arrangements for participation in the preparation and implementation of GEF policies and programs. The specialized agencies are dissatisfied with rotational representation by a single observer at Council meetings. At the project level, arrangements for collaboration between the three GEF implementing agencies and other executing agencies (regional banks, UN agencies, bilateral development agencies, national institutions, NGOs, private sector entities, and academic institutions) was to be considered further at the Council meeting in January 1995.

(6) The Information Base

The emphasis placed by the CSD in 1994 on sustainable development indicators, and reiterated in virtually all of the related inter-governmental fora, underscores their use in qualitative evaluation—of conditions and trends and of the policy and operational initiatives meant to address them—and as a simplified means of comparing progress achieved. In the UN secretariat, this issue is tackled by the Department of Economic and Social Information and Policy Analysis, in collaboration with the DPCSD. The World Bank hosted a major meeting on sustainable development indicators in September, and several government-sponsored and private initiatives are also contributing to these efforts. The aim was to have a full set of indicators by 1996 for use by national governments in submitting national progress reports to the CSD in 1997.

The Information and Analysis Department advanced toward an integrated database on economic and social information in 1994—the "Development Watch" contemplated in Agenda 21—and issued its first combined "World Economic and Social Survey." It contracted for an inventory of data held by the regional commissions, in order to enhance the division of labor between headquarters and regional levels and to improve the quality, timeliness, availability, and productivity of that data. In an unprecedented collaborative effort with the World Bank, the International Monetary Fund, OECD, and the European Union, the department produced a "System of National Accounts" as a framework for governments to quantify sustainable development, poverty, employment and compensation for women, and informal sector activities. These improved data systems are being applied to enhance research and to better meet government needs and strengthen national capabilities.

On a more technical level, the International Conference on Chemical Safety, reinforced by CSD endorsement of its Priorities for Action, decided to review and expand existing data on chemical risk assessment and to promote harmonized classification and labelling of chemicals. The objective is to consolidate this data for use on computer and other electronic communications media by 1997.

International institutions not only synthesize and analyze information on the problems of sustainable development, they may also help identify solutions. They play a catalytic and substantive role in refining assessment techniques (environmental and socio-economic), helping document and synthesize best practices, and disseminating the results. Several UN agencies are seeking to develop information on environmentally sound technologies. The CSD requested in 1994 that the results of a UN inter-agency survey and assessment on information systems for environmentally sound technologies be submitted in 1995. The UN General Assembly endorsed further consultations on the feasibility of developing a Small Islands Development States (SIDS) NET, endorsed in the SIDS Programme of Action, to improve skills and access in the SIDS for using global computer communications technologies. The establishment of a clearinghouse mechanism to facilitate the exchange of information and services has received renewed attention in inter-governmental discussions of biodiversity and protection of the marine environment from land-based activities.

As these database and clearinghouse initiatives evolve, they raise issues about the extent to which they serve not only as switchboards for information exchange, but take on a brokering role between suppliers and requesters, and whether and how to ensure some measure of assessment and quality control among suppliers. The IACSD has undertaken the task of conducting an inventory of existing global and regional clearinghouses and information exchange systems on technology needs and transfer and assessing their usefulness and recommending improvements. It has cautioned that information systems should not be developed without specifying their purpose, and that technology transfer should be dealt with in the specific context in which it arises.

(7) The Secretariat Role

The DPCSD acquired follow-up responsibility to support implementation of the SIDS Programme of Action throughout the UN system. A new unit within the department was expected to be established in 1995. DPCSD also supports the World Summit for Social Development (Copenhagen, March 1995) and the Conference on Women (Beijing, September 1995). Support for Habitat II (Istanbul, June 1996) is provided by Habitat in Nairobi. The General Assembly has requested that ECOSOC consider in 1995 secretariat support and coordination arrangements for UN system follow-up to the Population Conference, and it will be up to the first CoP of the Desertification Convention to determine secretariat support arrangements for that convention.

The Biodiversity CoP, at its first meeting in November, decided that UNEP should serve as permanent secretariat, although the location of the office has yet to be determined. UNEP convened a meeting in March on coordination of secretariats of environmental conventions, which was attended by representatives of UNEP-administered conventions (Conservation of Migratory Species, Basel, Ozone, International Trade in Endangered Species, and Biodiversity) and by observers from the Climate

Change, World Heritage, and Ramsar conventions. The CSD noted the need for coordination and more efficient structural arrangements among secretariats of conventions related to sustainable development.

(8) The Involvement of Non-Governmental Actors

As discussions of non-governmental actor participation evolve in many international fora, they increasingly distinguish involvement and partnerships with non-governmental actors in operational activities from contributions to policies and program planning. At the policy level and program level, NGOs do not yet participate in any significant way in the governing bodies of the international financial institutions. In the United Nations, they do not take part in the Security Council. The General Assembly, in an exceptional case, accepted the International Committee of the Red Cross in 1991 as an observer. Proposals to accept additional observers prompted some discussion of criteria during the 1994 General Assembly. A wide-ranging review of UN arrangements for consultation with NGOs is to be presented to ECOSOC in 1995 (*see* 4 *YbIEL* 103 (1993)). Two meetings of the open-ended working group were held during 1994, and a basis for discussion is on the table for the February 1995 meeting.

In a major departure for the financial institutions, the GEF Council agreed in November that NGOs may attend Council meetings as observers. Based on criteria to be approved in January 1995, and the principle of self-selection among the NGOS of a representative group, 10 NGOS will be invited to Council meetings, with the costs of travel and accommodation paid for four individuals from recipient nations. Executive sessions of the Council will not be open to NGOs. As for the practice of consultations with NGOs during GEF meetings, which evolved during the pilot phase, the January 1995 Council meeting will consider further their scope, financial implications, and modalities. Pending a final decision, the practice will continue.

With respect to on-the-ground development activities, the World Bank, as noted above, issued best practices on the involvement of the social sector in 1994. A UN Joint Inspection Unit report (*see* 4 *YbIEL* 104 (1993)) urges UN agencies involved in operational activities to distill guidelines based on experience, policies, and requirements to facilitate collaboration in the field with NGOs and to share their experiences with such collaboration.

The enlarged scope of those included within the terms "major groups" or "NGOs" has raised additional questions. Recent UN discussions have emphasized that the UN system should draw on private, for-profit organizations and on membership bodies like labor unions and political parties as well as more traditional NGOs. Modalities to promote the involvement of community groups and indigenous peoples are under discussion in both UN and international treaty fora. Grass roots groups and NGOs have already been added to UN lists as a result of UNCED and subsequent global conferences. This has prompted some discussion of whether and/or how to distinguish among non-governmental actors for the purpose of participation in intergovernmental fora.

Given the sheer number and diversity of non-governmental actors, alternative modalities and procedures for participation are also under consideration. These seek to ensure that in addition to international NGOs, local, national, and regional NGOs, particularly those from the South, are able to present their views. Another concern is ensuring that NGO participants, by their numbers, do not unduly delay or dominate the proceedings. GEF consideration of different modalities for NGO participation, and its experience with NGO consultations at global, regional, and national levels, have provided useful bases to be used in elaborating future directions. The hearings convened in 1994 on the Secretary-General's "Agenda for Development" offer another model for obtaining a spectrum of non-governmental actor views. Also in the UN context, it has been suggested that participation in conference processes be distinguished from participation in the work of ongoing inter-governmental bodies.

Another development that bears watching is the renamed Commission on International Investment and Transnational Corporations. ECOSOC installed it as an advisor to the Trade and Development Board in 1994 and gave it a new lease on life. The Commission is to promote an exchange of views among governments, inter-governmental organizations, NGOs, trade unions, private business, and other experts, and to encourage participation in its activities by these entities. This development follows the shift of the UN program on transnational corporations from New York to UNCTAD in Geneva in 1993 (*see* 4 *YbIEL* 103 (1993)).

The 21-member Earth Council, set in motion by UNCED Secretary-General Maurice Strong, held its second meeting in November at its Costa Rican headquarters. Its plans for 1995 include an "Earth Report," with an index of sustainability and country rankings, modeled on the index presented in the UNDP "Human Development Report"; a draft outline of an "Earth Charter"; a study of environmental harm caused by government subsidies and other economic policies; and a progress report on the establishment of national councils of sustainable development. The Council will continue to study the feasibility of an "ombudsman" function to respond to complaints regarding environmental responsibilities.

Lee A. Kimball

2. TRANSBOUNDARY ENVIRONMENTAL COOPERATION

A. PRIOR INFORMATION/CONSULTATION/ ENVIRONMENTAL IMPACT ASSESSMENT

(1) International Agreements

(a) Bi- and Tri-lateral Agreements

(i) Mexico-United States

The Agreement between Mexico and the United States concerning the establishment of a Border Environment Cooperation Commission (BECC) and a North American Development Bank (NADbank) entered into force on 1 January 1994. The BECC coordinates environmental infrastructure projects in the border area. BECC certifies applications for financing of these projects to be filed with the NADbank (Art. I, §2). Each such project "having significant transboundary environmental effects" requires an environmental assessment as part of the application process and will not be certified for funding application until it is determined to be able "to achieve a high level of environmental protection for the affected area" (Art. II, §3).

(ii) France, the Netherlands, and Belgium

On 26 April 1994, the governments of France, the Netherlands, and the three Belgian regions of Brussels (Capital), Flanders, and Wallonia signed two separate (➔) accords for the protection of the Meuse and Scheldt rivers, respectively. Both treaties were agreed to in "the spirit of" the March 1992 Helsinki Convention on Transboundary Watercourses and in light of the September 1992 Paris Convention on the Protection of the Marine Environment of the North-East Atlantic. The Helsinki Convention specifically encouraged the conclusion of agreements between parties which share transboundary waters.

To accomplish each treaty's purpose, the parties established two international commissions for the protection of the respective rivers (Art. 2). Article 3 of each treaty enumerates the principles of cooperation as precaution, prevention, pollution reduction at the source through the use of best available technology and best environmental practices, and polluter pays. The respective commissions are given identical tasks, namely to serve as a center for the exchange of information on projects that are subject to environmental impact assessment (EIA) and that have significant transboundary impact; to promote cooperation on scientific research and best technologies; to organize transboundary cooperation on emergency notification, and promote exchanges of information to prevent and combat accidental pollution; to report annually to the public; and to define, collect, and evaluate information from the parties regarding their territories in order to identify pollution sources that have a significant impact on water quality (Art. 5).

(b) Multilateral Agreements

(i) Energy Charter Treaty

The Energy Charter Treaty, signed in Lisbon on 17 December 1994, was negotiated pursuant to the European Energy Charter, adopted in December 1991 at the Hague. Its purpose is to establish a legal framework for promoting among its signatories "long-term co-operation in the energy field." Article 19, in addressing environmental aspects, refers to, *inter alia*, the principles of precaution, polluter pays, sustainable development, non-distortion of trade, and cost-efficiency. Parties are to strive to "minimize in an economically efficient manner harmful environmental impacts" whether they occur within or outside their areas of jurisdiction. They agree to promote and share environmentally sound energy policies and technologies, cooperate in research, and cooperate in "transparent assessment at an early state and prior to decision, and subsequent monitoring, of environmental impacts of environmentally significant energy investment projects." The Treaty defines environmental impact to mean "any effect caused by a given activity on the environment" including human health and safety, climate, historical monuments, and cultural or social-economic heritage.

(ii) Convention on Cooperation for the Protection and Sustainable Use of the Danube

The (→) Convention on Cooperation for the Protection and Sustainable Use of the Danube River Basin was opened for signature on 29 October 1994 in Sofia, Bulgaria. Its preamble refers specifically to the 1992 Helsinki Convention on Transboundary Watercourses and to the 1992 Convention on the Protection of the Black Sea. Its objectives include cooperation to strengthen, harmonize, and coordinate domestic and international measures and planned measures aimed at sustainable development and environmental protection of the Danube (Art. 3). Article 18 establishes the International Commission for the Protection of the Danube River.

Forms of cooperation include consultation on joint activities of the Commission and exchange of information on agreements and legal measures and other matters relating to water quality. Further information exchange duties are spelled out in Art. 12 regarding, *inter alia*, accidents, emission data, taken and planned measures to prevent, control and reduce transboundary impact, and best available techniques. Parties are to consider potential effects on water quality of "planned activities and ongoing measures" (Art. 6), such as waste water discharges, water construction works, reservoirs, and the like. They are subject to the Convention to the extent they cause or are likely to cause transboundary impacts. Reporting obligations are detailed in Art. 10; the resulting exchange of information forms the basis for consultations (Art. 11) on planned activities likely to cause transboundary impacts. Such consultations will generally be held within the framework of the Commission.

Control of effluents draws on EIA "in line with supranational and international regulations" (Art. 7(5)(f)) and advance permitting of discharges (Art. 7(5)(b)). Also, in planning, licensing, and implementing measures, parties must consider the risk of accidents by providing for preventive measures (Art. 7(5)(g)) and by coordinating communication, warning, and alarm systems basin-wide for emergencies (Art. 16).

(iii) Law of the Sea Convention

The controversial provisions of the United Nations Convention on the Law of the Sea on exploring and exploiting seabed minerals were modified by the July 1994 (➔) Agreement Relating to the Implementation of Part XI of the United Nations Convention on the Law of the Sea of 10 December 1982. In a detailed Annex (§1.6(a)(i)), the Agreement regulates exploration of the seabed, by making approval of work plans dependent on, *inter alia*, "an assessment of the potential environmental impacts of the proposed activities" and a program for oceanographic and baseline environmental studies in keeping with rules adopted by the Seabed Authority (§1.7).

(iv) International Tropical Timber Agreement

The (➔) International Tropical Timber Agreement was signed at Geneva on 26 January 1994. Each member state is to furnish information on timber, trade, and activities aimed at achieving sustainable management of timber-producing forests as well as other relevant information requested by the Council. The International Tropical Timber Organization itself is to compile and publish statistical information on production, supply, trade, the extent of timber resources, and the management of timber-producing forests (Art. 29).

(v) Desertification Convention

The (➔) United Nations Convention to Combat Desertification in those Countries Experiencing Serious Drought and/or Desertification, Particularly in Africa was signed on 17 June 1994. National action programs form the core basis for combatting desertification, together with subregional and regional action programs for sustainable management of transboundary natural resources and scientific and technical cooperation (Art. 11). The parties, according to their abilities, agree to coordinate "collection, analysis and exchange" of short- and long-term data "to ensure systematic observation of land degradation" (Art. 16). Each party must report to the conference of the parties on measures it has taken to implement the

Convention (Art. 26). Under the regional implementation annex for Africa (Annex I), African parties will cooperate to prepare and implement subregional action programs, addressing, *inter alia*, the exchange of information, experience and know-how. Similar provisions appear in the regional implementation annex for Asia (Annex II).

(vi) Convention on the Safety of Life at Sea

In January 1994, the 1991 amendments to the Convention on the Safety of Life at Sea entered into force. Chapter VI contains requirements regarding provision of cargo information to other parties. Under Regulation 7-1, any dangerous good lost overboard must be reported to the nearest coastal state.

(2) Activities of International Organizations

(a) United Nations International Conference on Population and Development

The final statement of the September 1994 conference, which was held in Cairo, Egypt, recommends various measures to help governments "achieve population and environmental integration," including the carrying out of EIAs.

(b) International Coral Reef Initiative

The International Coral Reef Initiative intends to establish a global coral reef management network through the International Oceanographic Commission and to support regional coral reef monitoring and assessment programs. During the First Meeting of the Conference of the Parties to the Biodiversity Convention, (*see* the (➔) Report on the First Meeting of the Conference of the Parties to the Biodiversity Convention), Australia, France, Jamaica, Japan, the Philippines, the United Kingdom, and the United States jointly announced this initiative.

(c) The European Environment Agency

The European Environment Agency presented its first formal report to the European Commission in July 1994 in the form of 10 proposed programs with more than 90 projects over the next five years. The Agency is charged with reporting every three years on the state of the European environment.

(d) Summit of the Americas

At the Summit of the Americas, held in December 1994 in Miami, United States, Central American states and the United States signed (➔) Conjunto Centroamerica-USA Panama, Costa Rica, Nicaragua, Honduras, El Salvador, Guatemala, and Belize. The general agreement provides for the exchange of environmental information that is not proprietary in nature. A Declaration of Principles contained in the Agreement urges cooperative action on conservation and sustainable use of Central America's biodiversity.

(e) United Nations Environment Programme

The Governing Council of the United Nations Environment Programme (UNEP) held its fourth special session on 18 June 1994. One Decision adopted by the Governing Council contains the Instrument for the Establishment of the Restructured Global Environment Fund (GEF). The principles of cooperation among the implementing agencies, II.11(b), appear in Annex D to the instrument. Under these principles, UNEP will provide guidance on relating the GEF-financed activities to global, regional, and national environmental assessments; policy frameworks and plans; and to international environmental agreements.

(f) UNEP/International Chamber of Commerce (ICC)

In April 1994, UNEP and the ICC announced a campaign to promote corporate guidelines for sustainable development. The Business Charter for Sustainable Development, drafted in 1991, includes principles of assessing the environmental impact of projects before their implementation.

(3) Activities of Regional Organizations

(a) European Union

On 16 March, the Commission of the European Union adopted a proposal to clarify the 1985 Environmental Impact Assessment Directive while retaining its dual category structure: EIAs would remain mandatory for category I projects (large public and private projects, *e.g.*, oil refineries, airports, freeways, waste incinerators, and chemical factories) and, at the member states' discretion, for category II projects (resorts and hotels). The Directive would continue to be a planning aid; neither category requires action to be taken if in fact the EIA foresees environmental damage. The proposed clarifications would standardize at the Union level the information to be provided by the developer, and the criteria (location, accident risk, size) to be used by members in determining if a category II project needs an EIA. Further, the proposal promotes greater cooperation between states when projects have transboundary effects, and urges assessment of any category II project with a likely significant impact on specially protected areas.

On 29 April, the Commission adopted Regulation No. 1091/94 on forests. The Regulation lays down detailed rules for the implementation of Council Regulation (EEC) No. 3528/86 on the protection of the Union's forests against atmospheric pollution. The 1994 Regulation requires a network of permanent forest observation plots to be installed by member states, 50 percent by 30 June 1994, to obtain detailed data on the evolution of forest ecosystems in the Community. The information is to be forwarded to the Commission in standardized form by 31 December 1996.

On 8 June, the Commission adopted a Recommendation for a Council Decision authorizing the Commission to negotiate agreements with certain countries regarding waste shipments into and out of the Union pursuant to Council Regulation (EEC) No. 259/93, which entered into force on 6 May 1994. The Recommendation also provides for temporary enabling arrangements for certain shipments to continue pending such agreements.

(b) European Court of Justice

The European Court of Justice (ECJ) ruled that Luxembourg had failed to implement the European environmental impact assessment Directive (*Commission v. Luxembourg*, C-313/93, 13 April 1994). The Commission of the European Union had brought the matter to the ECJ in 1993 following Luxembourg's delays and inadequate responses to repeated Commission requests for progress reports on legislation implementing the 1985 directive. The Court held that by failing to meet the deadline of 3 July 1988 for implementing the Directive, Luxembourg did not meet its obligations under the Treaty of Rome. Luxembourg finally adopted implementing legislation in March 1994, just before the Court's final decision.

(4) Decisions of National Courts/National Legislation

(a) Germany

The Upper Administrative Court for the German state of Rheinland-Pfalz issued a preliminary injunction on 29 December 1994 halting construction of highway A60, in large part because the required EIA for the project had not been produced. The decision is appealable to the Berlin Federal administrative court.

In mid-1994, 18 months after the deadline of 1 January 1993, Germany implemented the 1987 European Union Directive on Access to Environmental Information. The Directive entitles any person to access to environmental information in the possession of either any public official with environmental responsibilities or certain private parties that, under the supervision of public authorities, carry out public functions related to the environment. No particularized interest or legal right need be shown. Restrictions on access can be imposed only for reasons of national security, public safety, and trade secrets. Two of Germany's new states (Mecklenburg–Vorpommern and Sachsen) recognize a constitutional right of access to environmental information.

(b) Uruguay

Uruguay's Senate approved a new environmental bill in January 1994, containing requirements for EIA for a broad range of construction and development projects, including highways, bridges, airports, gas and oil pipelines, and major urban projects.

(c) Ecuador

In April 1994, the government of Ecuador established Unidad de Coordination Ambiental to supervise EIA of projects that multilateral lending agencies such as the World Bank and the Inter-American Development Bank support.

(d) Hidrovía Project

The Hidrovía inland waterway project, which would involve Argentina, Bolivia, Brazil, Paraguay, and Uruguay, received US$7 million in 1994 from the Inter-American Development Bank for the carrying out of an EIA.

(e) The Netherlands

The Netherlands revised Ch. 7 of its Environmental Management Act to bring national legislation in line with the European EIA Directive (85/337). Additional categories of projects, such as oil and gas production and dike reinforcement, are now subject to EIA, as are activities likely to have major transboundary effects, while food processing and chemical industrial projects may be subject to EIA on a case-by-case basis.

(f) United States

In October, in *Public Citizen v. Kantor*, 864 F.Supp. 208, a federal district court, following a line of recent decisions, held that the National Environmental Policy Act (NEPA) does not require an environmental impact statement for GATT negotiations. Further, as the President was free to renegotiate the GATT, the court held that the GATT proceedings were not "final agency action" within the meaning of the Administrative Procedure Act (APA). The APA did not therefore provide a basis for judicial review, and the court lacked jurisdiction to direct the Office of the US Trade Representative "to promulgate 'methods and procedures' to comply with NEPA when preparing future trade agreements."

(g) Canada

In February, the Canadian Supreme Court ruled that the National Energy Board (NEB) could impose environmental conditions on electricity imports to the United States, including EIAs for future generating facilities even if they would export only part of the power generated. In so deciding, the Supreme Court reversed the Court of Appeals, which had found that the NEB had exceeded its jurisdiction by subjecting Hydro-Quebec's application for an export license to an EIA requirement (Case No. 22705, 24 February 1994).

In 1994, Canada enacted a new environmental assessment law which creates the Canadian Environmental Assessment Agency, provides for greater funding of intervenors in public assessment processes and expands the role of mediation in resolving issues raised by an EIA.

Volker Röben

B. INTERNATIONAL/TRANSBOUNDARY CONTINGENCY PLANNING/EMERGENCY ASSISTANCE

(1) United Nations General Assembly

In continuation of its earlier work (*see* 4 *YbIEL* 112 (1993)), at its 49th session, the UN General Assembly dealt with contingency planning and emergency assistance in a number of resolutions. Two resolutions were adopted on "Strengthening of the Coordination of Humanitarian and Disaster Relief Assistance of the United Nations, including Special Economic Assistance." One resolution took note of the Report of the Secretary-General on "Strengthening of the Coordination of Emergency Humanitarian Assistance of the United Nations" (A/49/177 and Add. 1). The measures outlined by the Secretary-General for strengthening field coordination of humanitarian assistance were welcomed. These included in particular measures to be taken in advance of complex emergencies, *e.g.*, early warning; and measures to be taken when complex emergencies arise. Furthermore, the resolution stressed the need for the Inter-Agency Standing Committee to serve as the primary mechanism for inter-agency coordination under the leadership of the Emergency Relief Coordinator and the need for the cooperation of all operational agencies with the Department of Humanitarian Affairs. The resolution underlined the usefulness of the Central Emergency Revolving Fund in enhancing the operational agencies' capacities to address promptly the urgent requirements of the initial phase of natural disasters and other emergencies.

A second resolution dealt with the "participation of volunteers, 'White Helmets,' in activities of the United Nations in the field of humanitarian relief, rehabilitation and technical cooperation for development." It welcomed the establishment of volunteer corps on the national level for emergency assistance. Furthermore, it requested the Secretary-General to submit a report to the UN Economic and Social Council "on ways and means of strengthening national and regional stand-by arrangements, including the establishment and full utilization of national volunteer corps, in the area of emergency humanitarian assistance, as well as in the promotion of a smooth transition from relief to rehabilitation, reconstruction and development."

A resolution on the "International Decade for Natural Disaster

Reduction" (Res. 49/22) endorsed the results of the World Conference on Natural Disaster Reduction, which was held in Yokohama, Japan, 23-27 May, and called for a Second World Conference on Natural Disaster Reduction not later than the year 2000, to carry out an overall review of the accomplishments of the International Decade for Natural Disaster Reduction and map a strategy for continued disaster reduction activities into the 21st century. Moreover, a resolution entitled "Early Warning Capacities of the UN system with regard to Natural Disasters" requested, *inter alia*:

> the Secretary General to report to the General Assembly at its fiftieth session on early warning capacities within the United Nations system and to make proposals on how they may be improved and better coordinated in order to provide for an adequate response to natural disasters and similar disasters with an adverse impact on the environment and, in this context, also to make concrete proposals on the transfer of technologies related to early warning, in particular to developing countries, taking into account chapter 34 of Agenda 21, as well as the Principles of the Yokohama Strategy for a Safer World.

(2) International Law Commission (ILC)

At its 36th session, the ILC considered the question of contingency planning and emergency assistance in the context of "the law of the non-navigational uses of international watercourses" and "international liability for injurious consequences arising out of acts not prohibited by international law."

Part V of the (➔) "draft Articles on the Law of the Non-navigational Uses of International Watercourses and Resolution on Confined Transboundary Groundwater"—which was recommended to the General Assembly for elaboration in a convention—is entitled "Harmful Conditions and Emergency Situations." Article 27 provides that "watercourse States shall, individually or jointly, take all appropriate measures to prevent or mitigate conditions that may be harmful to other watercourse States, whether resulting from natural causes or human conduct, such as flood or ice conditions, waterborne diseases, siltation, erosion, salt-water intrusion, drought or desertification." Article 28 deals with the obligation of watercourse states in responding to actual emergency situations. A watercourse state shall, without delay and by the most expeditious means available, notify other potentially affected states and competent international organizations of any emergency originating within its territory. It shall, in cooperation with potentially affected states and, where appropriate, competent international organizations, immediately take all practicable measures necessitated by the circumstances to prevent, mitigate, and eliminate harmful effects of the emergency. When necessary, watercourse states shall jointly develop contingency plans for responding to emergencies, in cooperation, where appropriate, with other potentially affected states and competent international organizations.

In regard to its work "on international liability for injurious consequences arising out of acts not prohibited by international law," the ILC adopted provisionally on first reading draft articles concerning "measures to prevent and minimize the risk" (Art. 14), "notification and information" (Art. 15) and "exchange of information" (Art. 16) (*see* 4 *YbIEL* 112 (1993)). Furthermore, the ILC adopted an article on "consultations on preventive measures" (Art. 18) that provides that "States concerned shall enter into consultations, at the request of any of them and without delay, with a view to achieving acceptable solutions regarding measures to be adopted in order to prevent or minimize the risk of causing significant transboundary harm, and cooperate in the implementation of these measures." If no agreement is reached between the states concerned, the state of origin may proceed at its own risk, without prejudice to the right of any state withholding its agreement.

(3) International Atomic Energy Agency

Article 16 of the (➔) Convention on Nuclear Safety which was opened for signature on 20 September 1994 addresses the issue of emergency preparedness. According to para. 1 each contracting party is obliged to take appropriate steps to ensure that on-site and off-site emergency plans are established for nuclear installations, and that such plans are tested routinely. States must also ensure that their own population and the competent authorities of other states in the vicinity of nuclear installations are provided with appropriate information for emergency planning and response, insofar as they are likely to be affected by a radiological emergency (para. 2). Para. 3 extends the obligation for preparing and testing of emergency plans to potentially affected contracting parties which do not have a nuclear installation on their territory.

Gerhard Loibl

B. DISPUTE AVOIDANCE AND SETTLEMENT

[Editors' Note: No significant developments in 1994]

3. LIABILITY AND COMPENSATION

A. INTERNATIONAL LIABILITY AND COMPENSATION

[Editors' Note: No significant developments in 1994]

B. CIVIL LIABILITY AND OTHER FORMS TRANSNATIONAL ACCOUNTABILITY

[Editors' Note: No report received for Volume 5]

4. PROTECTION OF THE ENVIRONMENT THROUGH CRIMINAL LAW

1994 saw important developments in environmental criminal law, mainly in the form of legislative proposals addressed to the United Nations and its members by legal experts. This report highlights the most significant recommendations that were presented and published in 1994.

(1) The Portland Report and Model Law

On 23 March, experts from 27 countries, meeting on behalf of the United Nations Crime Prevention and Criminal Justice Branch, the International Centre for Criminal Law Reform and Criminal Justice Policy (Canada), the Portland Organizing Committee, and the United Nations Interregional Crime and Justice Research Institute in Portland, Oregon, adopted a Report of the International Meeting of Experts on the Use of Criminal Sanctions in the Protection of the Environment, Internationally, Domestically and Regionally (Portland Report). The Portland Report provides a concise assessment of the relevant existing regional and international laws and legislative drafts, such as the recent North American Free Trade Agreement's side agreement on environmental cooperation, and the proposed Council of Europe Convention for the Protection of the Environment through Criminal Law. While recognizing the strengths of proactive measures and the limits of criminal law, the report strongly recommends an extension of the scope of criminal law for environmental protection. To assist the various governments in achieving the goals of legislative change and international cooperation, the report provides a comprehensive and well-articulated three-tier package: a possible convention on transnational offences; a model domestic criminal statute; and a structure of regional enforcement.

The Report suggests that hard-core offenses against the environment should be defined as international crimes and be included in a Code of Crimes against the Peace and Security of Mankind, thereby enforcing the International Law Commission's draft Code of Crimes of 1991. Specifically, it recommends that a convention be created to cover four categories of international environmental crimes: the intentional causation of widespread, long-term, or severe pollution; the intentional unauthorized discharge of hazardous substances that is likely to severely pollute the environment; the intentional and illegal disposal, export, or import of hazardous waste; and the intentional and illegal operation of a hazardous installation or the intentional and illegal handling of specified radioactive, hazardous chemical, or biological materials.

Significantly, the Portland Report presents a model Domestic Law of Crimes Against the Environment, which is the first model law of its kind.

The model law is distinctive in at least four aspects. First, instead of trying to distinguish "core" crimes and "less serious" crimes, it proposes a division between generic offences and specific offences. The basic distinction lies in the fact that a violation of regulation is not required for conviction of a generic offence. Consequently, the definition of environmental crime is very inclusive: whether or not in violation of a statute or regulation, anyone who knowingly, recklessly, or negligently causes or contributes to serious damage or a substantial risk of serious damage to the local or regional environment, or who causes death, serious illness, or severe personal injury to a human being by releasing a pollutant, commits a crime against the environment.

Second, the model law is distinctive in that it recommends that legal entity liability apply in addition to personal liability, but does not require the identification of any individual agent. A legal entity is criminally responsible for such an offence on the ground of "faulty risk management" or violation of a regulatory provision. In essence, this provision suggests that legal-entity liability could be direct and purely objective. The model law thus attempts to bridge the wide gap that exists between civil-law and common-law countries in this area. Third, the model law does not recognize government immunity, although many specifics remain untouched in this respect. Last, in addition to traditional criminal sanctions, the model law permits the removal of illegally obtained economic benefits by imposing sanctions such as forfeiture of property and dissolution or winding up of the business.

Taking into consideration various existing models, the Portland Report recommends a realistic structure for a regional enforcement regime. In the short term, given the difficulties in transnational enforcement, regional institutions have to be complementary to domestic enforcement and focus on inspections, information gathering, monitoring, auditing, and dispute settlement. Nonetheless, the Report urges states to ensure that individuals and organizations in one state are accorded the right to initiate prosecution for environmental crimes committed by persons or entities of another state. Such proceedings should not be subject to the rule of exhaustion of local remedies. There should not be any discrimination based on residence or nationality.

(2) The UN Economic and Social Council (ECOSOC) Resolution

The Portland Report was subsequently distributed for consideration by a number of UN institutions. At its third session (26 April to 6 May), the UN Commission on Crime Prevention and Criminal Justice adopted a resolution requesting that the report be officially published as a United Nations document and be included in the documentation prepared for the 9th UN Congress on the Prevention of Crime and the Treatment of Offenders scheduled to be held in Cairo, 29 April to 12 May 1995.

ECOSOC later approved this request in its June 1994 resolution entitled "The Role of Criminal Law in the Protection of the Environment." Furthermore, as an Annex of the resolution, ECOSOC adopted the Recommendations of the 1993 Vienna *Ad Hoc* Expert Group Meeting on More Effective Forms of International Co-operation against Transnational Crime, including Environmental Crime. The Recommendations urge states to implement in their specific environmental legislation principles of the 1992 Rio Declaration on Environment and Development. The document recommends the use of a wide array of measures, including criminal sanctions, to ensure compliance with environmental protection laws. It emphasizes that a key function of environmental criminal law is to control and prohibit hazardous activities such as the establishment of hazardous installations and the illegal movements and disposal of hazardous materials. States are urged to criminalize "at least certain core criminal offences" in this area, including deliberate, reckless, or negligent offences that cause imminent risks of serious damage or danger to the environment. The wording of the Recommendations, however, is apparently less specific in terms of definitions and principles. For example, while promoting the concept of corporate criminal liability, no definition of the concept *per se* is formulated. This lacuna is filled, however, by the Portland model law.

Interestingly, the Recommendations encourage the introduction of a variety of relatively new concepts into national laws, including class actions and citizen suits, collaboration of governments with non-governmental organizations in crime prevention at an international level, the establishment of a permanent international criminal court for the prosecution of environmental crimes, and the idea that crimes against the environment are crimes against the peace and security of mankind. The last two ideas endorse the recommendation of the International Law Commission in its draft Code of Crimes against the Peace and Security of Mankind and the draft Statute for the International Criminal Court.

(3) The Rio Recommendations

The International Association of Penal Law held its 15th International Congress in Rio de Janeiro, 4–10 September. Over 1,000 jurists from 62 countries examined recommendations of the 1992 Ottawa Preparatory Colloquium, the 1993 *Ad Hoc* Expert Group meeting, the 1994 Portland meeting, the June 1994 ECOSOC resolution, and other recent international and regional developments in the area of environmental criminal law. The goal of the meeting was to formulate clear guidelines for the application of general criminal law principles to environmental crimes. Taking the different legal systems into account, the participants discussed key issues regarding the applicability of conventional penal principles to this type of unconventional crime, the criminal responsibility of legal entities, and the need to establish an international criminal justice system for the protection of the environment.

The 15th International Congress adopted a resolution entitled "Crime against the Environment—Application of the General Part," which presents a series of recommendations and recognizes criminal law as the last resort to ensure observance of the principle of sustainable development and the precautionary principle. In comparison with the Portland model law, the Rio Recommendations avoid some of the details, but confirm most of the principles. For example, the resolution broadly defines crimes against the environment as "culpable acts or omissions that cause serious harm" or "a real and imminent (concrete) endangerment to the environment or human beings," with the mental element as intent, knowledge, recklessness, or culpable negligence. This formulation is understandable, because while the Portland model law was aimed at national governments framing domestic legislation, the Rio recommendation had an international and inter-governmental focus.

The criminal responsibility of legal entities was a central topic. Several legislative models were discussed, and the Portland model is recommended in the resolution. In principle, the resolution states that an entity should be held criminally liable if serious harm to the environment results as a consequence of the failure of its managers and directing authorities to properly discharge their supervisory responsibility to prevent the harm. The identification of an individual for a faulty decision, however, is not a prerequisite to prosecution of a private entity for an offence against the environment. The same principle of direct liability applies to public entities, provided that the national law recognizes their criminal responsibility. Nonetheless, given the fact that public entities are normally immune from criminal sanctions in most jurisdictions, the resolution recommends that at the least, the criminally responsible human agents should be prosecuted for serious harm caused by the entities.

The 15th International Congress urged states to specify in their penal codes core crimes against the environment, *i.e.*, crimes that are *sui generis* and do not depend on other laws for their content. Core crimes affecting more than one state should be recognized as international crimes under conventions. A transborder offence against the environment should come under the jurisdiction of any state where it is committed, wholly or in part, or where the harm or serious risk of harm arises. Where the offence causes harm or serious risk of harm in the global commons, jurisdiction should be determined in the following order: the flag principle; the principle of nationality; the principle of extradite or prosecute; and, in the case of international crime, the principle of universality. The resolution also recommends that serious offences be made extraditable and suggests that the proposed international criminal court be given jurisdiction over environmental crimes against the global commons.

(4) Other Developments

In 1990, the European Ministers of Justice had adopted a resolution requesting the Council of Europe to produce a draft European Convention on the Role of Criminal Law in the Protection of the Environment (Resolution No. 1, the 17th Conference of European Ministers of Justice, Istanbul, 1990). In 1994, the Council continued its efforts to complete this draft. According to the 1990 resolution, the draft convention should include a list of criminal offences, apply the concept of endangerment offences (which requires no actual damage), define the relationship between criminal law and administrative law in the environmental sphere, and provide common guidelines for legislative and other measures for the investigation and prosecution of these offences. In principle, the current draft provides for both intentional and negligent offences, as well as individual and corporate criminal liability. Other key issues raised in the ongoing drafting process included group participation in proceedings, jurisdiction, and judicial assistance.

Illegal trafficking of hazardous wastes continued to be a major concern. In March, the Second Conference of the Parties to the Basel Convention adopted Decision II/10, requesting stringent national legislation and strengthened international cooperation to control transboundary movements of hazardous wastes. In May, the Second Meeting of the Interpol Working Party on Environmental Crime was held in Lyons, France. Interestingly, the agenda included transboundary movement and dumping of waste products, illegal traffic in radioactive substances, and illegal traffic in species of wild flora and fauna, to reflect the mandate of the three subgroups established in 1993. The Interpol Working Party urges its members to improve the exchange of information, study the patterns of environmental crimes, and establish an international network of knowledgeable enforcement contacts.

In September, the UN General Assembly decided to refer the International Law Commission's (ILC) draft Code of Crimes Against the Peace and Security of Mankind to the Sixth Committee. The Code, published in 1991, provides a special article (Art. 26) on wilful and severe damage to the environment, which reads: "An individual who wilfully causes or orders the causing of widespread, long-term and severe damage to the natural environment shall, on conviction thereof, be sentenced [to...]." In its commentary, the ILC insists that "particularly serious attacks" against the environment should be defined as international crimes under the proposed Code. In December, the Sixth Committee recommended to the General Assembly the adoption of two draft resolutions: the first addressed to the ILC Code and the second to the establishment of an international criminal court.

The first resolution (Draft Resolution I) urges the ILC, at its 47th session, to resume its work on the draft Code so that the second reading of the draft Code may be completed before the end of the present term of office. The approval of such a Code is necessary because it is the basis of the jurisdiction of the proposed international criminal court. Accordingly, the companion resolution (Draft Resolution III) establishes an *ad hoc* committee to review the major substantive and administrative issues arising out of the ILC's draft statute for an international criminal court and, in the light of that review, to consider arrangements for the convening of an international conference of plenipotentiaries, to begin and complete that work in 1995 with a view toward submitting its report to the General Assembly at the beginning of its 50th session. The resolution also calls for inclusion in the provisional agenda of the 50th session of an item entitled "establishment of an international criminal court" in order to study the report of the *ad hoc* committee and to decide on the convening of an international conference of plenipotentiaries to conclude a convention on the establishment of such a court.

Compared to the models developed in Portland and Rio, Art. 26 provides a much narrower definition of environmental crime. As the commentary indicates, Art. 26 requires three essential elements. First, it requires actual damage to the natural environment, thereby excluding endangerment. Second, the damage must be "widespread, long-term and severe." Third, the damage must be "wilful," which indicates an express aim or specific intention, so that mere knowledge, recklessness, and negligence are excluded.

The issue of corporate criminal liability with respect to environmental protection was also discussed at the 8th Annual Conference of the Society for the Reform of Criminal Law, held in Hong Kong in December. The "corporate culture" test as the basis for liability was the subject of much debate by the delegates from 26 countries. It will also be discussed by a panel of experts representing the principal legal systems of the world at the 9th UN Congress.

(5) Conclusion

From the 1991 ILC draft Code of Crimes to the 1994 Rio Recommendations, the trend of evolution favors a rapid extension of the scope of criminal law for the protection of the environment. Still, to what extent this will become a change in real law remains to be seen. Indeed, discussion on the strengths and limitations of criminal law will continue during the 9th UN Congress on the Prevention of Crime and the Treatment of Offenders. According to the agenda, the 9th UN Congress will open a workshop on environmental protection at the national and international levels to discuss the potential and limits of criminal justice in this area. Focusing on the problem of pollution, the workshop will once again consider recommendations of the Portland meeting, the *Ad Hoc* Group meeting and the Rio conference, as well as the ILC's draft Art. 26 on crimes against the environment. The most interesting component of this workshop will likely be publication of the results of an empirical study on criminal justice responses to pollution incidents in 11 developing and industrialized countries. This type of study may help to define the appropriate scope of environmental criminal law.

Vincent Cheng Yang
Daniel C. Préfontaine
Mohan Prabhu

5. ARMED CONFLICT AND THE ENVIRONMENT

(1) International Committee of the Red Cross (ICRC)

The main focus of the ICRC's work in 1994 on armed conflict and the environment was on the finalisation of its Guidelines for Military Manuals and Instructions on the Protection of the Environment in Times of Armed Conflict. The Guidelines were first introduced in the UN General Assembly in 1993. Although intended as a dissemination text of practical instructions, several of the provisions are declaratory of existing international customary or treaty law and therefore are already binding on states. UN General Assembly Resolution 48/30 (1993) had urged all states to review and comment on the Guidelines and requested the ICRC to present a new version in light of those comments. According to the ICRC, five states submitted comments on the 1993 Guidelines.

The revised Guidelines are similar to the 1993 version, containing sections on general principles of international law, specific rules on the protection of the environment, and a final section on the implementation and dissemination of the Guidelines. One change is in relation to the applicability of peacetime international environmental law to circumstances of armed conflict. The 1993 Guidelines indicated that such rules "should" continue to apply, whereas the 1994 version now reads "may" continue. Obligations regarding the protection of the environment of states not party to an armed conflict and of areas beyond national jurisdiction were, in the 1993 version, not affected "unless stipulated otherwise," while in the revised Guidelines they are not affected "to the extent they are not inconsistent with the applicable law of armed conflict." In cases where the natural environment is destroyed, and where this is not justified by military necessity, the 1993 Guidelines indicated that such destruction might be punishable as a violation of international law. The revised Guidelines now indicate that under certain circumstances such cases may be punishable as a "grave breach of international humanitarian law," which can trigger individual criminal responsibility (as indicated in both the 1993 and 1994 versions).
During 1994, the ICRC did not convene expert meetings specifically on the protection of the environment during armed conflict as it had in recent

years. It did, however, contribute to discussions on this topic at international meetings organised by other organisations, such as the Doha Conference on International Legal Issues arising under the United Nations Decade of International Law, organised by the Asian-African Legal Consultative Committee, and the Meeting of Experts on Human Rights and the Environment, organised by the Sierra Club Legal Defense Fund and held in Geneva. The ICRC also was involved in the preparations for the first Review Conference to the 1980 Convention on Prohibitions or Restrictions on the Use of Certain Conventional Weapons, by organising meetings of experts, drawing up documents, and making recommendations. The ICRC is of the view that a meeting of governmental experts specifically on the protection of the environment in times of armed conflict is not necessary at this stage (as had been suggested in UN General Assembly Resolution 48/30), but indicated that the topic will be considered in the context of its follow-up work to the 1993 International Conference for the Protection of War Victims.

(2) The United Nations

(a) UN Decade of International Law

On the recommendation of the Sixth (Legal) Committee, the UN General Assembly adopted without a vote Resolution 49/50, "United Nations Decade of International Law" on 9 December. The resolution calls on states, *inter alia*, to "disseminate widely" the revised ICRC Guidelines and to "give due consideration to the possibility of incorporating them into their military manual and other instructions addressed to their personnel." This call is repeated in the Programme for the Activities for the third term (1995-96) of the UN Decade of International Law under the heading "Encouragement of the Teaching, Study, Dissemination and Wider Appreciation of International Law." The ICRC is also invited to report on its activities and those of others relevant to the protection of the environment during armed conflict, which will be included in the UN Secretary-General's 1995 Report on the progressive development and codification of international law.

(b) Chemical Weapons Convention

The Convention on the Prohibition of the Development, Production, Stockpiling and Use of Chemical Weapons and on their Destruction, which opened for signature on 13 January 1993, is an ambitious blueprint for the prohibition of these environmentally hazardous weapons (*see* 4 *YbIEL* 131 (1993) for an overview). Although 154 nations signed the Convention, it has yet to enter into force; the earliest date it can enter into force is 13 January 1995, with the deposit of 65 instruments of ratification or accession. In 1994,

Albania, Australia, Bahamas, Bulgaria, Cook Islands, Germany, Maldives, Mexico, Saint Kitts and Nevis, Spain, Sri Lanka, and Tanzania deposited instruments of ratification. This brings the total number of ratifications to 16. There had been no accessions by the end of 1994.

(c) Comprehensive Nuclear Test Ban Treaty

In 1994, the Conference on Disarmament began negotiation of a Comprehensive Nuclear Test Ban Treaty, in response to UN General Assembly Resolution 48/70 of 16 December 1993. Two Working Groups were established: one on verification and one on institutional and legal questions. A "rolling test" was reported to exist. This effort is considered to have real prospects for success, especially given US President Clinton's support for the result and the extended US moratorium on nuclear testing until September 1995.

(d) International Law Commission (ILC)

In 1994, the ILC adopted the final text of its (➔) Draft Articles on the Law of the Non-Navigational Uses of International Watercourses. The Draft Articles represent a comprehensive set of provisions relating, *inter alia*, to the protection of the environment of such watercourses. Article 29 states that international watercourses and related installations, facilities, and other works enjoy the protection of the rules of international law applicable during armed conflict. The commentary to the provision indicates that during armed conflict, the obligations contained in the Draft Articles to protect and use international watercourses and related works continue to remain in effect. The intent of Art. 29 appears to be to supplement such protection with the law of armed conflict.

The ILC also elaborated a draft statute for an international criminal court, and recommended that the UN General Assembly convene an international conference of plenipotentiaries to study and conclude a convention. The statute is largely procedural and adjectival and does not purport to define or codify international crimes. Article 20 lists crimes within the jurisdiction of the court as (a) genocide, (b) aggression, (c) "serious violations of the laws and customs applicable in armed conflict," (d) crimes against humanity, and (e) crimes pursuant to a list of treaty provisions annexed "which constitute exceptionally serious crimes of international concern." The third category, "serious violations" of the law of armed conflict, is particularly relevant in that, according to the commentary, it is to be distinguished from "grave breaches" under international humanitarian law. Reference is made to Art. 22 of the ILC Draft Code of Crimes against the Peace and Security of Mankind, which deems the employment of "methods or means of warfare which are intended or may be expected to cause widespread, long-term and severe damage to the natural environment" to be "an exceptionally serious war crime." This is significant because the annex of suggested treaty provisions referred to in category (e) does not contain the provisions most directly applicable to environmental protection of the 1977 Additional Protocol 1 to the 1949 Geneva Convention, and Relating to the Protection of Victims of International Armed Conflicts or the 1977 UN Convention on the Prohibition of Military or Any Other Hostile Use of Environmental Modification Techniques.

(e) International Court of Justice (ICJ)

Pursuant to Resolution WHA46.40, adopted by the World Health Assembly in 1993, an Advisory Opinion from the ICJ on the following question had been requested: "In view of the health and environmental effects, would the use of nuclear weapons by a State in war or other armed conflict be a breach of its obligations under international law including the World Health Organisation (WHO) Constitution?"

The ICJ had set a deadline of 20 September 1994 for the WHO and its member states that are entitled to appear before the Court to submit written statements. By that time, the following states had filed written submissions: Australia, Colombia, Costa Rica, Finland, France, Germany, India, Ireland, Islamic Republic of Iran, Italy, Japan, Kazakhstan, Lithuania, Malaysia, Mexico, Moldova, Nauru, Netherlands, New Zealand, North Korea, Norway, Papua New Guinea, Philippines, the Russian Federation, Rwanda, Samoa, Saudi Arabia, Solomon Islands, Sri Lanka, Sweden, Uganda, Ukraine, United Kingdom, and the United States.

These statements are not yet publicly available, by virtue of Art. 106 of the Rules of the Court, which states that such statements may be made public on or after the opening of oral proceedings. But a letter dated 17 June 1994 to the UN Secretary General from the Permanent Representative of India, released as a UN document but later withdrawn, indicated that the use of nuclear weapons would constitute a crime against humanity and be a violation of international humanitarian law. In a "Press Guidance" released by the US State Department, the argument was made that the WHO lacked the jurisdiction to request the opinion and the long-standing American view was reiterated that international law does not prohibit nuclear weapons per se, but that each specific instance must be considered against the fundamental principles of international humanitarian law.

On 15 December, the UN General Assembly adopted Resolution 49/75K, pursuant to Art. 96(1) of the UN Charter, requesting the ICJ "urgently to render its advisory opinion on the following question 'is the threat or use of nuclear weapons in any circumstances permitted under international law?'"

Richard G. Tarasofsky

II. AIR AND ATMOSPHERE

1. TRANSBOUNDARY AIR POLLUTION

(1) Introduction

The main developments in the field of transboundary air pollution occurred in relation to the UN Economic Commission for Europe (ECE) region. There were also signs, however, of attention being given to the matter in Asia, as China and Japan concluded an Environmental Cooperation Agreement (including the field of acidification). While work on a World Bank/Asian Development Bank project on "Acid Rain and Emission Reductions in Asia" continued, the effects of forest fires became a new subject in the field of transboundary pollution.

(2) The Geneva Executive Body of the Convention on Long Range Transboundary Air Pollution

(a) New Sulphur Protocol

On 13 June, 26 countries of the ECE region signed a new (➔) Protocol on the further reduction of Sulphur Emissions (doc. ECE/EB.AIR/40) in Oslo. Thirteen parties to the 1979 Convention did not sign, including Ireland, Lithuania, Portugal, Romania, Turkey, and the United States (which is not a party to the 1985 sulphur dioxide (SO_2) Protocol either).

The most innovative aspect of the 1994 Protocol is the introduction of an approach using scientifically based critical loads. Annex 1 to the Protocol includes a map of critical loads based on an EMEP-grid (150 km x 150 km) covering the entire area over which the Convention applies. The application of this new approach has led to differentiated SO_2-emissions reduction percentages for each of the respective Parties (Art. 2). The required reductions (ranging from 22 to 80 percent) must be achieved in the year 2000, 2005, or 2010 (Annex II). The target years 2005 and 2010 were specifically introduced to offer a number of Central and Eastern European countries the possibility of becoming parties to the Convention. For Canada a special regime applies.

The Protocol also contains a new provision on compliance (Art. 7): On the basis of a decision by the Ministers, the text on the "structure and functions of the implementation, as well as procedures for its review of compliance" attached to the decision will be adopted at the first session of the Executive Body after the entry into force of the Protocol (doc. ECE/EB.AIR/40, pp. 30-32). Dispute settlement is to be achieved "by negotiation or by any other method of dispute settlement acceptable to the parties to the dispute" (Art. 9(1)). Article 9(2) allows parties to accept in writing dispute settlement through submission to the International Court of Justice or through arbitration, recognizing the applicability of this provision "as compulsory *ipso facto* and without agreement in relation to any Party accepting the same obligation." Where two parties to a dispute have not accepted the same approach to dispute settlement under Art. 9(2), a Conciliation Commission can be created at the request of one of the parties. The Commission "shall render a recommendatory award, which the parties shall consider in good faith."

(b) Oslo Ministerial Declaration

By declaration, the Ministers committed themselves to further air pollutant abatement. They declared that every effort should be made

> to accelerate the negotiations on a second step to the 1988 Protocol concerning the Control of Emissions of Nitrogen Oxides or their Transboundary Fluxes to further reduce the emissions the nitrogen compounds, including ammonia, and, if appropriate, volatile organic compounds in view of their contribution to photochemical pollution, acidification and eutrophication, and their effect on human health, the environment and materials, by addressing all significant emission resources.

In light of this declaration, the Executive Body, at its 12th session, adopted a timetable for the preparation of strategies to address multi-pollutants/multi-effects, and to elaborate an approach based on critical loads for the next protocol to be negotiated (doc. ECE/EB.AIR/38, Annex para. 8).

(c) Persistent Organic Pollutants

Negotiations on persistent organic pollutants and on heavy metals from anthropogenic activities that pose a risk to human health and the environment, including the sensitive Arctic environment, are now under consideration. It has been suggested, however, that persistent organic pollutants may be more properly a matter for a global legal instrument than a protocol to the 1979 Geneva Convention.

(d) Results of 1985 SO_2 Protocol

Reviewing the results of the 1985 SO_2 Protocol, the "1994 Major Review on Strategies and Policies for Air Pollution Abatement" comes to the provisional conclusion:

> Taken as a whole, the 21 Parties to the 1985 Helsinki Protocol reduced 1980 sulphur emissions by 46% by 1993 (using the latest available figure, where no data were available for 1993). In the whole of Europe, including non-Parties to the Protocol, that sum of emissions is just below 30,000 kt which corresponds to a reduction of 43% compared to 1980.

(Doc. EB.AIR/R87, para. 58.)
In evaluating these reductions, the industrial recession, especially in Central and Eastern Europe, should be taken into account.

(3) Bilateral Developments

(a) Environmental Cooperation Treaty between the People's Republic of China and Japan

On 20 March, China and Japan signed an Environmental Cooperation Treaty calling for efforts to combat environmental problems. The Treaty covers, *inter alia*, joint research on acidification and the extension of Japanese air pollution management technologies to China, as emission of air pollutants in China contribute to acidification in Japan.

(b) Agreement between Singapore and Indonesia

Forest fires caused by, *inter alia*, the clearing of forests for agricultural purposes and commercial logging in Indonesia (Borneo, Sumatra) have affected environmental and health conditions in Singapore and Malaysia. On 15 October, Singapore and Indonesia reached an agreement pursuant to which Indonesia will take measures to limit the burning of leftovers of tree cutting and engage in educational efforts to reduce emissions, and Singapore will provide early detection information on forest fires obtained by weather satellites to help prevent their spread.

(c) Agreement between Finland and the Russian Federation

Negotiations between these countries resulted in an agreement to reduce sulphur emissions by 50 percent by 1997, based on 1980 levels. Further reductions are to be considered on the basis of critical loads.

(4) Other Developments

In July 1992, researchers in Europe, the United States, and Asia began a collaborative project to study the effects of sulphur deposition in Asia. The project will aid in the development of a methodology and a PC-based software tool to assess the consequences of emission reduction strategies. RAINS-ASIA is based on the framework of a pioneering acid raid model for Europe (RAINS). Currently, RAINS-ASIA is being developed by integrating modeling strategies with the available data. The data include energy use, emission of sulfur dioxide, abatement techniques of emissions, long-range transport and deposition, and environmental effects. National and international bodies and research institutions will use the results to facilitate discussions on acid rain and sulfur deposition. The project, which is funded by a multi-national trust fund through the World Bank and the Asian Development Bank, could form the starting point for an agreement on the monitoring and evaluation of acid rain in Asia comparable to the European Monitoring and Evaluation Programme established under the 1979 Geneva Convention.

Willem Kakebeeke

2. OZONE LAYER

(1) Introduction

In order to present the full range of events that occurred in 1994 under the ozone-depletion regime, it may be useful to concentrate on the meetings of four different bodies closely related to the Montreal Protocol on Substances that Deplete the Ozone Layer: (1) the Open-ended Working Group (July 1994), (2) the Executive Committee of the Multilateral Fund (September 1994), (3) the Implementation Committee (3 October 1994), and (➔) (4) the Sixth Meeting of the Parties (6–7 October 1994).

(2) The Open-ended Working Group

The Open-ended Working Group learned from Ms. Dowdeswell, Executive Director of the United Nations Environment Programme that the worldwide production of chlorofluorocarbons (CFCs) had declined by 60 percent since 1988 and that 137 states had ratified the Protocol (with 88 states also being party to the London Amendment and 28 states party to the Copenhagen Amendment).

The Group's substantive work focussed at first on the review of the financial mechanism and the link between approval and implementation of projects supported by the Multilateral Fund and the reporting of data by developing-country members. These countries voiced their concern that an adequate supply of controlled substances should be at their disposal in order to meet their basic domestic needs. Accordingly, the Group proposed to adapt existing information procedures on transfers in order to make such movements more transparent.

A long debate took place over the classification and reclassification of countries as "members operating under Art. 5 para. 1" (developing countries), each classificatory decision being dependent on adequate date reporting and linked to both eligibility for assistance from the Fund and financial contributions to the Fund. In this context, mention was also made of the difficulties that countries in transition encountered in complying with their phase-out obligations and duties with respect to the Multilateral Fund. Nominations for essential uses of halons and other controlled substances also took up a major part of the discussion. These nominations will be reflected in the various annexes to the Group's report and thus constitute exceptions to the general reduction commitments.

From a legal perspective, attention had to be paid to the listing of products containing controlled substances from Annex B. According to Art. 4 para. 3 bis of the Montreal Protocol, such a list has to be established in order to allow for import bans vis-à-vis non-parties. In view of the tightening of the respective phase-outs, the Working Group concluded that such a list would have little practical consequence and that the work related to it would be disproportionate to its environmental benefits. The Chairman of the Legal Drafting Group suggested that Art. 4 para. 3 *bis* could be terminated by simple consent of the parties, without formal amendment procedures. The Working Group did not take a formal stand on the problem of termination and satisfied itself with a reference to the already-mentioned practical considerations. It is at least unclear whether this provision can be terminated by a simple decision of the Meeting of Parties or whether the amendment rules of the Vienna Convention should be applied. An alternative to a formal amendment would be "desuetudo," the long-term non-application of the respective rule.

(3) The Executive Committee of the Multilateral Fund

The Multilateral Fund's Executive Committee mainly had to deal with the problem of arrears in the 1991-1994 contributions. Of the 46 countries supposed to contribute to the Fund, nine had not made any payments at all, a situation that persuaded the Committee that some moral pressure would have to be exerted. Several members of the Committee were of the opinion that public attention should be drawn to these notorious non-payers. The United Nations Development Programme and the United Nations Industrial Development Programme, the implementing agencies, presented their general work programmes, as well as their specific country programmes (Bangladesh, Mauritania, and Venezuela). The Committee devoted a disproportionately long debate to the administrative cost of the financial mechanisms, during which complex problems such as the transparency of project implementation and related costs were raised.

(4) The Implementation Committee

The Implementation Committee, established under the Non-Compliance Procedure of the Montreal Protocol, met briefly in early October before the Meeting of the Parties. Some parties that were considered as benefitting from the Fund while not fulfilling their corresponding obligations to report necessary data had been invited to this conference to justify their non-compliance: Algeria, Antigua and Barbuda, Central African Republic, Iran, Lebanon, Swaziland, and Syrian Arab Republic. Some of these countries, however, submitted last-minute reports to the Committee and were therefore omitted from further scrutiny.

An interesting legal question arose regarding the transfer of production rights from Romania to a company in Greece, because Greece was a party operating under Art. 2 rather than under Art. 5. Although there was no final settlement of the issue, the Committee's chair was of the view that a country without production limits could not transfer production rights to a country with limits. Poland raised another problem: whether a party could join together the CFC-limits for two years and import the maximum possible in these two years in order to satisfy its industry, which could not possibly change immediately to substitutes. As the solution to this problem would have led the Committee well beyond the Montreal Protocol, no direct reply to the Polish request was possible; however, once Poland has ratified the Copenhagen Amendment, it will be free under that amendment's non-compliance procedure to justify its performance in terms of its conformity with its obligations.

(5) The Sixth Meeting of the Parties to the Montreal Protocol

Finally, the Sixth Meeting of the Parties to the Montreal Protocol took place 6–7 October 1994. The Executive Director again appealed to parties that had not fulfilled their reporting requirements, and noted an alarming trend of still outstanding contributions to the Multilateral Fund. She could also report, however, that by the end of 1993, developed countries had completely ceased production and consumption of halons were now expected to eliminate the production and consumption of CFCs by the end of 1995. A main feature of the debate following the Executive Director's introduction was the considerable number of complaints, by developing countries in particular. They criticized, *inter alia,* attempts allegedly made to impose earlier phase-out dates, the lack of progress made toward ozone-benign and safe substitutes and alternatives, the unavailability of relevant technology to developing countries, and the assumption that such technology would be transferred from industrialized to developing countries in a one-way transactional process, rather than jointly developed with the developing countries in order to be tailor-made to their unique problems. Another set of complaints related to the poor state of the Multilateral Fund. Donors were allegedly delaying their contributions, thereby delaying the implementation of projects in developing countries. The Fund's Executive Committee was suspected of limiting developing countries' access to available financial resources by interpreting the terms of reference of the Fund too restrictively, with the suspected goal of reducing the outflow of funds and therefore also the need for the inflow of contributions. In consequence, developing countries stated that until the requisite funds were forthcoming, they would have great difficulty implementing their phase-out plans.

Representatives of economies in transition complained that the amendments to the Protocol would commit their countries to financial obligations that they could not meet, and that their countries should be given a special status according to their actual capabilities. Various countries also pointed out that the use of CFCs was actually increasing in certain sectors, that CFCs were important transitional substances, and that any effort to restrict their use would place an undue burden on developing countries. Methyl bromide, however, continued to be considered indispensable for agricultural production and quarantine purposes.

Among the 20 decisions adopted by the Meeting of Parties are the following:

- Parties were reminded that the timely reporting of data was a legal obligation.
- Developing countries were reminded, with respect to their provisional classification as Art. 5 parties, that they would lose that preferential status if they did not report their data within one year of the approval of their country programme and of their institutional strengthening through actions of the Fund.
- For the benefit of developed countries, certain essential-use nominations of controlled substances were approved as exceptions to general commitments.
- As regards methyl bromide, broad definitions were given for "quarantine applications" and "preshipment applications"; for these purposes, the transfer technologies that are not ozone depleting should be improved through support from the Fund.
- It was decided not to elaborate further the list specified in Art. 4 para. 3 *bis* of the Montreal Protocol; the legal status of this decision was left open.
- Assessment panels were invited to evaluate the technical and economic feasibility as well as the environmental, scientific and economic implications of alternatives to hydrochlorofluorocarbons and methyl bromide.
- Information obligations were stipulated in order to better control the transfer of controlled substances that are required to meet the domestic needs of developing countries.
- Both the nature and the legal status of the Fund as a body under international law were clarified. As to the latter, the pertinent decision states that "[T]he Multilateral Fund shall enjoy such legal capacity as is necessary for the exercise of its functions and the protection of its interests, in particular the capacity to enter into contracts, to acquire and dispose of movable and immovable property and to institute legal proceedings in defence of its interests."

As regards the Fund's privileges and immunities, reference was made to an agreement with the host state, Canada. The conferment of legal personality on an institution previously established by amendment, without additional amendment of the Protocol, is a relatively new technique. Whether this decision is fully within the mandate of the Meeting of Parties and whether it constitutes itself a valid source of international law remains to be seen.

(6) Concluding Observations

On the legal side of the ozone-depletion regime, treaty obligations were viewed as capable of being undone by simple decisions. Such decisions were also considered sufficient to confer upon an institution legal personality under international law, including privileges and immunities. On the political side, the North-South relationship, including the funding of technology transfer, remains a weak point that will have to be addressed at future meetings.

Winfried Lang

3. GLOBAL CLIMATE

(1) UN Framework Convention on Climate Change

(a) General

The UN Framework Convention on Climate Change (FCCC) entered into force on March 21, 1994. As a result, the First Conference of the Parties (CoP) was to be held in Berlin from 28 March to 7 April 1995. Among those that became parties to the Convention by the end of 1994 were the Russian Federation, Saudi Arabia, and Kuwait, bringing the total number of parties to 116.

(b) Unresolved Issues

According to the Convention, the first CoP must make decisions on a range of difficult issues relating to the Convention's implementation. To prepare for the CoP, the Intergovernmental Negotiating Committee for a Framework Convention on Climate Change (INC/FCCC) continued to meet on an interim basis. The INC held two substantive meetings during 1994: its ninth session (INC 9) in Geneva from 7–18 February; and its tenth session (INC 10) in Geneva from 22 August to 2 September. At these meetings some progress was made on the adequacy of commitments, with little movement on other contentious issues. To the extent that the INC cannot resolve these questions in its final meeting on 6–17 February in New York, CoP I will have a difficult and antagonistic agenda.

(i) Adequacy of Commitments

The first CoP is charged with reviewing the adequacy of these commitments in light of the objective of the Convention and the most recent information on emissions trends and climate science, and with taking "appropriate action, which may include the adoption of amendments" to these provisions (Art. 4, para. 2(d)). Accordingly, during INC 9, the INC finally tackled the key topic of the commitments made by industrialized countries to reduce their emissions of greenhouse gases, contained in Art. 4, paras. 2(a) and (b) of the Convention. The discussion proceeded with much more ease than expected.

Referring to current scientific understanding, the view was expressed that the commitments in Arts. 4.2(a) and (b) should be considered inadequate for the long term and that further action may be required to make satisfactory progress toward achieving the objective of the Convention. The need for broader action which would have an impact in the period beyond 2000 was highlighted.

(A/AC/WG.1/L.17/Rev.1.) If, at the CoP, the commitments are found to be inadequate, the following options for further action would be available: an amendment to the Convention; a protocol or protocols to the Convention to be negotiated before, at, or subsequent to CoP I; and a resolution or decision by the parties at CoP I that would clarify or interpret the relevant text, provide guidance to the parties in implementing the article, or reflect a political statement of will by the parties. The Interim Secretariat was asked to prepare a paper for INC 10, compiling the interventions at INC 9 on the adequacy of commitments.

INC 10 moved at a much slower pace on this issue. German attempts at advancing the debate by circulating a paper on targets and timetables received no support from other Organisation for Economic Cooperation and Development (OECD) countries. Interventions by the United States and European Union (EU) on adequacy actually slowed down progress even further by calling for a review of "how to promote and recognize the efforts of an increasing number of countries, beyond those currently identified in Annex I, to play a greater role in solving this global problem." (US statement on the "adequacy of commitments" under Art. 4, paras. 2(a) and (b), 23 August 1994) The US statement put many developing countries on the defensive and caused a rift in the negotiations, as there was uncertainty as to which countries the United States was targeting.

Another key development in the adequacy of commitments debate was the submission of a protocol to the Interim Secretariat on 21 September by the Alliance of Small Island States (AOSIS). AOSIS is a group of developing countries that share common objectives on environmental and sustainable development matters. The AOSIS Protocol would require that each of the Annex I parties reduce its 1990 level of anthropogenic emissions of carbon dioxide (CO_2) by at least 20 percent by the year 2005; adopt specific targets and timetables to limit or reduce other greenhouse gases not controlled by the Montreal Protocol; develop a coordination mechanism for measures developed to achieve the objective of the Convention; and ensure that the best available technologies, practices, and processes in all relevant climate sectors be expeditiously transferred to developing-country parties to this Protocol. ((➔) Draft Protocol to the UNFCCC on Greenhouse Gas Emission Reduction). This Protocol was followed, on 22 September, by a paper from the German delegation, welcoming the AOSIS Protocol and footnoting it in its section on basic commitments.

(ii) National Communications

The FCCC requires each party included in Annex I to submit, within six months of the entry into force of the Convention, information as specified in Arts. 4, paras. 2(b) and 12. The INC agreed on guidelines that promote consistency, transparency, and comparability among communications (*see* A/AC.237/55, Annex I, decision 9/2) for the preparation of the first communications by Annex I parties. By year's end, 18 parties were required to submit communications to the Interim Secretariat: Australia, Austria, Canada, Czech Republic, Denmark, European Union, Germany, Iceland, Japan, Netherlands, New Zealand, Norway, Portugal, Spain, Sweden, Switzerland, United Kingdom, and the United States. All except the European Union, Iceland, and Portugal submitted their communications on time.

The INC requested the Interim Secretariat to prepare a compilation and synthesis of the national communications for consideration at INC 11 and for subsequent submission to the first CoP. The synthesis is designed to provide an overview of the implementation of the Convention across reporting parties, noting trends and patterns, areas of convergence or divergence, data gaps, and the overall effects of policies and measures. (A/AC.237/81.)

(iii) Joint Implementation

The criteria governing the joint implementation of treaty obligations among countries was once again a contentious topic on which the INC was unable to reach consensus in 1994. The central issue remains whether the industrialized countries listed in Annex I of the Convention should be able to receive credit toward their emission reduction obligations for activities they undertake in developing countries. The INC was unable to conclude anything more than that "the discussions held on joint implementation led to a better understanding of the positions presented by member States, and were indicative of an emerging need for a consensus on the criteria to be defined in development of the concept of joint implementation." (INC, Conclusions on Joint Implementation) The Committee requested the Interim Secretariat to provide yet further documentation on the issue for INC 10. INC 10 surveyed that documentation, but was unable to reach consensus on any criteria for a potential pilot phase. "Taking into account the complexity as well as the far-reaching political implications of the subject, the Committee agreed to continue discussion on this matter at its next session, with a view to deciding on a recommendation to CoP I." (A/AC.237/WG.I/L.24.)

Critics of joint implementation (including the EU and most developing countries) cited the lack of a global cap on emissions and the responsibility of industrialized countries to take domestic action; supporters (including most other OECD countries) argued that environmental benefits would be maximized by minimizing the economic cost of emission cuts. Since the CoP is expected to set requirements for many aspects of a pilot phase (preliminary guidelines, participation, length of pilot phase, reporting by parties on joint implementation pilot projects, registration of joint implementation pilot projects, and organization of a pilot phase), INC 11 will be faced with a grand task. In order to propel the discussion further, a number of countries have initiated their own joint implementation programs. Those countries include the United States, Canada, and Norway, with Germany administering a study of the potential use of joint implementation.

(iv) Financial Mechanism

The INC made little progress in 1994 in determining how the Convention's financial mechanism would operate. The lack of guidance from the Participants' Meeting of the Global Environment Facility (GEF) in Cartagena, which focused on the restructuring and replenishment of the GEF, affected the debate on funding under the FCCC during INC 9. Developing countries strongly objected to the view that only projects yielding "global benefits" be eligible, arguing that such limitation would preclude funds for adaptation measures, which they believe are guaranteed by Art. 4, paras. 3 and 4 of the Convention.

One noteworthy development during INC 9 was the adoption of language stating that "consistency should be sought and maintained between activities, including those related to funding, relevant to climate change undertaken outside the framework of the financial mechanism and the policies, programme priorities and eligibility criteria for activities as relevant, established by the CoP." (A/AC.237/L.20/Add.2.) This calls on the Secretariat to develop options to promote consistency and to develop a monitoring system to review the activities of the World Bank and other lending institutions. INC 10 witnessed deadlock over the collection of information, with widespread concern by developing countries that this could lead to scrutiny of internationally financed projects. The working group did make progress on funding of adaptation measures, by agreeing on a three-stage approach, beginning with impact studies, options identifications, and capacity building. The Interim Secretariat was requested to present a paper on technology transfer for INC 11. Much of the text from INC 10 was forwarded, with brackets and italics, to INC 11. Those "problem points" included the relationship between the financial mechanism, its operational entities, and the CoP; the definition of "full incremental costs;" and how funding levels would be determined.

(v) Other Issues

Other key issues included the roles of the Subsidiary Body for Implementation and the Subsidiary Body for Scientific and Technological Advice (A/AC.237/64)); and the rules of procedure for the CoP (A/AC.237/58).

(2) Intergovernmental Panel on Climate Change (IPCC)

During 1994, the three working groups of the IPCC continued their work programs for the IPCC's Second Assessment Report (SAR). In October, a workshop was convened in Forteleza, Brazil, on the adequacy of the FCCC's commitments, in light of its ultimate objective as set forth in Art. 2. Since the SAR will not be completed in time for use by the first CoP, a special report on science is being prepared by Working Group I. The IPCC Special Report will consist of:

- A summary for policymakers of the Working Group I report on the radiative forcing of climate change, approved by the Working Group at its fourth session (Maastricht, 13-15 September 1994), and its underlying report accepted by the Working Group at the same session;
- IPCC Guidelines for National Greenhouse Gas Inventories, developed by Working Group I and approved by the Working Group in Maastricht;
- A summary for policymakers of Working Group III's evaluation of the IPCC IS92 emission scenarios, and its overall report, approved by the Working Group at its second session (Geneva, 27-28 September 1994);
- The IPCC Technical Guidelines on Climate Change Impacts and Adaptations, developed by Working Group II and approved by the Working Group at its second session (Nairobi, 8 November 1994).

The IPCC Report on Radiative Forcing of Climate Change, prepared by Working Group I, finds that "stabilization of current global emissions of CO_2 does not lead to stabilization of CO_2 concentrations by 2100." It goes on to state that "stabilization at any of the concentration levels studied (350 to 750 ppmv) could be attained only with global anthropogenic emissions that eventually drop to substantially below 1990 levels." Working Group II organized its work program for the SAR around four subgroups, each exploring the impacts of climate change on a different sphere of the environment or human activity. Subgroup A is focusing on industry, air quality, and human health; Subgroup B is examining marine ecosystems, coastal zones, and storm intensity; Subgroup C is concentrating on natural terrestrial ecosystems and hydrology; and Subgroup D is dealing with desertification, agriculture, forestry, and water resources. In addition, Working Group II is cooperating with Working Group I on understanding "ecological limits" for climate change, including quantitative interpretation of the objective of the Convention. Working Group III is evaluating models for assessing the socio-economics of climate change, including ways of calculating the costs and benefits of different policy responses, the role of technological change, and internationally coordinated response strategies such as joint implementation.

(3) *Naples Group of 7 Summit*

The Group of Seven (G-7) industrialized countries addressed a number of climate-related matters at their annual summit in Naples in July. In their (➔) Communique, the G-7 leaders agreed to speed up implementation of their climate action plans and to report on what they have achieved at 1995's Halifax Summit. Moreover, the G-7 recognized the need to develop steps for the post-2000 period, noted the importance of investments in energy efficiency and improvements to protect the environment, and urged multilateral development banks to make more progress in incorporating environmental considerations and local citizen participation in their programs.

(4) *National and Regional Developments*

(a) *Developments in the United States*

In September 1994, the Administration's Climate Change Action Plan (CCAP) was submitted to the Interim Secretariat. In general, the CCAP is made up of modest proposals promoting voluntary actions on the part of businesses, industries, and households. This year it has become evident that the CCAP is in serious jeopardy. The US Congress, even before the November elections, failed to provide full funding for the CCAP initiatives. Meanwhile, US carbon emissions rose 28 million metric tons (mmt), or 2.1 percent, in 1993, and emissions in the first quarter of 1994 were up over 4 percent compared to the same period the previous year. A shortfall of approximately 80mmt is expected. (Geller, *Hotline* vol. 1, no. 3) The United States is not on track for returning greenhouse gas emissions to 1990 levels by 2000, let alone making the large absolute emissions reductions necessary over the long run.

"Car Talks," a year-long policy review process to address the transportation sector, began 28-29 September with a two-day meeting of a selected Advisory Committee, which is to "develop recommendations on the sets of policies that would, if adopted, most cost-effectively obtain a return to 1990 levels of greenhouse gas emissions from personal motor vehicles by the years 2005, 2015, and 2025, with no upturn thereafter." The Administration also created an interagency "Climate Change Post-2000 Deputies Task Force" to establish a long-term strategy and examine policies and measures that could impact greenhouse gas emission levels beyond the year 2000. The task force is charged with preparing a 1994 year-end report synthesizing available results and recommending next steps. It is likely that the report will not be issued until mid-1995.

(b) *Developments in Europe*

The meeting of EU environment ministers on 15-16 December saw the final burial of a unified EU tax on carbon dioxide emissions, largely the result of Britain's opposition to any EU-wide energy tax. The CO_2 tax controversy had dragged on for almost three years. At the end of the year, all EU countries except Britain appeared willing to adopt a voluntary tax with Denmark, Belgium, and the Netherlands ready to move forward within an EU framework. A number of European national plans that were based on the adoption of an EU CO_2 energy tax are now unlikely to achieve their stabilization goals.

By year's end it remained thus unclear whether the EU would reach its target, reconfirmed at the December meeting, to "limit CO_2 emissions and other greenhouse gases by year 2000 at 1990 levels," as agreed to under the Convention. The Council of Ministers agreed that "the CoP should, at a minimum, initiate negotiations on the further development, in a protocol, of the commitments in the Convention. A mandate for this purpose should contain specific elements regarding content and set a deadline for the conclusion of the negotiations. (Third CoP, 1997)" (EU Council Conclusions, 15-16 December 1994). Ten member states issued a joint statement on gasoline mileage of cars, asking the Commission to present a directive proposal by the next European Council.

Jennifer L. Morgan

III. FRESH WATER

INTERNATIONAL RIVERS AND LAKES/GROUND-WATER

(1) Europe

(a) European Union

Controversy continued to engulf the European Union (EU) drinking-water standards. The British government complained that the costs of meeting the drinking-water standards, set in the Directive on Urban Waste Water Treatment, would be prohibitive. Spain is expected to have difficulty in meeting the 1999 deadline for compliance with the Directive. However, in January, the EU Environment Commissioner and the European Parliament's Environment Committee Chairman denied that there would be any reduction in EU drinking-water standards. The European Commission also proposed stricter standards for analyzing and monitoring bathing water quality, despite continued improvement, in the quality of bathing water in EU member states in 1994. For example, in France, over 85 percent of areas tested complied with the EU Directive on Bathing Water Quality. Eighty percent of British bathing spots met the Directive's standards.

The Netherlands, France, and Belgium concluded agreements to protect the Maas and Scheldt rivers against pollution (*see* (➔) Accord concernant la protection de la Meuse; and (➔) Accord concernant la protection de l'Escaut). The Maas provides drinking water for 5 million people in the three countries, and both rivers are heavily polluted.

(b) Eastern Europe

Hungary has begun destroying the preparatory works it had completed on the Nagymaros dam, its portion of the partially completed Gabcikovo-Nagymaros project. The dam project is the legacy of a 1977 agreement between Hungary and Czechoslovakia to build a series of dams and other works for cooperative energy production, flood protection, and navigational improvement. Hungary unilaterally suspended work under the agreement in 1989, citing environmental concerns. Hoping to keep the project alive, Slovakia diverted water through the project's bypass canal to preserve the integrity of the canal lining, which would have otherwise been permeated by plant life. Environmentalists have been concerned about aquatic life in the region of the bypass canal and harm to groundwater. The aquifer in question acts as a natural filtration system, producing high-quality drinking water for the population in the area.

The two countries submitted the dispute over continuation of the dam project to the International Court of Justice. The issues before the Court include whether Hungary had the right to halt construction unilaterally on its share of the project in 1989 and "terminate" the 1977 Treaty in 1992, and whether Slovakia is internationally responsible for the diversion of water from the Danube into the bypass canal and hydroelectric plant on its territory in 1992. The Court's decision is not expected until late 1996 or 1997.

In January, the Environment Ministers of France and Ukraine agreed to cooperate on water management in the former Soviet republic. A new water agency will be established in Ukraine, modeled after France's current water management system. Under the French system, water management is organized by drainage basins, rather than according to established government boundaries.

(c) The Danube Convention

The (➔) Convention on Cooperation for the Protection and Sustainable Use of the Danube River was concluded in Sofia, on 29 October. The Convention consists of 31 articles arranged in four parts, and five Annexes that form an integral part of the Convention (Art. 20).

Article 2 sets forth a number of "objectives and principles of cooperation," including sustainable and equitable water management, control of hazards originating from accidents, the urgency of water pollution abatement measures, sustainable development and environmental protection, and the precautionary principle. The scope of the Convention includes both planned and ongoing measures specified in Art. 3 insofar as they cause or are likely to cause transboundary impacts. "Transboundary impact" is defined in Art. 1(c), in part, as "any significant adverse effect on the riverine environment resulting from a change in the conditions of the waters caused by human activity and stretching out beyond an area under the jurisdiction of a Contracting Party." The "changes" may be to "life and property, safety of facilities and aquatic ecosystems concerned." Article 4 is entitled "Forms of Cooperation." The forms envisaged are consultations and joint activities within the framework of the International Commission, and exchange of information on agreements, regulations, etc., on water management, exchange of legal documents, and other forms of exchange of information and experience.

Part II, entitled Multilateral Cooperation, comprises Arts. 5–17. Perhaps contrary to the impression given by the title, these articles lay down a number of obligations concerning action by individual states. The obligations concern primarily the adoption of legislation and regulations but also relate to compilation of inventories, monitoring, and the provision of information to the public. Part III establishes the International Commission for the

Protection of the Danube River (Art. 18) as a framework for cooperation between the contracting parties. The Commission, whose structure, procedures, and competence are set forth in Annex IV, may also elaborate proposals and recommendations for consideration by the parties. Among the five Annexes, Annex I summarizes "best available techniques" and "best environmental practice"; Annex II provides a list of industrial sectors and industries and a "guiding list" of hazardous substances; Annex III provides guidance on water quality objectives and criteria; Annex IV contains the statute of the International Commission; and Annex V lays out the procedure for arbitration pursuant to Art. 24 of the Convention.

The Convention is a rather ambitious attempt to provide for the sustainable use and development, and clean-up, of one of the world's most intensively used international watercourses. Its provisions are largely in keeping with current thinking as well as other international instruments in the fields of international environmental and watercourses law.

(2) Middle East

Israel and Jordan made significant strides toward a resolution of their freshwater problems. Article 6 and Annex II of the Treaty of Peace of 26 October deal with water. Article 6 sets out terms for the allocation of waters from the Jordan and Yarmouk Rivers, as well as Araba/Arava groundwater. The Treaty calls for a Joint Water Committee composed of three members each from Jordan and Israel to oversee its implementation. Specific quantities of water are allotted in Annex II to each country from the two rivers, and the countries agree to cooperate in finding new sources of fresh water to meet their respective needs. A dam is to be constructed on the Yarmouk river, using joint funds, to store water as well as improve the diversion efficiency into the King Abdullah Canal of Jordan. Jordan and Israel also agree to prohibit the disposal of untreated waste into the Yarmouk and Jordan Rivers, and to jointly monitor water standards as set by the Joint Water Committee.

British scientists have identified Saddam Hussein's destruction of marshes in southern Iraq as one of the worst ecological disasters of our time. They believe the region may turn into a desert within a decade, displacing indigenous peoples and affecting wildlife. The marshes provide a winter home for 134 species of birds, including the goliath heron and the sacred ibis. Hussein has been trying to flush out rebel forces living among the marshes by destroying the flora that conceals them. Sixty percent of the marshes have been eliminated since 1984. Salty shores are all that is left of fresh water marshes that have sustained life for thousands of years.

(3) Asia

(a) Lake Aral

In 1960, Lake Aral was the world's largest fresh water body. By 1994, it was half its original size, due largely to misguided Soviet irrigation policies. Additionally, salinity tripled and the receding shoreline left a salty desert that provokes dust storms. Pesticides that washed into the lake after years of agriculture are left on the shore and swept up into the air, causing health problems. A once thriving fishing industry has disappeared.

In 1994, the countries of the region launched a 20-year project to rescue the Aral Sea from further shrinkage. The objectives of the rescue project are to improve the management of international waters in the Aral basin, to rehabilitate the disaster zone as soon as possible, to stabilize the environment, and to improve the regional institutions involved in the plan. The project is expected to cost $220 million over the first three years, the funds provided by, *inter alia*, the Global Environment Facility. Each of the five countries surrounding the Aral sea—Kazakhstan, Kirghizstan, Tajikistan, Turkmenistan, and Uzbekistan—has pledged one percent of its national budget to economic and environmental development.

(b) The Three Gorges Project

International environmental groups are concerned about the long-term environmental effects of China's massive Three Gorges dam project on the Yangtze River. When complete, it will be the world's largest hydroelectric facility. Given its enormous size, damage to the environment is inevitable. The Yangtze is almost two kilometers wide at the Three Gorges site. The project is expected to displace approximately 1.2 million people, and cost US$10.5 billion. The Three Gorges project is being touted by the Chinese government as an environmentally sound project, despite persistent objections from environmental groups concerned about the massive displacement of people and flooding of unique scenic areas. China has taken steps to ensure that the rare Chinese Sturgeon, which is protected by the government, will not be affected by the dam project.

The dam is expected to be a tremendous economic boon for China, bringing foreign investment, providing power, easing intra-China shipping, and controlling floods along the Yangtze River. The project is slated to generate 18.2 million kilowatts of electricity annually. The dam is scheduled to begin generating electricity in 1997 and the final completion date is scheduled for 2009.

(c) Other Developments

The World Bank was considering financing for the construction of a major dam in Nepal. Nepal is in desperate need of electricity, and the Arun River has excellent hydroelectric potential due to its size and swift current. The major environmental concern over the project is a loss of biodiversity. The dam might also endanger some rare animal and fish species—such as the Clouded Leopard and the Snow Trout—and cause wide deforestation.

According to Bangladeshi officials, India has diverted such a large volume of water from the Ganges that desertification has become a significant problem in one-third of Bangladesh territory. Attempts to convince India to sign a water-sharing agreement have been unsuccessful since the last agreement expired in 1988. Bangladesh's Agriculture Minister has pleaded for international pressure on India to conclude a new agreement.

(4) South-East Asia

Malaysia has agreed to ship fresh water to the Middle East via converted oil tankers. Experts say the water will be of higher quality than that produced by desalinization plants currently in use. An 80km pipeline is being laid from Kenyir Lake to the Malaysian coast at Serating, Marang, where the water will pass through a treatment plant before being shipped. The effect on Malaysian lakes and rivers is expected to be negligible.

Plans by Thailand to dam the picturesque Salween River have met with resistance from Burmese and Thai ethnic groups. Currently, two hydroelectric projects are in the works, a response to Thailand's rapid industrialization and increasing power needs. The Salween is the longest river in Southeast Asia, and has many indigenous communities on its banks. The Karen community is particularly concerned, as its base is in a large watershed region along the Salween.

(5) Africa

The South African government launched its first long-term river clean-up program in January. The initial target is the Jukeski River, which has considerable bacteria pollution, particularly near the township of Alexandria. Initial cleanup efforts have already produced impressive results, via sewer cleanup, prevention of dumping, and construction of ablution blocks.

(6) North America

Mexico has adopted a new system of water regulations, patterned after the water administration rules set up by the US Environmental Protection Agency. The new regulations set penalties for polluters and call for an extensive review of current water policies, hydroelectric projects, and water pollution control programs. Previously, water regulations had been implemented by a hodge-podge of agencies. By bringing all water regulations under one federal agency, the Mexican government hopes to exercise greater influence over polluters and eliminate waste.

Negotiations continued with regard to plans for an international wastewater treatment plant on the US-Mexican border along the Tijuana river.

The impetus for the plan was a state-of-emergency declared by California in 1993, because of the volume of raw sewage flowing across the border. The Sierra Club sued the US Environmental Protection Agency over the border wastewater treatment plant, alleging a failure to develop the required environmental impact statement for the project. Additionally, the Sierra Club complains of an inadequate design and a violation of the US Clean Water Act.

Canada announced a six-year plan to clean up contaminants in the Great Lakes—the Great Lakes 2000 Program—which supplants the five-year Great Lakes Action Plan. The objective of the Plan is to eliminate persistent toxic substances identified by the International Joint Commission (Canada—US) as problematic.

(7) South America

The Argentine Wildlife Foundation called the binational Paraguayan-Argentine Yacyreta dam project an "environmental disaster." The planners are said not to have taken potentially negative environmental impacts into account when designing and building the international dam project. Recognizing the existence of environmental problems, the World Bank was trying to remedy some of the damage and avert future problems.

Stephen McCaffrey[1]

[1] I am grateful to Timothy M. Harris, University of the Pacific, McGeorge School of Law class of 1995, for his assistance in preparing this report.

IV. OCEANS

1. REGIONAL SEAS

(1) Introduction

The major new developments within the United Nations Environment Programme's (UNEP's) Regional Seas Programme reflect the broad programmatic emphases of Agenda 21. In many cases, in fact, the United Nations Conference on Environment and Development (UNCED) process has led to a review of both the action plans and the legal agreements adopted in the different regions to better take into account the principles, objectives, and priorities in the field on the protection and sustainable development of the marine and coastal environment and its resources that emerged at UNCED. Moreover, a number of initiatives were started to enhance the effective implementation of the agreements adopted as well as to improve the exchange of information among the countries involved.

As far as other regional seas are concerned, neither of the revised Conventions adopted in 1992, respectively in Paris for the protection of the marine environment of the North-East Atlantic, and in Helsinki for the protection of the marine environment of the Baltic Sea area, had entered into force by the end of the year.

(2) UNEP's Regional Seas Programme

(a) Mediterranean Region

A meeting of legal and technical experts to examine the amendments to the Barcelona Convention and its related Protocols and to the Action Plan was held in Barcelona, 14–18 November. Participants recognized that both the scope and the objectives of the legal agreements and of the Mediterranean Action Plan needed to be revised to incorporate the principles that emerged at UNCED. The UN Convention on the Law of the Sea, which entered into force in 1994, constituted another important point of reference in this review. The meeting provided an exchange of views on the proposed revision of the Action Plan and on all the legal agreements adopted for the Mediterranean Sea, with the exception of the Protocol on emergency situations, for which no proposal for amendments were made.

On 14 October, in Madrid, a Conference of plenipotentiaries adopted the (➔) Protocol for the Protection of the Mediterranean Sea against Pollution Resulting from Exploration and Exploitation of the Continental Shelf and the Seabed and its Subsoil. The Protocol will remain open for signature until 14 October 1995. It consists of 32 articles, 7 annexes, and one appendix. The annexes cover (I) prohibited or noxious substances and material the disposal of which is prohibited in the Protocol area; (II) harmful or noxious substances and materials the disposal of which is subject to a special permit in the Protocol area; (III) factors to be considered for the issue of the permits; (IV) environmental impact assessment; (V) oil and oily mixtures and drilling fluids and cuttings; (VI) safety measures; and (VII) contingency plan.

Pursuant to Art. 3 of the Protocol the parties commit themselves—individually or jointly—to prevent, abate, combat, and control pollution in the Protocol area resulting from activities, by ensuring, *inter alia*, the use of best available techniques that are both environmentally effective and economically appropriate. All activities in the Protocol area are subject to an authorization regime that sets out safety and environmental requirements as well as monitoring procedures. The parties also undertake to cooperate as soon as possible on adopting rules and procedures on liability and compensation for damage resulting from activities covered in the agreement. Pending the adoption of such rules, the parties further agree to ensure that operators will be held liable and have and maintain insurance coverage or other financial security to guarantee prompt and adequate compensation.

In 1994, negotiations on an additional protocol on the prevention of pollution of the Mediterranean Sea resulting from the transboundary movements of hazardous wastes and their disposal continued. After a first meeting in Cervia, Italy, 23–25 April 1993, a second meeting of Mediterranean experts took place in Rome, 21–24 September 1994. The meeting recognized that despite the measures taken at the global level with the adoption of the Basel Convention, there had been no decrease in transboundary movements of hazardous wastes in the Mediterranean. Most experts therefore agreed that an *ad hoc* legal instrument for the region—fully consistent with the Basel Convention but reflecting a more stringent regional approach—was necessary to strengthen the objectives of the Basel Convention.

As of the end of the year, the draft Protocol contained two interesting provisions: a commitment by the parties to provide appropriate information to the public, and a verification procedure to be administered by the body that will carry out the secretariat functions. The draft Protocol was to be reviewed at the next meeting of the Bureau in January 1995.

(b) Caribbean Region

The seventh intergovernmental meeting on the Action Plan for the Caribbean Environment Programme (CEP) and fourth meeting of the contracting parties to the Convention for the Protection and Development of the Marine Environment of the Wider Caribbean region approved a series of measures within the Action Plan of the Caribbean Environment Programme. These measures include assistance to governments of the region for the review, development, and enactment of national legislation in compliance with the Cartagena Convention, its Protocols, and other international environmental agreements of relevance for the region. Furthermore, the Regional Coordinating Unit was in the process of: developing a strategy for providing technical assistance to the CEP countries in legal matters; strengthening capabilities for the implementation of international agreements at the national level; exploring the possibility of developing control measures and appropriate sanctions to improve compliance; and organizing *ad hoc* training workshops and enhancing the exchange of information in the region.

As far as the status of the Cartagena Convention and its related protocols is concerned, by year's end only two countries were parties to the Protocol on specially protected areas and wildlife, namely the Netherlands, which ratified the Protocol on 19 November 1990, and St. Vincent and the Grenadines, which acceded on 26 July 1991.

(c) West and Central African Region

The basic legal framework for marine protection in this region is still the 1981 Abidjan Convention on Cooperation in the Protection and Development of the Marine and Coastal Environment of the West and Central African Region and its related Emergency Protocol, to which 10 states are contracting parties. By year's end, the agreement establishing the Regional Co-ordinating Unit for the Action Plan covering the marine environment of the West and Central African Region and the related legal agreements of Abidjan had not been signed.

No meeting of the governing bodies took place in 1994. Within the framework of the Action Plan, however, a project on integrated coastal areas management focusing on training and development of national capabilities for planning and management was being developed. The project was expected to include Côte d'Ivoire, Gambia, Ghana, Guinea, Nigeria, Senegal, and Togo.

As financial problems of the countries of the region remained critical, in 1994 only two of the 21 states covered by the Action Plan contributed to the trust fund established to support regional activities.

(d) North West Pacific Region

On 14 September, Japan, the Peoples' Republic of China, the Republic of Korea, and the Russian Federation adopted the Action Plan for the Protection, Management, and Development of the Marine and Coastal Environment of the North West Pacific Region. The Action Plan is complemented by three resolutions concerning, respectively, its implementation and related institutional and financial arrangements.

The basic goal of the Plan is summarized as the "wise use, development and management of the coastal and marine environment so as to obtain the utmost long-term benefits for the human population of the region while protecting human health, ecological integrity, and the region's sustainability for future generations." Regular intergovernmental meetings, to be held annually in one of the participating countries on a rotational basis, will provide policy guidance and make decisions on issues arising under Action Plan. The governments decided also to establish a Regional Co-ordinating Unit (RCU), and pending the full functioning of the RCU, to entrust UNEP with the coordination of the implementation of the Action Plan. Implementing activities will be financed mainly through contributions from governments and international and non-governmental organizations. For this purpose, participating governments decided also to establish a trust fund, initially for 1994–1997, to which each of the member states will contribute.

(e) East Asian Seas Region

A meeting of plenipotentiaries on the East Asian Seas Action Plan was held in Bangkok, 27 October, on which occasion the governments of Australia, the Kingdom of Cambodia, the Republic of China, the Republic of Korea, and the Socialist Republic of Vietnam decided to join Indonesia, Malaysia, the Philippines, Singapore, and Thailand in the East Asian Seas Action Plan. The meeting also provided an opportunity to update the existing programmatic and operational framework, resulting in a revised Action Plan for the protection and sustainable development of the marine and coastal areas of the East Asian region.

(f) South Pacific Region

In September 1994, the South Pacific Regional Environment Programme (SPREP) office launched an initiative to facilitate the exchange of information on the implementation of environmental agreements in the region. It circulated draft guidelines for a standardized format for national reports by the parties to both the 1986 Noumea Convention and the 1976 Apia Convention on the Conservation of Nature in the South Pacific. By year's end, SPREP was reviewing comments on these draft guidelines for a revision of the proposed format.

(g) Black Sea Region

The 1992 Convention for the Protection of the Black Sea against Pollution entered into force in April 1994.

(3) The European Community

The Council of Ministers' adoption of EC Regulation No. 1973/92 on 21 May 1992 concerning the creation of LIPE, a financial environmental instrument, marked the end of the individual regional seas activities entitled Medspa, Norspa, and Acnat that the Community had initiated in 1991. LIPE, whose purpose is to support development and implementation of

Community environmental policy and legislation, provides financing for, *inter alia*: priority actions in the field of the environment within the Community; actions for technical assistance to third countries of the Mediterranean region or to coastal third countries of the Baltic Sea; and exceptionally, actions concerning global or regional environmental problems envisaged in international conventions.

In 1994, the Commission issued communication (94/C/139) which identifies as "priority actions" for 1995, including the protection of habitats and of nature (including actions to halt coastal erosion and to protect the marine environment) within the Community. The Commission lists technical assistance to establish policies and programmes of action in the field of environment as the only priority action outside the Community for 1995.

Maria Marotta

2. MARINE POLLUTION

A. LAND-BASED POLLUTION (RIVERS/AIR)

(1) Preparations for the Washington Program of Action

The Meeting of Government-Designated Experts Focusing on the 1985 Montreal Guidelines for the Protection of the Marine Environment from Land-Based Sources of Marine Pollution took place in Montreal, 6-10 June. This was the second meeting in the preparatory process leading up to the Intergovernmental Conference on Protection of the Marine Environment from Land-Based Activities, which will take place in November 1995 in Washington DC. This conference should result in the adoption of a global program of action on land-based pollution. The Meeting's main task was to consider the future role of the 1985 Montreal Guidelines, a question arousing considerable controversy. The Meeting reviewed the Guidelines in general terms and offered suggestions for improving some of them as a basis for further work. It was not decided whether, or in what form, the Montreal Guidelines would survive after adoption of the global program of action in 1995.

It was further decided to develop a framework for the global program of action. The Meeting accepted as a basis for further work a draft outline prepared by a working group. This outline was to be further refined in the intersessional period leading up the final preparatory meeting in Reykjavik in March 1995.

(2) Small Island States

The UN Global Conference on the Sustainable Development of Small Island Developing States met in Bridgetown, Barbados, 25 April to 6 May

((→) *see* Report of the Global Conference). Sustainable development of coastal and marine resources, including prevention of marine degradation from land-based activities, was one of its focal points. The Conference adopted two main documents. The first of these, the Barbados Declaration, says that small island states share with all nations "a critical interest in the protection of coastal zones and oceans against the effects from land-based sources of pollution." The Declaration is drafted in general terms and does not elaborate on the 1992 Rio Declaration on Environment and Development.

The second document, the Programme of Action for the Sustainable Development of Small Island Developing States, defines environment and development priorities to be addressed jointly by small island states and other states in a number of priority areas, including coastal and marine resources. The Programme of Action envisages several policies on the national, regional, and global levels, with strong emphasis on coastal zone management and improved information gathering.

(3) The North-East Atlantic

The Sixteenth Joint Meeting of the Oslo and Paris Commissions (OSPARCOM) took place in Karlskrona, Sweden, 13–17 June. Because only the Netherlands, Spain, Sweden, and Switzerland had ratified the 1992 Convention for the Protection of the Marine Environment of the North-East Atlantic at the time of the meeting, the Commission technically continued to operate (as far as land-based pollution is concerned) under the 1974 Convention on the Protection of the North-East Atlantic against Pollution from Land-Based Sources. In practice, however, OSPARCOM put most of its effort into developing standards for "best available techniques" for point sources and "best environmental practices" for nonpoint sources, pursuant to the 1992 Convention.

OSPARCOM adopted nine recommendations relating to land-based sources. It established best available techniques for new aluminum electrolysis plants, the organic chemical industry, and wet processes in the textile-processing industry. It adopted best available techniques and best environmental practices for the integrated and non-integrated sulphite paper pulp industry and the kraft pulp industry, and it adopted best environmental practices for the reduction of inputs of potentially toxic chemicals from aquacultural use and of pesticides from agricultural use.

The Commission also adopted two recommendations on the controversial issue of nuclear discharge. The first concerns environmental impact resulting from discharges of radioactive substances and the second concerns the management of spent nuclear fuel. These recommendations were induced by concern by some contracting parties over the operation of the THORP installation in the United Kingdom. Both France and the United

Kingdom contest OSPARCOM's competence, asserting that the issue is covered by the Euratom Treaty, and for this reason, maintained their reservations to Recommendation 93/5 concerning increases in radioactive discharges from nuclear reprocessing plants. Other delegations urged France and the United Kingdom to reconsider their positions and comply with the provisions of this Recommendation.

One or more states entered reservations to virtually every new recommendation, and several parties maintained reservations to older decisions. Further, several draft instruments submitted to OSPARCOM could not be agreed upon, including one on phasing out short-chained chlorinated paraffins, which is critical to the Action Plan's objective of eliminating inputs of organohalogens to the marine environment. The Commission continues to adopt best available technologies in the form of legally non-binding recommendations rather than as legally binding decisions.

With the growth in the number of recommendations and decisions that OSPARCOM has adopted, the organization is increasingly focusing on contracting parties' compliance. The procedures for assessing compliance were found to be in need of improvement. The Working Group on Industrial Sectors had not been able to assess the level of compliance with a long list of recommendations "because of the nature and the complexity of the requirements." The Commission discussed ways to improve and harmonize the quality of the drafting of decisions and recommendations. It also considered issuing new guidelines for the preparation of implementation reports.

(4) The Baltic Sea

The Baltic Marine Environment Protection Commission (Helsinki Commission) held its 15th Meeting in Helsinki, 8–11 March. Pending the ratification and entry into force of the 1992 Convention on the Protection of the Marine Environment of the Baltic Sea Area, the Helsinki Commission continued to prepare and adopt specific recommendations for priority pollution sources and sectors on the basis of the 1974 Helsinki Convention.

Significantly, at a time when land-based pollution (LBP) is increasingly considered part of the broader phenomenon of marine degradation, the Commission adopted two recommendations relating to the protection of nature from these land-based activities. (➔) Recommendation 15/1 on protection of the coastal strip recommends that the contracting parties establish protected zones seaward of at least 100 to 300 metres from the mean water line, in which potentially harmful activities such as mining and construction should not be allowed. It also recommends that the parties establish a zone of at least 3 kilometers landward from the mean water line, where activities must be preceded by appropriate planning, including environmental impact assessment. Recommendation 15/5 recommends the establishment of a system of coastal and marine Baltic Sea protected areas, and provides some guidance for management plans for such areas.

The Commission adopted two further recommendations specifically relating to LBP. (➔) Recommendation 15/2 on pollution load compilation aims to improve the availability of reliable data on the waterborne load of pollutants to the Baltic Sea from land-based sources. (➔) Recommendation 15/3 recommends measures aimed at the reduction of discharges from marine fish farming and is particularly relevant in view of the importance of nutrients from marine fish farms as LBP. Draft recommendations relating to paper mills and municipal sewage treatment plants were still pending at year's end.

(5) The Wider Caribbean Region

The Second Meeting of Experts on Land-Based Sources of Marine Pollution in the Wider Caribbean Region convened in San Juan, Puerto Rico, 21–25 March. It was agreed that the LBP strategy would consist of three main steps: first, the development of an Action Plan to support the formulation and implementation of the protocol on LBP; second, the completion and adoption of the protocol itself by 1996; and third, the ensuring that there is adequate financial support for developing and implementing the protocol.

The protocol, as outlined at the Meeting, will generally follow the structure of other recent instruments on LBP, with general principles and obligations to be included in the protocol and the annexes for source categories and related substances. The Meeting of Experts made numerous suggestions, including application of best available techniques and best management practices (with emphasis on clean production and pollution prevention), timetables for implementation that may be adjusted to the economic and technical capacity of each country, water quality and environmental quality criteria, environmental impact assessment, nondiscrimination and education.

The Meeting's recommendations have been adopted as guidelines for a protocol of the Seventh Intergovernmental Meeting on the Action Plan for the Caribbean Environment Programme and the Fourth Meeting of the Contracting Parties to the Convention for the Protection of Development of the Marine Environment of the Wider Caribbean Region, which convened in Kingston, 12–14 December. The next steps in the process will be the convening of a regional meeting of legal, policy, and technical experts to develop a draft protocol in August 1995, and a regional meeting to negotiate the draft protocol in December 1995.

André Nollkaemper

B. VESSEL SOURCE POLLUTION

(1) Introduction

In 1994, states addressed vessel source pollution through the work of the International Maritime Organization (IMO), regionally, and nationally. Work continued within the IMO to strengthen and implement the provisions of both the International Convention for the Prevention of Pollution from Ships 73/78 (MARPOL) and the Safety of Life at Sea Convention (SOLAS). Port-state control measures were enacted to focus on the problem of substandard ships, and the issue of the human element as a contributing cause in maritime casualties remained a focus for the IMO. The International Convention on Oil Pollution Preparedness, Response and Co-operation (OPRC) was accepted by the requisite number of countries to enter into force in 1995. Regional programs and policies were developed for the East Asian Sea and in the European Union to address vessel source pollution. Additionally, France, New Zealand, and the United States adopted specific domestic measures to deal with the issue.

(2) IMO

(a) MARPOL

In 1994, the IMO's Marine Environment Protection Committee (MEPC) approved a Manual on Reception Facilities to assist in the implementation of three of MARPOL's five Annexes. It also approved guidelines on the implementation of Regulation 13G to the oil Annex on the prevention of oil pollution from existing tankers. Additionally, the MEPC continued to consider the development of new MARPOL Annexes to address air pollution from ships and the prevention of the introduction of unwanted aquatic organisms and pathogens from ships' ballast water and sediment discharge. The Manual on Reception Facilities applies to the Annexes on oil, noxious liquids carried in bulk, and garbage. It provides advice on waste-management strategies and the planning and choice of location for the reception facilities. The Manual describes the types and quantities of ship-generated wastes; the alternatives to the collection, storage, and treatment of wastes; and recycling and options for final disposal.

Regulation 13G, which will enter into force on 6 July 1995, applies to existing crude oil tankers of at least 20,000 deadweight tons and existing product carriers of at least 30,000 deadweight tons. All such vessels, not later than 30 years after the date of delivery, must comply with Regulation 13F, which requires double hulls for new tankers or another method of protecting the cargo that provides the equivalent level of protection. Tankers built before 1983, when MARPOL entered into force, must be fitted with double sides and bottoms to cover at least 30 percent of the cargo tank area no later than 25 years after the date of delivery. Other structural or operational arrangements, however, may be acceptable as alternatives to this requirement if such alternatives ensure the same level of protection against oil pollution in the event of collision or stranding and are based on the 1994 guidelines. In developing these guidelines, the MEPC considered three alternatives, but only the hydrostatically balanced loading method will be considered an acceptable alternative. The US delegation reserved its position on the guidelines because of inconsistencies with its Oil Pollution Act of 1990.

At its October meeting, the MEPC agreed that the draft Annex to MARPOL on the prevention of air pollution from ships would be the major focus of its next meeting in 1995 since several key issues required further discussion. These issues include establishment of the permitted sulphur content of fuel oil, application of requirements for nitrogen oxides to existing engines, procedures for the delineation of special areas, and the requirements for fuel oil quality. The legal procedures necessary to make the Annex mandatory will also be discussed at the next MEPC meeting.

Contamination of ballast water by unwanted aquatic organisms and pathogens remained an issue of major concern to the IMO. An MEPC Working Group was reconvened to continue work on this issue and discuss further the possibility of a new Annex to MARPOL. A circular that the Committee sent out to governments recognized the need to research this issue and develop improved ballast water management and treatment options. Studies and symposiums on this problem are being conducted in several countries, including Australia, Germany, and the United States.

(b) SOLAS

In 1994, the IMO Maritime Safety Committee (MSC) continued to work on two amendments to SOLAS in response to a growing concern of coastal states to protect their marine environment and minimize or prevent shipping accidents. In May 1994, the SOLAS contracting parties adopted a new Regulation V/8-1 on ship reporting systems, which will become effective on 1 January 1996. The Regulation provides that a ship reporting system, when adopted and implemented in accordance with the guidelines and criteria developed by the IMO, shall be used by all ships, certain categories of ships, or ships carrying certain cargoes. The MSC adopted Guidelines and Criteria for Ship Reporting Systems in December. They provide that such systems should be considered for adoption if supported by a demonstrated need to address one or more of the following: the improvement of the safety of life at sea; the safety and efficiency of navigation; and to increase the protection of the marine environment.

The Committee prepared an amendment to SOLAS Chapter V, Regulation 8 on ships' routing and authorized it to be circulated to the contracting parties. This amendment recognizes that ships' routing systems contribute to the safety of life at sea, the safety and efficiency of navigation, and/or the protection of the marine environment. Significantly, it provides that such systems are recommended for use by, and may be made mandatory for, all ships, certain categories of ships, or ships carrying certain cargoes. This amendment was expected to be adopted at the MSC's May 1995 meeting.

In December 1994, the MSC adopted the proposals by Egypt and the United States, subject to confirmation by the Assembly, for areas to be avoided (ATBA). These ATBAs were designed to protect nationally designated marine protected areas.

(c) Port State Control

In 1994, the contracting parties to MARPOL and SOLAS adopted amendments to strengthen port-state control over substandard ships. The amendments make it possible for port state control officers inspecting foreign ships to check operational requirements when there are clear grounds for believing that the master or crew are not familiar with essential shipboard procedures relating to the safety of ships or the prevention of pollution by oil, noxious liquids carried in bulk, harmful substances carried in packaged form, or garbage. An IMO resolution on this issue recognized the need for port states to be able to monitor not only the way in which foreign vessels comply with IMO standards, but also to assess the ability of ships' crews to perform operational requirements relevant to their duties, in particular with regard to passenger ships and ships that may present a special hazard. In July 1994, the US Coast Guard announced a port-state control initiative to identify and eliminate the operation of substandard ships in US waters. The initiative uses a risk-management approach and targets those foreign vessels that potentially pose the greatest threat to the safety of US ports and the marine environment.

In September 1994, each of the signatories to the Paris Memorandum of Understanding on Port State Control agreed to inspect 25 percent of the ships entering its ports and to coordinate inspections on a regional level. These states deemed it necessary to increase the use of port-state control measures to eliminate the operation of substandard ships that present a threat to the marine environment and maritime safety.

(d) Human Element

Since human error is estimated to be a contributory cause in 60 to 85 percent of maritime accidents, it remained a focus for the IMO. Substantial work was done on completely revising the 1978 International Convention on Standards of Training, Certification and Watchkeeping for Seafarers. A diplomatic conference to adopt the amended instrument was scheduled for 1995. The amendments will address such issues as requiring seafarers to be provided with ship-specific instructions to ensure that they are familiar with equipment, procedures, and other arrangements before being assigned to any safety or pollution-prevention duties. Another issue that the amendments will address is the procedures, including the necessary training and successful completion of examinations and skills assessment, that must be followed by contracting parties before issuing certificates or licenses to seafarers.

In May 1994, the SOLAS contracting parties adopted a new chapter to make mandatory the International Safety Management Code, which was previously set forth in an Assembly resolution. The chapter will enter into force on 1 June 1998. The Code requires a shipowner or any person who has assumed responsibility for a ship to establish a safety-management system. This system should include a safety and environmental protection policy, instructions and procedures to ensure environment protection and safety, procedures for reporting accidents, and procedures for responding to emergencies.

(e) OPRC Convention

On 13 May 1994, the requisite number of countries deposited instruments of accession to the OPRC Convention to allow entry into force in May 1995. The Convention's objective is to provide a global framework for international cooperation in preparing for and combatting oil pollution emergencies posing a threat to the marine environment or related interests of states. The Convention requires ships, offshore installations, and ports and oil handling facilities to have updated oil pollution emergency plans. These plans are to be integrated into national and regional contingency plans to enable prompt and effective response to emergencies. Additionally, contracting parties are to establish stockpiles of emergency response equipment, conduct training exercises, and develop detailed plans to deal with oil pollution emergencies. The parties have agreed to cooperate and render assistance at the request of other parties to deal with oil pollution incidents. The Convention further provides for the establishment of an Oil Pollution Coordination Centre at the IMO.

(f) Other Developments

During the meetings of the MEPC, a Working Group focussed on determining the IMO's strategy for follow-up action to the United Nations Conference on Environment and Development and Agenda 21. The Working Group drafted a report, which the MEPC approved, to send to the Commission on Sustainable Development. Guidelines for the application of the precautionary approach within the work of the IMO were also considered by the Working Group.

The Code for the Safe Carriage of Irradiated Nuclear Fuel, Plutonium and High-Level Radioactive Wastes in Flasks On Board Ships (INF Code) was discussed in various IMO bodies. The Assembly resolution adopting the Code called on the MSC and the MEPC to keep the Code under regular review and consider, as a matter of high priority, relevant transportation aspects that are complementary to the Code and submit a report on the progress of work to the Assembly in 1995. The MSC and MEPC agreed to support the hiring of a consultant to prepare an information document that would facilitate consideration of emergency preparedness and response processes associated with the marine transportation and related handling of irradiated nuclear fuel and other radioactive material. In December, the MSC also placed this issue on the agendas of the Subcommittee of the Carriage of Dangerous Goods and the Subcommittee on Radiocommunications, and requested that they consider requirements for equipment and devices that will facilitate the location and salvage of ship and cargo in the event of a maritime incident. The Subcommittee on the Safety of Navigation was requested to consider credible route planning and route restrictions and exclusions for vessels carrying INF Code materials. The MSC also agreed to refer the issue of routing restrictions to the Legal Committee for advice.

(3) Regional issues

(a) East Asia Pollution Prevention Project

The IMO was selected as the executing agency of an $8 million project for the prevention and management of marine pollution in the East Asia Sea. The program is funded by the the United Nations Development Programme and the Global Environment Facility. It is designed to address land- and sea-based pollution.

(b) European Parliament Shipping Measure

In November 1994, the European Parliament approved legislation offering financial incentives to use environmentally safer oil tankers with segregated ballast tanks. Segregated ballast tanks have separate ballast pumping and piping systems for the intake and discharge of ballast water from and to the sea. This system, although better for the marine environment, reduces the load carrying capacity of a ship. In some ports in the European Union, ships with segregated ballast tanks and those without are charged the same port and harbor fees. The legislation changes this to provide an incentive to use the more environmentally friendly system.

(4) Domestic Issues

(a) France

In June 1994, the French Parliament approved legislation to give French authorities greater powers to inspect and detain commercial ships suspected of violating international and French maritime rules. The legislation was in response to two incidents in which dangerous cargoes washed ashore after being lost from ships. These cargoes included toxic solid pesticides and explosive detonators, and resulted in the closure of French beaches. The law is intended to improve enforcement in such areas as the protection of the coastal environment, the safety of marine navigation, and the prevention of illegal fishing by foreigners in French waters.

(b) New Zealand

In November 1994, New Zealand adopted maritime legislation that will allow it to ratify MARPOL. Ratification will probably not take place until 1995 because the legislation must be supplemented by implementing regulations, which requires public consultation.

(c) United States

The US Oil Pollution Act required shipowners trading with the United States to have Certificates of Financial Responsibility (COFRs) by 28 December 1994. COFRs are issued for the purpose of demonstrating that shipowners and operators have the financial ability to pay for removal costs and damages resulting from oil spills or hazardous substance releases. As of 14 December 1994, 1,343 vessels demonstrated financial responsibility in accordance with the rule.

Lindy S. Johnson[1]

C. OCEAN DUMPING

(1) The London Convention

As of October 1994, 73 states were parties to the 1972 Convention on the Prevention of Marine Pollution by Dumping of Wastes and Other Matter (LC 1972). In 1994, Barbados and the Republic of Korea acceded to the Convention. Furthermore, South Africa accepted the Amendments concerning the Settlement of Disputes (LC 17/2), thereby bringing the total number of ratifications up to 19, 30 short of the ratifications required for their entry into force (LC 17/14 para. 2 and LC 17/2).

Representatives of 37 contracting parties, Hong Kong, the International Atomic Energy Agency, the UN, the United Nations Environment Programme (UNEP), as well as observers from five states, the Organisation for Economic Cooperation and Development, and seven non-governmental organizations attended the seventeenth consultative meeting (CM), October

[1] The views expressed in this report are solely those of the author, and do not necessarily represent the position of NOAA.

3–7 (LC 17/14 para. 1).

(a) 1993 Amendments

Australia submitted a declaration to the 1993 Resolution on the dumping of industrial waste (Res. LC 49(16)), indicating that with the exception of jarosite waste, it would prohibit all dumping of industrial wastes as of January 1, 1996 as required by the Resolution. Dumping of jarosite waste will not be permitted beyond December 31, 1997. During 1994, South Africa followed the prior report procedure with regard to a permit to dump obsolete ammunition (LC/SG 17/7/1). Only one contracting party provided information on alternative options. The CM did not decide whether or not obsolete ammunition is to be considered industrial waste within the meaning of the 1993 Resolution (LC 17/14, paras. 4.17 to 4.18).

The Russian Federation submitted a declaration to the 1993 Resolution on the dumping of radioactive matter (Res. LC 51(16)) indicating that it did not accept the Resolution.

(b) Review of LC 1972

In accordance with a decision of the 16th CM, further consideration was given to the overall review of LC 1972, which is to be completed in 1996. As to the format of the amendments, a protocol was referred to as the "preferred working hypothesis" (LC 17/14, para. 5.3). The report of the second meeting of the amendment group (LC/AM 2/8) and the report of the CM (LC 17/14, para. 5) clearly indicate that many issues remained undecided and "much more consideration was necessary to meet the goal in 1996 of a revised London Convention 1972" (LC 17/14, para. 5.41).

The issues to be decided included whether to replace the present prohibition and restriction lists by a so-called "reverse list"; whether to include among the general duties of contracting parties, under Art. 1 of LC 1972, the "elimination" of pollution of the marine environment or whether to retain the present wording, which refers to the "prevention" of pollution of the marine environment; whether Art. 1 should refer to all sources of marine pollution or only to dumping; whether the precautionary principle should be included in the body of the Convention, in an annex, or in both; whether to include the polluter pays principle in the Convention; whether the abandonment of materials related to the exploration and exploitation of offshore oil and gas should be covered by the Convention; whether marine internal waters should be covered by the Convention; and what the content of the provision on the export of waste should be. In addition, the CM did not consider many of the topics on which the amendment group had prepared alternative texts (*e.g.*, implementation, compliance and enforcement, and scientific and technical cooperation) (*see* Annex 2, to LC/AM 2/8). Among the few amendment proposals agreed to by the CM were the need for a provision on the export of waste and an amended definition of "pollution," which reads:

> "pollution" means the introduction, directly or indirectly, by human activity, of wastes or other matter or energy into the sea which results or is likely to result in such deleterious effects as harm to living resources and marine ecosystems, hazards to human health, hinderance to marine activities, including fishing and other legitimate uses of the sea, impairment of quality for use of sea water and reduction of amenities.

(LC 17/14, Annex 4, p. 3.)

(c) Technical Cooperation

The CM acknowledged the need for a technical cooperation program (LC 17/14, para. 7.8) and identified results of the Global Waste Survey as a "key consideration in the design and implementation" of such a program (LC 17/14, para. 7.1). It also adopted the objectives and a management scheme for the program (LC 17/14, paras. 7.11 to 7.12, Annex 5). Whether the financial means for realizing an effective program will be available, however, remains unclear. So far, means of financing have been identified only in general terms. Furthermore, Decision II/6 of the Open-Ended Committee on the Implementation of the Basel Convention with respect to the Global Waste Survey clarifies that the financial means for the continuation of the Survey within the framework of the Basel Convention—as agreed—still needed to be secured. The Decision thus casts doubts on the continuation of work on the much praised Global Waste Survey. Discontinuation of the Global Waste Survey would be regrettable, as it is an example of a project that, by working with local experts, enables countries themselves to develop the necessary tools and expertise to deal with environmental problems and thus to implement the obligations that they have undertaken at global level.

(d) Radioactive Waste

The Russian Federation reported that it had refrained from dumping radioactive wastes at sea and that it would endeavour to do so in future. It also indicated, however, that the situation concerning the handling of low-level radioactive waste was worsening and that further technical and financial cooperation was urgently needed (*see* Annex, 6 to LC 17/14). The report provides that although the quantity of radioactive waste to be handled in Murmansk is increasing and most storage sites are full, no new repositories are being built due to lack of funds. An agreement signed between Japan and the Russian Federation providing for the construction of a processing facility in the Eastern region of the Russian Federation may ameliorate this situation.

(e) United Nations Convention on the Law of the Sea (UNCLOS)

The CM expressed the view that the reference in Art. 210 of UNCLOS to "global rules and standards" referred to the rules and standards of the LC 1972. Several delegations were of the opinion that parties to UNCLOS were not only bound to apply the current LC 1972, but also future amendments to the Convention (LC 17/14, para. 2.5). The CM decided that the amendment group should take into account Art. 208(5) of UNCLOS, which requires states to "establish global and regional rules, standards and recommended practices and procedures to prevent, reduce and control" pollution from sea-bed activities subject to national jurisdiction (LC 17/14, para. 2.9).

(2) Baltic Sea

During 1994, the *Ad Hoc* Working Group on Dumped Chemical Munition held its fourth meeting. The Group assesses the effects of a possible relocation of the dumped materials and the effects or hazards that the materials may pose to the marine environment, living resources, and human activities. The Group also and identifies any gaps in knowledge and how these may be filled. It is estimated that 12,000 tons of warfare agents, including about 40,000 tons of chemical munition, were dumped into the Baltic Sea after World War II. Most of these materials, except for viscous mustard gas and compounds containing arsenic, are assumed not to pose a long-term threat to the marine environment. These substances can linger in the marine environment for a long time and occur in locally elevated concentrations in sediments. So far, none of the substances have been found in edible fish.

(3) Black Sea

The 1992 Convention on the Protection of the Black Sea against Pollution (Bucharest Convention) has now been ratified by all Black Sea coastal states. The Commission and Secretariat, as referred to in Art. 5 of the Bucharest Convention, however, have not yet been established due to lack of financial resources.

(4) North-East Atlantic

The parties to the 1972 Convention on the Prevention of Marine Pollution by Dumping from Ships and Aircraft (Oslo Convention) met jointly with the parties to the Convention for the Prevention of Marine Pollution from Land-Based Sources (Paris Convention), June 13-17. States that were not parties to either of these two Conventions but were signatories to the 1992 Convention for the Protection of the Marine Environment in the North-East Atlantic (OSPAR Convention) attended the meeting as observers. By year's end, the OSPAR Convention had been ratified by Germany, the Netherlands, Spain, Sweden, and Switzerland.

The Commission decided to delete from its agenda the entry into force of the Protocol Amending the Geographical Coverage of the Oslo

Convention (to include internal waters), as the Protocol had been superseded by the OSPAR Convention (OSPAR 16/13/1, para. 2.10). The Commission discussed the subject of "dumping under sovereign immunity" (OSPAR 16/13/1, paras. 3.88 to 3.93). Greenpeace reported that during the intersessional period, obsolete ammunition had been dumped without it being reported to the Oslo Commission or to the CM of LC 1972. The question was discussed whether contracting parties should be required to report dumping activities that take place under sovereign immunity. Opinions varied as to the appropriateness of adopting a legally binding decision on this topic. France and the United Kingdom indicated that they would prefer such a reporting requirement to be in the form of a recommendation. A proposal for a legally binding decision was submitted by the Netherlands and it was agreed that contracting parties should submit their views on this text during the intersessional period. In addition, it was agreed that on a voluntary basis, parties should submit reports on their practice with regard to dumping under sovereign immunity.

Ellen Hey

V. ENERGY

1. NUCLEAR ENERGY

A. POWER SAFETY

(1) The Nuclear Safety Situation in 1994

The opening for signature of the (➔) Nuclear Safety Convention in September was the main nuclear safety-related event of 1994. It opened new perspectives in the field of nuclear safety at the international level. Nevertheless, the daily efforts to improve the situation, especially in the Central and East European (CEE) countries, still proved to be cumbersome. As safety culture is a multi-faceted issue, technical, economic, legal, and human factors as well as existing legal lacunae continued to pose significant challenges.

(a) Programmes on Retrofitting Soviet-Type Reactors

The improvement of the safety of nuclear power plants in the newly independent states (NIS) of the former Soviet Union and in the states of Central and Eastern Europe remained one of the major problems confronting the states in transition to democratic and market-oriented economic systems. In response, the 1992 Munich Economic Summit had launched a multinational nuclear safety programme. By 1994, implementation of the programme, which was approved by the G-24 states, had made good progress, with NIS and CEE states contributing through efforts of their own with varying degrees of success.

The Munich Summit safety programme was based on the assumption that nuclear power plants of the types RBMK and VVER-440/230 could not be up-graded to an acceptable level of safety at reasonable expenditure, whereas the more modern plants of the VVER-440/213 and VVER-1000 type could be retrofitted at reasonable costs. Putting aside the question of whether to replace nuclear energy in the region in the long run, the G-24 set in motion a Nuclear Safety Assistance Coordination (NUSAC) to provide interim assistance with, *inter alia*, improvement of day-to-day operational safety; short-term technical improvements on the basis of safety assessments; and the establishment of new, and the strengthening of existing, regulatory bodies. NUSAC also assumed an umbrella function for other safety support programmes such as PHARE (the European Union's programme for CEE states) and TACIS (the European Union's programme for NIS) as well as the technical assistance activities of the International Atomic Energy Agency (IAEA). As a major step, participants to Munich Summit also had agreed to strengthen their respective bilateral programmes in the field of retrofitting nuclear installations in the NIS and CEE states. This package of measures was endorsed, once again, at the 1994 Naples Summit.

By the end of 1994, the aggregate amount available under the programmes concerned was 640 million ECU, consisting of 540 million ECU from bilateral programmes, the rest from the special Nuclear Safety Account set up at the European Bank for Reconstruction and Development.

(b) Obstacles to Implementing the Nuclear Safety Programmes

Major portions of the money for the nuclear safety programmes apparently never reached the target states. Considerable sums undoubtedly were spent on questionable missions by Western consultants to NIS and CEE states (some consultants proved to be inexperienced or not sufficiently qualified). The most important obstacle to effective aid, however, continued to be the inadequacy of existing regulatory regimes in a majority of the recipient states, and, in particular, the absence of appropriate licensing, monitoring, and civil liability provisions. Western suppliers and consultants therefore showed continued reluctance to engage in activities involving NIS and CEE states, fearing being held liable for damage caused by incidents at installations for which they might supply goods and services (*see* 3 *YbIEL* 266 (1992); 4 *YbIEL* 182 (1993)).

Progress in the legal field was slow, although, by 1994, all NIS and CEE states had at least developed draft nuclear legislation, and some states had actually passed such legislation. Also, an increasing number of NIS and CEE states acceded to the 1963 Vienna Convention on Civil Liability for Nuclear Damage: Armenia (1993), Bulgaria (1994), Croatia (1992), Czech Republic (1994), Hungary (1989), Lithuania (1992), Poland (1990), Romania (1992), and Slovenia (1992). The Convention provides for the so-called "legal channelling of liability solely onto the operator of the nuclear installation," which solves the liability problems of suppliers perfectly. Not all of these states, however, had enacted the necessary implementing legislation, so it remained unclear which law would be applied in case of a nuclear incident.

Russia and the Ukraine still gave cause for major concern. By year's end, neither state had acceded to the Vienna Convention, although both states had developed draft laws, the latest one being a comprehensive bill on the use of nuclear energy, including liability provisions, which was introduced in the Ukrainian parliament in December. In order to solve the liability exposure problems of suppliers, Western governments and companies tried to reach indemnification agreements with, or obtain equivalent declarations from, the two countries. On 16 December 1993, the United States and the Russian Federation concluded an agreement on operational safety enhancements, risk reduction measures, and nuclear safety regulations for civil nuclear facilities in the Russian Federation. Article IV of this agreement commits Russia to indemnify the US government and its contractors and sub-contractors from any liability claims. The United States and Ukraine had concluded a similar agreement on 25 October 1993. Representatives of US industry, however, noted that these agreements did not provide sufficient protection of suppliers' interests. Nevertheless, by the end of 1994, the Commission of the European Union was negotiating a similar agreement with the government of the Russian Federation.

To improve the legal situation in NIS and CEE states, the IAEA, the Nuclear Energy Agency of the Organisation for Economic Cooperation and Development (OECD), the European Union, and Western states continued to organize seminars on nuclear law. These seminars introduce experts from the recipient states, including members of parliaments and of the governments, to the basic principles of nuclear legislation, the major elements of nuclear licensing and supervision systems, and the nuclear liability regime, with special emphasis on the implementation of the Vienna Convention.

(2) Radiation Protection

In 1994, the six international organizations—IAEA, the Food and Agriculture Organization, the International Labour Organisation, the Nuclear Energy Agency of the OECD, the Pan American Health Organization and the World Health Organization—that took the lead in redrafting basic radiation standards finalized their discussions. The result is a new version of the "International Basic Safety Standards for Protection Against Ionizing Radiation and for the Safety of Radiation Sources" (IAEA Doc. GOV/2715, 11 April 1994). The document has been submitted to the governing bodies of the six sponsoring international organizations. It is probable that the adoption procedure will be finalized by spring 1995.

(3) The Nuclear Safety Convention

The Convention on Nuclear Safety, which was adopted on 17 June 1994 (IAEA Doc. INFCIRC/449), has been recognized as a milestone in the development of international nuclear energy law, representing the first global instrument on nuclear safety. The scope of application of the Convention is restricted to land-based commercial nuclear power plants. Following the 1979 Convention on Physical Protection of Nuclear Material, the 1986 Convention on Early Notification of a Nuclear Accident and the 1986 Convention on Assistance in the Case of a Nuclear Accident or Radiological Emergency, the Nuclear Safety Convention is the latest member of a growing family of nuclear safety Conventions. Indeed, in para. (ix) of the preamble of the Convention, the contracting parties affirm "the need to begin promptly the development of an international convention on the safety of radioactive waste management as soon as the ongoing process to develop waste management safety fundamentals has resulted in broad international agreement."

The Convention consists of a preamble and 35 articles. It covers both future and existing nuclear installations. According to Art. 2(i):

"nuclear installation" means for each Contracting Party any land-based civil nuclear power plant under its jurisdiction including such storage, handling and treatment facilities for radioactive materials as are on the same site and are directly related to the operation of a nuclear power plant. Such a plant ceases to be such a nuclear installation when all nuclear fuel elements have been removed permanently from the reactor core and have been stored safely in accordance with approved procedures and the decommissioning programme has been agreed to by the regulatory body.

Contracting parties are obliged to take, within the framework of their respective national laws, the legislative, regulatory, and administrative measures and other steps necessary for implementing their obligations under the Convention. To enhance compliance, Art. 5 requires contracting parties to submit for review, prior to each meeting referred to in Art. 20, a report on measures taken to implement each of the obligations of the Convention. Article 7 lists among these obligations the establishment and maintenance of a legislative regulatory framework, national safety requirements and regulations, and a licensing system for nuclear installations (permission principle). Contracting parties, moreover, must set up a system of inspection and assessment to ascertain compliance with the applicable regulations and the terms of the licence (supervision principle).

Article 8 requires each contracting party to establish or designate a regulatory body entrusted with the implementation of the legislative and regulatory framework and provided with adequate authority and power, including financial and human resources, to fulfil its assigned responsibilities. It also requires them to ensure an effective separation between the functions of the regulatory body and those of any other bodies or organisations concerned with the promotion or utilization of nuclear energy. Article 9, finally, commits each contracting party to ensure that the holder of the relevant licence has prime responsibility for the safety of nuclear installations.

Articles 10–16 address general safety concerns: The capabilities and limitations of human performance have to be taken into account throughout the life of a nuclear installation (Art. 12). Quality assurance programmes have to be established and implemented with a view to providing confidence that the specified requirements for all activities important to nuclear safety are satisfied (Art. 13). Furthermore, each contracting party is to take appropriate steps to ensure that comprehensive and systematic safety assessments are carried out and that there is verification by analysis, surveillance, testing, and inspection to ensure that the physical state and the operation of a nuclear installation continues to accord with the requirements (Art. 14).

Article 15 focuses on radiation protection, raising the "as low as reasonably achievable" principle to the level of an express legal obligation. Article 16 lists emergency-preparedness obligations. Interestingly, it requires contracting parties that do not have a nuclear installation on their territory, but are likely to be affected in the event of a radiological emergency in a nuclear installation in its vicinity, to prepare and test emergency plans for their own territories. Finally, Arts. 17-19, respectively, address siting, design and construction, and operation of nuclear installations.

A critical provision is Art. 20, which obliges the contracting parties to hold meetings for the purpose of reviewing the reports submitted pursuant to Art. 5 in accordance with procedures yet to be adopted under Art. 22. Given the importance of the structure and the procedure of the review meetings to the success of the Convention, the respective articles proved to be among the most sensitive topics of the negotiations on the Convention. The Convention's principle of "peer group review" signals the introduction of an entirely novel concept into international nuclear energy law. Because of the dearth of international experience with this type of compliance control approach, the final text of the Convention provides a skeletal outline rather than a comprehensive set of detailed rules. The implementation of these framework provisions was left to a preparatory meeting of the contracting parties that is, *inter alia*, to develop and adopt guidelines on the form and structure of the reports to be submitted pursuant to Art. 5, their submission, and the procedure for their review. Additionally, an annex to the Final Act of the diplomatic conference, entitled "Some Clarification With Respect to Procedural and Financial Arrangements, National Reports and the Conduct of Review Meetings, Envisaged in the Convention on Nuclear Safety" (IAEA Doc. INFCIRC/449/Add.1), outlines a rough scheme for national reports and the conduct of review meetings.

Article 24 of the Convention requires contracting parties to attend the review meetings and to be represented at such meetings by one delegate and by such alternates, experts, and advisors as it deems necessary. An express obligation of this kind was deemed a necessary complement to the obligation to report and to submit the reports for review at the meetings. Summaries of the issues discussed and conclusions reached during the meetings are to be made available to the public (Art. 25).

The Convention was opened for signature on 20 September. On 6 December, 53 states signed the Convention and Norway deposited its instrument of ratification with the IAEA. The Convention will enter into force on the 90th day after the 22d instrument of ratification is deposited with the IAEA, including the instruments of 17 states that each have at least one nuclear installation which has achieved criticality in a reactor core (Art. 31). The IAEA will perform the secretariat functions for the meeting of the contracting parties (Art. 28).

(4) Miscellaneous Activities of the International Atomic Energy Agency

During its 38th regular session (19–23 September), the IAEA General Conference again considered a number of items related to nuclear safety, radiological protection, and radioactive waste management. There was a consensus on the necessity of a future convention of the safe management and disposal of radioactive waste. The General Conference also underlined the vital necessity for the IAEA to continue, promote, coordinate, and strengthen international cooperation in the field of radioactive waste management. It specifically invited the IAEA Board of Governors and the Director General to start preparations for an international Convention.

In 1994, the IAEA continued its efforts to strengthen nuclear safety at the international level by sending missions to various countries to assess national safety policies and implementation at individual installations. Again, special attention was paid to the Chernobyl nuclear power plant, which was visited in March by an international expert safety-assessment team that found numerous safety deficiencies in the two units of the plant that remain operational, especially in Unit 1. A major problem is the accelerating deterioration of the encasing of the destroyed Unit 4 reactor, the collapse of which would have serious consequences.

At the request of the government of the People's Republic of China, a IAEA regulatory review team analyzed the Chinese regulatory process governing nuclear power activities in April-May. The review team's findings were positive, but recommended some improvements, such as the development of a strong safety culture not only at the National Nuclear Safety Administration but throughout the Chinese nuclear community. It also called attention to the Chinese authorities' insufficient use of operational experience feedback systems in accident prevention.

Norbert Pelzer

B. NUCLEAR WASTE MANAGEMENT

(1) Convention on the Safety of Radioactive Waste Management

With the (→) Convention on Nuclear Safety concluded and opened for signature, the General Conference of the International Atomic Energy Agency (IAEA), at its meeting in September, agreed to commence preparatory work on a convention on the safety of radioactive waste management. At its December meeting, the IAEA Board of Governors planned an open-ended working group of technical and legal experts in early 1995 to discuss a convention agenda.

(2) The Amendment of the Convention on the Prevention of Marine Pollution by Dumping of Wastes and Other Matter (London Convention)

Resolution LC.51 (16), adopted by the Sixteenth Consultative Meeting of the Parties to the London Convention, came into force on 20 February. The resolution amended the annexes to the London Convention to ban the ocean dumping of all radioactive waste, except for exempt quantities, as determined by the IAEA. The amendment was accepted by all parties to the London Convention, even those that had abstained in its adoption, except for the Russian Federation, which stated that it did not have the financial or technical capacity to dispose safely of all its radioactive waste on land and requested international assistance in this regard.

At their Seventeenth Consultative Meeting, the parties to the London Convention discussed the report of the Technical Assistance Advisory team that had been established to explore the possibilities of international cooperation and assistance for the Russian Federation regarding the implementation of alternative land-based treatment and disposal of radioactive waste. In this connection, Japan advised the parties that Japan and Russia had signed an agreement concerning the construction of a processing facility in the eastern region of the Federation, scheduled to begin before the end of 1994. In addition, the parties were notified that there was ongoing discussion between Russia, the United States, and Norway for the expansion and upgrading of an existing plant, and that other countries had expressed an interest in this project.

(3) Basic Safety Standards for Radiation Protection

The Board of Governors of the IAEA approved the revised Basic Safety Standards (BSS) at its meeting in September. Other sponsoring agencies are the International Labor Organization, the World Health Organization, and the Organisation for Economic Cooperation and Development Nuclear Energy Agency (NEA). The BSS include standards for radiation protection in relation to exposure to radioactive waste. Although the standards are recommendatory only, many countries incorporate them in their domestic legislation. The BSS were issued provisionally in English only so that they may be used immediately. When the other sponsoring agencies formally approve the standards, they will be published in the six UN languages.

(4) Radioactive Waste Safety Standards (RADWASS)

Progress was made on the Radioactive Waste Safety Standards (RADWASS) (*see* 4 *YbIEL* 190 (1993)). The Radioactive Waste Safety Standards

Fundamentals document was revised, but not approved, in the fall of 1994, due to remaining technical changes which were to be discussed at the International Nuclear Waste Advisory Committee meeting in January 1995. The Safety Fundamentals document will be used as the basis for the radioactive waste safety convention. Although not legally binding in themselves, the RADWASS documents are written in such a way as to be easily transformed into domestic legislation or regulations.

(5) Draft Nuclear Safety Protocol to the European Energy Charter Treaty

The European Energy Charter Treaty was signed in December, but the Nuclear Safety Protocol had not yet been completed. It was unclear whether it had been superseded by the Nuclear Safety Convention, but the Protocol is more comprehensive and more detailed, covering every aspect of nuclear safety, including that related to the management of radioactive waste. Furthermore, as part of the Energy Charter Treaty, the Protocol serves a different purpose, being directed specifically to the safety of nuclear activities in Central and Eastern Europe and the former Soviet Union.

(6) Protocol on Liability and Compensation to the Basel Convention on the Control of Transboundary Movements of Hazardous Wastes and Their Disposal

During the negotiations on the Basel Convention Liability Protocol in October, the question arose again whether the Protocol should cover compensation for damage caused by radioactive waste. Some parties believed that the IAEA guidelines, standards, and regulations on the safe management of radioactive waste, and the Code of Practice on Transboundary Movements do not cover low-level radioactive waste. The matter was referred to the *Ad Hoc* Meeting of the Parties in December.

At the *Ad Hoc* Meeting, a representative of the IAEA explained the work of the Agency on the safe management of radioactive waste and spoke to the issue of exempt quantities of waste. True low-level radioactive waste is subject to IAEA recommendations. Although some radioactive waste is exempt from regulatory requirements, the amount of radioactivity involved does not present a hazard. Therefore, such waste would not be included within the scope of the Basel Convention or the extension of the liability Protocol unless it possessed some other hazard characteristic, such as chemical toxicity. A representative of the World Health Organization informed the attending delegates that it was prepared to advise any member state that has a problem managing any radioactive wastes resulting from diagnostic care or medical research activities. Because the discussion was inconclusive, the issue was to be addressed again at the Third Meeting of the Parties in September 1995.

(7) *Draft International Maritime Organization Convention on Liability and Compensation for Damage in Connection with the Carriage of Hazardous and Noxious Substances by Sea (HNS Convention)*

States negotiating the HNS Convention still have not decided whether it will cover liability for damage caused by the maritime carriage of radioactive waste. Although the current draft contains an exclusion clause for when liability for the damage in question is covered by either the Paris or Vienna Conventions on nuclear liability or by equally favorable national legislation, there are a number of other proposals on the table. A working group discussed the question at the 71st session of the International Maritime Organization Legal Committee and work will continue by correspondence.

Louise de La Fayette[1]

2. OTHER ENERGY ISSUES

(1) *Introduction*

In 1994, legal developments in the energy field focused on the improvement of monitoring and information institutions and the promotion of alternative energy sources that minimize harmful environmental effects. Internationally, the UN Framework Convention on Climate Change entered into force and the Convention Secretariat began review of National Climate Plans. On a regional basis, important multinational energy agreements were signed between the Russian Federation and the United States, China and Japan, and among Southeast Asian nations bordering the Mekong River. Nationally, Australia and the United States announced plans to support cleaner energy sources.

(2) *International Developments*

(a) *National Action Plans Reviewed by Climate Change Convention Secretariat*

In December 1994, the Secretariat for the Framework Convention on Climate Change released its first review of signatory parties' national action plans. Preparation and submission of these plans was required under the terms of the Framework Convention. In these plans, nations evaluated their domestic sources of carbon dioxide (CO_2) emissions and the extent of these emissions, and set forth specific strategies for reduction.

In its review, the Secretariat found that fuel combustion was the largest source of CO_2 emissions and that managed forests accounted for most estimated CO_2 sinks. It also noted that of the 15 countries included in the

[1] Any opinions expressed are personal and do not necessarily reflect those of the Canadian Department of Foreign Affairs and International Trade.

initial review, nine countries projected an increase in emissions by the year 2000 in the absence of additional measures, while six projected stabilization or a decrease by the year 2000.

(b) GATT Panel Ruling on US Auto Fuel Efficiency Standards

On September 29, 1994, a General Agreement on Tariffs and Trade (GATT) Dispute Panel issued its ruling in a challenge to US taxes on automobile fuel economy standards. The challenge, brought by the European Union (EU), alleged that the US standards discriminated against foreign automakers and therefore violated GATT's free-trade requirements. The GATT issued a mixed decision. While it conceded that the primary purpose of the fuel economy standards was to promote energy efficiency and to reduce air pollution, it concluded that the US accounting procedures were designed to deliberately disadvantage European automakers. Rather than declaring outright that the US standards violated GATT, the panel determined that they would be consistent with GATT if the accounting procedures were modified. The Clinton administration had not announced plans to modify the law by year's end.

(c) Mekong River Commission

In December 1994, the Mekong River Commission, composed of all the Mekong riparian nations, unveiled a framework agreement to develop and industrialize the Mekong River Basin. The agreement calls for extensive hydro-electric development. Laos alone is proposing to build 58 new dams by the year 2020, mostly to feed the growing demand for energy in neighboring Thailand. These plans pose considerable environmental and economic threats to Cambodia and Vietnam, which rely on heavy river flows for their agriculture and fisheries. Among the many arguments against rapid hydro-electric development is that dams will decrease downstream fertility and risk increased intrusions of salt water. While Cambodia and Vietnam will try to protect their interests within the framework of the multinational Mekong River Commission, most observers believe that the proposed development plans will move forward because of Thailand's economic influence in the region.

(d) International Geosphere-Biosphere Project to Monitor Asian Methane Emissions

Asian rice paddies may account for over a third of total global anthropogenic methane emissions. One of the main obstacles facing Asian countries wishing to reduce their national methane emissions is the lack of reliable information and monitoring institutions. Responding to this problem, the International Geosphere-Biosphere Project has helped initiate a new Asian methane network. This network, with headquarters at India's National Physical Laboratory in Delhi, will offer assistance on measurement techniques and help distribute modern monitoring equipment and technology. In September 1994, 55 researchers from 17 countries in the Asian region convened in Delhi to receive hands-on training in methane emissions assessment.

(e) Russia-US Carbon Sequestration Project

Russia and the United States reported successful results from their first joint carbon-offset forestry project, RUSAFOR (Russia/USA Forestry and Climate Change Project). The project, which is co-directed by the US Environmental Protection Agency and the Russian Federal Forest Service, calls for tree planting on 500 hectares of marginal farmland in Saratov, which is 700 kilometers southeast of Moscow. This tree planting creates carbon "credits" which both American and Russian companies can use to offset economic activities that add to the global carbon load. RUSAFOR's directors maintain that many companies should find carbon/forestation projects an economically attractive investment, both for the low cost of the offsets and for the opportunity to develop a point of entry into Russian markets.

(f) China-Japan Treaty on Acid Rain and Air Pollution

In May, China and Japan signed a bilateral environmental protection treaty. The agreement developed largely out of Japanese concern over the impact of Chinese industry on East Asian air quality. More specifically, recent studies by Japan's Electric Power Research Institute indicated that Chinese coal-burning power plants were causing acid rain to fall on forests in Japan and the Korean Peninsula. Under the terms of the new treaty, Japan will help subsidize Chinese installation of desulphurization equipment.

(g) European Union Proposal for Community-Wide CO_2 Tax

Faced with continued resistance from the European Union's less economically developed countries, the EU shelved its proposal for an EU-wide energy tax. Instead, it was expected to seek to develop a common framework to encourage voluntary national CO_2 taxes. Disappointed with the EU's decision, several European nations initiated their own bilateral energy tax agreements. Belgium and the Netherlands, for example, announced they would introduce a common energy tax in their respective countries. Denmark, Germany, and Luxembourg may join the Belgium-Netherlands effort.

(3) National Developments

(a) Australia Comprehensive Biomass Energy Plan

As part of its national greenhouse response strategy, the Australian government announced a new plan to help develop the country's ethanol fuel and biomass energy industries. These alternative sources, derived from waste organic materials such as woody feedstocks, require minimal energy to produce fuel. Under the new plan, the government will subsidize domestically produced ethanol for use as a transport fuel.

(b) US Municipal CO_2 Emission Reduction Plans

Frustrated by the failure of state and federal governments to initiate stringent air quality programs, some US cities have developed their own CO_2 emission reduction plans. Minneapolis and St. Paul, Minnesota, and Portland, Oregon, for example, have proposed municipal strategies to reduce emissions by 20 percent below 1998 levels by 2010. These plans were developed with the assistance of the Canada-based International Council for Local Environmental Initiatives.

(c) Great Britain "Eco-Star" Energy Rating Scheme for Autos

In April, the United Kingdom (UK) Greener Motoring Forum (GMF) proposed a new automobile energy rating system. The GMF is a policy consortium composed of auto-makers, the oil industry, environmentalists, and government officials. Under the proposed scheme, called "Eco-Star," the British government would rank automakers and car models according to their fuel efficiency and emission standards. The Eco-Star rating system is intended to provide consumers with accurate and reliable information about the environmental standards of different automobiles. The proposed UK scheme is similar to an EU-wide auto energy rating system currently being developed by the European Federation for Transport and Environment, a Brussels-based environmental non-governmental organization (NGO).

(4) Policy/Research Developments

(a) Electric Vehicles

In a May 1994 report, the New York-based World Resources Institute (WRI) argued that electric vehicles are the best means for reducing greenhouse gas emissions and smog-producing pollutants. The WRI report, which called for the development and implementation of electric vehicle technology, also concluded that natural gas, methanol, and ethanol were poor choices to replace gasoline in cars and trucks.

WRI's findings have helped encourage the development of electric vehicles in California. In 1990, California adopted a Zero Emission Vehicles law. This law applies to all auto manufacturers selling more than 35,000 vehicles a year in the state. It requires that by 1998, at least two percent of the cars offered for sale by such manufacturers will have to be zero-emission vehicles. Several auto manufacturers asked the California Environmental Protection Agency's Air Resources Board to delay the 1998 deadline on the grounds that electric vehicle technology needs more time to mature. In late May, the Board rejected the auto manufacturers' request, stating that requirements remain "technologically feasible in the time-frame provided."

(b) Wind Power

Wind power has proven a divisive issue in the environmental community. Although almost all acknowledge its value as an efficient alternative energy source, many environmentalists have blocked the development of wind farms by convincing communities that wind turbines are a blight on the landscape and a disruption to the feeding and migratory habits of birds. To help counter these claims and maintain support for high-quality wind power projects, Friends of the Earth (UK Office) published new comprehensive guidelines in 1994 for wind power developers and local planners. These guidelines set forth standards for project siting and environmental impact assessment and recommend processes for consulting communities and assessing public opinion.

These guidelines should help further the expansion of established (though small) national wind energy programs in China, Denmark, Great Britain, Greece, and the United States. In 1994, the United States moved in this direction by allowing private utilities to earn tax credits—available between 1994 and 1999—for research and investment in wind power.

(c) US Energy Information Administration Study

On December 28, the US Energy Information Administration released a new report on global energy consumption and carbon emissions which concludes that as of 1992, 52 percent of the world's CO_2 emissions were generated by non-Organisation for Economic Cooperation and Development (OECD) countries. These figures represent a significant change from the 1970 figures, in which OECD countries accounted for 57 percent of emissions, and non-OECD countries contributed 43 percent of emissions.

Armin Rosencranz
Paul Stanton Kibel

VI. INTERNATIONAL HAZARD MANAGEMENT OTHER THAN NUCLEAR

1. BIOTECHNOLOGY

From the inception of the negotiations for the United Nations Convention on Biological Diversity, concern was expressed about the potential impact of biotechnologies on biodiversity conservation. While there was no consensus on either the precise nature of the threats posed or the means by which to address them, one manifestation of this concern is the Convention's provisions on the use and release of "living modified organisms" (LMOs).

Article 8(g) of the Convention calls on parties to regulate domestically the risks associated with the use and release of LMOs resulting from biotechnology. Article 19, para. 3 provides the basis for international action on the safe transfer, handling, and use of LMOs. It provides:

> The Parties shall consider the need for and modalities of a protocol setting out appropriate procedures, including, in particular, advanced informed agreement, in the field of the safe transfer, handling and use of any living modified organism resulting from biotechnology that may have adverse effect on the conservation and sustainable use of biological diversity.

In May 1993, the Governing Council of the United Nations Environment Programme, in its decision 17/30, established the Intergovernmental Committee for the Convention on Biological Diversity (ICCBD) to help prepare for the first meeting of the Conference of the Parties (CoP). The ICCBD devoted considerable time to discussing what process it could recommend to the COP to implement Art. 19, para. 3—what came to be known as the "biosafety" provision. There was consensus on the need for international cooperation to explore the ways and means of enhancing biosafety. The Group of 77 and China stressed the need for immediate work on a biosafety protocol under the Convention. (*See* (➔) Report of the Intergovernmental Committee on the Convention on Biological Diversity, UNEP/CBD/COP/1/4, pp. 47–48, paras. 226–227.) Several representatives, however, favored technical guidelines on biosafety to promote building the national capacity necessary to deal with risk assessment, management, and oversight, and to enable experience to be gained before introduction of a protocol. The US representative asserted that a protocol was not warranted under the Convention. Positions were firmly held and the ICCBD was ultimately able to reach agreement only on the recommendation that the issue of biosafety be on the agenda on the first meeting of the CoP.

The first meeting of the CoP was held from 28 November through 9 December 1994 in Nassau, the Bahamas. As with the negotiations and ICCBD preceding it, the discussions on the need for, and modalities of, a biosafety protocol were controversial and intense.

The CoP dealt with biosafety in the context of its decision adopting a medium-term programme of work for 1995–1997. The programme and the budget adopted to implement it reveal the tension between the urgency sensed by most countries and the reluctance felt by some donor countries. The feeling that there is a need for urgent action is reflected in the establishment of an *ad hoc* working group of government-appointed experts to report to the CoP at its second meeting and to consider:

> the needs for and modalities of a protocol setting out appropriate procedures, including, in particular, advance informed agreement, in the field of the safe transfer, handling and use of any living modified organism resulting from biotechnology that may have an adverse effect on the conservation and sustainable use of biological diversity.

The CoP requested that the Secretariat of the Convention establish a panel of 15 government-nominated experts in order to prepare for the meeting of the *ad hoc* working group. The fact that the budget that the CoP adopted allocated no money for this task reflects the reluctance felt predominantly by donor countries. The Secretariat has been forced not only to organize and administer these meetings, but to source the funds for them as well.

At its second meeting in Indonesia in November 1995, the CoP will consider the report of the *ad hoc* working group and determine how to proceed with implementation of Art. 19, para. 3 of the Convention on Biological Diversity.

Susan H. Bragdon
Kalemani Mulongoy

2. HAZARDOUS SUBSTANCES AND WASTE

A. INTERNATIONAL TRANSFER OF RESTRICTED OR PROHIBITED SUBSTANCES, REGULATION OF CHEMICALS

The most important events in the field of the international regulation of chemicals during 1994 were the International Conference on Chemical Safety, held in Stockholm in April, which resulted in the establishment of a permanent Intergovernmental Forum on Chemical Safety, and the adoption, under the auspices of the United Nations Environment Programme (UNEP), of a (→) Code of Ethics on the International Trade in Chemicals.

In addition to those events, this report will also review the ongoing work of UNEP for the development of a legally binding instrument for the application of the prior informed consent (PIC) procedure and a number of relevant measures of the European Community.

(1) The International Conference on Chemical Safety

The International Conference on Chemical Safety, organized jointly by UNEP, the World Health Organization (WHO), and the International Labour Organisation (ILO), and hosted by the Swedish government, was held in Stockholm, 25–29 April. This conference was convened pursuant to a recommendation of the United Nations Conference on Environment and Development (UNCED), contained in Ch. 19 of Agenda 21 (para. 19.76), inviting the executive heads of the three UN agencies to arrange an intergovernmental meeting to consider proposals for the establishment of an intergovernmental mechanism for the coordination of national and international activities relating to the assessment and management of chemical risks. The interest of governments in this initiative proved high, since as many as 114 countries were represented at the Stockholm meeting. The results of the conference are laid down in two resolutions which were adopted by consensus, one establishing a permanent "Intergovernmental Forum on Chemical Safety" (IFCS) and setting forth its organizational arrangements and terms of reference, and the other determining priorities for action in the implementation of the recommendations in Ch. 19 of Agenda 21, which effectively constitutes the work programme of the Forum for the next few years. Using an original procedural formula to jump-start the activities of this new international forum, the first resolution "[d]eclares that, for the purpose of commencing the work of the Forum, [the 1994 Stockholm] Conference shall, at its completion, be considered as though it were the first session of the Forum" (Final Report of the International Conference on Chemical Safety, Stockholm, Sweden, 25–29 April 1994, Doc. IPCS/ICCS/94.8).

The conference went out of its way to stress that the IFCS is not conceived as a new intergovernmental organization on a par with existing agencies such as WHO, UNEP, and ILO, nor is it intended to take over or duplicate the work of those agencies in the field of chemical safety. The Forum is explicitly defined as "a non-institutional arrangement whereby representatives of governments meet...to consider and to provide advice and, where appropriate, make recommendations to governments, intergovernmental bodies and nongovernmental organizations involved in chemical safety on aspects of chemical risk assessment and environmentally sound management of chemicals." Yet one cannot fail to notice that, for all its "non-institutional" character, the IFCS is well-endowed with institutional features. The Forum is to hold plenary sessions every few years; two such sessions are scheduled before the year 2000. In between plenary sessions, an Intersessional Group composed of representatives of 26 governments elected by the Forum will meet "as often as necessary and appropriate." The Forum or the Intersessional Group may decide to establish *ad hoc* working groups to undertake specific tasks. It shall have a president and other elected officers as well as a permanent secretariat, which will be integrated in, "but functionally different from," the secretariat of the International Programme on Chemical Safety, and will probably be hosted by WHO, in cooperation with the other intergovernmental organizations participating in this Programme. A Trust Fund financed by voluntary contributions is to be established to cover the costs of the Forum's activities, including those of the Secretariat.

The arrangements regarding participation are rather unique for an intergovernmental forum: the IFCS does not have formal membership, but rather three categories of "participants." The first category is that of Government Participants, composed of the representatives of all member states of the UN and its specialized agencies. In addition to the Government Participants, the Forum also has Intergovernmental Participants and Nongovernmental Participants. The former category comprises representatives of relevant UN bodies and other intergovernmental organizations, including regional groupings, "involved in the field of chemical safety." The latter category is composed of representatives of international non-governmental organizations "concerned with health, workers' interests, the environment, consumers and industry," that have consultative status or other official relations with any of the intergovernmental organizations participating in the Forum. While the Intergovernmental and Nongovernmental Participants are entitled to participate fully in all activities of the Forum and its subsidiary bodies, only the Government Participants have the right to vote. Decisions are to be made "by consensus among the Government Participants."

According to its terms of reference, the primary role of the IFCS is to "provide policy guidance" to governments and intergovernmental organizations and develop strategies for the implementation of Ch. 19 of Agenda 21. More specifically, the Forum is mandated to "identify priorities for cooperative action on chemical safety" and "recommend concerted international strategies" for the assessment and management of chemical risks. The Forum's coordinating role is particularly emphasized in several paragraphs of the terms of reference. One of its main functions is to "promote cooperation among governmental, intergovernmental and nongovernmental organizations and encourage the appropriate distribution of work" among them, in order to "avoid any duplication of effort" in the area of chemical safety. Another important function of the Forum will be to contribute to the strengthening of "national capabilities and capacities for chemicals management," especially in developing countries.

Although the development of international law in the field of chemical safety is not specifically mentioned in the terms of reference as one of the general functions of the Forum, legal aspects will obviously have to be considered as one element of the "cooperative action" and "concerted international strategies" to be developed in the framework of the IFCS. Some specific tasks assigned to the Forum necessarily involve a legal component. Such is the case where the Forum is mandated to "promote international agreements and commitments on harmonized classification and labelling of chemicals" and to "advise governments in their work on chemical safety with particular reference to legislative aspects."

A more precise picture of the activities to be undertaken by the IFCS in the coming years can be gathered from the conference resolution on "Priorities for Action in Implementing Environmentally Sound Management of Chemicals." This resolution outlines priorities for action by the Forum and its participants in each of the six programme areas identified in Ch. 19 of Agenda 21. In the area of chemical risk assessment, the resolution calls for the harmonization of "general principles for establishing guidelines for exposure limits" for chemicals. If this effort is successful at the technical level, it is conceivable that it may eventually lead to the elaboration of some form of international instrument. An international standard-setting initiative is explicitly envisaged in the programme area relating to the harmonization of classification and labelling requirements for chemicals. The resolution states that "[a]n international framework for translating the result of the technical work on harmonization into an instrument or recommendations applicable legally at the national level should be established at an appropriate time." As regards information exchange on toxic chemicals, the resolution calls for the full implementation of the UNEP/UN Food and Agriculture Organization (FAO) PIC procedure and specifically recommends the development of "effective international legally binding instruments concerning the PIC procedure." No specific regulatory initiatives are as yet announced in the section of the resolution dealing with "risk reduction programmes," but some activities in this programme area may eventually lead to the elaboration of international instruments on such topics as pollutant emission registers or risk reduction measures for particular chemicals of international significance (such as those currently under consideration within the OECD).

(2) The Code of Ethics on the International Trade in Chemicals

The drafting of a Code of Ethics on the International Trade in Chemicals was completed in April. This effort was undertaken under the auspices of UNEP, pursuant to its Governing Council decision 16/35 of 31 May 1991, with the subsequent endorsement of UNCED in Ch. 19 of Agenda 21 (para. 19.50(a)). In this instance, UNEP acted as a facilitator of voluntary self-regulation by the private sector. Indeed, the Code was not formally adopted by any organ of UNEP, but is the result of informal consultations between the "various private sector parties involved in the international trade in chemicals" which, according to the terms of decision 16/35, were "invited" by the Executive Director of UNEP to "enter into commitments" and to "prepare a code of ethics on the international trade in chemicals in consultation with the international organizations concerned."

In accordance with the instructions of the Governing Council, the Executive Director invited representatives of various national and international chemical industry associations to an informal meeting in Geneva in May 1992 to consider the modalities for the development and adoption of a code of ethics. The industry associations responded positively and requested UNEP to "continue to provide an international forum for consultation by private sector parties concerned with the preparation of the code" (UN Doc. UNEP/PIC/CONS.2/1/4, para. 39(e)). Accordingly, UNEP hosted three further meetings from 1992 to 1994. At the conclusion of the fourth and final meeting in Geneva in April, which completed the drafting work, the Code "was considered agreed upon by the parties that had participated in its preparatory process" (UN Doc. UNEP/PIC/CONS.2/4/3, para. 15). The UNEP Executive Director communicated the Code of Ethics to the second meeting of the Commission on Sustainable Development in May, which "appreciate[d]" it and "stress[ed] that it should be widely applied by industry in all countries without delay" (UN Doc. E/CN.17/1994/20, para. 166).

The Code is intended to complement UNEP's London Guidelines for the Exchange of Information on Chemicals in International Trade. While the Guidelines are addressed to governments and focus on information exchange and PIC procedures, the Code is addressed to industry and other private-sector parties and is broader in scope, covering "the production and management of chemicals in international trade, taking into account their entire life cycle." Thus, the nature of the new Code of Ethics also differs fundamentally from that of the FAO International Code of Conduct on the Distribution and Use of Pesticides, which, though also addressed to industry, includes many recommendations primarily addressed to governments. As defined in the Code of Ethics, the concept "private sector parties" covers not only industry, but also "workers and their representatives, environmental and consumer groups and other non-governmental organizations, and the public" (para. 2(d)). But by their nature, most guidelines in the code are addressed primarily to industry. A footnote stipulates that in countries with a government-owned chemical industry, the terms "industry" and "private sector parties" may be read as referring to "enterprises." It should be noted that representatives of state-owned chemical industries (*e.g.*, from China) also participated in drafting the Code.

Private-sector parties are invited to subscribe voluntarily to the Code of Ethics, more specifically to "make a commitment to undertake self-regulatory measures to meet the standards of conduct set out" in the Code (para. 4), independent of any legal obligations and government policies. The introduction stresses that adhering to the Code "is a voluntary action of the private sector parties" and does not require any government approval (para. 11). In making such a voluntary commitment, the private sector recognizes its "shared responsibility, along with the governments of chemical exporting and importing countries, for the protection of human health and the environment" (para. 5). Parties are to publish a written statement to this effect and notify UNEP of their decision. UNEP will maintain and regularly publish a list of those private-sector parties that have entered into a commitment to apply the Code (para. 38(a)).

The core of the Code of Ethics consists of a set of "general principles" followed by "standards of conduct" providing "guidance" for the implementation of the principles. The basic substantive principle requires private-sector parties "to take appropriate actions to protect human health and the environment from adverse effects from the production and management of chemicals in international trade" (para. 11). More specifically, industry is called upon to "develop management systems to enable the proper production and management of chemicals, taking into account their entire life cycle" and, "to the extent practicable" do business only with other private-sector parties "who meet applicable safety, health and environmental criteria" (para. 12). The first set of standards of conduct relates to risk reduction. Chemical producers have a general responsibility "to minimize adverse health and environmental effects from chemicals being manufactured and managed" (para. 18(a)(i)). This implies, *inter alia*, the development of safer packaging and labelling practices as well as a cradle-to-grave approach, "following chemicals to the ultimate consumer," in order to keep track of and take remedial action for any problems that may arise in the management of those chemicals (para. 18(a)(iii)). More importantly, however, producers are required to "voluntarily take corrective action" when "safe manufacture and management of a chemical...does not seem possible" (para. 18(b)) and to "halt manufacturing and trade, and recall products when appropriate," whenever there are "unacceptable risks associated with the product" (para. 18(c)). These provisions are somewhat ambiguous, as they suggest that production and trade must not necessarily be stopped when it is impossible to ensure the safety of a chemical, but that other, unspecified "corrective action" may suffice as long as the risk is not judged to be "unacceptable." Another important clause in the section on risk reduction provides that industry should, as a general rule, "endeavour to reduce the quantity of hazardous chemicals used [whenever] possible" (para. 20(a)).

The basic standard in the area of risk assessment urges chemical producers and formulators to "produce and commercialize only the chemicals that are known to have gone through a process of testing and assessment that is conducted in accordance with national laws and regulations or internationally accepted procedures" (para. 22(a)). Where risk evaluations have been carried out, they shall be made available to government authorities and taken into account in informing the users through labelling and advertising. The provisions of the Code of Ethics relating to quality assurance implicitly condemn double standards in the production of chemicals by requiring producers and formulators to "ensure, to the extent possible, that chemicals manufactured or formulated by a subsidiary company or a contract manufacturer meet appropriate human health and environmental requirements which are consistent with the requirements of the country of manufacture as well as those of the parent or contracting company" (para. 23(b)). Though somewhat tempered by the proviso "to the extent possible" and the qualification "appropriate," this provision imposes a special responsibility on transnational corporations.

The Code also spells out the responsibilities of industry with respect to information about chemicals. The basic principle is that producers and formulators should "provide information and instructions in a form and language which will ensure safe and effective use of a chemical" to all parties, including transporters, traders, occupational users, consumers, and government authorities (para. 27(a)–(b)). In particular, industry is expected to "make reasonable efforts to ensure that the information relevant to health and environmental protection from harmful effects of chemicals reaches the occupational users or traders in importing countries" (para. 28(a)) and, on request, to provide information to government authorities in such countries "concerning banned or severely restricted chemicals and alternatives to such chemicals" (para. 28(b)). It should be noted in this connection that another provision (para. 19) specifically requires industry to cooperate with government authorities "in order to ensure implementation of the export notification procedures for banned or severely restricted chemicals, where applicable" and, as regards those chemicals subject to the PIC procedure, to comply with the PIC decisions of importing countries. Finally, the Code also contains standards of conduct relating to classification, packaging, and labelling of chemicals; education and training of workers and users; and advertising and marketing. It is worth noting that the provisions on advertising and marketing practices of the new Code of Ethics are significantly less detailed than those of the FAO Code of Conduct on the Distribution and Use of Pesticides.

(3) *UNEP Work Toward a Binding Legal Instrument on the Prior Informed Consent Procedure*

The work undertaken by UNEP pursuant to Governing Council decision 16/35 of 31 May 1991, with a view toward "strengthening the legal basis of the amended London Guidelines," proceeded at a rather slow pace in 1994, with a second meeting of the task force to "consider modalities for a legally binding instrument for the mandatory application of the PIC procedure," followed by the fourth session of the *ad hoc* Working Group of Experts on the Implementation of the Amended London Guidelines.

The task force further elaborated on the "elements which might be included in a legally binding instrument" and recommended to the working group that the outcome of its work be used as a basis for drafting legal language for the proposed instrument (UN Doc. UNEP/PIC/TF.2/4, para. 24(a)). While industry representatives once more expressed their skepticism about the need for a legally binding instrument on PIC, there was a growing consensus among states that the development of such an instrument was desirable and that the elements elaborated by the task force, as amended by the working group, constituted a basis for commencing negotiations. It was clear, however, that there was as yet "no clear mandate for the development and subsequent negotiations for a legally binding instrument" and that guidance from the UN Commission on Sustainable Development (CSD) and/or the UN General Assembly would be necessary (UN Doc. UNEP/PIC/WG.1/4/5, para. 85). Accordingly, the working group recommended that the Executive Director of UNEP report to the second session of the CSD in May for guidance (*id.*, para. 89(d)).

The CSD considered this matter as part of its review of the implementation of the recommendations of Agenda 21 relating to toxic chemicals and hazardous wastes. The Commission "welcome[d]" the progress achieved by the UNEP *ad hoc* working group and, endorsing the recommendations of the International Conference on Chemical Safety, "recommend[ed] that UNEP, together with FAO and in close consultation with other international organizations, continue to evaluate and address problems with the implementation of the voluntary PIC procedure and to develop effective legally binding instruments concerning the PIC procedure" (UN Doc. E/CN.17/1994/20, para. 165). The CSD did not, however, provide a clear mandate to UNEP for initiating formal negotiations, nor did it decide on the forum, procedure, and time frame of such negotiations or the role of other interested UN agencies, such as FAO, in the process. Nor did the Commission recommend that the General Assembly do so, as the FAO representative at the third meeting of the *ad hoc* working group in 1993 had suggested earlier. Rather, the high-level meeting of the Commission added to the confusion by suggesting that the matter of a legally binding instrument should be considered by "the inter-sessional meeting of the Intergovernmental Forum on Chemical Safety and other relevant bodies" (*Id.*, at 53, para. 11). Moreover, the Chairman's summary of that meeting also notes the "strong sentiment...expressed by participants" that the proposed instrument should not only make the PIC procedure legally binding, but "subsequently ban the export of domestically prohibited chemicals" from OECD to non-OECD countries (*Id*). This may signal a new round of discussion on the proper scope of the proposed legal instrument, which the UNEP *ad hoc* working group agreed in 1993 should be limited to the PIC procedure (UN Doc. UNEP/PIC/WG.1/3/5, para. 103.12). The indecision of the CSD left the whole issue floating in mid-air until December 1994, when UNEP and FAO jointly organized an informal consultative meeting of government experts and representatives of various intergovernmental and non-governmental organizations to consider the substantive and procedural issues of developing a legally binding instrument, and to formulate recommendations for submission to the next regular session of the UNEP Governing Council, which is scheduled to be held in May 1995. Meanwhile, the FAO Council at its November 1994 session had endorsed cooperation with UNEP for the purpose of elaborating an international legal instrument for the application of the PIC procedure. The informal consultative meeting recommended that the Executive Director of UNEP seek a formal mandate from the UNEP Governing Council to start negotiations "with a view to the conclusion of such an instrument possibly by 1997." (UN Doc. UNEP/PIC/CONS.5/L.1/Rev. 1, para.58).

(4) Implementation and Amendment of European Community (EC) Regulation 2455/92 on Prior Informed Consent

EC Regulation 2455/92, which determines the export notification and PIC procedures for exports of hazardous chemicals from the European Union (*see* 3 *YbIEL* 284 (1992)), was amended twice in 1994. The first amendment was made in January, by a Commission Regulation that at last laid down the first entries to Annex II of Regulation 2455/92, listing a number of chemicals subject to the PIC procedure and decisions of participating importing countries with respect to those chemicals (Commission Regulation (EC) No. 41/94, amending Annex II of Council Regulation (EEC) No. 2455/92 concerning the export and import of certain dangerous chemicals, OJ 1994, L 8/1). As a result of this regulation, which entered into force on 12 February, Community exporters are now required to comply with the decisions of a number of non-participating countries banning the import of such pesticides as aldrin, dieldrin, DDT, dinoseb, fluoroacetamide, and HCH. On 25 August 1992, FAO/UNEP officially notified all governments and the European Commission of these decisions, taken within the framework of the joint UNEP/FAO PIC scheme. Thus, it was only 18 months after the adoption of Regulation 2455/92 that the Community took the necessary legislative action to make the PIC provisions of the regulation operational.

It should also be noted that the action taken by the end of 1994, covering six substances only, is insufficient for the EC to fulfil its commitments under the FAO/UNEP PIC scheme, as 17 chemicals had already been made subject to the PIC procedure internationally.

The second amendment of Regulation 2455/92 was adopted by the Council in December and adds a number of pesticides (including PCP, ethylene oxide, dinoseb, captafol, and dicofol) and industrial chemicals to Annex I of Regulation 2455/92's list of chemicals banned or severely restricted in the Community, which are subject to export notification requirements (Council Regulation (EC) No. 3135/94 of 15 December 1994 amending Annex I of Council Regulation (EEC) No. 2455/92 concerning the export and import of certain dangerous chemicals, OJ 1994, L 332/1).

Marc Pallemaerts

2. HAZARDOUS SUBSTANCES AND WASTE

B. TRANSBOUNDARY MOVEMENT OF HAZARDOUS WASTE

(1) Introduction

During 1994 there were several major developments regarding environmentally sound management of hazardous wastes and their transboundary movements. These took place mainly within the framework of the Basel Convention on the Control of Transboundary Movements of Hazardous Wastes and other Wastes and their Disposal (1989) (*see* (→) Report of the Second Meeting of the Parties to the Basel Convention); the UN Commission on Sustainable Development; the London Convention on the Prevention of Marine Pollution by the Dumping of Wastes and other Matter (1972); the Organisation for Economic Cooperation Development (OECD); the European Union (EU); the Mediterranean Region; and the South Pacific Region.

(2) The Basel Convention

As of December 1994, the Basel Convention on the Control of Transboundary Movements of Hazardous Wastes and other Wastes and their Disposal had 80 parties, including the European Union. The number of ratifications shows that governments are ready to cooperate in the field of environmentally sound management of hazardous wastes and also that they now recognize this problem as one of importance.

The second meeting of the Conference of the Parties (CoP), held from 21–25 March 1994 in Geneva, decided that the exports of hazardous wastes from OECD to non-OECD member states for final disposal is prohibited with immediate effect. In order to respond comprehensively to the needs of non-OECD countries, the decision was adopted to phase-out and prohibit by 31 December 1997 all transboundary movements from OECD to non-OECD countries of hazardous wastes that are destined for recycling or recovery operation. This transitional phase has been seen as necessary to enable interested actors to take measures consistent with the environmentally sound management of such wastes. The ban should provide a strong incentive to efforts by countries to reduce transboundary movements of hazardous wastes. In addition, it should consolidate policies aimed at treating and disposing of those wastes as close as possible to their source of generation, and it should act as an incentive to promote the introduction of cleaner production methods in industrial processes, thus minimizing the generation of hazardous wastes.

The parties adopted a detailed and comprehensive work program containing legal, technical, and financial components. The legal working group continues to work on a protocol on liability and compensation to be submitted to the next meeting of the COP scheduled for fall 1995. The Conference adopted an implementation manual for the Convention and a strategy to prevent and monitor illegal traffic in hazardous wastes. It has also accepted model national legislation in order to assist parties and non-parties in revising their national legislation related to the management of hazardous waste. The parties made plans for new technical guidelines for the environmentally sound management of hazardous wastes and the further elaboration of criteria for such wastes destined for recovery operations. The following subject areas received special consideration during 1994:

(a) Prevention and Monitoring of Illegal Traffic in Hazardous Wastes

The parties to the Basel Convention are moving toward implementing a comprehensive strategy to combat illegal traffic. This strategy contains key elements such as the need for countries to promulgate or develop stringent national or domestic legislation pertaining to the control of transboundary movements of hazardous wastes. In order to build the capacity for an effective response to the issue of illegal traffic, the strategy calls for strengthening regional or sub-regional cooperation.

(b) Controls at Border Points

Controls at border points is an essential and critical part of the global regulatory regime of the Basel Convention. Indeed, it is important that adequately trained customs officers be able to exercise full control over the hazardous wastes being moved across frontiers in order to make sure that the material being inspected corresponds to both the transport manifest and the movement document that accompany the waste, or to reveal cases of illegal traffic in such wastes. To achieve this, the Commission of the European Union and the OECD worked in close cooperation in 1994.

(c) Environmentally Sound Management of Hazardous Waste

The CoP adopted four sets of technical guidelines on priority waste streams and the framework document on the preparation of technical guidelines in 1994, as well as three sets of technical guidelines on disposal operations that served as guidance for the countries that were in the process of preparing waste-management plans or developing their capacity for treatment and disposal of wastes.

(d) Technical Assistance and Training

The 1994 CoP requested the Secretariat of the Basel Convention to assist parties and regions to develop training programs, including curricula at the national level, and to organize national and regional seminars or workshops on the environmentally sound management of hazardous wastes and the implementation of the Basel Convention.

Based on the identification of the specific needs of the different regions and subregions for training and technology transfer, the parties agreed that the selection of sites for the establishment of regional centers should be undertaken. In 1994, feasibility studies were carried out for Asia and the Pacific, Latin America and the Caribbean, and Eastern and Central Europe. Taking into account the outcome of these feasibility studies, the second meeting of the Open-ended *Ad Hoc* Committee for the Implementation of the Basel Convention (December 1994) decided on the location or establishment of some of the regional and sub-regional centers.

(e) Bilateral, Multilateral, and Regional Agreements or Arrangements

In 1994, as part of the implementation of Art. 11 of the Convention, the parties decided that when they have entered into bilateral, multilateral, or regional agreements or arrangements they shall notify the open-ended *ad hoc* committee responsible for facilitating the implementation of the Convention. The notification should refer to the conformity of such arrangements with the provisions of the Basel Convention, taking into consideration a list of specific questions that the Committee developed.

As of 1994, the Secretariat received Art. 11 notifications about seven bilateral agreements with non-parties (mainly between OECD countries, with one between Germany and Romania), one regional agreement (the Convention on the Protection of the Black Sea against Pollution), and one multilateral arrangement (the OECD Decision on the Control of Transboundary Movements of Wastes destined for Recovery Operations).

Several parties reported to the Secretariat on their decisions regarding a complete or partial ban on imports or exports of hazardous wastes. By the end of 1994, 56 contracting parties established their focal point for the Basel Convention and 60 established their competent authorities. One party reported the signing of a bilateral agreement with a neighboring country banning any export and import of hazardous wastes from and to each other, even prohibiting transit of hazardous wastes through their territories, on the way to one of these countries (Poland and Ukraine).

(f) Protocol on Liability and Compensation for Damage Resulting from the Transboundary Movement of Hazardous Wastes and their Disposal

The CoP requested the legal working group to make all efforts to finalize the draft articles of the Protocol on Liability and Compensation for Damage Resulting from the Transboundary Movements of Hazardous Wastes and their Disposal, in order to present it for consideration and possible adoption by the third meeting of the CoP. The same working group was also asked to consider elements that would be required for establishing an emergency fund and the relationship between such an emergency fund and the Protocol on Liability and Compensation.

Accordingly, the second meeting of the legal working group met in Geneva, 1014 October, to continue to negotiate a text for a draft Protocol on Liability and Compensation. The working group undertook a detailed second reading of the Protocol, dealing with the objectives, definitions, scope of application, liability, forms of compensation, and the financial and time limits of liability under the proposed Protocol. The session heard the opinion of insurance companies in relation to the Article on "insurance and other financial guarantees."

(g) Evaluation and Monitoring of the Implementation of the Convention and its Effectiveness

The second session of the Open-ended *Ad Hoc* Committee for the Implementation of the Basel Convention (December 1994) decided that the evaluation of the effectiveness of the Basel Convention should be prepared for the next meeting of the CoP to the Basel Convention.

(h) Information Exchange

Information exchange was recognized as a necessary condition for the effective implementation of conventions. In the case of the Basel Convention, effective exchange of information between countries is exceedingly important because the Convention is predicated not only on the control of transboundary movement of hazardous wastes and their disposal but also on international technical cooperation in the field of environmentally sound management of hazardous wastes and minimization of their generation. As of November 1994, as many as 31 parties had responded to the Secretariat's request for information.

(i) Enhancement of the Role of the Bureau of the CoP

The 1994 Conference decided to expand its Bureau, when convened between two meetings of the CoP, to include additional governmental representatives who served as officers of the previous Bureau of the CoP, to guarantee its continuity. New tasks were added for the expanded Bureau that include: policy guidance for implementation; advice on the preparation of agendas and other requirements of the meetings; and oversight of the development and execution of SBC's budget as derived from the Trust Fund and other sources.

(3) United Nations Commission on Sustainable Development (CSD)

At its second session in New York May 1994, the CSD considered the implementation of Chapter 20 of Agenda 21 on hazardous wastes, based on a report prepared by the United Nations Environment Programme. The Commission noted with concern that many countries face severe and urgent health and environmental problems due to the production and mismanagement of hazardous wastes by industrial and other economic activities, as a result of the lack of environmentally sound waste treatment facilities and appropriate technologies, of information and expertise, of preventive approaches, of financial resources to cover the enormous costs of treatment and remedial action, and of the illegal traffic in hazardous wastes both nationally and across boundaries.

The Commission endorsed decisions that the parties to the Basel Convention took. This included the immediate prohibition on all transboundary movement of hazardous wastes destined for final disposal from OECD states to non-OECD states. It also included the phase-out by 31 December 1997 of all transboundary movement from OECD states to non-OECD states of hazardous wastes that are destined for recycling and recovery. Finally, it endorsed decisions taken by the International Maritime Organization on marine pollution by hazardous waste dumping.

The CSD emphasized that particular attention should be given to the prevention of hazardous wastes and a minimization of their toxicity through the development, dissemination, and application of an integrated cleaner-production approach in all planning. The Commission also directed attention to the use of an appropriate mix of institutional and regulatory measures, as well as economic instruments, and to the development of environmentally sound management and disposal of wastes with a view to ensuring the principle of proximity and self-sufficiency.

(4) The London Convention on the Prevention of Marine Pollution by the Dumping of Wastes and Other Matters

In February 1994, the amendments to the Annex to the Convention on the Prevention of the Marine Pollution by Dumping of Wastes and other Matter (London Convention, 1972) entered into force. As a result of the adoption of these amendments, the incineration at sea of industrial wastes and sewage sludge is prohibited, and special permits are required to incinerate other wastes at sea. The amendments also include a prohibition of sea disposal of industrial and radioactive wastes.

In 1994, phase two of the Global Waste Survey on the development of national waste management profiles was completed. Eighteen countries submitted profiles. Phase three of the project, the case-study phase, was initiated in early 1994. The case studies will focus on priority issues in technical cooperation.

(5) The Organisation for Economic Development and Cooperation

In 1994, the Waste Management Policy Group (WMPG) continued to implement OECD Council Acts concerning transfrontier movements of wastes, in particular Council Decision C(92)30, which established the OECD system to control transfrontier movements of wastes destined for recovery operations. The November meeting of the OECD Pollution Prevention and Control Group and the December meeting of the Environmental Policy Committee opted for a further extension of the mandate of WMPG.

(6) The European Union

Regulation No. 259/93 on the supervision and control of shipments of wastes within, into and out of the European Community entered into force for all EU members in May 1994. The Regulation provides for prior notification regarding intra-Community shipments and prohibits exports except to European Free Trade Agreement (EFTA) countries.

In December, the European Council approved the hazardous wastes list (94/904/EC). The Commission also launched a proposal to control exports of recyclable wastes. Accordingly, the Directorate-General I, which handles trade issues, dispatched a letter to many states asking whether they would be ready to accept Green List waste shipments of wastes from European Union countries. The hazardous wastes list adopted 236 specific classes of wastes, as opposed to the criteria-based list originally proposed by the Commission.

In 1994, the Council adopted the Directive on the incineration of hazardous wastes and the Directive on the elimination of polychlorinated biphenyls and terphenyls. Because the European Parliament voted against the Directive, however, the proposed legislation needed to be adopted unanimously by the Council. The Council also adopted the Directive on packaging and packaging waste which covers all packaging and all packaging waste, regardless of the material used. It includes specific articles on preventive measures and re-use systems, and sets quantitative targets for recovery and recycling of packaging waste. In June, the Council approved the Directive on the landfill of wastes. Its aim is to harmonize environmental and technical standards and classes of waste, set requirements to be met by different categories of landfills to avoid pollution, define types of waste prohibited from landfill, and set out the conditions and procedures necessary before a site can be formally closed.

The Annex to the European Economic Area Agreement, which came into force on 1 January 1994, contains a list of EU environmental provisions directly applicable to the EFTA countries, which includes provisions on hazardous waste management. Austria accordingly amended its own Green List of wastes destined for recovery operations, but informed the EU that, because its Green List was more restrictive than the EU's, Austria would need a transitional period for full implementation of the EU shipment regulation.

(7) Mediterranean Region

The second meeting of Mediterranean Experts on the Preparation of a Protocol on the Prevention of Pollution of the Mediterranean Sea Resulting from the Transboundary Movements of Hazardous Wastes and their Disposal took place in Rome in September 1994. The meeting reviewed the Annexes that were not considered at the first meeting in 1993. Some delegations (EU, France, and Spain) still had reservations to the articles of the Protocol, particularly related to Art. 2 on scope of the Protocol.

(8) South Pacific Region

The South Pacific Forum member states met in November 1994 and reviewed the text of the Draft Regional Convention on Hazardous Wastes. Some of the main points that were extensively discussed during the meeting concerned the scope of the Convention (Art. 2), general obligations (Art. 4), and notification procedures for transboundary movement of hazardous wastes between parties (Art. 6). It is expected that the Convention will be adopted in Papua New Guinea in September 1995, after a final working group meeting, which will take place in Suva, Fiji, in April 1995.

Iwona Rummel-Bulska

VII. INTERNATIONAL COMMONS/AREAS BEYOND NATIONAL JURISDICTION

1. HIGH SEAS/SEA-BED AND OCEAN FLOOR

(1) The (➔) Agreement Relating to the Implementation of Part XI of the United Nations Convention on the Law of the Sea (UNCLOS)

UNCLOS entered into force on 16 November 1994. On 28 July 1994, the UN General Assembly adopted by Resolution 48/263 an Agreement relating to the Implementation of Part XI of the Convention. The Agreement was drafted after informal negotiations were convened by the UN Secretary-General from 1990 to 1994 in order to achieve universal participation in the Convention. In 1992 it was decided to remove environmental issues from the list of the outstanding issues, since they were no longer considered to be controversial in the context of deep seabed mining (*see* UN Doc. A/48/950 of 9 June 1994, para. 9 of the Report by the Secretary-General).

The Agreement sets forth several modifications to Part XI, "The Area," of the Convention, since "political and economic changes, including in particular a growing reliance on market principles, have necessitated the reevaluation of some aspects of the regime for the Area and its resources" (Res. 48/263, preamble). Under Art. 1 of the Agreement, the parties undertake to implement Part XI of the Convention in accordance with the Agreement and its Annex. The provisions of the Agreement and Part XI of the Convention are to be interpreted and applied together as a single instrument. In the event of any inconsistency between the Agreement and Part XI, the provisions of the Agreement are to prevail (Art. 2 of the Agreement).

In the preamble of the Agreement the parties declare themselves "mindful of the importance of the Convention for the protection and preservation of the marine environment and of the growing concern for the global environment." Section 1, para. 5, of the Annex provides that between the entry into force of the Convention and the approval of the first plan of work for exploitation, the Authority is to concentrate on a number of activities, including:

(g) adoption of rules, regulations and procedures incorporating applicable standards for the protection and preservation of the marine environment;

(h) promotion and encouragement of the conduct of marine scientific research with respect to activities in the Area and the collection and dissemination of the results of such research and analysis, when available, with particular emphasis on research related to the environmental impact of activities in the Area;

(i) acquisition of scientific knowledge and monitoring on the development of marine technology relevant to activities in the Area, in particular technology relating to the protection and preservation of the marine environment;...

(k) timely elaboration of rules, regulations and procedures for exploitation, including those relating to the protection and preservation of the marine environment.

The Secretariat of the Authority is to perform the functions of the Enterprise until it begins to operate independently. These functions include (§2, para. 5, of the Annex):

(b) Assessment of the results of the conduct of marine scientific research with respect to activities in the Area, with particular emphasis on research related to the environmental impact of activities in the Area;...

(d) Assessment of technological developments relevant to activities in the Area, in particular technology relating to the protection and preservation of the marine environment.

The Agreement also provides that applications "for approval of a plan of work shall be accompanied by an assessment of the potential environmental impacts of the proposed activities and by a description of a programme for oceanographic and baseline environmental studies in accordance with the rules, regulations and procedures adopted by the Authority" (§1, para. 7, of the Annex). In the field of technology transfer, "as a general rule, States Parties shall promote international technical and scientific cooperation with regard to activities in the Area either between the parties concerned or by developing training, technical assistance and scientific cooperation programmes in marine science and technology and the protection and preservation of the marine environment" (Section 5, para. 1c, of the Annex).

(2) The Work of the Prepcom in 1994

Work on the topic of protection and preservation of the marine environment from activities in the Area, by Special Commission 3 of the Preparatory Commission for the International Sea-Bed Authority (Prepcom) was previously summarized in earlier volumes of the *Yearbook* (*see* 1 *YbIEL* 167 (1990); 2 *YbIEL* 181 (1991); 3 *YbIEL* 295 (1992); 4 *YbIEL* 223 (1993)). No substantive developments occurred in 1994.

During the discussion on the periodic reports of the registered pioneer investors submitted by the certifying States (France (on behalf of

Ifremer/Afernod), India, Japan (on behalf of Dord), China (on behalf of Comra), Poland (on behalf of IOM)), the view was expressed that these reports should indicate the impact of the activities of the pioneer investors on the marine environment (UN Doc. LOS/PCN/T.114/Rev. 1, 8 March 1994, para. 5).

Prepcom also considered a report by a Group of Technical Experts on the state of deep seabed mining and on the issue of when commercial production might be expected to begin (UN Doc. LOS/PCN/L.114/Rev. 1, 8 March 1994, paras. 7–10). While the Group attached great importance to the protection of the environment with regard to deep seabed mining activities, it also noted the uncertainty as to exactly when such mining might begin.

Tullio Scovazzi

2. OUTER SPACE

(1) Space Technology and Agenda 21

In connection with a discussion on the possible holding of a Third United Nations Conference on the Exploration and Peaceful Uses of Outer Space (A/AC.105/575 of 9 May 1994), UNCOPUOS again made reference to Agenda 21 and the contribution that space technology could make to environmental monitoring and sustainable development, especially with regard to land planning and management, deforestation, desertification, water resource assessment, and the study of environmental dynamics. The UN Office for Outer Space Affairs prepared a detailed analysis of the applications of space technology to Agenda 21 in 1993 (A/AC.105/547 and Add.1).

(2) Space Debris

The problem of space debris has been comprehensively analyzed in a Position Paper on Orbital Debris compiled by an *Ad Hoc* Expert Group of the International Academy of Astronautics Committee on Safety, Rescue, and Quality, dated 8 March 1993. The paper notes that after nearly 35 years of outer space activity, almost 22,000 objects have been catalogued, with about one-third of them still in orbit. Orbital debris is defined as:

> any man-made Earth-orbiting object which is non-functional with no reasonable expectation of assuming or resuming its intended function or any other function for which it is or can be expected to be authorized, including fragments and parts thereof. Orbital debris includes non-operational spacecraft, spent rocket bodies, material released during planned space operations, and fragments generated by satellite and upper stage breakup due to explosions and collisions.

Objects included in the database of the United States Space Command's Space Surveillance Network are objects larger than 10–50 centimeters in diameter in low earth orbits and one meter in diameter in higher orbits. The paper contains detailed scientific information on the problem of space debris and stresses the need for preventive action with specific recommendations. It concludes:

> Now, as the realities of the orbital debris problem start to become clear, it is evident that the most challenging task might well be how to develop regulations, accepted practices, or treaties that serve to control the growth of this hazard. Nearly 800 papers, articles, newsletters, and books have been written on this topic, but not one binding agreement has been reached on how to mitigate and minimize orbital debris. For this reason, we believe that the most important documents to be written concerning space debris do not yet exist.

The Scientific and Technical Subcommittee of UNCOPUOS decided to structure its consideration of space debris as a new separate agenda item at its next session by focusing on the acquisition and understanding of data on the characteristics of the space debris environment (UN GAOR 49th Sess. Supp. (No. 20) at 14-15, UN Doc. A/49/20 (1994)). It also plans to develop a specific multi-annual plan for its work on the item. The following definition of space debris was proposed to be adopted by the Committee:

> Space debris are all man-made objects in Earth orbit or re-entering the dense layers of the atmosphere which are non-functional with no reasonable expectation of assuming or resuming their intended functions or any other functions for which they are or can be authorized, including their fragments and parts.

The acceptance of such a definition was, however, opposed by some delegations as being premature. Similar opposition was accorded to the suggestion to add the subject of space debris to the agenda of the Legal Subcommittee.

After eight years of work, the 66th Conference of the International Law Association, held in Buenos Aires in August, finally adopted the (➔) Draft International Instrument on the Protection of the Environment from Damage Caused by Space Debris. The 16 articles of the draft, which is to be circulated to UNCOPUOS and other relevant bodies, includes definitions (Art. 1), a general obligation to cooperate (Art. 3), obligations to prevent, inform, consult, and negotiate in good faith (Art. 4), rules on international responsibility and liability (Arts. 5–8), and rules on dispute settlement (Art. 9).

(3) Use of Nuclear Power Sources in Outer Space

No initiative for a revision of the 1992 Principles Relevant to the Use of Nuclear Power Sources in Outer Space was taken at the 1994 meeting of UNCOPUOS. The emphasis remained on the call for national and international research on the safety of orbiting space objects with nuclear power sources and the danger of the collision of such objects with space debris.

The United Kingdom, Russia, and Sweden submitted a number of new working papers to the Scientific and Technical Subcommittee.

(4) Environmental Remote Sensing from Outer Space

At its 1994 session, the Scientific and Technical Subcommittee of UNCOPUOS gave priority consideration to matters relating to remote sensing of the Earth by satellites. The value of remote sensing systems for environmental monitoring and the need for the international community to utilize remote-sensing data to implement Agenda 21 was stressed, but there were no significant new policy developments.

The Secretariat of UNCOPUOS prepared an instructive study entitled "Global Change: Participation of Developing Countries and Possibilities of Enhancing It" (A/AC.105/590 of 24 November 1994). It gives a good outline of the International Geosphere-Biosphere Programme (IGBP), the objective of which is to comprehend the "interactive physical, chemical and biological processes that regulate the total Earth system, the unique environment that it provides for life, the changes that are occurring in this system and the manner in which they are influenced by human activities." The results of this programme are relevant to the Intergovernmental Panel on Climate Change and the scientific support to the political process, including the UN Framework Convention on Climate Change. Earth observation technologies, such as remote sensing of the environment and natural resources and meteorological and climatic observations of the surface and atmosphere, are of particular importance to IGBP.

Peter Malanczuk

3. ANTARCTICA

(1) Introduction

This report covers the results of the 18th Antarctic Treaty Consultative Meeting (ATCM) (Kyoto, Japan, 11–22 April 1994). It also reports on the Legal Experts Meeting on Liability (the Hague, 6–10 November 1994). It summarizes developments at the 13th meeting of the Commission and the Scientific Committee established by the Convention on the Conservation of Antarctic Marine Living Resources (CCAMLR), which took place at CCAMLR headquarters in Hobart, Tasmania (24 October to 4 November 1994). Finally, it summarizes developments at the 49th United Nations General Assembly.

(2) Antarctic Treaty Regime

There were no new accessions to the Antarctic Treaty. There remain 26 consultative parties (ATCPs) and 15 non-consultative parties.

(a) XVIIIth ATCM

Meeting in Kyoto at the XVIIIth ATCM, the 26 ATCPs adopted a recommendation that contained two important documents relating to tourism and non-governmental activities in Antarctica, namely, "Guidance for Visitors to the Antarctic" and "Guidance for Those Organizing and Conducting Tourism and Non-governmental Activities in the Antarctic." The guidance documents are a practical compilation of the requirements of the Antarctic Treaty System, including those of the Protocol on Environmental Protection (the Madrid Protocol), that are applicable (or in the case of the Protocol, will be applicable upon entry into force) to non-governmental visitors and organizers of non-governmental activities. The recommendation calls on all treaty parties to circulate the guidance documents as widely and quickly as possible, and to urge all those intending to visit or organize visits in the Antarctic to act in accordance with them.

The XVIIIth ATCM also agreed on a significant change in the organization of future meetings as part of the transition to the expected entry into force of the Madrid Protocol. The meeting agreed to create a transitional environmental working group beginning with the XIXth ATCM, that would meet during the first week of the ATCM to give advice and recommendations on items that under Art. 12 of the Protocol will be dealt with by a Committee on Environmental Protection to be established when the Protocol enters into force.

The meeting considered various technical issues related to creating a treaty Secretariat, but did not agree on a location, means for funding, or the legal status for that body. The ATCM also developed an agreed checklist for states to follow in carrying out inspections of national facilities in Antarctica, drawing on a recommendation that the Scientific Committee for Antarctic Research and the Council of Managers of National Antarctic Programs prepared. The ATCM agreed that the next ATCM would be held in Seoul 8–19 May 1995.

(b) Meeting of Experts on Liability

A second meeting of legal experts was held in the Hague to continue discussion of an annex or annexes on liability to the Madrid Protocol, as called for in Article 16 of the Protocol. The meeting was limited to representatives of the treaty parties. Prof. Rüdiger Wolfrum again chaired the session. The experts had before them a "Second Offering" in the form of a revised draft annex that Prof. Wolfram circulated shortly before the meeting. As with the first legal experts meeting in Heidelberg in 1993, the meeting was largely devoted to a wide-ranging general discussion of the issues raised. The Chairman proposed that the third meeting of the experts take place during the first week of the XIXth ATCM in 1995, for which he would prepare a "Third Offering."

(c) *Protocol on Environmental Protection to the Antarctic Treaty (Madrid Protocol)*

The ATCPs Australia, China, Germany, Netherlands, New Zealand, and Sweden deposited instruments of ratification to the Madrid Protocol in 1994, bringing the total number of accessions to 12. By the end of 1994, a total of six countries, Australia, China, Germany, New Zealand, Peru, and Spain, had approved Annex V on area protection and management, which was adopted as a recommendation at the XVIth ATCM in Bonn on 17 October 1991.

(d) *Convention on the Conservation of Antarctic Marine Living Resources*

Ukraine became a party to CCAMLR in 1994. The total number of parties is now 29. There were no new applications to join the CCAMLR Commission.

The 13th annual meeting of the CCAMLR Commission at Hobart, Australia, adopted a number of conservation measures and resolutions. The Commission working group on krill reported on its continued work on refining estimates of potential yield for krill. The CEMP and krill working groups were officially combined to form a single new working group on ecosystem monitoring and management. It was reported that the 1993/94 longline fishery for Patagonian toothfish (*Dissostichus eleginoides*) was conducted according to a quota of one vessel at a time for each of five 55-day periods. Each vessel carried a CCAMLR International Scientific Observer, and carried out scientific depletion experiments. No crab fishing took place in the 1993/1994 season, but one vessel has obtained a license to fish in the 1994/1995 season. The conservation measures on new and exploratory fisheries and on experimental harvesting regimes adopted at the 12th meeting were again adopted with no substantive changes.

The Commission adopted a plan consisting of several measures to address the continuing problem of avian mortality associated with toothfish longline fishing, particularly a decline in albatross populations. Measures would require fishermen to use only thawed bait (which sinks more quickly), to set longlines only at night (when albatrosses do not feed), to not discard food products during the setting of longlines, and to use streamer lines to scare off birds. The fishery will only be open during the Antarctic winter, when night hours are maximized and the number of birds in the area minimized. CCAMLR international observers will continue to be present to observe incidental bird mortality during fishing operations. The Commission also agreed to communicate with organizations managing fisheries outside the Convention area regarding incidental bird mortality and corrective steps they are taking, and to distribute educational material to fishermen.

The use of cables with trawl net monitors was prohibited in the Convention area. The Commission also considered a vessel monitoring system and a vessel hail system involving electronic transponders to facilitate tracking of vessels in the Convention area and to assist monitoring and enforcement efforts.

(e) Convention on the Regulation of Antarctic Mineral Resource Activities

There was no action on this Convention, which has not entered into force and has been superseded by the Madrid Protocol, which prohibits Antarctic mineral resource activities indefinitely.

(f) Convention on the Conservation of Antarctic Seals

There was no action on this Convention.

(3) 49th Session of the United Nations General Assembly

The United Nations General Assembly (UNGA) made a major change in its consideration of Antarctica, fully endorsing the Antarctic Treaty and the Madrid Protocol for the first time, and ending years of resolutions adopted without the participation of the ATCPs. The 49th UNGA adopted a consensus resolution with the participation of all the ATCPs (Resolution 49/80). The resolution recognizes that the Antarctic Treaty is in furtherance of the purposes and principles of the UN Charter. It welcomes the Madrid Protocol's designation of Antarctica as a "natural reserve devoted to peace and science," its environmental protection procedures, and its prohibition of mineral resource activities. The resolution calls on the ATCPs to invite the Executive Director of the United Nations Environment Programme to ATCMs, as has been their practice, rather than the UN Secretary General as called for in previous resolutions. The resolution urges "all countries whose nationals undertake activities in Antarctica to ensure that all such activities are carried out in a manner consistent with the principles of the [Madrid] Protocol." Finally, the resolution calls for the UNGA to take up the "question of Antarctica" on its agenda at its 51st session in 1996, rather than annually as had been its practice.

Jeffrey D. Kovar[1]

[1] This report reflects the views of the author and not necessarily those of the US Department of State or the US government.

4. ARCTIC

(1) Introduction

Several positive developments stood out in 1994. On 29 September, the United States announced its long-anticipated new Arctic policy; effective 31 October, Canada appointed Mary M. Simon, past president of the Inuit Circumpolar Conference (ICC), to the newly established position of Ambassador for Circumpolar Affairs; and on 16 December, US Vice President Al Gore and Russian Prime Minister Viktor Chernomyrdin signed the (➔) Agreement on Prevention of Pollution in the Arctic.

The year was also marked by environmental insecurity in the region. Broken oil pipelines in the Komi Republic of Russia's vast Arctic region prompted the Russian Federation to invite the assistance of a team of experts from the United Nations. It was the first time Russia sought such assistance, and it was also the first time that the United Nations Environment Programme and the Department of Humanitarian Affairs (DHA) combined their expertise to send an assessment team to an environmental emergency. The team concluded that the extent of the spilled oil was more than five times the official estimate, with at least 79,000 tons still remaining on the land in December, and that this had resulted from multiple spills occurring over years, with increasing frequency in 1994.

The Komi spill was discovered within months of the 23 June 1994 signing of a Memorandum of Understanding between the Minerals Management Service of the US Department of the Interior and the Committee of the Russian Federation on Geology and the Use of Underground Resources, which lays the foundation for cooperative development of offshore oil and gas resources in the adjacent US and Russian waters of the Chukchi Sea. The prospect of such offshore oil and gas development is opposed by a variety of indigenous, commercial fishing and environmental organizations, including the World Conservation Union (IUCN).

The practical limitations inherent in attempting to address comprehensive Arctic environmental security from the useful, but nonobligatory and largely unfunded forum of the Arctic Environmental Protection Strategy (AEPS), which focuses primarily on data collection and research, assessment, information exchange, and cooperation, became increasingly apparent in 1994. The need for response mechanisms and enforceable agreements to be in place was more widely recognized. By the end of the year, Canada publicly supported the idea of turning the AEPS into a legally binding international Arctic instrument.

(2) Arctic Environmental Protection Strategy

(a) Arctic Monitoring and Assessment Program (AMAP)

The AMAP Working Group held its fifth and sixth meetings in 1994 at Tromsø, Norway (28 February to 4 March), and in Arlington, Virginia (26–28 October). They coincided with associated experts meetings.

In 1994, AMAP activities focused on achieving progress on an assessment report and data handling. The AMAP Assessment Report is to offer a comprehensive technical and scientific compilation of all available, validated data on pollutants in the Arctic environment. The Report will address, *inter alia*, health and ecological risks associated with Arctic contamination from persistent organic pollutants, heavy metals, and radioactivity; integrated pollution effects; pollutant pathways; acidification and Arctic haze; sub-regional stress factors, such as oil pollution and eutrophication; global climate change and ozone depletion; and human health. Publication of the Report is scheduled for December 1996.

Two thematic data centers were established in 1994 to handle AMAP marine and atmospheric monitoring data, namely at the International Council for the Exploration of the Sea, and the Norwegian Air Research Institute, respectively.

The disparity in Arctic nations' contributions to AMAP's budget—out of an overall budget for the year of $850,000, Norway provided over $500,000—remained a matter of concern in 1994. National efforts to secure funds to meet assessment-report commitments and to maintain sampling, analysis, and updating of implementation plans for the monitoring program, continued. Notably, in the summer of 1994, a $6.5 million contaminant study was initiated in Greenland involving marine, freshwater, and terrestrial sampling, and human health studies in four hospitals.

(b) Conservation of Arctic Flora and Fauna (CAFF)

The Third Annual meeting of the CAFF Working Group took place in Reykjavik, Iceland, 26–28 September. At the meeting, the final version of *The State of Protected Areas in the Circumpolar Arctic 1994*, CAFF Habitat Conservation Report No. 1, which describes 280 protected areas classified by IUCN Categories I–V, was presented. The Report contains no commonly agreed definition of the Arctic, however, it instead provides information on types of habitat classification and an overview of the protected area system by habitat type in each country. It also contains a Directory of Protected Areas of the Arctic on a country-by-country basis and identifies serious gaps in Arctic protected-area coverage. The meeting agreed to establish an *Ad Hoc* Working Group to draft the CAFF plan for a Protected Area Network under the joint leadership of Russia and Norway. Recognizing that resources are limited, the CAFF meeting set priorities for the 1994-95 work schedule, the objectives of which were grouped under five main headings: habitat conservation; species conservation; regional implementation of the Biodiversity Convention; integration of Indigenous Peoples and their knowledge into the CAFF program; and CAFF Program Management.

The CAFF Secretariat will continue to be located in Canada, but will be funded by all countries through cost sharing in the 1994-95 work year.

(c) Emergency Prevention Preparedness and Response (EPPR)

The EPPR Working Group met 28 June to 1 July in Anchorage, Alaska. Part of the meeting was taken up by a tabletop exercise involving a nuclear accident and a maritime incident. Participants drafted conclusions and recommendations at the end of the exercise, but did not discuss them at this meeting. A compilation of national responses on Arctic risk assessment was presented in the form of a qualitative risk assessment matrix, and was updated following discussion. Participants decided to postpone plans for a consolidated inventory and instead to request supplementary information from all nations, particularly in relation to the EPPR's emergency prevention mandate. In addition, they decided to approach AMAP, CAFF, and Protection of the Arctic Marine Environment (PAME) working groups for data on sensitive or vulnerable areas and areas of special conservation interest to carry out the risk assessment and recommend preventive measures. The EPPR Working Group also determined that it would be useful to elaborate an Arctic manual that would contain the basic information needed for cooperation in accident situations. It further decided to establish an Arctic Accident Action Plan for this purpose by the next EPPR Meeting, and to prepare a field guide to response measures in Arctic waters.

(d) Protection of the Arctic Marine Environment (PAME)

The PAME Working Group, whose principal focus is on chronic marine pollution from land and sea-based sources, met for the first time in Oslo, 3–5 May. Elaborating on informal talks in March within the International Maritime Organization's Marine Environmental Protection Committee (MEPC), the Group concluded that it would be premature to propose to the MEPC that it designate ice-covered sea areas of the Arctic as "Particularly Sensitive Sea Areas." The Group also agreed that its work should be guided by the precautionary approach; that the focus would be on activities and sources of pollution and associated impacts on the environment; that pollution from fishing activities was within its scope, but the taking of living resources was not; that all sources of pollution affecting the Arctic marine environment, including those outside of the Arctic, should be covered; that it was not presently useful to agree on a specific geographical definition of the Arctic; and that any such reference used by the Working

Group should not be used as a precedent for international legal purposes. The second meeting of the PAME Working Group was held in London, 29–30 September, to discuss progress on preparations of the Report to Ministers to be presented at the Third Ministerial Conference. Another issue before the Working Group was persistent organic pollutants (POPs). Because semivolatile POPs migrate from southern latitudes toward the Arctic Ocean, where they bioaccumulate and biomagnify, Sweden and Canada led the effort to develop a POP protocol under the auspices of the UN Economic Commission for Europe (UN ECE) and to open a dialogue with the non-UN ECE nations whose emissions and discharges may effect the Arctic. In 1994, these efforts persuaded the Group to convene an international meeting of experts to focus and accelerate global regulator action on POPs, to be held in Vancouver in March 1995.

The Group also reviewed the adequacy of existing legal and other instruments concerning prevention and remediation of Arctic marine pollution. Its Report to Ministers will discuss existing mechanisms and gaps in national, regional, and global instruments related to the Arctic marine environment, and recommend whether further action or legal instruments are needed.

(e) Task Force on Sustainable Development and Utilization

The first meeting of the Task Force, which is to prepare reports and make recommendations on sustainable development of the Arctic to the Ministers at the Third AEPS Ministerial Conference, was held in Yellowknife, Canada, 30–31 August. The meeting produced a work plan for 1994-96 featuring specific projects that include reviews of: the decline of the seal skin market (Canada and ICC); trade policies; opportunities and barriers related to sea mammal products; infrastructure limitations as barriers to trade, such as sea routes, air transport, and satellite communications; means of enhancing education, communication, and information sharing on sustainable development and use in the Arctic, to include economic valuation of subsistence hunting, trapping, and fishing; Prudhoe Bay oil fields; the 1973 Polar Bear Convention; and opportunities and problems with Arctic tourism development. The Task Force was also to comment on the draft analysis of Agenda 21 from a circumpolar indigenous perspective that ICC had produced, and to decide on its use as the basis of an AEPS document.

(f) Indigenous Peoples

The AEPS Indigenous Peoples Secretariat in Copenhagen was established in 1994. The objective of the Secretariat is to support participation of indigenous peoples organizations (IPOs) in the AEPS process. In 1994 there were three IPOs accredited as permanent observers to the AEPS: the Association of Indigenous Minorities of the North, Siberia and the Far

East of the Russian Federation; the Inuit Circumpolar Conference; and the Saami Council. A Seminar on Integration of Indigenous Peoples Knowledge in relation to the AEPS, held at Reykjavik, 20–23 September, sought to clarify how indigenous knowledge is applicable to the AEPS, identify strategies and pragmatic proposals for its integration, and identify the contribution that indigenous knowledge can make to sustainable development. The Seminar adopted several recommendations, which are part of the *Report on the Seminar on Integration of Indigenous Knowledge*, a 225-page AEPS report available from the AEPS Indigenous Peoples Secretariat.

(g) Environmental Impact Assessment (EIA)

At the May 1994 meeting of Senior Arctic Affairs Officials (SAAOs), Finland proposed that experts from Arctic countries discuss the possible need for new Arctic-specific EIA procedures extending beyond the provisions of the UN ECE Convention on Environmental Impact Assessment in a Transboundary Context (Espoo Convention). The proposal received an unenthusiastic response; the United States and others balked at the idea of creating new procedures without it being clear that Arctic conditions justify an approach different from the Espoo Convention. The United States asserted that wide-spread implementation of the Espoo Convention would probably result in better protection than the establishment of Arctic EIA procedures would. It should be noted, however, that the Espoo Convention does not apply to international waters in the Arctic area, to activities without significant adverse transboundary impact, to military activities, or to activities related to national security interests.

The first Workshop on EIA in the Arctic was held at Inari, Finland, 7–9 September. It emphasized EIA as a critical tool to protect the Arctic environment and recognized that improvements to practices were required to take into account the special features of the Arctic region.

(h) Financial Strategies

At the May 1994 SAAO Meeting, countries that currently fund parts of AEPS (Norway, Canada, and Denmark) called for some cost-sharing arrangement. The meeting agreed that Canada would coordinate a paper describing expenditures of each country for AEPS-related activities to assess the costs associated with Arctic environmental protection.

(3) Outlook

The outlook for the progressive development of international law for protecting the Arctic environment is positive, if one takes a long-term view. So too, is the prospect for sustainable development in the Arctic, and the international rights of indigenous peoples. One important factor in this is the new US Arctic Policy which seeks to strengthen cooperation towards environmentally sustainable development in the region, and "to create a more formal policy forum through which Arctic nations can oversee implementation of Arctic strategy." This may bode well for the proposal to establish an Arctic Council, composed of Canada, Denmark, Finland, Iceland, Norway, Russia, Sweden, and the United States, which would function as the permanent intergovernmental policy forum to address and manage the full range of common Arctic concerns.

Evelyn M. Hurwich

VIII. NATURAL RESOURCE MANAGEMENT AND CONSERVATION

1. NATURE CONSERVATION: NATURAL LANDS AND BIOLOGICAL DIVERSITY

[Editors' Note: This report features two separate entries by different authors.]

A. GENERAL REPORT

(1) Convention on Wetlands of International Importance (RAMSAR Convention)

The Ramsar Convention had 83 parties by the end of 1994, with the addition of Estonia, the Philippines, and Turkey. Malaysia deposited its instrument of accession late in 1994 and was finally to become a party on 31 March 1995. Tadjikistan, which made a declaration of succession in 1992, still had not designated a site for the Ramsar List of Wetlands of International Importance and cannot become a party until it has done so. There were 686 sites on the List at the end of 1994, covering 44 million hectares. Some sites that the Soviet Union had designated were removed from the List, as the new states in which they are located have not yet made a declaration of succession. There are 64 sites on the Record of Ramsar Sites where changes in ecological character have occurred, are occurring, or are likely to occur (also called the "Montreux Record," for the Swiss city where it was initially adopted.)

The amendments to the Convention that had been adopted by the Third Session of the Conference of the Parties in Regina, Canada, came into force on 1 May, after ratification by two-thirds of the states that were parties to the Convention at the time of their adoption in 1987. Of particular importance among these now binding amendments are those that empower the Conference of the Parties to adopt the Convention budget and to establish compulsory financial contributions from the parties.

Several regional meetings of the parties were held in 1994: in Nakuru, Kenya, for Africa; in Tunis for North Africa; in Budapest for Eastern Europe; and in Papua New Guinea for Oceania. Other regional meetings will be held in 1995. The next meeting of the Conference of the Parties will take place in Brisbane, Australia, in early 1996.

(2) Convention Concerning the Protection of the World Cultural and Natural Heritage (World Heritage Convention)

Four new states became parties to the World Heritage Convention in 1994, Azerbaijan, Kazakhstan, Myanmar, and Turkmenistan, bringing the total membership to 140.

Twenty-one new cultural sites were added to the World Heritage List, as well as eight new natural sites. There were also three extensions of cultural sites and two extensions of natural ones. Altogether, there were 440 sites in 100 different countries on the list at the end of 1994, of which 326 were cultural, 97 were natural, and 17 were "mixed." The eight new natural sites are the Australian Fossil Mammal Sites (Riversleigh, Naracoorte), the Los Katios National Park in Colombia, the Doñana National Park in Spain, the Bwindi Impenetrable National Park and the Ruwenzori Mountains National Park in Uganda, the Arabian Oryx Sanctuary in Oman, and the Halong Bay in Vietnam.

The Virunga National Park in Zaire has been inscribed on the World Heritage In Danger List.

(3) Convention on the Conservation of Migratory Species of Wild Animals (Bonn Convention)

The Philippines and the Czech Republic became parties to the Convention in 1994, bringing the total number of parties to 44, including the European Union. Slovakia deposited its instrument of accession on 14 December and was to formally become a party in early 1995.

(a) Fourth Meeting of the Conference of the Parties

The Fourth Meeting of the Conference of the Parties to the Convention met in Nairobi from 711 June. The Conference added three species to Appendix I of the treaty: the Scimitar-horned Oryx (*Oryx dammah* or Sahelian antelope); the White-headed Duck (*Oxyura leucocephala*), and the middle-European population of the Greater Bustard (*Otis tarda*). Appendix I lists endangered migratory species that parties have a strict obligation to protect. The Conference also adopted a resolution calling on parties to undertake concerted actions for a select number of species listed in Appendix I and to review the results at its next meeting. Fifty species of waterbirds and the European free-tailed bat (*Tatarida teniotis)*, were added to Appendix II, which lists species for which the Range States are encouraged to enter into specific agreements for their conservation and management. The Conference added these bird species to facilitate the conclusion of a comprehensive agreement under the Convention on African-Eurasian waterbirds. The bat was the only European species in this class of mammals that was not already listed in that appendix.

The conference considered a key paper entitled "Strategy for the Future Development of the Convention," which the Secretariat had prepared. The Strategy reviews the past performance of the Convention and makes recommendations aimed at improving its effectiveness in several key areas, such as geographic and taxonomic coverage implementation measures and the conclusion of agreements under the Convention and institutional arrangements. The Conference accepted the Strategy and identified a number of priorities for action.

Another matter that the Conference considered was the need to avoid discrepancies between agreements concluded under the Convention and the resulting need to formulate guidelines for their harmonization. The Conference examined an expert report on the matter and decided that after review by the Convention Standing Committee, the report will be submitted for adoption to the next meeting of the Conference of the Parties. It recommended that in the meantime the elements contained in the report immediately be taken into account in the elaboration of further agreements. The Conference also adopted an increased budget, thus allowing for a strengthening of the personnel capacity of the Secretariat, which, at its present level, is clearly unable to carry out the tasks required for the preparation of new agreements.

(b) Agreements in Force

The Agreement on the Conservation of Bats in Europe entered into force on 16 January. There were nine parties to the Agreement at the end of the year: the Czech Republic, Denmark, Germany, Hungary, Luxembourg, the Netherlands, Norway, Sweden, and the United Kingdom. The United Kingdom provides an interim secretariat. The first meeting of the parties was expected to take place in 1995.

The Agreement on the Conservation of Small Cetaceans of the Baltic and North Seas entered into force on 29 March. There were six parties to the Agreement at the end of the year: Belgium, Denmark, Germany, the Netherlands, Sweden, and the United Kingdom. The Secretariat is located in Cambridge, United Kingdom. The first meeting of the parties took place in Stockholm, 26-28 September. It considered national reports from parties and non-parties, discussed a potential extension of the agreement area to cover Irish waters, and held a debate on by-catches of small cetaceans in the course of fishing activities. Many organizations dealing with marine mammals were present as observers, including the International Whaling Commission, the North Atlantic Marine Mammal Commission, the Inter-American Tropical Tuna Commission and several non-governmental organizations (NGOs).

The informal Memorandum of Understanding concerning Conservation Measures for the Siberian Crane has been accepted by India, the Islamic Republic of Iran, Pakistan, and the Russian Federation. A technical meeting was planned for early 1995.

In 1994, Georgia and Uzbekistan signed the Memorandum of Understanding concerning Conservation Measures for the Slender-Billed Curlew (*Numenius tenuirostris*), which follows the same lines as its sister agreement on the Siberian Crane. Hungary joined the agreement later in the year.

(c) Agreements in Preparation

A revised version of the Draft Agreement on the Conservation of Small Cetaceans of the Mediterranean and Black Seas was circulated in September for comments by Range States and other interested bodies.

The proposed Draft Agreement on African-Eurasian Migratory Waterbirds was examined at a first inter-governmental session convened for that purpose in Nairobi, 12–14 June. General agreement was expressed on the structure and contents of the draft, subject to some amendments. Following the meeting, an amended text was circulated to all concerned. A formal negotiating meeting to conclude the Agreement was to be held in The Hague, the Netherlands, 12–17 June 1995.

The Agreement on the Conservation of Asian-Australasian Waterbirds was still in a preliminary stage of preparation at year's end.

(4) Convention on the Consertation of European Wildlife and Natural Habitats (Berne Convention)

Moldova and Monaco acceded to the Berne Convention in 1994, bringing the number of parties to 31, including the European Union. It was expected that several other countries, including the Czech and Slovak Republics, would join the Convention in 1995. The Standing Committee of the Convention did not meet in 1994. Its next meeting is scheduled for March 1995.

An intergovernmental symposium was organized in Monaco in September to discuss the role of the Berne Convention in the implementation of the Convention on Biological Diversity. The symposium was attended by almost all parties and a large number of observers from non-party states and international organizations. It provided a unique opportunity to hold a substantive debate on the strategic, scientific, technical, institutional, and financial aspects of the implementation of both conventions in Europe. The symposium adopted a formal declaration (the Monaco Declaration) on the role of the Berne Convention in the implementation of worldwide international instruments for the protection of biodiversity. The Declaration recognizes that the Berne Convention is an instrument of major importance for the conservation of biological diversity at the regional level. It also recognizes that the Convention's scope is broad enough to deal with many aspects of the Convention on Biological Diversity. Recommendations dealing with all of these aspects are accordingly addressed to Berne Contracting Parties and to the Standing Committee, with a view to improving the effectiveness of the Convention. The Declaration also recommends the establishment of appropriate coordination mechanisms with the Convention on Biological Diversity, "so that both instruments may be applied and elaborated on together in matters relating to the conservation of biological diversity and the sustainable use of its components." It is expected that the Standing Committee will consider these recommendations at its next meeting.

(5) Protocol to the Alpine Convention of 1991, In the Field of Nature Protection and Landscape Maintenance

This Protocol is one of several that the parties to the Alpine Convention had committed themselves to conclude. It was signed at Chambéry on 20 December, together with the Protocols on Mountain Agriculture and Mountain Forestry.

Membership of the Protocol is restricted to the parties to the Convention, *i.e.*, Austria, the European Union, France, Germany, Italy, Liechtenstein, Slovenia, and Switzerland. A special protocol was adopted, however, to enable the principality of Monaco to become a party to the Convention. As a result, Monaco was also able to sign the Protocol.

(a) Objectives and General Obligations

The objective of the Protocol is to lay down international rules aimed at guaranteeing the functioning of ecosystems, the conservation of landscape elements and wild species and the diversity, originality, and beauty of natural and rural landscapes (Art. 1). As a result, parties plan to take necessary measures to ensure the protection, management and, where required, restoration of nature and landscapes, including species of wild fauna and flora, their diversity, and their habitats throughout the Alpine area (Art. 2). They agree to cooperate for that purpose and, in particular, to promote transboundary cooperation (Art. 3), take into consideration the objectives of the Protocol in all their other policies (Art. 4), and provide for the participation of local authorities in the preparation and implementation of conservation policies and measures (Art. 5).

Under Art. 10, parties have a general obligation to endeavour to reduce the degradation of nature and landscapes in the whole Alpine area. They must also ensure that any form of land use in that area is exercised in a way that spares nature and landscapes. Protection, conservation, and management measures are to be carried out, wherever appropriate, through agreements concluded with landowners or tenants and the provision of adequate incentives or compensation. Support measures for farming, forestry, and other land uses must be further developed with a view to achieving the conservation measures set out by the Protocol. The Protocol lays down a number of very innovative obligations for a conservation treaty. These relate to inventories, landscape planning, and activities resulting in impairment to nature and landscapes.

(b) Inventories

Under Art. 6, parties undertake to submit, three years after the entry into force of the Protocol, and thereafter at least every 10 years, a full review of the state of nature protection and landscape maintenance in the Alpine part of their territory. Annex I to the Protocol provides a comprehensive and detailed list of elements that are to be taken up in that review. These include a review of the status of wild fauna and flora, habitats, landscapes, farming, forestry, hunting, fishing, protected areas, and protected habitat types. Information must also be provided on the administration of nature protection, wardening, conservation NGOs, NGO participation, including standing to sue, penalties, nature protection funds, nature protection planning and activities, wild species management including captive breeding, species and area monitoring, financing, and public information.

(c) Landscape Planning

Article 7 establishes an obligation for parties to prepare, within five years from the entry into force of the Protocol, guidelines or plans setting out requirements and measures for the achievement of the objectives laid down by that instrument. These guidelines or plans must include a review and an evaluation of the state of nature conservation and landscape maintenance in the Alpine area, a statement on the desired state that should be reached, and a list of measures that are necessary to achieve this desired state. These measures must include both general and specific measures for the protection and management of particular elements of nature or the landscape and of animal and plant species. Pursuant to Art. 8, the parties must, under their landscape planning system, take measures for the preservation and improvement of the habitats of wild animal and plant species and of other characteristic elements of natural and rural landscapes.

(d) Impairment of Nature ("Eingriff" in the German version; "atteinte" in the French version of the Protocol)

Article 9 requires parties to provide for the assessment of direct and indirect impacts on the natural balance and landscape of public and private measures and projects that are likely to significantly or lastingly impair nature and landscapes. The results of these assessments must be taken into consideration when permits are granted or when the measures or projects concerned are carried out. All avoidable impairments must be prevented. Unavoidable impairments must be compensated by other conservation measures. Where compensation is not possible, impairments can be authorized only if, after a balancing of all interests concerned, conservation requirements do not prevail. Other conventional obligations relate to the protection of areas, habitat types, and species, as well as to research and monitoring.

(e) Protected Areas

Parties undertake to conserve, manage, and, as appropriate, enlarge existing protected areas and, as far as possible, designate new ones (Art. 11). They have the obligation to establish a national and transboundary network of protected areas and to harmonize the objectives and measures applicable to transboundary protected areas (Art. 12).

(f) Habitat Types

A specific provision (Art. 13) is devoted to the protection of natural and semi-natural habitat types. Parties must take the necessary measures to guarantee the long-term conservation of these habitats in sufficient numbers throughout their range.

(g) Species

There is a general provision on the conservation of species (Art. 14). Parties are to take appropriate measures to conserve the diversity of animal and plant species in sufficiently large populations and must ensure that habitats of sufficient size are maintained for that purpose. Lists of habitat types and of species requiring special conservation measures will be prepared within the two years following the entry into force of the Protocol. Parties must also, within the same time period, designate animal and plant species the taking of and trade in which shall be prohibited (Art. 15). Parties must promote the re-establishment of native species (Art. 16), prevent the introduction of alien species (Art. 17), and ensure that the introduction of genetically modified organisms shall not constitute a hazard for humans and the environment (Art. 18).

(h) Research and Monitoring

Research and monitoring programmes must be harmonized and joint research programmes developed. Research and monitoring results are to be integrated into a common system for the monitoring of the state and evolution of the Alpine area. The public has a right to access to these results (Art. 20). Priority research themes are listed in Annex II to the Protocol.

(i) Institutions

The Protocol does not provide for any particular institutional mechanism of its own, as it will use those set up by the Alpine Convention. For the time being, the Convention does not have a secretariat, but the Conference is empowered to establish one if it thinks fit.

(j) Implementation and Compliance

Provisions on compliance include an obligation for the parties to report on a regular basis to the Convention Standing Committee on the measures they have taken to implement the Protocol. These reports must also deal with the effectiveness of these measures. The Standing Committee must examine these reports and verify that the parties have discharged their obligations under the Protocol. It may request additional information from the parties or other sources. The Committee must in turn submit a report to the Alpine Conference on the parties' compliance with the Protocol's obligations. If the Conference finds that a party has not complied with its obligations, the Conference may adopt a recommendation addressed to that party (Art. 23). Parties must also periodically review and assess the effectiveness of the provisions of the Protocol and consider any amendments that may be required. Local authorities must be associated to this review. NGOs may only be consulted (Art. 24).

(k) Final Clauses

The Protocol is only open to parties to the Alpine Convention. Denunciation of the Convention automatically results in the denunciation of the Protocol (Art. 25). The Protocol will come into force after the deposit of the third instrument of ratification or accession. The depositary is Austria (Art. 26).

(6) UNESCO Biosphere Reserve Network

There are now 324 biosphere reserves in 82 countries. An international conference was to be held in Seville in March 1995, to examine and evaluate the Action Plan for Biosphere Reserves adopted in 1984 and to elaborate a new Action Plan to be submitted for adoption to the International Coordinating Council of the Man and Biosphere Programme. It was expected that the conference would also approve draft statutes for the International Network of Biosphere Reserves, including criteria for the acceptance of reserves into the network and a periodic review of the status of the reserves after they have been accepted. The statutes, after approval by the conference, will also be submitted for adoption to the International Coordinating Council.

Cyrille de Klemm

B. CONVENTION ON BIOLOGICAL DIVERSITY

(1) Intergovernmental Committee on the Convention on Biological Diversity

After the difficult first session of the Intergovernmental Committee on the Convention on Biological Diversity (ICCBD) in October 1993, the interim period prior to the first meeting of the Conference of the Parties (CoP) continued in 1994 with two intergovernmental meetings. The Open-ended Intergovernmental Meeting of Scientific Experts on Biological Diversity was held in Mexico City, 11–15 April. A one-time event called for by the Intergovernmental Committee, the meeting was held in lieu of establishing an interim scientific and technical advisory committee as a forerunner to the Subsidiary Body for Scientific, Technical and Technological Advice. There were two significant outputs. The first was a series of indicative lists of technology related to biodiversity conservation and techniques to promote its development and transfer (UNEP/CBD/IC/2/11). The second was a preliminary agenda for scientific and technological research on biodiversity conservation and sustainable use (UNEP/CBD/IC/2/Inf.2). The work will provide the basis for future work by the CoP.

The second intergovernmental meeting of 1994 was the second session of the Intergovernmental Committee (ICCBD II), held in Nairobi from 20 June to 1 July. The second ICCBD focused its work on those agenda items that would directly contribute to the CoP's preparation, namely those topics that had to be acted on pursuant to the Convention at the first meeting. The Intergovernmental Committee's recommendations were forwarded to the CoP for its consideration, but were not binding upon it.

(2) (➔) First Meeting of the Conference of the Parties to the Convention on Biological Diversity

The First Meeting of the Conference of Parties, the third and final intergovernmental meeting of 1994, opened the Convention's formal implementation period. The Bahamas hosted the meeting in Nassau, from 28 November to 9 December. The primary purpose of CoP I was the initial institutionalization of the Convention. In fact, institutionalization dominated those actions specified in the Convention for action by the CoP at its first meeting.

The meeting was attended by 128 states. Ninety-four were parties or states that had deposited their instruments of ratification but for which the Convention had not yet entered into force. Thirty-four states were represented as observers, most notably the United States, which, in spite of its status, still managed to play a key role throughout the negotiations. With 107 non-governmental organizations in attendance, non-governmental activities contributed greatly to the depth of the meeting. The Global Biodiversity Forum met before hand and focused on techniques for priority setting and marine biodiversity issues. A biodiversity technology fair provided many organizations with the opportunity to share information and ideas on biodiversity conservation and sustainable use.

(a) Rules of Procedure

A critical issue left unresolved by the ICCBD was the rules of procedure for the Conference. By the time of the informal consultations on 27 November, it was unclear whether there would be agreement on rule 4(1) (periodicity of meetings of the CoP), rule 21 (Bureau for the CoP), and rule 40 (decisions involving the financial mechanism).

The Bureau for the CoP was most crucial to the meeting's smooth operation. In the ICCBD, developing countries argued for a larger Bureau to ensure adequate political representation, while developed countries, thinking in terms of efficiency and cost, wanted the standard five-officer Bureau. In addition, because of their special circumstances, the Small Island Developing States wanted guaranteed representation on the Bureau. In the end, the CoP agreed on a Bureau composed of one president, nine vice-presidents, and one rapporteur, with elections having due regard for equitable representation of the Small Island Developing States.

The CoP decided to meet annually, but there was no movement on the voting issue. The European Union insisted that decisions related to the financial mechanism be taken by consensus without a voting contingency where consensus could be reached. Developed countries remained concerned that a CoP dominated by developing countries could take decisions with regard to the extent or nature and form of the financial contributions of the contracting parties, instead of just the amount of total resources needed for the mechanism. Resolution was inextricably linked to the debate on the institutional structure to oversee the financial mechanism, which, it was hoped, would itself be resolved during the course of the first meeting. As result of the impasse, the CoP was forced to adopt its rules of procedure without rule 40(1). It remained in square brackets for resolution at the CoP's second meeting (UNEP/CBD/COP/1/L.12).

(b) Financial Resources and Mechanism

The CoP considered and decided a number of financially related issues, some of which were based on the recommendations of the ICCBD II. Pursuant to Art. 21(2), the CoP adopted policy, strategy, programme priorities, and eligibility criteria for access to and utilization of financial resources made available under Art. 20. A list of developed-country parties that will contribute financial resources, and those parties that voluntarily assume the obligations of the developed-country parties, was also adopted pursuant to Art. 20(2).

In addition, the CoP decided that the restructured Global Environment Facility (GEF) would continue as the institutional structure operating the financial mechanism until the CoP takes a decision at its second meeting. The CoP instructed the GEF to support programmes, projects, and activities consistent with the CoP's newly adopted policy, strategy, programme priorities, and eligibility criteria. The decision on the GEF reflected a compromise in the ongoing debate between developing and developed countries over the financial mechanism's operation and whether a separate fund should be established under the authority of the CoP. It seems evident, however, that the new opportunities for participation in the restructured GEF, and the firm insistence of developed countries, make it a foregone conclusion that GEF will continue in its role at least for the foreseeable future. An interesting development to watch will be the United States' influence over the Convention as a non-party and its participation in GEF as the largest contributor.

(c) Clearing-House Mechanism for Technical and Scientific Cooperation

Despite recommendations from the Intergovernmental Committee to create a clearing house or houses made up of a decentralized network of existing national, regional, and global centres or nodes (UNEP/CBD/COP/1/4), and a well drafted proposal by the Interim Secretariat on how to establish such a mechanism (UNEP/CBD/COP/1/8), the CoP made little progress on the issue. It merely called upon the Secretariat to prepare a comprehensive, costed study on how to establish the clearing house, and decided that any such medium would operate under CoP authority with funding from the Secretariat's budget and voluntary contributions.

(d) Selection of a Competent International Organization to Carry Out the Functions of the Secretariat

As regards the institutional set-up, the CoP first designated the United Nations Environment Programme to carry out the Secretariat functions (UNEP/CBD/COP/1/L.7). Second, it acknowledged the offers of other international organizations to support and cooperate with the Secretariat and requested the Executive Secretary to coordinate with them as required. The CoP also requested the Executive Secretary to contact and establish appropriate lines of cooperation with other conventions dealing with biodiversity-related issues. This action will be important for capturing the synergies between the Biodiversity Convention and other conventions.

(e) Financing of and Budget for the Convention

An important issue with direct implications for the functioning of the Convention Secretariat and, therefore, the implementation and fulfillment of the CoP's work programme, was the budget and its accompanying financial rules. Because of their interrelated nature, negotiations on these two issues and the CoP's medium term work programme were entrusted to an open-ended contact group of the Committee of the Whole. A very ambitious medium term work programme and a 1995 budget of US$4.7 million—approximately US$1.7 million dollars less than the Interim Secretariat had proposed—were ultimately adopted. It is too early to tell whether this first exercise portends a future of under-funded work programme mandates and an impotent Secretariat.

In its discussions on the financial rules, the CoP decided that contributions to the budget would be mandatory. However, outstanding issues as to adjustments to the scale of assessment in terms of specified limits on contributions and regarding the method for reaching agreement on the scale of assessment and the budget, whether solely by consensus or with a double majority voting system in instances where consensus cannot be reached, proved unresolvable. On the first issue, Brazil was adamant that no developing country should be required to pay more than any developed country. Concerning the second issue, some developed countries were in favour of consensus without contingent voting.

(f) Medium-Term Work Programme

The CoP established an initial three-year programme period with standing and rolling subject areas. Intensive detailed negotiations focused on the topics for inclusion and the timing of their treatment. Developing countries wanted access to genetic resources, technology transfer, capacity-building, intellectual property rights, and indigenous and local communities treated immediately within the first two years. Developed countries generally wanted conservation-oriented topics discussed immediately. These included thematic areas such as marine biodiversity and terrestrial biodiversity, threats to the components of biological diversity, and identification and monitoring. The adopted programme reflects a compromise (UNEP/CBD/COP/1/L.11 and Corr. 1), though governments side-stepped the forests issue.

The most difficult issue to resolve was how to treat the biosafety protocol. In the end, the CoP decided to immediately establish an open-ended *ad hoc* group of government-nominated experts to consider the need for and modalities of a protocol. This group will hold a one week meeting in 1995 to consider existing knowledge, experience, and legislation in the field. In preparation for the open-ended group, the Secretariat was directed to establish a panel of 15 experts nominated by governments to prepare background documentation for the *ad hoc* group. Funding for these meetings will be voluntarily provided by the parties.

(g) Subsidiary Body on Scientific, Technical and Technological Advice

Though the Convention does not actually call for the CoP to take action on the Subsidiary Body on Scientific, Technical and Technological Advice (SBSTTA) at it first meeting, the ICCBD noted that the SBSTTA was fundamentally important to the CoP's work. It recommended that the CoP consider operationalizing the SBSTTA as soon as possible.

The CoP decided that the SBSTTA will operate pursuant to the terms of reference provided at Art. 25(2) until they are further elaborated by the CoP and will report to the CoP at each of its ordinary meetings (UNEP/CBD/COP/1/L.4). For its second meeting, the CoP directed the

SBSTTA to consider its *modus operandi* and propose a medium-term work programme for the CoP's second meeting based on the CoP's medium-term work programme.

The CoP elected the SBSTTA's first two chairpeople. Malawi will chair for 1995. Norway will chair for 1996. An organizational meeting was held to prepare the SBSTTA's first meeting scheduled for 4-8 September 1995, at the UN Economic and Social Commission headquarters in Paris.

(h) Location of the Secretariat

Perhaps the most politically contentious issue of the entire meeting, next to the biosafety issue, was the location of the future Secretariat. By the time of the second meeting of the ICCBD in July, three governments—Kenya, Spain, and Switzerland—had expressed interest in hosting the permanent Secretariat. However, the ICCBD made no recommendations to the CoP on how to decide between these offers and entertain others (UNEP/CBD/COP/1/9). In the end, the CoP postponed consideration of the issue until its second meeting, scheduled for November 1995 (UNEP/CBD/COP/1/L.13). Parties were invited to submit their offers by 31 March 1995 and criteria were provided to guide the offers.

Lyle Glowka
Françoise Burhenne-Guilmin

2. COASTAL ZONE MANAGEMENT

(1) International Meetings and the Development of Global Guidelines and Agreements on Integrated Coastal Zone Management (ICZM)

(a) United Nations Global Conference on the Sustainable Development of Small Island Developing States

The 1992 United Nations Conference on Environment and Development (UNCED) and para. 17.131 of Agenda 21 urged the Global Conference on Sustainable Development of Small Island Developing States (Barbados Conference) to develop and strengthen national, regional, and interregional cooperation and information exchange to promote sustainable development. Because coastal and marine resources play a central role in the sustainable development of small island developing states (SIDS), Barbados Conference agreements have great implications for ICZM. The Barbados Conference, held in Bridgetown, Barbados, 25 April to 6 May, attempted to translate Agenda 21 into specific policies and actions to enable SIDS to attain sustainable development. Representatives of over 100 governments and 200 observer non-governmental organizations (NGOs) attended the meeting.

The Conference adopted the political principles set forth in the (➔) Declaration of Barbados (A/CONF.167/9) that was developed by the host country. This declaration recognized that SIDS are responsible for a significant portion of the world's oceans and many important ecological corridors that link major areas of biodiversity throughout the world. These nations are especially vulnerable to natural disasters and the adverse effects of global climate change and sea-level rise. Moreover, SIDS have a particular interest in protecting their coastlines and oceans from land-based pollution. Limited land and water resources place inordinate pressure on SIDS' coastal zones and marine environments and constrain sustainable development. Given the realities that SIDS face, the Declaration calls on the international community to cooperate with the (➔) Programme of Action for the Sustainable Development of Small Island Developing States "by providing effective means, including adequate, predictable new and additional financial resources in accordance with Chapter 33 of Agenda 21."

The Preamble to the Programme of Action (A/CONF.167/9) recognizes that many SIDS are entirely or predominantly coastal in nature and, therefore, their sustainable development requires effective and integrated management of these resources. The Programme of Action proposes measures at the national, regional, and international levels to promote sustainable development in SIDS in the following priority areas: climate change and sea-level rise; natural and environmental disasters; waste management; coastal and marine resources; fresh water resources; land use; energy; tourism; and biodiversity. Chapter IV (Coastal and Marine Resources) identifies the following national actions that would promote sustainable development of coastal resources: establishment or strengthening of institutional, administrative, and legislative arrangements for developing and implementing ICZM plans, including integrating them with national development plans; comprehensive monitoring programs for coastal and marine resources, and application of traditional knowledge and ecologically sound management practices as a basis for integrated coastal-zone planning. Regional institutions should develop methodologies for ICZM that are appropriate to SIDS, especially small, low elevation, and coralline islands.

Recommended international actions include: assistance with the establishment and strengthening of new institutional and administrative arrangements for the development of ICZM plans; application of the results from the World Coast Conference 1993 and the United Nations Environment Programme (UNEP) Regional Seas Programme to assist SIDS with the development and implementation of ICZM, and building ICZM capacity through strengthening regional and international networks; increasing public participation; ensuring NGO participation; and enhancing training and educational activities.

The Main Committee of the Barbados Conference agreed to the final language on finance late in the Conference. Chapter XV.c.1 noted that "[t]he implementation of the Programme of Action will require . . . new and additional financial resources by the international community." Nevertheless, there was no indication that donor nations were willing to commit new funds. Rather, donor nations supported "better and more efficient use of ODA [official development assistance] and other existing external sources of finance." The Barbados Conference adopted the Programme of Action and recommended to the UN General Assembly that it endorse both the Declaration of Barbados and the Programme of Action.

(b) Convention on Biological Diversity

The First Meeting of the Parties to the Convention on Biological Diversity met in Nassau, the Bahamas, 28 November to 9 December (*see* (→) Report of the First Meeting). The parties adopted an action plan, the Medium-Term Programme of Work of the Conference of the Parties 1995–1997, whose item 5.3.1 commits the parties to address coastal and marine biological diversity. At the next meeting, to be held 6–17 November 1995, in Bali, Indonesia, the parties will share national experiences on biodiversity, including marine and coastal environmental issues.

(c) World Coast Conference 1993 (WCC '93)

A report on the World Coast Conference at the Hague, the Netherlands, in November 1993, entitled "Preparing to Meet the Coastal Challenges of the 21st Century," was published in 1994. The report synthesizes information that was presented at the WCC '93 and the two preparatory workshops. Chapter 2 of the report discusses the economic and environmental benefits of ICZM and the urgent need for this type of planning. The document analyzes 46 vulnerability assessments for coastal areas to sea-level rise. These vulnerability case studies use a common methodology that specifies three variables: global climate change; socio-economic developments; and response options. The case studies assess vulnerability of population, agricultural production, and economic and social assets to a sea-level rise of 30 to 100cm before the year 2100. Chapter 3 surveys ongoing ICZM planning and implementation experiences and searches for their common elements and obstacles. The final chapter highlights the national and international opportunities for strengthening ICZM.

(2) *Development of Regional ICZM Guidelines, Agreements, and Important Program Developments*

(a) *UNEP Regional Seas Programs*

(i) *Black Sea*

In June, a Black Sea Environmental Programme (BSEP) ICZM Working Party meeting was held in Novorossysk, Russia. This meeting was instrumental in the establishment of the ICZM Activity Center in Novorossysk and the ICZM network. Subsequently, the BSEP Program Coordinating Unit sponsored the ICZM Coordinating Meeting in Istanbul, Turkey, on 2–21 October, with the aim of fostering closer cooperation and coordination among members. Representatives from the World Bank, the Commission of the European Community, and the Netherlands attended. In 1994, the World Bank sponsored an infrastructure rehabilitation and development project in the Republic of Georgia that focuses on the capital of Tbilisi and two coastal cities, Batumi and Poti. The World Bank will use an integrated management approach to assist the coastal cities with environmental issues (such as wastewater treatment), landfills, and coastal water quality. The European Union sponsored a Black Sea Environmental Impact Assessment Project, PHARE/TACIS Programme, that promotes sustainable development of the coastal areas of Bulgaria, Georgia, Romania, Russia, and the Ukraine. The project will provide extensive training to resource managers on environmental impact assessments and ICZM strategies for sustainable use of coastal resources. In collaboration with the Netherlands government, the BSEP sponsored the Integrated Resources Management of the Azov Sea: An Environmental Analysis. This project supports Russian and Ukrainian administrators in their analysis of environmental policy options. Guidelines and methodologies will be developed to aid effective resource management decisions.

Finally, a major achievement for the Black Sea ICZM was the signing on 6 July, by President Boris Yeltsin, of a decree adding the natural resources of the Black and Azov Sea coastal zones to a list of federal natural resources, thereby adding them to a 1994-1996 comprehensive coastal zone management program for the region.

(ii) *Mediterranean Sea*

On 1 November, Tunisia hosted the Mediterranean Conference on Sustainable Development. Preceded by two preparatory meetings in May and October 1994, this conference produced four inter-governmental resolutions adopted by the conference participants. The first, the Tunis Declaration, reaffirmed the commitments made at UNCED. Regional leaders pledged to achieve sustainable development in the Mediterranean region. The participants also adopted a resolution on the Mediterranean Commission for Sustainable Development, which will be an integral part of the Mediterranean Action Plan (MAP) and its existing Science and Technical and Socio-Economic Committees. Delegates also approved a resolution entitled "Agenda MED 21." Agenda MED 21 follows the UNCED Agenda 21 format but is tailored to the Mediterranean environment and its special needs. Chapter XVII addressed the protection of the sea and coastal areas and suggested measures that Mediterranean countries should follow. Item 7 specifically called for "policies of integrated ecologically sound coastal management" that will be adopted by decision-makers. Item 18 called on local authorities to use economic incentives to better manage their coastal zones. The fourth conference resolution addressed land-use policies and their application in the protection and conservation of the coastal zone.

The revision of the Convention for the Protection of the Mediterranean Sea Against Pollution (Barcelona Convention) and the sections related to MAP continued during November with a meeting of Contracting Parties in Barcelona. A follow-up meeting was to be held in February 1995 with final decisions to be made at the Ninth Meeting of the Contracting Parties to the Barcelona Convention in June 1995. In December, the Priority Action Programme/Regional Activity Centre (PAP/RAC) hosted a workshop in Split, Croatia, on economic analyses for use in Mediterranean coastal areas. Nations submitted country reports and evaluations. Recommendations from this workshop encouraged PAP/RAC to continue application of economic analyses and prepare guidelines that could assist other countries.

During 1994, MAP strengthened the Coastal Areas Management Programs (CAMPs) by focusing on integrated coastal and marine areas management methodologies previously developed (*see* 4 *YbIEL* 254 (1993)). The PAP/RAC manages 50 percent of all CAMP activities. In addition, PAP/RAC is developing coastal management plans for all CAMP centers. PAP/RAC integrates coastal development with environmental protection and accounts for the different needs of varying sectoral activities. The PAP/RAC is also preparing coastal management plans for Sfax (Tunisia), the area of Fuka-Matrouh (Egypt), and Lebanon. During 1994, progress continued at two other CAMP centers. On January 18–19, the United Nations Development Programme (UNDP) sponsored a meeting in Tirana regarding the CAMP Albania center that united potential project donors. In June, MAP coordinated a workshop on "Management of Albanian Coastal Lagoons" in Tirana, attended by the CAMP National Coordinator and PAP/RAC staff. In September, another project meeting was held that outlined development and environmental scenarios for Albanian coasts. MAP continued its plans to use remote sensing capabilities in coastal regions. The Environment Remote Sensing Regional Activity Center plans to match older maps with recent satellite images to compare changes to the coastal environment.

The second program in progress is CAMP Kastela Bay. Final results were presented at a meeting held in Split, Croatia, on 3–4 February 1994, by the Ministry of Building and Environment and the Croatian Chamber of Commerce. The meeting evaluated the MAP program and recommended continued support in this region.

(iii) Wider Caribbean

The Caribbean Environment Program's (CEP's) Regional Programme on Integrated Planning and Institutional Development for the Management of Marine and Coastal Resources (IPID) implements a number of activities in coastal zone protection and management. IPID's activity in environmental planning and management of heavily contaminated bays and coastal areas continued to implement assistance programs for Cartagena (Colombia), Havana (Cuba), Santo Domingo littoral (Dominican Republic), Kingston (Jamaica), and Point Lisas (Trinidad and Tobago). A new plan of assistance was prepared for Bluefields (Nicaragua) in 1994.

In 1994–1995, IPID's Environmentally Sound Tourism Development activity is preparing a number of ecotourism case studies that will focus on socio-economic benefits to local communities. An additional IPID activity on the development of pilot integrated management plans for small islands and coastal areas aims to prepare a regionally appropriate methodological framework for ICZM and present the framework at a 1995 workshop. Pilot case studies from a number of Caribbean Basin countries (Antigua and Barbuda, Colombia, Dominican Republic, Guatemala, Nicaragua, and Venezuela) will comprise the informational base of the framework. IPID is presently providing technical assistance for the preparation of integrated coastal development plans for Surinam, St. Lucia, St. Vincent and the Grenadines, and the La Caleta-San Pedro de Macoris sector of the Dominican Republic.

(b) European Union

On 6 May, the Council of the European Union adopted a Resolution on a Community Strategy for Integrated Coastal-Zone Management (37 OJ Eur. Comm. (No. C 135) 2 (1994)). The resolution emphasizes the need for a Community strategy on ICZM, based on the principle of sustainability and sound environmental practices, and invites the Commission to propose a strategy for the entire Community coastline that will establish a framework for sustainable use and conservation while taking into account the specific problems and potentials of specific areas. The resolution also invites member states to strengthen their own efforts to protect their coastal zones.

(c) World Bank

The World Bank's Environmental Department (Land, Water and Natural Habitats Division) and Africa Technical Department developed a Framework for Integrated Coastal Zone Management for Sub-Saharan Africa. This document recommends the cross-sectoral ICZM approach as the preferred management strategy for sustainable development in Sub-Saharan Africa, and is part of a larger World Bank effort, called the "Post UNCED Strategy Towards Environmentally Sustainable Development in Sub-Saharan Africa (SSA)." The World Bank is to publish a discussion paper in 1995 on the different scenarios for sustainable development in Africa that will include the Framework for Integrated Coastal Zone Management for Sub-Saharan Africa.

(3) Major Policy Statements Concerning International ICZM Activities

As suggested by Agenda 21 of UNCED, coral reef ecosystems require an integrated management approach for sustainable use. On 10 January 1994, the US Department of State sponsored a Coral Reef Consultation Day with the goal of establishing a strategy for the US Coral Reef Initiative. The resulting interagency task force will focus its efforts on national and international activities that potentially threaten coral reefs, and specifically on the development and integration of research and management strategies that conserve and protect coral reefs and their associated environments. The US Coral Reef Initiative supports an integrated management approach that incorporates land-use and urban planning into coral reef management. Seven other nations (Australia, France, Jamaica, Japan, the Philippines, Sweden, and the United Kingdom) have since joined the United States' effort to develop an International Coral Reef Initiative (ICRI) that adopts a broad coastal zone management perspective. The ICRI has established liaisons with other coral reef nations, non-governmental organizations (the World Conservation Union, the Alliance of Small Island States), multilateral banks (World Bank, Inter-American Development Bank), UN organizations (UNDP, UNEP, the UN Economic and Social Council), and intergovernmental organizations (South Pacific Regional Environment Program, Coordinating Body for the Seas of East Asia). The ICRI plans various workshops for 1995 and establishment of a Global Coral Reef Monitoring network through the International Oceanographic Commission.

Daniel O. Suman
Lynette Cardoch

3. TRADE IN ENDANGERED SPECIES

(1) Meeting of the Parties—CITES

The Ninth Conference of the Parties to the Convention on International Trade in Endangered Species of Wild Fauna and Flora (CITES) was held in Ft. Lauderdale, Florida. In November 1994, 119 national representatives and 221 non-governmental observers gathered to discuss the listing of species and the administration of treaty obligations.

From its beginning, this conference was more subdued, in contrast to the sharp, confrontational nature of the previous meeting in Kyoto *(see* Favre, "Debate within the CITES Community: What Direction for the Future?" 33 *NRJ* 875 (1993)). No potentially embarrassing resolutions, such as those exposing lack of enforcement efforts, were proposed. For example, while the conditions of the tiger and rhino were lamented by all, no proposals were introduced that would have singled out states that were lax in their enforcement obligations. Those resolutions actually proposed were conservative and did not represent radical policy shifts.

The parties discontinued a form used to report the shipping conditions of live animals due to the lack of interest. A recommendation for the creation of a committee of law enforcement personnel to aid in CITES enforcement was rejected.

Among the species-listing decisions made at the conference were:

- the box turtle was added to Appendix II;
- the white rhino of South Africa was down-listed from Appendix I to Appendix II, but trade was allowed only in live animals and sport hunting trophies (it is not clear whether the treaty allows the live and dead specimens of the same species to be placed on different appendices);
- the red-knee tarantula was added to Appendix II due to extensive demand in the pet trade;
- the sale of stockpiled Vicuña wool from Peru was approved;
- bigleaf mahogany received a majority vote for listing on Appendix II, but not the two-thirds required for adoption, and therefore remains unprotected under CITES;
- Norway's proposal to down-list the Minke whale to Appendix II so it could sell commercial whale meat to Japan was rejected 11–48.

Of prime importance at this conference was the adoption of a resolution setting forth new species-listing criteria, an idea that had been growing in popularity since the 1992 Kyoto meeting. The new resolution, Com.0.17, creates a more detailed frame of reference for the phrase "are or may be affected by trade" in Art. 2 of CITES. Com.9.17 also sets forth biological criteria for determining whether a species is endangered. In earlier drafts, specific numbers had been given as listing thresholds. For example, the definition of "population" states that "a figure of less than 5,000 mature individuals has been found to be an appropriate guideline of what constitutes a small wild population." Annex 4 of Com.9.17 sets out a number of rules for decision-making. For example, in case of unreliable or uncertain information about species, the parties must "act in the best interest of the conservation of the species."

There was some confusion among the delegates on the interrelation of CITES and other international treaties. For example, CITES has always accorded deference to the International Whaling Commission on issues dealing with whales. However, the parties seemed uncertain about how CITES should interact with the Convention on Biodiversity, the International Tropical Timber Agreement, or the General Agreement on Tariffs and Trade, particularly on the issue of trade sanctions. Given the steady proliferation of international treaties, this difficulty in reconciling conflicting treaties is likely to increase. There was, at the end of 1994, no international mechanism designed to address this problem.

At the Ft. Lauderdale conference, CITES's Standing Committee was expanded. Whereas in the past, each of the six regions of the world had one representative on the committee, the number of regional representatives is now determined by the number of CITES members in the region. North America, with three states parties, will continue to have only one representative, but Africa, with 41 states parties, will now have three. The effect will be to shift the balance of power within the committee toward developing countries. Therefore, the new committee will likely be more reluctant to request the imposition of trade sanctions on states parties than was the previous committee (*see* 4 *YbIEL* 260 (1993)).

In an effort to eliminate conflicting provisions, remove outdated material, and provide a simple reference source, the Secretariat prepared a series of resolutions combining all of the previously adopted resolutions in force and effect. Com.9.20 presented the Parties with 10 consolidation resolutions. With some minor changes, these were all adopted.

The next Conference of the Parties will be held in Zimbabwe in 1997. In the interim, there will be a study on how to improve the Convention's effectiveness. The total number of Parties to CITES will reach 126 in early 1995 with the addition of Mali, Romania, Eritrea, and Sierra Leone.

(2) Enforcement Developments

A new approach to international enforcement has been developed by six African states. With the quiet support of the United Nations Environment Programme and others, Kenya, South Africa, Swaziland, Tanzania, Uganda, and Zambia signed an agreement on 9 September 1994 referred to as the (➔) Lusaka Agreement on Co-operative Enforcement Operations

Directed at Illegal Trade in Wild Fauna and Flora. Under this agreement, a task force made up of personnel and resources from the signatory states will focus on violations of domestic law that lead to or support illegal international traffic in wildlife products. At the CITES meeting, this Agreement came under criticism as unnecessary and as an inappropriate delegation of sovereign authority. Nevertheless, the Agreement may encourage regional enforcement of international agreements, which is seriously lacking at present. Under the terms of the Lusaka Agreement, the task force will have the power to investigate criminal actions across state borders. In this author's opinion, it is doubtful that the agreement will ever be ratified or implemented.

The United States, for the first time, exercised its power under the Pelly Amendment. On 11 April 1994, President Clinton imposed trade sanctions against Taiwan, prohibiting the importation into the United States of wildlife specimens or products from Taiwan (59 Fed. Reg. 22043, 28 Apr. 1994). Of primary concern was the importation and sale of rhino horn, ivory, and tiger parts. At the end of 1994, these trade sanctions remained in place, despite new legislation that had been adopted in Taiwan in October 1994.

(3) Rhino and Ivory

The Middle East continues to be a source of demand for illegal rhino horn, which is used to make culturally valuable knives. In late 1994, Oman banned the importation of rhino horn and promised to ban the sale of rhino horn at a later date.

Although it has been substantially reduced, illegal trade in ivory continues. For example, in October, customs authorities in Taiwan seized 272 tusks and 139 tusk pieces with a total weight of more than 2000 kg. In July, officers in Zambia confiscated 216 elephant tusks.

Delegates at the Ninth Conference of the Parties of CITES attribute the reduction in elephant poaching to its listing on Appendix I, and to the banning of the commercial sale of ivory. By contrast, the decline of all but the white rhino continues unchecked. The states party passed another resolution about the illegal rhino trade, but it covers no new legal ground.

David S. Favre

4. FISHERIES/MARINE MAMMALS

(1) Straddling Fish Stocks and Highly Migratory Fish Stocks

The United Nations Conference continued in two sessions (March and August) during 1994, in response to Agenda 21's call for an intergovernmental meeting to address provisions of the United Nations Convention on the Law of the Sea (UNCLOS), particularly those on "straddling" fish stocks (those that occur both within and beyond exclusive economic zones (EEZs)) and highly migratory fish stocks. More than 100 states met at the UN headquarters in New York.

During the August session, a consensus began to form that the result of the Conference should be a binding agreement, although some distant-water fishing countries have not yet accepted that stipulation. The chairman's revised negotiating text was drafted in treaty form.

Important issues have been refined, including: whether the section of the text addressing general principles should apply within EEZs; how interim measures should be devised if disputes arise over differing measures for EEZ and high seas fishing; what participatory rights new members of a regional organization should have in a fully utilized fishery; whether a dispute settlement mechanism beyond those contained in UNCLOS is necessary; and how to deal with vessels whose flag states are unable or unwilling to investigate and prosecute high seas violations.

The UN General Assembly set dates for two more sessions of the Conference: March 27–April 12 and July 24–August 4, 1995.

(2) *Code of Conduct for Responsible Fishing*

The UN Food and Agriculture Organization (FAO) Committee on Fisheries (COFI) continued to work on a voluntary code of conduct, but became embroiled in debate on the relationship between the code and the product of the UN Conference. A technical consultation was held in Rome in late September 1994; COFI was to consider the code further at its March 1995 session. The code will address general principles, fishing operations, fishery management practices, fair trade practices, aquaculture development, fishery research, and integrated coastal areas management.

One portion of the operations section of the code of conduct is already complete: The Agreement to Promote Compliance with International Conservation and Management Measures by Fishing Vessels on the High Seas was adopted by the FAO Conference in November 1993. The Agreement will enter into force upon acceptance by 25 parties.

(3) *The Convention on International Trade in Endangered Species of Wild Fauna and Flora (CITES)*

The Ninth Conference of the Parties to CITES met in Florida in November 1994. The Conference dealt with several issues relating to fish and marine mammals.

Norway's proposal to downlist two stocks of minke whales from Appendix I to Appendix II was revised in favor of a proposal postponing downlisting until scientific evidence from the International Whaling Commission (IWC) showed that the populations were at harvestable levels.

This revised proposal was defeated, however, and Norway resumed its commercial hunt for minke whales in 1993 and 1994.

The Conference adopted a resolution recognizing the IWC's work on illegal trade in whale meat, calling for cooperation between the two organizations, and asking the IWC to report to the CITES Standing Committee on all related developments. Another resolution directs the CITES Animal Committee to review information about the trade and status of sharks and report to the Tenth Conference in 1997.

(4) Driftnet Moratorium

On January 1, 1993, a moratorium on fishing with large-scale driftnets (longer than 2.5 kilometers) took effect under UN General Assembly resolution 46/215. Compliance with the moratorium in the Pacific has been excellent.

At the end of 1993, the European Union's (EU's) Council of Fisheries Ministers turned down France's request for an extension of an exception for its tuna fishery in the Bay of Biscay for using driftnets under five kilometers, but agreed to review an environmental/economic study of the fishery. France announced in May 1994 that it would enforce the EU's 2.5 kilometer limit.

The United Kingdom promptly prosecuted minor violations by two British tuna vessels in the Bay of Biscay last summer. Italy stepped up its enforcement efforts to ensure compliance with the EU limit and announced a program to convert its Mediterranean driftnet fleet to other types of fishing gear.

(5) Pollock Fishery in the Central Bering Sea

All six parties signed the (➔) Convention on the Conservation and Management of Pollock Resources in the Central Bering Sea by the end of 1994. American and Russian fishing interests have been greatly concerned about fishing in the Bering Sea "donut hole"—an enclave beyond the 200-mile zones of the United States and the Russian Federation in the central Bering Sea—by trawl vessels from South Korea, Japan, Poland, and the People's Republic of China, because harvests there have had an adverse impact on pollock resources in the US and Russian zones. At the tenth negotiating session in February 1994, the parties agreed on a permanent management regime for the "donut hole" area.

Experts from the six parties will meet in Seattle, Washington, in February 1995 to set rules and procedures for the annual conference and for the scientific and technical committee, and to consider scientific and enforcement issues. The first annual conference will be held in November, preceded by a meeting of the scientific and technical committee in October. The US Senate consented to ratification; the Convention was expected to come into force before the end of 1995. In the meantime, the voluntary suspension of fishing in the area during 1993 and 1994 was extended through 1995.

(6) International Whaling Commission

The 1994 meeting of the IWC in Puerto Vallarta, Mexico, created a vast, circumpolar sanctuary for whales in the southern ocean, which took effect December 7, 1994 (*see* (➔) International Whaling Commission, Chairman's Report of the 46th Annual Meeting.) As a result, even if the Commission eventually adopts the Revised Management Scheme (RMS) for commercial whaling, 1.8 million square miles of ocean in the Southern Hemisphere would still be closed to commercial whalers. Japan lodged an objection to establishment of the sanctuary.

The Commission passed a resolution accepting the work of the Scientific Committee on the Revised Management Procedure, completing the main scientific component of the RMS. An *ad hoc* working group discussed the other major component, a supervision and control system, during the annual meeting and in much greater detail at an intersessional meeting in Norway in January 1995. The purpose, scope, and financing of the scheme are still at issue, along with most details of its operation.

Another resolution called on IWC members to enforce their obligations under the Convention and under CITES concerning whaling and trading in whale products, to observe earlier resolutions prohibiting import of whale products from non-IWC member countries, to use products from research whaling for domestic consumption only, and to report annually on developments relevant to trade in whale meat or products.

The Commission considered three proposals for lethal research, including a new program by Japan in the North Pacific. Japan again requested a quota of 50 minke whales for small-type coastal whaling, but its resolution was defeated.

Quotas were agreed to for aboriginal subsistence whaling: 204 bowheads to be landed during 1995-98 by natives in 10 Alaska villages, with a decreasing number of strikes allowed each year; 140 gray whales for Russian natives; continuation of the quotas for minke whales off East Greenland and for fin whales off West Greenland for three years; and a total of 450 minke whales struck off West Greenland for 1995–97. The Commission also adopted a resolution instructing the Scientific Committee to investigate potential management regimes for aboriginal whaling.

The Workshop on Whale Killing Methods was to be convened in conjunction with the May 1995 annual meeting in Dublin.

Iceland, which dropped out of the IWC several years ago, is now considering whether to resume commercial whaling and whether to rejoin the Commission.

(7) Atlantic Highly Migratory Species

At its November 1994 meeting, the International Commission for the Conservation of Atlantic Tunas (ICCAT), adopted a resolution to establish a mechanism that could lead to multilateral trade measures against non-member countries deemed to have diminished the effectiveness of ICCAT conservation measures.

New quotas for bluefin tuna in the western Atlantic were established for 1995 and 1996, and a schedule developed for allocating increases or decreases in this quota among the United States, Japan, and Canada. The Commission also agreed that the current fishing mortality rate for bluefin tuna in the eastern Atlantic and the Mediterranean must be reduced. ICCAT members fishing there in 1995 are to prevent any increase in the mortality rate. Beginning in 1996, they are to reduce catches by 25 percent by 1998. Country quotas were set for the major nations fishing for swordfish in the North Atlantic.

(8) Pacific Tuna Management

Distant-water fishing nations joined the 16 members of the Forum Fisheries Agency for a conference on management of South Pacific tuna fisheries in Honiara, Solomon Islands, in December 1994. The participants agreed to hold technical consultations on scientific research, data collection, and vessel-monitoring systems, and a workshop on dockside fisheries enforcement. A recent meeting between Japan and the United States resulted in an agreement to establish an interim scientific committee for tuna and tuna-like species in the North Pacific. The committee will hold its first meeting in Japan in December 1995, with other governments and organizations invited to participate.

(9) Anadromous Species

The United States and Canada, after nearly a decade of negotiations, reached an interim agreement for the conservation and management of Canadian-origin salmon in the Yukon River drainage in December 1994. Under the aegis of the Pacific Salmon Treaty, a Yukon River panel will be established to coordinate management and administer a fund to rebuild depleted salmon stocks for the benefit of both countries. Allocation issues had not been resolved by year's end. Other negotiations under the Treaty in 1994 also failed to settle intractable disputes between the two parties.

Margaret F. Hayes

5. FORESTS

The third substantive session of the UN Commission on Sustainable Development (CSD) in April 1995 was to review progress on the implementation of the Forest Principles and the forest-related chapters of Agenda 21. This review was seen potentially as a major step forward on the issue of forests, and its importance was reflected in the many forest initiatives that took place throughout 1994.

(1) (➔) International Tropical Timber Agreement 1994

The fourth session of the UN Conference for the Renegotiation of the International Tropical Timber Agreement of 1983 was held in Geneva, 10-26 January. The successor to the 1983 Agreement, the International Tropical Timber Agreement of 1994 (ITTA 1994) was adopted and opened for signature on 1 April. It will enter into force when 12 producing countries holding 55 percent of the votes and sixteen consuming countries holding 70 percent of the votes sign "definitively" or ratify. The Agreement provides for provisional entry into force after 1 February 1995 on less onerous requirements if these conditions have not been met by that date. By year's end, two consuming countries (Japan and the United States) and 11 producing countries (mainly the small producers/exporters except for Indonesia) had signed the ITTA 1994.

The main objective of the 1983 Agreement was to provide an effective framework for cooperation and consultation between tropical-timber producing and consuming countries on all aspects of the tropical-timber economy and the expansion and diversification of trade in tropical timber. Although the main framework of the 1983 Agreement remains intact, there are a number of important changes in the ITTA 1994, partly in response to the adoption by the UN Conference on Environment and Development (UNCED) of the Non-Legally Binding Authoritative Statement of Principles for a Global Consensus on the Management, Conservation and Sustainable Development of all Types of Forests (the Forest Principles) and the relevant chapters on forests of Agenda 21. The ITTA 1994 emphasizes among its objectives the process of sustainable development; the promotion of non-discriminatory timber-trade practices; the promotion of processing in producer countries; the development of mechanisms to provide new and additional financial resources; and the promotion of access to, and the transfer of, technology, including concessional and preferential terms.

Although the ITTA 1994 retains its focus on tropical timber, its objective is to provide an effective framework for consultation, international cooperation, and policy development between producers and consumers with regard to all aspects of the world timber economy. However, widening the scope of the ITTA 1994 to encompass timber from all forests, a change strongly favoured by producers, failed to materialize. The consumers believed that this would mean negotiating a global forests convention beyond the mandate of the ITTA. However, the ITTA 1994 is to be reviewed four years after entering into force, which allows for the reintroduction of the debate on the inclusion of temperate and boreal timber.

Another contentious issue was the inclusion to the ITTA 1994 of the non-binding political commitment known as the Bali Commitment, or "Target 2000." In Bali in 1990, members of the International Tropical Timber Organization (ITTO) had agreed that by the year 2000, all exports of tropical-timber products should come from sustainably managed sources. The producers were not prepared to accept this commitment in a legally binding text and the final Agreement contains only weak obligations by producers to enhance their capacity to attain sustainable forest management by the year 2000 (Art. 1 para. (d); Art. 21 para. 4(a); preamble). In a separate Formal Statement, the consumers committed themselves to implementing guidelines for sustainable management of their forests comparable to those developed by the ITTO and to achieving sustainable management of their forests by 2000. They also affirmed that appropriate resources should be provided to developing consumer countries to achieve sustainable forest management. This Statement is to be circulated with the final text of the ITTA 1994.

To assist producers in making the necessary investments by the year 2000, the ITTA 1994 created the Bali Partnership Fund (Arts. 18 and 21), to be sustained by voluntary contributions from members and income earned from the project funding account. The International Tropical Timber Council (ITTC) will oversee the Fund and endeavour to obtain additional resources, taking into account the special needs of those countries whose economies are adversely affected by the implementation of Target 2000. The ITTA 1994 expressly recognized that the ability of such countries to implement Target 2000 will be influenced by the availability of resources from the Fund. After the adoption of the ITTA 1994, Brazil suggested that the Fund provide producers with new and additional finances in order to meet the full incremental costs of attaining Target 2000.

The concern that the ITTA 1994 would provide a justification for discriminatory or restrictive trade measures was directly addressed in Art. 36. The trade provisions in the Forest Principles were unacceptable to the consumers, partly due to their desire to avoid establishing a precedent on the role of trade measures in the operative part of a legally binding environmental instrument.

A number of delegates voiced reservations to the Agreement after its adoption, among them Brazil, the European Union, and China.

(2) 16th Session of the International Tropical Timber Council (ITTC)

At its 16th Session in Cartagena, Colombia, 16–23 May, the ITTC heard reports from the three Permanent Committees on Economic Information and Market Intelligence, Reforestation and Forest Management, and Forest Industry and from other members on the progress being made toward the Year 2000 Objective. Indonesia became the first country to formally accede to the ITTA 1994.

The main decisions adopted by the ITTC were: approval of projects, including a sustainable forestry scheme in Bolivia, rehabilitation of fire-affected forests in East Kalimantan, and the establishment of a Forest Statistical Information System; certification of all timber and timber products, with a detailed study of the market for certified timber commissioned and recognition that certification schemes should neither be discriminatory nor a basis for trade measures incompatible with General Agreement on Tariffs and Trade; and listing of internationally traded species in the appendices of the Convention on International Trade in Endangered Species of Wild Fauna and Flora (CITES), thus encouraging members to adopt a consistent approach to both the ITTA and CITES, and to consult the ITTO before making formal proposals for listing in the CITES Appendices.

(3) Convention on International Trade in Endangered Species of Wild Fauna and Flora

The 9th meeting of the Conference of the Parties to CITES was held in Fort Lauderdale, Florida, 7–18 November. The Netherlands' proposal to list mahogany as an Appendix II species was rejected 50 to 33 votes (the proposal needed a two-thirds majority for passage). An Appendix II listing would have permitted the parties to monitor the volume of international trade to prevent over-exploitation. The Secretariat recommended that mahogany be included in Appendix II with the condition that CITES enforcement be restricted to saw logs, sawed wood, and veneer.

A proposal for the establishment of a temporary working group to improve the parties' implementation of the Convention for tree species was approved. The group will address the technical and practical problems associated with implementation of tree listings, define its relationship with international organizations addressing the problem of sustainable forestry, and consider other matters referred to it by the Plants Committee, the Standing Committee, or the Secretariat, and report back at the next meeting of the Conference of the Parties.

(4) European Union Developments

An amended proposal for a Council Regulation on operations to promote tropical forests was submitted by the Commission on 10 June. Under this regulation, the Community would support actions to promote the conservation and sustainable management of tropical forests and biodiversity by providing financial and technical expertise. Particular consideration would be given to the conservation of primary tropical forests, their biodiversity, and regeneration; defining a certification system; supporting indigenous populations; research; capacity-building; and the development of buffer zones and forest management plans. All actions would be subject to prior environmental, social, economic, and cultural impact assessments. Other Community policy would have to be developed so as not to impact negatively on the conservation of tropical forests.

In relation to the Community's own forests, a regulation extending the regulation to establish a European forestry information and communication system was adopted in February. This regulation extends the setting-up period for the system until 1997. A resolution of the European Parliament on urgent measures to save European forests was adopted on 11 March. The Parliament advocated a forestry policy balancing economic uses and environmental function, stressing the need to safeguard biodiversity by restricting monocultures, reducing atmospheric pollution, imposing heavier penalties for infringement of forestry legislation, and increasing public awareness of the importance and usefulness of forests.

(5) Commission on Sustainable Development

The third substantive session of the CSD, scheduled for April 1995, was to review progress on implementation of the Forest Principles and the forest-related chapters of Agenda 21. All governments were to submit national reports on these themes to the CSD by November 1994.

At the second session of the CSD in May 1994, it became evident that forests would be a priority issue in 1995. In preparation for its April 1995 session, the CSD decided to establish an inter-sessional *ad hoc*, open-ended working group whose mandate would be: to review Chapter 11 of Agenda 21 and the Forest Principles, taking account of inputs from other forums; to take stock of inter-session activity organized by governments or international organizations on forests; to group together initiatives underway on this issue; to convey the results of inter-sessional work to the Commission; and to make recommendations on the organization of the Commission's discussions. The working group was to meet from 27 February to 3 March 1995, and consolidate work done by that time.

(6) Intergovernmental Working Group on Global Forests (IWGGF)

The First Meeting of the IWGGF, jointly organized by the Governments of Canada and Malaysia, was held in Kuala Lumpur, 18–21 April. It was attended by some 100 representatives from 15 governments, as well as several intergovernmental and non-governmental organizations (NGOs). The objective of the IWGGF is to facilitate dialogue and consolidate approaches to the management, conservation, and sustainable development of the world's forests. The consultations are not aimed at developing legally binding proposals but are intended to facilitate the review of forest related issues by the CSD at its third session in April 1995.

At its First Meeting, the IWGGF considered five key issues: forest conservation, enhancing forest cover, and the role of forests in meeting basic human needs; criteria and indicators for sustainable forest management; trade and environment; approaches to mobilizing financial resources and technology transfer; and institutional linkages. Subsequently, two additional issues were identified: participation and transparency in forest management and comprehensive cross-sectoral integration, including land use planning and management; and the influence of policies external to the traditional forest sector. These issues were further discussed and synthesis papers were produced at the Second Meeting of the IWGGF in Ottawa in October.

(7) Toward Sustainable Forestry: Preparing for the Commission on Sustainable Development 1995

An international workshop in New Delhi was hosted by India and the United Kingdom, with assistance from UN Food and Agriculture Organization (FAO), 25-27 July, in preparation for the third session of the CSD. It was attended by 39 countries, the UN Department of Policy Coordination and Sustainable Development (UN/DPCSD), and other UN international and NGOs.

The Workshop adopted a "Framework for National Reporting to the Third Session of the CSD 1995" and recommended that the Secretariat of the UN/DPCSD use this framework document when formulating the guidelines to be issued to countries in preparing their national reports. The framework is designed to assist countries by providing information about their implementation of the Forest Principles and Agenda 21 (particularly Ch. 11.)

(8) 107th Session of the FAO Council

A report on proposals for strengthening the normative role of FAO in sustainable forest management and its cooperative role in the follow-up to UNCED was presented at the 107th Session of the FAO Council, 15–24 November in Rome. The report notes with concern the increasing number of bodies pursuing action along parallel lines and, at times, working in areas within FAO's mandate. It stresses that optimum deployment of limited resources must be ensured and dispersal and duplication of efforts among diverse international institutions avoided. Accordingly, the report suggests FAO's strategy for post-UNCED forestry activities should focus on: promoting international cooperation; coordination and policy reforms;

"greening" of the world; supporting sustainable forestry by the harmonization of codes of practice, criteria, indicators, and certification systems; supporting capacity-building; and human resources development. By year's end, actions already underway to strengthen FAO's role and to receive extra funding included: a strategy that refocuses FAO's priorities for the CSD review in 1995; a meeting of experts, which advised on future FAO forestry policy; a Ministerial meeting (together with a meeting of NGOs and the private sector) in March 1995, in conjunction with the 12th session of the Committee on Forestry to advise on FAO strategy; continued priority to the Tropical Forests Action Programme; and reorientation of FAO's work towards adopting a cross-sectoral approach.

(9) First Expert Level Follow-up Meeting of the Helsinki Conference

In June 1993, in Helsinki, 33 European countries signed resolutions to commit to implementing guidelines for the sustainable management of European forests (Resolution H1) and for the conservation of their biodiversity (Resolution H2). The First Expert Level Follow-up Meeting of the Helsinki Conference, held in Geneva, 23–24 June, approved a list of six criteria for sustainable forestry in European conditions and a list of the 20 most suitable quantitative indicators to demonstrate achievement of these criteria. The six criteria (with examples of indicators in parentheses) are: maintenance and enhancement of forest resources and their contribution to global carbon cycles (area of forest, changes in volume of growing stock, total carbon storage); forest ecosystem health and vitality (amount of air pollution depositions over five years, change in defoliation); productive functions of forests, wood and non-wood (balance between growth and removals of wood over 10 years); biological diversity in forest ecosystems (change in number of threatened species); protective functions in forest management, notably soil and water; and other socio-economic functions and conditions (provision of recreation). New indicators will be added to the list as soon as new scientific information is gained, and descriptive indicators to measure the existence and effective implementation of a policy framework are being elaborated.

(10) Seminar of Experts on Sustainable Development of Boreal and Temperate Forests

After the 1993 Montreal Seminar of Experts on sustainable Development of Boreal and Temperate Forests, organized under the auspices of the Conference on Security and Cooperation in Europe, there were three follow-up meetings during 1994 in New Delhi, Olympia, and Tokyo. An agreement was reached at the Tokyo meeting on seven measurable criteria and indicators of sustainable forest management. Areas of convergence with the Helsinki process were explored at the Olympia meeting, although further steps towards a merging of these two processes had not yet been taken at year's end. A final meeting was to be held in Santiago in early 1995 when a resolution should have been passed for the formal adoption of the criteria and indicators.

(11) World Bank Forest Policy Implementation Review

The United Kingdom Tropical Forest Forum hosted the European consultation of the World Bank Forest Policy Review on 3 May, in London. This meeting was one of a series of consultations being held on several continents to discuss the Bank's Draft Review Paper. Key issues that emerged from the review were: the need to expand and sustain stakeholder participation in projects; the need to integrate forestry projects into the wider poverty reduction; natural resource management strategies; and the need to improve environmental and social assessment procedures, as well as the conservation and utilization of tropical forests when Bank policy restricted financing of commercial logging. The need for a policy on dry, temperate, and boreal forests, as current policy is tropical-forest orientated, was recognized. The Bank accepted that its policy provided insufficient detail and guidance in many geographic and subject areas, insufficient technical expertise, and a restricted ability to lend only to governments.

NGOs criticized the Bank's Review Paper for failing to examine the impact of the Bank's non-forest sector lending, its review methodology, poor analysis of land tenure issues and forest conservation projects, weak treatment of indigenous peoples and temperate forest lending, and a flawed approach to plantations.

(12) World Commission on Forests and Sustainable Development

Efforts to establish an independent World Commission on Forests and Sustainable Development continued in 1994. Rather than seeking a UN mandate for the Commission, the Inter-Action Council of Former Heads of State and Government was invited to serve as a moral and political launching pad for the Commission. At its 12th annual session, the Council appointed two Co-Chairs, former Minister of Environment and Population of Indonesia, Prof. Emil Salim, and former Prime Minister of Sweden, Ambassador Ola Ullsten. The Council also listed the purposes of the Commission as increasing awareness about the environmental and socio-economic roles of forests; promoting consensus on data, science, and policy; and building confidence between North and South on forest issues. The Co-Chairs were in the process of selecting members of the Commission and establishing the Secretariat (to be based in Geneva) at year's end. It was hoped that the Commission's operations would begin in early 1995 and that its report will be completed by 1996 in time for the five-year review of UNCED.

(13) Forest Stewardship Council (FSC)

The FSC, officially inaugurated in October 1993 and based in Oaxaca, Mexico, aims to promote forest stewardship through a voluntary accreditation program for certifiers of forest products. The FSC evaluates, accredits, and monitors certifiers based on their adherence to the FSC Principles and Guidelines. The Principles are designed to ensure that all forests are managed in ways that are environmentally appropriate, socially beneficial, and economically viable. The FSC also encourages the development of national and regional forest management standards, as well as national certification capacity, by encouraging the development of certification initiatives worldwide.

At the FSC Board Meeting on 7 June in Oaxaca, the final drafts of the FSC Principles and Guidelines, the statutes, membership criteria, and the certifier accreditation procedures document were reviewed. The statutes were approved and ratified in August, although further consultation remained necessary on Principle 10 relating to plantations. NGO concern that membership criteria might not prevent bad operators from joining appears to have been eased by requiring prospective members to provide written evidence in support of the FSC and its aims.

The year saw growing collaboration with other certification bodies, such as LEMBAGA, the ecolabelling institute of Indonesia, asking for assistance from the FSC in drawing up forest-management standards and in developing procedures for accrediting Indonesian certifiers. A certifier program was in an early stage of development in Bolivia, and programs were being considered in the Solomon Islands, Sweden, and Mexico. Four certifiers applied for FSC accreditation, and a first draft of FSC's accreditation protocol was produced.

(14) Centre for International Forestry Research (CIFOR)

CIFOR, an autonomous international research organization registered with the UN, was established in March 1993. At its headquarters in Bogor, Indonesia, staff with global expertise will work to define the issues and design strategic research to solve forest problems in the tropics and subtropics of the developing world. CIFOR aims to improve the scientific basis for balanced forest management and develop policies and technologies for sustainable use and management of forest goods and services. During 1994, CIFOR progressed in forming international partnerships for strategic forest research, developing programs, and refining its future role in world forestry through world-wide consultations.

Amanda Wells
Ruth Mackenzie
Farhana Yamin

6. SOIL/DESERTIFICATION

(1) Introduction

Local, regional, and national economies depend on natural or managed ecosystems as a fundamental resource for obtaining food and materials. Soil and land are at the heart of agricultural production, mineral extraction, waste disposal, and human settlements. Their use, quality, and scale of protection are influenced by laws enacted to address not only soil or land but also other concerns such as air or water quality, waste disposal, product specifications, climate change, and biological resources.

1994 was marked by a growing awareness, both at the international and the domestic levels, of the urgency of soil protection generally, and of addressing desertification specifically. Desertification is a broad term referring to a decline in soil fertility and structure and the degradation of soil, rangelands, and irrigated cropland. Desertification affects 70 percent of all drylands and one-quarter of the total land area of the world.

(2) Multilateral Conventions

(a) Desertification Convention

Eighty-five countries and the European Union signed the (➔) United Nations Convention to Combat Desertification in Those Countries Experiencing Serious Drought and/or Desertification, Particularly in Africa on 14–15 October. The Convention acknowledges the strong link between land management, sustainable agriculture, and desertification, and the need to change land-management practices. As the first post-Rio "sustainable development convention," it is notable for its innovative approach in recognizing the physical, biological, and socio-economic aspects of desertification; the importance of demand-driven technology transfer; and the involvement of local populations in the development of national, subregional, and regional action programs.

A 26-paragraph preamble acknowledges that desertification and drought are problems of global dimensions, affecting all regions of the world. Therefore, joint action of the international community is needed to "combat desertification and/or mitigate the effects of drought." It also notes that the problems are more prevalent in developing countries, particularly the least developed ones. The preamble reaffirms the commitments of developed countries outlined in Ch. 33 of Agenda 21, including the need to provide other governments new and additional funding and access to technology.

Pursuant to Art. 4, all parties undertake to adopt an integrated approach to address the physical, biological, and socio-economic aspects of the problem and to give due attention to the situation of affected developing country parties with regard to international trade, marketing arrangements, and debt, with a view to establishing an enabling international economic environment conducive to the promotion of sustainable development. Obligations of affected country parties (Art. 5) include giving due priority to combating those phenomena by allocating resources and establishing strategies, promoting awareness and facilitating participation of local populations, strengthening existing legislation or enacting new laws, and establishing long-term policies. Article 6 obliges developed country parties to actively support the efforts of affected developing country parties; to provide substantial financial resources and other forms of support to assist them in developing and implementing their own long-term plans and strategies; to encourage the mobilization of funding from the private sector and other non-governmental sources; and to promote and facilitate access to appropriate knowledge, know-how, and technology. Article 7 gives priority for action to Africa.

Part III of the Convention calls for extensive cooperation on technical, scientific, and institutional matters among affected parties at the regional and subregional levels. Specifically, parties also agree to undertake to promote, finance, and/or facilitate the financing of the transfer, acquisition, adaptation, and development of environmentally sound, economically viable, and socially acceptable technologies.

Articles 20 and 21 on financial resources and financial mechanisms, respectively, may be the two most important articles of the Convention and were the cause of intense consultations throughout the negotiations. In Art. 20, parties undertake to make every effort to ensure that adequate financial resources are available for programmes. Article 21 establishes a Global Mechanism to promote the mobilization and channelling of substantial financial resources, including the transfer of technology, on grant and/or concessional terms, to affected developing country parties.

Part IV of the Convention establishes a Conference of the Parties, Permanent Secretariat to the Convention, and Committee on Science and Technology (Arts. 22, 23, and 24, respectively).

Part V of the Convention ("Procedures") provides, *inter alia*, for the parties to the Convention to report on activities they have undertaken to implement their obligations, the resolution of questions with regard to implementation, and the settlement of disputes. It also addresses the status of annexes, the procedure for amendments to the Convention and to annexes, and voting.

The Convention contains regional implementation annexes for Africa, Asia, Latin America and the Caribbean, and the Northern Mediterranean. There was no annex for the Australian or North American continents. The four annexes differ quite substantially in their content as they reflect different regional realities, although they cover the same range of issues. All describe the particular conditions of their regions followed by specific points for action. The 19-article annex for Africa is the most elaborate and the only one to articulate concrete commitments for financial contributions. It notes the high proportion of arid, semi-arid, and dry sub-humid areas in that continent, stresses that the large number of affected countries are landlocked and that because of the widespread poverty prevalent in most of those countries, significant amounts of external assistance is required to allow them to pursue their development objectives.

(b) The Alpine Convention

The Alpine Convention came into force in 1994 upon ratification by Austria, Germany, and Liechtenstein. By the end of the year, Austria, Germany, Liechtenstein, and Switzerland had approved the text of a draft Protocol on the protection of natural landscapes, which includes provisions on soil protection. With governments of the other Alpine countries expected to ratify in 1995, the Protocol was expected to be adopted in 1995.

(3) The United Nations

(a) Habitat II

The first session of the Preparatory Committee (PrepCom) for the Second United Nations Conference on Human Settlements (Habitat II) took place 11–22 April. The overriding objective of Habitat II, which will be held in Istanbul in June 1996, is to increase global awareness of the problems and potentials of human settlements as important vectors of social progress and economic growth, and to commit world leaders to making cities, towns, and villages healthy, safe, and sustainable. By year's end, more than 50 countries had established, or were in the process of establishing, national preparatory committees for the Conference. Participating countries are to design, adopt, and begin implementing national action plans that address the issue of human settlements in both urban and rural areas, taking into consideration environmental issues. Countries also are to strengthen the capacity of institutions at all levels to monitor shelter conditions and urbanization processes using a minimum set of substantially uniform and consistent indicators.

In December 1994, the UN General Assembly adopted a resolution that approved the recommendations of the first PrepCom and gave additional support to the process, including the convening of an additional session of the Preparatory Committee early in 1996, beyond the second session scheduled for 24 April to 5 May 1995.

(b) Commission on Sustainable Development

During the second session of the UN Commission on Sustainable Development (CSD), 16–27 May, delegates examined implementation of several Agenda 21 chapters relating to soil and land, including Chs. 7

(human settlements), 19 (toxic chemicals), 20 (hazardous wastes), 21 (solid wastes and sewage), and 22 (radioactive wastes). The CSD adopted decisions on protecting and promoting human health, human settlements, toxic chemicals, hazardous wastes, freshwater, and radioactive wastes. The CSD also adopted a decision on intersessional work, which calls for the establishment of an *ad hoc* open-ended intersessional working group to examine lands, desertification, forests, and biodiversity. The CSD was to address these sectoral issues in 1995.

The CSD recommended that governments strengthen the sound management of chemicals throughout their life-cycles; identify toxic, persistent, and bio-accumulative chemicals; and coordinate the work on chemical safety by concerned sectors. The United States and Canada each made separate proposals on air pollutants that eventually affect soil quality. The United States proposed a global phase-out of leaded gasoline and Canada wanted special reference to long-range transport of air pollution to the Arctic, but the CSD accepted neither proposal.

(4) The "Helsinki Process"

The "Helsinki Process," or the Ministerial Conference for the Protection of Forests in Europe, a forum used by industrialized countries since 1990, developed general guidelines for the sustainable management of forests in Europe. A core set of criteria and indicators to evaluate progress toward sustainable forestry was adopted at the first expert level follow-up meeting in June 1994. The criteria included: (1) maintenance and appropriate enhancement of protective functions in forest management (notably soil and water); (2) maintenance, conservation, and appropriate enhancement of biological diversity in forest ecosystems; and (3) maintenance and appropriate enhancement of forest resources and their contribution to global carbon cycles.

(5) European Union

The European Community (EC) continued its efforts to restrict or regulate farm practices, especially the use of fertilizers and other agricultural chemicals. The challenge is to devise farming and forestry systems in harmony with the soil and prevailing climate. Some soils are subject to inappropriate use or management practices, thereby causing environmental problems such as nitrate leaching. Intensive application of manure has led to water pollution and eutrophication of inland waters and coastal zones of the North Sea. Under the 1987 Rhine Action Plan and the 1990 North Sea Action Plan, EC countries agreed to seek 50 percent reductions in the nitrogen and phosphate levels in rivers and the North Sea by 1995, using 1985 as a baseline. Implementation of these programs has been slow in the agricultural sector, which accounts for over two-thirds of the nutrient inputs within the North Sea watershed.

(6) *National Developments*

(a) *Belgium*

The European Court of Justice (ECJ) held that Belgium had failed to fulfill its obligations under Council Directive 86/278/EEC on Sewage Sludge Used in Agriculture (*Commission v. Belgium*, C-260/93). The ECJ decision came nearly five years after the June 1989 date of entry into force of the Directive. Though the regional governments of Flanders and Brussels had implemented the Directive, the Walloon region and the national government had failed to do so.

(b) *France*

In January, France proposed a framework law on the protection of the rural environment that would provide tax breaks to farmers participating in regional land management programs. In June, the Environment Ministry noted that it was developing a framework soil law to be presented in 1995. The law will address prevention, management, and clean-up of contaminated sites. France was also continuing its program to identify local contaminated sites and establish a priority clean-up list at the national level. Each *département* was to furnish the central government with a description of currently known contaminated sites within their jurisdictions. This list will complement the inventory of contaminated sites that was published in January 1993.

(c) *Germany*

A new draft Federal Soil Protection Act (*Bundesbodenschutzgesetz*) would require polluters to clean up contaminated sites. Land owners would have to ensure that installations do not pose a risk to the soil, and preventive action would have to be taken against possible future contamination. The bill does not create new licensing or authorization procedures. It does, however, provide uniform standards for assessing soil pollution that take prospective land use into consideration.

(d) *Japan*

Advisors to the Environment Agency recommended establishment of soil and water standards for 15 additional chemicals and metals, including benzene, tiobenkalb (a pesticide), selenium, and several chlorinated ethanes. In February 1994, the standards for lead and copper were strengthened. When contaminants exceed the official tolerances, however, the Environment Agency cannot order a business or individuals to take remedial action; instead, it may merely "instruct" them to do so. Nevertheless, the stronger regulations caused an increase in clean-up technology imports from the United States and Germany and an increase in domestic companies working on soil-cleaning technologies and systems.

(e) The Netherlands

The first parts of the Soil Protection Act (*Wet Bodenscherming*) entered into force on 15 May. The Act, which incorporates the Interim Soil Cleanup Act of 1983 and the Soil Protection Act of 1986, imposes responsibility for investigation and clean-up of contaminated sites on the polluters or owners of the sites. Provinces now are authorized to issue a "clean-up order" in cases where companies refuse to act, and standards for soil clean-up have been clarified and made more stringent.

Dutch industry was continuing a five-year voluntary Soil Clean-up of Operative Industrial Sites program, with over 5,000 companies making commitments to take remedial action or isolate contaminated sites. As of 1994, the industry program was operating in all 12 provinces.

(f) The Russian Federation

Russia and Mongolia agreed to develop sustainable land-use programs for the Lake Baikal watershed, a 150 million-acre region encompassing parts of Mongolia and three Russian provinces. The plans call for 25 different zoning categories, ranging from industrial park to scientific reserve. In November, Russia and China began negotiations on a similar agreement for the Ussuri River basin. The Altai Republic in Siberia also started work on an "ecological-economic zone" concept. If adopted and enforced, these programs will protect a combined area more than twice the size of California. The projects are modeled after the Adirondack State Park in New York, the first area in the United States to have a regional land-use plan.

On 17 August, Russia and Germany concluded an agreement on cleaning up contaminated sites in both countries. The bilateral program will also support the search for solutions to disposal of hazardous mercury waste, recycling of toxic industrial byproducts, and development of dioxin-free production technologies; it will also help secure jobs for scientists and technicians in Russia and Eastern Germany, and clean up sites polluted under the communist regime.

(g) The United Kingdom (UK)

To review policy options with regard to land clean-up, the relationship between a statutory framework and common law, and extension of strict liability, the Department of Environment published two papers in 1994, called "Paying for our Past," and "Framework for Contaminated Land." The former paper reviews arrangements for a contaminated lands registry and the creation of a national priority list of contaminated sites. It supports a clean-up policy that deals "with unacceptable actual or perceived threats to health, safety, or the environment, taking into consideration the actual or intended use of the site." If the category of use changes, further clean-up at that time would be required. This "suitable for use" doctrine was carried over into the later "Framework" policy paper, however, the idea of a national registry was rejected. The UK has 187,000 acres of contaminated land.

The UK was modifying its rural and sub-urban land-use regulations. New national planning guidelines were issued to limit the scale of out-of-town developments. Housing and transport planning to favor pedestrian and bicycles would be encouraged, leading to reduced reliance on private cars. The program is designed to help implement the UK's international commitments under Agenda 21 and the UN Climate Change Convention.

(h) The United States

The US Department of Agriculture's Soil Conservation Service was renamed the Natural Resource Conservation Service. Although its mandate remained essentially unchanged, the renaming may signal a shift in future federal agricultural land policy.

At the state level, bills were introduced in over 30 state legislatures to protect private property rights against excessive regulation. In order to protect human and environmental health and safety, many federal, state, and local laws restrict or regulate the types of activities that may be conducted on private land. These restrictions may lead to a decline in property values, an action that could be considered a government "taking" of property. Several new laws require state agencies to ensure that new rules and regulations do not constitute a "taking" of land, however, by year's end no state had approved a formula for compensating landowners when regulations cause the value of property to fall.

Eric S. Howard

7. POPULATION: THE UNITED NATIONS POPULATION FUND (UNFPA)

(1) Introduction

Much attention during 1994 was focused on the Fund's participation in the preparation for, and organization of, the International Conference on Population and Development (ICPD) in Cairo from 5–13 September. In addition to ICPD, the UNFPA continued its activities as part of the UN system follow-up to the United Nations Conference on Environment and Development (UNCED), in Rio de Janeiro in June 1992, and its support of the country programmes that are key in assisting governments to develop strategies and action programmes that integrate population concerns and sustainable development.

(2) International Conference on Population and Development

The third and last session of the Preparatory Committee for the ICPD took place in New York from 4-22 April. With about 95 percent of the text of the draft Programme of Action approved, the remaining parts were negotiated at the ICPD itself. The ICPD preparatory process embraced numerous other activities at the regional and sub-regional levels involving vast numbers of non-governmental organizations (NGOs) and public and private institutions of various kinds. The resulting Programme of Action of the International Conference on Population and Development (*see* (➔) Report of the International Conference on Population and Development, A/CONF.171/13, 18 October 1994) has several outstanding features. It is more consciously people-focused than earlier documents of its kind. The center of attention is the improvement of the quality of life of all people. It places population issues firmly in the centre of all efforts at sustainable development, and is thus a further advance on Agenda 21. By placing the concept of reproductive health, including family planning, at its center, it is the most comprehensive and inclusive document on population ever adopted. It further recognizes the need to empower women with knowledge, skills, and self-confidence necessary to participate fully in the development process.

Environmental issues are dealt with in Ch. 3, "Interrelationship between population, sustained economic growth and sustainable development," of the ICPD Programme of Action. There is a close affinity between this chapter and Ch. 5 of Agenda 21, "Demographic dynamics and sustainability." Each document refers to the other, as, for example, when section C of the ICPD declares its objectives to be consistent with those of Agenda 21. Although the two chapters have a slightly different emphasis, the main thrust of both is similar and mutually reinforcing. Agenda 21 has the environment at the centre of its focus, whereas people and population issues stand at the centre of the ICPD Programme of Action. This is reflected in the sections A, B, and C of Ch. 3, which are entitled respectively "Integrating population and development strategies," "Population, sustained economic growth and poverty," and "Population and environment."

Three more general aspects of the ICPD process of relevance to international affairs should also be noted. First, together with earlier and future UN sponsored conferences such as UNCED, the human rights conference, and the forthcoming conferences on women in Beijing in 1995 and on human settlements (Habitat II) in Istanbul in 1996, the ICPD has been instrumental in shaping the international agenda for many years ahead. Second, under the new conditions brought about by the disappearance of the Cold War, questions have been asked about how rights, obligations, and responsibilities should be divided between the constituent members of the international community, including international organizations and NGOs, and what the international order should look like. Together with other UN conferences, the ICPD has potentially lent a helping hand in defining issues and allocating responsibilities, and perhaps above all, in building consensus about goals and policies at the international level. Last, like other UN conferences, the ICPD process has also contributed to the mobilization and participation of civil society and the private sector in the affairs of the international community, and thus helped foster transparency and accountability at the international level.

(3) The Follow-Up to UNCED

UNFPA contributed to a number of reports on the progress of the implementation of various chapters and clusters of chapters of Agenda 21 at the second substantive session of the Commission on Sustainable Development (CSD) in New York in May. UNFPA authored the report on Ch. 5 of Agenda 21. These reports will be incorporated into a comprehensive report by the UN Secretary-General, who will submit it to the next meeting of the CSD in April 1995.

(4) Global Activities

The UNFPA continued its work on a major, multi-year project to examine the relationship between poverty, environmental degradation, and population pressures in different habitats. The results of the project will assist UNFPA in providing governments in the developing world with policy advice and recommendations.

UNFPA also granted support to a number of new projects during 1994, including projects on environmental refugees, population, land management and environmental change, integrating population factors in strategies for sustainable development, and the relationships between environment, consumption, and population.

(5) Regional and National Activities

(a) Asia and the Pacific

The South Pacific Regional Environment Programme continued work on the population-environment project that UNFPA funded in the South Pacific (*see* 4 *YbIEL* 280 (1993); 3 *YbIEL* 337 (1992)). UNFPA also contributed to the development of Natural Environmental Management Strategies in several of the island states of the South Pacific. In the country programme of Thailand, several projects started in 1993 continued into 1994. These included projects on urbanization and migration; women, population, and development; and an international seminar on population and environmental protection. As in 1993, UNFPA projects in the Philippines focused on awareness-raising activities and education targeting strategic groups. Similar awareness-raising activities in Nepal continued to receive UNFPA support during 1994.

(b) Latin America and the Caribbean

A major project that UNFPA initiated in 1993 on women, population, and environment at the local level in El Salvador and Honduras continued during 1994. Regional workshops on population and environment issues also received UNFPA support.

(c) Arab States, Europe, and Africa

A significant population-environment project dealing with environment, internal migration, and the spatial distribution of the population commenced in Morocco in 1994. A colloquium on population-environment issues in the Maghreb states was organized with UNFPA support. Several projects with significant population-environment content were started in Africa.

(6) Conclusions

With the ICPD Programme of Action as a base, UNFPA began a review of its activities, including those in the field of population and environment. The Fund will gradually increase the scope and range of these activities with the aim of contributing significantly to the common store of knowledge and understanding of the complicated relationship between population, environment, and sustainable development.

Jyoti Shankar Singh

IX. INTERNATIONAL ECONOMY AND THE ENVIRONMENT

1. INTERNATIONAL TRADE RULES, WORLD MARKET CONDITIONS, AND ENVIRONMENTAL EFFECTS

There was considerable activity in 1994 relating to international trade institutions and the impact of trade rules on the environment. The most notable activity took place in respect to the World Trade Organization (WTO), which on January 1, 1995, succeeded the General Agreement on Tariffs and Trade (GATT) as the international organization principally responsible for governance of the multilateral trading system.

(1) Environment-Related Matters and the GATT-WTO

On April 15, the Final Act Embodying the Results of the Uruguay Round of Trade Negotiations was signed by Ministers at Marrakesh. The Final Act included the texts of the new WTO-related agreements. The WTO agreements with specific implications for the environment have been described in prior *Yearbook* reports on this subject.

(a) The Marrakesh (➔) Decision on Trade and Environment

The Ministers took a Decision on Trade and Environment in connection with the Marrakesh signing of the WTO. In this Decision, the Ministers directed

> the first meeting of the General Council of the WTO to establish a Committee on Trade and Environment open to all members of the WTO to report to the first biennial meeting of the Ministerial Conference after the entry into force of the WTO when the work and terms of reference of the Committee will be reviewed, in light of the recommendations of the Committee. . . .

The Marrakesh Decision stated that the Trade Negotiating Committee Decision of December 15, 1993 (*see* 4 *YbIEL* 283 (1993)), would constitute the terms of reference of the Committee. The Decision said that within such terms of reference, the Committee would address a number of matters, including the relationship between the international trading system, on the one hand, and taxes for environmental purposes, technical standards, and packaging and labelling requirements, on the other. The Committee would also consider transparency, the relationship between dispute settlement mechanisms in the multilateral trading system and multilateral environmental agreements, and the effect of environmental agreements on market access (especially in relation to developing countries). The Committee would further consider the work program envisaged by the Decision on Trade in Services and the Environment, and the relevant provisions of the TRIPS Agreement, as well as arrangements for relations with intergovernmental and non-governmental organizations.

(b) GATT Dispute Settlement Panels

Two GATT dispute settlement panel decisions concerning environment-related measures were rendered in 1994. Neither of these decisions was made under the new WTO dispute settlement procedure and neither was adopted in 1994 by the GATT Executive Council. The United States has objected to adoption of the Tuna II panel report, and the European Union has objected to adoption of the CAFE Standards panel report. The status of these decisions under the WTO may engender controversy, and the Preparatory Committee established to consider GATT-WTO transitional issues may have this status issue as one of its agenda items.

(i) (➔) United States-Restrictions on Imports of Tuna (Tuna II) Panel Report

This case involved a complaint by the European Economic Community (EEC) and Netherlands, as co-complainants, against the United States. The complaint of the EEC and Netherlands was brought following the decision of the government of Mexico not to seek adoption of the panel report on the same subject matter rendered in its favor in 1991 (*Tuna I*). In *Tuna II*, the complainants again challenged the GATT-legality of the US Marine Mammal Protection Act (MMPA). This legislation, *inter alia*, requires the imposition of restrictions on the import of tuna from nations harvesting in the Eastern Tropical Pacific when their harvesting practices yield an unacceptably high mortality rate for marine mammals (including dolphins). It also requires the imposition of a secondary embargo on nations that import tuna from nations subject to the primary embargo.

As in *Tuna I*, the panel concluded that US MMPA import restrictions should not be considered internal regulations applied at the nation's border pursuant to GATT Art. III and Note ad Art. III since the United States was not attempting to regulate tuna as a product, but rather was attempting to regulate tuna harvesting methods that could not "have any impact on the inherent quality of tuna as a product" (para. 5.9). The panel found that MMPA embargoes are import restrictions prohibited by GATT Art. XI. It then addressed US arguments that its measures are justifiable, even if inconsistent with Art. XI, because they are taken under Art. XX(g) to conserve dolphins (an exhaustible natural resource), or because they are necessary under Art. XX(b) to protect the life and health of dolphins.

Distinguishing *Tuna II* from *Tuna I*, both the United States and the co-complainants sought to use the negotiating history, terms, and practice of states with respect to treaties other than the GATT to aid in interpretation of Art. XX(b) and (g), and to address whether those provisions permit the imposition of extraterritorial measures. The panel, however, rejected these arguments on the basis of the rules of interpretation of the Vienna Convention on the Law of Treaties. According to the panel, since the parties to the GATT and the parties to the other referenced treaties are not coextensive, the other treaties could not be used as general GATT interpretative sources. The panel noted that a number of the referenced treaties were entered into after the GATT. It also said that practice under the various other treaties could not be used to generally interpret the GATT since practice under other treaties was not practice under the GATT. The panel finally noted that the other referenced treaties and their negotiating history could not be used as a supplementary interpretative source since: (a) the use of supplementary sources is confined to situations that the panel did not consider present in this case; and (b) none of the references cited by the disputing parties appeared to the panel to provide clear support for any particular contention.

The panel found that US embargo measures were not taken with the primary purpose of conserving exhaustible natural resources since the embargo measures would not be effective in controlling dolphin mortality unless harvesting countries changed their policies and practices. The panel said that while parties to the GATT are permitted to take trade measures to implement policies relating to conservation within their own jurisdictions, the balance of rights and obligations among parties to the GATT would be seriously impaired if parties were permitted to take trade measures to force changes to policies within the jurisdiction of other nations. The panel concluded that since the US measures were directed to forcing other countries to change their policies, and not directed primarily to the conservation of resources, they were not justifiable under Art. XX(g).

The United States and EEC agreed that protection of the life of dolphins could come within the scope of necessary measures under Art. XX(b), but differed as to whether measures could be taken to protect the life of living things outside the territory of a party. The panel noted that under certain other provisions of the GATT, parties could accord different treatment to products of different origin. The panel found that "[i]t could not therefore be said that the GATT proscribed in an absolute manner such measures" (para. 5.32). The panel also noted that under general principles of international law, states are not prohibited from regulating the conduct of their own nationals with respect to the treatment of animals outside their own territory. The panel concluded that US policies, insofar as they related to US nationals and vessels, fell within the range of policies covered by Art. XX(b).

The panel went on to examine whether the primary and secondary embargo measures of the United States were "necessary" to protect the life and health of dolphins. The panel referred to prior GATT panel decisions that took a narrow view of the Art. XX "necessary" standard, requiring parties that rely on the exception to take the least GATT-inconsistent measures reasonably available to them. The panel followed the same reasoning with respect to Art. XX(b) as it had with respect to Art. XX(g), finding that the United States was relying on forced changes to the policies and practices of other nations in order to make its own policies succeed. The panel found that while Art. XX(b) did not expressly prohibit such conduct, trade measures taken by one GATT party to force changes to the policies of other parties within their own jurisdictions would seriously impair the objectives of the GATT. The panel recommended that the United States bring its measures into conformity with its obligations under the GATT.

Although there are subtle differences in the reasoning of the *Tuna I* and *Tuna II* panels, from the perspective of environmental non-governmental organizations (NGOs) there does not appear any significant advance in *Tuna II* toward permitting countries in the GATT-WTO to maintain unilateral extraterritorial measures.

(ii) US CAFE Standards Panel Report

The Corporate Average Fuel Economy (CAFE) Standards dispute involved a claim by the European Community (EC) against the United States. The EC alleged that the US luxury tax on automobiles, the US gas-guzzler tax, and US legislation governing automobile fleet fuel economy, discriminate against automobiles imported into the United States from the EC. The luxury tax is imposed on the retail sale of automobiles. The tax rate is 10 percent of the amount by which the sales price of the automobile exceeds $30,000 (which base, per a 1993 amendment to the legislation, is indexed for inflation). The gas-guzzler tax is imposed on manufacturers whose automobiles within designated model types fail to achieve specified fuel economy standards (*i.e.*, that exceed a base fuel economy threshold). The tax is imposed with respect to each automobile and is disclosed to the consumer. CAFE legislation requires manufacturers and importers of automobiles to achieve certain fuel economy standards across the range of their US production/sales (but not exports), as well as their imports. Corporate fleet fuel economy is determined through a series of complex measures established by the US Environmental Protection Agency (EPA). For companies that are both manufacturers in the United States and importers, average fuel economy is calculated separately for imported and US-produced automobiles.

The EC contended that the luxury tax was inconsistent with US obligations under GATT Art. III:2, which requires equivalent treatment of "like products" of domestic and foreign manufacture. The EC contended that automobiles above and below the indexed $30,000 threshold are "like products," that the threshold is not based on objective standards, and that it has the effect of discriminating against EC producers that tend to export automobiles exceeding the threshold to the United States.

The panel decided that the principal criterion to be used in determining whether different and less favorable treatment applied to imported products (with similar characteristics to domestic products) is whether the distinction is made "so as to afford protection to domestic production" (referring to GATT Art. III:1) (para. 5.9). This criterion was held to be inconsistent with Art. III:2. The panel observed that the term "so as to afford protection" suggested both "aim and effect." "Aim" indicates a desired outcome as opposed to an incidental consequence, and "effect" refers to according greater competitive opportunities to domestic products. The panel said that the "effect of a measure in terms of trade flows was not relevant for the purposes of Art. III, since a change in the volume or proportion of imports could be due to many factors other than government measures" (para. 5.10). The panel found that, despite statements by some US legislators suggesting a protectionist intent, the establishment of the $30,000 threshold was consistent with the aim of raising revenues from the sale of "luxury" products, and that there was considerable uncertainty as to the impact of the tax on domestic as opposed to foreign products. The panel also found that there was not conclusive evidence that a change in conditions had occurred favoring US producers, and that EC manufacturers could export less expensive automobiles to the United States if they so chose. The panel concluded that the luxury tax was not adopted so as to afford domestic protection and that automobiles above and below the threshold could not, for the purposes of the luxury tax, be considered "like products." The luxury tax was not inconsistent with Art. III:2.

The EC claimed that the gas-guzzler tax is also inconsistent with GATT Art. III:2 because automobiles with different fuel consumption characteristics are nevertheless "like products," and because the gas-guzzler tax falls disproportionately on EC produced automobiles. The United States argued that the tax was based on objectively justifiable distinctions aimed at a policy other than protection of domestic production. It further said that even if the tax was inconsistent with Art. III:2, it was justified under Art. XX(g) as related to the conservation of fossil fuels.

The panel invoked the criterion it used in respect to the luxury tax, *i.e.*, whether the measure was adopted so as to afford protection to domestic production. The panel noted that even though the tax affected few cars (since it was complementary to the CAFE standards), and that other more efficient measures might have been used for conservation purposes, that the measure did not target foreign automobiles. The panel noted that at the time the tax was adopted, US manufacturers could not achieve the relevant fuel consumption threshold. The panel also found that the tax did not have the effect of protecting domestic production because EC manufacturers had the technology to meet the relevant threshold. The panel concluded moreover that the methodology used by the United States in determining fuel economy did not have the aim or effect of protecting domestic production, and that the exclusion of certain types of vehicles (*e.g.*, light trucks) did not have such aim or effect (even though including all vehicles might have advanced fuel conservation policies). In light of its determination regarding Art. III, the panel did not consider the US argument concerning Art. XX(g) with respect to the gas-guzzler tax.

The panel examined the claim of the EC that US CAFE standards are inconsistent with GATT Art. III:2 and :4. The EC contended the CAFE standards are inherently discriminatory since specialized manufacturers of imported cars may not use the fuel economy of cars that meet the requisite CAFE standards to offset the fuel consumption of cars that fail to meet these standards, as may their US counterparts. The EC argued that its manufacturers suffered a disproportionate impact from the regulations. The United States asserted that its regulations did not afford protection to domestic production, and that there was in fact no disproportionate impact.

The panel decided that US CAFE standards are a regulatory requirement affecting the internal sale of a product within the meaning of GATT Art. III:4, and not a tax within the meaning of Art. III:2. The panel found that the part of the CAFE standards that requires separate fleet accounting for foreign and domestic products places imported cars at a competitive disadvantage. It precludes US manufacturers of large cars from including small foreign-produced cars in their fleet calculations (thus discriminating against foreign small-car manufacturers), and likewise precludes foreign manufacturers of large cars from including US-produced small cars in their averaging (thus discriminating against foreign large car manufacturers). The panel said the possible adverse impact of the regulations on US large-car manufacturers (because they may not average with small foreign cars) could not be used to counterbalance the discriminatory impact imposed on foreign manufacturers. The panel decided that separate foreign and domestic fleet accounting was inconsistent with GATT Art. III:4. The panel similarly concluded that CAFE regulations that distinguished between products based on the foreign or US ownership of the manufacturer could not be consistent with GATT Art. III:4 since the distinctions in the regulations are not directly related to cars as "products."

The panel then addressed whether the provisions found contrary to Art. III:4 could be justified by the United States under Art. XX(g). It found that conservation of gasoline was within the range of policies mentioned in that article. The panel observed that the question whether the US measures were primarily related to the conservation of resources was not addressed to

CAFE standards in general, but only to the discriminatory elements the panel had found to be inconsistent with Art. III:4. The panel found that separate foreign and domestic fleet accounting did not serve conservation objectives (moreover, evidence suggested that by reducing imports of small foreign cars, separate accounting was contrary to the conservation objectives). The panel noted that CAFE regulations might apply to the fleets of foreign manufacturers in the absence of separate foreign and domestic fleet accounting, and that a CAFE arrangement that excluded separate fleet accounting and applied to import car manufacturers may, if properly designed, meet the conservation objectives of Art. XX(g). The panel rejected a further EC claim that the combined effect on EC products of the luxury tax, gas-guzzler tax, and CAFE standards constituted an additional inconsistency under Art. III.

In summary, the panel found only the separate domestic and foreign fleet accounting provisions of the CAFE standards to be inconsistent with the General Agreement. It may be hoped that this decision will alleviate some of the concerns that environmental NGOs have expressed with respect to the impact of the GATT on progressive environmental regulation.

(c) Subcommittee on Trade and Environment

In addition to the Marrakesh Decision and the panel reports, environment-related activity at the GATT in 1994 included several meetings of the Sub-Committee on Trade and Environment (the Subcommittee will be formally transformed into the Committee on Trade and Environment at the first meeting of the WTO General Council in 1995). The initial meetings of the Sub-Committee were largely devoted to administrative matters and the formulation of a work program. There also were important substantive discussions, however, in particular at the meeting of 15–16 September. Sub-Committee members debated the subject of charges and taxes for environmental purposes, including the application of border tax adjustments. They discussed the trade effects of environment-related product regulations, including recycling and reuse requirements, as well as eco-labelling measures. The role of NGOs in the Committee's activities was also actively debated. The United States took the lead in urging an enhanced role for NGOs, including their participation in meetings. Although most delegations appeared to recognize the need to increase transparency at the WTO, there was clear resistance to a participatory role from a majority of Committee members. The Chair of the Committee was authorized to hold informal consultations on this important issue.

(d) Ratification of the WTO in the United States

On environment-related issues, debate concerning approval of ratification of the WTO Agreement in the United States Congress mirrored the debate concerning approval of ratification of the North American Free Trade Agreement (NAFTA) in 1993. Congress approved the WTO and its related agreements in December 1994 in the face of intense opposition from numerous environmental NGOs, likewise mirroring the outcome of the NAFTA debate. Perhaps more so than in respect to the NAFTA, the WTO approval debate in the United States focused on the alleged extent to which the sovereignty of the US government, and Congress in particular, would be undermined by the new WTO dispute settlement procedure. The new WTO dispute settlement procedure involves the quasi-automatic approval by WTO Members of the reports of dispute settlement panels and the creation of a new appellate body. Under the former GATT procedure, a consensus of all parties was required before a panel decision became the formal and binding judgment of the organization. Under the former GATT procedure, any party could block the adoption of a panel report, and thus in essence protect itself against an adverse decision. Environmental NGOs argued unsuccessfully to the Congress that the new quasi-automatic WTO dispute settlement procedure would put US environmental regulations at the mercy of a small number of dispute settlement panel members connected with the WTO who might not be sympathetic to the maintenance of high levels of environmental protection.

(2) The NAFTA and Western Hemispheric Integration

The NAFTA and the North American Agreement on Environmental Cooperation (NAAEC) entered into force on 1 January 1994. NAFTA-related activities with respect to the environment in 1994 centered largely on the establishment of administrative arrangements, such as the creation of the North American Commission on Environmental Cooperation (NACEC). The NACEC is based in Montreal, and the Executive Director of its Secretariat (Victor Lichtinger) has been appointed. As of the end of 1994, rules regarding implementation of the NAAEC complaint process were still under consideration. It does not appear that any formal demands for Secretariat factual determinations were made by private groups during 1994. Some environmental NGOs have expressed disappointment with the slow pace of NAFTA organizational efforts.

The NAFTA provides in Art. 103 that it takes priority over the GATT and other existing agreements to which the parties are party (other than certain environmental agreements per Art. 104). Article 103 does not specifically refer to GATT successor agreements, and this raises the issue whether NAFTA environment-related rules will take priority over comparable WTO rules. NAFTA rules will likely continue to take priority over those WTO rules that are continuations of prior GATT rules. However, it may be some time before this question is definitively answered.

During 1994, the US Congress refused to extend fast-track authorization for negotiation of Chile's accession to the NAFTA, at least partially on the basis of Republican Party demands that its accession not include agreements such as the NAFTA supplemental agreements on labor and the environment. The Summit of the Americas Declaration, adopted in December 1994 by the Heads of State and Government of virtually all Western Hemisphere countries (*see* (➔) Conjunto Centroamerica-USA), calls for conclusion of the negotiation of a Free Trade Area of the Americas by 2005. The Declaration calls for the creation of partnerships to promote environmental objectives and sustainable development. The governments support the convening of other regional meetings on sustainable development. The Summit of Americas Plan of Action recognizes the need to make trade liberalization and environmental policies mutually supportive.

Frederick M. Abbott

2. MULTILATERAL LENDING ACTIVITIES

During 1994, international financial institutions faced continued pressure to reshape their operational practices in order to increase transparency and embrace the goals of sustainable development. Among the most important reforms, particularly from an international law perspective, were the creation of independent inspection panels at the World Bank and several of the regional multilateral development banks (MDBs).

(1) The World Bank Group

(a) Is 50 Years Enough?

This year marked the 50th anniversary of the signing of the Bretton Woods agreements creating the World Bank. Both the World Bank and its critics launched major efforts to evaluate, and reevaluate, the Bank's record and its ability to face today's challenges. In the largest coordinated challenge to the development model pursued by the World Bank, the "Fifty Years Is Enough" campaign, consisting of approximately 300 environmental, social, and development groups from around the world, questioned the efficacy of current development models for moving the poorest countries out of poverty and toward ecologically sustainable development. The Bank countered in what is proving to be a battle over both the history of the Bank and the future of development lending. This highly publicized and politicized debate will continue at least through 1996, when the Bank will celebrate its 50th year of operation.

(b) The World Bank Inspection Panel

On September 1, the World Bank's Inspection Panel began operations. The panel is authorized to receive claims about the bank's failure to comply with its own policies and procedures, including its failure to enforce related loan conditions. Claims can be filed by any affected party (other than an individual) in the borrower's territory. The affected party's local representative, the Bank's board of Executive Directors, or, in some cases, any one Executive Director is also eligible to file a claim. In an attempt to limit the role of non-governmental organizations (NGOs), non-local representatives can represent affected parties only in "exceptional cases" where "appropriate representation is not locally available."

Upon receiving a completed request for inspection that is within the panel's authority, the panel will register the claim in a public registry, notify the claimant and the executive directors, and forward a copy to bank management, which has 21 days to respond. The panel then has 21 days to review management's response, seek clarification from management or the claimant, and make recommendations to the executive directors, who must authorize any further investigation. The panel's recommendation must include a clear explanation setting forth reasons for the recommendation and including copies of the claim, management's response, advice from the bank's legal department, statements of minority views of the panel, and any other relevant information.

The first test of the panel was the adoption of operating procedures in August. In general, the operating procedures clarified the resolution creating the panel in important ways, making the panel easier to use and more accessible to less well-organized citizens. The operating procedures explicitly recognized the need to conduct preliminary studies as part of the initial review of a claim. The panel also created the public registry, developed a two-page form for requesting inspections, and explicitly required that inspection work plans be provided to the public, thus increasing the panel's ultimate transparency and effectiveness.

(c) The Arun III Controversy

For several years now, the Bank's proposal to develop a 200-Megawatt hydroelectric facility in the Arun Valley in Nepal has been extremely controversial. Nepal, one of Asia's poorest countries, undoubtedly needs electricity, but the expensive energy path that Arun III represents is being heavily criticized. On October 24, a Nepalese organization called the Arun Concerned Group filed the first claim before the Inspection Panel. The claim alleged that the Bank had violated several policies and procedures in preparing the $175 million loan for the project. After reviewing the Bank Management's response and conducting a preliminary investigation in Nepal, the Panel issued its initial report on December 16. The Panel found that each of the claimant's allegations were true, and requested from the Board of Executive Directors authority to conduct a more thorough investigation.

(d) Implementation of the Information Policy

In response to growing concerns over a lack of transparency and accountability, the World Bank substantially revised its information disclosure policy, now codified in Bank Procedure No. 17.50 (B.P. 17.50). As part of the policy, the Bank opened a Public Information Center in Washington, DC, to facilitate public access to Bank documents. Although a broad review of the Bank's implementation of its information policy is not yet available, initial reports from NGOs in developing countries suggest that information required to be disclosed under the information policy is not widely available in those countries.

(2) The International Finance Corporation

The International Finance Corporation (IFC) began updating its 1988 industrial pollution abatement standards; the first group of eight standards was due to be released in mid-1995.

In July, the IFC Board of Directors adopted its first information policy, which still has some notable gaps although it improves the amount of information available. Publicly available information about IFC's activities may now be obtained at the Bank's Public Information Center, described above. According to the policy, the IFC will now make available a Summary of Project Information (SPI), if Project sponsors agree. The SPI contains basic factual information about proposed IFC investments. It must be released at least 30 days before consideration by the Board of Directors. Environmental assessments will be released 60 days before Board consideration of projects. This section still does not meet the requirements in §521 of the US International Development and Finance Act of 1989 (the Pelosi Amendment). The Pelosi Amendment requires the US Secretary of Treasury to instruct the US Executive Directors of each MDB to abstain or vote against any action that would significantly affect the human environment, unless an environmental assessment has been made available to the board of directors at least 120 days before the vote. At least a summary of the assessment must also be made available to the public. The Department of Treasury continues to argue that the IFC is not an MDB, and thus, that the Pelosi Amendment does not apply.

(3) The Global Environment Facility (GEF)

The restructured GEF continues funding of projects in the same four focal areas as before: climate change, conservation of biological diversity, protection of international waters, and ozone depletion. Incremental costs of activities concerning, for example, land degradation, such as desertification and deforestation, will be eligible for funding only to the extent they relate to one of the four issues. The restructured GEF is governed by an

Assembly, a Council, and a Secretariat. The Assembly, consisting of representatives of all GEF participants will meet once every three years to review and evaluate the GEF's operations and to accept by consensus any amendments to the GEF structure recommended by the Council. The Council will consist of 32 members representing constituency groupings. It will meet semi-annually and will have primary authority for the operation and direction of the GEF. The GEF Secretariat will be primarily responsible for implementing the policies and decisions of the Assembly and the Council. The Secretariat will continue to be supported administratively by the World Bank, but will operate in a "functionally independent and effective manner." The Chief Executive Officer, who heads the Secretariat, is selected for a three-year term by the Council on the recommendation of the implementing agencies, *i.e.*, the World Bank, the United Nations Environment Programme, and the United Nations Development Programme.

(4) The International Monetary Fund

Despite a growing recognition of the relationship among environmental and social issues and macroeconomic policies, the International Monetary Fund (IMF) is still extremely slow to adopt even minor changes in the way it conducts business. The IMF still refuses to consider long-term environmental and natural resource issues in determining its macroeconomic policies toward a country. Increased pressure from donor countries has led the IMF to prepare an information policy that will make at least some minimal information available to the public. Because of its relatively backward approach to transparency and public participation issues, the IMF is becoming a major focus of environmental and social reform efforts.

(5) The Asian Development Bank (ADB)

The ADB proposed the creation of a new standing committee of the Board of Directors to review initial requests for inspection in conjunction with a panel of outside experts. The Board Inspection Committee (BIC) will supervise inspections and provide expertise on the Bank's policies and procedures. The BIC will consist of six members of the Bank's Board of Directors: four regional members; three hailing from borrower countries; and two non-regional members. The President will appoint members to the BIC after consultation with the Board. Members will serve a term of two years.

Applications for inspection may only be filed by communities, organizations, and other groups residing in the borrower member country in which the project in dispute is located. Applicants must present reasonable evidence that their rights or interests have been or are likely to be directly, materially, and adversely affected by an action or omission of the Bank as a result of the Bank's failure to follow its operational policies and procedures in connection with a proposed or ongoing Bank project. The Board of Directors, or in some instances a single Director, may also authorize inspection of an ongoing Bank project on request of three or more Directors. In the event that the panel and Board agree to changes in the scope or implementation of an ongoing project, management must implement these recommendations within a period designated by the Board. For ongoing projects, the Bank can suspend disbursements pending an investigation. The Board can also direct management to request the borrower's consent to stop the project temporarily. After the inspection, the full text of the panel's report, management's response, the BIC's recommendation and the Board decision will be made available to the applicant and the general public.

(6) The European Bank for Reconstruction and Development (EBRD)

Under the new leadership of Jacques de Larosière, the EBRD successfully streamlined operations and reduced its administrative costs. This has generally restored confidence within the donor community that the EBRD will use funds more judiciously. The change in leadership has not translated into any environmental gains, however, as the Bank still lacks any meaningful plan for operationalizing its mandate to promote sustainable development.

The EBRD found itself mired in two particularly controversial projects: the Ziar nad Hronom aluminum smelter in Slovakia (rejected for financing from the World Bank on economic grounds) and the Mochovce nuclear power project. The Ziar loan was approved, but only after a delay caused by the Bank's failure to conduct any public hearings. The Mochovce nuclear power plant project remains controversial, generating opposition from the Austrian government and Slovak and international NGOs.

(7) The Inter-American Development Bank (IDB)

(a) IDB Inspection Mechanism

In June, the IDB's Board of Directors created an "independent inspection mechanism" to "further the transparency, accountability and effectiveness of the Bank's performance in its operations." Like the inspection panel at the World Bank, the IDB's inspection mechanism is intended to protect affected citizens in borrowing countries. Any "organization, association, society or other grouping of individuals" can request an inspection by offering "reasonable evidence that its rights or interests have been or are likely to be directly and materially affected by an action or omission of the Bank as a result of a failure of the Bank to follow its operational policies or norms." By the end of the year, the IDB had yet to name any of the roster members from which panel member would be chosen, nor had any claims been filed with the President.

(b) IDB Information Disclosure Policy

On September 28, the IDB adopted an information disclosure policy that applies to all Bank documents generated, and loan proposals negotiated, after January 1, 1995. The IDB Disclosure Policy is designed to facilitate the disclosure of information about the Bank's operational activities when there is no compelling reason to keep information confidential. As part of this effort, the IDB will open Public Information Facilities at IDB Headquarters, each Country Office, and the Special Office in Europe. The policy is subject to review by Bank Management and the Board of Executive Directors after two years.

The new policy establishes a complicated set of criteria for release of basic project documents. Separate provisions apply to environmental documents. Environmental briefs containing summaries of environmental impact assessments and recommendations for addressing environmental issues during project preparation will be available at the discretion of the Executive Directors. Complete environmental impact assessments and environmental analyses should "be made available at some public place accessible to affected groups and local NGOs." Once released locally and officially submitted to the Bank, such assessments and analyses should be made available at the newly created Public Information Facilities unless the borrower objects to dissemination of the assessment or analysis outside of the country. Environmental reports containing staff conclusions and recommendations pertaining to mitigation measures will also generally be available at the Public Information Facilities.

(8) The African Development Bank

The African Development Bank (AfDB) released a proposal to create an Inspection Panel on October 3. In general terms, the draft follows the structure of the World Bank's Inspection Panel. There will be a permanent three-member panel that will receive complaints from affected citizens alleging AfDB failure to comply with its own policies and procedures.

The AfDB proposal is weaker in several critical ways than the World Bank panel. The AfDB's proposal includes no specific time-tables to ensure that claims move efficiently through the process. It also includes no conditions on the composition of the panel that would help to ensure that selected members are independent of the staff (except an inexplicable provision that all panel members should be over 50 years old). The proposal also failed to ensure that the inspection process would be transparent, thus threatening its independence and credibility from the beginning.

(9) The Border Environment Cooperation Commission and the North American Development Bank

On October 27, 1993, the United States and Mexico created two new organizations: the Border Environment Cooperation Commission (BECC) and the North American Development Bank (NADBank) to facilitate environmental cleanup along their 2,000-mile border and to provide additional support for community adjustment and investment related to the North American Free Trade Agreement. The BECC is designed to work with border states, local communities, and NGOs to design, coordinate, and finance environmental infrastructure projects. Once a project has been certified by the BECC, it is eligible for NADBank financing. Jointly and equally capitalized by the United States and Mexico, the NADBank's capital shares of $450 million paid-in capital (over four years) and $2.55 billion callable capital envision the ability to make $2-3 billion in loans and guarantees. Both the BECC and NADBank have been slow to start operation. By the end of 1994, neither had selected their primary staff nor established a specific work plan.

(10) Organisation for Economic Cooperation and Development (OECD) and Export Credit Agencies

The United States is leading efforts to have the OECD adopt uniform, minimum guidelines for export credit agencies. In part, this is due to US concerns that its export credit agency, the Export-Import Bank (Ex-Im Bank), will lose competitiveness as a result of new environmental protection guidelines required by the US Congress.

The Ex-Im Bank adopted its first permanent environmental policy on December 16. The policy establishes environmental screening and review procedures consistent with the Bank's export promotion objectives. The policies will be tested during a one-year trial implementation period. The Ex-Im Bank's environmental guidelines subject long-term projects and project finance transactions with significant adverse environmental impacts to mandatory environmental review. Medium-term transactions (defined as principal liability of $10 million or less with a repayment term of seven years), credit guarantee facilities, export credit insurance, and working capital guarantees are exempt from environmental reviews. Applicants for loans for long-term projects will be required to provide sufficient environmental information to enable the Ex-Im Bank to conduct its initial screening of the project. Depending on the project's potential impacts and its proximity to important ecological areas, the project will be reviewed against minimum industry-specific standards. Projects that significantly affect the quality of the human environment of the United States, its territories or possessions, or Antarctica, must comply with the US National Environmental Policy Act's environmental assessment requirements.

The environmental guidelines establish minimum quantitative and qualitative measures that should be attained in projects applying for Ex-Im Bank financing. The Ex-Im Bank's environmental guidelines set forth minimum environmental objectives for air quality, water use and quality, management of hazardous materials and waste, natural hazards, social and cultural effects, ecological resources, and noise protection. Projects that do not achieve the minimum environmental standards set for the specific industry group will be reviewed on a case-by-case basis. Ultimately, financing may be conditioned upon implementation of mitigation measures.

David Hunter
Amy McCrae

X. COUNTRY/REGION REPORTS

1. UNITED STATES OF AMERICA

(1) Introduction

In 1994, the pace of international environmental activity in the United States was significantly slower than during the previous year. The likelihood of ratification of the Biodiversity Convention and the Law of the Sea Convention diminished considerably as the year ended. While the Clinton Administration proposed a number of new policies, few were implemented. The Senate confirmed William Nitze to head the Environmental Protection Agency's (EPA) Office of International Activities, which had been without a director for more than 18 months. Prior to his appointment, interest in international environmental affairs had been waning at EPA. Under Nitze, it announced plans to shift from a program-based to an ecosystem-based approach within the next five years. The Clinton Administration also announced a new policy identifying four situations in which the United States would consider trade sanctions unilaterally against a country harming the environment: when trade sanctions are required by an international environmental treaty to which the United States is a party; when the detrimental environmental impact is partially within US jurisdiction and there is a reasonable scientific basis for concern; when a species, wherever located, is scientifically considered endangered or threatened; and when the effectiveness of a scientifically based international environmental or conservation standard is being diminished.

(2) The North American Free Trade Agreement (NAFTA)

On January 1, 1994, NAFTA went into effect in the United States; nevertheless, implementation of the side agreements intended to safeguard the environment proceeded slowly. By the end of the year, the Border Environmental Cooperation Commission (BECC) and the North American Development Bank were not yet in operation. Disagreements between the United States and Mexico over which country would lead each agency and how they would work have slowed down the process. The only clear sign of progress was President Clinton's naming of three officials to sit on the BECC.

The North American Commission for Environmental Cooperation (NACEC) met for the first time in July 1994. It heard from public interest groups about their concerns regarding the adverse effects on air quality along the Mexico/Texas border of emissions from a coal-fired plant, Carbon II, and its sister unit near the southern border of Texas. NACEC also approved a modest budget for 1994 of $2.1 million. In addition, the

Clinton Administration established two advisory committees to advise the EPA Administrator in her role as NACEC counsel member.

(3) United States/Mexico Border Issues

Most activity aimed at the resolution of environmental problems last year was between individual US states and Mexico. Colorado and Mexico signed an agreement encouraging businesses in each state to exchange technical environmental information and personnel. The governors of the US and Mexican states of California set up an alliance to address infrastructure needs along the border. They agreed to build an international wastewater treatment plant along the border to treat Tijuana River wastes and to create a laboratory to test pesticide residues. Also, governors from Mexican and US border states met in May and issued a statement on a broad range of environmental issues related to NAFTA, with proposals for funding environmental training and monitoring.

An EPA official said steps were being taken to create binational air quality districts along the border to allow for emissions trading. EPA also announced a cooperative enforcement plan that is expected to focus on protecting ecosystems and endangered species.

Finally, EPA issued 95 US companies with manufacturing plants along the border subpoenas requesting data on release of chemicals into the New River basin. EPA is seeking to determine whether the facilities are contaminating the New River in California.

(4) General Agreement on Tariffs and Trade (GATT)

In May, ruling on a petition by the European Union (EU) and the Netherlands, a GATT panel concluded that the secondary embargo by the United States on imports of tuna from intermediary nations was inconsistent with its GATT obligations because the ban was too attenuated to the preservation of dolphins to be "necessary" to protect the life or health of dolphins, or to be "related to" conserving dolphins. The US trade representative indicated the United States would ask for a full review or reconsideration of the (➔) GATT panel report, citing the failure to provide a fair hearing and due process through public hearings which allowed non-governmental organizations to participate. In July, Japan and the EU, among others, demanded that the United States lift its ban. Mexico and the United States continued to try to bilaterally work out their problems involving the primary ban on tuna imports previously found to be inconsistent with GATT by another panel.

A GATT dispute settlement panel rejected an EU claim that US fuel conservation and tax measures were discriminatory against European auto imports. The EU had challenged the US corporate average fuel economy (CAFE) requirements, the "gas guzzler" tax, and the luxury tax on cars over $30,000. The decision upheld these taxes and the 19-year-old CAFE standards, but the panel agreed with the EU that the CAFE accounting rules, which established separate domestic and import fleets for determining overall fuel economy, were discriminatory.

Despite opposition from environmental and consumer groups as well as some local governments, Congress approved implementing legislation for the Uruguay Round of the GATT near the end of the year. Environmentalists expressed concern that the GATT implementing legislation, unlike NAFTA's, contains no environmental provisions and therefore leaves US conservation laws open to attack as unfair trade barriers.

A suit filed by public interest groups to require the Office of the US Trade Representative to prepare an environmental impact statement for the Uruguay Round of GATT was dismissed by the District of Columbia federal district court (*Public Citizen v. Kantor*, 864 F.Supp. 208 (D.D.C. 1994)). The court relied on *Public Citizen v. US Trade Representative*, 5 F.3d 549 (1993), *cert. denied*, 114 S. Ct. 685 (1994), in which a federal appeals court had dismissed a similar challenge to NAFTA because there was no "final agency action" to trigger judicial review under the Administrative Procedure Act.

(5) Arctic/Antarctic

A bill introduced in November in the United States House of Representatives to implement provisions of the 1991 Madrid Protocol to the 1959 Antarctic Treaty failed to pass by the end of the year. As introduced, HR 3532 would have allowed citizen suits for environmental damage caused by US activities in the Antarctic.

On December 16, the United States and the Russian Federation signed (➔) an Agreement on Cooperation in the Prevention of Pollution of the Environment in the Arctic.

(6) Protection of Endangered Species and Biodiversity

In 1994, the United States Senate failed to ratify the UN Convention on Biological Diversity despite the support of President Clinton. Key members of Congress continued to question how the Convention would affect biotechnology and pharmaceutical industries. Because the Senate did not consent to the Convention, the United States was unable to participate as a voting party at the first meeting of the conference of the parties in November 1994.

For the first time, the United States imposed trade sanctions to protect endangered species. In April, the Clinton administration announced that it would impose penalties against Taiwan for its failure to stop the trade in tiger and rhinoceros products. While the sanctions—a ban on American imports of wildlife products from Taiwan—will cut off approximately $20 million in trade, Taiwan's total exports to the United States are valued at $25 billion.

At the Conference of the Parties of the Convention on International Trade in Endangered Species (CITES), the United States supported South Africa's successful proposal to permit limited trade in white rhinos, with a continuing prohibition on trade in rhino horn. The United States, the world's largest importer of mahogany, also voted in favor of a defeated proposal to list mahogany on Appendix II. Among other actions, the conference restricted trade in American box turtles, including three Florida varieties.

In the International Whaling Commission, the United States voted to establish a sanctuary around Antarctica that will permanently bar commercial whaling, even if the existing worldwide moratorium on whale hunting is lifted. The measure was approved over objections from Japan and Norway.

(7) Atmosphere

The Clinton Administration continued to work on its October 1993 Climate Change Action Plan. As of October 4, the Administration began accepting joint implementation proposals from domestic businesses to offset greenhouse gas emissions in other countries as part of a pilot initiative developed by the State Department. The pilot program is expected to serve as a model for global and domestic joint implementation programs in other nations. To meet the greenhouse gas emissions goal of reaching 1990 levels by the year 2000, the federal government may have to spend $1.9 billion. Greenhouse gas emissions in 1992 increased slightly over the 1990 ones. The Administration suggested that no emissions offsets gained through joint implementation would count toward the year 2000 goal.

Joint United States/Canadian efforts to reduce acid rain pollution appear to be having a favorable impact, according to a report released by the two governments. The report concludes that emissions of sulfur dioxide, nitrogen oxides, and volatile organic compounds are either declining or leveling out in both countries.

As an outgrowth of unsuccessful trade talks, the United States and Japan signed an agreement to engage in joint research on climate change and air pollution. The talks also led to a commitment by Japan to contribute $1 billion in loans and credits to help Eastern and Central European countries clean up their environments.

With respect to ozone depletion, EPA exempted products such as aircraft cleaning fluids and portable fire extinguishers from the ban on nonessential goods made with hydrochloroflurocarbons (58 Fed. Reg. 69638 (Dec. 30, 1993)). The agency also issued a proposed exemption from labeling rules for ozone-depleting substances for parties under the Montreal Protocol using approved destruction technologies (58 Fed. Reg. 69568

(Dec. 30, 1993)). In a final rule issued in March, EPA set up a Significant New Alternatives Policy (SNAP) to assess the use of safe substitutes for substances slated to be phased out under the Montreal Protocol. Although the final rule covered substitutes even if produced for export only, in December EPA announced it would delay coverage of chemicals for export for three months while reconsidering whether such chemicals should be subject to the SNAP program (59 Fed. Reg. 63255 (Dec. 8, 1994)). A coalition of companies and trade associations had filed for exemption under the proposed SNAP rule, and had also filed suit against EPA in the US Circuit Court for the District of Columbia. In other action, EPA also added several compounds to the list of safe substitutes (59 Fed. Reg. 44240 (Aug. 26, 1994)).

(8) Sustainable Development

At the Summit of the Americas in December, the United States signed a joint agreement (➔) (the Conjunto Centroamerica USA) with Belize, Costa Rica, El Salvador, Guatemala, Honduras, Nicaragua, and Panama establishing a framework for sustainable development. The participating nations also agreed to phase out leaded gasoline. In October, the Chairman of the President's Council on Sustainable Development announced that the Council would make its policy recommendations in April 1995.

(9) Hazardous Materials

Efforts by the Administration to develop and pass implementing legislation for the 1989 Basel Convention on the Transboundary Movement of Hazardous Wastes and their Disposal stalled after treaty parties agreed to an international ban on the shipment of hazardous waste from Organisation for Economic Cooperation and Development (OECD) countries to non-OECD countries ((➔)(Decision II/12)).

A South African company, Thor Chemicals, bowed to political pressure and sent a shipment of waste mercury back to Borden Chemicals in the United States. The Department of Justice later brought charges against Borden for, among other alleged violations, shipping over 300,000 pounds of hazardous waste to South Africa without notifying EPA, as required by the Resource Conservation and Recovery Act. In December, EPA proposed a rule that would forbid the import of virtually all fluids and transformers containing polychlorinated biphenyls from Canada. (59 Fed. Reg. 62875 (Dec. 6, 1994)).

Canada, Mexico, and the United States entered into several new emergency response agreements. In July, the United States and Canada signed a contingency plan to deal with environmental accidents along their border. Sister cities along the US/Mexico border agreed to collaborative planning to promote preparedness for chemical emergencies. Officials from all three countries also agreed to a plan of action for bringing each country's Emergency Response Guidebook into harmony with those of its neighbors. The Guidebook also deals with shipment of hazardous materials across borders.

(10) Nuclear Energy and Waste

The United States and the Russian Federation agreed to cooperate in developing improved processing and storage of Russian liquid radioactive waste as a means to help protect the Arctic environment. In August, Russian and American scientists met for three weeks to exchange information on nuclear waste cleanup technologies.

In an unusual arrangement, a Japan-US energy and environmental consulting group will begin offering services in China. The group will initially collect data and later give advice on both coal-burning and nuclear power plants. It will also provide environmental impact assessments for nuclear fuel facilities.

(11) Water and Ocean Pollution

The United States signed (➔) the Agreement Relating to the Implementation of Part XI of the United Nations Convention on the Law of the Sea (UNCLOS). Congress continued to express concerns, however, about US access to deep sea minerals. While the agreement had been expected to lead to the United States' signing and ratifying UNCLOS early in 1995, by year's end, the newly elected, Republican-dominated Congress made prospects for adoption uncertain.

By year's end, the US Coast Guard was set to begin enforcing provisions of the 1990 Oil Pollution Prevention Act vis-a-vis any oil tanker navigating US waters. The Coast Guard also promulgated a final rule requiring all US flag vessels over 400 tons and all US flag oil tankers over 150 tons to carry approved oil spill response plans (59 Fed. Reg. 51332 (Oct. 7, 1994)).

A report by the International Joint Commission (IJC), recommending a consensus plan to achieve eventual elimination of manufacture, use, and disposal of persistent toxic substances that threaten the Great Lakes Ecosystem, generated controversy in the United States. While the governments of Canada and Ontario signed agreements to implement the IJC's recommendations, the State of Michigan found a 30-year phase-out of chlorinated compounds possible, but not under the IJC's regulatory scheme.

Linda A. Malone

2. CANADA

[Editors' Note: The Canada report features two separate reports by two different authors]

A. INTERNATIONAL DEVELOPMENTS

While Canada continued to be an active player at all major international environmental negotiations in 1994, the frenetic pace of the first years of the 1990s was gone. Canadian international environmental law activities became more focussed on the implementation of existing agreements or the furtherance of objectives already well established by Canada, as opposed to the pursuit of many new initiatives. Implementation activities focussed on the North American Agreement on Environmental Cooperation, the two United Nations Conference on Environment and Development (UNCED) conventions, and trade in hazardous wastes under the Basel Convention. Work on existing objectives included, in particular, the Canadian High Seas Fishing initiative and the further development of international law relating to the forestry sector.

(1) The North American Free Trade Agreement (NAFTA) and the North American Agreement on Environmental Cooperation (NAAEC)

Following the coming into force of both the NAFTA and the NAAEC on January 1, 1994, environmental efforts focussed on the implementation of the two Agreements. Canadian internal consultations were designed to ensure that environmental interests were more adequately represented in the trade discussions. Generally, however, Canada remained conservative in its approach to trade and environment linkages. Indeed, sources close to the Summit of the Americas negotiations indicated that the decision to endorse the environmental and labour side agreements as part of the "package" for extending the NAFTA to Central and South American countries was taken by the Prime Minister of Canada against the advice of the Minister for International Trade. Canada's primary concern of not seeing unilateral environmental measures becoming disguised trade weapons, particularly in the natural resources sector, continued to dominate the trade and environment agenda. This was supported by an almost ideological devotion in some circles to the principle of not establishing any new trade barriers, a result often seen as an inevitable consequence of pursuing the environmental aspect of the trade and environment debate with any vigour.
Implementation of the NAAEC included three distinct elements. First, as regards the operationalization of the Commission, Victor Lichtinger of Mexico was appointed as the Executive Director of the Commission for Environmental Cooperation; Montréal was selected as the home of the Secretariat to the Commission; and the Commission's Rules of Procedure were adopted, but had not been published by year's end. Second, legislation to implement the dispute resolution provisions of the NAAEC specifically applicable to Canada (*see* Canada, 4 *YbIEL* 304-305 (1993)) was adopted in February 1994. (*An Act to Amend the Crown Liability*

Proceedings Act, Statutes of Canada, 42-43 Elizabeth II, 1994, Ch. 11.) This legislation ensures that the Commission has both the legal personality and the authority to initiate action necessary to make a panel determination under Part Five of the NAAEC enforceable by Canadian courts against the responsible Minister. It also ensures that any such action will not lead to a review of the findings of the Panel, and will not itself be subject to further judicial review or appeal, including on grounds of excess of jurisdiction. Third, Canada is required to notify the other parties which of its provinces and territories have agreed to be covered by the rights and obligations of the Agreement. (NAAEC, Annex 41). In order to promote the inclusion of all these sub-national governments, a federal/provincial/territorial agreement was concluded in 1994 (*see Inside NAFTA*, May 18, 1994, at 17). This agreement provides for the establishment of a Governmental Committee, as provided for in Art. 18 of the NAAEC, and includes a series of prescriptions for decision-making within that Committee. For the first time in respect of international environmental negotiations, the agreement provides for a possible veto by a participating province on the articulation of a Canadian position at the Commission. It also sets out the process by which Canadian delegations to Commission meetings will be chosen, as well as the participants in any working groups of the Commission. The agreement is undoubtedly the most far reaching one of its type ever concluded in Canada. By the end of 1994, however, no provinces or territories had signed on to the agreement, making it non-operational (and non-public in any official version.) Similarly, no provinces or territories had agreed to participate in the NAAEC up to that point.

(2) The Climate Change and Biodiversity Conventions

Canada submitted its first national reports pursuant to the two UNCED Conventions. *The National Report on Biodiversity,* developed after an extensive federal/provincial and multi-stakeholder consultation process, was reasonably complete by year-end. Some environmental groups, however, were critical of the lack of new legislation to implement the Convention, as opposed to the government's reliance on pre-existing federal/provincial/territorial legislation.

Canada's *National Report on Climate Change, 1994*, shows a considerable gap, estimated at 12–15 percent, between the net emissions of greenhouse gases estimated by the year 2000 under existing and planned programs, and the Convention target of a return to 1990 levels by that year. Intergovernmental and multi-stakeholder consultations to address this gap continued. A related issue of high concern to Canada has been the development of the joint implementation provisions of the Convention.

(3) Basel Convention

Canada continued its participation in implementing the Basel Convention in 1994, maintaining its previous designation by environmental groups as one of the "dirty seven" hazardous-waste trading countries. The particular target of the environmental non-governmental organization epitaph was Canada's active resistance to the proposed (➔) Decision at the Second Conference of the Parties on the banning of all trade in hazardous wastes from Organisation for Economic Cooperation and Development (OECD) to non-OECD countries, including for recycling. Based more on the "principle" of avoiding trade barriers for environmental reasons than preserving the actual trade that Canada was engaged in, which was virtually none in recent years, a trade-focussed delegation was dispatched to head off the expected ban at the Geneva meeting. Canada remained one of the final three countries to surrender its opposition to the ban, but ultimately did join the consensus decision to ban all North-South trade in hazardous waste by 1997.

(4) Continuing Objectives: Fish and Forests

International agreement on obligations for the conservation and sustainable management of highly migratory and straddling fish stocks was an initial objective of UNCED. The UN Conference on Straddling Fish Stocks and Highly Migratory Fish Stocks in 1993, as called for at UNCED, was seen as the means to achieve these objectives by the end of 1994. In 1994, Canadian efforts directed at this goal continued to go unfulfilled. (*See* Fauteux, "The Canadian Legal Initiative on High Seas Fishing," 4 *YbIEL* 51 (1993), for a complete history of the Canadian interests and objectives.) Additional sessions of the Conference were scheduled for the spring and summer of 1995. In a related development, Canada became the first country to ratify the 1993 UN Food and Agriculture Organization Agreement to Promote Compliance with International Conservation and Management Measures by Fishing Vessels on the High Seas, in May 1994.

The most controversial development in 1994 in relation to international environmental law was Canada's decision to amend the Coastal Fisheries Protection Act (May 25, 1994.) (*See* 33 *ILM* 1383 (1994).) The amendments allowed the prescribing of classes of ships by regulation that could be detained or seized on the high seas for fishing in violation of conservation regulations also enabled by the amendments. Subsequent regulations established stateless and flag-of-convenience vessels as the target ships. This new legislation essentially overrides international limits on conservation and arrest jurisdiction on the high seas by putting a limit on the freedom to fish as reiterated in the 1982 Law of the Sea Convention. The introduction of the legislation was, as a result, accompanied by a largely defensive posture that sought to emphasize the limited target range of the statutory amendment when read with the regulations, and the need to take measures to control these type of rogue fishing vessels in the face of vanishing stocks. Canada's defensiveness was highlighted by the fact that it amended its acceptance of the compulsory jurisdiction of the International Court of Justice under Art. 36 of the Court's Statute, exempting from the Court's jurisdiction any issue related to the amendments. This type of limitation by Canada of the Court's jurisdiction has a precedent in relation to another controversial enactment, the 1970 Arctic Waters Pollution Prevention Act, by which Canada unilaterally extended its jurisdiction to 100 miles offshore for the purpose of protecting the fragile environment of Arctic waters. That limitation to the Court's jurisdiction was removed in 1985, three years after the conclusion of the United Nations Convention on the Law of the Sea.

It is noteworthy that the introduction of the Act was not accompanied by any reference to the principles of sustainable development to justify the need for action to protect fish stocks from disappearing completely. Subsequent comments by Brian Tobin, the responsible Minister of Fisheries and Oceans, did, however, invoke this justificatory sword.

Forestry continued to be a major preoccupation of Canada at the international level, as Canada participated in the negotiations of the renewed (➔) International Tropical Timber Agreement of January 1994. Bilaterally, Canada established a new program on forestry cooperation with Mexico. Canada continued to promote the possibility of future negotiations on an international forestry convention that would lead to the definition of sustainable forestry standards and criteria. Canadian efforts seek to ensure the pursuit of a multilateral process for reaching such standards, and thereby to avoid imposition of unilateral standards that would create trade barriers of a legal or non-legal type.

(5) Other issues

Canada adopted legislation to implement the Copenhagen Amendments to the Montreal Protocol, which were ratified by Canada in March 1994. The legislation also updates and consolidates most of the measures necessary to continue implementing the Protocol itself and its previous amendments. (Ozone Depleting Substances Regulations, SOR/94-408, Canada Gazette II, Vol. 128, No. 12, June 15, 1994.) The new Regulation addresses all bulk ozone-depleting substances. Products containing these substances will be regulated by the Ozone Depleting Substances Products Regulations. (SOR/94-406, Canada Gazette II, Vol. 128, No. 12, June 15, 1994.)

Canada's focus on environmental quality issues of particular concern to the Arctic was reflected in the initiatives, both within the UN Economic Commission for Europe and the Commission on Sustainable Development

(CSD), to highlight the need to address the continued introduction of persistent organic pollutants (POPs) into the environment. Used as pesticides and industrial chemicals, and originating as unwanted by-products of industrial and waste management processes, POPs demonstrate a long-term persistence in the environment, bio-accumulation through the food chain, and a level of volatility that allows them to move repeatedly between land, air, and water. Canada was one of the countries that led an effort to have the Economic Commission for Europe (ECE) address POPs through a protocol to the Long-Range Transboundary Air Pollution Agreement of 1979. The ECE continued to work on this initiative. Canada also initiated, following its intervention in the CSD, an international meeting to increase global awareness of the scientific evidence relating to POPs and the range of possible means for addressing their continued release into the environment. The meeting, to be held in 1995, will be cosponsored by the Philippines.

Howard Mann

B. DOMESTIC DEVELOPMENTS

(1) Environmental Assessment (EA)

During 1994, Canada completed the tasks necessary to implement the federal Canadian Environmental Assessment Act (CEAA). Canada promulgated four sets of regulations in October 1994. The delay resulted from the lengthy process of developing the key regulations necessary to define the Act's scope of application and to prescribe projects for which full EA is mandatory. Essentially, these regulations specify the projects and activities to which the Act applies and those projects for which comprehensive study will be required without preliminary screening.

As part of the CEAA implementation process, the Act was amended on December 13, to add provisions designed to minimize unnecessary duplication in the EA process. Another amendment places a duty on the responsible Minister to establish a participant funding program to encourage citizens to participate in hearings conducted by review panels at the public-review stage of the process. When federal authorities decide that projects assessed and publicly reviewed are not likely to cause significant adverse environmental effects that cannot be mitigated or justified under the circumstances, the amendments subject the authorities' findings to the approval of the Federal Cabinet.

The Act specifically addresses environmental assessment of projects likely to have interjurisdictional environmental effects. Agreements for EA by joint review panels may be made with other jurisdictions that have responsibility for conducting EAs, including provincial governments, assessment authorities established under aboriginal land-claims agreements, governments or subdivisions of foreign states, and international organizations of states or their institutions. Such joint assessment agreements must require that EA include consideration of the factors listed under CEAA, that members of EA panels be expert and impartial, and that there be an opportunity for public participation in the panel's assessment.

There are similar provisions for cooperative EA where a project within Canada is likely to have significant adverse transboundary environmental effects. In the case of projects that may cause significant adverse effects outside federal lands or outside Canada, the Ministers of the Environment and of Foreign Affairs may refer the project for mediation or panel review. The government of a potentially affected foreign state or a subdivision of that state may request such a referral. Prior notice of intent to refer such a project for public review must be given to the proponent and to the governments of affected provinces and foreign states.

Environmental assessment was a focus in 1994 of the Canadian Council of Ministers of the Environment's (CCME's) continuing efforts to harmonize environmental management in Canada. A discussion draft of a federal-provincial Environmental Management Framework Agreement that CCME circulated for comment in late 1994 included a draft schedule on EA. This agreement will, when finalized, establish national standards and specify lead federal, provincial, or aboriginal land-settlement agency roles for assessment of projects in prescribed categories.

The Supreme Court of Canada rendered a decision in 1994 that has important implications for the environmental assessment of national and international energy projects and activities. In *Attorney General v. Canada (National Energy Board)*, the Court held that the National Energy Board (NEB) has the power to attach conditions to licenses for the export of electricity from Canada that were granted to Hydro-Québec for future construction. These planned facilities are part of the James Bay hydro-electric project, located in Northern Quebec. In imposing these conditions, the NEB was carrying out its responsibilities as an "initiating department" under the Federal Environmental Assessment and Review Process (EARP) Guidelines Order, the predecessor of the CEAA.

In principle, having regard to the court's concern about unduly narrowing the scope of EA in the detailed regulatory process, its conclusions in this case appeared to apply to natural gas export license applications. The implication was that the EARP process may reach downstream to include EA of future drilling, production, and transportation facilities necessary to meet export commitments under natural gas export licenses. It may, however, be significant that in the case of natural gas export applications, there is no provision in the NEB Act like the electricity-export section that the court relied on, for designating applications as license applications with public review and, in making such designation decisions, for taking into account the environmental impact of the proposed exportation on the environment.

The NEB recognized this issue by ordering review of its recent decision to issue natural gas export licenses and license amendments to five companies. The NEB initiated this review, based on written submissions in relation to the scope of EA, following a request by a regional environmental group. The Board concluded that it does have jurisdiction to consider the environmental and directly related social effects of upstream facilities and activities, but only where there is a necessary connection between those upstream matters and the proposal to export natural gas. Thus, the Board's assessment will relate only to new drilling production, processing, or transportation facilities required by an applicant to undertake the export, and not to all of its activities related to creation of the gas supply pool from which it fulfills all of its contractual commitments including exports.

Subsequent electricity and natural gas export applications will not trigger federal EA. The CEAA Law List Regulations make this clear by omitting the relevant NEB decision powers from the list of federal powers the exercise of which requires EA. One consequence is that for natural gas exports, the EA battle has now shifted to the provincial forum. Environmental intervenors will argue that the Alberta Energy Resources Conservation Board must conduct a full EA of all upstream exploration activities and the necessary production and transportation facilities, in forthcoming Board hearings on applications for permits to remove natural gas from the province.

Another 1994 judicial decision that defines and potentially restricts EA of energy projects is that of the Alberta Court of Appeal in *Syncrude Environmental Assessment Coalition v. Alberta Energy Resources Conservation Board*. The Court held that the Alberta Environmental Protection and Enhancement Act (AEPEA) does not operate retroactively, and therefore does not apply to Syncrude's application to expand its oil-sands production facility. Consequently, the Energy Resources Conservation Board was entitled to hear and determine Syncrude's application under the Oil Sands Conservation Act without reference to AEPEA's contaminant-discharge permitting and EA requirements.

A case concerning EA of proposed expansion of the Sunshine Ski Area in Banff National Park has important implications for federal EA. In *Sunshine Village Corporation v. Canadian Parks and Wilderness Society*, the Federal Court held that once a project has cleared the Federal Environmental Assessment Review Process (EARP) and received the necessary regulatory approvals, it is beyond the Minister's discretion to require full public review on "public concern" grounds. The Court emphasized that this discretion under s.13 of the EARP Guidelines Order must be exercised according to law, and not whimsically.

The Federal Court also rejected an application for orders requiring that a federally funded project involving construction in a marsh area be referred for EA under the federal EARP process (*Friends of Oak Hammock Marsh Inc. v. Canada*). The applicants had unsuccessfully attempted to stop the project in the Manitoba Courts. When the case reached the Federal Court, the project was complete and operating and all necessary provincial licenses and permits had been granted. Under these circumstances, the court held that even though the grant of federal funds would trigger the EARP process, orders to require federal EA would be futile.

(2) Protected Spaces and Species

New legislation and a series of regulatory decisions show the increasing levels of protection provided for natural areas and wildlife species. Decisions of the Alberta Energy Resources Conservation Board and the British Columbia Utilities Commission are landmarks in the protection of ecological systems threatened by natural resource exploration and development activities. New forest legislation in British Columbia addresses the ecologically harmful effects of forestry operations. At the federal level, the first step toward new legislation aimed at protection of endangered species was taken in 1994.

The Energy Resources Conservation Board (ERCB) denied an application by Amoco Canada Petroleum Company for a license to drill an exploratory well in the Whaleback Ridge area of southwestern Alberta. Although well licenses have occasionally been denied on grounds that may be characterized as environmental protection, this decision was unprecedented in its explicit recognition of the authority of provincial regional integrated resource plans and natural area protection policies. The Board's reasons for denying the application included the fact that the proposed well was not in conformity with the relevant sub-regional local integrated resource plan (IRP) established under the Public Lands Act, and that the area was a candidate for protection under Special Places 2000. Special Places 2000 is Alberta's proposed protected-areas strategy, drafted in response to the Brundtlund Commission's recommendation that at least 12 percent of each country be given protected status. Implementation of Special Places 2000 will increase the proportion of protected lands in Alberta from 8.5 to 12 percent.

The IRPs are not legally enforceable. Special Places 2000 is merely a policy proposal for designation and protection of categories of representative natural ecosystems in the province. One of the increasingly rare ecological categories is the montane, which includes the Whaleback Ridge area. The ERCB recognized that the protective instruments were not binding. Nevertheless, the purposes of its governing statute, the Energy Resources Conservation Act, require the Board to determine whether proposed energy projects are in the public interest, having regard to their social, economic, and environmental effects. The Board considered that it was required to assess the impacts and appropriateness of a proposed energy project for the affected area in light of these policies. This led to its conclusion that the proposed well was not in the public interest.

In British Columbia, the provincial cabinet rejected the "Kemano Completion Project" on the recommendation of the British Columbia Utilities Commission. The project would have required a second major diversion tunnel and additional electricity generating facilities to be built to further utilize water from a reservoir constructed in the first phase of the project. Under special discretionary powers in the Utilities Commission Act, the proposed project was subjected to lengthy review, including public hearings by the Commission under its energy project review process. Primarily because of likely damage to fish resources, the Commission recommended that the project be rejected. The cabinet agreed, and now faces compensation claims by the proponent based on a 1987 agreement between it and the federal and provincial governments.

Another instrument for area and habitat protection is the British Columbia Forest Practices Code, enacted in 1994. The Code establishes operational planning requirements and guidelines for specific forest practices, including soil conservation and remediation. A Forest Practices Board established under the Code is charged with overseeing compliance and government enforcement of forest-practice requirements. The Board also has the power to investigate complaints from members of the public and report its conclusions and recommendations to the complainant, the party investigated, and the responsible Ministers. Amid continuing criticisms of British Columbian forest industry practices, regulations are being developed so that the Code can be brought into force.

On November 17, 1994, Environment Canada released a discussion paper on endangered species legislation in Canada. The paper discusses current federal and provincial policies and legislation, identifies problem areas, and proposes alternatives for a federal component of a national framework for endangered species protection. It notes that a major perceived shortcoming of existing federal and provincial legislation is that it does not compel the governments to develop a national endangered species list or implement species recovery plans. The existing national listing system is only a policy; no legal consequences attach to the listing. Critical habitat is not explicitly protected.

According to the discussion paper, an ideal federal act would establish definitions and criteria for assessment and listing of endangered species nationally and trigger the EA process. It should also provide guidelines and direction for actions to promote recovery of species designated as endangered. Further, this federal law must reflect Canada's international obligations, particularly those under the Convention on the International Trade in Endangered Species and the Convention on Biodiversity. All of this is on the assumption that there would be full harmonization with provincial legislation and implementation arrangements. The discussion paper may be the first step toward comprehensive federal endangered species legislation. This would be a significant change from the existing situation, in which a variety of federal laws address certain aspects of endangered species protection, which is otherwise treated as largely a provincial responsibility.

(3) Contaminated Site Liability

Development and refinement of statutory requirements for contaminated site remediation and liability for the cost of such actions continued in 1994. Most significant are the new provisions of the British Columbia Waste Management Act. These were enacted in 1993 and were scheduled to come into force in 1995. During 1994, work continued on regulations necessary to implement these provisions.

The new provisions establish a very advanced régime for contaminated-site liability and remediation requirements. Certain features differ fundamentally from the comparable provisions in other Canadian jurisdictions, and more closely resemble features of the US Comprehensive Environmental Response, Compensation, and Liability Act. In particular, definition of contaminated sites is based on prescribed quantitative criteria, rather than an exercise of discretionary powers, as is common elsewhere in Canada. A "contaminated site" is defined as an area of land in which the soil or underlying groundwater contains prescribed substances in excess of criteria, standards, or conditions established by regulation. Also, liability for contaminated-site remediation is imposed directly on any responsible private person or government agency, rather than on the basis of failure to comply with a regulatory remediation order.

The provisions establish a unique process to facilitate resolution of disputes about remedial responsibility without resort to judicial processes. Included are disputes concerning whether parties are responsible persons, and if so, whether they are minor contributors; the proportionate contribution of responsible persons to contamination of sites; and the share of remediation costs attributable to particular responsible persons. For this purpose, a group of up to 12 expert "allocation advisors" may be appointed by the Minister.

At the request and expense of any person, an official designated under the Act may appoint allocation panels consisting of three allocation advisors to consider and issue opinions on any of these responsibility or allocation issues. Allocation panels must take into account listed factors, including degree of involvement or diligence.

The Ontario Environmental Appeal Board that individual investors in a bankrupt Ontario company must take specified actions to protect human health and the environment against hazardous wastes left on the company's premises, as required by prevention and waste removal orders issued under Ontario's Environmental Protection Act. (*Re 724597 Ontario Ltd.*) The Board upheld the orders, holding that the investors' involvement and influence in the management of the business constituted "charge management or control" under the terms of the Act. It adopted a "negligent investment" approach, which takes into account market realities, standards of conduct prevailing at the time the risk was created, the balance of competing interests, fair allocation of responsibility, and the impact of personal liability.

(4) Public Participation and Public-Interest Standing

In 1986, the Supreme Court of Canada had concluded in *Finlay v. Canada (Minister of Finance)* that a court has discretion to accord public-interest standing. This discretion is structured according to whether there is a justiciable issue; a genuine interest in the subject matter of the decision, even in the sense of established concern and advocacy actions; and no other reasonable and effective manner of bringing the matter before the courts. In 1994, a number of cases emerged relating to whether individuals and public groups have status to participate in decision processes of environmental and natural resource regulatory agencies. The results suggest a relatively strict and formal judicial and regulatory approach to interpretation of tribunal standing provisions and a disinclination to adopt the *Finlay* criteria for public-interest standing.

In *Canadian Union of Public Employees v. WMI Waste Management*, the Alberta Court of Queen's Bench held that a right of appeal to the Public Health Advisory and Review Board (PHARB) by persons "directly affected" does not mean that all persons affected by a decision of a public health authority have a right to appeal the decision to the Board. Something more than the effects suffered by all members of the public is required.

The same court followed the *Canadian Union* approach in *Friends of the Athabasca Environmental Association v. Alberta Public Health Advisory and Review Board*, which also involved the PHARB. Here, the court was asked to follow *Friends of the Island Inc. v. Canada (Minister of Public Works)*, a 1993 decision of the Federal Court that the words "directly affected" in the Federal Court Act should be interpreted as allowing discretionary public-interest standing under the *Finlay* test. The argument in *Athabasca* was that the words "directly affected" in the Alberta Public Health Act similarly provide for discretionary public-interest standing in appeals to the PHARB. The court rejected this argument on the ground that the interpretation in *Island* operated only in the special context of statutory changes in the division of jurisdiction between the Trial and Appeal Divisions of the Federal Court. The court concluded that it must give "directly affected" a restricted meaning, namely having a direct and personal interest in the subject of the appeal.

The Alberta Environmental Appeal Board, in a series of decisions (particularly *Ross v. Director, Alberta Environmental Protection*), developed a similar interpretation of the "directly affected" criterion in its empowering statute. Its analysis resulted in a test for direct affectation based on proximity to and causal connection with the proposed development to which the disputed environmental approval relates.

This follows closely the reasoning of another Alberta tribunal, the Natural Resources Conservation Board (NRCB) in a series of decisions concerning interpretation of the term "directly affected" in relation to eligibility for intervenor costs in Board hearings. In *Hazardous Waste Importation Review Committee v. NRCB*, the court concluded, after reviewing the NRCB's consideration of claimed effects of the proposed hazardous waste importation and disposal project, that there was no error in the Board's reasoning that led to the conclusion that members of an environmental coalition were not directly affected.

A similar narrow approach was taken by the Alberta Energy Resources Conservation Board to intervenor funding eligibility based on ownership or occupation of property that "is or may be directly and adversely affected by a decision of the Board." It denied an advance of costs to an environmental coalition that included an individual local resident who resided within the Emergency Planning Zone (EPZ) for a proposed exploratory well. The Board considered that the location of the land within the EPZ was not reason in itself to qualify the owner for intervenor costs (*Amoco Canada, Whaleback Ridge Area, Advance Local Intervener Funding Memorandum of Decision*).

Public interest group participation was also a matter of controversy before the NEB. The Rocky Mountain Ecosystem Coalition was initially granted intervenor status in Board hearings on applications for natural gas export licenses, but was denied the opportunity to make representations on the upstream environmental effects associated with the proposed exports. Only after the Supreme Court of Canada's decision in *Hydro Québec v. Canada (National Energy Board)* suggested that assessment of such environmental effects was required did the Board schedule a review of its decision to grant the licenses. The group had in the meantime sought leave of the federal Court of Appeal to appeal the Board's licensing decisions. The leave to appeal application was dismissed, however, after the Board concluded, following its review, that it was required to asses the environmental effects of new facilities causally related to the proposed exports, and required the licensees to file additional EA information.

As a counterpoint to this trend toward restricting public participation in natural resource environmental regulatory processes, there was evidence in 1994 of broader public participation rights and even expanded rights to intervenor funding in other Canadian jurisdictions and contexts. The Ontario Environmental Bill of Rights, which includes extensive procedural rights to participate in regulatory decisions as well as in development of new policies, statutes, and regulations, was proclaimed in force in 1994. At the federal level, extensive opportunities are provided for public participation at the panel review stage of assessment under the CEAA. 1994 amendments to CEAA, noted above, place a duty on the Minister of the Environment to establish an intervenor funding program for this purpose.

Alastair R. Lucas

3. CARIBBEAN

A. THE BAHAMAS, BELIZE, & JAMAICA

(1) The Bahamas

Draft regulations for air and water pollution have been prepared under the Environmental Health Act but had not yet been implemented by the end of 1994. The Bahamas has signed the Conventions on Biological Diversity and Climate Change, but not the Cartagena Convention or its protocols. It acceded to the Basel Convention on 12 August 1992 and ratified the Law of the Sea Convention on 29 July 1983. A Commission on Science, Environment, and Technology was established in 1994 and is expected to become operational in 1995.

(2) Belize

Of the many legal environmental initiatives undertaken in Belize in 1994, the preparation of a Forest Act, new Forest Regulations, and a Fisheries Act stand out. Both the draft Forest Act and the draft Fisheries Act will require that environmental considerations be taken into account in the use of natural resources.

Draft General Environment Impact Assessment Regulations and Effluent Limitation Regulations under the Environmental Protection Act were subject to extensive public discussions and detailed review by non-governmental agencies. They are expected to be implemented in 1995. A new draft Land Utilization Act has also been prepared, which would impose environmental restrictions on certain types of land subdivisions and would require environmental assessment for leases of national lands. In addition, Belize enacted comprehensive new Mining Regulations in 1994, which impose environmental restrictions on mining operations in Belize along with requirements for environmental impact assessment for certain types of mining activities.

Revisions to the National Parks Systems Act and the Wildlife Protection Act that would expand the categories of protected areas were also under consideration. Legislation was also drafted for the establishment of a Protected Areas Conservation Trust fund for the management of protected areas and the enhancement of the environmental protection of Belize. Finally, a draft National Environmental Action Plan was being prepared in 1994 and was expected to be completed in 1995.

(3) Jamaica

Jamaica has acceded to the UN Convention on Biological Diversity as well as the Climate Change Convention. By 1994, regulations were being prepared under the Natural Resources Conservation Authority Act for implementing the Convention on Trade in Endangered Species.

Winston McCalla

B. REST OF CARIBBEAN

(1) The Caribbean Region in General

In 1994, Caribbean countries acceded to several international environmental conventions. Barbados, Trinidad and Tobago, and Grenada all ratified the UN Framework Convention On Climate Change. Dominica and Grenada ratified the Convention on Biological Diversity—Saint Lucia, Antigua and Barbuda, and St. Kitts and Nevis having ratified it in 1993. St. Kitts and Nevis also acceded to the Convention on International Trade in Endangered Species of Wild Fauna and Flora (CITES). Barbados, Saint Lucia, and Saint Vincent had previously acceded to CITES. The Basel Convention on the Control of Transboundary Movement of Hazardous Wastes and Their Disposal entered into force in both Saint Lucia and Saint Kitts and Nevis during 1994.

Another development of special significance was the formation of an Environmental Committee by the Caribbean Hotel Association to supply hoteliers with important information and resources for protecting the environment. The effort was supported by the International Hotel Association and the United Nations Environmental Programme. The Committee also worked in conjunction with the recommendations of the First Environmental Conference on Health and Sustainable Tourism, which took place during 1993. An abstract of the Caribbean Hotel Association's Environmental Manual was prepared.

(2) Barbados

Barbados introduced significant new legislation in the form of the Shipping (Oil Pollution) Act 1994 and Shipping Regulations 1994. The new Shipping Oil Pollution Act provides a comprehensive scheme for the regulation of ships registered under the Barbados flag and establishes a code of regulations, enforcement procedures, and liabilities for the discharge of oil by any ships in Barbados waters and for the discharge of oil anywhere in the world by Barbados-registered ships. The Shipping and Shipping (Oil Pollution) Acts are both modelled on United Kingdom legislation and are supplemented by Schedules of Applied Regulations that in most cases consist of regulations adopted by the United Kingdom authorities and incorporated by reference in the Schedules. As new or amended United Kingdom legislation is adopted, the Minister responsible for Maritime Affairs may make them applicable to the Shipping or Shipping (Oil Pollution) Acts by way of publication in the Official Gazette.

Another significant development was the publication in 1994 of the Barbados National Building Code (1993 Edition). The Code's comprehensive scope, which covers building design and management, structural requirements, fire safety, health and amenity, services, and equipment, has obvious environmental implications. The Code is based on the Caribbean Uniform Building Code (CUBIC) published in 1985. CUBIC was prepared under the aegis of the Caribbean Community Secretariat through a project funded by the Caribbean Development Bank and the United States Agency for International Development. The Barbados Code has developed the CUBIC provisions by refining and simplifying the technical provisions applying to various classes of buildings. The Barbados Code takes into account administrative arrangements peculiar to Barbados and creates a regime for promoting compliance.

(3) British Virgin Islands

In March of 1994, the Merchant Shipping (Adoption of United Kingdom Legislation) Act went into effect. The Act has wide-ranging provisions, some of which relate to environmental protection and management.

(4) Cayman Islands

The Cayman Islands government introduced three pieces of legislation with environmental implications. First, the Marine Conservation (Marine Parks) (Amendment) Regulations 1994 under the Marine Conservation Law 1978 add a new replenishment zone in the Victoria House—Sand Cay Apartments Marine Park by amending the principal 1986 regulations. The effect of the new replenishment zone is to relax the prohibitions on anchoring and fishing that applied in the area of the new zone when it was part of the Victoria House—Sand Cay Apartments Marine Park. Second, the Water Authority (Amendment) Regulations 1994 provide legal mechanisms and appropriate fees for owners of premises, and non-owners of Caymanian and non-Caymanian status to connect to the West Bay Sewage Scheme. Third, the Animals (Amendment) Regulations 1994 establish a fee structure for the issue of export and import licences for specified animals. The licensing procedure is essentially a legal mechanism to ensure that environmental and health standards are maintained by the exclusion or inclusion, subject to quarantine, of certain animals from particular locations.

(5) Saint Lucia

St. Lucia introduced elaborate Fisheries Regulations 1994 that apply to any fishing vessel or other vessel capable of being used for fishing within "the fishery waters at a distance greater than three miles from the nearest land." They provide for certain equipment to be carried by every vessel. Provision is also made for a Fisheries Advisory Committee, fishery conservation measures, and the granting of various fishing and fish-processing licences.

(6) Saint Vincent and the Grenadines

The Merchant Shipping (Amendment) Act 1994 amended §9(1) of the principal Act by reducing the age of a seaworthy ship capable of registration from 40 to 25 years. Also in 1994, a Reef Monitoring Scheme was installed in the Tobago Cays Reef as part of the Tobago Cays National Marine Park Project.

(7) Trinidad and Tobago

In Trinidad and Tobago, a Land Acquisition Bill was laid in Parliament on 22 February 1994. The Bill is divided into six parts and seeks to reform the law governing compulsory acquisition of land for public purposes and to repeal and replace the Land Acquisition Act.

A new Environmental Management bill was put out for public comment. The Bill seeks to create a new environmental management authority, an environmental trust fund, and an environmental commission as a superior court of record. After a process of public consultation, the bill was revised in the latter half of 1994 for introduction in Parliament in early 1995.

(8) Turks and Caicos

The National Parks (Amendment No. 2) Regulations 1994 seek to better regulate the operation of dive and charter vessels operating within a national park or nature reserve. Returns are now required within seven days of the end of the preceding calendar month. Such returns must be on prescribed forms and sent to the Director of Planning.

Finally, the Providenciales Marine Biology Education Centre Development Order 1994 provides for the construction of a centre on Providenciales Islands to encourage environmental education and awareness within Turks and Caicos.

Trevor A. Carmichael
Susan D. Mohan

4. MEXICO

(1) Introduction

Compared with the prior three years, Mexico was less involved in international environmental negotiations in 1994. During 1994, much of Mexico's work in environmental law concerned domestic implementation and enforcement of treaties and agreements signed in the previous years.

(2) Multilateral Issues

(a) (➔) Convention to Combat Desertification

Mexico participated in all the meetings of the Intergovernmental Negotiating Committee of a Convention to Combat Desertification. Mexico called for a convention of universal character, although it acknowledged the special problems of the African countries.

Mexico was one of the countries opposed to the inclusion of the concept of "assistance" in the Desertification Convention, arguing that it was against the commitments adopted during the Rio Summit. Instead, Mexico proposed the inclusion of the concepts of "cooperation" and adoption of obligations in accordance with the principle of common but differentiated responsibility. During 1994, Mexico participated actively in the preparation of the Regional Annex for Latin America, which was adopted, together with the Convention itself on October 15, 1994.

(b) Organisation for Economic Cooperation and Development

In 1994, Mexico adhered to the Organisation for Economic Cooperation and Development (OECD). There were strong political criticisms concerning the government's decision to become a member of OECD, the thrust of which was that many social imbalances were not yet resolved and should be addressed before aspiring to such membership. At a more formal level, Mexico's adherence to OECD implied a pronunciation of the government concerning the Council documents.

As part of the proceedings for its acceptance to OECD, Mexico presented a position memorandum explaining the various ways in which it would comply with the obligations and activities the organization requires. This document makes a thorough review of Mexico's cultural and institutional background, which enables the country to be a member of OECD. The chapter on environment, which Mexico prepared jointly with various governmental agencies, as well as private and academic institutions, explains that Mexico's commitment toward protecting the environment and conserving natural resources goes beyond its potential activities within OECD. It states further that Mexico was already implementing several of OECD's decisions and recommendations before becoming a member of the organization.

OECD's activities regarding the environment are strongly concentrated in the area of chemicals management, but they cover other areas such as economics and environment, coastal areas, energy use, urban development and environment, and transboundary pollution. Mexico adopted, without any reservation, the OECD Council's 41 recommendations on the environment. But it was necessary to make observations regarding the implications, mechanisms, timing, and resources needed to adopt and implement the 13 decisions on chemical substances and hazardous wastes.

Among the decisions that Mexico adopted with reservations are those regarding the mutual acceptance of data on assessment of chemical substances (C(91)30(Final)), the minimum data on assessment of chemical products before their commercialization (C(82)196(Final)), principles on good laboratory practices (C(90)87(Final)), future measures on environmental protection through control of polychlorinated biphenyls (PBCs) (C(87)2(Final)), exchange of information on accidents that may cause transboundary damage (C(88)84(Final)), provision of information to the public and public participation on prevention and response to accidents involving chemical substances (C(88)85(Final)), systematic research of existing chemical substances (C(87)90(Final)), and control of transboundary movements of wastes for recovery operations (C(92)39(Final)).

The implementation of these decisions means that regulations and programs will have to be established to impose requirements on facilities that undertake related activities within Mexico. These requirements could be such things as a notification system to assess hazardous chemicals, procedures to be followed by laboratories which assess hazardous chemicals, or banning of PBCs and control of present uses.

The implementation of all the above decisions and recommendations will be under the surveyance of the OECD, which publishes every two years a Report on the State of the Environment in Countries Members. On September 1994, officials of the OECD Secretariat visited Mexico, and through interviews with government officials, filled in thorough questionnaires on the environmental conditions of air, freshwater resources, soils, forests, wildlife, energy uses, transport, industry, agriculture, and environmental management in general.

(3) Regional Issues

The North American Commission for Environmental Cooperation met for the first time in regular session, on July 26, 1994. The governing body of the Commission (the Council) approved its priority activities for the first year. Activities were approved in the following seven areas: conservation and ecosystem protection, North American Free Trade Agreement effects and consultation, enforcement, pollution prevention, environmental policy instruments, technology cooperation and capacity-building, and trans-boundary environmental issues.

The Council also adopted the rules and procedures for the Joint Public Advisory Committee (JPAC). These rules aim at ensuring that the Council operates in an open and transparent manner and that the JPAC will be able to effectively provide advice. In general, the JPAC is charged with providing advice to the Commission on implementing the Environment Agreement and may provide the Council with relevant technical, scientific, or other information.

JPAC members decided to meet regularly, four times a year, in the early stages and to advise the Council on all aspects of the Commission's work. The members will draw on their expertise in a wide rage of activities. The Committee's membership, totaling 15 members with five from each country, reflects the diverse range of interests that the public of all three countries has regarding the work of the Commission. The members will help ensure that the Commission's activities achieve the goals of the Agreement.

(4) Bilateral Issues

No new environmental agreements were adopted at a bilateral level. The activities concentrated on creating and implementing specific projects, either as a result of agreements adopted in previous years, or simply as part of the international cooperation activities of Mexico. During 1994, Mexico initiated specific projects with the following countries:

- Belize: cooperation on mining, eco-tourism, and ecological zoning;
- Bolivia: cooperation on air quality;
- Canada: cooperation on law enforcement, hazardous substances management, and natural protected areas;
- Chile: cooperation on air quality in urban areas;
- Costa Rica: cooperation on air quality, water quality, and solid wastes management;
- El Salvador: cooperation on information and data management, environmental impact assessment, air quality, environmental education, and ecological zoning;
- Germany: cooperation on residual waters, and on restoration and sustainability of ecosystems;

- Great Britain: cooperation on air quality in industrial corridors;
- Guatemala: cooperation on ecological zoning;
- Japan: cooperation on air quality in Mexico City and establishment of a National Center on Environmental Research and Training;
- Nicaragua: cooperation on environmental education and on environmental impact assessment in urban areas;
- Panama: cooperation on natural protected areas;
- Spain: cooperation on ecological zoning and environmental impact assessment; and
- Venezuela: cooperation on environmental education.

Diana L. Ponce-Nava

5. CENTRAL AMERICA

(1) Regional Activities and Declarations

On 12 October, presidents from Central America, Panama, and Belize met in Managua, Nicaragua, for the Central America Ecological Summit for Sustainable Development, where they adopted a holistic strategy for sustainable development in the region, called the Alliance for Sustainable Development. A Declaration embodying the Alliance includes a definition of sustainable development that takes into account the characteristics of the Central American region, the principles in which this strategy is grounded, the bases needed to make it happen, the objectives and the tools. It defines sustainable development as:

> a process of gradual change in the quality of life of people that sees them as the center and the pivotal subject of development, through economic growth with social fairness and through the transformation of the means of production and of the consumption patterns, all grounded in the region's ecological equilibrium and vital support. This process implies the respect for the regional ethnic and cultural diversity, both national and local, and the strengthening and full participation of their citizens, in peaceful coexistence and in harmony with nature, without detriment to, and assuring, the quality of life of future generations.

The Declaration defines its guiding principles as respect for life in all its expressions; improvement of the quality of human life; respect for, and sustainable use of, the vitality and diversity of the land; promotion of peace and democracy as basic forms of human coexistence; respect for the region's cultural pluralism and ethnic diversity; attainment of greater degrees of economic integration among the countries in the region, and of these with the world; and intergenerational responsibility for sustainable development. The Declaration states that it is based on democracy, sociocultural development, sustainable economic development, sustainable management of natural resources, and improvement of environmental quality.

It includes an Annex that spells out the specific objectives.

The Declaration also promotes the establishment of national councils for sustainable development as instruments of implementation. The councils are to implement the Declaration with the aid of the public and private sectors and of the Central American Council for Sustainable Development, composed of the Central American Presidents and the Prime Minister of Belize.

On the occasion of the Declaration's adoption, at the foot of the Masaya volcano, the parties also signed the Commitments Regarding the Environment and Natural Resources, Masaya Volcano, Nicaragua. These Commitments set out specific actions, with well-defined and stringent timetables, for carrying out the basic objectives of the Alliance for Sustainable Development.

(2) Summit of the Americas

Thirty-four presidents came together at the hemisphere's most important political event of 1994, the Summit of the Americas, held in Miami, 9–11 December. The Summit issued two documents. The first of these, the Declaration of Principles: Agreement for Development and Prosperity: Democracy, Free Trade, and Sustainable Development in the Americas, aims to achieve four objectives: to preserve and strengthen the community of democracies of the Americas; to promote prosperity through the integration of the economies and through free trade; to uproot poverty and discrimination in the hemisphere; and to guarantee sustainable development and preserve the environment for future generations. The second document, the Plan of Action, lists certain groups of objectives in organizational terms, namely as the Alliance for the Sustainable Use of Energy, the Alliance for Biodiversity, and the Alliance for the Prevention of Pollution. It thereby emphasizes the participants' belief that the realization of the objectives concerned requires broad participation of both the public and private sectors, although the principal responsibility for carrying out the Plan lies with governments, individually and collectively.

The Summit of the Americas openly subscribed to the Central American Alliance for Sustainable Development, and thus provides important political support in its attempt to strengthen regional democracies through the promotion of social and economic prosperity and rational environmental management.

(3) Convenio Entre Centroamerica y Estados Unidos de America ((➔) CONCAUSA—Agreement between Central America and the United States)

At the Summit of the Americas, the CONCAUSA Declaration was signed. Through this document, the United States became the first partner from outside the Alliance for Sustainable Development region. The Agreement's Plan of Action specifies the individual responsibilities of the governments of the United States and the Central America countries.

The CONCAUSA Plan of Action includes the following elements: identification, preservation, and sustainable use of the region's unique biodiversity; promoting clean and efficient energy use; strengthening legal and institutional frameworks and environmental implementing legislation and improving and harmonizing environmental protection norms; and sustainable economic development. In addition to the specific components of its Plan of Action, CONCAUSA also voices general support for carrying out the Alliance for Sustainable Development.

(4) Regional and National Perspectives

There has been a proliferation of environmental legislation in the region, with national actions and initiatives taking shape within the Central American framework. Regional and national legal instruments provide insight into a number of general development perspectives embedded in public participation, including participation by native communities, indigenous groups, and other groups at the fringe of society in environmental decisions; environmental impact assessment; and natural resource management.

Natural resource management expanded in a variety of ways. For example, regional and national legal instruments establish requirements and procedures for management plans, certification of timber-yielding products from sustainable forests, contingency plans for forest fires, and participation of municipalities and local authorities in forest administration.

Similarly, biodiversity took on an ever-increasing importance in the region. Since the signing of the Agreement on the Conservation of Biodiversity and the Protection of Prime Wilderness Areas in Central America in June 1992, regional projects such as the Central American Biological Corridor, a linkage of protected areas for the conservation and migration of species, have taken shape. Also notable are the establishment of centers of biodiversity and botanical gardens and the preparation of a Central American list of endangered species of wild flora and fauna. Other regional priorities include energy, transportation, the management and conservation of water resources, control and prevention of air and water pollution, and uniformity in classification of lands and strategies for protecting and restoring exhausted and polluted soils.

Finally, a consensus has developed in Central America regarding the need to apply environmental legislation at both the international and national levels. All the regionally developed documents therefore contain political commitments to ratify regional and international agreements on the environment and natural resources, and to develop the institutional capacity to make their implementation possible.

(5) Ratification of International Agreements

During 1994, Guatemala ratified the Central American Regional Agreement on Forests (Convenio Regional para el Manejo y Conservación de los Ecosistemas Naturales Forestales y el Desarrollo de Plantaciones Forestales). All the current regional agreements are in force in Guatemala, except the one on climate change. Costa Rica and Guatemala both ratified the Basel Convention on the Control of the Transboundary Movements of Hazardous Wastes. Nicaragua ratified the Protocol of the International Convention for the Prevention of Pollution by Ships.

The agreements signed at UNCED in 1992 received strong support from the Central American countries. In December, Costa Rica, El Salvador, Honduras, and Panama all ratified the Biodiversity Convention, and Costa Rica, El Salvador, and Honduras joined the UN Climate Change Convention as parties.

As of year's end, the regional agreements on Biodiversity, Climate Change, Transboundary Movements of Hazardous Waste and Forests were on national legislative agendas. It was expected that the ratification process would be expedited in 1995 in response to the political commitments assumed in the Alliance.

(6) Other Developments and Initiatives with International Dimensions

(a) Constitutional Reform in Costa Rica

Costa Rica approved the reform of Art. 50 of its Political Constitution to include the right to a healthy and ecologically balanced environment.

(b) Court Decisions

Panama's Third Court of the Supreme Court of Justice handed down an important decision holding that the National Association for the Conservation of Nature (ANCON—Asociación Nacional para la Conservación de la Naturaleza), a non-governmental organization, had standing to challenge the granting of a forest license by submitting its "opposition" to the National Institute of Renewable Natural Resources. Costa Rica's Constitutional Court of the Supreme Court of Justice reiterated its position that for purposes of environmental law, the procedural assumption of standing allows any person to sue. Based on this argument, the Court heard a case brought by a minor against a local government that allegedly had been violating the plaintiff's "constitutional right to a healthy environment" through the unlawful disposal of solid wastes.

Patricia Madrigal Cordero

6. SOUTH AMERICA

A. ARGENTINA

In 1994, several significant developments took place with regard to international environmental treaties, national legislation (particularly the new National Constitution), and Southern Cone Common Market (MERCOSUR) environmental norms.

(1) International Treaties

The UN Convention on Biological Diversity was ratified by Law of Congress No. 24.375 on 7 September, and promulgated by the Executive Office on 3 October. The Convention had been signed by Argentina during the Earth Summit in 1992. The International Convention on the Protection of New Varieties of Plants, originally adopted in 1961 and revised in 1972 and 1978, was ratified by Law of Congress No. 24.376 on 21 September and promulgated on 20 October.

(2) National Legislation of International Significance

(a) The National Constitution

On 22 August, Argentina adopted a new National Constitution, based on the previous Constitution (1853/1860), which incorporates such environmental concepts as the right to a healthy, balanced, and adequate environment for human development; a general duty to preserve the environment; intergenerational equity; the obligation of authorities to guarantee these rights; the rational use of natural resources; the preservation of natural and cultural heritage and biological diversity; and the state's duty to provide environmental education and information.

The Constitution also includes a special clause banning imports of hazardous, potentially hazardous, and radioactive waste. The practical effects of this provision remain to be seen. Other nations may adopt reciprocal bans, and Argentine waste may not be accepted for treatment and final disposal abroad, even if no adequate facilities are available in Argentina. Wastes generated in border areas may have to be transported to facilities in the industrial areas of the country, rather than exported to nearer foreign facilities. This would create new domestic environmental and health risks. The ban may also preclude the option of waste management arrangements with other countries, such as Brazil, that already have a waste treatment infrastructure that is better than Argentina's. (A similar clause exists in the new Constitution of the Province of Buenos Aires (Art.28) whereby waste may not be introduced into its territory from other jurisdictions.)
Significantly, the Constitution provides for the supremacy of international

treaties over national laws, so that environmental treaties will trump inconsistent statutory provisions.

(b) The National Space Plan

By Executive Decree 2076 of 28 November, the Government adopted a National Space Plan to be executed from 1995 to 2006. The Plan covers terrestrial infrastructure, satellite systems, information systems, access to space, and institutional development. The Plan also touches on environmental concerns in that it is expected to provide the National Space Commission with knowledge on the state of the environment and the ecology of the country. In addition, it will be an excellent system for collecting environmental data on the MERCOSUR countries as well as other parts of the world.

(3) MERCOSUR Environmental Norms

MERCOSUR, the single market area created by Argentina, Brazil, Paraguay, and Uruguay, came into effect on 1 January 1995. It includes a region of great biological and cultural diversity, ranging from the largest tropical forest in the world, the Brazilian Amazon, to the grasslands of the Argentine and Uruguayan Pampas, to the wetlands of the Brazilian and the Paraguayan Pantanal and the River Plate Basin five-country system, to the Argentine Cordillera de los Andes mountain range, to the Argentine Patagonia steppes and the sub-Antarctic forest. Thus, MERCOSUR presents an enormous opportunity for setting minimum environmental standards to ensure fair competition in the four-country single market. It also presents, however, the challenge of guaranteeing sound environmental policies and legislation for each type of economic development envisioned in the new economic union.

MERCOSUR established a "Specialized Conference on the Environment" (REMA) to develop environmental harmonization strategies. During 1994, REMA proposed to the Common Market Group (equivalent to the EEC Commission) "Basic Directives on Environmental Policy" ((➔) *Directrices Basicas en Materia de Politica Ambiental.*) The Group adopted the document by Resolution No. 10 of 1994. The Directives include 11 paragraphs on harmonizing environmental legislation and on principles of common environmental policy and management. In 1995, REMA's focus will be on environmental institution building, harmonization criteria and techniques, common environmental policy and law-making, programmes of action, and environmental technical support as part of dispute resolution mechanisms.

It should be noted that Art. 75, §24, of the new Argentine Constitution allows the Argentine Congress to approve integration treaties pursuant to which law-making powers are delegated to supranational organizations, and allows for norms adopted within such regimes to be granted supremacy over Argentine legislation.

Pedro Tarak

B. BOLIVIA

(1) International Developments

(a) International Agreements

In 1994, Bolivia became a party to a number international agreements bearing on environmental protection. By Law No. 1570 of 12 July, Bolivia ratified the 1982 Law of the Sea Convention; by Law No. 1572 of the same date, it ratified the Amazonian Cooperation Agreement with Peru; by Law No. 1576 of 25 July, Bolivia approved of the UN Climate Change Convention, which it had signed during the United Nations Conference on Environment and Development in 1992. Bolivia also became a party to the international ozone layer protection regime by acceding to the Vienna Convention and the Montreal Protocol, its 1990 London Amendment, and its 1992 Copenhagen Amendments, by Law No. 1584 of 3 August.

Also, by Law No. 1589 of 12 August, Bolivia ratified an agreement with Paraguay on environmental and natural resource management, which the two countries had signed in Asunción on 15 March 1994. The agreement promotes, *inter alia*: environmental cooperation through exchange of information on environmental protection methods and techniques and on legislation; coordination of efforts related to protection of the Chaco ecosystem; joint planning for the conservation and sustainable use of biodiversity resources and integrated water management in common frontier areas; and strict control of trade in animals and plants, as well as their products, through enforcement of the Convention on International Trade in Endangered Species of Wild Fauna and Flora (CITES). The agreement calls for the creation of a binational council and working groups for the implementation of the objectives of the agreement. On 17 March, Bolivia and Argentina signed an agreement on cooperation in the field of environmental protection (which was approved and ratified by Law No. 1592 of 12 August). The agreement covers air, soil, water, biological diversity, hazardous wastes, environmental effects of energy production, mining and other industrial activities, and urban pollution. It also provides for an institutional framework for cooperation. Also on 12 August, Law No. 1595 approved and ratified an agreement that the Bolivian and Swiss governments had signed on 2 March 1993, pursuant to which Switzerland grants Bolivia sf. 5.2 million for biodiversity conservation purposes.

On 26 April the Presidents of Bolivia, Argentina, and Paraguay signed a 10-point agreement in Formosa, Argentina (Formosa Declaration), concerning the tri-national management of the Pilcomayo River. The Declaration emphasizes environmental protection and sustainable development of the region, and establishes a tripartite commission, composed of two representatives of each nation that will coordinate the Pilcomayo project and search for international funding. The accord set in motion activities to reduce the intense erosion in the upper reaches of the Pilcomayo watershed, regulate water flows to Paraguay and Argentina, control flooding of the river basin and the uncontrolled migration of the river channel, and promote rational use of waters. The core of the project is the proposed Caipipendi Dam on the Pilcomayo River in Bolivia above Villamontes. The dam will regulate water flows to the downstream states (Paraguay and Argentina), provide water for 100,000 hectares of irrigated land in Bolivia and 200,000 hectares in Argentina and Paraguay and generate 210 megawatts of electricity.

To counter the increasing environmental degradation of Lake Titicaca, the Organization of American States and the governments of Bolivia and Peru signed a technical cooperation agreement in December that initiated the Environmental Planning Project of the Titicaca-Desaguadero-Popopó-Salar de Coipsa System. This project is the first environmental management initiative undertaken in the Lake Titicaca Basin. Its objectives include the preparation of zoning plans, development of information systems, strengthening of institutional arrangements, and feasibility studies of priority environmental management projects.

(b) *Hidrovía Waterway Project*

In March, the Inter-American Development Bank allocated an initial $7 million to the Hidrovía Project, a 3,400km inland navigable waterway that would create river access to the Atlantic Ocean through the Río de la Plata, Paraguay, and Paraná Rivers in four nations members of Mercosur (Argentina, Brazil, Paraguay, and Uruguay), as well as Bolivia. Local environmentalists expressed concern that the Hidrovía Project would have a potentially negative impact on the region's ecosystems, especially the 200,000km^2 Pantanal wetlands in Paraguay and Brazil. The Hidrovía Project advanced to a new phase after a 24-25 September meeting of the Presidents of Bolivia, Paraguay, and Peru, during which the chief executives recognized the need to consider the project's ecological impacts during its planning and development phase. At the 16th Meeting of the Intergovernmental Hidrovía Committee (CIH) in October, delegates from Argentina, Bolivia, Brazil, Paraguay, and Uruguay adopted a resolution that appeared to strengthen environmental protection in the Hidrovía planning process. The CIH delegated the responsibility for developing preventive and mitigation measures to a Technical Environmental Group. Nevertheless, by the end of the year, public concern over the potential environmental impact of the Hidrovía Project continued to mount.

(c) *Bolivia-Brazil Border Cooperation*

The Second Binational Border Meeting was held in April in Guayará-Mirim (Brazil) between business and political delegates of the Beni

Department (Bolivia) and Rondônia State (Brazil). The Meeting addressed, *inter alia*, cooperation in environmental protection. Delegates advocated construction of a 1,800km paved road between Pôrto Velho (Brazil) and Tambo Quemado (Bolivia), a project that could facilitate export of Brazilian products to Pacific ports. An additional recommendation of the meeting focused on integrated sustainable development of this border region, which contains a significant percentage of the natural resources of both countries.

(d) CITES

The vicuña, a South American cameloid, had been listed in Appendix I of CITES since 1975. In 1987, however, Note 106 to the Appendix I listing of *Vicugna vicugna* removed processed wool (but not the animal itself) from certain vicuña populations in Peru and Chile from that appendix. At the Ninth Meeting of the Contracting Parties to CITES in November 1994, Bolivia opposed a change in the protected status of the vicuña. In the end, the Conference downlisted the vicuña populations in Chile and Peru, but retained those of Bolivia and Argentina on Appendix I. While this action facilitates the export of processed vicuña fiber from Peru and Chile, it can also exacerbate illegal hunting, sale, and export activities involving Bolivian vicuñas. In response, in September, the Ministry of Sustainable Development and Environment took direct administrative responsibility for the Ulla National Wildlife Reserve, a principal refuge for the vicuña in Bolivia. Local communities, as well as the "ecological battalion" of the Bolivian Army specifically organized to protect the vicuña, assist in managing the reserve.

The illegal harvesting and export of the American Mahogany or "mara" (*Swietenia macrophylla*) continued to be a topic of intense debate this year. Bolivian environmental organizations supported listing mara on CITES Appendix II. At the Eighth Conference of the Contracting Parties to CITES in 1992, the Bolivian delegation had opposed the listing of mara on Appendix II. The Bolivian delegation adopted a similar position at the Ninth Conference, arguing that the management activities of the Ministry of Sustainable Development and the imminent approval of the Forestry Law would be sufficient to control the exploitation and commercialization of this species. In the end, the Conference failed to approve the Appendix II listing.

(2) Domestic Developments

(a) General Environmental Law

In June, the Ministry of Sustainable Development announced that it would create Departmental Environmental Councils in Bolivia's nine departments. The Councils will include representatives, public institutions, business groups, and non-governmental organizations. The principal Council function will be to identify activities that cause negative environmental impacts in each jurisdiction and suggest remedial policies to address the problems. Five multi-sectoral technical commissions continued to develop regulations pursuant to Bolivia's General Environmental Law (Law No. 1333, 27 April 1992), namely on environmental impact evaluation, water pollution, solid wastes, and toxic substances. The regulations will provide economic incentives for environmental protection as well as sanctions for environmental crimes. Five sets of regulations were expected to be presented to Congress, adopted, and implemented in 1995.

(b) National Council on Sustainable Development

In May, the government set up the National Council on Sustainable Development, an inter-ministerial body that is to focus on integration of environmental protection with social and economic development and on governance. The Council, which represents the ministries of Sustainable Development, Human Development, Economic Development, National Defense, and Foreign Affairs, is presided by the President.

(c) National Plan to Combat Soil Degradation

In September, the Secretariat of Renewable Natural Resources of the Ministry of Sustainable Development launched a National Plan to Combat Soil Degradation that seeks to integrate agro-ecology with socio-economic realities. Under this plan, Bolivia will develop strategies to be presented to a future meeting of the conference of the parties to the (_) Convention on Desertification.

(d) Forests

The proposed Forestry Law (*see* 3 *YbIEL* 378 (1992); 4 *YbIEL* 330 (1993)) passed the Chamber of Deputies in late February but stalled in the Senate for the remainder of the year due to controversies with Native communities and the timber industry. Timber interests lobbied for legislative modifications that would allow for private property rights and lower taxes on the 40-year timber concessions. Opposition from Native Peoples focused on what they considered to be restricted forestry use by local communities and their limited ability to block forestry concessions on the lands they inhabit.

The Secretariat of Ethnic Affairs of the Ministry of Human Development and the Secretariat of Natural Resources of the Ministry of Sustainable Development gave timber companies 120 days to remove logging equipment from the Chimán Forest located in lands belonging to Native Peoples. The legal basis for this action was Supreme Decree 22611 of 1990, which prohibits commercial forestry activities in the Chimán Forest and declared the Forest to be indigenous territory (*see* 3 *YbIEL* 377 (1992)).

Daniel O. Suman
Patricia Mariaca Zárate

D. CHILE

(1) Domestic Legal Developments

On 9 March, Chile enacted a first framework environmental law, the *Ley General de Bases de Medio Ambiente* (Law 19,300). The Law introduces novel concepts into Chilean environmental law, such as environmental impact assessment (EIA); environmental management and clean-up; protection of private natural lands; public participation in environmental decision-making at the municipal level; and environmental litigation. It also provides for a new procedure for enacting ambient quality and emission standards; and creates a new environmental institution, CONAMA.

Among the regulations implementing the framework law, two—on EIA and on the environmental standard-setting procedure—are especially noteworthy. The regulations that establish the system of EIA provide for a single-step process: in its approval of a project or activity, CONAMA will jointly grant all relevant environmental permits from the various regulatory authorities concerned in a single step. CONAMA will also set environmental conditions for the granting of future permits. Once CONAMA authorizes a project or activity, therefore, no other public authority will be able to oppose it on environmental grounds.

The new procedure for setting primary and secondary environmental quality and emissions standards provides for a series of stages—a review of pertinent scientific and economic data, input from the affected community, and the approval of CONAMA's board of directors—before the any new standard can be enacted. Until recently, the secretaries of the different ministries autonomously set environmental standards.

(2) International Developments

In 1994, Chile ratified the Convention on Biodiversity. By the end of the year, the government was pressing ahead with plans to initiate negotiations to accede to the North American Free Trade Agreement, which would have important repercussions on Chile's environmental laws.

Eduardo J. Astorga

E. COLOMBIA

(1) Ratification of the Biodiversity Convention

In 1994, the Colombian Congress ratified the Biodiversity Convention, which Colombia had originally signed in Rio de Janeiro in 1992 (Law 162 of 1994).

(2) Judicial Decision Concerning International Toxic Trade

In February 1993, industrial toxic waste allegedly to be used as fuel for an electric power plant had been imported into Colombia from Croatia in violation of Art. 92 of the Colombian Constitution. After identifying several violations of the law in the importation process, the Health and the Environment Ministers ordered the importer to re-export the material. The importer, however, failed to comply, pleading a lack of economic means. After several months of inaction, a group of concerned citizens sued for a constitutional injunction against the shipping company, Croatia Line, whose vessel, the *Triglav*, had brought the waste to Colombia and was about to return to Cartagena as part of the company's regular commercial service. In 1994, the Court of Appeals of Santa Marta issued an order against Croatia Line obliging the *Triglav* to reload the waste material and take it out of the country. The company complied with the judicial order within 24 hours. The Colombian Supreme Court affirmed the decision of the Court of Appeals, which had held that the importation of toxic waste violated fundamental rights of Santa Marta citizens and that the shipping company was liable to remove the materials from Colombian soil.

(3) Environmental Impact Assessment

Decree 1753 of 1994, which implements Law 99 of 1993, provides for the issuance of permits for activities that may significantly affect the environment. Any such activities are now subject to environmental impact assessment. The permits specify obligations and conditions that the applicant must comply with so as to prevent, mitigate, compensate, and manage environmental effects of the activity. Under the Decree, the Ministry of the Environment, regional environmental authorities, and municipal authorities are authorized to issue environmental permits as well as to enforce permit conditions.

Germán Sarmiento Palacio

F. ECUADOR

(1) Petroleum

Ecuador signed an agreement in April 1994 with the Latin American Organization of Energy (OLADE) that will help reconcile petroleum exploitation with environmental protection. OLADE will prepare a technical document that will define the petroleum technologies most consistent with environmental protection. The organization will also develop technical parameters for environmental impact statements, environmental management plans, and plans for termination of activities in areas of operation.

The Ministry of Energy and Mines announced that it will establish strict environmental controls in contracts that result from the Seventh Round of Petroleum Bids. Successful companies will have to perform environmental audits before and after conducting operations. If the audits indicate environmental damage, the company will have to indemnify the state.

In 1994, the Minister of Energy and Mines conducted two dialogues with representatives of Amazon Indian organizations. Upon proposal by the Confederation of Indigenous Nationalities of the Ecuadorian Amazon and the Confederation of Indigenous Nationalities of Ecuador, the Minister agreed to the formation of an Environmental Monitoring Commission. The Commission will include representatives of Petroecuador, the armed forces, local Amazon governments, environmental groups, and Native peoples' organizations.

(2) Alleged Environmental Damage by Texaco, Inc.

(a) Class Action Suit Against Texaco

In November 1993, a group of Ecuadorian Indians brought a class action law suit against Texaco in the US District Court for the Southern District of New York (*Aguinda v. Texaco, Inc.*, No. 93-7257-CIV (VLB)) (*See* 4 *YbIEL* 337 (1994)). The plaintiffs alleged that Texaco had engaged in environmental abuse, including large-scale disposal of inadequately treated hazardous wastes and destruction of the tropical rain forest habitat where the plaintiffs live. The outcome of this case could have great implications for the manner in which multinational corporations operate in developing countries, the technologies they adopt, and the fora in which foreign plaintiffs file complaints.

In 1994, Texaco moved to dismiss the complaint on several grounds, including *forum non conveniens*. Another ground for dismissal, according to Texaco, is that the Ecuadorian government is an indispensable party in the action but cannot be joined because of sovereign immunity. The Ecuadorian government submitted an amicus brief that supported Texaco's motion to dismiss the action and argued that exercise of jurisdiction in this case would provide a disincentive to US firms considering investment in Ecuador. Moreover, Ecuador stressed that according to the 1992 Rio Declaration on Environment and Development, it maintained a sovereign right to exploit its own natural resources pursuant to its own environmental policies and laws.

On April 11, 1994, Judge Broderick delivered a memorandum addressing these issues and temporarily reserved decision on Texaco's motions while the plaintiffs pursued discovery. The Court allowed discovery of events relating to harm alleged by the plaintiffs to have occurred in the United States. The judge also allowed discovery concerning events that occurred outside the United States as long as this information could be obtained voluntarily through Texaco officials in the United States. Discovery will give the plaintiffs access to information that may demonstrate that Texaco headquarters made decisions in the United States that negatively affected the Ecuadorian environment. Judge Broderick divided the case into two parts: (1) monetary damages to the persons affected by Texaco's actions and (2) injunctive relief. The Court strongly hinted, without deciding, that the damages suit could better be tried in Ecuadorian courts (Sucumbíos). Although reserving judgment, the Court was more positive on the likelihood that US courts could take jurisdiction over the issue of injunctive relief.

Some sectors of the Ecuadorian government reacted negatively to the Court's opinion. Ecuador's ambassador to the United States accused the Ecuadorian Indians of undermining the nation's sovereignty.

On April 25, Texaco requested that the Court reconsider its April 11 order. But on April 29, Judge Broderick denied Texaco's request for dismissal. In the interim, Texaco had made no commitment to satisfy the requirement that it fully submit to the jurisdiction of Ecuadorian courts and that Ecuadorian courts exercise jurisdiction over plaintiffs' claims.

On December 29, 1994, a group of Peruvian Indians filed a similar complaint with the court (*Ashanga v. Texaco, Inc.*, No. 94-9266-CIV (VLB)). An estimated 25,000 Peruvians who live along the Napo River could comprise this class. The complaint alleges that the petroleum released by Texaco into the environment in Ecuador subsequently flowed into Peru and generated similar health problems among native peoples in the Peruvian Amazon.

(b) Environmental Audit: The Texaco/Ecuador Agreement

In 1991, the Ministry of Energy and Mines had solicited foreign environmental auditors (the Canadian firm HBT Agra) to evaluate the environmental impact of Texaco's Amazon operations. The audit was supposed to be completed by September 1993. In January, the Ministry of Energy and Mines announced that the audit would remain confidential. By mid-1994, dissatisfaction with HBT Agra's environmental audit process to consider the social impacts on Native communities, destruction of forests, and pollution of rivers and lagoons, led the newly formed Environmental Monitoring Commission to disapprove the study. By July, the Minister of Energy and Mines rejected the audit and instead appointed a technical commission to perform its own environmental inventory of the region.

By August, the Ecuadorian government dropped its threat to sue Texaco for environmental damages after the company agreed to restore the Amazonian environment that had been damaged between 1968 and 1990. The Minister of Energy and Mines proposed that Texaco build a hospital in the Amazon region, clean up oil lagoons and oil wells, reinject production waters, implement reforestation projects, and pay damages to the local populations in affected areas. While Texaco agreed to assume the entire cost of the environmental reparation in a 400,000 hectare area, it refused to acknowledge the social consequences of its activities and thus refused to construct a hospital, distribute monies to local communities, and contribute to other social causes.

(3) Amazon Basin

The Sixth Assembly of the Amazonian Parliament convened in June 1994 in Quito, Ecuador, with the participation of over 50 parliamentarians from Bolivia, Brazil, Colombia, Ecuador, Guyana, Peru, Surinam, and Venezuela. The Assembly reviewed environmental protection programs undertaken pursuant to the Treaty for Amazon Cooperation. The legislators agreed to a project under which national laws will be analyzed in an attempt to harmonize environmental regulations and norms, on the assumption that harmonization could advance protection of the Amazon's natural resources, promote sustainable use of biological diversity, and help consolidate national sovereignty in the region.

The Assembly condemned environmental degradation in the Amazon Basin and demanded adoption of immediate and effective measures to end the continuing erosion of biological diversity and degradation of Amazon ecosystems. It denounced the polluting activities of petroleum companies in the Amazon Basin, as well as indiscriminate logging activities, and recommended that all Amazon governments conduct environmental audits of petroleum activities with the active participation of native peoples.

Ecuador and seven other member states of the Treaty for Amazon Cooperation met in Lima, Peru, from October 10-11 to discuss ways to protect both Amazon biodiversity and ethno-cultural groups while pursuing sustainable development.

(4) Toxics

In July 1994, the ship *Triglav* sailed from Cartagena, Colombia, for Guayaquil, Ecuador, carrying eight containers with 575 drums, or 97 tons, of PVC, heavy metal, and pharmaceutical residues originating in Croatia. Upon notification of the shipment, President Durán-Ballén reiterated Ecuador's absolute prohibition on the importation of hazardous wastes. Referring to the Basel Convention on the Control of Transboundary Movements of Hazardous Wastes and their Disposal, the Ecuadorian Defense Minister announced that the Navy would prohibit the *Triglav* from entering Ecuadorian territorial waters. After the governments of Peru and Chile also prohibited the *Triglav* from unloading at their ports, the ship returned to Croatia.

(5) Galapagos Islands

Early in the year, the government granted permits for two cruise liners from the United States to visit the Galapagos Archipelago, which the United Nations Education, Scientific, and Cultural Organization (UNESCO) had declared a Natural Patrimony of Mankind in 1978. Environmental groups and local tourist operators criticized this authorization. As a result of the protests, the government commissioned studies to determine the impact of tourism on the islands.

In May 1994, President Durán-Ballén announced, in an executive decree, a plan for the controlled development of tourism in the Galapagos Archipelago. The program will consider the economic condition of Galapagos residents and at the same time regulate fishing and tourism activities.

The World Bank approved a $7.2 million grant to be coordinated through the Global Environment Facility. Funds will be used to protect biodiversity in Ecuador, especially in the Galapagos Islands. At the end of the year, the Japanese government also granted $600,000 to support existing management plans at the Galapagos National Park on conservation and administration of tourism and on administration of the Marine Resources Reserve. The Inter-American Development Bank will administer these funds.

In September, an Ecuadorian patrol boat captured a Japanese fishing boat with twenty tons of shark fins north of Isabela Island in the Galapagos Archipelago. The fishing vessel was detained in an area where all fishing was restricted. Moreover, a prohibition on commercial fishing of shark is in effect in all Ecuadorian waters. Ecuadorian officials admitted that enforcement of fishing regulations is difficult and surmised that for every foreign boat captured, dozens escape enforcement operations.

The continued degradation of the Galapagos ecosystem led the Ecuadorian government to suspend all concessions for tourist operations and all permits to construct new tourist facilities in September 1994. The government also reinforced its prohibitions on commercial and industrial fishing activities. The suspensions will last until detailed studies show how tourism can continue without degrading the islands' environment. President Durán-Ballén also announced the expansion of the Galapagos Marine Resource Reserve from 15 to 40 miles measured from the coastline. Another government initiative to protect the Galapagos will be its petition to the International Maritime Organization to declare the waters adjacent to the Galapagos Islands as sensitive to traffic in hydrocarbons and noxious substances. Such a declaration would lead to restrictions on vessel traffic.

During a December 1994 meeting in Thailand, UNESCO's World Patrimony Committee postponed for a year its decision to include the

Galapagos Islands on a list of patrimonies in danger. This postponement will give the Ecuadorian government an opportunity to take steps to reduce the threats to the Galapagos Islands. At this meeting, the Committee also rejected the Ecuadorian request to extend the designation of Natural Patrimony of Mankind to the Galapagos Marine Resources Reserve. The World Patrimony Committee requested further evidence of the effectiveness of Ecuador's actions to conserve the Galapagos marine resources. The Committee cited the damage to the marine ecosystem caused by continuing legal and illegal fishing of shark, lobster, and sea cucumber in these waters as the basis for its decision.

(6) Endangered Species

At the November 1994 Conference of the Parties to the Convention on International Trade in Endangered Species of Wild Fauna and Flora held in Fort Lauderdale, United States, Ecuador requested that the black caiman (*Melanosuchus niger*) be moved from Appendix I to Appendix II. The Ecuadorian proposal reported the existence of "extensive" populations of the black caiman in the Amazon Region (Napo, Lagartococha, and Yasuní Rivers) and expressed interest in encouraging the export of skins. Up to 1,500 black caiman newborns and eggs would be collected and raised in ranches.

Daniel O. Suman
Efraín Pérez

G. GUYANA

(1) Introduction

In 1994, Guyana made little progress in the areas of domestic and international environmental law. The government still had not finalised comprehensive environmental protection legislation expected to be presented to Parliament by the end of the year. From an international legal point of view, the most significant development was the ratification of the Convention on Biological Diversity, which Guyana had signed at the United Nations Conference on Environment and Development in 1992.

(2) National Developments

(a) National Environmental Action Plan and National Environmental Policy

In June, Parliament approved the National Environmental Action Plan (NEAP) and the National Environmental Policy (NEP). The NEAP was developed by the government with technical assistance from the World Bank. It identifies the major environmental problems in Guyana and formulates appropriate policies to address the causes and effects of these problems. NEP is a guidance document to promote sound environmental management and sustainable development. NEP states, *inter alia*, that in order to conserve and improve the environment, the government will endeavor to achieve a balance between the use and conservation of the nation's resources to meet the needs of economic development and improved standards of living.

(b) Legal and Institutional Arrangements

During 1994, efforts accelerated to finalise existing draft environmental legislation. By December, a draft Environmental Protection Act based primarily on draft legislation developed by the Commonwealth Secretariat in 1990, and other draft environmental laws patterned after Canadian legislation, had been developed with the assistance of the Inter-American Development Bank (IDB). By year's end, the Government and other relevant parties were reviewing the 1994 draft Act. The overall aim of the 1994 draft Act is to "regulate the management, conservation, protection and improvement of the environment, the prevention or control of pollution and the assessment of the environmental impact of economic development and the sustainable use of natural resources." Moreover, the draft Act proposes the establishment of an Environmental Protection Agency (EPA) that would, *inter alia*, coordinate environmental management activities, regulate prevention and control of pollution, promote public awareness, and advise on policy matters.

Legal reform, in particular the development of environmental protection legislation and the strengthening of the future EPA, figured high on the agenda of several ongoing or proposed projects, such as the Government of Guyana/World Bank/IDB Project on Environmental and Natural Resources Management. The UNDP/IDB Institutional Strengthening Project, initiated in 1993, continued to provide assistance to the government in the areas of environmental impact assessment (EIA) and pollution monitoring, and resulted in draft EIA Guidelines that were still being reviewed by the government by the end of the year.

(c) Coastal Zone Management

In April, IDB, jointly with the government of Guyana, launched a five-year Shore Zone Management Programme. The major objectives of this programme are to reduce and/or control loss of land due to erosion and flooding, promote environmentally sound land use, and strengthen national capacity for integrated coastal zone management. So far, the Programme has identified several problems, such as outdated and nonexistent laws and regulations and a lack of institutional capacity and capability in key environmental institutions.

(d) Biodiversity

In collaboration with the Secretariat of the Treaty of Amazonian Cooperation (TAC), the government prepared a draft National Strategy for the Conservation and Sustainable Use of Biodiversity. In October, this draft document was reviewed at a public consultation. A second consultation was planned for March 1995. It is envisaged that the Strategy will form the basis for a comprehensive national policy framework for promoting the conservation and sustainable use of biodiversity and biological resources. Indeed, the Strategy is expected to provide valuable guidance in implementing the objectives of the Convention on Biological Diversity.

Also, at the request of the Secretariat of the TAC, a study was undertaken on the laws governing patent and intellectual property rights in Guyana, with specific reference to the Convention on Biological Diversity. The study concludes, *inter alia*, that the current scope of national legislation is inadequate and outdated, and therefore does not promote the conservation and sustainable use of Guyana's biodiversity. It includes specific recommendations to improve the present situation.

(e) Forestry

In 1994, the government reiterated its commitment to the sustainable development of forest resources in Guyana. Most significantly, it decided to cease granting new forest and timber concessions until existing monitoring and management capabilities are strengthened.

Various forestry and land use projects, as proposed, included an offer of technical assistance to Guyana. For example, a proposed British Overseas Development Administration Project would provide assistance to the Guyana Forestry Commission monitoring and enforcement, training, developing a National Forestry Policy, and revising forestry legislation. Similarly, a World Bank/Government of Guyana workshop held in November discussed the establishment of a National Protected Areas System (NPAS) to be funded by the Global Environment Facility. The NPAS is a component of the proposed Project on Environmental and Natural Resources Management, and would sponsor research, data gathering, and the development of relevant legislation. Finally, to redress the present absence of an integrated land-use policy in Guyana, the government and the German Agency for Technical Cooperation (GTZ) discussed the possibility of jointly developing such policy and relevant legislation. In January 1995, a workshop was to be held by GTZ to examine the institutional responsibilities for the management of national parks in Guyana. The Carter Center has also proposed to hold a Land Use Planning Workshop in 1995.

(f) Wildlife

A 1993 governmental ban on all exports of wildlife (except aquarium fish and orchids) was lifted in November 1994. The government, however, recognises that there are several problems with the trade in wildlife (such as a lack of data and public awareness of applicable regulations) which need to be addressed, especially inadequate implementation of and compliance with the Convention on the International Trade in Endangered Species.

(g) Natural Resources Management

In 1994, it was widely accepted that the management of Guyana's vast natural resources suffered from critical social-institutional shortcomings including the country's archaic laws; its weak institutional capacity and capability; a lack of human, technical and financial resources; weak monitoring and enforcement of laws and regulations; and a general lack of public awareness of the issues.

Several projects were proposed to redress these problems. The government, in collaboration with the World Bank and the IDB, began discussions on an Environmental and Natural Resources Management Project that would support the government in implementing the goals and priorities identified in the NEAP. The Project is divided into three main components: legislative reform and development; institutional restructuring and development; and the establishment of a National Protected Areas System. The legislative component seeks to streamline and strengthen environmental and natural resources legislation. In a similar vein, the governments of Guyana and the Federal Republic of Germany signed an Agreement for the development of a Natural Resources Management Plan. The GTZ was to hold a workshop to define the goals and objectives of this pin early 1995.

(3) Other Significant Developments

In 1994, Guyana hosted for the first time the Annual General Meeting and Conservation Congress of the Caribbean Conservation Association, 23-26 August. The Meeting discussed several issues under the theme "Sustainable Development—Putting People First," and recommended, *inter alia*, that draft environmental legislation and national environmental plans should be circulated and discussed publicly prior to their adoption by the respective governments of the region.

At the invitation of Amerindian groups, a Greenpeace vessel visited Guyana as part of a tour of the Caribbean and South America. The short visit provided a forum for the discussion of a number of issues, including biodiversity and indigenous peoples' rights.

(4) International Developments

On August 29, Guyana ratified the Convention on Biological Diversity. Ratification allowed the country to participate, with full party status, in the first meeting of the Conference of the Parties in Nassau, the Bahamas, 28 November to 9 December 1994. Also in 1994, Guyana became a member of the World Intellectual Property Organisation.

Fiona Pompey

H. PERU

(1) Introduction

Peru ended 1994 in preparation for the presidential and congressional elections scheduled for April 1995, which will signal the return of the democratic order interrupted by the so-called "auto-coup" of President Fujimori in 1992. A grouping of environmental and development non-governmental organizations (NGOs) began to organize an ecological forum at which candidates for presidential and congressional elections would be invited to outline their plans for future sustainable development in Peru.

In 1994, environmental issues took on a new dimension in Peru's national affairs. While the legislature was less active in the promulgation of environmental legislation than in 1993, the government took important steps to consolidate the advances of recent years, culminating in the creation of a national environmental authority to coordinate the activities of Ministries. Furthermore, sectoral authorities improved their conformance with environmental obligations in 1994. This happened under increased scrutiny by a civil society anxious to secure enforcement of public-interest rights. As a consequence, the private sector is showing concern to meet both the spirit and the letter of the law. During 1994, there was also a growing trend toward wider participation by the civil society in the formulation of environmental policy and in decision-making processes.

(2) National Legislation

The most important environmental legislation enacted in 1994 was Law No. 26420 of December 22, which established a national environmental authority, the Consejo Nacional del Ambiente (CONAM). The need for the creation of this authority had been highlighted by a number of prominent Peruvian environmentalists for more than 15 years, even before the development of Peru's main environmental movement. This pressure, which has been growing in intensity in recent years, has now borne fruit with the establishment of a public, decentralized institution under the President of the Council of Ministers. This new institution is responsible for the planning, promotion, coordination, and control of environmental affairs and the natural patrimony of the nation. CONAM's mandate is to seek a balance between socio- economic development, sustainable use of natural resources, and conservation of the environment, as well as to coordinate environmental actions of Ministries.

CONAM's organizational structure envisions a "Consejo Directivo" made up of representatives of the public and private sectors; a Secretariat that will provide technical advice and a Consultative Commission composed of representatives of the public and private sectors. Although the law makes no direct reference to the NGO community, the "private sector" in Latin America is often interpreted to include all actors not in the public sector. The Inter-American Development Bank offered financial assistance for the preparation of implementing regulations, and it is to be hoped that this secondary legislation will be drafted in a manner that secures the participation of NGOs and other interested groups in CONAM. One of CONAM's most important and pressing tasks will be to oversee establishment of environmental standards to regulate private-sector activities.

There is concern within the NGO community that CONAM, as created, has not been given sufficient powers to enable it to ensure development and enforcement of an integrated national environmental policy and processes for its implementation and policing. There is hope, however, that the current confusion in the environmental management system may progressively be resolved and that sustainable development principles will take on a greater role in national decision-making processes. Decentralization of CONAM will not be easy due to the policies of the current government, in which centralization of power has become the norm, in contrast to the trend in neighboring countries. Although all presidential candidates have made decentralization part of their election platforms, their true commitment to this end will only emerge after the election.

(a) Environmental Impact Assessment (EIA)

Peru's environmental impact assessment legislation has brought about the establishment of numerous EIA enterprises, both national and foreign, to meet the need for preparation of environmental impact studies. There have been complaints about the lack of guidelines for preparation of EIAs and there is a feeling that in some cases the EIAs are being approved in principle before their completion. The Ministry of Fisheries, however, declared that all the plans provided by existing fishery operations on their proposed actions to bring their activities into accordance with environmental obligations were inadequate, thereby refuting the claims that the existing legislation and lack of standards encouraged blanket approval for projects.

The petroleum industry started to show greater awareness of the need to confer with indigenous and local communities. But the Ministry of Energy and Mining has not encouraged the preparation of comprehensive EIAs.

The Ministry accepted an EIA that Mobil Oil prepared for activities in the Tambopata-Candamo Reserve despite concerns of the Directorate of Protected Areas of the National Institute of Natural Resources as to the manner in which it was prepared. The oil industry is concerned that lack of guidance by the state and failure to define the scope of legal obligations may leave it open to legal actions by environmentalists and indigenous peoples.

(b) Protected Areas

A national participatory project to develop a "Plan Director" (master plan) for natural protected areas was carried out in 1994. This project has as its objective the establishment of a system of protected areas and a long-term plan for their governance and management. It is intended to apply to all protected areas and would include an institutional and legal framework, recategorization, exploitation of natural resources, bio-prospecting, preservation of pristine ecosystems, sustainable development projects with local communities, and planning for activities such as eco-tourism. The Plan Director is due to be completed by July 1995 and will be promoted for adoption under law as the policy for protected areas management.

(c) Judicial Activity

Actions in defence of the Pantanos de Villa, an important wetland on the outskirts of Lima, have been initially successful. An important *habeas data* action is currently before the courts in order to secure access to information regarding disposal of mine tailings and a landslide which killed eight field workers. The Sociedad Peruana de Derecho Ambiental brought this action, the first of its kind, which is seen as a precedent-setting case with regard to the public's right to access information held by government bodies.

(d) TEXACO Class Action Suit

Indigenous peoples of the Northern Peruvian Amazon have filed a class-action suit in the United States seeking damages for environmental damage caused by TEXACO's operations in Ecuador. This action follows a similar action filed by Ecuadorian indigenous peoples (*see* 4 *YbIEL* 336 (1993)).

(e) Privatization

Anticipation of the April 1995 presidential and congressional elections had an impact on the government's privatization program as well as on proposed legislation. The government delayed the sale of PetroPeru, the state oil company. It also delayed the promulgation of a controversial new water privatization law that has been the subject of much criticism for its failure to either protect water quality or to ensure adequate potable and irrigation water supplies for the poorer sectors of society.

(3) Implementation of International Law Obligations

Peru has established national commissions, with representation of the state, universities, indigenous peoples, NGOs, the private sector, and relevant institutions to help formulate policy and legislative proposals relevant to the Climate Change Convention, the Convention on Biological Diversity, (➔) the Desertification Convention, and Agenda 21. A national commission has also been created to discuss the issue of mountainous ecosystems and Peru will host the first Latin American regional meeting on this topic during the second quarter of 1995. NGOs and indigenous peoples have also been invited to participate in a working group preparing national regulations for plant breeders' rights.

(a) Biodiversity Convention

Peru has been an active participant in the work of the International Committee on the Convention on Biological Diversity, where the national delegation has led the call for examination of the implications of intellectual property rights for realization of the Convention's objectives. This was done with the support of the G-77 and various northern delegations. Peru hosted the Latin American Conference on the Convention on Biological Diversity before the first Conference of the Parties, in October 1994, at which it presented a draft resolution for the Conference that called for action by recipient countries to protect the interests of countries of origin of genetic resources.

Peru has been selected for one of three United Nations Environment Programme grants for establishment of national databases of biological diversity. It is one of two regional vice-presidents to the Conference of the Parties for 1995.

(b) (➔) International Tropical Timber Agreement (ITTA)

On January 26, 1994, Peru signed the International Tropical Timber Agreement (ITTA). The ITTA promotes having all tropical timber come from sustainably managed forests after the year 2000. The failure to broaden this Agreement to cover all sources of timber is likely to undermine its effectiveness. Developing countries, which are home to the worlds largest tropical timber stands, view the Agreement as another example of inequity and double standards imposed under pressure from consumer countries in the North. Peru stands close to Brazil on forestry issues and opposes the establishment of a Convention on Forests, if it were to be taken outside of the sustainable development debate within the Commission on Sustainable Development.

(c) International Labour Organisation (ILO) Convention 169

ILO Convention 169 promises to be an important tool for ensuring that development of Peru's Amazonian territories is carried out in a manner respectful of the moral and legal rights of the indigenous inhabitants of this region. While implementing legislation has not yet been promulgated, the Convention became, in accordance with the Constitution of 1993, part of national law. As such, indigenous peoples may call on it in defence of their interests. The recognition of indigenous territorial rights, a centerpiece of Convention 169, is now becoming central to the environmental debate, and efforts to secure indigenous land rights will increase as calls to colonize Peru's border threaten to increase the pressures on indigenous peoples' territorial integrity.

(d) Andean Pact

The Andean Pact is currently negotiating a decision to establish a common regime to regulate access to genetic resources. This debate is focusing its work on a legislative proposal prepared by the governments of Colombia and Venezuela and a technical report on possible elements for inclusion in such a regime prepared by the World Conservation Union's Environmental Law Center and the Sociedad Peruana de Derecho Ambiental. The Peruvian delegation has adopted a strong position with regard to the need to include measures to secure protection of indigenous peoples' intellectual property rights over their innovations, practices, and knowledge.

(e) Convention to Combat Desertification

Peru signed the Convention to Combat Desertification in Paris on October 15, 1994.

Jorge Caillaux
Brendan Tobin

I. SURINAME

(1) Legal Developments

On 26 May the Council of Ministers of Suriname approved the Biodiversity Convention. By year's end, the Convention was still awaiting formal ratification by the National Assembly. In the interim, the Minister of Public Works established an environmental working group for the purpose of following up on and implementing the United Nations Conference on Environment and Development instruments.

The National Assembly, however, did give its consent to ratification of the Vienna Convention for the Protection of the Ozone Layer, and the Montreal Protocol on Substances that Deplete the Ozone Layer, as well as the London Amendment thereto. During the discussions in the Assembly, the Minister of Foreign Affairs expressed concern about the potential environmental impact of propellants used in launching rockets from the European space centre at Kourou, in neighboring French Guiana.

On the domestic legal front, the government agreed to create a central environmental protection agency with full jurisdictional powers and thus to do away with the traditional system in which jurisdiction over environmental protection matters was split among the various ministries. Because of upcoming elections in 1995 and the ongoing implementation a structural adjustment program that produced some institutional disruption, the government took few other environmental initiatives in 1994.

(2) Other Developments

The European Commission gave 50 million Suriname guilders to the Center for Agriculture Research in Suriname as seed money to investigate rain forest ecosystems and to enable the government to develop strategies for better use and management of the rain forests.

In June, the Caribbean Institute for Organic Agriculture, of which Suriname is a member, met to: develop biological agriculture at local, regional, and national levels, as well as in the Caribbean region; promote agro-forestry; work on management and protection of the natural eco-system; and establish an organization for control and certification of organic production methods. Implementation of these program objectives, however, was deemed to be dependent on foreign funding.

(3) Activities related to Biodiversity

March marked the beginning of the "Biodiversity Prospecting Project in Suriname," in the course of which Conservation International Suriname carries out field work with indigenous and Maroon communities. BGVS (a government owned pharmaceutical company), the Missouri Botanical Garden, the Virginia Polytechnic Institute and State University, and Bristol Meyers-Squibb Pharmaceutical agreed to enter into a bio-prospecting partnership in Suriname.

In September, a round-table conference focused on a proposal for a Global Environment Facility-funded Suriname biodiversity project called "Community Integration in National Park Rehabilitation and Management." Conservation International Suriname set up a policy group to assist, in cooperation with several national and international organizations, in the preparation of an environmental profile for the country, a national tropical forestry action plan, a national policy for agrarian reform and rural development, a review of intellectual property rights and biodiversity, a national strategy for the conservation of biodiversity, and measures implementing the Biodiversity Convention.

Reggy Nelson

K. URUGUAY

(1) Domestic Legal Developments

With the approval of Law 16.466 of January 19, 1994, on environmental impact assessment (EIA), Uruguay established a general system of environmental impact assessment for certain public and private projects. The regulations under the new EIA law were approved on September 21, 1994, by decree 435/994. Until the enactment of this law, EIA was called for only in special cases such as the construction of nuclear power plants (Art. 215 of law 16.226 of October 29, 1991) and private port activities (Art. 46 of the Port Regulations Law, Law 16.246 of April 8, 1992).

As regards the scope of application, the Uruguayan EIA system establishes a non-exclusive list of activities, construction projects, and works, the execution of which are subject to prior environmental authorization (known as "AAP", its Spanish acronym) by the Ministry of Housing, Land Use Management, and Environment (Environment Ministry). The Environment Ministry must process the request for authorization, taking into account the environmental impact study submitted by the interested party. The Environment Ministry may obtain advice from other agencies, hold public hearings, and provide for other forms of public access to information and participation in the procedure.

(2) Ratification of International Agreements

By Law 16.517 of July 22, 1994, Uruguay approved the United Nations Framework Convention on Climate Change. An inventory of gas emissions contributing to the greenhouse effect is scheduled to be compiled in 1995.

As a member of the Antarctic Treaty, by Law 16.518 of July 22, 1994, Uruguay approved the Madrid Protocol on Environmental Protection and its attachments, which it had originally signed on October 4, 1991.

Similarly, being a party to the Inter-American Convention on Human Rights, by Law 16.519 of July 22, 1994, Uruguay approved the 1988 Additional Protocol on Economic, Social, and Cultural Rights, known as the San Salvador Protocol. Article 11 of this Protocol acknowledges the right of all persons to live in a healthy environment and obligates the parties to promote environmental protection, conservation, and improvement.

(3) Regulations Implementing International Agreements

To strengthen the existing country program on protection of the ozone layer, Uruguay by decree 308/994 of June 29, 1994, established a national halons program. As Uruguay is not a producer, the program establishes strict foreign trade and domestic commerce regulations for the substances included in Group II of Schedule A to the Montreal Protocol, as well as mixtures or items containing any of these substances (Arts. 2 through 5). It also provides for the creation of a National Halons Bank, involving a registry and one or more physical storage sites, to create an inventory and to concentrate these substances under appropriate conditions.

(4) Regional Cooperation

During 1994, the four member states of the 1991 Asunción Treaty (Argentina, Brazil, Paraguay, and Uruguay) worked towards implementing MERCOSUR (the common market of the southern cone states of Latin America), to be established on January 1, 1995.

The most important decision adopted in the environmental area was undoubtedly the approval by the Common Market Group, in resolution No. 10/94, of a document entitled "Basic Environmental Policy Guidelines" (➔) (Directrices Básicas en Materia de Política Ambiental). These guidelines, which were drawn up during the third session of the specialized meeting on the environment, held in Brasilia, Brazil, from June 27 to 29, 1994, are to facilitate the development of joint environmental management strategies by the four countries.

The 12 basic guidelines emphasize issues instrumental to the integration process. Guideline 1 addresses the need to harmonize environmental legislation of the member states, subject to the caveat that harmonization does not imply establishment of a single body of laws, but rather the taking into account of actual compliance with existing legislation. The guidelines also focus on equity, specifically in relation to conditions of economic competition among member states. Guideline 2 thus recommends inclusion of environmental costs in the costs of production. To guarantee the adoption of sustainable management and use of renewable natural resources, the guidelines seek to ensure that all member states use a system of environmental licensing or permit forms, of which EIA is an obvious example (Guidelines 3 through 8). Finally, the guidelines accord priority to the establishment of common environmental criteria for the negotiation and implementation of international instruments (Guideline 9), and to the strengthening of national institutions for environmentally sustainable management. For these purposes, they recommend greater access to information; improvement of environmental assessment; and upgrading of training, educational, and research institutions.

Marcelo J.Cousillas

L. VENEZUELA

(1) International Issues

(a) Multilateral Treaties

In 1994, Venezuela adopted implementing legislation for a number of important environmental treaties. The Congress enacted the Convention on

Biological Diversity, including Annexes I and II, on September 30; on November 30, the International Convention on Oil Pollution Preparedness, Response and Cooperation, signed in London in 1990; and on December 27, the UN Framework Convention on Climate Change.

(b) Biodiversity: Action by the Cartagena Agreement Commission

The Cartagena Agreement Commission, by Decision No. 345 of 18 January, took a vital step toward the conservation of plant resources in Bolivia, Colombia, Ecuador, Peru, and Venezuela by establishing a Common Regime for the Protection of Plant Varieties Breeders. The Commission had also been requested to enact a Decision on a common regime on access to genetic resources and on biosecurity in the Andean Pact subregion, as called for in the Biodiversity Convention, by December 31, 1994. Authorities in the subregion were unable to meet the deadline, however, because the proposal for such a regime, as presented by the World Conservation Union and the Peruvian Environmental Law Society, was strongly criticized by environmental non-governmental organizations and peasant, indigenous, and black communities, as well as government organizations. Critics demanded restrictions on access to genetic resources and to the knowledge of local communities, an administrative procedure that guarantees public participation and food security and respects the sovereign rights of the countries of the subregion over their natural resources.

(c) Inter-American Centre for the Development of Environmental Research

On September 30, the Ministry for External Relations published Instrument No. 142 on the Inter-American Program OEA/CIDIAT, which amends and extends an agreement between the Venezuelan government and the Secretariat of the Organisation of American States, and ensures continuation of the Inter-American Centre for the Development of Environmental Research. The Centre trains public employees from the member countries, performs environmental research, provides technical assistance, and cooperates with other public institutions on environmental matters.

(2) National Legal Issues

One of the most important regulations adopted in 1994 was Decree No. 125, which regulates water discharges from industrial activities. Also, the Ministry of the Environment and Natural Renewable Resources established new regulations on sustainable management and breeding of wild species such as Baba (*Caiman crocodilus*) and Chiguire (*Hydrochaeris hydrochaeris*).

In response to the country's economic crisis, in 1994 the government started an intense campaign to increase gold and diamond mining.

Unfortunately, this has led to harmful environmental impacts and has threatened energy security and the water supply in the country. A distressing related development was the enactment by the Ministry of Energy and Mines of regulations that declare confidential all reports and legal studies related to mining concessions and contracts in that Ministry. Thus, the government is infringing on the civil right to participate in public decision-making related to activities that can harm the environment. Furthermore, the government's present position appears to be in violation of the provisions of the Organic Environmental Law of 1976, and others, as well as the right of citizens to a healthy environment.

Alberto Blanco-Uribe Quintero

7. NORDIC COUNTRIES AND BALTIC STATES

A. NORWAY

(1) National Legislation and Practice

(a) General, Including Implementation of European Economic Area (EEA) Treaty Obligations

1994 saw fewer and less remarkable developments in national law than most previous years. No major environmental legislation or significant amendments to existing acts were passed. However, a number of new regulations were passed, several of them regarding compliance with Norway's obligations as a member of the EEA, for example, on noise limits for bulldozers, caterpillars, transportable compressors, and lawn-mowers.

In December 1994, the government proposed a bill to bring the general provisions on environmental impact assessment (Ch. VII-a of the Planning and Building Act 1985) into conformity with EEC Directive 85/337, which is binding on Norway under the EEA Treaty.

(b) Waste

Following two White Papers on waste management policies that the Government presented to Parliament in 1989 and 1992, a number of new regulations were laid down under either the Product Control Act or the comprehensive 1981 Pollution Control Act. Municipalities are required to set up a waste management plan by 1996 pursuant to the Pollution Control Act (§33a, added to the Act in 1993). By 1995, they were to introduce waste management fees at a level sufficient to cover all their expenses on collection and management of household waste (§34 of the Act, as amended in 1993). Recycling is encouraged for certain kinds of waste. For this purpose, regulations were adopted in 1994 concerning discarded tires and brown paper.

New regulations on hazardous waste (19 May 1994) have replaced the former regulations of 1984. The new regulations cover hazardous waste of 15 different categories, including waste oil, paint, and varnish; waste containing cyanide, mercury, cadmium, or other toxic metals or metallic compounds; and pesticides. Moreover, the State Pollution Control Authority is empowered to decide in individual cases that the regulations should also apply to hazardous waste that falls outside the categories defined by the regulations. Any person in possession of hazardous waste must ensure that the waste is managed in a proper manner that does not cause risk of pollution (§5 of the Regulations). This includes an obligation not to mix hazardous waste with other waste, such as ordinary household waste. It is for the municipalities to provide adequate facilities to receive small quantities of hazardous waste from households and other sources. Enterprises that possess more than one kilogram of any category of hazardous waste must deliver it to an authorized management plant at least once a year (§8). Anyone who operates an enterprise for the management of hazardous waste must have a permit from the pollution control authorities (§§6–7). The regulations also seek to prevent inadequate management of hazardous waste from insolvent enterprises by requiring, when insolvency proceedings have been instituted, that the appointed administrator notify the county governor of any hazardous waste that has been left behind (§9).

Special regulations may apply to certain sources or kinds of hazardous waste. In 1994, the 1990 regulations on batteries and accumulators harmful to the environment were amended with special attention to mercury and cadmium batteries. Regulations on amalgam discharge water and waste from dentistries were introduced (23 September 1994).

(c) Gene Technology

The provisions of the Gene Technology Act of 1993 on deliberate release of genetically modified organisms (GMOs) entered into force in 1993. Under these provisions, the Ministry of Environment granted four approvals for release of genetically modified plants in greenhouses for research purposes. The Norwegian authorities rejected three applications originating from European Union countries under the EEA Treaty, including one for the marketing of a genetically modified species of oil-seed rape. In 1994, the remainder of the Act, dealing with contained use of GMOs, also became operative, and the necessary regulations were issued on 11 February.

(d) Conservation of Natural and Cultural Heritage and Compensation Issues

Conservation plans for coniferous forests (mainly Norwegian spruce and pine) were being implemented under the Nature Conservation Act 1970.

The scope of the plans, which cover a total area of 700 km^2 (of which 280 km^2 is productive forest), was subject to much debate and criticism. Landowners are entitled to compensation for nature reserves created under the plans and, with a few modifications, compensation is to be paid in accordance with the law on the taking of property.

Under the Planning and Building Act of 1985, traditional architecture and townscapes may be protected as part of the cultural heritage, mainly through local zoning. Development projects, begun in accordance with old plans that are subsequently modified by municipal authorities in order to preserve a traditional environment, have raised the question of the developer's right to be compensated for project expenses that turn out to be of no use. The Supreme Court decided one such case (*see* Norsk Retstidende (NRt) 1994, p. 813). In following the reasoning applied with respect to compensation for restrictions on land use in general (which allows for compensation in exceptional circumstances only), the Court dismissed the developer's claim, partly because it was based on an old development plan that, as the developer must have realized, was no longer in keeping with current trends and values as reflected in local public opinion and municipal policies.

(e) Reform of Water Law

The Watercourses Act of 1940 is still the basic legal framework for freshwater management, even though important matters such as regulation of watercourses for energy production, water pollution, and inland fish and fisheries are dealt with by other legislation. The 1940 Act was the result of a committee report submitted in 1918 and now appears rather outdated from both a technical and a substantive viewpoint. A law reform committee submitted its report in 1994 (NOU 1991:12) proposing an entirely new draft bill. The draft bill retains private property rights to watercourses but otherwise represents a shift from a private-law system to public-law measures, including a permit system. It also includes provisions on groundwater resources and increased emphasis on environmental considerations. The draft bill has provisions to ensure legal protection against any development of watercourses which are protected against hydropower development by plenary decision of Parliament. Altogether, 324 objects of varying size, representing 35 TWh or 20 percent of Norway's total hydropower potential, have been protected by parliamentary decisions. The legal status of these decisions, however, is uncertain. Moreover, there are provisions for the sustainable management of other freshwater resources. It is not expected that a bill will be presented to Parliament before 1996.

(2) International Activities

At the global level, Norway initiated a debate on sustainable consumption at the first meeting of the UN Commission on Sustainable Development, and hosted an international symposium on this topic in Oslo. Norway asserted that a change in the consumption pattern of industrialised countries was needed to facilitate global sustainable development.

As regards climate change, Parliament (Stortinget) adopted a preliminary target of stabilizing carbon dioxide (CO_2) emissions by the year 2000 at the 1989 level. Norwegian charges on CO_2 emissions are among the highest in the world and cover approximately 60 percent of the total Norwegian CO_2 emissions. Still, under current conditions, emissions are expected to rise 13 percent by 2000. The government is preparing a national plan to curb emissions of climate gases. Norway will also continue to pursue joint implementation with other countries at the international level.

By year's end, Norway was in full compliance with the requirements of the Montreal Protocol on Substances that Deplete the Ozone Layer. Norway had even adopted more stringent reductions with regard to certain substances than required by the Protocol. The government was expected to present a national plan for the protection of biological diversity.

Management of fishing in the remaining area of high seas in the Barents Sea (known as the "loophole") remains unresolved. Norway has participated actively on the UN Conference on Straddling Fish Stocks and Highly Migratory Fish Stocks and has had regular consultations with Iceland, which allows unregulated fishing in this area. This conflict has had a spillover effect in bringing increased attention to the disputed legal status of the 200-mile zone around the Norwegian archipelago Svalbard (Spitsbergen). Norway has, under reference to its reservation, continued whaling despite the moratorium adopted by the International Whaling Commission. A quota of 301 minke whales, including 95 whales for research purposes, has been adopted.

Removal of oil installations on the Norwegian continental shelf, as required by the 1958 Continental Shelf Convention (Art. 5(5)) and the 1982 UN Convention on the Law of the Sea (UNCLOS) (Art. 60(3)), is an increasingly pertinent issue. It has been estimated that removing the 70 existing or planned installations will cost approximately US$5-6 billion. In 1994, Norway was preparing ratification of UNCLOS.

At the regional level, a significant development was the signing of (➔) the Protocol on Sulphur Emissions to the 1979 Convention on Long-Range Transboundary Air Pollution on 14 June 1994. This Protocol represents the first in a new generation of environmental treaties in the sense that pollution reductions are based on critical biological levels, and that different reduction requirements apply to different states. These reductions will improve the living conditions for fish and other organisms in Norway's lakes and rivers and limit the risk of damage to forests, but stricter reductions are needed.

Environmental protection of the Arctic continued to be pursued through the Arctic Environmental Protection Strategy (the Rovaniemi Process), the Barents Euro-Arctic Regional Council, and within the context of the 1992 bilateral environmental treaty between Norway and Russia. Of special concern to Norway has been the safety of Russian nuclear power plants, disposal of nuclear waste, and acid emissions from the Kola Peninsula.

Following a Norwegian referendum on 28 November, Norway will not become a member of the European Union, but will remain a member of the 1992 Agreement on an European Economic Area.

Inge Lorange Backer
Geir Ulfstein

B. FINLAND

(1) Environmental Impact Assessments

The Finnish Act on Environmental Impact Assessment (EIA) Procedure (*Laki ympäristövaikutusten arviointimenettelystä-Lag om förfarande vid miljökonsekvensbedömning*) entered into force on 1 September (Official Gazette SSK 10.6.1994/468). The goal of the Act is to prevent harm to man and to the environment while promoting sustainable development. It encourages taking the environment into account in planning and decision-making, and recognizes the important role the private sector plays in planning and impact assessment. It also establishes a general obligation to assess environmental impacts, within a coherent permit procedure and other decision-making processes. The new Act is a flexible instrument that complements existing special legislation regarding planning and licensing procedures. The EIA procedure is to be applied to projects with a potentially significant environmental impact.

The types of projects to which EIA will routinely apply are listed in a separate Decree on Environmental Impact Assessment Procedure, which also entered into force on 1 September (SSK 25.8.1994/792). The Decree's list follows the enumeration of major projects in the EEC Council Directive of 27 June 1985 (85/337/EEC) and the ECE Convention on Environmental Impact Assessment in a Transboundary Context. EIAs for projects not listed in the Decree and major changes in already-completed projects may be required on a case-by-case basis. The Ministry of the Environment, which decides these individual cases, is to take into the account the size of the projected environmental effect, its location, its effects, and the possibility of combined effects with other projects (in order to avoid fragmentation of projects). An EIA will be required where a project is uncommonly large for the type of activity, close to environmentally sensitive or important areas or international borders, particularly complex, or potentially very harmful.

(2) Compensation for Environmental Damage

A new Act on Compensation for Environmental Damage (Laki ympäristövahinkojen korvaamisesta-Lagen om ersättning för miljöskador SSK 19.8.1994/737) was adopted on 8 August and was to enter into force on 1 June 1995. The Act complements special legislation such as the Water Act and the Mining Act. The Act applies, *inter alia*, to damage caused by water, air, and soil pollution, as well as pollution caused by noise, vibration, light, heat, and radiation (§1). Damage is to be compensated under the Act where there is a probable causal link. Economic loss is to be compensated only when the damage is significant. Costs incurred by preventive measures are to be compensated (§6).

(3) Water Pollution

On 1 August, amendments to the Water Act entered into force (SSK 28.6.1994/553), speeding up the processing of permit applications, especially with regard to on-site inspections and separating compensation issues from the licensing procedure. The old scheme of advance compensation was abandoned in favor of obliging the applicant to present bank guarantees or other security.

(4) Nuclear Energy

On 3 January 1995, the maximum liability of an operator of a Finnish nuclear installation was to increase from 100 to 150 million SDRs (SSK 28.6.1994/588). On 6 May, Parliament, in adopting the Government Statement on the Energy Policy (Valtioneuvoston energiapoliittinen selonteko Eduskunnalle syksyllä 1993) urged a stop to spent nuclear-fuel shipments from the two reactors in the Loviisa plant to Chelyabinsk in Russia. These shipments will, however, be permitted until November 1996, when the transport agreement between the operator IVO and Techsnabexport (formerly Atomenergoexport) expires. An absolute prohibition on re-exports of nuclear wastes under the Nuclear Energy Act was to take effect on 1 January 1995 (new §6a, SSK 29.12.1994/1420); the Act was to also ban storage nuclear wastes produced abroad "in a manner that is meant to be permanent."

(5) International Developments

(a) Multilateral Treaties

Amendments to Annex III (Regulations for the Prevention by Harmful Substances Carried by Sea in Packaged Form) of the 1978 Protocol Relating to the 1973 London Convention for the Prevention of Marine Pollution from Ships, adopted 30 October 1992, became binding on Finland on 2 March (SSK 25.2.1994/175). On that day, the amendments adopted in London on 12 November 1993 to the 1972 London Convention on the Prevention of Marine Pollution by Dumping of Wastes and other Matter entered into force for Finland (SSK 25.2.1994/176). The Copenhagen amendments to the 1987 Montreal Protocol on Substances that Deplete the Ozone Layer became effective for Finland on 14 June (SSK 3.6.1994/426). On 3 October, Finland deposited the instrument of acceptance of the 1988 Joint Protocol Relating to the Application of the Vienna Convention and the Paris Convention (on Nuclear Liability). The 1976 Protocol to the International Convention on the Establishment of an International Fund for Compensation for Oil Pollution Damage entered into force for Finland on 24 November. The UN Framework Convention on Climate Change entered into force in Finland on 1 August; the Convention on Biological Diversity on 26 October. The Finnish Ministry for Foreign Affiars declared that Part XI of the 1982 Law of the Sea Convention and the (➔) Agreement relating to the Implementation of Part XI was to be applied temporarily beginning 16 November, until both treaties enter into force for Finland (SSK 3.6 1994/426).

(b) Bilateral Treaties

In addition to previous environmental treaties between Finland and the Russian Federation, a Treaty on the Implementation of Environment Protection Projects in the Carelian Republic; the Oblasts of Murmansk, Novgorod, and Pskov; and St. Petersburg became operative on 10 December. On 14 September, the Estonian-Finnish Treaty in the Field of Air Pollution Control entered into force, as did, on 13 November, the Estonian-Finnish Treaty in the Field of Water Pollution Abatement.

Frank Horn

8. WESTERN EUROPE

A. AUSTRIA

(1) International Agreements

In 1994, Austria ratified the UN Framework Convention on Climate Change, the UN Convention on Biological Diversity, and the Convention for the Protection of the Alps. Austria participated at the Third Alpine Conference in the elaboration of protocols implementing the last Convention. Work on only three of the five planned protocols was finished in time for the meeting (environmental planning, agricultural economy of mountainous regions, and protection of the countryside.) No agreement could be reached on protocols concerning tourism and traffic. Austria did not sign the three completed protocols because it did not consider the existing protocols a well-balanced package without the protocol on traffic. The obstacle to reaching an agreement on a traffic protocol is the issue of new high-capacity roads through the Alps.

Austria also signed the (➔) Second Sulphur Protocol to the ECE Convention on Long-Range Transboundary Air Pollution and the (➔) Convention on the Protection of the Danube.

(2) Treaty of Accession to the European Union

The Treaty of Accession to the European Union, pursuant to its Art. 69, grants Austria a transitional period of four years from the date of accession (1 January 1995) regarding a number of provisions that are listed in Annex VIII concerning "standards and environment." During this transitional period, Austria is to keep its higher environmental standards; such provisions have also been included in the treaty of accession in favor of Finland and Sweden. The relevant provisions will be reviewed during this period in accordance with EC procedures.

In a "Joint Declaration on standards for the protection of environment, health and product safety," the contracting parties emphasize the great importance of promoting a high level of environmental protection as part of Community action, in conformity with the objectives and in accordance with the criteria laid down in the Treaty on European Union. Furthermore, note is taken of the attachment of the new Member States to the preservation of the standards they have implemented in certain fields, owing in particular to their special geographical and climatic conditions. The Contracting Parties have agreed, exceptionally and for specific cases, on a procedure for examining the existing "acquis communautaire," with the full participation of the new Member States, under the terms and conditions laid down in the Accession Treaty.

Article 69 and the Joint Declaration underline, without prejudice to the outcome of the agreed examination procedure, that "at the end of the transitional period, the entire 'acquis communautaire' will be applicable in the new Member States under the same conditions as in the present Member States of the Union."

(3) Judicial Decisions

The Constitutional Court dealt with the question of national implementation of Art. 4, para. 2(e) of the Basel Convention on the Control of Transboundary Movements of Hazardous Wastes and Their Disposal in the form of Art. 35 of the Law on the Disposal of Wastes (AWG-Abfallwirtschaftsgesetz [BGB1. 1990/325 as amended]). Article 35 AWG determines the criteria for granting an export permit for wastes, and, specifically, appears to require "environmentally sound management of the wastes" in the importing state. The question was raised whether the competent Austrian authority—the Minister for the Environment—is obliged to make enquiries concerning the facilities for waste management outside Austria. The Constitutional Court held in regard to Art. 35 AWG that no independent inquiry of the facilities in the importing state had to be made by the Minister. In the administrative proceedings, the Austrian authority only has to examine whether legal regulations exist in the importing country which provide for an environmentally sound management of waste and whether the importer has a proper permit.

Gerhard Loibl

B. GERMANY

(1) Multilateral Cooperation

In 1994, the Federal Republic of Germany ratified the Convention on the Control of Transboundary Movements of Hazardous Wastes and their Disposal (Basel Convention). The law on ratification entered into force on 15 October (Bundesgesetzblatt 1004 Vol. II, p. 2703). An additional law on implementation (Bundesgesetzblatt 1994 Vol. I, Pl 2771) was adopted to address all those issues that had not yet been regulated in European Economic Community (EEC) Regulation 259/93 of 1 February 1993, and entered into force on 6 May 1994. The law provides for priority of domestic disposal. It also requires the establishment of an insurance policy for export of those wastes for which notification is required. In cases of re-importation, all parties involved in the export transaction are jointly liable. "Waste brokers" need a license for their operations. Illegal transboundary shipments of wastes are subject to criminal sanctions.

On 25 November, Germany ratified the 1991 Protocol to the Antarctic Treaty on Environment Protection (*Umwelt und Entwicklung*, December 1994, p. 25). In June 1994, the federal parliament adopted the laws on ratification and on implementation. The law on implementation specifies that any activity originating in Germany requires a permit and an environmental impact assessment (EIA). This development is particularly relevant to tourist activities, which increased considerably in recent years to about 7,500 visitors annually. The Federal Minister of Environment also distributed non-binding "Guidelines for Visitors to Antarctica" (*UMWELT* 10/1994, p. 367).

Germany ratified the Convention on the Protection of the Alps on 5 December. By year's end, the Convention, which is a framework convention to be implemented by protocols, had also been ratified by Austria and Liechtenstein and thus was to enter into force 5 March 1995. Additionally, during 1994, Germany signed several unilateral environmental protection instruments. On 2 February, the federal government initiated the parliamentary process for ratification of the UN Economic Commission for Europe Convention on the Protection and Use of Transboundary Watercourses and International Lakes (*UMWELT* 4/1994, p. 140). On 29 June, Germany signed the (➔) International Convention on the Protection of the Danube. Other signatories were Austria, Bulgaria, Croatia, Czech Republic, the European Union, Hungary, Moldova, Romania, Slovakia, Slovenia, and Ukraine. On 20 September, Germany signed the (➔) IAEA Convention on Nuclear Safety (*UMWELT* 12/1994. p.470). The Convention is the first international instrument to provide for binding safety standards. On 14 October, Germany signed the (➔) International Convention on Combatting Desertification (*UMWELT* 12/1994, p. 450). Germany announced the provision of an additional 5 million deutschmarks to assist affected countries (existing projects were said to amount to 1.835 billion deutschmarks, *UMWELT* 12/1994, p. 450). Finally, on 30 November, Denmark, Germany, and the Netherlands signed a memorandum declaring the Wadden Sea a "transboundary cooperation area." The three countries agreed on harmonizing their protection standards "at a high level." Protected zones will be established on the basis of uniform criteria. Outside protected zones, economic activities, including the production of gas, will continue to be permitted (*see Umwelt und Entwicklung*, December 1994, p. 22).

(2) Bilateral Cooperation

On 6–7 April, the German-Polish Environmental Council held its 4th session at Schwerin. At the meeting, the Ministers of the Environment of the two countries signed a new Agreement on Cooperation in Environmental Protection. The Agreement, which replaces a similar agreement of 1989, provides for cooperation on air pollution control, water resources management, and nature conservation with particular attention given to transboundary issues. The parties agree on transboundary EIA, including prior transboundary information and consultation, with regard to projects with significant environmental impact potential. They agree on transboundary information and cooperation in cases of emergencies. Liability for damages resulting from transboundary pollution "is subject to the existing law of each Contracting Party"; however, each party agrees to provide citizens of the other party "unhindered and equal access to its courts subject to its existing law, including binding international agreements" (text of Agreement in *UMWELT* 6/1994, p. 224).

On 26 September, Germany signed an Agreement on Environmental Cooperation with China (*UMWELT* 12/1994, p. 448). Areas of cooperation include air pollution control, water resource management, and waste disposal. Germany also strengthened its cooperation with Russia. A new

Agreement on Monitoring Ionizing Radiation in the Vicinity of Nuclear Power Plants was signed at the beginning of the year (*UMWELT* 3/1994, p. 118). On the basis of the existing Agreement on Environmental Cooperation, the German Federal Ministry of Environment supported the cooperation of a German non-governmental organization and two Russian environment groups in the Lake Baikal area (*UMWELT* 12/1994, p. 453).

(3) European Union Relations

Several 1994 decisions of the European Court of Justice concerned the relationship between German environmental legislation and the environmental policy of the European Union. In its judgment of 17 May 1994 (*France v. Commission*, Case 41/93) the Court declared null and void a decision of the Commission affirming the validity of Germany's pentachlorophenol (PCP) legislation, which is stricter than Directive 91/173/EEC. The Court's main objection was that the Commission, which must affirm a country's stricter standards according to Art. 100a of the European Community Treaty, had failed to give sufficient justification for its decision approving the German legislation. On 14 September, the Commission reaffirmed Germany's PCP legislation, ruling that the German regulation was justified on substantive grounds and that it did not constitute an act of arbitrary discrimination or a disguised restriction on trade between member states.

The judgment of the Court of 9 August 1994 (*Bund Naturschutz in Bayern v. State of Bavaria*, Case 396/92) implicated Germany's implementation of the EEC Directive on EIA (Directive 85/337/EEC). Germany had failed to implement the Directive by 3 July 1988, as required. The Court ruled that projects for which the Directive required an EIA and that were started after 3 July 1988 must comply with the Directive; there was no room for exceptions during the transition period between 3 July 1988 and the entry into force on 1 August of the German EIA law that belatedly implemented the Directive. Based on this judgment, on 29 December, a German domestic court ruled that highway construction in the Eifel mountains that began after 3 July 1988 without an EIA had to be stopped (Oberverwaltungsgericht Koblenz, Decision 10903/02.)

(4) National Legislation of International Significance

On 16 July, the Law on Environmental Information implementing Directive 90/313/EEC on Free Access to Environmental Information (Official Journal 1990 No. L 158) entered into force (Bundesgesetzblatt 1994, Vol. I, p. 1490.) In 1994, Germany extended its territorial waters up to a distance of 12 nautical miles, effective 1 January 1995. This decision was motivated mainly by environmental protection and maritime traffic safety concerns. At the same time, Germany declared a 200-mile economic zone.

(5) Policy Developments

In August 1994, the federal government published "Environment 1994: A Policy for Environmentally Sustainable Development" (available from the Federal Ministry of Environment, Bonn.) The report describes Germany's environmental policy positions at the national, European, and international level. In June, the federal government's scientific council on global environmental change presented a report entitled "Global Change/Soils in Danger" ("Welt im Wandel/Die Gefährdung der Böden," Economica Verlag, Bonn) which describes major trends in global change (climate, biological diversity, desertification) and discusses the threats to soils worldwide. Another 1994 governmental report focuses on the implementation of the Convention on the International Trade in Endangered Species in the Federal Republic of Germany ("Durchführung des Washingtoner Artenschutzübereinkommens in der Bundesrepublik Deutschland," April 1994.) It compiles all relevant laws and regulations and describes the practice of German authorities and courts under the Convention. Finally, a comprehensive "Report on the State of Water Protection in the Federal Republic of Germany" was released in November 1994 (reproduced in *UMWELT* 12/1994, Special Section.)

(6) Other Developments

A long-lasting dispute was eventually settled in 1994 by Germany agreeing to re-import hazardous substances that had been exported to Albania in 1991/92. In March, the German Federal Minister of the Environment claimed to accept back 460 tons of pesticides for "humanitarian and political reasons," arguing that as the original export to Albania had not been illegal, there was no legal obligation to re-import the substances to Germany (*UMWELT* 12/1994, p. 465).

Lothar Gündling

C. FRANCE

In 1994, France ratified the UN Framework Convention on Climate Change (instrument of ratification deposited on 25 March), the UN Convention on Biological Diversity (instrument of ratification deposited on 1 July), and Amendments of 28 May 1987 to the Convention on Wetlands of International Importance Especially as Waterfowl Habitat (instrument of ratification deposited on 1 July).

France also signed the following agreements in 1994: (➔) Agreement on the Protection of the River Meuse (signed at Charleville Mézières on 28 April); (➔) Agreement on the Protection of the River Escaut (signed at Charleville Mézières on 28 April); (➔) ECE Protocol on the Further

Reduction of Sulphur Emissions (signed in Oslo on 14 June); (➔) UN Convention on Desertification (signed in Paris on 14 October); Protocol on the Accession of the Principality of Monaco to the Convention on the Protection of the Alpes; Protocol on the Application of the Alpine Convention of 1991 in the Field of Nature Protection; Protocol on the Application of the Alpine Convention of 1991 in the Field of Land Use Planning and Sustainable Development; and Protocol on the Application of the Alpine Convention of 1991 in the Field of Agriculture (all Protocols signed at Chambéry on 20 December.)

Pascale Kromarek
Lothar Gündling

D. SPAIN

(1) Institutional Developments

An important development in 1994 was the creation of the Consultative Council for the Environment by Royal Decree 223/1994. The goal of this new body is to foster the participation of representative social-interest organizations in the elaboration and implementation of environmental policy for sustainable development. Although the Consultative Council composition is not yet well balanced, it represents a new direction in environmental policy in Spain. One function of the Council is to propose measures to comply with international agreements in the field of the environment and sustainable development.

(2) International Developments

(a) International Conventions

Spain ratified the Convention on Biological Diversity and the Convention on Climate Change in 1993. The Conventions became effective domestically upon publication of the texts in the Boletin Oficial del Estado (BOE) 1 February 1994.

To comply with the obligations of Art. 6(a) of the Biodiversity Convention, the Ministry for Public Works, Transport, and the Environment (MOPTMA) began preparing a National Program on Biodiversity that was expected to be completed in the first quarter of 1995. The Convention's requirements concerning *in-situ* conservation are to be fulfilled through implementation of the European Council Directive on the conservation of natural habitats and flora and fauna habitats. The Directive contains similar obligations regarding the designation of protected areas. Spain has applied to host the Biodiversity Convention Secretariat in Seville.

Given significant implications of climate change for the territory of Spain, preparation of a National Program on Climate Change, which was to be published in 1995, was a high-priority item on MOPTMA's agenda. Some parts of the budget for research and development, which stem from the third Research and Development European Union Framework Program for the Environment, will be used to assess the effects of climate change. The MOPTMA was also preparing an international seminar on Climate Change to be held in early 1995.

In February 1994, Spain ratified the 1992 Convention for the Protection of the Marine Environment in the North-East Atlantic (OSPAR), which will replace both the Convention for the Prevention of Marine Pollution by Dumping from Ships and Aircraft 1972 (the Oslo Convention) and the Convention for the Prevention of Marine Pollution from Land-Based Sources 1974 (the Paris Convention). To enter into force, the OSPAR Convention must be ratified by all of the signatories of the Oslo and Paris Conventions. On 15 October, Spain signed the (➔) International Convention to Combat Desertification in Those Countries Experiencing Serious Drought and/or Desertification, Particularly Africa. This Convention contains four regional implementation annexes for Africa, Asia, Latin America, and the Northern Mediterranean. During the negotiations, Spain led the group that lobbied for the adoption of the annex on desertification in the Northern Mediterranean region.

During the year, Spain published the Amendments to the Montreal Protocol on Substances that Deplete the Ozone Layer adopted in the Third Meeting of the Parties, and the Adjustments and Amendments to the Montreal Protocol adopted at the Fourth Meeting of the Parties (BOE, 29 March 1994). It also published the Protocol Relating to Intervention on the High Seas in Cases of Pollution by Substances other than Oil, 1993 (BOE n. 112, 11 May 1994); and the Conservation Measures 18/IX and the Annex, adopted by the Commission on Antarctic Marine Living Resources at its IX Plenary Meeting in Hobart (BOE n. 165, 12 July 1994).

(b) Financial Mechanisms

Spain's participation in the Global Environment Facility (GEF) was authorized by Act 7/1994, 11 May 1994 (BOE n. 113, 12 May). The Spanish contribution to the GEF amounts to 10.000.000 Special Drawing Rights.

(3) Regional Developments

(a) Water Issues

Spain experienced one of the worst droughts of the century, a situation that makes water issues one of the priorities of environmental policy. To comply with Council Directive 91/271/EEC, of 21 May, concerning urban wastewater treatment provisions, the MOPTMA drafted a Drainage and Purification National Plan. The plan, which will be implemented cooperatively with the Spanish Autonomous Communities and municipalities, will be partly financed by the European Community's (EC's) Cohesion Fund (*see* European Commission Decision 94/708/EEC, OJ L 291, 11 November 1994, on the concession of financial assistance from the Cohesion Fund for the project related to purification and minimization of wastewater in Spain). In a related development, by the end of the year, the MOPTMA and the Ministry of Industry and Energy (MINER) were jointly preparing the White Book on Ground Water, which was expected to be published in February 1995. By taking into account Council Directive 80/68/EEC on the protection of groundwater against pollution caused by certain dangerous substances, the White Book develops a strategy to avoid water pollution from diffuse sources such as agriculture.

(b) Freedom of Access to Information on the Environment

Council Directive 90/313/EEC of 7 June 1990 on freedom of access to information on the environment established 31 December 1993 as the deadline for national implementation. As of 1994, the Directive had not been properly transposed into Spanish Law, even though Act 30/1992 on Administrative Procedures recognizes a citizen's right of access to public administrative records and archives.

(c) Genetically Modified Organisms

Council Directive 90/219/EEC on the contained use of genetically modified micro-organisms and Council Directive 90/220/EEC on the deliberate release into the environment of genetically modified organisms were implemented through Act 15/1994, 3 June 1994 (BOE n. 133, 4 June 1994). The Act transposes only the substantive rules of the two Directives, however. Additional regulations will still be necessary to implement the procedural aspects of the Directives.

(d) Environmental Impact Assessment (EIA)

Council Directive 85/337 on environmental impact assessment was implemented by Royal Legislative Decree 1302/1986, 28 June, and by Royal Decree 1131/1988, 30 September. In 1994, after a complaint by Greenpeace to the European Commission, it became clear that the EIA procedures needed modification. By year-end, a proposal was pending to change the EIA procedure to allow greater public participation and to extend the number of projects subject to EIA. The draft law was taking into account the European Union (EU) Commission proposal to revise the EIA Directive (COM(93)575).

One of the most controversial debates in 1994 centered on the construction of the Itolz dam in the north of Spain. Although the project had passed through the required EIA procedure, environmentalist non-governmental organizations opposed the project, arguing that it did not comply with the provisions of Council Directive 79/409 on the conservation of wild birds. Following a complaint to the European Commission, the Spanish government suspended construction. In the end, however, the Commission did not accept the complaint.

(e) *Instruments of Environmental Policy: Eco-Labelling and the Eco-Management and Audit Scheme*

Council Regulation 880/1992 on a community award scheme for an eco-labelling system was implemented through Royal Decree 598/1994, 8 April. During the year, the MOPTMA and the MINER worked to finalize arrangements to make operative Council Regulation 1836/93 of 29 June 1993 on voluntary participation by companies in the industrial sector in a Community eco-management and audit scheme, before the deadline for implementation, April 1995. The Ministries were also working on the system for environment verifiers accreditation.

(f) *Nature Conservation*

Council Directive 92/43/EEC on the conservation of natural habitats and flora and fauna habitats was implemented by means of a series of administrative measures. A coordination team composed of representatives of the Spanish Nature Conservation Institute (ICONA) and of the Autonomous Communities worked on the identification of significant community areas to be include in the Natura 2000 Network. To compile the ecosystem inventory of Annex 1 of the Directive, a scientific team of 300 specialists, cofinanced with the EU financing environment mechanism, LIFE (Council Regulation 1973/92/EEC, OJ L 206), was assembled.

The sustainable use of marine living resources and the application of the EC common fisheries policy were also an important issue during 1994. Spain continued to maintain its long-standing policy of opposing the use of driftnets, a practice forbidden by national legislation under Ministerial Orders of 21 November 1981 and 22 October 1990 (with some exceptions for coastal fishing in the Mediterranean). In pursuance of this policy, Spain called for an amendment of EEC Regulation 345/92 on technical measures for the conservation of fishery resources, before the so-called "tuna and anchovies war" broke out in the summer of 1994, involving serious incidents at sea, mainly between French and Spanish boats. The Council of Ministers on Fisheries did not adopt a Spanish proposal presented to it on 28 September, calling for a total ban of driftnets by 1 January 1995, despite its endorsement by the European Parliament. At year's end the Commission was considering a proposal to ban the use of driftnets. An agreement reached on 22 December 1994 with the EU, will permit complete integration of Spanish policies with the EU common fisheries policy by 1 January 1996.

(g) The Cohesion Fund

Spain, together with Greece, Ireland, and Portugal, qualify for financial aid for infrastructure and environment projects from the Cohesion Fund, which was created by the Maastricht Treaty as a part of the EU's social and economic cohesion policy. During 1994, the European Commission gave approval to several Spanish environmental projects to use this Fund. Together with the water project mentioned above, the Commission approved an industrial waste management project (Decision 94/710 EEC), a waste oils management project (Decision 94/711/EEC), and a land restoration project (Decision 94/713/EEC).

(4) Bilateral Cooperation

In April 1994, Spain and the Russian Federation signed an agreement on environmental cooperation (BOE n. 298, 14 December). Spain also has signed several bilateral scientific and technical cooperation agreements with European, African, Asian, and American partners where cooperation in the field of the environment is paramount. The focus of cooperation is principally on biotechnology and natural resources research, nature conservation, air pollution, land degradation, water management, and waste studies.

Ana Barreira López
José Juste Ruiz

E. UNITED KINGDOM

(1) Developments Relating to Global Environmental Concerns

During 1994, the United Kingdom published four strategy documents to fulfil obligations it took on at the UN Conference on Environment and Development in 1992. The documents address the UK strategies on sustainable development, climate change, biodiversity, and sustainable forestry. The United Kingdom also published a paper outlining its strategy for reducing volatile organic compounds (VOCs) and ground-level ozone formation in response to the UN Economic Commission for Europe (UNECE) Protocol concerning the control of VOC emissions and their transboundary fluxes, which the United Kingdom signed in November 1991 and ratified in June 1994.

The United Kingdom also became a signatory of the new UNECE (➔) Protocol on reducing sulphur emissions, which commits the country to reducing sulphur dioxide emissions to 50 percent of 1980 levels by the year

2000, 70 percent by 2005, and 80 percent by 2010. Regulations to implement EC Directive 92/72/EEC on ozone pollution came into force in the United Kingdom during February of 1994, allowing the establishment of ozone-measuring stations and prescribing the reference methods for its measurement. Important new provisions on marine pollution in the Merchant Shipping (Salvage and Pollution) Act 1994 made it possible to implement the 1990 International Convention on Pollution Preparedness, Response and Cooperation and the 1982 UN Convention on the Law of the Sea. The Salvage and Shipping Act makes the owner of a ship from which oil escapes liable for certain types of damage except in specified circumstances, thereby extending to all merchant ships the liability regime that already applied to laden oil tankers.

(2) Other Developments of International Interest

The United Kingdom issued several regulations during 1994 that gave effect to various EC directives. The Waste Management Licensing Regulations 1994 implemented the EC Waste Framework Directive (75/442/EEC, as amended by 91/156/EEC). The regulations incorporate the principle of "directive waste" as specified in the Directive and deal with the requirements for waste management licensing. The Transfrontier Shipment of Waste Regulations 1994 gave full effect to EC Regulation No. 259/93 on the supervision and control of shipments of waste within, into, and out of the European Community (EC), which in turn implemented within the EC the requirements of the 1989 Basel Convention on the Control of Transboundary Movements of Hazardous Wastes and their Disposal.

New regulations that established waste water treatment plants for significant centres of population or industry, provided a timescale for implementing collection and treatment systems, and specified the level of treatment required implemented the requirements of the EC Urban Waste Water Treatment Directive in England and Wales and in Scotland. In anticipation of the new EC Directive on Packaging and Packaging Waste, representatives from the packaging industry put forward a plan for recovering 58 percent of packaging waste by the year 2000, and proposed that a levy be put on one or more of packers/fillers, retailers, or wholesalers. The government proposed legislation to support such an industry-led scheme.

The British Standards Institution published a revised Environmental Management Systems Standard (BS7750) in 1994. It sets out how companies can implement environmental policies and objectives. The Standard is intended to be compatible with the EC Eco-Audit and Management Regulation. Also, the government implemented new regulations in both England and Scotland to give further effect to Council Directive 85/337/EEC on assessing the environmental effects of specified public and private developments. Wind generators, motorway service areas, and coast protection work all now require an environmental assessment.

The United Kingdom also promulgated legislation in 1994 detailing the requirements for notifying relevant authorities that one tonne or more per year of a new chemical substance is to be placed on the UK market. A "new" substance is one that does not appear on the European Inventory of Existing Commercial Chemical Substances (EINECS). EC Regulation No. 793/93 concerning the notification requirements for existing, rather than new, EINECS substances became applicable in the United Kingdom on 28 June 1994. A recent government publication explained this regulation and set out how UK-based producers and importers of existing chemical substances can comply with the reporting requirements. The government also issued regulations to enforce compliance with the EC Regulation. Three sets of regulations, applicable to Northern Ireland only, implemented various parts of EC Directive 89/677/EEC on the marketing and use of certain dangerous substances and preparations.

The government introduced the Nitrate Sensitive Areas Regulations 1994 to comply with EC Regulation No. 2978/92 on agriculture methods compatible with environmental protection and the maintenance of the countryside. The regulations apply to England only and provide for aid payments to farmers in designated nitrate-sensitive areas in exchange for their modifying their farming practices to reduce nitrate leaching. The Batteries and Accumulators (Containing Dangerous Substances) Regulations 1994 prohibit the marketing of batteries containing dangerous substances, require separate collection of spent batteries and accumulators for recovery and disposal, and mandate appropriate marking of appliances that contain such batteries. The marking requirement does not apply, however, to appliances marketed before 31 December 1995 if they were manufactured or imported into the Community before 1 January 1994. The regulation implements EC Directive 91/157/EEC relating to batteries and accumulators containing dangerous substances.

The Conservation (Natural Habitats etc.) Regulations 1994 provide for the implementation of EC Directive 92/43/EEC on the conservation of natural habitats and wild flora and fauna. The regulations provide for the selection, registration, management, and protection of sites to be protected under the Directive "European Sites." The regulations also protect designated species of animals and plants. A new Land Drainage Act also placed emphasis on the environment and conservation during land drainage and flood defence operations.

(3) National Legislation

Proposals for a new Environment Act were produced during the latter part of 1994. The proposals provide for the establishment of new environmental regulatory agencies for England and Wales and for Scotland, and would merge the present regulatory agencies. The proposals also detail a new regime that includes provisions for identifying and remediating contaminated land; preparing waste strategies; establishing producer responsibility for prescribed products and materials in order to promote or increase their reuse, recovery, or recycling; establishing independent National Park Authorities for the 10 National Parks in England and Wales; protecting important hedgerows; and prohibiting water pollution from abandoned mines. The new contaminated-land proposals are the result of a lengthy consultation between the government and interested parties, which has been a source of intense debate. A similar EC debate has arisen out of the EC Green Paper on Remedying Environmental Damage ((COM/93)47 final), some aspects of which have been incorporated into the proposed legislation.

Paul Smith

9. EAST CENTRAL EUROPE

A. POLAND

(1) International Developments

(a) Bilateral Agreements

Poland and Ukraine signed two bilateral agreements dealing with the protection of the environment during a meeting of their environmental ministers in Warsaw on 24 January 1994. The instruments involved are a treaty between the governments on cooperation in the field of the protection of environment and an inter-ministerial agreement on the transfer of hazardous wastes.

The main objective of the Treaty on Environmental Cooperation, which replaces a similar 1989 Polish-Soviet agreement, is to promote sustainable development, and to improve the environment, enhance environmental security, and prevent pollution (Art. 1). The Treaty stresses the importance of achieving these objectives in the border areas (Art. 2), goals that are to be realized through increased control of the sources of transboundary pollution, abatement of existing pollution, application of the polluter pays principle, strengthening of the protection of fauna and flora and their habitats, and streamlining of environmental and technological transfer of information.

Bilateral cooperation pursuant to the Treaty covers exchange of information on environmental management systems and legal regulations, protection of all media of the environment against pollution, protection and preservation of endangered species of fauna and flora, environmental monitoring, disposal of wastes, control of transboundary shipments of hazardous waste and illegal transfers, exchange of information and consultation on planned activities that are likely to have adverse effects on the territory of the other party, environmental impact assessment (EIA), information on environmental emergencies (especially those involving nuclear installations), mutual assistance in case of environmental emergency, and environmental education (Art. 3). Article 3 also calls for rules and procedures on liability for damage to the environment or to one of the parties caused by an accident originating in the territory of the other to be developed in a separate agreement. Article 4 allows for the settlement of disputes by submission to international arbitration in accordance with UNCITRAL rules if direct negotiations between the parties do not resolve the dispute within six months. Article 5 provides for the establishment of a Joint Commission for Cooperation in the field of the environment, to be chaired by the environmental ministers of the both countries. The other interesting feature of the Treaty is a commitment of the parties to support direct environmental cooperation between regional and local governments, various institutions, enterprises, and non-governmental organizations (NGOs) (Art. 6).

The Inter-Ministerial Agreement on the Transfer of Hazardous Waste covers cooperation to limit the amount of hazardous waste being transported through and into the territory of the two states. The parties recognize the need to inform each other about legal restrictions imposed on transboundary transfers of hazardous waste and any amendments to such restrictions (Art. 2). In Art. 3, the parties commit themselves to undertake all possible measures to prevent the transfer of waste into the territory of the other party, provided that the waste concerned is considered hazardous in the territory of either party. The Agreement entered into force on the date of its signing and runs for an indefinite period.

In addition, Poland concluded two agreements with countries from outside the Central and Eastern European region: an Agreement between the Ministry of Environmental Protection, Natural Resources, and Forestry of the Republic of Poland and the Ministry of the Environment of the Kingdom of Denmark on cooperation in the field of environmental protection, signed in Warsaw on 1 June; and a Memorandum of Understanding between the Minister of Environmental Protection, Natural Resources, and Forestry of the Republic of Poland and the Department of the Environment of Canada and the Department of Industry of Canada, signed on 12 September, in Ottawa.

(b) Multilateral Agreements

In 1994, Poland became a party to the UN Framework Convention on Climate Change. The Convention entered into force for Poland on 26 October. On 13 June, Poland signed the (➔) Protocol to the 1979 Convention on Long-range Transboundary Air Pollution on Further Reduction of Sulphur Emissions.

(2) National Developments

As regards national environmental legislation, two important developments can be reported for 1994. First, a new Land Use Planning Act was adopted on 7 July, which replaces the old land-use legislation of 1984. The new Act, effective 1 January 1995, provides for EIA for investments and local land use plans. Second, Poland adopted a new Geological and Mining Act and 17 accompanying executive regulations on 4 February. The Act, which took effect 1 September, replaces the 1960 Geological Act and the 1953 Mining Decree. In specifying terms and conditions for performing geological work and the extraction of minerals, the Act incorporates pollution prevention, rational use of natural resources, and the polluter pays principles.

Stanislaw Wajda

B. CROATIA

(1) Domestic Developments

(a) Environmental Protection Act

On October 27, 1994, the Croatian Parliament adopted the Environmental Protection Act (Official Gazette of the Republic of Croatia, hereinafter OGRC, No.82/94), an umbrella act containing general environmental obligations and embodying general environmental protection principles. Its main purpose is to lay down the foundation for systematic legislation, which would give effect to the main objective of sustainable development and overcome the present fragmentation and lack of coordination between numerous sectoral regulations treating environmental protection. The basic objectives and principles of the Act are pollution prevention; use of ecologically acceptable technologies, substances and activities; preservation of biological diversity; the polluter pays principle; and the right to information. The Act specifies the indispensable tools for achieving these objectives: environmental impact assessment; monitoring; setting of environmental quality standards; physical planning; eco-labeling; establishment of an environmental information system; and contingency planning. As for liability for environmental harm, the Act provides for the principle of strict liability and requires mandatory insurance or other financial guarantees for environmental risks. An environmental protection inspection process is envisaged at county and state levels. The Act entrusts the newly established State Directorate for Environment with all matters of environmental protection, the environmental sector thus no longer being a part of the Ministry of Civil Engineering and Environmental Protection.

(b) Maritime Code

On January 27, 1994, the Croatian Parliament adopted the Maritime Code (OGRC, No. 17/94), a comprehensive legal act consisting of 1,056 articles divided into 13 sections that also contains provisions relevant to environmental protection. These include a special regime for a narrow belt of the coast and the sea falling within the category of the "public domain" and provisions on liability for pollution damage. Disposal of all substances likely to contaminate the public domain is absolutely prohibited. As for marine pollution, the Code provides for strict liability of the vessel owner for oil pollution damage from tankers. The defenses available include acts of God, acts of war, intentional acts or omissions of third parties, governmental negligence regarding navigational aids, and the injured parties' negligent acts or omissions. The scope of recoverable damage comprises costs of preventive measures, material damage, economic loss, and injury to natural resources. Liability is capped according to vessel size. As for liability for marine pollution by other noxious substances, the Code provides for strict liability of the vessel owner as well as the operator of the ship. The defenses are limited to negligence of port authorities or bodies responsible for navigational aids.

(c) CORINAIR 90 Project

At the beginning of 1994, the Republic of Croatia started the implementation of the CORINAIR 90 Project (International Air Pollutants Information System), encompassing the emission calculation of eight pollutants for the entire country's territory. This project is an indispensable prerequisite for any action aimed at air quality protection and promotion.

(2) International Cooperation

In 1994, the Republic of Croatia ratified the 1989 Basel Convention on the Control of Transboundary Movements of Hazardous Wastes and Their Disposal.

The Republic of Croatia continued its active participation in regional Mediterranean activities within the framework of the Mediterranean Action Plan. Croatian delegates attended several meetings of the Mediterranean coastal states. Their task was to examine the revision of the 1976 Barcelona Convention, its related protocols, and the Mediterranean Action Plan.

The Republic of Croatia also participated in several meetings of the Danube river basin countries and signed the Declaration on the Protection of the Environment of the Danube River Basin, adopted on 6 December 1994 at the ministerial conference in Bucharest. At the same conference, the Strategic Action Plan for the Danube River Basin was also adopted.

Budislav Vukas
Maja Serčić

C. REPUBLIC OF SLOVENIA

[Editors' Note: This report focuses exclusively on developments in the field of conservation]

(1) National Legislation in the Field of Nature Conservation

Based on such strategic documents as Caring for the Earth, the Global Biodiversity Strategy, and the Council of Europe's Nature Conservation in Europe, Slovenia prepared a long-term nature conservation strategy for activities on international, national, and local levels in 1994. This framework document sets out basic legislative and institutional policies on protected areas, and in particular, on area management, species and habitat conservation, and integration of nature conservation principles into other policies.

The major development in 1994 was the reorganization of the state administration, with responsibility for nature conservation passing from the Ministry of Culture to the Ministry of Environment and Physical Planning. At year's end, basic legislative measures (accession to international treaties, adoption of framework laws and by-laws) were held up by a delay in implementing the decision on reorganization and ministerial responsibilities.

A governmental Decree for the protection of the *Autochthonous fungi* came into force in June 1994. The Decree seeks to prevent overcollecting and the commercial use of the fungi and to temporarily remedy ineffective existing legislation until adoption of more comprehensive conservation legislation in the future.

(2) International Legislation

In December, Slovenia signed three protocols to the 1991 Alpine Convention and started the procedure for ratifying the Convention. Proposals for accession to the Bern, Bonn, and Washington Conventions were prepared, but no formal procedure was started because of the pending reorganization issues. A similar delay occurred regarding the ratification of the Biodiversity Convention.

Peter Skoberne

10. COMMONWEALTH OF INDEPENDENT STATES

A. RUSSIAN FEDERATION

(1) Introduction

Given the scope and dimension of environmental problems in Russia, there was no significant progress in this area in 1994. The state of the environment continued to be alarming, due to various negative political and economic factors, including significant inflation and lack of necessary financial resources. Ironically, however, a constant decrease in industrial output (more than 20 percent during 1994 and more than 50 percent since 1990) resulted in an apparent reduction in air and water pollution by industrial emissions and wastes. On the other hand, there remain serious problems such as radioactive contamination and an aging industrial infrastructure, which is particularly dangerous in the oil and petrochemical sectors. The risk to the environment was evidenced by a number of industrial accidents, including the oil spill from a deteriorated pipeline near Usinsk in northern Russia. The spill, which according to remarkably contradictory estimates varies from 15 to 150 thousand tons, could seriously endanger not only nearby areas, but adjacent Arctic territories as well.

Notwithstanding a host of political and economic problems that continued to trouble Russia in 1994, however, certain efforts on the part of the government to cope with the current environmental situation have been undertaken on both the international and domestic levels.

(2) *International Developments*

(a) *Multilateral Cooperation*

The Russian Parliament ratified two important environmental conventions: the 1989 Basel Convention on the Control of Transboundary Movements of Hazardous Wastes and their Disposal (25 November) and the 1992 UN Framework Convention on Climate Change (4 November). Their implementation will require a number of regulatory, administrative, and organizational measures.

The ratification of the Basel Convention was a significant step toward protecting the Russian environment against pollution by hazardous substances arising from the illegal movement of industrial wastes and their disposal, as existing regulations and administrative mechanisms were inadequate for preventing and banning completely such activities. Several cases involving both Russian and foreign companies have already been reported. Along with the ratification of the Basel Convention, the government decided, *inter alia*, to prepare a list of hazardous and other wastes the entry or disposal of which would be prohibited; to review existing rules; and to enact new legislation regarding the treatment, movement, and disposal of dangerous wastes and substances.

The implementation of the UN Framework Convention on Climate Change began even prior to its formal approval by Parliament. In January, the government decided to create the Inter-Agency Commission on the Problems of Climate Change, which was established three months later. The Commission was asked to coordinate actions of various ministries and other agencies toward mitigating the adverse effects of economic activities on the climate and preventing possible negative consequences of climate change on the environment and the national economy. The Commission will supervise the implementation of the Convention on Climate Change and participate in the drafting of new regulations regarding this problem.

For Russia to achieve one of the Convention's main objectives—the return by the year 2000 to the 1990 level of the anthropogenic emissions of carbon dioxide (CO_2) and other greenhouse gases—might not be as difficult as is generally believed. The decrease in industrial production and the consequent decline in energy consumption have already resulted in the reduction of these emissions. Expected future economic growth will not necessarily require a significant increase in the production of electricity. Rather, this growth could be better achieved through a radical improvement in the efficiency of power use.

The reduction of CO_2 levels can be facilitated also by the enormous capacity of the Russian natural environment to provide greenhouse gas sinks and reservoirs. According to some scientific estimates, the former Soviet Union and the United States each annually produced about 20 percent (1.2 out of 6 gigatons) of the total quantity of CO_2 emissions produced worldwide. Russia's share of this total was about 0.8 Gt of CO_2, 50 percent of which was absorbed by the swamp ecosystems and the remaining 50 percent absorbed by forests. Notably, the absorbing potential of Russian forests, if managed properly, could be doubled, considerably surpassing the total CO_2 emissions produced within its territory. This would not only allow Russia to meet its conventional obligations, but could also give it certain advantages with respect to possible "joint implementation" of the Convention and envisaged trade in emission permits.

Two multilateral agreements in force for Russia—the 1971 Ramsar Convention on Wetlands of International Importance, Especially as Waterfowl Habitat, and the 1973 Convention on the International Trade in Endangered Species of Wild Fauna and Flora (CITES)—became the subjects of recent decisions by the Russian government. With respect to the Ramsar Convention, the government approved a List of Wetlands of International Importance located on Russian territory. The List includes 35 such areas, which require a special regime for their use and protection. As to CITES, the Ministry of the Protection of the Environment was designated as the Management Authority under the Convention responsible for export and import permits. The Ministry was also requested to prepare a list of endangered species and to adopt new regulations concerning their export and import.

The 1991 UN Economic Commission for Europe Convention on the Environmental Impact Assessment in Transboundary Context was signed by the Soviet Union in 1991 and is in force for Russia as its successor state.

To implement the provisions of this treaty, the Ministry of the Environment issued regulations regarding environmental impact assessment (EIA). The regulations contain detailed rules, requirements, and procedures relating to EIA; specify rights, obligations, and responsibilities of all parties involved in the project under evaluation; and provide for public participation in the assessment process.

Among other important developments in 1994 was the signing and ratification (16 December) of the (➔) Convention on the Conservation and Management of Pollock Resources in the Central Bering Sea. The Convention resulted from a series of conferences and negotiations between coastal (Russia and the United States) and high-seas fishing (Japan, Poland, Korea, and China) states aimed at establishing an international legal fishing regime in the Bering Sea "donut hole."

On 14 June, Russia signed the (➔) 1994 Protocol to the 1979 Convention on Long-Range Transboundary Air Pollution on the Further Reduction of Sulphur Emissions.

To implement the decisions of the 1993 Kirkenes Conference, the Russian government established a national Inter-Agency Commission on the Development of Cooperation in the Barents Euro-Arctic Region. The Commission's mandate is broad enough to encompass various aspects of international cooperation and state policy in this part of the Arctic, including questions of social and economic development, environmental protection, regimes of navigation and state borders, etc.

Finally, the growing cooperation between Russia and multilateral financial institutions regarding the environment is worth noting. The Russian government's decision of 13 September paved the way for its formal participation in the activities of the restructured Global Environment Facility (GEF). The World Bank approved a $110 million environmental loan for Russia the World Bank on 8 November, the largest such credit to be directed exclusively for cleaning up the environment. The loan is a part of a Russian environmental management project that will cost a total of $194.8 million. The Russian government ($9.8 million) and a group of Russian banks and companies ($75 million) will provide the remainder of the funds. The project will consist of about $50 million in technical assistance and nearly $150 million of investments in an estimated 30 clean-up programs, the main targets of which are water and air pollution. The technical assistance, comprising mainly training and scientific know-how, is aimed at helping the regional authorities in the Ural region, Upper Volga, and North Caucasus to establish regulatory agencies and train appropriate personnel over the next five years.

(b) Cooperation between Commonwealth of Independent State (CIS) Members

The fifth session of the Inter-State Ecological Council (IEC) was convened in Moscow in September. It was attended by the heads of environmental protection agencies and experts from Armenia, Belarus, Kazakhstan, Kirgizia, Russia, Tadjikistan, and Uzbekistan. Three new members—Azerbaijan, Georgia, and Moldova—were added to the IEC. The session was attended also by the representatives of the United Nations Environment Programme, the Organisation for Economic Cooperation and Development, and other international organizations. A number of decisions promoting further environmental cooperation between the members of the CIS were adopted. Among them are the new regulations of the Inter-State Ecological Fund and the multilateral Agreement on the Protection and Utilization of the Migratory Species of Birds and Mammals and Their Habitats.

(c) Bilateral Cooperation

In 1994, Russia continued to cooperate in the area of environmental protection on a bilateral level, primarily with its neighbours. In June, Russia and Belarus signed the Agreement on Cooperation in the Protection of the Environment—the first bilateral agreement of its kind between the former Soviet republics. It contains, in particular, obligations to improve the environmental situation in the respective adjacent territories of the two countries and a commitment to collaborate in the joint utilization of the shared basins of the rivers Dnieper, Western Dvina, and Sozh.

A similar Agreement on Cooperation in the Field of the Protection of the Environment between Russia and Ukraine was still being negotiated by year's end. Russia also concluded agreements on Cooperation in the Prevention of Industrial Accidents, Natural Disasters and Elimination of their Consequences with Armenia and Moldova, two other CIS Members. Russia also achieved significant progress in its relations with the United States. A number of bilateral instruments were signed, including an Agreement on Cooperation in the Field of the Environment and Natural Resources. Russia and the United States also undertook to study jointly the impact of radiation on human health and to combat radioactive contamination of the environment and to implement their earlier commitments regarding creation of the international park "Beringia" on the Russian and American coasts of the Bering Strait.

Other bilateral environmental instruments that Russia signed in 1994 include:

- Agreement on Notification about Nuclear Accidents and Exchange of Information Regarding Nuclear Installations; and Agreement on Cooperation in the Prevention of Industrial accidents, Natural Disasters and Elimination of their Consequences, with Finland;
- Agreement on Cooperation in the Field of the Protection of the Environment, with Spain;

- Agreement on Cooperation in the Protection of the Environment and Natural Resources, with India;
- Agreement on Cooperation Against Pollution by Oil of the Barents Sea, with Norway;
- Agreement on Cooperation in the Prevention of Industrial Accidents, Natural Disasters and Elimination of their Consequences; and Agreement on the Protection and Utilization of Transboundary Waters, with Mongolia;
- Agreement on Cooperation in the Protection, Regulation and Reproduction of the Water Resources of the Boundary Rivers Amur and Ussuri; and Agreement on Cooperation in the Phytosanitary Field and Protection of Plants, with China;
- Agreement on Notification about Nuclear Accidents, Exchange of Information Regarding Nuclear Installations, and Cooperation in the Field of Nuclear Safety and Protection against Radiation, with Poland;
- Agreement on Cooperation in the Field of Conservation and Utilization of the Fishery Resources of the Lakes Chudskoe, Tyoploe and Pskovskoe, with Estonia;
- Agreement on Cooperation in the Phytosanitary Field and Protection of Plants, with the Czech Republic; and
- Agreement on Cooperation in the Phytosanitary Field and Protection of Plants, with Romania.

(3) Domestic Developments

The most important national document defining the long-term environmental policy in Russia is the Main Provisions of the State Strategy of Environmental Protection and Sustainable Development, endorsed by Presidential Decree No. 236 of 4 February 1994. The document sets out the general directives of Russian environmental policy and contains special references to the documents of the UN Rio Conference on Environment and Development. Four areas are designated as the most significant: environmentally secure sustainable development within a market economy; protection of the human environment; restoration of damaged ecosystems in environmentally impaired regions of Russia; and participation in solving global environmental problems.

On 18 May, the government adopted a first element in implementing the Environmental Strategy, the Action Plan for the Protection of the Environment in 1994–1995. The Plan contains an impressive list of legislative proposals, technical and scientific programmes, and organizational and economic measures. They include, *inter alia*, amendments to the Law on the Protection of the Environment, as well as new legislation on protection and conservation of wild fauna and flora, protection of the atmosphere, protection of the population in emergency situations, payments for the use of natural resources, status of federal natural resources, protection of the population against radiation, treatment of radioactive wastes, industrial wastes, exclusive economic zone, fishing and fishery resources, specially protected natural territories, and protection of Lake Baikal. A number of programmes and projects specifically target such critical areas as the Black, Baltic, Azov, and Caspian Seas; Lake Baikal; the Volga river; and the Ural region, and such important problems as improvement of soil productivity, pollution by dioxins, creation of a comprehensive automated system to monitor environmental radioactivity, and development of a system of notification and contingency plans for emergency situations. The Action Plan pays special attention to international cooperation with respect to global environmental problems, including climate change, ozone layer depletion, deforestation, and environmentally secure elimination of chemical and nuclear weapons.

Presidential Decree No. 2099 of 22 November 1994 On the Activities of Russian Physical and Juridical Persons in Exploration and Exploitation of the Seabed Mineral Resources Beyond the Limits of the Continental Shelf was adopted in response to the recent multilateral (➔) Agreement Relating to the Implementation of Part XI of the 1982 UNCLOS. According to the Decree, the state enterprise *Yuzhmorgeologia* was designated as the developer of mineral resources within specially defined zones of the seabed. The government was directed to draft legal regulations regarding seabed mineral resources activities conducted by Russian companies and individuals.

Presidential Decree No. 1470 of 6 July 1994 on the Natural Resources of the Black and Azov Seas Coasts has as its primary objective the establishment of specially protected territories for recreational purposes. It authorizes the federal government, in cooperation with local authorities, to include certain natural resources (areas) located on the coasts of the Black and Azov Seas in the category of federal natural resources, which have special status under the 1993 Presidential Decree on the Federal Natural Resources.

On 26 September, the government approved new regulations regarding the control of export of human, animal, and plant pathogens; their forms; fragments of genetic material; and equipment that can be used for the development of bacteriological (biological) and toxin weapons. In accordance with these regulations, the export of such listed objects to countries that violate the 1972 Convention on the Ban of the Bacteriological (Biological) and Toxin Weapons and the 1925 Geneva Protocol on the Prohibition of the Use of Poisonous Gases is prohibited. Export of these materials is subject to a strict licensing procedure, requiring both a special permit for each contract and prior approval of import by the competent authority in the importing country.

By year's end, the State Duma (lower house) of the Federal Parliament had on its agenda an impressive list of draft legislation on such issues as land use, environmental impact assessment, environmental security, protection of Lake Baikal, state policy in the management of radioactive wastes, protection of the population against radiation, specially protected natural territories, solid wastes, protection, and the use of water.

Sergei V. Vinogradov[1]

B. BELARUS

(1) Bilateral Cooperation in the Field of Environment Protection

In 1994, Belarus concluded a number of bilateral agreements on friendly relations and cooperation that focus, *inter alia*, on the rational use of natural resources and environmental protection. For example, an agreement with Romania places special emphasis on the development of bilateral relations in the field of development of natural resources, minimization and redress of the consequences of the Chernobyl nuclear accident, and prevention of future catastrophes such as Chernobyl. An agreement with Bulgaria also addresses cooperative measures to overcome the consequences of the Chernobyl accident. Similarly, Belarus and Moldova have agreed to close cooperation in the field of environmental protection and rational use of natural resources; at the same time, the parties noted that efforts of the international community as a whole, including the United Nations and its agencies, would be necessary to minimize the effects of the Chernobyl disaster.

In implementation of the 1992 Commonwealth of Independent States (CIS) Agreement on Cooperation in the Field of Ecology and Environmental Protection, Belarus concluded corresponding intergovernmental environmental protection agreements with the Russian Federation (5 July) and Ukraine (16 December). These agreements lay out the basic direction and form of cooperation. Beyond this, the Russian-Belarussian Agreement provides for each party's responsibility in the case of adverse transboundary effects on the environment of the other party, and sets out procedures for financing and settling accounts related to contractual works undertaken within the framework of this Agreement.

Finally, an important contribution to the development of friendly relations with the Baltic states was the signing of the Belarussian-Latvian Agreement on Cooperation in the Field of Environmental Protection, which outlines areas and forms of cooperation as well as principles of compensation for ecological damage.

[1] The author would like to express his gratitude to Dr. M. Brinchuk, Director of the Environmental Law Centre of the Institute of State and Law, Russian Academy of Sciences, for his assistance in preparing this report.

(2) New Constitution of the Republic of Belarus

The Constitution of the Republic of Belarus, adopted by the Supreme Soviet on 15 March, recognizes for the first time the right of every person living in the Republic to a healthy environment and to compensation for damage incurred through a violation of that right (Art. 46). On the other hand, Art. 55 imposes on every person a duty to protect the natural environment. Within two years following adoption of the Constitution, specific implementing legislation must be enacted. In accordance with the Law on the Procedure for the Entry Into Force of the Constitution, the transition to operational effectiveness is to be accomplished within five years of the entry into force of the relevant laws.

Thus, the Constitution has laid the foundations for the further development of environmental legislation and for the review of its implementation in practice. Efforts to implement the 1992 Law on the Protection of the Environment have resulted in a number of new laws and government programmes.

(3) Other Domestic Developments

(a) The State Programme for the Protection and Rational Use of Land

To improve land use and soil protection, on 17 October the Cabinet of Ministers adopted a State Programme for the Protection and Rational Use of Land. This action was prompted by the rapid decline in agriculturally cultivated land. The 9,353,600 hectares of agricultural land in in use in 1965 was reduced by 1.5 million hectares by 1994, while the Republic's total land area is 20,759,600 hectares. The amount of arable land per capita has fallen from 0.74 to 0.59 hectares, largely as a result of the conversion of productive land to industrial and civil construction use and the contamination of land by radionuclides.

The State Programme sets out the basic direction for the protection and rational use of land by calling for: improved land monitoring and thereby information on the conditions, ways of use, and changes in use of land; maximum conservation of agricultural land; measures to improve the condition of protected areas around water reservoirs; the clean-up of polluted lands, including territories contaminated by nuclear fallout; and improvement of both the ecological and the economic efficiency of remedial measures.

(b) Legislation on Production and Disposal of Wastes

A Law on the Production and Disposal of Wastes, which entered into force on 22 January, seeks to maximize recycling and reuse of waste as a supplementary source of raw materials (at present, about 15 million tons of wastes are being generated in the Republic, of which only 2 million tons are being reused). The Law defines waste in broad terms and applies to all economic actors that engage in activities on the Republic's territory, irrespective of the form of ownership of the property involved.

Pursuant to Art. 10, storage, processing, and disposal of waste are allowed only at special sites or facilities. For the first time, fees must be paid for introducing waste into the natural environment. The government establishes the rates and procedures for collecting payments. The Law forbids discharge of waste into overflow drainage, water reservoirs, marshes, water protection areas, and water-mains, as well as onto the territory of preserves, conservation areas, national parks, and other protection zones. Even stronger restrictions are imposed on the disposal of hazardous wastes. The Government is vested with the power to approve a list of dangerous wastes. Control and supervision of production, processing, packaging, storage, transportation, use, and disposal of waste is exercised by the Ministry of Natural Resources and Environment Protection, whose decisions are binding on all ministries, enterprises, and organizations. Economic actors are given the right to appeal to the courts against decisions made by environmental protection authorities imposing restrictions on their waste-management activities. At the same time, the Law imposes a number of obligations on economic actors that must be fulfilled in carrying out waste management. In particular, they must: introduce ecologically clean, low-waste, and waste-free technological processes; conduct waste-management activities in an ecologically justified manner; exercise laboratory control over the quality of the environment at dump sites and at intermediate storage sites; inform state authorities about accidental discharges of hazardous wastes into the environment and measures taken to mitigate consequences; and compensate all damage to the environment, health, and the property of natural and legal persons resulting from a violation of the Law.

(c) Legislation on Specially Protected Areas and Natural Objects

The Law on Specially Protected Areas and Natural Objects of 20 October lays down basic principles for identifying and protecting natural lands and objects. Specially protected natural areas and objects are considered national property. The term "specially protected areas and objects" includes preserves, reservations, national parks, and natural monuments. Preserves and natural monuments can be assigned either national or local significance or value. Establishment of specially protected areas and recognition of certain natural objects as natural monuments are to be performed in accordance with the Plan for the Rational Management of Protected Areas of the Republic that is to be approved by the Cabinet of Ministers. The Plan is to ensure an optimal ratio between lands used for economic purposes and those excluded from such use.

(d) Administrative and Legal Measures to Strengthen Environmental Protection

With the adoption of the Law on the Protection of the Environment and other environmental legislation, the need to hold violators accountable increased sharply. By 1994, legal liability had been established for such environmental legal violations as the unauthorized use of natural resources, and the pollution of lands and forests by dumping of household and industrial waste. Persons accused of infringing ecological laws now can be called to account directly by state environmental protection inspectors. Penalties vary depending on whether the offender is an official or an ordinary citizen as well as on the character and size of the environmental damage in question. Full compensation for damage is a separate aspect of liability, and is not dependent on the size of the penalty imposed by the state inspector.

Nikolai Storozhev
Viktor M. Zarkov

C. UKRAINE

(1) Introduction

In 1994, Ukraine elected a new President and Supreme Council. Environmental concerns were not a priority on the Ukrainian agenda, as the government was primarily preoccupied with the worsening economic crisis and with the task of designing a new state policy. In 1994, inflation in Ukraine reached 8,940 percent. According to a report of the International Labour Organisation, Ukraine has the highest level of unemployment in Eastern and Central Europe, the lowest minimum wage, and possibly the greatest degree of poverty.

(2) International Developments

In January, the Ministers of Environment of Ukraine and Poland signed an agreement in Warsaw on cooperation in controlling shipments of hazardous waste. The treaty with Poland is important for Ukraine, because there are no strong domestic laws for controlling shipments of hazardous wastes across Ukraine's borders. The treaty includes a clause on prevention of transit of hazardous waste via the territories of the two countries.

Also in January, Ukraine entered into a bilateral agreement with France on water resources management (signed 26 January). Under the agreement, France will assist with the establishment of an experimental water management agency on the southern portion of the Bug River in Ukraine. France will also assist with a comprehensive analysis of the state of the region's environment. The agreement also paves the way for further cooperation in other environmental fields, such as energy conservation, waste treatment and recovery, prevention of industrial accidents, and nature conservation.

Ukraine participated in the June 1994 Economic Commission for Europe conference to finalize the (➔) Protocol on Further Reduction of Sulphur Emissions, which was held in Oslo, Norway, and was among the first signatories of the Protocol. On 20 September, Ukraine signed the (➔) International Convention on Nuclear Safety, the first legal instrument that directly addresses the issue of the safety of nuclear power plants worldwide.

The issue of whether or not to close the Chernobyl nuclear power station remained the most controversial issue on the Ukrainian agenda in 1994 and was of major concern to the European and international community. According to a report of the International Atomic Energy Agency, produced by eight nuclear safety experts from the United States, Europe, and the Russian Federation in spring 1994, "numerous safety deficiencies" still remain at the Chernobyl nuclear power station, and "international levels of safety are not being met." The decision to close the power station by the end of 1994 was cancelled by the Ukrainian parliament because of a continuing energy shortage. In April 1994, the United States and Ukraine signed an agreement according to which Ukraine agreed to cease operation of the Chernobyl plant once it had secured alternative sources of energy to replace the plant's nuclear electricity. The European Union also promoted closure of Chernobyl, in part through persuading the Group of Seven leading industrial countries to work out a financial agreement with Ukraine to facilitate closure. Despite these efforts, the Chernobyl nuclear power plant continued to operate at year's end.

(3) Domestic Developments

Two new environmental laws were enacted during 1994, replacing former laws that had been developed in the late 1980s. The two laws, one on forests and the other concerning the subsoil, contain general provisions on public participation in the protection, use, and restoration of the natural resources covered. However, neither contains specific provisions on how this general obligation is to be implemented.

The new Forestry Code of Ukraine (21 January) outlines the jurisdiction of the various state authorities over the use of forest resources, establishes environmental conditions for industrial and other uses of forest resources, and sets out rules for restoration. The Code also introduces economic incentives for the protection of forest resources, sanctions for the violation of legal requirements, and remedies for damage.

The Subsoil Code of Ukraine (27 July) regulates the protection and use of the subsoil. According to the Code, subsoil resources are exclusive state property, but can be made available by state bodies to different users for development for a fee. For the first time, this Code introduces licensing of subsoil resources.

The Law on Measures for Sanitary-Epidemiological Welfare of the Population of Ukraine was enacted on 24 February. It specifies the authority and responsibilities of state sanitary-epidemiological services and outlines the rights and duties of citizens and enterprises in the area of sanitary-epidemiological welfare. The law not only acknowledges the citizen's right to a safe natural environment, but, as a first for any Ukrainian environmental law, introduces substantive enforcement provisions. Thus, the law contains direct provisions concerning administrative and financial remedies that can be imposed on the violators.

On 22 September, the Supreme Council of Ukraine adopted a decree on specially protected areas in Ukraine, which outlines a new policy for expanding protected areas around the country. By year's end, several draft environmental laws were pending before the Supreme Council for adoption in 1995; among them were laws on the use of nuclear energy and nuclear safety, the safe treatment of radioactive wastes, ecological emergency zones, ecological assessment, and water conservation and management. There were also plans to amend the leading environmental law, the Act on Protection of the Natural Environment, during 1995.

Tatiana Zaharchenko

D. KAZAKHSTAN

(1) The Environmental Situation in 1994

With a territory of 2.7 million square kilometers, Kazakhstan is the second largest successor state to the former Soviet Union. Geographically, Kazakhstan straddles the boundary between Europe and Asia. As of 1994, the environmental situation in this part of the world could only be characterized as catastrophic.

As in the past, significant environmental and public health risks resulted from nuclear tests that were conducted in 1994 at Lop-Nor, China, located only a few hundred kilometers from the Kazakh border. Thus far China has not renounced testing, arguing that because its nuclear weapons are less developed than those of other weapons states, such tests are needed.

The environmental threat is of special concern in the area of Semipalatinsk, where nuclear tests were conducted for 40 years—from 1949 to 1963 above ground and in the atmosphere and from 1964 to 1989 underground. During this series of tests, radionuclides with a total activity of approximately 45 million Curies were released into the atmosphere. According to the Kazakh Ministry of the Environment, 190,570 persons were suffering from various radiation-induced illnesses in 1994.

Besides radioactive contamination, reckless development activities and unsound economic planning in the former Socialist Soviet republic are major causes of the catastrophic environmental situation now facing the country. An illustration of the gravity is the continuing drying up of Lake Aral, which has prompted authorities to declare an ecological emergency in the entire region. Every year, including 1994, 70 million tons of salt are freed from the dry lakebed and spread by wind into neighboring regions over thousands of square kilometers, entailing in its wake local climate change, increased salinity of the soil, and a gradual withering away of fauna and flora. Moreover, in 1994 the number of health effects related to this pollution phenomenon increased significantly among the population, and in particular among children.

West Kazakhstan is affected by the continuing rise of the level of the Caspian Sea (its level has risen by 2 meters since 1978) leading to the flooding of shore areas up to 20 to 30 kilometers from the original coastline. This has resulted in a significant worsening of the pollution of the Caspian Sea, the habitat of 90 percent of all sturgeon worldwide. Regional ecological problems are exacerbated by a general acute shortage of water and the concentration of oil and gas industry in West Kazakhstan.

The East and Central Kazakh cities of Ust-Kamenogorsk and Leninogorsk deservedly have the reputation of being the most polluted cities of the country. Each year the 265 local industrial enterprises release 270 tons of toxic pollutants into the air, resulting in an environmental concentration of zinc, copper, beryllium, and cadmium that is 10 times the maximum permissible level. A similar situation prevails in the cities of Pavlodar, Karaganda, Temirtau, and Ekibastus.

In the South, phosphate mining has caused serious groundwater pollution, with phosphate concentration three times the maximum permissible level for groundwater. Additionally, air quality, in particular in Almaty, has deteriorated very significantly. The area's natural pattern of air circulation—Almaty is situated in a basin—has been completely disrupted by uncoordinated and uncontrolled construction activity.

(2) Measures Taken in 1994 to Address the Ecological Crisis

(a) Domestic Measures

The major emphasis of the government's environmental policy measures was on enforcing strict compliance by commercial and industrial enterprises with the country's environmental protection laws and regulations. On the one hand, the government offered subsidies and tax relief for environmental protection investments; on the other hand, it imposed environmental charges on enterprises for using natural resources and polluting the environment.

The legal bases for the government's increased environmental protection efforts were the Environmental Protection Law of 1991 and the state's "Ecology" program. To further the implementation of the Environmental Protection Law, in 1994 the Council of Ministers adopted two regulations (N 1112 and N 1113). During the year, the Ministry of the Environment proposed a draft regulation on a uniform system of environmental monitoring. The Ministry has already compiled a medical-ecological atlas of the Republic.

During 1994, Kazakhstan sought to make its investment legislation both "greener" and more attractive to foreign nationals, thereby pursuing both foreign capital as well as the introduction of modern environmental technologies.

(b) Activities within the Framework of the Commonwealth of Independent States (CIS)

In 1994, Kazakhstan participated in two meetings: the Intergovernmental Ecological Council (IEC) and the CIS (4th Meeting of the Council, Minsk, April; 5th Meeting of the Council, Moscow, September). The meetings resulted in approval of the Statutes of the working bodies of the Council and produced an agreement to compile data (in the form of a book) on endangered species of fauna and flora in the CIS. A number of expert meetings within the framework of the IEC also took place.

(c) Other International Activities

In 1994, Kazakhstan became a party to UN Convention on Biological Diversity. To implement the Convention, the Council of Ministers promulgated Regulation N 918 of 10 August. On 15 October, Kazakhstan signed the (➔) Convention on Desertification. During the year, experts from Kazakhstan actively participated in environmental protection-oriented meetings of international organizations such as the UN, the Organisation for Economic Cooperation and Development, and the UN Economic Commission for Europe. In September, Kazakhstan, with the assistance of the International Union for the Conservation of Nature, hosted an international seminar on biodiversity.

Bakhytjan Chenguelbaev[1]

[1] The author gratefully acknowledges funding for this report from the Daimler-Benz Foundation, and information supplied by the Kazakh Ministry of the Environment.

11. SOUTHERN EUROPE/TURKEY

A. ALBANIA

(1) International Legal Instruments

Following Albania's accession to a number of international environmental agreements in 1993, there were few developments in 1994. One notable exception is Albania's active negotiations with neighboring countries within the framework of the Convention on the Protection and Use of Transboundary Watercourses and International Lakes, which focused in particular on the shared management of the Ohrida and Prespa Lakes.

Decision No. 413 of the Council of Ministers of 22 August formally proclaimed the Eivjaka-Karavastra lagoon and park as an area to be proposed for inclusion in the List of Wetlands of International Importance under the Ramsar Convention.

(2) Domestic Environmental Legislation

With the main environmental protection law in place since 1993, only specific natural resource sectors were the subject of legislation in 1994. A new wildlife management law, adopted on 23 November, allows hunting by permit on the basis of wildlife management plans to be prepared and periodically updated. It also allows foreign investment in the field of ecotourism, hunting, and related infrastructure. The Forestry Department adopted legislation to implement the law. A moratorium on hunting that was established in 1993 was lifted in 1994. The Forestry Department also prepared a draft law to regulate grazing on state lands that are part of the forest estate. Agricultural areas are excluded from the draft law's application of the draft law.

The Fisheries Department finalized a draft fisheries law to regulate both marine and inland fisheries, which had been widely discussed within the country. One section of the law is devoted to aquaculture, a growing activity in Albania. Parliament was expected to examine the draft early in 1995. By year's end, the Department had begun to prepare detailed implementing legislation.

Finally, establishment of some communal forests (*i.e.*, parcels of state forest handed over to communal administrations for management) pursuant to the Forest Law of 1992 was expected by the end of the year. The experience gained in the process will serve as a basis for the adoption of the necessary subsidiary legislation on communal forests.

Maria Teresa Cirelli

B. ROMANIA

(1) Introduction

In 1994, Romanian efforts in the field of environmental protection focused on the Balkan Peninsula and Europe. Although Romania made no significant headway in its domestic legislation and regulations, it did participate in a meaningful way at both the regional and the European levels in attending conferences and reaching agreements, along with other nations of Eastern Europe. This increasing participation evidences Romania's desire to become a full member of the European Community.

Despite Romania's regional efforts at pollution control, pollution within Romania continued to worsen in 1994. Water and air pollution continued to increase with measurable effects. For example, 7 percent of the forests in Romania are now ecologically dead. Romania still accepts toxic waste from abroad for a fee, putting a greater strain on the land dedicated as dump sites. The Copsa Mica and Silistra-Calarasi regions remain ecological wastelands.

As a result of its continuing economic difficulties, Romania is unable to tackle its current environmental problems. Romania continues to rely on nuclear power as a source of electricity, thereby adding to the problem of nuclear waste disposal in the region. Further, Romania is unable to pay for desulfurization and nitrogen oxides reduction programs in those industries that continue to use fossil fuels, as such programs are currently beyond Romania's economic means.

(2) European Efforts

On 5 October, the Romanian Environmental Minister, along with other environmental ministers from Eastern Europe, attended a meeting of the European Union's environment ministers in Luxembourg. The purpose of the meeting was to develop a plan for eliminating obstacles to membership in the European Union. The result of the meeting was a series of recommendations on the environment that are intended to guide Central and Eastern European countries toward successful entry into the European Union.

(3) Regional Efforts

Romania participated in several important conferences that took place regarding environmental protection in the Balkan region. On 22 April, Romania attended the first inter-parliamentary environmental conference, held in Prague. The discussions focused on pollution control in Southeastern Europe. Romania also attended the Central Asia and Environmental Conference, held in Istanbul on 4 July. The purpose of the

Conference was to implement on a regional level decisions and recommendations of the United Nations Conference on Environment and Development. Romania also participated in the Conference on Environmental Protection of the Carpathian Basin, held in Debrcen on 30 July. Finally, members of the Romanian Green Party attended a meeting of Balkan Green Parties, held on 6 November in Sofia. The attendees decided to table the "Balkan Environmental Charter" as an official document of the European Parliament.

(4) Bilateral Efforts

On 10 January, Romania and Denmark signed an Environmental Cooperation Agreement that focuses, *inter alia*, on air pollution by power and industrial plants, water management and protection of underground water resources, sea pollution, waste administration, and nature preservation.

Romania's environmental disputes with neighboring Bulgaria continued in 1994. In August 1994, the Secretary-General of the European Trade Union Confederation received a letter from the coordinating council of the Confederation of Independent Trade Unions in Silistra, Bulgaria, requesting action on environmental issues in the Silistra-Calarasi region of Romania and Bulgaria. This region was also on the agenda of an inter-governmental committee meeting between Romania and Bulgaria on the environment, held on 6 October in Calarasi.

George C. Summerfield

C. TURKEY

(1) National Developments and Fulfillment of International Obligations

(a) National Policies

In 1994, in order to conform to United Nations Conference on Environment and Development instruments, certain revisions were made to Turkish environmental law. Turkey believes that effective implementation of Agenda 21 at the national level requires the review of development plans and programs with a view to integrating environmental concerns at all levels of policy-making. Turkey's main action was to prepare the seventh Five-Year Development Plan (1995–2000) which, according to the Turkish Constitution, is binding on the public sector and serves as a guidance document to the private sector. For all socio-economic sectors, 62 expert commissions were created, one of which is devoted to environmental concerns. In addition, certain sectors such as tourism, industry, energy, transport, and agriculture were given special instructions to integrate relevant environmental considerations into their work.

(b) *Water-Related Issues*

In 1994, the Water Pollution Control Regulation of 1988 was revised. Serious water pollution problems have arisen in certain regions of Turkey in recent years and protection of water resources against pollution has become increasingly important for Turkey, particularly since a large share of ground water resources has already become depleted.

In 1994, the Southeastern Anatolia Project—a large-scale, multi-sectoral regional development project—took a significant step towards full realization. The project, which envisages the construction of 22 dams and 19 hydro-power plants, aims at developing the Euphrates and Tigris basins, which contribute approximately 30 percent to the total flow of streams in Turkey. The water will be used mainly for irrigation, production of hydro-electric power, and urban consumption. Both rivers are international watercourses: the Euphrates flows into Syria, the Tigris into Iraq. Technical arrangements have been made with these countries in connection with the waters of the rivers. In November 1994, water was drawn from Ataturk Dam to irrigate areas of Southeastern Turkey. Ataturk Dam is the sixth largest dam in the world in terms of volume of embarkment and the 20th largest in terms of reservoir capacity. To minimize the environmental impact and to prevent undue agricultural activity in the region, the Ministry of Agriculture and the Ministry of Environment jointly began a large-scale environmental impact assessment process.

(c) *Climate Change and the Ozone Layer*

The London Amendment to the Montreal Protocol on Substances that Deplete the Ozone Layer was ratified by Turkey and went into force on 28 December. The Copenhagen Amendments are still awaiting approval in the Committee of the Grand National Assembly.

In 1994, Turkey continued to refuse to sign the UN Framework Convention on Climate Change. Under the Convention, Turkey is grouped together with "developed countries," and consequently would be required to reduce its carbon dioxide (CO_2) emissions to 1990 levels by the year 2000. Furthermore, Turkey would have to contribute to funds being provided to developing countries. Since Turkey's CO_2 emissions are very low compared to those of developed countries proper, the obligation to keep emissions at 1990 levels would impose a heavy and troublesome burden on energy production and development. As a result, in 1994, the government set up a National Climate Program Committee which is to present the Turkish viewpoint in the various international fora.

(d) *Waste Management*

In addition to rapid population growth, Turkey is experiencing dramatic urbanization. Municipal and industrial solid wastes produced by developing industrial sectors are among the most serious challenges faced by major cities and tourist regions. In response to this adverse trend in solid waste management, Turkey enacted amendments to the Regulation on the Control of Solid Wastes (1991) which entered into force on 2 November. Also, after a one-year trial period, the Regulation on the Control of Chemical and Hazardous Substances and Wastes (1993), entered into force on 11 July.

Finally, the Basel Convention on the Control of Transboundary Movements of Hazardous Wastes and their Disposal became effective for Turkey in September.

(e) Natural Resource Management and Conservation

In order to protect its flora and fauna and their natural habitats, Turkey signed and ratified various international conventions in 1994: The Convention on Wetlands of International Importance especially as Waterfowl Habitats was ratified on 17 May, as was the Convention on International Trade in Endangered Species on 27 September. Turkey signed the (➔) Convention to Combat Desertification on 15 October.

(2) Regional Activities

(a) Mediterranean Action Plan

In October 1993, in accordance with the rules of procedure of the Barcelona Convention, Turkey was elected President of Bureau until June 1995. In 1994, three Bureau meetings were held in Ankara, Tunisia, and Morocco under the Presidency of the Turkish Minister for the Environment. Within this framework, the program on mapping and monitoring of soil erosion processes was carried forward throughout 1994.

In November 1994, Turkey participated in a conference on "Agenda 21 for the Mediterranean" in Tunis. Mediterranean countries believe that cooperation within the Mediterranean Basin could serve as a model for the rest of the world for the implementation of Agenda 21.

(b) Environmental Management of the Black Sea

The Convention on the Protection of the Black Sea against Pollution (Bucharest Convention) and its three Protocols—the ultimate objective of which is to eliminate environmental pollution and degradation of the Black Sea—were signed by representatives of the six coastal states on 21 April 1992 and entered into force on 15 January 1994. On 7 February, the environmental management project document for the protection of the Black Sea was officially opened in Istanbul to accelerate the action plan for the Black Sea. Turkey launched a "pollution monitoring network" involving universities and other public institutions in 1994 to assist the Secretariat, which is located in Istanbul.

(c) Cooperation with Central Asian Countries

Environmental cooperation with and between Central Asian states, a process that Turkey helped launch, continued in 1994. To improve regional cooperation on environmental matters, Turkey hosted a first conference of Central Asia and Balkan Republics Ministers of Environment on 4-5 July. The Ministers of the Environment of Albania, Azerbaijan, Kazakhstan, Kyrgystan, Macedonia, Tajikistan, Turkey, the Turkish Republic of Northern Cyprus, and Uzbekistan, as well as the Ambassador of Bosnia-Herzegovina in Turkey attended. The participants signed three non-binding documents, and signatory countries decided to create a follow-up committee to prepare a regional action plan within the framework of Agenda 21.

(3) Bilateral Activities

A protocol to implement the 1993 bilateral framework agreement between Azerbaijan and Turkey was signed on 6 July. The protocol establishes pollution control and prevention strategies for the Hzer Sea, as well as the Aras and Kura rivers. It also calls for Turkey to provide technological aid, as well as assistance with environmental impact assessment, solid waste management, and measures regarding specially protected areas.

On 11 April, Turkey and Israel signed an Agreement on Environmental Problems and Protection of Nature. The Agreement is expected to contribute significantly to comprehensive environmental security in the region.

Hilel Zilelioglu Elver

D. MALTA

(1) International Developments

(a) Ratification of Multilateral Conventions

Malta ratified the UN Framework Convention on Climate Change on 15 March 1994. It entered into force with regard to Malta in June 1994. Malta also ratified the Council of Europe's Revised European Convention on the Protection of the Archaeological Heritage, done in Valleta on 16 January 1992, on 24 November.

(b) Barcelona Convention

On 14 October, Malta, together with Croatia, Cyprus, Greece, Israel, Italy, Monaco, Spain, and Tunisia, signed the (➔) Protocol for the Protection of the Mediterranean Sea Against Pollution Resulting From Exploration and Exploitation of the Seabed and its Subsoil. This is the fifth Protocol to the Barcelona Convention for the Protection of the Mediterranean Sea Against Pollution.

Malta participated in the April meeting of the contracting parties of the Barcelona Convention, which the Government of Tunisia called to discuss the relationship between the Convention and the principle of sustainable development enshrined in Agenda 21. Malta also participated in the November meeting of legal and technical experts that was called to examine amendments to the Barcelona Convention and its related Protocols and amendments to the Mediterranean Action Plan. At both meetings Malta submitted a number of amendments to update the Convention by taking into consideration developments at the United Nations Third Conference on the Law of the Sea and the United Nations Conference on Environment and Development. The proposed amendments were to be discussed by the contracting parties in Barcelona in 1995 during their ninth ordinary meeting.

(2) National Legislation

(a) Environment Protection Act

Under the Environment Protection Act of 1991, the Minister of Environment issued Legal Notice 1 of 1994 concerning environmental protection (including preventive and remedial measures), which authorizes the Director of the Department for the Protection of the Environment to monitor compliance with the provisions of the Act and all regulations and codes of practice enacted thereunder.

Legal Notice 87 of 1994 sets out the procedure to be followed before the "Authority of Review," an independent body established under the Environment Protection Act, whose function it is to hear objections to regulations of the Ministry of the Environment. The Authority has only advisory powers and can only offer suggestions to the Minister to amend or delete regulations enacted pursuant to the Environment Protection Act. In 1994, the Authority heard a number of objections in connection with hunting regulations enacted in 1993 following Malta's accession to the Council of Europe's Berne Convention on the Conservation of European Wildlife and Natural Habitats (1979).

On 6 September, the Minister for the Environment issued Legal Notice 103 of 1994, declaring the use of non-refillable glass containers for non-alcoholic beverages to be harmful to the environment.

(b) Development Planning Act

The Development Planning (Use Classes) Order 1994, Legal Notice 53 of 1994, groups together those uses of land and buildings that have broadly similar environmental implications. The order provides that a change from one use within a class to another in the same class does not require a development permit. It also indicates those uses that do not fall into any use class and will thus invariably require development permits.

Hilal Zilelioglu Elver

12. NEAR EAST

A. ISRAEL

(1) National Policy Developments

(a) Water and Sewage Purification

1994 was marked by large government investment in sewage purification plants and the publication of tender offers for the construction of such plants. Construction was also underway at year's end in several local communities for area-wide sewage treatment plants. On the administrative level, the government decided that water and sewage should be separated from local municipal administration and be placed in the hands of water and sewage companies, owned by local municipalities but operated in a closed economic system. The government has seen to the establishment of several such water and sewage companies, even on a regional basis.

(b) Solid Waste Landfills

The government also embarked on a national plan for solid waste landfill sites. The National Planning Council determined that five such sites would be located in different geographic regions throughout Israel. In 1994, the government published two international tenders for the planning, construction, and operation of two landfills, one in the northern and the other in the southern part of Israel. It is projected that the 400 local and regional solid waste landfills will gradually be closed and replaced by the five national sites. Very little was done in 1994, however, to implement the Recycling Law that the Ministry of Environment passed in 1993.

(2) Water Management

In 1994, there was increased government activity to restore and beautify Israel's streams. The major achievements in this field were not on the legislative level, but in the practical implementation of local and national policy. Israel created a Rivers Administration, however, that, although without legislative authority, has encouraged drainage boards and other stream authorities to protect and attempt to beautify their streams.

The Yarkon River Authority, Israel's oldest river authority, which was created in 1989, embarked on a master plan for the protection of the Yarkon river and archaeological and architectural sites along its banks. In 1994, it issued a tender offer for the preparation of an outline plan to protect the river for future generations. The Authority also published a new by-law forbidding the pollution of, or damage to, the banks of the Yarkon River. The prohibition is enforceable with punitive sanctions.

A second such management system, the Kishon River Authority, was established on 4 September within the framework of the Streams and Springs Authorities Law. The new Authority's function will be to prevent new, and abate existing, pollution of the Kishon River, a highly polluted stream carrying waste from the Haifa Bay region; and to transform the area into a recreational site. For that purpose the Authority is, *inter alia*, empowered to set licensing conditions designed to prevent negative impacts from industrial plants on the river, and to require the preparation and submission of detailed plans to planning authorities to prevent further degradation of the Kishon. In addition, the Authority may appoint inspectors and levy fees on corporations and local authorities to enable it to fulfill its mandate.

Authority members include representatives of government ministries, local authorities, public corporations (such as the Jewish National Fund), green organizations, tourism, water and transport authorities, and riparian land owners. The Authority will operate through an administrative board appointed by the Minister of the Environment. Like that of the Yarkon River Authority, the Kishon River Authority's jurisdiction extends only 25 meters from the river's banks, which severely limits its operation.

(3) Government Legislation

(a) Dangerous Substances

In 1994, the Ministry of the Environment continued to publish regulations consolidating its authority over the handling of dangerous substances. Regulations were implemented for dangerous substances and for the registration of insecticides. An insecticide is defined under the law as "any material which is used to destroy insects or rodents that may cause damage to persons, their homes, their businesses or their premises, other than such material used on a person's body." The regulations require that all such substances be registered with the Ministry of Environment before their production, distribution, or importation. Prior to registration, a manufacturer or distributor of such a substance must prove to the satisfaction of the Ministry of Environment that the insecticide is effective and has been registered in other countries. The regulations also require that a sample of the insecticide's packaging be presented for inspection and that evidence be presented showing that a full toxicological study of the components of the insecticide has been completed, showing its effect on humans and the environment, including plants and animals. Furthermore, the regulations require the submission of a material safety data sheet for the active ingredients and each of its parts, and other relevant information that is required in order to register the insecticide. A request to register a new insecticide is filed before a committee of three representatives of the Ministry of Environment and three representatives of the Ministry of Health.

The Ministry of Environment also produced regulations for the dumping of dangerous solid waste in order to bring it in line with previous regulations published by the Ministry. These regulations require that the definition of dangerous substances meet the definition previously published by the Ministry under the special order for commodities and services and the transportation of solid waste.

(b) Open Spaces

Israel enacted an important piece of legislation on national parks, nature reserves, archaeological sites, and monuments in 1992 (*see* 3 *YbIEL* 425 (1992)). 1994, however, was marked by the publication of a law that is basically anti-environment: the Law on the Concession of the Dead Sea (Planning and Building) (Construction of Certain Works) 5764-1994. The Law reduces the involvement of the planning authorities in granting construction permits to the Dead Sea Works in the area defined in its concession. The area, however, has been very broadly defined to include thousands of kilometers. Therefore, the effect of the law will be to reduce the ability of those objecting to industrialization in the Dead Sea to operate under the normal terms of the Planning and Building Law.

More in line with enlightened environmental policy is the amendment to the Planning and Building Law No. 37 of 1994. This amendment requires the preparation of a road plan for roads in Israel. In addition, the law requires that no road may be planned without preparation of an environmental impact assessment by the Environmental Adviser to the District Planning Commission.

(c) Air Pollution

Israel published no legislation in the field of air pollution in 1994, but the Ministry of Environment was busy updating the present legal framework for air pollution prevention. It was expected that new regulations or legislation would be passed in 1995 to enable the Ministry of Environment to prevent air pollution by land-use measures rather than by attacking the pollution after it has occurred.

Richard Laster

B. KUWAIT

(1) Local Developments—General Environmental Policy Document

A working group charged with revising Kuwait's General Environmental Policy Document submitted an amended version that integrates into its text the principles and concepts of the 1992 Rio Declaration and Agenda 21. After obtaining input from relevant organizations, the Environmental Protection Council's (EPC's) subcommittee entrusted with the follow-up to

Agenda 21, reviewed the revised final draft. The Legal Committee was to review this draft by the end of the year, before submission to the EPC and then to the Council of Ministers for formal approval. The amendments add several new chapters to the Document, namely on agriculture, training and manpower development, public education, biodiversity and nature reserves, promotion of environmental research, and international environmental affairs.

(2) Regional Developments

In 1994, the EPC represented the State of Kuwait at various meetings of the Gulf Cooperation Council's (GCC's) Environmental Affairs Committee. These meetings aimed at coordinating environmental policies in the region generally, and, more specifically, at coordinating governmental views on the issues of environment and energy, and the economic implications of emerging energy policies related to concerns over global warming, especially the proposed carbon tax.

An EPC delegation headed by the Chairman of the Council also participated in the meetings of the Executive Office of the Arab Council of Ministers Responsible for the Environment as well as the Ministerial Conference that followed. The EPC, in cooperation with the GCC Secretariat and the World Conservation Union, also organized a Regional Workshop on Biodiversity in the GCC countries, which focused on the costs and benefits and legal and administrative requirements of joining the Biodiversity Convention.

(3) International Level

In 1994, Kuwait ratified the UN Framework Convention on Climate Change. Also, the EPC recommended ratification of the (→) Desertification Convention. The recommendation awaited approval by the Council of Ministers at year's end.

The Environmental Protection Council planned to attend a United Nations Environment Programme meeting scheduled to be held in the Netherlands in August 1995, which is to prepare a Convention for the Protection of Migratory Birds.

Mahmood Y. Abdulraheem

C. WEST ASIA REGION (REST OF)

(1) Bahrain

(a) National Legislation

The continuous depletion of fish stocks in regional waters caused concern among Bahrain and other Gulf States. In response to this concern, Bahrain in November adopted several amendments to its Fishing Law No. 5 of 1981. Decree No. 14 of 1994 prohibits ships not registered in Bahrain from fishing in territorial waters and the economic zone. Decree No. 15 of 1994 suspended issuance of any new fishing licenses for 1995 and 1996. Decree No. 16 of 1994 requires the presence of a Bahraini Sea Pilot on ships in the traditional shipping sector. And Decree No. 17 of 1994 standardized the length and size of various types of fish and shrimps that may be caught or sold in Bahrain.

In September, the Council of Ministers discussed the proposed draft law for the Protection of Wildlife and the Conservation of Biodiversity. The law's stated objective is to establish and develop a plan of action and policies necessary to protect all types of wildlife from any harmful effects arising from human activities. The proposed law calls for the formation of a national committee for the protection of wildlife. It also includes several articles for setting up mechanisms to coordinate these activities with other concerned bodies and for the imposition of fines. The Council of Ministers decided to study further the proposed draft law and was expected to approve it early in 1995.

(b) Conventions/Protocols

In December, Bahrain ratified the UN Framework Convention on Climate Change. Bahrain is also currently studying the UN Convention on Biological Diversity (Biodiversity Convention) and the Ramsar Convention. On the regional level, Bahrain continued to coordinate its environmental activities with other members of the Gulf Cooperation Council (GCC). Bahrain adopted both the GCC Unified Code for Management and Disposal of Radioactive Material and also the General Environmental Code in 1994, and at the end of the year was still considering a third GCC Unified Code for the Management of Hazardous Waste.

(c) Other Environmental Issues

In 1994, depletion of water resources was of major concern to Bahrain. As with other countries of the region, Bahrain's water resources are very scarce. A recent study showed that underground water resources are being depleted faster than expected. Extraction of groundwater in 1993 was equivalent to 194 million cubic meters, with an estimated inflow of only 112 million cubic meters to the aquifer. This imbalance has contributed to the existing deterioration of groundwater quality and may cause the aquifer to be completely depleted in less than 20 years. Bahrain uses water from desalination plants to supplement and lower the salinity of groundwater for domestic use. Bahrain initiated a major awareness campaign for water conservation, and is also contemplating other actions such as the gradual lifting of subsidies, privatization of water management, and the increased use of non-conventional water resources such as treated wastewater in both agricultural and industrial sectors.

Finding alternatives to ozone-depleting substances (ODS) was also important in 1994. Bahrain is covered by Art. 5 of the Montreal Protocol, and since it is an importer of ODS, it initiated an ambitious programme to reduce consumption and convert to alternative substances and formed a national committee for ozone affairs to design a national strategy to phase out the use of ODS. Bahrain also received assistance from the Ozone Multilateral Fund to prepare its country programme and organized a national training workshop for ODS Alternatives in the Refrigeration Sector. Another workshop, on halons management, was to be held in 1995.

(2) Jordan

(a) National Legislation

In 1994, Jordan's Council of Ministers passed the Environmental Protection Bill and submitted it to the National Assembly. During its sessions in October and November, the Legislation Commission of the National Assembly started debate on the bill and approved a number of its articles. The bill was expected to win approval by the National Assembly in 1995.

The Department of Environment at the Ministry of Municipalities, Rural Affairs and Environment, with the assistance of UNEP/ROWA, prepared six draft environmental regulations in 1994. The draft regulations cover general cooperation for environmental protection, protection of water resources and the marine ecosystem, prevention and control of air pollution, control and disposal of hazardous wastes, and protection and conservation of soil and protected areas. These regulations will be ready for implementation once Jordan adopts the Environmental Protection Bill.

(b) Conventions/Protocols

In November 1993, Jordan ratified the UN Framework Convention on Climate Change and the Biodiversity Convention. By the end of 1994, it was in the process of ratifying the (➔) Desertification Convention.

(c) Other Environmental Issues

In early 1994, Jordan started a programme for monitoring the ambient air in Amman, completed a study on assessing hazardous waste generation in the country, and established a database on toxic chemicals used in the country.

(3) Lebanon

(a) National Legislation

Lebanon is still trying to recover from two decades of civil strife. In 1993, Lebanon's Parliament passed a law establishing the Ministry of Environment as the decision-making body responsible for environmental affairs in the country, however, the Ministry still lacks the funds and personnel to carry out its mandate. In collaboration with the UNDP, Lebanon is implementing a national environmental management programme. An Inter-Agency Working Group on Environment, which involves representatives of the UN Development Programme, the UN Food and Agriculture Organization, the UN Children's Fund, the UN Industrial Development Organization, the World Health Organization, the UN Environment Programme (UNEP), the Ministry of Environment and other governmental institutions, is overseeing the programme's development and implementation. UNEP will be involved in both drafting environmental legislation and setting up regulations.

(b) Conventions/Protocols

Lebanon ratified the Desertification Convention. On 15 December, Lebanon also ratified the Convention on Biological Diversity and the UN Framework Convention on Climate Change, and on 21 December it ratified the Basel Convention on the Control of Transboundary Movements of Hazardous Wastes and Their Disposal.

(c) Other Environmental Issues

Between 1987–88, during the civil strife, several industrial countries, including Italy and Germany, transported over 17,000 barrels of toxic waste to Lebanon, which were buried all over the country. During 1993 and 1994, the government received several reports of chemical contamination of ground and surface water, as well as widespread reports of human and animal poisoning. A committee of the Parliament and a judicial committee undertook investigations that revealed that toxic waste sites are widespread. Lebanon is making efforts to locate and recover the toxic waste and avoid further damage to the environment.

(4) Oman

(a) National Legislation

In 1994, Oman drafted a new environmental law. Several national committees are reviewing the draft law, and UNEP/ROWA is assisting in the process of reevaluation. Oman also adopted two ministerial decrees dealing with noise pollution. Decree No. 79/1994 dealt with public places and Decree No. 80/1994 dealt with the work place. Consultation meetings to further redefine the National Strategy for the Protection of Environment continued throughout 1994. The new strategy will include an extensive number of projects for environmental protection, policy guidelines and implementation mechanisms to ensure the preservation of natural resources and sustainable development, and economic evaluation of Oman's natural resources. The strategy was expected to be finalized and ready for approval during 1995.

Oman considers wildlife preservation a high priority. A study by the World Conservation Union showed that Oman remained home to several endangered wild Arabian animals such as the oryx, tigers, and other desert wildlife. Within Oman's marine environment, 13 species of dolphins and whales can be found in territorial waters and over 400 species of migratory and indigenous birds and five species of turtles nest on the country's shoreline. In 1994, Oman passed Royal Decree No. 4 to deal with a special demarcation for the Arabian Oryx reserve.

(b) Conventions/Protocols

Special committees carried out detailed reviews of several international agreements in 1994, with specific emphasis on Oman's financial and technical obligations after ratification. Among these agreements are the Basel Convention on the Control of Transboundary Movements of Hazardous Wastes, the Biodiversity Convention, the Vienna Convention and Montreal Protocol for the Control of Ozone Depleting Substances, and the UN Framework Convention on Climate Change. The Committees have recommended their ratification.

(c) Other Environmental Issues

Oman is making every possible effort to prevent its 1700km shoreline from becoming contaminated with oil from oil tankers criss-crossing the Gulf waters. It is estimated that over 120 oil tankers pass through the Strait of Hormuz every day, each disposing of its contaminated ballast water as it enters the Gulf. Oman has put into action a contingency plan to protect its shoreline by imposing heavy fines on polluters. A well-established network of surveillance aircraft and coastguard boats continuously monitor Oman's shoreline. Deep concerns were raised when two oil tankers collided near the eastern shores of the United Arab Emirates, spilling over 17,000 tons of crude oil. Oman's contingency plan was put into action to control the oil slick.

(5) Qatar

(a) National Legislation

The most important environmental event in Qatar of 1994 was the Amiri Decree No. 13 of 1994, which amended Law No. 4 of 1981. The amendment transferred the Environmental Protection Committee and its Technical Secretariat from the Ministry of Public Health to the Ministry of Municipal Affairs and Agriculture. This amendment set the Ministerial representation in the committee at the Director level or equivalent, with approval of the Council of Ministers. The amendment calls for the establishment of a Department for the Environment within the Ministry to assist the Technical Secretariat in carrying out its duties and following up on the implementation of the Committee's decisions and recommendations.

(b) Conventions/Protocols

The Committee's working group for environmental legislation and international agreements completed a detailed study of the Biodiversity Convention and the Vienna Convention for the protection of the Ozone layer and the Montreal Protocol in 1994. Ratification of these instruments was expected during 1995. The Committee also completed a detailed study of the UN Framework Convention on Climate Change, and will submit it for ratification in 1995.

(c) Other Environmental Issues

In 1994, Qatar carried out several activities to develop wildlife reserves, as for example in Ras Usherg. It also promoted the planting and protection of mangrove in special areas, and a wide-scale campaign to plant trees and shrubs throughout the country.

(6) Syria

(a) National Legislation

In 1993, the Ministry of State for Environmental Affairs completed a draft environmental law for Syria, which Syria's Council of Ministers approved. By the end of 1994, however, the General Assembly had not taken action on the bill. Meanwhile, the Ministry continued to expand its technical staff and reorganize its administrative structure, including the strengthening of provincial environmental departments.

Syria also completed a study to establish a 590-hectare wildlife reserve on Thoura Island, and proposed two other reserves: Um Al-Toyor in Latakia Province, and Al Sharah in the Arab Mountains.

(b) Conventions/Protocols

Syria ratified the Desertification Convention in 1994. The Ministry completed the preliminary preparation for submission of the UN Framework Convention for Climate Change, to be ratified by the Syrian authorities.

(c) Other Environmental Issues

Division of the Euphrates River water between Turkey and Syria remains one of the most serious problems between the two countries. Plans to construct a network of dams are underway in Turkey, and the resulting decrease in water flow is expected to drastically affect the agricultural output of Syria and Iraq, since the Euphrates River is a major source of water for both countries.

Syria has initiated a major plan to assess and mitigate the effect of water pollution in the country. A major wastewater treatment plant is being constructed in Damascus. Upon completion, this plant will prevent the disposal of industrial and other untreated wastewater directly into the Barada River. At the end of 1994, a study was also underway to assess the quality of the Asi River's water and propose solutions to prevent further deterioration in water quality from industrial sources.

(7) United Arab Emirates (UAE)

(a) National Legislation

The UAE is a confederation of seven Emirates. Environmental institutions in the Emirates are not equally developed. Therefore, one of the most important environmental events of 1993 was the UAE's creation of the Federal Environment Agency (FEA). Throughout 1994, the FEA strengthened its administrative and institutional structure, drafting six regulations dealing with, among other things, hazardous waste, the marine environment, and air and water resources. For many years, the Emirate of Dubai has been developing and expanding its environmental department within the Municipality Council, and has implemented environmental regulations dealing with, *inter alia*, hazardous waste and air and water pollution. In 1994, the Emirates of Abu-Dhabi and Sharjah both established environmental departments within their Municipal Councils and formed Environmental Protection Committees for coordination. Other Emirates are in the process of following suit.

(b) Conventions/Protocols

By year's end, the UAE was in the process of ratifying the UN Framework Convention on Climate Change and was reviewing the Biodiversity and Desertification Conventions.

(c) Other Environmental Issues

Pollution of the seas by oil is one of the main environmental problems facing the UAE and other Gulf countries. Besides the discharge of contaminated ballast water, another source of oil pollution is spillage caused by maritime collisions. In 1994, approximately 15 collisions involving oil tankers were reported near UAE shores. One of the worst accidents was the collision near the Emirate of Fujairah on the eastern shores of the UAE, which caused the spillage of over 17,000 tons of crude oil. The spill caused extensive damage to sandy beaches, fishing areas, and coral reefs. Large numbers of marine life, including sea turtles and fish, were washed ashore. By year's end, the UAE was considering ratifying the MARPOL 73/78 Convention.

(8) Yemen

(a) National Legislation

For several months in 1994, Yemen was burdened with civil strife. Consequently, the environmental bill that Yemen's Council of Ministers passed was still pending at the end of the year, and Parliament had taken no action to approve it. Other regulations still pending at the end of the year include the National Strategy for Environmental Protection, the proposed standards for drinking water, an environmental impact assessment regulation, and a regulation declaring the Island of Socatres a wildlife reserve.

(b) Conventions/Protocols

Yemen issued Ministerial Decrees in 1993 to accede to the Vienna Convention and the Montreal Protocol, the Biodiversity Convention, the UN Framework Convention on Climate Change, and the Basel Convention on Hazardous Waste. Parliamentary approval of ratification was still pending.

Fouad Kanbour

13. IRAN AND AFGHANISTAN

[Editors' Note: No report received for Volume 5]

14. SOUTH ASIA

A. INDIA

(1) International Developments

(a) UN Summit on Tiger Conservation

In March 1994, India hosted the first-ever ministerial conference in Asia, aimed at devising fresh strategies to end the slaughter of tigers. Environment ministers from Bhutan, Burma, India, and the Russian Federation, and experts from Cambodia, China, Indonesia, Laos, Nepal, Thailand, and Vietnam attended the conference, which India organized in cooperation with the United Nations Environment Programme. Tigers in India, which numbered about 40,000 in 1947, have dwindled to around 3,750, with most restricted to 19 national reserves. The participating countries agreed to set up a Global Forum of Tiger Range States to pool their efforts to save the tiger from extinction.

(b) Desertification Convention

In 1994, India signed the (➔) UN Convention to Combat desertification, adopted in June 1994. The Convention resulted from the efforts of the Intergovernmental Negotiating Committee for the Convention to Combat Desertification, which was set up in the aftermath of the Rio Conference. Desertification affects about 900 million people in over 100 countries. Recent estimates put the amount land affected at approximately 1.2 billion hectares worldwide—about the size of China and India combined.

(2) Denotification of Sanctuaries

In 1994, in a climate of economic liberalization and industrial growth, there was an increase in the trend toward removing sanctuaries and other protected areas from protected status ("denotification") in favor of various industrial projects. The Narayan Sarovar sanctuary in Gujarat is a case in point. The area designated by the Gujarat State Government in 1981 for the original sanctuary was roughly 765 square kilometers. The same government issued a Notification, the effect of which will reduce the sanctuary to under 100 square kilometers and open the rest of the area to limestone quarrying and the cement industry. The denotification has been challenged by activists and at year's end the issue was pending before the Gujarat High Court. Similarly, the Maharashtra Government proposed to denotify about one-third of the Melghat Tiger Reserve to permit large-scale felling of teak trees, a large-scale program of construction, and the building of a dam across the Tapi River. The Bhittarnika Sanctuary in Orissa was proposed to be opened to trawling operations. Plans were also afoot to denotify the Pirotan Marine Park in Gujarat (the first marine ecosystem in India to be protected) in order to locate a petrochemical project by Reliance Industries in the area. Large-scale mining operations continued in Sariska Sanctuary in Rajasthan.

Apart from being *prima facie* illegal on several grounds, the assault on sanctuaries, forests, and other protected areas through denotifications is in breach of the spirit of the Biodiversity Convention, of which India is a signatory. The Director of the World Conservation Monitoring Centre has, in fact, requested that the Narayan Sarovar denotification be reconsidered, and has stated that "the international community will be watching to ensure that India does implement in full its obligations under the Convention."

(3) Environmental Impact Assessment (EIA) Notification and Amendment to the Environment Protection (EP) Rules

In 1994, a Notification dealing with mandatory Environment Impact Assessment was issued under Rule 5 of the EP Rules, 1986. The introduction for the first time in India of provisions relating to EIA, if strictly enforced, is clearly a positive development. The Notification mandates an EIA or Environment Management Plan to be prepared and submitted for clearance to an Impact Assessment Agency. The Notification also provides for reference to a committee of experts in certain cases. Access to relevant documents is to be provided to members of the public, and public hearings are expected to be held in cases having severe environmental ramifications. The central government's approach, however, has not been encouraging. The original Notification of 27 January 1994 was amended by a Notification dated 4 May that diluted requirements regarding public participation and public access to relevant material. The amendment was effected without inviting suggestions and objections, by reliance on Rule 5 of the EP Rules, as amended, which provides that notice may be dispensed with "in the public interest." The amendment was challenged in the Bombay High Court by the Bombay Environment Action Group (BEAG). The petition was admitted by the Court, but since no stay was granted, the operation of the amendment remained effective. The BEAG presented a special leave petition to the Supreme Court contesting the High Court's refusal to grant the appropriate interim relief.

(4) The Taj Mahal

In 1993, the Supreme Court of India had ordered the closure of more than 212 industries in the Agra region whose emissions endangered this monument (*see* 4 *YbIEL* 418 (1993)). On 11 April 1994, the Supreme Court directed the Indian Ministry of Environment and Forests to establish a special council to develop a green belt around the Taj Mahal. The Court directed the planting of greenery to commence within two weeks and also ordered the Ministry to file an affidavit of compliance thereafter. Also in April, the Supreme Court directed the Ministry of Environment and Forests to appoint an expert authority to undertake a survey of the Taj Trapezium and submit a report of the area's pollution, control measures, and polluting industries. The Taj Trapezium is the geographical limit covering 10,400 square kilometres in the form of a regular trapezoid, around the Taj Mahal, within which the location of new polluting industries was prohibited and existing industries were to be strictly controlled to further reduce the pollution load.

(5) Sardar Sarovar Project

The struggle against the Sardar Sarovar Project (more commonly known as the Narmada Project) continued through 1994. Although work on the dam continues, opponents of the project have had some successes. The Chief Minister of Madhya Pradesh (MP) suggested that the height of the dam be reduced from 138.68 meters as MP faces the unwelcome prospect of losing the most land to submergence, and, consequently, of having to resettle the largest number of displaced persons. This reduction in the height of the dam is expected to save 6242 hectares out of the 20,722 hectares (30 percent) that would otherwise be submerged. The Chief Minister claimed that as many as 38,000 out of the original 150,000 persons would be spared displacement.

Meanwhile, the resettlement of displaced persons continued to be a human rights issue that all participating state governments seemed to overlook. Large numbers of displaced persons have not been resettled, and most of those who have resettled are forced to live under very adverse conditions. Adequate resettlement, according to Prime Minister Narasimha Rao, remained a precondition for continuation of the work on the dam.

(6) Ganga Water Pollution

In response to heavy pollution of the Ganga (Ganges) River by tanneries and by untreated effluents and sewage, in December 1993, the Supreme Court of India had ordered the closure of thirteen industries in Uttar Pradesh that had flouted the Court's earlier directives and failed to install effluent treatment plants. In January 1994, the Court issued similar orders to similar industries in Bihar and West Bengal, states in eastern India. The Court also called on local authorities to submit reports on their sewage treatment and on the use of the millions of rupees that the Ganga Authority, a unit set up by the Central Government for the specific purpose of cleaning up the river, had given them.

Armin Rosencranz
Shiraz Rustomjee
T. Mohan
Nandan Nelivigi

B. SRI LANKA

In 1994, Sri Lanka ratified the 1982 UN Convention on the Law of the Sea (at the instance of the Minister of Finance) and the UN Framework Convention on Climate Change (at the instance of the Minister of Environment).

During the year, the Ministry of Environment was very much in the forefront of environmental law-related activities with the setting up of a legal department within the Ministry. With United Nations Environment Programme assistance, the Ministry also set up a National Task Force to revise and codify environmental legislation in Sri Lanka. This process has been open and transparent, with several sub-committees being established, comprising representatives of the state, non-governmental organizations, the private sector, and members of the public. The Task Force submitted its interim report for public comment for a period that ended 31 December 1994.

The Ministry of Environment also drafted implementing legislation for the 1989 Basel Convention, to which Sri Lanka is a signatory. Regulations for the implementation of the 1987 Montreal Protocol were enacted under the National Environmental Act, No. 47 of 1980. They prohibit the use of 20 ozone-depleting substances. The use of these substances for the limited purpose of servicing equipment or industrial plants already in operation or to be installed prior to 2000, however, will be permitted until 2005. Sri Lanka also published National Environmental (Ambient Air Quality) Regulations in 1994.

In 1994, environmental impact assessment (EIA) finally became an established feature of the Sri Lankan legal process. Pursuant to the National Environmental Act, several EIAs and initial environmental examinations were tabled for the compulsory 30-day public inspection and comment period. Some projects drew objections (for example, the proposed Colombo-Katunayaka Expressway Project drew approximately 600 objections), while others drew none. A number of public hearings were held. The very first administrative appeal by a developer whose project had been rejected in response to an EIA was heard by the Secretary of the Ministry of Transport, Environment, and Women's Affairs. As the EIA process began gathering steam, the Ministry of Fisheries and Aquatic Resources' attention was drawn to the increasing environmental and social problems caused by unauthorized shrimp farms in Northwest Sri Lanka, prompting the Ministry to publish a paper notice informing all unauthorized shrimp farms to close down immediately or face legal action.

In response to litigation by persons affected by industrial pollution, in 1994 Sir Lanka adopted legislation to provide potentially affected persons with a forum to present objections to the issuance or renewal of an Environmental Protection License. The National Environmental (Appellate Procedure) Regulations, 1994, now specify the procedure for appeals in relation to Environmental Protection Licenses under the National Environmental Act. The Regulations provide an opportunity to appeal against the refusal, refusal to renew, suspension, or cancellation of a license and, conversely, provide for the appellate authority to require comments on appeal from any persons or bodies who were parties to any hearing or inspection carried out by the authority authorized to issue the license.

Lalanath de Silva
G. L. Anandalal Nanayakkara

C. BANGLADESH

(1) Introduction

In 1994, Bangladesh witnessed several efforts to enhance protection of the environment, including the first instance of public interest environmental litigation. Further, the deadlock in developing the country's health service was terminated by court action, a draft bill on environmental conservation was approved by the Cabinet, and non-governmental organizations (NGOs) developed new programmes and public awareness campaigns. While pressure for re-designing the country's law and policy-making processes increased, steps were also taken toward greater openness and public participation in public sector development activities.

(2) Policy Developments

(a) Forest Policy and Master Plan

The Cabinet approved a forest policy aimed at encouraging "participatory or social forestry" at all possible sites to ensure maximum output on a sustainable basis. The Government also prepared a 20-year Forestry Master Plan, implementation of which was expected to begin in 1995. Through public and private efforts, the Plan seeks to expand forest cover to at least 20 percent of the country's total land area. At present, less than eight percent of the country's land area is forested. The Plan has components for social forestry, agro-based forestry, and utilization of marginal agricultural lands for these purposes. It provides for the creation of a separate "Social Forestry Directorate," and suggests amendments to existing forest legislation.

(b) Ban on Polyethylene

In 1993, a decision had been taken to ban the production of polyethylene beginning 18 January 1994. On 16 January, the proposed ban was lifted and the Cabinet subsequently approved the postponement of the implementation of the ban on production and marketing of polyethylene shopping bags, without specifying any future date for its entry into force.

(c) Participatory Planning and Public Participation

In 1994, the Ministry of Planning agreed to public participation in the preparation of the national Five Year Plan. The public was also involved in the preparation of the National Environmental Management Action Plan. The objectives, priorities, and strategies of the development plan are to be determined at the local level and will be formulated in the light of local problems and resources. The next plan is expected to emphasize, *inter alia*, poverty alleviation, employment, human resource development, health, education, environment conservation, and the participation of women in development.

(3) Legislative Developments

(a) Acquisition and Requisition of Immovable Property (Amendment) Act, 1994.

A number of changes were made to the original 1982 Act. These have been designed to minimize the delay in the acquisition of land for the implementation of development projects. The Act enhanced the power of the revenue authority to acquire land, but has also extended the amount of compensation to be paid.

(b) Coast Guard Act, 1994

This Act establishes a Coast Guard Force, to be headed by a Director-General, for maintaining law and order in coastal areas and to prevent hostile acts against the economy of the country in adjacent maritime areas. The Act is also intended to address the unregulated and illegal activities of foreign fishing vessels in Bangladesh maritime zones, which have posed an increasingly significant threat to fishery resources. The Coast Guard's functions include, *inter alia*, prevention of illegal fishing in the territorial waters, contiguous zone, continental shelf, conservation zone, and exclusive economic zone; investigation of activities in the maritime zone of Bangladesh that might pollute the environment; and enforcement of preventive measures.

(c) Environment Conservation Bill, 1994

An Environment Conservation bill received final approval from the Cabinet, and will go to Parliament in 1995. It will repeal the Environment Pollution Control Ordinance, 1977. The Bill was reviewed by NGOs, thus representing the first time in Bangladesh that a bill of national interest has been debated outside the traditional law-making procedure.

(4) Public Interest Environmental Action and Litigation

The Bangladesh Environmental Lawyers Association served a Legal Notice on persons responsible for deleting three paragraphs from the official record of the Prime Minister's speech to the 1992 Second Conference on the Flood Action Plan, held under the auspices of the Flood Plan Coordinating Organization, and the World Bank Resident Flood Action Plan Coordinator. The deleted paragraphs supported public participation in project planning. As a result of this threat, the authorities reprinted and re-distributed the full text, including the relevant paragraphs that had been omitted. Other new cases include *Bangladesh Environmental Lawyers Association v. The Election Commission & Others*, the first instance of public interest environmental litigation in Bangladesh.

(5) International

At the FAO's 10th Council Session in November 1994, Bangladesh urged the FAO to take action against the illegal export of toxic materials to developing countries, including the development of a legally binding instrument for the mandatory application of the prior informed consent procedure, to protect developing countries from such toxic dumping. This issue was the subject of significant domestic interest as a result of the unlawful import into Bangladesh by three companies of approximately 6,000 tons of fertilizer containing high amounts of toxic lead and cadmium under an agreement with the Bangladesh Agricultural Development Corporation, a statutory public agency created under the Ministry of Agriculture. By year's end, negotiations continued on the re-export of these toxic materials to the United States.

In other international fora, including the Sixth Committee of the UN General Assembly, Bangladesh continued to reiterate its right to have an equitable share of the waters of the Ganges River (shared with India and Nepal). As a lower riparian state, Bangladesh faces severe environmental hazards resulting from the withdrawal of waters upstream in violation of international norms and standards. The Cabinet agreed to sign the (➔) UN Convention to Combat Desertification.

Mohiuddin Farooque
Syeda Rizwana Hasan

D. NEPAL

Unresolved environmental issues spilled over from 1993, with major hydroelectric projects continuing to occupy centre stage.

(1) Hydropower Development

Nepal has an installed power capacity of 241 megawatts and an estimated exploitable capacity of at least 35,000 megawatts. It is the world's fourth poorest country, with an annual per capita income of US$180. Fewer than 10 percent of its people have access to electricity. In 1994, Nepal formulated a hydroelectric development policy and enacted legislation that gives foreign and domestic private investors 20- to 30-year licenses to develop and operate hydroelectric power projects. The regulation gives especially favorable concessions on income tax and import duty compared to the ordinary foreign investment regulation, creating one of Asia's most generous legal environments for investment.

Nepal has not yet resolved the question of whether to go in for small to medium projects or mega projects. Smaller projects involve low financial risk for the government, offer the advantage of encouraging local technology and expertise, and pose less of an environmental threat. Mega projects involve great financial risk, centralization, major inundation and displacement of people, and potentially large environmental harm. Nothing typifies this situation better than the Arun III project, which has been in the pipeline since 1985. The Arun III hydroelectric project, involving a project outlay of US$764 million, is expected to generate 201 megawatts and to be completed by 2002. If the project proceeds, it will entail the construction of 11 bridges, numerous dams, a 122-kilometer road in a hitherto inaccessible region, and the clearing of virgin forest. It was initially to be funded by the World Bank, the Asian Development Bank, Germany, and other donor countries. Nepal has spent more than US$15 million on feasibility studies, has cut public subsidies on power supply, and has pruned its workforce at the Nepal Electricity Authority by 1,200 people at the behest of the World Bank. It has now begun to pay the price for neglecting environmental concerns and smaller alternatives.

In mid-December 1994, a newly constituted World Bank independent panel, responding to a petition by Nepali citizen groups, advised that bank terms may have been breached in implementing the project. The panel observed, "[t]he cost of the project, greater than one year's budget for the kingdom of Nepal, will have an extensive impact on living conditions throughout the country." The panel also found enough evidence that the project may violate Bank policies on information disclosure, indigenous peoples, involuntary resettlement, and environmental and social impacts to warrant "further investigation," and sought authorization from the World Bank's executive board for such an investigation.

Earlier, Martin Karcher, the head of population and human resources in the World Bank department that includes Nepal, tendered his resignation over the proposed Bank funding of the project. The independent panel endorsed Karcher's view that the project was not viable economically because of the heavy investment (at US$3,800 per megawatt, it is believed to the most expensive power scheme in the world) and unrealistic projections that the Nepalese population would be willing to pay up to 53 cents per kilowatt (while consumers in many parts of the United States pay 6–8 cents). The panel found that the project violated Bank policy on information disclosure. Significantly, in January 1994, the Arun Concerned Group, an independent group that has been in the forefront of the anti-dam movement, sued the Nepali Government in the Supreme Court of Nepal to force it to open all project information to public scrutiny.

Environmentalists hope that the panel's finding that the Bank has not devoted enough attention to alternatives to the Arun III project, as urged by the non-governmental organizations (NGOs), would force the Bank to abandon the project. They charge the Bank management with misrepresenting the panel's finding to the Bank's Executive Board. NGOs assert that the Bank is exerting pressure on the newly elected Communist-led government in Kathmandu to push ahead with the project despite the findings of its own appointed panel.

(2) Forest Conservation

In April 1994, the Government of Nepal gave the Annapurna Conservation Area Project (ACAP) responsibility for managing 4,000 square kilometres. Launched in 1987 to protect the Annapurna region of the Himalayas, the ACAP features a host of innovative approaches to protect forest resources that were being destroyed to meet the annual demands of over 40,000 tourists. The ACAP's jurisdiction now encompasses 7,000 square kilometres—home to more than 100,000 people of numerous different ethnic communities. Over the past 30 years, most of the country's forests have been logged for building material and fuelwood or cleared for agriculture. This deforestation has led to soil erosion, resulting in the destruction of terraces and in avalanches of mud and rock into valleys. Scientists estimate that more than 264 million tons of topsoil erode from the hills of Nepal every year. This topsoil erosion has caused many rivers in Central Nepal to be heavily sedimented with lime. Some 13 percent of the country's watersheds are degraded to the point of no return. Irrigation drawn from such rivers chokes off plant life. With tree cover gone, droughts are prolonged and floods more frequent. Despite heavy use of fertilizers, the topsoil erosion causes a progressively lower yield of food crops.

In the ACAP, forest cover and wildlife population have been slowly increasing. Laws ag`ainst poaching, hunting, logging, and the collection of herbs are strict. Anyone not abiding by the laws is punished by the villagers—a system that encourages people to police themselves.

(3) Pesticides

In October 1994, Pro-Public, a public interest environmental law group, sued the Government in the Supreme Court of Nepal, seeking to cancel importation from Indonesia of the pesticide DDT for violating the country's Pesticide Act. The Supreme Court stayed the import. The Pesticide Act, enacted in July 1994, requires government and private groups to register the pesticides they want to import with the government's Pesticide Board. The Board had refused to register DDT. Green groups also accused the government of violating national environmental guidelines (*see* 4 *YbIEL* 425 (1993)) that require the Ministry of Health to assess the environmental impact of the use of DDT.

Armin Rosencranz
T. Mohan

15. SOUTHEAST ASIA/ASEAN COUNTRIES

(1) Association of Southeast Asian Nations (ASEAN)

The ASEAN Ministerial Meeting on the Environment was held in April in Brunei Darussalam. The Meeting adopted the Bandar Seri Begawan Resolution, which spells out ASEAN's commitment to implement the following measures to promote sustainable development: (1) an ASEAN Strategic Plan of Action on the Environment, which is a response to specific recommendations of Agenda 21; (2) adoption, in each ASEAN member state, of similar environmental quality standards for air and river water quality by the year 2000; and (3) strengthening of cooperation among ASEAN countries to ensure the effective management and control of transboundary movements of hazardous wastes into and within the region. On the same occasion, it was suggested that air pollution in urban and industrialized areas not exceed 200 on the pollutant standards index, while river water quality standards were set at 6.0-8.5pH, two milligrams per litre of dissolved oxygen or more, 10 milligrams or less per litre of biochemical oxygen demand, and 200 milligrams or less per litre of total suspended solids.

The ASEAN Strategic Plan of Action on the Environment, an "ASEAN green plan," commits governments to address environmental implications of increased investments arising from the move to set up a free trade area. Under the five-year green plan, the six-member ASEAN will integrate sound environmental policies with the ambitious 15-year program objectives of the Asean Free Trade Area (AFTA). It is envisaged that tariffs on 15 groups of manufactured products covering 40,000 items will be lowered to between zero and five percent under AFTA. This prompted Malaysia's Environment Minister to remark:

The process of economic integration in ASEAN, initiated by AFTA, requires that environmental management be mutually supportive for increased trade and not emerge as a non-tariff barrier. We need to make projections on the volume of intra-ASEAN trade, the pattern of growth of manufacturing industries, resource usage, technology requirements and hence, their overall impact on the environment.

Finally, a meeting of government-supported Southeast Asian "think tanks" urged an expansion of ASEAN (currently, Brunei, Indonesia, Malaysia, Philippines, Singapore, and Thailand) to include Cambodia, Laos, Myanmar, and Vietnam. The European Union was unmistakably the model in the proposed plan to make Southeast Asia a community. The Manila meeting declared that this community should be a major political, economic, cultural, and moral entity on the world stage in the 21st century, the Manila meeting declared. Participants asked for the statement to be endorsed at the 1995 ASEAN summit in Bangkok.

(2) The Philippines

The Department of Environment and Natural Resources (DENR) Administrative Order No. 02 to implement the country's National Integrated Protected Areas Law entered into force in 1994. The basic policy of the rules and regulations as laid down in Administrative Order No. 02 is to ensure recognition of the customs and traditions of indigenous cultural communities in their ancestral domains and the importance of promoting indigenous ways, such as ecologically sound traditional practices, for the sustainable management of natural resources. In furtherance of this policy, indigenous communities are to exercise general supervision and control over the management of their claimed ancestral domains, including the resources found therein. For this purpose, the council of elders of each community is recognized as the decision-making and management body within the domain. Implementation of government programs under the control of the DENR requires the consent of the indigenous cultural community concerned, written and signed on its behalf by a majority of its recognized leaders. Once such consent is given, the community must be allowed to participate in the planning, implementation, and maintenance of the program. The rules and regulations require the preparation of a comprehensive, ancestral-domain management plan by each indigenous community that takes into consideration indigenous land use and systems of tenure including customary laws, beliefs, and traditional practices. Also to be considered are the question of indigenous community participation in the protection, conservation, development, and maintenance of indigenous communities' rights over their sources of livelihood as well as the question of the provision of supplemental sources of livelihood.

DENR Administrative Order No. 11 (1994), providing for a programmatic compliance procedure within the environmental impact assessment (EIA) system, also took effect during the year. The procedure, as set out in Environmental Management Bureau guidelines, covers programs consisting of a series of similar projects or a project subdivided into several phases and/or stages, whether situated in a contiguous area or geographically dispersed, such as energy projects, projects consisting of several components or a cluster of projects all located in a designated area such as an industrial estate or export processing zone, and the expansion of a program or project that may have significant impact on the environment.

By year's end, the following environmental legislative proposals were pending before the Congress of the Philippines: (1) a bill to establish a "final forest line," harmonizing it with a possible ancestral-lands bill as well as with other land-use related bills with the goal of ensuring that no permanent forest is converted to farmland or other uses; (2) a revision of the Forestry Code to bring it in line with the goals of sustainable development;

(3) a proposal for revisions to the National Building Code that would insert specific provisions on waste management, pollution control, energy efficiency, and conservation measures; (4) measures aimed at prohibiting the use of pesticides banned in other countries; (5) amendments to the Fishery Code and to both the Philippine-Japanese and the Philippine-Taiwanese treaties relating to fisheries and coastal zone management; (6) a National Policy on Coastal and Ocean Resources Management, including the banning of organohalogen compounds and toxic chemicals in coastal areas; and (7) amendment to the law on the Oil Price Stabilization Fund that would set aside funds for air quality management.

(3) Malaysia

In 1994, Malaysia's tremendous economic growth placed the country on the verge of being classified as a developed country. In anticipation of major development projects that will be carried out across the country from 1996 to 2000 under the Seventh Malaysia Plan, the Department of Environment released a new set of guidelines on siting and zoning of factories for implementation by state governments. The guidelines were issued for the purpose of ensuring systematic planning of industrial estates with criteria being based on the type of industries and their impact on residents nearby. Specifically, the guidelines will help state governments to identify buffer zones between industrial and housing sites providing, *inter alia*, that pollution factories should not be allowed to be located next to food manufacturers and that factories generating toxic wastes should not be located upstream of catchment areas. The government will set basic regulations or provide economic incentives, while leaving the specifics of compliance to the private sector. For instance, as of 1995, Malaysia will impose a tax differential to spur use of unleaded gasoline and catalytic converters on motor vehicles. The Ministry of Science, Technology and Environment also drew up a new system of environmental audits to provide feedback on the effectiveness of environmental protection measures to the appropriate authorities. State governments have been asked to consult with the Federal Government before enacting any environmental laws, particularly on land use, in order to avoid confusion and duplication in enforcement.

Also in 1994, the Department of Environment (DOE) disclosed the results of a study on reasons for rejection of EIAs for development projects over the last three years. The reasons included poor project description; failure to provide an environmental monitoring programme; absence of effective mitigating measures; lack of baseline data on environmental quality; poor quantitative predictions; lack of alternatives for siting, production technology, and pollution control; and inconsistency in reported information. To remedy the situation, the Ministry of Science, Technology and Environment considered allowing only environmental consultants registered with the DOE to prepare EIAs, while the DOE outlined certain criteria for the registration of individual consultants and consulting firms which began in July 1994.

Environmental control regulations in Malaysia that were expected to be introduced in 1995 cover the following topics: (1) limitation of storage time for toxic wastes produced and kept at prescribed premises; (2) control of all types of noise pollution; (3) stiffer penalties for dumping rubbish in illegal dumping grounds; and (4) conduct of EIAs by logging companies. Bills were also tabled to amend the Environmental Quality Act of 1974 (calling for, *inter alia*, stricter control over land use and stiffer penalties for violators); the Strata Title Act (requiring the original owner to maintain a certain percentage of the building/units as well as requiring mandatory formation of management cooperatives for condominiums/apartments); and the Land Conservation Act of 1960 (defining hill land and establishing variants for hill slopes, based on the geology and gradient).

(4) Thailand

Thailand's Pollution Control Department announced two types of new water quality standards (ambient standards and source standards) to regulate the quality and amount of wastewater discharged by hospitals, large residential units, government agencies, and commercial enterprises. Both sets of standards will be implemented under the 1992 National Environmental Quality Act. Ambient standards for coastal water and groundwater quality are based on the use of the various bodies of water—rivers, canals, lakes, reservoirs and lagoons. Five grades of fresh water quality will be established, while seven grades will be set up for coastal areas. Ambient standards—as against source standards—will not be used for enforcement purposes but, rather, are to serve as guidelines to governmental agencies.

Consonant with the government's Seventh National Economic and Social Development Plan (1992-96) which identifies the reduction of air and water pollution from industrial sources as priority targets for the country's environmental management, the Office of Environmental Policy and Planning proposed stricter maximum emission levels for sulfur dioxide and other pollutants released by manufacturing plants, as well as tougher standards for industrial wastewater effluents. In anticipation of stricter air pollution control regulations, a Thai company (Pholasith) signed an agreement with a US research and development firm (American Electric Car Technology) for the latter to supply 5,900 battery-powered electric vehicles to replace "tuk tuks," Thai three-wheeled taxis notorious for their noxious fumes, over the next three years.

Thailand was preparing ratification of the 1981 Ramsar Convention on Wetlands of International Importance Especially Waterfowl Habitat. Thailand will identify the Kham Sam Roi Yot National Park and Talee Noi wetlands as Ramsar sites. In a related matter, the Environmental Law Study Centre asked the Appeals Court to rule against the Prime Minister and another government official in its suit for negligence in the construction of a Revenue Department office building in the Phyathai wetlands area that allegedly destroyed the latter's ecological system. The Centre claimed that construction of the office building in the wetland was tantamount to violating the right of the community to a good quality of life.

Finally, in 1994, proposals were made to develop environmental law in two areas. The first proposal was for the formulation of guidelines on eco-tourism in 14 Southern Thailand provinces. The second proposal sought to limit coastal zone reclamation to projects that involve national security or that benefit the general public (such as the construction of deep-sea ports).

(5) Indonesia

After more than 10 years of experience with Indonesia's 1982 Environmental Preservation Law, there were increasing calls for the law to be amended make it more effective vis-à-vis corporate polluters. To some of the country's environmental law experts, the government appeared to be reluctant to mete out administrative sanctions against companies polluting the environment for fear that sanctions, such as closure could lead to social unrest. On the other hand, it was also deemed possible that some companies would welcome closure in order to free themselves from obligations toward their employees or banks and other lending institutions. Also under consideration in this debate were economic incentives (*e.g.*, tax credits and tax exemptions) to companies that faithfully comply with environmental rules and regulations, and environmental auditing to enhance compliance with environmental laws.

By year's end, a national law on conservation of biological diversity was expected to be enacted to pave the way for Indonesia's ratification of the Convention on Biological Diversity. Indonesia signed the Convention but wanted ratification to be preceded by a law that spells out the national strategy for conservation of biodiversity, including the appropriate national authority for purposes of the Convention as well as the role of a number of government agencies which will be involved in Convention-based conservation efforts.

A major development in Indonesia during 1994 was the government's announcement that a new forest management system will be introduced that will convert the current scheme of Forest Concession Rights into Production Forest Concession Units. The new system will reduce the number of concessionaires from the present 500, a number that covers concessions granted over the last 20 years ranging from 49,400 acres to 4.94 million acres. Within 25 years, all licenses will be converted into Production Forest Concession Units. It is hoped that the reduction of concessions and the tightening of regulations will help sustain the country's tropical forests.

On 13 September, 11 environmental groups led by the Indonesian Forum for Environment won an unexpected approval of an administrative court to sue the President of the Republic of Indonesia for diverting $185 million intended for rain-forest preservation to a controversial state-owned aircraft maker, Industri Pesawat Terbang Negara. This was the first time non-governmental organizations were given the legal right to file suit to challenge the President's administrative authority.

(6) Brunei Darussalam

In 1994, Brunei introduced unleaded petrol, the use of which surged to 67 percent within a month. By 1 January 1995, all new motor vehicles were to be required to meet the emission standards of the countries of origin of the vehicle's design, which will result in importation of many car models equipped with catalytic converters. In an effort to further reduce air pollution, an air quality monitoring programme will be carried out at two sites in the country to measure total suspended particulates, particulate matter less than 10 microns in diameter, lead, sulphur dioxide, nitrogen oxides, carbon monoxide, and ozone.

Guidelines or codes of good practice for water-quality management were to be developed by the Ministry of Health for use by other agencies in their review of development projects. These guidelines were expected to include the requirement that septic tank overflows be connected to sewers and "soakways" be provided in areas not yet serviced by sewers; and that an ambient water-quality monitoring network be established.

Amado S. Tolentino, Jr.

16. INDOCHINA

A. KINGDOM OF CAMBODIA

In November, representatives of the governments of Cambodia, Laos, Thailand, and Vietnam initialed a "Draft Agreement on the Cooperation for the Sustainable Development of the Mekong River Basin." When the respective governments formally approve the Agreement, it will officially establish the Mekong River Commission to replace the Interim Mekong Committee, which was established in 1978. The Commission will play a significant role in the allocation of water resources in the region, as a cooperative vehicle for nations bordering the lower Mekong River to make decisions regarding use, management, and conservation of the resources of the Mekong River Basin. Although the Kingdom of Cambodia was not a member of the Interim Mekong Committee, Cambodia will be a full participant in the Mekong Commission. The United Nations Development Programme mediated the Agreement over a two-year period.

Cambodia's Ministry of Environment, with the assistance of the United Nations Environment Programme, was preparing a draft law on environmental protection for review by the Juridical Council and Council of Ministers and, ultimately, for submission to the National Assembly. At the end of 1994, the draft was still in a preliminary stage, and substantial revisions are anticipated before any draft is enacted into law.

B. SOCIALIST REPUBLIC OF VIETNAM

(1) Domestic Law Developments

On 10 January, the President of the Socialist Republic of Vietnam issued an order promulgating the Environmental Protection Law, which the National Assembly of the Socialist Republic of Vietnam had passed on December 27, 1993.

Chapter I of the statute states that "[a]ll acts causing environmental degradation, environmental pollution or environmental incidents, are strictly prohibited," and requires those who cause environmental damage to pay compensation. Chapter II addresses the prevention of environmental harm, setting forth the responsibilities of various actors for the preservation of nature and the prevention of environmental pollution. The Chapter requires preparation of environmental impact assessment reports for certain activities, and strictly prohibits the burning and destruction of forests, uncontrolled exploitation of minerals, discharge of noxious substances or radioactivity, discharge of toxic or infectious substances into water sources, and burial of toxic substances exceeding permissible limits. Chapter III addresses liability and remedies.

Vietnam issued implementing regulations on October 18 as Decree No. 175-CP On the Implementation of Instructions for the Law on Environmental Protection. The Decree apportions responsibility for execution of the environmental law, listing the relevant obligations of the Ministry on Science, Technology and the Environment (MoSTE); other ministries, ministerial offices, and governmental offices; city and provincial People's Committees; state offices and mass organizations; and production and business organizations. MoSTE, in collaboration with related ministries and industries, must develop environmental standards in 21 separate areas. Production and business organizations must comply with regulations regarding environmental impact appraisals, compliance with environmental standards, and prevention of pollution and environmental degradation, and must "contribute financially to environmental protection," compensate for damage to the environment, and provide full information to investigators and inspectors.

The Decree sets forth a wide range of circumstances in which environmental impact appraisals are required. Based on the results of an evaluation of an environmental impact appraisal report for an existing project, a previously existing project may be required to suspend operation, change technology, or invest in waste processing technology, as appropriate.

(2) Regional Law Developments

In November, the Socialist Republic of Vietnam initialed the "Draft Agreement on the Cooperation for the Sustainable Development of the Mekong River Basin." The Agreement officially establishes the Mekong River Commission, which succeeds the Interim Mekong Committee as the vehicle by which the Lower Mekong nations can make cooperative decisions regarding use, management, and conservation of the Mekong River's water resources.

(3) International Law Developments

During 1994, the Socialist Republic of Vietnam became a signatory to a number of international agreements on environmental issues, including the Convention on International Trade in Endangered Species of Wild Fauna and Flora (CITES), the Vienna Convention for the Protection of the Ozone Layer, and the Montreal Protocol on Substances that Deplete the Ozone Layer. The regulations promulgated under the Law on Environmental Protection make specific reference to Vietnam's compliance with its obligations under CITES.

Margaret Raymond

17. NORTHEAST ASIA

A. JAPAN

(1) Introduction

While Japan's political leadership underwent drastic changes in 1994 (from Prime Minister Hosokawa to Mr. Hata and then to Mr. Murayama, a socialist, who now heads the coalition government), the basic governmental policy has remained unchanged as far as its commitment to the protection of the environment is concerned. Mr. Yohei Kono, Deputy Prime Minister and Minister for Foreign Affairs stressed, in a speech to the UN General Assembly on September 27, 1994, that "Japan, for its part, is actively engaged in environmental protection efforts." He went on to illustrate: "For example, [Japan] is working to strengthen the international framework for such efforts, to transfer relevant technologies to developing countries, and to expand and strengthen its official development assistance in environmental areas." Nevertheless, the level of environment-related activity, both governmental and non-governmental, has been somewhat lower due to a shift from attractive law-making and regime-building proposals to day-to-day efforts aimed at implementation and regime-maintenance. The environment has also been less prominent in media coverage compared with that of previous years.

(2) Treaty Practice and Implementing Legislation

On December 20, Japan accepted the Copenhagen Amendment to the Montreal Protocol on Substances that Deplete the Ozone Layer. It will enter into force for Japan on March 20, 1995. In order to allow Japan to ratify the Amendment, the Diet amended its law concerning Protection of the Ozone Layer through Control of Certain Substances (Law No. 53 of 1988), the statute implementing the Montreal Protocol. The new law was promulgated on June 29, 1994 and entered into effect on September 30, 1994.

On July 15, Japan withdrew its reservation to the listing of the species *Eretmochelys imbricata* (a sea turtle with the Japanese name "Taimai") listed in Appendix I of the Convention on International Trade in Endangered Species (CITES) (Official Gazette, No. 1445 of July 20, 1994). This withdrawal became effective on July 29, 1994, thus binding Japan to the regulation of trade in this species under Art. 3 of CITES. With the exception of certain whales, Japan has now withdrawn all its reservations entered against species listed in Appendix I of CITES.

On October 14, 1994, Japan signed the (➔) United Nations Convention to Combat Desertification in Those Countries Experiencing Serious Drought and/or Desertification, Particularly in Africa.

(3) International Conferences

From April 11–22, 1994, the 18th Antarctic Treaty Consultative Meeting was held in Kyoto, Japan. Mr. Shozo Azuma, Parliamentary Vice-Minister for Foreign Affairs, outlined the major pending issues with regard to the Antarctic Treaty system and reminded attending state delegates of the importance of implementing the provisions of the Madrid Protocol on Environmental Protection—even before its entry into force, where possible. As to the latter, he stated that Japan had already conducted observations with regard to marine pollution, waste disposal and other activities in accordance with the spirit of the Protocol. Mr. Azuma added that, despite the difficulties involved, Japan had also committed itself to the establishment of a system of liability for environmental damage, an important part of the Protocol. He also stressed the importance of restricting the growing tourism and non-governmental activity in the Antarctic area, with a view toward minimizing adverse environmental impact.

At the First Conference of the Parties to the Convention on Biological Diversity, held in Nassau, the Bahamas, Ambassador Hisashi Owada, at its session on December 8, 1994, described Japan's domestic and international efforts as follows:

Japan since prior to its adoption of the Convention, has consistently pursued efforts for the conservation and sustainable use of biological diversity through effective implementation of the laws and regulations on the domestic front, such as the Nature Conservation Law, the Natural Parks Law, the Wildlife Protection Law, Forest Law, the Preservation of Marine Resources Law, and the Law for the Protection of Copyright Cultural Properties. Under these legislations, the Government of Japan has established a system of protected areas to promote the protection of ecosystems and natural habitats. Since the entry into force of the Convention, the Government of Japan established an inter-ministerial coordinating body in January 1994 to promote implementation of the Convention, and in April this year, it initiated the Biodiversity Survey, the purpose of which is to present a comprehensive picture of the distribution of fauna and flora in Japan.

With regard to international cooperation, Japan, as the largest donor of official development assistance in the world, makes environmental aid one of its highest priorities. During the past two years, Japan has provided assistance of over 500 billion yen in the field of environment. The conservation of biodiversity is one of the most important goals within this field. In order to promote our efforts in this field, Japan has been carrying out cooperation for in-situ conservation in countries such as Kenya and Tanzania, as well as assistance for ex-situ conservation in countries such as China, Sri Lanka and Chile.

In the same speech, Ambassador Harada noted that Japan had reached agreement with the United States on cooperation on a biodiversity conservation programme in Indonesia. Under this project, Japan will assist Indonesia in the construction of conservation facilities for biological specimens and research facilities for the improved management of national parks, and in the collection of information relating to biological diversity and the transfer of technology related to conservation and research.

The non-governmental Tokyo Conference on Global Environmental Action was held on October 24-26, 1994, to consider a number of issues, including the impact of population on the environment, citizen-level cooperation in environmental protection, trade and the environment, and funding mechanisms. It was designed as a follow-up to the Eminent Persons' Meeting on Financing Global Environment and Development, held in Tokyo in April 1992, two months before the Earth Summit in Rio de Janeiro. It was suggested that the next conference take place in 1997, just before the special UN General Assembly session on the environment, so that the outcome of the meeting will be reflected in the work of the Assembly.

(4) Judicial Decisions

On January 31, 1994, the Sendai District Court rejected a plea by fourteen local residents to halt operations of Tohoku Electric Power Company's nuclear power plant in Onagawa, Miyagi Prefecture. In December 1981, the residents had requested an injunction on the basis that the power plant posed the danger of a major accident either from human error or from natural disasters such as earthquakes or tidal waves. The court stated that a certain amount of routine radioactive leakage could not be avoided, thus posing a danger to residents that, in the opinion of the court, was not beyond tolerable limits. The court also set a legal precedent by ruling that nuclear plants such as the Onagawa operation are necessary to ensure a stable supply of electricity. However, recognizing the Onagawa facility's potential risk, the court stated that the burden was on the defendants to establish that the plant was safe. If it did not meet this burden, the court said, it must be assumed that the power company had failed to carry out the necessary safety measures. By year's end, the case was pending before the Sendai High Court.

On January 25, 1994, Yokohama District Court's Kawasaki Branch, found 12 industrial firms jointly responsible for causing air pollution and were ordered to pay a total of ¥463 million in damages to 106 local residents suffering from asthma and bronchitis. However, the court rejected the plaintiffs' claims against the state and the Metropolitan Expressway Public Corporation that their health had also been damaged by automobile emissions containing nitrogen dioxide on the basis that no causal relationship had been established between the auto emissions and the respiratory diseases. It also rejected the plaintiffs' request that the companies be ordered to keep discharges of pollutants such as sulfur dioxide below certain levels. In a similar air pollution case, Okayama District Court, on March 23, 1994, ordered eight companies to pay ¥190 million in compensation to 41 residents for health injuries caused by the emission of nitrogen dioxide from the Mizushima industrial complex in Kurashiki, Okayama Prefecture. But the court rejected a demand by the plaintiffs that the firms stop emitting pollutants in excess of environmental standards, because the plaintiffs did not specify what methods the companies should take to curb such emissions.

With regard to noise pollution from military bases, a clear trend in court rulings developed. While the courts award monetary damages for the residents' proven past sufferings, they will not award any compensation for future injuries or grant injunctions to halt flights. This is generally in line with the Supreme Court decision of February 25, 1993 (*see* 4 *YbIEL* 435

(1993)). Thus, while on February 24, the Naha District Court ordered the state to pay ¥807.45 million in compensation to 768 residents around the US Kadena Air Base for noise pollution, the court ruled against the request for an advance payment for future damages and the demand to suspend night flights. The key issue in determining the state's liability was the setting of the noise tolerance level. It was measured by the weighted equivalent continuous perceived noise level that the International Civil Aviation Organization has set. Similarly, on March 30, 1994, the Tokyo High Court ordered the state to pay ¥710 million in compensation to 56 residents around US Yokoto Air Base, while rejecting compensation for future noise pollution and the request to ban night flights. In a rare move, the presiding judge, after rendering the judgment, called on the government and residents to work out an agreement aimed at reducing noise from the flights. Finally, the Nagoya High Court's Kanazawa Branch on December 26, 1994, awarded ¥180 million in compensation to 213 residents living near the Komatsu Air Base, which is used by the US Air Force and Japan's Air Self-Defense Force. This court, like the others discussed above, refused to order future damage compensation or a halt to the flights.

Shinya Murase

B. CHINA

(1) Introduction

Although the People's Republic of China's (PRC's) transition from a tradition of a centrally planned economy to the unfamiliar market economy has led to notable economic growth in 1994, considerable environmental costs remain unaccounted for. It has been estimated that pollution and related harm to natural resources cost the national economy up to 100 billion Renminbi (RMB). The National Environmental Protection Agency (NEPA) of the PRC acknowledges that whilst economic development is essential for the well-being of the Chinese nation as a whole, rapid economic growth has also undermined efforts to protect and conserve China's natural resources. In order to redress these ecological problems, the state has sought to enshrine environmentally sustainable objectives within the existing legal framework and to enforce environmental law more effectively.

This 1994 update focuses on four basic legal areas of international significance: (1) the implementation of the PRC's international environmental obligations in accordance with the outcome of the United Nations Conference on Environment and Development (UNCED); (2) the development of conservation measures with respect to major infrastructure projects; (3) the enactment of domestic environmental regulations relating to foreign and domestic economic law; and (4) current administrative and judicial decisions in the environmental law field that impact upon both foreign and local interests.

(2) International Obligations

In response to the international environmental obligations that emerged from UNCED in 1992, China has published two important policy documents relating to Agenda 21 and the Convention on Biological Diversity.

(a) Agenda 21 of China

The issuance of *Agenda 21 of China—the White Book of China on Population, Environment and Development in the 21st Century* by the State Council on 25 March 1994 is the most significant new development in environmental policy and law in China in 1994. *Agenda 21 of China* is a comprehensive and operational strategic plan that aims at providing guidance for the middle-term (1996–2000) and long-term (2000–2010) social and economic development plans of China.

Agenda 21 of China underlines the determination of China to establish and implement a strategy of sustainable development. Sustainable development is described as an essential element of the current reform of the Chinese system. According to the report, the strategy of sustainable development for China consists of three integrated parts: a sustainable economy; a sustainable society; and sustainable natural resources.

Agenda 21 of China emphasizes that the state must recognize economic development as the principal national priority and must encourage an appropriately high rate of economic growth in order to eliminate poverty and meet the basic material and cultural needs of the people. The report asserts that an 8–9 percent annual rate of growth in gross national product for the remaining years of the 20th century would be satisfactory. According to the report, only a national strategy promoting economic growth can provide the necessary capacity and conditions for attainment of sustainable development. Consequently, *Agenda 21 of China* proposes that only through the continued implementation of the present economic reforms will a gradual transition to a policy of sustainable development be possible.

According to *Agenda 21 of China*, sustainable social development requires the state to carry out a number of important public welfare policies. These policies include population growth control and population quality improvement, equitable distribution of social wealth, continuation of China's moral and cultural tradition, the reinforcement of public security, the development of education and professional training, and the improvement of general welfare conditions such as housing and medical care. *Agenda 21 of China* also emphasizes the need to educate the people and relevant governmental officials on the meaning and importance of sustainable development.

Finally, *Agenda 21 of China* stresses the importance of using natural resources sustainably, setting forth four general goals to be achieved by the year 2000: (1) the reduction and control of environmental pollution; (2) the enforcement of appropriate environmental quality objectives in the major cities; (3) the reversal of the tendency to accept ecological deterioration; and (4) the gradual harmonization of economic, social, and environmental development. The report underscores the importance of addressing environmental problems including soil erosion and desertification. *Agenda 21 of China* also emphasizes the PRC's intention to participate fully in the establishment and development of a viable international environmental legal system. The report stresses, however, that international legal authorities must take into account the social and economic tensions between developing and developed countries (*e.g.*, poverty, international trade, and environmentalism) when examining issues of sustainable development.

Agenda 21 of China highlights five principles that must be part of any international cooperation regarding sustainable development. They include: (1) the right of all states to participate equally; (2) the importance of national sovereignty when considering policies concerning economic development, environmental protection, and biological diversity; (3) the development of an international environmental law which takes into account the various geographic, economic, and cultural differences between developing and developed countries; (4) the notion of just and differentiated responsibility in light of a developed country's greater responsibility and more extensive duties regarding global sustainable development; and (5) the provision of support, including capital and technology, from the international community to developing countries so as to enhance their ability to achieve development. Finally, the *Agenda 21 of China* declares China's willingness to participate actively in global environmental protection programmes including the control of greenhouse gas emissions and the elimination of dangerous substances such as chlorofluorocarbons, toxic chemicals, and hazardous wastes. The United Nations Development Programme (UNDP) and other international organizations supported and sponsored *Agenda 21 of China*'s preparation.

(b) Biodiversity Conservation Action Plan of the PRC

On 13 June 1994, China promulgated its State Action Plan for Biodiversity Conservation (BAP), an undertaking necessary for fulfillment of China's obligations under the Convention on Biological Diversity. The purpose of China's BAP is to integrate the goals of biodiversity conservation with the country's social and economic development plans. Nevertheless, the effectiveness of the BAP and its various conservation measures will ultimately depend on the extent to which the government, at national, provincial, and local levels, enforces the plan's directives.

The BAP is divided into three parts: the overall objective; specific objectives; and major actions with respect to biodiversity conservation. The overall objective is to set in place, as soon as possible, measures for avoiding further ecological damage, and to mitigate or reverse damage already done in the long run. Specifically, the BAP is to: improve basic research on biodiversity in China; improve the national network of nature reserves and other protected areas; conserve wild species that are significant for biodiversity; conserve genetic resources related to crops and domestic livestock; protect in-situ conservation outside nature reserves; establish a nation-wide information and monitoring network for biodiversity conservation; and coordinate biodiversity conservation and sustainable development. At the core of the BAP is in-situ protection, which is complemented by ex-situ protection.

To achieve its overall objectives, the BAP sets out seven areas for action: legislation and policy; institutional measures; scientific research; technical dissemination and demonstration; publicity and education; the identification of sources of finance; and increased international cooperation. Preparation of the BAP had been supported by a number of international organizations, including the World Bank, UNDP, and the Global Environment Facility.

(c) Other Developments

In addition to *Agenda 21 of China* and the BAP, on 7 July, China published its first list of priority projects for implementing the *Agenda 21 of China*, featuring 62 projects divided into environmental education, standards, and facilities; sustainable agricultural policies; cleaner industrial production; clean energy and transportation; conservation of natural resources; water pollution, solid waste, and hazardous waste; poverty alleviation and regional development; population and health; and global change and biodiversity. Those projects will be integrated into the middle-term and long-term social and economic development plans of China.

The Third Meeting of the China Council for International Cooperation on Environment and Development was held in Beijing in September. It outlined *Agenda 21 of China* and China's efforts to revise environmental laws and the environmental legislative plan.

As regards the implementation of China's obligations under the Framework Convention on Climate Change, the environmental monitoring station of Beijing finished a two-year study on the reduction of greenhouse gas emissions in the city of Beijing and published the first local greenhouse gas emission inventory for China in early October. The study was supported by the Ministry of Environment of Canada.

By year's end, China had signed a number of bilateral agreements on environmental protection, namely the Sino-Japanese Agreement on

Cooperation in Environmental Protection (20 March), the Sino-Russian Agreement on Cooperation in Environmental Protection (27 May), and the Memorandum on Friendship and Cooperation between the Environmental Protection Bureau of Zhejiang Province of the PRC and the Federal and British Columbian Environmental Departments of Canada (17 October).

Finally, the PRC government criticized the British Hong Kong government's Strategic Sewage Disposal Scheme, a HK$20 billion project to discharge wastewater into the South China Sea. The PRC government complained that Hong Kong neither informed nor consulted the PRC about the project, which could have a detrimental environmental impact to the chinese coastal city of Zhanjiang. No final decisions had been reached on the project by year's end.

(3) National Law and Policy

(a) Conservation Measures With Respect to Major Infrastructure Projects

The Three Gorges Dam Construction Corporation (TGDCC) announced the inauguration of construction work on its project. Prime Minister Li Peng formally opened the project on 14 December, explaining that the dam is central to China's economic reconstruction. He pointed out that the effectiveness of the project will depend both on the capacity to relocate over one million people whose residences will be adversely affected by construction and on the establishment of an economic open zone in the area. The project, which is expected to be completed in 2009, is to provide hydroelectric power for the region, control flooding, and improve marine transportation. In June, the government's Three Gorges Environment Inspection Group identified several issues concerning implementation of the environmental impact assessment (EIA) for the project. It suggested that the environmental measures proposed by the EIA must be improved by: establishing a high-level environmental decision-making and coordinating organ; relocating towns and populations based strictly on the guidance supplied by the EIA and expert environmental planners; strengthening environmental regulations covering the construction of the dam; and reinforcing the water pollution control system in place to protect the upstream areas of the Yangtze River. In September, the TGDCC and the Environmental Protection Bureau of Yichang City issued environmental protection and management standards for Three Gorges Dam construction area to control air, water, and noise pollution as well as solid waste, while safeguarding public health and ensuring reforestation.

By year's end, the State Council had approved a plan to establish a nature reserve for endangered fishery resources in the upstream section of the Yangtze River. Officials from the Ministry of Agriculture and the

Ministry of Water Conservancy reiterated the need to initiate the project as early as possible.

Finally, administrative measures were taken to address serious water pollution problems in the Huaihe River basin. Mr. Song Jian, a State Council official, personally inspected the river basin in May. Official tests revealed that 82 percent of the waterway water pollution exceeded quality objectives, especially during the dry season. During an on-site meeting in Anhui Province in June, it was decided that the relevant provinces must take firm action to control the pollution sources that affect the basin. As a first-stage measure, polluters were required to reduce their discharge by 70 percent.

(b) New Legislation

Consistent with the aims of *Agenda 21 of China*, the NEPA, the Customs Administration (CA), and the Ministry of Foreign Trade and Economic Cooperation (MFTEC) jointly enacted Provisions on the Environmental Management of First-Time Importation of Chemicals and Import and Export of Toxic Chemicals on 16 March. The Provisions implement the 1989 London Guidelines on the Exchange of Information on International Trade in Chemicals. They establish the authority of NEPA, the CA and the MFTEC to regulate the import and export of dangerous chemicals and set forth procedures for product registration and management as well as provisions bearing on pollution prevention and sanctions.

On 12 May, the Standing Committee of the National People's Congress (NPC) passed the Foreign Trade Law of the PRC. It prohibits the import or export of goods banned under domestic legislation in foreign countries on the basis that the goods may cause harm to human health or damage the environment. Additionally, goods that are banned under rules of international conventions and agreements that the PRC has ratified are prohibited from being imported to or exported from the PRC. Also on 12 May, the Standing Committee passed revised regulations concerning the administration of public security and punishment. These regulations provide guidelines for administrative detention and the imposition of fines and warnings for the manufacture, sale, storage, transport, or use of explosives, poisonous, flammable, or radioactive materials.

Rules for the Implementation of the mineral resources law of the PRC, enacted on 26 March, reconfirm that the state retains ownership of all mineral resources within the jurisdiction of the PRC. The law requires registrations and licenses for mineral resources surveys and mineral extractions, and establishes penalties for infractions. The State Council promulgated Regulations Governing the Collection of Compensation Fees for Mineral Resources on 27 February and enacted Regulations on Primary Farmland Protection in September. The latter entered into force on 1 October. The land-use regulations aim at preventing and controlling pollution and soil erosion of primary farmland by setting forth control standards. They also provide for monitoring and controlling the conversion of primary farmland into non-agricultural land. Finally, State Council Regulations Governing the Breeding of Livestock and Poultry of 15 April authorize the State to regulate the breeding of livestock and poultry, with special protection given to endangered species of livestock and poultry.

On 16 August, the National Planning Committee of the State Council and NEPA jointly enacted Environmental Protection Plan Management Provisions that implement the 1989 Environmental Protection Law of the PRC. The latter requires planners to integrate environmental protection strategies into the local and national social and economic development plans.

(c) Legislation Pending by Year's End

The Standing Committee of the NPC announced plans to revise a number of environmental protection laws within the next three years. They include the Law on Air Pollution Prevention and Control, the Law on Water Pollution Prevention and Control, the Law on Marine Environmental Protection, and the Environmental Protection Law. The Committee also announced plans for several new laws on solid and radioactive wastes, noise prevention, and nature conservation.

The Tenth Meeting of the Standing Committee of the Eighth NPC (21-26 October) reviewed and discussed the bill amending the Air Pollution Prevention and Control Law, which the Environment and Resources Committee (ERC) of the NPC had submitted. The Standing Committee, however, did not pass the bill, deciding instead to consider it at its next meeting in 1995. Also in 1994, the NEPA and the ERC began to prepare amendments to the Law on Water Pollution Prevention and Control.

(d) Enforcement

(i) Administration

Although a considerable number of environmental law violations were prosecuted in 1994, officials admit that enforcement is not as strict as it should be. In order to improve enforcement, the NPC decided to expand its supervisory role over enforcement efforts by organizing inspection groups to investigate the enforcement activities of provinces and autonomous regions. Similar inspection teams were also established at the provincial level to improve enforcement. These inspections revealed that about one-fourth of the 4,000 enterprises inspected were violating environmental laws. Strict fines and punishments were imposed.

(ii) Judicial and Administrative Decisions

Recent judicial and administrative decisions also demonstrated China's greater willingness to enforce its environmental laws. For example, on 30 September, the Wenzhou City Environmental Protection Bureau of

Zhejiang Province fined a local enterprise 50,000 RMB for illegally importing 233 containers of commercial and domestic waste from abroad. In another incident, Daye Black Metals Corporation, a large-scale, state-owned corporation located in Hubei Province, was found liable for serious crop damage in neighbouring areas caused by its factories' sulphur dioxide (SO_2) emissions. The court required the company to pay 510,000 RMB to local farmers in damages. Finally, the Environmental Protection Bureau of Jinzhou City in Liaoling Province found that SO_2 emissions from the Jinzhou Copper Smelter, a joint venture between a large state-owned corporation and a Hong Kong company, caused serious damage to crops and threatened the health of neighbouring farmers. The court ordered the factory to halt operation until appropriate pollution-control devices were installed, compensate the neighborhood farmers for the harm they suffered to their property, and pay a fine of 2,000 RMB.

Wang Xi
Bryan Bachner

C. HONG KONG

(1) Introduction

As the deadline approaches for the transfer of Hong Kong from the United Kingdom to the People's Republic of China, it is clear that the government of Hong Kong is anxious to complete its plan to combat pollution in the territory, which it first published in a White Paper called "A Time To Act" in June 1989. 1994 therefore saw another active year on the Hong Kong legislative calendar with a number of important developments in environmental law. Hong Kong published a second environmental White Paper, largely in response to calls by the 1992 United Nations Conference on Environment and Development (UNCED) for the publication of domestic environmental strategies, and announced an ambitious plan for legislation that, when enacted, will add considerably to the body of environmental law that already exists in Hong Kong.

(2) International Environmental Law

Hong Kong completed the second review of the original White Paper in November of 1993. The resulting report, entitled "The Hong Kong Environment: A Green Challenge for the Community," was in part a response to the above-mentioned call by UNCED for governments to publish policy statements about issues such as sustainable development, global warming, biodiversity, and the protection of rain forests. The document is a comprehensive report intended to educate and inform, set out future programmes designed to build upon efforts initiated following the original

White Paper, and deal with new environmental challenges. One chapter of the 11-chapter report is devoted exclusively to Hong Kong's global environmental responsibilities.

The report states that the government is "determined to adopt the standards set out at [UNCED]" and to fulfil all international obligations that Hong Kong is required to meet. The report asserts that the decision by the government's Energy Efficiency Advisory Committee to move toward natural gas power generation is evidence of Hong Kong's commitment to the UN Framework Convention on Climate Change. Further, the government has organized a Coordination Group on Global Climate Change to advise the government and coordinate action on the Convention.

As for the Convention on Biological Diversity, the government states that conservation policy is enforced through the implementation of the Country Parks Ordinance, the Town Planning Ordinance, and administrative environmental impact requirements. Concerning the Statement on Forest Principles, the government has prohibited, in government contracts, the use of hardwood for site hoardings, false work, and the shoring of trenches and pits. The government asserts that it is working to integrate the broad principles of sustainable development found in Agenda 21 and the Rio Declaration within its larger environmental policy. The report also states that Hong Kong has enacted the Ozone Layer Protection Ordinance to ensure the enforcement of objectives of the Montreal Protocol on Substances that Deplete the Ozone Layer. The government has also stated its intention to seek application to Hong Kong of the Basel Convention on the Control of Transboundary Movements of Hazardous Wastes and Their Disposal, which both China and the United Kingdom have ratified. According to the report, Hong Kong has also undertaken to fulfil requirements under the Convention for the Prevention of Pollution from Ships, the Convention on the Prevention of Marine Pollution by Dumping of Wastes and Other Matters, the Convention on International Trade in Endangered Species of Wild Fauna and Flora, the Convention on the Conservation of Migratory Species of Wild Animals, and the Convention on Wetlands of International Importance Especially as Waterfowl Habitat.

(3) Local Environmental Law

Late in 1994, the Secretary for Planning, Environment, and Lands announced the legislative programme for 1994-1995, which includes amendments to the Town Planning Ordinance and the Marine Parks Ordinance and the introduction of chemical waste and landfill charges, the control of vehicular emissions and construction site dust, and noise control.

In 1994, heightened public awareness of the environmental problems confronting the territory was, *inter alia*, evidenced by launching of two independent associations, the Hong Kong Environmental Law Association and the Hong Kong Waste Management Association. Both organisations aim at promoting awareness of environment-related issues.

The government's intent to apply the polluter pays principle inspired legislation, most obviously the Sewage Services Bill, which was introduced on 6 July 1994. This legislation will introduce a charging scheme for sewage disposal so that everyone that generates domestic or industrial sewage must pay toward the costs of its disposal and treatment. It will enable the operating costs of sewage treatment and services to be recovered from the users. The proposed charging scheme will consist of a fixed and a variable charge. The fixed charge will be determined by the category of user, which will be specified in appropriate regulations enacted under the proposed Ordinance. The variable charge will depend on the volume of water supplied to the premises by the Water Authority. Commercial enterprises, including both trade and manufacturing, that produce waste effluents will be required to pay a surcharge. The proposed legislation will give wide powers of access to the appropriate authority to verify information needed to determine the charges and surcharges and to measure the volume of wastewater consumed by the user.

In addition to the proposed sewage services legislation, on 1 July, a series of laws and regulations aiming at tightening control over livestock farming and livestock waste in Hong Kong were enacted. On 1 November, parts of Victoria Harbour, the harbors at Kwun Tung (East) and Tsuen Wan and Kwai Chung (West), were constituted as the "Victoria Harbour Water Control Zone." This development marks the beginning of a process by which the whole of Victoria Harbour—one of the pollution black spots in Hong Kong—will become a water control zone, making it the 10th and final such zone pursuant to the 1980 Water Pollution Ordinance. Once an area is designated as a water control zone, any discharge of waste or polluting matter into that area is an offence unless the discharge is in accordance with the terms and conditions of a licence. Licences are normally granted for two-year periods and licence fees vary with the volume and type of discharge.

In response to an outbreak of cholera, the Food Business (Regional Council) by-laws were amended. They now specify a minimum water quality for keeping live fish or shellfish intended for human consumption.

In addition to legislation and regulations introduced in 1994 to consolidate and bolster existing environmental laws, by year's end several significant legislative initiatives were underway, namely on dumping at sea, marine parks and reserves, and environmental impact assessment. Separate bills were introduced to address the marine environmental issues, while a mere consultation paper was published on environmental impact assessment setting out the proposed legislation.

Martin G. David
Rona H. Westgate
Terri Mottershead
Bryan Bachner

D. TAIWAN

(1) General Background

Over the years, concern for the environment at home and abroad has prompted authorities in Taiwan to place environmental protection in tandem with economic development. Yet international pressure for environmental conservation has also highlighted the fact that Taiwan's embarrassing international legal status impedes its meaningful participation in the formation and implementation of international environmental norms.

(2) International Agreements

By the end of 1994, Taiwan had not yet signed any multilateral environmental treaty. However, on June 27, Taiwan and Sweden concluded an agreement on technical cooperation in the field of environmental protection, which was signed by the President of the Swedish Trade Council and the Representative of the Taipei Mission in Sweden, a format first developed in a Taiwan-US agreement of the same nature concluded in 1993. The Agreement calls for the establishment of cooperative programs between the environmental protection agencies of the parties.

(3) Asia-Pacific Economic Cooperation (APEC)

Although, in general, Taiwan (Chinese Taipei) has encountered problems in participating in the work of regional organizations, Taiwan plays a role in APEC, and in 1994 actively participated in APEC's environment-oriented activities. Taiwan (Chinese Taipei) attended the First Environment Ministerial Meeting in Vancouver, Canada, in March, which focused on environment and sustainable development issues. In August, Taiwan and Canada co-hosted the APEC Environmental Experts Meeting in Hualien to follow-up on agreements of the APEC Environment Ministerial Meeting and the conclusions of the APEC Senior Official Meeting. The purpose of the Experts Meeting was to integrate environmental and sustainable development considerations into the workplans of APEC.

(4) National Legislation

In December, the Legislative Yuan passed the Environmental Impact Assessment (EIA) Act. Like most existing EIA regimes in the world, the Act includes provisions on information disclosure and public participation. The Act also authorizes, however, the Environmental Protection Administration (EPA) to reject development projects of other agencies if the EIA review committee of EPA finds that the targeted projects might cause significant impacts on the environment. Moreover, government policies are also subject to EIA. This policy review feature, which was added during the second reading of the bill, was expected to bring environmental concerns to the forefront at an early stage of governmental decision-making. The scope and content of this requirement, however, remain controversial.

(5) Regulatory Measures Directed Toward Compliance with International Environmental Agreements

(a) Ozone Depletion

Although Taiwan was unsuccessful in its efforts to become a contracting party to the international ozone regime, the government reiterated its intention to abide by all relevant international agreements. By the end of 1993, Taiwan had already reduced the use of products containing chlorofluorocarbons to 37.4 percent as measured against the 1986 level. Based on Taiwan's compliance with the terms of the Montreal Protocol, several countries, including Australia, Japan, and the United States, as well as the European Union (EU), announced that they would not restrict trade in ozone-depleting substances with Taiwan. The EU even went so far as to establish a "Taiwan" article (Art. 13) in its 1994 (➔) Council Regulation on substances that deplete the ozone layer.

Taiwan's Industrial Technology and Research Institution attended the Sixth Meeting of the Conference of the Parties to Montreal Protocol in October as a non-governmental organization (NGO) observer.

(b) Wildlife Conservation and International Trade

Taiwan has been accused of being sluggish in curbing illegal trade in the products of rhinoceros, tiger, and other endangered species. Following a process of investigation and discussion, the United States imposed trade sanctions on Taiwan pursuant to the Pelly Amendment. Facing pressure at home and abroad, the government cracked down on the smuggling of wildlife products and revised the Wildlife Conservation Law. The amendments strengthen regulatory measures and impose higher penalties on violators.

The Industrial Technology and Research Institution and SWAN International, acting as NGO observers from Taiwan, attended the First Meeting of the Conference of the Parties to the Biodiversity Convention in November.

(c) Climate Change

In 1994, the government continued to promote energy sources, such as LNG and nuclear power, to lower carbon dioxide emissions; strengthen the campaign for energy conservation through regulation and education; and enhance technological innovation.

Taiwan's failure to become a party to the UN Framework Convention on Climate Change has entailed uncertainty as to the country's regulatory status. If Taiwan's obligations were the same as those of developed countries, the costs of compliance would be staggeringly high. Even so, the government decided to submit a national report on domestic measures to reduce greenhouse gas emissions for consideration by the Conference of the Parties.

(6) Institutional Arrangements

On August 12, the Executive Yuan established a Global Change Policy Guidance Task Force which is divided into six sub-groups, namely on ozone-depletion, wildlife protection, climate change, transboundary hazardous waste, Agenda 21 and sustainable development, and trade and environment. Members of the Task Force include the ministers of relevant departments, experts, and scholars. The EPA serves as the Secretariat to the Task Force. The Task Force's first mission was to review and approve a national action plan on the issue of global change. The National Science Council, in cooperation with various academic institutions, completed a five-year research plan on global change issues.

Jiunn-rong Yeh

E. REPUBLIC OF KOREA (SOUTH KOREA)

(1) International Activities

In 1994, Korea signed, ratified, and acceded to several environment-related treaties. The London Convention on the Prevention of Marine Pollution by Dumping of Waste and other Matter, the Amendment to the Annex of London Convention, and the United Nations Framework Convention on Climate Change, all of which Korea acceded to or adopted in 1993, entered into force for Korea on 21 January, 20 February, and 15 March, respectively. Korea acceded to the Basel Convention on the Control of Transboundary Movements of Hazardous Wastes and their Disposal on 28 February; it entered into force on May 28. Furthermore, on 5 July, Korea concluded an agreement on environmental cooperation with the Russian Federation pursuant to Art. 7(3) of the Treaty on Basic Relations between the Republic of Korea and the Russian Federation. The agreement specifically provides for the contracting parties to cooperate and exchange information and techniques in the field of environmental protection and sustainable development, and to establish a Joint Committee on Environmental Cooperation. Korea has endeavored to secure a bilateral cooperative treaty system with neighboring countries since 1992. With agreements on environmental coöperation concluded with Japan (29 June 1993) and China (27 November 1993), the agreement with Russia will play an important role in regional environmental protection.

Under an Agreement between the Republic of Korea and the Russian Federation on the Protection of Migratory Birds, also of 5 July, the contracting parties recognized that many species of birds migrate between, and seasonally live in, both countries and that certain species are endangered. The parties thus agreed to a variety of cooperative measures for protection of migratory birds and their habitat as well as for the prevention of extinction of certain birds.

In accordance with Art. 24(2) of the Convention on the Conservation of Antarctic Marine Living Resources (CCAMLR) and the system for international observation adopted at the 11th annual meeting of the CCAMLR Commission in 1993, on 29 January 1994, the governments of Korea and the United Kingdom agreed to an arrangement for placing scientific observers on board fishing vessels in the area that the CCAMLR covers. On 25 March, by an exchange of notes, a 1982 fisheries agreement between the United States and the Republic of Korea was extended for an additional two-year period, until 31 December 1995.

In February 1994, the Republic of Korea and the International Bank for Reconstruction and Development (IBRD) signed an agreement whereunder the IBRD provides a loan equivalent to US$2 million for a training program for professional technicians and environmental improvement projects in Korea. Also in 1994, a Memorandum of Understanding between the Ministry of Health and Social Problems of the Republic of Korea, the International Labor Organization, the United Nations Environmental Programme (UNEP), and the World Health Organization established a program of comprehensive cooperation on chemical safety.

By year's end, Korea had entered, or hoped to enter, into cooperative relationships with major international organizations in the field of environmental protection. For example, in December 1994, Korea became an Executive Director Member of UNEP for four years. Korea was also preparing to join the Organisation for Economic Cooperation and Development (OECD). In this connection, Korea began a review of 71 OECD environmental documents (15 regulations, 49 recommendations, and 7 declarations) with a view to domestic implementation, a step that would enable Korea to participate in the Environment Committee of OECD even before full accession to the OECD.

Regionally, Korea made a vigorous effort to engage neighboring Asian countries in joint environmental protection activities. The government sponsored the fourth meeting of Experts and National Focal Points of the North-West Pacific Action Plan (NOWPAP). Subsequent to the meeting, the participants (IBRD, the International Maritime Organization, South

Korea, Japan, Russia, the People's Republic of China, and UNEP) adopted an action plan and three resolutions regarding the establishment of a secretariat for regional cooperation, the priority of projects, the institutional mechanism of NOWPAP, and financial issues. The Korean government pledged US$100,000 in support and suggested a survey of the extent of pollution of the Yellow Sea. North Korea, which had participated in the previous meetings, made no appearance.

(2) National Activities

In December 1994, the Ministry of Environment was elevated to cabinet rank. This reorganization had been helped by a major pollution incident involving the Nakdong River of April 1994, which brought the people's attention to the seriousness of environmental pollution in Korea.

New legislation on nuclear waste management and on special funding of environmental improvement was enacted on 5 January 1994. Moreover, in 1994, existing legislation was amended in the areas of tap water, sewage system (to establish overall responsibility for water quality management in the Ministry of Environment); protection of birds and beasts, hunting, and the preservation of the environment (to adapt domestic laws to the Convention on International Trade in Endangered Species of Wild Fauna and Flora); and hazardous chemicals and soil erosion.

Jae-Gon Lee

18. NORTH AFRICA

EGYPT

On February 3, Egypt enacted comprehensive legislation on the environment—Law No. 4 of 1994. In laying the basic legal groundwork for protecting the environment, the Law represents a milestone in Egypt's environmental efforts. Without implementing executive regulations, however, much of the Law's very sound objectives will remain unrealized. By year's end, most necessary implementing regulations still needed to be adopted.

Law No. 4 supersedes almost all preexisting environmental legislation (one notable exception is Law No. 48 of 1982 on the protection of the Nile). The Law tightens land-use regulations by providing, *inter alia*, for environmental impact assessment for construction projects. It also addresses nature preservation, air quality, pollution of the marine environment, and hazardous wastes. For example, the new Law requires that all entities engaged in the production, use, disposal, or handling of hazardous materials obtain a license. It establishes an almost complete ban on waste imports into Egypt. The Law itself is vague in its definition of what constitutes hazardous material or waste, and leaves clarification to a list of hazardous wastes that the authorities are to jointly issue. Also, the procedures for obtaining the requisite licenses, as well as the administrative authorities authorized to issue such licenses, remain ill-defined. Clarifying executive regulations were likely to be adopted in 1995.

The Law also incorporates provisions on liability, and establishes detailed penalties—including fines as well as criminal sanctions for certain violations of the Law—and enforcement procedures. Significantly, it recognizes a right of enforcement on the part of individuals and non-governmental organizations. While Egypt's green movement is still in its infancy, this provision is potentially very significant as it opens up violators to effective scrutiny by private citizens and organizations.

One of the Law's most significant features is its consolidation of implementation and enforcement measures through the creation of a single executive agency, the Agency for Environmental Affairs (AEA). The AEA is managed by a board of directors that consists of 20 members and is chaired by the Minister of the Environment. Unlike its predecessor, the AEA disposes of its own budget and has the power to create its own independent branches throughout the country as it deems appropriate. Thus, the AEA need not rely on other government organizations for funding or manpower to enforce its mandate.

Samir M. Hamza

19. SUB-SAHARAN AFRICA

A. KENYA

(1) International Environmental Law

(a) Lusaka Agreement

In 1994, Kenya was among the six countries of East, Central, and Southern Africa that signed the (➔) Lusaka Agreement on Cooperative Enforcement Operations Directed at Illegal Trade in Wild Fauna and Flora at a Ministerial Meeting in Lusaka, Zambia, on 9 September. The other countries were South Africa, Swaziland, Uganda, the United Republic of Tanzania, and Zambia. The Agreement aims at reducing and ultimately eliminating illegal trade in wild fauna and flora on the African continent. It establishes a permanent multinational task force responsible for undertaking cross-border investigations and law enforcement with regard to illegal trade. Contracting parties are required to establish national bureaus to coordinate with the task force's investigations involving illegal trade. The functions of the task force include facilitating cooperative activities among the national bureaus in carrying out investigations; investigating violations of national laws; collecting, processing, and disseminating information on illegal trade; and providing information to the parties relating to the return to the country of original export, or country of re-export, of confiscated wild fauna and flora.

The Agreement is a regional response to the enormous continental problem of large-scale poaching, illegal harvesting, and trade in African biological resources. African governments consider regional cooperation and collaboration essential to combat illegal trade in wild fauna and flora. The Agreement is a significant complement to the regime of the Convention on the International Trade in Endangered Species, which governs international trade in endangered species of wild fauna and flora and provides an important framework for the implementation of some of the provisions of the 1968 African Convention on the Conservation of Nature and Natural Resources, Algiers, and the 1992 Convention on Biological Diversity, Rio de Janeiro, at a regional level. The Agreement is open for signature to all African States.

(b) Lake Victoria

On 30 June 1994, the governments of Kenya, Uganda, and Tanzania adopted the Convention for the Establishment of the Lake Victoria Fisheries Organization at a Conference of Plenipotentiaries convened under the auspices of the Food and Agriculture Organization (FAO) in Kisumu, Kenya. The Convention is a response to the recognition by the three countries of the need for continued cooperation in the sustainable utilization of Lake Victoria and its resources. Thus, the objectives of the organization "shall be to foster cooperation among the contracting parties, harmonize national measures for the sustainable utilization of the living resources of the Lake and to develop and adopt conservation and management measures." The functions of the organization include promoting the proper management and optimal use of the fisheries and other resources of the Lake; enhancing capacity-building of existing institutions; facilitating research concerning the waters of the Lake; advising on the effects of the introduction of any non-indigenous aquatic animals or plants into the waters of Lake Victoria; and coordinating and undertaking training and extension activities in all aspects of fisheries.

The Convention establishes both a Fisheries Management Committee and a Scientific Committee. The Fisheries Management Committee is responsible for, *inter alia*, reviewing stock assessment, monitoring, harvest, and enforcement data; identifying emerging problems in fisheries; ensuring the conservation of indigenous species; and developing management policies. The Scientific Committee is charged with initiating, facilitating, and coordinating applied and innovative research pertinent to the management of the living resources of Lake Victoria. The adoption, effective enforcement, and harmonization of national laws and regulations, is an important element in the scheme of the Convention. Indeed, the organization is required to establish an appropriate system to keep under review the laws, regulations and other measures adopted by the contracting parties in the pursuit of the objectives of the Convention. The Director-General of the FAO is the depositary of the Convention.

(2) National Developments

In June, the government of Kenya adopted its National Environment Action Plan (NEAP). The NEAP process provided an opportunity for reexamination of existing environmental policies, laws, and institutional arrangements. The NEAP Report concludes that whereas there are over 77 statutes dealing with the management and conservation of the environment and natural resources, the legal framework is characterized by important lacunae, the absence of legally defined environmental quality criteria and standards, and inadequate enforcement of legal provisions by relevant authorities. The institutional framework for the management of the environment and natural resources contains significant gaps and overlaps in agency mandates, making law enforcement a difficult task. The Report stresses that the need to review existing laws; establish a framework of laws and regulations that would facilitate the integration of environmental issues in socio-economic development, require prior environmental impact assessment of new investments, maintain ecosystems and ecological processes, control pollution, and improve waste management; and enact legislation that would establish a new institutional framework to coordinate, enable and, where necessary, enforce environmental policy and legislation. Implementation of the NEAP began in November 1994.

Dan Bondi Ogolla

B. SOUTH AFRICA

The most significant event in South Africa during 1994, if not this century, was the coming into force of the new Interim Constitution (the Constitution of the Republic of South Africa Act, 200 of 1993). It put an end to the apartheid era and put into place South Africa's first democratically elected government. The main implications of this historic event for international environmental law were reviewed in 4 *YbIEL* 455-57 (1993). The new constitution is interim in nature and is to be replaced after five years by a final constitution. The final constitution must be drawn up by 1997. The Constitutional Assembly has already taken initial steps toward its formulation. Among the changes already submitted to the Assembly are suggested improvements to the environmental clause that appears in the Fundamental Rights chapter of the interim constitution.

The current clause states that "[e]very person shall have the right to an environment which is not detrimental to his or her health or well-being." It would be desirable to widen the ambit of this clause to promote the environment, but the legal challenge is to ensure that it is drafted as a justiciable right, with real and practical import.

(1) The 1982 United Nations Law of the Sea Convention (UNCLOS)

Although South Africa has not ratified the UNCLOS, which it signed in December 1984, it was an observer at the 12th Session of the LOSC Preparatory Commission (Prepcom) held in Kingston, Jamaica, during 1994. South Africa also attended the informal consultations held in New York during 1994 on the question of implementation of Part XI of UNCLOS relating to deep-seabed mining. Consequently, in October 1994, South Africa signed the (➔) Agreement Relating to the Implementation of Part XI of UNCLOS, and is currently considering ratifying UNCLOS.

The road toward ratification has to some extent been paved by parliament's passing of the Maritime Zones Act (15 of 1994) during 1994. This Act repeals the Territorial Waters Act (87 of 1963) and replaces it with a system of maritime zones for South Africa much in conformity with the UNCLOS. Among the zones claimed by the South African Act are an exclusive economic zone of 200 nautical miles and a contiguous zone extending up to 24 nautical miles from the baseline.

(2) The 1989 Convention on the Control of Transboundary Movement of Hazardous Waste and Their Disposal (the Basel Convention)

On 5 May 1994, South Africa acceded to the Basel Convention, which entered into force in South Africa on 4 August, 90 days from the date of accession, pursuant to Art. 25(2) of the Convention. Although South Africa had not passed legislation to give the Convention domestic effect by year's end, it published a draft Policy on the Transboundary Movement of Hazardous Waste (Government Gazette No. 15987, 30 September 1994) to elicit public comment and debate on the proposed domestic legislation.

The rather ambiguously worded draft policy elicited a storm of protest from non-governmental organizations representing the total spectrum of South African society. Public hearings on the draft policy were subsequently initiated in some provinces. The Department of Environmental Affairs and Tourism, the promoter of the policy, has as a result postponed publishing draft regulations to give the policy legislative effect until the matter has been given a more thorough public airing. The chief point of contention is that the draft policy does not explicitly ban the importation of hazardous waste into South Africa. A further difficulty is the approach that should be taken regarding importation of hazardous substances that are not imported for final disposal, but for reprocessing in South Africa.

Much public attention was paid in South Africa in 1994 to the criminal prosecution of Thor Chemicals (the South African subsidiary of a British company) and some of its officers for allegedly causing the death of two workers and injury to others as a result of mercury contamination. The company had been importing catalytic converters for reprocessing in South Africa and allegedly contaminated area watercourses during this process. The trial had not yet been finalised at the end of 1994.

(3) The 1971 Convention on Wetlands of International Importance Especially as Waterfowl Habitats (the Ramsar Convention)

South Africa ratified the Ramsar Convention in 1975 but has not passed specific implementing legislation. Rather, the conservation authorities have relied on general conservation legislation such as the National Parks Act (57 of 1976) and the various Nature Conservation ordinances that apply in the different provinces to give the Convention domestic effect.

A private members bill, the Wetlands Conservation Bill (B3-95), was tabled in parliament toward the end of 1994 and was to be considered in 1995. The bill gives wide discretionary power to the Minister of Environmental Affairs and Tourism to prohibit certain activities in wetlands and to provide for their protection. This bill was probably introduced to force the Minister's hand in the controversial application for a mining permit to exploit the heavy mineral sands in an ecologically sensitive area in KwaZulu/Natal province.

Jan I. Glazewski

C. NAMIBIA

[Editors' Note: Since this is the first report in the *Yearbook* on Namibia, it refers to a number of antecedent events as a background to developments in 1994.]

(1) Introduction

Namibia gained independence in 1990 and since then has embarked on a steady course of revising and replacing the laws that it inherited from its colonial past. Apart from the need to review and revise Namibia's environmental laws, which in some cases inappropriately reflected the country's colonial legacy, legislation also needed to be aligned with international environmental law developments insofar as these are relevant to Namibia. This report accordingly summarises the most significant international environmental legal developments that have occurred between the coming into force of the Namibian constitution on 21 March 1990 and the end of 1994.

(2) The Constitution

The stage for the development of environmental law in Namibia was set by the constitution itself, which includes an environmental provision. Chapter 11 lays down "Principles of State Policy" and includes a provision on "Promotion of the Welfare of the People" (Art. 95). This article includes a sub-article calling upon the state to actively promote and maintain the welfare of the people by adopting policies aimed at "maintenance of ecosystems, essential ecological processes and biological diversity of Namibia and utilisation of living natural resources on a sustainable basis for the benefit of all Namibians, both present and future," and by providing "measures against the dumping or recycling of foreign nuclear and toxic waste on Namibian territory" (Art. 95(l)).

Although this clause has not been formally invoked in court proceedings, it has been harnessed in political debates and issues relating to the utilisation of Namibia's natural resources. For example, it is relevant to an ongoing debate in Namibia regarding its policy of importation of waste and its approach to the possible adoption of the Basel and Bamako Conventions; it was also relevant to a controversial seal-culling programme as well as the alleged over-harvesting of pilchards, a mainstay of Namibia's fishing resources.

The question of succession to international conventions entered in to by South Africa prior to Namibian independence is dealt with in the constitution (Art. 143). It provides that all existing international agreements binding on Namibia shall remain in force unless decided otherwise by parliament. In the current context, this implies that Namibia succeeds to those international environmental conventions which had been entered into by South Africa.

(3) Namibia's Green Plan

Soon after independence the Ministry of Wildlife, Conservation and Tourism (since renamed the Ministry of Environment and Tourism) published Namibia's Green Plan. This is a comprehensive document reviewing Namibia's natural resource base and laying down its environmental priorities in the African and global contexts. It is essentially a state of the Namibian environment report and was tabled at the 1992 UN Conference on Environment and Development. The Namibian Green Plan is complemented by a 12-point plan for Integrated and Sustainable Environmental Management drawn up by the Directorate of Environmental Affairs. It sets out Namibia's environmental priorities for the first five years of its independence.

(4) Environmental Legislation Project

A number of other initiatives have been taken by the Ministry of Environment and Tourism since independence, such as the launching of a number of environmental research and policy development programmes. Included here is a programme to review and revise Namibia's environmental laws in the context of changed political, economic, and ecological circumstances. Like many countries, Namibian environmental laws are un-coordinated, disparate and in need of integration. But in addition, Namibia inherited a body of law from its colonial apartheid past that in certain cases reflected South Africa's interests, rather than its own. The formalities for this three-year programme were completed in 1994 and the newly appointed project manager is to take up his position in 1995.

(5) Fisheries and the 1982 UN Convention on the Law of the Sea (UNCLOS)

The United Nations Council for Namibia, which had been formally recognised by the UN General Assembly as the legitimate authority for Namibia in 1968, signed and subsequently ratified UNCLOS prior to independence. The recognition by UNCLOS of a 200 nautical mile exclusive economic zone was particularly relevant to Namibia as it has abundant pelagic and demersal fish resources off its coastline. For decades these resources had been exploited by foreign fishing interests that cashed in on the political impasse around the status of the territory and its waters. Little benefit accrued to Namibia. The hake resource was to some extent regulated by the 17-member International Commission on South East Atlantic Fisheries (ICSEAF), but Namibia was not represented on it. ICSEAF became largely redundant after the recognition of state jurisdiction over 200 mile exclusive economic zones. Newly independent Namibia quickly took control of its fishery resources by enacting the Territorial Sea and Exclusive Economic Zone of Namibia Act (3 of 1990). Since the entry into force of the Act, a number of foreign vessels have been arrested and successfully prosecuted for illegal fishing in Namibia's waters.

(6) Terrestrial Resources

Namibia plays host to a number of internationally significant but diminishing wildlife species, including Africa's most endangered pachyderm, the rhinoceros. Its rhino dehorning programme, an attempt to reduce losses to poachers who export horn to lucrative Far East markets, has received international attention in both scientific and conservation circles.

Namibia is a member of the 1973 Convention on International Trade in Endangered Species of Wild Fauna and Flora (CITES), having acceded to it in 1990. It has been an active participant in the bi-annual Conference of the Parties (CoP) where it has been a vigorous proponent of the notion of sustainable utilisation of resources rather than their preservation. Thus at the 1994 CoP held in Fort Lauderdale, Florida, a resolution proposed by Namibia to expedite the export and import of lawfully acquired hunting trophies was adopted. It was also elected to the CITES Standing Committee as an African representative.

As regards the elephant, Namibia is a founding member of the Southern African Centre for Ivory Management, along with four other southern African states, whose overall objective is to promote the marketing of ivory on a sustainable basis. Namibia was a party to the group of southern African states that suggested the transfer of the Elephant from Appendix I to Appendix II of CITES in order to reap some financial benefit from its policy of sustainable development.

(7) Biodiversity

Namibia was a signatory to the 1992 Convention on Biological Diversity at the Rio Summit and is considering ratifying it. To this end it initiated an inter-sectoral biodiversity programme during 1994 to coordinate and develop Namibia's biodiversity policy. This committee coordinates research and legislative initiatives in this regard.

(8) Pollution and Waste Management

Because of its wide open tracts of arid land, low population density, and geological make-up, Namibia has been considered by foreign states as a promising repository for their toxic waste. But as pointed out above, Namibia has specifically prohibited any such importation in its constitution. Furthermore, while Namibia has adopted neither the 1991 Organization of African Unity Convention on the Ban of Import into Africa and the Control of Transboundary Movement and Management of Hazardous Waste within Africa (Bamako), nor the 1989 Convention on the Control of Transboundary Movements of Hazardous Waste and their Disposal (Basel), it is considering adopting the latter. Namibia has actively participated in United Nations Environment Programme meetings in this regard.

Namibia has acceded to the 1985 Vienna Convention for the Protection of the Ozone Layer and ratified the 1987 Montreal Protocol on Substances that deplete the Ozone Layer. It was also considering ratifying the 1990 London Amendment to the Montreal Protocol.

(9) General

(a) Commission on Sustainable Development

Namibia has been an active participant on this Commission and held the office of vice-chair of the Bureau of the Commission during 1994.

(b) Other Environmental Conventions

Namibia is considering ratifying or acceding to a number of other international conventions, including the 1971 Convention on Wetlands of International Importance, Especially as Waterfowl Habitat (Ramsar); the 1979 Convention on the Conservation of Migratory Species of Wild Animals (Bonn); the UN Framework Convention on Climate Change, which it signed at the Rio summit, parliament having resolved to ratify it during its 1994 session August; the 1994 (➔) Convention on Desertification, which is particularly relevant to Namibia; and a regional Convention on Fisheries Cooperation among African States bordering the Atlantic Ocean. Namibia will have to ensure that its domestic laws are in conformity with these conventions. Developments in this regard will no doubt be reported on in future editions of the *Yearbook*.

Jan I. Glazewski

20. INDIAN OCEAN ISLAND STATES

(1) Introduction

Sensitive habitats, fragile island ecosystems, and unique and endangered flora and fauna are found throughout the island states of the Indian Ocean region. For many years Comoros, Madagascar, Maldives, Mauritius, and Seychelles have relied on the pristine nature of their environments for economic and social well-being. But growing environmental problems resulting from recent development now threaten the resource base upon which these states' future economic growth depends. With limited technical and financial resources at their disposal, the island states are fostering greater regional and international cooperation as a means of addressing some of their more pressing environmental problems.

The high level of participation by the Indian Ocean island states at the UN Global Conference on the Sustainable Development of Small Island Developing States (*see* (➔) Report of the Global Conference) is an indication of their recognition that their environmental and development problems can only be overcome with the assistance and support of the international community. Additionally, the island states of the Indian Ocean are seeking to develop comprehensive legal frameworks to address these problems. In this respect, the island of the region made considerable progress during the year. Seychelles passed a revised Environment Protection Act, Comoros enacted a new Environment Act, and guidelines were established during 1994 to give effect to the Environmental Protection and Preservation Act that Maldives enacted in April 1993.

(2) Multilateral Legal Developments

Preparations for and participation in the UN Global Conference on the Sustainable Development of Small Island Developing States featured prominently on the national environmental agendas of the island states of the Indian Ocean region. High-level delegations from Comoros, Madagascar, Maldives, Mauritius, and Seychelles attended the Conference in Bridgetown, Barbados, from 25 April to 6 May.

The Governments of Maldives, Mauritius, and Seychelles played an active role in the preparatory process for the Conference. The Association of Small Island States, to which all three states belong, prepared an action paper that formed the basis for discussion at the two regional technical meetings held during 1993 in Port Vila, Vanuatu, and Port-of-Spain, Trinidad and Tobago. The "Programme of Action" that ultimately formed the basis for discussion during the Conference itself was largely based on recommendations made during the two technical meetings of experts. Representatives from Maldives, Mauritius, and Seychelles attended the technical meeting of experts from the Pacific and Indian Ocean regions.

In promoting the development of disaster-preparedness programmes at the national and regional level, regional delegates to the Conference highlighted the major risk of oil spills that tankers passing through the region present. The island states are located along the most densely used oil transportation artery in the world. There are over 5,000 tanker voyages through the sensitive coastal waters of Comoros and Madagascar each year, passing close to the World Heritage Site of Aldabra atoll in Seychelles. Over 232 million tons of crude oil pass yearly through and near the sensitive coral atolls of Maldives. On average, there are over 220 oil tankers in transit through the coastal waters of the small island states every day.

The small island states are particularly vulnerable to oil spills because of their economic dependence on tourism and fishing. Delegates from the island states thus stressed the urgent need to establish an effective oil-spill response capability within the region. They recognised that individual island states will never have the capability to effectively react in the event of a major maritime accident and that establishment of regional oil spill response and coordination capacity is necessary for effective protection. The states maintained that a regional response centre should be established along the lines of the international action plan for response to marine pollution incidents proposed under various international agreements such as the International Convention on Oil Spill Preparedness, Response and Cooperation; the Convention for the Protection, Management and Development of the Marine and Coastal Environment of the Eastern Africa Region; and the Protocol Concerning Co-operation in Combating Marine Pollution in Cases of Emergency in the Eastern African Region.

Delegates from the Indian Ocean Commission, which represents all the island states of the Western Indian Ocean region, met during the Conference and agreed to seek the assistance of the international community in the development and implementation of a Regional Oil Spill Contingency Programme.

(3) National Legislation—Seychelles

On 13 September, the National Assembly of the Republic of Seychelles passed a revised Environment Protection Act. Formulated after a broad-based consultation process, the Act is intended to provide for the protection, preservation, and improvement of the environment; the control of hazardous substances; the integration of environmental considerations into the development process; and the coordination, implementation, and enforcement of national policies on environmental management. The Act repeals the Environment Protection Act of 1988.

Section 4 of the Act grants a variety of powers and responsibilities to the Environment Authority and imposes certain restrictions on its powers in matters of public health and matters under the control of other government Ministries. Section 5 mandates the creation of a National Environmental Advisory Council, consisting of representatives of government agencies, non-governmental organizations, and environmental associations.

Part III of the Act deals with the prevention, control, and abatement of environmental pollution. Section 6 provides that the Minister of Environment may prescribe standards relating to air, water, or soil quality; effluents from new and existing point sources of water pollution; noise and odour emissions; and pesticide residues. Under §7, the Minister may establish regulations for the preservation of fishing areas, aquatic areas, drinking water sources, and other areas where water resources may require special protection. Regulations may provide for carrying out any work necessary to prevent, control, or abate water pollution from natural causes or from abandoned works or projects. The Act prohibits the discharge of contaminants into the soil and of polluting or hazardous substances into any watercourse or into territorial waters.

Section 8 provides that the Minister may declare any area an "air pollution control area," within which control measures may be prescribed for the use of any fuel or substance that may cause air pollution. Section 9 governs noise emission standards and noise abatement measures. Section 10 provides that the Environmental Authority may undertake studies and make recommendations concerning any substance or activity that may reasonably be anticipated to harm the ozone layer to the Minister, who may control them by regulation.

Section 11 provides for the survey of Seychelles' coastal zone and the preparation of an "Integrated Coastal Zone Management Plan." It also allows the Minister to issue regulations to ensure that activities in the coastal zone do not damage the environment and to provide such measures as are necessary to prevent, reduce, and control pollution in the coastal zone.

Regarding waste management, §12 provides that the Minister may prescribe standards for the classification and analysis of waste and for treatment and disposal methods. It mandates promulgation of regulations for the introduction, production, possession, handling, storage, transportation, segregation, and disposal of hazardous waste. It prohibits importation of hazardous waste. Section 12(9) requires the Environment Agency to monitor environmental contamination and degradation arising from the operation of any waste disposal site. The Act seeks to promote recycling, waste reduction, and the use of cleaner technologies.

Part IV of the Environment Protection Act establishes a legal basis for the implementation of an environmental impact assessment process. Section 15 provides that any person who commences, proceeds with, carries out, executes, or conducts any "prescribed project or activity" without carrying out an environmental impact assessment study and subsequently obtaining authority to proceed, shall be guilty of an offence. The Act specifies the required contents of environmental impact statements.

The project proponent is responsible for the preparation of the environmental impact assessment, its submission to the Authority, and the public inspection and commentary process, while the Authority is responsible for monitoring and ensuring that any conditions are implemented. Work on a project may be suspended by an order of the Authority under specified conditions. Section 15(9) provides that where any project brings about a change in the physical environment, the project proponent shall provide compensation for any resulting loss or damage to the environment.

Part V of the Act provides for enforcement, and gives powers to the Administrator to issue "enforcement," "prohibition," "variation," and "withdrawal" notices where necessary. Powers of entry, inspection, and seizure are granted to authorised officers, together with powers to take samples of air, water, soil, or any other substance.

Section 23 of the Act provides that the Minister may declare an environmental emergency where pollution occurs or is expected to occur due to any accident or other unforeseen act or event, or where there is, in the opinion of the Minister, an imminent risk of serious pollution to the environment. In cases where an environmental emergency has been declared, an authorised officer may, without warrant, arrest a person reasonably suspected of violating the Act.

Part VI of the Act specifies criminal and civil penalties, including fines and imprisonment, for particular offences. It also provides for civil liability for environmental harm, and requires compensatory damages for any costs relating to the prevention, control, abatement, or mitigation such harm.

(4) National Legislation—Comoros

On 22 June, in spite of the continued, unstable political climate, the Federal Islamic Republic of Comoros enacted the "Loi Cadre Relative à l'Environnement," an act providing for the protection and management of the environment.

Part I provides for the preservation of biodiversity in Comoros and the promotion of sustainable development. Comoros is to prohibit all activities under its control, within its territory, or in regions under its jurisdiction that are likely to cause environmental degradation in other states. The Act also provides for the creation of natural parks and reserves. Management policies for forests are to be established. A Cabinet Decree is to determine the measures required for the protection of forests, while taking into account the preservation of local communities' user rights. A number of activities are prohibited, including campfires in forest areas, clearcutting, deforestation programmes, and farming activities, except where expressly permitted.

Part II creates the Environment Division, the main administrative body in charge of managing the environment. The government is to establish environmental policies, while the Environment Minister is to ensure the application of the Act, except where another authority expressly has jurisdiction. Part III addresses environmental assessments. Section 11 requires individuals and corporations to submit environmental assessment reports with applications for administrative approval of construction and development projects. A Cabinet Decree establishes a list of projects that do not require environmental assessment and outlines the requirements for the submission of environmental assessment reports, their review by the Administration, and the public information process.

Part IV establishes a trust fund to help finance programmes created by the Environment Division and other associations. The structures and operation of the Trust are to be established by Cabinet Decree. Part V provides that the Environment Division may order the cessation of any activity that is likely to endanger any component of the natural environment, including soil and subsoil; water resources, including the marine environment; atmosphere, and biodiversity. Section 22 provides that any undertaking involving the use of the soil, whether for private, agricultural, industrial, or urban purposes, must receive prior approval by the Environment Minister. Such approval is also required for any research or exploitation project of subsoil natural resources. Section 23 specifies the conditions for approval.

Section 24 requires the approval of both the Water Resources Management Minister and the Environment Minister for all undertakings carried out on watercourses, their beds, or their banks that are likely to impact water flow or jeopardize the local ecological balance. Section 29 prohibits any discharges into watercourses or their surroundings that are likely to produce adverse effects on water quality. All agricultural and industrial facilities, including wastewater treatment facilities, that discharge wastewaters into a watercourse must obtain prior approval from the Environment Minister.

Part V also provides measures for protecting the marine environment. All development undertakings and projects must receive prior approval from the appropriate Minister and the Environment Minister. Ships are prohibited from discharging untreated wastewaters into the marine environment and waters under Comoros' jurisdiction, and fishing is governed by a Cabinet Decree that prohibits industrial fishing in the territorial waters. Further, the removal of material from the seashore is strictly prohibited.

Section 38 provides for the regulation and prohibition of releases of harmful substances into the atmosphere. This section also provides for the promotion of alternate technologies and the decrease in the import, production, consumption, and export of substances that alter the Earth's climatic stability.

Sections 39-45 aim at preserving biodiversity. The Act also provides for the creation of natural parks and reserves, and requires management policies for forests to be established. A Cabinet Decree is to determine the measures required for the protection of forests, taking into account the preservation of local communities' user rights. A number of activities are prohibited, including campfires in forest areas, clearcutting, deforestation programmes, and farming activities, except where expressly permitted.

Part VI of the Act provides for the protection of the human environment, particularly through control and regulation of urban planning. Any project covered by the Planning Code must take environmental protection into consideration and have the Environment Minister's prior approval. The Environment Division may order the cessation of any activity that is likely to endanger the quality of human life and health.

Section 59 defines "wastes" and §60 imposes a general obligation to collect and dispose of wastes. Local authorities are responsible for the disposal of household wastes, while owners or occupiers of industrial and agricultural facilities must manage their wastes and report to the Environment Division the nature, quantity, and place of storage of such wastes. The import, export, and transit of hazardous waste may only be authorized by the Environment Minister if the transport and disposal does not endanger the environment. Section 67 of the Act regulates hazardous substances and calls on the Cabinet to establish a list of hazardous substances for which import, export, transit, production, sale, and distribution is prohibited except with the prior approval of the Environment Minister.

Finally, the Act establishes a classification system for facilities that an environmental assessment has identified either as constituting a source of serious harm to public health and safety, as endangering the preservation of the natural environment and its resources, or as affecting the protection of architectural and cultural heritage.

George H. de Berdt Romilly
Nathalie F. Bernard

21. OCEANIA

[Editors' Note: Because the 1993 *Yearbook* did not contain a report on Oceania, this report includes developments in 1993 and 1994.]

(1) South Pacific Forum

The 25th South Pacific Forum took place in Brisbane, Australia, 31 July to 2 August 1994. Its central theme was "Managing Our Resources," concentrating on human resources, forestry and fishery resources, land use, and tourism. The heads of governments of Australia, Cook Islands, Federated States of Micronesia, Fiji, Kiribati, Nauru, New Zealand, Niue, Papua New Guinea, Republic of the Marshall Islands, Solomon Islands, Tonga, Tuvalu, Vanuatu, and Western Samoa attended. One of the keys to the gathering's success was the opportunity for informal discussions at a leader's retreat.

The main environmental outcome of the 25th Forum, as reflected in the Communiqué, concerned forests. The Prime Ministers of Australia, Fiji, New Zealand, Papua New Guinea, Solomon Islands, and Vanuatu agreed to work toward developing a common code of conduct governing logging of indigenous forests, to which companies operating in their countries will have to adhere. They also agreed to increase monitoring of timber exports and logging. The 25th Forum further called for early agreement on a process for negotiating one or more protocols to the UN Framework Convention on Climate Change. Small island countries' concerns resulted in a call for industrialized countries to ensure that joint implementation complement, and not replace, action at home. The 25th Forum also agreed to promote multilateral approaches to the sustainable use of fish stocks within the region.

(2) Regional Forestry Code

Senior officials of Australia, Fiji, New Zealand, Papua New Guinea, Solomon Islands, and Vanuatu met in Suva, Fiji, at the end of October 1994 to commence drafting the Code of Conduct for Logging of Indigenous Forests in Selected South Pacific Countries. A technical group began work on this process in December 1994. In addition, the Melanesian Spearhead Group (Fiji, Papua New Guinea, Solomon Islands, and Vanuatu) undertook to examine the development of uniform legislation, procedures, and practices for forest resources management.

Vanuatu, in a parallel development, introduced a logging ban on the Island of Erromango and a ban on the export of roundlogs. Papua New Guinea hired an international consulting group to monitor logging operations to ensure that operations met sustainability criteria and that government royalties due on logs could be effectively audited.

(3) South Pacific Regional Environment Programme

The Plenipotentiary Meeting of the South Pacific Regional Environment Programme (SPREP), held in Apia, Western Samoa, 14–16 June 1993, concluded an agreement establishing SPREP as an international organization separate from the South Pacific Commission, of which SPREP had been a subsidiary since its inception in 1982. The agreement provides a framework clarifying the legal status, role, and functions of the SPREP Inter-Governmental Meeting and SPREP Secretariat, and confers on SPREP the same legal status as other South Pacific organizations. It also ensures SPREP's effective operation and enables it to fulfil its role in regional environmental protection and management. As of the end of 1994, 15 members of SPREP had signed the Agreement and eight had ratified it. The Agreement requires 10 ratifications for entry into force.

During 1994, conceptual and planning work for a South Pacific Biodiversity Conservation Programme proceeded. In 1993, the Global Environment Facility (GEF) had agreed to provide SPREP funding in the order of US$10 million for 11 projects. The projects are intended to implement sustainable development through the management of multiple-use conservation areas on land and in marine environments.

(4) Forum Fisheries Agency

The 25th Forum agreed to promote multilateral approaches to the sustainable exploitation of fish stocks within the region and, to this end, to define sustainable catch levels based on the precautionary principle, cooperatively enhance monitoring and policing efforts, and obtain fair prices and increased value-added production for fisheries resources. Forum leaders also agreed to pursue multilateral agreements with distant-water fishing states. During 1994, the Forum Fisheries Agency (FFA) sought to develop multilateral access arrangements similar to the Treaty on Fisheries Between the Governments of Certain Pacific Island States and the Government of the United States of America (1987, renewed 1992), already in force for the United States.

The 13th Annual Meeting of the Parties to the Nauru Agreement Concerning Cooperation in the Management of Fisheries of Common

Interest (1982) took place on 29 April. Kiribati, Marshall Islands, Micronesia, Nauru, Palau, Papua New Guinea, Solomon Islands, and Tuvalu are parties to the Nauru Agreement (and are also members of the FFA). The Meeting decided to reduce the number of foreign purse seine vessels allowed access to fish in the Central and Western Pacific region in order to promote both greater regional management and control of the fishery and also the development of direct participation in the fishery by the region's nationals and domestic fishing industries. To this end, the Meeting considered a draft preferential access arrangement, which Micronesia, Kiribati, the Marshall Islands, Nauru, Solomon Islands, Papua New Guinea, and Tuvalu adopted on 30 November. The Arrangement, known as the Federated States of Micronesia Arrangement for Regional Fisheries Access, is subsidiary to the Nauru Agreement.

At its meeting of 1–9 December 1994, the Forum Fisheries Committee established a Sub-Committee on Future Management Arrangements to establish more effective arrangements for conserving the region's tuna resources, with a view to maximizing the benefit to FFA member countries from the harvest of those resources while ensuring sustainable management. In a related development, the FFA is actively examining using satellite transponders to enforce regional fisheries conservation and management laws. In 1994, the FFA commenced research on a transponder development programme, with funding for a five-year Integrated Regional Fisheries Surveillance and Management Programme from the Commission of the European Communities. Information and input from the programme will be disseminated through the Maritime Surveillance Communications Network, which has been implemented since 1991 with support from the Australian Defence Cooperation Programme.

(5) High Seas Fisheries

Through the FFA, the region maintains an active input to the UN Conference on Straddling Fish Stocks and Highly Migratory Fish Stocks. With control over tuna stocks in mind, it has formulated a regional strategy that seeks to ensure that the principle of sovereign coastal-state rights over highly migratory species within areas of national jurisdiction is not weakened. The FFA plans to hold a high-level multilateral fisheries conference following the UN Conference to examine its implications for bilateral and multilateral access in the region.

(6) Regional Hazardous Wastes Convention

At the 23rd South Pacific Forum, in Honiara, Solomon Islands, in 1992, Papua New Guinea had proposed a regional convention to ban the import of and control the movement and management of hazardous wastes, and agreed that it should forward the proposed convention to the SPREP for technical evaluation and comment. A Technical Working Group was established and met in Suva, Fiji, in March 1993, to give the proposal careful technical evaluation. The Technical Working Group reported to the 24th South Pacific Forum in Nauru in 1993, which agreed that technical consultations and negotiations on a regional convention complementary to relevant global regimes should commence by March 1994, with the aim of concluding them by the 26th Forum. Two Forum working group meetings, in March and November 1994, made good progress on negotiating a draft text. The current draft seeks to ban the import into Pacific Island Countries of all hazardous wastes generated outside the proposed convention area, and to ensure that transboundary movements of hazardous wastes within the South Pacific area are completed in a controlled and environmentally sound manner. Its provisions are complementary to those of the 1989 Basel Convention on Transboundary Movements of Hazardous Wastes and Their Disposal, although it is not yet determined whether the regional convention might extend beyond the Basel Convention by clearly covering radioactive wastes. The working group also considered the question of a secretariat for the proposed convention. Given its mandate and technical capabilities, it was agreed that SPREP should undertake this role, although a final decision on this will require the endorsement of SPREP's membership.

The 25th Forum noted the (➔) decision in March 1994 of the Parties to the Basel Convention to ban all exports of hazardous wastes from Organisation for Economic Cooperation and Development (OECD) to non-OECD countries. It welcomed the progress made in the negotiation of the regional convention, which will ban the importation into Forum island countries of hazardous wastes and control their transboundary movement and management within the South Pacific region. The Forum directed officials to make every effort to ensure that the convention would be completed in time for signature at the 26th South Pacific Forum. The 25th Forum encouraged members to become involved in these negotiations and endorsed the recommendation that SPREP act as the Secretariat under the convention. This initiative met the call of para. 24.A(viii) concerning hazardous wastes in the (➔) Program of Action for the Sustainable Development of Small Island States adopted at Barbados in May 1994 (discussed below).

The Republic of the Marshall Islands proposed to establish a radioactive waste disposal facility on one or more islands contaminated by radiation from the United States' atomic bomb testing in the 1940s and 1950s. The proposal has given rise to some concern from other South Pacific countries and, at the end of 1994, had not yet reached preliminary feasibility study stage.

(7) Global Environment Treaty Participation

South Pacific Island countries made substantial progress in ratifying international environmental agreements in 1994. The UN Convention on the Law of the Sea (1982) came into force on 16 November 1994, and by the end of the year Australia, Fiji, Micronesia, and the Marshall Islands had ratified the Convention. Also at the end of 1994, the UN Framework Convention on Climate Change (1992) had been ratified by Australia, Cook Islands, Fiji, Micronesia, Marshall Islands, Nauru, New Zealand, Papua New Guinea, and Tuavalu. The Convention on Biological Diversity (1992) had been ratified by Australia, Cook Islands, Fiji, Micronesia, Marshall Islands, Nauru, New Zealand, Papua New Guinea, and Vanuatu.

(8) Small Island Developing States Conference

South Pacific Island countries were active in preparations for and during the Global Conference on the Sustainable Development of Small Island Developing States, which concluded in Barbados in May 1994. SPREP hosted a regional technical meeting for the Indian and Pacific Oceans from 31 May to 4 June 1993. The Global Conference adopted the Program of Action for the Sustainable Development of Small Island States. Chapter X of the Program of Action concerns regional institutions and technical cooperation for sustainable development and Ch. XV, Part D, covers institutional arrangements for implementation of the Program. The 25th South Pacific Forum emphasized the importance of effective implementation of the Global Conference's Program of Action and decided to establish a regional mechanism for consultation on implementation, in accordance with para. 132 of the Program. The consultative mechanism is to consist of support units in the Pacific Operations Centre of the UN Economic and Social Commission for Asia and Pacific and in SPREP, together with an Advisory Committee consisting of senior policy officials. At its annual meeting in October 1994, SPREP presented a report recommending that the support units be activated without delay and that the Advisory Committee meetings coincide with and report to annual SPREP meetings. These recommendations were adopted.

(9) Global Environment Facility

The Restructured GEF includes a GEF Council consisting of representatives of regional or voluntary constituencies. Upon the Restructured GEF's establishment, Pacific Island countries, Indonesia, and the Philippines formed a joint GEF Council constituency. Participation of these two larger island countries may enhance GEF Council consideration of Pacific Island concerns. When, at its meeting in 1994, the GEF Council considered how its programme funds for environmental protection of international waters are used, it interpreted the scope of this programme area broadly, seeking to ensure that funds are directed to projects that cover more than one of the four GEF programme areas (*i.e.*, climate change, biodiversity conservation, ozone layer, and international waters). The approach is expected to produce benefits for the small island States of Oceania, which are seeking economic development while preserving marine and terrestrial environments.

Gregory Rose

22. NEW ZEALAND

(1) Introduction

New Zealand's international environmental policy reflects its enthusiasm for environmental issues, but also acknowledges New Zealand's limited influence and resources. New Zealand has, despite its small size, made a significant impact on international environmental issues as diverse as ozone depletion, whaling, sustainable forestry, and the emerging concern for reconciliation of trade and environment policies. New Zealand has also contributed to the negotiations on climate change and the transfer of technology. Of particular focus for New Zealand is the South Pacific where, as one of the larger states in the region, it has often played a leading role.

(2) Environment 2010 Strategy

As an element of its commitment to the United Nations Conference on Environment and Development's (UNCED's) Agenda 21, New Zealand's Ministry for the Environment published a statement of its strategy for the environment, titled "Environment 2010 Strategy," in October 1994. It is a statement of broad strategic direction rather than specific policies that is intended to guide the government's policies and priorities in relation to the environment into the next century. The overall guiding vision outlined in the Strategy calls for "a clean, healthy, and unique environment, sustaining nature and people's needs and aspirations." The vision seeks to maintain an environment that safeguards the life-supporting capacity of air, water, soil and ecosystems and conserves biological diversity and spectacular scenery. The Strategy stresses that a basis must be provided for sustainable development that meets the needs of present and future generations; natural, renewable resources should not be consumed faster than they can regenerate. In addition, people must be able to meet their needs, especially for employment, food, clothing, shelter, and education; and leisure and recreational opportunities must be provided for those who enjoy the outdoors. Finally, Maori natural treasures or taonga are protected and their cultural practices associated with the environment are provided for.

The Strategy identifies the major threats to New Zealand's biophysical environment and sets out an action plan for those that are of the highest priority. The Strategy also establishes a number of environmental goals and delineates responsibilities among stakeholders. It recognizes that all decisions will have to be made within the framework of a market economy. Finally, the Strategy establishes an agenda for action.

(3) Trade and the Environment

The links between trade policies and environmental policies have raised a number of important issues for New Zealand. As a small nation reliant on trade for a quarter of its gross national product, New Zealand is wedded to the idea of liberalized international trade. New Zealand also produces mainly agricultural products, with their consequent impact on the environment. There is also an increasing dependence on tourism in the economy. New Zealand's indigenous people, the Maori, have also become concerned that new international trade rules will impact on their interests, particularly in the protection of their intellectual property rights.

New Zealand has based its position on the principles agreed by the international community at UNCED and, in particular, the belief that international trade and environmental protection should and can be mutually supportive. The government is committed to an open, non-discriminatory, and equitable trading system, seeking multilateral solutions to environmental problems of a transboundary or global nature.

New Zealand opposed the action taken by the United States to ban the import of Mexican tuna. In its submission to the General Agreement on Tariffs and Trade (GATT) Tuna/Dolphin II Dispute Panel, New Zealand argued that the United States (or, for that matter, any other country) should not be able to prescribe the environmental polices other countries had to adopt in order to trade with it, especially when based only on unilateral action. (*See* (➔) Report of the GATT Dispute Settlement Panel.)

An example of the difficulties involved in reconciling New Zealand's interests in free trade and environmental protection occurred when a leading New Zealand company requested that the government ban the import of freezers and refrigerators that used chlorofluorocarbons. Other countries, such as Australia had implemented a ban. The government considered whether the environmental benefits arising from such a ban would outweigh the possible costs to the New Zealand economy from any trade impacts and decided that it was not appropriate to implement a ban at that time.

New Zealand participated actively in various international fora dealing with trade and the environment, but focused its efforts on the GATT/World Trade Organization Committee and the Organisation for Economic Cooperation and Development (OECD) Joint Experts Group. In

November 1994, the New Zealand Ministry of Foreign Affairs and Trade published a report titled "The GATT Uruguay Round: Trade and Environment."

(4) Protection of the Atmosphere

(a) Ozone Depletion

New Zealand has been a leader in the scientific efforts being undertaken to understand and preserve the ozone layer. The government has also been engaged fully in negotiations on international agreements, with New Zealand also encouraging and supporting the participation of representatives from Pacific island countries.

At the national level, New Zealand implemented its international obligations through the Ozone Layer Protection Act 1990, as amended, and the timetable set by the international community. In 1994, New Zealand was ahead of the international timetable in the early phase-out of halons. As New Zealand does not produce any controlled substances listed under the Montreal Protocol, the phase-out dates have required New Zealand to ban the imports of virgin substances.

(b) Climate Change

It is expected that the impact of climate change will have an adverse effect on New Zealand's economy, infrastructure, and society. The threat to the South Pacific island neighbors from sea level rise is expected to be even more significant. Consequently, New Zealand has been involved fully in the international processes that seek to address climate change. New Zealand scientists participated in the Intergovernmental Panel on Climate Change, at times taking a leading role. New Zealand submitted its national communication to the Framework Convention on Climate Change in September 1994.

New Zealand also worked to implement the New Zealand Climate Change Strategy, which is a comprehensive long-term strategy that deals with the issues involved in climate change. Because of the impact of the energy sector, the New Zealand Climate Change Strategy consists mainly of a package of measures that seek to reduce energy-based carbon emissions. They include legislative and regulatory reform proposals in the energy sector, the Energy Efficiency Strategy, cooperative energy efficiency programs between the Energy Efficiency and Conservation Authority and the private and public sectors, renewable-energy measures, and specific transport-sector measures.

The 1994 budget set aside $8.4 million for work on energy efficiency, which would help lower emissions by improving energy efficiency standards in the Building Code, improve the energy efficiency of household electrical appliances, and improve energy use.

In negotiations to further develop the Climate Change Convention, New Zealand supported additional commitments to reduce emissions in recognition of the fact that current commitments will not achieve the goals of the Convention. New Zealand has supported valuative approaches that take into account all greenhouse gases, as well as their sinks/reservoirs, and those that recognize the differentiation in obligations that arise from the unequal responsibilities between various countries. New Zealand has supported approaches favoring internationally agreed economic instruments and global least-cost abatement, as well as the direct involvement of business in negotiations.

(5) Land Resources

(a) Sustainable Agriculture

New Zealand had a major role at UNCED in the completion of the chapter on sustainable agriculture and rural development. Chapter 14 is one of the largest of Agenda 21, covering 11 program areas. While many of the activities listed in Ch. 14 were promoted in 1994, there is still much to be done to shift existing agricultural practices to a more sustainable footing. Nevertheless, there have been a number of encouraging signs, including the strong interest of the farming community. New Zealand's approach emphasises eliminating production-orientated subsidies in agriculture.

(b) Sustainable Forestry

New Zealand participated actively in the international efforts to advance the agreement forged at UNCED on Forest Principles. It was represented at the Montreal, Helsinki, and at intergovernmental working groups on forests, and worked with other countries in preparing for the review of land management and forestry that was planned for 1995 by the UN Commission on Sustainable Development. Some countries, including New Zealand, sought the preparation of an international convention governing forestry management worldwide.

New Zealand is deeply concerned about the impact of unsustainable forestry activities in Pacific island countries. For instance, some island nations will have no commercially available forests left within a decade at current rates of exploitation. Degradation caused by deforestation is itself a major environmental concern. In some countries of the region it is having a serious impact on river and coastal systems. At the 25th Session of the South Pacific Forum, held in August 1994, a communique was issued, in part concerning forests. The Forum expressed concern at the way in which forests throughout the region and the world were being harvested in a highly destructive manner. It welcomed initiatives being taken at the national level with the aim of achieving sustainable forestry practices and noted international negotiations on the subject.

New Zealand played an active role in implementing the outcomes of the Forum meeting and supported reforestation and forest management programs in a number of Pacific island countries as part of its overseas development assistance program.

(6) Biodiversity and Species Conservation

(a) Biodiversity

New Zealand is very dependent on the maintenance of biological diversity. New Zealand's farming, horticultural, and forestry industries are almost completely dependent on less than 50 species introduced from overseas. A large proportion of New Zealand's 50,000 or so native species are found nowhere else. While this biodiversity has been the basis of New Zealand's tourism industry for some time, it is now also attracting the attention of overseas pharmaceutical companies.

Much of New Zealand's biodiversity is, however, under threat. Since Maori and European arrival in New Zealand, biodiversity has been reduced to only 23 percent of its original amount through the effects of settlement, pastoral farming, drainage, hunting, and competition from the introduction of exotic species.

New Zealand has a range of legislation that is seeking to protect and sustain remaining biodiversity, and in 1994 proposed the Hazardous Substances and New Organisms Bill. The Hazardous Substances and New Organisms Bill will, when enacted, amend and consolidate the 22 laws currently governing the import, registration, and use of potentially harmful substances and organisms. The Act is designed to mesh with the Resource Management and Biosecurity Acts to provide integrated environmental management of hazardous substances and new organisms. The Bill will improve New Zealand's ability to control the introduction of new organisms that might compete with endemic flora and fauna.

In addition, key environmental principles have been incorporated into a new Fisheries Bill 1994 that seeks to reform and restate the law relating to fisheries in New Zealand. Clause 8(b) of the bill requires that persons exercising functions under the new legislation must have regard to the "principle that biological diversity within the aquatic environment ought to be conserved."

(b) Possums

A report by the New Zealand Parliamentary Commissioner for the Environment titled "Possum Management in New Zealand" was tabled in Parliament during May 1994. The report emphasized the seriousness of the possum problem in New Zealand, and in particular the considerable damage that possums do to unique native species. It also pointed out the contribution of possums to the spread of bovine tuberculosis (with its accompanying risk of raising non-tariff barriers in overseas markets against New Zealand's meat and dairy exports). The report argued that ongoing possum control over as much as 37 percent of New Zealand is required and at this stage no other method was more cost-effective than the aerial application of 1080 poison. Some environmental groups in New Zealand, however, are opposed this measure.

(c) Whales and Other Cetaceans

In 1994, the International Whaling Commission (IWC) voted to establish a southern ocean whale sanctuary. This circumpolar sanctuary extends from the Antarctic ice edge to points between 40 and 55 degrees south latitude, surrounding much of New Zealand's Exclusive Economic Zone (EEZ). The sanctuary was adopted with the overwhelming support of IWC members (23 in favor, including New Zealand, 1 against, and 6 abstentions). New Zealand lent its full support to the southern ocean whale sanctuary proposal. Within New Zealand's own EEZ, whales and other cetaceans are fully protected by the Marine Mammals Protection Act 1978.

(7) Oceans, Coastal Areas, and Marine Pollution

(a) Living Marine Resources

As a significant fishing nation with strong interests in the sustainable utilization of fish stocks, New Zealand was an active participant in many of the multilateral processes that sought to address the conservation of living marine resources. This includes the work New Zealand undertakes in the International Whaling Commission for the protection of whales and other cetaceans and in the Convention on the Conservation of Antarctic Marine Living Resources. During 1993, New Zealand, Japan, and Australia also concluded an important agreement for the management of southern bluefin tuna, which in recent years have come under increasing stress. The first meeting of the Commission established under this agreement was held in 1994.

New Zealand also took on a prominent role at the UNCED deliberations on the oceans chapter of Agenda 21 and, in 1994, played a significant part in the United Nations Conference on Straddling Fish Stocks and Highly Migratory Fish Stocks. New Zealand was also a key player during the international debate on driftnet fishing. New Zealand has ratified the Convention for the Prohibition of Fishing with Long Drift Nets in the South Pacific, known as the Wellington Convention.

(b) Law of the Sea Convention

In November 1994, the United Nations Convention on the Law of the Sea came into force. Although New Zealand signed the Convention on 10 December 1982, New Zealand had not yet ratified it at year's end.

Legislation necessary for New Zealand to ratify the Convention was being drafted during 1994, and it was expected that New Zealand would be in a position to ratify it toward the end of 1995.

(c) Sustainable Development of Small Island States

New Zealand also played a significant role in preparation for the Global Conference on the Sustainable Development of Small Island States (GCS-DSIDS), which was held in Barbados from 25 April to 6 May 1994. New Zealand made a financial contribution to the Conference that was used to assist Pacific island representatives attend meetings, to co-fund with Australia a second to the UN Secretariat to undertake preparatory work, and to contribute to the UN Trust Fund for GCSDSIDS. The major accomplishment of the Conference was agreement on a Program of Action for the sustainable development of SIDS. The program is a small Agenda 21 for islands, comprising 15 chapters and providing a policy blueprint specifying measures to be taken at national, subregional, regional, and international levels. (*See* (➔) Report of the Global Conference.)

(d) Coastal Zone Management

New Zealand has a very extensive coastline compared to its overall geographic area, and thus considers coastal zone management matters very seriously. The need to protect coastal zones received attention at the Global Conference on the Sustainable Development of Small Island States in 1994. The South Pacific Regional Environment Programme (SPREP) applied considerable resources to coastal zone management, including the convening of regional meetings and the organization of a number of country projects.

New Zealand's foreign policy regarding coastal zones focused particularly on the problems faced by the small island states of the Pacific. New Zealand assisted the SPREP in its work on coastal zone protection, and provided $100,000 for a SPREP conference aimed at developing regional capacity. New Zealand also supported a number of coastal zone country projects.

Within New Zealand, the Minister of Conservation is responsible under the Resource Management Act 1991 (RMA) for the coastal environment. In accordance with the RMA, the Minister of Conservation prepared a New Zealand Coastal Policy Statement, which was completed in May 1994. The New Zealand Coastal Policy Statement provides for:

- the preservation of the natural character of the coastal environment;
- the protection of the characteristics of the coastal environment of special value to tangata whenua;
- activities involving the subdivision, use, or development of areas of the coastal environment;

- Crown interests in Crown land in the coastal environment;
- the matters to be included in regional coastal plans in order to preserve the natural character of the coastal environment;
- the implementation of New Zealand's international obligations affecting the coastal environment; and
- the procedures and methods to be used to review these policies and to monitor their effectiveness.

Also in 1994, the Department of Conservation issued a Guideline of New Zealand's International Obligations Affecting the Coastal Environment.

(e) Marine Pollution

During 1993–1994, considerable amendments were made to the Convention on the Prevention of Marine Pollution by Dumping of Wastes and Other Matter (the London Convention), which New ratified on 30 April 1975. New Zealand was closely involved in the amendment process and was instrumental in obtaining the bans on the dumping of radioactive and industrial wastes at sea and on the incineration of wastes at sea.

New Zealand has not yet signed or ratified the International Convention for the Prevention of Pollution from Ships (1973) and its associated Protocol (1978), although the Transport Law Reform Act 1994 seeks to provide the legislative framework that will enable the government to ratify the Convention very soon.

(8) Wastes and Toxic Substances

(a) The Basel Convention

At the Second Meeting of the Basel Convention, held in March 1994, in Geneva, the parties adopted a resolution that totally banned all transboundary movements of hazardous wastes, including those intended for recycling from OECD to non-OECD countries. This ban is to come fully into force on 31 December 1997. New Zealand has signed, but not yet ratified the Basel Convention.

The government is being cautious about ratifying the Convention because of the obligations involved and the domestic measures that must be put in place to meet those obligations. Nevertheless, the government is actively considering ratification and introduced the Hazardous Substances and New Organisms Bill (HSNO) in late 1994 to provide for ratification.

The aim of the HSNO legislation is to provide a comprehensive and consistent approach to the management of all hazardous substances and new organisms in New Zealand, which at present are regulated by a variety of different Acts. The HSNO establishes a new statutory body, the Environmental Risk Management Authority, which will have responsibilities to assess and develop controls for the importation, manufacture, development, and release within New Zealand of hazardous substances and new organisms. Controls under the HSNO will principally take the form of performance standards prescribed in regulations. Some economic instruments, including transferable permits and environmental user charges, may also be used to control the harmful effects from hazardous substances.

(b) Exports of Polychlorinated biphenyls (PCBs)

Polychlorinated biphenyls were used in New Zealand as dielectrics in transformers and capacitors until concern arose in the 1960s that they were accumulating in the environment. Although PCBs were removed from use and stored, there is no facility in New Zealand that can safely dispose of them. After considering various options, the government decided that the best option for environmentally sound disposal was to send the PCBs to a high temperature incineration facility in France. As neither France nor New Zealand are parties to the Basel Convention, a bilateral arrangement was concluded in February 1994 and is valid for one year.

(c) The South Pacific Hazardous Wastes Convention

Negotiations during 1994 have aimed at producing a regional convention dealing with hazardous wastes in time for the 1995 meeting of the South Pacific Forum at Port Moresby in Papua New Guinea. The aims of the proposed convention are to ban the import of hazardous and radioactive waste generated outside the region into Forum island countries and to control the movement of these types of wastes within the region. New Zealand supports this regional proposal and has been actively participating in its formulation.

(d) Radioactive Wastes

New Zealand strongly believes in the importance of global consensus on the handling and disposal of nuclear waste, and that legally binding rules are essential. New Zealand has therefore supported the concept of an International Convention on Nuclear Wastes and worked within the International Atomic Energy Agency structure to develop such a convention.

(9) Antarctica

New Zealand signed the Protocol on Environmental Protection to the Antarctic Treaty (the Madrid Protocol) in October 1991. Parliament passed legislation to enable New Zealand to ratify the Protocol in November 1994, with ratification expected to take place early in 1995. New Zealand strongly supports the aims of the Protocol and has already obtained an environmental audit on its Antarctic Program.

(10) Nuclear Weapons—World Court Submission

The New Zealand government filed a submission with the International Court of Justice, which has been asked to rule on the question of whether the use of nuclear weapons is illegal. A number of countries are challenging the jurisdiction of the Court and others are asking the court to decline to hear the matter. The New Zealand submission at this stage simply expresses New Zealand's active support of the disarmament process, especially as it relates to nuclear weapons, and stresses the importance that any opinion of the Court should not undermine current disarmament efforts. The submission preserves the option of making more extensive submissions should the Court in fact decide to take the case.

Irrespective of what the Court decides to do, the New Zealand government has stated that it will continue to support multilateral negotiations for a Comprehensive Test Ban Treaty and the review of the Non-Proliferation Treaty. New Zealand is concerned that a finding by the Court that the use of nuclear weapons is legal in certain circumstances, such as self defence, will be damaging to the multilateral disarmament process.

Grant Hewison

23. AUSTRALIA

(1) Antarctic: Madrid Protocol

On 6 April, Australia ratified the 1991 Protocol to the Antarctic Treaty (also known as the Madrid Protocol). Ratification was the culmination for Australia of an Australia-France joint diplomatic initiative that led to acceptance of this comprehensive regime for the protection of the world's largest wilderness area. Over the preceding two years, Australia amended the Antarctic Treaty (Environment Protection) Act and regulations that enabled Australia to be the eighth party to ratify the Protocol.

In March, the Australian Government made regulations under the Antarctic Treaty (Environment Protection) (Waste Management) Regulations in order to address its obligations under the Madrid Protocol. The regulations provide for the planning and conduct of waste minimization and management; the storage, removal, and disposal of waste; and the cleaning up of waste disposal sites and abandoned work sites.

(2) Marine Environment

(a) Law of the Sea Convention

On 5 October, Australia ratified the UN Convention on the Law of the Sea (UNCLOS). The Convention entered into force on 16 November. Australia had been active in the UN Secretary-General's informal consultations on Part XI (deep sea bed mining), which will assist in the process of ratification of the Convention by the major industrialized countries.

Australian ratification was preceded by passage of the Maritime Legislation (Amendment) Act 1994 (see below). This Act completed the process of bringing Australia's maritime zones into line with those to which Australia is entitled under international law, as reflected in UNCLOS. The Act contains provisions declaring sovereign rights and jurisdiction in an exclusive economic zone (EEZ) and rights of control in a contiguous zone. It incorporates into the Seas and Submerged Lands Act 1973 a new definition of the continental shelf, based on that in the UNCLOS. The Act mirrors the Convention's obligations to ensure, through proper conservation and management, that the living resources in the EEZ are protected and preserved.

(b) Exclusive Economic Zone

In August, Australia declared an EEZ around the Australian mainland and Australia's external territories, including the Australian Antarctic Territory, by virtue of the Maritime Legislation Amendment Act 1994, amending the Seas and Submerged Lands Act 1973, the Fisheries Management Act 1991, and the Whale Protection Act 1980. The effect of the Act around the Australian mainland is minimal, because of the control that Australia already exercises within the 200 nautical mile Australian Fishing Zone established in 1979 under the former Fisheries Act 1952.

The Maritime Legislation (Amendment) Act 1994 further provides that the Whale Protection Act 1980, which had previously applied within the Australian Fishing Zone, now also applies within the EEZ, including the EEZ off the Australian Antarctic Territory. The Whale Protection Act applies in relation to all, including foreign, persons, aircraft, and vessels. However, the Act notes that it has effect subject to Australia's obligations under international law, including obligations under any agreements between Australia and another country or countries. The actual effect of the extension of the Australian Fishing Zone to the EEZ off the Australian Antarctic Territory is limited to the control of the activities of Australian nationals and Australian vessels.

(3) Whales: Southern Ocean Whale Sanctuary

Australia played a key role in the (➔) International Whaling Commission's decision of 26 May to establish a circumpolar sanctuary for whales in the Southern Ocean south of latitude 40 degrees south. The sanctuary will cover almost all the migration routes of most of the great whales in Australia's region. It is contiguous with the existing Indian Ocean sanctuary. The combination of the two sanctuaries covers a vast area.

(4) Fisheries

During 1994, Australia, together with members of the South Pacific Forum Fisheries Agency, took an active role as a well-organized regional bloc in the UN Conference on Straddling Fish Stocks and Highly Migratory Fish Stocks. In these negotiations Australia argued for an effective regime to address the problems of over-exploitation of straddling fish stocks and highly migratory species and unregulated high seas fishing. In particular, Australia supported improved standards of flag-state responsibility; development of precautionary approaches to fisheries conservation and management; improved mechanisms for effective monitoring, control, and surveillance; and compulsory and binding dispute settlement.

(5) Hazardous Wastes

(a) Basel Convention on Transboundary Movements of Hazardous Wastes and Their Disposal

The second Conference of Parties of the Basel Convention, held in Geneva, 21-25 March decided to prohibit immediately the export of hazardous wastes for final disposal from Organization for Economic Cooperation and Development (OECD) states to non-OECD states and to phase out by the end of 1997 all exports of hazardous wastes destined for recycling or recovery operations from OECD to non-OECD states. (*See* (➔) Report of the Second Meeting of the Parities.) Australia and some other industrialized parties had originally argued against the decision, mainly because of its failure to include a reference to exports for recovery operations conducted in a fully environmentally sound manner and because of the artificial nature of the categorization of countries as "OECD" and "non-OECD." At the conference, the decision was strongly supported by the G-77, including a number of Australia's key non-OECD trading partners in the region. At the 11th hour, Australia joined the consensus.

While Australia does not allow exports of hazardous wastes for disposal, the Government indicated that it would not take a decision on the second part of the decision (the phase out of hazardous recyclables) until consultations took place with Australia's regional trading partners. These consultations began with bilateral talks in October in Beijing, Delhi, Manila, Seoul, and Tokyo.

The Australian Government decided in 1994 to amend the Hazardous Wastes (Import and Export) Act 1989 to bring it into conformity with Australia's obligations under the Basel Convention. The present Act fails to properly regulate hazardous wastes destined for recycling or recovery operations. Extensive consultations with industry, non-governmental organizations (NGOs), and the Australian States and Territories were conducted on the shape of the amendments through 1994. The new amendments are likely to involve the creation of an independent Technical Group comprising scientific and other experts, which will provide advice to the Environment Minister as to which materials are considered to constitute hazardous wastes within the ambit of the Basel Convention. To provide additional certainty to traders in this field, a list of materials considered to constitute hazardous wastes will be included in a schedule to the Act.

(b) Waigani Convention

Australia took an active part in the negotiations of the South Pacific Hazardous Wastes Convention (Waigani Convention), conducted under the auspices of the South Pacific Forum in Suva, Fiji, in March and November. The aim is to have this Convention ready for adoption at the September 1995 meeting of the South Pacific Forum to be held in Port Moresby, Papua New Guinea.

Australia supported inclusion in the Convention of an obligation that would prohibit the export of hazardous wastes (including recyclables) to small island developing states. It was argued that this formulation was more appropriate than an OECD/non-OECD ban, given the existence of OECD countries or territories in the region (*e.g.*, American Samoa and French Polynesia). Australia also made a proposal to simplify the notification requirements under the Convention, which may pose particular difficulties for island countries with limited resources.

(6) Australia's Biodiversity Strategy

A National Strategy for the conservation of Australia's biological diversity was completed in 1994 after several years of negotiation and consultation.

(7) (➔) Desertification Convention

In October, Australia signed the Desertification Convention. Australia is one of the few industrialized countries that face serious droughts and desertification. The Convention is seen, among other things, as an opportunity to share and sell Australian expertise and technology in the field of land degradation.

A key provision of the Convention, the elaboration of national action programs by developing countries to combat desertification, was based largely on an Australian proposal. While the preparation of national action programs to combat desertification is not mandatory under the Convention, the National Farmers Federation of Australia has lobbied the government to declare that no such action program will be prepared, and ratification of the Convention remains controversial.

(8) South Pacific Forum

In July, in Brisbane, Australia hosted the meeting of the 22 heads of state of the South Pacific Forum. Australia proposed the theme of "Managing our Natural Resources" for the meeting. The Forum Communiqué included an agreement to begin negotiating a Code of Conduct for Logging of Indigenous Forests in Selected South Pacific Countries.

(9) Development Assistance

The component of Australia's development assistance program devoted to funding environment activities increased to A$120 million for 1994 as part of a total budget of A$1,486 million for 1994–95. This includes an additional A$5.7 million as Australia's contribution to the Global Environment Facility (GEF).

(10) Treaty Debate

Throughout 1994, the federal Opposition Liberal and National Party attacked the Labor Government for allegedly eroding Australia's sovereignty by signing on to environment conventions that, it was claimed, were imposed on Australia in an "undemocratic" fashion. These attacks were most vociferous in relation to the Desertification and Climate Change Conventions, the Basel Conference ban, and action under the World Heritage Properties Conservation Act 1983 to protect the environmental values of Hinchinbrook Island in the State of Queensland (part of a World Heritage listing).

The Opposition advocated a greater role for the Parliament in relation to treaty-making and greater weight being given to Australia's trade interests in the context of environment conventions. The Government responded to these claims by pointing out that most major treaty obligations would require implementing legislation that, depending on the subject matter, may be passed by the Commonwealth, States, or Territories (or all). Australia's practice was not to become a party to a treaty until the (democratically elected) Parliament enacted such legislation. The Government also undertook to table treaties that were signed but not ratified in the Senate for discussion, rather than approval. The Government also reiterated its commitment to consult with industry and environment NGOs as part of the process of forming Australian Government negotiating positions on proposed conventions.

In October, the Government published a comprehensive information kit entitled "Australia and International Treaty Making." This kit sets out, among other things, the process by which the government enters into treaties after consulting with the governments of the States and Territories, as well as with industry and other interest groups.

(11) Sustainability Conference

Late in 1994, the Australian federal Department of the Environment held a major conference on the theme of ecologically sustainable development, entitled "Sustainability: Principles to Practice." The Conference accepted the principle that environmental costs should be internalized (in effect a more sophisticated version of the polluter pays principle.) The Conference and its background documents constitute further steps to the realization of the policy goals of the Australian Government relating to the achievement of sustainability across all economic sectors.

Ben Boer
Peter Lawrence

XI. REPORTS FROM INTERNATIONAL COURTS AND TRIBUNALS

INTERNATIONAL COURT OF JUSTICE (ICJ)/INTERNATIONAL TRIBUNALS

(1) Introduction

Environmental issues remain squarely on the agenda of the ICJ. The parties to the case concerning the Gabcikovo/Nagymaros Dispute exchanged two sets of pleadings, 35 states submitted written observations on the advisory opinion request by the World Health Organization (WHO), and the UN General Assembly requested an advisory opinion on the legality of the threat or use of nuclear weapons, in terms similar but not identical to the WHO's 1993 request. The European Court of Justice decided a number of cases relating directly to the environment.

(2) International Court of Justice (ICJ)

(a) Case Concerning Gabcikovo/Nagymaros Dispute

After submission of Memorials and Countermemorials by Hungary and Slovakia, the ICJ ordered each state to submit Replies to the Counter-Memorials June 1995.

(b) Request by the World Health Organization for an Advisory Opinion on the Legality of the Use of Nuclear Weapons

In respect to the WHO's request for an advisory opinion on the question "[i]n view of the health and environmental effects, would the use of nuclear weapons by a State in war or other armed conflict be a breach of its obligations under international law including the WHO's Constitution," and following the request of several states, the Court extended the date for the submission of the written statements to 20 September 1994. The Court also fixed 20 June 1995 as the date by which states and organizations that presented written statements must submit written comments on the other written statements. By 20 September, 34 states had filed written statements. The WHO did not file a written statement, which was the first time an international organisation making a request for an advisory opinion failed to submit observations.

(c) Request by the UN General Assembly for an Advisory Opinion on the Legality of the use or threat of use of nuclear weapons

On 15 December, the UN General Assembly adopted Resolution 49/75K

("Request for an Advisory Opinion from the International Court of Justice on the Legality of the Threat or Use of Nuclear Weapons"), which asked the Court "urgently to render its advisory opinion on the following question: Is the threat or use of nuclear weapons in any circumstances permitted under international law?" The resolution, submitted to the Court on 19 December, was adopted by 78 states voting in favor, 43 against, 38 abstaining, and 25 not voting. By year's end the Court had not decided how to proceed with the request, including whether, and if so how, to link it to the proceedings relating to the WHO request in 1993.

(d) Chamber for Environmental Matters

The ICJ extended until 6 February 1995 the mandate of the members of the Chamber for Environmental Matters, established in 1993. With Judge Carl-August Fleischhauer replacing former judge Jens Evensen, the Chamber is now composed of Mohammed Bedjaoui (President), Stephen M. Schewebel (Vice-President), Mohamed Shahabuddeen, Christopher G. Weeramantry, Raymond Ranjeva, Géza Herczegh, and Carl-August Fleischhauer. None of the cases currently before the Court which directly or indirectly raise environmental issues have been submitted to the Chamber.

(3) European Court of Justice (ECJ)

The ECJ handed down a number of judgments with important implications for environmental law.

(a) The Wild Birds Directive

On 19 January, in Case C-435/92, *Association pour la Protection des Animaux Sauvages and Others v. Préfet de Maine-et-Loire and Préfet de la Loire-Atlantique*, the Court considered the proper interpretation of Art. 7(4) of Council Directive 79/409/EEC of 2 April 1979 on the conservation of wild birds. Various environmental protection associations brought the case against the Prefects of Maine-et-Loire and Loire-Atlantique for their decision to fix dates for hunting in the 1992–1993 season. Plaintiffs argued that the decisions did not comply with the Directive's provisions for the protection of migratory birds returning to their rearing grounds.

The Court held, *inter alia*, that the closing dates for the hunting season must be based on a system that ensures complete protection during the period of pre-mating migration, citing Case C-157/89, *Commission v. Italy* [1991] ECR I-57. Consequently, any method that allowed some birds to escape such protection did not comply with Art. 7(4). The court held that in order to implement the objectives of Art. 7(4), the member state must fix the same closing date for all species concerned, based on that fixed for the species that migrates the earliest. Staggered closing dates for the hunting season according to species were found to be unacceptable unless evidence showed that such staggering did not impede the complete protection of the species of birds likely to be affected. The Court further held that the Directive permitted the fixing of closing dates varying between different parts of a member state's territory, provided that the complete protection of the species was guaranteed.

(b) The "Direct Effect" of the Framework Waste Directive

On 23 February, the ECJ decided Case C-236/92, *Comitato di Coordinamento per la Difesa della Cava and Others v. Regione Lombardia and Others*, concerning the legality of decisions by authorities in the Italian region of Lombardy to site a solid urban waste tip. Plaintiffs claimed that the decisions undermined their rights to environmental protection. In 1992, the regional administrative court of Lombardy asked to the ECJ for a preliminary ruling on five questions on the interpretation of a Council Directive on waste. The ECJ decided it needed only address the question whether "Community environmental law, in particular Art. 4 of Council Directive 75/442/EEC of 15 July 1975 on waste, grant[ed] to individuals 'subjective rights' which the national court is required to protect?" Article 4 provides: Member States shall take the necessary measures to ensure that waste is disposed of without endangering human health and without harming the environment, and in particular

- without risk to water, air, soil, and plants and animals,
- without causing a nuisance through noise or odors,
- without adversely affecting the countryside or places of special interest.

The ECJ held that Art. 4 did not confer right on individuals rights that a national court must safeguard. According to the Court, the provisions of Art. 4 are neither unconditional nor sufficiently precise to be capable of conferring rights on which individuals might rely against the state. (A provision is unconditional where it is not subject to the taking of any measure either by the Community institutions or by member states. A provision is sufficiently precise where the obligations that it imposes are set out in unequivocal terms.) The ECJ found that Art. 4 merely indicated a programme to be followed by member states regarding the treatment of waste and set out the objectives that member states must observe in the performance of the more specific obligations imposed on them by Arts. 5-11 of the Directive on planning, supervision, and monitoring of waste disposal operations.

(c) National Environmental Standards v. Free Movement of Goods

The Case C-41/93, *France v. Commission of the European Communities* presented the ECJ with the first opportunity to consider the compatibility of national measures with Art. 100a(4) of the EEC Treaty, which allows member states, on grounds of "major needs" to apply stricter national standards than those agreed to at the Community level. In 1989, the Federal Republic of Germany had adopted a regulation restricting the use of pentachlorophenol (PCP) as a pesticide and preservative. The German legislation was more restrictive than Community legislation subsequently adopted on the basis of Art. 100a, namely, Council Directive 91/173/EEC amending for the ninth time Directive 76/769/EEC on the approximations of the laws, regulations, and administrative provisions of the member states relating to restrictions on the marketing and use of certain dangerous substances and preparations, including PCP. In accordance with Art. 2 of Directive 91/173, which requires member states to communicate to the Commission the text of the main provisions of national law that they adopt in the field covered by the Directive, Germany notified the Commission of its decision, based on Art. 100a(4), to continue to apply its more restrictive national provisions concerning the use of PCP as a pesticide and preservative instead of Directive 91/173. Over the opposition of France, Italy, and Greece, which were concerned about the impact the ban would have on German imports of leather goods, the Commission, in 1992, adopted a decision approving the more stringent German restrictions. France challenged this decision by applying for judicial review under Art. 173 of the EEC Treaty, claiming that the decision violated Art. 100a(4) of the Treaty because it had not been demonstrated that the German measures restricting the use of PCP were justified on the grounds of major needs or relating to the protection of the environment or working environment, and because the Commission had violated Art. 190 of the Treaty by not proving that the conditions in Art. 100a(4) for confirmation had been fulfilled.

On 17 May 1994, the Court annulled the Commission's decision on the second, procedural ground, thereby avoiding the substantive issue. The Court held that by confining itself to describing in general terms the content and aim of the German rules and to stating that these rules were compatible with Art. 100a(4) without explaining the reasons of fact and law, the contested decision did not satisfy the obligation to state reasons as required by Art. 190 of the Treaty.

(d) The Legal Basis for the Regulation on Shipments of Waste

On 28 June, the ECJ decided Case C-187/93, *European Parliament v. Council of the European Union*, an application brought by the European Parliament to annul Council Regulation (EEC) No. 259/93 of 1 February 1993, on the supervision and control of shipments of waste within, into, and out of the European Community ("the Regulation"). The Commission had originally proposed that the Regulation be based on Arts. 100a and 113, which would have given the Parliament a greater involvement in the legislative process. In support of its application, the Parliament asserted that the aim and purposes of the Regulation were to regulate movements of waste within the Community and foreign trade in waste between the Community and third countries, and that, therefore, the Regulation should be based on Arts. 100a and 113 of the EEC Treaty. The Council, however, adopted the Regulation under Art. 130s, which limits the Parliament's right to consultation.

The Court held the action admissible insofar as it contested the fact that the Regulation was based on Art. 130s rather than Art. 100a, but inadmissible to the extent it was based on Art. 113, citing Case C-316/91, *Parliament v. Council* [1994] ECR I-625, which held that an action for annulment by the Parliament was admissible provided it sought only to safeguard the Parliament's prerogatives and was founded exclusively on submissions alleging their infringement. The Court found that Art. 113 did not provide for the Parliament to be involved in any way in the drawing up of the acts envisaged by that Article, so that its exclusion from the legal basis of the Regulation was not such that it would prejudice its prerogatives.

As to the substance of the case, the Court relied on Case C-155/91, *Commission v. Council* [1993] ECR I-939, which found that the legal basis for an act must be determined with regard to its own aim and content. The aim of the Regulation is to establish a supervision and control system for shipment of wastes between member states, reflecting the need to preserve, protect, and improve the quality of the environment while protecting human health and the environment. The Regulation's conditions governing shipments of waste between member states and the procedure to be followed for their authorization had all been adopted with a view toward ensuring the protection of the environment through the principles of proximity, priority for recovery, and self-sufficiency. Consequently, the Court concluded that the Regulation fell within the framework of the environmental policy pursued by the Community and could not be regarded as seeking to implement the free movement of waste within the Community.

(e) Obligations under the Environmental Impact Assessment (EIA) Directive

On 9 August, in Case C-396/92, *Bund Naturschutz in Bayern e.V., Richard Stahnsdorf and Others v. Freistaat Bayern*, the ECJ reviewed Council Directive 85/337/EEC of 27 June 1985 on the assessment of the effects of certain public and private projects on the environment. The case arose from proceedings before the Bavarian Higher Administrative Court against the State of Bavaria, and concerned the conformity with the requirements laid down in the Directive of the German consent procedure for construction plans for a new federal highway in Bavaria. The German Law implementing the Directive came into force on 1 August 1990. Under its transitional provision, an EIA was to be carried out for projects that had not been publicly notified before the Law came into force. In the national proceedings, the developer (the Bavarian Highways Department) had lodged permit applications after the deadline for transposition of the Directive—3 July 1988—but before the implementing law entered into force. The Government of Lower Bavaria had approved the projects without an EIA. The plaintiffs thereupon asserted a procedural deficiency, claiming that the Directive did not permit national transitional rules and that approval of the projects had been given after the date by which the Directive was to be implemented.

The ECJ held that the Directive did not permit a member state, by a transitional provision, to exempt projects and waive its obligations to carry out an EIA, where the consent procedure was initiated before the entry into force of the national law but after the deadline for transposition.

(f) Actions brought by the Commission for Member States' Failure to Implement Properly

The Court also considered a number of applications brought by the Commission for a declaration that a member state had failed to transpose a Directive into national law.

In Case C-291/93, *Commission of the European Communities v. Italian Republic*, decided on 9 March 1994, the Court declared that the Italian Republic had failed to fulfil its obligations under the Treaty by failing to adopt within the prescribed period the measures necessary to comply both with Council Directive 78/659/EEC of 18 July 1978 on the quality of fresh waters needing protection or improvement in order to support fish life, and with the Court's judgment of 12 July 1978 in Case 322/86 *Commission v. Italy* [1988] ECR 3995. The Commission found Italy's adopted legislation insufficient to give full effect to the Court's judgment and submitted that Italy had still not complied with its obligation to designate certain waters or to establish programmes in order to reduce water pollution. Italy did not deny its failure to fulfil its obligations.

In Case C-313/93 *Commission of the European Communities v. Grand Duchy of Luxembourg*, decided on 13 April, the Court declared that Luxembourg had failed to fulfil its obligations under the Treaty by failing to comply with Council Directive 85/337/EEC of 27 June 1985 on the assessment of the effects of certain public and private projects on the environment. In Case C-260/93 *Commission for the European Communities v. Kingdom of Belgium*, judgment of 3 May 1994, the Commission brought an action against Belgium for failing to transpose Council Directive 86/278/EEC of 12 June 1986 on the protection of the environment, and in particular of the soil, when sewage sludge is used in agriculture at the federal level and in the Walloon Region. Belgium did not dispute the complaint and indicated that the procedure for implementing the directive was in progress. On 5 October, the Court decided Case C-255/93 *Commission of the European Communities v. French Republic*, holding that France failed to draw up and communicate within the prescribed period the programmes laid down by Art. 3 of Council Directive 85/399/EEC to reduce the tonnage and/or volume of beverage containers to be disposed of in household waste. The French authorities maintained that six voluntary agreements concluded between the public authorities and the businesses concerned amounted to the reduction programmes required by the Directive. The Court, however, held that only one of the agreements complied with the requirement of setting out quantitative objectives and that none of the agreements drew up time-tables for completion of the programmes, nor did they guarantee that they would be regularly revised and updated every four years.

(4) GATT Dispute Settlement Panels

Reports adopted by two GATT Dispute Settlement Panels have important implications for environmental protection: a (➔) Panel Report on United States Restrictions on Imports of Tuna (Tuna II), and a Panel Report on Corporate Average Fuel Economy Standards. (*See* Parts IX.1 and XIII.1. of the *Yearbook*.)

Philippe Sands
Ruth Khalastchi

XII. REPORTS FROM ORGANIZATIONS

1. INTERNATIONAL ORGANIZATIONS AND BODIES

A. ASIAN-AFRICAN LEGAL CONSULTATIVE COMMITTEE (AALCC)

During 1994, the Asian-African Legal Consultative Committee's focus continued to be on follow-up matters related to the decisions taken at the 1992 United Nations Conference on Environment and Development (UNCED). For the AALCC's Tokyo session, held in January 1994, the Secretariat prepared studies reviewing the progress made at the first session of the Commission on Sustainable Development and in respect of the Convention on Biological Diversity and the Framework Convention on Climate Change. A detailed report on the outcome of the second session of the Intergovernmental Negotiating Committee for the Elaboration of an International (➔) Convention to Combat Desertification in those countries Experiencing Serious Drought and/or Desertification, particularly in Africa, was also set out in the Secretariat study. The Secretariat worked in close cooperation with the Organisation of African Unity and prepared a draft text of a Convention on Combatting Desertification and Mitigation of Drought. At the Tokyo session, it was decided that the Secretariat should continue to monitor the developments in these areas and submit a progress report for the consideration of member governments at the AALCC's next session, scheduled to be held in Doha in April 1995.

The Government of the State of Qatar and the AALCC jointly organized, in cooperation with the United Nations, an international conference on legal issues arising under the United Nations Decade of International Law, which was held in Doha 22–25 March 1994. Among the items discussed in the conference were environmental law, law of the sea, and the follow-up to UNCED.

The AALCC was represented at the second annual session of the United Nations Commission on Sustainable Development, held in New York 16-27 May 1994, and the 10th session of the Intergovernmental Negotiating Committee for Framework Convention on Climate Change, held in Geneva in August 1994.

The United Nations General Assembly considered an item entitled "Co-operation between the United Nations and the Asian-African Legal Consultative Committee" at its 49th session. Several delegations recognized the role of the AALCC in promoting ratification of the environmental conventions. Resolution A/49/8, which the General Assembly adopted on 25

October 1994, noted the AALCC's involvement in field of environment and sustainable development with appreciation.

Tang Chengyuan

B. COUNCIL OF EUROPE

In 1994, Andorra became the 33d nation to join the Council of Europe (CE). The CE's recent expansion is likely to continue, given that applications for full membership have been received from Albania (1992), Belarus (1993), Croatia (1992), Latvia (1991), the Former Yugoslav Republic of Macedonia (1992), Moldova (1993), the Russian Federation (1992), and Ukraine (1992). These eight Central and Eastern European countries currently have special guest status with the CE, as does Bosnia-Herzegovina. Special guest status entitles countries to send parliamentary delegations to meetings of the CE Parliamentary Assembly. Requests for special guest status from Armenia (1991), Azerbaijan (1992), and Georgia (1993) were pending at year's end.

(1) Convention on Civil Liability for Damage Resulting from Activities Dangerous to the Environment (Lugano Convention)

In 1994, the CE Secretariat focused its Lugano Convention-related efforts on the task of obtaining a sufficient number of signatures and ratification to make the Convention a significant legal instrument. Whereas eight countries—Cyprus, Finland, Greece, Iceland, Italy, Liechtenstein, Luxembourg, and the Netherlands—signed the Lugano Convention in 1993, no additional signatures were received in 1994. However, in the autumn of 1994, Austria's Parliament adopted a resolution asking the government to prepare for ratification of the Convention, and the Government accepted. The Convention requires only three ratifications, including two from Council of Europe countries, before it comes into force.

(2) Draft Convention on the Protection of the Environment Through Criminal Law

In 1994, the Committee of Experts on the Protection of the Environment through Criminal Law (PC-EN) actively worked on a draft text for a convention on environmental crimes. At the end of the year, the PC-EN's discussions concerning the draft text were still at a formative stage, and the text remained restricted.

The draft text includes a chapter defining types of offenses against the environment that may be necessary to establish as criminal offenses under domestic law. These include "intentional offenses," *inter alia*, the discharge, emission, or introduction of a quantity of substances or radiation into the environment "which causes a serious damage to persons or which creates a danger of such damage." An infringement of a law, administrative regulation, or decision by a competent authority that "causes serious damage or deterioration to a component of the protected environment, or which is likely to cause such damage to persons," may also be considered a criminal offense. The draft text thus recognizes the difference between a real and present threat of damage and the likelihood that damage might be caused. By allowing for the possibility of abstract endangerment of persons to be subject to criminal penalty, it appears that the PC-EN intends to afford a higher level of protection for human beings. The draft chapter on offenses also recognizes criminal sanctions for gross negligence and negligence.

Among sanctions for environmental offenses, the draft text acknowledges such measures as imprisonment or other forms of deprivation of liberty, pecuniary sanctions, reinstatement of the environment, and confiscation. Early proposals to make some sanctions obligatory were not adopted. Instead, it was decided to make such measures optional, in recognition of the fact that in some jurisdictions, these sanctions are either considered civil law remedies or do not exist at all.

The draft text recognizes the priority of the territorial principle. It states that a party is to have jurisdiction over an offense committed in its territory, on board a vessel or aircraft flying its flag, or by one of its national "if the offence is punishable where it was committed."

The draft text includes an article on corporate liability that expressly provides for parties to adopt measures that impose criminal or administrative sanctions "on legal persons on whose account an offense covered [by the draft Convention] has been committed by its organs . . . or other representatives."

The chapter on international cooperation is consistent with earlier regional conventions on criminal matters in the inclusion of articles on the obligation of parties to afford each other mutual legal assistance in prosecuting offenses under the convention, on direct communication between judicial authorities, and on extradition.

The draft convention was not expected to be circulated publicly for wider consultation outside of the CE framework before summer 1995.

(3) Standing Committee on the Convention on the Conservation of Wildlife and Natural Habitats (Bern Convention)

In 1994, Moldova and Monaco acceded to the Bern Convention, bringing the total number of parties to 31. Slovakia and Lithuania both signed the Convention in 1994, but had not yet completed the process of accession by year's end.

The Standing Committee, which monitors application of the Bern Convention, did not meet in 1994 because of a conflict in international meeting dates. From a legal point of view, the most significant activity in 1994 was an inter-governmental symposium in Monaco from 26-28 September 1994. The symposium considered the future role of the Bern

Convention with regard to the UN Convention on Biological Diversity and the European Union's Directive 92/43/EEC on the conservation of natural habitats and of wild fauna and flora (Habitats Directive). At the conclusion of the symposium, participants issued the *Monaco Declaration on the Role of the Bern Convention in the Implementation of Worldwide International Instruments for the Protection of Biodiversity* (Monaco Declaration). The Monaco Declaration will be presented for possible adoption at the next meeting of the Standing Committee, scheduled for 22-24 March 1995.

According to the Monaco Declaration, the Bern Convention "constitutes a fundamental regional instrument for the application of provisions of the Convention on Biological Diversity." The Declaration acknowledges the fundamental role of the Council of Europe in implementing, at a regional level, the principles and obligations adopted at the global level for the protection of biodiversity. It recommends, *inter alia*, that the Standing Committee include in its activity program the measures appropriate for the Bern Convention deriving from the Convention on Biological Diversity.

The Monaco Declaration recommends that the Secretariat regularly review the national policies of the contracting parties to the Bern Convention for implementing the parts of both the Bern Convention and the Convention on Biological Diversity that are relevant to the conservation of biological diversity. It also recommends that the Secretariat continue to use its procedure for enforcing the Bern Convention (including general and special reports, and the case-file system).

The provisional procedure for enforcement of the Bern Convention proposed by the Secretariat in 1993 will most likely remain provisional because of concern over possible jurisdictional conflict with the European Union's powers of enforcing relevant European Union legislation such as the Habitats Directive.

At the end of 1994, the Secretariat was preparing to take further steps with regard to the Standing Committee's 1993 declaration that Greece had not fulfilled its obligations under the Convention. A CE delegation was to visit Greece in January 1995 to discuss the protection of *Caretta caretta* in Laganas Bay, Zakynthos, and to warn that other contracting parties are prepared to file a dispute against Greece on the basis of Art. 18(2). If other parties proceed against Greece in this manner, the Bern Convention's provision on settlement of disputes would be used for the first time. It would also bring the CE into conflict with the European Union, which is proceeding with its own enforcement action against Greece on the basis of the Habitats Directive.

(4) Committee of Ministers

The Committee for the Conservation and Management of the Environment and Natural Habitats (CPDE) leads the Committee of Ministers' work with regard to nature conservation. The CPDE has assumed significant responsibilities for implementing the Rio initiatives. It has also taken the lead with regard to nature conservation issues in preparation for the autumn 1995 meeting of European Environment Ministers in Sofia, Bulgaria. For example, in response to a request made at the 1993 Lucerne Conference, work was proceeding on an inventory of legal, regulatory, and other instruments and means designed to develop and effectively manage non-protected natural areas.

The CPDE also administers the European Diploma, an award recognizing specially protected sites of particular importance for the conservation of the European natural common heritage. In 1994, the CPDE awarded three European Diplomas for the first time to sites in Austria (1) and the Russian Federation (2). It renewed European Diplomas for sites in Germany (1), Greece (1), Spain (1) and the United Kingdom (2).

In 1994, the Committee of Ministers adopted two Recommendations related to environmental protection: Recommendation No. R(94)6 for the sustainable development and use of the countryside with a particular focus on the safeguarding of wildlife and landscapes (Recommendation on Landscapes); and Recommendation No. R(94)7 on a general policy for a sustainable and environment-friendly tourism development (Recommendation on Tourism). An appendix to the Recommendation on Landscapes sets forth important principles and measures for bringing about sustainable development of the countryside, including compulsory environmental impact assessments; spatial planning rules that take account of preconditions for ecological balance; use of a range of economic mechanisms; and ecological management on a contractual basis between farmers, landowners, governments, and/or voluntary organizations.

The Recommendation on Tourism also features an appendix that sets forth principles and recommends that national authorities implement those principles through a number of different measures, including controls over tourist demand and flow, and possible penal sanctions for activities harmful to the environment, including sufficient levels of compensation paid by developers to repair damage caused by development.

(5) Parliamentary Assembly

The Parliamentary Assembly is the CE's deliberative body, consisting of 236 members from the 33 national parliaments of its member states, as well as "special guest" delegations from Central and Eastern European countries. In 1994, the Parliamentary Assembly considered a number of environment-related reports. With regard to those reports, it adopted, *inter alia*, the following resolutions and recommendations: Resolution 1024 (1994) on European environmental policy (1992-93); Recommendation 1233 (1994) on European environmental policy (1992-93); Resolution 1021 (1994) on the preservation and development of the Danube basin; Resolution 1038 (1994) on a common European policy for the polar regions; Resolution 1045 (1994) on the energy-environment interface; and Recommendation 1249 (1994) on cooperation in the Mediterranean basin.

Particularly relevant from the point of view of environmental law was the *Report on the Application of Conventions Concerning the Environment* (ADOC7076/21 April 1994, Rapporteur: Mr. Hardy). The Parliamentary Assembly adopted Recommendation 1241 (1994) on the application of conventions concerning the environment, which called on the CE's Committee of Ministers to increase the budgetary and human resources allocated to the Standing Committee of the Bern Convention, in order to enable it to undertake its responsibilities with regard to the Rio Convention on Biological Diversity.

(6) Congress of Local and Regional Authorities

In 1994, following decisions reached at the October 1993 Vienna Summit of Heads of State and Government, the CE's Standing Conference of Local and Regional Authorities of Europe became the Congress of Local and Regional Authorities of Europe (CLRAE). In addition to this change in title, the CLRAE's political status was significantly reinforced. Though it is not yet on a par with the CE's Committee of Ministers and the Parliamentary Assembly, it is well on the way to becoming the third political leg of the CE. The CLRAE's purpose is to strengthen democratic structures at the local level.

At the reorganized CLRAE's first session, 31 May to 3 June 1994, it examined two reports on the environment in Central and Eastern Europe and in the Eastern Baltic Region and adopted a resolution and a recommendation concerning these reports. Henceforth, the CLRAE's environment-related work will be carried out in the form of special projects coordinated by *ad hoc* working groups. Its schedule of work for 1995 includes preparation of a report for the 1995 Plenary Session on Local Fiscal Incentives for Environmental Protection, organization of two colloquies on the theme of the European Nature Conservation Year, preparation of a manual on good practice on nature conservation by local authorities, and preparation of a European Landscape Charter, building on the Charter for the Mediterranean Landscape.

A colloquy at La Grande Motte focused on preparatory work toward a European Landscape Charter. The colloquy emphasized the need to reverse the trend of devitalization of the countryside, and instead to develop stronger regional economic autonomy, encouraged by more integration of economic, environmental, and cultural policies.

(7) Cooperation with Central and Eastern Europe: Model Act on Protection of the Environment

In 1994, within the framework of the CE's program of cooperation with the emerging democracies of Central and Eastern Europe, the CE issued a *Model Act on the Protection of the Environment* (Model Act). According to the Environment Division of the CE Secretariat, the governments of both the Russian Federation and Slovakia have taken the Model Act under serious consideration for possible adoption as framework environmental legislation.

A group of independent experts prepared the Model Act's 11 parts. Part I, "Definitions," defines such terms as "environment," "risk," "danger," "administrative procedure," and "wastes." Part II, "General Provisions," contains articles on the right to a stable environment, the precautionary principle, substitution, maintenance of biodiversity, and the polluter pays principle.

Part III, "The Organizational System of Environmental Protection," prescribes that every state's legal framework should provide for an organizational system that includes a policy and planning function, an executive and inspection function, a coordinating function, and an advisory function. Under the policy function, the Model Act provides for the government to produce a document describing the principal policy objectives to be achieved and the means for achieving those objectives. The executive and inspection function is described in terms of 18 responsibilities, including promoting amendments to environmental protection legislation, revocation of licenses and authorizations, and the undertaking of remedial action. Concerning the advisory function, the Model Act provides for a National Environmental Council to advise the government on environmental matters and to comment on relevant draft legislation, programs, policies, and proposed activities prepared by all ministries, government departments, and other public bodies.

Part IV provides, briefly, for "Distribution of Responsibilities Among Different Tiers of Government." Part V, "Financing of Environmental Protection," states that the cost of measures designed to protect the environment under the Act shall be borne by the budgets of the state, regional, and local authorities, as well as by those who create a risk, danger, or damage to the environment. Authorities may establish environmental funds financed by special taxes or charges, the proceeds from fines and penalties for violations of environmental laws, and regular payments from the general budget.

Part VI, "Right to Information and Public Participation in the Protection of the Environment," provides that everyone has the right to receive environmental information from public authorities. Conditions with respect to giving information include the right of persons who have provided information to authorities to the protection of their personal and trade secrets. A person whose request for information has been unreasonably refused may seek a judicial or administrative review of the decision.

Part VII, "Proceedings in Environmental Matters," requires the completion of a "participation procedure," based on an environmental impact assessment (EIA), before a public authority takes a decision that is likely to affect the environment and concerns a large number of persons. The participation procedure covers immobile, or stationary, facilities that are listed in the Annex to the Act or are likely to have a significant impact on the environment. The procedure is to afford an opportunity to be heard for those whose rights, freedom, or interests may be affected by a decision. Other parties to the proceedings are the applicant and his counterpart, the person to whom the administrative decision will be addressed, and "persons who according to national law have the right to claim a specific collective interest that is likely to be affected by the administrative act even though it is not addressed to them." If important and controversial issues are raised by the project, the authority is to publish a draft decision and give objectors 14 days in which to comment in writing on that draft decision.

Part VIII, "Regulatory Devices," provides that limit values and guide values are to be set by regulation for concentrations of substances in air, water, and soil, and for noise and radioactivity levels. Insofar as these limit values and guide values are not designed to protect against health risks, they can be set differently according to a particular area's need. Requirements for precautions against risks to health or the environment are to be proportionate to the existing or possible risk, and based on best available technology not entailing disproportionate costs.

The production, marketing, transport, storage, use, and disposal of certain hazardous substances or certain hazardous preparations can be prohibited or restricted by regulation. Special regulations are to cover the transport, import, and export of hazardous substances and wastes. In addition, territories of the state can be classified, in order to establish different degrees of restrictions over human activities, as set forth in a special law on protected areas.

Individual activities potentially harmful to health and the environment may also be controlled through authorization, notification, prohibition, or limitation. Activities subject to authorization include immobile facilities subject to the EIA requirement, mobile facilities such as motor vehicles and railway engines, and "particularly hazardous" substances or preparations, including plant protection products and other biocides, and fuels.

Part VIII requires charges to be set on the emissions and residual substances of immobile facilities subject to authorization, the rate of such charges to be based on the kind and extent of the adverse effect on the environment. Charges can be offset against expenses for construction of a facility or equipment that is expected to substantially reduce emissions. The Model Act specifies conditions under which environmental subsidies may be granted, and provides for the establishment of an environmental audit scheme to promote continuous improvements in the environmental performance of industrial activities.

Part IX, "Enforcement," provides for designated officials to be charged with responsibility for monitoring observance of the Act. These officials are to be given inspection powers, including right of entry where reasonably necessary to perform their duties. Proceedings for implementation and enforcement are also detailed.

Part X, "Sanctions and Enforcement Measures," lists a number of measures that can be taken against persons responsible for non-compliance, including, *inter alia*, modification or revocation of authorizations, administrative fines and penalties, prohibitions or limitations of an activity, and remedial action for restoration of the environment. Monetary sanctions are to be in reasonable proportion to the extent of the damage done as well as the intended impact of the penalty's imposition. The possibility of criminal sanctions is noted.

Finally, Part XI, "Civil Liability and Compensation for Damage to the Environment," simply incorporates by reference rules based on the 1993 Lugano Convention on Civil Liability for Damage Resulting from Activities Dangerous to the Environment.

In addition to issuing the Model Act, the CE also organized a seminar on Protection of the environment and the new technologies used in agriculture in Dijon, France, 13–17 September 1994, in liaison with the Association international des entretiens écologiques. A pan-European colloquy on the protection of Adriatic coastlines took place in Tirana, Albania, 27–29 October 1994. The colloquy was organized by the CE, in association with the Albanian Ministry of Health and the Environment. A particular emphasis was on Albanian coastal regions not yet polluted or developed.

(8) Landmark European Court of Human Rights Ruling

For the first time in the 44 years since the establishment of the European Convention of Human Rights, a complaint about environmental pollution was successfully brought under Art. 8 of the Convention, which states: "Everyone has the right to respect for his private and family life, his home, and his correspondence." On 9 December 1994, the European Court of Human Rights (ECHR) unanimously ruled that Spain had violated a family's right of privacy when local authorities allowed operation of a waste treatment plant just a few meters from the family's home. The ECHR ordered the Spanish government to pay 5.5 million pesetas (US$42,000) in damages and legal fees. The court's ruling in (➔) *López Ostra v. Spain* (Case No. 41/1993/436/515) cannot be appealed.

Although the ECHR found a violation of Art. 8, it rejected the argument that Art. 3 of the Convention had also been violated. Article 3 states: "No one shall be subjected to torture or to inhuman or degrading treatment or punishment." Previous environment-related cases decided by the ECHR had been based on other articles, such as those guaranteeing speedy access to objective judicial hearings.

Gretta Goldenman

C. UNITED NATIONS COMMISSION ON SUSTAINABLE DEVELOPMENT

(1) Introduction

The United Nations Commission on Sustainable Development (CSD) was established as a functional commission of the United Nations Economic and Social Council (ECOSOC) by United Nations General Assembly resolution 47/191. Sixteen new members were elected to begin their three-year terms on 1 January 1994 (ECOSOC decision 1993/218). The full 53 members of the CSD in 1994 were Algeria, Antigua and Barbuda, Australia, Austria, Barbados, Belarus, Belgium, Benin, Bolivia, Brazil, Bulgaria, Burkina Faso, Canada, Chile, China, Colombia, Cuba, Czech Republic, Egypt, France, Gabon, Germany, Guinea, Hungary, Iceland, India, Indonesia, Italy, Japan, Malawi, Malaysia, Mexico, Morocco, Namibia, Netherlands, Nigeria, Norway, Pakistan, Philippines, Poland, Republic of Korea, Russian Federation, Singapore, Sri Lanka, Tunisia, Turkey, Uganda, United Kingdom of Great Britain and Northern Ireland, United Republic of Tanzania, the United States, Uruguay, Vanuatu, and Venezuela.

(2) Second Session

The CSD held its second session in New York, 16–27 May 1994. The report of this session is contained in document E/CN.17/1994/20 of 12 July 1994. Among the many contributions made in preparation for this session were nine international meetings that were organized in response to the CSD's agenda and hosted by national governments. The meetings included two on technology transfer (United Nations Conference on Trade and Development and the government of Norway, in Oslo; the governments of Colombia and the United States, in Cartagena); one on sustainable consumption (government of Norway, in Oslo); one on finance (governments of Japan and Malaysia, in Kuala Lumpur, Malaysia); one on health (government of Denmark, in Copenhagen); one on international law (government of Austria, in Baden bei Wien, Austria); and one on chemical safety

(United Nations Environment Programme (UNEP), International Labour Organisation, World Health Organization, and the government of Sweden, in Stockholm). In addition, the Commission itself held two *ad hoc*, open-ended working groups on technology transfer and on financial flows and mechanisms, in New York, in February and March of 1994.

In the second session, the members elected Germany's Minister for the Environment, Nature Conservation, and Nuclear Safety, Mr. Klaus Töpfer, as its new Chairman.

Consistent with the multi-year thematic programme of work adopted at its first session, the Commission reviewed designated chapters of Agenda 21, including the following cross-sectoral issues: trade, environment, and development; consumption patterns; institutions and legal instruments; the roles of major groups; financial resources and mechanisms; and technology cooperation, transfer, and capacity-building. Sectoral issues were dealt with in two clusters; the first being health, human settlements, and freshwater; the second being toxic chemicals and hazardous wastes.

(a) Cross-sectoral Issues

(i) Trade, Environment, and Sustainable Development

Trade, environment, and sustainable development (Ch. 2) received considerable attention, particularly coming in the wake of the successful conclusion of the Uruguay Round of multilateral trade negotiations. The CSD supported the (➔) decision taken at the Marrakesh Ministerial Meeting in April 1994 to establish a Committee on Trade and Environment, and indicated its intention to interact with the new World Trade Organization. It reiterated Principle 12 of the Rio Declaration and Agenda 21, para. 2.22, to ensure that environment-related regulations or standards, including those related to health and safety standards, do not constitute a means of arbitrary or unjustifiable discrimination or a disguised restriction on trade. The Commission noted the importance of developing a framework to facilitate the assessment of the environmental impact of trade policies and of a number of concepts and principles, such as the polluter pays principle, the precautionary principle, and life-cycle management. It agreed to review annually developments in the area of trade, development, and the environment. It also recommended that the Secretary-General, through ECOSOC, seek views on an analytical study to be undertaken on the relationship of environmental protection to international competitiveness, job creation, and development.

(ii) Changing Consumption Patterns

With the United Nations Conference on Environment and Development, the issue of changing consumption patterns (Ch. 4) was for the first time formally placed on the agenda for multilateral negotiations. It drew significant attention from the CSD, which recommended at its second session that steps be taken to change consumption and production patterns, especially in developed countries, *inter alia*, by appropriate instruments, information, and education. Emphasis was placed on the differentiated responsibilities among countries and the need to offset adverse impacts on vulnerable groups. Governments were encouraged to intensify data collection and analysis regarding the interrelationship between consumption patterns, production structures and techniques, economic growth, employment, population dynamics, and environmental stress. It was agreed that the Secretary-General would request the views of governments to formulate elements of a possible work programme for sustainable consumption and production patterns by the third session of the CSD, in 1995.

(iii) International Legal Instruments

Focussing on institutional and international legal instruments (Chs. 38 and 39), the Commission recommended that relevant international treaty regimes should contain effective machinery for consensus-building and dispute settlement. It emphasized the importance of full participation of all interested parties in negotiation of international agreements relating to sustainable development and called on the relevant bodies to promote financing for this purpose. Non-legally binding agreements were encouraged as a first step in the preparation of international regulations. The need for improved coordination and more efficient structural arrangements among the secretariats of conventions related to sustainable development was noted, as was consistency among the concepts, requirements, and implications of sustainable development and international law. Countries were called on to create national legal frameworks for the implementation of Agenda 21.

(iv) Major Groups

The CSD recognized the indispensable role that major groups (Chs. 23–32) and their representatives play in the implementation of Agenda 21 and encouraged them to engage in creating multi-stakeholder partnerships and to carry out concrete partnership projects. Continued value was placed on the involvement of major groups in the meetings of the Commission itself and as an important source of information for both the inter-sessional activities and the documentation for the CSD.

(v) Financial Resources

As in the first session, there was a concern that financial resources (Ch. 33), including official development assistance, were falling short both of expectations and requirements to move toward sustainable development. The CSD reiterated that overseas development assistance levels should be brought in line with the 0.7 percent target, and it welcomed the restructuring of the Global Environment Facility (GEF) and its replenishment of US$2 billion as a "first step at a minimum level" (para. 60). During the preparatory meetings for this discussion, a number of innovative financial mechanisms, policy instruments, and reforms were proposed, including, *inter alia*, tradable permits, emission taxes, and air travel taxes. These were discussed, and the CSD requested the Secretary-General to determine their feasibility, socio-economic consequences, impact on the environment and administrative arrangements, and report on these issues at the third session.

(vi) Technology Transfer

The discussion on technology transfer, cooperation and capacity building (Chs. 34 and 37) emphasized three main themes: access to and dissemination of reliable information on environmentally sound technologies (ESTs); institutional development and capacity-building; and financial and partnership arrangements. The Commission requested a survey on and assessment of available sources of information on selected technologies, case studies on national technology needs, and concrete modalities and usefulness of a number of specific and innovative technology transfer mechanisms benchmarking the management of venture capital funds for ESTs and joint ventures. Concrete recommendations on these issues are to be submitted to the Commission at its third session. The Secretary-General was requested to examine the feasibility of establishing a consultative group on environmental technology centres.

(b) Sectoral Issues

All of the sectoral issues had elements in common, specifically with respect to cross-sectoral issues. Full participation from major groups, technology innovation and transfer, capacity-building, partnerships between public and private entities and, where relevant, with local communities; the use of economic instruments as internal financing mechanisms; and the provision of external financial resources were all emphasized. The importance of integrated management and the use of comprehensive environmental impact assessment at decision-making and project levels were noted. In addition, the Commission drew attention, *inter alia*, to health, human settlements, and fresh water, and to toxic chemicals and hazardous wastes, as discussed below.

(i) Health, Human Settlements, and Fresh Water

In discussing health and sustainable development (Ch. 6), the CSD noted the need to tie population issues and food security with health concerns and to enhance efforts to prevent and eradicate communicable diseases. Five issues were identified as priority areas to be the focus of the 1997 review: supporting countries in the development of national environmental health plans as part of national sustainable development programmes; extending scientific and public understanding of the cumulative human health effects of chemicals in consumer products, plant and animal-based food, water, soil, and air; determining mechanisms that identify and control newly emerging infectious diseases and their possible environmental linkages; providing a status report on the health implications of the depletion of the ozone layer, based on epidemiological studies; and developing an effective and efficient environmental health information system.

Much of the international discussion concerning human settlements (Ch. 7) took place within the preparatory process for the Second United Nations Conference on Human Settlements (Habitat II), and the CSD called for support for this process. The Commission urged the application of land-use planning and management strategies, called for best practice in delivery mechanisms and the dissemination of effective models, and invited organizations of the UN system to launch a demonstration initiative for environmentally friendly urban transport and to consider the feasibility of integrated demonstration projects for human settlements in three megacities. The CSD called for support to local, small, and micro-enterprises, more attention to management of solid waste, joint programming specifically focussed on urban services and urban poverty and their linkages with health and the environment, and alliances with local authorities, as well as other major groups.

The decision of the Commission regarding freshwater (Ch. 18) urged that special attention be given to the integrated management of water, river, and lake basins; the implementation of the polluter pays principle and pricing water to equal its full costs; the encouragement of partnership projects; promotion of a gender perspective in water resources management; promotion of education programmes; greater efficiency of sustainable water use, water conservation and protection, particularly in agriculture, and the increased application of rainwater-harvesting techniques; and the conservation and sustainable management of forests, including their use as a means of halting soil degradation and increasing moisture retention. The Commission requested that countries include in their 1997 national reports a specific section on national goals and strategies in the field of drinking water and environmental sanitation, including, as appropriate, target dates. Organizations of the UN system were called on to complete a comprehensive assessment of freshwater resources in time for the special session of the General Assembly in 1997.

(ii) Toxic Chemicals and Hazardous Wastes

The Commission endorsed the Intergovernmental Forum on Chemical Safety, established by the International Conference on Chemical Safety (Sweden, July 1994), as well as the priorities for action adopted by that Conference. In reviewing environmentally sound management of toxic chemicals (Ch. 19), it called for the development of effective legally binding instruments for the application of the prior informed consent procedure (PIC), stressed that the (_) Code of Ethics on the International Trade in Chemicals be widely applied by industry in all countries without delay, and recognized the need to identify persistent and bioaccumulative chemicals with a view to phasing out or banning such chemicals.

In its discussion of hazardous wastes (Ch. 20), the Commission suggested that the parties to the Basel Convention on the Control of Transboundary Movements of Hazardous Wastes and their Disposal (1989) consider the feasibility of developing non-compliance procedures. The CSD urged that high priority be given to halting the illegal disposal of tanker sludge and ballast water into marine waters and that such waters be made subject to the relevant requirements of the appropriate international conventions. It also urged governments to take action to implement fully the decision of the UNEP Governing Council (decision 17/5) on the application of environmental norms by the military establishment. Governments were asked to establish the legal, regulatory, and other institutional and national plans to manage hazardous waste. Industry was encouraged to develop voluntary codes of conduct for the use of clean technologies and the safe management of hazardous waste in all countries where they operate.

The subject of radioactive wastes (Ch. 22) was discussed separately. The Commission urged governments to apply the precautionary principle in decisions concerning new or extended activities that generate radioactive wastes. CSD called on governments to ensure that radioactive wastes arising from military activities be subject to the same types of strict safety and environmental regulations as those arising from civilian activities. The Commission urged governments to begin promptly, in the context of the International Atomic Energy Agency, after the finalization of the (_) Nuclear Safety Convention, to work on the development of an international convention on the safety of radioactive waste management, including consideration of the total life-cycle management of nuclear materials. The export of radioactive wastes to countries without the technical, economic, legal, and administrative resources for their management was considered inadmissible.

(3) Inter-sessional Activities

In determining its activities between the second and third sessions, the Commission decided to retain its inter-sessional *ad hoc* open-ended working group on finance and to establish an inter-sessional *ad hoc* open-ended working group on land, desertification, forests, and biodiversity. The CSD decided not to organize a separate working group on technology transfer during this period, but to address technology issues in the context of the other two working groups. The CSD also welcomed a number of national initiatives to host inter-sessional meetings on specific topics in preparation for the third session in 1995.

The high-level segment opened on 26 May, with over 40 ministers and high-level officials in attendance. Those participating underscored the high political profile of the Commission and the need to demonstrate political leadership in order to serve as an effective catalyst for sustainable development. Discussion centered primarily on issues of trade and environment, consumption patterns, financing and technology transfer, and the application of PIC to the export of banned or severely restricted chemicals. Support was given to the monitoring and reviewing role of the Commission and, in that context, to the ongoing work on the elaboration of sustainable development indicators.

(4) Conclusion

The second session of the CSD was successful in moving the international agenda for sustainable development forward, particularly in those areas in which intersessional meetings had provided a clear focus for both expert and political consideration. It was felt that the work of the Commission could have a broader impact if delegations to its sessions reflected the interministerial character of sustainable development and not place undue emphasis only on environmental representation.

Mary Pat Williams Silveira

D. EUROPEAN UNION

A review of the main developments in European Union environmental law in 1994 reveals two contrasting trends. First, partly because of the principle of subsidiarity, many member states are anxious to re-nationalize several areas that existing Council Directives already regulate and to circumscribe Community actions by restricting the latter to a few framework laws. Second, most states and many industrial sectors consider it essential that the rules governing trade and competition should be the same for everyone and as fully defined and precise as possible. These two tendencies are not always mutually compatible. Seen in conjunction with the lengthy and tortuous nature of decision-making procedures, they explain a certain degree of paralysis within the Community.

1994 was not characterized by any particularly significant events. From the very beginning of the year, the Community institutions lacked the determination to develop an ambitious programme. One reason for this was that the Parliament had already been considering numerous proposals for several months that were due to be subjected to the new decision-making rules that the Maastricht Treaty established. In addition, the Commission was entering the last year of its tenure. The fact that its members were due to be replaced at the end of 1994 was not conducive to an atmosphere of creativity. The Commission's legislative programme was not very far-reaching. In response to the economic crisis that was raging in most states within the Union, the Commission designed its legislative programme primarily to strengthen industry's competitiveness in the Community and to promote better use of industrial potential for innovation, research, and technological development. The Commission indicated that it would continue to base its actions on a global and voluntary approach aimed at transparency and improving the integration of environmental considerations into other areas of policy.

(1) Institutional Developments

(a) Community Institutions

The new commissioners of the Commission were announced in September 1994. The nominations were to take effect in January 1995. The European Parliamentary elections in June 1994 did not bring about any major changes, as the Socialist Party retained its majority: the Environmental Commission is still under the presidency of the representative of the English Labour Party. The strengthening of the Parliament's role was of much greater significance. The Parliament not only gave its decision on the nominations to the new Commission, but also insisted on reviewing all draft texts that were adopted pursuant to Arts. 189b or 189c following the entry into force of the Maastricht Treaty. The Parliament had to re-examine a large number of texts, because under the Maastricht Treaty, the vast majority of environmental directives must now be adopted by qualified majority vote of the member states under the procedures of "cooperation" (Art. 189b) or "co-decision" (Art. 189c) with the European Parliament. The Parliamentary review covered those directives that had originally been examined under the old regime and in respect of which Parliament had simply been "consulted." Any amendments voted by the Parliament during this second reading must now be taken into consideration by the Council and the Commission. For the first time in the environmental field, the "conciliation procedure," which is necessary where the Council refuses to accept Parliamentary amendments, had to be invoked for two draft directives.

(b) Accessions

In 1994, Austria, Sweden, and Finland decided to join the European Union, bringing the number of its members to 15. Norway rejected accession to the Union. An agreement on the environmental aspects of this enlargement had to be concluded due to the differences between environmental protection rules in the European Union and the new member states, whose rules are more stringent in some circumstances. The agreement provides that the incoming countries may retain environmental protection standards that are stricter than Community norms for four years. The allowable derogations mainly relate to legislation dealing with hazardous substances. In order not to impede the working of the internal market, the members agreed that the application of stricter national rules must not entail any border controls. At the end of this four-year transitional period, which may be extended, Community rules will apply to all states but will have to be reassessed in the interest of achieving the highest possible norms. This clearly shows that the new member states of the European Union are determined to play a leading role in the preparation of European environmental legislation and to contribute decisively to establishing more rigorous controls.

(2) *Actions*

(a) *Waste*

(i) *Hazardous waste*

In 1994, the final step in making Directive No. 91/689 on hazardous waste of 12 December 1991 operational finally took place. Its entry into force was contingent on the compilation of a list of hazardous wastes that a Council Decision of 22 December 1994 adopted. The Directive was to enter into force on 27 June 1995. Pursuant to the Directive, the hazardous waste covered must be included in a list drawn up on the basis of three criteria. To qualify, the waste must be produced by certain categories of activities defined in the Annex to the Directive; it must contain hazardous substances listed in another annex; and it must possess hazardous properties as defined by Directive No. 67/548 (as amended) on the classification, labelling, and packaging of chemical products. Whilst all waste on the list is considered hazardous in principle, the materials listed therein only constitute "waste" if the holder of the material at issue actually does, wishes to, or is required to dispose of it.

Although the classification "hazardous waste" is not left to the discretion of member states, they may determine, on the basis of documentary proof supplied by the holder of specified waste, that such waste does not possess hazardous properties and is consequently not hazardous. States must notify the Commission of any exceptions to the Community list of hazardous waste made in this way.

(ii) *Packaging*

The Council adopted Directive No. 94/62 of 20 December 1994 on packaging and packaging waste after three years of discussions. The text will go down as the most intensively lobbied instrument in the history of the European institutions. The proposal was governed by the cooperation procedure before the Maastricht Treaty entered into force. After 1 November

1993, however, the Directive became subject to the Maastricht Treaty's co-decision procedure and therefore had to go back to the Parliament for a further reading. The Commission accepted virtually all the amendments that the Parliament proposed, but the two bodies were unable to reach a common position on one provision. The text was accordingly submitted to a conciliation procedure between the Parliament and the Council and was then voted on a third time by the Parliament before being adopted by the Council by qualified majority. States have until 30 June 1996 to transpose this Directive into national law.

The Directive's primary objective is to prevent the production of packaging waste. States are required to draw up national programmes for this purpose and must promote the re-use of packaging. Failing this, states must take measures to attain specific waste-recovery and recycling targets by 30 June 2001 at the latest. Greece, Ireland, and Portugal may decide to attain lower targets. Other states may exceed these targets if they have sufficient internal capacity and the Commission decides that such measures avoid distortions of the internal market.

A process of standardization is to be carried out for the classification and uniform labelling of packaging, to replace national symbols that are currently placed on packaging in certain countries. States may make use of economic instruments to promote the selective collection, recycling, reuse, or prevention of waste. The Directive also establishes maximum concentration levels of heavy metals in packaging.

The Directive was based on Art. 100a, which covers rules from which states may not, in principle, derogate. However, the Directive still does not remove all risks of obstacles to trade or distortion of competition. On the one hand, it sets ambitious targets, most notably the requirements to recycle a minimum of 15 percent by weight of each packaging material and the requirement that states wishing to go beyond the Directive's recovery targets have appropriate recycling and recovery capacities within their own territory. On the other hand, these recovery targets are very broad and it is just as possible to derogate downwards as upwards.

The practical implementation of this Directive is likely to be difficult, particularly in view of these recycling targets and the organisational changes and administrative structures that will be necessary to achieve them.

(iii) Incineration of Hazardous Waste

The Council adopted Directive No. 94/67 of 16 December 1994 on the incineration of hazardous waste after two and a half years of negotiations. Since the European Parliament rejected the text that the Commission had proposed, on its second reading, this Directive had to be adopted by the Council unanimously.

The Directive defines hazardous waste by reference to Directive No.

91/689 and the list of hazardous waste. Municipal waste and combustible liquid wastes, including waste oils, however, are excluded from the scope of the Directive if their combustible properties only result in negligible noxious emissions.

Under the Directive, the operation of new and existing incineration plants and plants that burn hazardous waste as additional fuel are subject to permitting, as are discharges of aqueous waste resulting from the cleaning of exhaust gases. Plants must be designed, equipped, and operated with combustion technologies as specified in the Directive. Plant emissions must not exceed the emission limit values corresponding to those obtainable by using best available technology. Operators must control the quantity and type of waste that they receive and take continuous measurements of specified quantitatively significant emissions. Other emissions are to be monitored monthly. The emission limit values are to be revised before 31 December 2000, on the basis of experience gained and technical progress made.

(b) Air

(i) Volatile Organic Compounds (VOCs)

Also in 1994, the Community adopted the Directive on Volatile Organic Compounds emanating from the storage of petrol and its distribution between terminals and service stations. The Directive aims to reduce loss through evaporation at every stage of the storage and distribution chain, except the refuelling of motor vehicles at service stations. It lays down highly technical measures that will come into force under a detailed timetable, phased in accordance with the types of installations concerned and their output. The Directive constitutes the first step in a programme to reduce the 10 million tonnes of VOCs that the Community emits annually, of which 200,000 tonnes originate from the 137,000 service stations within the European Union. This programme will also include measures relating to emissions from the use of solvents and motor vehicles. Motor vehicle refuelling emissions will be covered by the separate "State 2" VOC Directive, which had been in preparation for over a year at the end of 1994.

(ii) Other Instruments

The draft text amending the Large Combustion Plants Directive was still under consideration at the end of 1994. The Commission had also submitted a draft directive on ambient air quality.

(iii) International Commitments

The Council signed the 1994 Oslo (➔) Protocol on Further Reduction of Sulphur Emissions, concluded under the auspices of the Convention on Long Range Transboundary Air Pollution of 1979. This Protocol calls on its 25 signatory countries to reduce their emissions in proportion to the amount of damage done by each country to its own ecosystem. It is consequently for individual states to fix their own reduction targets and the measures they wish to adopt. Germany, including the former East Germany, has gone furthest in this direction by aiming for emission levels to be reduced to 87 percent of their 1980 levels by the year 2005.

With regard to the ozone layer, the Council adopted the 1992 Amendment (Copenhagen) to the Montreal Protocol. The Regulation for its implementation (*see* (➔) Council Regulation (EC) No. 3093/94) sets more stringent standards for, *inter alia*, chlorofluorocarbons, hydrochlorofluorocarbons, and methyl bromide and requires these to be enforced earlier than is called for under the Copenhagen Amendment.

(c) Nature

In the area of nature conservation, certain disputes that had dragged on for years were finally settled. Several species of wild birds that used to be fully protected under Directive No. 79/409 on the protection of migratory birds living in the wild may now be hunted if states so decide. This applies to birds that are considered to be pests in certain states, such as magpies, crows, starlings, and some species of raven.

The need to develop more precise criteria for fixing hunting seasons has become apparent in view of the repeated violations of the prohibition on hunting migratory species during their reproductive period and their journeys to their nesting places, which have regularly been punished by the Court of Justice of the Community.

(d) Chemical Products

It is in the area of chemical products and hazardous substances that differences in national environmental protection standards are felt most acutely, partly because this directly affects the internal market. The 14th amendment to Directive No. 76/769 on placing specified hazardous substances and compounds on the market conflicts with existing national rules. Several states now intend to apply Art. 100a4 of the Treaty of Rome, as twice amended, which would allow them to retain more stringent regulations than those established under Community legislation. In addition, the Parliament has proposed amendments to the draft Directive by adding 15 substances whose use should be prohibited or significantly restricted.

The pentachlorophenol (PCP) case (*French Republic v. Commission of the European Communities*, Case C-41/93) highlights the absence of any clear policy on this subject within the Community. In that case, the Court of Justice held that the Commission had not given adequate reasons for its decision to uphold Germany's total prohibition on the placing on the market and use of products containing PCPs. The Commission was therefore obliged to adopt a new decision, based on the conclusions of a Swedish scientific report. The same question has now arisen in the Netherlands and Denmark, which both banned using or placing PCPs on the market. Denmark has also prohibited the sale of packaging containing PCPs within its borders.

A proposal to eliminate all polychlorinated biphenyls by the year 2010 is now under consideration. This would require all equipment containing those substances to be decontaminated by that deadline.

Finally, with regard to risk evaluation, the Commission has adopted a regulation ((➔) Regulation (EC) No 1488/94) establishing the first list of priority substances to be evaluated pursuant to Council Regulation No. 793/93 on the evaluation and control of existing substances. Regulation No. 793/93 aims to allow the systematic evaluation of risks that substances listed in the European Inventory of Existing Commercial Substances pose, on the basis of information that manufacturers and importers are to supply. The new regulation lists 42 substances requiring urgent investigation. The Commission has assigned each substance to a member state for evaluation.

(e) Transport by Sea

The Greek Presidency during the first half of 1994 identified the strengthening of safety at sea as one of its priorities. The majority of measures taken or proposed relate to the transportation of petrol by sea. The Commission adopted a regulation to implement the International Maritime Organization's resolution on oil tankers with separate fuel tanks. Such tankers, which pose less environmental risk, will be able to obtain reductions on their port taxes, whereas they were previously penalised in comparison with traditional petrol tankers because of their greater weight.

(f) Trade

Two cases that came before the Court of Justice of the European Community in 1994 reveal the difficulties of managing trade and environment issues within the European Union. In the first case, the European Parliament brought proceedings against the Council for basing Regulation No. 259/93 on the transboundary movement of waste on Art. 130s instead of Art. 100a. The Parliament claimed that the Council should use the provision on the internal market whenever there is any movement of goods or products. The Court of Justice held that the case related to environmental rather than internal market issues, which meant that Art. 130s was the correct legal basis for the Regulation (decision of 28 June 1994, Case No. C187/93). This ruling means that states may take more stringent environmental protection measures on the basis of Art. 130t and thereby impede the free movement of waste products within the Union. This ruling contrasts to an earlier Court ruling that had held that waste products are goods that must be allowed to move freely.

It should be noted that national initiatives have already made their mark in the area of waste. Some states ban the entry into their territory of waste originating from other countries. Whilst Wallonia was forbidden to prohibit the import of household waste into its territory from any source (*see* judgment of the Court of Justice of 9 July 1992, Case No. C 2/90, ECR 1992, 1 4431), Denmark has now banned the entry of German household waste into its territory.

In a second case, the Court made an opposite ruling in favour of free movement in the context of nature protection. In its Decree on protected species, Germany had prohibited the import of live freshwater crayfish of European species, whether they originated from member states or third countries. Imports were only permitted for purposes of research or education. The court held that this prohibition violated Arts. 30 and 36 of the Treaty of Rome, which established the principle of the free movement of goods. The Court held that there were less restrictive methods of protecting these gravely endangered native crayfish.

(g) Tax on Carbon Dioxide and Energy

After more than two and a half years, the 12 Environment Ministers reached agreement in the last Council of Ministers of 1994 to allow countries to introduce a carbon dioxide tax unilaterally. The Commission is to determine parameters that will be submitted to the Finance Ministers, rather than the Environment Ministers. These parameters will need to take account of the use of existing systems of excise duties and the importance of avoiding negative impacts on competitiveness. This solution could put a stop to states' procrastination over the proposed tax and mollify national sensitivities. It also effectively buries the Commissions's draft Directive on the tax, albeit perhaps only temporarily. At the end of 1994, the European Parliament, which may well not endorse this new development, had yet to be consulted. To replace this tax, the Commission is now developing a proposal to increase the rate of excise duties and extend them to carbon dioxide and gas. This would lead to a steep rise in the price of fuel, which could have a similar effect to the measure on energy efficiency/carbon dioxide taxation.

(h) Financial Assistance

The European Union provides assistance through three main mechanisms. First, the LIFE Programme for 1995 is providing 96 million Ecus to finance 233 national schemes in the areas of nature and habitat conservation, the development of clean technology, the urban environment, monitoring networks, and training. Second, the Cohesion Funds to finance transport and environment programmes in Greece, Ireland, Portugal, and Spain approved 20 projects in Greece and 9 in Ireland in April 1994, for a total of 135 million Ecus, and approved a Spanish project costing more than 10 million Ecus in October. The majority of these projects relate to the provision of drinking water. Third, the PHARE Programme, which is concerned only with eastern European countries and comprises many elements, chiefly focused on research and training.

These programmes are complemented by budgets for research and targeted assistance that have been provided under the structural funds, particularly in the fields of energy, the renewal of regions affected by the decline in industry, urban areas, and employment. These budgets support some projects of an environmental nature.

(3) Texts in the Course of Preparation

(a) Water

Proposals have been made to amend the Directives on the quality of bathing water and drinking water, largely in response to the principle of subsidiarity. The second of these proposals will have significant financial ramifications if states agree to lower the lead content in drinking water to 10 microgrammes/litre.

A draft directive on the ecological quality of water was under consideration at the end of 1994. This text is effectively no more than a list of some guidelines and basic rules that leaves states free to adopt "measures to combat the pollution of surface waters in order to maintain and improve the ecological quality" of these waters. The objective is to achieve "good" or "high" water quality. These terms are defined by reference to specifications for representative elements of the aquatic ecosystem in question. Best available technology and best environmental practices must also be taken into account.

(b) Industrial Installations

The draft revised version of the Seveso Directive on the prevention of major accidents was still under consideration at year's end. It has given rise to severe criticism concerning the extension of its field of application and the tightening of certain of its provisions.

The proposal on integrated pollution prevention and control has been amended several times in response to the growing momentum in favour of subsidiarity, which makes it unlikely for the time being that any real integration of licensing procedures for polluting activities, or even any harmonization of existing procedures, will take place. The cross-media approach is wholly logical and necessary for the environment, but proves extremely difficult to translate into concrete terms and make legally enforceable. The debate about the respective merits of emission limit values and environmental quality standards (EQS), which dates back to the very first Community Environmental Action Programmme (1973), returned to centre stage during the negotiations over this proposed text. One burning question is the role that the Community should play in setting emissions limit values and EQS.

(c) Environmental Impact Assessments

The draft Directive amending Directive No. 85/337 on the assessment of the effects of certain public and private projects on the environment was still under discussion at the end of 1994.

(d) Eco-Labelling

Community efforts concerning eco-labels were fairly unsuccessful. The Commission drew up criteria for the labelling of washing machines, dishwashers, cosmetic and hygienic paper products, and floor cleaning products. In 1994, it decided to delegate the formulation of labelling criteria in the future to the European Environmental Agency in Copenhagen.

Pascale Kromarek

E. GENERAL AGREEMENT ON TARIFFS AND TRADE (GATT)

[Editors' Note: *See* report XIII.1]

F. INTERNATIONAL LABOUR ORGANISATION (ILO)

The ILO's work in relation to the environment continued on three fronts: international labour standards, programmatic work, and technical cooperation.

(1) ILO Instruments

(a) Proposed Standards on Safety and Health in Mines

At its 81st Session in June 1994, the International Labour Conference adopted a draft convention and recommendation on safety and health in mines, which will be examined again at the 82nd Session in 1995. The draft instruments address national policy on the subject and call for national laws and regulations regarding, among other matters, mine inspection and preventive and protective measures.

(b) Maritime Labour Standards

The ILO held a Tripartite Meeting on Maritime Labour Standards in Geneva from 28 November to 9 December 1994, at which representatives of governments, trade unions, and employers' organizations from 30 seafaring countries examined draft revised ILO instruments on the placement of seafarers; inspection of vessels; and manning, hours of work, and wages of seafarers. Also on the agenda was a proposed protocol to the Merchant Shipping (Minimum Standards) Convention, 1976 (No. 147), which contains a port-state control provision. The issues of port-state control, inspection of vessels, and avoidance of fatigue caused by excessive working hours all have a relationship to the prevention of accidents and the pollution they can cause. The Tripartite Meeting's conclusions will be discussed by a future session of the International Labour Conference, with a view toward the adoption of revised conventions and recommendations on those subjects.

In 1994, the ILO pointed out to the United Nations Division for Ocean Affairs and the Law of the Sea those articles in the Law of the Sea Convention that involve the competence of the ILO. They relate to matters addressed in ILO conventions and recommendations on maritime labour standards, particularly those on job safety and inspection of vessels and those pertinent to labour conditions under the jurisdiction of the International Seabed Authority.

(c) Other Activities

Among other activities, the ILO contributed to reports of the UN Commission on Sustainable Development, including a report on international legal instruments related to Agenda 21 and the Rio Declaration, which encompasses ILO conventions and recommendations related to the social aspects of Agenda 21 as well as the working environment. The ILO has voiced its particular concern regarding the involvement of non-governmental organizations (and hence Major Groups) in follow-up to Agenda 21. This concern reflects international labour standards on freedom of association, consultation of workers' and employers' organizations, indigenous peoples, and other topics.

The ILO's regular work concerning the application of international labour standards, including those most relevant to environmental concerns, continued as in past years. The ILO Governing Body approved a new cycle for the frequency of future government reports on ratified conventions under Art. 22 of the ILO Constitution.

(2) Convocation of the International Conference on Chemical Safety

Together with the United Nations Environment Programme (UNEP) and the World Health Organization (WHO), the ILO co-convened the International Conference on Chemical Safety in Stockholm from 25 to 29 April 1994. The Conference was held at the request of the United Nations Conference on Environment and Development (UNCED), to consider proposals for the establishment of an intergovernmental mechanism for chemical risk assessment and management. The Government of Sweden hosted the Conference, representatives from 114 countries and various inter-governmental and non-governmental organizations attended. The ILO delegation included one employer and one worker expert nominated by the employers' and workers' groups of the ILO Governing Body.

The Conference adopted a resolution and a set of priorities for action. It also resolved to establish an Intergovernmental Forum on Chemical Safety, a "non-institutional mechanism" that is to meet periodically, and approved its terms of reference. Government participants will have the right to vote in the Forum, which provides for representation on a regional basis in the Intersessional Group. Provision is made for non-voting participation in the Forum by inter-governmental organizations and international non-governmental organizations that are concerned with health, workers' interests, the environment, consumers, and industry and that are involved in the field of chemical safety. The Conference expected that members of the Intersessional Group of the Forum would establish active networks of information and consultation among countries of their regions or subregions.

The Conference also adopted a set of priorities for action for the effective implementation of six programme areas as defined by UNCED in Chapter 19 of Agenda 21, as follows: expanding and accelerating the international assessment of chemical risks; harmonizing the classification and labelling of chemicals; information exchange on toxic chemicals and chemical risks; establishing risk-reduction programmes; strengthening national capabilities and capacities for the management of chemicals; and preventing illegal international traffic in toxic and dangerous products. The Conference recommended that by 1997 no fewer than 25 additional countries should have implemented systems for preventing major industrial accidents in accordance with international principles such as those contained in the Prevention of Major Accidents Convention, 1993 (No. 174), and the UN Economic Commission for Europe Convention on Transboundary Effects of Industrial Accidents. It also urged that by that date, 50 more countries should have introduced national systems for emergency preparedness and response, including a strategy for educating and training personnel, with the aid, *inter alia*, of the APELL Programme and the ILO Code of Practice on the Prevention of Major Industrial Accidents (1991). Further, it recommended that comprehensive guidelines for chemical legislation and enforcement be elaborated as soon as possible, taking into account, *inter alia*, the principles in the ILO Chemicals Convention, 1990 (No. 170).

(3) Strengthening and Expanding the International Programme on Chemical Safety

In response to the calls made at UNCED and the 1994 Stockholm Conference for greater coordination among inter-governmental organizations, negotiations were held throughout the year for the purpose of establishing an expanded and strengthened International Programme on Chemical Safety (IPCS). The current IPCS is a joint effort of UNEP, ILO and WHO, governed by the Memorandum of Understanding (MOU) that they signed in 1980 and have renewed several times since (most recently on 21 April 1994). Discussions involving these and other inter-governmental organizations led to the view that there should be two new MOUs, one to update the current IPCS MOU, for the carrying out of substantive work, and another to establish an expanded coordinating mechanism. Accordingly, UNEP, ILO, WHO, the United Nations Food and Agriculture Organization, the United Nations Industrial Development Organization, and the Organisation for Economic Co-operation and Development negotiated a new MOU to establish an Inter-Organization Programme for the Sound Management of Chemicals in 1994. This MOU is now being circulated for signature by the executive heads of these organizations and would enter into force once four organizations have accepted its terms. The purpose of this programme would be to promote coordination of the policies and activities pursued by the participating organizations, jointly and separately, to achieve the sound management of chemicals in relation to human health and the environment. The ILO played an active role in the negotiation of this MOU.

(4) Governing Body Action

At its 259th Session in March 1994, the ILO Governing Body's Committee on Employment and Social Policy reviewed the ILO contribution to environmentally sound and sustainable development (G.B.259/ESP/3/3). The document concluded:

The ILO is continuing its efforts to integrate relevant environment and sustainable development considerations within its regular programmes and technical cooperation activities. At the same time, particular priority is being given to supporting the special needs of the ILO's tripartite constituents to enable them to play an effective role in these matters.

In 1994, the Governing Body also reviewed the Activities of the International Occupational Safety and Health Information Centre in 1992-93 (GB. 259/14/10), the Report of the symposium on Workers' Education and the Environment (GB.259/ESP/4/1), and a summary on the work of the International Conference on Chemical Safety (GB.261/ESP/INF.1).

(5) Project on Environment, Sustainable Development, and the World of Work

In 1994, the ILO launched work on an interdepartmental project involving the environment, sustainable development, and the world of work. It has articulated the priority concerns for the ILO with regard to these interlinked issues and has launched a series of national studies and meetings. In 1994, one of two "tripartite plus" (government, trade unions, and employers' organizations, plus environmental groups) roundtables was held to examine environmental law issues in relationship to the world of work. A second roundtable will be held in the Philippines in 1995. The project is examining how 25 countries are implementing Agenda 21 as regards the world of work, and is also organizing missions to encourage ratification and implementation of selected ILO Conventions, particularly the Chemicals Convention, 1990 (No. 170) and the Prevention of Major Industrial Accidents Convention, 1974 (No. 174).

Anne M. Trebilcock

G. THE INTERNATIONAL LAW COMMISSION (ILC)

(1) International Watercourses

At its 1994 session, the ILC adopted on second reading a complete set of 33 (➔) Draft Articles on the Law of the Non-Navigational Uses of International Watercourses. The Commission also adopted a (➔) Resolution on Transboundary Confined Groundwater. Both the Draft Articles and the Resolution were submitted to the UN General Assembly with the Commission's recommendation that a convention on international watercourses be elaborated by the Assembly or by an international conference of plenipotentiaries on the basis of the Draft Articles.

In their final version, the Draft Articles are similar in most respects to those the Commission adopted on first reading in 1991. Several important changes were made, however. These modifications, together with the Resolution on Confined Groundwater, enhance the Commission's contribution to the law in this field.

The draft contains 33 articles organized in six parts: Part I, Introduction (Arts. 1–4); Part II, General Principles (Arts. 5–10); Part III, Planned Measures (Arts. 11-19); Part IV, Protection, Preservation and Management (Arts. 20–26); Part V, Harmful Conditions and Emergency Situations (Arts. 27 and 28); and Part VI, Miscellaneous Provisions (Arts. 29–33). The draft is intended to serve as a framework instrument, setting forth principles and rules of general applicability that may be used in agreements between states sharing international watercourses (referred to in the Draft Articles as "watercourse states"). Article 2 defines "watercourse" broadly to mean "a system of surface waters and groundwaters constituting by virtue of their physical relationship a unitary whole and normally flowing into a common terminus." An "international watercourse" is defined as "a watercourse, parts of which are situated in different states." The draft would thus apply not only to the main stem of a river or stream forming or crossing an international boundary, but also, *e.g.*, to tributaries of such watercourses, boundary-straddling lakes, and groundwater that is connected with other parts of an international watercourse, whether or not the groundwater is intersected by a boundary.

Part II of the Draft Articles is entitled "General Principles." This part contains two articles, the focus of much debate, that define the most fundamental rights and obligations of states sharing international watercourses: Article 5 on equitable and reasonable utilization of international watercourses, and Art. 7 on the obligation not to cause significant harm to other riparian states. (*See, e.g.*, UN Doc. A/CN.4/447 p. 44 (1993); and McCaffrey, "The Law of International Watercourses: Some Recent Developments and Unanswered Questions," 17 *Denver JILP* 505, 508-513 (1989)). Discussion focused on which of these principles should prevail in the event they come into conflict, for example, if the no-harm rule prevailed, and a later-developing upstream state was not permitted to construct a dam that would cause significant harm to its downstream neighbor. If the equitable utilization doctrine took precedence, harm to the downstream state would need to be taken into account in determining whether the dam would be permissible. The draft adopted on first reading in 1991 had accorded primacy to the no-harm rule. The new special rapporteur proposed reversing that regime. However, his proposed text would have raised, in effect, a rebuttable presumption that a use causing significant pollution is inequitable and unreasonable. The final version of the draft does not reverse the primacy of the no-harm rule, but softens the regime by making two important changes to Art. 7. The first change is the introduction of a "due diligence" standard. Many observers have concluded that this change only makes express what was already implied, since there is scant support in state practice for an obligation of result—*i.e.*, a virtual guarantee that significant harm will not occur—in this context.

The second major change in the articles is the addition of a paragraph that directly addresses the relationship between the equitable utilization and no-harm principles. This paragraph strongly suggests that a state's use that causes significant harm is not *per se* a breach of the state's international obligations. Instead, it recognizes the possibility that the states concerned will already have agreed to the use, in which case there would be no obligation to consult. Failing such an agreement, it requires that the states involved enter into consultations over the matters there indicated. By requiring consultations, the article enhances the possibility that the states concerned will resolve the problem by agreement. If consultations do not resolve the problem, the draft's new article on dispute resolution would apply. This requirement to have recourse to third-party dispute resolution is an important and useful addition to the Draft Articles, especially in view of the importance of establishing the facts in such cases and because of the many factors that must be assessed.

The approach adopted by the Commission to reconciling Arts. 5 and 7 softens the absolute priority given the no-harm rule under the 1991 articles, a priority that does not appear to accord with state practice and could well give rise to more problems than it resolves, especially by inhibiting states' efforts to develop. The revised text is also more likely to lead to a satisfactory resolution of conflicts in uses because of its requirement that the states concerned enter into consultations and ultimately have recourse to the draft's dispute-resolution procedures. The adjustment of conflicting uses of an international watercourse, especially where the watercourse is "successive" in character, is a highly complex matter, the accomplishment of which is not likely to be supported by the no-harm rule.

Part III of the draft addresses a subject that has been problematic in the practice of states, that of "new uses," specifically, the obligations of a state that is planning a change in its use of an international watercourse. While initially somewhat controversial within the Commission itself, the question was resolved in 1988 in a detailed set of provisions regulating the rights and obligations of both the state contemplating the change and the state or states likely to be affected by it. This regime essentially requires the state planning to undertake a change that "may have a significant adverse impact" upon other states to notify such states in a timely fashion of its plans. If within six months of the notification it has received no reply from the notified states it may implement its plans (subject always to its obligations of equitable utilization and harmless use). If the notifying state does receive a response in which the notified states object to the planned change, the states concerned are to "enter into consultations and, if necessary, negotiations with a view to arriving at an equitable resolution of the situation." Specifically, the notified states must find that the change would violate the notifying state's obligations of equitable utilization or harmless use and provide the notifying state within six months of the initial notification with a "documented explanation setting forth the reasons for the finding." If so requested by the notified state when making its reply, the notifying state must suspend implementation of its plans for six months to permit consultation and negotiation. Thus, the entire process could take 12 months or longer if the states concerned have not completed good-faith consultations and negotiations within the second six-month period. If the matter is not resolved to the satisfaction of any of the states concerned, the dispute settlement procedures of Art. 33 would be applicable.

Part IV of the draft addresses not only water pollution, but more widely, the protection and preservation of international watercourse ecosystems. Its first article, Art. 20, was modelled after Art. 192 of the UN Convention on the Law of the Sea and reflects recognition of the importance of the protection of ecosystems to sustainable development. Subsequent articles in Part IV deal with water pollution, exotic species, and protection of the marine environment against pollution from international watercourses. Part IV also contains provisions on water installations, measures to regulate watercourses, and the cooperative management of international watercourses.

Part V contains provisions on harmful conditions, including floods, and emergency situations like chemical spills. Part VI contains articles on armed conflict, indirect procedures, data vital to national security, and non-discrimination, as well as a new article on dispute resolution. The article on non-discrimination has been modified since the first reading. It requires states to grant private persons equal access, regardless of nationality or residence, to judicial or other procedures for compensation or other relief for injuries from watercourse-related activities. The new article on dispute settlement applies to "any watercourse dispute concerning a question of fact or the interpretation or application of the present articles." It provides for a series of stages of dispute settlement, beginning with consultations and negotiations through existing joint watercourse institutions. If, after six months, the states concerned have not resolved the dispute they must submit it to an impartial fact-finder or mediator. The article contains provisions for the establishment of a fact-finding commission, its procedure, powers, report, and expenses. The states concerned "may by agreement" submit their dispute to arbitration or judicial settlement if the dispute has not been resolved through the aforementioned procedures within specified time limits.

The Resolution on Confined Transboundary Groundwater was added at the second reading stage to address, if only indirectly, a subject not covered by the draft adopted on first reading. The definition of the term "watercourse" adopted on first reading included groundwater only to the extent that it interacts in some way with surface water. The Commission was unwilling at that stage to include "confined" groundwater, which groundwater that is not related in some way to surface water. The Commission took this position, despite the importance of transboundary aquifers, because members generally had not had this form of groundwater in mind during the elaboration of the Draft Articles. During the second reading of the draft the new special rapporteur, Robert Rosenstock, proposed that confined groundwater be included in the draft. In an apparent compromise, the ILC adopted a resolution expressing its "view that the principles contained in its draft articles . . . may be applied to transboundary confined groundwater."

In the fall of 1994, the General Assembly convened "a Working Group of the Whole, open to States Members of the United Nations or members of specialized agencies, . . . to elaborate a framework convention on the law of the non-navigational uses of international watercourses on the basis of the draft articles adopted by the International Law Commission . . . ." Debates in the Sixth (Legal) Committee of the General Assembly over the years suggest many states' beliefs that the draft strikes a good balance between the upper and lower riparian states. As the new special rapporteur noted, however, the utility of a framework convention will depend on the strength and depth of its acceptance.

Regardless of the outcome, the Commission's draft represents a significant milestone. The Helsinki Rules on the Uses of the Waters of International Rivers, adopted by the International Law Association (ILA) in 1966, were an influential attempt to codify and progressively develop rules of international law in the field, but they are now nearly 30 years old and do not deal with what are key issues today. Furthermore, the ILA did not have the benefit of government comment during the Rules' elaboration. States will undoubtedly look to the Commission's Draft Articles and commentaries for guidance as to their rights and obligations and may use the draft as a model for agreements with other riparian states. At the least, the ILC's Draft Articles will have made an important contribution toward reconciling the often divergent interests of riparian states and toward the protection and preservation of international watercourses.

(2) International Liability

The Commission once again made significant progress in its work on International Liability for Injurious Consequences Arising out of Acts Not Prohibited by International Law. It adopted eleven articles and three definitions, together with commentaries, bringing the total number of articles adopted on first reading to 14.

The articles adopted in 1994 constitute, according to the ILC, "a complete set of provisions on prevention . . . ." They include: Art. 1 (Scope of the Present articles); paras. (a), (b), and (c) of Art. 2 (Use of Terms); Art. 11 (Prior Authorization); Art. 12 (Risk Assessment); Art. 13 (Pre-Existing Activities); Art. 14 (Measures to Prevent or Minimize the Risk); Art. 14 *bis* [20 *bis*] (Non-Transference of Risk); Art. 15 (Notification and Information); Art. 16 (Exchange of Information); Art. 16 *bis* (Information to the Public); Art. 17 (National Security and Industrial Secrets); Art. 18 (Consultations on Preventive Measures); Art. 19 (Rights of the States Likely to be Affected); and Art. 20 (Factors Involved in an Equitable Balance of Interests).

These provisions conform in the main with provisions on the respective subjects contained in other general instruments in the field of international environmental law. In particular, a number of the liability articles (*e.g.*, Arts. 15, 16, 17, 18, and 19) parallel corresponding provisions in the Commission's Draft articles on international watercourses.

Another general point of interest has to do with the Commission's increasing reliance on the concept of "due diligence." This standard was used in Art. 7 of the watercourses draft, as noted above, and is also employed in the Commission's explanation of the "standard of the obligation of States to take preventive measures" under Art. 14. Thus, the obligation of prevention is one of "conduct" rather than of "result," presumably meaning that if a state has satisfied its due diligence obligation . . . *i.e.*, if it has taken reasonable measures to prevent harm . . . it would not be "liable" for an injurious consequence that nonetheless occurs in another state. While the due diligence standard is doubtless a flexible one, the Commission notes in its commentary that "a State's economic level cannot be used to discharge a State from its obligation under this article."

This raises the question of whether, or to what extent, the draft articles on liability will take into account the position of developing countries. While none of the adopted articles directly addressed the special situation of developing countries, the Commission's report indicates that the ILC intends to address this issue in a provision to be located in the chapter on general provisions that would be applicable to the entire set of draft articles.

In addition to the draft articles adopted on first reading, the ILC's 1994 report contains an interesting summary of the Commission's discussion of the special rapporteur's 10th report (UN Doc. A/CN.4/459 (1994) covering issues relating to the scope of the topic and to the direction in which future work should proceed. Considered were three major issues: (1) whether "prevention *ex-post*" was within the scope of the topic; (2) the special rapporteur's proposals to date on the question of liability; and (3) "procedural channels" (the need to create "a single forum like a mixed claims commission where all kinds of claims involving States and private individuals could be heard and adjudicated.") On the central question of liability, the special rapporteur postponed an examination of the "content of the remedial measures, which could be other than monetary compensation." He dealt instead with two issues, the relationship between state liability and civil liability and civil liability itself, including liability of the operator; the obligation to purchase insurance; the competent court; non-discrimination; causality; enforcement of judgments; exceptions to liability; and the statute of limitations. It remains to be seen whether the Commission will now be prepared to endorse a comprehensive set of provisions on private remedies of this kind, an approach it was unwilling to take in the Draft Articles on international watercourses.

Stephen McCaffrey

H. INTERNATIONAL MARITIME ORGANIZATION (IMO)

(1) The IMO Legal Committee

As in recent years, the IMO Legal Committee in 1994 focused mainly on the elaboration of the International Convention on Liability and Compensation for Damage in Connection with the Carriage of Hazardous and Noxious Substances by Sea (HNS). It was agreed that there would be a two-tier system with post-event contributions by ship owners in the first tier and by importers or "receivers" of hazardous and noxious substances in the second tier. The discussions were greatly assisted by the submission of a proposal on the second tier prepared by Australia, Canada, and Norway. After considerable debate, it was decided that there would be a general account divided into two sectors, plus only two special accounts. Receivers of substances in the special accounts would not have to contribute to the compensation for damage caused by substances in the other accounts. Some countries, including Japan in particular, pressed for more special accounts.

The substances covered are those referred to in the definitions sections of existing instruments. These include Annexes I and II of the International Convention for the Prevention of Marine Pollution from Ships (MARPOL 73/78); the International Maritime Dangerous Goods Code; solid bulk materials possessing hazardous chemicals covered by Appendix B of the Code of Safe Practice for Solid Bulk cargoes; and the London Convention 1972. The Convention will apply to accidents occurring during domestic as well as international voyages and will require compensation for damage caused by hazardous wastes on their way to a dump site. Any damage caused by a dumping operation or its aftermath would be dealt with under the London Convention 1972.

The principal remaining issues to be settled at what is expected to be the final negotiating session in April 1995 are the relationship of the HNS Convention to other liability regimes, particularly the 1976 Convention on the Limitation of Liability of Maritime Claims, and the question of to what extent the HNS Convention will cover damage caused by radioactive substances. In relation to the latter problem, a correspondence group led by the United States is studying five options intersessionally. At the October meeting of the Committee, the United States tabled the "umbrella convention" on nuclear liability that it had presented to the Intersessional Working Group of the Standing Committee of the International Atomic Energy Agency (IAEA) that is working on the revision of the Vienna Convention on Civil Liability for Nuclear Damage.

(2) The IMO Marine Environment Protection Committee (MEPC)

In 1994, MEPC met twice, on 7–11 March (MEPC 35) and on 31 October to 4 November (MEPC 36).

(a) MARPOL 73/78

(i) Revision of Annexes

A correspondence group that MEPC 34 established continued its work on the examination of amendments to the United States' proposed amendment to MARPOL Annex V on placards, waste management plans, and refuse record-keeping. MEPC 36 reviewed the draft amendments and requested the Secretary-General to circulate them, with a view to their adoption in 1995. A completely revised version of Annex I, which a correspondence group led by Norway prepared, was only partly discussed. Comments are to be sent to the leader of the correspondence group.

(ii) Ballast Water Working Group

MEPC 36 approved the report of the Ballast Water Working Group, in particular the conclusions and recommendations concerning a possible new annex to MARPOL to minimize the introduction of unwanted aquatic organisms and pathogens from ships' ballast water and associated sediment discharges. The Working Group was reconvened and requested to continue its work on the prospective new annex. After discussing the necessary elements of such an annex, the Working Group requested the IMO Secretariat to prepare a first draft to serve as a working document for further deliberations.

(iii) Air Pollution Annex

Work continued on the draft air pollution annex to MARPOL and a text was submitted to MEPC 36, which decided that further work on both substance and editing was necessary. A correspondence group was created to effect the editing, however, decisions on substance were left for MEPC 37 in 1995. Policy decisions are required on the application of nitrogen oxides requirements for existing engines, a 5 percent cap for the sulphur content of fuel oil, the extent of special areas, and requirements for fuel-oil quality. MEPC 36 postponed a decision on the designation of the Baltic Sea as a special area, as the Baltic Sea states had proposed. A discussion on the legal framework required for the adoption of the new annex was inconclusive, and MEPC 36 requested the secretariat to prepare a paper setting forth different options for the adoption of the new annex.

(iv) Regulations 13F and 13G of Annex I

Regulations 13F and 13G of MARPOL Annex I make obligatory the use of a double-hull design or a mid-deck design or any equally effective construction measures to reduce the risk of pollution. By resolution MEPC.64(36), the Committee adopted the Guidelines for Approval of Alternative Structural or Operational Arrangements under regulation 13G of MARPOL Annex I. A drafting group finalized the Draft Interim Guidelines for the Approval of Alternative Tanker Designs under regulation 13F of Annex I. The draft was circulated to member governments for comment, with a view to their adoption at MEPC 37 in 1995.

(v) Shipboard Waste Management

MEPC considered the text of a manual on shipboard waste management and formed a small working group to make the manual consistent with the existing manual on port reception facilities, with the new amendments to MARPOL Annex V and with the International Safety Management Code. A draft was to be submitted to MEPC 37 in 1995. The provision of reception facilities is essential for the implementation of MARPOL, for if ships are not to dump at sea, they must have somewhere to discharge the wastes and other substances cited in the annexes.

(b) MEPC Response to Agenda 21

MEPC adopted a report for the UN Commission on Sustainable Development on IMO's implementation of Agenda 21. During consideration of the report, a number of delegations led by Sweden voiced their opposition to the conclusions on degradation of the marine environment by offshore oil and gas platforms, in particular, the statement that IMO saw no compelling need to develop further global environmental regulations. The Committee decided to retain the existing text.

The Working Group on Agenda 21 developed draft guidelines to be used as a basis for further deliberations on the development of a precautionary approach for IMO.

(c) Sub-Committee on Flag State Implementation

The Sub-Committee decided to give top priority to the creation of a ship casualty database, in order to provide an overview of ship casualties; provide statistical support for the evaluation of IMO regulations; assist in the identification of problem areas with respect to casualty types, causes, and consequences; and provide information for the work of all IMO committees. MEPC established a correspondence group with Greenpeace International acting as coordinator to determine a definition of "severe pollution" for the purpose of developing the database on casualties. The Sub-Committee decided to develop a code of conduct on port-state control and to prepare a set of requirements for the training and qualifications of port-state surveyors. Further, a correspondence group was created to amalgamate all Assembly resolutions on port-state control.

(d) Joint Maritime Safety Commission (MSC)/MEPC Working Group on the Human Element

MEPC accepted the Joint MSC/MEPC Working Group's recommendation that the sub-committees developing various shipboard emergency plans use the Shipboard Oil Pollution Emergency Plan Guidelines as a model. Furthermore, a correspondence group was established to prepare a draft of a possible integrated structure of such plans, in order to avoid the proliferation of different, perhaps inconsistent, emergency plans.

Consistent with the previous decision of the MSC, MEPC approved the establishment of a correspondence group to develop guidelines for Administrations on the implementation of the International Safety Management Code, taking into account the guidelines already issued by the International Chamber of Shipping and the International Shipping Federation, and focusing on certification, verification, and control.

(e) Steering Committee on the International Ship Information Database (ISID)

IMO is considering the establishment of an International Ship Information Database that would receive and provide data relating to ships' identification (the core of the whole system), port-state control, casualties, and marine pollution. The Committee has agreed in principle that governments and classification societies acting on their behalf with respect to their own ships should provide and have access to the information in the database. Legal issues being discussed include liability, privacy, and intellectual property rights.

Because the Steering Committee on ISID had found it necessary to hold an additional unscheduled meeting in September, its final report was not available for the consideration of MEPC 36. After an exchange of views, the Committee decided that before taking a decision, it required more information. Therefore, it agreed to request the Council to authorize the Secretary-General to hire a contractor to conduct a detailed needs-assessment for the ISID and to evaluate the legal implications. When the final report of the Steering Committee and the contractor are available in 1995, MEPC will decide whether or not to create the ISID.

(f) Spills of Dangerous Goods

In response to maritime incidents resulting in the loss of dangerous cargo that subsequently washed up on its coasts, France proposed that certain parts of the Code of Safe Practice for Cargo Stowage and Securing and the International Maritime Dangerous Goods Code be made compulsory and that ships carrying dangerous goods be required to maintain a shipboard emergency plan.

(g) International Convention on Oil Pollution Response and Co-operation (OPRC) Working Group

The OPRC will come into force in May 1995. The Working Group for the Implementation of the OPRC continued its work on the development and revision of a number of manuals and guidelines related to OPRC implementation, some of which were approved for publication. The MEPC agreed on the further development of course materials on oil pollution preparedness and response, as well as on the initial pilot testing of some courses already prepared.

The Netherlands proposed the development of a protocol to extend the OPRC to cover hazardous substances while still allowing states to become party only to the existing Convention. Rather than adopting a separate protocol, some states preferred simply to amend the OPRC Convention to include hazardous substances other than oil. Furthermore, some states wished the adoption of the HNS Convention to be a prerequisite for extending the OPRC Convention, while other states disagreed. MEPC 36 called for comments on the proposal for consideration at its next meeting. Under Assembly resolution A.748(18), the MSC and the MEPC, together with the IAEA, were requested to study aspects of the transport of irradiated nuclear fuel (INF) and other nuclear materials that were related to the INF Code. MEPC agreed with the IAEA to expedite work on the question of preparedness and response processes associated with the marine transport of INF and other nuclear material for consideration at MEPC 37. The Committee decided to engage a consultant to prepare an information document. Supported by Singapore, Greenpeace stated that a Working Group on INF transportation be established and that shipments of INF substances should be suspended until the Working Group had presented its report.

(h) Particularly Sensitive Sea Areas

MEPC established a correspondence group on Particularly Sensitive Sea Areas (PSSAs) to be coordinated by Friends of the Earth International, with a mandate to assess the need to revise the PSSA Guidelines to include a definition of PSSAs in MARPOL 73/38 Annex I, taking into account documents MEPC 36/21/4 and MEPC 36/21/1, and to report to MEPC 38.

(i) Compensation for Pollution from Ships' Bunkers

Australia suggested that MEPC consider the possibility of the elaborating an international regime for compensation for damage caused by pollution from ships' bunkers. As there was strong support for this proposal, MEPC decided that the issue should be referred to the Legal Committee for consideration.

(3) Maritime Safety Committee

In 1994, the MSC met twice, on 16–25 May (MSC 63) and on 5-9 December (MSC 64).

(a) Ship Reporting Systems

Expanded to include all the parties to the International Convention on the Safety of Life at Sea (SOLAS), MSC 63 adopted new regulation 8-1 to Ch. V of the Convention, which deals with the safety of navigation. Regulation 8-1 makes the use of an IMO-approved ship reporting system mandatory for all ships or certain classes of ships when entering areas covered by the ship reporting system. Ship reporting systems provide, gather, and exchange information through radio reports to be used for vessel traffic services, search and rescue, weather forecasting, and the prevention of marine pollution. When entering the system, ships will have to provide information on their position, identity, and sailing plans. The information that the ship provides will enable the journey to be tracked, so that the ship may be warned if it begins to go off course or if there is a danger of collision or grounding. In addition, ships are required to report incidents that have caused or may cause marine pollution.

Guidelines and criteria for the implementation of this regulation were developed and approved by MSC 64. They will be submitted for adoption by the IMO Assembly in 1995.

(b) International Convention on Standards of Training, Certification, and Watchkeeping (STCW) 1978

IMO engaged in a complete revision of the STCW Convention, with the new Convention expected to be adopted in July 1995. The revised Convention will be confined to provisions on general principles and legal arrangements, while the substance will be placed in a new Code containing technical details that will be incorporated in the Convention by reference. The STCW Convention, which deals with the training and certification of shipboard personnel, is important to environmental protection because casualties and pollution incidents are caused by human error. In principle, it has been agreed that seafarers must be provided with ship-specific instructions before they are assigned to any duties involving ship safety or pollution prevention.

MSC 64 considered the texts of the new draft STCW Convention, the STCW Code, and the associated conference resolutions and approved them for circulation to the 1995 Conference of the Parties.

(4) Conventions and Diplomatic Conferences

(a) International Convention for the Safety of Life at Sea 1974

In May 1994, at a diplomatic conference, SOLAS was amended to include a new Ch. IX: Management for the Safe Operation of Ships, designed to make mandatory the International Safety Management Code. The Code sets forth safety management objectives and requires a safety management system (SMS) to be established by "the Company," defined as the ship-owner or any person who has assumed responsibility for managing the ship. The SMS should include a number of functional requirements, including:

- a safety and environment protection policy;
- instructions and procedures to ensure safety and environmental protection;
- defined levels of authority and lines of communication between and amongst shore and shipboard personnel;
- procedures for reporting accidents, etc.;
- procedures for responding to emergencies; and
- procedures for internal audits and management review.

Responsibility for ensuring that companies comply with the Code rests with the government of the state party. Companies that conform to the Code should be provided with a certificate of compliance that will be kept on board the ship.

A new Ch. X deals with Safety Measures for High Speed Craft, while new Ch. XI adopts a number of special measures to enhance safety in four regulations. Regulation 1 of Ch. XI states that organisations entrusted by an Administration with the responsibility for carrying out surveys and inspections shall comply with the guidelines that IMO adopted in resolution A.739(18) in November 1993. Regulation 2 extends to bulk carriers the enhanced programme of surveys for tankers more than five years old introduced under MARPOL 73/78. Regulation 3 requires all ships above a certain tonnage to be issued an IMO identification number. Finally, regulation 4 provides that port-state control officers may check compliance with operational requirements "where there are clear grounds for believing that the master or crew are not familiar with essential shipboard procedures relating to the safety of ships."

(b) MARPOL 73/78

Pursuant to the decisions of MEPC 34 and the 18th IMO Assembly, IMO convened a Conference of the Parties to MARPOL 73/78 in November 1994. The purpose of the Conference of the Parties was to consider and adopt amendments to MARPOL permitting port-state control to be exercised in respect of operational requirements. In order that they might take effect fairly rapidly, in accordance with the tacit acceptance procedure, the amendments were made to Annexes I, II, III, and V rather than to the text of the Convention itself. The substance of the amendments is the same as that adopted in regulation 4 of the new Ch. XI of SOLAS, referred to above, entitling port-state control officers to check compliance with operational requirements.

(5) Special Questions: Navigation in the Turkish Straits

In recent years, there has been severe congestion in the Turkish Straits (the Strait of Istanbul, the Strait of Canakkale, and the Marmara Sea) involving very large oil tankers and ships carrying dangerous cargo. This has lead to an increasing number of accidents and collisions resulting in pollution damage. In response, in January 1994, Turkey adopted regulations for safe navigation in the Straits under national law, which came into force on 1 July 1994. Turkey also submitted to MSC 63 for approval draft rules for navigation that were a version of its national regulations. Although the Turkish draft was rejected, MSC 63 adopted Rules and Recommendations on Navigation through the Strait of Istanbul, the Strait of Canakkale, and the Marmara Sea, which were circulated as SN/Cir.166 of 1 June 1994. They came into force on 24 November 1994.

At the October meeting of the Legal Committee, a number of states led by Russia criticized the Turkish domestic regulations as being inconsistent with the IMO recommendations; the 1936 Montreux Convention, which governs navigation through the Straits; and the United Nations Convention on the Law of the Sea. The Turkish government took the position that as the IMO was not a judicial body, it had no right to judge the validity of Turkey's regulations under international law.

During discussion in the Legal Committee, there was general recognition that Turkey had acted in good faith out of concern for the safety of navigation and the protection of the marine environment. Nevertheless, a significant number of delegations (Bulgaria, France, Germany, Greece, Italy, Mexico, Poland, Romania, the United Kingdom, and the United States) believed that the Turkish regulations were too restrictive. Since the Legal Committee considered that it was not competent to judge the technical aspects of the regulations, it decided to request IMO Council to refer the matter to the MSC for a technical review.

IMO Council acceded to this request. By the time the question reached MSC 64, the regulations had come into force and Turkey had adopted a set of instructions to its local authorities for their implementation. During the discussion, the Russian Federation advised the Committee that its vessels were experiencing delays at the entrance to the Straits and that its masters were unsure as to which regulations applied. Yet it was prepared to consider the explanations given by the Turkish delegation and suggested that the practical application of the IMO Rules and Recommendations be considered at the next meeting of the MSC.

The United States declared that its concerns about the Turkish national regulations had been laid to rest by the instructions for implementation, which it had studied carefully. Further, it noted that not enough time had passed since the IMO Rules and Recommendations had come into force to evaluate them. Most other states had not had an opportunity to examine the Turkish instructions, but there was general agreement to postpone consideration of all aspects of the question until MSC 65 in 1995.

Louise de La Fayette

I. ORGANISATION FOR ECONOMIC COOPERATION AND DEVELOPMENT (OECD)

At its 834th Session, 28–29 July, the OECD Council adopted three decisions relating to various aspects of the transfrontier movement of wastes, all of which had been proposed by the Environment Policy Committee.

Decision C(94)152 amends Decision C(88)90 of 27 May 1988 on "Transfrontier Movements of Hazardous Wastes," the Annex of which provides for definition and classification of hazardous wastes according to a series of seven tables. When the Basel Convention on the Control of Transboundary Movements of Hazardous Wastes and their Disposal was adopted on 22 March 1989, it incorporated two tables of Decision C(88)90: the "core list of wastes to be controlled" (Table Y) and the "list of hazardous characteristics" (Table 5). The Convention made some modifications to these tables to reflect the Convention's scope. Since the modifications introduced minor differences between the Convention and Decision C(88)90 that might create confusion in their implementation, and since most OECD member countries are now parties to the Basel Convention, Decision C(94)152 amends the relevant tables in Decision C(88)90 to conform them to the corresponding tables in the Convention.

Decision C(94)153 amends Decision C(92)39 of 30 March 1992 concerning the "Control of Transfrontier Movements of Wastes destined for Recovery Operations," as amended by Decision C(93)74 of 23 July 1993, with respect to the Green List of Wastes. Decision C(92)39 instructed the OECD Environment Committee, in cooperation with other relevant OECD bodies, in particular the Trade Committee, to review periodically the control system and the lists of wastes set out in Annex 1, taking into account the criteria listed in Annex 2, and to make any proposal it deems necessary for revisions of Annex 1. As a result of the review conducted in 1993–94, Decision C(94)153 further amends the lists of wastes set out in Decision C(92)39 by adding one additional item to the Green List and by replacing entries GM 010 to GM 060 in that list with a general entry dealing with wastes from the agro-food industry.

Decision C(94)154 concerning the "Document for Transfrontier Movements of Wastes" also amends Decision C(92)39. The preamble of Decision C(94)154 is interesting in that it recalls several of the important steps in the international effort to control transfrontier movements of waste, in which the OECD played a pioneering role, and highlights the inter-relationship between the instruments that the three main regional and global organizations active in this field elaborated:

- OECD Decision-Recommendation C(83)180 of 1 February 1984, which required member countries to control transfrontier movements of hazardous waste;
- the Basel Convention on the Control of Transboundary Movements of Hazardous Wastes and their Disposal, adopted on 22 March 1989 under the aegis of the United Nations Environment Programme, to which most OECD member countries and the European Community have become parties; and
- European Council (EC) Regulation 259/93 of 1 February 1993 on the Supervision and Control of Shipments of Waste within, into and out of the European Community.

The implementation of the control system that Decision C(92)39 established called for the development of a uniform document to provide the information required for notification and tracking of transfrontier movements of wastes destined for recovery operations within the OECD area. The Decision originally envisaged that the uniform document would be mandatory. OECD member countries, however, subsequently expressed the wish that the uniform document be developed so that it could be used for movements controlled by the Basel Convention and the EC Regulation as well as those controlled by the Decision. In order for this to happen, use of the uniform document could not be made mandatory. Similarly, the Commission of the European Communities was also proposing to use the uniform document for transfrontier movements to be controlled by the EC Regulation.

As a result of these developments, Decision C(94)154 amends Decision C(92)39 to provide that "it is recommended that" member countries use the uniform Document for Transfrontier Movement of Wastes to provide the information required to control transfrontier movements of wastes destined for recovery operations within the OECD area. Decision C(94)154 also requests the Secretary-General of the OECD to pursue discussions with the Secretariat of the Basel Convention to assess whether the uniform Document for Transfrontier Movement of Wastes could also be used for transfrontier movements to be controlled by the Convention.

Paul Fauteux

J. ORGANIZATION OF AFRICAN UNITY (OAU)

[Editors' Note: No report received for volume 5]

K. REGIONAL DEVELOPMENT BANKS: ASIAN DEVELOPMENT BANK

(1) Environment as a Strategic Development Objective

In his May 1994 address to the Board of Governors of the Asian Development Bank (ADB), President Mitsuo Sato indicated that "protecting the environment" is among five interrelated "strategic development objectives to be pursued by the ADB" to help attain "sustainable development of the Asian and Pacific Region." These objectives "include promoting efficient economic growth, reducing poverty, protecting the environment, facilitating progress in population planning and enhancing the role of women in development." The President stated that he was "pleased to report that at least half of all [ADB]-financed projects address social or environmental concerns."

(2) *Improving Project Quality and Reorganizing the Office of the Environment*

A January 1994 ADB Report of the Task Force on Improving Project Quality indicated that the ADB will give greater emphasis to "social and environmental dimensions," such as "poverty reduction, human resource development, women-in-development and environmental rehabilitation." Partly in response to a key recommendation in the Task Force Report to realign the Bank's Office of the Environment and the Social Dimensions Unit, the ADB's Board of Directors approved, on 17 November 1994, a "revised organization structure" creating an Office of Environment and Social Development, which reports directly to the President and consists of an Environment Division and a Social Development Division.

(3) *Classification of Loan Projects in Terms of ADB's Strategic Development Objectives*

In April 1994, the ADB published *The Environmental Program of the Asian Development Bank: Past, Present and Future* (*ADB Environmental Program*), which indicates a proposed project mix for 1994 to 1996 with less than 50 percent of the number of loan projects in the traditional growth category and more than 50 percent "directly aimed at social concerns," "at the environment," or "[at] growth-oriented projects having secondary features to address social and/or environmental concerns." Criteria for categorizing a project as having either a primary or a secondary environmental concern, which by year's end were still under review, classify a project as falling into the first category if its primary aim is to protect or improve the environment, conserve natural resources (excluding minerals), or promote nonconventional renewable energy; and if one or more components specifically related to environmental protection/improvement, conservation of natural resources, or promotion of nonconventional renewable energy account for at least 50 percent of the total project costs. This category excludes the mitigation or offsetting of incremental adverse effects since this is now mandatory for all Bank-financed projects.

A project would be classified as having the environment as its secondary objective if the effect of "the project case" is beneficial to the environment and if a secondary objective of the project is either to achieve a measurable environmental improvement, or protect the environment from further deterioration; or if one or more components specifically related to environmental protection/improvement, conservation of natural resources (excluding minerals), or promotion of non-conventional renewable energy account for at least 20 percent of the total project costs. As with the primary-objective category, the secondary-objective category excludes the mitigation of incremental adverse effects since this is now mandatory.

(4) Environmental Loan Program

In 1994, the ADB approved four loans totalling about US$462.1 million for environment-oriented projects including one with primary environmental purposes amounting to $157 million for the Beijing Environmental Improvement Project in the People's Republic of China (PRC). ADB also made loans for three projects with secondary environmental concerns: $165 million for the Qitaihe Thermal Energy and Environmental Improvement Project; $62.2 million for the Third Punjab On-Farm Water Management Project; and $77 million for the Yannan Simas Forestation and Sustainable Wood Utilization Project.

(5) Technical Assistance

In 1994, the ADB approved $12,636,000 for six technical assistance grant projects and four regional technical assistance projects with an environmental focus, and $900,000 for two regional technical assistance projects dealing with social dimensions. The ADB technical assistance grants with an environmental focus consisted of: $500,000 to the PRC for a Legislative Reform for Protecting the Environment and Natural Resources Project; $550,000 to Cambodia for a Strengthening Environmental Impact Assessment Procedures and Capabilities Project; $600,000 to Vietnam for a Strengthening Environmental Planning and Environmental Impact Assessment (EIA) Capabilities Project; $250,000 to Thailand for Preparation and Implementation of a National Sustainable Development Strategy (Agenda 21); $850,000 to Pakistan for Implementation of a National Conservation Strategy for Pakistan; and $500,000 to Nepal to Strengthen Inter-Ministerial Capability for Implementing EIA Guidelines.

The ADB's 1994 regional technical assistance grant program with an environmental focus consisted of a supplemental $600,000 for Coastal and Marine Environmental Management in the South China Sea; $99,000 for the Strengthening of the Regional Environmental and Natural Resources Information Center; $450,000 for a Ministerial Level Conference on Environment and Development and Preparation of a State of the Environment Report; and $8,237,000 for a Least-Cost Greenhouse Gas Abatement Strategy for Asia. In the last-mentioned project, the Global Environment Facility (GEF), acting through the United Nations Development Programme, provided a grant of $8,137,000 for technical assistance to be administered by the ADB in Bangladesh, India, Indonesia, the Democratic People's Republic of Korea (DPRK), Mongolia, Myanmar, Pakistan, PRC, Philippines, Thailand, and Vietnam, while the ADB provided a grant of $100,000 to co-finance technical assistance in the Republic of Korea. Since the DPRK is not a member of the ADB, the ADB agreed to subcontract implementation of GEF-financed technical assistance in

DPRK to the United Nations Economic and Social Commission for Asia and the Pacific (ESCAP).

(6) *Staff Instructions*

On 15 February 1994, President Sato issued Staff Instructions as "interim arrangements, pending . . . Board discussion and approval of policies on these subjects" on four subjects relevant to environmental issues, which are discussed in the following sub-sections: (a) good governance, (b) involuntary resettlement, (c) indigenous peoples and (d) population. Additionally, on 22 November 1994, Staff Instructions on Confidentiality and Disclosure of Information were issued.

(a) *Good Governance*

On the matter of good governance, the Staff Instruction emphasizes as the "principal issues" public sector management, accountability, legal framework for development, and transparency and information. Paragraphs 6 and 7 highlight the "importance of the rule of law for economic development for predictability and stability in regulatory frameworks" and of "[a]ccess to information (about the economy in general, market conditions and government policies), and of transparency of decision-making processes as prerequisites for both accountability and the rule of law." With respect to the activities to be addressed by staff, para. 8(iii) lists "improving compliance with financial (accounts and audit) covenants," while para. 8(v) includes "providing advisory technical assistance in such areas as capacity building, regulatory frameworks, and privatization."

(b) *Involuntary Resettlement*

The Staff Instruction on Involuntary Resettlement states in part in that "[w]here large-scale population displacement is unavoidable, a detailed resettlement plan should be prepared along with a timetable and a budget for implementation of the plan." Among other elements to be included in the plan are, *inter alia*, legal mechanisms for the resolution of conflicts and appeals procedures and provisions on the valuation of compensation for lost assets, on land ownership, tenure, acquisition, and transfer. The Involuntary Resettlement Staff Instruction commits the ADB to assist developing member countries in designing and assessing national resettlement policies, strategies, laws, regulations, and plans.

(c) *Indigenous Peoples*

The Staff Instruction defines "indigenous peoples" as including "'indigenous and ethnic minorities', 'tribal groups', and 'scheduled tribes' who have a social and cultural identity distinct from the dominant society which makes them vulnerable to being disadvantaged in the development process." Defining characteristics of indigenous peoples under this provision include "close attachment to ancestral territories and to the natural resources in those areas" and "customary social and political institutions." The Staff Instruction reiterates that the ADB's policy on indigenous peoples will be to ensure that "the development process facilitates their informed participation and fosters full respect for their dignity, human rights and cultural uniqueness," while recognizing that "orienting and strengthening the social, legal and technical skills of government institutions responsible for dealing with indigenous peoples" is a critical element in this process.

(d) Population

The Staff Instruction on Population indicates in part that:

Demographic perspectives have . . . to be reflected in all COSS [Country Operation Strategy Studies] and country analytical documents, looking at the impact of population growth on economic growth, poverty and the environment; and analyzing the spatial and age distribution of the population and its implications for Bank assistance in regional development and social sectors.

(e) Confidentiality and Disclosure of Information

The Staff Instructions on Confidentiality and Disclosure of Information are based on the ADB's new policy on disclosure and procedures for its implementation, including a revised classification system for documents relating to the public and private sector operations of the Bank. While recognizing important practical and legal constraints, the ADB's new policy provides for the greatest possible degree of transparency and disclosure in all areas of its operations. It emphasizes a presumption in favor of disclosure where disclosure would not materially harm the interests of the ADB, its membership, borrowers, and private sector clients.

The new policy, which was to become effective on 1 January 1995, distinguishes between full disclosure, openness, and transparency with respect to the ADB's operations and policies on the one hand, and disclosure of information provided by others on the other hand. Any disclosure regarding the latter must be subject to safeguards. Information supplied on a confidential basis or information of a proprietary nature generally cannot be released without the consent of the supplier or legal owner. Similarly, information received prior to the policy becoming effective cannot be disclosed without appropriate consent or authorization. The new policy also protects the integrity of the deliberation and decision-making process of the ADB's Board of Directors.

(7) Social Dimensions Handbook

In May 1994, the ADB's Social Dimensions Unit published a *Handbook for Incorporation of Social Dimensions in Projects*. Designed as a supplement to the "Guidelines for Incorporation of Social Dimensions in Bank Operations" (described in 4 *YbIEL* 528 at pp. 532–533 (1993)), the *Handbook* contains brief chapters on social analysis and project design as well as initial social assessment plus subsector checklists on irrigation, flood control and drainage, fisheries and coastal zone management, micro-finance and development of micro-enterprises, forestry and watershed management, integrated rural development, tree crops and plantations, livestock, urban and rural water supply and sanitation, population, health, education and training, roads and road transport, airports, ports and shipping, railways, telecommunications, and power.

(8) Climate Change

In July 1994, the ADB published nine volumes of a study on *Climate Change in Asia*. One volume provided an Executive Summary of the study, while the other eight volumes consisted of country reports concerning Bangladesh, India, Indonesia, Malaysia, Pakistan, Philippines, Sri Lanka, and Vietnam. The nine volumes were financed under the ADB's Regional Study on Global Environmental Issues, which received support from the Governments of Australia, Japan, and Norway. Topics covered in each country report included assessment of impacts, adaptation and mitigation options, and a national response strategy including research and technical assistance needs as well as investment packages.

In February 1994, the ADB published the proceedings of the Second Asia Pacific Seminar on Climate Change held in ESCAP headquarters from 29 to 31 March 1993 in Bangkok, Thailand. The seminar was financed by the Japan Environment Agency and the ADB and included discussion of the current work of the Intergovernmental Panel on Climate Change, impacts of sea level rise and response strategies in Japan, and emission inventories and mitigation measures.

(9) Biodiversity

From 6 to 8 June 1994, the ADB organized with the International Union for the Conservation of Nature a regional conference on biodiversity conservation, held at ADB's Manila Headquarters. A portion of the conference was devoted to the political and legal dynamics of implementing the Convention on Biological Diversity in the Asia and Pacific Region. The ADB was to publish a book containing a record of the proceedings of the conference, entitled *Biodiversity Conservation in the Asia and Pacific Region*, soon after.

(10) Financing Environmentally-Sound Development

In December of 1994, the ADB published a book entitled *Financing Environmentally-Sound Development*, which consists primarily of contributions from experts who attended the ADB-sponsored Regional Meeting on the Financing of Environmentally-Sound Development held in Bangkok, Thailand, from 15 to 17 June 1993. Chapters of the book discuss major environmental problems and costs of abatement, sources of funds for environmental management, market-based instruments in the Asian and Pacific region, structural adjustment and sustainable development, the market for environmental goods and services, privatization and sustainable development, and implications for regional institutions.

John A. Boyd

K. REGIONAL DEVELOPMENT BANKS: EUROPEAN BANK FOR RECONSTRUCTION AND DEVELOPMENT

(1) Introduction

According to Art. 2(1.vii) of the agreement establishing the European Bank for Reconstruction and Development (EBRD), the Bank must "promote in the full range of its activities environmentally sound and sustainable development." Launched as a state-of-the-art multilateral financing institution, the EBRD has had four troubled years of operation, during which environmentalists have criticised it for significant gaps in its environmental policies and procedures.

(2) Specific Projects Raise Doubts about EBRD Environmental Policy

A number of particularly controversial projects exposed difficulties with the Bank's environmental assessment procedures. In particular, the completion of the Mochovce nuclear power plant and the ZSNP/SLOVALCO Aluminum plant, both in the Slovak Republic, focused public and non-governmental organization (NGO) attention on gaps in the EBRD's ability to effectively implement its environmental policies and procedures. Critics have accused the Bank of failing to follow its own public participation procedures or to properly take environmental costs into account when assessing least-cost options to investment activities. The ZSNP/SLOVALCO Aluminum Plant is one example of the difficulties the Bank has had ensuring effective public participation in project selection. In September 1993, the EBRD approved a loan for $100 million for a new aluminum smelter at the plant despite environmental and economic problems. Although such a project would normally require a full environmental assessment, the EBRD announced that it would not follow public participation procedures due to time constraints. Under NGO pressure, the project sponsors eventually held two brief public meetings that were criticised as allowing insufficient opportunity to air the issues. Seeking to make amends, the EBRD proposed to give the public a role in monitoring the project to make sure that all agreed remediation and mitigation measures were being followed. The NGOs, however, feeling that the Bank had effectively excluded them from the planning phase, refused to take part in the monitoring to avoid giving legitimacy to the project.

Construction of the Mochovce nuclear power plant in Slovakia, 150km from Vienna, was originally halted in 1991 due to lack of financing. As of the end of 1994, however, the EBRD was attempting to provide financing to a new sponsor. Local and international NGOs, as well as Austria, attempted to block the loan by publicizing that the reactor contained design defects. Critics claimed it lacked a proper containment facility and had inadequate protection from external hazards like plane crashes, earthquakes, and sabotage. They also challenged the official estimated costs of the plant's operation, particularly the costs of risks of accidents and environmental externalities.

NGOs and others have criticised the Bank's approval of the project for failing to comply with the EBRD's energy operations policy, which provides that "it is environmentally and economically better to reduce the existing excessive demand for electricity than to build new facilities that continue the old wasteful ways." Environmental groups have put forward alternatives that they argue would be far cheaper than the completion of Mochovce Units 1 and 2. The final fate of the project has not yet been determined.

(3) The Baltic Sea Programme

The EBRD took part in the Baltic Sea Environmental Programme in 1994 by promoting a coordinated approach among the concerned countries. The Bank performed some pre-feasibility and area studies in Kalingrad, Russia, as well as region-wide studies of agricultural run-off and airborne pollution. The Bank also initiated project identification studies, including the Baltic pulp and paper sector study and the Latvian forest sector master plan. The EBRD has increasingly concentrated on financing priority investments in a few cities, and has set up water and wastewater management projects in Estonia and hazardous waste management projects in Latvia.

In July, the EBRD made its first loan (DM 44.4 million) for an environmental infrastructure project that combines financing from Finland and the European Community EC-PHARE programme. The project concerns the Tallin Water and Sewerage Municipal Enterprise (TWSME) in Estonia. Its objective is to rehabilitate the existing system, develop new groundwater well fields, and expand the wastewater treatment plant in order to improve the reliability of water supply services and drinking water quality, as well as reduce waterborne pollution from Tallin to the Gulf of Finland in the Baltic sea. Additionally, the Bank entered into a twinning arrangement with the Helsinki Waterworks to restructure TWSME into a self-managed and self-financed water utility enterprise independent of any state or municipal subsidies.

(4) New Energy Operations Policy

In July, the EBRD also issued a new energy operations policy that provides considerable guidance on environmental issues. It focuses on conservation, energy efficiency, least-cost planning, and renewable energy sources. The policy's overall objective is to help countries reorient sector development away from supply expansion to a broader "least-cost" focus on energy efficiency and resource conservation.

On the supply side, the Bank set up Emergency Energy Investment projects in the Baltic sea countries. The Polish Power Grid Company project, signed on 8 July, included a loan of Ecu 31.4 million and involves the upgrading of thermal power stations and district heating stations to improve combustion efficiencies, and the repairing of the power and heating distribution system.

(5) Restructuring the Environmental Advisory Council

The Environmental Advisory Council (ENVAC) is an advisory board of 17 environmental experts from Central and Eastern Europe and Organisation for Economic Cooperation and Development countries. It meets twice a year, and is intended to provide the EBRD with expertise on environmental protection and natural resource management at the national, regional, and local levels. It also advises the EBRD on strategic policy implications of global environmental issues.

After a controversial suspension of ENVAC's activities in September 1993, the Bank re-established it in 1994 and directed it to continue as an expert, external, independent group. At the end of 1994, ENVAC advised the EBRD that it should ensure full public participation before funding investment projects. It stated that energy and transport policies should focus on demand-side management and innovative projects such as alternative energy sources. As for the Mochovce Nuclear Power Plant, ENVAC stressed the importance of public participation, including input from countries bordering Slovakia, and urged careful consideration of all options, including the option not to act.

(6) Development of Environmental Training

The EBRD sought to maintain a proactive environmental stance by providing environmental analysis training for professionals. It developed a training course in environmentally sound banking and sector-specific environmental impact assessment (EIA). The training is designed to accelerate the successful implementation of EIA.

During 1994, the EBRD was also setting up training for public participation to assist administrators, investors, and financial institutions with public meetings and conflict resolution techniques. The Bank teaches modern techniques in environmental management and audits as well.

The Bank implemented some specific environmental training projects in 1994. It demonstrated a Hungarian pilot training module at an international workshop in Budapest. In January, the EBRD's Operations Committee approved a project that focuses on environmental assessment training for transport specialists. Workshops are to take place in Belarus, Kazakhistan, Russia, and Ukraine. The training is to provide senior officials in Ministries of Transport with an understanding of the environmental issues associated with transport in general. It emphasises the use of EIA as a planning tool, and explores methods and techniques for assessing environmental impacts.

Jacob Werksman

K. REGIONAL DEVELOPMENT BANKS: EUROPEAN INVESTMENT BANK

(1) European Investment Bank

The European Investment Bank's (EIB's) massive resources and expanding activities in environmentally volatile areas of Eastern Europe and the developing world have begun to attract increased attention from the environmental community. The EIB also appears to be gaining greater responsibilities in shaping the European Union's (EU's) infrastructural investment policies. The Bank did not issue the much-anticipated comprehensive review of its environmental policy in 1994.

The EIB began implementation of a number of legal and policy initiatives on development and the environment in the EU in 1994. As the EU's primary financial institution, the EIB plays a central role in implementing these initiatives by carrying out the relevant provisions of the Maastricht Treaty and the European Community (EC) Commission's December 1993 "White Paper on Growth, Competitiveness and Employment" (White Paper).

The Maastricht Treaty both confirms and broadens the EIB's key role in the implementation of Community development policy. It assigns to the EIB the protection and improvement of the environment as well as the promotion of the Trans-European Networks (TENs) for transportation, energy, and telecommunications.

Under the White Paper, drafted to help implement the Treaty, the EIB and the Commission established two new financial instruments—the Cohesion Fund and the European Investment Fund—designed to stimulate economic activity within the EU. Both the Bank and the Commission are to coordinate the activities of the Funds, which will help finance TENs and EU initiatives to encourage small-scale and medium-scale enterprises.

The EIB began to take part in programming the community structural support operations (CSFs) covering the period 1994 to 1999. CSF resources during this five-year period should amount to ECU 164.3 billion. The EIB, with the cooperation of the European Community (EC) Commission, is to directly or indirectly allocate these funds, which will be concentrated on the poorer regions of the EU.

The Edinburgh Facility allocated a further ECU 7 billion to the EIB to speed up the financing of large infrastructure projects, improve the environment, and help small-scale and medium-scale enterprises. In this context, the European Council, at its 1993–1994 meetings in Copenhagen, Brussels, Corfu, and Essen, asked the EIB to assist the EC Commission in coordinating the funding of these activities.

(2) Trans-European Networks

The White Paper establishes that TENs, and in particular transportation network investment, are the EU's main development priority. In order to guide TENs investment, in December 1993 the European Council of Ministers set up a Special Group of Representatives of Heads of States and Governments, known as the Christophersen Group. The EIB provides technical expertise to assist the Group in assessing and prioritising projects. The Christophersen Group and the EIB defined selection criteria for projects on the basis of the EC Commission's proposals. Eligible transportation infrastructure projects must be of exceptional scale, of common interest, economically viable, and must facilitate connections both within the EU and between the EU and neighbouring countries.

Following these guidelines, the EIB provided technical, economic, and financial assessments of 14 transportation projects that the Council approved. Over ECU 10 billion is to finance high-speed trains in Belgium and motorways in Spain, Greece, Finland, and Portugal, and accelerate the financing of 150 large infrastructure schemes. TENs investments were beginning to reach into neighbouring Eastern Europe as well. The EIB's implementation of large-scale projects under the TENs drew praise for promoting public transportation and improving electronic communication networks, but received criticism for investing too heavily in motorways and supply-side oriented electrical power grid investments.

TENs, like all EIB projects, must comply with EC environmental legislation, which requires environmental impact assessments. The Christophersen Group stated that, as a result of the attention to environmental protection, 88 percent of the total investments will be dedicated to railways. By reducing travel time between European centres, it is hoped that these projects will encourage passengers and freight shippers to switch from the road to the more environmentally friendly rail.

The pressure on the EIB and the Commission to more carefully take into account the potential environmental impacts of large-scale transportation investment grew during 1994, and a Council meeting highlighted the need to integrate consideration for the environment into national and European transportation policies. To this end, the EU is to work in close cooperation with United Nations in its preparations for the 1996 Conference "Transports and Environment," organised by the UN Economic Commission for Europe.

At its meeting in Essen in December, the Council established a "Special Window" within the Bank, which is to provide financing for environmental aspects of TENs projects. Finally, the Council requested the Christophersen Group to examine the extent to which the TENs approach could be applied to the funding of projects with specific environmental objectives.

(3) Lending to Mediterranean Countries

The EIB supports productive investment to aid in the development of Mediterranean countries, with a particular focus on environmental protection and private-sector growth. The Bank's environmental activity concentrates on water resources management, such as developing drinking-water reserves and supply facilities and establishing sewerage and water treatment plants. The EIB has, for example, helped to clean up the Gulf of Gabes in Tunisia and set up wastewater collection and treatment facilities in coastal towns in Morocco, the Greater Algiers area, Cairo, Israel, and Jordan. The EIB and the World Bank were in the process of implementing the Mediterranean Environmental Technical Assistance Programme, of which the first objective is to prepare viable investment projects in both EU and non-EU Mediterranean countries. Twenty studies on pilot projects had been conducted thus far and 30 other projects were in preparation.

(4) Lending to African, Caribbean, and Pacific Countries

The EIB also plays a role in implementing the EU's obligations to assist the development of African, Caribbean, and Pacific states under the fourth Lom Convention. Apart from productive investment in mining, tourism, and agriculture, the EIB contributes to the setting up of basic infrastructure such as urban water management, transport, and energy production and distribution.

(5) Lending to Asian and Latin American Countries

Two 1994 projects in Costa Rica and India concerning electricity generation and supply attracted EIB loans of over ECU 99 million. The EIB also provided ECU 750 million for February 1993-1995 for projects in Asian and Latin American countries that have signed cooperation agreements with the EU.

(6) Lending to Central and Eastern Europe

The EIB became involved in the international programme for protecting the Elbe River basin, supervising studies on the upper basin in order to identify possible investment projects. The Bank also participated in preparatory discussions on multilateral action for the environmental rehabilitation of the Danube River basin.

With the accession of Finland and Sweden to the EU, the Community will be directly concerned with the problem of pollution of the Baltic Sea. The EIB has therefore taken part in international cooperation programmes aimed at preserving the Baltic Sea and its main rivers.

Some major projects dealing with urban wastewater collection and treatment and with atmospheric pollution were expected to be ready for financing in 1995 in most Eastern European countries.

Jacob Werksman

K. REGIONAL DEVELOPMENT BANKS: INTER-AMERICAN DEVELOPMENT BANK

(1) Introduction

During 1994, the Inter-American Development Bank (IDB) received a substantial increase in its working capital; the eighth in its 34-year history. The capital increase calls upon the Bank to raise the priority given to projects that: reduce poverty; promote social equity, economic modernization, and integration; and strengthen civil society. As in the previous capital increases, the Bank's commitment to private sector initiatives and the environment was reaffirmed. In addition to ensuring that all its operations are environmentally sustainable, the Bank will raise the social impact and economic efficiency of its programs and projects. Project design will also take into consideration the global benefits of sustainable environmental management.

(2) Internal Reorganization

In order to carry out the mandates of the eighth capital increase and to better adapt the organization to the needs of its borrowing countries, the Bank's Board of Directors authorized a reorganization of the institution's operating departments. The reorganization implied a significant change in the treatment accorded to environmental issues. The most important of these affects the preparation of operations the main purpose of which is to contribute to the resolution of environmental or natural resources problems. Before the reorganization, technical responsibility for preparing these operations rested solely with the Environment Protection (ENV) and Sanitation and Urban Development (SUD) Divisions in the Project Analysis Department. This function has now been transferred to separate Environment and Natural Resource Management Divisions within each of the three new Regional Operations Departments. In addition to the functions previously performed by ENV and SUD, the new regional environment divisions now also perform functions previously assigned to the Agriculture Division.

An Environment Division (SDS/ENV) was also created within the new Social Programs and Sustainable Development Department (SDS). This new division is charged with environmental quality enhancement and the development of environmental policies, strategies, guidelines, and conceptual papers. It also assists the Environment Committee (CMA) in the environmental quality control of all Bank operations. In addition, the new division is responsible for maintaining inter-institutional ties, developing training programs, and providing technical advice to the three Regional Operations Departments. As is the case with the regional environment units, this new division also deals with urban and rural environmental issues, natural resources management and conservation, and agriculture and sustainable rural development. In addition, it is responsible for promoting energy conservation and use of alternative energy sources.

Recognizing the increasing importance of indigenous and resettlement issues, the reorganization resulted in the creation of an Indigenous Peoples and Community Development unit within SDS. The Bank will actively seek innovative projects to foster the ethno-development of indigenous peoples and to address resettlement in more comprehensive and creative ways.

The duties of the Regional Environmental Advisors stationed throughout Latin America and the Caribbean have not changed as a result of the reorganization. They continue to be responsible for field monitoring and follow-up of the environmental requirements of approved operations. The number of Regional Environmental Advisors will increase until the needs of all the Country Offices are adequately addressed. For the time being, the six existing Regional Advisors are being assisted by local environmental consultants.

(3) Major Focus Areas of Environmental Project Financing

Since 1990, total lending for projects specifically designed to address environmental and natural resources problems has risen at an average annual rate of 35.7 percent, totaling $4.8 billion between 1990 and 1994. In 1994, the Bank approved four natural resources conservation operations (Ecuador, Colombia, Honduras, and Barbados), four urban environment operations (Ecuador, Mexico, Brazil, and Peru), one sociocultural loan (Ecuador), and one loan to strengthen environmental institutions (Bolivia). In addition, a tourism development loan for Brazil contained a large (73 percent of the total loan) environmental component.

Eighteen technical cooperation and small projects dealing with environment and natural resources were also approved in 1994. The technical cooperation totaled $19.4 million, the bulk of which went to natural resources conservation. In addition, the Multilateral Investment Fund approved $1.5 million in lending to benefit the environment and natural resources.

(a) Natural Resources Conservation

Natural resource projects include watershed management, coastal management and marine resources, and forestry and biodiversity. Natural resources lending in 1994 was concentrated in marine resources and coastal management projects, including technical cooperation to initiate an environmental development project in Ecuador's Galapagos Islands, technical cooperation to prepare a coastal management project in Guyana, an environmental management project for the Bay Islands of Honduras, and a sustainable development project for Colombia's Pacific Coast.

(b) Forestry and Biodiversity

At the time of the eighth increase in Bank capital, the Board accepted several principles related to the conservation-oriented management of forest resources. The Bank will finance forestry activities only when the borrowing country government has shown a firm commitment to sustainable forest management. It will also support investments that foster such commitment and strengthen the institutional capacity of responsible governmental and non-governmental entities to engage in the management of forest resources.

During 1994, the Bank approved several projects with important forestry components, including investments to rehabilitate land (such as reforestation and afforestation, as well as agroforestry activities), promote soil conservation, and encourage the appropriate management of watersheds.

(c) Urban Environment and Pollution Control

The biggest share of Bank lending for the environment goes to urban projects, including air and water pollution control, potable water supply, and sewerage. The Bank approved four projects in 1994 totaling $747 million. Included were two potable water and sewerage loans (one for Quito, Ecuador, and the other for Guadalajara, Mexico), a drainage program for

Sao Paulo, Brazil, and a project to support the basic sanitation sector in Peru.

(d) Institutional Strengthening and Regulatory Framework

During 1994, the Bank approved one loan and five technical cooperation projects on institutional strengthening totaling $23.75 million. The loan for $19 million will assist the Bolivian government in strengthening its ability to address sustainable development and environmental problems. The program includes institutional strengthening, data development, environmental quality control, public participation, and privatization.

The Bank will continue to work with member countries to strengthen environmental legislation and establish regulations and systems of incentives and sanctions aimed at promoting environmental conservation and improving the management of institutions responsible for the environment and natural resources. A significant effort must be made to establish efficient institutional mechanisms to address environmental matters. These will entail the coordination of the decision-making process and the promotion of participatory processes through local public and private organizations. Environmental management at the local level can play a fundamental role in allowing the population to take part in creating a better environment.

(e) Energy Conservation and Efficiency

In 1994, the Bank continued to assist member countries in carrying out structural reforms of their energy sectors in order to provide a more appropriate institutional framework and enhance the financial position and operational efficiency of utility companies.

(f) Environmental Features of Operations in Other Sectors

In addition to the areas listed above, the Bank financed operations in other areas that included important environmental components. For example, operations in the transportation sector require environmental components to avoid or mitigate the potentially negative environmental impacts of road construction works. Furthermore, three agricultural sector reform programs (in Ecuador, Colombia, and Nicaragua) included institutional components. These programs will create and strengthen environmental management and the reclamation of degraded areas among national and sectoral institutions.

(4) Environmental Quality Control in IDB Operations

As in previous years, the Bank has made important strides in ensuring the environmental quality of all operations. In 1994, 30.2 percent of the operations that the CMA reviewed were in categories that required environmental impact assessments. It is estimated that approximately $150 million was spent on measures to improve the environmental quality of non-environmental operations.

The Bank's internal reorganization led to a restructuring of the CMA to take into account the increase in the number of Bank departments with responsibility for environmental matters. The CMA's primary responsibility for internal coordination, particularly the approval of documents dealing with the environmental quality of operations, however, has not changed.

The reorganization also led to a necessary revision in the Bank's operations and procedures manual, including the environmental procedures. The most important change is the move toward preparation of tailor-made environmental briefs for each operation. This is expected to replace the previous assignment of environmental categories. Existing experience now makes it possible to propose measures specifically suited to the needs of each particular project. If the existing categorization will thus be replaced, it is no longer necessary to establish generic or standardized measures according to categories of projects without relation to the specifics of a particular situation. The new environmental quality procedures are expected to be approved in early 1995.

(5) Information Disclosure Policy

In October 1994, the Board of Directors approved the new information access policy, which is aimed at allowing the general public and interested parties greater access to information on Bank policies and projects, including environmental information. The policy is based on the premise that the effectiveness of projects supported by the Bank will be strengthened by public access to information and consultation with affected populations, and that transparency and accountability will increase public support for the Bank.

The Bank will make available (at Headquarters and in all Country Offices) factual and technical information on the environmental impact of all projects throughout the preparation and implementation period, including environmental briefs and reports prepared by Bank staff. Before the Bank proceeds to an operation's analysis mission, the environmental impact assessment (EIA) is made available in the member country at a public place accessible to affected groups and local non-governmental organizations (NGOs). Once the EIA is released locally and officially submitted to the Bank, it is made available to the public at IDB Headquarters and Country Offices. If the country objects to the release of the EIA outside its country, the matter is taken to the Board of Directors.

(6) Independent Investigation Mechanism

In August 1994, the Board of Directors approved the establishment of the independent investigation mechanism. In addition to the existing system of internal controls and safeguards, the introduction of this mechanism will provide a safety net to those groups in the borrowing country that might be affected by Bank-supported operations. It may investigate complaints of affected parties in the territory of a borrower country alleging that the Bank has failed to follow its own operational policies or norms (including enforcement of compliance with borrower's obligation) in the design, analysis, or implementation of proposed or ongoing operations, when material adverse effects might or have occurred.

If the Board of Directors determines that an investigation is warranted, a panel, named from an independent permanent roster of 10 investigators, shall submit its findings to the Board of Directors. The Board shall subsequently determine what preventive or corrective action, if any, should be taken.

(7) Environmental Training

To enhance the environmental knowledge and awareness of Bank staff and pertinent regional, national, and institutional audiences, the Environment Division of SDS hosts training seminars. In December 1994, following the reorganization, the Environment Division of SDS organized in-house training for Bank staff with new environmental responsibilities focusing on environmental procedures, the evaluation of EIAs, a general review of international environmental law, and other key ecological issues. On an *ad hoc* basis, divisional staff also arrange informal workshops in the several departments of the Bank covering special environmental issues of common interest that have a direct connection to the Bank's developmental objective.

In early 1994, the Bank published in Spanish and English "Agenda 21 and Latin America: The Challenge of Implementing Environmental Law and Policy." This publication contains the proceedings of the Bank sponsored seminar on the same subject in Santiago, Chile, in May 1993.

(8) Interagency Cooperation

In 1994, the Bank and the United Nations Development Program reactivated the Latin American and Caribbean Commission on Development and Environment. The Commission and expert advisory groups met several times during the year to develop the joint recommendations published as "Our Common Agenda for the Americas" for the Americas Summit, held in December in Miami.

The Bank continued to cooperate with the World Bank on the environmental issues surrounding joint projects. In addition, the Bank and the other Regional Development Banks continued to negotiate with the World Bank on an agreement that would ensure their participation in the Global Environment Facility (GEF). However, in late October, the Bank informed the GEF that it prefers not to conclude an agreement but rather would coordinate GEF financing for its member countries through *ad hoc* cofinancing with the World Bank or the United Nations Development Program.

The Bank continues to cooperate with the Organization of American States and other regional agencies active in environmental issues.

(9) Relationship with Non-Governmental Organizations

Bank cooperation with NGOs takes place at two levels. One of these is through NGO participation in Bank operations. Consultation with local populations is now the rule in bank operations. The number of operations carried out by NGOs or other local community organizations has also increased substantially. The second type of relationship with NGOs consists of an ongoing dialogue. The Bank and NGOs consult on particular or general aspects of Bank policies and strategies as they are applied in the region or when the NGOs feel that the Bank can intervene in some environmental aspects in the member countries.

The Bank and environmental NGOs held their fifth consultative meeting in Barbados from May 30 to June 1, 1994. Discussions centered on community and NGO participation in sustainable development projects in the Caribbean.

Dana V. Martin
Gil Nolet

L. UNITED NATIONS ENVIRONMENT PROGRAMME (UNEP)

[Editors' Note: Because of space limitations, this report is intended to provide only an overview of UNEP activities. For details on any of the issues referred to, the reader should turn to the specific subject-matter entries.]

(1) Montevideo II

At the 1992 United Nations Conference on Environment and Development, Agenda 21 stressed the need for UNEP and its Governing Council to have an enhanced and strengthened role, including UNEP's involvement in the development and implementation of environmental law, in addition to UNEP's performance of Secretariat duties for major environmental conventions.

By Decision 17/25 (1993) of the Governing Council, the "Programme for the Development and Periodic Review of Environmental Law for the 1990s," commonly referred to as "Montevideo II," was adopted, which outlines objectives, strategies, and activities relating to the general development of international environmental law, and addresses areas such as effective state participation, implementation of international law, adequacy of existing international instruments, dispute avoidance and settlement, and mechanisms for the prevention and redress of environmental damage. The following are the activities that UNEP undertook in 1994 with respect to a number of the subjects listed in Montevideo II.

(a) *Liability and Compensation for Environmental Damage from Military Activities*

In 1994, the UNEP Environment Law and Institutions Programme Activity Centre (ELI/PAC), in close cooperation with the Foundation for International Environmental Law and Development, initiated a project focused on defining environmental damage caused by military activities. The need for such an undertaking arose when UN Security Council Resolution 687 established the UN Compensation Commission in April 1991 to hear claims of environmental damage and depletion of natural resources caused by military activities. The Resolution did not define these terms or provide any guidance to the Commission as to how compensation is to be assessed. By 1 February 1997, which is the final date for the presentation of claims for damage, the Commission is likely to be faced with a range of petitions that may require a variety of methods for assessing damage and raise questions regarding "reasonableness" of compensation for environmental damage and the appropriate method for assessing and valuing environmental damage and depletion of natural resources. In 1994, UNEP embarked upon the study with the aim of providing a practical contribution to the work of the UN Compensation Commission and other relevant UN bodies, while at the same time further developing the law in this area. A working group of international experts in the field was to convene in February 1995 to begin deliberations on the issue. A background paper, which will serve as the basis for discussion at the first working group meeting, was circulated to the invited experts.

(b) *Application of Environmental Norms to Military Establishments*

In 1994, UNEP initiated a process for convening regional meetings to discuss the application of environmental norms to military establishments. This initiative was launched in response to Governing Council Decision 17/5, which requests UNEP to collect information on this subject. The report is to address the conformity of military establishments' hazardous waste policies to national environmental norms and the military's contribution of the achievement of national environmental policies, and to assess environmental damage caused by military activities and the feasibility of restorative efforts.

(c) *Compliance with UNEP-Administered Treaties*

In 1994, ELI/PAC commenced an empirical study on states' implementation of and compliance with UNEP-administered international environmental conventions, with particular attention to the operation of trade provisions. Also to be examined in this connection are liability and compensation for environmental damage and dispute avoidance and settlement. The goal is to identify and promote legal elements that are consistent with sustainable development, thereby facilitating the coherent development of law in that direction.

(2) International Environmental Conventions

(a) Biological Diversity

The first meeting of the Conference of the Parties (CoP) to the Biological Diversity Convention, took place in Nassau, the Bahamas, 29 November to 9 December. UNEP was selected to provide the permanent Secretariat for the Convention (the decision on the location of the Secretariat was deferred to the second meeting of the CoP).

(b) Ozone Depletion: The Vienna Convention and Montreal Protocol

At the sixth meeting of the parties to the Montreal Protocol, in Nairobi, 6–7 October, the parties made several requests of the technology and economic assessment panel. At the 13th Meeting of the Executive Committee of the Multilateral Fund in Montreal, 25-27 July, the Executive Committee reviewed financial reports and approved recent requests for bilateral assistance projects. At the 14th meeting of the Executive Committee in Nairobi, 28-30 September, the Executive Committee agreed that US$4 million should be earmarked for the six-month pilot phase for small projects that can be approved through the expedited approval process. It also approved requests for bilateral cooperation projects and several country programmes.

(c) Transboundary Movement of Hazardous Wastes and Their Disposal: The Basel Convention

At the Second Meeting of the CoP, held in Geneva, 21–25 March, the CoP decided to establish an immediate prohibition of all transboundary movements of hazardous wastes that are destined for final disposal from Organisation for Economic Cooperation and Development (OECD) to non-OECD countries. The transboundary movement of hazardous wastes destined for recycling or recovery operations is to be phased out by 31 December 1997. The CoP agreed that it was imperative to render such prohibition effective and decided on a control system through regular reporting on implementation of the decision.

(d) United Nations Framework Convention on Climate Change

During the Ninth Session of the Intergovernmental Negotiating Committee (INC), in Geneva, 7–18 February, it was decided that Annex I parties should, on a provisional basis, use the Intergovernmental Panel on Climate Change Draft Guidelines for National Greenhouse Gas Inventories in preparing their first communications pursuant to the Convention. The INC agreed on criteria for projects funded through the financial mechanisms and called for consistency between activities undertaken within and outside the framework of the financial mechanism. The 10th Session of the Intergovernmental Negotiating Committee took place 22 August to 2 September.

(e) Convention on the Conservation of Migratory Species of Wild Animals

The Fourth Meeting of the CoP was held at UNEP Headquarters in Nairobi, 7–11 June. The meeting was the best attended to date, with 70 parties and non-parties participating. The fourth CoP meeting was followed by a very successful intergovernmental meeting to discuss a draft Agreement on the Conservation of African Eurasian Migratory Waterbirds. Considerable progress was made in reaching an informal agreement on the text and basic structure of the Agreement.

(f) Convention on International Trade in Endangered Species of Wild Fauna and Flora (CITES)

The Ninth Meeting of the Conference of Parties was held 7–18 November 1994, in Fort Lauderdale, Florida. The CoP adopted decisions such as proposals to improve the enforcement of CITES, guidelines for the disposal of confiscated live animals, a convention on trade in rhino and tiger, new criteria to amend Appendices I and II, standard nomenclature, and increased participation of producer countries in CITES Committees.

(g) Coordination of Secretariats of Environmental Conventions

In March 1994 in Geneva, Switzerland, UNEP convened the First Meeting on Coordination of Secretariats of Environmental Conventions, which representatives of secretariats attended and UNEP and several other secretariats present as observers administered. At the meeting, a number of issues common to the Secretariats were discussed, such as concepts and mechanisms of implementation of the Conventions, and trade-related provisions of environmental conventions. Also discussed were modalities for coordination among Convention Secretariats aimed at the effective implementation of the respective Conventions. The participants to the meeting considered the concept of coordination, and agreed to institutionalize coordination meetings on a regular basis, with the possibility of more frequent informal sectoral consultations.

(h) Chemicals in International Trade

(i) (➔) Code of Ethics on International Trade in Chemicals

UNEP issued a Code of Ethics on International Trade in Chemicals on 9 August to guide the private sector in enhancing safety in international trade in chemicals. The Code of Ethics was developed in response to a 1991 decision of the UNEP Governing Council and Ch. 19 of Agenda 21. It is complementary, though broader in scope, to a 1989 set of guidelines targeted at governments known as the Amended London Guidelines for the

Exchange of Information on Chemicals in International Trade. The Code is a voluntary guide to standards of conduct in chemical production and management. It takes into account the entire life cycle of chemical production, transport, use, and disposal, and has been developed with the purpose of reducing health and environmental risks. The International Conference on Chemical Safety, which 114 Governments attended in late April 1994 in Stockholm, recommended wide application of the Code. The second session of the UN Commission on Sustainable Development in May 1994 also called for the Code's application on as wide a scale as possible, and reinforced the industry's role as a major player in furthering the objectives of Agenda 21.

(ii) Prior Informed Consent

In March, a task force met to consider a possible convention on the concept of prior informed consent (PIC). The Commission on Sustainable Development at its second session in New York, 16–27 May, recommended that UNEP and the UN Food and Agriculture Organization (FAO) continue to evaluate and address problems with the implementation of the voluntary PIC procedure and to develop effective legally binding instruments concerning the PIC procedure. UNEP and FAO convened an informal consultative meeting in Geneva, 1–2 December, to consider major issues related to the development of a PIC Convention. It is envisioned that such a convention would provide, in addition to the PIC procedure, a means of capacity-building in the management of chemicals in those countries without adequate infrastructure for the implementation of the Convention.

(iii) Inter-Agency Memorandum of Understanding

A Memorandum of Understanding concerning the establishment of a programme for the sound management of chemicals was agreed upon at an inter-agency meeting held in Paris, 10-11 November. Representatives of UNEP, the International Labour Organisation, the FAO, the World Health Organization, the United Nations Industry and Development Organization, and the OECD attended the meeting. The programme arose from the need for a coordinated and holistic approach to strengthen partnerships among these organizations.

(i) Marine Pollution from Land-Based Sources

A meeting of government-designated experts focusing on the 1985 Montreal Guidelines for the Protection of the Marine Environment from Land-Based Sources of Pollution was held in Montreal, 6–10 June. UNEP is coordinating inter-sessional work on a draft programme of action prior to the final preparatory meeting in Reykjavik, Iceland, in March 1995. The Reykjavik meeting will review and revise the programme in preparation for the two-week intergovernmental conference, to be held in Washington, DC, in November 1995, for the purpose of adopting the programme of action.

(j) Lusaka Agreement

After six months of formal negotiations, six Eastern and Southern African states—Kenya, South Africa, Swaziland, Uganda, the United Republic of Tanzania, and Zambia—signed the (➔) Lusaka Agreement on Co-operative Enforcement Operations Directed at Illegal Trade in Wild Fauna and Flora in Lusaka, Zambia, on 9 September. Lesotho and Mozambique accepted the text but were unable to attend the signing ceremony. UNEP played a leading role in furthering the development of this first regional agreement on enforcement measures to counter the trade in wildlife in Africa, and the first multilateral agreement of its kind to be signed by the new South African Government. The Agreement is aimed at easing the administrative difficulties currently hampering cross-border efforts to restrict the trade. The objective of the Agreement is to reduce and ultimately eliminate illegal trade in wild fauna and flora. A task force will be established to investigate violations of national laws pertaining to illegal trade in all wildlife, combat international syndicates smuggling wildlife out of the region, and disseminate information on activities relating to the illegal trade. It will have an international legal character and be responsible to a Governing Council made up of the Parties to the Agreement.

(3) Capacity-Building at the National Level

(a) Technical Assistance

In 1994, UNEP provided technical assistance to almost 30 countries worldwide. ELI/PAC helped prepare draft legislation for Burundi, Cambodia, Chad, Ghana, Malawi, Nigeria, São Tomé and Principe, Sri Lanka, Sudan, Trinidad and Tobago, and Zambia. ELI/PAC staff members undertook scoping missions to Kiribati, Lebanon, Morocco, Mozambique, Oman, Tanzania, and Uganda. Workshops and conferences on various issues of environmental law and institutions assisted by ELI/PAC input were held in Kazakhstan, Kenya, Lesotho, Mexico, and Tanzania. ELI/PAC expertise was also provided to an intergovernmental meeting held among Kenya, Tanzania, and Uganda to discuss the environmental management of the Lake Victoria Basin.

(b) UNEP/United Nations Development Programme (UNDP) Joint Project on Environmental Law in Africa

The UNEP/UNDP joint project on environmental law in Africa, funded by the government of the Netherlands with a US$5 million Trust Fund established at UNEP, is designed to assist selected African countries to formulate and enact national environmental legislation and establish and enhance related institutional structures to improve environmental management for sustainable development. The second meeting of the Steering Committee of the project was held at the UNEP Regional Office in Geneva on 30 September 1994. The Steering Committee, consisting of representatives of UNEP, UNDP, the World Bank, FAO, and the World Conservation Union considered reports from earlier needs-assessment missions to countries that had sought inclusion in the project, and approved projects in a number of these countries to be implemented in the first phase.

(c) Model Framework Environmental Impact Assessment Law

UNEP is currently developing a model framework law on environmental impact assessment (EIA) with a commentary and implementing regulations. ELI/PAC has been compiling existing examples of national EIA legislative provisions, and work has begun on drafting a model law. A model workshop on EIA was held in Nairobi, 5–7 September.

(d) Inter-Agency Cooperation in Capacity-Building

In 1994, UNEP assisted UNDP in preparing the first of a monograph series on capacity-building that UNDP initiated. UNDP asked UNEP to prepare the first of this series on capacity-building in the field of environmental law. The monographs are intended to serve as resource tools for professionals involved in environment and natural resource management.

(e) Training in Environmental Law and Policy

In partnership with the Industry and Environment Programme Activity Centre (IE/PAC) and the Regional Office for Asia Pacific, ELI/PAC organized a Regional Workshop on Institutional Capacity Building for Industrial Environmental Compliance and Enforcement Response in Rapidly Advancing Economies in Asia, which was held in Beijing and Beihai, China, 13–19 November. UNEP and the National Environmental Protection Agency of China jointly sponsored the workshop.

The objective of the Workshop was to contribute to the sustainable development of countries in the Asia Pacific region in the area of industrial environmental compliance and enforcement as set out in Agenda 21. The Workshop dealt with a wide range of legal and institutional issues relating to industrial compliance and enforcement, including designing enforcement programs, developing permit systems, monitoring compliance, and developing an inspection scheme. The participants—senior government officials from China, India, Indonesia, Malaysia, the Philippines, the Republic of Korea, Singapore, and Thailand—developed outlines for enhancing the system of compliance and enforcement in their respective countries, which will serve as a basis for a programme of follow-up action.

(f) International Environmental Law Information

In 1994, UNEP completed the development of the Computerized Environmental Law Information Base (CELIB), which became accessible on INTERNET. CELIB contains legal and institutional information and is available to the public free of charge. The information base includes material regarding international environmental legal instruments and international environmental law in general. Information on international environmental conventions includes the 1993 Register of International Treaties and Other Agreements in the Field of the Environment, and 60 texts of international conventions or agreements in the field of the environment.

ELI/PAC launched a new publication, the Biannual Bulletin of Environmental Law, in 1994. The publication provides information about UNEP's activities in environmental law and institutions. The Bulletin was developed by ELI/PAC in partnership with Convention Secretariats, other in-house Units and Programme Activity Centres, and Regional and Outposted offices of UNEP. It details UNEP's major activities in the legal and institutional fields.

The first volume of the UNEP National Environmental Legislation Series was being prepared at year's end. National environmental management and EIA laws and regulations of developing countries and countries with economies in transition were being collected and an index of all major provisions was being compiled. Upon completion, the information will also be made available in the electronic media through CELIB. The volume was expected to be released in May 1995.

UNEP also developed the first draft of a Training Manual in Environmental Law and Institutions. The Manual will contain a comprehensive, integrated, and adaptable set of training modules. It is intended to serve as a pool of training materials from which requisite sections may be drawn for use in a range of workshop programs. It covers both international and national environmental legal issues.

UNEP began work in 1994 on a publication of the progressive development of environmental law, at both the international and national levels, in the context of sustainable development in the post Rio period. The emphasis will be on UNEP's contributions to the field.

Regional delivery of UNEP's Environmental Law Programme commenced for the West Asia Region with the preparation of an Arabic Compendium of International Environmental Law. The compendium will include the texts of regional and international environmental agreements affecting countries in the West Asian region. Work was undertaken in 1994 to select the appropriate instruments for inclusion to translate them, as necessary, into Arabic. The Compendium was scheduled for release in 1995.

Lal Kurukulasuriya

M. UNITED NATIONS FOOD AND AGRICULTURE ORGANIZATION (FAO)

(1) FAO Restructuring

In order to adjust to an evolving world where new concerns and priorities have emerged, FAO's Secretariat is undergoing structural changes that are meant to reinvigorate the organization and enhance its efficiency. The main elements of restructuring are the newly created Department of Sustainable Development, the transformation of the Development Department into the Technical Cooperation Department, and the strengthening of the regional offices and the establishment of subregional offices.

To give shape to these changes and to provide a sharpened priority focus, two new programs were initiated: the "Food Production in Support of Food Security in Low-Income Food-Deficit Countries" to tackle the food security and malnutrition problem, and the "Emergency Prevention System to Combat Transboundary Animal Pests and Diseases." To ensure an integrated corporate approach and independent review of the Organization's relevant programs, various committees and panels were set up: two internal steering committees, one for the World Food Summit (1996), and the other for the Food Security Programme; and three external oversight panels, for food security, sustainable development, and economic and social activities, respectively.

(2) FAO, the Commission on Sustainable Development (CSD) and the United Nations Conference on Environment and Development (UNCED)

FAO was designated task manager for various chapters of Agenda 21, including those on land resources (Ch. 10), deforestation (Ch. 11), sustainable mountain development (Ch. 13), and agriculture (Ch. 14). As regards freshwater (Ch. 18) and oceans (Ch. 17), two sub-committees with a rotating chairmanship were established. Until September 1994, the sub-committee on water resources, which prepared a report on Ch. 18 for the second substantive session of the CSD in May 1994, was chaired by FAO. The sub-committee on oceans and coastal resources, which will be preparing a report on Ch. 17 for the 1996 session of the CSD, will be chaired by FAO up to this session. In addition, FAO provides technical inputs to the World Health Organization, the United Nations Economic and Social Council, and the United Nations Industrial Development Organization on their committees dealing with health, education, and biotechnology, respectively.

As task manager, FAO convened two inter-agency meetings in 1994 to which UN entities, other intergovernmental organizations, and non-governmental organizations were invited. At the meeting on Ch. 10 (integrated approach to the planning and management of land resources), in Rome, 10-11 October, the main priority identified was the development of a holistic framework to facilitate the cooperation of all institutions and stakeholders in meeting conflicting demands on land resources while avoiding land degradation. At the meeting on Ch. 14 (managing fragile ecosystems: sustainable mountain development) in Rome, 21–22 March, the main proposals for action included promoting the formulation and negotiation of regional cooperative agreements on mountains, possibly leading to the development of a global mountain charter and action plan.

FAO also contributed actively to the implementation of UNCED agreements, in particular, by providing technical and legal advice to the Interim Secretariat of the Convention on Biological Diversity and to the Intergovernmental Negotiating Committee of the (➔) International Convention to Combat Desertification. FAO acted as technical secretariat and provided documentation for the three sessions of the UN Conference on Straddling and Highly Migratory Fish Stocks. It also contributed to the UN Global Conference on the Sustainable Development of Small Island Developing States (Barbados, 25 April to 6 May). In addition, the organization prepared a monograph on capacity-building in agriculture, forestry, and fisheries, to assist in the development of the United Nations Development Program in these sectors.

(3) Plant Genetic Resources

Although the Convention on Biological Diversity deals with the conservation and sustainable use of biological resources, two outstanding matters were left pending: access to *ex-situ* collections and farmers' rights. In view of this, it was agreed that the FAO 1983 International Undertaking on Plant Genetic Resources be revised accordingly in the light of the Convention. To this end, FAO was asked to provide a forum for intergovernmental negotiations. In November, at the first extraordinary session of the FAO Commission on Plant Genetic Resources, the view was widely expressed that the revised Undertaking should become a protocol to the Biodiversity Convention. Later that month, however, during the FAO Council meeting, it was agreed that the issue required further discussion before a decision could be reached.

Consideration was also given to a possible widening of the mandate of the FAO Commission on Plant Genetic Resources. The Commission serves as a forum for governments to address policy and legal issues within the field of competence of the organization. These issues include the implementation of the International Undertaking on Plant Genetic Resources, access to plant genetic resources, plant breeders' rights, farmers' rights, intellectual property rights related to biotechnologies, and the relevant codes of conduct. In its present form, the Commission's mandate is sufficient to deal with plant genetic resources. However, analogous jurisdictional arrangements are needed to allow FAO to discharge its international obligations regarding other genetic resources. One way to achieve this would be to broaden the Commission's mandate to cover genetic resources for food and agriculture in general, which would include plant, livestock, and fisheries. This possibility was examined at the last session of the FAO Council in November. No specific objections to the principle of broadening the mandate of the Commission were raised, but it was agreed that a cautious process was needed in dealing with this matter and that further consideration of the financial, institutional, and administrative implications would be required before an appropriate decision could be made by the FAO Conference.

(4) Prior Informed Consent (PIC)

In 1989, the FAO Code of Conduct on the Distribution and Use of Pesticides, originally adopted in 1985, was amended to included provisions for the PIC procedure. PIC refers to the principle that international shipment of a pesticide that is banned or severely restricted in order to protect human health or the environment should not proceed without the agreement or contrary to the decision of the importing country. A similar process was established by the United Nations Environment Programme (UNEP) in 1989: The 1987 London Guidelines for the Exchange of Information on Chemicals in International Trade were amended to include PIC, with a view to assisting governments in the process of increasing chemical safety through the exchange of information on chemicals in international trade. UNEP and FAO thereafter established a joint program on the implementation of PIC in 1990.

As of September, 125 states had designated national authorities to be responsible for the operation of PIC procedures and were cooperating in the global program. A joint FAO/UNEP group of experts on PIC provided advice on the implementation of the procedure and met seven times. Twelve pesticides are presently included in the procedure, and countries have been requested to make decisions on these. Compilations of import decisions were sent to designated national authorities; the latest compilation was sent in July.

However, PIC procedures under both the FAO Code of Conduct and the UNEP London Guidelines are voluntary. Hence, the recommendation in Ch. 19 of Agenda 21 for the conclusion of a legally binding instrument on PIC was reiterated at the International Conference on Chemical Safety (Stockholm, April 1994), as well as during the second session of the Commission on Sustainable Development (New York, May 1994).

FAO is working closely with UNEP in preparing the elements that might be included in a legal instrument for the mandatory application of PIC.

FAO's main concern is that issues relating to pesticides, for which it has primary responsibility in the operation of the PIC procedure, are effectively taken into account. The last FAO Council (November 1994) agreed that the Secretariat should proceed with the preparation of this instrument as part of the joint FAO/UNEP program. It was noted that it should apply to all sources of supplies of pesticides. The Council also agreed that an appropriate balance should be sought between the responsibilities of importing and exporting countries and that an agreement should not unduly limit trade. It was considered that a draft instrument be ready for adoption in 1997.

(5) Forestry

The restructuring of the organization included a priority resource shift to forestry to allow FAO to play a leading role in the implementation of UNCED follow-up for the forestry sector. Accordingly, an additional allocation of resources was made to FAO's programs on forestry. Furthermore, a number of actions were taken to strengthen the normative role of FAO in sustainable forest management, which included the adoption of a strategy that refocuses FAO's priorities to address the requirements of preparations for CSD in 1995, and reorientation of FAO's work toward a cross-sectoral approach to forestry development focused on sustainability, with greater emphasis on the interaction between agriculture and forestry and on poverty and population concerns.

A High Level Panel of External Experts was convened at FAO Headquarters, 19–21 October, to advise on how FAO might more effectively provide leadership in the international dialogue on forests and forest-related issues, as well as assistance to member nations in the formulation and implementation of sustainable national forestry action plans and programs. The Panel concluded that FAO's reputation in the international forestry community had suffered in past years, that the Organization had not been visibly active and open to interact with other organizations, and that it should move much more effectively and proactively in the international dialogue on forests and forest-related issues. The Panel recommended that the Tropical Forests Action Program's (TFAP's) scope should be broadened to include other types of forests and that the TFAP should be integrated into normal planning and programming activities, typically at the initial stages of the FAO's continuum of services in forestry at the national level.

As task manager on Ch. 10 of Agenda 21, as well as the major UN agency with technical capacity in forestry, FAO assists the UN Department for Policy Coordination and Sustainable Development and serves as its principal adviser on matters related to forestry. FAO was also assisting the CSD Secretariat in the preparation of the review of forests. In support of the 1995 CSD session, FAO helped prepare guidelines for national reporting, as well as other documents that the CSD required. In addition, FAO has prepared a publication entitled *Putting UNCED to Work in Forestry*, designed to be an overall guide to major UNCED decisions on forests and on broad strategies for follow-up action. It has also published *The Road from Rio: Moving Forward in Forestry*, for a broader audience.

In 1994, FAO increasingly assisted countries in developing or adapting their forestry policies and strategies, especially in order to combine the economic importance of forests and trees with their roles in social equity and ecological integrity. Interdepartmental working groups focused on integrating cross-sectoral programs. The new Department of Sustainable Development was expected to facilitate joint work on programs such as agroforestry, forestry/agriculture interactions in overall land use, and forestry linkages with fisheries under programs for integrated management of coastal areas.

Resources information is essential in the planning of sustainable management and use of forests. The FAO Forest Resources Assessment Program continued to provide reliable information for making policy decisions on forest conservation and development. With the publication of results of the assessment of the status of forest resources in the non-tropical developing countries in late 1994, FAO completed its 1990 global Forest Resources Assessment.

(6) Water

In 1994, FAO hosted two significant events on water law: a regular meeting of the Water Resources Committee of the International Law Association, 10–12 February, and a Symposium on "Water Law and Administration in Italy: Present State and Pointers for the Future" (15–16 March.) The latter event was organized by the International Association for Water Law.

In support of its technical advisory assistance to member countries in the field of water law and its administration, FAO published in 1994 "Preparing National Regulations for Water Resources Management: Principles and Practice," No. 52 in the FAO Legislative Study series. This publication consists of a manual providing conceptual material for use in the preparation of national regulations for the management, development, use, and protection of freshwater resources.

(7) Fisheries

Development by FAO of the International Code of Conduct for Responsible Fishing progressed during 1994 through wide-ranging consultation and review. The Code of Conduct will provide comprehensive guidance to states and promote responsible behavior among all those involved in fisheries. It will implement and complement the UN Convention on the

Law of the Sea, as well as other international instruments on the conservation and development of fisheries. A first draft of the general principles was considered at an informal working group of government-nominated experts that met in February at FAO Headquarters. This was followed by a technical consultation on the Code of Conduct for Responsible Fishing, which met in Rome, 26 September to 5 October. It undertook a thorough review of the draft Code and provided directions for its further elaboration. A revised version of the draft Code was subsequently prepared by the Secretariat, and was to be submitted to the FAO Committee on Fisheries in March 1995, the FAO Council in June, and the Conference in November.

Mohamed Ali Mekouar

N. UNITED NATIONS GENERAL ASSEMBLY

(1) Introduction

The 49th session of the UN General Assembly (GA) discussed issues concerning the environment under various aspects: Strengthening of the Coordination of Humanitarian and Disaster Relief Assistance of the United Nations, Including Special Economic Assistance (agenda item 87); Sustainable Development and International Economic Cooperation (agenda item 88); Environment and Sustainable Development (agenda item 89); and Non-Navigational Uses of International Watercourses (agenda item 137).

(2) Plenary: Humanitarian and Disaster Relief Assistance of the UN

Resolution 49/139A approves further measures to strengthen coordination in the area of humanitarian disaster and relief assistance provided through the UN (Emergency Relief Coordinator), emphasizing in particular coordination in the field and the mechanisms of the Central Emergency Revolving Fund.

Resolution 49/139B encourages voluntary and regional actions aimed at providing the UN system, on a stand-by basis, with specialized human (volunteer corps, so-called "White Helmets") and technical resources for emergency relief and rehabilitation.

Resolution 49/22B requests that the Secretary-General make proposals to improve and better coordinate early warning capacities within the UN system for natural disasters and similar disasters with an adverse impact on the environment. This resolution, without specifically addressing the issue of manmade disasters, is a potential step toward broadening the capabilities of the UN system for early warning.

Resolution 49/22, entitled "International Decade for Natural Disaster Reduction," endorses the Yokohama Strategy for a Safer World: Guidelines for Natural Disaster Prevention, Preparedness, and Mitigation (adopted at the World Conference on Natural Disaster Reduction, Yokohama, 23 to 27 May), its Plan of Action, and the mid-term review of the implementation of the International Framework of Action for the International Decade for Natural Disaster Reduction (ECOSOC Res. 1994/31). It calls on all participants in the Decade to support, financially and technically, the implementation of the International Framework of Action, particularly with a view toward translating the Yokohama Strategy and the Plan of Action into concrete disaster reduction programmes and activities.

(3) Second Committee

(a) Report of the Commission on Sustainable Development (CSD)

Resolution 49/111 deals with the "report of the Commission on Sustainable Development on its second session," which was held in New York from 16–27 May 1994. It expresses deep concern that the financial recommendations and commitments of Agenda 21 fall short of expectations and requirements and that the current financing of sustainable development and limited new and additional financial resources will constrain the effective implementation of Agenda 21 and could undermine the basis of the global partnership for sustainable development. It stresses the critical need to provide the means of implementation, especially "new and additional financial resources and the transfer of environmentally sound technology to developing countries on favourable terms, including concessional and preferential terms."

The resolution also underlines the role of the CSD as a unique international forum for fostering multilateral negotiations and promoting action in the area of changing consumption and production patterns. The resolution notes the need for close cooperation between the CSD and the General Agreement on Tariffs and Trade/World Trade Organization (GATT/WTO), the United Nations Conference on Trade and Development (UNCTAD), and the United Nations Environment Programme (UNEP), and recommends that the CSD, UNCTAD, UNEP and the UN Food and Agriculture Organization (FAO) continue to be represented at the Committee on Trade and Environment of WTO.

Resolution 49/111 further stresses the importance of the CSD's decisions on, *inter alia*, health, human settlements, freshwater, toxic chemicals, and hazardous wastes, as concrete steps in the implementation of the sectoral clusters of Agenda 21.

In order to increase its effectiveness in monitoring the implementation of

Agenda 21 and other United Nations Conference on Environment and Development decisions, the CSD is to develop close relationships with other relevant international organizations and entities (*e.g.*, the conferences of parties to the UN Framework Convention on Climate Change, the Convention on Biological Diversity, the (➔) Convention to Combat Desertification, and the Global Environment Facility).

(b) Climate Change

Resolution 49/120 welcomes the entry into force of the UN Framework Convention on Climate Change on 21 March 1994, and urges the Intergovernmental Negotiating Committee (INC), during its 11th session (6–17 February 1995), to complete its plan of preparatory work for the first session of the Conference of the Parties to the Convention, which will be held in Berlin from 28 March to 7 April 1995. As financial and technical assistance will be necessary for developing country parties to enable them to comply with their commitments under the Convention, the resolution invites contributions to the extra-budgetary funds established under Res. 45/212 and maintained in accordance with Res. 47/195.

(c) Desertification and Drought

Resolution 49/784, entitled "Elaboration of an International Convention to Combat Desertification in Those Countries Experiencing Serious Drought and/or Desertification, particularly in Africa," welcomes the adoption of the (➔) Convention and of Committee resolution 5/1 on urgent action for Africa, in Paris on 17 June 1994. It decides that the INC shall continue its function, *inter alia*, in order to prepare for the first session of the Conference of the Parties of the Convention, to facilitate the implementation of Committee resolution 5/1, and to initiate identification of an organization to house the global mechanism to mobilize and channel financial resources.

The work of the Committee and the Interim Secretariat is to continue to be funded through existing UN budgetary resources and voluntary contributions. The resolution welcomes the proposal of the Administrator of the United Nations Development Programme (UNDP) to support implementation worldwide, with particular attention to Africa, and invites UNDP and the UN Sahelian Office to seek the necessary financial resources. Furthermore, it requests that the Chairman of the INC submit a progress report to the GA, the CSD and other appropriate bodies of the UN. 17 June was proclaimed World Day to Combat Desertification and Drought (Res. 49/115).

(d) Fisheries

Resolution 49/116 deals with the detrimental impact of "unauthorized fishing in zones of national jurisdiction and its impact on the living marine resources of the world's oceans and seas." It calls on states to take measures to ensure that no fishing vessels under their flags fish in zones under the jurisdiction of other states unless authorized by the competent organs of the coastal state concerned. Development assistance organizations are to support efforts of developing coastal states to improve the monitoring of fishing activities and the enforcement of fishing regulations through financial and/or technical assistance.

Resolution 49/118 deals with the problem of "fisheries bycatch and discards and their impact on the sustainable use of the world's living marine resources." Continued and effective response to this problem is necessary to ensure the long-term sustainable development of fisheries, taking into account the relevant principles contained in the Rio Declaration. The resolution invites the FAO to formulate fisheries bycatch and discard provisions in its international code of conduct for responsible fishing. It also invites the UN Conference on Straddling Fish Stocks and Highly Migratory Fish Stocks to elaborate fisheries bycatch and discard provisions.

In Resolution 49/121 the GA notes the progress made by the UN Conference on Straddling Fish Stocks and Highly Migratory Fish Stocks and approves two further sessions of the Conference (27 March to 12 April 1995 and 24 July to 4 August 1995). It urges the Conference to complete its work before the 50th session of the GA and requests the Secretary-General to submit the final report of the Conference to this session.

The GA also adopted a resolution on "large-scale drift-net fishing and its impact on the living marine resources of the world's oceans and seas," reaffirming the necessity of compliance with Res. 46/215 and calling for full implementation of a global moratorium on all large-scale pelagic drift-net fishing on the high seas. Since there were still reports of conduct inconsistent with the terms of Res. 46/215, the GA urges members to ensure full compliance.

(e) Sustainable Development of Small Island Developing States

Resolution 49/122 endorses the Declaration of Barbados and the Programme of Action adopted by the "Global Conference on Sustainable Development of Small Island Developing States," held in Barbados from 25 April to 6 May 1994 ((➔) Report of the Conference A/CONF.167/9). It calls on governments, international organizations, and non-governmental organizations "to implement all commitments reached and recommendations made at the Conference and to take the action necessary for effective follow-up to the Programme of Action, including ensuring the provision of the means of implementation under [its] chapter XV [Implementation, Monitoring, and Review]."

UNDP is invited to initiate the implementation of the technical assistance programme specified in para. 106 of the Programme of Action (directory of experts, feasibility study, information network). The resolution also requests the CSD to make arrangements for monitoring and reviewing the implementation of the Programme of Action and to carry out an initial review of the progress achieved in 1996. In the context of its overall review of Agenda 21, the CSD shall also recommend specific modalities for a full review of the Programme of Action in 1999, including the question of a second global conference.

The resolution further requests that the Secretary-General to establish a clearly identifiable entity within the Department of Policy Coordination and Sustainable Development to support the system-wide implementation of the Programme of Action in accordance with para. 123.

Resolution 49/100 on "specific measures in favour of island developing countries" takes note of the Secretary-General's report on a development strategy for island developing countries (A/49/277 and Adds. 1 and 2), and invites the CSD to convene, during its 1996 session, a high-level panel to discuss the challenges faced by island developing countries and to assist the Commission in its review of the implementation of the Programme of Action agreed at the Barbados Conference. It also invites UNCTAD to organize that panel in cooperation with the Department for Policy Coordination and Sustainable Development. The resolution further requests the Secretary-General to continue to monitor and review in a coordinated manner within the Inter-Agency Committee on Sustainable Development and the Secretariats of the Commission on Sustainable Development and UNCTAD, the concerns and needs of island developing countries. It also requests the Secretary-General to report to the 51st GA on the implementation of this resolution and to take measures to provide for integrated reporting on these issues in recognition of the complementarity of the follow-up to the Barbados Conference and the ongoing island developing country programmes.

(f) Trade and Development

Resolution 49/99 on "international trade and development" emphasizes in its preamble the role of a favourable international economic environment and positive investment climate for the recovery and growth of the world economy, in particular for the sustained economic growth and sustainable development of developing countries. It underlines the importance of the full integration of countries with economies in transition into the multilateral trading system. It also stresses the need to promote, facilitate, and finance access to, and the transfer of, environmentally sound technology and corresponding know-how, in particular to developing countries, under favourable terms, taking into account the protection of intellectual property rights, as well as the needs of the developing countries for the implementation of Agenda 21.

In its operative paragraphs, the resolution stresses the need for trade liberalization and improved access to the markets of all countries, in particular those of the developed countries, in order to generate global economic growth and sustainable development. In this context it also emphasizes the need for continued evaluation of the implementation of the Uruguay Round agreements to ensure the expansion of world trade. The resolution "deplores any attempt to bypass or undermine multilaterally agreed measures of trade liberalization through resort to unilateral actions, over and above those agreed to in the Uruguay Round," and reaffirms that environmental and social concerns should not be used for protectionist purposes. It recognizes that, "in order to promote sustained economic growth and sustainable development, environment and trade policies should be made mutually supportive."

The resolution reaffirms UNCTAD's role as the focal point within the UN for the integrated treatment of development in the area of trade and sustainable development and:

> requests UNCTAD to continue its role in the field of trade and environment, including policy analysis, conceptual work and consensus-building, with a view to ensuring transparency and coherency in making environmental and trade policies mutually supportive, taking into account the work done by the GATT and other competent and regional economic institutions.

(g) Food and Agricultural Development

Resolution 49/103 deals mainly with the importance of freshwater resources for food production, especially in developing countries. It stresses the importance of the full implementation of the decisions of the CSD in the area of freshwater resources. It requests that the United Nations system and the multilateral financial institutions assist interested developing countries in the formulation and implementation of national water policies. It also asks the relevant regional and international organizations to assist the cooperative efforts of developing countries in the area of conservation, sustainable use, and integrated water management. It further requests the Secretary-General to submit to the 51st GA a report on the implementation of this resolution, focusing on the use of freshwater resources, as well as on the effects of the results of the Uruguay Round on food production.

(h) Human Settlement (Habitat II)

Resolution 49/109 recommends that the sustainable human settlements issues as contained in Ch. 7 of Agenda 21 be included in the Agenda for Development, which is being prepared pursuant to GA Res. 47/181 and 48/166, and "reaffirms that the overall human settlement objective is to improve the social, economic and environmental quality of human settlements and the living and working environments of all people, in particular the urban and rural poor."

(4) Sixth Committee

With regard to the (➔) Draft Articles on the Law of Non-Navigational Uses of International Watercourses transmitted by the International Law Commission (ILC) and the Commission's thereto related recommendations, the GA decided that the Sixth Committee should convene as a Working Group of the Whole at the beginning of its 51st session, in order to elaborate a framework convention on the basis of the ILC draft articles, and in the light of the written comments and observations of states and views expressed in the debate at the 49th session of the GA.

Lilly Sucharipa-Behrmann

O. UNITED NATIONS ECONOMIC COMMISSION: ASIA AND THE PACIFIC

In 1994, upon admission of Armenia, membership of the United Nations Economic and Social Commission for Asia and the Pacific (ESCAP) increased to 49 members and 10 associate member countries.

(1) (➔) International Convention to Combat Desertification

ESCAP, in cooperation with the United Nations Environment Programme, convened a regional meeting in Bangkok, 7–9 March 1994, to provide Asian inputs to the International Negotiating Committee on Desertification during its fourth session at Geneva. The meeting was attended by countries of the ESCAP region and some Asian countries outside ESCAP, as well as institutional representatives such as the Director General of the Arab Centre for the Studies of Arid Zones and Drylands. The meeting provided the basic inputs for the development of an Asian annex to the International Convention to Combat Desertification.

(2) Framework Convention on Climate Change

In 1994, ESCAP was implementing a project entitled "Regional Cooperation on Global Climate Change," aimed at developing a regional strategy to address implications of climate change in the region and developing a regional network of institutions involved with policy analysis, formulation, and research in fields related to climate change. These activities relate to the provisions of the Framework Convention on Climate Change concerning information exchange, public awareness, technical and international cooperation, and capacity-building.

(3) Basel Convention on Transboundary Movements of Hazardous Wastes

In support of the Basel Convention on the Control of Transboundary Movements of Hazardous Wastes and their Disposal, the Secretariat undertook an inter-country project on the preliminary assessment of illegal traffic in toxic and dangerous products and wastes in the region. The study, which involved 13 countries, collected information on national legislation, regulations, mechanisms, and manpower capabilities for the implementation of the Convention. A workshop was held in Tokyo in March 1994 to examine the existing situation and make recommendations for effectively tackling the problem in future.

(4) The Convention on Wetlands of International Importance (Ramsar Convention)

In order to assist the countries in effectively meeting their international obligations, ESCAP conducted a review of the status of implementation of the Ramsar Convention. The review covered 24 countries in the Asian and Pacific region, examined the main constraints in implementation of the Convention at national level, and made recommendations to overcome these constraints.

(5) Institution-Building

In order to promote regional initiatives for a balanced consideration of environment and development concerns in the process of further development of international law on sustainable development, ESCAP, in cooperation with the World Conservation Union, developed a proposal for the establishment of a regional law centre at the National University of Singapore. This centre, once established, is to provide training and assist in enhancing national capacities toward this end.

Seiko Takahashi

O. UNITED NATIONS ECONOMIC COMMISSION: EUROPE

In 1994, the membership of the United Nations Economic Commission for Europe (ECE) increased to 55 countries with the admittance of Tajikistan. Twenty-six of the current members are countries in transition.

(1) Convention on Long-Range Transboundary Air Pollution

With the accession of Latvia and Lithuania in 1994, the 1979 Convention on Long-Range Transboundary Air Pollution (E/ECE/1010) had 39 parties at year's end. The Protocol on Long-term Financing of the Cooperative Programme for Monitoring and Evaluation of the Long-range Transmission of Air Pollutants in Europe (EMEP) (ECE/EB.AIR/11), which entered into force on 28 January 1988, has been ratified by 35 Parties to the Convention. The Protocol on the Reduction of Sulphur Emissions or their Transboundary Fluxes by at least 30 percent (ECE/EB.AIR/12), which entered into force on 2 September 1987, has been ratified by 21 parties to the Convention. With the ratifications by Ireland and Liechtenstein in 1994, the Protocol concerning the Control of Emissions of Nitrogen Oxides or their Transboundary Fluxes (ECE/EB.AIR/21), which entered into force on 14 February 1991, has now been ratified by 25 parties. The Protocol concerning the Control of Emissions of Volatile Organic Compounds or their Transboundary Fluxes (ECE/EB.AIR/30), which was adopted in Geneva on 18 November 1991, has been signed by 23 parties, and by the end of 1994, 11 parties to the Convention had ratified this Protocol. In 1994, (➔) the Protocol on further Reduction of Sulphur Emissions (ECE/EB.AIR/40), which was adopted on 14 June in Oslo, was signed by 28 parties to the Convention.

The Convention on Long-range Transboundary Air Pollution is one of the central means for protecting the European environment. Over the years, it has served as a bridge between different political systems and as a factor of stability in years of political change. It has substantially contributed to the development of international environmental law and has created the essential framework for controlling and reducing the damage to human health and the environment caused by transboundary air pollution. It is an outstanding example of what can be achieved through intergovernmental cooperation. The Convention constitutes a framework within which the contracting parties identify the problems posed by transboundary air pollution and accept their responsibility to undertake appropriate abatement action.

Besides laying down the general principles of international cooperation for air pollution abatement, the Convention sets up an institutional framework bringing together research and policy. The Convention sets out the following major principles: the recognition that air pollution is a major problem; the declaration that contracting parties determined "to protect man and his environment against air pollution" would "endeavour to limit and, as far as possible, gradually reduce and prevent air pollution;" the commitment of contracting parties to, "by means of exchanges of information, consultation, research and monitoring, develop without undue delay policies and strategies which shall serve as a means of combating the discharge of air pollutants, taking into account efforts already made at national and international levels;" and the intention to use "the best available technology which is economically feasible" to meet the objectives of the Convention.

The Executive Body for the Convention, which includes representatives of all the contracting parties, meets at least once a year to review the implementation of the Convention and to adopt a work plan for its activities. The second level of the institutional framework established by the Executive Body under the Convention deals with specific areas of the work plan and consists at present of six intergovernmental bodies, open to all parties to the Convention and other interested ECE member countries.

The Executive Body for the Convention on Long-Range Transboundary Air Pollution at its 12th session (28 November-1 December) reiterated its previous decision that, after finalization of the second sulphur protocol, highest priority should be given to the development of a strategy for the second step to the nitrogen oxides Protocol. The Executive Body also decided to prepare preliminary elements for possible protocols on persistent organic pollutants and on heavy metals.

In 1994, Volume 10 in the Air Pollution Studies series was published. It contains chapters on strategies and policies for the abatement of air pollution, the condition of forests in Europe, and the abatement of air pollution from fossil fuels combustion processes.

(2) Committee on Environmental Policy

In 1994, the ECE endorsed the name change of the Senior Advisers to ECE Governments on Environmental and Water Problems to the "Committee on Environmental Policy" and approved the terms of reference of the Committee. At its first session, the Committee gave its general approval to the Guidelines on Integrated Environmental Management in Countries in Transition, which has been published under symbol ECE/CEP/5. The Working Group of Senior Governmental Officials, as the central coordinating body for the further development of the "Environment for Europe" process, is involved in the substantive preparations for the next Ministerial Conference which was to be held in October 1995 in Sofia. Further development of the Environmental Programme for Europe, facilitation of financing environmental investments, public participation, compliance with environmental conventions, integration of environmental and sectoral policies, and the use of economic instruments for environmental policies are considered possible topics for the Sofia Conference. As a follow-up to the second European Conference on Environment and Health, held in Helsinki in June, the Committee supported the establishment of a European Environment and Health Committee for the implementation of the Environmental Health Action Plan for Europe, and nominated four representatives to participate in its work. In order to strengthen environmental management capabilities, the Committee decided to assess the region-wide implications of improving environmental performance in the countries in transition. Progress has been made in the ECE programme of country environmental performance reviews including the pilot ECE review of Estonia and cooperation with the Organisation for Economic Cooperation and Development (OECD) in pilot OECD reviews of Poland and Bulgaria. At its first session in 1994, the Committee also adopted soft-law regulations in the form of recommendations to ECE Governments on environmentally sound technology and products, environmental product profiles and the financing of environmental policies.

(a) Convention on Environmental Impact Assessment in a Transboundary Context

With the ratification by Austria and the Republic of Moldova in 1994, six governments have now ratified the 1991 ECE Convention on Environmental Impact Assessment in a Transboundary Context (E/ECE/1250). Information on policies and strategies promoting environmental impact assessment (EIA) in the ECE region was analyzed with a view to further examine ways and means of harmonizing these policies and strategies. The analysis indicates that in the ECE region, EIA is being increasingly used in a transboundary context as an instrument promoting an integrated approach to environmental protection and management, as it requires a comprehensive assessment of the impacts of a proposed activity and its alternatives on the environment, and brings facts and information on impacts to the attention of the decision makers and the public. It thereby strengthens the achievement of sustainable development. In 1994, it was also decided to publish the reports on policies and strategies, on legal and administrative aspects, and on methodological aspects of EIA in a transboundary context together as a new volume in the ECE Environmental Series.

(b) Convention on the Transboundary Effects of Industrial Accidents

In 1994, Albania, Hungary, Luxembourg, the Republic of Moldova, and the Russian Federation deposited their instruments of ratification, accession, approval, or acceptance regarding the 1992 Convention on the Transboundary Effects of Industrial Accidents (E/ECE/1268), which six governments have now ratified. The third meeting of signatories, open to all ECE member countries, was convened in 1994 and reviewed relevant policies and strategies, the use of points of contacts for the ECE accident notification system and ways and means to strengthen the ability of countries in transition to prevent, prepare for, and respond to industrial accidents. The meeting also established two ECE regional coordinating centres for the purposes of the Convention; one for industrial accident training and exercises (Warsaw, Poland) and one for the prevention of industrial accidents (Budapest, Hungary) together with an intergovernmental steering group to coordinate and oversee their functions and activities.

(c) Convention on the Protection and Use of Transboundary Watercourses and International Lakes

With the ratification of Albania, Hungary, Luxembourg, Portugal, and the Republic of Moldova in 1994, eight countries have now ratified the Convention on the Protection and Use of Transboundary Watercourses and International Lakes (E/ECE/1267). A series of activities was undertaken, such as monitoring and assessment of conditions of transboundary waters, control of water pollution from point and diffuse sources, and legal and administrative issues of the Convention. It was also decided to publish the reports on policies and strategies for the protection and use of transboundary waters as a new volume in the ECE Water Series. Recommendations to ECE governments on the prevention of water pollution from hazardous substances were also adopted in 1994.

(3) Inland Transport Committee

With the accession of Liechenstein, Romania, and the Russian Federation in 1994, the 1957 European Agreement concerning the International Carriage of Dangerous Goods by Road (ADR; ECE/TRANS/110; UNTS 619/77; 774/368; 828/518; 883/174; 907/158; 921/284; 922/282; 926/114; 951/433; 982/313; 987/435; 1003/249; 1023/462; 1035/330; 1074/352; 1107/269; 1161/461; 1162/437; 1259/407; 1279/307; and 1297/406) now has 28 parties. A revision of the European provisions concerning the international carriage of dangerous goods by inland waterway is under preparation, which will lead to a new publication to be finalized in 1996. The development of a formal agreement is also under consideration. There were no changes during 1994 in the status of the 1989 Convention on Civil Liability for Damage caused during Carriage of Dangerous Goods by Road, Rail and Inland Navigation Vessels (CRTD; ECE/TRANS/79), which has not yet entered into force. So far, Germany and Morocco have signed but not yet ratified this Convention. With the succession of Croatia in 1994, the 1958 Agreement concerning the Adoption of Uniform Conditions of Approval and Reciprocal Recognition of Approval for Motor Vehicles Equipment and Parts (E/ECE/324-E/ECE/TRANS/505/Rev.1; UNTS 335/211; 516/378; 609/290 and 1059/404) now has 25 parties. In the framework of this Agreement, a new regulation concerning the approval of compression ignition engines to be installed in agricultural and forestry tractors was adopted in 1994 and was expected to enter into force in 1995. A new regulation was adopted on the uniform provisions concerning the approval of passenger cars equipped with internal combustion engines, with regard to the measurement of the emission of carbon dioxide and fuel consumption, which will replace existing Regulation

No. 84 of the Agreement (measurement of fuel consumption.) This method is identical to that being used within the EC.

Wiek Schrage[1]

P. UNITED NATIONS INSTITUTE FOR TRAINING AND RESEARCH (UNITAR)

UNITAR continued to strengthen its training programmes for the implementation of international environmental agreements and policy initiatives. Training programmes for which formal cooperation agreements were in place with responsible UN secretariats and bodies include, *inter alia*, the UN Framework Convention on Climate Change, the Basel Convention on the Transboundary Movement for Hazardous Wastes and Their Disposal, and the London Guidelines for the Exchange of Information on Chemicals in International Trade. Other emerging programmes at UNITAR focus on the implementation of specific international policy initiatives related to the sound management of chemicals. These programmes are conducted as UN Conference on Environment and Development follow-up activities pursuant to Ch. 19 of Agenda 21, which addresses the sound management of chemicals.

(1) Training Programmes on the Implementation of International Agreements and Policy Initiatives in the Area of Chemical and Waste Management

(a) The London Guidelines

The United Nations Environment Programme (UNEP)/UNITAR Training Programme on the Implementation of the London Guidelines on the Exchange of Information on Chemicals in International Trade was established in 1991 to assist developing countries in their efforts to implement the London Guidelines and to strengthen their chemical management schemes. It is a joint venture between UNEP's International Register of Potentially Toxic Chemicals and UNITAR. The UNEP/UNITAR Training Programme has two main objectives: (1) to assist developing countries in the implementation of the Prior Informed Consent (PIC) procedure, and (2) to strengthen the establishment of National Information Systems for the Sound Management of Chemicals. In 1994, the programme conducted workshops and training seminars on: Chemicals Management in Mexico in the Context of the London Guidelines, the Organisation for Economic Cooperation and Development (OECD), and the North American Free Trade Agreement (Mexico City, Mexico, June); the Implementation of PIC

[1] The views expressed are those of the author and do not necessarily coincide with those of UN/ECE.

and related Issues of Chemicals Management (Santa Marta, Colombia, June/July); and Strengthening National Information Systems for Chemicals Management in India, Malaysia, the Philippines, Sri Lanka, and Thailand.

(b) Pilot Studies on the Establishment of Pollutant Release and Transfer Registers in Developing/Industrializing Countries

In 1993, several international organizations began to cooperate on the development of "emission inventories" as outlined in Ch. 19 of Agenda 21. The OECD has taken steps to develop a guidance document for the establishment of what is now titled "Pollutant Release and Transfer Registers." An informal coordination group was established with the participation of several international organizations and other interested parties, in which UNITAR is responsible for training, outreach, and pilot studies. In 1994, parallel to the work of OECD, UNITAR initiated a series of "Pilot Studies on the Establishment of Pollutant Release and Transfer Registers [PRTRs] in Developing/Industrializing Countries." Pilot studies were ongoing in Mexico, Egypt, and the Czech Republic. The first results of the pilot studies are expected in early 1996. At this point all three participating countries are expected to have developed a final national PRTR concept/assessment.

(c) National Reference Documents/Profiles in the Area of Chemical Management and Safety

In April, the International Conference on Chemical Safety adopted "Priorities for Action" for the implementation of Programme E of Agenda 21, Ch. 19. The Conference recommended that "[n]ational profiles to indicate current capabilities and capacities for management of chemicals and the specific needs for improvement should be elaborated as soon as possible and not later than 1997." Taking this recommendation into consideration, UNITAR, in co-operation with the secretariat of the Intergovernmental Forum on Chemical Safety, initiated a project to strengthen the capability of developing countries to create comprehensive national reference documents/profiles for chemical management and safety. Once available, national reference documents/profiles should become the official reference point for national action and priority needs for external technical assistance. 1994 efforts focussed on draft guidance material on the structure and substantive scope of national profiles and the preparation of national profiles through participation. The guidance material was to be tested in a few pilot study countries during the second half of 1995.

(d) The Basel Convention

In October, the UNEP/Secretariat of the Basel Convention (SBC) and UNITAR signed a Memorandum of Agreement for a Training Programme to Strengthen Capabilities in Developing Countries and Countries in

Economic Transition to implement the Basel Convention. Under the European Community-supported joint cooperation, SBC takes primary responsibility for the technical supervision of all activities, while UNITAR, in close consultation with SBC, will be responsible for developing training components, organizing workshops, and preparing training material, the content of which will be assessed and cleared by SBC. The planned programme is composed of two complementary programme areas: (1) assessment of hazardous waste management infrastructure and related training and technical assistance needs, and (2) capacity-building to assist countries on implementation of the Basel Convention and preparation of national hazardous waste management plans.

(2) CC:TRAIN-UNITAR Training Programme to Implement the UN Framework Convention on Climate Change

The Training Programme to Promote the Implementation of the United Nations Framework Convention on Climate Change was established in 1993 as a joint effort by the Convention's Interim Secretariat and UNITAR, in collaboration with the secretariats of the Global Environment Facility, the Intergovernmental Panel on Climate Change, and the United Nations Development Programme, with the assistance of the Information Unit on Climate Change. These organizations constitute the Steering Group of the training programme. The programme is designed to strengthen the institutional capacity of both developing countries and those in economic and political transition to address the causes and effects of climate change and to undertake activities in pursuit of the objective of the Convention. During the pilot phase, the training programme is developing a model for initiating multi-sectoral policy dialogue as input into future capacity-building, policy development, and project coordination activities. The three pilot-phase countries are Lithuania, Vietnam, and Zimbabwe. In 1994, the training programme implemented three-quarters of the full training cycle in the three pilot phase countries. Several seminars for country teams and a number of consultative roundtable meetings took place and the formulation of a national strategy to implement the Convention got underway, the objective being to present these draft strategies to high-level decision makers at national conferences in 1995. The process of selecting the countries to participate in phase 2 of CC:TRAIN also began. By the end of 1994, about 50 countries had registered their requests for consideration.

In October 1994, preparations were begun for the CC:TRAIN Training Package. It will comprise two modules: the first will provide guidelines on organizing workshops and presentations, the second will deal with developing a national implementation strategy on climate change and the Convention.

(3) UNEP/UNITAR Training Programme in Environmental Law and Policy in Association with HABITAT

The objective of this programme is to inform and train environmental lawyers from developing countries and countries in transition about the legal and institutional developments at international and national levels in the field of environmental law. The training is conducted by experts from UNEP and other UN agencies, representatives of Environmental Convention Secretariats, the World Bank, and experts in the field of environmental law and policy. 1994 was devoted to the preparation of the second global training programme in environmental law and policy, which was to take place 27 March through 13 April 1995 at UNEP Headquarters in Nairobi, accommodating 30 government-nominated participants. Preparation was based on the evaluation of the first global training programme, held in December 1993. The training material was further developed and transformed into a user-friendly manual that contains background and reference material, as well as practical exercises and case studies.

Achim A. Halpaap

Q. WORLD BANK

The World Bank consists of four closely associated institutions: the International Bank for Reconstruction and Development (IBRD), the International Development Association (IDA), the International Finance Corporation (IFC), and the Multilateral Investment Guarantee Agency. Unless otherwise specified, the "World Bank" as used in this report refers to the IBRD and IDA only. IFC activities are summarized in section 2 below.

(1) Operational Policies and Procedures

The World Bank's field activities are subject to a series of operational policies (OPs), bank procedures (BPs) and good practices (GPs). Of these, the following new texts issued in 1994 are environmentally relevant.

(a) OP 4.02, BP 4.02, and GP 4.02 on Environmental Action Plans (EAPs)

The World Bank issued these documents in October. They aim at providing support and guidance to borrowing countries in the preparation and implementation of EAPs. The OP specifically notes that preparing and implementing EAPs is the borrower's responsibility. In this context, the OP and BP outline some of the key elements for a sound EAP, including public participation, diagnosis of the country's most pressing environmental problems, recommendations, and monitoring and evaluation. In addition, the GP provides useful suggestions on how to prepare an EAP.

(b) OP 4.20 on The Gender Dimension of Development

Issued in April, this OP states the Bank's policy on gender issues. The Bank supports efforts to reduce gender disparities to "enhance women's participation in the economic development of their countries." To this end, the Bank assists its borrowers in reviewing and modifying borrowers' policies affecting women's access to assets and services. The Bank also assists its borrowers in providing training for country officials and in obtaining financing for specific programs.

(c) OP 10.04 on Economic Evaluation of Investment Operations

The World Bank issued OP 10.04 on Economic Evaluation of Investment Operations in April. Paragraph 8 states that some projects may have cross-border or global externalities. Cross-border externalities are effects on neighboring countries, whereas global externalities affect the entire world. The economic evaluation of Bank-financed projects takes into account cross-border externalities. Global externalities are normally identified in the Bank's sector work and in the environment assessment process. The Bank's Environment Department provides guidance on analyzing, ranking, and physically quantifying global externalities and on taking them into account in project selection and justification. A project's global externalities are considered in these economic analyses when a country has actually made commitments for global environmental action through international agreement or when the Global Environment Facility finances projects or project components.

(2) International Finance Corporation

Separate from the IBRD's and IDA's lending activities, the IFC provides direct project financing for private investment in developing countries not guaranteed by member governments. During fiscal 1994, the Environment Division in IFC's Technical and Environment Department increased its staff to accommodate its growth. As a result, the IFC strengthened the monitoring and supervision of projects during the year. The IFC also took steps toward following through on its commitment to greater transparency in the environmental issues that its investments raise, and revised its environmental review procedure for proposed projects. Key changes involve expanded public disclosure requirements for category A and B projects, including release of environmental information about projects through the World Bank's new Public Information Center. During fiscal 1994, the IFC received more than 100 expressions of interest in financial participation in environmental projects, of which 40 were considered appropriate for possible IFC involvement.

(3) Global Environment Facility—World Bank as Implementing Agency and Trustee

With the three-year pilot phase of the Global Environment Facility (GEF) scheduled to end in 1994, negotiations to restructure the GEF in March concluded successfully when representatives of 73 states accepted the Instrument for the Establishment of the Restructured Global Environment Facility (the Instrument). The GEF's three implementing agencies (the United Nations Development Programme, the United Nations Environment Programme, and the World Bank) then adopted the Instrument. The restructured GEF is to provide new and additional grant and concessional funding to meet the agreed incremental costs of measures to achieve agreed global environmental benefits in the focal areas of climate change, biodiversity, international waters, and ozone-layer depletion. Also eligible for funding are the agreed incremental costs of activities concerning land degradation, primarily desertification and deforestation, as they relate to the focal areas.

The World Bank's Executive Directors adopted the Instrument in Washington, DC, on May 24, and the Bank's Board of Governors adopted Resolution No. 487, "Protection of the Global Environment" on July 7, approving Bank cooperation with other international organizations, as appropriate, to achieve the purposes of the GEF. The World Bank also serves as Trustee of the GEF Trust Fund. To date, the Bank's GEF Work Program consists of 52 investment projects totalling US$454.95 million, 37 of which have been approved for a total of US$327.25 million. In addition, the Bank's pre-investment preparation fund for GEF projects has supported 30 projects at approximately US$12.85 million.

(4) Montreal Protocol—Multilateral Fund

The World Bank continues to serve, administer, and manage the Ozone Projects Trust Fund (OTF), including the preparation, appraisal, and supervision of projects under the OTF. The Bank's portfolio of Montreal Protocol investment operations has grown to almost US$100 million, and projects that have been given permission to proceed now amount to over US$20 million.

In 1994, the OTF financed a grant agreement with the Philippines (US$15 million), an "umbrella" grant agreement with the Kingdom of Thailand (US$40 million), the first ozone-related grant agreements with Tunisia, and a US$17 million umbrella grant agreement with Indonesia. Based on Multilateral Fund Executive Committee (MFEC) approvals to date, about US$5 million is available for implementation of eight projects under the new agreement with Thailand. The MFEC considered additional project proposals at its December meeting. In addition, the Bank cleared the second India Project (umbrella grant agreement of US$50 million) for negotiations, as well as the third China Project (umbrella grant agreement of US$60 million.)

(5) Rainforest Trust Fund

The Bank made substantial progress with regard to the Rain Forest Trust Fund (RFT) in 1994. Brazil and the Bank negotiated and signed the following RFT Projects: Demonstration Project; Science Centers and Directed Research; Extractive Reserves; and Natural Resources Policy Project. In 1995 at least two RFT Projects are expected to be prepared: Environmental Education and National Forests.

(6) Technical Assistance

The Legal Department of the World Bank, through its Environment Unit, provided technical assistance with regard to environmental legislation, regulation, and institutional capacity- building in 32 countries in Africa, Asia, the Caribbean and Latin America, Eastern Europe, the Middle East and North Africa, and the Pacific region. The Department provided this assistance in the context of Bank-sponsored National Environment Action Plans, which the Bank, GEF, and other trust funds finance.

(7) Desertification Convention

During the negotiation and drafting stage, the World Bank was actively involved in supporting the (➔) Convention to Combat Desertification.

Charles E. Di Leva
Mohammed A. Bekhechi
Alberto Ninio

R. WORLD HEALTH ORGANIZATION (WHO)

[Editors' Note: No significant developments in 1994.]

2. NON-GOVERNMENTAL ORGANIZATIONS

A. CENTER FOR INTERNATIONAL ENVIRONMENTAL LAW (CIEL), WASHIGNTON, D.C.

(1) Biodiversity and Wildlife Program

The Center for International Environmental Law's Biodiversity and Wildlife Program develops and coordinates non-governmental positions and strategies, and prepares position papers and draft coalition statements.

CIEL played a coordinating role in the debate over US ratification of the Biodiversity Convention. CIEL's work included advice to non-governmental organizations (NGOs) regarding ratification and implementation of the Biodiversity Convention. CIEL also provided comments to the US Senate Foreign Relations Committee on legal questions involving the Biodiversity Convention. In addition, CIEL participated in international meetings concerning the Biodiversity Convention, *inter alia,* as the NGO representative on the official US delegation at the 1994 Conference of the Parties, where CIEL sponsored a workshop on incentives for biodiversity conservation.

CIEL continued to provide law and policy advice to governments and NGOs on commercial uses of biodiversity and benefit sharing. For instance, CIEL helped scientists and activists draft proposed guidelines for sharing the benefits of commercial use of biodiversity for distribution to some of the world's leading scientists involved in conservation.

During 1994, CIEL began a study of the effect of economic policies in the United States on biodiversity conservation, including policies that encourage destruction of biodiversity and those that encourage conservation. At the invitation of the U.S. delegation, CIEL presented its findings to the Organization for Economic Cooperation and Development (OECD) experts group on economic aspects of biodiversity in November. CIEL also worked with the NGO Conservation International to develop introductory materials on economic incentives and biodiversity for policy-makers in Latin America.

Finally, CIEL participated in the December Conference of the Parties to the Convention on the International Trade in Endangered Species.

(2) Trade and Environment

CIEL remains committed to promoting transparency and public accountability and participation in trade policy-making. In 1994, CIEL analyzed the rules, policies, procedures, and customs that affect public participation in trade policy institutions and identified existing opportunities for public participation. For example, CIEL worked to create an environmental advisory committee to the OECD that would parallel existing advisory bodies such as the business and industry advisory committee. CIEL is also actively participating in the International Standards Organization's effort to develop and strengthen environmental management, packaging, and labelling standards.

During 1994, CIEL continued its efforts to improve implementation of the North American Free Trade Agreement (NAFTA), working in partnership with other US NGOs and NGOs from Mexico and Canada. Working with Defenders of Wildlife, CIEL drafted an Executive Order on public oversight and participation in the US implementation of NAFTA, which, after slight modification, President Clinton signed. As part of its support of the United Nations Environment Program's Trade and Environment Program, CIEL published a comprehensive study of NAFTA's lessons for future trade agreements. CIEL President Durwood Zaelke serves on the NAFTA National Advisory Board—the body advising the U.S. in its participation in the North American Commission for Environmental Cooperation. CIEL held parallel conferences in Washington, D.C. and Santiago, Chile, relating to the potential expansion of NAFTA to Chile.

In 1994, CIEL completed an extensive analysis of six key multilateral environmental agreements (MEAs) in light of the trade disciplines established by the GATT, including the Final Act of the Uruguay Round and relevant reports of GATT dispute resolution panels. The analysis discusses the relationship between new trade rules and the following MEAs: the Montreal Protocol on Substances that Deplete the Ozone Layer, the United Nations Framework Convention on Climate Change, the Basel Convention on the Control of Transboundary Movements of Hazardous Wastes and Their Disposal, the Convention on International Trade in Endangered Species, the Convention on Biological Diversity, and the London Convention on the Prevention of Marine Pollution by Dumping of Wastes and Other Matter. The study was to be published in early 1995.

(3) Global Commons Program

CIEL continued its work on the Global Environment Facility (GEF) by testifying before the US House Banking Committee on behalf of a number of environmental groups regarding US involvement with the GEF. CIEL also began work on a project to identify mechanisms for the GEF to mobilize private sector investment in energy efficiency and renewable sources of energy.

In 1994, CIEL was the fiscal sponsor for Ozone Action, a new NGO aimed at stimulating and coordinating a broader response to the threats of ozone depletion. Along with Ozone Action and several other groups, CIEL organized a roundtable of scientists and lawyers to discuss the factual and legal requirements for holding manufacturers of ozone-destroying substances responsible.

(4) Increasing Accountability at the Multilateral Development Banks (MDBs)

As part of its ongoing efforts to monitor MDBs, CIEL has launched a multi-year effort to increase accountability at the MDBs by promoting, monitoring, and using the MDBs' new inspection panels. In addition, CIEL continued its work to monitor the European Bank for Reconstruction and Development.

(a) The New Inspection Panels

CIEL, along with other NGOs, was instrumental in pushing for the creation of the World Bank's precedent-setting Inspection Panel. In 1994, along with International Rivers Network, CIEL prepared "model" procedures for the Panel, which heavily influenced the final procedures. CIEL monitored the implementation of those procedures in the first claim brought before the Panel—including the Arun III dam project in Nepal. In addition, CIEL worked with other US and foreign environmental, human rights, and development groups to inform affected parties in developing countries of their new rights under this panel. CIEL is currently assisting affected parties in India, Brazil, Slovakia, and other countries in analyzing potential claims to bring before the panel. CIEL is actively promoting the development of similar inspection functions at the regional MDBs as well.

(b) European Bank for Reconstruction and Development (EBRD)

In November 1994, CIEL released a draft of its Environmental Progress Report on the EBRD, which evaluates the first four years of the EBRD's operation. The EBRD was the first MDB to include an explicit sustainable development mandate in its charter. The draft report concludes that the EBRD has yet to live up to its commitment to sustainable development and democracy. It also makes a series of concrete proposals to improve the EBRD's environmental performance, including the establishment of a sustainable development policy and criteria, environmental department veto power over projects that could adversely affect the environment, public notification requirements at the earliest stage in project development, and an independent inspection panel.

(5) Regional Programs

In Central and Eastern Europe and the newly independent states of the former Soviet Union, CIEL continued to provide legal and technical assistance to NGOs and governments. This included completing a report on privatization and environment, developing implementing legislation for a national conservation strategy in Slovakia and Bulgaria, conducting environmental impact assessment training seminars in Bulgaria, providing assistance to increase the capabilities and effectiveness of grassroots environmental groups in several countries, and reviewing environmental laws in Kazakhstan and Georgia. To better provide such assistance in the region, CIEL opened a Moscow office in August 1994 now has one full-time attorney stationed there.

CIEL also continued its efforts to assist public interest environmental lawyers in Latin America. CIEL continued its support and assistance to the Centro Mexican de Derecho Ambiental, Mexico's first public interest environmental law firm. In Chile, Argentina, and Brazil, CIEL has provided technical and legal support to NGO leaders, public interest lawyers, and government officials. In November, CIEL hosted "Haiti and Environmental Restoration: Toward an Environmentally Sustainable Society," a conference that examined proposals for long-term environmentally sustainable investment and development assistance in Haiti.

CIEL's activities in Asia included developing a training course on environmental law enforcement for judges, assisting the Cambodian Ministry of Environment with drafting a framework environmental law and an environmental impact assessment law, and completing a feasibility study on collecting and analyzing environmental laws from 14 Asia-Pacific Countries.

(6) Environmental Information Alliance

In 1994, CIEL formed the Environmental Information Alliance, which is designed to increase electronic access to environmental information. The Alliance is a partnership of CIEL, EcoNet, the World Resources Institute, and Island Press. The Alliance is also working with the Public Information Exchange, a nonprofit public utility of digital information and communications dedicated to public access.

(7) Joint Research Program

During 1994, CIEL continued its Joint Research Program with the American University's Washington College of Law. This joint program trains lawyers from around the world, particularly from developing countries, in international and comparative environmental law. As part of the program, CIEL arranges for scholarships, facilitates exchanges of law professors, and sponsors conferences on pressing environmental issues.

David Hunter
Claudia Saladin

B. CENTRO DE DERECHO AMBIENTAL Y DE LOS RECURSOS NATURALES (CEDARENA), SAN JOSÉ, COSTA RICA

(1) Objective, Mission, and Programs

The Environmental and Natural Resources Law Center (CEDARENA) is a non-profit, non-political association of attorneys, law students, interns, and volunteers based in San José, Costa Rica. CEDARENA has established a permanent center for environmental law research, information exchange, and education, and has initiated projects for action and advocacy leading to improved environmental law and policy in Costa Rica and

Central America. Its objective is to strengthen the capacity of the Central American people to resolve environmental problems and improve their quality of life. Its mission is to introduce, develop, and consolidate the ecological variable as a fundamental element within the legislative and judicial order.

CEDARENA's current work encompasses public policy, international collaboration, distribution of legal information and resources, and community services. Within these programs, CEDARENA has established several projects. The Public Policy Program Land Tenure and Land Use Planning Pilot Project on the Osa Peninsula, conducted with the Neotrópica Foundation's BOSCOSA project, has continued with a land-titling process in the Peninsula. Its purpose is to facilitate the adoption and acceptance of forest management plans in the region. Two of the pilot project's greatest accomplishments have been its beneficiaries' acceptance of the project and their recognition of it as part of a larger program for land tenure and land-use planning in the Peninsula.

The Talamanca-Caribbean Biotic Corridor Project seeks to stimulate and coordinate local and external efforts to protect the relationship between man and the environment within the Biotic Corridor. An inter-institutional committee, on which CEDARENA represents the legal component, coordinates the project.

CEDARENA's Coastal and Marine Resources Project aims to empower coastal communities by broadening citizen participation in the control and protection of coastal resources through knowledge of relevant legislation and through the development of coastal management plans. An important result has been CEDARENA's publication of a Manual for the Conservation of Coastal Resources.

The Tortuguero Biological Corridor litigation process, intended to protect the biological corridor between Tortuguero National Park and Barra del Colorado Wildlife Refuge from illegal occupation, was still continuing at year's end. In a very significant development, the Agrarian Appeals Court recognized the concept of "ecological possession," which for the first time recognized the protection of the natural state as a valid land use under law.

(2) International Collaboration Program

Under its Mesoamerican Environmental Law Project, CEDARENA program attorneys, with the support of a second grant from the North-South Center, began their second applied research project in the region, focusing on the difficult issues involved in property tenure (including wildlife and intellectual property) on indigenous lands in the region. At the end of 1994, planning was underway to host a second roundtable meeting of attorneys, policymakers, managers, donors, and scientists to discuss management issues surrounding the bi-national management of the Río San Juan.

The Mesoamerican Environmental Law Project assisted the Caribbean Conservation Corporation in hosting a side meeting of the delegates from Costa Rica, Nicaragua, and Panama to the Conference of the Parties to the Convention on the International Trade in Endangered Species. The delegates discussed issues related to the management of marine turtles.

(3) Community Service Program

CEDARENA is involved in several community service programs. The Environmental Law Consultancy continues to offer legal advice to associations, institutions, and persons interested in the solution of ecological problems. To date, more than 200 consultations have been given. The Consultancy is pursuing more complex cases closely, due to the heightened possibility of their negative impact on the environment. CEDARENA also provides training courses in environmental law as part of its community service program. Since it began the program, it has offered more than 20 legal training courses for preventing and reporting environmental crimes to 390 participants representing 123 organizations.

Project REFORMA aims to decrease the deforestation rate and augment forest cover in Talamanca, San Carlos, and the Osa Peninsula. CEDARENA is in charge of the legal component of the project and is pursuing this end by monitoring all complaints of illegal logging and educating organizations involved in monitoring such complaints. These educational efforts are aimed at judges, representatives of the regional offices of the General Forest Bureau, and private organizations located in the three zones covered by the project.

At the end of 1994, CEDARENA's project for education on forest-fire legislation was in its first phase, which consisted primarily of analysis of the legal options for preventing forest fires in the Guanacaste region of Costa Rica. As part of this phase, CEDARENA published two important manuals, the Manual on Legislation and Institutional Competences relating to Forest Fires in Guanacaste, and the Manual on Legislation on Burnings and Forest Fires. These manuals are directed toward public functionaries and the general public, respectively. An important contribution of the project has been the drafting of a decree regulating agricultural burnings for the first time. The decree has already been signed and published.

Zdenka Piskulich
Rodrigo Barahona

C. EARTH COUNCIL, SAN JOSÉ, COSTA RICA

(1) Introduction

The United Nations Conference on Environment and Development, commonly known as the Earth Summit, developed the blueprint for a sustainable future. Each UN member country was to carry out implementation, create national councils on sustainable development and develop local ways to implement Agenda 21. By the end of 1994, over 100 countries had created a national council or an equivalent body, and the UN had created the Commission on Sustainable Development (CSD).

The Earth Summit endorsed the creation of the Earth Council, which has provided an important international forum for focusing on the Earth Summit's work and assisting national councils and local grassroots organizations in acting more effectively in respect to sustainable development. Among the Earth Council's key strategies are the development of alliances and partnerships, avoiding duplication of effort, and maximizing resources. Working with national councils and providing a forum for their joint efforts has become the key element of the Earth Council's programme. National councils are the only recognized bodies in each country in which the various societal sectors have the mandate to work together to determine how to develop in a sustainable manner. By helping national councils, the Earth Council will promote and institutionalize non-governmental groups' participation in policy formulation at the national level.

In October, the Earth Council organized and hosted the first regional meeting of national councils, in cooperation with the United Nations Environment Programme, the United Nations Development Programme, the Department of Policy Coordination on Sustainable Development, and the Inter-American Institute for Cooperation on Agriculture. Two other regional meetings of national councils were to take place in Asia and Africa in 1995, and discussions were underway at year's end regarding a global forum of national councils and international networks of major groups.

(2) Earth Council Programmes and Activities

The Earth Council focuses on four priority areas: monitoring of and reporting on the overall progress of sustainable development; facilitating local initiatives regarding sustainable development; developing an Earth Charter to define the principles of sustainable development; and creating public awareness and information. Each programme is guided by the need to produce concrete and definable results and to encourage dialogue and cooperation among civil society members and government, particularly with those whose views and voices are too often unheard or unheeded.

(a) Earth Monitoring and Reporting Programme

This programme provides user-friendly tools for implementing, monitoring, and reporting on the progress made toward achieving sustainable development. Its goal is to highlight international successes, remaining challenges, and the gaps between promises and performances. The core of the programme is the *Earth Report*, which provides decision-makers with insights and practical experiences of civil society. To support the *Earth Report*, the Earth Council is preparing sector assessments in collaboration with other organizations. The economics/financing sector assessment, the first of the four sector assessments that the Earth Council has selected, focusses on economic incentives. A proposal has been prepared on this issue, and the first phase of the assessment was expected to be completed in 1995. The goal of the trade sector assessment is to establish links between trade and environment. This initiative has greatly benefitted from the cooperation of the International Institute for Sustainable Development and the World Economic Forum. The energy assessment focuses on the promotion of energy-efficient policies and the use of renewable energy resources. This assessment is being developed by Energy 21, an organization affiliated with the Earth Council. During 1994, Energy 21 carried out the first study on implementation in this area. Finally, an Inter-American group of experts created an agriculture/natural resources assessment. These experts met three times in 1994 and prepared a final draft on "Agriculture and Natural Resources in the Americas."

(b) Facilitating People's Initiatives

Facilitating People's Initiatives focuses on promoting sustainable development activities among civil society institutions and groups and helping to ensure their input into decision-making processes, especially at the global level. The Earth Council has undertaken numerous activities in this regard. With the World Resources Institute and the Natural Resources Defense Council, it published the first directory of national councils and presented it to the CSD in 1994.

With regard to educational tools, the Earth Council participated in a number of ventures in 1994. It created arrangements with partner organizations to produce information kits and educational tools to enable civil institutions and major groups to monitor progress toward sustainable development. The International Council of Scientific Unions, the Third World Academy of Sciences, and the Earth Council joined to integrate and broaden work on sustainable development in the "Lectureships and Professorships in Science and Sustainable Development Programme." The World Travel and Tourism Council and the World Travel Organization similarly agreed to collaborate on the preparation of the "International

Agenda 21 for the Travel and Tourism Industry" and "The Green Globe Programme." Parliamentarians for Global Action joined in the preparation and mailing of a pamphlet and diskettes on the Earth Summit agreements and the directory of the national councils for sustainable development. And the Earth Council initiated a pilot project to consult those involved in the Costa Rican Earth Charter process, along with developing a series of teaching materials entitled "Pedagogia para el Desarrollo Sostenible." Discussions are also underway for a partnership with the International Association of Universities and the International Institute for Sustainable Development to advance Agenda 21 with emphasis on the role of universities.

In 1994, the Earth Council held 10 workshops with indigenous peoples on biodiversity and sustainable development. It produced a booklet called "Dialogue on the Bio-Diversity Convention" in Spanish and English, and issued a bulletin for Indigenous People's Exchange, called "Life, Wisdom and Future."

By year's end, the Earth Council had been involved in eight international youth events and had installed a database including information on more than 700 youth organizations. The Youth Programme, together with Peach Child International and the Secretariat of the CSD, were launching an international process to assess the implementation of Agenda 21 from a youth perspective. Three issues of the information bulletins "INTERaccion Juvenil" and "INTERcambio Juvenil" have been produced. More than 150 organizations had provided feedback by year's end.

(c) The Earth Charter

In 1994, the Earth Council, in partnership with the Green Cross International and with the support of the Netherlands Government, launched the Earth Charter initiative. The Charter is to represent a universally accepted set of principles, building on governmental and non-governmental efforts started during the Earth Summit. The target is to establish the foundations for the Charter in time for the 50th Anniversary of the United Nations in June 1995. The Earth Council has established a steering committee to support the Earth Charter process.

(d) Ombudsman Function

At its Inaugural Meeting in November 1993, the Earth Council decided that one of its priority areas should be establishing an ombudsman-type function. During the Second Annual Meeting in November, the Earth Council defined some initial criteria for issues to be taken up by the ombudsman. Eligible issues must involve alleged damage that creates a serious risk to human rights, human health, and well-being; important ecological systems or resources; or endangered species. They must also have an international cross-boundary aspect and not be amenable to effective redress otherwise.

Alicia Bárcena

D. THE ENVIRONMENTAL DEFENSE FUND (EDF), WASHINGTON, D.C.

(1) Introduction

In 1994, EDF was involved in multi-disciplinary research and advocacy in a variety of international fora. EDF continued to promote environmental and institutional reforms in the multilateral development banks (MDBs), the restructured Global Environment Facility, and the US Export-Import Bank. EDF also continued its commitment to promote effective implementation of key international environmental treaties, including the UN Framework Convention on Climate Change, the Montreal Protocol, and the Convention on Biodiversity, and began a new initiative on population growth and consumption patterns.

(2) Environmental Treaties

(a) UN Framework Convention on Climate Change

EDF was represented at the Ninth and Tenth Meetings of the Inter-Governmental Negotiating Committee (INC). At the Ninth INC Meeting in Geneva, EDF pushed for tighter scrutiny of the implications of MDB energy lending for achieving the goals of reducing carbon dioxide and other greenhouse gases. As a result, the Ninth Meeting of the INC resolved to establish an oversight mechanism among the parties to the Climate Convention to monitor the energy lending activities of the MDBs with respect to achieving the goals of the Convention.

EDF encouraged stronger commitments on the part of developed countries, while proposing a practical mechanism for joint implementation of the Convention's goals by industrialized and developing nations. The proposed mechanism consists of an emissions credit trading program that provides a cost-effective means of compliance for developed countries while promoting sustainable development in developing countries.

(b) Convention on Biodiversity

EDF continued to work toward establishing a closer integration of the goals of the Convention on Biological Diversity and its interim financial mechanism, the Global Environment Facility (GEF). At the First Meeting of the Conference of the Parties of the Biodiversity Convention in December 1994, EDF played a key role in obtaining government support for a survey of international financial institutions and the compatibility of their programs, policies, and projects with the goals of the Convention (*see* (➔) Report of the First Meeting).

(c) Montreal Protocol on Substances That Deplete The Ozone Layer

EDF participated in scientific and financial discussions regarding the Montreal Protocol and its Multilateral Fund. EDF advocated the inclusion of alternatives for hydrochlorofluorocarbons and methyl bromide into the technical and economic assessment panel study during the Open Ended Working Group Meeting and at the Sixth Meeting of the Parties to the Montreal Protocol held in Nairobi, 6–7 October (*see* (➔) Report of the Sixth Meeting). EDF also attended the Executive Committee Meeting to the Multilateral Fund, held in Montreal in July 1994, and monitored the status of the Fund and its role as the financial mechanism. EDF's contributions to two Multilateral Fund reviews will be useful in 1995 as parties discuss acceleration of phase-out schedules and inclusion of methyl bromide as a controlled substance.

(3) UN Commission on Sustainable Development (CSD)

In collaboration with the Consortium for Action to Protect the Earth 2000, EDF focused the attention of the governments and non-governmental organizations (NGOs) attending the CSD meetings on four key initiatives: phase-out of lead in gasoline; clean-up of freshwater sources; ratification and implementation of the Basel Convention on Hazardous Wastes; and protection of pristine rivers.

A major accomplishment of the CSD in 1994 was the decision by participating governments to acknowledge the health and environmental dangers of lead, including leaded gasoline. EDF's research and advocacy for global phase-out of lead positively influenced the decision and helped prompt US Environmental Protection Agency (EPA) Administrator Carol Browner and US Undersecretary of State for Global Affairs Timothy Wirth to call for a global phase-out of lead.

Following extensive work on freshwater issues at the 1992 Dublin Water Conference and the Earth Summit, EDF successfully influenced the CSD to take up freshwater issues at its opening meeting in 1994. In May 1994, EDF figured prominently in the freshwater discussions at the CSD meeting and submitted a position paper proposing a global initiative: Clean Water 2000. The initiative called for partnerships among government, the private sector, NGOs, and communities to clean up a particular polluted river or waterbody, to foster "demonstration projects" for pollution control and water conservation, and to develop joint management plans among countries sharing transboundary water resources. Portions of the initiative were integrated in the CSD's final resolution.

(4) Public Lending Institutions

In 1994, EDF continued to work collaboratively with NGOs around the world to improve the accountability and environmental performance of public lending institutions through research, outreach, media campaigns, and discussions with policymakers.

(a) US Export Import (Ex-Im) Bank

Through testimony to the US Congress, EDF influenced policy decisions specifically related to the Ex-Im Bank. EDF was successful in persuading the Clinton Administration and the Congress to request that the Bank develop a new policy on the environment. EDF submitted comments on drafts of the environmental policy, many of which were reflected in the final version. EDF documented and opposed the Bank's flagship environmental project—the Mt. Apo geo-thermal project—which poses a threat to the endangered Philippine Eagle and would disturb ancestral land.

(b) The World Bank and Other MDBs

EDF continued to monitor the activities of and promote positive changes in each of the regional development banks: the Inter-American Development Bank, the Asian Development Bank, the African Development Bank, and the European Bank for Reconstruction and Development.

1994 marked the 50th anniversary of the United Nations Monetary and Financial Conference in Bretton Woods, New Hampshire, where representatives of 44 countries drafted and endorsed the charters of the World Bank and International Monetary Fund (IMF). In late 1993, EDF and five other US NGOs formed a coalition which has campaigned aggressively for fundamental reforms in the operations, role, financing and power of the World Bank and IMF, while favoring equitable, participatory, and sustainable development. By the end of 1994, the "50 Years is Enough" campaign had grown to include some 135 US environmental, development, religious, labor, women's, and student organizations, as well as about 170 international groups in over 40 countries, both industrialized and developing. As part of the effort to raise public awareness and debate about the World Bank, EDF distributed educational materials to academics and organizations around the world, including fact sheets and a timeline revealing the neglect of social and environmental impacts in Bank lending.

EDF produced and widely distributed a background paper on the environmental and social implications of forcible resettlement in Bank-financed projects. EDF helped mobilize NGOs and governments around the issue, motivating the Bank to make public its internal resettlement study in April, which revealed the Bank's failure in almost all cases to fully comply with a 1980 Bank policy on resettlement.

EDF testimony before the US Senate Foreign Relations Subcommittee in March on MDB performance contributed to unprecedented action by the US Congress; 50 percent of fiscal year 1995 appropriations were made contingent on certification from the Treasury Department on April 1, 1995, that the Bank has made satisfactory progress implementing improvements in the areas of resettlement, overall project quality, and public access to information.

EDF was also involved in motivating the Bank to set up an independent inspection panel to look into citizen complaints about projects. Similar bodies are currently being considered and established at some of the regional multilateral development banks as well.

Finally, EDF co-authored a report on the World Bank's failure to comply with its energy policies. The report, "Power Failure," examined the entire pending World Bank power loan portfolio, some 44 loans totalling over $7 billion to 33 countries.

(c) Global Environment Facility

Although the GEF restructuring process was formally concluded in March 1994, many critical issues of how the GEF will address environmental problems in its four focal areas (biodiversity, climate change, international waters, and ozone-layer protection) remain unresolved. An important piece of progress was achieved when EDF, together with other environmental organizations was able to obtain observer status for NGOs at GEF Council meetings as of February 1995. EDF continues to provide critical analysis of GEF policy papers that determine the way GEF projects will be managed, such as the GEF's proposal for a project cycle concept and its follow up to the December 1993 Independent Evaluation Report.

(5) Population

Recognizing the complexity, urgency, and connection of population growth with environmental degradation, EDF launched the Project on Population, Consumption, and Sustainable Development. In 1994, the project primarily focused on preparation for and participation in the International Conference on Population and Development, which was held in September in Cairo. EDF was an active participant at the Conference, spearheading a coalition effort to bring the concerns of community groups and grassroots activists into the negotiations process.

(6) Regional Activities

EDF initiated a three-year project to clean the air in the Paso del Norte region of the Texas-Mexico border. EDF works closely with government and businesses on both sides of the border on several projects designed to reduce emissions and facilitate the transfer of technology and skills. Efforts to create a binational governance structure also continued with US EPA and State Department. Work also began on drafting guidelines for awarding emission reduction credits under the Clean Air Act for transboundary investment in pollution control projects.

In March, EDF participated in a workshop convened by the US Asia Environmental Partnership in Manila, Philippines, to address opportunities for NGO-business networking. The workshop was based on presentation of several case studies in which NGOs and businesses had worked together to achieve improvements in the environmental performance of the business partner. Representatives from EDF and McDonald's Corporation presented as a case study their joint Waste Reduction Task Force, which led to the implementation of dozens of steps to reduce packaging and waste from McDonald's restaurants, distribution centers, and supply network. Other case studies were drawn from a range of Asian countries.

Throughout 1994, EDF worked with the Panara indians and a consortium of Brazilian NGOs in support of the Panara initiative to re-occupy 488,000 hectares of their tropical forest homeland. On December 14, the Brazilian National Indian Foundation published the identification of the territory in the Brazilian Federal Registry, the first step toward legal demarcation.

Bruce Rich

E. ENVIRONMENTAL LAW INSTITUTE (ELI), WASHINGTON, D.C.

(1) Sustainable International Law

(a) Summit of the Americas

Through participation in the December 1994 Summit of the Americas and its preparatory process, ELI has continued to help build the legal and institutional framework for environmental protection in the Western Hemisphere. ELI promoted initiatives such as non-governmental organization (NGO) participation in the Summit process, inclusion of biodiversity and conservation issues on the Summit agenda, development of stronger national frameworks for environmental protection, and public participation in environmental management.

(b) Revitalizing the Western Hemisphere Convention

ELI has begun work with partners in the United States and Latin America, and has sponsored a series of workshops and seminars, to revitalize the 1940 Convention on Nature Protection and Wildlife Preservation in the Western Hemisphere.

(c) Implementing the Biodiversity Convention

In January 1994, ELI and its partners developed a new project for implementing the Biodiversity Convention that will examine existing national laws throughout the Western Hemisphere regulating access to genetic resources.

(d) Improving Ecosystem Management for the Great Lakes Basin

In 1994, ELI undertook a project to evaluate the work of the International Joint Commission (IJC), to determine how the IJC can address Great Lakes pollution. Under the Boundary Waters Treaty and the Great Lakes Water Quality Agreement, the IJC protects the boundary waters between the United States and Canada. The initial report was to be available in mid-1995.

(2) Regional Strengthening of Environmental Law

(a) Latin America

Since 1989, ELI's Inter-American Program has been forging a partnership among the nations of the Americas to protect the hemisphere's environment. As part of its efforts to strengthen the national environmental institutions, ELI completed a research paper on improving implementation of the legal framework for Brazil's extractive reserve system, which Brazil established in 1990 to protect traditional ways of life in the rainforest.

The Inter-American Program worked with ELI's partners in Mexico on two separate research projects. The first analyzed government policies and institutional structures that encourage tropical and temperate forest destruction in Mexico. The second analyzed the environmental laws and institutions of five Mexican states in an effort to strengthen state and local environmental policy-making and enforcement.

ELI also assisted in individual national environmental law efforts through information exchanges. In Argentina, ELI sponsored a workshop to assist several provinces and the federal government as they considered constitutional amendments to guarantee environmental protection. At the request of Brazil's federal government, ELI co-sponsored a conference to assist in the process of preparing a new environmental code. Finally, ELI worked with partners in Colombia on a seminar to promote legislation allowing citizen suits for environmental protection.

(b) Central and Eastern Europe

Since 1988, ELI's Environmental Program in Central and Eastern Europe has assisted partners in the region as they develop more effective environmental protection systems. In 1994, ELI was especially active in Romania and Slovakia. ELI assisted Romania in revising its draft general environmental law and participated in a workshop discussing the law with members of the Romanian Parliament. ELI also worked closely with a Ministerial team on developing a new Water Law. ELI similarly worked with Slovakia's Environment Ministry on how to improve implementation and enforcement of environmental laws within its existing legal and regulatory framework. In addition, ELI provided detailed comments on, and comparative research relating to, the draft Slovak Water Law. During this period, ELI also provided the Polish Ministry of Environment with comments on its draft law protecting the environment against emergencies and provided the Bulgarian Ministry of Environment with comments on its draft Clean Air Act.

ELI continued its close work with the NGO community in Central and Eastern Europe and encouraged an open exchange of information through its Visiting Scholar and Study Tour programs. On the regional level, ELI focused on promoting public participation in environmental decision-making, especially through participating in seminars and conferences in Romania, Bulgaria, and Slovakia.

In 1994, ELI met with the Russian Ministry of Environmental Protection to discuss future law-drafting assistance and participated in an international conference on legal mechanisms for preservation of Lake Baikal. ELI also began collaboration with Moscow-based Ecojuris, the first public interest environmental law firm in Russia, and with EcoPravo, a similar group in Ukraine.

(c) The Middle East

In September 1994, ELI's Middle East Program Office relocated from Washington, D.C., to Jerusalem. During the fall of 1994, ELI presented its proposed strategies for regional environmental management at the Middle East/North Africa Economic Summit in Casablanca, and at the Conference on Promoting Regional Cooperation in the Middle East in Vouliagmeni, Greece.

ELI joined with Palestinian attorneys and scientists in law-drafting efforts. The transition to Palestinian self rule in the West Bank and Gaza Strip calls urgently for environmental safeguards to ensure that economic development does not damage environmental resources, especially scarce fresh water supplies. ELI also assisted environmental law reform efforts in Israel and Jordan. In Jordan, ELI served as coordinator of preparations for the World Bank-sponsored Marine Pollution Action Plan for the Gulf of Aqaba.

(3) International Training Programs

In 1994, ELI's Inter-American Program held a series of training courses on different aspects of environmental law, policy, and management. ELI provided training for Brazilian federal and state judges, public prosecutors, and lawyers and engineers. ELI also sponsored an enforcement course for the office of the Mexican Attorney General for the Environment, a legal skills workshop for community activists in Southern Mexico, and a course on corporate environmental management for Mexican environmental managers. ELI co-sponsored a series of training workshops in environmental impact assessment in Argentina for participants from governmental organizations, private entities, and universities. Finally, ELI held a two-week environmental law training course for lawyers and judges from the Russian Federation.

Susan Casey-Lefkowitz

F. FOUNDATION FOR INTERNATIONAL ENVIRONMENTAL LAW AND DEVELOPMENT (FIELD), LONDON

(1) International Law and Sustainable Development

During 1994, FIELD's sustainable development programme followed up on particular aspects of the various themes that had emerged from the 1993 FIELD-sponsored Consultation on International Law in the Field of Sustainable Development. Particular emphasis was placed on procedural aspects, especially liability for environmental damage, dispute resolution, and the integration of environmental and human rights norms concerning the laws of war and armed conflict.

Regarding liability, FIELD continued to actively participate in the work of the International Atomic Energy Agency Standing Committee on Liability for Nuclear Damage as counsel to Greenpeace International. Documents were circulated addressing a new US proposal intended to break the five-year negotiation deadlock. Together with the United Nations Environment Programme (UNEP), FIELD made preparations to convene a Working Group of Experts on Liability for Environmental Damage caused by Military Activities, which is to meet in early 1995. The Group is to prepare recommendations for UNEP that might assist the UN Compensation Commission with implementing its obligations under Security Council Resolution 687 (1991), which held Iraq liable for environmental damage and the depletion of natural resources as a result of its unlawful invasion and occupation of Kuwait. The Group was expected to report in mid-1996.

FIELD began to work with the Secretariat of the Permanent Court of Arbitration (PCA) and Professor Alfred Rest on the PCA's possible contribution to the resolution of disputes relating to environment and sustainable development. A working group was to be convened in 1995 to review existing arrangements, identify gaps, and propose possible new institutional arrangements.

FIELD is assisting two governments from the South Pacific region with their written observations in response to the World Health Organization's request that the International Court of Justice give an advisory opinion on the legality of nuclear weapons, given their effects on human health and the environment. FIELD has also been asked to assist these governments with a similar request that the UN General Assembly made in December 1994.

(2) Climate Change and Energy

FIELD's work on climate change has continued to grow with the entry into force of the UN Framework Convention on Climate Change and in anticipation of the first meeting of the Conference of the Parties (CoP) in early 1995. FIELD staff provided advice on legal and policy matters and assisted governments, non-governmental organisations (NGOs), and intergovernmental organisations.

FIELD staff attended the International Negotiating Committee (INC) for a Framework Convention on Climate Change (FCCC) in February. FIELD assisted in the preparation of materials on the legal and institutional aspects of funding for the global environment to be submitted to the INC. Working closely with the Convention's secretariat, and with the assistance of the United Kingdom (UK) Economic and Social Research Council, FIELD prepared a document on compliance procedures for the Convention. At the Intergovernmental Panel on Climate Change (IPCC) Working Group III's Workshop on Equity and Social Considerations, FIELD presented a paper on "Principles of Equity in International Environmental Agreements with Special Reference to the Climate Change Convention" and was asked to be a lead author on Working Group's chapter on Equity for the IPCC's Second Assessment Report.

In cooperation with the Secretariat of the FCCC, FIELD organised workshops on the Climate Change and Biodiversity Conventions at the UN Global Conference for the Sustainable Development of Small Island Developing States, for which it developed financial proposals, specifically concerning adaptation costs. FIELD received a mandate from the Alliance of Small Island States (AOSIS) to research ways to increase funding by securing commitments from major donors through the Global Environment Facility (GEF). FIELD also assisted AOSIS with a paper on joint implementation presented to the INC in August 1994 and with a Carbon Dioxide Reduction Protocol (*see* (➔) (AOSIS) Draft Protocol) to be considered at the 1995 Berlin CoP.

FIELD was invited to participate in a meeting organised by the Rockefeller Brothers Foundation (RBF) and the Kendall Foundation at Kykuit, the Rockefeller Family Estate, to discuss the current state of science, policy, and law on climate change; the structure of the Convention; and improvements to it. In May, the Royal Geographical Society and FIELD co-hosted a conference on the FCCC followed by a round-table discussion on improving compliance with international environmental agreements.

FIELD advised the UN Development Programme, AOSIS, and, informally, the G-77 countries on the restructuring of the GEF, and it was the only NGO invited to contribute a paper on the relationship between the FCCC and the GEF to an international symposium of government representatives and intergovernmental organisations, held at the Woods Hole Research Center in the United States. FIELD completed energy efficiency work for the UK Office of the Electricity Regulator and submitted final papers in 1994. FIELD and the Conservation Law Foundation organized several meetings of energy efficiency and renewable energy advocates from American and European NGOs to share information on energy industry structures within Europe and the United States.

(3) Trade, Environment, and Sustainable Development

In 1994, FIELD embarked on a collaborative project with the Natural Resources Defense Council (NRDC) entitled "Environmental Priorities for the New World Trade Organisation" funded by the RBF and the US German Marshall Fund. Recommendations from a round-table discussion, co-hosted by FIELD and the NRDC in May, were presented to the Trade and Environment Committee to begin the process of integrating environmental concerns into the General Agreement on Tariffs and Trade (GATT). The joint report was published for wide circulation.

FIELD was invited to send a delegate to regular meetings of trade and environment experts from governments, industry, and other NGOs at the Organisation for Economic Cooperation and Development (OECD), and was preparing a research report for the OECD on dispute settlement.

A major new trade and environment study, the Global Environmental Trade Study, was established in collaboration with the Yale Center for Environment and Policy and the Institute for Agriculture and Trade Policy, with funding obtained from the Pew Foundation and the RBF, to research trade and environment policy-making. A second initiative, sponsored by Harvard-MIT, the Trade and Environment Policy Dialogue, brought together a group of academics and experts to stimulate further debate on the newly created GATT Trade and Environment Committee.

(4) Access to Justice

Research and reports continue to be published under FIELD's Access to Justice Programme. Work was done for the European Court of Justice on improving compliance with international environmental agreements, implementing environmental principles for the Australian Government, providing access to information under EC law, and reconciling human rights and the environment. In collaboration with the Sierra Club Legal Defense Fund, FIELD provided expert advice on human rights and the environment to the UN Special Rapporteur. FIELD staff also held a number of lectures throughout the year.

(5) Education and Training

FIELD expanded the LLM options in international environmental law at the School of Oriental and African Studies, University of London, by offering a course in International Economic Law. FIELD staff continued to supervise PhD students, and welcomed interns and volunteers from the United States and Europe, alongside British trainee lawyers on secondment and Visiting Scholars from Australia, Europe, and Palestine.

The new three-year training project, under the UK Department of the Environment's Darwin Initiative, was established for training and research in the implementation of the Biodiversity Convention. Four lawyers, from Cook Islands, Kenya, Malaysia, and Mexico were appointed as Darwin Fellows for 1994-1996. FIELD also became involved in a UN Institute for Training and Research pilot project on climate change training in Lithuania, Vietnam, and Zimbabwe and assisted in developing a training module for the UN Conference on Trade and Development called "International Environmental Law for Negotiators of International Agreements."

(6) Publications

Now in its fourth year, *The Review of European Community and International Environmental Law* featured articles on Access to Environmental Justice, Financial Mechanisms for the Protection of the Environment, and Environmental Rights and Access to Justice.

(7) Other Activities

FIELD was offered an increasing range of consultancy work, and won a worldwide tender by the Asian Development Bank to advise the Environmental Protection Committee of the National Peoples Congress of China on legislative planning and procedures on environmental law in that country.

At the 9th CoP to the Convention on the International Trade in Endangered Species, held in Fort Lauderdale, Florida, FIELD was elected to represent the European NGOs on the Working Group created to negotiate the new listing criteria. FIELD also aided in preparing a legal opinion for the Environmental Investigation Agency on issues arising at the CoP.

Roger Wilson

G. FUNDACIÓN AMBIENTE Y RECURSOS NATURALES (FARN), BUENOS AIRES

[Editors' Note: This report includes information on FARN activities prior to 1994, since this is the first report of FARN to appear in the Yearbook]

(1) Introduction

FARN is a non-partisan, environmental non-profit organization dedicated to environmental and natural resources policy, law, economics, and institutional organization. The Foundation involves itself in research, publications, information, consulting, and training, as well as the promotion of environmental policy and legal issues and information.

Since its foundation in 1984, FARN has conducted numerous national and international studies on environmental policy and legal issues in the Western Hemisphere. Among the international organizations that FARN has collaborated with are the United Nations Environmental Program (UNEP) and the International Union for the Conservation of Nature (IUCN). FARN has also actively organized and participated in international conferences, meetings, and training courses. Consistent with its non-partisan philosophy, FARN has played an advisory role as a consultant to both non-governmental organizations (NGOs), business, and local and national governments.

(2) FARN's Different Roles: Training and Outreach

Apart from its investigative activities, FARN is dedicated to informing, educating, and training NGOs, governments, and business in Latin America on environmental institutional issues. In 1993, FARN's Center for Institutional Training on Sustainable Development conducted its first month-long training course for 33 representatives from Latin American environmental agencies, NGOs, and universities.

FARN's "Dialogues with World Leaders on Environmental Policy" program offers a yearly series of conferences, seminars and lectures on environmental policy issues conducted by renowned international environmental experts, primarily from Europe and North America. In 1991, FARN expanded its Dialogues program to include Brazil, Chile, Paraguay, and Uruguay.

FARN also developed a "Luncheon for Business Leaders" program, funded by *Apertura* magazine, which seeks to inform business leaders on the importance of environmental policy and legal responses through a series of lectures and presentations.

(3) Publications

During 1994, FARN continued to publish its bimonthly newspaper on environmental policy issues, which the Canadian Government funds, and resumed the publication of its quarterly environmental legal magazine, which had operated from 1984 to 1991. The magazine, in Spanish and in English, is produced jointly with the United Nations Environmental Program in Mexico. Recently, FARN started the first Argentine *Environmental Law Reporter*, jointly published by Editorial La Ley, the largest legal publisher in Argentina.

(4) International Environmental Law Information Center

FARN also operates a full time Environmental Law Information Center containing environmental laws and literature related to environmental policy, economics, legislation, and institutional organization available to the public (governments, businesses, NGOs, students, etc.), free of charge. By the end of 1994, the Center had computerized over 30 percent of its library and had developed specialized databases for coastal zone legislation in Patagonia, environmental standard setting in Argentina, and legislative harmonization of environmental laws of the four Southern Cone Common Market (MERCOSUR) member states.

(5) Regional International Integration

One of FARN's principle objectives, outlined in its Strategic Plan, is to foster greater participation and integration among Latin American and Hemispheric organizations in joint projects on environmental and sustainable development policy and law. To this end, FARN has served as a leader in coordinating and facilitating projects within the region involving the partnership of different organizations and governments in Latin America, as well as in North America and Europe.

FARN designs its projects to involve partner organizations from other countries, to ensure that different parties play different roles in the project and that the results benefit all participating countries.

(6) Philosophy in Action: The MERCOSUR Project

During 1994, FARN conducted a two-year project related to the harmonization of environmental standards and requirements within the framework of the MERCOSUR, the common market encompassing Argentina, Brazil, Paraguay, and Uruguay, to be established by 31 December 1994, pursuant to the Treaty of Asunción. The project, which is supported by the W. Alton Jones Foundation and involves four attorneys affiliated with NGOs in Argentina, Brazil, Paraguay, and Uruguay, aims at the compilation of environmental standards and other legal requirements of the countries concerned according to a matrix specially prepared by FARN. The Information Center at FARN has created a special data bank for that purpose for any governmental or non-governmental user from the four countries. One of the final products of the project will be a publication containing a legislative chart outlining environmental asymmetries among the four countries and the basis for a "standard harmonization regime" for MERCOSUR. The publication was to be presented to the governments, NGOs, and business leaders of Argentina, Brazil, Paraguay, and Uruguay in April 1995.

During 1992 and 1993, FARN also served as an international facilitating agency to the Bolivian government, overseeing a three-year environmental project that sought to revise and improve the nation's environmental policy, legislation, and regulations as well as its ability to implement environmental laws. In 1991, to facilitate a regional position in preparation for the Earth Summit, FARN organized a Latin American NGO conference. For the same purpose, FARN also facilitated various sub-regional workshops and seminars and held a series of press briefings on environmental issues having an impact on the Latin American region.

(7) Funding for FARN

Funding for institutional development and for FARN's projects comes from individual and corporate contributions; local, provincial, and foreign governments; local and foreign foundations; and fees collected for consulting rendered by FARN.

The above is only a brief selection of the many different projects which FARN has undertaken in the last 10 years. During 1994, FARN coordinated more than 60 projects in 7 countries.

Pedro Tarak

H. THE WORLD CONSERVATION UNION (IUCN), BONN

(1) Introduction

In January, IUCN held the triennial IUCN General Assembly in Buenos Aires, which adopted a new strategy of decentralizing and regionalizing all of its activities. At the same time, attending IUCN members adopted several resolutions requiring IUCN's Environmental Law Programme (Law Programme) to continue focusing a major part of its efforts on global and international activities. With the arrival of a new Director-General in April, IUCN took its first major step toward implementing the new strategy. That strategy included expanding the Commission on Environmental Law, which by year's end had over 200 members in 73 countries, and cooperating with other IUCN partner organizations to further develop the Law Programme's regional orientation.

(2) Legal Research and Development

(a) International

During 1994, IUCN substantially completed The Draft International Covenant on Environment and Development, which it had begun developing in 1989, and commenced work on an article-by-article commentary. During the General Assembly, the Law Programme, in collaboration with the Ethics Working Group of IUCN's Commission on Environmental Strategies and Planning, held a workshop to discuss the Covenant in the context of ethical aspects of environmental issues and their integration into international law. The Draft Covenant was to be presented for the first time at the United Nations Conference on Public International Law in New York City in March 1995.

The Law Programme also collaborated intensively in 1994 with the secretariats of several international environmental agreements. The Secretariat of the Bonn Convention on the Conservation of Migratory Species of Wild Animals requested assistance in preparing four documents for submission to the conference of the parties to the Bonn Convention. These documents included a revision of the Draft Agreement on the Conservation of African/Eurasian Migratory Waterbirds, revisions of two Species Action Plans, and guidelines for the preparation of future agreements. In June, the Law Programme delivered an analysis of national implementing legislation in 45 states in Europe and Africa, requested by the Secretariat of the Convention on International Trade in Endangered Species of Wild Flora and Fauna. The Law Programme also provided technical assistance to the Tunis Centre in revising the Protocol on Mediterranean Protected Areas. In light of the entry into force of the Law of the Sea Convention, the Law Programme updated its Chart on Required Initiatives and Responsibilities under the 1982 UN Convention on the Law of the Sea.

(b) Regional Capacity Building

The Law Programme and IUCN's Biodiversity Programme organized a regional conference on biodiversity conservation, held in Manila, 6-8 June, co-sponsored by the Asian Development Bank (ADB). Its objectives were to: identify socioeconomic incentives for developing country members (DCMs) of the ADB to invest in conserving biodiversity; help DCMs gain a clear understanding of available alternative financial and technical assistance options; address the significance of integrating conservation with economic development; and identify specific priority investments for conserving biodiversity in selected DCMs.

IUCN also provided technical support for a workshop on biodiversity in the Gulf Cooperation Council (GCC) countries, which was held in Kuwait, 24–26 September. One major issue the workshop addressed was ratification of the Convention on Biological Diversity by the GCC countries.

(3) The Environmental Law Service (ELS)

ELS continues to provide technical legal assistance to developing countries. ELS undertook five projects that involved drafting legislation in 1994. It drafted legislation for Guinea Bissau on protected areas and protection of mangroves; revised Mauritania's Wildlife Law and Forestry Code; drafted environmental protection regulations under Nepal's Environmental Protection Bill, which ELS helped draft in 1993; drafted a law for Pakistan on provincial environmental protection; and drafted a new wildlife law for Panama. ELS also undertook a review of Fiji's international agreements and a review of Lebanon's existing legislation and administrative structures. ELS further undertook a capacity- building project in Argentina that examined technical legal aspects of a public education campaign on constitutional provisions on the environment, as part of Argentina's constitutional reform process. Another capacity-building project consisted of a regional workshop on biodiversity in Central Asia, with particular emphasis on environmental legislation.

ELS began a four-year project in 1994 designed to assist developing countries with implementing legislation for the UN Convention on Biological Diversity. The Commission of the Cartagena Accord (Andean Pact) requested ELS technical assistance for the pre-governmental phase of development of a regional decision on access to genetic resources. The Sociedad Peruana de Derecho Ambiental was ELS's regional partner for this project. At the request of the Andean Pact, ELS presented an archetypical technical report with accompanying commentary. ELS submitted the final report in October. The political phase of the process of adopting a regional decision was to begin in early 1995 and continue through at least mid-year.

Preliminary planning began in 1994 for a four-year UN Environment Programme/UN Development Programme (UNEP/UNDP) Joint Project on Environmental Law and Institutions in Africa, which the government of the Netherlands is to fund. IUCN, the UN Food and Agriculture Organization and the World Bank are partners with UNEP and UNDP in this project. Five countries (Burkina Faso, Malawi, Mozambique, Sao Tomé and Principe, and South Africa) and one region (East Africa: Kenya, Tanzania, and Uganda) were selected for the first phase of the project. Activities were to begin in 1995.

Patricia F. Moore

I. THE MEKONG REGION LAW CENTER, BANGKOK

The Mekong Region Law Center (MRLC), formed in 1994, is a network of lawyers and legal professionals from Cambodia, Lao PDR, Thailand, and Vietnam. It arose from a long-standing discussion within the region about law reform and the need for training, research, and information to support that reform. The MRLC was discussed at two major regional meetings held in 1992 and 1993, and was formally initiated at an inaugural conference held in Phnom Penh, Cambodia, that representatives from the governments of the participating countries attended. The MRLC is intended to be a truly regional organization, governed by a Board of Trustees that includes representation from each member country.

The MRLC's goal is to further the role of law and promote the regional legal community's development by coordinating, supporting, and developing programs in law training, law development, research, and information sharing. It serves as a clearinghouse for information regarding legal education and training, conferences and meetings, and publications. It circulates a monthly newsletter advising of relevant activities in and regarding the Mekong region. Although still in the formative stage, the MRLC anticipates that it can play a significant and useful role in advancing the rule of law by working to make law training, development, and other activities in the region less duplicative and more responsive to regional needs.

The MRLC focuses on four main areas: business, finance, and international trade law; legal aspects of resource management; international law and dispute resolution; and administration of justice. To assist the MRLC in assessing needs and developing its programs in the area of legal aspects of resource management, the MRLC, along with the Ministry of Justice, Lao PDR, and the Thailand Development Research Institute, held a conference called "Current Issues in Environmental Law in the Mekong Region: Preparing for the Future," in Vientiane, Lao PDR, 15-17 December. The conference was the first international meeting that the Ministry of Justice hosted. At the conference, representatives from each of the participating countries, delegates from the Mekong Secretariat, and other interested participants from the region discussed striking the balance between environmental regulation and development and developing innovative mechanisms for environmental enforcement. A brainstorming session developed an agenda for further activities in the area. These activities include additional workshops in sectoral areas, research on comparative environmental impact assessment, and research and training on the significance of international environmental law and its implications for national law.

The MRLC is partially funded through a grant from The Asia Foundation.

Margaret Raymond

J. SOCIEDAD PERUANA DE DERECHO AMBIENTAL (SPDA), LIMA

(1) *Introduction*

In response to its rapid institutional growth and the concomitant need for a clear definition of operational priorities, SPDA in 1994 launched a program of strategic planning and administrative review. SPDA's vision statement entitled "A Present with a Future: Towards a Sustainable Society" reflects the organization's inherent belief in the capacity of mankind to secure sustainable development and, consequently, in the fundamental need to protect and conserve the environment as a step toward securing improved quality of life for society as a whole. The SPDA is now organized into six primary program areas: environmental law and policy; public interest defense; industry; commerce and environment; conservation; international affairs; and information services. It also supports an autonomous education program (EDUCA-21).

To promote sustainable development, in 1994, SPDA maintained its policy of offering no-fee consultancies on legislative proposals to national governmental agencies. In a significant step toward self-sufficiency, SPDA also undertook a number of consultancies for international institutions on issues of both national and international significance.

(2) *SPDA Involvement in National Issues*

(a) *Assistance on Legislation and Consultancies*

On 22 December, by Congressional Law No. 26410, Peru established a National Environmental Commission (CONAM). By the end of the year, SPDA was working with relevant state bodies, the private sector, and the non-governmental community, to develop draft regulations to ensure timely adoption of implementing legislation to make CONAM operative. SPDA also provided support to the Ministry of Fisheries in preparing implementing regulations for the General Law on Fishing.

SPDA prepared a report entitled "Legal Analysis of the National System of Natural Protected Areas" and acted as legal consultant to the interdisciplinary team responsible for the preparation of a proposal for a national plan for the administration and maintenance of protected areas. SPDA also prepared a draft proposal on behalf of the National Chamber of Tourism to enforce legal provisions on private-sector ecotourism activities. Similarly, SPDA worked with national conservation organizations and the Peruvian Association of Adventure Tourism and Ecotourism on proposals to regulate ecotourism in three national protected areas: Manu National Park; Huascarán National Park; and Macchu Picchu Historic Sanctuary.

In 1994, SPDA was one of three elected representatives of the Peruvian

Environmental Network which sits on the board of PROFONANPE, a mixed government, non-governmental organization (NGO), and international assistance organization, founded to administer a Global Environment Facility-financed trust fund for the protection and management of the National System of Protected Areas. SPDA also provided legal services to PROFONANPE.

(b) Public Interest Litigation

In the first action of its kind, under new provisions of the Constitution of 1993, SPDA initiated an access-to-information action against the Ministry of Energy and Mining. It also brought an administrative action to prevent the renewal of forestry concessions in northern Peru, which had previously been revoked following exposure of illegalities in the original grants of concession. Through judicial actions at the Superior Court level, SPDA helped stop illegal logging activities in the forests of the Peruvian jungle in the region of Pucallpa. SPDA also brought criminal proceedings against shrimp companies in northern Peru to prevent the occupation of the National Sanctuary Manglares de Tumbes and the construction of reproduction pools within this protected area. Finally, SPDA was also successful in legal proceedings aimed at the preservation of Pantanos de Villa, an important wetlands area in Lima that was being threatened by construction and development activities.

SPDA's capacity to carry out public-interest defense work was strengthened during 1994 with the hiring of new staff members and as a result of an internal reorganization that allowed more time to be allocated to the promotion of greater public awareness of environmental rights and obligations and the preparation and prosecution of cases.

(c) Indigenous Peoples

SPDA continued its involvement in various projects to strengthen ties between indigenous peoples and the environmental law community. These projects are part of a program of capacity- building for lawyers, indigenous leaders, and their advisers in order to examine the interfaces between environmental law and realization of indigenous rights and aspirations. The projects' intent is to develop mutual respect and confidence as the basis for more sensitive practice of environmental law and for greater awareness of its utility to protecting indigenous interests. For example, SPDA received funding for a project to consolidate land use and land rights for five Tacana indigenous communities residing in the buffer zone of the National Park of Madidi, Bolivia. SPDA is a partner to CEDPA, a Bolivian NGO, which provides legal support and advice for this initiative.

SPDA addressed a conference on "Indigenous Peoples, Biodiversity and Intellectual Property" organized by the Coordinator of Indigenous

Organizations of the Amazonian Basin and the United Nations Development Programme in Santa Cruz, Bolivia, in September. A proposed "Certificate of Origin" system to protect local communities' rights to indigenous knowledge and practices was well received. The final conference report characterized the idea as deserving of further investigation in the search for equitable protection of indigenous interests.

(d) Education, Capacity-Building, Informational Services

SPDA organized two legal seminars in different regions of the country (Piura and Arequipa) as part of a two-year regional capacity-building program for lawyers and students. In 1994, 45 lawyers and law students attended these courses and six of the participants were awarded one-month internships at SPDA's offices. Staff members also participated in the teaching of environmental law at Universidad Catolica del Perú as well in seminars for forestry and biology students organized jointly with the Universidad Nacional Agraria and the Natural History Museum of the Universidad de San Marcos. Finally, SPDA continued its EDUCA-21 program, which, at the level of primary education, seeks to promote conservation of natural resources. EDUCA-21 also provides instruction manuals to teachers in rural areas on how to incorporate environmental concerns into everyday classroom activities.

The SPDA organized its environmental law and policy and educational materials, including videos, into a public-access lending and reference library. SPDA also provides access to electronic mail conference materials and is helping to extend knowledge of and access to E-mail services to regional universities as part of an effort to encourage and facilitate greater regional participation in national and international debates.

(3) SPDA's International Activities

SPDA participated in a joint technical project with the World Conservation Union's (IUCN's) Environmental Law Centre to provide the Andean Pact countries with a proposal for a regional instrument on access to genetic resources. A meeting of regional and international legal, genetic, agricultural experts and indigenous peoples representatives (Lima, May), and a workshop convening NGOs, indigenous peoples, and local community representatives, as well as governmental experts (Colombia, August), discussed a working paper on the proposed elements for this instrument. In October, the result of these consultations—draft elements for a law on access—was communicated to the Andean Pact governments. By year's end, the Pact countries were negotiating the content of the future law, and SPDA had been invited to act as advisors to the Peruvian delegation for the remainder of this process. SPDA was also invited to join a national working group on implementing regulations for Decision 345 of the Andean Pact, which establishes a plant breeder's rights regime for Andean Pact countries, as well as to act as advisors to the Peruvian delegation to the Andean Pact debate on this topic.

The Amazonian Co-operation Treaty contracted a member of the SPDA to prepare a proposal for a draft treaty to regulate transboundary pollution of the Amazon river, for consideration by contracting parties. The Inter-American Development Bank contracted SPDA to assist in the preparation of a draft General Law of the Environment for Panama for consideration by the Congress of Panama. SPDA was also closely involved in the preparatory process for a World Resources Institute-sponsored project "Action for a Sustainable Amazonia" which is to be coordinated by the Secretariat of the Amazon Cooperation Treaty. The project is to design a methodology for identifying sustainable development projects in Amazonia through a cooperative process involving public, private, and independent actors of the region. Finally, SPDA actively participated in the Forest Stewardship Council's working group on criteria and indicators for natural resources, and in the national coordinating committee of the Latin-American forests network as well as in the follow-up of a number of international initiatives on forestry issues, such as the formation of a World Forest Commission.

A comparative study of Latin-American legislation relating to wetlands, commissioned by the Wetlands for the Americas project, was completed in 1994.

SPDA attended the second meeting of the International Committee of the Convention on Biological Diversity in Nairobi, as well as the Conference of the Parties to the Convention on Biological Diversity held in Nassau, Bahamas (*see* (➔) Report of the First Meeting of the Conference of the Parties). An open workshop, organized by the SPDA together with Conservation International and the Center for International Environmental Law, was held at the Bahamas meeting on access to genetic resources, which included a presentation of the ELC-IUCN/SPDA proposed elements for inclusion in a common regime for access to genetic resources, prepared for the Andean Pact countries.

Two members of the SPDA were invited by the Secretariat of the General Agreement on Tariffs and Trade (GATT) to participate in the meeting of NGOs and the GATT on trade and the environment issues in Geneva in June. SPDA also partook in seminars to prepare for the Summit of the Americas, including a pre-meeting workshop on Environment and Sustainable Development in October and a meeting of NGOs of the Americas.

Manuel Pulgar-Vidal

XIII. SPECIAL REPORTS

1. THE GENERAL AGREEMENT ON TARIFFS AND TRADE IN 1994

(1) Introduction

By far the most significant development in 1994 was the long-awaited completion of the Uruguay Round of multilateral trade negotiations. As far as work on trade-related environmental issues was concerned, 1994 was marked by both continuity regarding the substantive work already begun, and institutional development in preparation for the new World Trade Organization (WTO). Thus, the Group on Environmental Measures and International Trade (EMIT) continued to study such issues as "border tax adjustment" and "unnecessary obstacles to international trade" (Art. 2.1, Tokyo Round Agreement on Technical Barriers to Trade, TBT Code) and, as part of the United Nations Conference on Environment and Development (UNCED) follow-up, prepared its report to the Secretariat of the UN Commission on Sustainable Development (CSD) on the progress governments had made through the General Agreement on Tariffs and Trade (GATT) in the past 12 months in implementing the recommendations contained in Agenda 21. EMIT also drew up a work programme on trade and environment for the Marrakesh Ministerial meeting of April 1994, pursuant to the Trade Negotiating Committee's Decision on Trade and Environment of 15 December 1993.

(2) Work of the EMIT Group

At its 13th meeting on 27 January, its first of 1994, EMIT prepared its report to the forthcoming Council meeting on UNCED follow-up and continued work under its regular three agenda items: (1) trade provisions contained in Multilateral Environmental Agreements (MEAs); (2) transparency of trade-related environmental measures; and (3) possible trade effects of environmental packaging and labelling requirements. EMIT considered this work in itself to be an important GATT contribution to the UNCED follow-up.

(a) UNCED Follow-Up

There was wide agreement that the successful conclusion of the Uruguay Round was the single most important contribution GATT had made toward sustainable development, both in terms of greater market access for all contracting parties and in view of the promotion of development and concomitant protection for the environment. Some representatives thought that the Agenda 21 follow-up exercise was a global commitment that gave general guidance on achieving the aims of sustainable development, and that GATT work should both remain closely linked with Agenda 21 follow-up and complement the CSD's work. Some took the view that Agenda 21's main principles and objectives should be taken as a basis for future work on fostering international cooperation and consensus and on avoiding unilateral, extraterritorial, and trade protectionist actions when dealing with environmental challenges. Others had already proposed specific issues for the post-Marrakesh process of examination, including production and process methods and points (d), (e), (g), and (i) of Ch. 2.22. Still others cautioned against using environmental concerns as a reason for de-emphasizing some countries' comparative advantage in the pursuit of development or sustainable development.

(b) Agenda Item 1

(i) Article XX(h) GATT

Some EMIT representatives commented on Art. XX(h) GATT, which deals with measures taken pursuant to international commodity agreements. Of particular concern were the similarities between Art. XX(h) and measures taken pursuant to MEAs.[1] In this context, the suggestion was made to discuss the possibilities and difficulties with Art. XX(h) in relation to MEAs in the future work on trade and environment in the GATT and the WTO.

(ii) Border Tax Adjustment

At the 13th meeting, some consideration was also given to the issue of border tax adjustment on the basis of a factual note that the GATT Secretariat issued in response to a request EMIT made at its meeting of 5-6 October 1993 (TRE/W/20, 11 January 1994). One delegation that described the issue as central to any analysis of the relationship between trade and environment policies noted that the trade implications were important if the domestic use of environmentally motivated product taxes were to be expanded and applied to imported products in accordance with the rules of the trading system.

In examining issues such as which taxes are eligible for adjustment and whether tax adjustments are optional under the GATT, the note draws largely on the conclusions of the 1968 Working Party on Border Tax Adjustment (BISD 18S/97)[2] and on certain panel findings[3] with regard to relevant GATT articles (I, II, III, VI, VII, and XVI).

[1] The Havana Charter's definition in Ch. VI of what constituted an MEA: (1) open to all members on equal terms; (2) adequate participation by countries with an interest in the importation or consumption of a commodity; and (3) fair treatment to members that did not participate.

[2] According to an Organisation for Economic Cooperation and Development (OECD) definition, border tax adjustment is:

any fiscal measures which put into effect, in whole or in part, the destination principle (*i.e.*, which enables exported products to be relieved of some or all of the tax charged in the

(iii) Unnecessary Obstacles to International Trade

Another Secretariat note (TRE/W/21, 17 January 1994) that EMIT requested contains a review of the drafting history of Art. 2.1 of the Tokyo Round Agreement on Technical Barriers to Trade (TBT Code)[4] as well as an examination of subsequent practice under that provision and of relevant developments since 1979.

(3) The Uruguay Round Agreements

(a) Overview

While trade and environment issues were not as such among the subjects of negotiations, they were to some extent adumbrated in several Uruguay Round Agreements and Understandings. Thus, according to the preamble of the agreement establishing the WTO, the WTO will pursue a variety of goals "while allowing for the optimal use of the world's resources in accordance with the objective of sustainable development." Other Uruguay Round texts contain similar references. The preamble to the Agreement on Agriculture refers to "the need to protect the environment," and the Agreement on Sanitary and Phytosanitary Measures refers to "relevant ecological and environmental conditions" (para. 17). The Agreement on Technical Barriers to Trade recognizes "urgent problems of . . . environmental protection" as exempt from notification requirements regarding national standards (Arts. 2.10. and 5.7.), while the Agreement on Subsidies and Countervailing Measures treats assistance for the adaptation of existing facilities to new, legally prescribed environmental requirements as

exporting country in respect of similar domestic products sold to consumers on the home market and which enable imported products sold to consumers to be charged with some or all of the tax charged in the importing country in respect of similar domestic products).

[3] On the distinction between "other duties or charges" imposed "on or in connection with importation" (Art. II:1(b)) and "internal taxes or charges" (Art. III:2), see the Panel Report on EEC—Regulation on Imports of Parts and Components, BISD 37S/132. On the "equivalence" of an importation charge (Art. II:2(a)) to an internal tax (Art. III:2), see the Panel Report on United States—Taxes on Petroleum and Certain Imported Substances, BISD 34S/136, paras. 5.2.7 to 5.2.8. On the link between tax adjustments and consistency with Art. III, see the Panel Report on United States—Restriction on Imports of Tuna, DS21/R, 3 Sept. 1991, not yet adopted. On the link between tax adjustments for like products and consistency with Art. III, see Panel Reports on Japan—Customs Duties, Taxes and Labelling Practices on Imported Wines and Alcoholic Beverages, BISD 34S/83, para. 5.2.4., and on United States—Measures Affecting Alcoholic and Malt Beverages, DS23/R, paras. 5.24 to 5.25 and 5.71 to 5.72.

[4] "Parties . . . shall . . . ensure that neither technical regulations nor standards themselves nor their application have the effect of creating unnecessary obstacles to international trade."

"non-actionable" subsidies (Art. 8.2(c)). In contrast, none of the three new agreements, the General Agreement on Trade and Services, Trade Related Intellectual Property Rights, and TRIMS, refer to "sustainable development" *eo nomine*, and only two of them refer to the environment at all.

(b) Agreements, Understandings, and Decisions: Substantive Limitations

(i) Agreement on Agriculture

Under the Agreement on Agriculture, which deals specifically with agricultural subsidies, members are committed to phased reduction of domestic support measures. Certain types of environmental subsidies, however, are exempt from the support-reduction commitment. Generally speaking, these exemptions concern government payments pursuant to environmental and conservation programmes and those made to withdraw agricultural land and resources from production.

The preamble to the Agreement states that commitments under the reform programme should be made in an equitable way among all members, "having regard to non-trade concerns, including . . . the need to protect the environment."

Annex 2 exempts from the reduction commitments regarding domestic support, *inter alia*, government expenditures (or revenue foregone) for "research in connection with environmental programmes" and "infrastructural works associated with environmental programmes." Under specific conditions, payments under environmental or conservation programmes are also exempt. Similarly, Annex 5 exempts members from Art. 4:2's obligation not to "maintain, resort to, or revert to any measures of the kind which have been required to be converted into ordinary customs duties" in respect of primary agricultural products subject to special treatment reflecting factors of non-trade concerns, such as environmental protection.

(ii) Agreement on the Application of Sanitary and Phytosanitary Measures (SPS)

The SPS Agreement concerns food safety as well as animal and plant health regulations. Like the TBT Agreement, it is limited in application to production and process methods related to the characteristics of products. The SPS Agreement expressly recognizes the right of governments "to take sanitary and phytosanitary measures necessary for the protection of human, animal or plant life or health" (para. 5). It is based on a modified "least trade restrictive" test, whereby a protective measure is prohibited if there is another measure "reasonably available taking into account technical and economic feasibility, that achieves the appropriate level of protection and is significantly less restrictive to trade" (para. 21). The SPS Agreement also requires regulations to be based on existing international standards such as the *Codex Alimentarius*, however, it allows higher national standards if they are scientifically justifiable, provided that the standards are not inconsistent with any other provision of the TBT Agreement (para. 11) and that members avoid arbitrary or unjustifiable distinctions that result in discrimination or a disguised restriction on international trade (para. 20). Moreover, measures falling within the SPS Agreement must both be necessary to protect human, animal, or plant life or health and be based on scientific principles (para. 6).

In November, an Informal Contact Group on Agriculture recommended format and procedures for notifications of SPS measures in conformity with Art. 7 and Annex B of the SPS Agreement, for consideration by the Committee on Sanitary and Phytosanitary Measures. Regarding the requirement that notifications "take place at an early stage, when amendments can still be introduced and comments taken into account" (Art. 5(b) of Annex B, SPS Agreement), the Informal Contact Group recommended a 60-day notification period, while encouraging longer time limits.

(iii) Agreement on Technical Barriers to Trade

The TBT Agreement embodies significant changes in the area of product standards. Its main objective is to strike a balance between preserving national standard-setting authority for the protection of legitimate health, safety, and environmental objectives[5] and ensuring that such standards do not arbitrarily impede free trade.[6] To achieve this, the TBT Agreement encourages members to use international standards where appropriate, while applying the so-called "least trade restrictive" test to national technical regulations that "shall not be more trade-restrictive than necessary to fulfil a legitimate objective" (Art. 2.2). If international standards are used, the exporting country challenging them bears the burden of proof of showing that they are inconsistent with the TBT Agreement. Furthermore, assessments of imported products' conformity with national regulations "shall not be more strict or be applied more strictly than is necessary to give the importing Member adequate confidence that products conform with the applicable technical regulations or standards, taking account of the risks non-conformity would create." (Art. 5.1.2). The TBT Agreement also applies to production and process methods, but only to those that relate to the characteristics of products, such as hygiene requirements in slaughterhouses affecting meat quality.

A member may omit notifying interested other members in order to cope with urgent problems of safety, health, environmental protection, or

[5] "[N]o country should be prevented from taking measures necessary to ensure the quality of its exports, or for the protection of human, animal or plant life or health, of the environment." Preamble, para. 5.

[6] *I.e.,* "arbitrary or unjustifiable discrimination between countries . . . or a disguised restriction on international trade." *Id.*

national security in some circumstances. Such non-notification is allowed in the absence of a relevant international standard or where the technical content of a proposed regulation is not in accordance with that of relevant international standards, even if the technical regulation may have a significant effect on trade of other members.

The TBT Agreement also contains binding requirements with respect to conformity-assessment procedures to determine whether products conform to technical regulations and standards. Central governments are obliged to use existing international guides or recommendations except where this would be inappropriate for, *inter alia*, reasons such as the protection of the environment (Art. 5.4.). Likewise, in the absence of an international guide or recommendation or where the technical content of a proposed conformity-assessment procedure is not in accordance with international standards, members may omit publishing the conformity procedures in draft form. They must, however, notify other members through the WTO Secretariat and establish procedures for reviewing complaints about the operation of the system if they consider such omission necessary because of urgent problems of environmental protection (Art. 5.7). Central governments must also take measures reasonably available to them to secure compliance with the TBT Agreement by sub-national government units (Arts. 3.1, 4.1, and 7.1).

The scope of the TBT Agreement also encompasses standards dealing with packaging, marking, or labelling requirements applicable to a product, as well as process or production methods. Thus, the Agreement would appear to cover a regulation on characteristics of packaging material, *e.g.*, one prescribing the use of recycled material. The TBT Agreement would presumably not cover a ban on such material, however, if it were based on the manner in which the packaging material was made, *e.g.*, a ban on aluminum cans due to high energy consumption in the production of aluminum.[7]

Mandatory labelling requirements are covered, but voluntary eco-labelling sought by firms is presumably only covered where there is a certain degree of government involvement. While purely private labelling schemes do not appear to be covered, governments must still take reasonable steps to have non-governmental bodies adopt a Code of good practice for the preparation, adoption, and application of standards in Annex 3 to the TBT Agreement (Art. 4.1). Conceivably, therefore, certification procedures leading to the granting of eco-labels may in certain instances be subject to TBT disciplines.[8]

[7] V. Rege, *GATT Law and Environment-Related Issues Affecting the Trade of Developing Countries*, 28 JWT No. 3. (June 1994).

[8] C.S. Pearson, *Trade and Environment*, Paper presented at the ESCAP/UNDP/KDI Regional Symposium on the Uruguay Round Agreements, Seoul, Korea, 30 Nov. to 3 Dec.

(iv) Agreement on Subsidies and Countervailing Measures

Under the 1979 Tokyo Round Subsidies Code, signatories recognized that non-export subsidies are important, widely used instruments for the promotion of social and economic policy objectives, and therefore exempted some of them from countervailing duties. Thus, the right of signatories to use such "non-actionable" subsidies to achieve certain desirable goals remained unrestricted. Amongst such desirable objectives was that of the "redeployment of industry in order to avoid congestion and environmental problems."[9]

The 1994 Agreement on Subsidies and Countervailing Measures limits the concept of "subsidy" to financial contributions by governments. It also goes further than the 1979 Subsidies Code in two important respects. First, while the Tokyo Round Code had relatively few signatories, all members of the WTO will be obliged to observe its subsidies provisions. Second, the 1994 Agreement establishes certain environmental subsidies as non-actionable. Assistance to promote the adaptation of existing facilities to new, legally prescribed environmental requirements that result in greater constraints and financial burden on firms is treated as non-actionable under certain conditions.[10] Similarly, financial assistance for research activities conducted by firms or by higher education or research establishments on a contract basis with firms is treated as non-actionable if the government assistance covers no more than 75 percent of the costs of industrial research or 50 percent of the costs of pre-competitive development activity.[11]

[9] Art. 11(1)(f) of the Agreement on interpretation and application of Arts. VI, XVI, and XXIII of the GATT.

[10] Article 8.2(c) lists as conditions that the assistance: (i) is a one-time non-recurring measure; (ii) is limited to 20 percent of the cost of adaptation; (iii) does not cover the cost of replacing and operating the assisted investment, which must be fully borne by firms; (iv) is directly linked to and proportionate to a firm's planned reduction of nuisances and pollution, and does not cover any manufacturing cost savings that may be achieved; and (v) is available to all firms that can adopt the new equipment and/or production processes.

[11] Such assistance, however, will be non-actionable only if it is limited exclusively to (i) personnel costs (researchers, technicians and other supporting staff employed exclusively in the research activity); (ii) costs of instruments, equipment, land, and buildings used exclusively and permanently (except when disposed of on a commercial basis) for the research activity; (iii) costs of consultancy and equivalent services used exclusively for the research activity, including bought-in research, technical knowledge, patents, etc.; (iv) additional overhead costs incurred directly as a result of the research activity; and (v) other running costs (such as those of materials, supplies and the like) incurred directly as a result of the research activity.

(v) Trade Related Intellectual Property Rights (TRIPS)

The TRIPS Agreement seeks to fill a gap in the multilateral framework of trade rules by establishing principles, rules, and disciplines providing minimum standards for the protection and enforcement of intellectual property rights. It also deals with international trade in counterfeit goods, a growing source of friction in international economic relations. Essentially, it consists of phased commitments of members to provide copyright, trademark, and patent protection. It represents a new trend toward harmonizing domestic policies.

Under the TRIPS Agreement, members can invoke the need to avoid serious harm to the environment as a ground for excluding patentability of inventions the commercial exploitation of which they wish to prevent (Art. 27(2)). They may likewise exclude from patentability "plants and animals other than microorganisms, and essentially biological processes for the production of plants or animals other than non-biological and microbiological processes" (Art. 27(3)(b)).

(vi) General Agreement on Trade in Services

A Decision concerning Art. XIV para. (b) of the GATS authorizes, like Art. XX(b) GATT, "measures necessary to protect human, animal or plant life or health." Due to the rejection of the "environment" as one of the exceptions in Art. XX GATT, however, the "environment" is also not an exception under Art. XIV GATS. The Decision in effect acknowledges that measures necessary to protect the environment may conflict with the provisions of the Agreement, but leaves the decision whether to extend Art. XIV para. (b) beyond the typical exemptions for the protection of human, animal, or plant life or health to the future Council for Trade in Services.

Accordingly, the latter is required to set up a working party to examine and make recommendations on the relationship between the services trade and the environment, including the issues of sustainable development and of pertinent international agreements. It will report in 1998.

(c) Agreements, Understandings, and Decisions: Procedural and Institutional Provisions

(i) Understanding on Dispute Settlement (DSU)

The new DSU incorporates a single, integrated, exclusive dispute-settlement system under which members are required to solve their disputes solely by recourse to the rules and procedures of the DSU (Art. 23.1). As a single "integrated dispute settlement system" of the WTO, it is applicable to the WTO Agreement (§1.1 DSU; Appendix 1) and to all "covered agreements."[12]

[12] Covered agreements comprise the "multilateral trade agreements" (Agreements on Trade in Goods; General Agreement on Trade in Services; Agreement on

The DSU provides, *inter alia*, that "panels may seek information from any relevant source and may consult experts" and, "with respect to a factual issue concerning a scientific or other technical matter raised by a party to a dispute . . . may request an advisory report in writing from an expert review group" (§13.2.). Such expert evidence may also be solicited in disputes involving trade-related environmental measures. Indeed, future DSU panels, conscious of the possibility of being overruled by the newly created Appellate Body, might more readily be prepared to support their reasoning with considerations of trade and environmental policy.

(ii) Ministerial Decision on Trade and Environment

The Marrakesh (➔) Ministerial Decision of 14 April 1994 (MTN.TNC/45(MIN), Annex II), which was adopted on the occasion of the signing the Final Act embodying the results of the Uruguay Round of Multilateral Trade Negotiations, seeks to ensure that the WTO will give priority to the linkages between trade policies, environmental policies, and sustainable development.

The Decision directs the WTO General Council to establish formally a new Committee on Trade and Environment, open to all WTO members, with a broad remit covering all sectors of the multilateral trading system—goods, services, and intellectual property rights. Pending the establishment of that Committee, its work is to be carried out by a Sub-Committee of the Preparatory Committee of the WTO. The creation of the Sub-Committee was an important step in the efforts GATT contracting parties had been making to cope with the tasks required by the Rio Principles and Agenda 21 that resulted from UNCED.

Much of the Ministerial Decision confirms the position that safeguarding an open, non-discriminatory, and equitable multilateral trading system need not conflict with protecting the environment and promoting sustainable development. To show the WTO's commitment to sustainable development, the Decision makes reference to the preamble to the Agreement establishing the WTO. Nonetheless, expectations are dampened that this will herald a profound transformation of the "new GATT." Indeed, while coordination of respective policies in the field of trade and environment is desirable, the WTO must respect the scope of its competence, which is limited to trade policies and those trade-related aspects of environmental policies that may result in significant trade effects. The Decision entrusts the future Committee on Trade and Environment with the task "to identify the

Trade-Related Aspects of Intellectual Property Rights, including Trade in Counterfeit Goods, Appendix 1, Annexes 1A, 1B, 1C); the "plurilateral trade agreements" (the Agreements on Trade in Civil Aircraft; Government Procurement; International Dairy Arrangement; Arrangement Regarding Bovine Meat, Annex 4); and the DSU itself.

relationship between trade measures and environmental measures, in order to promote sustainable development," and, where appropriate, to recommend modifications of the multilateral trading system.

The Committee on Trade and Environment's initial work programme comprises seven areas within which "any relevant issue may be raised." Areas one, two, three, and five deal with the relationships between, respectively: (1) the provisions of the multilateral trading system and trade measures for environmental purposes, including those pursuant to MEAs; (2) environmental policies relevant to trade and environmental measures with significant trade effects and the provisions of the multilateral trading system; (3) the provisions of the multilateral trading system and (a) charges and taxes for environmental purposes and (b) requirements for environmental purposes relating to products, including standards and technical regulations, packaging, labelling, and recycling; and (5) the dispute-settlement mechanisms in the multilateral trading system and those found in MEAs. Area four is concerned with the provisions of the multilateral trading system with respect to the transparency of trade measures used for environmental purposes and environmental measures and requirements which have significant trade effects. Area six involves the effect of environmental measures on market access (especially in relation to developing countries, in particular to the less developed countries) and the environmental benefits of removing trade restrictions and distortions. Area seven concerns exports of domestically prohibited goods.

(4) Post-Marrakesh Developments

(a) Work of the Sub-Committee on Trade and Environment

(i) First Meeting

At its first meeting on 11 May, the Sub-Committee considered various organizational matters, including requests for observer status from governments not members of the WTO Preparatory Committee and from intergovernmental organizations that had registered their interest in following GATT work on the subject of trade and environment.

(ii) Second Meeting

The second meeting, on 12 July, was dedicated both to a review of the work programme contained in the Decision on Trade and Environment and of the work that the EMIT Group and the Committee on Trade and Development (CTD) had accomplished.

EMIT achieved most progress regarding the first item of the work programme, the relationship between trade provisions contained in MEAs and the rules of the multilateral trading system. It had identified difficulties potentially arising from the use of trade measures in MEAs and had examined various approaches to dealing with them, including the idea of a collective interpretation of Art. XX GATT and the development of a waiver procedure. To Brazil, the real goal was to find an equilibrium between promoting recourse to multilateral solutions when dealing with environmental problems and ensuring that WTO members would not be arbitrarily affected either by disguised protectionism or the imposition of environmental values through trade policy action. Korea considered that further elaboration should take place within the WTO framework of internationally accepted principles on trade measures for environmental purposes, such as the avoidance of unilateral measures, the least trade-restrictive principle, and proportionality. Korea also thought the WTO should address the two challenging questions of extra-jurisdictional action and of the application of the trade provisions of MEAs to non-parties. It was also pointed out that certain issues such as restrictive trade practices applied between members of a given agreement were outside the GATT's competence, as they were negotiated among countries that were responsible for their own actions. Some wanted eco-labelling to be analysed in-depth, particularly the points of transparency, non-discrimination, and access to certification.

The third item, which Austria considered a priority area, consists of a cluster of issues generally intended to cover the use of economic instruments to realize environmental goals. Although the EMIT Group's work on packaging and labelling could be built on, additional documentation was needed on energy taxes, border tax adjustments, emission charges, tradable permits, recycled content requirements, waste management, the role of life-cycle analysis, and possibly measures related to road traffic policies. Austria considered that all these measures could be related to the concept of "cost internalization," which refers to the actual occurrence of external costs triggered by an economic activity. The internalization process could, in turn, be facilitated by using the polluter pays principle.

Sweden, on behalf of the Nordic countries, considered that charges and taxes for environmental purposes did not, at present, pose a serious problem to the trading system, since they were in most cases levied at quite a low level and thus did not lead to competitive advantages or disadvantages. It also considered that the concept of welfare gains from liberalized trade, compatible with sustainable development, accentuated the need to internalize environmental costs. According to some experts, this might best be achieved through increased use of environmental taxes, which in turn leads to the question of how this could be done with the least effect on trade.

Several delegations considered the sixth item, the effect of environmental measures on market access, an important cross-cutting issue. These delegations saw this item as being related both to the trade impact of trade restrictive measures and to the contribution that improved trading opportunities could play in furthering sustainable development. Some advocated a clear division of work or close collaboration with the CTD, which had earlier taken up this issue.

(iii) Third Meeting

The third meeting of the Sub-Committee on Trade and Environment took place on 15–16 September and was devoted to the third set of issues of the Ministerial Decision on Trade and Environment. Of particular interest was the relationship between the provisions of the multilateral trading system and requirements for environmental purposes relating to products.[13] Many delegations shared the view that charges and taxes for environmental purposes are an efficient form of policy intervention to tackle environmental externalities. Many also stressed, however, that WTO member governments had a sovereign right to decide on the way and the extent to which they would approach the internalisation of domestic environmental costs, citing Principle 16 of the Rio Declaration,[14] which endorses the use of charges and taxes as a means of promoting sustainable development.

Mexico advocated carrying out a full analysis of the economic and environmental effects of such charges and taxes before relating them to GATT disciplines. In Mexico's view, four considerations needed to be taken into account. These included: (1) valuation to determine the tax rate, although in the view of other delegations such valuation could be impossible in some cases, such as valuation of costs of species extinction; (2) the considerable diversity of tax rates due to national variations in environmental costs attributable to special conditions and social preferences; (3) an appraisal of the effectiveness of product taxes and charges for combatting consumption pollution at the source; and (4) their impact on relative competitiveness.

In this regard, the Sub-Committee on Trade and Environment discussed the established GATT rules on border tax adjustment and the abovementioned Report of the Working Party of 1970. Accordingly, taxes such as excise duties and sales and value added taxes that are directly levied on products are eligible for adjustment at the border irrespective of the tax's purpose, but those not directly levied on products, such as social security charges, payroll, and income taxes, are not adjustable. If properly applied, border tax adjustment of environmental taxes and charges would not alter equal opportunity in the conditions of competition between domestic and imported products. It was the object and purpose of Art. III GATT to protect these conditions, as confirmed in many dispute Panel Reports (*e.g.*, 7S/64). Some delegations, however, pointed out that GATT rules permit border tax adjustment regarding incorporated inputs of final products but

[13] For a detailed summary see *Trade and Environment*, TE 010, 11 Oct. 1994.

[14] Principle 16 advocates the internalization of environmental costs and the application of the principle that the polluter bear the cost of pollution.

not regarding unincorporated production and process methods, mainly because these are in practice difficult to verify. Korea pointed to another difficulty of taxing unincorporated production and process methods, namely the risk of undermining trade neutrality, because the imposition of production taxes or charges on the exported product might amount to double taxation where an exporter had already had incurred environmental costs through complying with local environmental regulations. Brazil considered taxing overseas production methods an unacceptable interference with a country's sovereign rights to determine and internalize their domestic environmental costs. Many agreed that the best way of tackling problems of transboundary or global production pollution would be through international cooperation and agreements.

The discussion also embraced the economic rationale of GATT rules on border tax adjustment, particularly the effectiveness of environmental taxes and charges for attaining environmental objectives and their analysis from a fiscal point of view. New Zealand added the trade dimension to the discussion on the effectiveness of environmental taxes and charges by distinguishing four types of environmental externalities: local production and consumption externalities and global/transboundary production and consumption externalities.

Some delegations suggested taking up the issue of the justification for different treatment of taxes and charges on products as opposed to production methods, including the question of the definition of "like product." Sweden expressed concern that the current GATT Rules on border tax adjustment might unduly influence the formulation of environmental policy. The European Union (EU) took the view that the rules should be interpreted in the light of a tax's environmental aim, taking into account the preamble of the WTO Agreement, which refers to environmental protection and sustainable development. The United States cautioned against a hasty conclusion that the GATT rules and jurisprudence on border tax adjustment prevented adjustment of taxes on production methods, and Austria identified as a central issue the question of how a tax on production methods could be translated into a tax on the final product.

Discussions of environmental product requirements were able to draw on a good deal of work EMIT had already done on packaging and labelling requirements.

While the United States felt that uncertainties regarding which measures were covered by the TBT Agreement should be eliminated as a first step, the EU preferred gaining some experience with the revised TBT Agreement before considering additional rules for environmental products. Sweden felt that important areas such as recycling and waste management requirements were not covered by the TBT Agreement. Further, Argentina thought that the TBT Agreement might not entirely cover eco-labelling schemes that incorporate life-cycle analysis to the extent that they include evaluations of unincorporated production and process methods, which many members felt did not justify discrimination between products at the border. Canada suggested that the relative effectiveness of environmental product requirements such as labelling and packaging requirements that play an important part in environmental policies should be further analysed. It also indicated characteristics of life-cycle analysis and recommended further study on a case-by-case basis. Egypt identified two principles that should be observed in developing eco-labelling schemes, namely full and effective participation of developing countries in the selection of criteria, particularly for exports of interest to them, and full compliance with the TBT Agreement, to ensure full transparency and to prevent trade barriers by according imported products less favourable treatment. This view was echoed by Argentina, which said that if it were possible to assimilate requirements on allowable types of packaging materials into technical regulations, they would then be covered by the TBT Agreement. Furthermore, in order to minimize the negative trade effects of many different systems for the recovery, re-use, or disposal of packaging, Argentina said that these should be subject to obligations similar to those of the TBT Agreement for technical regulations and standards. Argentina noted that there is a distinction between requirements regulating the recyclability of a product or its packaging, an externality at the consumption stage, and those regulating the recycled content that a product or its packaging must contain, an externality at the production stage that should not, therefore, have extraterritorial application. Argentina also indicated criteria for these measures and wished to see consensus to enable them to be legitimately applied extraterritorially.

(iv) Fourth Meeting

The fourth meeting of the Sub-Committee on Trade and Environment on 26–27 October focused on the first item of the work programme: "the relationship between the provisions of the multilateral trading system and trade measures for environmental purposes, including those pursuant to multilateral environmental agreements." Delegations continued their examination of the potential advantages and disadvantages of *ex ante* and *ex post* approaches to establishing the relationship of these measures to the provisions of the multilateral trading system.

The central question was whether a WTO rule should be developed to exempt trade measures taken by one or more parties to an MEA with regard to one or more GATT contracting parties or WTO members that are not parties to that MEA, or whether such trade measures in MEAs should be subject to "*ex-post*" WTO "approval" on a case-by-case basis. The Sub-Committee also agreed to extend observer status to those intergovernmental organizations that had enjoyed observer status in EMIT, including, apart from the UN, the UN Conference on Trade and Development, the World Bank, and the International Monetary Fund (which already had observer status in the Sub-Committee), the United Nations Environment Programme, the UN Food and Agriculture Organization, the International Trade Centre, the United Nations Development Programme, the Organisation for Economic Cooperation and Development, and the European Free Trade Agreement. Requests by others are to be taken up on a case-by-case basis.

(v) Fifth Meeting

The fifth and last meeting of the Sub-Committee on Trade and Environment on 23–24 November focused on the sixth item of the Ministerial work programme: the effect of environmental measures on market access (especially in relation to developing countries, particularly less developed countries) and the environmental benefits of removing trade restrictions and distortions. This involved further examination of such issues as the effects of tariff escalation; non-trade barriers and trade-distorting subsidies on the environment; export diversification and its relationship to environmental protection; market opportunities for environmentally friendly products, particularly from developing countries; and the importance of technology transfer and technical and financial assistance in the pursuit of sustainable development. Many delegations remarked that this was a cross-cutting issue related to other items of the work programme, including transparency and charges, taxes, and product requirements that serve environmental purposes. Several delegations also reverted to items one and three of the work programme, particularly to the use of trade measures pursuant to MEAs.

(b) Panel Reports

(i) United States—Restrictions on Imports of Tuna

In July 1992, the Council had established a Panel to examine the European Community's and the Netherlands' complaint.

On 20 May 1994, the Panel submitted its (➔) report to the parties to the dispute. After a thorough analysis of the facts of the case and arguments of the parties, the Panel found that the US policy to conserve dolphins in the Eastern Tropical Pacific Ocean, which the United States pursued within its jurisdiction over its nationals and vessels, fell within the range of policies covered by GATT Art. XX(b) and (g). It concluded, however, that the US import prohibitions on tuna and tuna products under §101(a)(2) and §305(a)(1) and (2) of the Marine Mammal Protection Act (the primary nation embargo) and under §101(a)(2)(C) of that Act (the intermediary nation embargo)[15] did not meet the requirements of the Note ad Article

[15] The term "intermediary nation" means a nation that exports yellowfin tuna or

III,[16] were contrary to Art. XI:1, and were not covered by the exceptions in Art. XX(b)[17], (g), or (d) of the General Agreement. Central to the Panel's deliberations was Art. XX of the GATT and the exceptions contained therein. With regard to Art. XX(g) (relating to the conservation of an exhaustible natural resource) the Panel shared the view of a previous panel that "relating to" should be read as "primarily aimed at," on the understanding that the words "primarily aimed at" referred not only to the purpose of the measure but also to its effect on the conservation of the natural resource. The Panel's view on the interpretation of Art. XX is set out in the following terms:

> If however Article XX was interpreted to permit contracting parties to take trade measures so as to force other contracting parties to change their policies within their jurisdiction, including their conservation policies, the balance of rights and obligations among contracting parties, in particular the right of access to markets, would be seriously impaired. Under such an interpretation the General Agreement could no longer serve as a multilateral framework for trade among contracting parties.

(Para. 5.26.)

As regards the interpretation of Art. XX(b), the Panel stressed that the text of this provision "does not spell out any limitation on the location of the things to be protected." It also noted "that the statements and drafting changes made during the negotiation of the Havana Charter and the General Agreement did not clearly support any particular contention of the parties with respect to the location of the living thing to be protected under Article XX(b)." The Panel added its view that the "prohibition on imports

yellowfin tuna products to the United States and that imports yellowfin tuna or yellowfin tuna products that are subject to a direct ban on importation into the United States pursuant to §101(a)(2)(B).

[16] Note ad Art. III GATT:

> Any internal tax or other internal charge, or any law, regulation or requirement of the kind referred to in paragraph 1 which applies to an imported product and the like domestic product and is collected or enforced in the case of the imported product at the time or point of importation, is nevertheless to be regarded as an internal tax or other internal charge, or a law, regulation or requirement of the kind referred to in paragraph 1, and is accordingly subject to the provisions of Article III.

[17] Art. XX(b) GATT:

> Subject to the requirement that such measures are not applied in a manner which would constitute a means of arbitrary or unjustifiable discrimination between countries where the same conditions prevail, or a disguised restriction on international trade, nothing in this Agreement shall be construed to prevent the adoption or enforcement by any contracting party of measures:
>
> * * *
>
> (b) necessary to protect human, animal or plant life or health.

of tuna into the United States taken under the intermediary nation embargo could not, by itself, further the United States conservation objective." The Panel also observed that:

> both the primary and intermediary nation embargoes on tuna were taken by the United States so as to force other countries to change their policies with respect to persons and things within their own jurisdiction, since the embargoes required such changes in order to have any effect on the protection of the life or health of dolphins.

In its concluding observations, the Panel set out the key issues in the dispute in these terms:

> The Panel noted that the objective of sustainable development, which includes the protection and preservation of the environment, has been widely recognized by the contracting parties to the General Agreement. The Panel observed that the issue in this dispute was not the validity of the environmental objectives of the United States to protect and conserve dolphins. The issue was whether, in the pursuit of its environmental objectives, the United States could impose trade embargoes to secure changes in the policies which other contracting parties pursued within their own jurisdiction. The Panel therefore had to resolve whether the contracting parties, by agreeing to give each other in Article XX the right to take trade measures necessary to protect the health and life of plants, animals and persons or aimed at the conservation of exhaustible natural resources, had agreed to accord each other the right to impose trade embargoes for such purposes. The Panel had examined this issue in the light of the recognized methods of interpretation and had found that none of them lent any support to the view that such an agreement was reflected in Article XX.

The Panel concluded its report by recommending that the contracting parties request the United States to bring the measures in question into conformity with its obligations under the General Agreement. By the end of 1994 the Panel Report had not yet been adopted.

(ii) United States—Taxes on Automobiles

On 12 May 1993, the Council had established a Panel to examine the complaint by the European Community. It issued its decision to the parties to the dispute on 30 September and to the contracting parties on 11 October 1994. The Panel examined three US measures affecting imported automobiles: the luxury tax, the Corporate Average Fuel Efficiency (CAFE) regulation, and the so-called gas-guzzler tax.

The EC contended, *inter alia*, that CAFE was a civil penalty that imposed a discriminatory special tax on top-of-the-line cars that favoured large, integrated, full-line car producers and worked to the detriment of limited-line producers operating at the top of the market, such as those that many European car manufacturers export to the United States. Such discrimination, it claimed, was contrary to Art. III GATT. It also contended that the fuel-economy standard of the gas-guzzler tax was not based on any objective or reasonable criteria and discriminated against imported cars, contrary to Art. III GATT.

The Panel Report concluded that neither the luxury tax nor the gas-guzzler tax was inconsistent with Art. III:2 GATT,[18] but that the CAFE regulation was inconsistent with Art. III:4[19] and, to the extent that it was based on separate foreign fleet accounting, could not be justified under Art. XX(g) or (d).[20] The Panel, therefore, recommended that the contracting parties request the United States to bring that part of the CAFE regulation found to be inconsistent with the GATT into conformity with its GATT obligations. By the end of 1994 the Panel Report had not yet been adopted.

Friedl Weiss

[18] Art. III:2 GATT:

The products of the territory of any contracting party imported into the territory of any other contracting party shall not be subject, directly or indirectly, to internal taxes or other internal charges of any kind in excess of those applied, directly or indirectly, to like domestic products. Moreover, no contracting party shall otherwise apply internal taxes or other internal charges to imported or domestic products in a manner contrary to the principles set forth in paragraph 1.

[19] Art. III:4 GATT:

The products of the territory of any contracting party imported into the territory of any other contracting party shall be accorded treatment no less favourable than that accorded to like products of national origin in respect of all laws, regulations and requirements affecting their internal sale, offering for sale, purchase, transportation, distribution or use. The provisions of this paragraph shall not prevent the application of differential internal transportation charges which are based exclusively on the economic operation of the means of transport and not on the nationality of the product.

[20] Art. XX(d), (g) GATT:

Subject to the requirement that such measures are not applied in a manner which would constitute a means of arbitrary or unjustifiable discrimination between countries where the same conditions prevail, or a disguised restriction on international trade, nothing in this Agreement shall be construed to prevent the adoption or enforcement by any contracting party of measures:

* * *

(d) necessary to secure compliance with laws or regulations which are not inconsistent with the provisions of this Agreement, including those relating to customs enforcement, the enforcement of monopolies operated under paragraph 4 of Article II and Article XVII, the protection of patents, trade marks and copyrights, and the prevention of deceptive practices;

* * *

(g) relating to the conservation of exhaustible natural resources if such measures are made effective in conjunction with restrictions on domestic production or consumption.

2. THE PROCESS "ENVIRONMENT FOR EUROPE"

(1) Introduction

Following the political changes in Central and Eastern Europe (CEE) in the late 1980s and early 1990s, concern about the critical state of the environment in many states of the former Eastern Block soon came to occupy an important place on the emerging pan-European political agenda. Accordingly, plans were made for a multilateral effort to help restore the environment in Central and Eastern Europe, to promote environmental protection in the region, and to coordinate Western assistance in this field.

(2) "Environment for Europe": An Overview

The first Ministerial Conference on "Environment for Europe," held in June 1991 at Dobris Castle (Czech Republic), called for the elaboration of three fundamental documents: (1) an Environmental Action Programme for Central and Eastern Europe, which would identify the environmental priorities for the region and set out a strategy and action programme; (2) a comprehensive report on the state of the environment in Europe (subsequently known as the Dobris Assessment); and (3) a longer-term Environmental Programme for Europe, extending to the whole continent. The follow-up to these decisions proceeded at varying paces. The Environmental Action Programme (EAP), elaborated by different expert groups and drafted under the guidance of the World Bank, was ready for submission to the second Ministerial Conference on "Environment for Europe," convened in April 1993 at Lucerne (Switzerland).[1] The 600-page Dobris Assessment was drafted under the auspices of the European Commission. Because of delays in its publication, it will now be submitted to the third Ministerial Conference on "Environment for Europe" in October 1995 at Sofia (Bulgaria).[2] The Environmental Programme for Europe (EPE) should build upon the Dobris Assessment. An outline and some basic elements were prepared under the guidance of the UN Economic Commission for Europe (UN/ECE). Drafting of the EPE was in progress at year's end, and it was intended to be ready for adoption by the Sofia Conference.

The 1993 Lucerne Conference adopted a Ministerial Declaration,

[1] *Environmental Action Programme for Central and Eastern Europe*, 2 Vols. *See also* the abridged version of the document, endorsed by the Lucerne Ministerial Conference.

[2] A published version of the Dobris Assessment is not yet available.

endorsing the EAP and giving guidance for the follow-up process.[3] It established three international bodies to deal with different aspects of the further development of the process "Environment for Europe": The UN/ECE *Ad Hoc* Working Group of Senior Governmental Officials, charged with the overall coordination of the follow-up to Lucerne and the substantive preparation of the Sofia Conference; the Task Force, charged with facilitating the implementation of the EAP (with the Organisation for Economic Cooperation and Development providing secretariat functions); and the Project Preparation Committee (PPC), charged with the coordination of international assistance to Central and Eastern European countries in the field of environmental protection (with the European Bank for Reconstruction and Development (EBRD) providing secretariat functions). The Council of Europe, together with World Conservation Union, was put in charge of the work in the field of nature conservation. This includes the elaboration of a work programme, as well as liaising with local authorities and organizations.

Virtually all member countries of the UN/ECE are currently involved in the process "Environment for Europe," albeit to varying degrees. Whereas membership of the PPC is limited to donor countries and international financial institutions, the Task Force is open to all countries as well as international organizations and non-governmental organizations (NGOs). The relevant bodies are convened at regular intervals, generally every few months.

The discussions in many areas show a considerable gap between the Central European states and the Newly Independent States of Eastern Europe. Whereas work in the various fields addressed by the process "Environment for Europe" is reasonably well advanced in most Central European countries, in particular the so-called Vizegrad states (Poland, Hungary, and the Czech and Slovak Republics), the Newly Independent States are in many ways still at the beginning of the process.

(3) The Environmental Action Programme for Central and Eastern Europe

The EAP probably constitutes the most tangible result of the process "Environment for Europe" thus far. Designed to provide guidance for environmental protection activities at all levels, it constitutes a basis for CEE countries to identify and develop their own environmental programmes. The facilitation of the adaptation of the EAP to national needs constitutes one of the major functions of the Task Force. Accordingly, the EAP has been translated into most Central European languages. Translation into

[3] *See* Declaration by the Ministers of the Environment of the region of the UN/ECE and the Member of the Commission of the European Communities responsible for the Environment, 30 April 1993.

Russian was under preparation at year's end. Under the auspices of the Task Force and with the assistance of the Regional Environmental Centre for Central and Eastern Europe, in Budapest (Hungary), most Central European states are in the process of developing and implementing their own National Environmental Action Programmes based on the EAP. In the Newly Independent States of Eastern Europe, this process has yet to get underway.

The EAP takes into account the results of the 1992 United Nations Conference on Environment and Development. It also attempts to adopt a realistic approach; due to the continuing lack of funding as well as the absence or deficiencies of competent institutional mechanisms in most CEE countries, all environmental problems cannot be addressed at once. The EAP therefore identifies priority areas on which action should be focused, as well as approaches that should ensure the best results with minimum investment. It also provides guidance to countries on how to set their individual priorities.

Immediate priority is given to those issues that have the most direct impact on human health in CEE countries. These include air pollution through emissions from industrial enterprises, heating, and transport (*e.g.*, lead, airborne dust, sulfur dioxide and nitrogen oxides); water pollution (*e.g.*, due to nonexistent or inappropriate waste water treatment); and unsound management of toxic chemicals and wastes that leads to contamination of food and water. Depletion of natural resources and loss of biological diversity, although not directly relevant to human health, are also identified as priority areas.

In addition to substantive priority areas, the EAP proposes instruments and mechanisms to be used in addressing environmental problems. These include environmental objectives as integral elements of the ongoing privatization process in CEE countries; economic instruments to achieve environmental objectives (*e.g.*, "green taxes," pollution charges, emission permits, and deposit-fund schemes); a regional approach to environmental protection (addressing local problems at the local level); "win-win" policies (*e.g.*, the abolishment of state subsidies that encourage the excessive use of energy or water, investments in energy and water conservation, low-waste technologies, and good housekeeping); and an institutional and legal framework for the adoption and implementation of environmental policies.

The priority areas and mechanisms that the EAP identified have considerable practical significance. In addition to serving as a basis for environmental activities undertaken by competent authorities of CEE states, the EAP is also used as a guideline by many Western states when designing and implementing their bilateral environmental assistance programmes for Central and Eastern Europe.

(4) The Environmental Programme for Europe

Taking into account the findings of the Dobris Assessment, the EPE is to provide a longer-term environmental programme for the entire European continent. Based on previously defined criteria, the Dobris Assessment singled out 12 environmental problems that were considered to merit priority treatment. The UN/ECE Working Group in 1994 proposed a provisional outline for the EPE. After addressing the results of the Dobris Assessment (including the issue of priority problems) and analysing current policies affecting the environment in Europe, the EPE is to set out the following main elements on which future environmental action in Europe is to be based: (1) General issues (information, public participation, cooperation among competent national authorities, involvement of industry, capacity building, and the wider economic context of environmental efforts); (2) cleaner production and efficient use of energy and materials; (3) sustainable consumption patterns; (4) use of natural resources; (5) biodiversity; and (6) sustainable agriculture, forestry, and fisheries. Financial mechanisms are to be addressed under a separate heading in the EPE.

(5) Toward the 1995 Sofia Ministerial Conference on "Environment for Europe"

Efforts undertaken in 1993 and 1994 within the bodies set up pursuant to the Lucerne Conference proceeded in accordance with the decisions taken at Lucerne. Initial difficulties in getting work underway gave rise to the question whether the Sofia Conference should be postponed. By year's end, however, there appeared to be general agreement that October 1995 was a feasible target.

The UN/ECE Working Group, the Task Force, and the PPC initially experienced some problems establishing a clear focus for their work. These difficulties have since been resolved to a considerable extent. The UN/ECE Working Group concentrates mainly on the agenda for Sofia and the finalization of the EPE. Within the PPC, the process of "matchmaking" between the individual donors is now well established. In practice, this consists almost entirely in the contribution by Western donor countries to major projects in CEE that are administered and managed by the World Bank and the EBRD. To facilitate the exchange of information between donors and to avoid duplication of efforts, the PPC has adopted a format for the reporting of environmental projects in CEE countries to the Secretariat. The Task Force, besides promoting the implementation of the EAP at the national level, is sponsoring separate discussions on important issues related to its work. These include financial mechanisms to implement environmental activities (including the question of "soft loans" for environmental projects), and the involvement of industry in environmental protection activities.[4]

Although the different bodies have different objectives, discussions have increasingly focused on the agenda for the Sofia Ministerial Conference, and the future of the process "Environment for Europe." Under the heading "Partners in Cooperation," the Sofia Conference is to consider issues concerning environmental assistance to CEE countries by Western states. These include progress in the implementation of the EAP and the National Environmental Action Programmes, the role of industry, financial mechanisms, the setting of new priorities, and the continuation of the process "Environment for Europe" after Sofia. The second major part of the agenda is to be devoted to issues concerning the future of environmental protection efforts in Europe as a whole. The main points to be addressed under this heading are the consideration of the Dobris Assessment and the adoption of the EPE. The Conference is expected to adopt a Ministerial Declaration, which by the UN/ECE Working Group is also drafting. Separate meetings parallel to the Sofia Conference are planned, which are to bring together environmental NGOs and the business community, respectively.

Katharina Kummer

[4] *See* the respective reports of the UN/ECE Working Group, the Task Force, and the PPC.

PART 3

LITERATURE REVIEW

A. BOOK REVIEWS

Daniel C. Esty, *Greening the GATT: Trade, Environment, and the Future* (Washington: Institute for International Economics, 1994), 319 pages.

Within the past four years, trade and the environment has leaped from being an unmapped concern to being a hot topic in both trade law and international environmental law. Daniel C. Esty's *Greening the GATT* is not the first book on the subject, but it is the most comprehensive and readable. Esty, now an associate professor at Yale Law School and the Yale School of Forestry and Environmental Studies, was a policy official in the U.S. Environmental Protection Agency during the Bush Administration and was a negotiator of the North American Free Trade Agreement.

Greening the GATT presents a vivid portrayal of the views of the trade policy community and of environmentalists, and shows why these two groups began to clash in the early 1990s. There have been misunderstandings, Esty explains, but there are other philosophical, cultural, and institutional factors that have led to real conflicts between the goals of free trade and environmental protection.

Esty is an internationalist and a consensus builder. He is at his best in pointing out the mutually reinforcing goals of "free traders" and "environmentalists." Both camps seek to improve the efficiency of resource use and to add to worldwide social welfare. Good trade policy and good environmental policy complement each other.

The book contains several insights. The most important is Esty's recognition that an institutional contribution of the General Agreement on Tariffs and Trade (GATT) can be applied to environmental politics. Esty explains the history of the GATT and highlights what trade law theorist E.U. Petersmann calls the "constitutional" function of the GATT. So viewed, the GATT fulfills more than its obvious roles as a facilitator of trade liberalization and as a forum for settling disputes. The GATT also "provides a mechanism for addressing the collective-action problems that plague domestic policymaking."

The syndrome of trade policy being shaped by rent-seeking, special-interest groups has been well documented since E.E. Schattschneider's landmark study of 1935. Using the work of contemporary political economists, Esty explains how the GATT responds through international rules that help lawmakers resist protectionist pressures. There have been countless occasions when members of the U.S. Congress have responded to pleas for import protection by saying that they would really like to help, but cannot because of the GATT.

Esty claims that a similar mechanism could help lawmakers resist special interest pleading on the environment. In a play on words, he calls this "GATTing the greens." Quoting Gifford Pinchot's warning that "special interests" could "nullify the will of the majority," Esty suggests that environmental policymaking is often warped, not only by polluters, but also by over-eager environmental groups. To remedy this, Esty calls for "an institutional structure to protect the environment the way the GATT guards free trade." He calls it the Global Environmental Organization or GEO.

Esty's portray is accurate, but he draws only part of the picture. The GATT was established to deal with government failure, not market failure. Protectionism is a non-cooperative government policy — bad for the nation doing it and bad for that nation's trading partners. Environmental problems, on the other hand, are largely the result of market failure.

Viewing environmental problems mainly as manifestations of government failure, because governments do not regulate properly, oversimplifies the issue. The GATT is a set of negative directives — for example, do not enact tariffs that discriminate between countries. Surely, some negative directives are needed for the environment, but more needed are positive directives (*e.g.*, cost internalization).

Unlike other social problems, like unemployment, underdevelopment, and pollution, the problem of trade protectionism can theoretically be solved on a permanent basis. Environmental policy is far more complex. No permanent solution is imaginable. Thus, the GATT analogy does not take us as far as we need to go.

Esty is right to perceive institutional problems in international environmental governance, and his recommendation for a GEO is very timely in that regard. But he weakens his own case in describing the GEO as a "counterweight" to GATT's "market-access oriented rules." The best reasons for a GEO are the points that Esty lays out elsewhere in the book. He explains that the international environmental regime remains thin (UNCED notwithstanding), and notes that there is no institution where concepts like life-cycle analysis, pollution prevention, the precautionary principle, and cost internalization can be debated and turned into operational standards.

Esty discusses the existing international environmental institutions, like UNEP and the Commission on Sustainable Development, and notes their weaknesses. However, he does not help the reader understand why the institutions were created with such weaknesses. In other words, he offers little analysis of the political forces that have engendered the current incoherence in international environmental governance and that will continue to stand in the way of reform proposals such as a GEO.

The thinness of governance for the environment is not as exceptional as Esty sometimes implies. There is very little global governance at all. If one looks at the major forces driving the world economy such as the flows of money, information, services, and products, it is noteworthy how much of this occurs without international rules. Esty might also have devoted more discussion to the supervisory and assistance roles of the International Monetary Fund. Some "IMFing" of the greens may be needed as well as the "GATTing" of them.

Esty examines the compatibility of environmental taxes, regulations, and trade restrictions with the GATT, and points out where the use of these measures might clash with GATT rules. He is not a promoter of trade restrictions; Esty notes that they "are a poor substitute for proper environmental policies", but that in some cases they may be the best option available. His explanation of GATT's complex rules is lucid and informative. He is critical of recent GATT panel decisions that seek to require that trade measures be based on product characteristics and disallow trade measures based on the process by which a product is made. According to Esty, this artificial distinction "makes no sense in an ecologically interdependent world, where pollution spillovers in the manufacturing process can have global consequences."

He is also critical of the way that GATT panels have narrowed the treaty's general exception for human, animal, or plant life or health. He calls the "least-GATT-inconsistent" test in GATT Article XX (which contains the exceptions for health and conservation) an "inappropriately high hurdle" for ascertaining GATT legality, "since there are almost always policy mechanisms available that would be less inconsistent with the GATT." One minor criticism: Esty himself takes too narrow a view of GATT Article XX when he says that its scope "fails to cover important natural resources such as the atmosphere, the oceans, the ozone layer, and other elements of the global commons." The recent decision by GATT's Tuna-Dolphin II panel clarified Article XX a bit in this regard.

In a very ambitious effort, Esty presents a new juridical framework for how the GATT should handle complaints about environmental measures. Borrowing from U.S. Constitutional jurisprudence under the interstate commerce clause, Esty would have the GATT (or the GEO) "weigh the commercial benefits of trade against competing environmental ends." Esty introduces a number of new tests to balance the two interests. There is an "intent and effect" test, an "environmental legitimacy" test, and a "clearly disproportionate" test. For environmental legitimacy, Esty would ask panels to use "science" to separate what he calls "bona fide environmentalism" from "moral choices" like dolphin-safe tuna. Esty seems to side more with the tuna fishermen than with the dolphins in that dispute. That may be a reasonable position. Yet it is hardly more "scientific" than the pro-dolphin position.

The "clearly disproportionate" test is the most innovative of the three tests. Esty wants the GATT to act like the U.S. Supreme Court or the European Court of Justice when they determine the legality of internal trade barriers, but recognizing that the GATT would be making judgments about sovereign nations, Esty would give nations the benefit of the doubt. As he explains: "close calls are not second-guessed; only obvious off-base decisions are overturned."

Of course, one person's off-base call may be another person's close call. Esty suggests that the U.S. Corporate Average Fuel Economy (CAFE) program would fail his test as "disproportionate to the significant trade impacts on European automakers." Yet a recent GATT panel rejected an identical argument by the European Union. Esty would also have the GATT rule against the U.S. EPA's ban on asbestos as being too costly to Canadian asbestos producers. The total ban may have been too blunt an instrument — it was overturned by the U.S. Court of Appeals — but it is not clear that the GATT should be judging the bluntness of non-discriminatory national laws.

Esty devotes an entire chapter to the controversial issue of economic competitiveness and the "race to the bottom." He points out that there is little evidence that high environmental standards degrade competitiveness. Instead of stopping there, as many analysts have done, Esty goes on to explain that perceptions may be just as important as reality. If corporations are worried that higher environmental standards will make then uncompetitive, and if they transmit this worry to policymakers, then a phenomenon Esty calls "political drag" will occur, as countries settle for suboptimal standards. This situation results in part from the interest group lobbying noted above. But it also results from the fact that nations may have to pay the full costs of their environmental regulation even though some of the benefits may spill over to other countries.

Esty discusses several policy proposals to deal with political drag including eco-taxes, border tax adjustments, green subsidies, eco-labeling, and harmonization. He sees some benefit in all of these proposals when implemented in a multilaterally-agreed way.

The book is lucidly written, well-documented, and moderate in tone. Esty argues persuasively that growing ecological interdependence calls for the GATT and the new World Trade Organization to be updated to reflect global realities. Shortly after its publication, the book drew two critical reviews in *The Economist* (July 9, 1994) and the *Financial Times* (July 21, 1994). Both argue that Esty strays too much from economic orthodoxy and take him to task for recommending changes in GATT rules. The two reviews should become exhibits in the next edition of Esty's book. They show how resistant the trade camp is to meeting the environmental camp even halfway.

Greening the GATT also contains chapters on "offensive" trade measures for the environment and on the particular problems of developing countries. The book is a goldmine of information including an 18-page appendix providing short descriptions of all the important trade and environment cases (*e.g.*, tuna-dolphin, Danish bottles, etc.) and a 22-page bibliography on trade and environment, the most extensive one compiled so far. The book is very well organized, in the style of all books from the Institute for International Economics. The policy recommendations are highlighted throughout the book and everything is summed up in a detailed final chapter.

At a time when world politics and international law have largely succeeded in safeguarding the integrity of territorial borders, it is ironic that this security has been somewhat negated by the permeability of national borders to environmental threats. *Greening the GATT* is a very useful book because it tries to develop a framework for thinking about the interaction between economic and environmental spillovers. The management of these problems will remain a critical issue for several years at least.

Steve Charnovitz

Serge Pannatier, *L'Antarctique et la protection internationale de l'environnement* (Zürich: Schulthess Polygraphischer Verlag, 1994), 323 pages.

In its thirty-five years of history, the Antarctic Treaty System has undergone considerable transformation and expansion. From a security arrangement designed to prevent competing territorial claims from creating international conflicts, it has evolved into a complex regulatory network of scientific cooperation, resource management, conservation and, more recently, environmental protection and institutional development. Antarctica is becoming a microcosm of international legal issues ranging from sovereignty claims, jurisdiction, law of the sea, and, naturally, environmental protection. It is not surprising that the process has attracted increasing attention from international legal scholars, including those from countries that do not have a long history of presence in Antarctica or specific national interests in its legal-political regime. This development must be welcomed. It signals the importance of the Antarctic legal regime to the international community as a whole, beyond the restricted circle of specially concerned States. It also contributes to the intellectual pluralism that is needed to expand and strengthen the acceptance and legitimacy of the Antarctic Treaty regime worldwide.

Pannatier's book, published as a doctoral dissertation in Switzerland, reflects this trend. Switzerland only recently acceded to the Antarctic

Treaty, but it is rapidly producing a body of doctrinal contributions in line with its distinguished tradition of international legal studies.[1]

The stated objective of the book is to offer an overview of the development of international environmental law and of the tendencies that influence its progress, in order to assess the effectiveness of the legal regime applicable to protecting the Antarctic environment. To achieve this objective, the author organizes the volume in three parts. The first, consisting of six chapters, examines international environmental law with almost no reference to Antarctica. The second part examines in four chapters the Antarctic Treaty System and includes, at the end, a short appendix of the Swiss contribution to the System. The third part, in five chapters, addresses general problems of international law, notably the global character of the environment, the relevance of the common heritage of mankind, international responsibility for environmental harm, the interaction between environment and development, and new techniques for improving the effectiveness of law-making and implementation of environmental rules.

Overall, Dr. Pannatier's book represents a commendable effort at concisely treating two very complex subjects: international environmental law and Antarctica. For the reader, this approach presents some unquestionable advantages: each of the three parts and, indeed, each of the fifteen chapters may be read independently. This makes the book a useful for quick reference and for teaching individual subjects in an introductory course in international environmental law. The fluid language and the extreme clarity of the French text enhance the qualities and potential use of the book.

The structure also has its shortcomings. It is lamentable that the treatment of Antarctica in the second part is totally divorced from the treatment of international environmental law in the first and third parts. It appears as if the author began writing a concise manual of international environmental law and then decided to juxtapose a free-standing portion on Antarctica. The lack of harmonization of the parts is aggravated by the absence of an adequate system of cross-references and by the omission of important precedents and information on Antarctica in the chapters dealing with general problems of international environmental law. For example, when the author discusses the international law response to massive environmental disasters, he lists major cases of oil spills, from the *Amoco Cadiz* to *Exxon Valdez*, but ignores the 1989 *Bahia Paraiso* accident. One does not need to be privy to the Antarctic Treaty negotiations to be aware

[1] *See particularly* L. Caflisch & F. Tanner, *The Polar Regions and Their Strategic Significance* (1989); L. Caflisch, "L'Antarctique: nouvelle frontière sans frontières," in Melange Virally: *Le droit international au service de la paix, de la justice et du développement* 157 (1991); and *id.*, "The Interaction of Science and Politics in the Field of International Relations: The Case of Antarctica," 28 *Polar Record* 159 (1992).

of the importance of this accident in orienting the Antarctic Treaty Parties towards a ban on mineral activities and the adoption of the comprehensive environmental regime embodied in the 1991 Madrid Protocol.

Equally unrelated to Antarctica is the treatment of international responsibility for environmental harm. In Chapter 14, the author revisits at length the work of the International Law Commission on the subject. However, he neglects to examine what implications this work could have for a liability regime in Antarctica. This is particularly surprising in light of the 1992 establishment of a group of experts within the Antarctic Treaty System to develop a liability instrument pursuant to article 16 of the Madrid Protocol. The results of the discussions within the working group, including the chairman's draft articles, offer useful insights for the treatment of this subject.[2]

Due to its compartmentalized structure, the book also fails to address a fundamental issue arising from the current development of specific environmental legislation within the Antarctic Treaty: the relationship between such legislation and multilateral treaties on the protection of the environment which either expressly or by implication are applicable to the Antarctic Treaty area. These include such universal instruments as the United Nations Law of the Sea Convention, general conventions on marine pollution such as MARPOL, and more specialized instruments such as the 1989 Basel Convention on Transboundary Movement of Hazardous Waste and instruments on the conservation of marine living resources. Doctrinal analysis is needed to clarify this issue and to indicate which principles should govern the relationship between the Antarctic Treaty System and the general instruments of international environmental law. Several principles might be tested: subsidiarity, application of the Vienna Convention on the Law of Treaties, priority of Antarctic legislation. Unfortunately, none are discussed in the book.

Despite the above reservations, Dr. Pannatier's book remains a useful and practical tool for those who want to orient themselves to the increasing complexities of Antarctic legislation and to the ever-expanding body of international environmental law. The book is based on thorough research and on a wealth of bibliographic information in many languages including German, Italian and Spanish. In this respect, it is an example to follow for young (and less young) international lawyers who unfortunately seem to believe that the study of international law today permits ignorance of literature in languages other than English.

Francesco Francioni

[2] The author makes only cursory reference to these negotiations in Chapter 9, p. 178, saying that "...les Parties Consultatives ne montrent pas un veritable empressement à les mener à terme."

L. Campiglio, L. Pineschi, D. Siniscalco, T. Treves (eds.), *The Environment After Rio: International Law and Economics* (London/Dordrecht/Boston: Graham & Trotman/Martinus Nijhoff 1994) 285 pages.

This volume contains revised and updated versions of papers presented at the Congress on "The Environment after Rio" held at Courmayeur (Italy), 11–13 February 1993. These collected papers are interesting in part because Courmayeur was one of the first meetings to debate the political, economic and legal implications of the 1992 Rio Conference on Environment and Development (UNCED). In fact, the book contains more than a broad, interdisciplinary review of the results of the Rio Summit and of issues related to "sustainable development." It also lays the foundation for further analysis of post-UNCED progress in international cooperation to ensure compatibility between protection of the environment and economic growth. Both scholars and practitioners will greatly benefit from the contributions that appear in the volume.

Following the programme of the Courmayeur Congress, the book is divided into four parts. Part One, titled "The Rio Conference between Policy and Law" studies the pre-UNCED negotiations. The opening piece is A. Adede's "The Road to Rio: The Development of Negotiations." Contributions by S. Hajost, M. Bruscasco-Mackenzie and C. Mensah then discuss the political role in the Rio process of the United States, the European Communities and the developing countries. Analysis of the negotiating positions of the major players is especially useful for understanding the difficulties confronting UNCED and the reasons behind its shortcomings. The latter were often due to the need to reconcile opposite views and concerns by recourse to the lowest common denominator. In this respect, the paper by Hajost should be noted for its critical appraisal of the U.S. Government's attitude towards UNCED during the Bush administration contrasted with the commitment of the Clinton-Gore administration to more dynamic action for the protection of the global environment.

Part Two ("The Declarations and the Conventions Adopted in Rio") examines the UNCED legal instruments, namely the Rio Declaration on Environment and Development (A. Kiss), the Authoritative Non-legally Binding Statement of Principles on Forests (A. Szekely), the Framework Convention on Climate Change (J. F. Pulvenis), and the Convention on Biological Diversity (A. Boyle). These contributions reach different conclusions in evaluating the various documents. According to Kiss, the Rio Declaration should be praised not only because "it confirms several international environmental rules and reinforces emerging ones", but also because it establishes a definitive link between environmental protection and development, and reveals the emergence of non-political movements and groups as active participants in some areas of the international law-making process. By contrast, Szekely's article on the Statement on Forests is highly skeptical of its impact on states' behavior and the future development of international legislation. In his view, the content of this instrument "falls one hundred per cent short of providing even the most elementary basis for an international regime for the protection of the world's forests". Substantial criticisms of the treaty texts are also made by Pulvenis and Boyle. Pulvenis's criticism of the Framework Convention on Climate Change is tempered by optimism that the Intergovernmental Negotiating Committee operating during the interim period (prior to the Conference of the Parties) will adequately address crucial issues such as the definition of parameters for response measures, the provision of financial means and the transfer of technology.

Some of the most important chapters of "Agenda 21" are examined in Part Three ("Prospects for the Future in the Light of Agenda 21 and of the Evolving Principles of International Environmental Law"). This Part includes contributions from H. Smets on the so-called "polluter-pays principle", S. McCaffrey on the management of fresh water resources, T. Treves on the protection of the oceans and L. Pineschi on the protection of mountain areas. The prominence that Courmayeur gave to various chapters of "Agenda 21" is justified by the fact that this action programme represents perhaps the most significant "product" of the Conference, as it has rapidly shown its impact on states' conduct and the elaboration of new instruments and rules relating to sustainable development.

Treves's comments on Chapter 17 ("Protection of the oceans, all kinds of seas, including enclosed and semi-enclosed seas and coastal areas and the protection, rational use and development of their living resources") are of special interest, as they are centered on some of the program areas where "Agenda 21" has given evident impulse to developing further interstate cooperation. These comments relate, in particular, to the conflict of interests at the source of the mandate of the UN Conference on Straddling Stocks and Highly Migratory Fish Stocks, convened pursuant to Programme Area D of Chapter 17. The Conference, opened in 1993, will hold its fifth and sixth sessions in 1995. Treves also notes the special ecological vulnerability of small islands, addressed by Programme Area D, and the consequent decision of the 47th General Assembly to convene a "Global Conference on the Sustainable Development of Small Island Developing States," held in Barbados in 1994.

Part Four ("Environment, Development and Interdependence") examines economic issues. The first topic is the concept of sustainability (P. Hammond), followed by the relationship between economic growth, technical progress, and the environment (I.Musu). Other subjects are the influence of the current patterns of North-South trade on environmental protection (G. Chichilnisky), and the value of rationality and ethics in the process of global environmental change (S. Zamagni). Additional contributions relate to the question of poverty and the environment (P. Dasgupta), the interface between urbanization, energy, and environmental protection (S. Allal), and the role of international institutions in promoting sustainable development (Y.Berthelot). Some of the more stimulating comments are those of Chichilnisky on the need to adapt traditional concepts and policies of international trade, and those of Berthelot on ways to enhance the role of international institutions, including the U.N. Commission on Sustainable Development. As a whole, the "economic section" of the volume complements the political and legal analysis of the Rio documents, providing a broad perspective to the discussions and ample material for further reflection.

Mauro Politi

Harald Hohmann, *Precautionary Legal Duties and Principles of Modern International Environmental Law* (London/Dordrecht/Boston: Graham & Trotman/Martinus Nijhoff 1994), 377 pages.

This book is an update and translation from the German of Hohmann's doctoral dissertation first published in 1992 (Harald Hohmann, *Präventive Rechtspflichten und -prinzipien des modernen Umweltvölkerrechts*, Duncker & Humblot, Berlin). Hohmann seeks "to determine whether there has been a change of perspective in international environmental law from the predominantly economic, traditional perspective to a predominantly ecological approach" (p. 4-5). The main feature of an ecological approach is precaution which, Hohmann suggests, can clearly be observed in national environmental law in Germany and "in other industrialized nations of Europe" (p. 5). German environmental law is briefly described to demonstrate that "since 1986" a change of paradigm has occurred and that "out of the previous economic- and maximum distribution-oriented regulations pertaining to natural resources has emerged an ecological, precautionary law oriented toward long-term optimum resource conservation" (p. 11). This observation is generally correct in that elements of precautionary thinking, such as environmental planning or environmental impact assessment (EIA), can be found in German law as in the laws of other jurisdictions. It is also true, though, that the precautionary principle has always played a major role in German environmental law as evidenced by the long-standing controversies over the meaning and implications of the principle.[3]

[3] *See e.g.* E. Rehbinder, *Das Vorsorgeprizip im internationalen Vergleich* (1991).

Hohmann's inquiry ends with the conclusion that "modern international environmental law is largely precautionary" (p. 203). International environmental law, he suggests, contains "far-reaching precautionary duties which are . . . triggered by risk potential" (*ibid.*) "Risk potential" is understood as a stricter concept than "concrete danger," requiring action also in cases of scientific uncertainty about cause-effect relationships. Hohmann is somewhat concerned about the "lack of commitment to emission standards," the "vague planning and prevention duties," the "low standard of technology," and "a near lack of financial incentives." These "detract from the precautionary character of international environmental law." He remains convinced, however, that at least in Europe and North America there can be no doubt about the precautionary nature of international environmental law:

> Only the modern European/North American customary law of the environment can be called precautionary. It avoids almost all of these shortcomings (except for the economic dependence of technology). At the global level, protection of resources is relatively weak because, at present, the duty of optimal sustainable productivity has not yet been inferred from the now recognized intergenerational equity principle; this situation is apparently different in the case of European/North American customary law (*ibid.*).

Hohmann finds evidence of the precautionary character of international environmental law in the declarations, guidelines, standards, resolutions, codes of conduct, and similar instruments adopted in international organizations. He does not argue that these instruments, generally referred to as "legally non-binding" or "soft law", are binding as such. Rather, he believes that "declarations, guidelines, etc. initiate, confirm, specify and/or establish duties of customary law" (p. 184). Most international lawyers would agree with this general position, although the crucial questions remain to be answered. For example, what are the criteria by which such a duty can be considered part of binding international customary law; what are the specific implications of the largely abstract principle of precautionary action; and, finally, is there sufficient evidence in state practice to consider these implications part of customary law?

One may agree with the four characteristics Hohmann identifies for the evolution of a general customary rule of law (tightening of the rule through continual use; no regional limitation; adoption by the community of nations; and subsequent citation in agreements and declarations (p.172-173). One can also agree with his nine "principles of precaution and resource conservation," fundamental commandments of international environmental protection, namely to recognize the intrinsic value of nature; to act not only in cases of "concrete danger" but also in cases of "risk potential;" not to insist on full scientific proof of environmental damage; to protect environmental media, take into account cross media issues and intergenerational equity; to cooperate regionally and globally; to grant transboundary access to administrative and judicial procedures; to provide for environmental planning, EIA procedures, emission standards and the use of best available technology (BAT); and to prevent pollution at the source (p. 189–190).

Readers will find it difficult, however, to agree with Hohmann's analysis of state practice and his conclusions. He asserts that the practice of states within international organizations in adopting (non-binding) declarations, guidelines or similar instruments offers sufficient evidence to consider the nine principles part of binding international law. Although Hohmann himself questions the general acceptance of the cross-media and intergenerational approaches and discusses whether planning, EIA, emission standards and BAT are binding customary law, in the end, he affirms the customary legal nature of all the principles. These conclusions are questionable. Hohmann misinterprets the practice of states. States do take international organizations seriously; they battle "over every word and comma" as Hohmann rightly observes (p. 173). States do so, however, not so much because they believe that the declarations, guidelines or resolutions as agreed to contain binding obligations. States fight over words and commas to avoid creating precedents which might initiate developments leading to eventual legal obligations to protect the environment.

Another problem is that state practice within international organizations and international treaty practice cannot be considered separately. Hohmann deals with major international agreements as if there were no links between treaty law and customary law. Yet, the interplay between the two sources of international law is, self-evidently, crucial. Treaty law may contribute to the formation of customary international law. In this context it is important to look not only at the text of a treaty but also to the practice of states with regard to the treaty in question. Finding evidence of a customary law rule is always a complicated undertaking, particularly in the field of environmental protection; a multi-factor analysis is required which considers a broad variety of international instruments including both binding and non-binding ones as well as the practice of states under the respective instruments.

The main criticism of Hohmann's book is thus a methodological one: It is not sufficient to quote a number of declarations, guidelines or resolutions of international organizations to establish that a rule has become part of customary law. A deeper analysis is necessary. Hohmann does not do justice to his own criteria of a customary law rule. He inexplicably fails to analyze each of his principles of precaution and resource conservation in the light of continual use, exclusion of regional limitations, adoption by the community of nations and subsequent citation. A hard look at state practice leads to different conclusions and more sobering results.

The book has been written with many good intentions and reflects a true commitment to environmental protection. Hohmann is concerned with the role that international law can play in protecting the environment. He is particularly interested in clarifying the contributions of international organizations, which have adopted hundreds of resolutions, declarations, guidelines, codes of conducts and other instruments. As many others have done in the past, he attempts to demonstrate that these "soft law" instruments are not irrelevant in international environmental law. However, his analysis remains superficial and his conclusions are simply too optimistic. International environmental law — "largely precautionary"? One could only wish that were so.

Lothar Gündling

B. BIBLIOGRAPHY

I. GENERAL DEVELOPMENTS

1. Internationalization of Natural Resource Management

a. Transboundary Risk of Harm

b. Emerging Intergenerational Equity and Sustainable Development Standards

Beckerman, "'Sustainable Development': Is it a Useful Concept?" 3 *EnvV* 191 (1994).

Baram, "Multinational Corporations, Private Codes, and Technology Transfer for Sustainable Development," 24 *EnvL* 33 (1994).

J. de Castro, *The Internalization of External Environmental Costs and Sustainable Development* (Geneva: UNCTAD 1994).

W. Futrell, *The Transition to Sustainable Development Law* (Washington, D.C.: Environmental Law Institute 1994).

Jacob, "Sustainable Development and Deep Ecology: an Analysis of Competing Traditions," 18 *EnvM* 477 (1994).

Karp, "Sustainable Development: Toward a New Vision," 13 *VaELJ* 239 (1994).

M. Redclift & C. Sage (eds), *Strategies for Sustainable Development: Local Agendas for the Southern Hemisphere* (Chichester: John Wiley & Sons Ltd. 1994).

L. Starke (ed), *State of the World 1994: A Worldwatch Institute Report on Progress Toward a Sustainable Society* (New York: Worldwatch Institute/W.W. Norton & Co. Inc. 1994).

E. Swanson, *Putting Sustainable Development to Work: Implementation Through Law and Policy* (Edmonton: Environmental Law Centre 1994).

Upreti, "Environmental Conservation and Sustainable Development Require a New Development Approach," 21 *EnvC* 18 (1994).

J. Young, *The Next Efficiency Revolution: Creating a Sustainable Materials Economy* (Washington, D.C.: Worldwatch Institute 1994).

c. Human Rights

Abraham, "Expanding Community Right to Know and Participate: Citizens Negotiate New Rights with Petrochemicals Companies in Texas," 1 *EnvLNI* 18 (1994).

Führs, et al., "Access to Justice: Legal Standing for Environmental Associations in the European Community," 1 *EnvLNI* 3 (1994).

de Lucas, "El principio de solidaridad como fundamento del derecho al medio ambiente," 12 *RevDA* 51 (1994).

Mateo, "The Right to Environmental Information," 1 *JEnvPLLAC* 47 (1994).

B. Nagy, et al. (eds), *Manual on Public Participation in Environmental Decisionmaking: Current Practice and Future Possibilities in Central and Eastern Europe* (Budapest, Hungary: The Regional Environmental Center for Central and Eastern Europe 1994).

Pugh & Moor "Access to Environmental Information in the UK: A Silk Purse or a Pig's Ear?" 3 *RECIEL* 26 (1994).

Richardson, Craig & Boer, "Indigenous Peoples and Environmental Management: A Review of Canadian Regional Agreements and Their Potential Application to Australia—Part 1," 11 *EnvPlanLJ* 320 (1994).

R. Salazar Cambronero & R. Saborío Valverde, *Manual Sobre Derechos Humanos y Ambiente* (San José, Costa Rica; Fundación Ambio / Academia Costarricense de Derecho Ambiental 1994).

Van Dyke & Brennan, "A Proposal to Introduce the Right to a Healthy Environment into the European Convention Regime," 13 *VaELJ* 323 (1994).

Wheeler, "The Right to Know in the European Union," 3 *RECIEL* 1 (1994).

Zaidi, "Human Health Effects of Oil Development in the Ecuadorian Amazon: A Challenge to Legal Thinking," 14 *EnvIAR* 337 (1994).

Symposium, "Endangered Peoples: Indigenous Rights and the Environment," 5 *CoJIELP* 23 (1994).

- Hitchcock, "International Human Rights, the Environment, and Indigenous Peoples," 1;
- Rubin & Fish, "Biodiversity Prospecting: Using Innovative Contractual Provisions to Foster Ethnobotanical Knowledge, Technology, and Conservation," 23;
- Suagee & Stearns, "Indigenous Self-Government, Environmental Protection, and the Consent of the Governed: A Tribal Environmental Review Process," 59;
- Stavroupoulou, "Indigenous Peoples Displaced from their Environment: Is there Adequate Protection?," 105;
- LaDuke, "Traditional Ecological Knowledge and Environmental Futures," 127.
- Asiema & Situma, "Indigenous Peoples and the Environment: The Case of the Pastoral Maasai of Kenya," 149;
- O'Connor, "'We Are Part of Nature': Indigenous Peoples' Rights as a Basis for Environmental Protection in the Amazon Basin," 193;
- Chiropolos, "Inupiat Subsistence and the Bowhead Whale: Can Indigenous Hunting Cultures Coexist with Endangered Animal Species?," 213;
- Rohrbough, "On Our Way to Ten Billion Human Beings: A Comment on Sustainability and Population," 235;

2. Institutional Developments/UNCED

Cano, "Agenda 21: Latin America and the Caribbean," 1 *JEnvPLLAC* 29 (1994).

Casey-Lefkowitz, "The Road from Rio: Next Steps," *EnvL* (Cosponsored by the

Environmental Law Institute and The Smithsonian Institution), February 17, 1994.

Freestone, "The Road from Rio: International Law After the Earth Summit," 6 *JEnvL* 193 (1994).

French, "Strengthening International Environmental Governance," 3 *JEnvDev* 59 (1994).

Handl, "Controlling Implementation of and Compliance with International Environmental Commitments: The Rocky Road from Rio," 5 *CoJIELP* 305 (1994).

Rest, "Need for an International Court for the Environment?: Underdeveloped Legal Protection for the Individual in Transnational Litigation," 24 *EnvPL* 173 (1994).

B. Spector, G. Sjöstedt & W. Zartman, *Negotiating International Regimes: Lessons Learned from the UN Conference on Environment and Development (UNCED)* (London/Dordrecht/Boston: Graham & Trotman/Martinus Nijhoff 1994).

J. Scherr, et al., *Four in '94: Assessing National Actions to Implement Agenda 21: A Country-by-Country Progress Report* (New York: Natural Resources Defense Council Publications 1994).

Tarasofsky, "Significant British Practice in Relation to UNCED," 43 *ICLQ* 432 (1994).

O. Young, *International Governance: Protecting the Environment in a Stateless Society* (Ithaca and London: Cornell University Press 1994).

3. Transboundary Environmental Cooperation

Carraro, Lanza & Tudini, "Technological Change, Technology Transfer, and the Negotiation of International Agreements," 6 *IEA* 203 (1994).

Mumme, "Enforcing International Environmental Agreements: Lessons from U.S.-Mexico Border," 3 *EnvPlanLJ* 71 (1994).

a. Environmental Information/Consultation/Impact Assessment

Bakkenist, "Notification of Transnational Environmental Impacts," 3 *RECIEL* 7 (1994).

"Case Law Analysis: Redressing the Late Implementation of the Environmental Protection Assessment Directive," 6 *JEnvL* 351 (1994).

Cook & Hearn, "Putting Together the Pieces: A Comprehensive Examination of the Legal and Policy Issues of Environmental Auditing," 7 *TulaneELJ* 545 (1994).

Jiménez Jaén, "Evaluación de impacto ambiental y procedimiento administrativo," 12 *RevDA* 29 (1994).

Kakonge, "Monitoring of Environmental Impact Assessments in Africa," 14 *EnvIAR* 295 (1994).

Karl, "Better Environmental Future in Europe through Environmental Auditing?" 18 *EnvM* 617 (1994).

Kimerling, "Recent Development: The Environmental Audit of Texaco's Amazon

Oil Fields: Environmental Justice or Business as Usual?," 7 *Harvard HRJ* 199 (1994).

Leeson, "EIA and the Politics of Avoidance," 11 *EnvPlanLJ* 71 (1994).

Liniger & Martens, "Die Umweltmanagement—und Audit—Verordnung der Europäischen Union: Analyse und Umsetzung," 8 *UmweltPrax* 301 (1994).

Penney, "Assessing CEAA: Environmental Assessment Theory and the Canadian Environmental Assessment Act," 4 *JEnvLPrac* 243 (1994).

Spedding, "Environmental Auditing and International Standards," 3 *RECIEL* 14 (1994).

Thompson & Wilson, "Environmental Auditing: Theory and Applications," 18 *EnvM* 605 (1994).

E. Wathern, *Environmental Impact Assessment Legislation in the EC* (London: Belhaven Press 1994).

Winter, "Access of the Public to Environmental Data from Satellite Remote Sensing," 6 *JEnvL* 43 (1994).

b. International/Transboundary Contingency Planning/Emergency Assistance

Vera-Morales, "Dumping in the International Backyard: Exportation of Hazardous Wastes to Mexico," 7 *TulaneELJ* 353 (1994).

c. Dispute Avoidance and Settlement (Equal Right of Access, Fact-finding, etc.)

Natural Resources and International Dispute Settlement (London: Foundation for International Environmental Law and Development (FIELD)/ Frere Cholmeley Bischoff 1994).

Kahn, "Resolving Environmental Disputes: Litigation, Mediation and the Courting of Ethical Community," 3 *EnvV* 211 (1994).

4. Liability and Compensation

a. International Liability/Compensation

Kummer, "Providing Incentives to Comply with Multilateral Environmental Agreements: An Alternative to Sanctions?" 3 *EurEnvLR* 256 (1994).

Martin, "La responsabilité civile pour les dommages à l'environnement et la Convention de Lugano," No. 2/3 *RJE* 121 (1994).

Murphy, "Prospective Liability Regimes for the Transboundary Movement of Hazardous Waste," 88 *AJIL* 24 (1994).

Scherer, "Restoration and Prevention of Environmental Damage Through Joint Compensation Systems," 3 *EuELR* 161 (1994).

b. "Civil Liability" and other Forms of Transnational Accountability

Bianchi, "The Harmonization of Laws on Liability for Environmental Damage in Europe: An Italian Perspective," 6 *JEnvL* 21 (1994).

Cabanillas Sánchez, "El daño ambiental," 12 *RevDA* 9 (1994).

Brans, "Liability for Ecological Damage Under the 1992 Protocols to the Civil Liability Convention and the Fund Convention, and the Oil Pollution Act of 1990," 3-4 *TMA* 61, 85 (1994).

Jones, "Remedying Environmental Damage: The European Commission's Green Paper," 1 *TMA* 1 (1994).

Marshall, "Environmental Impairment — Insurance Perspectives," 3 *RECIEL* 153 (1994).

Martin, La responsabilité civile pour les dommages à l'environnement et la Convention de Lugano," 2-3 *RJE* 121 (1994).

McIntyre & Robbins, "Can the EU Afford a Superfund Programme?," 3 *RECIEL* 143 (1994).

M. Müller, *Die internationale Zuständigkeit bei grenzüberschreitenden Umweltbeeinträchtigungen* (Basel: Helbing & Lichtenhahn 1994).

Organisation for Economic Co-Operation and Development, Nuclear Energy Agency, *Liability and Compensation for Nuclear Damage: An International Overview* (OECD: Paris 1994)

Posner, "Environmental Impairment Liability and the Chemical Industry" 3 *RECIEL* 160 (1994).

S. Pritchard, *Managing Environmental Risks and Liabilities* (Cheltenham: Stanley Thornes (Publishers) Ltd. 1994).

Thieffrey, "L'opportunité d'une responsabilité communautaire du pollueur: les distorsions et les enseignements de l'expérience américaine," 46 *RevIDC* 103 (1994).

Wetterstein, "Current Trends in International Civil Liability for Environmental Damage," 1 *Annual Survey of Int'l & Comp. L.* 181 (1994).

5. Protection of the Environment through Criminal Law

"Crimes Against the Environment: General Part. Preparatory Colloquium, Section 1. Ottawa, November 2–6, 1992," 65 *IntRevPenL* 633 (1994).

A. Eser & G. Heine, *Umweltstrafrecht in England, Kanada und den U.S.A.* (Freiburg im Breisgau: Eigenverlag Max-Planck-Institut für ausländisches und internationales Strafrecht 1994).

Hughes, "Sentencing Environmental Offenders: Objectives and Principles," 4 *JEnvLPrac* 185 (1994).

Minister, "Federal Facilities and the Deterrence Failure of Environmental Law: The Case for Criminal Prosecution of Federal Employees," 18 *Harvard ELR* 185 (1994).

6. Environment and Armed Conflict

Adede, "Protection of the Environment in Times of Armed Conflict," 1 *Annual Survey of Int'l & Comp. L.* 161 (1994).

7. International Environmental Law in General

Agenda 21 and Latin America: The Challenge of Implementing Environmental Law and Policy (Washington, D.C.: Inter-American Development Bank 1994).

Timoshenko, "Agenda 21 and the Development of International Environmental Law," 34;

Vergara Larraín, "Agenda 21: Legislation, Economic Instruments, the Rights of Women and of Indigenous Populations," 46;

Handl, "International Environmental Law: Promises and Perils of Agenda 21," 51;

Rummel-Bulska, "The Basel Convention: A Global Approach for the Management of Hazardous Waste," 65;

Mateo, "The Basel Convention on Transboundary Movements of Hazardous Wastes and their Disposal," 77;

Eglin, "International Economics, International Trade, International Environmental Protectionism," 89;

Hazael Mendoza, "The General Agreement on Tariffs and Trade 'GATT' and the Environment Seminar on Environmental

Law," 102;

Futrell, "Public Access and Judicial Review: A Viewpoint from the United States," 290;

Bell, "Exporting Environmental Protection" 23 *ELR* 10701 (1994).

H. Bergesen & G. Parmann (eds), *Green Globe Yearbook of International Cooperation on Environment and Development 1994* (New York: Oxford University Press 1994).

Standford, "International Environmental Treaty Secretariats: Stage-hands or Actors?" 17;

Markussen, "Deep Seabed Mining and the Environment: Consequences, Perceptions and Regulations," 31;

Peet, "International Cooperation to Prevent Oil Spills at Sea: Not Quite the Success it Should Be," 41;

Barden, "Combating the Illegal Timber Trade—Is there a Role for ITTO?" 55;

de Klemm, "The Problem of Migratory Species in

International Law," 67;

Toulmin, "Combating Desertification: Encouraging Local Action within a Global Framework," 79;

Herttrich, "International Cooperation to Promote Nuclear- Reactor Safety in the Former USSR and Eastern Europe," 89;

Khor, "The Commission on Sustainable Development: Paper Tiger or Agency to Save the Earth?" 103;

Bárcena, "An Overview of Follow-up of Agenda 21 at the National Level," 127;

Juma, "Promoting International Transfer of Environmentally Sound Technologies: The Case for National Incentive Schemes," 137;

U. Beyerlin & T. Marauhn, *Abrüstung und Umweltschutz—eine völkerrechtliche Interessenkollision?* (Bochum: UVB Universitätsverlag Dr. N. Brockmeyer 1994).

Boyle, "Environmental Change and International Law: New Challenges and Dimensions," 9 *IJMCL* 118 (1994).

T. Brenton, *The Greening of Machiavelli: The Evolution of International Environmental Politics* (London: The Royal Institute of International Affairs, Energy and the Environment Programme 1994).

Drago, "Droit de l'environnement: L'épreuve de l'alternace," 110 *Revue de Droit Public et de la Science Politique en France et à l'Étranger* 1165 (1994).

Dwivedi, "An Ethical Approach to Environmental Protection: A Code of Conduct and Guiding Principles," 35 *CanPA* 363 (1994).

A. Freeman, *The Measurement of Environmental and Resource Values: Theory and Methods* (Washington, D.C.: Resources for the Future 1994).

B. Gebers & J. Jendroska (eds), *Environmental Control of Products and Substances: Legal Concepts in Europe and the United States* (Frankfurt am Main: Verlag Peter Lang 1994).

T. Gehring, *Dynamic International Regimes: Institutions for International Environmental Governance* (Frankfurt am Main: Verlag Peter Lang 1994)

Hohmann, "Cross-Media Pollution and International Environmental Law," 34 *NRJ* 535 (1994).

Hunter, Sommer & Vaughan, "Concepts and Principles of International Environmental law: An Introduction" 2 *ET* 1 (1994).

A. Kiss & D. Shelton, *International Environmental Law—1994 Supplement* (Irvington: Transnational Publishers 1994).

Kloepfer, "Is There the Threat of an Authoritarian Ecological State?" 3 *EuELR* 112 (1994).

Lerch, "Property Rights und Biologische Vielfalt," 3 *ZUPUR* 289 (1994).

T. O'Riordan & J. Cameron (eds), *Interpreting the Precautionary Principle* (London: Cameron May Ltd. 1994)

K. Pickering & L. Owen, *An Introduction to Global Environmental Issues* (London: Routledge 1994).

M. Prieur & S. Doumbé-Billé, *Droit de l'environnement et développement durable* (Limoges: Presses Universitaires de Limoges (PULIM) 1994).

"Conclusions et propositions de Rio 92 des Juristes de l'Environnement," 19;

Leme Machado, "Les principes généraux de droit international de l'environnement et la politique brésilienne de l'environnement," 33;

Romi, "Les problèmes d'effectivité du droit international: Le rôle des organisations non-gouvernementales en droit de l'environnement," 65;

Real Ferrer, "El principio de solidaridad en la declaración de Río," 77;

Tinker, "The Global Conventions: The Biodiversity Convention," 85;

Bosselmann, "Governing the Global Commons: The Ecocentric Approach to International Environmental Law," 93;

Untermaier, "La convention de Rio sur la conservation et l'utilisation," 103;

Kabala, "Aperçu sur la problèmatique concernant la diversité biologique dite 'biodiversité'," 125;
Winter, "Biotechnology Principles," 143;
Kamto, "La desertification: Aperçu écologique et esquisse pour une convention sur les zones désertiques, arides, semi-arides et sèches subhumides," 149;
Prieur, "Pollutions transfrontières et transferts de déchets radioactifs," 170;
Doumbé-Billé, "L'Agenda 21 et les eaux douces," 196;
Bouraqui, "Les politiques et mécanismes de promotion de la femme travers l'Agenda 21," 211;
Logan, "Basic Countermeasures for the Global Environmental Issues," 217;
Carreño Peralta, "Education ambiental espiritualidad y derecho ambiental," 221;

Rose, "Given-ness and Gift: Property and the Quest for Environmental Ethics," 24 *EnvL* 1 (1994).
Sands, "The 'Greening' of International Law: Emerging Rules and Principles," 1 *Ind. J. Global Leg. Stud.* 293 (1994).
P. Sands (ed), *Greening International Law* (New York: The New Press 1994).
Shearer, "International Environmental Law and Development in Developing Nations: Agenda Setting, Articulation, and Institutional Participation," 7 *TuELJ* 391 (1994).
Stitt, "Plastic Trees and Plastic Houses: The Formulation of Environmental Law and Policy to Address Imitation of Cultural Heritage," 11 *EnvPlanLJ* 155 (1994).
G. Teubner, L. Farmer & D. Murphy, *Environmental Law and Ecological Responsibility: The Concept and Practice of Ecological Self-Organization* (Chichester: John Wiley & Sons Ltd. 1994).

II. AIR AND ATMOSPHERE

1. Transboundary Air Pollution

Betlem, "Cross-Border Pollution: Two Dutch Cases," 1 *EnvLNI* 48 (1994).
Grant, "Transboundary Air Pollution: Can NAFTA and NAAEC Succeed Where International Law Has Failed?" 5 *CoJIELP* 439 (1994).
Holzinger, "A Surprising Success in EC Environmental Policy: The Small Car Exhaust Emission Directive of 1989," *Successful Environmental Policy* 214 (1994).
P. Nieuwenhuis & P. Wells (eds), *Motor Vehicles in the Environment: Principles and Practice* (Chichester: John Wiley & Sons Ltd. 1994).

2. Ozone Layer

Kupferberg, "Fixin' a Hole: Recent Attempts by the European Community to Preserve the Ozone Layer," 17 *BostCICLR* 165 (1994).
Lieberman, "Stratospheric Ozone Depletion and the Montreal Protocol: A Critical Analysis," 2 *BuffELJ* 1 (1994).

3. Global Climate

Aspinall & Matthews, "Climate Change Impact on Distribution and Abundance of Wildlife Species: An Analytical Approach Using GIS," 86 *EnvP* 217 (1994).

Bella, Jacobs & Li, "Ecological Indicators of Global Climate Change: A Research Framework," 18 *EnvM* 489 (1994).

Fish & South, "Industrialized Countries and Greenhouse Gas Emissions," 6 *IEA* 14 (1994).

Loske & Oberthür, "Joint Implementation Under the Climate Change Convention," 6 *IEA* 45 (1994).

J. Pernetta, et al. (eds), *Impacts of Climate Change on Ecosystems and Species: Implications for Protected Areas* (Gland: IUCN 1994).

J. Pernetta, et al. (eds), *Impacts of Climate Change on Ecosystems and Species: Marine and Coastal Ecosystems* (Gland: IUCN 1994).

K. Ramakrishna (ed), *Criteria for Joint Implementation under the Framework Convention on Climate Change—Report of a Workshop* (Woods Hole: The Woods Hole Research Center 1994).

P. Read, *Responding to Global Warming: The Technology, Economics and Politics of Sustainable Energy* (London: Zed Books Ltd. 1994).

III. FRESH WATER

du Bois, "Water Rights and the Limits of Environmental Law," 6 *JEnvL* 73 (1994).

S. Burchi, *Preparing National Regulations for Water Resources Management: Principles and Practice*, FAO Legislative Study No. 52 (Rome: FAO 1994).

Dellapenna, "Treaties as Instruments for Managing Internationally-Shared Water Resources: Restricted Sovereignty vs. Community of Property," 26 *CaseWRJIL* 27 (1994).

1. International Rivers and Lakes

Barston, "The Helsinki Convention (1992): New Approaches," 22 *OCM* 249 (1994).

Williams, "International Environmental Dispute Resolution: The Dispute Between Slovakia and Hungary Concerning Construction of the Gabcikovo and Nagymaros Dams, " 19 *ColumbJEL* 1 (1994).

Wilson, "A Fish Out of Water: A Proposal for International Instream Flow Rights in the Lower Colorado River," 5 *CoJIELP* 249 (1994).

2. Groundwater

Petersen, "Bodenschutz und Property Rights: Grundwasserprobleme durch Landwirtschaft in zwei amerikanischen Bundesstaaten" 2 *ZUPUR* 133 (1994).

IV. OCEANS

1. Regional Seas

Agniel, "L'adoption de la Convention Portant Création du Programme Régional Océanien de l'Environnement: Les limites de l'autonomie du droit régional," 98 *RGDIP* 89 (1994).

Scovazzi, "International Law of the Sea as Applied to the Mediterranean," 24 *OCM* 71 (1994).

Zrajevskij, "UNEP's Future Regional Seas Programme with Special Reference to the Black Sea and the North-West Pacific," *Papers from the Advisory Committee on Protection of the Sea submitted to the Conference on Assessment of Land-based Sources of Marine Pollution in the Seas Adjacent to the Commonwealth of Independent States (CIS)* 131 (London: ACOPS 1994).

2. Marine Pollution

Barston, "International Dimensions of Coastal Zone Management," 23 *OCM* 93 (1994).

Gosseries, "Marine Pollution in the North Sea: The Position in International Law," 3 *EurELR* 53 (1994).

Grose, "Oil Spills, Tourism and the Great Barrier Reef—An Unpalatable Mix: The Role of Regulation and Self-regulation," 1195 *EnvPlanLJ* 395 (1994).

Ijlstra, "The 1993 Copenhagen Intermediate Ministerial Meeting: North Sea Cooperation at a Turning Point?" 9 *IJMCL* 173 (1994).

Littmann-Martin, "L'Article 22 de la Loi du 3 Janvier 1992 et la protection des milieux aquatiques," No. 2/3 *RJE* 137 (1994).

Torrens, "Protection of the Marine Environment in International Law: Toward an Effective Regime of the Law of the Sea," 19 *QLJ* 613 (1994).

a. Land-based Pollution (Rivers/Air)

Teitz, "Assessing Point Source Discharge Permit Trading: Case Study in Controlling Selenium Discharges to the San Francisco Bay Estuary," 21 *ELQ* 79 (1994).

b. Vessel Source and Offshore Platform Pollution

E. Owens, *Canadian Coastal Environments, Shoreline Processes, and Oil Spill Cleanup* (Ottawa: Environment Canada 1994).

"Regime Design Matters: Intentional Oil Pollution and Treaty Compliance," 48 *IO* 425 (1994).

c. Ocean Dumping

Canfield, "Soviet and Russian Nuclear Waste Dumping in the Arctic Marine Environment: Legal, Historical, and Political Implications," 6 *GeoIELR* 353 (1994).

V. ENERGY SYSTEMS

1. Nuclear Energy

a. Power Safety

Gureghian, "Medzamor: Weighing the Reopening of Armenia's Unstable Nuclear Power Plant and the Duties of the International Community," 5 *VillELJ* 163 (1994).

Hague Academy of International Law, Centre for Studies and Research in International Law and Relations, *The Hazards Arising out of the Peaceful Use of Nuclear Energy* (Dordrecht/Boston/London: Martinus Nijhoff Publishers 1994).

Jankowitsch, "The Convention on Nuclear Safety," 54 *NucLBull* 9 (1994).

Schmitz & Foxworth, "Coping with the New Russian Nuclear Threat: A Legal Alternative to Environmental Extortion," 6 *GeoIELR* 445 (1994).

b. Nuclear Waste Management

"Case Law Analysis: A Harpoon for Greenpeace?: Judicial Review of the Regulation of Radioactive Substances," 6 *JEnvL* 351 (1994).

McReynolds, "Visiting Warships in Canadian Harbours and Nuclear Liability," 4 *JEnvLPrac* 271 (1994).

Rabe, Gunderson, Frazer & Gillroy, "Nimby and Maybe: Conflict and Cooperation in the Siting of Low-level Radioactive Waste Disposal Facilities in the United States and Canada," 24 *EnvL* 67 (1994).

2. Other Energy Issues

Redgwell, "Energy, Environment and Trade in the European Community," 12 *JENRL* 128 (1994).

Roggenkamp, "Implications of GATT and EEC on Networkbound Energy Trade in Europe," 12 *JENRL* 59 (1994).

VI. INTERNATIONAL HAZARD MANAGEMENT

1. Transboundary Industrial Risks, Generally

B. le Blansch & D. Pearson, *Industrial Relations and the Environment: Case Studies* (Luxembourg: Office for Official Publications of European Communities 1994).

2. Biotechnology

Nion, "Biotechnology and Environmental Law in Europe" 34 *JJLST* 317 (1994).

S. Soumastre, *Droit et génie génétique: Premier bilan international et européen des réglementations et des nouvelles politques* (Paris: Elsevier 1994).

3. Hazardous Substances and Waste

Biggs, "Latin America and the Basel Convention on Hazardous Wastes," 5 *CoJIELP* 333 (1994).

Rummel-Bulska, "The Basel Convention: A Global Approach for the Management of Hazardous Wastes," 1 *JEnvPLLAC* 1 (1994).

Singh, "Integrating Economic Development and Waste Management in Small Island States," *EcoDecision* No. 11 (1994).

a. International Transfer of Restricted or Prohibited Substances

Kwiatkowska & Soons, "Comment. Plutonium Shipments—A Supplement," 25 *ODIL* 419 (1994).

b. Transboundary Movement of Hazardous Waste

Clapp, "Africa, NGOs, and the International Toxic Waste Trade," 3 *JEnvDev* 17 (1994).

Fluck, "The Term 'Waste' in EU Law," 3 *EuELR* 79 (1994).

Hall, "'Carried by the Wind Out to Sea'—Ireland and the Isle of Man v. Sellafield: Anatomy of a Transboundary Pollution Dispute," 6 *GeoIELR* 639 (1994).

Murphy, "Prospective Liability Regimes for the Transboundary Movement of Hazardous Wastes," 88 *AJIL* 24 (1994).

Sánchez, "International Trade in Hazardous Wastes: A Global Problem with Uneven Consequences for the Third World," 3 *JEnvDev* 137 (1994).

A. Tolentino, *Guidelines for the Development of a National Legal and Institutional Framework to Prevent Illegal Traffic in Toxic and Dangerous Products and Wastes* (New York: United Nations 1994).

Weinstein, "The Impact of Regulation of Transport of Hazardous Waste on Freedom of Navigation," 9 *IJMCL* 135 (1994).

Winter, "Die neue Abfallverbringungs—Verordnung der EG," 5 *UP* 161 (1994).

c. Regulation of Chemicals

VII. INTERNATIONAL COMMON/AREAS BEYOND NATIONAL JURISDICTION

1. High Seas/Seabed and Ocean Floor

P. Bautista Payoyo (ed), *Ocean Governance: Sustainable Development of the Seas* (Tokyo: United Nations University Press 1994).

Hayashi, "Activities Linked to the Entry into Force of the United Nations Convention on the Law of the Sea," 9 *IJMCL* 261 (1994).

Knecht, "Essay: Emerging International Goals and Principles and Their Influence on National Ocean Governance," 22 *CoastMgt* 177 (1994).

Larson, "Customary, and Consensual Law in the United Nations Convention on the Law of the Sea," 25 *ODIL* 75 (1994).

Lester, "Contemporary Federalism and New Regimes of Ocean Governance: Lessons from the Case of Outer Continental Shelf Oil Development," 23 *OCM* 7 (1994).

O'Keefe & Nafziger, "The Draft Convention on the Protection of the Underwater Cultural Heritage," 25 *ODIL* 391 (1994).

Rothwell & Kaye, "Law of the Sea and the Polar Regions: Reconsidering the Traditional Norms," 18 *MP* 41 (1994).

2. Outer Space

3. Antarctica

Andersen, "Leading International Efforts to Improve Environmental Controls in Antarctica While Navigating National Politics," 6 *GeoIELR* 303 (1994).

Angelini & Mansfield, "A Call for US Ratification of the Protocol on Antarctic Environmental Protection," 21 *ELQ* 163 (1994).

Bauer & Diggins, "Tourism in Antarctica, Yes or No?" 22 *HA* 32 (1994).

Orrego Vicuña, "The Protocol on Environmental Protection to the Antarctic Treaty: Questions of Effectiveness," 7 *GeoIELR* 1 (1994).

S. Pannatier, *L'Antarctique et la protection internationale de l'environnement* (Zürich: Schulthess Polygraphischer Verlag 1994).

4. Arctic

Rothwell, "Polar Lessons for an Arctic Regime," 29 *C+C* 55 (1994).

VIII. NATURAL RESOURCE MANAGEMENT AND CONSERVATION

1. Nature Conservation: Natural Lands and Biological Diversity

Anglada Gotor & Mateos Guilarte, "Informe sobre parques nacionales y organización del Estado en la Europa Comunitaria," 133 *RevAP* 529 (1994).

Caillaux, "Between Two Fires: Intellectual Property Rights over Biological Resources and the Convention on Biological Diversity," 1 *JEnvPLLAC* 1 (1994).

Charlez, "Dommages causés par les espèces sauvages et indemnisation," 192 *BMONC* 67 (1994).

The Crucible Group, *People, Plants and Patents: The Impact of Intellectual Property on Biodiversity, Conservation, Trade, and Rural Society* (Ottawa: International Development Research Centre 1994).

T. Davis, (ed), *The Ramsar Convention Manual: A Guide to the Convention on Wetlands of International Importance, Especially as Waterfowl Habitat* (Gland: Ramsar Convention Bureau 1994).

Diaz, "Permanent Sovereignty over Natural Resources," 24 *EnvPL* 157 (1994).

Emmenegger & Tschentscher, "Taking Nature's Rights Seriously: The Long Way to Biocentrism in Environmental Law," 6 *GeoIELR* 545 (1994).

IUCN/WRI/UNEP/ACTS, *Report of the Global Biodiversity Forum* (Gland: IUCN 1994).

A. Krattiger, et al. (eds), *Widening Perspectives on Biodiversity* (Gland: IUCN 1994).

Lees, "Lessons from the Pacific: Linking the Traditional Ownership, Development Needs and Protected Areas," 4 *Parks* 41 (1994).

D. O'Halloran, et al., *Geological and Landscape Conservation: Proceedings of the Malvern International Conference 1993* (London: The Geological Society 1994).

D. Pearce & D. Moran, *The Economic Value of Biodiversity* (London: Earthscan Publications Ltd. 1994).

V. Sánchez & C. Juma (eds), *Biodiplomacy: Genetic Resources and International Relations* (Nairobi: ACTS Press 1994).

- Sánchez, "The Convention on Biological Diversity: Negotiations and Contents," 7;
- Okidi, "International Environmental Law and National Interests," 19;
- Svarstad, "National Sovereignty and Genetic Resources," 45;
- Shiva, "Farmers' Rights and the Convention on Biological Diversity," 107;
- Posey, "International Agreements for Protecting Indigenous Knowledge," 119;
- Achanta & Ghosh, "Technology Transfer and the Environment," 157;
- Illescas, "Intellectual Property Institutions and Technological Cooperation," 195;
- Brown & Moran, "Valuing Biodiversity: The Scope and Limitations of Economic Analysis," 213;

Yusuf, "Technology and Genetic Resources: Is Mutually— Beneficial Access Still Possible?" 233;

Reid, " Biodiversity Prospecting: Strategies for Sharing Benefits," 241;

Friis-Hansen, et al., "Financial Mechanisms and Biotechnology Transfer," 271;

Hendrickx, et al., "Access to Genetic Resources: A Legal Analysis," 139;

Juma et al., "Access to and Transfer of Biotechnology: Blind Alleys and Windows of Opportunity," 139;

Wells, "The Global Environment Facility and Prospects for Biodiversity Conservation," 6 *IEA* 69 (1994).

Wetlands for the Americas, *Conserving Wetlands for a Sustainable Future: Profile 1991–01994* (Manomet: Wetlands for the Americas 1994).

D. Whitmeyer & M. Strauss (eds.), *Building Global Cooperation: Conservation of Plant Genetic Resources and the United Nations Convention on Biological Diversity* (Washington, D.C.: The American Association for the Advancement of Science 1994).

Wils, "The Birds Directive 15 Years Later: A Survey of the Case Law and a Comparison with the Habitats Directive," 6 *JEnvL* 220 (1994).

2. Coastal Zone Management

Ballinger, Smith & Warren, "The Mangement of the Coastal Zone of Europe," 22 *OCM* 45 (1994).

Barston, "International Dimensions of Coastal Zone Management," 23 *OCM* 93 (1994).

Lakhan, "Planning and Development Experiences in the Coastal Zone of Guyana," 22 *OCM* 169 (1994).

3. Trade in Endangered Species

Mofson, "Protecting Wildlife from Trade: Japan's Involvement in the Convention on International Trade in Endangered Species," 3 *JEnvDev* 91 (1994).

4. Fisheries/Marine Mammals

Bergin & Haward "The Last Jewel in a Disintegrating Crown: The Case of Japanese Distant Water Tuna Fisheries," 25 *ODIL* 187 (1994).

W. Burke, *The New International Law of Fisheries: UNCLOS 1982 and Beyond* (Oxford: Oxford University Press 1994).

Burke, Freeberg & Miles, "United Nations Resolutions on Driftnet Fishing: An Unsustainable Precedent for High Seas and Coastal Fisheries Management," 25 *ODIL* 127 (1994).

Davies, "Legality of Norwegian Commercial Whaling under the Whaling Convention and its Compatibility with European Community Law," 43 *ICLQ* 270 (1994).

Fauteux, The Canadian Legal Initiative on High Seas Fishing," 4 *YbIEL* 51 (1993).

Gwilliam & Lugten, "Norway and the European Union: Fishing for Compliments," 24 *EnvPL* 254 (1994).

Hawes, "Norwegian Whaling and Pelly Amendment: A Misguided Attempt at Conservation," 3 *MinnJGT* 97 (1994).

Joseph, "The Tuna-Dolphin Controversy in the Eastern Pacific Ocean: Biological, Economic, and Political Impacts," 25 *ODIL* 1 (1994).

Mclaughlin, "UNCLOS and the Demise of the United States' Use of Trade Sanctions to Protect Dolphins, Sea Turtles, Whales, and Other International Marine Living Resources," 21 *ELQ* 1 (1994).

Shibles, "Implications of an International Legal Standard for Transboundary Management of Gulf of Maine-Georges Bank Fishery Resources," 1 *OCLJ* 1 (1994).

Young, et al., "Subsistence, Sustainability, and Sea Mammals: Reconstructing the International Whaling Regime," 23 *OCM* 117 (1994).

Stein, "Whales Swim for Their Lives as Captain Ahab Returns in a Norwegian Uniform: An Analysis of Norway's Decision to Resume Commercial Whaling," 8 *TICLJ* 155.

UNEP, *The Impact of the Climate on Fisheries* (Nairobi: UNEP 1994).

5. Forests

C. Barber, N. Johnson & E. Hafild, *Breaking the Logjam: Obstacles to Forest Policy Reform in Indonesia and the United States* (Washington, D.C.: World Resources Institute 1994).

Breton, Les aspects juridiques de la gestion des ressources naturelles et de la conservation des zones protégées en milieu forestier tropical (l'exemple du Congo)," 1 *RJE* 37 (1994).

Castilleja, "Changing Trends in Forest Policy in Latin America: Chile, Nicaragua and Mexico," 44 *Unasylva* 29 (1994).

Hadley, "Forests Biodiversity. Diversity and the Management of Tropical Forests," *EcoDecision* No. 13 (1994).

Lagarde, "Réflexions sur l'élaboration des codes forestiers," 3 *Revff* 275 (1994).

Schally, "Forests: Toward An International Legal Regime?" 4 *YbIEL* 30 (1993).

6. Soil

Guttieres, Sikabonyi & Hellenbrand, "Contaminated Land. A Comparative Study of Italy and Luxembourg," 3 *EuELR* 103 (1994).

H. Lee, "Planung und Bodenschutz in der Republik Korea im Vergleich zu Deutschland und anderen europäischen Staaten," 3 *ZUPUR* 383 (1994).

Scannell & Thylstrup, "Contaminated Land: A Comparative Survey of Ireland and Denmark," 3 *EuELR* 15 (1994).

Untermaier, "Les carrières, l'environnement et la Loi du 4 Janvier 1993," 1 *RJE* 5 (1994).

7. Population

R. Hardaway, *Population, Law, and the Environment* (Westport: Praeger 1994).

S. Johnson, *World Population—Turning the Tide: Three Decades of Progress* (London, New York: Graham & Trotman/Martinus Nijhoff 1994).

Ketover, "Fouling Our Own Nest: Rapid Population Growth and Its Effect on the Environment," 7 *TuELJ* 431 (1994).

IX. INTERNATIONAL ECONOMY AND THE ENVIRONMENT

1. International Trade Rules, World Market Conditions and Environmental Effects

Abbott, "The NAFTA Environmental Dispute Settelement System as a Prototype for Regional Economic Integration Arrangements," 4 *YbIEL* 3 (1993).

Aldaraca, "The North American Agreement on Environmental Co-operation," 3 *RECIEL* 98 (1994).

Carlson, "The Montreal Protocol's Environmental Subsidies and GATT: A Needed Reconciliation," 29 *TexasILJ* 211 (1994).

Charnovitz, "Environmental Trade Sanctions and the GATT: An Analysis of the Pelly Amendment on Foreign Environmental Practices," 9 *AmUJILP* 751 (1994).

Charnovitz, "Green Roots, Bad Pruning: GATT Rules and their Application to Environmental Trade Measures," 7 *TulaneELJ* 299 (1994).

Chase, "Tropical Forests and Trade Policy: The Legality of Unilateral Attempts to Promote Sustainable Development under the GATT," 17 *HastICLR* 349 (1994).

C. Dawkins, *Balancing: Policies for Just and Sustainable Trade* (Minneapolis: Institute for Agriculture and Trade Policy 1994).

Duerkop, "Trade and Environment: International Trade Law Aspects of Proposed EC Directive Introducing a Tax on Carbon Dioxyde Emissions and Energy," 31 *CMLRev* 807 (1994).

D. Esty, *Greening the GATT: Trade, Environment and the Future* (Washington, D.C.: Institute for International Economics 1994).

S. Fletcher & M. Tiemann, *Trade and Environment: GATT and NAFTA* (Washington, D.C.: Congressional Research Service—The Library of Congress 1994).

Jeffrey, "The Environmental Implications of NAFTA: A Canadian Perspective," 26 *UL* 31 (1994).

Jeffery, "The Legal Framework for Environmental Regulation Under the North American Free Trade Agreement," 11 *EnvPlanLJ* 382 (1994).

Kennedy, "Reforming US Trade Policy to Protect the Global Environment: A Multilateral Approach," 18 *Harvard ELR* 185 (1994).

International Institute for Sustainable Development (IISD), *Trade and Sustainable Development Principles* (Winnipeg: IISD 1994).

Kublicki, "The Greening of Free Trade: NAFTA, Mexican Environmental Law and Debt Exchanges for Mexican Environmental Infrastructure Development," 19 *ColumbJEL* 59 (1994).

Lesser, "Institutional Mechanisms Supporting Trade in Genetic Materials: Issues under the Biodiversity Convention and GATT / TRIPs," 4 *ET* (1994).

Love, "International Trade Agreements and Domestic Environmental Policy: The NAFTA Example," 19 *NCJILCR* 353 (1994).

Lucas, "Natural Resources Trade Under NAFTA: the Interface with International Environmental Treaties," 12 *JENRL* 175 (1994).

McConnell, "North American Free Trade Agreement: Trading Natural Resource Goods and Protecting the Environment," 12 *JENRL* 151 (1994).

McLaughlin, "Free Trade, GATT, and Ocean Governance" 23 *OCM* 65 (1994).

Menotti, "Trade Measures as Part of the Solution: How Compensatory Tariffs Can Help Save Endangered Sea Turtles," 3 *JEnvDev* 97 (1994).

von Moltke, "The World Trade Organization: Its Implications for Sustainable Development," 3 *JEnvDev* 43 (1994).

Muñoz, "The 'Green" vs Trade Debate in the Americas," 3 *JEnvDev* 110 (1994).

O'Connell, "Using Trade to Enforce International Environmental Law: Implications for the United States," 1 *Ind. J. Global Leg. Stud.* 273 (1994).

Organisation for Economic Co-operation and Development, *The Environmental Effects of Trade* (Paris: OECD Publications 1994).

Organ & Williams, "NAFTA and the Environment; the "Greening" of Mexico," 4 *DukeEL&P* 62 (1994).

Pathak, "International Trade and Environmental Development: A View from India," 1 *Ind. J. Global Leg. Stud.* 325 (1994).

Repetoo, "Trade and Sustainable Development" 1 *ET* 1 (1994).

Saunders, "GATT, NAFTA and North American Energy Trade: A Canadian Perspective" 12 *JENRL* 4 (1994).

Saunders, "NAFTA and the North American Agreement on Environmental Cooperation: A New Model for International Collaboration on Trade and the Environment," 5 *CoJIELP* 273 (1994).

N. Shaw & A. Cosbey, *GATT , the WTO and Sustainable Development: Positioning the Work Program on Trade and Environment* (Winnipeg: International Institute for Sustainable Development (IISD) 1994).

Shaw & Cosbey, "GATT, the World Trade Organization, and Sustainable Development," 6 *IEA* 245 (1994).

Smith & Cluchey "GATT, NAFTA and North American Energy Trade: A US Perspective" 12 *JENRL* 27 (1994).

Sucharipa-Behrmann, "Austrian Legislative Efforts to Regulate Trade in Tropical Timber and Tropical Timber Products," 46 *AJPIL* 283 (1994).

Van Pelt, "Countervailing Environmental Subsidies: A Solution to the Environmental Inequities of the North American Free Trade Agreement," 29 *TexILJ* 123.

Ward, "Trade and Environment in the Round—and After," 6 *JEnvL* 263 (1994).

W. Watson, *Environmental and Labor Standards in the NAFTA* (Toronto: C. D. Howe Institute 1994).

Winham, "Enforcement of Environmental Measures: Negotiating the NAFTA Environmental Side Agreement," 3 *JEnvDev* 29 (1994).

Williams, "Environmental Law and Democratic Legitimacy" 4 *DukeEL&P* 1 (1994).

Wilson, "Ecodumping: A Compromise to the Conflict of International Free Trade and Environmental Responsibility," 42 *Kansas L. Rev.* 709 (1994).

Wirth, "International Trade and the Environment," *Environmental Law* (Co-sponsored by the Environmental Law Institute and The Smithsonian Institution), February 17, 1994.

Wynne, "The Impact of NAFTA on the U.S./Mexico Border Environment," 26 *UL* 11 (1994).

2. Multilateral Lending Activities/Development Assistance and Sustainable Development

Fox-Przeworski, "Development Co-operation and the Environment: The Role of the OECD Development Assistance Committee," 3 *RECIEL* 111 (1994).

Johnston, "Debt Conversion and Environmental Protection," 3 *RECIEL* 88 (1994).

Kublicki, "Green Finance: Problems and Solutions Concerning Alternative Environmental Debt Exchanges," 18 *Vermont L. Rev.* 313 (1994).

Jordan & Werksman, "Additional Funds, Incremental Costs and the Global Environment," 3 *RECIEL* 81 (1994).

Di Leva, "The World Bank and Environmental Law: A Post-Rio Summary of Activities," *Environmental Law* (Co-sponsored by the Environmental Law Institute and The Smithsonian Institution), February 17, 1994.

K. Ramakrishna (ed), *The Financial Mechanism of the Framework Convention on Climate Change: Operational Issues* (Woods Hole: The Woods Hole Research Center 1994).

B. Rich, *Mortgaging the Earth: The World Bank, Environmental Impoverishment, and the Crisis of Development* (Boston: Beacon Press 1994).

Robins, "European Community Funding for the Environment in Developing Countries," 3 *RECIEL* 127 (1994).

P. Sand, *Trusts for the Earth: New Financial Mechanisms for International Environmental Protection* (Hull: The University of Hull Press 1994).

Sarkar, "Debt Relief for Environment: Experience and Issues," 3 *JEnvDev* 123 (1994).

Tucker, "A Proposed Debt-for-Nature Swap in Madagascar and the Larger Problem of LDC Debt," 6 *IEA* 59 (1994).

Webb, "Debt for Nature Swaps: The Past, the Present and Some Possibilities for the Future," 11 *EnvPlanLJ* 222 (1994).

Wee, "Debt-for-Nature Swaps, A Reassessment of their Significance in International Environmental Law," 6 *JEnvL* 57 (1994).

Wilkinson, "Using the European Union's Structural and Cohesion Funds for the Protection of the Environment," 3 *RECIEL* 119 (1994).

3. International Business Activities and Changing Global Environmental Legal Framework

Fandell, "Foreign Investment, Logging, and Environmentalism in Developing Countries: Implications of Stone Container Corporations's Experience in Honduras," 35 *Harvard ILJ* 499
(1994).

Fees & Hohmann, "Aktuelle Tendenzen im Umweltrecht und ihre Auswirkungen auf Unternehmen," in H. Kreikebaum, E. Seidel & H. Zabel (eds), *Unternehmenserfolg durch Umweltschutz. Rahmenbedingungen, Instrumente, Praxisbeispiele* 83 (Wiesbaden: Gabler 1994)

Hadlock, "Multinational Corporations and the Transfer of Environmental Technology to Developing Countries," 6 *IEA* 149 (1994).

Organisation of Economic Co-Operation and Development, *Environment and Taxation: The Cases of the Netherlands, Sweden and the United States* (Paris: OECD 1994).

Tuohy, "Neglect of Market Incentives in Local Environmental Planning: A Case Study in the National Estuary Program," 22 *CoastMgt* 81 (1994).

L. Urbani & C. Rubin, *Transnational Environmental Law and its Impact on Corporate Behavior* (Irvington: Transnational Juris 1994).

X. COUNTRY/REGION REPORTS

1. USA

Austing, "The National Oceanic and Atmospheric Administration's Proposed Rules for Natural Resource Damage Assessment under the Oil Pollution Act," 18 *Harvard ELR* 549 (1994).

Ayorinde, "Inconsistencies Between OPA '90 and MARPOL 73/78: What is the Effect on Legal Rights and Obligations of the United States and Other Parties to MARPOL 73/78?" 25 *JMLC* 55 (1994).

Barr, Mosk, Williams & Farber, "Culpability, Restitution, and the Environment: The Vitality of Common Law Rules," 21 *ELQ* 549 (1994).

Bloch, "Preserving Biological Diversity in the United States: The Case for Moving to an Ecosystems Approach to Protect the Nation's Biological Wealth," 10 *PaceELR* 175 (1994).

Blumm, "Public Choice Theory and the Public Lands: Why `Multiple Use' Failed," 18 *Harvard ELR* 405 (1994).

Blumm, "The Clinton Wetlands Plan: No Net Gain in Wetlands Protection," 9 *JLandUEL* 203 (1994).

Bondareff, "Congress, Reform, and Oceans Policy," 22 *CoastMgt* 147 (1994).

Brauchler, "United States Environmental Policy and the United States Army in Western Europe," 5 *CoJIELP* 479 (1994).

Crolikowski, "A Sovereign in a Sovereignless Land? The Extraterritorial Application of United States Law," 19 *NCJILCR* 333 (1994).

DeVeau, "The Taking of Threatened Species under the Endangered Species Act: Fund for Animals v. Turner," 30 *ILR* 109 (1994).

Feld, H, "Saving the Citizen Suit: The Effect of Lujan v. Defenders of Wildlife and the Role of Citizen Suits in Environmental Enforcement," 19 *ColumbJEL* 141 (1994).

Feldman, "The Supreme Court's New Sovereign Immunity Doctrine and the McCarran Amendment: Toward Ending State Adjudication of Indian Water Rights," 18 *Harvard ELR* 433 (1994).

Fink, "The National Wildlife Refuges: Theory, Practice and Prospect," 18 *Harvard ELR* 1 (1994).

Gibbons, "NAFTA vs. The Environment: The Court's Mandate to Require the Preparation of Environmental Impact Statements for Trade Agreements," 15 *HamJPLP* 101.

Goldfarb, "Watershed Management: Slogan or Solution?" 21 *BostCEALR* 483 (1994).

Hardt, "Federal Land Management in the Twenty-First Century: From Wise Use to Wise Stewardship," 18 *Harvard ELR* 345 (1994).

Klavens, "At the Edge of Environmental Adjudication: An Administrative Takings Variance," 18 *Harvard ELR* 277 (1994).

G. McGregor, *Environmental Law and Enforcement* (Boca Raton: Lewis Publishers, Inc. 1994).

Meese, Rothman, Ellickson, Turley & Stewart, "Liberty, Property, and Environmental Ethics," 21 *ELQ* 387 (1994).

Mostlow, "Reassessing the Scope of Federal Biotechnology Oversight," 10 *PaceELR* 227 (1994).

Needleman, "Hazardous Waste Recycling under the Resource Conservation and Recovery Act: Problems and Potential Solutions," 24 *EnvL* 971 (1994).

Ragsdale, "The Buffalo River: A Jurisprudence of Preservation," 21 *BostCEALR* 429 (1994).

Randolph, Doniger, Chayes, Merrill & Stone, "International Law, Global Environmentalism, and the Future of American Environmental Policy," 21 *ELQ* 475 (1994).

Smith, Gray, Lazarus, Huber & Sunstein, "Public versus Private Environmental Regulation," 21 *ELQ* 431 (1994).

Steiger, "The Consultation Provision of Section 7(a)(2) of the Endangered Species Act and its Application to Delegable Federal Programs," 21 *ELQ* 243 (1994).

2. Canada

Kwasniak, "Private Conservancy: The Path to Law Reform," *Proceedings and Additional Material from: Environmental Law Centre's Private Conservancy Conference* (Edmonton: Environmental Law Centre 1994).

3. Caribbean

4. Mexico

5. Central America

Arellano, "Regimen jurídico de la protección ambiental," *Revista de la Universidad de Mariano Gálvez de Guatemala* 42 (1994).

6. South America

Batmanian, "The Pilot Program to Conserve the Brazilian Rainforests," 6 *IEA* 3 (1994).

M. Cousillas, *Evaluación del impacto ambiental: Analisis de la ley 16/466 de 19 de enero de 1994* (Montevideo: Instituto de Estudios Empresariales de Montevideo 1994).

Friedman, Nield & Weed, "Community Involvement in the Protection of a Threatened Latin American Ecosystem: The Antisana Ecological Reserve," 3 *JEnvDev* 153 (1994).

F. del Giudice, *Guía ambiental de la Argentina* (Buenos Aires: Editorial Espacio 1994).

Moran, "The Law, Politics, and Economics of Amazonian Deforestation," 1 *Ind. J. Global Leg. Stud.* 397 (1994).

Piccirillo, "The Metamorphosis: Expected Changes in the Brazilian Debt-for-Nature Swap Process and Policy Implications," 17 *FordhamILR* 547 (1994).

Weed & Karren, "Environmental Politics in Latin America: Moving the Policy Agenda Forward?" 3 *JEnvDev* 163 (1994).

7. Nordic Countries/Baltic States

K. Cornils & G. Heine, *Umweltstrafrecht in den Nordischen Ländern* (Freiburg im Breisgau: Eigenverlag Max-Planck-Institut für ausländisches und internationales Strafrecht 1994).

Henry, "Comment l'adhésion des pays nordiques à l'Europe va changer votre environnement," 1531 *EM* 74 (1994).

Hjorth, "Baltic Sea Environmental Cooperation: The Role of Epimistic Communities and the Politics of Regime Change," 29 *C+C* 11 (1994).

Riggs, "Fisheries and Coastal Management in the Republic of Estonia," 22 *CoastMgt* 25 (1994).

8. Western Europe

Alberti, "Regional Integration and Environmental Policy in Europe: The Need for a Pan-European Approach," 14 *EnvIAR* 137 (1994).

Ballard & Keating, "Is There an Ocean of Difference?: A Comparison of the European Community's and United States' Environmental Regulations Protecting Air and Water Quality," 5 *VillELJ* 115 (1994).

Ballinger, Smith & Warren, "The Management of the Coastal Zone of Europe," 22 *OCM* 45 (1994).

Barthod & Touzet, "De Strasbourg à Helsinki: les deux premières Conférences Ministérielles pour la Protection des Forêts en Europe," 46 *RevFF* 319 (1994).

Beuttler, "Marine Nature Reserves in France: Legal Framework, Management, and Comparative Notes of the US Marine Sanctuary Program," 22 *CoastMgt* 1 (1994).

Caravita, "Potenzialità e limiti della recente Legge Sulle Aree Protette," 9 *RG Ambiemte* 1 (1994).

Devos, et al., "Les forêts privées en Europe: Cadre juridique et financier," 98 *FE* 9 (1994).

A. Gregory, *Conservation Law in the Countryside* (Croydon: Tolley Publishing Co. Ltd. 1994).

Hochreiter, "The Austrian Packaging Ordinance and Packaging Waste Recycling Target Ordinance," 1 *EnvLNI* 40 (1994).

M. Holden, *The Common Fisheries Policy: Origin, Evaluation and Future* (Oxford: Fishing News Books/Blackwell Scientific Publications Ltd. 1994).

Huglo, "L'application par les Etats Membres des normes communautaires en matière d'environnement," 3 *RevTDE* 451 (1994).

Lagarde, "L'évolution de la législation forestière en 1992: 4e partie," 4 *RevFF* 387 (1994).

London, Llamas, "Packing Laws in France and Germany," 6 *JEnvL* 1 (1994).

Nielsen, "Participation in Fishery Management Policy Making: National and EC Regulation of Danish Fishermen," 18 *MP* 28 (1994).

J. Salter, *European Environmental Law* (London, New York: Graham & Trotman/Martinus Nijhoff, 1994).

Simoncini, "Italy: Protected areas and the 'Caracas Action Plan'," 24 *EnvPL* 95 (1994).

Skaerseth, "The Climate Policy of the EC: Too Hot to Handle," 32 *JCMS* 25 (1994).

S. Tromans & R. Turrall-Clarke, *Contaminated Land* (London: Sweet & Maxwell, 1994).

9. East Central Europe

Andrews, Paroha, Vozab & Sauer, "Decentralized Environmental Management in the Formerly Communist States: A Case Study of Decin, Czech Republic," 14 *EnvIAR* 111 (1994).

Baumgartl, "'Only' a Guideline: The Environmental Action Program for Central and Eastern Europe," 14 *EnvIAR* 147 (1994).

Branis, "A System of Certified Environmental Impact Assessment Experts in the Czech Republic," 14 *EnvIAR* 203 (1994).

Branis & Kruzikova, "The Environmental Impact Assessment Act in the Czech Republic: Origins, Introduction, and Implementation Issues," 14 *EnvIAR* 195 (1994).

Cummings, "Environmental Protection and Privatization: The Allocation of Environmental Responsibility and Liability in Sale Transactions of State-Owned Companies in Poland," 17 *HastICLR* 551 (1994).

G. Goldenman, et al., *Environmental Liability and Privatization in Central and Eastern Europe* (London/Dordrecht/Boston: Graham & Trotman/Martinus Nijhoff 1994).

Jendroska & Sommer, "Environmental Impact Assessment in Polish Law: The Concept, Development, and Perspectives," 14 *EnvIAR* 169 (1994).

Kerekes & Bulla, "Environmental Management in Hungary," 14 *EnvIAR* 95 (1994).

Panayotou & Bluffstone, "Lemons and Liabilities: Privatization, Foreign Investment, and Environmental Liability in Central and Eastern Europe," 14 *EnvIAR* 157 (1994).

Vavrousek, "Environmental Management in Czechoslovakia and Succession States," 14 *EnvIAR* 103 (1994).

10. Commonwealth of Independent States

Brinchuk, Klovach, Sidorov, "Industrial Safety: The Statutory Framework in Russia," 1 *EnvILN* 42 (1994).

Kibel, "Russia's Wild East: Ecological Deterioration and the Rule of Law in Siberia," 7 *GeoIELR* 59 (1994).

Kiselev & Koroleva, "Liability for Damage from Marine Pollution: A Review of Legislation in Former Soviet Union and Legislation in the Russian Federation," *Papers from the Advisory Committee on Protection of the Sea Submitted to the Conference on Assessment of Land-Based Sources of Marine Pollution in the Seas Adjacent to the Commonwealth of Independent States (CIS)* 55 (1994).

Malone, "Discussion in the Security Council on Environmental Intervention in Ukraine," 27 *LoyLALR* 893 (1994).

Moynagh, "The Legacy of Chernobyl: Its Significance for the Ukraine and the World," 21 *BostCEALR* 709 (1994).

Rosen, "Balancing Economics and Ecology: Financing Mechanisms for the Cleanup of Ukraine," 18 *Harvard ELR* 235 (1994).

Woods, "International Environmental Aid to the States of the Former Soviet Union: A Case Study Focusing on Siberia's Lake Baikal," 5 *CoJIELP* 459 (1994).

11. Southeast Europe

12. Near East

S. Gabbay, *The Environment in Israel* (Jerusalem: Ministry of the Environment 1994).

13. Gulf States, Saudi Arabia, Yemen and Oman

14. Iraq, Iran and Afghanistan

15. South and Central Asia

V. Desai, *Forest Management in India: Issues and Problems* (New Delhi: Academic and Law Serials 1994).

Dias, "Judicial Activism in the Development and Enforcement of Environmental Law: Some Comparative Insights from the Indian Experience," 6 *JEnvL* 243 (1994).

V. Mishra, *Environmental Disasters and the Law* (Ashish Publishing House 1994).

R. Repetto, *The 'Second India' Revisited: Population, Poverty, and Environmental Stress over Two Decades* (Washington, D.C.: World Resources Institute 1994).

P. Trivedi, P. Sharma & K. Sudarshan, *Natural Environment and Constitution of India* (New Delhi: Ashish Publishing House 1994).

16. Southeast Asia/ASEAN Countries

Allen, "The Philippine Children' Case: Recognizing Legal Standing for Future Generations," 6 *GeoIELR* 713 (1994).

Hardaway & Dacres, "Tropical Forest Conservation Legislation and Policy: Focus on South-East Asia," 11 *EnvPlanLJ* 419 (1994).

Kessler, "Asian Rainforests: Death on the Installment Plan," 9 *SwRevWA* 29 (1994).

Ross, "Environmental Impact Assessment in the Philippines: Progress, Problems, and Directions for the Future," 14 *EnvIAR* 217 (1994).

Toh, Wong, & Lu, "Energy and Environmental Protection for Sustainable Development in Singapore: Regional Report—Singapore," 3 *JEnvDev* 123 (1994).

Tongeumpou & Harvey, "Implications of Recent EIA Changes in Thailand," 14 *EnvIAR* 271 (1994).

Valencia & van Dyke, "Vietnam's National Interests and the Law of the Sea," 25 *ODIL* 187 (1994).

17. Northeast Asia

Cole, "The Right to Demand: Citizen Activism and Environmental Politics in Japan," 3 *JEnvDev* 77 (1994).

18. China and Hong Kong

Bloch, "Conservation in a Concrete Jungle: Political, Legal and Societal Obstacles to Environmental Protection in Hong Kong," 6 *GeoIELR* 593 (1994).

Lo & Tang "Institutional Contexts of Environmental Management: Water Pollution Control in Guangzhou, China," 14 *PAdminDev* 53 (1994).

Roos-Collins, "Status of Tibet and China's International Responsibilities in Managing Tibet's Environment: Using Law and Politics to Protect Tibet's Environment—Part II," 4 *Tibet Brief* 10 (1994).

Roth, "China's Environomic Challenge: Regional Report—China," 3 *JEnvDev* 139 (1994).

Tang, "Maritime Jurisdiction of the People's Republic of China: Legal Framework, Recent Developments, and Future Prospects," 25 *JMLC* 251 (1994).

19. North Africa

20. Sub-Saharan Africa

Abate & Akhtar, "Information and Knowledge Inputs: Combatting Desertification in Africa and Transboundary Air Pollution," 24 *EnvPL* 71 (1994).

Asava, "Local Fishing Communities and Marine National Parks and Protected Areas in Kenya," 4 *Parks* 26 (1994).

Behnke, "Natural Resource Management in Pastoral Africa," 12 *DevPR* 5 (1994).

Eleri, "Africa's Decline and Greenhouse Policies," 6 *IEA* 133 (1994).

K. Makombe (ed), *Sharing the Land. Wildlife, People and Development in Africa* (Gland: IUCN 1994).

Mwenda, "Land Claims and Mineral Rights in Namaqualand: A Comparative Legal Study," 9 *P.L.* 81 (1994).

Nickerson, "The Environmental Laws of Zimbabwe: A Unique Approach to Management of the Environment," 14 *BostCTWLJ* 189 (1994).

United Nations Sudano—Sahelian Office (UNSO), *Poverty Alleviation and Land Degradation in the Drylands: Issues and Action Areas for the International Convention on Desertification* (New York: UNSO 1994).

21. Australia and New Zealand

Brunton, "Water Pollution Law in New South Wales and Victoria: Current Status and Future Trends," 11 *EnvPlanLJ* 39 (1994).

Buckley, "Cumulative Environmental Impacts: Problems, Policy and Planning Law," 11 *EnvPlanLJ* 344 (1994).

Cox, "Environmental Protection Policies in Western Australia: Establishing Statutory Environmental Objectives for Land Managers," 11 *EnvPlanLJ* 307 (1994).

Dixon, "Protection of Endangered Species: How Will Australia Cope?" 11 *EnvPlanLJ* 6 (1994).

Gardner, "Federal Intergovernmental Cooperation on Environmental Management: A Comparison of Developments in Australia and Canada," 11 *EnvPlanLJ* 104 (1994).

Meyers, "Divining Common Law Standards for Environmental Protection: Application of the Public Trust Doctrine in the Context of Reforming NEPA and the Commonwealth Environmental Protection Act," 11 *EnvPlanLJ* 289 (1994).

Murchison, "Environmental Law in Australia and the United States: A Comparative Overview, Parts 1–2," 11 *EnvPlanLJ* 179 (1994).

Phillipson, "Implementing Sustainable Development in New Zealand: The Resource Management Act of 1991," 4 *JEnvLPrac* 222 (1994).

Suter, "Shark Bay, Western Australia: A Case Study of a UNESCO, World Heritage Listing," 11 *EnvPlanLJ* 31 (1994).

Weir, "Putting the Environment into the Queensland Local Government (Planning and Environment) Act," 11 *EnvPlanLJ* 409 (1994).

22. Oceania

XI. INTERNATIONAL COURTS AND TRIBUNALS

Rosenblum, et al., "ITO: Economic Trends of an International Court of Justice Contrasting the Proposed ITO Arbitration Mechanisms with the Bilateral GATT Negotiations and Related Issues," 14 *NIULR* 471 (1994).

Schemmel & De Regt, "The European Court of Justice and the Environmental Protection Policy of the European Community," 17 *BostCICLR* 53 (1994).

XII. ORGANIZATIONS

1. International Organizations and Bodies

I. Bowles & G. Prickett, *Reframing the Green Window: An Analysis of the GEF Pilot Phase—Approach to Biodiversity and Global Warming and Recommendations for the Operational Phase* (Washington, D.C.: Conservation International and Natural Resources Defense Council 1994).

Dwyer, "EC Directive 91/173 Pertaining to Dangerous Substances: When May a Member State Impose Environmental Restrictions which are Stricter than Those Mandated by the European Community?," 17 *BostCICLR* 127 (1994).

Mertens, "Toward Accountability in the Restructured Global Environment Facility," 3 *RECIEL* 105 (1994).

I. Shihata, *The World Bank Inspection Panel* (New York: Oxford University Press 1994).

2. Non-Governmental Organizations (NGOs) and Other Non-State Actors

Peet, "The Role of (Environmental) Non-Governmental Organizations at the Marine Environment Protection Committee (MEPC) of the International Maritime Organization (IMO), and the London Dumping Convention (LDC)," 22 *OCM* 1 (1994).

PART 4
DOCUMENTS

Detailed Table of Documents

AGREEMENT BETWEEN THE GOVERNMENT OF THE UNITED STATES OF AMERICA AND THE GOVERNMENT OF THE RUSSIAN FEDERATION ON COOPERATION IN THE PREVENTION OF POLLUTION OF THE ENVIRONMENT IN THE ARCTIC

The Government of the United States of America and the Government of the Russian Federation (hereinafter referred to as the Parties),

Recognizing the sensitivity of the Arctic environment and our mutual commitment to protect the Arctic environment and to promote the social and economic interests of local, especially indigenous populations, including their traditional way of life;

Concerned over the potential threats posed by contaminants in the Arctic region to the health of the indigenous and local populations of the region as well as to its flora and fauna;

Convinced that cooperation and sharing of experience between the parties will contribute to understanding and effective response to any such threat both on a national basis and within broader international efforts to protect the Arctic environment;

Desiring to build upon the results of the American-Russian Summit held in Vancouver, April 3–4, 1993;

Noting the particular importance of relevant provisions of Part XII of the United Nations Convention on the Law of the Sea of 1982; the provisions of the Convention on the Prevention of Marine Pollution by Dumping of Wastes and Other Matter of 1972; and the provisions of the Arctic Environmental Protection Strategy of 1991;

Have agreed as follows:

Article 1

The Parties shall cooperate in the prevention, reduction and control of pollution in the Arctic marine and terrestrial environment resulting from the accidental or intentional introduction of contaminants into that environment.

To this end the Parties shall cooperate in research, monitoring, assessment and other activities, bilaterally and in the appropriate multilateral fora.

Article 2

1. The Parties shall cooperate in the conduct of scientific research, monitoring, and assessment activities to determine the potential impacts of contaminants in the Arctic environment, including, inter alia:

1) the pathways by which such contaminants reach and are dispersed within the Arctic environment;

2) the effects of such contaminants, including rates of bio-accumulation, upon Arctic flora and fauna, including fish populations; and

3) the effects of such contaminants upon human health in the Arctic environment, especially upon local and indigenous populations.

2. The Parties further shall cooperate in the monitoring and assessment of levels of hazardous contamination in the Arctic environment, including, inter alia:

1) exchange of data and information on the effects of disposal and release of such contaminants introduced directly or indirectly into the Arctic environment;

2) determination of the level, chemical composition, and patters of such contamination caused by releases from sites at which materials have been stored, processed or disposed; and

3) determination of the amount, concentrations and dynamics of transport of such contaminants introduced into the marine zone, including through rivers and other watercourses, natural or artificial, and via ice transport and ice rafted sediment.

3. The Parties shall consult with regard to technical solutions for the elimination of radioactive and other types of contamination impacts.

4. The Parties shall cooperate in the conduct of joint scientific research to predict ecological impacts of the existing disposals of radioactive waste and consult with regard to technical solutions for the elimination of disposals in places where ecological safety is not insured.

5. Cooperation between the Parties in scientific research and monitoring referred to in this Article shall take place bilaterally, and within the appropriate international, including regional, mechanisms, in particular the Arctic Monitoring and Assessment Program of the Arctic Environmental Protection Strategy of 1991 and the International Arctic Seas Assessment Program of 1993 the International Atomic Energy Agency. [sic]

Article 3

1. Each Party shall facilitate joint activities under Article 2 in areas that are under its jurisdiction in accordance with international law and that are or are believed to be contaminated, under such reasonable conditions as it may establish.

2. The Parties shall ensure that the data and information resulting from such research and monitoring are exchanged and made freely available on a reciprocal basis.

Article 4

The Parties shall promote the development of specific measures to give effect to this Agreement, including:

1) programs for the exchange of scientists, students and experts;

2) organization of seminars and meetings of experts;

3) organization of joint research activities, including marine scientific research cruises;

4) development of Geographic Information Systems, data bases and inventories on Arctic environmental data;

5) cooperation in emergency preparedness exercises and prompt exchange of information concerning major accidental releases of contaminants into the Arctic environment; and

6) exchange of information on technologies and assessment methodologies applicable within the framework of this Agreement and on relevant environmental protection legislation and regulations.

Article 5

Activities under this Agreement, including specific projects and programs, shall be carried out by responsible agencies of each Party in accordance with the Agreement Between the Government of the Union of Soviet Socialist Republics and the Government of the United States on Cooperation in Ocean Studies of 1990 and the Agreement between the Government of the United States and the Government of the Russian Federation on Cooperation in the Field of Protection of the Environment and National Resources of 1994 and under the overall coordination of the United States-Russian Commission on Economic and Technological Cooperation or under any other coordinating body as may be agreed by the Parties.

Article 6

1. All activities undertaken pursuant to this Agreement shall be conducted in accordance with the applicable laws, regulations, and procedures in both countries and shall be subject to the availability of funds and personnel.

2. Scientific and technological information resulting from cooperation under this Agreement, other than information which is not disclosed for national security, commercial or industrial reasons, shall be made freely available, unless otherwise agreed.

3. Issues of intellectual property created or furnished in the course of joint activities under this Agreement shall be governed by Annex II of the Agreement between the Government of the United States of America and the Government of the Russian Federation on Science and Technology Cooperation, signed at Moscow December 16, 1993.

Article 7

The Parties shall resolve by consultation any differences as to the interpretation or application of this Agreement.

Article 8

1. This Agreement shall enter into force upon signature and remain in force for a period of five years, and may be extended for additional five year periods upon written agreement of the Parties.

2. Either Party may terminate this Agreement by so notifying the other Party in writing. Such termination shall be effective six months from such written notification.

IN WITNESS WHEREOF, the undersigned, being duly authorized by their respective Governments, have signed this Agreement.

DONE at Moscow, in duplicate, this sixteenth day of December 1994, in the English and Russian languages, each text being equally authentic.

FOR THE GOVERNMENT OF THE UNITED STATES OF AMERICA:

FOR THE GOVERNMENT OF THE RUSSIAN FEDERATION:

UNITED NATIONS CONVENTION TO COMBAT DESERTIFICATION IN THOSE COUNTRIES EXPERIENCING SERIOUS DROUGHT AND/OR DESERTIFICATION, PARTICULARLY IN AFRICA

The Parties to this Convention,

Affirming that human beings in affected or threatened areas are at the centre of concerns to combat desertification and mitigate the effects of drought,

Reflecting the urgent concern of the international community, including States and international organizations, about the adverse impacts of desertification and drought,

Aware that arid, semi-arid and dry sub-humid areas together account for a significant proportion of the Earth's land area and are the habitat and source of livelihood for a large segment of its population,

Acknowledging that desertification and drought are problems of global dimension in that they affect all regions of the world and that joint action of the international community is needed to combat desertification and/or mitigate the effects of drought,

Noting the high concentration of developing countries, notably the least developed countries, among those experiencing serious drought and/or desertification, and the particularly tragic consequences of these phenomena in Africa,

Noting also that desertification is caused by complex interactions among physical, biological, political, social, cultural and economic factors,

Considering the impact of trade and relevant aspects of international economic relations on the ability of affected countries to combat desertification adequately,

Conscious that sustainable economic growth, social development and poverty eradication are priorities of affected developing countries, particularly in Africa, and are essential to meeting sustainability objectives,

Mindful that desertification and drought affect sustainable development through their interrelationships with important social problems such as poverty, poor health and nutrition, lack of food security, and those arising from migration, displacement of persons and demographic dynamics,

Appreciating the significance of the past efforts and experience of States and international organizations in combating desertification and mitigating the effects of drought, particularly in implementing the Plan of Action to Combat Desertification which was adopted at the United Nations Conference on Desertification in 1977,

Realizing that, despite efforts in the past, progress in combating desertification and mitigating the effects of drought has not met expectations and that a new and more effective approach is needed at all levels within the framework of sustainable development,

Recognizing the validity and relevance of decisions adopted at the United Nations Conference on Environment and Development, particularly of Agenda 21 and its chapter 12, which provide a basis for combating desertification,

Reaffirming in this light the commitments of developed countries as contained in paragraph 13 of chapter 33 of Agenda 21,

Recalling General Assembly resolution 47/188, particularly the priority in it prescribed for Africa, and all other relevant United Nations resolutions, decisions and programmes on desertification and drought, as well as relevant declarations by African countries and those from other regions,

Reaffirming the Rio Declaration on Environment and Development which states, in its Principle 2, that States have, in accordance with the Charter of the United Nations and the principles of international law, the sovereign right to exploit their own resources pursuant to their own environmental and developmental policies, and the responsibility to ensure that activities within their jurisdiction or control do not cause damage to the environment of other States or of areas beyond the limits of national jurisdiction,

Recognizing that national Governments play a critical role in combating desertification and mitigating the effects of drought and that progress in that respect depends on local implementation of action programmes in affected areas,

Recognizing also the importance and necessity of international cooperation and partnership in combating desertification and mitigating the effects of drought,

Recognizing further the importance of the provision to affected developing countries, particularly in Africa, of effective means, *inter alia* substantial financial resources, including new and additional funding, and access to technology, without which it will be difficult for them to implement fully their commitments under this Convention,

Expressing concern over the impact of desertification and drought on affected countries in Central Asia and the Transcaucasus,

Stressing the important role played by women in regions affected by desertification and/or drought, particularly in rural areas of developing countries, and the importance of ensuring the full participation of both men and women at all levels in programmes to combat desertification and mitigate the effects of drought,

Emphasizing the special role of non-governmental organizations and other major groups in programmes to combat desertification and mitigate the effects of drought,

Bearing in mind the relationship between desertification and other environmental problems of global dimension facing the international and national communities,

Bearing also in mind the contribution that combating desertification can make to achieving the objectives of the United Nations Framework Convention on Climate Change, the Convention on Biological Diversity and other related environmental conventions,

Believing that strategies to combat desertification and mitigate the effects of drought will be most effective if they are based on sound systematic observation and rigorous scientific knowledge and if they are continuously re-evaluated,

Recognizing the urgent need to improve the effectiveness and coordination of international cooperation to facilitate the implementation of national plans and priorities,

Determined to take appropriate action in combating desertification and mitigating the effects of drought for the benefit of present and future generations,

Have agreed as follows:

PART I

INTRODUCTION

Article 1

Use of terms

For the purposes of this Convention:

(a) "desertification" means land degradation in arid, semi-arid and dry sub-humid areas resulting from various factors, including climatic variations and human activities;

(b) "combating desertification" includes activities which are part of the integrated development of land in arid, semi-arid and dry sub-humid areas for sustainable development which are aimed at:
  (i) prevention and/or reduction of land degradation;
  (ii) rehabilitation of partly degraded land; and
  (iii) reclamation of desertified land;

(c) "drought" means the naturally occurring phenomenon that exists when precipitation has been significantly below normal recorded levels, causing serious hydrological imbalances that adversely affect land resource production systems;

(d) "mitigating the effects of drought" means activities related to the prediction of drought and intended to reduce the vulnerability of society and natural systems to drought as it relates to combating desertification;

(e) "land" means the terrestrial bio-productive system that comprises soil, vegetation, other biota, and the ecological and hydrological processes that operate within the system;

(f) "land degradation" means reduction or loss, in arid, semi-arid and dry sub-humid areas, of the biological or economic productivity and complexity of rainfed cropland, irrigated cropland, or range, pasture, forest and woodlands resulting from land uses or from a process or combination of processes, including processes arising from human activities and habitation patterns, such as:
  (i) soil erosion caused by wind and/or water;
  (ii) deterioration of the physical, chemical and biological or economic properties of soil; and
  (iii) long-term loss of natural vegetation;

(g) "arid, semi-arid and dry sub-humid areas" means areas, other than polar and sub-polar regions, in which the ratio of annual precipitation to potential evapotranspiration falls within the range from 0.05 to 0.65;

(h) "affected areas" means arid, semi-arid and/or dry sub-humid areas affected or threatened by desertification;

(i) "affected countries" means countries whose lands include, in whole or in part, affected areas;

(j) "regional economic integration organization" means an organization constituted by sovereign States of a given region which has competence in respect of matters governed by this Convention and has been duly authorized, in accordance with its internal procedures, to sign, ratify, accept, approve or accede to this Convention;

(k) "developed country Parties" means developed country Parties and regional economic integration organizations constituted by developed countries.

Article 2

Objective

1. The objective of this Convention is to combat desertification and mitigate the effects of drought in countries experiencing serious drought and/or desertification, particularly in Africa, through effective action at all levels, supported by international cooperation and partnership arrangements, in the framework of an integrated approach which is consistent with Agenda 21, with a view to contributing to the achievement of sustainable development in affected areas.

2. Achieving this objective will involve long-term integrated strategies that focus simultaneously, in affected areas, on improved productivity of land, and the rehabilitation, conservation and sustainable management of land and water resources, leading to improved living conditions, in particular at the community level.

Article 3

Principles

In order to achieve the objective of this Convention and to implement its provisions, the Parties shall be guided, *inter alia*, by the following:

(a) the Parties should ensure that decisions on the design and implementation of programmes to combat desertification and/or mitigate the effects of drought are taken with the participation of populations and local communities and that an enabling environment is created at higher levels to facilitate action at national and local levels;

(b) the Parties should, in a spirit of international solidarity and partnership, improve cooperation and coordination at subregional, regional and international levels, and better focus financial, human, organizational and technical resources where they are needed;

(c) the Parties should develop, in a spirit of partnership, cooperation among all levels of government, communities, non-governmental organizations and landholders to establish a better understanding of the nature and value of land and scarce water resources in affected areas and to work towards their sustainable use; and

(d) the Parties should take into full consideration the special needs and circumstances of affected developing country Parties, particularly the least developed among them.

PART II

GENERAL PROVISIONS

Article 4

General obligations

1. The Parties shall implement their obligations under this Convention, individually or jointly, either through existing or prospective bilateral and multilateral arrangements or a combination thereof, as appropriate, emphasizing the need to coordinate efforts and develop a coherent long-term strategy at all levels.

2. In pursuing the objective of this Convention, the Parties shall:

(a) adopt an integrated approach addressing the physical, biological and socio-economic aspects of the processes of desertification and drought;

(b) give due attention, within the relevant international and regional bodies, to the situation of affected developing country Parties with regard to international trade, marketing arrangements and debt with a view to establishing an enabling international economic environment conducive to the promotion of sustainable development;

(c) integrate strategies for poverty eradication into efforts to combat desertification and mitigate the effects of drought;

(d) promote cooperation among affected country Parties in the fields of environmental protection and the conservation of land and water resources, as they relate to desertification and drought;

(e) strengthen subregional, regional and international cooperation;

(f) cooperate within relevant intergovernmental organizations;

(g) determine institutional mechanisms, if appropriate, keeping in mind the need to avoid duplication; and

(h) promote the use of existing bilateral and multilateral financial mechanisms and arrangements that mobilize and channel substantial financial resources to affected developing country Parties in combating desertification and mitigating the effects of drought.

3. Affected developing country Parties are eligible for assistance in the implementation of the Convention.

Article 5

Obligations of affected country Parties

In addition to their obligations pursuant to article 4, affected country Parties undertake to:

(a) give due priority to combating desertification and mitigating the effects of drought, and allocate adequate resources in accordance with their circumstances and capabilities;

(b) establish strategies and priorities, within the framework of sustainable development plans and/or policies, to combat desertification and mitigate the effects of drought;

(c) address the underlying causes of desertification and pay special attention to the socio-economic factors contributing to desertification processes;

(d) promote awareness and facilitate the participation of local populations, particularly women and youth, with the support of non-governmental organizations, in efforts to combat desertification and mitigate the effects of drought; and

(e) provide an enabling environment by strengthening, as appropriate, relevant existing legislation and, where they do not exist, enact new laws and establishing long-term policies and action programme.

Article 6

Obligations of developed country Parties

In addition to their general obligations pursuant to article 4, developed country Parties undertake to:

(a) actively support, as agreed, individually or jointly, the efforts of affected developing country Parties, particularly those in Africa, and the least developed countries, to combat desertification and mitigate the effects of drought;

(b) provide substantial financial resources and other forms of support to assist affected developing country Parties, particularly those in Africa, effectively to develop and implement their own long-term plans and

strategies to combat desertification and mitigate the effects of drought;
(c) promote the mobilization of new and additional funding pursuant to article 20, paragraph 2 (b);
(d) encourage the mobilization of funding from the private sector and other non-governmental sources; and
(e) promote and facilitate access by affected country Parties, particularly affected developing country Parties, to appropriate technology, knowledge and know-how.

Article 7

Priority for Africa

In implementing this Convention, the Parties shall give priority to affected African country Parties, in the light of the particular situation prevailing in that region, while not neglecting affected developing country Parties in other regions.

Article 8

Relationship with other conventions

1. The Parties shall encourage the coordination of activities carried out under this Convention and, if they are Parties to them, under other relevant international agreements, particularly the United Nations Framework Convention on Climate Change and the Convention on Biological Diversity, in order to derive maximum benefit from activities under each agreement while avoiding duplication of effort. The Parties shall encourage the conduct of joint programmes, particularly in the fields of research, training, systematic observation and information collection and exchange, to the extent that such activities may contribute to achieving the objectives of the agreements concerned.

2. The provisions of this Convention shall not affect the rights and obligations of any Party deriving from a bilateral, regional or international agreement into which it has entered prior to the entry into force of this Convention for it.

PART III

ACTION PROGRAMMES, SCIENTIFIC AND TECHNICAL COOPERATION AND SUPPORTING MEASURES

Section 1: Action programmes

Article 9

Basic approach

1. In carrying out their obligations pursuant to article 5, affected developing country Parties and any other affected country Party in the framework of its regional implementation annex or, otherwise, that has notified the Permanent Secretariat in writing of its intention to prepare a national action programme, shall, as appropriate, prepare, make public and implement national action programmes, utilizing and building, to the extent possible, on existing relevant successful plans and programmes, and subregional and regional action programmes, as the central element of the strategy to combat desertification and mitigate the effects of drought. Such programmes shall be updated through a continuing participatory process on the basis of lessons from field action, as well as the results of research. The preparation of national action programmes shall be closely interlinked with other efforts to formulate national policies of sustainable development.

2. In the provision by developed country Parties of different forms of assistance under the terms of article 6, priority shall be given to supporting, as agreed, national, subregional and regional action programmes of affected developing country Parties, particularly those in Africa, either directly or through relevant multilateral organizations or both.

3. The Parties shall encourage organs, funds and programmes of the United Nations system and other relevant intergovernmental organizations, academic institutions, the scientific community and non-governmental organizations in a position to cooperate, in accordance with their mandates and capabilities, to support the elaboration, implementation and follow-up of action programmes.

Article 10

National action programmes

1. The purpose of national action programmes is to identify the factors contributing to desertification and practical measures necessary to combat desertification and mitigate the effects of drought.

2. National action programmes shall specify the respective roles of government, local communities and land users and the resources available and needed. They shall, *inter alia*:

(a) incorporate long-term strategies to combat desertification and mitigate the effects of drought, emphasize implementation and be integrated with national policies for sustainable development;
(b) allow for modifications to be made in response to changing circumstances and be sufficiently flexible at the local level to cope with different socio-economic, biological and geo-physical conditions;
(c) give particular attention to the implementation of preventive measures for lands that are not yet degraded or which are only slightly degraded;
(d) enhance national climatological, meteorological and hydrological capabilities and the means to provide for drought early warning;
(e) promote policies and strengthen institutional frameworks which develop cooperation and coordination, in a spirit of partnership, between the donor community, governments at all levels, local populations and community groups, and facilitate access by local populations to appropriate information and technology;
(f) provide for effective participation at the local, national and regional levels of non-governmental organizations and local populations, both women and men, particularly resource users, including farmers and pastoralists and their representative organizations in policy planning, decision-making, and implementation and review of national action programmes; and
(g) require regular review of, and progress reports on, their implementation.

3. National action programmes may include, *inter alia*, some of all of the following measures to prepare for and mitigate the effects of drought:

(a) establishment and/or strengthening, as appropriate, of early warning systems, including local and national facilities and joint systems at the subregional and regional levels, and mechanisms for assisting environmentally displaced persons;
(b) strengthening of drought preparedness and management, including drought contingency plans at the local, national, subregional and regional levels, which take into consideration seasonal to interannual climate predictions;
(c) establishment and/or strengthening, as appropriate, of food security systems, including storage and marketing facilities, particularly in rural areas;
(d) establishment of alternative livelihood projects that could provide incomes in drought prone areas; and

(e) development of sustainable irrigation programmes for both crops and livestock.

4. Taking into account the circumstances and requirements specific to each affected country Party, national action programmes include, as appropriate, *inter alia*, measures in some or all of the following priority fields as they relate to combating desertification and mitigating the effects of drought in affected areas and to their populations: promotion of alternative livelihoods and improvement of national economic environments with a view to strengthening programmes aimed at the eradication of poverty and at ensuring food security; demographic dynamics; sustainable management of natural resources; sustainable agricultural practices; development and efficient use of various energy sources; institutional and legal frameworks; strengthening of capabilities for assessment and systematic observation, including hydrological and meteorological services, and capacity building, education and public awareness.

Article 11

Subregional and regional action programmes

Affected country Parties shall consult and cooperate to prepare, as appropriate, in accordance with relevant regional implementation annexes, subregional and/or regional action programmes to harmonize, complement and increase the efficiency of national programmes. The provisions of article 10 shall apply *mutatis mutandis* to subregional and regional programmes. Such cooperation may include agreed joint programmes for the sustainable management of transboundary natural resources, scientific and technical cooperation, and strengthening of relevant institutions.

Article 12

International cooperation

Affected country Parties, in collaboration with other Parties and the international community, should cooperate to ensure the promotion of an enabling international environment in the implementation of the Convention. Such cooperation should also cover fields of technology transfer as well as scientific research and development, information collection and dissemination and financial resources.

Article 13

Support for the elaboration and implementation of action programmes

1. Measures to support action programmes pursuant to article 9 include, *inter alia*:

(a) financial cooperation to provide predictability for action programmes, allowing for necessary long-term planning;

(b) elaboration and use of cooperation mechanisms which better enable support at the local level, including action through non-governmental organizations, in order to promote the replicability of successful pilot programme activities where relevant;

(c) increased flexibility in project design, funding and implementation in keeping with the experimental, iterative approach indicated for participatory action at the local community level; and

(d) as appropriate, administrative and budgetary procedures that increase the efficiency of cooperation and of support programmes.

2. In providing such support to affected developing country Parties, priority shall be given to African country Parties and to least developed country Parties.

Articles 14

Coordination in the elaboration and implementation of action programmes

1. The Parties shall work closely together, directly and through relevant intergovernmental organizations, in the elaboration and implementation of action programmes.

2. The Parties shall develop operational mechanisms, particularly at the national and field levels, to ensure the fullest possible coordination among developed country Parties, developing country Parties and relevant intergovernmental and non-governmental organizations, in order to avoid duplication, harmonize interventions and approaches, and maximize the impact of assistance. In affected developing country Parties, priority will be given to coordinating activities related to international cooperation in order to maximize the efficient use of resources, to ensure responsive assistance, and to facilitate the implementation of national action programmes and priorities under this Convention.

Article 15

Regional implementation annexes

Elements for incorporation in action programmes shall be selected and adapted to the socio-economic, geographical and climatic factors applicable to affected country Parties or regions, as well as to their level of development. Guidelines for the preparation of action programmes and their exact focus and content for particular subregions and regions are set out in the regional implementation annexes.

Section 2: Scientific and technical cooperation

Article 16

Information collection, analysis and exchange

The Parties agree, according to their respective capabilities, to integrate and coordinate the collection, analysis and exchange of relevant short term and long term data and information to ensure systematic observation of land degradation in affected areas and to understand better and assess the processes and effects of drought and desertification. This would help accomplish, *inter alia*, early warning and advance planning for periods of adverse climatic variation in a form suited for practical application by users at all levels, including especially local populations. To this end, they shall, as appropriate:

(a) facilitate and strengthen the functioning of the global network of institutions and facilities for the collection, analysis and exchange of information, as well as for systematic observation at all levels, which shall *inter alia*:
  (i) aim to use compatible standards and systems;
  (ii) encompass relevant data and stations, including in remote areas;
  (iii) use and disseminate modern technology for data collection, transmission and assessment on land degradation; and
  (iv) link national, subregional and regional data and information centres more closely with global information sources;

(b) ensure that the collection, analysis and exchange of information address the needs of local communities and those of decision makers, with a view to resolving specific problems, and that local communities are involved in these activities;

(c) support and further develop bilateral and multilateral programmes and projects aimed at defining, conducting, assessing and financing the collection, analysis and exchange of data and information, including, *inter alia*, integrated sets of physical, biological, social and economic indicators;

(d) make full use of the expertise of competent intergovernmental and non-governmental organizations, particularly to disseminate relevant information and experiences among target groups in different regions;

(e) give full weight to the collection, analysis and exchange of socio-economic data, and their integration with physical and biological data;

(f) exchange and make fully, openly and promptly available information from all publicly available sources relevant to combating desertification and mitigating the effects of drought; and

(g) subject to their respective national legislation and/or policies, exchange information on local and traditional knowledge, ensuring adequate protection for it and providing appropriate return from the benefits derived from it, on an equitable basis and on mutually agreed terms, to the local populations concerned.

Article 17

Research and development

1. The Parties undertake, according to their respective capabilities, to promote technical and scientific cooperation in the fields of combating desertification and mitigating the effects of drought through appropriate national, subregional, regional and international institutions. To this end, they shall support research activities that:

(a) contribute to increased knowledge of the processes leading to desertification and drought and the impact of, and distinction between, causal factors, both natural and human, with a view to combating desertification and mitigating the effects of drought, and achieving improved productivity as well as sustainable use and management of resources;

(b) respond to well-defined objectives, address the specific needs of local populations and lead to the identification and implementation of solutions that improve the living standards of people in affected areas;

(c) protect, integrate, enhance and validate traditional and local knowledge, know-how and practices, ensuring, subject to their respective national legislation and/or policies, that the owners of that knowledge will directly benefit on an equitable basis and on mutually agreed terms from any commercial utilization of it or from any technological development derived from that knowledge;

(d) develop and strengthen national, subregional and regional research capabilities in affected developing country Parties, particularly in

Africa, including the development of local skills and the strengthening of appropriate capacities, especially in countries with a weak research base, giving particular attention to multidisciplinary and participative socio-economic research;

(e) take into account, where relevant, the relationship between poverty, migration caused by environmental factors, and desertification;

(f) promote the conduct of joint research programmes between national, subregional, regional and international research organizations, in both the public and private sectors, for the development of improved, affordable and accessible technologies for sustainable development through effective participation of local populations and communities; and

(g) enhance the availability of water resources in affected areas, by means of, *inter alia*, cloud-seeding.

2. Research priorities for particular regions and subregions, reflecting different local conditions, should be included in action programmes. The Conference of the Parties shall review research priorities periodically on the advice of the Committee on Science and Technology.

Article 18

Transfer, acquisition, adaptation and development of technology

1. The Parties undertake, as mutually agreed and in accordance with their respective national legislation and/or policies, to promote, finance and/or facilitate the financing of the transfer, acquisition, adaptation and development of environmentally sound, economically viable and socially acceptable technologies relevant to combating desertification and/or mitigating the effects of drought, with a view to contributing to the achievement of sustainable development in affected areas. Such cooperation shall be conducted bilaterally or multilaterally, as appropriate, making full use of the expertise of intergovernmental and non-governmental organizations. The Parties shall, in particular:

(a) fully utilize relevant existing national, subregional, regional and international information systems and clearing-houses for the dissemination of information on available technologies, their sources, their environmental risks and the broad terms under which they may be acquired;

(b) facilitate access, in particular by affected developing country Parties, on favourable terms, including on concessional and preferential terms, as mutually agreed, taking into account the need to protect intellectual property rights, to technologies most suitable to practical application for specific needs of local populations, paying special attention to the social, cultural, economic and environmental impact of such technology;

(c) facilitate technology cooperation among affected country Parties through financial assistance or other appropriate means;

(d) extend technology cooperation with affected developing country Parties, including, where relevant, joint ventures, especially to sectors which foster alternative livelihoods; and

(e) take appropriate measures to create domestic market conditions and incentives, fiscal or otherwise, conducive to the development, transfer, acquisition and adaptation of suitable technology, knowledge, know-how and practices, including measures to ensure adequate and effective protection of intellectual property rights.

2. The Parties shall, according to their respective capabilities, and subject to their respective national legislation and/or policies, protect, promote and use in particular relevant traditional and local technology, knowledge, know-how and practices and, to that end, they undertake to:

(a) make inventories of such technology, knowledge, know-how and practices and their potential uses with the participation of local populations, and disseminate such information, where appropriate, in cooperation with relevant intergovernmental and non-governmental organizations;

(b) ensure that such technology, knowledge, know-how and practices are adequately protected and that local populations benefit directly, on an equitable basis and as mutually agreed, from any commercial utilization of them or from any technological development derived therefrom;

(c) encourage and actively support the improvement and dissemination of such technology, knowledge, know-how and practices or of the development of new technology based on them; and

(d) facilitate, as appropriate, the adaptation of such technology, knowledge, know-how and practices to wide use and integrate them with modern technology, as appropriate.

Section 3: Supporting measures

Article 19

Capacity-building, education and public awareness

1. The Parties recognize the significance of capacity-building—that is to say, institution-building, training and development of relevant local and

national capacities—in efforts to combat desertification and mitigate the effects of drought. They shall promote, as appropriate, capacity-building:

(a) through the full participation at all levels of local people, particularly at the local level, especially women and youth, with the cooperation of non-governmental and local organizations;
(b) by strengthening training and research capacity at the national level in the field of desertification and drought;
(c) by establishing and/or strengthening support and extension services to disseminate relevant technology methods and techniques more effectively, and by training field agents and members of rural organizations in participatory approaches for the conservation and sustainable use of natural resources;
(d) by fostering the use and dissemination of the knowledge, know-how and practices of local people in technical cooperation programmes, wherever possible;
(e) by adapting, where necessary, relevant environmentally sound technology and traditional methods of agriculture and pastoralism to modern socio-economic conditions;
(f) by providing appropriate training and technology in the use of alternative energy sources, particularly renewable energy resources, aimed particularly at reducing dependence on wood for fuel;
(g) through cooperation, as mutually agreed, to strengthen the capacity of affected developing country Parties to develop and implement programmes in the field of collection, analysis and exchange of information pursuant to article 16;
(h) through innovative ways of promoting alternative livelihoods, including training in new skills;
(i) by training of decision makers, managers, and personnel who are responsible for the collection and analysis of data for the dissemination and use of early warning information on drought conditions and for food production ;
(j) through more effective operation of existing national institutions and legal frameworks and, where necessary, creation of new ones, along with strengthening of strategic planning and management; and
(k) by means of exchange visitor programmes to enhance capacity-building in affected country Parties through a long-term, interactive process of learning and study.

2. Affected developing country Parties shall conduct, in cooperation with other Parties and competent intergovernmental and non-governmental organizations, as appropriate, an interdisciplinary review of available capacity and facilities at the local and national levels, and the potential for strengthening them.

3. The Parties shall cooperate with each other and through competent intergovernmental organizations, as well as with non-governmental organizations, in undertaking and supporting public awareness and educational programmes in both affected and, where relevant, unaffected country Parties to promote understanding of the causes and effects of desertification and drought and of the importance of meeting the objective of this Convention. To that end, they shall:

(a) organize awareness campaigns for the general public;

(b) promote, on a permanent basis, access by the public to relevant information, and wide public participation in education and awareness activities;

(c) encourage the establishment of associations that contribute to public awareness;

(d) develop and exchange educational and public awareness material, where possible in local languages, exchange and second experts to train personnel of affected developing country Parties in carrying out relevant education and awareness programmes, and fully utilize relevant educational material available in competent international bodies;

(e) assess educational needs in affected areas, elaborate appropriate school curricula and expand, as needed, educational and adult literacy programmes and opportunities for all, in particular for girls and women, on the identification, conservation and sustainable use and management of the natural resources of affected areas; and

(f) develop interdisciplinary participatory programmes integrating desertification and drought awareness into educational systems and in non-formal, adult, distance and practical educational programmes.

4. The Conference of the Parties shall establish and/or strengthen networks of regional education and training centres to combat desertification and mitigate the effects of drought. These networks shall be coordinated by an institution created or designated for that purpose, in order to train scientific, technical and management personnel and to strengthen existing institutions responsible for education and training in affected country Parties, where appropriate, with a view to harmonizing programmes and to organizing exchanges of experience among them. These networks shall cooperate closely with relevant intergovernmental and non-governmental organizations to avoid duplication of effort.

Article 20

Financial resources

1. Given the central importance of financing to the achievement of the objective of the Convention, the Parties, taking into account their capabilities, shall make every effort to ensure that adequate financial resources are available for programmes to combat desertification and mitigate the effects of drought.

2. In this connection, developed country Parties, while giving priority to affected African country Parties without neglecting affected developing country Parties in other regions, in accordance with article 7, undertake to:

(a) mobilize substantial financial resources, including grants and concessional loans, in order to support the implementation of programmes to combat desertification and mitigate the effects of drought;

(b) promote the mobilization of adequate, timely and predictable financial resources, including new and additional funding from the Global Environment Facility of the agreed incremental costs of those activities concerning desertification that relate to its four focal areas, in conformity with the relevant provisions of the Instrument establishing the Global Environment Facility;

(c) facilitate through international cooperation the transfer of technology, knowledge and know-how; and

(d) explore, in cooperation with affected developing country Parties, innovative methods and incentives for mobilizing and channelling resources, including those of foundations, non-governmental organizations and other private sector entities, particularly debt swaps and other innovative means which increase financing by reducing the external debt burden of affected developing country Parties, particularly those in Africa.

3. Affected developing country Parties, taking into account their capabilities, undertake to mobilize adequate financial resources for the implementation of their national action programmes.

4. In mobilizing financial resources, the Parties shall seek full use and continued qualitative improvement of all national, bilateral and multilateral funding sources and mechanisms, using consortia, joint programmes and parallel financing, and shall seek to involve private sector funding sources and mechanisms, including those of non-governmental organizations. To this end, the Parties shall fully utilize the operational mechanisms developed pursuant to article 14.

5. In order to mobilize the financial resources necessary for affected developing country Parties to combat desertification and mitigate the effects of drought, the Parties shall:

(a) rationalize and strengthen the management of resources already allocated for combating desertification and mitigating the effects of drought by using them more effectively and efficiently, assessing their successes and shortcomings, removing hindrances to their effective use and, where necessary, reorienting programmes in light of the integrated long-term approach adopted pursuant to this Convention;

(b) give due priority and attention within the governing bodies of multilateral financial institutions, facilities and funds, including regional development banks and funds, to supporting affected developing country Parties, particularly those in Africa, in activities which advance implementation of the Convention, notably action programmes they undertake in the framework of regional implementation annexes; and

(c) examine ways in which regional and subregional cooperation can be strengthened to support efforts undertaken at the national level.

6. Other Parties are encouraged to provide, on a voluntary basis, knowledge, know-how and techniques related to desertification and/or financial resources to affected developing country Parties.

7. The full implementation by affected developing country Parties, particularly those in Africa, of their obligations under the Convention will be greatly assisted by the fulfilment by developed country Parties of their obligations under the Convention, including in particular those regarding financial resources and transfer of technology. In fulfilling their obligations, developed country Parties should take fully into account that economic and social development and poverty eradication are the first priorities of affected developing country Parties, particularly those in Africa.

Article 21

Financial mechanisms

1. The Conference of the Parties shall promote the availability of financial mechanisms and shall encourage such mechanisms to seek to maximize the availability of funding for affected developing country Parties, particularly those in Africa, to implement the Convention. To this end, the Conference of the Parties shall consider for adoption *inter alia* approaches and policies that:

(a) facilitate the provision of necessary funding at the national, subregional, regional and global levels for activities pursuant to relevant provisions of the Convention;

(b) promote multiple-source funding approaches, mechanisms and arrangements and their assessment, consistent with article 20;

(c) provide on a regular basis, to interested Parties and relevant intergovernmental and non-governmental organizations, information on available sources of funds and on funding patterns in order to facilitate coordination among them;

(d) facilitate the establishment, as appropriate, of mechanisms, such as national desertification funds, including those involving the participation of non-governmental organizations, to channel financial resources rapidly and efficiently to the local level in affected developing country Parties; and

(e) strengthen existing funds and financial mechanisms at the subregional and regional levels, particularly in Africa, to support more effectively the implementation of the Convention.

2. The Conference of the Parties shall also encourage the provision, through various mechanisms within the United Nations system and through multilateral financial institutions, of support at the national, subregional and regional levels to activities that enable developing country Parties to meet their obligations under the Convention.

3. Affected developing country Parties shall utilize, and where necessary, establish and/or strengthen, national coordinating mechanisms, integrated in national development programmes, that would ensure the efficient use of all available financial resources. They shall also utilize participatory processes involving non-governmental organizations, local groups and the private sector, in raising funds, in elaborating as well as implementing programmes and in assuring access to funding by groups at the local level. These actions can be enhanced by improved coordination and flexible programming on the part of those providing assistance.

4. In order to increase the effectiveness and efficiency of existing financial mechanisms, a Global Mechanism to promote actions leading to the mobilization and channelling of substantial financial resources, including for the transfer of technology, on a grant basis, and/or on concessional or other terms, to affected developing country Parties, is hereby established. This Global Mechanism shall function under the authority and guidance of the Conference of the Parties and be accountable to it.

5. The Conference of the Parties shall identify, at its first ordinary session, an organization to house the Global Mechanism. The Conference of the Parties and the organization it has identified shall agree upon modalities for this Global Mechanism to ensure *inter alia* that such Mechanism:

(a) identifies and draws up an inventory of relevant bilateral and multilateral cooperation programmes that are available to implement the Convention;
(b) provides advice, on request, to Parties on innovative methods of financing and sources of financial assistance and on improving the coordination of cooperation activities at the national level;
(c) provides interested Parties and relevant intergovernmental and non-governmental organizations with information on available sources of funds and on funding patterns in order to facilitate coordination among them; and
(d) reports to the Conference of the Parties, beginning at its second ordinary session, on its activities.

6. The Conference of the Parties shall, at its first session, make appropriate arrangements with the organization it has identified to house the Global Mechanism for the administrative operations of such Mechanism, drawing to the extent possible on existing budgetary and human resources.

7. The Conference of the Parties shall, at its third ordinary session, review the policies, operational modalities and activities of the Global Mechanism accountable to it pursuant to paragraph 4, taking into account the provisions of article 7. On the basis of this review, it shall consider and take appropriate action.

PART IV

INSTITUTIONS

Article 22

Conference of the Parties

1. A Conference of the Parties is hereby established.

2. The Conference of the Parties is the supreme body of the Convention. It shall make, within its mandate, the decisions necessary to promote its effective implementation. In particular, it shall:
(a) regularly review the implementation of the Convention and the functioning of its institutional arrangements in the light of the experience gained at the national, subregional, regional and international levels and on the basis of the evolution of scientific and technological knowledge;
(b) promote and facilitate the exchange of information on measures adopted by the Parties, and determine the form and timetable for

transmitting the information to be submitted pursuant to article 26, review the reports and make recommendations on them;

(c) establish such subsidiary bodies as are deemed necessary for the implementation of the Convention;

(d) review reports submitted by its subsidiary bodies and provide guidance to them;

(e) agree upon and adopt, by consensus, rules of procedure and financial rules for itself and any subsidiary bodies;

(f) adopt amendments to the Convention pursuant to articles 30 and 31;

(g) approve a programme and budget for its activities, including those of its subsidiary bodies, and undertake necessary arrangements for their financing;

(h) as appropriate, seek the cooperation of, and utilize the services of and information provided by, competent bodies or agencies, whether national or international, intergovernmental or non-governmental;

(i) promote and strengthen the relationship with other relevant conventions while avoiding duplication of effort; and

(j) exercise such other functions as may be necessary for the achievement of the objective of the Convention.

3. The Conference of the Parties shall, at its first session, adopt its own rules of procedure, by consensus, which shall include decision-making procedures for matters not already covered by decision-making procedures stipulated in the Convention. Such procedures may include specified majorities required for the adoption of particular decisions.

4. The first session of the Conference of the Parties shall be convened by the interim secretariat referred to in article 35 and shall take place not later than one year after the date of entry into force of the Convention. Unless otherwise decided by the Conference of the Parties, the second, third and fourth ordinary sessions shall be held yearly, and thereafter, ordinary sessions shall be held every two years.

5. Extraordinary sessions of the Conference of the Parties shall be held at such other times as may be decided either by the Conference of the Parties in ordinary session or at the written request of any Party, provided that, within three months of the request being communicated to the Parties by the Permanent Secretariat, it is supported by at least one third of the Parties.

6. At each ordinary session, the Conference of the Parties shall elect a Bureau. The structure and functions of the Bureau shall be determined in the rules of procedure. In appointing the Bureau, due regard shall be paid

to the need to ensure equitable geographical distribution and adequate representation of affected country Parties, particularly those in Africa.

7. The United Nations, its specialized agencies and any State member thereof or observers thereto not Party to the Convention, may be represented at sessions of the Conference of the Parties as observers. Any body or agency, whether national or international, governmental or non-governmental, which is qualified in matters covered by the Convention, and which has informed the Permanent Secretariat of its wish to be represented at a session of the Conference of the Parties as an observer, may be so admitted unless at least one third of the Parties present object. The admission and participation of observers shall be subject to the rules of procedure adopted by the Conference of the Parties.

8. The Conference of the Parties may request competent national and international organizations which have relevant expertise to provide it with information relevant to article 16, paragraph (g), article 17, paragraph 1 (c) and article 18, paragraph 2 (b).

Article 23

Permanent Secretariat

1. A Permanent Secretariat is hereby established.

2. The functions of the Permanent Secretariat shall be:
   (a) to make arrangements for sessions of the Conference of the Parties and its subsidiary bodies established under the Convention and to provide them with services as required;
   (b) to compile and transmit reports submitted to it;
   (c) to facilitate assistance to affected developing country Parties, on request, particularly those in Africa, in the compilation and communication of information required under the Convention;
   (d) to coordinate its activities with the secretariats of other relevant international bodies and conventions;
   (e) to enter, under the guidance of the Conference of the parties, into such administrative and contractual arrangements as may be required for the effective discharge of its functions;
   (f) to prepare reports on the execution of its functions under this Convention and present them to the Conference of the Parties; and
   (g) to perform such other secretariat functions as may be determined by the Conference of the Parties.

3. The Conference of the Parties, at its first session, shall designate a Permanent Secretariat and make arrangements for its functioning.

Article 24

Committee on Science and Technology

1. A Committee on Science and Technology is hereby established as a subsidiary body of the Conference of the Parties to provide it with information and advice on scientific and technological matters relating to combating desertification and mitigating the effects of drought. The Committee shall meet in conjunction with the ordinary sessions of the Conference of the Parties and shall be multidisciplinary and open to the participation of all Parties. It shall be composed of government representatives competent in the relevant fields of expertise. The Conference of the Parties shall decide, at its first session, on the terms of reference of the Committee.

2. The Conference of the Parties shall establish and maintain a roster of independent experts with expertise and experience in the relevant fields. The roster shall be based on nominations received in writing from the Parties, taking into account the need for a multidisciplinary approach and broad geographical representation.

3. The Conference of the Parties may, as necessary, appoint ad hoc panels to provide it, through the Committee, with information and advice on specific issues regarding the state of the art in fields of science and technology relevant to combating desertification and mitigating the effects of drought. These panels shall be composed of experts whose names are taken from the roster, taking into account the need for a multidisciplinary approach and broad geographical representation. These experts shall have scientific backgrounds and field experience and shall be appointed by the Conference of the Parties on the recommendation of the Committee. The Conference of the Parties shall decide on the terms of reference and the modalities of work of these panels.

Article 25

Networking of institutions, agencies and bodies

1. The Committee on Science and Technology shall, under the supervision of the Conference of the Parties, make provision for the undertaking of a survey and evaluation of the relevant existing networks, institutions, agencies and bodies willing to become units of a network. Such a network shall support the implementation of the Convention.

2. On the basis of the results of the survey and evaluation referred to in paragraph 1, the Committee on Science and Technology shall make

recommendations to the Conference of the Parties on ways and means to facilitate and strengthen networking of the units at the local, national and other levels, with a view to ensuring that the thematic needs set out in articles 16 to 19 are addressed.

3. Taking into account these recommendations, the Conference of the Parties shall:

(a) identify those national, subregional, regional and international units that are most appropriate for networking, and recommend operational procedures, and a time-frame, for them; and

(b) identify the units best suited to facilitating and strengthening such networking at all levels.

PART V

PROCEDURES

Article 26

Communication of information

1. Each Party shall communicate to the Conference of the Parties for consideration at its ordinary sessions, through the Permanent Secretariat, reports on the measures which it has taken for the implementation of the Convention. The Conference of the Parties shall determine the timetable for submission and the format of such reports.

2. Affected country Parties shall provide a description of the strategies established pursuant to article 5 and of any relevant information on their implementation.

3. Affected country Parties which implement action programmes pursuant to articles 9 to 15 shall provide a detailed description of the programmes and of their implementation.

4. Any group of affected country Parties may make a joint communication on measures taken at the subregional and/or regional levels in the framework of action programmes.

5. Developed country Parties shall report on measures taken to assist in the preparation and implementation of action programmes, including information on the financial resources they have provided, or are providing, under the Convention.

6. Information communicated pursuant to paragraphs 1 to 4 shall be transmitted by the Permanent Secretariat as soon as possible to the Conference of the Parties and to any relevant subsidiary body.

7. The Conference of the Parties shall facilitate the provision to affected developing countries, particularly those in Africa, on request, of technical and financial support in compiling and communicating information in accordance with this article, as well as identifying the technical and financial needs associated with action programmes.

Article 27

Measures to resolve questions on implementation

The Conference of the Parties shall consider and adopt procedures and institutional mechanisms for the resolution of questions that may arise with regard to the implementation of the Convention.

Article 28

Settlement of disputes

1. Parties shall settle any dispute between them concerning the interpretation or application of the Convention through negotiation or other peaceful means of their own choice.

2. When ratifying, accepting, approving, or acceding to the Convention, or at any time thereafter, a Party which is not a regional economic integration organization may declare in a written instrument submitted to the Depositary that, in respect of any dispute concerning the interpretation or application of the Convention, it recognizes one or both of the following means of dispute settlement as compulsory in relation to any Party accepting the same obligation:
   (a) arbitration in accordance with procedures adopted by the Conference of the Parties in an annex as soon as practicable;
   (b) submission of the dispute to the International Court of Justice.

3. A Party which is a regional economic integration organization may make a declaration with like effect in relation to arbitration in accordance with the procedure referred to in paragraph 2 (a).

4. A declaration made pursuant to paragraph 2 shall remain in force until it expires in accordance with its terms or until three months after written notice of its revocation has been deposited with the Depositary.

5. The expiry of a declaration, a notice of revocation or a new declaration shall not in any way affect proceedings pending before an arbitral tribunal or the International Court of Justice unless the Parties to the dispute otherwise agree.

6. If the Parties to a dispute have not accepted the same or any procedure pursuant to paragraph 2 and if they have not been able to settle their dispute within twelve months following notification by one Party to another that a dispute exists between them, the dispute shall be submitted to conciliation at the request of any Party to the dispute, in accordance with procedures adopted by the Conference of the Parties in an annex as soon as practicable.

Article 29

Status of annexes

1. Annexes form an integral part of the Convention and, unless expressly provided otherwise, a reference to the Convention also constitutes a reference to its annexes.

2. The Parties shall interpret the provisions of the annexes in a manner that is in conformity with their rights and obligations under the articles of this Convention.

Article 30

Amendments to the Convention

1. Any Party may propose amendments to the Convention.

2. Amendments to the Convention shall be adopted at an ordinary session of the Conference of the Parties. The text of any proposed amendment shall be communicated to the Parties by the Permanent Secretariat at least six months before the meeting at which it is proposed for adoption. The Permanent Secretariat shall also communicate proposed amendments to the signatories to the Convention.

3. The Parties shall make every effort to reach agreement on any proposed amendment to the Convention by consensus. If all efforts at consensus have been exhausted and no agreement reached, the amendment shall, as a last resort, be adopted by a two-thirds majority vote of the Parties present and voting at the meeting. The adopted amendment shall be communicated by the Permanent Secretariat to the Depositary, who shall circulate it to all Parties for their ratification, acceptance, approval or accession.

4. Instruments of ratification, acceptance, approval or accession in respect of an amendment shall be deposited with the Depositary. An amendment adopted pursuant to paragraph 3 shall enter into force for those Parties

having accepted it on the ninetieth day after the date of receipt by the Depositary of an instrument of ratification, acceptance, approval or accession by at least two thirds of the Parties to the Convention which were Parties at the time of the adoption of the amendment.

5. The amendment shall enter into force for any other Party on the ninetieth day after the date on which that Party deposits with the Depositary its instrument of ratification, acceptance or approval of, or accession to the said amendment.

6. For the purposes of this article and article 31, "Parties present and voting" means Parties present and casting an affirmative or negative vote.

Article 31

Adoption and amendment of annexes

1. Any additional annex to the Convention and any amendment to an annex shall be proposed and adopted in accordance with the procedure for amendment of the Convention set forth in article 30, provided that, in adopting an additional regional implementation annex or amendment to any regional implementation annex, the majority provided for in that article shall include a two-thirds majority vote of the Parties of the region concerned present and voting. The adoption or amendment of an annex shall be communicated by the Depositary to all Parties.

2. An annex, other than an additional regional implementation annex, or an amendment to an annex, other than an amendment to any regional implementation annex, that has been adopted in accordance with paragraph 1, shall enter into force for all Parties to the Convention six months after the date of communication by the Depositary to such Parties of the adoption of such annex or amendment, except for those Parties that have notified the Depositary in writing within that period of their non-acceptance o f such annex or amendment. Such annex or amendment shall enter into force for Parties which withdraw their notification of non-acceptance on the ninetieth day after the date on which withdrawal of such notification has been received by the Depositary.

3. An additional regional implementation annex or amendment to any regional implementation annex that has been adopted in accordance with paragraph 1, shall enter into force for all Parties to the Convention six months after the date of the communication by the Depositary to such Parties of the adoption of such annex or amendment, except with respect to:

(a) any Party that has notified the Depositary in writing, within such six month period, of its non-acceptance of that additional regional implementation annex or of the amendment to the regional implementation annex, in which case such annex or amendment shall enter into force for Parties which withdraw their notification of non-acceptance on the ninetieth day after the date on which withdrawal of such notification has been received by the Depositary; and

(b) any Party that has made a declaration with respect to additional regional implementation annexes or amendments to regional implementation annexes in accordance with article 34, paragraph 4, in which case any such annex or amendment shall enter into force for such a Party on the ninetieth day after the date of deposit with the Depositary of its instrument of ratification, acceptance, approval or accession with respect to such annex or amendment.

4. If the adoption of an annex or an amendment to an annex involves an amendment to the Convention, that annex or amendment to an annex shall not enter into force until such time as the amendment to the Convention enters into force.

Article 32

Right to vote

1. Except as provided for in paragraph 2, each Party to the Convention shall have one vote.

2. Regional economic integration organizations, in matters within their competence, shall exercise their right to vote with a number of votes equal to the number of their member States that are Parties to the Convention. Such an organization shall not exercise its right to vote if any of its member States exercises its right, and vice versa.

PART VI

FINAL PROVISIONS

Article 33

Signature

This Convention shall be opened for signature at Paris, on 14–15 October 1994, by States Members of the United Nations or any of its specialized agencies or that are Parties to the Statute of the International Court of Justice and by regional economic integration organizations. It shall remain open for signature, thereafter, at the United Nations Headquarters in New York until 13 October 1995.

Article 34

Ratification, acceptance, approval and accession

1. The Convention shall be subject to ratification, acceptance, approval or accession by States and by regional economic integration organizations. It shall be open for accession from the day after the date on which the Convention is closed for signature. Instruments of ratification, acceptance, approval or accession shall be deposited with the Depositary.

2. Any regional economic integration organization which becomes a Party to the Convention without any of its member States being a Party to the Convention shall be bound by all the obligations under the Convention. Where one or more member States of such an organization are also Party to the Convention, the organization and its member States shall decide on their respective responsibilities for the performance of their obligations under the Convention. In such cases, the organization and the member States shall not be entitled to exercise rights under the Convention concurrently.

3. In their instruments of ratification, acceptance, approval or accession, regional economic integration organizations shall declare the extent of their competence with respect to the matters governed by the Convention. They shall also promptly inform the Depositary, who shall in turn inform the Parties, of any substantial modification in the extent of their competence.

4. In its instrument of ratification, acceptance, approval or accession, any Party may declare that, with respect to it, any additional regional implementation annex or any amendment to any regional implementation annex shall enter into force only upon the deposit of its instrument of ratification, acceptance, approval or accession with respect thereto.

Article 35

Interim arrangements

The secretariat functions referred to in article 23 will be carried out on an interim basis by the secretariat established by the General Assembly of the United Nations in its resolution 47/188 of 22 December 1992, until the completion of the first session of the Conference of the Parties.

Article 36

Entry into force

1. The Convention shall enter into force on the ninetieth day after the date of deposit of the fiftieth instrument of ratification, acceptance, approval or accession.

2. For each State or regional economic integration organization ratifying, accepting, approving or acceding to the Convention after the deposit of the fiftieth instrument of ratification, acceptance, approval or accession, the Convention shall enter into force on the ninetieth day after the date of deposit by such State or regional economic integration organization of its instrument of ratification, acceptance, approval or accession.

3. For the purposes of paragraphs 1 and 2, any instrument deposited by a regional economic integration organization shall not be counted as additional to those deposited by States members of the organization.

Article 37

Reservations

No reservations may be made to this Convention.

Article 38

Withdrawal

1. At any time after three years from the date on which the Convention has entered into force for a Party, that Party may withdraw from the Convention by giving written notification to the Depositary.

2. Any such withdrawal shall take effect upon expiry of one year from the date of receipt by the Depositary of the notification of withdrawal, or on such later date as may be specified in the notification of withdrawal.

Article 39

Depositary

The Secretary-General of the United Nations shall be the Depositary of the Convention.

Article 40

Authentic texts

The original of the present Convention, of which the Arabic, Chinese, English, French, Russian and Spanish texts are equally authentic, shall be deposited with the Secretary-General of the United Nations.

IN WITNESS WHEREOF the undersigned, being duly authorized to that effect, have signed the present Convention.

DONE AT Paris, this 17the day of June one thousand nine hundred and ninety-four.

ANNEX I

REGIONAL IMPLEMENTATION ANNEX FOR AFRICA

Article 1

Scope

This Annex applies to Africa, in relation to each Party and in conformity with the Convention, in particular its article 7, for the purpose of combating desertification and/or mitigating the effects of drought in its arid, semi-arid and dry sub-humid areas.

Article 2

Purpose

The purpose of this Annex, at the national, subregional and regional levels in Africa and in the light of its particular conditions, is to:

(a) identify measures and arrangements, including the nature and processes of assistance provided by developed country Parties, in accordance with the relevant provisions of the Convention;

(b) provide for the efficient and practical implementation of the Convention to address conditions specific to Africa; and

(c) promote processes and activities relating to combating desertification and/or mitigating the effects of drought within the arid, semi-arid and dry sub-humid areas of Africa.

Article 3

Particular conditions of the African region

In carrying out their obligations under the Convention, the Parties shall, in the implementation of this Annex, adopt a basic approach that takes into consideration the following particular conditions of Africa:

(a) the high proportion of arid, semi-arid and dry sub-humid areas;

(b) the substantial number of countries and populations adversely affected by desertification and by the frequent recurrence of severe drought;

(c) the large number of affected countries that are land-locked;

(d) the widespread poverty prevalent in most affected countries, the large number of least developed countries among them, and their need for significant amounts of external assistance, in the form of grants and loans on concessional terms, to pursue their development objectives;

(e) the difficult socio-economic conditions, exacerbated by deteriorating and fluctuating terms of trade, external indebtedness and political instability, which induce internal, regional and international migrations;

(f) the heavy reliance of populations on natural resources for subsistence which, compounded by the effects of demographic trends and factors, a weak technological base and unsustainable production practices, contributes to serious resource degradation;

(g) the insufficient institutional and legal frameworks, the weak infrastructural base and the insufficient scientific, technical and educational capacity, leading to substantial capacity-building requirements; and

(h) the central role of actions to combat desertification and/or mitigate the effects of drought in the national development priorities of affected African countries.

Article 4

Commitments and obligations of African country Parties

1. In accordance with their respective capabilities, African country Parties undertake to:

(a) adopt the combating of desertification and/or the mitigation of the effects of drought as a central strategy in their efforts to eradicate poverty;

(b) promote regional cooperation and integration, in a spirit of solidarity and partnership based on mutual interest, in programmes and activities to combat desertification and/or mitigate the effects of drought;

(c) rationalize and strengthen existing institutions concerned with desertification and drought and involve other existing institutions, as appropriate, in order to make them more effective and to ensure more efficient use of resources;
(d) promote the exchange of information on appropriate technology, knowledge, know-how and practices between and among them; and
(e) develop contingency plans for mitigating the effects of drought in areas degraded by desertification and/or drought.

2. Pursuant to the general and specific obligations set out in articles 4 and 5 of the Convention, affected African country Parties shall aim to:
(a) make appropriate financial allocations from their national budgets consistent with national conditions and capabilities and reflecting the new priority Africa has accorded to the phenomenon of desertification and/or drought;
(b) sustain and strengthen reforms currently in progress towards greater decentralization and resource tenure as well as reinforce participation of local populations and communities; and
(c) identify and mobilize new and additional national financial resources, and expand, as a matter of priority, existing national capabilities and facilities to mobilize domestic financial resources.

Article 5

Commitments and obligations of developed country Parties

1. In fulfilling their obligations pursuant to articles 4, 6 and 7 of the Convention, developed country Parties shall give priority to affected African country Parties and, in this context, shall:
(a) assist them to combat desertification and/or mitigate the effects of drought by, *inter alia*, providing and/or facilitating access to financial and/or other resources, and promoting, financing and/or facilitating the financing of the transfer, adaptation and access to appropriate environmental technologies and know-how, as mutually agreed and in accordance with national policies, taking into account their adoption of poverty eradication as a central strategy;
(b) continue to allocate significant resources and/or increase resources to combat desertification and/or mitigate the effects of drought; and
(c) assist them in strengthening capacities to enable them to improve their institutional frameworks, as well as their scientific and technical capabilities, information collection and analysis, and research

and development for the purpose of combating desertification and/or mitigating the effects of drought.

2. Other country Parties may provide, on a voluntary basis, technology, knowledge and know-how relating to desertification and/or financial resources, to affected African country Parties. The transfer of such knowledge, know-how and techniques is facilitated by international cooperation.

Article 6

Strategic planning framework for sustainable development

1. National action programmes shall be a central and integral part of a broader process of formulating national policies for the sustainable development of affected African country Parties.

2. A consultative and participatory process involving appropriate levels of government, local populations, communities and non-governmental organizations shall be undertaken to provide guidance on a strategy with flexible planning to allow maximum participation from local populations and communities. As appropriate, bilateral and multilateral assistance agencies may be involved in this process at the request of an affected African country Party.

Article 7

Timetable for preparation of action programmes

Pending entry into force of this Convention, the African country Parties, in cooperation with other members of the international community, as appropriate, shall, to the extent possible, provisionally apply those provisions of the Convention relating to the preparation of national, subregional and regional action programmes.

Article 8

Content of national action programmes

1. Consistent with article 10 of the Convention, the overall strategy of national action programmes shall emphasize integrated local development programmes for affected areas, based on participatory mechanisms and on integration of strategies for poverty eradication into efforts to combat desertification and mitigate the effects of drought. The programmes shall aim at strengthening the capacity of local authorities and ensuring the

active involvement of local populations, communities and groups, with emphasis on education and training, mobilization of non-governmental organizations with proven expertise and strengthening of decentralized governmental structures.

2. National action programmes shall, as appropriate, include the following general features:

(a) the use, in developing and implementing national action programmes, of past experiences in combating desertification and/or mitigating the effects of drought, taking into account social, economic and ecological conditions;
(b) the identification of factors contributing to desertification and/or drought and the resources and capacities available and required, and the setting up of appropriate policies and institutional and other responses and measures necessary to combat those phenomena and/or mitigate their effects; and
(c) the increase in participation of local populations and communities, including women, farmers and pastoralists, and delegation to them of more responsibility for management.

3. National action programmes shall also, as appropriate, include the following:

(a) measures to improve the economic environment with a view to eradicating poverty:
  (i) increasing incomes and employment opportunities, especially for the poorest members of the community, by:
    – developing markets for farm and livestock products;
    – creating financial instruments suited to local needs;
    – encouraging diversification in agriculture and the setting-up of agricultural enterprises; and
    – developing economic activities of a para-agricultural or non-agricultural type;
  (ii) improving the long-term prospects of rural economies by the creation of:
    – incentives for productive investment and access to the means of production; and
    – price and tax policies and commercial practices that promote growth;
  (iii) defining and applying population and migration policies to reduce population pressure on land; and
  (iv) promoting the use of drought resistant crops and the application of integrated dry-land farming systems for food security purposes;
(b) measures to conserve natural resources:

(i) ensuring integrated and sustainable management of natural resources, including:
- agricultural land and pastoral land;
- vegetation cover and wildlife;
- forests;
- biological diversity;

(ii) training with regard to, and strengthening, public awareness and environmental education campaigns and disseminating knowledge of techniques relating to the sustainable management of natural resources; and

(iii) ensuring the development and efficient use of diverse energy sources, the promotion of alternative sources of energy, particularly solar energy, wind energy and bio-gas, and specific arrangements for the transfer, acquisition and adaptation of relevant technology to alleviate the pressure on fragile natural resources;

(c) measures to improve institutional organization:

(i) defining the roles and responsibilities of central government and local authorities within the framework of a land use planning policy;

(ii) encouraging a policy of active decentralization, devolving responsibility for management and decision-making to local authorities, and encouraging initiatives and the assumption of responsibility by local communities and the establishment of local structures; and

(iii) adjusting, as appropriate, the institutional and regulatory framework of natural resource management to provide security of land tenure for local populations;

(d) measures to improve knowledge of desertification:

(i) promoting research and the collection, processing and exchange of information on the scientific, technical and socio-economic aspects of desertification;

(ii) improving national capabilities in research and in the collection, processing, exchange and analysis of information so as to increase understanding and to translate the results of the analysis into operational terms; and

(iii) encouraging the medium- and long-term study of:
- socio-economic and cultural trends in affected areas;
- qualitative and quantitative trends in natural resources; and
- the interaction between climate and desertification; and

(e) measures to monitor and assess the effects of drought:

(i) developing strategies to evaluate the impacts of natural climate variability on regional drought and desertification and/or to utilize predictions of climate variability on seasonal to inter-annual time scales in efforts to mitigate the effects of drought;

(ii) improving early warning and response capacity, efficiently managing emergency relief and food aid, and improving food stocking and distribution systems, cattle protection schemes and public works and alternative livelihoods for drought prone areas; and

(iii) monitoring and assessing ecological degradation to provide reliable and timely information on the process and dynamics of resource degradation in order to facilitate better policy formulations and responses.

Article 9

Preparation of national action programmes and implementation and evaluation indicators

Each affected African country Party shall designate an appropriate national coordinating body to function as a catalyst in the preparation, implementation and evaluation of its national action programme. This coordinating body shall, in the light of article 3 and as appropriate:

(a) undertake an identification and review of actions, beginning with a locally driven consultation process, involving local populations and communities and with the cooperation of local administrative authorities, developed country Parties and intergovernmental and non-governmental organizations, on the basis of initial consultations of those concerned at the national level;

(b) identify and analyse the constraints, needs and gaps affecting development and sustainable land use and recommend practical measures to avoid duplication by making full use of relevant ongoing efforts and promote implementation of results;

(c) facilitate, design and formulate project activities based on interactive, flexible approaches in order to ensure active participation of the population in affected areas, to minimize the negative impact of such activities, and to identify and prioritize requirements for financial assistance and technical cooperation;

(d) establish pertinent, quantifiable and readily verifiable indicators to ensure the assessment and evaluation of national action programmes, which encompass actions in the short, medium and long terms, and of the implementation of such programmes; and

(e) prepare progress reports on the implementation of the national action programmes.

Article 10

Organizational framework of subregional action programmes

1. Pursuant to article 4 of the Convention, African country Parties shall cooperate in the preparation and implementation of subregional action programmes for central, eastern, northern, southern and western Africa and, in that regard, may delegate the following responsibilities to relevant subregional intergovernmental organizations:

(a) acting as focal points for preparatory activities and coordinating the implementation of the subregional action programmes;
(b) assisting in the preparation and implementation of national action programmes;
(c) facilitating the exchange of information, experience and know-how as well as providing advice on the review of national legislation; and
(d) any other responsibilities relating to the implementation of subregional action programmes.

2. Specialized subregional institutions may provide support, upon request, and/or be entrusted with the responsibility to coordinate activities in their respective fields of competence.

Article 11

Content and preparation of subregional action programmes

Subregional action programmes shall focus on issues that are better addressed at the subregional level. They shall establish, where necessary, mechanisms for the management of shared natural resources. Such mechanisms shall effectively handle transboundary problems associated with desertification and/or drought and shall provide support for the harmonious implementation of national action programmes. Priority areas for subregional action programmes shall, as appropriate, focus on:

(a) joint programmes for the sustainable management of transboundary natural resources through bilateral and multilateral mechanisms, as appropriate;
(b) coordination of programmes to develop alternative energy sources;
(c) cooperation in the management and control of pests as well as of plant and animal diseases;
(d) capacity-building, education and public awareness activities that are better carried out or supported at the subregional level;
(e) scientific and technical cooperation, particularly in the climatological,

meteorological and hydrological fields, including networking for data collection and assessment, information sharing and project monitoring, and coordination and prioritization of research and development activities;

(f) early warning systems and joint planning for mitigating the effects of drought, including measures to address the problems resulting from environmentally induced migrations;

(g) exploration of ways of sharing experiences, particularly regarding participation of local populations and communities, and creation of an enabling environment for improved land use management and for use of appropriate technologies;

(h) strengthening of the capacity of subregional organizations to coordinate and provide technical services, as well as establishment, reorientation and strengthening of subregional centres and institutions; and

(i) development of policies in fields, such as trade, which have impact upon affected areas and populations, including policies for the coordination of regional marketing regimes and for common infrastructure.

Article 12

Organizational framework of the regional action programme

1. Pursuant to article 11 of the Convention, African country Parties shall jointly determine the procedures for preparing and implementing the regional action programme.

2. The Parties may provide appropriate support to relevant African regional institutions and organizations to enable them to assist African country Parties to fulfil their responsibilities under the Convention.

Article 13

Content of the regional action programme

The regional action programme includes measures relating to combating desertification and/or mitigating the effects of drought in the following priority areas, as appropriate:

(a) development of regional cooperation and coordination of subregional action programmes for building regional consensus on key policy areas, including through regular consultations of subregional organizations;

(b) promotion of capacity-building in activities which are better implemented at the regional level;

(c) the seeking of solutions with the international community to global economic and social issues that have an impact on affected areas taking into account article 4, paragraph 2 (b) of the Convention;

(d) promotion among the affected country Parties of Africa and its subregions, as well as with other affected regions, of exchange of information and appropriate techniques, technical know-how and relevant experience; promotion of scientific and technological cooperation particularly in the fields of climatology, meteorology, hydrology, water resource development and alternative energy sources; coordination of subregional and regional research activities; and identification of regional priorities for research and development;

(e) coordination of networks for systematic observation and assessment and information exchange, as well as their integration into world-wide networks; and

(f) coordination of and reinforcement of subregional and regional early warning systems and drought contingency plans.

Article 14

Financial resources

1. Pursuant to article 20 of the Convention and article 4, paragraph 2, affected African country Parties shall endeavour to provide a macroeconomic framework conducive to the mobilization of financial resources and shall develop policies and establish procedures to channel resources more effectively to local development programmes, including through non-governmental organizations, as appropriate.

2. Pursuant to article 21, paragraphs 4 and 5 of the Convention, the Parties agree to establish an inventory of sources of funding at the national, subregional, regional and international levels to ensure the rational use of existing resources and to identify gaps in resource allocation, to facilitate implementation of the action programmes. The inventory shall be regularly reviewed and updated.

3. Consistent with article 7 of the Convention, the developed country Parties shall continue to allocate significant resources and/or increased resources as well as other forms of assistance to affected African country Parties on the basis of partnership agreements and arrangements referred to in article 18, giving, *inter alia*, due attention to matters related to debt, international trade and marketing arrangements in accordance with article 4, paragraph 2 (b) of the Convention.

Article 15

Financial mechanisms

1. Consistent with article 7 of the Convention underscoring the priority to affected African country Parties and considering the particular situation prevailing in this region, the Parties shall pay special attention to the implementation in Africa of the provisions of article 21, paragraph 1 (d) and (e) of the Convention, notably by:
   (a) facilitating the establishment of mechanisms, such as national desertification funds, to channel financial resources to the local level; and
   (b) strengthening existing funds and financial mechanisms at the subregional and regional levels.

2. Consistent with articles 20 and 21 of the Convention, the Parties which are also members of the governing bodies of relevant regional and subregional financial institutions, including the African Development Bank and the African Development Fund, shall promote efforts to give due priority and attention to the activities of those institutions that advance the implementation of this Annex.

3. The Parties shall streamline, to the extent possible, procedures for channelling funds to affected African country Parties.

Article 16

Technical assistance and cooperation

The Parties undertake, in accordance with their respective capabilities, to rationalize technical assistance to, and cooperation with, African country Parties with a view to increasing project and programme effectiveness by, *inter alia*:

(a) limiting the costs of support measures and backstopping, especially overhead costs; in any case, such costs shall only represent an appropriately low percentage of the total cost of the project so as to maximize project efficiency;
(b) giving preference to the utilization of competent national experts or, where necessary, competent experts from within the subregion and/or region, in project design, preparation and implementation, and to the building of local expertise where it does not exist; and
(c) effectively managing and coordinating, as well as efficiently utilizing, technical assistance to be provided.

Article 17

Transfer, acquisition , adaptation and access to environmentally sound technology

In implementing article 18 of the Convention relating to transfer, acquisition, adaptation and development of technology, the Parties undertake to give priority to African country Parties and, as necessary, to develop with them new models of partnership and cooperation with a view to strengthening capacity-building in the fields of scientific research and development and information collection and dissemination to enable them to implement their strategies to combat desertification and mitigate the effects of drought.

Article 18

Coordination and partnership agreements

1. African country Parties shall coordinate the preparation, negotiation and implementation of national, subregional and regional action programmes. They may involve, as appropriate, other Parties and relevant intergovernmental and non-governmental organizations in this process.

2. The objectives of such coordination shall be to ensure that financial and technical cooperation is consistent with the Convention and to provide the necessary continuity in the use and administration of resources.

3. African country Parties shall organize consultative processes at the national, subregional and regional levels. These consultative processes may:
   (a) serve as a forum to negotiate and conclude partnership agreements based on national, subregional and regional action programmes; and
   (b) specify the contribution of African country Parties and other members of the consultative groups to the programmes and identify priorities and agreements on implementation and evaluation indicators, as well as funding arrangements for implementation.

4. The Permanent Secretariat may, at the request of African country Parties, pursuant to article 23 of the Convention, facilitate the convocation of such consultative processes by:
   (a) providing advice on the organization of effective consultative arrangements, drawing on experiences from other such arrangements;
   (b) providing information to relevant bilateral and multilateral agencies concerning consultative meetings or processes, and encouraging their active involvement; and

(c) providing other information that may be relevant in establishing or improving consultative arrangements.

5. The subregional and regional coordinating bodies shall, *inter alia*:
(a) recommend appropriate adjustments to partnership agreements;
(b) monitor, assess and report on the implementation of the agreed subregional and regional programmes; and
(c) aim to ensure efficient communication and cooperation among African country Parties.

6. Participation in the consultative groups shall, as appropriate, be open to Governments, interested groups and donors, relevant organs, funds and programmes of the United Nations system, relevant subregional and regional organizations, and representatives of relevant non-governmental organizations. Participants of each consultative group shall determine the modalities of its management and operation.

7. Pursuant to article 14 of the Convention, developed country Parties are encouraged to develop, on their own initiative, an informal process of consultation and coordination among themselves, at the national, subregional and regional levels, and, at the request of an affected African country Party or of an appropriate subregional or regional organization, to participate in a national, subregional or regional consultative process that would evaluate and respond to assistance needs in order to facilitate implementation.

Article 19

Follow-up arrangements

Follow-up of this Annex shall be carried out by African country Parties in accordance with the Convention as follows:
(a) at the national level, by a mechanism the composition of which should be determined by each affected African country Party and which shall include representatives of local communities and shall function under the supervision of the national coordinating body referred to in article 9;
(b) at the subregional level, by a multidisciplinary scientific and technical consultative committee, the composition and modalities of operation of which shall be determined by the African country Parties of the subregion concerned; and
(c) at the regional level, by mechanisms defined in accordance with the relevant provisions of the Treaty establishing the African Economic Community, and by an African Scientific and Technical Advisory Committee.

ANNEX II

REGIONAL IMPLEMENTATION ANNEX FOR ASIA

Article 1

Purpose

The purpose of this Annex is to provide guidelines and arrangements for the effective implementation of the Convention in the affected country Parties of the Asian region in the light of its particular conditions.

Article 2

Particular conditions of the Asian region

In carrying out their obligations under the Convention, the Parties shall, as appropriate, take into consideration the following particular conditions which apply in varying degrees to the affected country Parties of the region:
(a) the high proportion of areas in their territories affected by, or vulnerable to, desertification and drought and the broad diversity of these areas with regard to climate, topography, land use and socio-economic systems;
(b) the heavy pressure on natural resources for livelihoods;
(c) the existence of production systems, directly related to widespread poverty, leading to land degradation and to pressure on scarce water resources;
(d) the significant impact of conditions in the world economy and social problems such as poverty, poor health and nutrition, lack of food security, migration, displaced persons and demographic dynamics;
(e) their expanding, but still insufficient, capacity and institutional frameworks to deal with national desertification and drought problems; and
(f) their need for international cooperation to pursue sustainable development objectives relating to combating desertification and mitigating the effects of drought.

Article 3

Framework for national action programmes

1. National action programmes shall be an integral part of broader national policies for sustainable development of the affected country Parties of the region.

2. The affected country Parties shall, as appropriate, develop national action programmes pursuant to articles 9 to 11 of the Convention, paying special attention to article 10, paragraph 2 (f). As appropriate, bilateral and multilateral cooperation agencies may be involved in this process at the request of the affected country Party concerned.

Article 4

National action programmes

1. In preparing and implementing national action programmes, the affected country Parties of the region, consistent with their respective circumstances and policies, may, *inter alia*, as appropriate:

(a) designate appropriate bodies responsible for the preparation, coordination and implementation of their action programmes;

(b) involve affected populations, including local communities, in the elaboration, coordination and implementation of their action programmes through a locally driven consultative process, with the cooperation of local authorities and relevant national and non-governmental organizations;

(c) survey the state of the environment in affected areas to assess the causes and consequences of desertification and to determine priority areas for action;

(d) evaluate, with the participation of affected populations, past and current programmes for combating desertification and mitigating the effects of drought, in order to design a strategy and elaborate activities in their action programmes;

(e) prepare technical and financial programmes based on the information derived from the activities in subparagraphs (a) to (d);

(f) develop and utilize procedures and benchmarks for evaluating implementation of their action programmes;

(g) promote the integrated management of drainage basins, the conservation of soil resources, and the enhancement and efficient use of water resources;

(h) strengthen and/or establish information, evaluation and follow-up and early warning systems in regions prone to desertification and drought, taking account of climatological, meteorological, hydrological, biological and other relevant factors; and

(i) formulate in a spirit of partnership, where international cooperation, including financial and technical resources, is involved, appropriate arrangements supporting their action programmes.

2. Consistent with article 10 of the Convention, the overall strategy of national action programmes shall emphasize integrated local development

programmes for affected areas, based on participatory mechanisms and on the integration of strategies for poverty eradication into efforts to combat desertification and mitigate the effects of drought. Sectoral measures in the action programmes shall be grouped in priority fields which take account of the broad diversity of affected areas in the region referred to in article 2 (a).

Article 5

Subregional and joint action programmes

1. Pursuant to article 11 of the Convention, affected country Parties in Asia may mutually agree to consult and cooperate with other Parties, as appropriate, to prepare and implement subregional or joint action programmes, as appropriate, in order to complement, and increase effectiveness in the implementation of, national action programmes. In either case, the relevant Parties may jointly agree to entrust subregional, including bilateral or national organizations, or specialized institutions, with responsibilities relating to the preparation, coordination and implementation of programmes. Such organizations or institutions may also act as focal points for the promotion and coordination of actions pursuant to articles 16 to 18 of the Convention.

2. In preparing and implementing subregional or joint action programmes, the affected country Parties of the region shall, *inter alia*, as appropriate:

(a) identify, in cooperation with national institutions, priorities relating to combating desertification and mitigating the effects of drought which can better be met by such programmes, as well as relevant activities which could be effectively carried out through them;

(b) evaluate the operational capacities and activities of relevant regional, subregional and national institutions;

(c) assess existing programmes relating to desertification and drought among all or some parties of the region or subregion and their relationship with national action programmes; and

(d) formulate in a spirit of partnership, where international cooperation, including financial and technical resources, is involved, appropriate bilateral and/or multilateral arrangements supporting the programmes.

3. Subregional or joint action programmes may include agreed joint programmes for the sustainable management of transboundary natural resources relating to desertification, priorities for coordination and other

activities in the fields of capacity-building, scientific and technical cooperation, particularly drought early warning systems and information sharing, and means of strengthening the relevant subregional and other organizations or institutions.

Article 6

Regional activities

Regional activities for the enhancement of subregional or joint action programmes may include, *inter alia*, measures to strengthen institutions and mechanisms for coordination and cooperation at the national, subregional and regional levels, and to promote the implementation of articles 16 to 19 of the Convention. These activities may also include:
(a) promoting and strengthening technical cooperation networks;
(b) preparing inventories of technologies, knowledge, know-how and practices, as well as traditional and local technologies and know-how, and promoting their dissemination and use;
(c) evaluating the requirements for technology transfer and promoting the adaptation and use of such technologies; and
(d) encouraging public awareness programmes and promoting capacity-building at all levels, strengthening training, research and development and building systems for human resource development.

Article 7

Financial resources and mechanisms

1. The Parties shall, in view of the importance of combating desertification and mitigating the effects of drought in the Asian region, promote the mobilization of substantial financial resources and the availability of financial mechanisms, pursuant to articles 20 and 21 of the Convention.

2. In conformity with the Convention and on the basis of the coordinating mechanism provided for in article 8 and in accordance with their national development policies, affected country Parties of the region shall, individually or jointly:
   (a) adopt measures to rationalize and strengthen mechanisms to supply funds through public and private investment with a view to achieving specific results in action to combat desertification and mitigate the effects of drought;
   (b) identify international cooperation requirements in support of

national efforts, particularly financial, technical and technological; and

(c) promote the participation of bilateral and/or multilateral financial cooperation institutions with a view to ensuring implementation of the Convention.

3. The Parties shall streamline, to the extent possible, procedures for channelling funds to affected country Parties in the region.

Article 8

Cooperation and coordination mechanisms

1. Affected country Parties, through the appropriate bodies designated pursuant to article 4, paragraph 1 (a), and other Parties in the region, may, as appropriate, set up a mechanism for, *inter alia*, the following purposes:

(a) exchange of information, experience, knowledge and know-how;
(b) cooperation and coordination of actions, including bilateral and multilateral arrangements, at the subregional and regional levels;
(c) promotion of scientific, technical, technological and financial cooperation pursuant to articles 5 to 7;
(d) identification of external cooperation requirements; and
(e) follow-up and evaluation of the implementation of action programmes.

2. Affected country Parties, through the appropriate bodies designated pursuant to article 4, paragraph 1 (a), and other Parties in the region, may also, as appropriate, consult and coordinate as regards the national, subregional and joint action programmes. They may involve, as appropriate, other Parties and relevant intergovernmental and non-governmental organizations in this process. Such coordination shall, *inter alia*, seek to secure agreement on opportunities for international cooperation in accordance with articles 20 and 21 of the Convention, enhance technical cooperation and channel resources so that they are used effectively.

3. Affected country Parties of the region shall hold periodic coordination meetings, and the Permanent Secretariat may, at their request, pursuant to article 23 of the Convention, facilitate the convocation of such coordination meetings by:

(a) providing advice on the organization of effective coordination arrangements, drawing on experience from other such arrangements;
(b) providing information to relevant bilateral and multilateral agencies concerning coordination meetings, and encouraging their active involvement; and

(c) providing other information that may be relevant in establishing or improving coordination processes.

ANNEX III

REGIONAL IMPLEMENTATION ANNEX FOR LATIN AMERICA AND THE CARIBBEAN

Article 1

Purpose

The purpose of this Annex is to provide general guidelines for the implementation of the Convention in the Latin American and Caribbean region, in light of its particular conditions.

Article 2

Particular conditions of the Latin American and Caribbean region

The Parties shall, in accordance with the provisions of the Convention, take into consideration the following particular conditions of the region:

(a) the existence of broad expanses which are vulnerable and have been severely affected by desertification and/or drought and in which diverse characteristics may be observed, depending on the area in which they occur; this cumulative and intensifying process has negative social, cultural, economic and environmental effects which are all the more serious in that the region contains one of the largest resources of biological diversity in the world;

(b) the frequent use of unsustainable development practices in affected areas as a result of complex interactions among physical, biological, political, social, cultural and economic factors, including international economic factors such as external indebtedness, deteriorating terms of trade and trade practices which affect markets for agricultural, fishery and forestry products; and

(c) a sharp drop in the productivity of ecosystems being the main consequence of desertification and drought, taking the form of a decline in agricultural, livestock and forestry yields and a loss of biological diversity; from the social pint of view, the results are impoverishment, migration, internal population movements, and the deterioration of the qualify of life; the region will therefore have to adopt an integrated approach to problems of desertification and drought by promoting sustainable development models that are in keeping with the environmental, economic and social situation in each country.

Article 3

Action programmes

1. In conformity with the Convention, in particular its articles 9 to 11, and in accordance with their national development policies, affected country Parties of the region shall, as appropriate, prepare and implement national action programmes to combat desertification and mitigate the effects of drought as an integral part of their national policies for sustainable development. Subregional and regional programmes may be prepared and implemented in accordance with the requirements of the region.

2. In the preparation of their national action programmes, affected country Parties of the region shall pay particular attention to article 10, paragraph 2 (f) of the Convention.

Article 4

Content of national action programmes

In the light of their respective situations, the affected country parties of the region may take account, *inter alia*, of the following thematic issues in developing their national strategies for action to combat desertification and/or mitigate the effects of drought, pursuant to article 5 of the Convention:

(a) increasing capacities, education and public awareness, technical, scientific and technological cooperation and financial resources and mechanisms;
(b) eradicating poverty and improving the quality of human life;
(c) achieving food security and sustainable development and management of agricultural, livestock-rearing, forestry and multipurpose activities;
(d) sustainable management of natural resources, especially the rational management of drainage basins;
(e) sustainable management of natural resources in high-altitude areas;
(f) rational management and conservation of soil resources and exploitation and efficient use of water resources;
(g) formulation and application of emergency plans to mitigate the effects of drought;
(h) strengthening and/or establishing information, evaluation and follow-up and early warning systems in areas prone to desertification and

drought, taking account of climatological, meteorological, hydrological, biological, soil, economic and social factors;

(i) developing, managing and efficiently using diverse sources of energy, including the promotion of alternative sources;

(j) conservation and sustainable use of biodiversity in accordance with the provisions of the Convention on Biological Diversity;

(k) consideration of demographic aspects related to desertification and drought; and

(l) establishing or strengthening institutional and legal frameworks permitting application of the Convention and aimed, *inter alia*, at decentralizing administrative structures and functions relating to desertification and drought, with the participation of affected communities and society in general.

Article 5

Technical, scientific and technological cooperation

In conformity with the Convention, in particular its articles 16 to 18, and on the basis of the coordinating mechanism provided for in article 7, affected country Parties of the region shall, individually or jointly:

(a) promote the strengthening of technical cooperation networks and national, subregional and regional information systems, as well as their integration, as appropriate, in world-wide sources of information;

(b) prepare an inventory of available technologies and know-how and promote their dissemination and use;

(c) promote the use of traditional technology, knowledge, know-how and practices pursuant to article 18, paragraph 2 (b), of the Convention;

(d) identify transfer of technology requirements; and

(e) promote the development, adaptation, adoption and transfer of relevant existing and new environmentally sound technologies.

Article 6

Financial resources and mechanisms

In conformity with the Convention, in particular its articles 20 and 21, on the basis of the coordinating mechanism provided for in article 7 and in accordance with their national development policies, affected country Parties of the region shall, individually or jointly:

(a) adopt measures to rationalize and strengthen mechanisms to supply funds through public and private investment with a view to achieving specific results in action to combat desertification and mitigate the effects of drought;

(b) identify international cooperation requirements in support of national efforts; and

(c) promote the participation of bilateral and/or multilateral financial cooperation institutions with a view to ensuring implementation of the Convention.

Article 7

Institutional framework

1. In order to give effect to this Annex, affected country Parties of the region shall:

(a) establish and/or strengthen national focal points to coordinate action to combat desertification and/or mitigate the effects of drought; and

(b) set up a mechanism to coordinate the national focal points for the following purposes:

(i) exchanges of information and experience;

(ii) coordination of activities at the subregional and regional levels;

(iii) promotion of technical, scientific, technological and financial cooperation;

(iv) identification of external cooperation requirements; and

(v) follow-up and evaluation of the implementation of action programmes.

2. Affected country Parties of the region shall hold periodic coordination meetings and the Permanent Secretariat may, at their request, pursuant to article 23 of the Convention, facilitate the convocation of such coordination meetings, by:

(a) providing advice on the organization of effective coordination arrangements, drawing on experience from other such arrangements;

(b) providing information to relevant bilateral and multilateral agencies concerning coordination meetings, and encouraging their active involvement; and

(c) providing other information that may be relevant in establishing or improving coordination processes.

ANNEX IV

REGIONAL IMPLEMENTATION ANNEX FOR THE NORTHERN MEDITERRANEAN

Article 1

Purpose

The purpose of this Annex is to provide guidelines and arrangements necessary for the effective implementation of the Convention in affected country Parties of the northern Mediterranean region in the light of its particular conditions.

Article 2

Particular conditions of the northern Mediterranean region

The particular conditions of the northern Mediterranean region referred to in article 1 include:

(a) semi-arid climatic conditions affecting large areas, seasonal droughts, very high rainfall variability and sudden and high-intensity rainfall;
(b) poor and highly erodible soils, prone to develop surface crusts;
(c) uneven relief with steep slopes and very diversified landscapes;
(d) extensive forest coverage losses due to frequent wildfires;
(e) crisis conditions in traditional agriculture with associated land abandonment and deterioration of soil and water conservation structures;
(f) unsustainable exploitation of water resources leading to serious environmental damage, including chemical pollution, salinization and exhaustion of aquifers; and
(g) concentration of economic activity in coastal areas as a result of urban growth, industrial activities, tourism and irrigated agriculture.

Article 3

Strategic planning framework for sustainable development

1. National action programmes shall be a central and integral part of the strategic planning framework for sustainable development of the affected country Parties of the northern Mediterranean.

2. A consultative and participatory process, involving appropriate levels of government, local communities and non-governmental organizations,

shall be undertaken to provide guidance on a strategy with flexible planning to allow maximum local participation, pursuant to article 10, paragraph 2 (f) of the Convention.

Article 4

Obligation to prepare national action programmes and timetable

Affected country Parties of the northern Mediterranean region shall prepare national action programmes and, as appropriate, subregional, regional or joint action programmes. The preparation of such programmes shall be finalized as soon as practicable.

Article 5

Preparation and implementation of national action programmes

In preparing and implementing national action programmes pursuant to articles 9 and 10 of the Convention, each affected country Party of the region shall, as appropriate:

(a) designate appropriate bodies responsible for the preparation, coordination and implementation of its programme;
(b) involve affected populations, including local communities, in the elaboration, coordination and implementation of the programme through a locally driven consultative process, with the cooperation of local authorities and relevant non-governmental organizations;
(c) survey the state of the environment in affected areas to assess the causes and consequences of desertification and to determine priority areas for action;
(d) evaluate, with the participation of affected populations, past and current programmes in order to design a strategy and elaborate activities in the action programme;
(e) prepare technical and financial programmes based on the information gained through the activities in subparagraphs (a) to (d); and
(f) develop and utilize procedures and benchmarks for monitoring and evaluating the implementation of the programme.

Article 6

Content of national action programmes

Affected country Parties of the region may include, in their national action programmes, measures relating to:

(a) legislative, institutional and administrative areas;
(b) land use patterns, management of water resources, soil conservation, forestry, agricultural activities and pasture and range management;
(c) management and conservation of wildlife and other forms of biological diversity;
(d) protection against forest fires;
(e) promotion of alternative livelihoods; and
(f) research, training and public awareness.

Article 7

Subregional, regional and joint action programmes

1. Affected country Parties of the region may, in accordance with article 11 of the Convention, prepare and implement subregional and/or regional action programmes in order to complement and increase the efficiency of national action programmes. Two or more affected country Parties of the region, may similarly agree to prepare a joint action programme between or among them.

2. The provisions of articles 5 and 6 shall apply *mutatis mutandis* to the preparation and implementation of subregional, regional and joint action programmes. In addition, such programmes may include the conduct of research and development activities concerning selected ecosystems in affected areas.

3. In preparing and implementing subregional, regional or joint action programmes, affected country Parties of the region shall, as appropriate:
(a) identify, in cooperation with national institutions, national objectives relating to desertification which can better be met by such programmes and relevant activities which could be effectively carried out through them;
(b) evaluate the operational capacities and activities of relevant regional, subregional and national institutions; and
(c) assess existing programmes relating to desertification among Parties of the region and their relationship with national action programmes.

Article 8

Coordination of subregional, regional and joint action programmes

Affected country Parties preparing a subregional, regional or joint action programme may establish a coordination committee composed of representatives of each affected country Party concerned to review progress in combating desertification, harmonize national action programmes, make recommendations at the various stages of preparation and implementation of the subregional, regional or joint action programme, and act as a focal point for the promotion and coordination of technical cooperation pursuant to articles 16 to 19 of the Convention.

Article 9

Non-eligibility for financial assistance

In implementing national, subregional, regional and joint action programmes, affected developed country Parties of the region are not eligible to receive financial assistance under this Convention.

Article 10

Coordination with other subregions and regions

Subregional, regional and joint action programmes in the northern Mediterranean region may be prepared and implemented in collaboration with those of other subregions or regions, particularly with those of the subregion of northern Africa.

PROTOCOL TO THE 1979 CONVENTION ON LONG-RANGE TRANSBOUNDARY AIR POLLUTION ON FURTHER REDUCTION OF SULPHUR EMISSIONS

and decision on the Structure and Functions of the Implementation Committee, as well as Procedures for its Review of Compliance

The Parties,

Determined to implement the Convention on Long-range Transboundary Air Pollution,

Concerned that emissions of sulphur and other air pollutants continue to be transported across international boundaries and, in exposed parts of Europe and North America, are causing widespread damage to natural resources of vital environmental and economic importance, such as forests, soils and waters, and to materials, including historic monuments, and, under certain circumstances, have harmful effects on human health,

Resolved to take precautionary measures to anticipate, prevent or minimize emissions of air pollutants and mitigate their adverse effects,

Convinced that where there are threats of serious or irreversible damage, lack of full scientific certainty should not be used as a reason for postponing such measures, taking into account that such precautionary measures to deal with emissions of air pollutants should be cost-effective,

Mindful that measures to control emissions of sulphur and other air pollutants would also contribute to the protection of the sensitive Arctic environment,

Considering that the predominant sources of air pollution contributing to the acidification of the environment are the combustion of fossil fuels for energy production, and the main technological processes in various industrial sectors, as well as transport, which lead to emissions of sulphur, nitrogen oxides, and other pollutants,

Conscious of the need for a cost-effective regional approach to combating air pollution that takes account of the variations in effects and abatement costs between countries,

Desiring to take further and more effective action to control and reduce sulphur emissions,

Cognizant that any sulphur control policy, however cost-effective it may be at the regional level, will result in a relatively heavy economic burden on countries with economies that are in transition to a market economy,

Bearing in mind that measures taken to reduce sulphur emissions should not constitute a means of arbitrary or unjustifiable discrimination or a disguised restriction on international competition and trade,

Taking into consideration existing scientific and technical data on emissions, atmospheric processes and effects on the environment of sulphur oxides, as well as on abatement costs,

Aware that, in addition to emissions of sulphur, emissions of nitrogen oxides and of ammonia are also causing acidification of the environment,

Noting that under the United Nations Framework Convention on Climate Change, adopted in New York on 9 May 1992, there is agreement to establish national policies and take corresponding measures to combat climate change, which can be expected to lead to reductions of sulphur emissions,

Affirming the need to ensure environmentally sound and sustainable development,

Recognizing the need to continue scientific and technical cooperation to elaborate further the approach based on critical loads and critical levels, including efforts to assess several air pollutants and various effects on the environment, materials and human health,

Underlining that scientific and technical knowledge is developing and that it will be necessary to take such developments into account when reviewing the adequacy of the obligations entered into under the present Protocol and deciding on further action,

Acknowledging the Protocol on the Reduction of Sulphur Emissions or Their Transboundary Fluxes by at least 30 per cent, adopted in Helsinki on 8 July 1985, and the measures already taken by many countries which have had the effect of reducing sulphur emissions,

Have agreed as follows:

Article 1

Definitions

For the purposes of the present Protocol,

1. "Convention" means the Convention on Long-range Transboundary Air Pollution, adopted in Geneva on 13 November 1979;

2. "EMEP" means the Cooperative Programme for Monitoring and Evaluation of the Long-range Transmission of Air Pollutants in Europe;

3. "Executive Body" means the Executive Body for the Convention constituted under article 10, paragraph 1, of the Convention;

4. "Commission" means the United Nations Economic Commission for Europe;

5. "Parties" means, unless the context otherwise requires, the Parties to the present Protocol;

6. "Geographical scope of EMEP" means the area defined in article 1, paragraph 4, of the Protocol to the 1979 Convention on Long-range Transboundary Air Pollution on Long-term Financing of the Cooperative Programme for Monitoring and Evaluation of the Long-range Transmission of Air Pollutants in Europe (EMEP), adopted in Geneva on 28 September 1984;

7. "SOMA" means a sulphur oxides management area designated in annex III under the conditions laid down in article 2, paragraph 3;

8. "Critical load" means a quantitative estimate of an exposure to one or more pollutants below which significant harmful effects on specified sensitive elements of the environment do not occur, according to present knowledge;

9. "Critical levels" means the concentration of pollutants in the atmosphere above which direct adverse effects on receptors, such as human beings, plants, ecosystems or materials, may occur, according to present knowledge;

10. "Critical sulphur deposition" means a quantitative estimate of the exposure to oxidized sulphur compounds, taking into account the effects of base cation uptake and base cation deposition, below which significant harmful effects on specified sensitive elements of the environment do not occur, according to present knowledge;

11. "Emission" means the discharge of substances into the atmosphere;

12. "Sulphur emissions" means all emissions of sulphur compounds expressed as kilotonnes of sulphur dioxide (kt SO_2) to the atmosphere originating from anthropogenic sources excluding from ships in international traffic outside territorial waters;

13. "Fuel" means any solid, liquid or gaseous combustible material with the exception of domestic refuse and toxic or dangerous waste;

14. "Stationary combustion source" means any technical apparatus or group of technical apparatus that is co-located on a common site and is or could be discharging waste gases through a common stack, in which fuels are oxidized in order to use the heat generated;

15. "Major new stationary combustion source" means any stationary combustion source the construction or substantial modification of which is authorized after 31 December 1995 and the thermal input of which, when operating at rated capacity, is at least 50 MW_{th}. It is a matter for the competent national authorities to decide whether a modification is substantial or not, taking into account such factors as the environmental benefits of the modification;

16. "Major existing stationary combustion source" means any existing stationary combustion source the thermal input of which, when operating at rated capacity, is at least 50 MW_{th};

17. "Gas oil"means any petroleum product within HS 2710, or any petroleum product which, by reason of its distillation limits, falls within the category of middle distillates intended for use as fuel and of which at least 85% by volume, including distillation losses, distils at 350° C;

18. "Emission limit value" means the permissible concentration of sulphur compounds expressed as sulphur dioxide in the waste gases from a stationary combustion source expressed in terms of mass per volume of the waste gases expressed in mg SO_2/Nm^3, assuming an oxygen content by volume in the waste gas of 3% in the case of liquid and gaseous fuels and 6% in the case of solid fuels;

19. "Emission limitation" means the permissible total quantity of sulphur compounds expressed as sulphur dioxide discharged from a combustion source or group of combustion sources located either on a common site or within a defined geographical area, expressed in kilotonnes per year;

20. "Desulphurization rate" means the ratio of the quantity of sulphur which is separated at the combustion source site over a given period to the quantity of sulphur contained in the fuel which is introduced into the combustion source facilities and which is used over the same period;

21. "Sulphur budget" means a matrix of calculated contributions to the deposition of oxidized sulphur compounds in receiving areas, originating from the emissions from specified areas.

Article 2

Basic obligations

1. The Parties shall control and reduce their sulphur emissions in order to protect human health and the environment from adverse effects, in particular acidifying effects, and to ensure, as far as possible, without entailing excessive costs, that depositions of oxidized sulphur compounds in the long term do not exceed critical loads for sulphur given, in annex I, as critical sulphur depositions, in accordance with present scientific knowledge.

2. As a first step, the Parties shall, as a minimum, reduce and maintain their annual sulphur emissions in accordance with the timing and levels specified in annex II.

3. In addition, any Party:
   (a) Whose total land area is greater than 2 million square kilometres;
   (b) Which has committed itself under paragraph 2 above to a national sulphur emission ceiling no greater than the lesser of its 1990 emissions or its obligation in the 1985 Helsinki Protocol on the Reduction of Sulphur Emissions or Their Transboundary Fluxes by at least 30%, as indicated in annex II;
   (c) Whose annual sulphur emissions that contribute to acidification in areas under the jurisdiction of one or more other Parties originate only from within areas under its jurisdiction that are listed as SOMAs in annex III, and has presented documentation to this effect; and
   (d) Which has specified upon signature of, or accession to, the present Protocol its intention to act in accordance with this paragraph,

shall, as a minimum, reduce and maintain its annual sulphur emissions in the area so listed in accordance with the timing and levels specified in annex II.

4. Furthermore, the Parties shall make use of the most effective measures for the reduction of sulphur emissions, appropriate in their particular circumstances, for new and existing sources, which include, *inter alia*:
   - Measures to increase energy efficiency;
   - Measures to increase the use of renewable energy;
   - Measures to reduce the sulphur content of particular fuels and to encourage the use of fuel with a low sulphur content, including the combined use of high-sulphur with low-sulphur or sulphur-free fuel;

– Measures to apply best available control technologies not entailing excessive cost,

using the guidance in annex IV.

5. Each Party, except those Parties subject to the United States/Canada Air Quality Agreement of 1991, shall as a minimum:

(a) Apply emission limit values at least as stringent as those specified in annex V to all major new stationary combustion sources;

(b) No later than 1 July 2004 apply, as far as possible without entailing excessive costs, emission limit values at least as stringent as those specified in annex V to those major existing stationary combustion sources the thermal input of which is above 500 MW_{th} taking into account the remaining lifetime of a plant, calculated from the date of entry into force of the present Protocol, or apply equivalent emission limitations or other appropriate provisions, provided that these achieve the sulphur emission ceilings specified in annex II and, subsequently, further approach the critical loads as given in annex I; and no later than 1 July 2004 apply emission limit values or emission limitations to those major existing stationary combustion sources the thermal input of which is between 50 and 500 MW_{th} using annex V as guidance;

(c) No later than two years after the date of entry into force of the present Protocol apply national standards for the sulphur content of gas oil at least as stringent as those specified in annex V. In cases where the supply of gas oil cannot otherwise by ensured, a State may extend the time period given in this subparagraph to a period of up to ten years. In this case it shall specify, in a declaration to be deposited together with the instrument of ratification, acceptance, approval or accession, its intention to extend the time period.

6. The Parties may, in addition, apply economic instruments to encourage the adoption of cost-effective approaches to the reduction of sulphur emissions.

7. The Parties to this Protocol may, at a session of the Executive Body, in accordance with rules and conditions which the Executive Body shall elaborate and adopt, decide whether two or more Parties may jointly implement the obligations set out in annex II. These rules and conditions shall ensure the fulfilment of the obligations set out in paragraph 2 above and also promote the achievement of the environmental objectives set out in paragraph 1 above.

8. The Parties shall, subject to the outcome of the first review provided for under article 8 and no later than one year after the completion of that review, commence negotiations on further obligations to reduce emissions.

Article 3

Exchange of technology

1. The Parties shall, consistent with their national laws, regulations and practices, facilitate the exchange of technologies and techniques, including those that increase energy efficiency, the use of renewable energy and the processing of low-sulphur fuels, to reduce sulphur emissions, particularly through the promotion of:

(a) The commercial exchange of available technology;
(b) Direct industrial contacts and cooperation, including joint ventures;
(c) The exchange of information and experience;
(d) The provision of technical assistance.

2. In promoting the activities specified in paragraph 1 above, the Parties shall create favourable conditions by facilitating contacts and cooperation among appropriate organizations and individuals in the private and public sectors that are capable of providing technology, design and engineering services, equipment or finance.

3. The Parties shall, no later than six months after the date of entry into force of the present Protocol, commence consideration of procedures to create more favourable conditions for the exchange of technology to reduce sulphur emissions.

Article 4

National strategies, policies, programmes, measures and information

1. Each Party shall, in order to implement its obligations under article 2:

(a) Adopt national strategies, policies and programmes, no later than six months after the present Protocol enters into force for it; and
(b) Take and apply national measures

to control and reduce its sulphur emissions.

2. Each Party shall collect and maintain information on:

(a) Actual levels of sulphur emissions, and of ambient concentrations and depositions of oxidized sulphur and other acidifying compounds, taking into account, for those Parties within the geographical scope of EMEP, the work plan of EMEP; and
(b) The effects of depositions of oxidized sulphur and other acidifying compounds.

Article 5

Reporting

1. Each Party shall report, through the Executive Secretary of the Commission, to the Executive Body, on a periodic basis as determined by the Executive Body, information on:

(a) The implementation of national strategies, policies, programmes and measures referred to in article 4, paragraph 1;

(b) The levels of national annual sulphur emissions, in accordance with guidelines adopted by the Executive Body, containing emission data for all relevant source categories; and

(c) The implementation of other obligations that it has entered into under the present Protocol,

in conformity with a decision regarding format and content to be adopted by the Parties at a session of the Executive Body. The terms of this decision shall be reviewed as necessary to identify any additional elements regarding the format and/or content of the information that are to be included in the reports.

2. Each Party within the geographical scope of EMEP shall report, through the Executive Secretary of the Commission, to EMEP, on a periodic basis to be determined by the Steering Body of EMEP and approved by the Parties at a session of the Executive Body information on the levels of sulphur emissions with temporal and spatial resolution as specified by the Steering Body of EMEP.

3. In good time before each annual session of the Executive Body, EMEP shall provide information on:

(a) Ambient concentrations and deposition of oxidized sulphur compounds; and

(b) Calculations of sulphur budgets.

Parties in areas outside the geographical scope of EMEP shall make available similar information if requested to do so by the Executive Body.

4. The Executive Body shall, in accordance with article 10, paragraph 2 (b), of the Convention, arrange for the preparation of information on the effects of depositions of oxidized sulphur and other acidifying compounds.

5. The Parties shall, at sessions of the Executive Body, arrange for the preparation, at regular intervals, of revised information on calculated and internationally optimized allocations of emission reductions for the States within the geographical scope of EMEP, with integrated assessment models, with a view to reducing further, for the purposes of article 2, paragraph

1, of the present Protocol, the difference between actual depositions of oxidized sulphur compounds and critical load values.

Article 6

Research, development and monitoring

The Parties shall encourage research, development, monitoring and cooperation related to:

(a) The international harmonization of methods for the establishment of critical loads and critical levels and the elaboration of procedures for such harmonization;

(b) The improvement of monitoring techniques and systems and of the modelling of transport, concentrations and deposition of sulphur compounds;

(c) Strategies for the further reduction of sulphur emissions based on critical loads and critical levels as well as on technical developments, and the improvement of integrated assessment modelling to calculate internationally optimized allocations of emission reductions taking into account an equitable distribution of abatement costs;

(d) The understanding of the wider effects of sulphur emissions on human health, the environment, in particular acidification, and materials, including historic and cultural monuments, taking into account the relationship between sulphur oxides, nitrogen oxides, ammonia, volatile organic compounds and tropospheric ozone;

(e) Emission abatement technologies, and technologies and techniques to enhance energy efficiency, energy conservation and the use of renewable energy;

(f) The economic evaluation of benefits for the environment and human health resulting from the reduction of sulphur emissions.

Article 7

Compliance

1. An Implementation Committee is hereby established to review the implementation of the present Protocol and compliance by the Parties with their obligations. It shall report to the Parties at sessions of the Executive Body and may make such recommendations to them as it considers appropriate.

2. Upon consideration of a report, and any recommendations, of the Implementation Committee, the Parties, taking into account the

circumstances of a matter and in accordance with Convention practice, may decide upon and call for action to bring about full compliance with the present Protocol, including measures to assist a Party's compliance with the protocol, and to further the objectives of the Protocol.

3. The Parties shall, at the first session of the Executive Body after the entry into force of the present Protocol, adopt a decision that sets out the structure and functions of the Implementation Committee as well as procedures for its review of compliance.

4. The application of the compliance procedure shall be without prejudice to the provisions of article 9 of the present Protocol.

Article 8

Reviews by the Parties at sessions of the Executive Body

1. The Parties shall, at sessions of the Executive Body, pursuant to article 10, paragraph 2 (a), of the Convention, review the information supplied by the Parties and EMEP, the data on the effects of depositions of sulphur and other acidifying compounds and the reports of the Implementation Committee referred to in article 7, paragraph 1, of the present Protocol.

2. (a) The Parties shall, at sessions of the Executive Body, keep under review the obligations set out in the present Protocol, including:
   (i) Their obligations in relation to their calculated and internationally optimized allocations of emission reductions referred to in article 5, paragraph 5; and
   (ii) The adequacy of the obligations and the progress made towards the achievement of the objectives of the present Protocol;
(b) Reviews shall take into account the best available scientific information on acidification, including assessments of critical loads, technological developments, changing economic conditions and the fulfilment of the obligations on emission levels;
(c) In the context of such reviews, any Party whose obligations on sulphur emission ceilings under annex II hereto do not conform to the calculated and internationally optimized allocations of emission reductions for that Party, required to reduce the difference between depositions of sulphur in 1990 and critical sulphur depositions within the geographical scope of EMEP by at least 60%, shall make every effort to undertake revised obligations;
(d) The procedures, methods and timing for such reviews shall be specified by the Parties at a session of the Executive Body. The first such review shall be completed in 1997.

Article 9

Settlement of disputes

1. In the event of a dispute between any two or more Parties concerning the interpretation or application of the present Protocol, the Parties concerned shall seek a settlement of the dispute through negotiation or any other peaceful means of their own choice. The Parties to the dispute shall inform the Executive Body of their dispute.

2. When ratifying, accepting, approving or acceding to the present Protocol, or at any time thereafter, a Party which is not a regional economic integration organization may declare in a written instrument submitted to the Depositary that, in respect of any dispute concerning the interpretation or application of the Protocol, it recognizes one or both of the following means of dispute settlement as compulsory *ipso facto* and without agreement, in relation to any Party accepting the same obligation:

(a) Submission of the dispute to the International Court of Justice;

(b) Arbitration in accordance with procedures to be adopted by the Parties at a session of the Executive Body as soon as practicable, in an annex on arbitration.

A Party which is a regional economic integration organization may make a declaration with like effect in relation to arbitration in accordance with the procedures referred to in subparagraph (b) above.

3. A declaration made under paragraph 2 above shall remain in force until it expires in accordance with its terms or until three months after written notice of its revocation has been deposited with the Depositary.

4. A new declaration, a notice of revocation or the expiry of a declaration shall not in any way affect proceedings pending before the International Court of Justice or the arbitral tribunal, unless the Parties to the dispute agree otherwise.

5. Except in a case where the Parties to a dispute have accepted the same means of dispute settlement under paragraph 2, if after twelve months following notification by one Party to another that a dispute exists between them, the Parties concerned have not been able to settle their dispute through the means mentioned in paragraph 1 above, the dispute shall be submitted, at the request of any of the Parties to the dispute, to conciliation.

6. For the purpose of paragraph 5, a conciliation commission shall be created. The commission shall be composed of an equal number of members appointed by each Party concerned or, where Parties in conciliation share

the same interest, by the group sharing that interest, and a chairman chosen jointly by the members so appointed. The commission shall render a recommendatory award, which the Parties shall consider in good faith.

Article 10

Annexes

The annexes to the present Protocol shall form an integral part of the Protocol. Annexes I and IV are recommendatory in character.

Article 11

Amendments and adjustments

1. Any Party may propose amendments to the present Protocol. Any Party to the Convention may propose an adjustment to annex II to the present Protocol to add to it its name, together with emission levels, sulphur emission ceilings and percentage emission reductions.

2. Such proposed amendments and adjustments shall be submitted in writing to the Executive Secretary of the Commission, who shall communicate them to all Parties. The Parties shall discuss the proposed amendments and adjustments at the next session of the Executive Body, provided that those proposals have been circulated by the Executive Secretary to the Parties at least ninety days in advance.

3. Amendments to the present Protocol and to its annexes II, III and V shall be adopted by consensus of the Parties present at a session of the Executive Body, and shall enter into force for the Parties which have accepted them on the ninetieth day after the date on which two thirds of the Parties have deposited with the Depositary their instruments of acceptance thereof. Amendments shall enter into force for any other Party on the ninetieth day after the date on which that Party has deposited its instrument of acceptance thereof.

4. Amendments to the annexes to the present Protocol, other than to the annexes referred to in paragraph 3 above, shall be adopted by consensus of the Parties present at a session of the Executive Body. On the expiry of ninety days from the date of its communication by the Executive Secretary of the Commission, an amendment to any such annex shall become effective for those Parties which have not submitted to the Depositary a notification in accordance with the provisions of paragraph 5 below, provided that at least sixteen Parties have not submitted such a notification.

5. Any Party that is unable to approve an amendment to an annex, other than to an annex referred to in paragraph 3 above, shall so notify the Depositary in writing within ninety days from the date of the communication of its adoption. The Depositary shall without delay notify all Parties of any such notification received. A Party may at any time substitute an acceptance for its previous notification and, upon deposit of an instrument of acceptance with the Depositary, the amendment to such an annex shall become effective for that Party.

6. Adjustments to annex II shall be adopted by consensus of the Parties present at a session of the Executive Body and shall become effective for all Parties to the present Protocol on the ninetieth day following the date on which the Executive Secretary of the Commission notifies those Parties in writing of the adoption of the adjustment.

Article 12

Signature

1. The present Protocol shall be open for signature at Oslo on 14 June 1994, then at United Nations Headquarters in New York until 12 December 1994 by States members of the Commission as well as States having consultative status with the Commission, pursuant to paragraph 8 of Economic and Social Council resolution 36 (IV) of 28 March 1947, and by regional economic integration organizations, constituted by sovereign States members of the Commission, which have competence in respect of the negotiation, conclusion and application of international agreements in matters covered by the Protocol, provided that the States and organizations concerned are Parties to the Convention and are listed in annex II.

2. In matters within their competence, such regional economic integration organizations shall, on their own behalf, exercise the rights and fulfil the responsibilities which the present Protocol attributes to their member States. In such cases, the member States of these organizations shall not be entitled to exercise such rights individually.

Article 13

Ratification, acceptance, approval and accession

1. The present Protocol shall be subject to ratification, acceptance or approval by Signatories.

2. The present Protocol shall be open for accession as from 12 December 1994 by the States and organizations that meet the requirements of article 12, paragraph 1.

Article 14

Depositary

The instruments of ratification, acceptance, approval or accession shall be deposited with the Secretary-General of the United Nations, who will perform the functions of Depositary.

Article 15

Entry into force

1. The present Protocol shall enter into force on the ninetieth day following the date on which the sixteenth instrument of ratification, acceptance, approval or accession has been deposited with the Depositary.

2. For each State and organization referred to in article 12, paragraph 1, which ratifies, accepts or approves the present Protocol or accedes thereto after the deposit of the sixteenth instrument of ratification, acceptance, approval or accession, the Protocol shall enter into force on the ninetieth day following the date of deposit by such Party of its instrument of ratification, acceptance, approval or accession.

Article 16

Withdrawal

At any time after five years from the date on which the present Protocol has come into force with respect to a Party, that Party may withdraw from it by giving written notification to the Depositary. Any such withdrawal shall take effect on the ninetieth day following the date of its receipt by the Depositary, or on such later date as may be specified in the notification of the withdrawal.

Article 17

Authentic texts

The original of the present Protocol, of which the English, French and Russian texts are equally authentic, shall be deposited with the Secretary-General of the United Nations.

IN WITNESS WHEREOF the undersigned, being duly authorized thereto, have signed the present Protocol.

DONE at Oslo, this fourteenth day of June one thousand nine hundred and ninety-four.

ANNEX I

Critical sulphur deposition

(5-percentile in centigrams of sulphur per square metre per year)

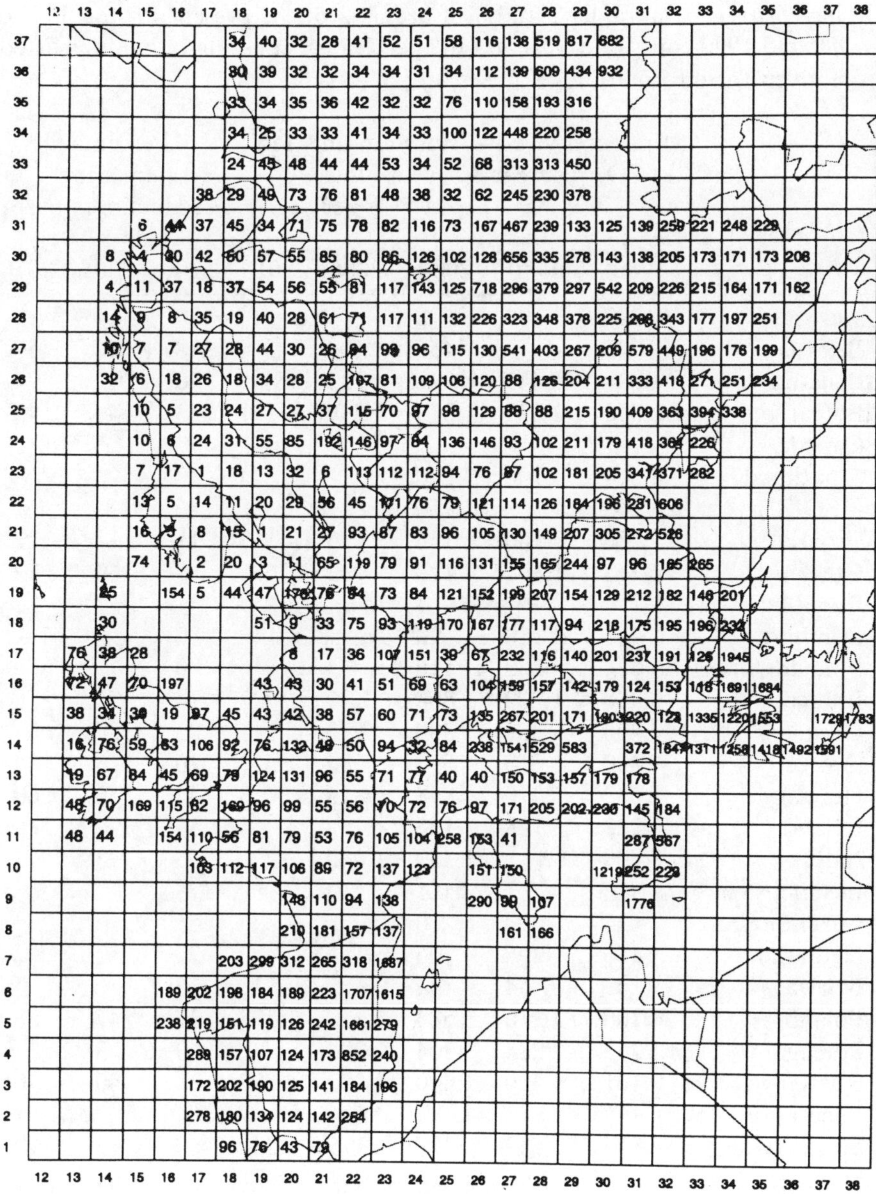

ANNEX II

Sulphur emission ceilings and percentage emission reductions

The sulphur emission ceilings listed in the table below give the obligations referred to in paragraphs 2 and 3 of article 2 of the present Protocol. The 1980 and 1990 emission levels and the percentage emission reductions listed are given for information purposes only.

	Emission levels kt SO_2 per year		Sulphur emission ceilings[a] kt SO_2 per year			Percentage emission reductions (base year 1980)[b]		
	1980	1990	2000	2005	2010	2000	2005	2010
Austria	397	90	78			80		
Belarus	740		456	400	370	38	46	50
Belgium	828	443	248	232	215	70	72	74
Bulgaria	2,050	2,020	1,374	1,230	1,127	33	40	45
Canada								
—national	4,614	3,700	3,200			30		
—SOMA	3,245		1,750			46		
Croatia	150	160	133	125	117	11	17	22
Czech Republic	2,257	1,876	1,128	902	632	50	60	72
Denmark	451	180	90			80		
Finland	584	260	116			80		
France	3,348	1,202	868	770	737	74	77	78
Germany	7,494	5,803	1,300	990		83	87	
Greece	400	510	595	580	570	0	3	4
Hungary	1,632	1,010	898	816	653	45	50	60
Ireland	222	168	155			30		
Italy	3,800		1,330	1,042		65	73	
Liechtenstein	0.4	0.1	0.1			75		
Luxembourg	24		10			58		
Netherlands	466	207	106			77		
Norway	142	54	34			76		
Poland	4,100	3,210	2,583	2,173	1,397	37	47	66
Portugal	266	284	304	294		0	3	
Russian Federation[c]	7,161	4,460	4,440	4,297	4,297	38	40	40
Slovakia	843	539	337	295	240	60	65	72
Slovenia	235	195	130	94	71	45	60	70

	Emission levels kt SO_2 per year		Sulphur emission ceilings[a] kt SO_2 per year			Percentage emission reductions (base year 1980)[b]		
	1980	1990	2000	2005	2010	2000	2005	2010
Spain	3,319	2,316	2,143			35		
Sweden	507	130	100			80		
Switzerland	126	62	60			52		
Ukraine	3,850		2,310			40		
United Kingdom	4,898	3,780	2,449	1,470	980	50	70	80
European Community	25,513		9,598			62		

[a] If, in a given year before 2005, a Party finds that, due to a particularly cold winter, a particularly dry summer and an unforeseen short-term loss of capacity in the power supply system, domestically or in a neighbouring country, it cannot comply with its obligations under this annex, it may fulfil those obligations by averaging its national annual sulphur emissions for the year in question, the year preceding that year and the year following it, provided that the emission level in any single year is not more than 20% above the sulphur emission ceiling.

The reason for exceedance in any given year and the method by which the three-year average figure will be achieved, shall be reported to the Implementation Committee.

[b] For Greece and Portugal percentage emission reductions given are based on the sulphur emission ceilings indicated for the year 2000.

[c] European part within the EMEP area.

ANNEX III

Designation of sulphur oxides management areas (SOMAs)

The following SOMA is listed for the purposes of the present Protocol:

South-east Canada SOMA

This is an area of 1 million km^2 which includes all the territory of the provinces of Prince Edward Island, Nova Scotia and New Brunswick, all the territory of the province of Quebec south of a straight line between Havre-St. Pierre on the north coast of the Gulf of Saint Lawrence and the point where the Quebec-Ontario boundary intersects the James Bay coastline, and all the territory of the province of Ontario south of a straight line between the point where the Ontario-Quebec boundary intersects the James Bay coastline and Nipigon River near the north shore of Lake Superior.

ANNEX IV

Control technologies for sulphur emissions from stationary sources

I. INTRODUCTION

1. The aim of this annex is to provide guidance for identifying sulphur control options and technologies for giving effect to the obligations of the present Protocol.

2. The annex is based on information on general options for the reduction of sulphur emissions and in particular on emission control technology performance and costs contained in official documentation of the Executive Body and its subsidiary bodies.

3. Unless otherwise indicated, the reduction measures listed are considered, on the basis of operational experience of several years in most cases, to be the most well-established and economically feasible best available technologies. However, the continuously expanding experience of low-emission measures and technologies at new plants as well as of the retrofitting of existing plants will necessitate regular review of this annex.

4. Although the annex lists a number of measures and technologies spanning a wide range of costs and efficiencies, it cannot be considered as an exhaustive statement of control options. Moreover, the choice of control measures and technologies for any particular case will depend on a number of factors, including current legislation and regulatory provisions and, in particular, control technology requirements, primary energy patterns, industrial infrastructure, economic circumstances and specific in-plant conditions.

5. The annex mainly addresses the control of oxidized sulphur emissions considered as the sum of sulphur dioxide (SO_2) and sulphur trioxide (SO_3), expressed as SO_2. The share of sulphur emitted as either sulphur oxides or other sulphur compounds from non-combustion processes and other sources is small compared to sulphur emissions from combustion.

6. When measures or technologies are planned for sulphur sources emitting other components, in particular nitrogen oxides (NO_x), particulates, heavy metals and volatile organic compounds (VOCs), it is worthwhile to consider them in conjunction with pollutant-specific control options in order to maximize the overall abatement effect and minimize the impact on the environment and, especially, to avoid the transfer of air pollution problems to other media (such as waste water and solid waste).

II. MAJOR STATIONARY SOURCES FOR SULPHUR EMISSIONS

7. Fossil fuel combustion processes are the main source of anthropogenic sulphur emissions from stationary sources. In addition, some non-combustion processes may contribute considerably to the emissions. The major stationary source categories, based on EMEP/CORINAIR 90, include:

(i) Public power, cogeneration and district heating plants:
  (a) Boilers;
  (b) Stationary combustion turbines and internal combustion engines;

(ii) Commercial, institutional and residential combustion plants:
  (a) Commercial boilers;
  (b) Domestic heaters;

(iii) Industrial combustion plants and processes with combustion:
  (a) Boilers and process heaters;
  (b) Processes, e.g. metallurgical operations such as roasting and sintering, coke oven plants, processing of titanium dioxide (TiO_2), etc.;
  (c) Pulp production;

(iv) Non-combustion processes, e.g. sulphuric acid production, specific organic synthesis processes, treatment of metallic surfaces;

(v) Extraction, processing and distribution of fossil fuels;

(vi) Waste treatment and disposal, e.g. thermal treatment of municipal and industrial waste.

8. Overall data (1990) for the ECE region indicate that about 88% of total sulphur emissions originate from all combustion processes (20% from industrial combustion), 5% from production processes and 7% from oil refineries. The power plant sector in many countries is the major single contributor to sulphur emissions. In some countries, the industrial sector (including refineries) is also an important SO_2 emitter. Although emissions from refineries in the ECE region are relatively small, their impact on sulphur emissions from other sources is large due to the sulphur in the oil products. Typically 60% of the sulphur intake present in the crudes remains in the products, 30% is recovered as elemental sulphur and 10% is emitted from refinery stacks.

III. GENERAL OPTIONS FOR REDUCTION OF SULPHUR EMISSIONS FROM COMBUSTION

9. General options for reduction of sulphur emissions are:

(i) Energy management measures:*

* Options (i) and (a) and (b) are integrated in the energy structure and policy of a Party. Implementation status, efficiency and costs per sector are not considered here.

(a) Energy saving

The rational use of energy (improved energy efficiency/process operation, cogeneration and/or demand-side management) usually results in a reduction in sulphur emissions.

(b) Energy mix

In general, sulphur emissions can be reduced by increasing the proportion of non-combustion energy sources (i.e. hydro, nuclear, wind, etc.) to the energy mix. However, further environmental impacts have to be considered.

(ii) Technological options:

(a) Fuel switching

The SO_2 emissions during combustion are directly related to the sulphur content of the fuel used.

Fuel switching (e.g. from high- to low-sulphur coals and/or liquid fuels, or from coal to gas) leads to lower sulphur emissions, but there may be certain restrictions, such as the availability of low-sulphur fuels and the adaptability of existing combustion systems to different fuels. In many ECE countries, some coal or oil combustion plants are being replaced by gas-fired combustion plants. Dual-fuel plants may facilitate fuel switching.

(b) Fuel cleaning

Cleaning of natural gas is state-of-the-art technology and widely applied for operational reasons.

Cleaning of process gas (acid refinery gas, coke oven gas, biogas, etc.) is also state-of-the-art technology.

Desulphurization of liquid fuels (light and middle fractions) is state-of-the-art technology.

Desulphurization of heavy fractions is technically feasible; nevertheless, the crude properties should be kept in mind. Desulphurization of atmospheric residue (bottom products from atmospheric crude distillation units) for the production of low-sulphur fuel oil is not, however, commonly practised; processing low-sulphur crude is usually preferable. Hydro-cracking and full conversion technology have matured and combine high sulphur retention with improved yield of light products. The number of full conversion refineries is as yet limited. Such refineries typically recover 80% to 90% of the sulphur intake and convert all residues into light products or other marketable products. For this type of refinery, energy consumption and investment costs are increased. Typical sulphur content for refinery products is given in table 1 below.

Current technologies to clean hard coal can remove approximately 50% of the inorganic sulphur (depending on coal properties) but none of the organic sulphur. More effective technologies are being developed which, however, involve higher specific investment and costs. Thus the efficiency of sulphur removal by coal cleaning is limited compared to flue gas desulphurization. There may be a country-specific optimization potential for the best combination of fuel cleaning and flue gas cleaning.

Table 1 *Sulphur content from refinery products* (S content (%))

	Typical present values	Anticipated future values
Gasoline	0.1	0.05
Jet kerosene	0.1	0.01
Diesel	0.05–0.3	<0.05
Heating oil	0.1–0.2	<0.1
Fuel oil	0.2–3.5	<1
Marine diesel	0.5–1.0	<0.5
Bunker oil	3.0–5.0	<1 (coastal areas)
		<2 (high seas)

(c) Advanced combustion technologies

These combustion technologies with improved thermal efficiency and reduced sulphur emissions include: fluidized-bed combustion (FBC): bubbling (BFBC), circulating (CFBC) and pressurized (PFBC); integrated gasification combined-cycle (IGCC); and combined-cycle gas turbines (CCGT).

Stationary combustion turbines can be integrated into combustion systems in existing conventional power plants which can increase overall efficiency by 5% to 7%, leading, for example, to a significant reduction in SO_2 emissions. However, major alterations to the existing furnace system become necessary.

Fluidized-bed combustion is a combustion technology for burning hard coal and brown coal, but it can also burn other solid fuels such as petroleum coke and low-grade fuels such as waste, peat and wood. Emissions can additionally be reduced by integrated combustion control in the system due to the addition of lime/limestone to the bed material. The total installed capacity of FBC has reached approximately 30,000 MW_{th} (250 to 350 plants), including 8,000 MW_{th} in the capacity range of greater than 50 MW_{th}. By-products from this process may cause problems with respect to use and/or disposal, and further development is required.

The IGCC process includes coal gasification and combined-cycle power generation in a gas and steam turbine. The gasified coal is burnt in the combustion chamber of the gas turbine. Sulphur emission control is achieved by the use of state-of-the-art technology for raw gas cleaning facilities upstream of the gas turbine. The technology also exists for heavy oil residues and bitumen emulsions. The installed capacity is presently about 1,000 MW_{el} (5 plants).

Combined-cycle gas-turbine power stations using natural gas as fuel with an energy efficiency of approximately 48% to 52% are currently being planned.

(d) Process and combustion modifications

Combustion modifications comparable to the measures used for NO_x emission control do not exist, as during combustion the organically and/or inorganically bound sulphur is almost completely oxidized (a certain percentage depending on the fuel properties and combustion technology is retained in the ash).

In this annex dry additive processes for conventional boilers are considered as process modifications due to the injection of an agent into the combustion unit. However, experience has shown that, when applying these processes, thermal capacity is lowered, the Ca/S ratio is high and sulphur removal low. Problems with the further utilization of the by-product have to be considered, so that this solution should usually be applied as an intermediate measure and for smaller units (table 2).

(e) Flue gas desulphurization (FGD) processes

These processes aim at removing already formed sulphur oxides, and are also referred to as secondary measures. The state-of-the-art technologies for flue gas treatment processes are all based on the removal of sulphur by wet, dry or semi-dry and catalytic chemical processes.

To achieve the most efficient programme for sulphur emission reductions beyond the energy management measures listed in (i) above a combination of technological options identified in (ii) above should be considered.

In some cases options for reducing sulphur emissions may also result in the reduction of emissions of CO_2, NO_x and other pollutants.

In public power, cogeneration and district heating plants, flue gas treatment processes used include: lime/limestone wet scrubbing (LWS); spray dry absorption (SDA); Wellman Lord process (WL); ammonia scrubbing (AS); and combined NO_x/SO_x removal processes (activated carbon process (AC) and combined catalytic NO_x/SO_x removal).

In the power generation sector, LWS and SDA cover 85% and 10%, respectively, of the installed FGD capacity.

Several new flue gas desulphurization processes, such as electron beam dry scrubbing (EBDS) and Mark 13A, have not yet passed the pilot stage.

Table 2 above shows the efficiency of the above-mentioned secondary measures based on the practical experience gathered from a large number of implemented plants. The implemented capacity as well as the capacity range are also mentioned. Despite comparable characteristics for several sulphur abatement technologies, local or plant-specific influences may lead to the exclusion of a given technology.

Table 2 also includes the usual investment cost ranges for the sulphur abatement technologies listed in sections (ii) (c), (d) and (e). However, when applying these technologies to individual cases it should be noted that investment costs of emission reduction measures will depend amongst other things on the particular technologies used, the required control systems, the plant size, the extent of the required reduction and the time-scale of planned maintenance cycles. The table thus gives only a broad range of investment costs. Investment costs for retrofit generally exceed those for new plants.

IV. CONTROL TECHNIQUES FOR OTHER SECTORS

10. The control techniques listed in section 9 (ii) (a) to (e) are valid not only in the power plant sector but also in various other sectors of industry. Several years of operational experience have been acquired, in most cases in the power plant sector.

11. The application of sulphur abatement technologies in the industrial sector merely depends on the process's specific limitations in the relevant sectors. Important contributors to sulphur emissions and corresponding reduction measures are presented in table 3 below.

12. In the sectors listed in table 3, process-integrated measures, including raw material changes (if necessary combined with sector-specific flue gas treatment), can be used to achieve the most effective reduction of sulphur emissions.

Table 3

Source	Reduction measures
Roasting of non-ferrous sulphides	Wet sulphuric acid catalytic process (WSA)
Viscose production	Double-contact process
Sulphuric acid production	Double-contact process, improved yield
Kraft pulp production	Variety of process-integrated measures

13. Reported examples are the following:
   (a) In new kraft pulp mills, sulphur emission of less than 1 kg of sulphur per tonne of pulp AD (air dried) can be achieved;**

** Control of sulphur-to-sodium ratio is required, i.e. removal of sulphur in the form of neutral salts and use of sulphur-free sodium make-up.

Table 2 *Emissions of sulphur oxides obtained from the application of technological options to fossil-fuelled boilers*

	Uncontrolled emissions		Additive injection		Wet scrubbing[a]		Spray dry absorption[b]	
Reduction efficiency (%)			up to 60		95		up to 90	
Energy efficiency ($kW_{el}/10^3\ m^3/h$)			0.1–1		6–10		3–6	
Total installed capacity (ECE Eur) (MW_{th})					194,000		16,000	
Type of by-product			Mix of Ca salts and fly ashes		Gypsum (sludge/waste water)		Mix of $CaSo_3 * \frac{1}{2} H_2O$ and fly ashes)	
Specific investment (cost ECU(1990)/kW_{el})			20–50		60–250		50–220	
	$mg/M^{3\ c}$	g/kWh_{el}	$mg/m^{3\ c}$	g/kW_{el}	$mg/m^{3\ c}$	g/kWh_{el}	mg/m^{3c}	g/kWh_{el}
Hard coal[d]	1,000–10,000	3.5–35	400–4,000	1.4–14	<400 (<200, 1% S)	<1.4 <0.7	<400 (<200, 1% S)	<1.4 <0.7
Brown coal[d]	1,000–20,000	4.2–84	400–8,000	1.7–33.6	<400 (<200, 1% S)	<1.7 <0.8	<400 (<200, 1% S)	<1.7 <0.8
Heavy oil[d]	1,000–10,000	2.8–28	400–4,000	1.1–11	<400 (<200, 1% S)	<1.1 <0.6	<400 (<200, 1% S)	<1.1 <0.6

	Ammonia scrubbing[b]		Wellman Lord[a]		Activated carbon[a]		Combined catalytic[a]	
Reduction efficiency (%)	up to 90		95		95		95	
Energy efficiency ($kW_{el}/10^3\ m^3/h$)	3–10		10–15		4–8		2	
Total installed capacity (ECE Eur) (MW_{th})	200		2,000		700		1,300	
Type of by-product	Ammonia fertilizer		Elemental S Sulphuric acid (99 vol.%)		Elemental S Sulphuric acid (99 vol.%)		Sulphuric acid (70 wt.%)	
Specific investment (cost ECU(1990)/kW_{el})	230–270 [e]		200–300 [e]		280–320[e f]		320–350[e f]	
	mg/m^3 [c]	g/kWh_{el}	mg/m^3 [c]	g/kW_{el}	mg/m^3 [c]	g/kWh_{el}	mg/m^3[c]	g/kWh_{el}
Hard coal[d]	<400 (<200, 1% S)	<1.4 <0.7	<400 (<200, 1% S)	<1.4 <0.7	<400 (<200, 1% S)	<1.4 <0.7	<400 (<200, 1% S)	<1.4 <0.7
Brown coal[d]	<400 (<200, 1% S)	<1.7 <0.8	<400 (<200, 1% S)	<1.7 <0.8	<400 (<200, 1% S)	<1.7 <0.8	<400 (<200, 1% S)	<1.7 <0.8
Heavy oil[d]	<400 (<200, 1% S)	<1.1 <0.6	<400 (<200, 1% S)	<1.1 <0.6	<400 (<200, 1% S)	<1.1 <0.6	<400 (<200, 1% S)	<1.1 <0.6

[a] For high sulphur content in the fuel the removal efficiency has to be adapted. However, the scope for doing so may be process-specific. Availability of these processes is usually 95%.
[b] Limited applicability for high-sulphur fuels.
[c] Emission in mg/m^3 (STP), dry, 6% oxygen for solid fuels, 3% oxygen for liquid fuels.
[d] Conversion factor depends on fuel properties, specific fuel gas volume and thermal efficiency of boiler (conversion factors (m^3/kWh_{el}, thermal efficiency: 36%) used: hard coal: 3.50; brown coal: 4.20; heavy oil: 2.80).
[e] Specific investment cost relates to a small sample of installations.
[f] Specific investment cost includes denitrification process.

The table was established mainly for large combustion installations in the public sector. However, the control options are also valid for other sectors with similar exhaust gases.

(b) In sulphite pulp mills, 1 to 1.5 kg of sulphur per tonne of pulp AD can be achieved;
(c) In the case of roasting of sulphides, removal efficiencies of 80 to 99% for 10,000 to 200,000 m^3/h units have been reported (depending on the process);
(d) For one iron ore sintering plant, an FGD unit of 320,000 m^3/h capacity achieves a clean gas value below 100 mg SO_x/Nm^3 at 6% O_2;
(e) Coke ovens are achieving less than 400 mg SO_x/Nm^3 at 6% O_2;
(f) Sulphuric acid plants achieve a conversion rate larger than 99%;
(g) Advanced Claus plant achieves sulphur recovery of more than 99%.

V. BY-PRODUCTS AND SIDE-EFFECTS

14. As efforts to reduce sulphur emissions from stationary sources are increased in the countries of the ECE region, the quantities of by-products will also increase.

15. Options which would lead to usable by-products should be selected. Furthermore, options that lead to increased thermal efficiency and minimize the waste disposal issue whenever possible should be selected. Although most by-products are usable or recyclable products such as gypsum, ammonia salts, sulphuric acid or sulphur, factors such as market conditions and quality standards need to be taken into account. Further utilization of FBC and SDA by-products have to be improved and investigated, as disposal sites and disposal criteria limit disposal in several countries.

16. The following side-effects will not prevent the implementation of any technology or method but should be considered when several sulphur abatement options are possible:
(a) Energy requirements of the gas treatment processes;
(b) Corrosion attack due to the formation of sulphuric acid by the reaction of sulphur oxides with water vapour;
(c) Increased use of water and waste water treatment;
(d) Reagent requirements;
(e) Solid waste disposal.

VI. MONITORING AND REPORTING

17. The measures taken to carry out national strategies and policies for the abatement of air pollution include: legislation and regulatory provisions, economic incentives and disincentives; as well as technological requirements (best available technology).

18. In general, standards are set, per emission source, according to plant size, operating mode, combustion technology, fuel type and whether it is a new or existing plant. An alternative approach also used is to set a target for the reduction of total sulphur emissions from a group of sources and to allow a choice of where to take action to reach this target (the bubble concept).

19. Efforts to limit the sulphur emissions to the levels set out in the national framework legislation have to be controlled by a permanent monitoring and reporting system and reported to the supervising authorities.

20. Several monitoring systems, using both continuous and discontinuous measurement methods, are available. However, quality requirements vary. Measurements are to be carried out by qualified institutes using measuring and monitoring systems. To this end, a certification system can provide the best assurance.

21. In the framework of modern automated monitoring systems and process control equipment, reporting does not create a problem. The collection of data for further use is a state-of-the-art technique; however, data to be reported to competent authorities differ from case to case. To obtain better comparability, data sets and prescribing regulations should be harmonized. Harmonization is also desirable for quality assurance of measuring and monitoring systems. This should be taken into account when comparing data.

22. To avoid discrepancies and inconsistencies, key issues and parameters, including the following, must be well defined:

(a) Definition of standards expressed as ppmv, mg/Nm^3, g/GJ, kg/h or kg/tonne of product. Most of these units need to be calculated and need specification in terms of gas temperature, humidity, pressure, oxygen content or heat input value;

(b) Definition of the period over which standards are to be averaged, expressed as hours, months or a year;

(c) Definition of failure times and corresponding emergency regulations regarding bypass of monitoring systems or shut-down of the installation;

(d) Definition of methods for back-filling of data missed or lost as a result of equipment failure;

(e) Definition of the parameter set to be measured. Depending on the type of industrial process, the necessary information may differ. This also involves the location of the measurement point within the system.

23. Quality control of measurements has to be ensured.

ANNEX V

Emission and sulphur content limit values

A. EMISSION LIMIT VALUES FOR MAJOR STATIONARY COMBUSTION SOURCES[a]

	(i) (MW_{th})	(ii) Emission limit value (mg SO_2/Nm^3 [b])	(iii) Desulphurization rate (%)
1. SOLID FUELS	50–100	2,000	
(based on 6% oxygen in flue gas)	100–500	2,000–400 (linear decrease)	40 (for 100–167 MW_{th}) 40–90 (linear increase for 167–500 MW_{th})
	>500	400	90
2. LIQUID FUELS	50–300	1,700	
(based on 3% oxygen in flue gas)	300–500	1,700–400 (linear decrease)	90
	>500	400	90
3. GASEOUS FUELS (based on 3% oxygen in flue gas)			
Gaseous fuels in general		35	
Liquefied gas		5	
Low calorific gases from gasification of refinery residues, coke oven gas, blast-furnace gas		800	

B. GAS OIL	Sulphur content (%)
Diesel for on-road vehicles	0.05
Other types	0.2

[a] As guidance, for a plant with a multi-fuel firing unit involving the simultaneous use of two or more types of fuels, the competent authorities shall set emission limit

values taking into account the emission limit values from column (ii) relevant for each individual fuel, the rate of thermal input delivered by each fuel and, for refineries, the relevant specific characteristics of the plant. For refineries, such a combined limit value shall under no circumstances exceed 1,700 mg SO_2/Nm^3.

In particular, the limit values shall not apply to the following plants:

- Plants in which the products of combustion area used for direct heating, drying, or any other treatment of objects or materials, e.g. reheating furnaces, furnaces for heat treatment;
- Post-combustion plants, i.e. any technical apparatus designed to purify the waste gases by combustion which is not operated as an independent combustion plant;
- Facilities for the regeneration of catalytic cracking catalysts;
- Facilities for the conversion of hydrogen sulphide into sulphur;
- Reactors used in the chemical industry;
- Coke battery furnaces;
- Cowpers;
- Waste incinerators;
- Plants powered by diesel, petrol and gas engines or by gas turbines, irrespective of the fuel used.

In a case where a Party, due to the high sulphur content of indigenous solid or liquid fuels, cannot meet the emission limit values set forth in column (ii), it may apply the desulphurization rates set forth in column (iii) or a maximum limit value of 800 mg SO_2/Nm^3 (although preferably not more than 650 mg SO_2/Nm^3). The Party shall report any such application to the Implementation Committee in the calendar year in which it is made.

Where two or more separate new plants are installed in such a way that, taking technical and economic factors into account, their waste gases could, in the judgement of the competent authorities, be discharged through a common stack, the combination formed by such plants is to be regarded as a single unit.

[b] mg SO_2/Nm^3 is defined at a temperature of 273° K and a pressure of 101.3 kPa, after correction for the water vapour content.

DECISION TAKEN BY THE EXECUTIVE BODY AT THE ADOPTION OF THE PROTOCOL

The Executive Body,

Having agreed upon and adopted the Protocol to the 1979 Convention on Long-range Transboundary Air Pollution on Further Reduction of Sulphur Emissions,

Resolved to act as early as possible to ensure effective monitoring of the operation of the new Protocol,

Decides, with reference to article 7, paragraph 3, of the new Protocol, to approve the attached text on the "Structure and Functions of the

Implementation Committee, as well as Procedures for its Review of Compliance"; and

Urges the Parties to the new Protocol to adopt the attached text at the first session of the Executive Body after the entry into force of the Protocol.

STRUCTURE AND FUNCTIONS OF THE IMPLEMENTATION COMMITTEE, AS WELL AS PROCEDURES FOR ITS REVIEW OF COMPLIANCE

1. The Committee shall consist of eight Parties. The Parties shall, at the first session of the Executive Body after the entry into force of this Protocol, elect four Parties to the Committee for a term of two years and four Parties for a term of one year. At each session thereafter they shall elect four new Parties for a term of two years. Outgoing Parties may be re-elected for one immediately consecutive term. The Committee shall elect its own chairman and vice-chairman.

2. The Committee shall, unless it decides otherwise, meet twice a year. The secretariat shall arrange for and service its meetings.

3. If one or more Parties have reservations about another Party's implementation of its obligations under the present Protocol, these concerns may be addressed in writing to the secretariat. Such a submission shall be supported by corroborating information. The secretariat shall, within two weeks of its receiving a submission, send a copy of that submission to the Party whose implementation of a particular provision of the Protocol is at issue. Any reply and information in support thereof are to be submitted to the secretariat and to the Parties involved within three months of the date of the dispatch or such longer period as the circumstances of any particular case may require. The secretariat shall transmit the submission, the reply and the information provided by the Parties to the Committee, which shall consider the matter as soon as practicable.

4. Where the secretariat, in particular upon reviewing the reports submitted in accordance with article 5, becomes aware of possible non-compliance by any Party with its obligations under the Protocol, it may request the Party concerned to furnish necessary information about the matter. If there is no response from the Party concerned within three months or such longer period as the circumstances of the matter may require or the matter is not resolved through administrative action or through diplomatic contacts, the secretariat shall inform the Committee accordingly.

5. Where a Party concludes that, despite having made its best bona fide efforts, it is or will be unable to comply fully with its obligations under the

present Protocol, it may address to the secretariat a submission in writing, explaining, in particular, the specific circumstances that it considers to be the cause of its non-compliance. The secretariat shall transmit such a submission to the Committee, which shall consider it as soon as practicable.

6. The Committee shall:
   (a) Subject to policy guidance by the Parties at sessions of the Executive Body, synthesize and evaluate the information reported by Parties in accordance with article 5 of the Protocol;
   (b) Subject to policy guidance by the Parties at sessions of the Executive Body, analyse and evaluate on a periodic basis, the progress that has been made in the implementation of the Protocol;
   (c) Consider any matter brought before it in accordance with paragraphs 3, 4 and 5 above with a view to securing a constructive solution of the matter; and
   (d) Ensure that the quality of data reported by a Party in accordance with article 5 (Reporting) is evaluated by the EMEP technical centres, and/or by an independent expert nominated by the Implementation Committee. In areas outside the geographic scope of EMEP, evaluation procedures appropriate to the particular circumstances of the Parties concerned shall be used.

7. The Committee may:
   (a) Request, through the secretariat, further information on matters under its consideration;
   (b) Undertake, upon the invitation of the Party concerned, information gathering in the territory of that Party; and
   (c) Consider any information forwarded by the secretariat concerning compliance with the provisions of the present Protocol.

8. The Committee shall report annually to the Parties at sessions of the Executive Body on its activities and in particular any recommendations it considers appropriate regarding compliance with the Protocol. Each such report shall be finalized by the Committee no later than ten weeks in advance of the session of the Executive Body at which it is to be considered.

9. Where a Party that is not a member of the Committee is identified in a submission under paragraph 3, or makes itself a submission under paragraph 5, it shall be entitled to participate in the consideration of that submission by the Committee.

10. No Party, whether or not a member of the Committee, involved in a matter under consideration by the Committee, shall take part in the elaboration and adoption of recommendations on that matter to be included in the report of the Committee.

COMMISSION REGULATION (EC) No 1488/94
of 28 June 1994
laying down the principles for the assessment of risks to man and the environment of existing substances in accordance with Council Regulation (EEC) No 793/93
(Text with EEA relevance)

THE COMMISSION OF THE EUROPEAN COMMUNITIES,

Having regard to the Treaty establishing the European Community,

Having regard to Council Regulation (EEC) No 793/93 of 23 March 1993 on the evaluation and control of the risks of existing substances[1] and, in particular, Article 10 (4) thereof,

Whereas Regulation (EEC) No 793/93 envisages a system of evaluation and control of the risk of existing substances and whereas Article 10 thereof requires that it shall be for the Member States to carry out such risk assessment on existing substances having priority;

Whereas, given that the responsibility for risk assessment lies with the Member States, it is, however, appropriate that the principles of such assessment be adopted at Community level to avoid disparities between Member States which would not only affect the functioning of the internal market but would also fail to guarantee the same level of protection of man and the environment;

Whereas the assessments of risks should be based on a comparison of the potential adverse effects of a substance with the known or reasonably foreseeable exposure of man and the environment to that substance;

Whereas, having regard to the classification of a given substance in accordance with Council Directive 67/548/EEC of 27 June 1967 on the approximation of the laws, regulations and administrative provisions relating to the classification, packaging and labelling of dangerous substances[2], as last amended by Commission Directive 93/105/EC[3], the assessment of risks to man should take account of the physico-chemical and toxicological properties of a substance;

[1] OJ No L 84, 5. 4. 1993, p. 1. [2] OJ No 196, 16. 8. 1967, p. 1.
[3] OJ No L 294, 30. 11. 1993, p. 21.

Whereas, having regard to its classification in accordance with directive 67/548/EEC, the assessment of risks to the environment should take account of the environmental effects of a substance;

Whereas the results of a risk assessment should be the principal basis of decisions under appropriate legislation to reduce the risks arising from manufacture, transport, storage, formulation into a preparation or other processing, use and disposal or recovery of existing substances;

Whereas it is appropriate to reduce to a minimum the number of animals used for experimental purposes in accordance with Council Directive 86/609/EEC of 24 November 1986 on the approximation of the laws, regulations and administrative provisions of the Member States regarding the protection of animals used for experimental and other scientific purposes[4];

Whereas the provisions of this Regulation shall be without prejudice to specific Community legislation concerning the safety and protection of health of workers at work, in particular Council Directive 89/391/EEC[5], which places an obligation on employers to evaluate the risks to the health and safety of workers arising from the use of new and existing chemical substances and, as necessary, to take measures to ensure an appropriate protection of workers;

Whereas the measures set out in this Regulation are in accordance with the opinion of the Committee set up pursuant to Article 15 of Regulation (EEC) No 793/93,

HAS ADOPTED THIS REGULATION:

Article 1

Objectives

This Regulation lays down general principles for the assessment of the risks posed by existing substances to man and the environment as required by Article 10 of Council Regulation (EEC) No 793/93.

Article 2

Definitions

1. The definitions contained in Article 2 of Regulation (EEC) No 793/93 are applicable to this Regulation.

[4] OJ No L 358, 18. 12. 1986, p. 1. [5] OJ No L 183, 29. 6. 1989, p. 1.

2. For the purposes of this Regulation:
   (a) 'hazard identification' is the identification of the adverse effects which a substance has an inherent capacity to cause;
   (b) 'dose (concentration)—response (effect) assessment' is the estimation of the relationship between dose, or level of exposure to a substance, and the incidence and severity of an effect;
   (c) 'exposure assessment' is the determination of the emissions, pathways and rates of movement of a substance and its transformation or degradation, in order to estimate the concentrations/doses to which human populations or environmental spheres (water, soil and air) are or may be exposed;
   (d) 'risk characterization' is the estimation of the incidence and severity of the adverse effects likely to occur in a human population or environmental sphere due to actual or predicted exposure to a substance, and may include 'risk estimation', i.e. the quantification of that likelihood.

Article 3

Principles of risk assessment

1. The risk assessment shall entail hazard identification and, as appropriate, dose (concentration)—response (effect) assessment, exposure assessment and risk characterization. It shall be based on the information on the substance submitted in accordance with Articles 3, 4, 7 (1) and (2), 9 (1) and (2) and 10 (2) of Regulation (EEC) No 793/93 and on other available information and shall normally be conducted in accordance with the procedures set out in Articles 4 and 5 of this Regulation.

2. Notwithstanding paragraph 1, in relation to particular effects, such as ozone depletion, for which the procedures set out in Articles 4 and 5 are impracticable, the risks associated with such effects shall be assessed on a case-by-case basis and the rapporteur shall include a full description and justification of such assessments in the written report submitted to the Commission in accordance with Article 6.

3. In conducting an exposure assessment, the rapporteur shall take into account those human populations or environmental spheres for which exposure to the substance is known or reasonably foreseeable in the light of available information on the substance, with particular regard to manufacture, transport, storage, formulation into a preparation or other processing, use and disposal or recovery.

4. Where a substance for which a risk assessment has already been carried out in accordance with Article 10 of Regulation (EEC) No 793/93

appears again on a priority list, the subsequent risk assessment shall take into account the previous risk assessment(s).

Article 4

Risk assessment: human health

For each substance appearing on the priority lists in accordance with Article 8 of Regulation (EEC) No 793/93, the rapporteur shall carry out a risk assessment in relation to its effects on human health, the first stage of which shall be hazard identification which shall address, at least, the properties and potential adverse effects specified in Annexes I A and II A. Having conducted the hazard identification, the rapporteur shall take the following sequence of actions, which shall be carried out in accordance with the guidelines set out in Annexes I B and II B:

(a) (i) dose (concentration)—response (effect)assessment, where appropriate;
(ii) exposure assessment for whichever human population-group (i.e. workers, consumers or man exposed indirectly via the environment) is exposed or likely to be exposed to the substance;

(b) risk characterization.

Article 5

Risk assessment: environment

For each substance appearing on the priority lists in accordance with Article 8 of Regulation (EEC) No 793/93, the rapporteur shall carry out a risk assessment in relation to its environmental effects, the first stage of which shall be hazard identification. Having conducted the hazard identification, the rapporteur shall proceed to the following sequence of actions which shall be carried out in accordance with the guidelines set out in Annex III;

(a) (i) dose (concentration)—response (effect) assessment, where appropriate;
(ii) exposure assessment for the environmental spheres exposed or likely to be exposed to the substance;

(b) risk characterization.

Article 6

Risk assessment report

Having carried out the risk assessment in accordance with Articles 4 and 5, the rapporteur shall prepare a report containing at least the information set out at Annex V together with all data relevant for the risk assessment. This report, together with a summary thereof, shall be forwarded to the Commission in accordance with Article 10 (3) of Regulation (EEC) No 793/93.

Article 7

Final provisions

This Regulation shall enter into force on the 60th day following its publication in the *Official Journal of the European Communities*.

This Regulation shall be binding in its entirety and directly applicable in all Member States.

Done at Brussels, 28 June 1994.

For the Commission
René STEICHEN
Member of the Commission

ANNEX I

RISK ASSESSMENT: HUMAN HEALTH (TOXICITY)

Part A

The risk assessment conducted in accordance with Article 4 shall take account of the following potential toxic effects and populations exposed or liable to be exposed:

EFFECTS

1. Acute toxicity
2. Irritation
3. Corrosivity
4. Sensitization
5. Repeated dose toxicity
6. Mutagenicity
7. Carcinogenicity

8. Toxicity for reproduction

HUMAN POPULATIONS

1. Workers
2. Consumers
3. Man exposed indirectly via environment

Part B

1. HAZARD IDENTIFICATION

The objective shall be to identify the effect(s) of concern and to review the (provisional) classification in the light of all data available.

2. DOSE (CONCENTRATION)—RESPONSE (EFFECT) ASSESSMENT

2.1. For repeated-dose toxicity and reproductive toxicity, the dose-response relationship shall be assessed and, where possible, the no observed adverse effect level (Noael) identified. If it is not possible to identify a Noael, the lowest dose/concentration associated with an adverse effect, i.e. the lowest observed adverse effect level (Loael), shall be identified.

2.2. For acute toxicity, corrosivity and irritation, it is not usually possible to derive a Noael or Loael on the basis of the results of tests conducted in accordance with the requirements of Directive 67/548/EEC. For acute toxicity, the LD50 or LC50 value or, where the fixed dose procedure has been used, the discriminating dose shall be derived. For the other effects, it shall be sufficient to determine whether the substance has an inherent capacity to cause such effects.

2.3. For mutagenicity and carcinogenicity, it shall be sufficient to determine whether the substance has an inherent capacity to cause such effects. However, if it can be demonstrated that a substance identified as a carcinogen is non-genotoxic, it will be appropriate to identify a Noael/Loael as described in paragraph 2.1.

2.4. With respect to skin sensitization and respiratory sensitization, in so far as there is no consensus on the possibility of identifying a dose/concentration below which adverse effects are unlikely to occur in a subject already sensitized to a given substance, it shall be sufficient to evaluate whether the substance has an inherent capacity to cause such effects.

2.5. Where toxicity data derived from observations of human exposure, e.g. information from poison centres or epidemiological surveys, are available, special consideration shall be given to those data when carrying out the risk assessment.

3. EXPOSURE ASSESSMENT

3.1. An exposure assessment shall be conducted for each of the human populations (workers, consumers and man liable to exposure indirectly via the environment) for which exposure to the substance is known or can reasonably be foreseen. The objective of the assessment shall be to make a quantitative or qualitative estimate of the dose/concentration of the substance to which a population is or may be exposed. Such estimation shall take account of spatial and temporal variations in the exposure pattern.

3.2 In particular, the exposure assessment, where appropriate, shall take account of:

(i) adequately measured exposure data;
(ii) the quantity in which the substance is produced and/or imported;
(iii) the form in which the substance is produced and/or imported and/or in which the substance is used (e.g. substance itself or as component of a preparation);
(iv) use pattern and degree of containment;
(v) process data, where relevant;
(vi) physico-chemical properties of the substance including, where relevant, those conferred by the process (e.g. aerosol formation);
(vii) breakdown products and/or transformation products;
(viii) likely routes of exposure and potential for absorption;
(ix) frequency and duration of exposure;
(x) type and size of specific exposed population(s) where such information is available.

3.3. Where adequately measured, representative exposure data are available, special consideration shall be given to them when conducting the exposure assessment. Where calculation methods are used for the estimation of exposure levels, adequate models shall be applied. Relevant monitoring data from substances with analogous use and exposure patterns of analogous properties shall then also be considered.

3.4. If a substance is contained in a preparation, consideration of exposure to the substance in that preparation shall be necessary if the latter is classified on the basis of the toxicological properties of the substance in accordance with Council Directive 88/379/EEC[1], or if there are other reasonable grounds for concern.

[1] OJ No L 187, 16. 7. 1988, p. 14.

4. RISK CHARACTERIZATION

4.1. Where, for any of the effects set out in Annex I A, a Noael or Loael has been identified, the risk characterization in relation to each of those effects shall entail comparison of the Noael or Loael with the estimate of the dose/concentration to which the population(s) will be exposed. If a quantitative estimate of exposure is available, an exposure level /N(L)oael ratio shall be derived. On the basis of the comparison between the quantitative or qualitative estimate of exposure and the N(L)oael, the rapporteur shall indicate the results of the risk characterization in relation to those effects.

4.2. Where, for any of the effects set out in Annex I A, a N(L)oael has not been determined, the risk characterization in relation to each of those effects shall entail an evaluation, on the basis of the quantitative and/or qualitative information on exposure relevant to the human populations under consideration, of the likelihood that the effect will occur[2]. Having made the evaluation, the rapporteur shall indicate the results of the risk characterization in relation to those effects.

4.3. When carrying out the risk characterization, the rapporteur shall take into account, *inter alia*:

(i) the uncertainty arising, among other factors, from the variability in the experimental data and intra- and inter-species variation;

(ii) the nature and severity of the effect;

(iii) the human population to which the quantitative and/or qualitative information on exposure applies.

5. INTEGRATION

In accordance with the provisions of Article 4, a risk characterization may be carried out in relation to more than one potential adverse effect or human population. The rapporteur shall judge the result of the risk characterization for each effect. Having completed the risk assessment, the rapporteur shall review the various results and produce integrated results in relation to the overall toxicity of the substance.

[2] Where, despite a N(L)oael not having been determined, the test results nevertheless demonstrate a relationship between dose/concentration and the severity of an adverse effect or where, in connection with a test method which entails the use of only one dose or concentration it is possible to evaluate the relative severity of the effect, such information shall also be taken into account in evaluating the likelihood of the effect occurring.

ANNEX II

RISK ASSESSMENT: HUMAN HEALTH (PSYCHO-CHEMICAL PROPERTIES)

Part A

Risk assessment in accordance with Article 4 shall take account of the potential adverse effects which may occur in the following human populations exposed or liable to be exposed to substances with the following properties.

PROPERTIES

1. Explosivity
2. Flammability
3. Oxidizing potential

HUMAN POPULATIONS

1. Workers
2. Consumers
3. Man exposed indirectly via the environment

Part B

1. HAZARD IDENTIFICATION

   The objective shall be to identify the effect(s) of concern and to review the (provisional) classification in the light of all data available.

2. EXPOSURE ASSESSMENT

   If risk characterization has to be conducted in accordance with Article 4, it shall be necessary to determine the known or the reasonably foreseeable conditions of use.

3. RISK CHARACTERIZATION

   The risk characterization shall entail an evaluation of the likelihood that an adverse effect will be caused under the known or the reasonably foreseeable conditions of use. The rapporteur shall indicate the results of the risk characterization.

4. INTEGRATION

In accordance with the provisions of Article 4, a risk characterization may be carried out in relation to more than one potential adverse effect or human population. The rapporteur shall judge the results of the risk characterization for each effect. Having completed the risk assessment, the rapporteur shall review the various results and produce integrated results.

ANNEX III

RISK ASSESSMENT: ENVIRONMENT

1. HAZARD IDENTIFICATION

The objective shall be to identify the effect(s) and/or property (properties) of concern and to review the (provisional) classification in the light of all data available.

2. DOSE (CONCENTRATION)—RESPONSE (EFFECT) ASSESSMENT

2.1. The objective shall be to predict the concentration of the substance below which adverse effects in the environmental sphere of concern are not expected to occur. This concentration is known as the predicted no effect concentration (PNEC). However, in some cases, it may not be possible to establish a PNEC and a qualitative estimation of the dose (concentration)—response (effect) relation would have to be made.

2.2. The PNEC may be calculated by applying an assessment factor to the values resulting from tests on organisms, e.g. LD50 (median lethal dose), LC50 (median lethal concentration), EC50 (median effective concentration), IC50 (concentration causing 50 per cent inhibition of a given parameter, e.g. growth), NOEL(C) (no observed effect level (concentration)), or LOEL(C) (lowest observed effect level (concentration)) or other appropriate methods.

2.3. An assessment factor is an expression of the degree of uncertainty in extrapolation from test data on a limited number of species to the real environment. Therefore, in general, the more extensive the data and the longer the duration of the tests, the smaller is the degree of uncertainty and the size of the assessment factor[1].

[1] An assessment factor of the order of 1,000 is typically applied to an L(E)C50 value derived from the results of testing for acute toxicity but that factor may be reduced in the light of other relevant information. A lower assessment factor is typically applied to an NOEC derived from the results of testing for long-term/chronic toxicity.

3. EXPOSURE ASSESSMENT

3.1. The objective of the exposure assessment shall be to predict the concentration of the substance which is likely to be found in the environment. That concentration is known as the predicted environmental concentration (PEC). However, in some cases, it may not be possible to establish a PEC and a qualitative estimation of exposure would have to be made.

3.2. A PEC or, where necessary, a qualitative estimation of exposure need only be determined for the environmental spheres to which emissions, discharges, disposal or distributions are known or are reasonably foreseeable.

3.3. The PEC or qualitative estimation of exposure shall be determined taking account of, in particular and if appropriate:

(i) adequately measured exposure data;
(ii) the quantity in which the substance is produced and/or imported;
(iii) the form in which the substance is produced and/or imported and/or in which the substance is used (e.g. substance itself or as component of a preparation);
(iv) use pattern and degree of containment;
(v) process data, where relevant;
(vi) physico-chemical properties of the substance, in particular melting point, boiling point, vapour pressure, surface tension, water solubility, partition coefficient n-octanol/water;
(vii) breakdown products and/or transformation products;
(viii) likely pathways to environmental spheres and potential for absorption/desorption and degradation;
(ix) frequency and duration of exposure.

3.4. Where adequately measured, representative exposure data are available, special consideration shall be given to them when conducting the exposure assessment. Where calculation methods are used for the estimation of exposure concentrations, adequate models shall be applied. Where appropriate, on a case-by-case basis, relevant monitoring data from substances with analogous use and exposure patterns or analogous properties shall then also be considered.

4. RISK CHARACTERIZATION

4.1. For any given environmental sphere, the risk characterization shall, as far as possible, entail comparison of the PEC with the PNEC so that a PEC/PNEC ratio may be derived. If the PEC/PNEC ratio is equal to or less than one, the risk characterization shall result that, at present, no further information and/or testing and no risk reduction measures beyond those which are being applied already are necessary. If the ratio is greater than one, the rapporteur shall judge, on the basis of the size of that ratio and other relevant factors, such as:

(i) indications of bioaccumulation potential;
(ii) the shape of the toxicity/time curve in ecotoxicity testing;
(iii) indications of other adverse effects on the basis of toxicity studies, e.g. classification as a mutagen, toxic or very toxic or as harmful with risk phrase R40 ('Possible risk of irreversible effects') or R48 ('Danger of serious damage to health by prolonged exposure');
(iv) data on structurally analogous substances;

if further information and/or testing are required to clarify the concern or if risk reduction measures are necessary.

4.2. If it has not been possible to derive a PEC/PNEC ratio, the risk characterization shall entail a qualitative evaluation of the likelihood that an effect is occurring under the current conditions of exposure or will occur under the expected conditions of exposure. Having made such an evaluation and taking into account relevant factors such as those listed in paragraph 4(1), the rapporteur shall indicate the results of the risk characterization in relation to those effects.

5. INTEGRATION

In accordance with the provisions of Article 5, a risk characterization may be carried out in relation to more than one environmental sphere. The rapporteur shall judge the results of the risk assessment for each sphere. Having completed the risk assessment, the rapporteur shall review the different results and produce integrated results in relation to the overall environmental effects of the substance.

ANNEX IV

OVERALL INTEGRATION OF RESULTS

1. The results produced in conformity with section 5 of Annex 1 B, section 4 of Annex II B and section 5 of Annex III shall be reviewed by the rapporteur and integrated in relation to the totality of risks identified in the risk assessment.

2. Further information/testing requirements or recommendations to consider risk reduction measures shall be justified.

ANNEX V

INFORMATION TO BE INCLUDED IN REPORT OF RISK ASSESSMENT

1. The written report submitted to the Commission of the European Communities in accordance with Article 6 shall include the following elements:
   (i) the results of the risk assessment produced in conformity with Annex IV;
   (ii) if there is need for further information and/or testing in relation to one or more potential adverse effect(s), human population(s) or environmental sphere(s), a description and justification of the further information and/or tests required and a proposal for the time limits within which that further information and/or the results of tests should be submitted;
   (iii) if there is at present no need for further information and/or testing and no need for risk reduction measures beyond those which are being applied already in relation to all potential adverse effects, human populations and environmental spheres, a statement that, on the basis of all available information, at present no further information/testing on the substance is needed and that at present no risk reduction measures beyond those being applied already, are necessary;
   (iv) if there is a need for limiting the risks and risk reduction measures are necessary in relation to one or more potential adverse effect(s), human population(s) and/or environmental sphere(s), a statement of the effect(s), human population(s) and/or environmental sphere(s) for which the risk needs to be reduced and an explanation of the need for risk reduction measures. Risk reduction measures which are already being applied shall be taken into account. A risk reduction strategy in accordance with Article 10 (3) of Regulation (EEC) No 793/93 shall be drawn up and be submitted to the Commission together with the risk assessment as foreseen under this Regulation.
2. Where risk characterization has entailed the use of exposure/effect ratios as described in section 4 of Annex I B and section 4 of Annex III or the use of assessment factors as described in section 2 of ANnex III, those

ratios or factors shall be stated and methods of calculation used shall be explained.

3. The data considered relevant and therefore chosen as the basis for the risk assessment by the rapporteur on each effect or property and each exposure group listed in Annexes I A and II A and for each environmental property and environmental sphere according to Annex III shall be submitted to the Commission of the European Communities using an appropriate computer program.

I

(Acts whose publication is obligatory)

COUNCIL REGULATION (EC) No 3093/94
of 15 December 1994
on substances that deplete the ozone layer

THE COUNCIL OF THE EUROPEAN UNION,

Having regard to the Treaty establishing the European Community, and in particular Article 103s (1) thereof,

Having regard to the proposal from the Commission[1],

Having regard to the opinion of the Economic and Social Committee[2],

Acting in accordance with the procedure laid down in Article 189c of the Treaty[3],

Whereas it is established that continued emissions of ozone-depleting substances at current levels cause significant damage to the ozone layer;

Whereas Council Regulation (EEC) No 594/91 of 4 March 1991 on substances that deplete the ozone layer[4] was amended by Regulation (EEC) No 3952/92[5]; whereas on the occasion of this amendment it is desirable, in the interests of clarity, to recast that Regulation;

Whereas in view of the Community's responsibilities for the environment and trade, all Member States and the Community have become Parties to the Vienna Convention for the Protection of the Ozone Layer and the Montreal Protocol on Substances that Deplete the Ozone Layer as amended by the Parties to the Protocol at their second meeting in London;

Whereas, in the light of recent scientific evidence, at their fourth meeting in Copenhagen, at which the Community and the Member States played a leading role, the Parties to the Montreal Protocol adopted a second amend-

[1] OJ No C 232, 28. 8. 1993, p. 6.
[2] OJ No C 52, 19. 2. 1994, p. 8.
[3] European Parliament opinion of 8 February 1994 (OJ No C 61, 28. 2. 1994, p. 114). Council common position of 27 July 1994 (OJ No C 301, 27. 10. 1994, p. 1). European Parliament decisions of 17 November 1994 (not yet published in the Official Journal).
[4] OJ No L 67, 14. 3. 1991, p. 1.
[5] OJ No L 405, 31. 12. 1992, p. 41.

ment to the Protocol comprising additional measures for the protection of the ozone layer;

Whereas it is necessary for action to be taken at Community level to carry out the Community's obligations under the Convention and the second amendment to the Protocol, in particular to control the production and supply of methyl bromide and hydrobromofluorocarbons and the supply and use of hydrochlorofluorocarbons within the Community;

Whereas in the light of scientific evidence in particular it is appropriate in certain cases to introduce control measures which are more severe than those of the second amendment to the Protocol;

Whereas a periodical review of the permitted uses of ozone-depleting substances by means of the committee procedure is desirable;

Whereas it is necessary to keep under review the evolution of the market in ozone-depleting substances, particularly in order to ensure sufficient supply for essential uses, and the state of development of appropriate substitutes, but also to keep to a minimum the imports of virgin, recovered and reclaimed ozone-depleting substances released for free circulation in the European Community;

Whereas it is appropriate to take all precautionary measures practicable to prevent leakages of ozone-depleting substances and to promote the recovery of such substances after use for recycling or safe destruction,

HAS ADOPTED THIS REGULATION:

CHAPTER I

INTRODUCTORY PROVISIONS

Article 1

Scope

This Regulation shall apply to the production, importation, exportation, supply, use and recovery of chlorofluorocarbons, other fully halogenated chlorofluorocarbons, halons, carbon tetrachloride, 1,1,1-trichloroethane, methyl bromide, hydrobromofluorocarbons and hydrochlorofluorocarbons. It shall also apply to the reporting of information on these substances.

Article 2

Definitions

For the purposes of this Regulation:

- 'Protocol' shall mean the Montreal Protocol on Substances that Deplete the Ozone Layer, whether in the original 1987 version as adjusted in 1990 and 1992, the amended 1990 version as adjusted in 1992, or the amended 1992 version,
- 'Party' shall mean any Party to the Protocol,
- 'State not Party to the Protocol' shall, with respect to a particular controlled substance, include any State or regional economic-integration organization that has not agreed to be bound by the control measures applicable to that substance,
- 'controlled substances' shall mean chlorofluorocarbons, other fully halogenated chlorofluorocarbons, halons, carbon tetrachloride, 1,1,1-trichloroethane, methyl bromide, hydrobromofluorocarbons and hydrochlorofluorocarbons, whether alone or in a mixture. This definition shall not cover any controlled substance which is in a manufactured product other than a container used for the transportation or storage of that substance, or insignificant quantities of any controlled substance, originating from inadvertent or coincidental production during a manufacturing process, from unreacted feedstock, or from use as a processing agent which is present in chemical substances as trace impurities, or that is emitted during product manufacture or handling;
- 'chlorofluorocarbons' shall mean the controlled substances listed in Group I of Annex 1, including their isomers,
- 'other fully halogenated chlorofluorocarbons' shall mean the controlled substances listed in Group II of Annex I, including their isomers,
- 'halons' shall mean the controlled substances listed in Group III of Annex I, including their isomers,
- 'carbon tetrachloride' shall mean the controlled substance specified in Group IV of Annex I,
- '1,1,1-trichloroethane' shall mean the controlled substance specified in Group V of Annex I,
- 'methyl bromide' shall mean the controlled substance specified in Group VI of Annex I,
- 'hydrobromofluorocarbons' shall mean the controlled substances listed in Group VII of Annex I, including their isomers,
- 'hydrochlorofluorocarbons' shall mean the controlled substances listed in Group VIII of Annex I, including their isomers,
- 'producer' shall mean any natural or legal person manufacturing controlled substances within the Community,

- ‘production’ shall mean the amount of controlled substances produced, less the amount destroyed by technologies approved by the Parties and less the amount entirely used as feedstock in the manufacture of other chemicals. No amount recovered and reclaimed shall be considered as ‘production’,
- ‘undertaking’ shall mean any natural or legal person who produces, recycles for placing on the market or uses controlled substances for industrial or commercial purposes in the Community, who releases such imported substances for free circulation in the Community, or who exports such substances from the Community for industrial or commercial purposes,
- ‘ozone-depleting potential’ shall mean the figure specified in the final column of Annex I representing the potential effect of each controlled substance on the ozone layer,
- ‘calculated level’ shall mean a quantity determined by multiplying the quantity of each controlled substance by its ozone-depleting potential as specified in Annex I and by adding together, for each group of controlled substances in Annex I separately, the resulting figures,
- ‘industrial rationalization’ shall mean the transfer either between Parties or within a Member State of all or a portion of the calculated level of production of one producer to another, for the purpose of optimizing economic efficiency or responding to anticipated shortfalls in supply as a result of plant closures,
- ‘recovery’ shall mean the collection and the storage of controlled substances from, for example, machinery, equipment and containment vessels during servicing or before disposal,
- ‘recycling’ shall mean the reuse of a recovered controlled substance following a basic cleaning process such as filtering and drying. For refrigerants, recycling normally involves recharge back into equipment as is often carried out on site,
- ‘reclamation’ shall mean the reprocessing and upgrading of a recovered controlled substance through such processes as filtering, drying, distillation and chemical treatment in order to restore the substance to a specified standard of performance, which often involves processing off site at a central facility.

CHAPTER II

PHASE-OUT SCHEDULE

Article 3

Control of production of controlled substances

1. Subject to paragraphs 8 to 12, each producer shall ensure that:

- the calculated level of his production of chlorofluorocarbons in the period 1 January to 31 December 1994 does not exceed 15% of the calculated level of his production of chlorofluorocarbons in 1986,
- he produces no chlorofluorocarbons after 31 December 1994.

However, subject to paragraphs 8 to 12, each producer in a Member State in which the calculated level of production of chlorofluorocarbons was less than 15,000 tonnes in 1986 shall ensure that:

- the calculated level of his production of chlorofluorocarbons in the period 1 January to 31 December 1994 and in the following 12-month period does not exceed 15% of the calculated level of his production in 1986,
- he produces no chlorofluorocarbons after 31 December 1995.

In the light of the nominations made by Member States the Commission shall, in accordance with the procedure laid down in Article 16, apply the criteria set out in Decision IV/25 of the Parties to the Montreal Protocol in order to determine every year any essential uses for which the production and importation of chlorofluorocarbons may be permitted in the Community after 31 December 1994 and those users who may take advantage of those essential uses or their own account. Such production and importation shall be allowed only if no adequate alternatives or recycled chlorofluorocarbons are available from any of the Parties to the Protocol.

The Commission shall issue licences to those users identified as laid down in the third subparagraph and shall notify them of the use for which they have authorization and the substances and the quantities of them that they are authorized to use.

A producer may be authorized by the competent authority of the Member State in which his relevant production is situated to produce chlorofluorocarbons after 31 December 1994 for the purpose of meeting the licensed demands presented by users identified as laid down in the third subparagraph. The competent authority of the Member State concerned shall notify the Commission in advance of its intention of issuing any such authorization.

2. Subject to paragraphs 8 to 12, each producer shall ensure that:

- the calculated level of his production of other fully halogenated chlorofluorocarbons in the period 1 January to 31 December 1994 does not exceed 15% of the calculated level of his production of other fully halogenated chlorofluorocarbons in 1989,
- he produces no other fully halogenated chlorofluorocarbons after 31 December 1994.

In the light of the nominations made by Member States the Commission shall, in accordance with the procedure laid down in Article 16, apply the criteria set out in Decision IV/25 of the Parties to the Montreal Protocol in order to determine every year any essential uses for which the production and importation of other fully halogenated chlorofluorocarbons may be permitted in the Community after 31 December 1994 and those users who may take advantage of those essential uses for their own account. Such production and importation shall be allowed only if no adequate alternatives or recycled other fully halogenated chlorofluorocarbons are available from any of the Parties to the Protocol.

The Commission shall issue licences to those users identified as laid down in the second subparagraph and shall notify them of the use for which they have authorization and the substances and the quantities of them that they are authorized to use.

A producer may be authorized by the competent authority of the Member State in which his relevant production is situated to produce other fully halogenated chlorofluorocarbons after 31 December 1994 for the purpose of meeting the licensed demands presented by users identified as laid down in the second subparagraph. The competent authority of the Member State concerned shall notify the Commission in advance of its intention of issuing any such authorization.

3. Subject to paragraphs 8 to 12, each producer shall ensure that he produces no halons after 31 December 1993.

In the light of the nominations made by Member States the Commission shall, in accordance with the procedure laid down in Article 16, apply the criteria set out in Decision IV/25 of the Parties to the Montreal Protocol in order to determine every year any essential uses for which the production and importation of halons may be permitted in the Community after 31 December 1993 and those users who may take advantage of those essential uses for their own account. Such production and importation shall be allowed only if no adequate alternatives or recycled halons are available from any of the Parties to the Protocol.

The Commission shall issue licences to those users identified as laid down in the second subparagraph and shall notify them of the use for which they have authorization and the substances and the quantities of them that they are authorized to use.

A producer may be authorized by the competent authority of the Member State in which his relevant production is situated to produce halons after 31 December 1993 for the purpose of meeting the licensed demands presented by users identified as laid down in the second subparagraph. The competent authority of the Member State concerned shall notify the Commission in advance of its intention of issuing any such authorization.

4. Subject to paragraphs 8 to 12, each producer shall ensure that:
– the calculated level of his production of carbon tetrachloride in the

period 1 January to 31 December 1994 does not exceed 15% of the calculated level of his production of carbon tetrachloride in 1989,
– he produces no carbon tetrachloride after 31 December 1994.

In the light of the nominations made by Member States the Commission shall, in accordance with the procedure laid down in Article 16, apply the criteria set out in Decision IV/25 of the Parties to the Montreal Protocol in order to determine every year any essential uses for which the production and importation of carbon tetrachloride may be permitted in the Community after 31 December 1994 and those users who may take advantage of those essential uses for their own account. Such production and importation shall be allowed only if no adequate alternatives or recycled carbon tetrachloride are available from any of the Parties to the Protocol.

The Commission shall issue licences to those users identified as laid down in the second subparagraph and shall notify them of the use for which they have authorization and the substances and the quantities of them that they are authorized to use.

A producer may be authorized by the competent authority of the Member State in which his relevant production is situated to produce carbon tetrachloride after 31 December 1994 for the purpose of meeting the licensed demands presented by users identified as laid down in the second subparagraph. The competent authority of the Member State concerned shall notify the Commission in advance of its intention of issuing any such authorization.

5. Subject to paragraphs 8 to 12, each producer shall ensure that:
- the calculated level of his production of 1,1,1-trichloroethane in the period 1 January to 31 December 1994 and in the following 12-month period does not exceed 50% of the calculated level of his production of 1,1,1-trichloroethane in 1989,
- he produces no 1,1,1-trichloroethane after 31 December 1995.

In the light of the nominations made by Member States the Commission shall, in accordance with the procedure laid down in Article 16, apply the criteria set out in Decision IV/25 of the Parties to the Montreal Protocol in order to determine every year any essential uses for which the production and importation of 1,1,1-trichloroethane may be permitted in the Community after 31 December 1995 and those users who may take advantage of those essential uses for their own account. Such production and importation shall be allowed only if no adequate alternatives or recycled 1,1,1-trichloroethane are available from any of the Parties to the Protocol.

The Commission shall issue licences to those users identified as laid down in the second subparagraph and shall notify them of the use for which they have authorization and the substances and the quantities of them that they are authorized to use.

A producer may be authorized by the competent authority of the Member State in which his relevant production is situated to produce 1,1,1-trichloroethane after 31 December 1995 for the purpose of meeting the licensed demands presented by users identified as laid down in the second subparagraph. The competent authority of the Member State concerned shall notify the Commission in advance of its intention of issuing any such authorization.

6. Subject to paragraphs 8 to 12, each producer shall ensure that:

– the calculated level of his production of methyl bromide in the period 1 January to 31 December 1995 and in each 12-month period thereafter does not exceed the calculated level of his production of methyl bromide in 1991,
– the calculated level of his production of methyl bromide in the period 1 January to 31 December 1998 and in each 12-month period thereafter does not exceed 75% of the calculated level of his production of methyl bromide in 1991.

The calculated level of each producer's production of methyl bromide under this paragraph shall not include the amount he produces for quarantine and pre-shipment applications.

7. Subject to paragraphs 10 to 12, each producer shall ensure that he produces no hydrobromofluorocarbons after 31 December 1995.

In the light of the nominations made by Member States the Commission shall, in accordance with the procedure laid down in Article 16, apply the criteria set out in Decision IV/25 of the Parties to the Montreal Protocol in order to determine every year any essential uses for which the production and importation of hydrobromofluorocarbons may be permitted in the Community after 31 December 1995 and those users who may take advantage of those essential uses for their own account. Such production and importation shall be allowed only if no adequate alternatives or recycled hydrobromofluorocarbons are available from any of the Parties to the Protocol.

The Commission shall issue licences to those users identified as laid down in the second subparagraph and shall notify them of the use for which they have authorization and the substances and the quantities of them that they are authorized to use.

A producer may be authorized by the competent authority of the Member State in which is relevant production is situated to produce hydrobromofluorocarbons after 31 December 1995 for the purpose of meeting the licensed demands presented by users identified as laid down in the second subparagraph. The competent authority of the Member State concerned shall notify the Commission in advance of its intention of issuing any such authorization.

8. To the extent permitted by the Protocol, the competent authority of the Member State in which a producer's relevant production is situated may authorize him to exceed the calculated levels of production laid down in paragraphs 1 to 6 in order to satisfy the basic domestic needs of Parties pursuant to Article 5 of the Protocol, provided that the additional calculated levels of production of the Member State concerned do not exceed those permitted for that purpose by Articles 2A to 2E and 2H of the Protocol for the periods in question. The competent authority of the Member State concerned shall notify the Commission in advance of its intention of issuing any such authorization.

9. To the extent permitted by the Protocol, the competent authority of the Member State in which a producer's relevant production is situated may authorize him to exceed the calculated levels of production laid down in paragraphs 1 to 5 and 7 in order to satisfy any essential uses of Parties at their request. The competent authority of the Member State concerned shall notify the Commission in advance of its intention of issuing any such authorization.

10. To the extent permitted by the Protocol, the competent authority of the Member State in which a producer's relevant production is situated may authorize him to exceed the calculated levels of production laid down in paragraphs 1 to 9 for the purpose of industrial rationalization within the Member State concerned, provided that the calculated levels of production of that Member State do not exceed the sum of the calculated levels of production of its domestic producers as laid down in paragraphs 1 to 9 for the periods in question. The competent authority of the Member State concerned shall notify the Commission in advance of its intention of issuing any such authorization.

11. To the extent permitted by the Protocol, the Commission may, in agreement with the competent authority of the Member State in which a producer's relevant production is situated, authorize him to exceed the calculated levels of production laid down in paragraphs 1 to 10 for the purpose of industrial rationalization between Member States, provided that the combined calculated levels of production of the Member States concerned do not exceed the sum of the calculated levels of production of their domestic producers as laid down in paragraphs 1 to 10 for the periods in question. The agreement of the competent authority of the Member State in which it is intended to reduce production shall also be required.

12. To the extent permitted by the Protocol, the Commission may, in agreement with both the competent authority of the Member State in which a producer's relevant production is situated and the government of the

third Party concerned, authorize a producer to combine the calculated levels of production laid down in paragraphs 1 to 11 with the calculated levels of production allowed to a producer in a third Party under the Protocol and that producer's national legislation for the purpose of industrial rationalization with a third Party, provided that the combined calculated levels of production by the two producers do not exceed the sum of the calculated levels of production allowed to the Community producer under paragraphs 1 to 11 and the calculated levels of production allowed to the third Party producer under the Protocol and his national legislation.

Article 4

Control of the supply of controlled substances

1. Subject to paragraph 10, each producer shall ensure that:
- the calculated level of chlorofluorocarbons which he places on the market or uses for his own account in the period 1 January to 31 December 1994 does not exceed 15% of the calculated level of chlorofluorocarbons which he placed on the market or used for his own account in 1986,
- he does not place any chlorofluorocarbons on the market or use any for his own account after 31 December 1994.

The competent authority of the Member State in which a producer's production is situated may authorize him to place chlorofluorocarbons on the market after 31 December 1994 for the purpose of meeting the licensed demands of those users identified as laid down in Article 3 (1).

2. Subject to paragraph 10, each producer shall ensure that:
- the calculated level of other fully halogenated chlorofluorocarbons which he places on the market or uses for his own account in the period 1 January to 31 December 1994 does not exceed 15% of the calculated level of other fully halogenated chlorofluorocarbons which he placed on the market or used for his own account in 1989,
- he does not place any other fully halogenated chlorofluorocarbons on the market or use any for his own account after 31 December 1994.

The competent authority of the Member State in which a producer's production is situated may authorize him to place other fully halogenated chlorofluorocarbons on the market after 31 December 1994 for the purpose of meeting the licensed demands of those users identified as laid down in Article 3 (2).

3. Subject to paragraph 10, each producer shall ensure that he does not place any halons on the market or use any for his own account after 31 December 1993.

The competent authority of the Member State in which a producer's production is situated may authorize him to place halons on the market after 31 December 1993 for the purpose of meeting the licensed demands of those users identified as laid down in Article 3 (3).

4. Subject to paragraph 10, each producer shall ensure that:

- the calculated level of carbon tetrachloride which he places on the market or uses for his own accounting the period 1 January to 31 December 1994 does not exceed 15% of the calculated level of carbon tetrachloride which he placed on the market or used for his own account in 1989,
- he does not place any carbon tetrachloride on the market or use any for his own account after 31 December 1994.

The competent authority of the Member State in which a producer's production is situated may authorize him to place carbon tetrachloride on the market after 31 December 1994 for the purpose of meeting the licensed demands of those users identified as laid down in Article 3 (4).

5. Subject to paragraph 10, each producer shall ensure that:

- the calculated level of 1,1,1-trichloroethane which he places on the market or uses for his own account in the period 1 January to 31 December 1994 and in the following 12-month period does not exceed 50% of the calculated level of 1,1,1-trichloroethane which he placed on the market or used or his own account in 1989,
- he does not place any 1,1,1-trichloroethane on the market or use any for his own account after 31 December 1995.

The competent authority of the Member State in which a producer's production is situated may authorize him to place 1,1,1-trichloroethane on the market after 31 December 1995 for the purpose of meeting the licensed demands of those users identified as laid down in Article 3 (5).

6. Subject to paragraph 10, each producer shall ensure that:

- the calculated level of methyl bromide which he places on the market or uses for his own account in the period 1 January to 31 December 1995 and in each 12-month period thereafter does not exceed the calculated level of methyl bromide which he placed on the market or used for his own account in 1991,
- the calculated level of methyl bromide which he places on the market or uses for his own account in the period 1 January to 31 December 1998 and in each 12-month period thereafter does not exceed 75% of the calculated level of methyl bromide which he placed on the market or used for his own account in 1991,

The calculated level of methyl bromide which each producer places on the market or uses for his own account under this paragraph shall not include any amounts he places on the market or uses for his own account for quarantine and pre-shipment application.

7. Subject to paragraph 10, each producer shall ensure that he does not place any hydrobromofluorocarbons on the market or use any for his own account after 31 December 1995.

The competent authority of the Member State in which a producer's production is situated may authorize him to place hydrobromofluorocarbons n the market after 31 December 1995 for the purpose of meeting the licensed demands of those users identified as laid down in Article 3 (7).

8. Subject to paragraph 10:

- the calculated level of hydrochlorofluorocarbons which producers and importers place on the market or use for their own account in the period 1 January to 31 December 1995 and in each 12-month period thereafter shall not exceed the sum of:
- 2.6% of the calculated level of chlorofluorocarbons which producers and importers placed on the market or used for their own account in 1989, and
- the calculated level of hydrochlorofluorocarbons which producers and importers placed on the market or used for their own account in 1989.

  To this end the Commission shall, in accordance with the procedure laid down in Article 16, assign a quota to each producer or importer when the total quantity which producers and importers place on the market or use for their own account reaches 80% of the quantity defined by the sum described above or at the latest on 1 January 2000, whichever comes first,
- the calculated level of hydrochlorofluorocarbons which a producer or importer places on the market or uses for his own account in the period 1 January to 31 December 2004 and in each 12-month period thereafter shall not exceed 65% of the quota assigned,
- the calculated level of hydrochlorofluorocarbons which a producer or importer places on the market or uses for his own account in the period 1 January to 31 December 2007 and in each 12-month period thereafter shall not exceed 40% of the quota assigned,
- the calculated level of hydrochlorofluorocarbons which a producer or importer places on the market or uses for his own account in the period 1 January to 31 December 2010 and in each 12-month period thereafter shall not exceed 20% of the quota assigned,
- the calculated level of hydrochlorofluorocarbons which a producer or importer places on the market or uses for his own account in the period 1 January to 31 December 2013 and in each 12-month period thereafter shall not exceed 5% of the quota assigned,
- no producer or importer shall place hydrochlorofluorocarbons on the market or use any for his own account after 31 December 2014.

The Commission may, in accordance with the procedure laid down in Article 16, revise the assigned quotas for hydrochlorofluorocarbons to the extent permitted by this Regulation.

9. The quantities referred to in paragraphs 1 to 7 shall apply to the amounts of virgin substances which a producer places on the market or uses for his own account within the Community.

The quantities referred to in paragraph 8 shall apply to the amounts of virgin substances which a producer or importer places on the market or uses for his own account within the Community and which were produced in or imported into the Community.

10. Any producer entitled to place a group of substances referred to in this Article on the market or use them for his own account may transfer his right in respect of all or any quantities of that group of substances fixed in accordance with this Article to any other producer of that group of substances within the Community. A producer acquiring such rights shall immediately notify the Commission. The transfer of the right to place on the market or use shall not imply the further right to produce.

At the request of a producer, the Commission may adopt measures to respond to any shortfalls in that producer's right to place hydrochlorofluorocarbons on the market or use them for his own account to the extent permitted by the Protocol.

Article 5

Control of the use of hydrochlorofluorocarbons

1. From the first day of the sixth month following that of the entry into force of this Regulation, the use of hydrochlorofluorocarbons shall be prohibited except:
- as solvents,
- as refrigerants,
- for the production of rigid insulating foams and integral-skin foams for use in safety applications,
- in laboratory uses, including research and development,
- as feedstock in the manufacture of other chemicals and
- as carrier gas for sterilization substances in closed systems.

2. From 1 January 1996 the use of hydrochlorofluorocarbons shall be prohibited:
- in non-contained solvent uses including open-top cleaners and open-top dewatering systems without cold areas, in adhesives and mould-release agents when not employed in closed equipment, for drain cleaning where

hydrochlorofluorocarbons are not recovered and aerosols, apart from use as solvents for reagents in fingerprint development on porous surfaces such as paper and apart from use as fixing agents for laser printers produced before 1 January 1996,

– in equipment produced after 31 December 1995 for the following uses:
  (a) as refrigerants in non-confined direct-evaporation systems;
  (b) as refrigerants in domestic refrigerators and freezers;
  (c) in car air conditioning;
  (d) in road public-transport air conditioning.

3. From 1 January 1998 the use of hydrochlorofluorocarbons in equipment produced after 31 December 1997 for the following uses shall be prohibited:

– in rail public-transport air conditioning,
– as carrier gas for sterilization substances in closed systems.

4. From 1 January 2000 the use of hydrochlorofluorocarbons in equipment produced after 31 December 1999 for the following uses shall be prohibited:

– as refrigerants in public and distribution cold stores and warehouses,
– as refrigerants for equipment of 150 kw and over, shaft input,

except where codes, safety regulations or other such constraints prevent the use of ammonia.

5. The importing, release for free circulation and placing on the market of equipment for which a use restriction is in force under this Article shall be prohibited from the date on which that use restriction comes into force. Equipment shown to be manufactured before the date of that use restriction shall not be covered by this prohibition.

6. The Commission may, in accordance with the procedure laid down in Article 16 and in the light of technical progress, add to, delete items from or amend the list set out in paragraphs 1 to 4.

CHAPTER III

TRADE

Article 6

Licences to import from third countries

1. The release for free circulation in the Community or inward processing of controlled substances shall be subject to the presentation of an import licence, whether the substances are virgin, recovered or reclaimed. Such licences shall be issued by the Commission after verification of compliance with Articles 6, 7, 8 and 12. The Commission shall forward a copy of each licence to the competent authority of the Member State into which the substances concerned are to be imported. Each Member State shall appoint a competent authority for that purpose.

2. A request for a licence shall state:
   (a) the names and the addresses of the importer and the exporter;
   (b) the country of exportation;
   (c) a description of each controlled substance including:
      – the commercial description,
      – the heading and the CN code,
      – the nature of the substance (virgin, recovered or reclaimed),
      – the quantity of the substance in kilograms;
   (d) the purpose of the proposed input (destruction by technologies approved by the Parties, recycling, feedstock use or other use of the controlled substance);
   (e) the place and date of the proposed importation, if known.

3. The Commission may require a certificate attesting to the nature of substances to be imported.

Article 7

Imports of controlled substances from third countries

1. Without prejudice to Article 4 (8) and unless the substances are intended for destruction by a technology approved by the Parties, for feedstock use in the manufacture of other chemicals or for quarantine and preshipment, the release for free circulation in the Community of controlled substances imported from third countries shall be subject to quantitative limits. Those limits shall be determined in accordance with the procedure laid down in Article 16.

2. The Community shall open the quotas set out in Annex II or in Article 4 (8) which shall be applicable for each 12-month period laid down in the Annex or in Article 4 (1) and allocate them to undertakings in accordance with the procedure laid down in Article 16.

3. The Commission may, in accordance with the procedure laid down in Article 16, alter the quotas set out in Annex II.

4. The Commission may allow the importation into the Community of controlled substances over and above the quantities set out in Article 4 (8) and Annex II to meet the licensed demands of users identified as laid down in Articles 3 (1) to (5) and (7).

5. The Commission may authorize undertakings to release for free circulation in the Community controlled substances which are intended for destruction by a technology approved by the Parties, for feedstock use in the manufacture of other chemicals or for quarantine and preshipment in accordance with the procedure laid down in Article 16.

Article 8

Imports of controlled substances from a State not Party

1. The release for free circulation in the Community of virgin, recovered or reclaimed chlorofluorocarbons, other fully halogenated chlorofluorocarbons, halons, carbon tetrachloride or 1,1,1-trichloroethane imported from any State not Party shall be prohibited.

2. One year after the date of the entry into force of the second amendment to the Protocol, the release for free circulation in the Community of virgin, recovered or reclaimed hydrobromofluorocarbons imported from any State not Party shall be prohibited. The Commission shall publish the date of the entry into force of that amendment in the *Official Journal of the European Communities.*

Article 9

Imports of products containing controlled substances from a State not Party

1. Subject to the decision referred to in paragraph 4, the release for free circulation in the Community of products containing chlorofluorocarbons or halons imported from any State not Party shall be prohibited.

2. Subject to the decision referred to in paragraph 4, the release for free circulation in the Community of products containing other fully

halogenated chlorofluorocarbons, carbon tetrachloride or 1,1,1-trichloroethane imported from any State not Party shall be prohibited.

3. Subject to the decision referred to in paragraph 4, the release for free circulation in the Community of products containing hydrobromofluorocarbons imported from any State not Party shall be prohibited.

4. The Commission may, in accordance with the procedure laid down in Article 16, add to, delete items from or amend the list set out in Annex V in the light of the lists established by the Parties.

Article 10

Imports of products produced using controlled substances from a State not Party

In the light of the decision of the Parties, the Council shall, on a proposal from the Commission, adopt rules applicable to the release for free circulation in the Community of products imported from any State not Party, produced from controlled substances, which can be positively identified as such but do not contain such controlled substances. The identification of such products shall comply with periodical technical advice given to the Parties. The Council shall act by a qualified majority.

Article 11

Exports of controlled substances to a State not Party

1. Exports of virgin, recovered or reclaimed chlorofluorocarbons, other fully halogenated chlorofluorocarbons, halons, carbon tetrachloride or 1,1,1-trichloroethane from the Community to any State not Party shall be prohibited.

2. One year after the date published in the *Official Journal of the European Communities* pursuant to Article 8 (2), exports of virgin, recovered or reclaimed hydrobromofluorocarbons from the Community to any State not Party shall be prohibited.

Article 12

Exceptional authorization to trade with a State not Party

By way of derogation from Articles 8, 9 (1), (2) and (3) and 11, trade with any State not Party in controlled substances and products which contain or are produced by means of one or more such substances may be authorized by the Commission, to the extent that the State not Party is determined by a meeting of the Parties to be in full compliance with Articles 2, 2A to 2E, 2G and 4 of the Protocol and has submitted data to that effect as specified in Article 7 of the Protocol. The Commission shall act in accordance with the procedure laid down in Article 16.

Article 13

Trade with a territory not covered by the Protocol

1. Subject to any decision taken under paragraph 2, Articles 8, 9 and 11 shall apply to any territory not covered by the Protocol as they apply to any State not Party.

2. Where the authorities of a territory not covered by the Protocol are in full compliance with Articles 2, 2A to 2E, 2G and 4 of the Protocol and have submitted data to that effect as specified in Article 7 of the Protocol, the Commission may decide that some or all of the provisions of Articles 8, 9 and 11 shall not apply in respect of that territory.

The Commission shall take its decision in accordance with the procedure laid down in Article 16.

CHAPTER IV

EMISSION CONTROL

Article 14

Recovery of used controlled substances

From the first day of the fourth month following that of the entry into force of this Regulation, chlorofluorocarbons, fully halogenated chlorofluorocarbons, halons, carbon tetrachloride, 1,1,1-trichloroethane, hydrobromofluorocarbons and hydrochlorofluorocarbons contained in:
- commercial and industrial refrigeration equipment and air-conditioning equipment,
- equipment containing solvents, and
- fire protection systems

shall be recovered if practicable for destruction by technologies approved by the Parties or by any other environmentally acceptable destruction technology, or for recycling or reclamation during the servicing and maintenance of equipment or before the dismantling or disposal of equipment.

Member States may define the minimum qualification requirements for the servicing personnel involved.

This provision shall be without prejudice to Council Directive 75/442/EEC of 15 July 1975[1] on waste or to Member States' measures transposing its provisions.

Before 31 December 1994 the Commission shall submit to the Council and the European Parliament a report on the implementation of the provisions of this Article by the Member States.

Article 15

Leakages of controlled substances

1. From the first day of the fourth month following that of the entry into force of this Regulation, all precautionary measures practicable shall be taken to prevent leakages of chlorofluorocarbons, other fully halogenated chlorofluorocarbons, halons, carbon tetrachloride, 1,1,1-trichloroethane, hydrobromofluorocarbons and hydrochlorofluorocarbons from commercial and industrial air-conditioning and refrigeration equipment, from fire-protection systems and from equipment containing solvents during manufacture, installation, operation and servicing. Member States may define the minimum qualification requirements for the servicing personnel involved.

2. From the first day of the fourth month following that of the entry into force of this Regulation, all precautionary measures practicable shall be taken to prevent leakages of methyl bromide from fumigation installations and operations in which methyl bromide is used. Member States may define the minimum qualification requirements for the servicing personnel involved.

3. From the first day of the fourth month following that of the entry into force of this Regulation, all precautionary measures practicable shall be taken to prevent leakages of controlled substances used as feedstock in the manufacture of other chemicals.

4. From the first day of the fourth month following that of the entry into force of this Regulation, all precautionary measures practicable shall be taken to prevent any leakage of controlled substances inadvertently produce in the course of the manufacture of other chemicals.

[1] OJ No L 194, 25. 7. 1975, p. 39. Directive as amended by Directive 91/156/EEC (OJ No L 78, 26. 3. 1991, p. 32) and by Directive 91/692/EEC (OJ No L 377, 31. 12. 1991, p. 48).

CHAPTER V

MANAGEMENT, REPORTING AND FINAL PROVISIONS

Article 16

Management

The Commission shall be assisted by a committee composed of representatives of the Member States and chaired by a representative of the Commission.

The representative of the Commission shall submit to the committee a draft of the measures to be taken. The committee shall deliver its opinion on that draft within a time limit which the chairman may lay down according to the urgency of the matter. Each opinion shall be delivered by the majority laid down in Article 148 (2) of the Treaty for decisions which the Council is required to adopt on a proposal from the Commission. The votes of the representatives of the Member States within the committee shall be weighted in the manner laid down in that Article. The chairman shall not vote.

The Commission shall adopt measures which shall apply immediately. If, however, those measures are not in accordance with the committee's opinion the Commission shall communicate them to the Council forthwith. In that event, the Commission may defer application of the measures on which it has decided for up to one month after the date of that communication.

The Council may, acting by a qualified majority, take a different decision within the time limit laid down in the third paragraph.

Article 17

Reporting

1. (a) Every year before 31 March, starting in 1995, each producer, importer and exporter of controlled substances shall communicate to the Commission, sending a copy of the competent authority of the Member State concerned:
   - his total production,
   - his production to meet the licensed demands of users identified as laid down in Articles 3 (1) to (5) and (7),
   - any increase in his production under Article 3 (8) to satisfy the basic domestic needs of Parties pursuant to Article 5 of the Protocol,
   - any increase in his production under Article 3 (9) to satisfy his essential uses of Parties,

- any increase in his production under Article 3 (10), (11) and (12) authorized in connection with industrial rationalization,
- any quantities recycled,
- any quantities destroyed by means of technologies approved by the Parties,
- any stocks,
- any quantities of imported virgin substances released for free circulation in the Community with separate figures for States Party and States not Party,
- any imports into the Community to meet the licensed demands of users identified as laid down in Article 3 (1) to (5) and (7),
- any exports of production from the Community, with separate figures for States Party and States not Party,
- any production placed in the market or used for the producer's own account within the Community,
- any quantities used for feedstock,

for each controlled substance in respect of the period 1 January to 31 December of the preceding year.

Notwithstanding the above obligations, the communication referred to in this paragraph for the period 1 January to 31 December 1993 shall be effected no later than the last day of the fourth month following that of the entry into force of this Regulation.

(b) For the purposes of Article 4 (8) on the last day of the quarter following that of the entry into force of this Regulation, and on the last day of each quarter thereafter, each producer or importer of hydrochlorofluorocarbons shall communicate to the Commission, sending a copy to the competent authority of the Member State concerned:

- his production of hydrochlorofluorocarbons placed on the market or used for his own account within the Community,
- his imports of hydrochlorofluorocarbons into the Community.

2. Every year before 31 March, beginning in 1996 for chlorofluorocarbons, other fully halogenated chlorofluorocarbons, halons and carbon tetrachloride and 1997 for 1,1,1-trichloroethane and hydrobromofluorocarbons, each user identified as laid down in Articles 3 (1) to (5) and (7) shall communicate to the Commission, sending a copy to the competent authority of the Member States in which he uses them, his use and the quantities he has used of those substances for which he has received authorization under the relevant paragraphs of Article 3.

3. Each producer, importer and exporter of methyl bromide in 1991 shall communicate to the Commission, sending a copy to the competent author-

ity of the Member State concerned, the information referred to in paragraph 1 in respect of that year not later than the last day of the fourth month following that of the entry into force of this Regulation. Each producer, importer and exporter shall also indicate any quantities which relate to quarantine and pre-shipment uses.

4. The Commission shall take appropriate steps to protect the confidentiality of the information submitted.

Article 18

Inspection

1. In carrying out the tasks assigned to it by this Regulation, the Commission may obtain all the information from the governments and competent authorities of the Member States and from undertakings.

2. When requesting information from an undertaking the Commission shall at the same time forward a copy of the request to the competent authority of the Member State within the territory of which the undertaking's seat is situated, together with a statement of the reasons why that information is required.

3. The competent authorities of the Member States shall carry out the investigations which the Commission considers necessary under this Regulation.

4. Subject to the agreement of the Commission and of the competent authority of the Member State within the territory of which the investigations are to be made, the officials of the Commission shall assist the officials of that authority in the performance of their duties.

5. The Commission shall take appropriate steps to protect the confidentiality of information obtained under this Article.

Article 19

Sanctions

Each Member State shall determine the penalties to be imposed in the event of any failure to comply with this Regulation or with any national measures taken to implement it.

Article 20

1. Regulation (EEC) No 594/91 shall be repealed.

2. References to the Regulation repealed under paragraph 1 shall be construed as references to this Regulation.

Article 21

Entry into force

This Regulation shall enter into force on the day following that of its publication in the *Official Journal of the European Communities.*

This Regulation shall be binding in its entirety and directly applicable in all Member States.

Done at Brussels, 15 December 1994.

For the Council
The President
A. MERKEL

ANNEX I

SUBSTANCES COVERED

Group	Substance		Ozone-depleting potential[1]
Group I	$CFCl_3$	(CFC- 11)	1,0
	CF_2Cl_2	(CFC- 12)	1,0
	$CF_2F_3Cl_3$	(CFC-113)	0,8
	$C_2F_4Cl_2$	(CFC-114)	1,0
	C_2F_5Cl	(CFC-115)	0,6
Group II	CF_3Cl	(CFC- 13)	1,0
	C_2FCl_5	(CFC-111)	1,0
	$C_2F_2Cl_4$	(CFC-112)	1,0
	C_3FCl-	(CFC-211)	1,0
	$C_3F_2Cl_6$	(CFC-212)	1,0
	$C_3F_3Cl_5$	(CFC-213)	1,0
	$C_3F_4Cl_4$	(CFC-214)	1,0

Group	Substance		Ozone-depleting potential([1])
	$C_3F_5Cl_3$	(CFC-215)	1,0
	$C_3F_6Cl_2$	(CFC-216)	1,0
	C_3F_7Cl	(CFC-217)	1,0
Group III	CF_2BrCl	(halon-1211)	3,0
	CF_3Br	(halon-1301)	10,0
	$C_2F_4Br_2$	(halon-2402)	6,0
Group IV	CCl_4	(carbon tetrachloride)	1,1
Group V	$C_2H_3Cl_3$([2])	(1,1,1-trichloroethane)	0,1
Group VI	CH_3Br	(methyl bromide)	0,7
Group VII	$CHFBr_2$		1,00
	CHF_2Br		0,74
	CH_2FBr		0,73
	C_2HFBr_4		0,8
	$C_2HF_2Br_3$		1,8
	$C_2HF_3Br_2$		1,6
	C_2HF_4Br		1,2
	$C_2H_2FBr_3$		1,1
	$C_2H_2F_2Br_2$		1,5
	$C_2H_2F_3Br$		1,6
	$C_2H_3FBr_2$		1,7
	$C_2H_3F_2Br$		1,1
	C_2H_4FBr		0,1
	C_3HFBr_6		1,5
	$C_3HF_2Br_5$		1,9
	$C_3HF_3Br_4$		1,8
	$C_3HF_4Br_3$		2,2
	$C_3HF_5Br_2$		2,0
	C_3HF_6Br		3,3
	$C_3H_2FBr_5$		1,9
	$C_3H_2F_2Br_4$		2,1
	$C_3H_2F_3Br_3$		5,6
	$C_3H_2F_4Br_2$		7,5
	$C_3H_2F_5Br$		1,4
	$C_3H_3FBr_4$		1,9
	$C_3H_3F_2Br_3$		3,1
	$C_3H_3F_3Br_2$		2,5

Group	Substance		Ozone-depleting potential(1)
	$C_3H_3F_4Br$		4,4
	$C_3H_4FBr_3$		0,3
	$C_3H_4F_2Br_2$		1,0
	$C_3H_4F_3Br$		0,8
	$C_3H_5FBr_2$		0,4
	$C_3H_5F_2Br$		0,8
	C_3H_6FBr		0,7
Group VIII	$CHFCl_2$	(HCFC- 21)	0,040
	CHF_2Cl	(HCFC- 22)	0,055
	CH_2FCl	(HCFC- 31)	0,020
	C_2HFCl_4	(HCFC-121)	0,040
	$C_2HF_2Cl_3$	(HCFC-122)	0,080
	$C_2HF_3Cl_2$	(HCFC-123)(3)	0,020
	C_2HF_4Cl	(HCFC-124)(3)	0,022
	$C_2H_2FCl_3$	(HCFC-131)	0,050
	$C_2H_2F_2Cl_2$	(HCFC-132)	0,050
	$C_2H_2F_3Cl$	(HCFC-133)	0,060
	$C_2H_3FCl_2$	(HCFC-141)	0,070
	CH_3FCl_2	(HCFC-141b)(3)	0,110
	$C_2H_3F_2Cl$	(HCFC-142)	0,070
	CH_3F_2Cl	(HCFC-142b)(3)	0,065
	C_2H_4FCl	(HCFC-151)	0,005
	C_3HFCl_6	(HCFC-221)	0,070
	$C_3HF_2Cl_5$	(HCFC-222)	0,090
	$C_3HF_3Cl_4$	(HCFC-223)	0,080
	$C_3HF_4Cl_3$	(HCFC-224)	0,090
	$C_3HF_5Cl_2$	(HCFC-225)	0,070
	$CF_3CF_2CHCl_2$	(HCFC-225ca)(3)	0,025
	CF_2ClF_2CHClF	(HCFC-225cb)(3)	0,033
	C_3HF_6Cl	(HCFC-226)	0,100
	$C_3H_2FCl_5$	(HCFC-231)	0,090
	$C_3H_2F_2Cl_4$	(HCFC-232)	0,100
	$C_3H_2F_3Cl_3$	(HCFC-233)	0,230
	$C_3H_2F_4Cl_2$	(HCFC-234)	0,280
	$C_3H_2F_5Cl$	(HCFC-235)	0,520
	$C_3H_3FCl_4$	(HCFC-241)	0,090
	$C_3H_3F_2Cl_3$	(HCFC-242)	0,130
	$C_3H_3F_3Cl_2$	(HCFC-243)	0,120
	$C_3H_3F_4Cl$	(HCFC-244)	0,140

Group	Substance		Ozone-depleting potential[1]
	$C_3H_4FCl_3$	(HCFC-251)	0,010
	$C_3H_4F_2Cl_2$	(HCFC-252)	0,040
	$C_3H_4F_3Cl$	(HCFC-253)	0,030
	$C_3H_3FCl_2$	(HCFC-261)	0,020
	$C_3H_3F_2Cl$	(HCFC-262)	0,020
	C_3H_6FCl	(HCFC-271)	0,030

(1) These ozone-depleting potentials are estimates based on existing knowledge and will be reviewed and revised periodically in the light of decisions taken by the Parties to the Montreal Protocol on Substances that Deplete the Ozone Layer.

(2) This formula does not refer to 1,1,2-trichloroethane.

(3) Identifies the most commercially-viable substance as prescribed in the Protocol.

ANNEX II

QUANTITATIVE LIMIT ON IMPORTS FROM THIRD COUNTRIES
(calculated levels expressed in tonnes)

Substance For 12-month periods from 1 January to 31 December	Group I	Group II	Group III	Group IV	Group V	Group VI	Group VII
1993	1,161	14	700	1,288	2,378		
1994	348	4	0	386	1,189		
1995	0	0		0	1,189	11,530	
1996					0	11,530	0
1997						11,530	
1998						8,648	
1999						8,648	
2000						8,648	
2001						8,648	
2002						8,648	
2003						8,648	
2004						8,648	
2005						8,648	
2006						8,648	
2007						8,648	
2008						8,648	
2009						8,648	
2010						8,648	
2011						8,648	

Substance For 12-month periods from 1 January to 31 December	Group I	Group II	Group III	Group IV	Group V	Group VI	Group VII
2012						8,648	
2013						8,648	
2014						8,648	
2015						8,648	
thereafter						8,648	

ANNEX III

COMBINED NOMENCLATURE (CN) CODES AND DESCRIPTIONS FOR THE SUBSTANCES REFERRED TO IN ANNEXES I AND II

CN code	Description
2903 40 10	– – – Trichlorofluoromethane
2903 40 20	– – – Dichlorodifluoromethane
2903 40 30	– – – Trichlorotrifluoroethane
2903 40 40	– – – Dichlorotetrafluoroethane
2903 40 50	– – – Chloropentafluoroethane
2903 40 61	– – – – Chlorotrifluoromethane, Pentachlorofluoroethane, Tetrachlorodifluoroethane, Heptachlorofluoropropane, Hexachlorodifluoropropane, Pentachlorotrifluoropropane, Tetrachlorotetrafluoropropane, Trichloropentafluoropropane, Dichlorohexafluoropropane or Chloroheptafluoropropane
2903 40 70	– – – Bromotrifluoromethane
2903 40 80	– – – Dibromotetrafluoroethane
2903 40 91	– – – Bromochlorodifluoromethane
2903 14 00	– – Carbon tetrachloride
2903 19 10	– – – 1,1,1-Trichloroethane
2903 30 33	– – – Bromomethane (methyl bromide)
ex 2903 40 98	– – – Hydrobromofluorocarbons
ex 2903 40 69	– – – Hydrochlorofluorocarbons
ex 3823 90 96	– – – – Mixtures containing substances falling within codes 2903 40 10, 2903 40 20, 2903 40 30, 2903 40 40, 2903 40 50 or 2903 40 61
ex 3823 90 97	– – – – Mixtures containing substances falling within codes 2903 40 70, 2903 40 80, 2903 40 91 or 3823 90 96
ex 3823 90 98	– – – Mixtures containing substances falling within codes 2903 14 00 or 2903 19 10

ANNEX IV

TOTAL QUANTITATIVE LIMITS ON PRODUCERS' AND IMPORTERS' PLACING HYDROCHLOROFLUOROCARBONS ON THE MARKET AND USING THEM FOR THEIR OWN ACCOUNT IN THE COMMUNITY

For the 12-month period from 1 January to 31 December	Group VIII(1)	
	Limit in ODP tonnes	Percentage of limit
1995	7,655	100%
1996	7,655	100%
1997	7,655	100%
1998	7,655	100%
1999	7,655	100%
2000	7,655	100%
2001	7,655	100%
2002	7,655	100%
2003	7,655	100%
2004	4,975	65%
2005	4,975	65%
2006	4,975	65%
2007	3,062	40%
2008	3,062	40%
2009	3,062	40%
2010	1,531	20%
2011	1,531	20%
2012	1,531	20%
2013	383	5%
2014	383	5%
2015	0	0%

(1) The limits consists of 2,6% of the CFC and 100% of the HCFC marketed by producers or used for their own account in 1989.

ANNEX V

COMBINED NOMENCLATURE (CN) CODES FOR PRODUCTS CONTAINING CONTROLLED SUBSTANCES[1]

1. Automobiles and truck air-conditioning units

CN codes
8701 20 10 – 8701 90 90
8702 10 11 – 8702 90 90
8703 10 10 – 8703 90 90
8704 10 11 – 8704 90 90
8705 10 00 – 8705 90 90
8706 00 11 – 8706 00 99

2. Domestic and commercial refrigeration and air-conditioning/heat-pump equipment

Refrigerators:

CN codes
8418 10 10 – 8418 29 00
8418 50 11 – 8418 50 19
8418 61 10 – 8418 69 99

Freezers:

CN codes
8418 10 10 – 8418 29 00
8418 30 10 – 8418 30 99
8418 40 10 – 8418 40 99
8418 50 11 – 8418 50 19
8418 61 10 – 8418 61 90
8418 69 10 – 8418 69 99

[1] These customs codes are given for the guidance of the Member States' customs authorities

Dehumidifiers:

CN codes
8415 10 00 – 8415 83 90
8424 89 00
8479 89 10
8479 89 80

Water coolers:

CN codes
8419 60 00
8419 89 80

Ice machines:

CN codes
8418 10 10 – 8414 29 00
8418 30 10 – 8418 30 99
8418 40 10 – 8418 40 99
8418 50 11 – 8418 50 19
8418 61 10 – 8418 61 90
8418 69 10 – 8418 69 99
8479 89 80

Air-conditioning and heat-pump units:

CN codes
8415 10 00 – 8415 83 90
8418 61 10 – 8418 61 90
8418 69 10 – 8418 69 99
8418 99 10 – 8418 99 90

3. Aerosol products, except medical aerosols

Food products:

CN codes
0404 90 11 – 0404 90 99
1517 90 10 – 1517 90 99
2106 90 91
2106 90 99

Paints and varnishes, prepared water pigments and dyes:

CN codes
3208 10 10 – 3208 10 90
3208 20 10 – 3208 20 90
3208 90 10 – 3208 90 99
3209 10 00 – 3209 90 00
3210 00 10 – 3210 00 90
3212 90 90

Perfumery, cosmetic or toilet preparations:

CN codes
3303 00 10 – 3303 00 90
3304 30 00
3304 99 00
3305 10 00 – 3305 90 90
3306 10 00 – 3306 90 00
3307 10 00 – 3307 30 00
3307 49 00
3307 90 00

Surface-active preparations:

CN codes
3402 20 10 – 3402 20 90

Lubricating preparations:

CN codes
3402 11 00
3402 10 10 – 3404 19 99
3403 91 00
3403 99 10 – 3403 99 90

Household preparations:

CN codes
3405 10 00
3405 20 00
3405 30 00
3405 40 00
3405 90 10 – 3405 90 90

Articles of combustible materials:

CN codes
3606 10 00

Insecticides, rodenticides, fungicides, herbicides, etc.:

CN codes
3808 10 10 – 3808 10 90
3808 20 10 – 3808 20 80
3808 30 11 – 3808 30 90
3808 40 10 – 3808 40 90
3808 90 10 – 3808 90 90

Finishing agents, etc.:

CN codes
3809 10 10 – 3809 10 90
3809 91 00 – 3809 93 00

Organic composite solvents, etc.:

CN codes
3814 00 10 – 3814 00 90

Prepared de-icing fluids:

CN codes
3820 00 00

Products of the chemical or allied industries:

CN codes
3823 90 10
3823 90 60
3823 90 70
3823 90 81 – 3823 90 98

Silicones in primary forms:

CN codes
3910 00 00

Arms:

CN codes
9304 00 00

4. Portable fire extinguished

CN codes
8424 10 10 – 8424 10 99

5. Insulation boards, panels and pipe covers

CN codes
3917 21 10 – 3917 40 90 3920 10 21 – 3920 99 90 3921 11 00 – 3921 90 90 3925 10 00 – 3925 90 80 3926 90 10 – 3926 90 99

6. Pre-polymers

CN codes
3901 10 10 – 3911 90 90

CONVENTION ON THE CONSERVATION AND MANAGEMENT OF POLLOCK RESOURCES IN THE CENTRAL BERING SEA

The Parties to this Convention,

Recognizing the urgent necessity to cooperate in taking measures for the conservation and management of pollock resources in the central Bering Sea consistent with international law, and

Noting the adoption of the United Nations Convention on the Law of the Sea in 1982,

Have agreed as follows:

Article I

This Convention applies to the high seas area of the Bering Sea beyond 200 nautical miles from the baselines from which the breadth of the territorial sea of the coastal States of the Bering Sea is measured (herinafter referred to as 'the Convention Area'), except as otherwise provided in this Convention. Activities under this Convention, for scientific purposes, may extend beyond the Convention Area within the Bering Sea..

Article II

The objectives of this Convention shall be:

1. to establish an international regime for conservation, management, and optimum utilization of pollock resources in the Convention Area;

2. to restore and maintain the pollock resources in the Bering Sea at levels which will permit their maximum sustainable yield;

3. to cooperate in the gathering and examining of factual information concerning pollock and other living marine resources in the Bering Sea; and

4. to provide, if the Parties agree, a forum in which to consider the establishment of necessary conservation and management measures for living marine resources other than pollock in the Convention Area as may be required in the future.

Article III

1. To achieve the objectives of this Convention, the Parties agree to:
   (a) convene an Annual Conference of the Parties; and
   (b) establish a Scientific and Technical Committee.

2. The Parties shall adopt and amend as necessary rules of procedure both for the Annual Conferences and the Scientific and Technical Committee.

Article IV

1. The functions of the Annual Conference shall be:
   (a) to establish the allowable harvest level for pollock in the Convention Area (hereinafter referred to as "the AHL") for the succeeding year;
   (b) to establish an individual national quota of pollock in the Convention Area (hereinafter referred to as "the INQ") for the succeeding year for each Party;
   (c) to adopt other appropriate conservation and management measures for the pollock resources in the Convention Area;
   (d) to establish a plan of work for the Scientific and Technical Committee (hereinafter referred to as "the Plan of Work");
   (e) to receive reports from each Party relating to measures taken to investigate and penalize violations of provisions of this Convention and measures adopt pursuant thereto;
   (f) to establish the terms and conditions for any trial fishing operations for pollock in the Convention Area and to determine the scope of any cooperative scientific research on living marine resources other than pollock covered by this Convention;
   (g) to discuss cooperative enforcement measures;
   (h) to consider the effectiveness of the Central Bering Sea Observer Program established pursuant to Article XI and to adopt a manual of the procedures for boarding and inspection referred to in Article XI;
   (i) to consider matters related to the conservation and management of living marine resources other than pollock in the Convention Area;
   (j) to discuss scientific data and conservation measures of the coastal States of the Bering Sea related to pollock fishing in the Bering Sea;
   (k) to discuss fishery support operations in the Convention Area, including the environmental impact of such operations;
   (l) to adopt amendments to the Annex to this Convention; and
   (m) to perform other functions as follow from provisions of this Convention or as are necessary to attain the objectives of this Convention.

2. The Party that hosts the Annual Conference shall publish and maintain a record of all conservation and management measures in force in the Convention Area.

3. In exercising its functions under paragraph 1 above, the Annual Conference shall take full account of the reports and recommendations of the Scientific and Technical Committee.

Article V

1. Each Party has one vote in making decisions at the Annual Conference.

2. Except as provided elsewhere in this Convention, decisions of the Annual Conference on matters of substance shall be taken by consensus. A matter shall be deemed to be of substance if any Party considers it to be of substance.

3. Decisions on matters other than those referred to in paragraph 2 above shall be taken by a simple majority of the votes of all Parties casting affirmative or negative votes.

Article VI

1. The Annual Conference shall be held in rotation among the Parties.

2. The site of the next Annual Conference shall be decided by the previous Annual Conference.

3. The Parties shall at the end of each Annual Conference elect a Chairperson and a Vice-Chairperson who shall serve until the end of the next Annual Conference.

Article VII

1. The Annual Conference shall establish by consensus the AHL for the succeeding year, based upon an assessment of the Aleutian Basin pollock biomass by the Scientific and Technical Committee.

2. If every effort to achieve consensus has failed, the AHL shall be determined in accordance with the provisions of Part 1 of the Annex.

Article VIII

1. The Annual Conference shall establish by consensus the INQ for the succeeding year for each Party, the total of which shall not exceed the AHL, with the understanding that an INQ shall not be transferred to any other Party or non-Party to this Convention.

2. If every effort to achieve consensus has failed, the Parties agree that fishing for pollock in the Convention Area shall take place pursuant to the provisions of Part 2 of the Annex.

Article IX

1. The Scientific and Technical Committee, which shall be comprised of at least one representative from each Party, shall compile, exchange, and analyze information on fisheries harvests, and pollock and other living marine resources covered by this Convention in accordance with the Plan of Work established by the Annual Conference, and shall investigate other scientific matters as may be referred to it by the Annual Conference. It shall also establish forms and procedures for the Parties to submit fisheries data as required by Article X.

2. The Scientific and Technical Committee shall hold a meeting prior to the Annual Conference and shall report to the Annual Conference the results of its meeting.

3. The Scientific and Technical Committee shall strive to adopt its reports by consensus. If every effort to achieve consensus has failed, the report shall include the differing views of the representatives of the Parties to the Scientific and Technical Committee.

4. The Scientific and Technical Committee shall make recommendations to the Annual Conference with respect to the conservation and management of pollock, including the AHL for the succeeding year.

5. The Scientific and Technical Committee may perform such functions as follow from other provisions of this Convention or as the Annual Conference may determine.

Article X

1. The Parties shall cooperate in the conduct of scientific research on the pollock resources and, as may be determined by the Annual Conference, on other living marine resources covered by this Convention, including research on the determination of migratory patterns of pollock within and beyond the Convention Area. The Parties shall also cooperate in exchanging scientific data on these resources and in adopting standardized methodologies for such scientific research.

2. The Parties shall annually submit fisheries data to the Scientific and Technical Committee including catch and effort statistics, time and area of fishing operations, incidental taking of anadromous species or other living

marine resources, or other biological and technical data as may be required to meet the objectives of this Convention.

3. Each Party shall, at the request of any other Party, consult bilaterally for the purpose of accommodating scientific observers from the requesting Party on board any fishing vessel of the requested Party in the Convention Area.

4. For any year in which the AHL is zero, the Annual Conference may authorize trial fishing operations for pollock in the Convention Area to be conducted by the fishing vessels of the Parties in accordance with a research plan that is submitted by any Party concerned and is approved by the Annual Conference, based upon the recommendations of the Scientific and Technical Committee. The terms and conditions for such operations shall be established by the Annual Conference.

Article XI

1. Each Party shall take all necessary measures to ensure that its nationals and fishing vessels flying its flag comply with the provisions of this Convention and measures adopted pursuant thereto. For purposes of this Convention, "fishing vessel" means any vessel used or intended for use for the purposes of the commercial exploitation of living marine resources, including mother ships and any other vessels directly engaged in such fishing operations.

2. Each Party shall:
   (a) ensure that its fishing vessels fish for pollock in the Convention Area only pursuant to specific authorization issued by that Party; and
   (b) ensure that fishing operations for pollock by its fishing vessels undertaken in violation of the provisions of this Convention or of such authorization constitute an offense under its national legislation.

3. Each Party shall require its fishing vessels that fish for pollock in the Convention Area:
   (a) to use real-time satellite position-fixing transmitters while in the Bering Sea;
   (b) to notify the other Parties of their intention to enter the Convention Area 48 hours prior to such entry, the procedures for which shall be established by the Annual Conference; and
   (c) to notify the other Parties of the location of any transshipments of fish and fish products to transport vessels 24 hours prior to such transshipment.

4. The Parties shall exchange:
   (a) information collected by real-time satellite position-fixing transmitters on a real-time basis through bilateral channels; and
   (b) catch data on a sufficiently regular basis, established by the Annual Conference, to ensure effective implementation of the relevant conservation and management measures.

5. The Parties shall establish a Central Bering Sea Observer Program in accordance with the following principles:
   (a) Each fishing vessel of the Parties that fishes for pollock in the Convention Area shall accept one observer of a Party other than its flag-State Party, upon request of such Party, under conditions established bilaterally sufficiently in advance by the Parties concerned. If such an observer is not available, the fishing vessel shall have on board one observer from its flag-State Party.
   (b) The observers shall be trained and certified in accordance with the procedures to be included in the Program.
   (c) The Program shall have as its objective a significant level of coverage by observers sent by non-flag-State Parties.
   (d) With respect to observers sent by non-flag-State Parties, each Party shall require its fishing vessels to bear the costs of meals and accommodation of such observers. Other matters relating to costs shall be arranged between the Parties concerned.
   (e) The activities of observers shall include monitoring the implementation of conservation and management measures adopted pursuant to this Convention (*e.g.*, measures relating to fishing activities, location thereof, incidental catch, and fishing gear) and reporting of their findings to the flag-State Party and observer's Party.

6. Each Party may enforce the provisions of this Convention within the Convention Area in accordance with the following:
   (a) Each Party consents to the boarding and inspection of fishing vessels flying its flag and located in the Convention Area by duly authorized officials of any other Party for compliance with this Convention or measures adopted pursuant thereto.
   (b) Such officials may inspect the vessel (other than crew quarters and engineering spaces), catch, fishing gear, and relevant documents and logbooks, and question the master, the fishing master, and other officers on board.
   (c) When conducting inspections, such officials shall present credentials issued by their Governments, minimize interference with and inconvenience to the operations of the fishing vessel undertaken pursuant to this Convention, and follow procedures set forth in a manual adopted by the Annual Conference.

7. Where an inspection of a fishing vessel undertaken under paragraph 6 above reveals evidence of a violation of the provisions of this Convention or of measures adopted pursuant thereto:

(a) The flag-State Party shall be notified promptly of alleged violations. The flag-State Party shall take appropriate measures in accordance with its national laws and regulations, including prompt investigation. The flag- State Party shall order the fishing vessel to cease operations in violation of the provisions of this Convention or of measures adopted pursuant thereto and, in appropriate cases, shall order the fishing vessel to leave the Convention Area immediately.

(b) In any case in which the fishing vessel has:

(i) engaged in fishing for pollock, other than authorized trial fishing, in the Convention Area in any year:

(1) in which the AHL is zero;

(2) while fishing for pollock is not allowed in accordance with the provisions of this Convention;

(3) after the total catch of pollock of the fishing vessel's Party has reached the INQ of that Party;

(ii) operated in the Convention Area without specific authorization from the flag-State Party; or

(iii) operated in the Convention Area without an observer or without an operable real-time satellite position-fixing transmitter, in circumstances set forth in a manual adopted by the Annual Conference;

and the flag-State Party is not in a position to take immediate control of or otherwise carry out its responsibility for the operation of the fishing vessel, the officials of the boarding Party may continue the boarding initiated under paragraph 6 above until officials of the flag-State Party board the fishing vessel or the flag-State Party otherwise carried out its responsibility for the operation of the fishing vessel. In such circumstances, the Parties concerned shall cooperate to ensure full compliance with this Convention and with conservation and management measures adopted pursuant thereto. In particular, the Parties concerned shall consult and take such practical steps as may be necessary to ensure such compliance.

(c) Only the authorities of the flag-State Party may try the offense and impose penalties therefore. The evidence necessary for establishing the offense, insofar as it is under the control of any of the Parties, shall be furnished, in accordance with the respective laws and regulations of the Parties, as promptly as possible to the Party having jurisdiction to try the offense and shall be taken into account, and utilized as appropriate, by the relevant authorities of that Party.

(d) Penalties provided for in the relevant laws and regulations of the Parties shall reflect the seriousness of the infractions.

Article XII

1. The Parties agree to invite the attention of any non-Party to this Convention to any matter relating to the fishing operations of its nationals, residents, or vessels flying its flag that could affect adversely the attainment of the objectives of this Convention.

2. The Parties shall, consistent with international law, encourage any non-Party to respect the provisions of this Convention and any conservation and management measures adopted pursuant thereto.

3. If fishing operations by nationals, residents, or vessels of any non-Party could affect adversely the attainment of the objectives of this Convention, the Parties shall take measures, individually or collectively, which are consistent with international law, and which they deem necessary and appropriate, to deter such operations.

4. Each Party shall take appropriate measures aimed at preventing fishing vessels registered under its laws and regulations from transferring their registration for the purpose of avoiding compliance with the provisions of this Convention or conservation and management measures adopted pursuant thereto.

5. The Parties may, by unanimous agreement, invite the representative of any non-Party to participate as an observer at the Annual Conferences.

Article XIII

If any dispute arises between two or more of the Parties concerning the interpretation or application of this Convention, those Parties shall consult among themselves with a view to having the dispute resolved by available peaceful means of their own choice.

Article XIV

1. The Annex to this Convention shall form an integral part of this Convention. All references to this Convention shall be understood as including the Annex.

2. The Annex to this Convention shall be considered amended upon the acceptance by the Governments of all Parties of a proposed amendment to

the Annex adopted by the Annual Conference in accordance with the provisions of subparagraph 1(1) of Article IV. An amendment to the Annex shall enter into force on the date upon which the Depositary receives notification in writing from all Parties of their acceptance of the amendment.

3. The Depositary shall notify all Parties of the date of receipt of each notification of acceptance of an amendment to the Annex.

Article XV

The official language of the Annual Conference and the Scientific and Technical Committee shall be English.

Article XVI

1. This Convention shall be open for signature at Washington by the People's Republic of China, Japan, the Republic of Korea, the Republic of Poland, the Russian Federation, and the United States of America.

2. This Convention shall enter into force on the thirtieth day following the date on which at least four signatory States, including the Russian Federation and the United States of America, which are the coastal States of the Bering Sea, have deposited their instrument of ratification, acceptance, or approval with the Depositary.

3. This Convention shall enter into force for each of the other signatory States on the thirtieth day following the date of deposit of that State's instrument of ratification, acceptance, or approval.

4. After the entry into force of this Convention, the Parties may, by unanimous agreement, invite other States whose nationals and fishing vessels wish to conduct fishing for pollock in the Convention Area to become Parties to this Convention. This Convention shall enter into force for any such other State on the thirtieth day following the date of deposit of the State's instrument of accession.

Article XVII

1. Any Party may at any time propose an amendment to this Convention other than the Annex by providing the text of such a proposal to the Depositary. The Depositary shall promptly circulate any such proposals to all Parties.

2. If one-half of the Parties request a meeting to discuss a proposed amendment, the Depositary shall call such a meeting, which shall take place

no sooner than sixty days following the date of circulation of the proposal pursuant to paragraph 1 above.

3. An amendment shall enter into force when the Depositary has received instruments of ratification, acceptance, or approval thereof from all Parties.

Article XVIII

After three years from entry into force of this Convention, any Party may withdraw from this Convention twelve months after the date on which it notifies the Depositary in writing of its intention to withdraw.

Article XIX

Nothing in this Convention nor any measures adopted pursuant thereto shall be deemed to prejudice the positions or views of any Party with respect to its rights and obligations under treaties and other international agreements to which it is Party or its positions or views with respect to the law of the sea.

Article XX

The original of this Convention shall be deposited with the Government of the United States of America, which shall be Depositary. The Depositary shall transmit certified copies thereof to all other signatory States and acceding States.

IN WITNESS WHEREOF the undersigned, being duly authorized thereto, have signed this Convention.

DONE AT Washington this sixteenth day of June, 1994, in a single original, in the English language.

FOR THE PEOPLE'S REPUBLIC OF CHINA:

FOR JAPAN:

FOR THE REPUBLIC OF KOREA:

FOR THE REPUBLIC OF POLAND:

FOR THE RUSSIAN FEDERATION:

FOR THE UNITED STATES OF AMERICA:

ANNEX

PART 1

Pursuant to paragraph 2 of Article VII, the AHL shall be determined as follows:

(a) Based on scientific and technical information reviewed by the Scientific and Technical Committee, one institution each designated by the Russian Federation and the United States of America, as the coastal states of the Bering Sea, shall jointly establish the Aleutian Basin pollock biomass.

(b) If there is insufficient scientific and technical information available to allow the two institutions designated pursuant to paragraph (a) above to establish the Aleutian Basin pollock biomass, the Parties agree that, for the purpose of this Convention, the pollock biomass for the Specific Area (note) as determined by the United States institution designated pursuant to paragraph (a) above shall be deemed to represent 60 percent of the Aleutian Basin pollock biomass.

(c) If the Aleutian Basic pollock biomass is less than 1.67 million metric tons, the AHL shall be zero and, therefore, there shall be no directed fishing on the Aleutian Basin pollock stock.

(d) If the Aleutian Basic pollock biomass is equal to or above 1.67 million metric tons, the AHL shall be determined in accordance with the following table:

Aleutian Basin pollock biomass	*AHL*
1.67 million metric tons or more but *less than 2.0 million metric tons*	*130,000 metric tons*
2.0 million metric tons or more but *less than 2.5 million metric tons*	*190,000 metric tons*
2.5 million metric tons or more	Determined by consensus at the *Annual Conference*

Note: The Specific Area is the area south of a straight line between a point at 55°46′N. and 170°00′W. and a point at 54°30′N. and 167°00′W., and between the meridian 167°00′W. and the meridian 170°00′W., and north of the Aleutian Islands and straight lines between the islands connecting the following coordinates in the order listed:

52°49.2′N. 169°40.4′W.,
52°49.8′N. 169°06.3′W.,
53°23.8′N. 167°50.1′W.,
53°18.7′N. 167°51.4′W.

INTERNATIONAL TROPICAL TIMBER AGREEMENT 1994

PREAMBLE

The Parties to this Agreement,

Recalling the Declaration and the Programme of Action on the Establishment of A New International Economic Order; the Integrated Programme for Commodities; A New Partnership for Development: the Cartagena Commitment and the relevant objectives contained in the Spirit of Cartagena,

Recalling the International Tropical Timber Agreement, 1983, and *recognizing* the work of the International Tropical Timber Organization and its achievements since its inception, including a strategy for achieving international trade in tropical timber from sustainably managed sources,

Recalling further the Rio Declaration on Environment and Development, the Non-Legally Binding Authoritative Statement of Principles for a Global Consensus on the Management, Conservation and Sustainable Development of all Types of Forests, and the relevant Chapters of Agenda 21 as adopted by the United Nations Conference on Environment and Development in June 1992, in Rio de Janeiro; the United Nations Framework Convention on Climate Change; and the Convention on Biological Diversity,

Recognizing the importance of timber to the economies of countries with timber-producing forests,

Further recognizing the need to promote and apply comparable and appropriate guidelines and criteria for the management, conservation and sustainable development of all types of timber-producing forests,

Taking into account the linkages of tropical timber trade and the international timber market and the need for taking a global perspective in order to improve transparency in the international timber market,

Noting the commitment of all members, made in Bali, Indonesia, in May 1990, to achieve exports of tropical timber products from sustainably managed sources by the year 2000 and *recognizing* Principle 10 of the Non-Legally Binding Authoritative Statement of Principles for a Global

Consensus on the Management, Conservation and Sustainable Development of all Types of Forests which states that new and additional financial resources should be provided to developing countries to enable them to sustainably manage, conserve and develop their forests, including through afforestation, reforestation and combating deforestation and forest and land degradation,

Noting also the statement of commitment to maintain, or achieve by the year 2000, the sustainable management of their respective forests made by consuming members who are parties to the International Tropical Timber Agreement, 1983 at the fourth session of the United Nations Conference for the Negotiation of a Successor Agreement to the International Tropical Timber Agreement, 1983 in Geneva on 21 January 1994,

Desiring to strengthen the framework of international cooperation and policy development between members in finding solutions to the problems facing the tropical timber economy,

Have agreed as follows:

CHAPTER I. OBJECTIVES

Article 1

Objectives

Recognizing the sovereignty of members over their natural resources, as defined in Principle 1 (a) of the Non-Legally Binding Authoritative Statement of Principles for a Global Consensus on the Management, Conservation and Sustainable Development of all Types of Forests, the objectives of the International Tropical Timber Agreement, 1994 (hereinafter referred to as "this Agreement") are:

(a) To provide an effective framework for consultation, international cooperation and policy development among all members with regard to all relevant aspects of the world timber economy;
(b) To provide a forum for consultation to promote non-discriminatory timber trade practices;
(c) To contribute to the process of sustainable development;
(d) To enhance the capacity of members to implement a strategy for achieving exports of tropical timber and timber products from sustainably managed sources by the year 2000;
(e) To promote the expansion and diversification of international trade in tropical timber from sustainable sources by improving the structural

conditions in international markets, by taking into account, on the one hand, a long-term increase in consumption and continuity of supplies, and, on the other, prices which reflect the costs of sustainable forest management and which are remunerative and equitable for members, and the improvement of market access;

(f) To promote and support research and development with a view to improving forest management and efficiency of wood utilization as well as increasing the capacity to conserve and enhance other forest values in timber-producing tropical forests;

(g) To develop and contribute towards mechanisms for the provision of new and additional financial resources and expertise needed to enhance the capacity of producing members to attain the objectives of this Agreement;

(h) To improve market intelligence with a view to ensuring greater transparency in the international timber market, including the gathering, compilation, and dissemination of trade-related data, including data related to species being traded;

(i) To promote increased and further processing of tropical timber from sustainable sources in producing member countries with a view to promoting their industrialization and thereby increasing their employment opportunities and export earnings;

(j) To encourage members to support and develop industrial tropical timber reforestation and forest management activities as well as rehabilitation of degraded forest land, with due regard for the interests of local communities dependent on forest resources;

(k) To improve marketing and distribution of tropical timber exports from sustainably managed sources;

(l) To encourage members to develop national policies aimed at sustainable utilization and conservation of timber-producing forests and their genetic resources and at maintaining the ecological balance in the regions concerned, in the context of tropical timber trade;

(m) To promote the access to, and transfer of, technologies and technical cooperation to implement the objectives of this Agreement, including on concessional and preferential terms and conditions, as mutually agreed; and

(n) To encourage information-sharing on the international timber market.

CHAPTER II. DEFINITIONS

Article 2

Definitions

For the purposes of this Agreement:

1. "Tropical timber" means non-coniferous tropical wood for industrial uses, which grows or is produced in the countries situated between the Tropic of Cancer and the Tropic of Capricorn. The term covers logs, sawnwood, veneer sheets and plywood. Plywood which includes in some measure conifers of tropical origin shall also be covered by this definition;

2. "Further processing" means the transformation of logs into primary wood products, semi-finished and finished products made wholly or almost wholly of tropical timber;

3. "Member" means a Government or an intergovernmental organization referred to in article 5 which has consented to be bound by this Agreement whether it is in force provisionally or definitively;

4. "Producing member" means any country with tropical forest resources and/or a net exporter of tropical timber in volume terms which is listed in annex A and which becomes a party to this Agreement, or any country with tropical forest resources and/or a net exporter of tropical timber in volume terms which is not so listed and which becomes a party to this Agreement and which the Council, with the consent of that country, declares to be a producing member;

5. "Consuming member" means any country listed in annex B which becomes a party to this Agreement, or any country not so listed which becomes a party to this Agreement and which the Council, with the consent of that country, declares to be a consuming member;

6. "Organization" means the International Tropical Timber Organization established in accordance with article 3;

7. "Council" means the International Tropical Timber Council established in accordance with article 6;

8. "Special vote" means a vote requiring at least two thirds of the votes cast by producing members present and voting and at least 60 per cent of the votes cast by consuming members present and voting, counted separately, on condition that these votes are cast by at least half of the producing members present and voting and at least half of the consuming members present and voting;

9. "Simple distributed majority vote" means a vote requiring more than half of the votes cast by producing members present and voting and more than half of the votes cast by consuming members present and voting, counted separately;

10. "Financial year" means the period from 1 January to 31 December inclusive;

11. "Freely usable currencies" means the deutsche mark, the French franc, the Japanese yen, the pound sterling, the United States dollar and any other currency which has been designated from time to time by a competent international monetary organization as being in fact widely used to make payments for international transactions and widely traded in the principal exchange markets.

CHAPTER III. ORGANIZATION AND ADMINISTRATION

Article 3

Headquarters and structure of the International Tropical Timber Organization

1. The International Tropical Timber Organization established by the International Tropical Timber Agreement, 1983 shall continue in being for the purposes of administering the provisions and supervising the operation of this Agreement.

2. The Organization shall function through the Council established under article 6, the committees and other subsidiary bodies referred to in article 26 and the Executive Director and staff.

3. The headquarters of the Organization shall be in Yokohama, unless the Council, by special vote, decides otherwise.

4. The headquarters of the Organization shall at all times be located in the territory of a member.

Article 4

Membership in the Organization

There shall be two categories of membership in the Organization, namely:
(a) Producing; and
(b) Consuming.

Article 5

Membership by intergovernmental organizations

1. Any reference in this Agreement to "Governments" shall be construed as including the European Community and any other intergovernmental organization having responsibilities in respect of the negotiation, conclusion and application of international agreements, in particular commodity agreements. Accordingly, any reference in this Agreement to signature, ratification, acceptance or approval, or to notification of provisional application, or to accession shall, in the case of such intergovernmental organizations, be construed as including a reference to signature, ratification, acceptance or approval, or to notification of provisional application, or to accession, by such intergovernmental organizations.

2. In the case of voting on matters within their competence, such intergovernmental organizations shall vote with a number of votes equal to the total number of votes attributable to their member States in accordance with article 10. In such cases, the member States of such intergovernmental organizations shall not entitled to exercise their individual voting rights.

CHAPTER IV. INTERNATIONAL TROPICAL TIMBER COUNCIL

Article 6

Composition of the International Tropical Timber Council

1. The highest authority of the Organization shall be the International Tropical Timber Council, which shall consist of all the members of the Organization.

2. Each member shall be represented in the Council by one representative and may designate alternates and advisers to attend sessions of the Council.

3. An alternate representative shall be empowered to act and vote on behalf of the representative during the latter's absence or in special circumstances.

Article 7

Powers and functions of the Council

1. The Council shall exercise all such powers and perform or arrange for the performance of all such functions as are necessary to carry out the provisions of this Agreement.

2. The Council shall, by special vote, adopt such rules and regulations as are necessary to carry out the provisions of this Agreement and as are consistent therewith, including its own rules of procedure and the financial rules and staff regulations of the Organization. Such financial rules shall *inter alia*, govern the receipt and expenditure of funds under the Administrative Account, the Special Account and the Bali Partnership Fund. The Council may, in its rules of procedure, provide for a procedure whereby it may, without meeting, decide specific questions.

3. The Council shall keep such records as are required for the performance of its functions under this Agreement.

Article 8

Chairman and Vice-Chairman of the Council

1. The Council shall elect for each calendar year a Chairman and a Vice-Chairman, whose salaries shall not be paid by the Organization.

2. The Chairman and the Vice-Chairman shall be elected, one from among the representatives of producing members and the other from among the representatives of consuming members. These offices shall alternate each year between the two categories of members, provided, however, that this shall not prohibit the re-election of either or both, under exceptional circumstances, by special vote of the Council.

3. In the temporary absence of the Chairman, the Vice-Chairman shall act in his place. In the temporary absence of both the Chairman and the Vice-Chairman, or in the absence of one or both of them for the rest of the term for which they were elected, the Council may elect new officers from among the representatives of the producing members and/or from among the representatives of the consuming members, as the case may be, on a temporary basis or for the rest of the term for which the predecessor or predecessors were elected.

Article 9

Sessions of the Council

1. As a general rule, the Council shall hold at least one regular session a year.

2. The Council shall meet in special session whenever it so decides or at the request of:

(a) The Executive Director, in agreement with the Chairman of the Council; or

(b) A majority of producing members or a majority of consuming members; or
(c) Members holding at least 500 votes.

3. Sessions of the Council shall be held at the headquarters of the Organization unless the Council, by special vote, decides otherwise. If on the invitation of any member the Council meets elsewhere than at the headquarters of the Organization, that member shall pay the additional cost of holding the meeting away from headquarters.

4. Notice of any sessions and the agenda for such sessions shall be communicated to members by the Executive Director at least six weeks in advance, except in cases of emergency, when notice shall be communicated at least seven days in advance.

Article 10

Distribution of votes

1. The producing members shall together hold 1,000 votes and the consuming members shall together hold 1,000 votes.

2. The votes of the producing members shall be distributed as follows:
(a) Four hundred votes shall be distributed equally among the three producing regions of Africa, Asia-Pacific and Latin America. The votes thus allocated to each of these regions shall then be distributed equally among the producing members of that region;
(b) Three hundred votes shall be distributed among the producing members in accordance with their respective shares of the total tropical forest resources of all producing members; and
(c) Three hundred votes shall be distributed among the producing members in proportion to the average of the values of their respective net exports of tropical timber during the most recent three-year period for which definitive figures are available.

3. Notwithstanding the provisions of paragraph 2 of this article, the total votes allocated to the producing members from the African region, calculated in accordance with paragraph 2 of this article, shall be distributed equally among all producing members from the African region. If there are any remaining votes, each of these votes shall be allocated to a producing member from the African region: the first to the producing member which is allocated the highest number of votes calculated in accordance with paragraph 2 of this article, the second to the producing member which is allocated the second highest number of votes, and so on until all the remaining votes have been distributed.

4. For purposes of the calculation of the distribution of votes under paragraph 2 (b) of this article, "tropical forest resources" means productive closed broad-leaved forests as defined by the Food and Agriculture Organization (FAO).

5. The votes of the consuming members shall be distributed as follows: each consuming member shall have 10 initial votes: the remaining votes shall be distributed among the consuming members in proportion to the average volume of their respective net imports of tropical timber during the three-year period commencing four calendar years prior to the distribution of votes.

6. The Council shall distribute the votes for each financial year at the beginning of its first session of that year in accordance with the provisions of this article. Such distribution shall remain in effect for the rest of that year, except as provided for in paragraph 7 of this article.

7. Whenever the membership of the Organization changes or when any member has its voting rights suspended or restored under any provision of this Agreement, the Council shall redistribute the votes within the affected category or categories of members in accordance with the provisions of this article. The Council shall, in that event, decide when such redistribution shall become effective.

8. There shall be no fractional votes.

Article 11

Voting procedure of the Council

1. Each member shall be entitled to cast the number of votes it holds and no member shall be entitled to divide its votes. A member may, however, cast differently from such votes any votes which it is authorized to cast under paragraph 2 of this article.

2. By written notification to the Chairman of the Council, any producing member may authorize, under its own responsibility, any other producing member, and any consuming member may authorize, under its own responsibility, any other consuming member, to represent its interests and to cast its votes at any meeting of the Council.

3. When abstaining, a member shall be deemed not to have cast its votes.

Article 12

Decisions and recommendations of the Council

1. The Council shall endeavour to take all decisions and to make all recommendations by consensus. If consensus cannot be reached, the Council shall take all decisions and make all recommendations by a simple distributed majority vote, unless this Agreement provides for a special vote.

2. Where a member avails itself of the provisions of article 11, paragraph 2, and its votes are cast at a meeting of the Council, such member shall, for the purposes of paragraph 1 of this article, be considered as present and voting.

Article 13

Quorum for the Council

1. The quorum for any meeting of the Council shall be the presence of a majority of members of each category referred to in article 4, provided that such members hold at least two thirds of the total votes in their respective categories.

2. If there is no quorum in accordance with paragraph 1 of this article on the day fixed for the meeting and on the following day, the quorum on the subsequent days of the session shall be the presence of a majority of members of each category referred to in article 4, provided that such members hold a majority of the total votes in their respective categories.

3. Representation in accordance with article 11, paragraph 2, shall be considered as presence.

Article 14

Cooperation and coordination with other organizations

1. The Council shall make arrangements as appropriate for consultations and cooperation with the United Nations and its organs, including the United Nations Conference on Trade and Development (UNCTAD) and the Commission on Sustainable Development (CSD), intergovernmental organizations, including the General Agreement on Tariffs and Trade (GATT) and the Convention on International Trade in Endangered Species of Wild Fauna and Flora (CITES), and non-governmental organizations.

2. The Organization shall, to the maximum extent possible, utilize the facilities, services and expertise of existing intergovernmental, governmental

or non-governmental organizations, in order to avoid duplication of efforts in achieving the objectives of this Agreement and to enhance the complementarity and the efficiency of their activities.

Article 15

Admission of observers

The Council may invite any non-member Government or any of the organizations referred to in article 14, article 20 and article 29, interested in the activities of the Organization to attend as observers any of the meetings of the Council.

Article 16

Executive Director and staff

1. The Council shall, by special vote, appoint the Executive Director.

2. The terms and conditions of appointment of the Executive Director shall be determined by the Council.

3. The Executive Director shall be the chief administrative officer of the Organization and shall be responsible to the Council for the administration and operation of this Agreement in accordance with decisions of the Council.

4. The Executive Director shall appoint the staff in accordance with regulations to be established by the Council. The Council shall, by special vote, decide the number of executive and professional staff the Executive Director may appoint. Any changes in the number of executive and professional staff shall be decided by the Council by special vote. The staff shall be responsible to the Executive Director.

5. Neither the Executive Director nor any member of the staff shall have any financial interest in the timber industry or trade, or associated commercial activities.

6. In the performance of their duties, the Executive Director and staff shall not seek or receive instructions from any member or from any authority external to the Organization. They shall refrain from any action which might reflect adversely on their positions as international officials ultimately responsible to the Council. Each member shall respect the exclusively international character of the responsibilities of the Executive Director and staff and shall not seek to influence them in the discharge of their responsibilities.

CHAPTER V. PRIVILEGES AND IMMUNITIES

Article 17

Privileges and immunities

1. The Organization shall have legal personality. It shall in particular have the capacity to contract, to acquire and dispose of movable and immovable property, and to institute legal proceedings.

2. The status, privileges and immunities of the Organization, of its Executive Director, its staff and experts, and of representatives of members while in the territory of Japan shall continue to be governed by the Headquarters Agreement between the Government of Japan and the International Tropical Timber Organization signed at Tokyo on 27 February 1988, with such amendments as may be necessary for the proper functioning of this Agreement.

3. The Organization may conclude, with one or more countries, agreements to be approved by the Council relating to such capacity, privileges and immunities as may be necessary for the proper functioning of this Agreement.

4. If the headquarters of the Organization is moved to another country, the member in question shall, as soon as possible, conclude with the organization a headquarters agreement to be approved by the Council. Pending the conclusion of such an Agreement, the Organization shall request the new host Government to grant, within the limits of its national legislation, exemption from taxation on remuneration paid by the Organization to its employees, and on the assets, income and other property of the Organization.

5. The headquarters agreement shall be independent of this Agreement. It shall, however, terminate:
   (a) By agreement between the host Government and the Organization;
   (b) In the event of the headquarters of the Organization being moved from the country of the host Government; or
   (c) In the event of the Organization ceasing to exist.

CHAPTER VI. FINANCE

Article 18

Financial accounts

1. There shall be established:

(a) The Administrative Account;
(b) The Special Account;
(c) The Bali Partnership Fund; and
(d) Such other accounts as the Council shall deem appropriate and necessary.

2. The Executive Director shall be responsible for the administration of these accounts and the Council shall make provision therefor in the financial rules of the Organization.

Article 19

Administrative Account

1. The expenses necessary for the administration of this Agreement shall be brought into the Administrative Account and shall be met by annual contributions paid by members in accordance with their respective constitutional or institutional procedures and assessed in accordance with paragraphs 3, 4 and 5 of this article.

2. The expenses of delegations to the Council, the committees and any other subsidiary bodies of the Council referred to in article 26 shall be met by the members concerned. In cases where a member requests special services from the Organization, the Council shall require that member to pay the costs of such services.

3. Before the end of each financial year, the Council shall approve the administrative budget of the Organization for the following financial year and shall assess the contribution of each member to that budget.

4. The contribution of each member to the administrative budget for each financial year shall be in the proportion which the number of its votes at the time the administrative budget for that financial year is approved bears to the total votes of all the members. In assessing contributions, the votes of each member shall be calculated without regard to the suspension of any member's voting rights or any redistribution of votes resulting therefrom.

5. The initial contribution of any member joining the Organization after the entry into force of this Agreement shall be assessed by the Council on the basis of the number of votes to be held by that member and the period remaining in the current financial year, but the assessment made upon other members from the current financial year shall not thereby be altered.

6. Contributions to administrative budgets shall become due on the first day of each financial year. Contributions of members in respect of the financial year in which they join the Organization shall be due on the date on which they become members.

7. If a member has not paid its full contribution to the administrative budget within four months after such contribution becomes due in accordance with paragraph 6 of this article, the Executive Director shall request that member to make payment as quickly as possible. If that member has still not paid its contribution within two months after such request, that member shall be requested to state the reasons for its inability to make payment. If at the expiry of seven months from the due date of contribution, that member has still not paid its contribution, its voting rights shall be suspended until such time as it has paid in full its contribution, unless the Council, by special vote, decides otherwise. If, on the contrary, a member has paid its full contribution to the administrative budget within four months after such contribution becomes due in accordance with paragraph 6 of this article, the member's contribution shall receive a discount as may be established by the Council in the financial rules of the Organization.

8. A member whose rights have been suspended under paragraph 7 of this article shall remain liable to pay its contribution.

Article 20

Special Account

1. There shall be established two sub-accounts under the Special Account:
   (a) The Pre-Project Sub-Account; and
   (b) The Project Sub-Account.

2. The possible sources of finance for the Special Account may be:
   (a) The Common Fund for Commodities;
   (b) Regional and international financial institutions; and
   (c) Voluntary contributions.

3. The resources of the Special Account shall be used only for approved pre-projects or projects.

4. All expenditures under the Pre-Project Sub-Account shall be reimbursed from the Project Sub-Account if projects are subsequently approved and funded. If within six months of the entry into force of this Agreement the Council does not receive any funds for the Pre-Project Sub-Account, it shall review the situation and take appropriate action.

5. All receipts pertaining to specific identifiable pre-projects or projects under the Special Account shall be brought into that Account. All expenditures incurred on such pre-projects or projects, including remuneration and travel expenses of consultants and experts, shall be charged to the same Account.

6. The Council shall, by special vote, establish terms and conditions on which it would, when and where appropriate, sponsor projects for loan financing, where a member or members have voluntarily assumed full obligations and responsibilities for such loans. The Organization shall have no obligations for such loans.

7. The Council may nominate and sponsor any entity with the consent of that entity, including a member or members, to receive loans for the financing of approved projects and to undertake all the obligations involved, except that the Organization shall reserve to itself the right to monitor the use of resources and to follow up on the implementation of projects so financed. However, the Organization shall not be responsible for guarantees voluntarily provided by individual members or other entities.

8. No member shall be responsible by reason of its membership in the Organization for any liability arising from borrowing or lending by any other member or entity in connection with projects.

9. In the event that voluntary unearmarked funds are offered to the Organization, the Council may accept such funds. Such funds may be utilized for approved pre-projects and projects.

10. The Executive Directive shall endeavour to seek, on such terms and conditions as the Council may decide, adequate and assured finance for pre-projects and projects approved by the Council.

11. Contributions for specified approved projects shall be used only for the projects for which they were originally intended, unless otherwise decided by the Council in agreement with the contributor. After the completion of a project, the Organization shall return to each contributor for specific projects the balance of any funds remaining pro rata to each contributor's share in the total of the contributions originally made available for financing that project, unless otherwise agreed to by the contributor.

Article 21

The Bali Partnership Fund

1. A Fund for sustainable management of tropical timber-producing forests is hereby established to assist producing members to make the investments necessary to achieve the objective of article 1 (d) of this Agreement.

2. The Fund shall be constituted by:
   (a) Contributions from donor members;
   (b) Fifty per cent of income earned as a result of activities related to the Special Account;

(c) Resources from other private and public sources which the Organization may accept consistent with its financial rules.

3. Resources of the Fund shall be allocated by the Council only for pre-projects and projects for the purpose set out in paragraph 1 of this article and approved in accordance with article 25.

4. In allocating resources of the Fund, the Council shall take into account:
   (a) The special needs of members whose forestry sectors' contribution to their economies is adversely affected by the implementation of the strategy for achieving the exports of tropical timber and timber products from sustainably managed sources by the year 2000;
   (b) The needs of members with significant forest areas who establish conservation programmes in timber-producing forests.

5. The Council shall examine annually the adequacy of the resources available to the Fund and endeavour to obtain additional resources needed by producing members to achieve the purpose of the Fund. The ability of members to implement the strategy referred to in paragraph 4 (a) of this article will be influenced by the availability of resources.

6. The Council shall establish policies and financial rules for the operation of the Fund, including rules covering the settlement of accounts on termination or expiry of this Agreement.

Article 22

Forms of payment

1. Contributions to the Administrative Account shall be payable in freely usable currencies and shall be exempt from foreign-exchange restrictions.

2. Financial contributions to the Special Account and the Bali Partnership Fund shall be payable in freely usable currencies and shall be exempt from foreign-exchange restrictions.

3. The council may also decide to accept other forms of contributions to the Special Account or the Bali Partnership Fund, including scientific and technical equipment or personnel, to meet the requirements of approved projects.

Article 23

Audit and publication of accounts

1. The Council shall appoint independent auditors for the purpose of auditing the accounts of the Organization.

2. Independently audited statements of the Administrative Account, of the Special Account and of the Bali Partnership Fund shall be made available to members as soon as possible after the close of each financial year, but not later than six months after that date, and be considered for approval by the Council at its next session, as appropriate. A summary of the audited accounts and balance sheet shall thereafter be published.

CHAPTER VII. OPERATIONAL ACTIVITIES

Article 24

Policy work of the Organization

In order to achieve the objectives set out in article 1, the Organization shall undertake policy work and project activities in the areas of Economic Information and Market Intelligence, Reforestation and Forest Management and Forest Industry, in a balanced manner, to the extent possible integrating policy work and project activities.

Article 25

Project activities of the Organization

1. Bearing in mind the needs of developing countries, members may submit pre-project and project proposals to the Council in the fields of research and development, market intelligence, further and increased wood processing in producing member countries, and reforestation and forest management. Pre-projects and projects should contribute to the achievement of one or more of the objectives of this Agreement.

2. The Council, in approving pre-projects and projects, shall take into account:

(a) Their relevance to the objectives of this Agreement;
(b) Their environmental and social effects;
(c) The desirability of maintaining an appropriate geographical balance;
(d) The interests and characteristics of each of the developing producing regions;
(e) The desirability of equitable distribution of resources among the fields referred to in paragraph 1 of this article;
(f) Their cost-effectiveness; and
(g) The need to avoid duplication of efforts.

3. The Council shall establish a schedule and procedure for submitting, appraising, and prioritizing pre-projects and projects seeking funding from

the Organization, as well as for their implementation, monitoring and evaluation. The Council shall decide on the approval of pre-projects and projects for financing or sponsorship in accordance with article 20 or article 21.

4. The Executive Director may suspend disbursement of the Organization's funds to a pre-project or project if they are being used contrary to the project document on in cases of fraud, waste, neglect or mismanagement. The Executive Director will provide to the Council at its next session a report for its consideration. The Council shall take appropriate action.

5. The Council may, by special vote, terminate its sponsorship of any pre-project or project.

Article 26

Establishment of Committees

1. The following are hereby established as Committees of the Organization:
   (a) Committee on Economic Information and Market Intelligence;
   (b) Committee on Reforestation and Forest Management;
   (c) Committee on Forest Industry; and
   (d) Committee on Finance and Administration.

2. The Council may, by special vote, establish such other committees and subsidiary bodies as it deems appropriate and necessary.

3. Participation in each of the committees shall be open to all members. The rules of procedure of the committees shall be decided by the Council.

4. The committees and subsidiary bodies referred to in paragraphs 1 and 2 of this article shall be responsible to, and work under the general direction of, the Council. Meetings of the committees and subsidiary bodies shall be convened by the Council.

Article 27

Functions of the Committee

1. The Committee on Economic Information and Market Intelligence shall:
   (a) Keep under review the availability and quality of statistics and other information required by the Organization;
   (b) Analyse the statistical data and specific indicators as decided by the Council for the monitoring of international timber trade;

(c) Keep under continuous review the international timber market, its current situation and short-term prospects on the basis of the data mentioned in subparagraph (b) above and other relevant information, including information related to undocumented trade;
(d) Make recommendations to the Council on the need for, and nature of, appropriate studies on tropical timber, including prices, market elasticity, market substitutability, marketing of new products, and long-term prospects of the international tropical timber market, and monitor and review any studies commissioned by the Council;
(e) Carry out any other tasks related to the economic, technical and statistical aspects of timber assigned to it by the Council;
(f) Assist in the provision of technical cooperation to developing member countries to improve their relevant statistical services.

2. The Committee on Reforestation and Forest Management shall:
(a) Promote cooperation between members as partners in development of forest activities in member countries, *inter alia*, in the following areas:
(i) Reforestation;
(ii) Rehabilitation;
(iii) Forest management;
(b) Encourage the increase of technical assistance and transfer of technology in the fields of reforestation and forest management to developing countries;
(c) Follow up ongoing activities in this field, and identify and consider problems and possible solutions to them in cooperation with the competent organizations;
(d) Review regularly the future needs of international trade in industrial tropical timber and, on this basis, identify and consider appropriate possible schemes and measures in the field of reforestation, rehabilitation and forest management;
(e) Facilitate the transfer of knowledge in the field of reforestation and forest management with the assistance of competent organizations;
(f) Coordinate and harmonize these activities for cooperation in the field of reforestation and forest management with relevant activities pursued elsewhere, such as those under the auspices of the Food and Agriculture Organization of the United Nations (FAO), the United Nations Environment Programme (UNEP), the World Bank, the United Nations Development Programme (UNDP), regional development banks and other competent organizations.

3. The Committee on Forest Industry shall:
(a) Promote cooperation between member countries as partners in the

development of processing activities in producing member countries, *inter alia*, in the following areas:
   (i) Product development through transfer of technology;
   (ii) Human resources development and training;
   (iii) Standardization of nomenclature of tropical timber;
   (iv) Harmonization of specifications of processed projects;
   (v) Encouragement of investment and joint ventures; and
   (vi) Marketing, including the promotion of lesser known and lesser used species;

(b) Promote the exchange of information in order to facilitate structural changes involved in increased and further processing in the interests of all member countries, in particular developing member countries;

(c) Follow up ongoing activities in this field, and identify and consider problems and possible solutions to them in cooperation with the competent organizations;

(d) Encourage the increase of technical cooperation for the processing of tropical timber for the benefit of producing member countries.

4. In order to promote the policy and project work of the Organization in a balanced manner, the Committee on Economic Information and Market Intelligence, the Committee on Reforestation and Forest Management and the Committee on Forest Industry shall each:

(a) Be responsible for ensuring the effective appraisal, monitoring and evaluation of pre-projects and projects;

(b) Make recommendations to the Council relating to pre-projects and projects;

(c) Follow up the implementation of pre-projects and projects and provide for the collection and dissemination of their results as widely as possible for the benefit of all members;

(d) Develop and advance policy ideas to the Council;

(e) Review regularly the results of project and policy work and make recommendations to the Council on the future of the Organization's programme;

(f) Review regularly the strategies, criteria and priority areas for programme development and project work contained in the Organization's Action Plan and recommend revisions to the Council;

(g) Take account of the need to strengthen capacity building and human resource development in member countries;

(h) Carry out any other task related to the objectives of this Agreement assigned to them by the Council.

5. Research and development shall be a common function of the Committees referred to in paragraphs 1, 2, and 3 of this article.

6. The Committee on Finance and Administration shall:
   (a) Examine and make recommendations to the Council regarding the approval of the Organization's administrative budget proposals and the management operations of the Organization;
   (b) Review the assets of the Organization to ensure prudent asset management and that the Organization has sufficient reserves to carry out its work;
   (c) Examine and make recommendations to the Council on the budgetary implications of the Organization's annual work programme, and the actions that might be taken to secure the resources needed to implement it;
   (d) Recommend to the Council the choice of independent auditors and review the independent audited statements;
   (e) Recommend to the Council any modifications it may judge necessary to the Rules of Procedure or the Financial Rules;
   (f) Review the Organization's revenues and the extent to which they constrain the work of the Secretariat.

CHAPTER VIII. RELATIONSHIP WITH THE COMMON FUND FOR COMMODITIES

Article 28

Relationship with the Common Fund for Commodities

The Organization shall take full advantage of the facilities of the Common Fund for Commodities.

CHAPTER IX. STATISTICS, STUDIES AND INFORMATION

Article 29

Statistics, studies and information

1. The Council shall establish close relationships with relevant intergovernmental, governmental and non-governmental organizations, in order to help ensure the availability of recent reliable data and information on the trade in tropical timber, as well as relevant information on non-tropical timber and on the management of timber-producing forests. As deemed necessary for the operation of this Agreement, the Organization, in cooperation with such organizations, shall compile, collate and, where relevant, publish statistical information on production, supply, trade, stocks, con-

sumption and market prices of timber, the extent of timber resources and the management of timber-producing forests.

2. Members shall, to the fullest extent possible not inconsistent with their national legislation, furnish, within a reasonable time, statistics and information on timber, its trade and the activities aimed at achieving sustainable management of timber-producing forests as well as other relevant information as requested by the Council. The Council shall decide on the type of information to be provided under this paragraph and on the format in which it is to be presented.

3. The Council shall arrange to have any relevant studies undertaken of the trends and of short- and long-term problems of the international timber markets and of the progress towards the achievement of sustainable management of timber-producing forests.

Article 30

Annual report and review

1. The Council shall, within six months after the close of each calendar year, publish an annual report on its activities and such other information as it considers appropriate.

2. The Council shall annually review and assess:
   (a) The international timber situation;
   (b) Other factors, issues and developments considered relevant to achieve the objectives of this Agreement.

3. The review shall be carried out in the light of:
   (a) Information supplied by members in relation to national production, trade, supply, stocks, consumption and prices of timber;
   (b) Other statistical data and specific indicators provided by members as requested by the Council;
   (c) Information supplied by members on their progress towards the sustainable management of their timber-producing forests;
   (d) Such other relevant information as may be available to the Council either directly or through the organizations in the United Nations system and intergovernmental, governmental or non-governmental organizations.

4. The Council shall promote the exchange of views among member countries regarding:
   (a) The status of sustainable management of timber-producing forests and related matters in member countries;

(b) Resource flows and requirements in relation to objectives, criteria and guidelines set by the Organization.

5. Upon request, the Council shall endeavour to enhance the technical capacity of member countries, in particular developing member countries, to obtain the data necessary for adequate information-sharing, including the provision of resources for training and facilities to members.

6. The results of the review shall be included in the reports of the Council's deliberations.

CHAPTER X. MISCELLANEOUS

Article 31

Complaints and disputes

Any complaint that a member has failed to fulfil its obligations under this Agreement and any dispute concerning the interpretation or application of this Agreement shall be referred to the Council for decision. Decisions of the Council on these matters shall be final and binding.

Article 32

General obligations of members

1. Members shall, for the duration of this Agreement, use their best endeavours and cooperate to promote the attainment of its objectives and to avoid any action contrary thereto.

2. Members undertake to accept and carry out the decisions of the Council under the provisions of this Agreement and shall refrain from implementing measures which would have the effect of limiting or running counter to them.

Article 33

Relief from obligations

1. Where it is necessary on account of exceptional circumstances or emergency or *force majeure* not expressly provided for in this Agreement, the Council may, by special vote, relieve a member of an obligation under this Agreement if it is satisfied by an explanation from that member regarding the reasons why the obligation cannot be met.

2. The Council, in granting relief to a member under paragraph 1 of this article, shall state explicitly the terms and conditions on which, and the period for which, the member is relieved of such obligation, and the reasons for which the relief is granted.

Article 34

Differential and remedial measures and special measures

1. Developing importing members whose interests are adversely affected by measures taken under this Agreement may apply to the Council for appropriate differential and remedial measures. The Council shall consider taking appropriate measures in accordance with section III, paragraphs 3 and 4, of resolution 93 (IV) of the United Nations Conference on Trade and Development.

2. Members in the category of least developed countries as defined by the United Nations may apply to the Council for special measures in accordance with section III, paragraph 4, of resolution 93 (IV) and with paragraphs 56 and 57 of the Paris Declaration and Programme of Action for the Least Developed Countries for the 1990s.

Article 35

Review

The Council shall review the scope of this Agreement four years after its entry into force.

Article 36

Non-discrimination

Nothing in this Agreement authorizes the use of measures to restrict or ban international trade in, and in particular as they concern imports of and utilization of, timber and timber products.

CHAPTER XI. FINAL PROVISIONS

Article 37

Depositary

The Secretary-General of the United Nations is hereby designated as the depositary of this Agreement.

Article 38

Signature, ratification, acceptance and approval

1. This Agreement shall be open for signature, at United Nations Headquarters from 1 April 1994 until one month after the date of its entry into force, by Governments invited to the United Nations Conference for the Negotiation of a Successor Agreement to the International Tropical Timber Agreement, 1983.

2. Any Government referred to in paragraph 1 of this article may:
   (a) At the time of signing this Agreement, declare that by such signature it expresses its consent to be bound by this Agreement (definitive signature); or
   (b) After signing this Agreement, ratify, accept or approve it by the deposit of an instrument to that effect with the depositary.

Article 39

Accession

1. This Agreement shall be open for accession by the Governments of all States upon conditions established by the Council, which shall include a time-limit for the deposit of instruments of accession. The Council may, however, grant extensions of time to Governments which are unable to accede by the time-limit set in the conditions of accession.

2. Accession shall be effected by the deposit of an instrument of accession with the depositary.

Article 40

Notification of provisional application

A signatory Government which intends to ratify, accept or approve this Agreement, or a Government for which the Council has established conditions for accession but which has not yet been able to deposit its instrument, may, at any time, notify the depositary that it will apply this Agreement provisionally either when it enters into force in accordance with article 41, or, if it is already in force, at a specified date.

Article 41

Entry into force

1. This Agreement shall enter into force definitively on 1 February 1995 or on any date thereafter, if 12 Governments of producing countries holding at least 55 per cent of the total votes as set out in annex A to this Agreement, and 16 Governments of consuming countries holding at least 70 per cent of the total votes as set out in annex B to this Agreement have signed this Agreement definitively or have ratified, accepted or approved it or acceded thereto pursuant to article 38, paragraph 2, or article 39.

2. If this Agreement has not entered into force definitively on 1 February 1995, it shall enter into force provisionally on that date or on any date within six months thereafter, if 10 Governments of producing countries holding at least 50 per cent of the total votes as set out in annex A to this Agreement, and 14 Governments of consuming countries holding at least 65 per cent of the total votes as set out in annex B to this Agreement have signed this Agreement definitively or have ratified, accepted or approved it pursuant to article 38, paragraph 2, or have notified the depositary under article 40 that they will apply this Agreement provisionally.

3. If the requirements for entry into force under paragraph 1 or paragraph 2 of this article have not been met on 1 September 1995, the Secretary-General of the United Nations shall invite those Governments which have signed this Agreement definitively or have ratified, accepted or approved it pursuant to article 38, paragraph 2, or have notified the depositary that they will apply this Agreement provisionally, to meet at the earliest time practicable to decide whether to put this Agreement into force provisionally or definitively among themselves in whole or in part. Governments which decide to put this Agreement into force provisionally among themselves may meet from time to time to review the situation and decide whether this Agreement shall enter into force definitively among themselves.

4. For any Government which has not notified the depositary under article 40 that it will apply this Agreement provisionally and which deposits its instrument of ratification, acceptance, approval or accession after the entry into force of this Agreement, this Agreement shall enter into force on the date of such deposit.

5. The Executive Director of the Organization shall convene the Council as soon as possible after the entry into force of this Agreement.

Article 42

Amendments

1. The Council may, by special vote, recommend an amendment of this Agreement to members.

2. The Council shall fix a date by which members shall notify the depositary of their acceptance of the amendment.

3. An amendment shall enter into force 90 days after the depositary has received notifications of acceptance from members constituting at least two thirds of the producing members and accounting for at least 75 per cent of the votes of the producing members, and from members constituting at least two thirds of the consuming members and accounting for at least 75 per cent of the votes of the consuming members.

4. After the depositary informs the Council that the requirements for entry into force of the amendment have been met, and notwithstanding the provisions of paragraph 2 of this article relating to the date fixed by the Council, a member may still notify the depositary of its acceptance of the amendment, provided that such notification is made before the entry into force of the amendment.

5. Any member which has not notified its acceptance of an amendment by the date on which such amendment enters into force shall cease to be a party to this Agreement as from that date, unless such member has satisfied the Council that its acceptance could not be obtained in time owing to difficulties in completing its constitutional or institutional procedures, and the Council decides to extend for that member the period for acceptance of the amendment. Such member shall not be bound by the amendment before it has notified its acceptance thereof.

6. If the requirements for the entry into force of the amendment have not been met by the date fixed by the Council in accordance with paragraph 2 of this article, the amendment shall be considered withdrawn.

Article 43

Withdrawal

1. A member may withdraw from this Agreement at any time after the entry into force of this Agreement by giving written notice of withdrawal

to the depositary. That member shall simultaneously inform the Council of the action it has taken.

2. Withdrawal shall become effective 90 days after the notice is received by the depositary.

3. Financial obligations to the Organization incurred by a member under this Agreement shall not be terminated by its withdrawal.

Article 44

Exclusion

If the Council decides that any member is in breach of its obligations under this Agreement and decides further that such breach significantly impairs the operation of this Agreement, it may, by special vote, exclude that member from this Agreement. The Council shall immediately so notify the depositary. Six months after the date of the Council's decision, that member shall cease to be a party to this Agreement.

Article 45

Settlement of accounts with withdrawing or excluded members or members unable to accept an amendment

1. The Council shall determine any settlement of accounts with a member which ceases to be a party to this Agreement owing to:
   (a) Non-acceptance of an amendment to this Agreement under article 42;
   (b) Withdrawal from this Agreement under article 43; or
   (c) Exclusion from this Agreement under article 44.

2. The Council shall retain any contribution paid to the Administrative Account, to the Special Account or to the Bali Partnership Fund by a member which ceases to be a party to this Agreement.

3. A member which has ceased to be a party to this Agreement shall not be entitled to any share of the proceeds of liquidation or the other assets of the Organization. Nor shall such member be liable for payment of any part of the deficit, if any, of the Organization upon termination of this Agreement.

Article 46

Duration, extension and termination

1. This Agreement shall remain in force for a period of four years after its entry into force unless the Council, by special vote, decides to extend, renegotiate or terminate it in accordance with the provisions of this article.

2. The Council may, by special vote, decide to extend this Agreement for two periods of three years each.

3. If, before the expiry of the four-year period referred to in paragraph 1 of this article, or before the expiry of an extension period referred to in paragraph 2 of this article, as the case may be, a new agreement to replace this Agreement has been negotiated but has not yet entered into force either definitively or provisionally, the Council may, by special vote, extend this Agreement until the provisional or definitive entry into force of the new agreement.

4. If a new agreement is negotiated and enters into force during any period of extension of this Agreement under paragraph 2 or paragraph 3 of this article, this Agreement, as extended, shall terminate upon the entry into force of the new agreement.

5. The Council may at any time, by special vote, decide to terminate this Agreement with effect from such date as it may determine.

6. Notwithstanding the termination of this Agreement, the Council shall continue in being for a period not exceeding 18 months to carry out the liquidation of the Organization, including the settlement of accounts, and, subject to relevant decisions to be taken by special vote, shall have during that period such powers and functions as may be necessary for these purposes.

7. The Council shall notify the depositary of any decision taken under this article.

Article 47

Reservations

Reservations may not be made with respect to any of the provisions of this Agreement.

Article 48

Supplementary and transitional provisions

1. This Agreement shall be the successor to the International Tropical Timber Agreement, 1983.

2. All acts by or on behalf of the Organization or any of its organs under the International Tropical Timber Agreement, 1983, which are in effect on the date of entry into force of this Agreement and the terms of which do not provide for expiry on that date shall remain in effect unless changed under the provisions of this Agreement.

IN WITNESS WHEREOF the undersigned, being duly authorized thereto, have affixed their signatures under this Agreement on the dates indicated.

DONE at Geneva, on twenty-six January, one thousand nine hundred and ninety-four, the text of this Agreement in the Arabic, Chinese, English, French, Russian and Spanish languages being equally authentic.

ANNEX A

List of producing countries with tropical forest resources and/or net exporters of tropical timber in volume terms, and allocation of votes for the purposes of article 41

Bolivia	21
Brazil	133
Cameroon	23
Colombia	24
Congo	23
Costa Rica	9
Côte d'Ivoire	23
Dominican Republic	9
Ecuador	14
El Salvador	9
Equatorial Guinea	23
Gabon	23
Ghana	23
Guyana	14
Honduras	9
India	34
Indonesia	170

Liberia	23
Malaysia	139
Mexico	14
Myanmar	33
Panama	10
Papua New Guinea	28
Paraguay	11
Peru	25
Philippines	25
Tanzania, United Republic of	23
Thailand	20
Togo	23
Trinidad and Tobago	9
Venezuela	10
Zaire	23
Total	1,000

ANNEX B

List of consuming countries and allocation of votes for the purposes of article 41

Afghanistan	10
Algeria	13
Australia	18
Austria	11
Bahrain	11
Bulgaria	10
Canada	12
Chile	10
China	36
Egypt	14
European Community	(302)
Belgium/Luxembourg	26
Denmark	11
France	44
Germany	35
Greece	13
Ireland	13
Italy	35
Netherlands	40

Portugal	18
Spain	25
United Kingdom	42
Finland	10
Japan	320
Nepal	10
New Zealand	10
Norway	10
Republic of Korea	97
Russian Federation	13
Slovakia	11
Sweden	10
Switzerland	11
United States of America	51
Total	1,000

REPORT OF THE SECOND MEETING OF THE CONFERENCE OF THE PARTIES TO THE BASEL CONVENTION ON THE CONTROL OF TRANSBOUNDARY MOVEMENTS OF HAZARDOUS WASTES AND THEIR DISPOSAL

Decision II/4

Illegal traffic in hazardous wastes and other wastes

The Conference,

Expressing its concern at the problems of illegal traffic in hazardous wastes and other wastes, in particular to developing countries and to the countries in transition,

Recalling decision I/15 of the First Meeting of the Conference of the Parties,

Having considered the report of the Secretariat contained in document UNEP/CHW.2/8,

Having further considered the Open-ended Ad Hoc Committee recommendations contained in its decision I/6 on "Illegal Traffic in Hazardous Wastes and other Wastes,"

1. *Requests* the Parties to promulgate or develop stringent national legislation on the control of transboundary movement of hazardous wastes taking into account the elements contained in document UNEP/CHW/C.1/1/7;

2. *Further requests* the Parties to incorporate in their legal systems, appropriate sanctions or penalties for the illegal traffic in hazardous wastes and other wastes;

3. *Requests* the regional commissions and secretariats of regional conventions and protocols to take an effective role in the monitoring and prevention of illegal traffic in hazardous wastes and other wastes and to coordinate their efforts and activities in this regard with the Secretariat of the Basel Convention;

4. *Requests* all Governments to promote interministerial coordination within their respective Governments to prevent and penalize illegal traffic in hazardous wastes and other wastes;

5. *Requests* the S ecretariat of the Basel Convention:
   (a) To assist Parties in developing national legislation to deal with illegal traffic and hazardous wastes and other wastes;
   (b) To assist Parties in capacity-building including the development of an appropriate infrastructure, with a view to the prevention and penalization of illegal traffic in hazardous wastes and other wastes and to ensure the involvement of national authorities and focal points for the Basel Convention in the prevention and monitoring of illegal traffic in hazardous wastes and other wastes;
   (c) To liaise with the various regional commissions and secretariats of regional conventions and protocols with a view to promoting the development of compatible regional mechanisms and systems;
   (d) To promote the implementation of the appropriate parts of chapter 20 of Agenda 21 related to the illegal traffic in hazardous wastes, in particular its section D. In this regard a report should be presented to the relevant substantive session of the United Nations Commission on Sustainable Development;
   (e) To continue its cooperation with the Customs Co-operation Council Secretariat, with a view to ensuring better control of the import and export of hazardous wastes and other wastes and, in particular, identifying hazardous wastes and other wastes subjected to the Basel Convention in the Harmonized System;
   (f) To include, in cooperation with the Governments concerned, the Customs Co-operation Council and the International Maritime Organization, the training of customs and ports officers in relation to the import and export of hazardous wastes and other wastes in its programme of training activities;
   (g) To receive, collate and disseminate information on illegal traffic in hazardous, wastes and other wastes promptly and systematically with a view to ensuring that hazardous waste detected and rejected by one country is not dumped in another;
   (h) To explore the possibility of cooperation with Interpol in cases of illegal traffic in hazardous wastes and other wastes;
   (i) To establish a well-defined reporting system on cases of illegal traffic in hazardous wastes and other wastes, which would:
      (i) Request Parties to report to the Secretariat on any cases of illegal traffic in hazardous wastes and other wastes as defined by the Basel Convention and the actions taken to monitor and prevent such cases;
      (ii) Include a submission by the Secretariat to the Conference of the Parties to the Basel Convention of reports, based on information received from the Parties, on cases of illegal traffic in hazardous wastes and other wastes and the publication of these reports;

(j) To enhance its cooperation in the prevention and monitoring of illegal traffic in hazardous wastes and other wastes with non-governmental organizations, industry and the private sector;

(k) To submit a report on the above-mentioned activities to the third meeting of the Conference of the Parties to the Basel Convention.

Decision II/10

Bilateral, multilateral and regional agreements or arrangements

The Conference,

Recalling that Article 11, paragraph 1, of the Basel Convention permits Parties to enter into bilateral, multilateral and regional agreements or arrangements regarding the transboundary movements of hazardous wastes or other wastes with Parties and non-Parties provided that such agreements or arrangements do not derogate from the environmentally sound management of hazardous wastes and other wastes as required by the Basel Convention and that these agreements or arrangements shall stipulate provisions which are not less environmentally sound than those provided for by the Convention, in particular taking into account the interest of developing countries,

Recalling that Article 11, paragraph 2, provides that the provisions of the Basel Convention shall not affect transboundary movements which are taking place pursuant to agreements concluded prior to the entry into force of the Basel Convention for the relevant Parties to such agreements provided that such agreements are compatible with the environmentally sound management of hazardous wastes and other wastes as required by the Basel Convention,

Recalling decision I/9 of the First Meeting of the Conference of the Parties,

Having considered the report of the Secretariat contained in document UNEP/CHW.2/9 on the implementation of decision I/9 referred to above,

Requests Parties which have entered, in accordance with Article 11, into bilateral, multilateral and regional agreements or arrangements to report, consistent with national laws and regulations, to the Open-Ended Ad Hoc Committee, through the Secretariat of the Basel Convention, on the conformity of such agreements or arrangements taking into consideration the list of questions annexed to the present decision.

ANNEX

Questions to be considered by Parties to bilateral, multilateral or regional agreements or arrangements when reporting on their conformity with the provisions of Article 11 of the Convention

In preparation of its report to the Conference of the Parties, the following questions could be used as a guide by a Party when it is reviewing one of its agreements which falls under Article 11. The questions would help the Party focus on particular issues, however it is important to note that the agreement must be viewed in its entirety and not strictly provision by provision. It is also recognized that the purpose of the said agreement and the geographic, legal and economic circumstances of the other Contracting Party(ies) constitute elements of this review. A Party's Report would have to indicate that the different requirements found in paragraph 1 or 2 of Article 11, as appropriate, are met in conformity with the Basel Convention.

1. Does the agreement address the control of the transboundary movement of hazardous wastes and other wastes subject to the Basel Convention?

2. Taking all practicable steps, will the management of hazardous wastes under the agreement or arrangement be such that it will protect human health and the environment against adverse effects?

3. How does the agreement or arrangement take into account the interests of developing countries?

4. Does the agreement or arrangement require prior notification?

5. Does the agreement or arrangement require prior consent?

6. Does the agreement or arrangement provide for the tracking of the wastes?

7. Does the agreement or arrangement provide for alternative measures for wastes which cannot be managed as planned?

8. Does the agreement or arrangement provide for the identification of authorities responsible for the implementation of such an agreement?

9. Are the obligations of the Article 11 Agreement or arrangement consistent with the control measures related to transboundary movements of hazardous wastes as provided for by the Basel Convention?

10. Are the wastes covered by the Article 11 agreement or arrangement consistent with the scope of the Basel Convention?

Decision II/12

The Conference,

Recalling the request of the Group of 77 countries at the First Meeting of the Conference of the Parties to the Basel Convention held in Uruguay, from 3 to 4 December 1992, for the total ban on all exports of hazardous wastes from OECD countries to non-OECD countries,

Recognizing that transboundary movements of hazardous wastes from OECD to non-OECD States run a high risk of not constituting an environmentally sound management of hazardous wastes as required by the Basel Convention,

1. *Decides* to prohibit immediately all transboundary movements of hazardous wastes which are destined for final disposal from OECD to non-OECD States;

2. *Decides also* to phase out by 31 December 1997, and prohibit as of that date, all transboundary movements of hazardous wastes which are destined for recycling or recovery operations from OECD to non-OECD States;

3. *Decides further* that any non-OECD State, not possessing a national hazardous wastes import ban, which allows the import from OECD States of hazardous wastes for recycling or recovery operations up to 31 December 1997, should inform the Secretariat of the Basel Convention that it would allow the import from an OECD State of hazardous wastes for recycling or recovery operations by specifying the categories of hazardous wastes which are acceptable for import, the quantities to be imported, the specific recycling/recovery process to be used, and the final destination/disposal of the residues which are derived from recycling/recovery operations;

4. *Requests* the Parties to report regularly to the Secretariat on the implementation of this decision, including details of the transboundary movements of hazardous wastes allowed under paragraph 3 above. Further requests the Secretariat to summarize and compile these reports for consideration by the Open-ended Ad Hoc Committee. After considering these reports, the Open-ended Ad Hoc Committee will submit a report based on the input provided by the Secretariat to the Conference of the Parties to the Convention;

5. *Requests* further the Parties to cooperate and work actively to ensure the effective implementation of the present decision.

Decision II/13

Technical guidelines for the environmentally sound management of wastes subject to the Basel Convention

The Conference,

Recalling decision I/19 of the First Meeting of the Conference of the Parties to the Basel Convention accepting the Framework Document on the Preparation of Technical Guidelines and the four Technical Guidelines on priority waste streams and extending the mandate of the Technical Working Group to review the three revised Draft Technical Guidelines on Disposal Operations and to prepare Technical Guidelines for other priority operations and waste streams subject to the Basel Convention,

Further recalling the decision I/7 of the Open-ended Ad Hoc Committee on Technical Guidelines for the Environmentally Sound Management of Wastes subject to the Basel Convention recommending that the Conference of the Parties adopt the three draft Technical Guidelines on Disposal Operations (Specially Engineered Landfill D5; Incineration on Land D10; Used Oil Re-refining or other Re-uses of Previously Used Oil R9) and extend the mandate of the Technical Working Group with the aim to continue the preparation of new technical guidelines as identified by the Group itself, namely on:

(a) First priority: D9 Physico-chemical treatment; R4 Recycling/reclamation of metals and metal compounds; Y17 Wastes resulting from surface treatment of metals and plastics;

(b) Second priority: Y1 Clinical wastes; D8 Biological treatment; R1 Use as fuel; R2 Solvent reclamation/regeneration,

Having considered the report of the Secretariat on the Implementation of decision I/19 which contains the Framework Document and the four Technical Guidelines on Priority Waste Streams (UNEP/CHW.2/10) and the three Technical Guidelines on Priority Disposal Operations (UNEP/CHW.2/10/Add.1),

Noting with appreciation the progress achieved by the Technical Working Group in the preparation of the Framework Document and the Technical Guidelines for Priority Waste Streams and Disposal Operations subject to the Basel Convention,

1. *Confirms* adoption of the Framework Document on the Preparation of Technical Guidelines for the Environmentally Sound Management of

Wastes Subject to the Basel Convention and the four Technical Guidelines, namely on Hazardous Wastes from the Production and Use of Organic Solvents (Y6), on Waste Oils from Petroleum Origins and Sources (Y8), on Wastes Comprising or Containing PCBs, PCTs and PBBs (Y10), and on Waste Collected from Household (Y46); and requests the Secretariat to publish and disseminate the Framework Document and the four Technical Guidelines between Parties and non-Parties together with a cover note explaining the nature of the document;

2. *Adopts* provisionally the three draft Technical Guidelines on: Specially Engineered Landfill (D5), on Incineration on Land (D10) and Used Oil Re-refining or other Re-uses of Previously Used Oil, subject to the additional comments to be provided to the Secretariat by States and concerned international organizations, and to publish and disseminate them to Parties and non-Parties;

3. *Extends* the mandate of the Technical Working Group with the aim that this Group further revise, as appropriate, the Draft Technical Guidelines adopted provisionally and continue the preparation of new technical guidelines as identified by the Technical Working Group, namely on:

(a) *First priority*:
- D9 Physico-chemical treatment
- R4 Recycling/reclamation of metals and metals compounds
- Y17 Wastes resulting from surface treatment of metals and plastics

(b) *Second priority*:
- Y1 Clinical wastes
- D8 Biological treatment
- R1 Use as a fuel
- R2 Solvent reclamation/regeneration.

Decision II/14

Transboundary movements of hazardous wastes destined for recovery operations

The Conference,

Recalling decision I/16 of the First Meeting of the Conference of the Parties to the Basel Convention requesting its Technical Working Group to review the issue and consider the views submitted by States and interested organizations and to present its recommendations to the Second Meeting of the Conference of the Parties,

Noting paragraph 20.33 (c) of UNCED Agenda 21, chapter 20, which calls upon countries "to promote the development of control procedures for the transboundary movements of hazardous wastes destined for recovery operations under the Basel Convention that encourage environmentally and economically sound recyclable options",

Also recalling decision I/7 of the Open-ended Ad Hoc Committee recommending to the Conference to extend the mandate of the Technical Working Group to further develop the draft paper on transboundary movements of hazardous wastes destined for recovery operations, and invite interested Parties and non-Parties, and as the case may be non-governmental organizations and/or the private sector, in association with the Secretariat of the Basel Convention, to prepare two or three case-studies related to recovery operations involving two countries in full respect of the environmentally sound management of hazardous wastes destined to such recovery operations,

Having considered the draft paper on transboundary movements of hazardous wastes destined for recovery operations annexed to the note of the Secretariat (UNEP/CHW.2/12),

1. *Welcomes* the draft paper on transboundary movements of hazardous wastes destined for recovery operations;

2. *Decides* to extend the mandate of the Technical Working Group to further develop the draft paper on transboundary movements of hazardous wastes destined for recovery operations, taking into account the comments formulated by States and interested organizations and to present a revised version of this document to the Third Meeting of the Conference of the Parties for adoption in consultation with the Open-ended Ad Hoc Committee;

3. *Requests* Parties together with non-Parties, and as the case may be non-governmental organizations, including the private sector, in association with the Secretariat of the Basel Convention, to prepare two or three case-studies along the lines developed in the terms of reference annexed to the present decision, related to recovery operations involving two countries in full respect of the environmentally sound management of the hazardous wastes destined to such recovery operations;

4. *Further requests* the Technical Working Group to develop guidelines to assist States on the question of hazardous wastes under the Basel Convention, including hazardous wastes destined for recovery operations and in cooperation with the Open-ended Ad Hoc Committee to present such guidelines to the Third Meeting of the Conference of the Parties for consideration.

ANNEX

Proposed terms of reference for the case-studies on the environmentally sound management of hazardous wastes destined for recovery operations

1. Identify the hazardous waste streams that are subject to recovery operations and the national/domestic infrastructure including legal and administrative arrangements that sustain such operations.

2. Describe the existing trade in wastes identified and the structure and characteristics of the industries involved.

3. Identify the technological options for the management of such wastes including their economic and technical aspects.

4. Carry out a practical assessment of the facilities which recover the hazardous wastes, how the residues arising from the process are being disposed of and their impact on health and the environment.

5. Compare environmental and economic aspects of the recovery of secondary raw material from hazardous wastes and their production from virgin materials taking into account the disposal of any residues generated through the process.

Decision II/15

Possible effects of the Basel Convention on transboundary movements of waste ozone-depleting chemicals, including halons, intended for recovery

The Conference,

Recalling Article 1 of the Basel Convention concerning the scope of the Convention, in particular its paragraph 1(a),

Having considered the report by the Secretariat on possible effects of the Basel Convention on transboundary movements of waste ozone-depleting chemicals, including halons, intended for recovery contained in document UNEP/CHW.2/11,

Also noting the consideration of the Technical Working Group in regard to its role in the case of a need for technical interpretation of the Convention,

1. *Requests* its Technical Working Group in close cooperation with the Ozone Secretariat to further work on the issue of the classification of the

waste ozone-depleting chemicals as hazardous wastes in accordance with the Basel Convention definition;

2. *Also requests* its Technical Working Group to perform the functions of its advisory body in case of a need for technical interpretation of the Convention;

3. *Further requests* its Technical Working Group to report on the issue of waste ozone-depleting chemicals and any cases involving a technical interpretation of the Convention to the Third Meeting of the Conference of the Parties.

Decision II/16

Documentation: Notification and Movement Document

The Conference,

Recalling decision I/21 of the First Meeting of the Conference of the Parties to the Basel Convention adopting, provisionally, the forms for both the notification and the movement documents and recommending to Parties to use these forms,

Noting that some delegations to the Open-ended Ad Hoc Committee emphasized the need to harmonize the forms of the Basel Convention with related forms being developed by the OECD and the EU (para. 16 of the report of the First Meeting of the Open-ended Ad Hoc Committee for the implementation of the Basel Convention),

Having considered the report of the Secretariat contained in document UNEP/CHW.2/14,

1. *Requests* the Parties to continue using the forms adopted provisionally and to inform the Secretariat on their experience in the use of these forms;

2. *Requests* the Secretariat to continue its work on the format of the notification and movement documents, based on the replies received and comments to be sent by the Parties and international organizations concerned to the Secretariat by June 1994;

3. *Instructs* the Secretariat to report on paragraphs 1 and 2 above to the Third Meeting of the Conference of the Parties in consultation with the Open-ended Ad Hoc Committee, and to present its recommendations for any changes to be made to the notification and movement documents.

Decision II/17

Transmission of information

The Conference,

Recalling Article 13 of the Basel Convention which stipulates that the Parties to the Convention shall, through the Secretariat, provide information to each other and in some cases also to non-Party States on a set of issues concerning transboundary movements of hazardous wastes and their disposal,

Further recalling decision I/11 of the First Meeting of the Conference of the Parties which requested the Secretariat to prepare an analytical summary of the reports submitted to it and to present the summary to its Open-ended Ad Hoc Committee for evaluation of the information contained therein and a report on its findings to the Second Meeting of the Conference of the Parties.

Having considered the information provided by the Parties to the Convention presented in documents UNEP/CHW.C.1/1/5, UNEP/CHW.2/15, UNEP/CHW/C.1/1/Inf.3, UNEP/CHW.2/Inf.5 and decision I/4 of the Open-ended Ad Hoc Committee,

1. *Urges* Parties to report, as soon as possible, to the Secretariat in accordance with Article 13, on activities undertaken in 1993, using the form provided by the Secretariat for this purpose;

2. *Also urges* those Parties who have already presented an interim report for 1993 to provide any complementary information, as necessary, well in time, in order to enable the Secretariat to prepare a comprehensive analytical summary of the information provided by the Parties for the whole of 1993 to be considered by the Open-ended Ad Hoc Committee for the Implementation of the Basel Convention at its next meeting;

3. *Further requests* the Secretariat to issue in one document all information received up to date and presented in various documents and distributed to Parties, non-Parties and non-governmental organizations.

Decision II/18

Establishment of the information management system of the Basel Convention in accordance with decision I/4 of the First Meeting of the Open-ended Ad Hoc Committee for the Implementation of the Basel Convention

The Conference,

Recalling decision I/4 of the First Meeting of the Open-ended Ad Hoc Committee inviting the Conference to consider the need to develop an electronic information system and integrated telecommunications network to improve data gathering, organization, treatment and dissemination, and to provide assistance to developing countries in the collection and processing of these databases on a detailed request by the Secretariat that includes relevant technical and financial requirements,

Having considered the report by the Secretariat on the establishment of the information management system of the Basel Convention contained in document UNEP/CHW.2/16,

1. *Requests* the Secretariat of the Basel Convention to develop the information management system of the Basel Convention based on the outcome of the preliminary review, and to report on progress to the Third Meeting of the Conference of the Parties in consultation with the Open-ended Ad Hoc Committee;

2. *Requests* the Parties to allocate adequate financial resources for a minimum period of two years (1994–1995), taking into account the costs estimated as indicated under paragraph 9, to allow the Secretariat to develop the Information Management System;

3. *Also requests* the Parties to make additional contributions for the budget for 1994 to allow starting the establishment of the information management system already in 1994, subject to the availability of resources.

CONVENTION ON NUCLEAR SAFETY

PREAMBLE

THE CONTRACTING PARTIES

(i) Aware of the importance to the international community of ensuring that the use of nuclear energy is safe, well regulated and environmentally sound;

(ii) Reaffirming the necessity of continuing to promote a high level of nuclear safety worldwide;

(iii) Reaffirming that responsibility for nuclear safety rests with the State having jurisdiction over a nuclear installation;

(iv) Desiring to promote an effective nuclear safety culture;

(v) Aware that accidents at nuclear installations have the potential for transboundary impacts;

(vi) Keeping in mind the Convention on the Physical Protection of Nuclear Material (1979), the Convention on Early Notification of a Nuclear Accident (1986), and the Convention on Assistance in the Case of a Nuclear Accident or Radiological Emergency (1986);

(vii) Affirming the importance of international cooperation for the enhancement of nuclear safety—through existing bilateral and multilateral mechanisms and the establishment of this incentive Convention;

(viii) Recognizing that this Convention entails a commitment to the application of fundamental safety principles for nuclear installations rather than of detailed safety standards and that there are internationally formulated safety guidelines which are updated from time to time and so can provide guidance on contemporary means of achieving a high level of safety;

(ix) Affirming the need to begin promptly the development of an international convention on the safety of radioactive waste management as soon as the ongoing process to develop waste management safety fundamentals has resulted in broad international agreement;

(x) Recognizing the usefulness of further technical work in connection with the safety of other parts of the nuclear fuel cycle, and that this work may, in time, facilitate the development of current or future international instruments;

HAVE AGREED as follows:

CHAPTER 1. OBJECTIVES, DEFINITIONS AND SCOPE OF APPLICATION

Article 1

Objectives

The objectives of this Convention are:

(i) to achieve and maintain a high level of nuclear safety worldwide through the enhancement of national measures and international co-operation including, where appropriate, safety-related technical co-operation;

(ii) to establish and maintain effective defences in nuclear installations against potential radiological hazards in order to protect individuals, society and the environment from harmful effects of ionizing radiation from such installations;

(iii) to prevent accidents with radiological consequences and to mitigate such consequences should they occur.

Article 2

Definitions

For the purpose of this Convention:

(i) "nuclear installation" means for each Contracting Party any land-based civil nuclear power plant under its jurisdiction including such storage, handling and treatment facilities for radioactive materials as are on the same site and are directly related to the operation of the nuclear power plant. Such a plant ceases to be a nuclear installation when all nuclear fuel elements have been removed permanently from the reactor core and have been stored safely in accordance with approved procedures, and a decommissioning programme has been agreed to by the regulatory body.

(ii) "regulatory body" means for each Contracting Party any body or bodies given the legal authority by that Contracting Party to grant licences and to regulate the siting, design, construction, commissioning, operation or decommissioning of nuclear installations.

(iii) "licence" means any authorization granted by the regulatory body to the applicant to have the responsibility for the siting, design, construction, commissioning, operation or decommissioning of a nuclear installation.

Article 3

Scope of application

This Convention shall apply to the safety of nuclear installations.

CHAPTER 2. OBLIGATIONS

(a) General Provisions

Article 4

Implementing measures

Each Contracting Party shall take, within the framework of its national law, the legislative, regulatory and administrative measures and other steps necessary for implementing its obligations under this Convention.

Article 5

Reporting

Each Contracting Party shall submit for review, prior to each meeting referred to in Article 20, a report on the measures it has taken to implement each of the obligations of this Convention.

Article 6

Existing nuclear installations

Each Contracting Party shall take the appropriate steps to ensure that the safety of nuclear installations existing at the time the Convention enters into force for that Contracting Party is reviewed as soon as possible. When necessary in the context of this Convention, the Contracting Party shall ensure that all reasonably practicable improvements are made as a matter of urgency to upgrade the safety of the nuclear installation. If such upgrading cannot be achieved, plans should be implemented to shut down the nuclear installation as soon as practically possible. The timing of the shutdown may take into account the whole energy context and possible alternatives as well as the social, environmental and economic impact.

(b) Legislation and regulation

Article 7

Legislative and regulatory framework

1. Each Contracting Party shall establish and maintain a legislative and regulatory framework to govern the safety of nuclear installations.

2. The legislative and regulatory framework shall provide for:
   (i) the establishment of applicable national safety requirements and regulations;
   (ii) a system of licensing with regard to nuclear installations and the prohibition of the operation of a nuclear installation without a licence;
   (iii) a system of regulatory inspection and assessment of nuclear installations to ascertain compliance with applicable regulations and the terms of licences;
   (iv) the enforcement of applicable regulations and of the terms of licences, including suspension, modification or revocation.

Article 8

Regulatory body

1. Each Contracting Party shall establish or designate a regulatory body entrusted with the implementation of the legislative and regulatory framework referred to in Article 7, and provided with adequate authority, competence and financial and human resources to fulfil its assigned responsibilities.

2. Each Contracting Party shall take the appropriate steps to ensure an effective separation between the functions of the regulatory body and those of any other body or organization concerned with the promotion or utilization of nuclear energy.

Article 9

Responsibility of the licence holder

Each Contracting Party shall ensure that prime responsibility for the safety of a nuclear installation rests with the holder of the relevant licence and shall take the appropriate steps to ensure that each such licence holder meets its responsibility.

(c) General Safety Considerations

Article 10

Priority to safety

Each Contracting Party shall take the appropriate steps to ensure that all organizations engaged in activities directly related to nuclear installations shall establish policies that give due priority to nuclear safety.

Article 11

Financial and human resources

1. Each Contracting Party shall take the appropriate steps to ensure that adequate financial resources are available to support the safety of each nuclear installation throughout its life.

2. Each Contracting Party shall take the appropriate steps to ensure that sufficient numbers of qualified staff with appropriate education, training and retraining are available for all safety-related activities in or for each nuclear installation, throughout its life.

Article 12

Human factors

Each Contracting Party shall take the appropriate steps to ensure that the capabilities and limitations of human performance are taken into account throughout the life of a nuclear installation.

Article 13

Quality assurance

Each Contracting Party shall take the appropriate steps to ensure that quality assurance programmes are established and implemented with a view to providing confidence that specified requirements for all activities important to nuclear safety are satisfied throughout the life of a nuclear installation.

Article 14

Assessment and verification of safety

Each Contracting Party shall take the appropriate steps to ensure that:

(i) comprehensive and systematic safety assessments are carried out before the construction and commissioning of a nuclear installation and throughout its life. Such assessments shall be well documented, subsequently updated in the light of operating experience and significant new safety information, and reviewed under the authority of the regulatory body;

(ii) verification by analysis, surveillance, testing and inspection is carried out to ensure that the physical state and the operation of a nuclear installation continue to be in accordance with its design, applicable national safety requirements, and operational limits and conditions.

Article 15

Radiation protection

Each Contracting Party shall take the appropriate steps to ensure that in all operational states the radiation exposure to the workers and the public caused by a nuclear installation shall be kept as low as reasonably achievable and that no individual shall be exposed to radiation doses which exceed prescribed national dose limits.

Article 16

Emergency preparedness

1. Each Contracting Party shall take the appropriate steps to ensure that there are on-site and off-site emergency plans that are routinely tested for nuclear installations and cover the activities to be carried out in the event of an emergency.

For any new nuclear installation, such plans shall be prepared and tested before it commences operation above a low power level agreed by the regulatory body.

2. Each Contracting Party shall take the appropriate steps to ensure that, insofar as they are likely to be affected by a radiological emergency, its own population and the competent authorities of the States in the vicinity of the nuclear installation are provided with appropriate information for emergency planning and response.

3. Contracting Parties which do not have a nuclear installation on their territory, insofar as they are likely to be affected in the event of a radiological emergency at a nuclear installation in the vicinity, shall take the appropriate steps for the preparation and testing of emergency plans for

their territory that cover the activities to be carried out in the event of such an emergency.

(d) Safety of Installations

Article 17

Siting

Each Contracting Party shall take the appropriate steps to ensure that appropriate procedures are established and implemented:

(i) for evaluating all relevant site-related factors likely to affect the safety of a nuclear installation for its projected lifetime;

(ii) for evaluating the likely safety impact of a proposed nuclear installation on individuals, society and the environment;

(iii) for re-evaluating as necessary all relevant factors referred to in sub-paragraphs (i) and (ii) so as to ensure the continued safety acceptability of the nuclear installation;

(iv) for consulting Contracting Parties in the vicinity of a proposed nuclear installation, insofar as they are likely to be affected by that installation and, upon request providing the necessary information to such Contracting Parties, in order to enable them to evaluate and make their own assessment of the likely safety impact on their own territory of the nuclear installation.

Article 18

Design and construction

Each Contracting Party shall take the appropriate steps to ensure that:

(i) the design and construction of a nuclear installation provides for several reliable levels and methods of protection (defense in depth) against the release of radioactive materials, with a view to preventing the occurrence of accidents and to mitigating their radiological consequences should they occur;

(ii) the technologies incorporated in the design and construction of a nuclear installation are proven by experience or qualified by testing or analysis;

(iii) the design of a nuclear installation allows for reliable, stable and easily manageable operation, with specific consideration of human factors and the man-machine interface.

Article 19

Operation

Each Contracting Party shall take the appropriate steps to ensure that:

(i) the initial authorization to operate a nuclear installation is based upon an appropriate safety analysis and a commissioning programme demonstrating that the installation, as constructed, is consistent with design and safety requirements;

(ii) operational limits and conditions derived from the safety analysis, tests and operational experience are defined and revised as necessary for identifying safe boundaries for operation;

(iii) operation, maintenance, inspection and testing of a nuclear installation are conducted in accordance with approved procedures;

(iv) procedures are established for responding to anticipated operational occurrences and to accidents;

(v) necessary engineering and technical support in all safety related fields is available throughout the lifetime of a nuclear installation;

(vi) incidents significant to safety are reported in a timely manner by the holder of the relevant licence to the regulatory body;

(vii) programmes to collect and analyse operating experience are established, the results obtained and the conclusions drawn are acted upon and that existing mechanisms are used to share important experience with international bodies and with other operating organizations and regulatory bodies;

(viii) the generation of radioactive waste resulting from the operation of a nuclear installation is kept to the minimum practicable for the process concerned, both in activity and in volume, and any necessary treatment and storage of spent fuel and waste directly related to the operation and on the same site as that of the nuclear installation take into consideration conditioning and disposal.

CHAPTER 3. MEETING OF THE CONTRACTING PARTIES

Article 20

Review meetings

1. The Contracting Parties shall hold meetings (hereinafter referred to as "review meetings") for the purpose of reviewing the reports submitted pursuant to Article 5 in accordance with the procedures adopted under Article 22.

2. Subject to the provisions of Article 24 sub-groups comprised of representatives of Contracting Parties may be established and may function during the review meetings as deemed necessary for the purpose of reviewing specific subjects contained in the reports.

3. Each Contracting Party shall have a reasonable opportunity to discuss the reports submitted by other Contracting Parties and to seek clarification of such reports.

Article 21

Timetable

1. A preparatory meeting of the Contracting Parties shall be held not later than six months after the date of entry into force of this Convention.

2. At this preparatory meeting, the Contracting Parties shall determine the date for the first review meeting. This review meeting shall be held as soon as possible, but not later than thirty months after the date of entry into force of this Convention.

3. At each review meeting, the Contracting Parties shall determine the date for the next such meeting. The interval between review meetings shall not exceed three years.

Article 22

Procedural arrangements

1. At the preparatory meeting held pursuant to Article 21 the Contracting Parties shall prepare and adopt by consensus Rules of Procedure and Financial Rules. The Contracting Parties shall establish in particular and in accordance with the Rules of Procedure:

(i) guidelines regarding the form and structure of the reports to be submitted pursuant to Article 5;

(ii) a date for the submission of such reports;

(iii) the process for reviewing such reports;

2. At review meetings the Contracting Parties may, if necessary, review the arrangements established pursuant to sub-paragraphs (i)–(iii) above, and adopt revisions by consensus unless otherwise provided for in the Rules of Procedure. They may also amend the Rules of Procedure and the Financial Rules, by consensus.

Article 23

Extraordinary meetings

An extraordinary meeting of the Contracting Parties shall be held:

(i) if so agreed by a majority of the Contracting Parties present and voting at a meeting, abstentions being considered as voting; or

(ii) at the written request of a Contracting Party, within six months of this request having been communicated to the Contracting Parties and notification having been received by the secretariat referred to in Article 28, that the request has been supported by a majority of the Contracting Parties.

Article 24

Attendance

1. Each Contracting Party shall attend meetings of the Contracting Parties and be represented at such meetings by one delegate, and by such alternates, experts and advisers as it deems necessary.

2. The Contracting Parties may invite, by consensus, any intergovernmental organization which is competent in respect of matters governed by this Convention to attend, as an observer, any meeting, or specific sessions thereof. Observers shall be required to accept in writing, and in advance, the provisions of Article 27.

Article 25

Summary reports

The Contracting Parties shall adopt, by consensus, and make available to the public a document addressing issues discussed and conclusions reached during a meeting.

Article 26

Languages

1. The languages of meetings of the Contracting Parties shall be Arabic, Chinese, English, French, Russian and Spanish unless otherwise provided in the Rules of Procedure.

2. Reports submitted pursuant to Article 5 shall be prepared in the national language of the submitting Contracting Party or in a single designated language to be agreed in the Rules of Procedure. Should the report be submitted in a national language other than the designated language, a translation of the report into the designated language shall be provided by the Contracting Party.

3. Notwithstanding the provisions of paragraph 2, if compensated, the secretariat will assume the translation into the designated language of reports submitted in any other language of the meeting.

Article 27

Confidentiality

1. The provisions of this Convention shall not affect the rights and obligations of the Contracting Parties under their law to protect information from disclosure. For the purposes of this Article, "information" includes, inter alia, (i) personal data; (ii) information protected by intellectual property rights or by industrial or commercial confidentiality; and (iii) information relating to national security or to the physical protection of nuclear materials or nuclear installations.

2. When, in the context of this Convention, a Contracting Party provides information identified by it as protected as described in paragraph 1, such information shall be used only for the purposes for which it has been provided and its confidentiality shall be respected.

3. The content of the debates during the reviewing of the reports by the Contracting Parties at each meeting shall be confidential.

Article 28

Secretariat

1. The International Atomic Energy Agency, (hereinafter referred to as the "Agency") shall provide the secretariat for the meetings of the Contracting Parties.

2. The secretariat shall:
   (i) convene, prepare and service the meetings of the Contracting Parties;
   (ii) transmit to the Contracting Parties information received or prepared in accordance with the provisions of this Convention.

The costs incurred by the Agency in carrying out the functions referred to in sub-paragraphs (i) and (ii) above shall be borne by the Agency as part of its regular budget.

3. The Contracting Parties may, by consensus, request the Agency to provide other services in support of meetings of the Contracting Parties. The Agency may provide such services if they can be undertaken within its programme and regular budget. Should this not be possible, the Agency may provide such services if voluntary funding is provided from another source.

CHAPTER 4. FINAL CLAUSES AND OTHER PROVISIONS

Article 29

Resolution of disagreements

In the event of a disagreement between two or more Contracting Parties concerning the interpretation or application of this Convention, the Contracting Parties shall consult within the framework of a meeting of the Contracting Parties with a view to resolving the disagreement.

Article 30

Signature, ratification, acceptance, approval, accession

1. This Convention shall be open for signature by all States at the Headquarters of the Agency in Vienna from 20 September 1994 until its entry into force.

2. This Convention is subject to ratification, acceptance or approval by the signatory States.

3. After its entry into force, this Convention shall be open for accession by all States.

4. (i) This Convention shall be open for signature or accession by regional organizations of an integration or other nature, provided that any such organization is constituted by sovereign States and has competence in respect of the negotiation, conclusion and

application of international agreements in matters covered by this Convention.

(ii) In matters within their competence, such organizations shall, on their own behalf, exercise the rights and fulfil the responsibilities which this Convention attributes to States Parties.

(iii) When becoming party to this Convention, such an organization shall communicate to the Depositary referred to in Article 34, a declaration indicating which States are members thereof, which articles of this Convention apply to it, and the extent of its competence in the field covered by those articles.

(iv) Such an organization shall not hold any vote additional to those of its Member States.

5. Instruments of ratification, acceptance, approval or accession shall be deposited with the Depositary.

Article 31

Entry into force

1. This Convention shall enter into force on the ninetieth day after the date of deposit with the Depositary of the twenty-second instrument of ratification, acceptance or approval, including the instruments of seventeen States, each having at least one nuclear installation which has achieved criticality in a reactor core.

2. For each State or regional organization of an integration or other nature which ratifies, accepts, approves or accedes to this Convention after the date of deposit of the last instrument required to satisfy the conditions set forth in paragraph 1, this Convention shall enter into force on the ninetieth day after the date of deposit with the Depositary of the appropriate instrument by such a State or organization.

Article 32

Amendments to the convention

1. Any Contracting Party may propose an amendment to this Convention. Proposed amendments shall be considered at a review meeting or an extraordinary meeting.

2. The text of any proposed amendment and the reasons for it shall be provided to the Depositary who shall communicate the proposal to the Contracting Parties promptly and at least ninety days before the meeting

for which it is submitted for consideration. Any comments received on such a proposal shall be circulated by the Depositary to the Contracting Parties.

3. The Contracting Parties shall decide after consideration of the proposed amendment whether to adopt it by consensus, or, in the absence of consensus, to submit it to a Diplomatic Conference. A decision to submit a proposed amendment to a Diplomatic Conference shall require a two-thirds majority vote of the Contracting Parties present and voting at the meeting, provided that at least one half of the Contracting Parties are present at the time of voting. Abstentions shall be considered as voting.

4. The Diplomatic Conference to consider and adopt amendments to this Convention shall be convened by the Depositary and held no later than one year after the appropriate decision taken in accordance with paragraph 3 of this Article. The Diplomatic Conference shall make every effort to ensure amendments are adopted by consensus. Should this not be possible, amendments shall be adopted with a two-thirds majority of all Contracting Parties.

5. Amendments to this Convention adopted pursuant to paragraphs 3 and 4 above shall be subject to ratification, acceptance, approval, or confirmation by the Contracting Parties and shall enter into force for those Contracting Parties which have ratified, accepted, approved or confirmed them on the ninetieth day after the receipt by the Depositary of the relevant instruments by at least three fourths of the Contracting Parties. For a Contracting Party which subsequently ratifies, accepts, approves or confirms the said amendments, the amendments will enter into force on the ninetieth day after that Contracting Party has deposited its relevant instrument.

Article 33

Denunciation

1. Any Contracting Party may denounce this Convention by written notification to the Depositary.

2. Denunciation shall take effect one year following the date of the receipt of the notification by the Depositary, or on such later date as may be specified in the notification.

Article 34

Depositary

1. The Director General of the Agency shall be the Depositary of this Convention.

2. The Depositary shall inform the Contracting Parties of:
   (i) the signature of this Convention and of the deposit of instruments of ratification, acceptance, approval or accession, in accordance with Article 30;
   (ii) the date on which the Convention enters into force, in accordance with Article 31;
   (iii) the notifications of denunciation of the Convention and the date thereof, made in accordance with Article 33;
   (iv) the proposed amendments to this Convention submitted by Contracting Parties, the amendments adopted by the relevant Diplomatic Conference or by the meeting of the Contracting Parties, and the date of entry into force of the said amendments, in accordance with Article 32.

Article 35

Authentic texts

The original of this Convention of which the Arabic, Chinese, English, French, Russian and Spanish texts are equally authentic, shall be deposited with the Depositary, who shall send certified copies thereof to the Contracting Parties.

IN WITNESS WHEREOF THE UNDERSIGNED, BEING DULY AUTHORIZED TO THAT EFFECT, HAVE SIGNED THIS CONVENTION.

Done at Vienna on the 20th day of September 1994.

THE LAW OF THE NON-NAVIGATIONAL USES OF INTERNATIONAL WATERCOURSES

Draft articles on The Law of Non-Navigational Uses of International Watercourses: titles and texts of articles 1 to 33 adopted by the Drafting Committee on second reading

THE LAW OF THE NON-NAVIGATIONAL USES OF INTERNATIONAL WATERCOURSES

PART I

INTRODUCTION

Article 1

Scope of the present articles

1. The present articles apply to uses of international watercourses and of their waters for purposes other than navigation and to measures of conservation and management related to the uses of those watercourses and their waters.

2. The use of international watercourses for navigation is not within the scope of the present articles except in so far as other uses affect navigation or are affected by navigation.

Article 2

Use of terms

For the purposes of the present articles:

(a) "international watercourse" means a watercourse, parts of which are situated in different States;

(b) "watercourse" means a system of surface waters and groundwaters constituting by virtue of their physical relationship a unitary whole and normally flowing into a common terminus;

(c) "watercourse State" means a State in whose territory part of an international watercourse is situated.

Article 3

Watercourse agreements

1. Watercourse States may enter into one or more agreements, hereinafter referred to as "watercourse agreements", which apply and adjust the provisions of the present articles to the characteristics and uses of a particular international watercourse or part thereof.

2. Where a watercourse agreement is concluded between two or more watercourse States, it shall define the waters to which it applies. Such an agreement may be entered into with respect to an entire international watercourse or with respect to any part thereof or a particular project, programme or use, provided that the agreement does not adversely affect, to a significant extent, the use by one or more other watercourse States of the waters of the watercourse.

3. Where a watercourse State considers that adjustment or application of the provisions of the present articles is required because of the characteristics and uses of a particular international watercourse, watercourse States shall consult with a view to negotiating in good faith for the purpose of concluding a watercourse agreement or agreements.

Article 4

Parties to watercourse agreements

1. Every watercourse State is entitled to participate in the negotiation of and to become a party to any watercourse agreement that applies to the entire international watercourse, as well as to participate in any relevant consultations.

2. A watercourse State whose use of an international watercourse may be affected to a significant extent by the implementation of a proposed watercourse agreement that applies only to a part of the watercourse or to a particular project, programme or use is entitled to participate in consultations on, and in the negotiation of, such an agreement, to the extent that its use is thereby affected, and to become a party thereto.

PART II

GENERAL PRINCIPLES

Article 5

Equitable and reasonable utilization and participation

1. Watercourse States shall in their respective territories utilize an international watercourse in an equitable and reasonable manner. In particular, an international watercourse shall be used and developed by watercourse States with a view to attaining optimal utilization thereof and benefits therefrom consistent with adequate protection of the watercourse.

2. Watercourse States shall participate in the use, development and protection of an international watercourse in an equitable and reasonable manner. Such participation includes both the right to utilize the watercourse and the duty to cooperate in the protection and development thereof, as provided in the present articles.

Article 6

Factors relevant to equitable and reasonable utilization

1. Utilization of an international watercourse in an equitable and reasonable manner within the meaning of article 5 requires taking into account all relevant factors and circumstances, including:
   (a) geographic, hydrographic, hydrological, climatic, ecological and other factors of a natural character;
   (b) the social and economic needs of the watercourse States concerned;
   (c) the dependency of the population on the watercourse;
   (d) the effects of the use or uses of the watercourse in one watercourse State on other watercourse States;
   (e) existing and potential uses of the watercourse;
   (f) conservation, protection, development and economy of use of the water resources of the watercourse and the costs of measures taken to that effect;
   (g) the availability of alternatives, of corresponding value, to a particular planned or existing use.

2. In the application of article 5 or paragraph 1 of this article, watercourse States concerned shall, when the need arises, enter into consultations in a spirit of cooperation.

Article 7

Obligation not to cause significant harm

1. Watercourse States shall exercise due diligence to utilize an international watercourse in such a way as not to cause significant harm to other watercourse States.

2. Where, despite the exercise of due diligence, significant harm is caused to another watercourse State, the State whose use causes the harm shall, in the absence of agreement to such use, consult with the State suffering such harm over:

(a) the extent to which such use has proved equitable and reasonable taking into account the factors listed in article 6;

(b) the question of ad hoc adjustments to its utilization, designed to eliminate or mitigate any such harm caused and, where appropriate, the question of compensation.

Article 8

General obligation to cooperate

Watercourse States shall cooperate on the basis of sovereign equality, territorial integrity and mutual benefit in order to attain optimal utilization and adequate protection of an international watercourse.

Article 9

Regular exchange of data and information

1. Pursuant to article 8, watercourse States shall on a regular basis exchange readily available data and information on the condition of the watercourse, in particular that of a hydrological, meteorological, hydrogeological and ecological nature, as well as related forecasts.

2. If a watercourse State is requested by another watercourse State to provide data or information that is not readily available, it shall employ its best efforts to comply with the request but may condition its compliance upon payment by the requesting State of the reasonable costs of collecting and, where appropriate, processing such data or information.

3. Watercourse States shall employ their best efforts to collect and, where appropriate, to process data and information in a manner which facilitates its utilization by the other watercourse States to which it is communicated.

Article 10

Relationship between different kinds of uses

1. In the absence of agreement or custom to the contrary, no use of an international watercourse enjoys inherent priority over other uses.

2. In the event of a conflict between uses of an international watercourse, it shall be resolved with reference to the principles and factors set out in articles 5 to 7, with special regard being given to the requirements of vital human needs.

PART III

PLANNED MEASURES

Article 11

Information concerning planned measures

Watercourse States shall exchange information and consult each other on the possible effects of planned measures on the condition of an international watercourse.

Article 12

Notification concerning planned measures with possible adverse effects

Before a watercourse State implements or permits the implementation of planned measures which may have a significant adverse effect upon other watercourse States, it shall provide those States with timely notification thereof. Such notification shall be accompanied by available technical data and information in order to enable the notified States to evaluate the possible effects of the planned measures.

Article 13

Period for reply to notification

Unless otherwise agreed:

(a) a watercourse State providing a notification under article 12 shall allow the notified States a period of six months within which to study and evaluate the possible effects of the planned measures and to communicate the findings to it;

(b) this period shall, at the request of a notified State for which the evaluation of the planned measure poses special difficulty, be extended for a period not exceeding six months.

Article 14

Obligations of the notifying State during the period for reply

During the period referred to in article 13, the notifying State shall cooperate with the notified States by providing them, on request, with any additional data and information that is available and necessary for an accurate evaluation, and shall not implement or permit the implementation of the planned measures without the consent of the notified States.

Article 15

Reply to notification

1. The notified States shall communicate their findings to the notifying State as early as possible.

2. If a notified State finds that implementation of the planned measures would be inconsistent with the provisions of articles 5 or 7, it shall communicate this finding to the notifying State within the period applicable pursuant to article 13, together with a documented explanation setting forth the reasons for the finding.

Article 16

Absence of reply to notification

1. If, within the period applicable pursuant to article 13, the notifying State receives no communication under paragraph 2 of article 15, it may, subject to its obligations under articles 5 and 7, proceed with the implementation of the planned measures, in accordance with the notification and any other data and information provided to the notified States.

2. Any claim to compensation by a notified State which has failed to reply may be offset by the costs incurred by the notifying State for action undertaken after the expiration of the time for a reply which would not have been undertaken if the notified State had objected within the period applicable pursuant to article 13.

Article 17

Consultations and negotiations concerning planned measures

1. If a communication is made under paragraph 2 of article 15, the notifying State and the State making the communication shall enter into consultations and, if necessary, negotiations with a view to arriving at an equitable resolution of the situation.

2. The consultations and negotiations shall be conducted on the basis that each State must in good faith pay reasonable regard to the rights and legitimate interests of the other State.

3. During the course of the consultations and negotiations, the notifying State shall, if so requested by the notified State at the time it makes the communication, refrain from implementing or permitting the implementation of the planned measures for a period not exceeding six months.

Article 18

Procedures in the absence of notification

1. If a watercourse State has serious reason to believe that another watercourse State is planning measures that may have a significant adverse effect upon it, the former State may request the latter to apply the provisions of article 12. The request shall be accompanied by a documented explanation setting forth its reasons.

2. In the event that the State planning the measures nevertheless finds that it is not under an obligation to provide a notification under article 12, it shall so inform the other State, providing a documented explanation setting forth the reasons for such finding. If this finding does not satisfy the other State, the two States shall, at the request of that other State, promptly enter into consultations and negotiations in the manner indicated in paragraphs 1 and 2 of article 17.

3. During the course of the consultations and negotiations, the State planning the measures shall, if so requested by the other State at the time it requests the initiation of consultations and negotiations, refrain from implementing or permitting the implementation of those measures for a period not exceeding six months.

Article 19

Urgent implementation of planned measures

1. In the event that the implementation of planned measures is of the utmost urgency in order to protect public health, public safety or other equally important interests, the State planning the measures may, subject to articles 5 and 7, immediately proceed to implementation, notwithstanding the provisions of article 14 and paragraph 3 of article 17.

2. In such cases, a formal declaration of the urgency of the measures shall be communicated to the other watercourse States referred to in article 12 together with the relevant data and information.

3. The State planning the measures shall, at the request of any of the States referred to in paragraph 2, promptly enter into consultations and negotiations with it in the manner indicated in paragraphs 1 and 2 of article 17.

PART IV

PROTECTION, PRESERVATION AND MANAGEMENT

Article 20

Protection and preservation of ecosystems

Watercourse States shall, individually or jointly, protect and preserve the ecosystems of international watercourses.

Article 21

Prevention, reduction and control of pollution

1. For the purposes of this article, "pollution of an international watercourse" means any detrimental alteration in the composition or quality of the waters of an international watercourse which results directly or indirectly from human conduct.

2. Watercourse States shall, individually or jointly, prevent, reduce and control pollution of an international watercourse that may cause significant harm to other watercourse States or to their environment, including harm to human health or safety, to the use of the waters for any beneficial purpose or to the living resources of the watercourse. Watercourse States shall take steps to harmonize their policies in this connection.

3. Watercourse States shall, at the request of any of them, consult with a view to establishing list of substances, the introduction of which into the waters of an international watercourse is to be prohibited, limited, investigated or monitored.

Article 22

Introduction of alien or new species

Watercourse States shall take all measures necessary to prevent the introduction of species, alien or new, into an international watercourse which may have effects detrimental to the ecosystem of the watercourse resulting in significant harm to other watercourse States.

Article 23

Protection and preservation of the marine environment

Watercourse States shall, individually or jointly, take all measures with respect to an international watercourse that are necessary to protect and preserve the marine environment, including estuaries, taking into account generally accepted international rules and standards.

Article 24 [26]

Management

1. Watercourse States shall, at the request of any of them, enter into consultations concerning the management of an international watercourse, which may include the establishment of a joint management mechanism.

2. For the purposes of this article, "management" refers, in particular, to:
   (a) planning and sustainable development of an international watercourse and providing for the implementation of any plans adopted; and
   (b) otherwise promoting rational and optimal utilization, protection and control of the watercourse.

Article 25 [27]

Regulation

1. Watercourse States shall cooperate, where appropriate, to respond to needs or opportunities for regulation of the flow of the waters of an international watercourse.

2. Unless otherwise agreed, watercourse States shall participate on an equitable basis in the construction and maintenance or defrayal of the costs of such regulation works as they may have agreed to undertake.

3. For the purposes of this article, "regulation" means the use of hydraulic works or any other continuing measure to alter, vary or otherwise control the flow of the waters of an international watercourse.

Article 26 [28]

Installations

1. Watercourse States shall, within their respective territories, employ their best efforts to maintain and protect installations, facilities and other works related to an international watercourse.

2. Watercourse States shall, at the request of any of them which has serious reason to believe that it may suffer significant adverse effects, enter into consultations with regard to:
   (a) the safe operation or maintenance of installations, facilities or other works related to an international watercourse; or
   (b) the protection of installations, facilities or other works from wilful or negligent acts or the forces of nature.

PART V

HARMFUL CONDITIONS AND EMERGENCY SITUATIONS

Article 27 [24]

Prevention and mitigation of harmful conditions

Watercourse States shall, individually or jointly, take all appropriate measures to prevent or mitigate conditions that may be harmful to other watercourse States, whether resulting from natural causes or human conduct, such as flood or ice conditions, water-borne diseases, siltation, erosion, salt-water intrusion, drought or desertification.

Article 28 [25]

Emergency situations

1. For the purposes of this article, "emergency" means a situation that causes, or poses an imminent threat of causing, serious harm to water-

course States or other States and that results suddenly from natural causes, such as floods, the breaking up of ice, landslides or earthquakes, or from human conduct, such as in the case of industrial accidents.

2. A watercourse State shall, without delay and by the most expeditious means available, notify other potentially affected States and competent international organizations of any emergency originating within its territory.

3. A watercourse State within whose territory an emergency originates shall, in cooperation with potentially affected States and, where appropriate, competent international organizations, immediately take all practicable measures necessitated by the circumstances to prevent, mitigate and eliminate harmful effects of the emergency.

4. When necessary, watercourse States shall jointly develop contingency plans for responding to emergencies, in cooperation, where appropriate, with other potentially affected States and competent international organizations.

PART VI

MISCELLANEOUS PROVISIONS

Article 29

International watercourses and installations in time of armed conflict

International watercourses and related installations, facilities and other works shall enjoy the protection accorded by the principles and rules of international law applicable in international and internal armed conflict and shall not be used in violation of those principles and rules.

Article 30

Indirect procedures

In cases where there are serious obstacles to direct contacts between watercourse States, the States concerned shall fulfil their obligations of cooperation provided for in the present articles, including exchange of data and information, notification, communication, consultations and negotiations, through any direct procedure accepted by them.

Article 31

Data and information vital to national defence or security

Nothing in the present articles obliges a watercourse State to provide data or information vital to its national defence or security. Nevertheless, that State shall cooperate in good faith with the other watercourse States with a view to providing as much information as possible under the circumstances.

Article 32

Non-Discrimination

Unless the watercourse States concerned have agreed otherwise for the protection of the interests of persons, natural or juridical, who have suffered or are under a serious threat of suffering significant transboundary harm as a result of activities related to an international watercourse, a watercourse State shall not discriminate, on the basis of nationality or residence or place where the injury occurred, in granting to such persons, in accordance with its legal system, access to judicial or other procedures or a right to claim compensation or other relief in respect of significant harm caused by such activities carried on under its jurisdiction.

Article 33

Settlement of disputes

In the absence of an applicable agreement between the watercourse States concerned, any watercourse dispute concerning a question of fact or the interpretation or application of the present articles shall be settled in accordance with the following provisions:

(a) If such a dispute arises, the States concerned shall expeditiously enter into consultations and negotiations with a view to arriving at equitable solutions of the dispute, making use, as appropriate, of any joint watercourse institutions that may have been established by them;

(b) If the States concerned have not arrived at a settlement of the disputes through consultations and negotiations, at any time after six months from date of the request for consultations and negotiations they shall at the request of any of them have recourse to impartial fact-finding or, if agreed upon by the States concerned, mediation or conciliation;

 (i) Unless otherwise agreed, a Fact-Finding Commission shall be established, composed of one member nominated by each State concerned and in addition a member not having the nationality of any of the States concerned chosen by the nominated members who shall serve as Chairman;

(ii) If the members nominated by States are unable to agree on a Chairman within four months of the request for the establishment of the Commission, any State concerned may request the Secretary-General of the United Nations to appoint the Chairman. If one of the States fails to nominate a member within four months of the initial request pursuant to paragraph (b), any other State concerned may request the Secretary-General of the United Nations to appoint a person who shall not have the nationality of any of the States concerned who shall constitute a single member Commission;

(iii) The Commission shall determine its own procedure;

(iv) The States concerned have the obligation to provide the Commission with such information as it may require and, on request, to permit the Commission to have access to their respective territory and to inspect any facilities, plant, equipment, construction or natural feature relevant for the purpose of its inquiry;

(v) The Commission shall adopt its report by a majority vote, unless it is a single member Commission, and shall submit that report to the States concerned setting forth its findings and the reasons therefor and such recommendations as it deems appropriate;

(vi) The expenses of the Commission shall be borne equally by the States concerned.

(c) If, after 12 months from the initial request for fact-finding, mediation or conciliation or, if a fact-finding mediation or conciliation Commission has been established, 6 months after receipt of a report from the Commission, whichever is the later, the States concerned have been unable to settle the dispute, any of them may, subject to the agreement of the States concerned, submit the dispute to a permanent or ad hoc tribunal or to the International Court of Justice.

ADDENDUM

DRAFT RESOLUTION ADOPTED BY THE DRAFTING COMMITTEE

The International Law Commission,

Having completed its consideration of the topic on the Law of the Non-Navigational Uses of International Watercourses,

Having considered in that context groundwater which is related to an international watercourse,

Recognizing that confined groundwater, that is groundwater not related to an international watercourse, is also a natural resource of vital importance for sustaining life, health and the integrity of ecosystems,

Recognizing also the need for continuing efforts to elaborate rules pertaining to confined transboundary groundwater,

1. *Expresses* its view that the principles contained in its draft articles on the Law of the non-navigational uses of watercourses may be applied to transboundary confined groundwater;

2. *Commends* States to be guided by the said principles, where appropriate, in regulating transboundary groundwater;

3. *Recommends* States to consider entering into agreements with the other State or States in which the confined transboundary groundwater is located;

4. *Recommends also* that, in the event of any dispute involving transboundary confined groundwater, the States concerned should consider resolving such dispute in accordance with the provisions contained in article 33 of the draft articles, or in such other manner as may be agreed upon.

RESOLUTION ADOPTED BY THE GENERAL ASSEMBLY

[without reference to a Main Committee (A/48/L.60 and Add.1)]

48/263. *Agreement relating to the implementation of Part XI of the United Nations Convention on the Law of the Sea of 10 December 1982*

The General Assembly,

Prompted by the desire to achieve universal participation in the United Nations Convention on the Law of the Sea of 10 December 1982[1] (hereinafter referred to as the "Convention") and to promote appropriate representation in the institutions established by it,

Reaffirming that the seabed and ocean floor and subsoil thereof, beyond the limits of national jurisdiction (hereinafter referred to as the "Area"), as well as the resources of the Area, are the common heritage of mankind,[2]

Recalling that the Convention in its Part XI and related provisions (hereinafter referred to as "Part XI") established a regime for the Area and its resources,

Taking note of the consolidated provisional final report of the Preparatory Commission for the International Seabed Authority and for the International Tribunal for the Law of the Sea,[3]

Recalling its resolution 48/28 of 9 December 1993 on the law of the sea,

Recognizing that political and economic changes, including in particular a growing reliance on market principles, have necessitated the re-evaluation of some aspects of the regime for the Area and its resources,

Noting the initiative of the Secretary-General which began in 1990 to promote dialogue aimed at achieving universal participation in the Convention,

[1] *Official Records of the Third United Nations Conference on the Law of the Sea*, vol. XVII (United Nations publication, Sales No. E.84.V.3), document A/CONF.62/122.

[2] General Assembly resolution 2749 (XXV) of 17 December 1970; article 136 of the United Nations Convention on the Law of the Sea.

[3] Documents LOS/PCN/130 and Add.1.

Welcoming the report of the Secretary-General on the outcome of his informal consultations,[4] including the draft of an agreement relating to the implementation of Part XI,

Considering that the objective of universal participation in the Convention may best be achieved by the adoption of an agreement relating to the implementation of Part XI,

Recognizing the need to provide for the provisional application of such an agreement from the date of entry into force of the Convention on 16 November 1994,

1. *Expresses its appreciation* to the Secretary-General for his report on the informal consultations;

2. *Reaffirms* the unified character of the United Nations Convention on the Law of the Sea of 10 December 1982;

3. *Adopts* the Agreement relating to the implementation of Part XI of the United Nations Convention on the Law of the Sea of 10 December 1982 (hereinafter referred to as the "Agreement"), the text of which is annexed to the present resolution;

4. *Affirms* that the Agreement shall be interpreted and applied together with Part XI as a single instrument;

5. *Considers* that future ratifications or formal confirmations of or accessions to the Convention shall represent also consent to be bound by the Agreement and that no State or entity may establish its consent to be bound by the Agreement unless it has previously established or establishes at the same time its consent to be bound by the Convention;

6. *Calls upon* States which consent to the adoption of the Agreement to refrain from any act which would defeat its object and purpose;

7. *Expresses its satisfaction* at the entry into force of the Convention on 16 November 1994;

8. *Decides* to fund the administrative expenses of the International Seabed Authority in accordance with section 1, paragraph 14, of the Annex to the Agreement;

9. *Requests* the Secretary-General to transmit immediately certified copies of the Agreement to the States and entities referred to in article 3 thereof, with a view to facilitating universal participation in the Convention and the Agreement, and to draw attention to articles 4 and 5 of the Agreement;

[4] A/48/950.

10. *Also requests* the Secretary-General immediately to open the Agreement for signature in accordance with article 3 thereof;

11. *Urges* all States and entities referred to in article 3 of the Agreement to consent to its provisional application as from 16 November 1994 and to establish their consent to be bound by the Agreement at the earliest possible date;

12. *Also urges* all such States and entities that have not already done so to take all appropriate steps to ratify, formally confirm or accede to the Convention at the earliest possible date in order to ensure universal participation in the Convention;

13. *Calls upon* the Preparatory Commission for the International Seabed Authority and for the International Tribunal for the Law of the Sea to take into account the terms of the Agreement when drawing up its final report.

101st plenary meeting
28 July 1994

ANNEX

AGREEMENT RELATING TO THE IMPLEMENTATION OF PART XI OF THE UNITED NATIONS CONVENTION ON THE LAW OF THE SEA OF 10 DECEMBER 1982

The States Parties to this Agreement,

Recognizing the important contribution of the United Nations Convention on the Law of the Sea of 10 December 1982[1] (hereinafter referred to as "the Convention") to the maintenance of peace, justice and progress for all peoples of the world,

Reaffirming that the seabed and ocean floor and subsoil thereof, beyond the limits of national jurisdiction (hereinafter referred to as "the Area"), as well as the resources of the Area, are the common heritage of mankind,

Mindful of the importance of the Convention for the protection and preservation of the marine environment and of the growing concern for the global environment,

Having considered the report of the Secretary-General of the United Nations on the results of the informal consultations among States held from 1990 to 1994 on outstanding issues relating to Part XI and related provisions of the Convention[4] (hereinafter referred to as "Part XI"),

Noting the political and economic changes, including market-oriented approaches, affecting the implementation of Part XI,

Wishing to facilitate universal participation in the Convention,

Considering that an agreement relating to the implementation of Part XI would best meet that objective,

Have agreed as follows:

Article 1

Implementation of Part XI

1. The States Parties to this Agreement undertake to implement Part XI in accordance with this Agreement.

2. The Annex forms an integral part of this Agreement.

Article 2

Relationship between this Agreement and Part XI

1. The provisions of this Agreement and Part XI shall be interpreted and applied together as a single instrument. In the event of any inconsistency between this Agreement and Part XI, the provisions of this Agreement shall prevail.

2. Articles 309 to 319 of the Convention shall apply to this Agreement as they apply to the Convention.

Article 3

Signature

This Agreement shall remain open for signature at United Nations Headquarters by the States and entities referred to in article 305, paragraph 1 (a), (c), (d), (e) and (f), of the Convention for 12 months from the date of its adoption.

Article 4

Consent to be bound

1. After the adoption of this Agreement, any instrument of ratification or formal confirmation of or accession to the Convention shall also represent consent to be bound by this Agreement.

2. No State or entity may establish its consent to be bound by this Agreement unless it has previously established or establishes at the same time its consent to be bound by the Convention.

3. A State or entity referred to in article 3 may express its consent to be bound by this Agreement by:
   (a) Signature not subject to ratification, formal confirmation or the procedure set out in article 5;
   (b) Signature subject to ratification or formal confirmation, followed by ratification or formal confirmation;
   (c) Signature subject to the procedure set out in article 5; or
   (d) Accession.

4. Formal confirmation by the entities referred to in article 305, paragraph 1 (f), of the Convention shall be in accordance with Annex IX of the Convention.

5. The instruments of ratification, formal confirmation or accession shall be deposited with the Secretary-General of the United Nations.

Article 5

Simplified procedure

1. A State or entity which has deposited before the date of the adoption of this Agreement an instrument of ratification or formal confirmation of or accession to the Convention and which has signed this Agreement in accordance with article 4, paragraph 3 (c), shall be considered to have established its consent to be bound by this Agreement 12 months after the date of its adoption, unless that State or entity notifies the depositary in writing before that date that it is not availing itself of the simplified procedure set out in this article.

2. In the event of such notification, consent to be bound by this Agreement shall be established in accordance with article 4, paragraph 3 (b).

Article 6

Entry into force

1. This Agreement shall enter into force 30 days after the date on which 40 States have established their consent to be bound in accordance with articles 4 and 5, provided that such States include at least seven of the States referred to in paragraph 1 (a) of resolution II of the Third United Nations Conference on the Law of the Sea[5] (hereinafter referred to as "resolution II") and that at least five of those States are developed States. If these conditions for entry into force are fulfilled before 16 November 1994, this Agreement shall enter into force on 16 November 1994.

2. For each State or entity establishing its consent to be bound by this Agreement after the requirements set out in paragraph 1 have been fulfilled, this Agreement shall enter into force on the thirtieth day following the date of establishment of its consent to be bound.

Article 7

Provisional application

1. If on 16 November 1994 this Agreement has not entered into force, it shall be applied provisionally pending its entry into force by:

(a) States which have consented to its adoption in the General Assembly of the United Nations, except any such State which before 16 November 1994 notifies the depositary in writing either that it will not so apply this Agreement or that it will consent to such application only upon subsequent signature or notification in writing;

(b) States and entities which sign this Agreement, except any such State or entity which notifies the depositary in writing at the time of signature that it will not so apply this Agreement;

(c) States and entities which consent to its provisional application by so notifying the depositary in writing;

(d) States which accede to this Agreement.

2. All such States and entities shall apply this Agreement provisionally in accordance with their national or internal laws and regulations, with effect from 16 November 1994 or the date of signature, notification of consent or accession, if later.

[5] *Official Records of the Third United Nations Conference on the Law of the Sea*, vol. XVII (United Nations publication, Sales No. E.84.V.3), document A/CONF.62/121, annex I.

3. Provisional application shall terminate upon the date of entry into force of this Agreement. In any event, provisional application shall terminate on 16 November 1998 if at that date the requirement in article 6, paragraph 1, of consent to be bound by this Agreement by at least seven of the States (of which at least five must be developed States) referred to in paragraph 1 (a) of resolution II has not been fulfilled.

Article 8

States Parties

1. For the purposes of this Agreement, "States Parties" means States which have consented to be bound by this Agreement and for which this Agreement is in force.

2. This Agreement applies *mutatis mutandis* to the entities referred to in article 305, paragraph 1 (c), (d), (e) and (f), of the Convention which became Parties to this Agreement in accordance with the conditions relevant to each, and to that extent "States Parties" refers to those entities.

Article 9

Depositary

The Secretary-General of the United Nations shall be the depositary of this Agreement.

Article 10

Authentic texts

The original of this Agreement, of which the Arabic, Chinese, English, French, Russian and Spanish texts are equally authentic, shall be deposited with the Secretary-General of the United Nations.

IN WITNESS WHEREOF, the undersigned Plenipotentiaries, being duly authorized thereto, have signed this Agreement.

DONE AT NEW YORK, this . . . day of July, one thousand nine hundred and ninety-four.

ANNEX

SECTION 1. COSTS TO STATES PARTIES AND INSTITUTIONAL ARRANGEMENTS

1. The International Seabed Authority (hereinafter referred to as "the Authority") is the organization through which States Parties to the Convention shall, in accordance with the regime for the Area established in Part XI and this Agreement, organize and control activities in the Area, particularly with a view to administering the resources of the Area. The powers and functions of the Authority shall be those expressly conferred upon it by the Convention. The Authority shall have such incidental powers, consistent with the Convention, as are implicit in, and necessary for, the exercise of those powers and functions with respect to activities in the Area.

2. In order to minimize costs to States Parties, all organs and subsidiary bodies to be established under the Convention and this Agreement shall be cost-effective. This principle shall also apply to the frequency, duration and scheduling of meetings.

3. The setting up and the functioning of the organs and subsidiary bodies of the Authority shall be based on an evolutionary approach, taking into account the functional needs of the organs and subsidiary bodies concerned in order that they may discharge effectively their respective responsibilities at various stages of the development of activities in the Area.

4. The early functions of the Authority upon entry into force of the Convention shall be carried out by the Assembly, the Council, the Secretariat, the Legal and Technical Commission and the Finance Committee. The functions of the Economic Planning Commission shall be performed by the Legal and Technical Commission until such time as the Council decides otherwise or until the approval of the first plan of work for exploitation.

5. Between the entry into force of the Convention and the approval of the first plan of work for exploitation, the Authority shall concentrate on:

(a) Processing of applications for approval of plans of work for exploration in accordance with Part XI and this Agreement;

(b) Implementation of decisions of the Preparatory Commission for the International Seabed Authority and for the International Tribunal for the Law of the Sea (hereinafter referred to as "the Preparatory Commission") relating to the registered pioneer investors and their certifying States, including their rights and obligations, in accordance with article 308, paragraph 5, of the Convention and resolution II, paragraph 13;

(c) Monitoring of compliance with plans of work for exploration approved in the form of contracts;

(d) Monitoring and review of trends and developments relating to deep seabed mining activities, including regular analysis of world metal market conditions and metal prices, trends and prospects;

(e) Study of the potential impact of mineral production from the Area on the economies of developing land-based producers of those minerals which are likely to be most seriously affected, with a view to minimizing their difficulties and assisting them in their economic adjustment, taking into account the work done in this regard by the Preparatory Commission;

(f) Adoption of rules, regulations and procedures necessary for the conduct of activities in the Area as they progress. Notwithstanding the provisions of Annex III, article 17, paragraph 2 (b) and (c), of the Convention, such rules, regulations and procedures shall take into account the terms of this Agreement, the prolonged delay in commercial deep seabed mining and the likely pace of activities in the Area;

(g) Adoption of rules, regulations and procedures incorporating applicable standards for the protection and preservation of the marine environment;

(h) Promotion and encouragement of the conduct of marine scientific research with respect to activities in the Area and the collection and dissemination of the results of such research and analysis, when available, with particular emphasis on research related to the environmental impact of activities in the Area;

(i) Acquisition of scientific knowledge and monitoring of the development of marine technology relevant to activities in the Area, in particular technology relating to the protection and preservation of the marine environment;

(j) Assessment of available data relating to prospecting and exploration;

(k) Timely elaboration of rules, regulations and procedures for exploitation, including those relating to the protection and preservation of the marine environment.

6. (a) An application for approval of a plan of work for exploration shall be considered by the Council following the receipt of a recommendation on the application from the Legal and Technical Commission. The processing of an application for approval of a plan of work for exploration shall be in

accordance with the provisions of the Convention, including Annex III thereof, and this Agreement, and subject to the following:

(i) A plan of work for exploration submitted on behalf of a State or entity, or any component of such entity, referred to in resolution II, paragraph 1 (a) (ii) or (iii), other than a registered pioneer investor, which had already undertaken substantial activities in the Area prior to the entry into force of the Convention, or its successor in interest, shall be considered to have met the financial and technical qualifications necessary for approval of a plan of work if the sponsoring State or States certify that the applicant has expended an amount equivalent to at least US$ 30 million in research and exploration activities and has expended no less than 10 per cent of that amount in the location, survey and evaluation of the area referred to in the plan of work. If the plan of work otherwise satisfies the requirements of the Convention and any rules, regulations and procedures adopted pursuant thereto, it shall be approved by the Council in the form of a contract. The provisions of section 3, paragraph 11, of this Annex shall be interpreted and applied accordingly;

(ii) Notwithstanding the provisions of resolution II, paragraph 8 (a), a registered pioneer investor may request approval of a plan of work for exploration within 36 months of the entry into force of the Convention. The plan of work for exploration shall consist of documents, reports and other data submitted to the Preparatory Commission both before and after registration and shall be accompanied by a certificate of compliance, consisting of a factual report describing the status of fulfilment of obligations under the pioneer investor regime, issued by the Preparatory Commission in accordance with resolution II, paragraph 11 (a). Such a plan of work shall be considered to be approved. Such an approved plan of work shall be in the form of a contract concluded between the Authority and the registered pioneer investor in accordance with Part XI and this Agreement. The fee of US$ 250,000 paid pursuant to resolution II, paragraph 7 (a), shall be deemed to be the fee relating to the exploration phase pursuant to section 8, paragraph 3, of this Annex. Section 3, paragraph 11, of this Annex shall be interpreted and applied accordingly;

(iii) In accordance with the principle of non-discrimination, a contract with a State or entity or any component of such entity referred to in subparagraph (a) (i) shall include arrangements which shall be similar to and no less favourable than those agreed with any registered pioneer investor referred to in subparagraph (a) (ii). If any of the States or entities or any components of such entities referred to in subparagraph (a) (i) are granted more favourable arrangements, the Council shall make similar and no less favourable arrangements with regard to the rights and obligations assumed by the registered pioneer investors referred to in subparagraph (a) (ii), provided that such arrangements do not affect or prejudice the interests of the Authority;

(iv) A State sponsoring an application for a plan of work pursuant to the provisions of subparagraph (a) (i) or (ii) may be a State Party or a State which is applying this Agreement provisionally in accordance with article 7, or a State which is a member of the Authority on a provisional basis in accordance with paragraph 12;

(v) Resolution II, paragraph 8 (c), shall be interpreted and applied in accordance with subparagraph (a) (iv).

(b) The approval of a plan of work for exploration shall be in accordance with article 153, paragraph 3, of the Convention.

7. An application for approval of a plan of work shall be accompanied by an assessment of the potential environmental impacts of the proposed activities and by a description of a programme for oceanographic and baseline environmental studies in accordance with the rules, regulations and procedures adopted by the Authority.

8. An application for approval of a plan of work for exploration, subject to paragraph 6 (a) (i) or (ii), shall be processed in accordance with the procedures set out in section 3, paragraph 11, of this Annex.

9. A plan of work for exploration shall be approved for a period of 15 years. Upon the expiration of a plan of work for exploration, the contractor shall apply for a plan of work for exploitation unless the contractor has already done so or has obtained an extension for the plan of work for exploration. Contractors may apply for such extensions for periods of not more than five years each. Such extensions shall be approved if the contractor has made efforts in good faith to comply with the requirements of the plan of work but for reasons beyond the contractor's control has been unable to complete the necessary preparatory work for proceeding to the

exploitation stage or if the prevailing economic circumstances do not justify proceeding to the exploitation stage.

10. Designation of a reserved area for the Authority in accordance with Annex III, article 8, of the Convention shall take place in connection with approval of an application for a plan of work for exploration or approval of an application for a plan of work for exploration and exploitation.

11. Notwithstanding the provisions of paragraph 9, an approved plan of work for exploration which is sponsored by at least one State provisionally applying this Agreement shall terminate if such a State ceases to apply this Agreement provisionally and has not become a member on a provisional basis in accordance with paragraph 12 or has not become a State Party.

12. Upon the entry into force of this Agreement, States and entities referred to in article 3 of this Agreement which have been applying it provisionally in accordance with article 7 and for which it is not in force may continue to be members of the Authority on a provisional basis pending its entry into force for such States and entities, in accordance with the following subparagraphs:

(a) If this Agreement enters into force before 16 November 1996, such States and entities shall be entitled to continue to participate as members of the Authority on a provisional basis upon notification to the depositary of the Agreement by such a State or entity of its intention to participate as a member on a provisional basis. Such membership shall terminate either on 16 November 1996 or upon the entry into force of this Agreement and the Convention for such member, whichever is earlier. The Council may, upon the request of the State or entity concerned, extend such membership beyond 16 November 1996 for a further period or periods not exceeding a total of two years provided that the Council is satisfied that the State or entity concerned has been making efforts in good faith to become a party to the Agreement and the Convention;

(b) If this Agreement enters into force after 15 November 1996, such States and entities may request the Council to grant continued membership in the Authority on a provisional basis for a period or periods not extending beyond 16 November 1998. The Council shall grant such membership with effect from the date of the request if it is satisfied that the State or entity has been making efforts in good faith to become a party to the Agreement and the Convention;

(c) States and entities which are members of the Authority on a provisional basis in accordance with subparagraph (a) or (b) shall apply the terms of Part XI and this Agreement in accordance with their national or internal laws, regulations and annual budgetary appropriations and shall have the same rights and obligations as other members, including:

(i) The obligation to contribute to the administrative budget of the Authority in accordance with the scale of assessed contributions;

(ii) The right to sponsor an application for approval of a plan of work for exploration. In the case of entities whose components are natural or juridical persons possessing the nationality of more than one State, a plan of work for exploration shall not be approved unless all the States whose natural or juridical persons comprise those entities are States Parties or members on a provisional basis;

(d) Notwithstanding the provisions of paragraph 9, an approved plan of work in the form of a contract for exploration which was sponsored pursuant to subparagraph (c) (ii) by a State which was a member on a provisional basis shall terminate if such membership ceases and the State or entity has not become a State Party;

(e) If such a member has failed to make its assessed contributions or otherwise failed to comply with its obligations in accordance with this paragraph, its membership on a provisional basis shall be terminated.

13. The reference in Annex III, article 10, of the Convention to performance which has not been satisfactory shall be interpreted to mean that the contractor has failed to comply with the requirements of an approved plan of work in spite of a written warning or warnings from the Authority to the contractor to comply therewith.

14. The Authority shall have its own budget. Until the end of the year following the year during which this Agreement enters into force, the administrative expenses of the Authority shall be met through the budget of the United Nations. Thereafter, the administrative expenses of the Authority shall be met by assessed contributions of its members, including any members on a provisional basis, in accordance with articles 171, subparagraph (a), and 173 of the Convention and this Agreement, until the Authority has sufficient funds from other sources to meet those expenses. The Authority shall not exercise the power referred to in article 174, paragraph 1, of the Convention to borrow funds to finance its administrative budget.

15. The Authority shall elaborate and adopt, in accordance with article 162, paragraph 2 (o) (ii), of the Convention, rules, regulations and procedures based on the principles contained in sections 2, 5, 6, 7 and 8 of this Annex, as well as any additional rules, regulations and procedures necessary to facilitate the approval of plans of work for exploration or exploitation, in accordance with the following subparagraphs:

(a) The Council may undertake such elaboration any time it seems that all or any of such rules, regulations or procedures are required for the conduct of activities in the Area, or when it determines that commercial exploitation is imminent, or at the request of a State whose national intends to apply for approval of a plan of work for exploitation;

(b) If a request is made by a State referred to in subparagraph (a) the Council shall, in accordance with article 162, paragraph 2 (o), of the Convention, complete the adoption of such rules, regulations and procedures within two years of the request;

(c) If the Council has not completed the elaboration of the rules, regulations and procedures relating to exploitation within the prescribed time and an application for approval of a plan of work for exploitation is pending, it shall none the less consider and provisionally approve such plan of work based on the provisions of the Convention and any rules, regulations and procedures that the Council may have adopted provisionally, or on the basis of the norms contained in the Convention and the terms and principles contained in this Annex as well as the principle of non-discrimination among contractors.

16. The draft rules, regulations and procedures and any recommendations relating to the provisions of Part XI, as contained in the reports and recommendations of the Preparatory Commission, shall be taken into account by the Authority in the adoption of rules, regulations and procedures in accordance with Part XI and this Agreement.

17. The relevant provisions of Part XI, section 4, of the Convention shall be interpreted and applied in accordance with this Agreement.

SECTION 2. THE ENTERPRISE

1. The Secretariat of the Authority shall perform the functions of the Enterprise until it begins to operate independently of the Secretariat. The Secretary-General of the Authority shall appoint from within the staff of the Authority an interim Director-General to oversee the performance of these functions by the Secretariat.

These functions shall be:

(a) Monitoring and review of trends and developments relating to deep seabed mining activities, including regular analysis of world metal market conditions and metal prices, trends and prospects;

(b) Assessment of the results of the conduct of marine scientific research with respect to activities in the Area, with particular emphasis on research related to the environmental impact of activities in the Area;

(c) Assessment of available data relating to prospecting and exploration, including the criteria for such activities;

(d) Assessment of technological developments relevant to activities in the Area, in particular technology relating to the protection and preservation of the marine environment;

(e) Evaluation of information and data relating to areas reserved for the Authority;

(f) Assessment of approaches to joint-venture operations;

(g) Collection of information on the availability of trained manpower;

(h) Study of managerial policy options for the administration of the Enterprise at different stages of its operations.

2. The Enterprise shall conduct its initial deep seabed mining operations through joint ventures. Upon the approval of a plan of work for exploitation for an entity other than the Enterprise, or upon receipt by the Council of an application for a joint-venture operation with the Enterprise, the Council shall take up the issue of the functioning of the Enterprise independently of the Secretariat of the Authority. If joint-venture operations with the Enterprise accord with sound commercial principles, the Council shall issue a directive pursuant to article 170, paragraph 2, of the Convention providing for such independent functioning.

3. The obligation of States Parties to fund one mine site of the Enterprise as provided for in Annex IV, article 11, paragraph 3, of the Convention shall not apply and States Parties shall be under no obligation to finance any of the operations in any mine site of the Enterprise or under its joint-venture arrangements.

4. The obligations applicable to contractors shall apply to the Enterprise. Notwithstanding the provisions of article 153, paragraph 3, and Annex III, article 3, paragraph 5, of the Convention, a plan of work for the Enterprise upon its approval shall be in the form of a contract concluded between the Authority and the Enterprise.

5. A contractor which has contributed a particular area to the Authority as a reserved area has the right of first refusal to enter into a joint-venture arrangement with the Enterprise for exploration and exploitation of that area. If the Enterprise does not submit an application for a plan of work for activities in respect of such a reserved area within 15 years of the commencement of its functions independent of the Secretariat of the Authority or within 15 years of the date on which that area is reserved for the Authority, whichever is the later, the contractor which contributed the area shall be entitled to apply for a plan of work for that area provided it offers in good faith to include the Enterprise as a joint-venture partner.

6. Article 170, paragraph 4, Annex IV and other provisions of the Convention relating to the Enterprise shall be interpreted and applied in accordance with this section.

SECTION 3. DECISION-MAKING

1. The general policies of the Authority shall be established by the Assembly in collaboration with the Council.

2. As a general rule, decision-making in the organs of the Authority should be by consensus.

3. If all efforts to reach a decision by consensus have been exhausted, decisions by voting in the Assembly on questions of procedure shall be taken by a majority of members present and voting, and decisions on questions of substance shall be taken by a two-thirds majority of members present and voting, as provided for in article 159, paragraph 8, of the Convention.

4. Decisions of the Assembly on any matter for which the Council also has competence or on any administrative, budgetary or financial matter shall be based on the recommendations of the Council. If the Assembly does not accept the recommendation of the Council on any matter, it shall return the matter to the Council for further consideration. The Council shall reconsider the matter in the light of the views expressed by the Assembly.

5. If all efforts to reach a decision by consensus have been exhausted, decisions by voting in the Council on questions of procedure shall be taken by a majority of members present and voting, and decisions on questions of substance, except where the Convention provides for decisions by consensus in the Council, shall be taken by a two-thirds majority of members present and voting, provided that such decisions are not opposed by a majority in any one of the chambers referred to in paragraph 9. In taking decisions the Council shall seek to promote the interests of all the members of the Authority.

6. The Council may defer the taking of a decision in order to facilitate further negotiation whenever it appears that all efforts at achieving consensus on a question have not been exhausted.

7. Decisions by the Assembly or the Council having financial or budgetary implications shall be based on the recommendations of the Finance Committee.

8. The provisions of article 161, paragraph 8 (b) and (c), of the Convention shall not apply.

9. (a) Each group of States elected under paragraph 15 (a) to (c) shall be treated as a chamber for the purposes of voting in the Council. The developing States elected under paragraph 15 (d) and (e) shall be treated as a single chamber for the purposes of voting in the Council.
(b) Before electing the members of the Council, the Assembly shall establish lists of countries fulfilling the criteria for membership in the groups of States in paragraph 15 (a) to (d). If a State fulfils the criteria for membership in more than one group, it may only be proposed by one group for election to the Council and it shall represent only that group in voting in the Council.

10. Each group of States in paragraph 15 (a) to (d) shall be represented in the Council by those members nominated by that group. Each group shall nominate only as many candidates as the number of seats required to be filled by that group. When the number of potential candidates in each of the groups referred to in paragraph 15 (a) to (e) exceeds the number of seats available in each of those respective groups, as a general rule, the principle of rotation shall apply. States members of each of those groups shall determine how this principle shall apply in those groups.

11. (a) The Council shall approve a recommendation by the Legal and Technical Commission for approval of a plan of work unless by a two-thirds majority of its members present and voting, including a majority of members present and voting in each of the chambers of the Council, the Council decides to disapprove a plan of work. If the Council does not take a decision on a recommendation for approval of a plan of work within a prescribed period, the recommendation shall be deemed to have been approved by the Council at the end of that period. The prescribed period shall normally be 60 days unless the Council decides to provide for a longer period. If the Commission recommends the disapproval of a plan of work or does not make a recommendation, the Council may nevertheless approve the plan of work in accordance with its rules of procedure for decision-making on questions of substance.
(b) The provisions of article 162, paragraph 2 (j), of the Convention shall not apply.

12. Where a dispute arises relating to the disapproval of a plan of work, such dispute shall be submitted to the dispute settlement procedures set out in the Convention.

13. Decisions by voting in the Legal and Technical Commission shall be by a majority of members present and voting.

14. Part XI, section 4, subsections B and C, of the Convention shall be interpreted and applied in accordance with this section.

15. The Council shall consist of 36 members of the Authority elected by the Assembly in the following order:

(a) Four members from among those States Parties which, during the last five years for which statistics are available, have either consumed more than 2 per cent in value terms of total world consumption or have had net imports of more than 2 per cent in value terms of total world imports of the commodities produced from the categories of minerals to be derived from the Area, provided that the four members shall include one State from the Eastern European region having the largest economy in that region in terms of gross domestic product and the State, on the date of entry into force of the Convention, having the largest economy in terms of gross domestic product, if such States wish to be represented in this group;

(b) Four members from among the eight States Parties which have made the largest investments in preparation for and in the conduct of activities in the Area, either directly or through their nationals;

(c) Four members from among States Parties which, on the basis of production in areas under their jurisdiction, are major net exporters of the categories of minerals to be derived from the Area, including at least two developing States whose exports of such minerals have a substantial bearing upon their economies;

(d) Six members from among developing States Parties, representing special interests. The special interests to be represented shall include those of States with large populations, States which are land-locked or geographically disadvantaged, island States, States which are major importers of the categories of minerals to be derived from the Area, States which are potential producers of such minerals and least developed States;

(e) Eighteen members elected according to the principle of ensuring an equitable geographical distribution of seats in the Council as a whole, provided that each geographical region shall have at least one member elected under this subparagraph. For this purpose, the geographical regions shall be Africa, Asia, Eastern Europe, Latin America and the Caribbean and Western Europe and Others.

16. The provisions of article 161, paragraph 1, of the Convention shall not apply.

SECTION 4. REVIEW CONFERENCE

The provisions relating to the Review Conference in article 155, paragraphs 1, 3, and 4, of the Convention shall not apply. Notwithstanding the provisions of article 314, paragraph 2, of the Convention, the Assembly, on the recommendation of the Council, may undertake at any time a review of the matters referred to in article 155, paragraph 1, of the Convention. Amendments relating to this Agreement and Part XI shall be subject to the procedures contained in articles 314, 315 and 316 of the Convention, provided that the principles, regime and other terms referred to in article 155, paragraph 2, of the Convention shall be maintained and the rights referred to in paragraph 5 of that article shall not be affected.

SECTION 5. TRANSFER OF TECHNOLOGY

1. In addition to the provisions of article 144 of the Convention, transfer of technology for the purposes of Part XI shall be governed by the following principles:
   (a) The Enterprise, and developing States wishing to obtain deep seabed mining technology, shall seek to obtain such technology on fair and reasonable commercial terms and conditions on the open market, or through joint-venture arrangements;
   (b) If the Enterprise or developing States are unable to obtain deep seabed mining technology, the Authority may request all or any of the contractors and their respective sponsoring State or States to cooperate with it in facilitating the acquisition of deep seabed mining technology by the Enterprise or its joint venture, or by a developing State or States seeking to acquire such technology on fair and reasonable commercial terms and conditions, consistent with the effective protection of intellectual property rights. States Parties undertake to cooperate fully and effectively with the Authority for this purpose and to ensure that contractors sponsored by them also cooperate fully with the Authority;
   (c) As a general rule, States Parties shall promote international technical and scientific cooperation with regard to activities in the Area either between the parties concerned or by developing training, technical assistance and scientific cooperation programmes in marine science and technology and the protection and preservation of the marine environment.

2. The provisions of Annex III, article 5, of the Convention shall not apply.

SECTION 6. PRODUCTION POLICY

1. The production policy of the Authority shall be based on the following principles:

(a) Development of the resources of the Area shall take place in accordance with sound commercial principles;

(b) The provisions of the General Agreement on Tariffs and Trade, its relevant codes and successor or superseding agreements shall apply with respect to activities in the Area;

(c) In particular,t here shall be no subsidization of activities in the Area except as may be permitted under the agreements referred to in subparagraph (b). Subsidization for the purpose of these principles shall be defined in terms of the agreements referred to in subparagraph (b);

(d) There shall be no discrimination between minerals derived from the Area and from other sources. There shall be no preferential access to markets for such minerals or for imports of commodities produced from such minerals, in particular:

(i) By the use of tariff or non-tariff barriers; and

(ii) Given by States Parties to such minerals or commodities produced by their state enterprises or by natural or juridical persons which possess their nationality or are controlled by them or their nationals;

(e) The plan of work for exploitation approved by the Authority in respect of each mining area shall indicate an anticipated production schedule which shall include the estimated maximum amounts of minerals that would be produced per year under the plan of work;

(f) The following shall apply to the settlement of disputes concerning the provisions of the agreements referred to in subparagraph (b):

(i) Where the States Parties concerned are parties to such agreements, they shall have recourse to the dispute settlement procedures of those agreements;

(ii) Where one or more of the States Parties concerned are not parties to such agreements, they shall have recourse to the dispute settlement procedures set out in the Convention;

(g) In circumstances where a determination is made under the agreements referred to in subparagraph (b) that a State Party has engaged in subsidization which is prohibited or has resulted in adverse effects on the interests of another State Party and appropriate steps have not been taken by the relevant State Party or States Parties, a State Party may request the Council to take appropriate measures.

2. The principles contained in paragraph 1 shall not affect the rights and obligations under any provision of the agreements referred to in paragraph 1 (b), as well as the relevant free trade and customs union agreements, in relations between States Parties which are parties to such agreements.

3. The acceptance by a contractor of subsidies other than those which may be permitted under the agreements referred to in paragraph 1 (b) shall constitute a violation of the fundamental terms of the contract forming a plan of work for the carrying out of activities in the Area.

4. Any State Party which has reason to believe that there has been a breach of the requirements of paragraphs 1 (b) to (d) or 3 may initiate dispute settlement procedures in conformity with paragraph 1 (f) or (g).

5. A State Party may at any time bring to the attention of the Council activities which in its view are inconsistent with the requirements of paragraph 1 (b) to (d).

6. The Authority shall develop rules, regulations and procedures which ensure the implementation of the provisions of this section, including relevant rules, regulations and procedures governing the approval of plans of work.

7. The provisions of article 151, paragraphs 1 to 7 and 9, article 162, paragraph 2 (q), article 165, paragraph 2 (n), and Annex III, article 6, paragraph 5, and article 7, of the Convention shall not apply.

SECTION 7. ECONOMIC ASSISTANCE

1. The policy of the Authority of assisting developing countries which suffer serious adverse effects on their export earnings or economies resulting from a reduction in the price of an affected mineral or in the volume of exports of that mineral, to the extent that such reduction is caused by activities in the Area, shall be based on the following principles:

   (a) The Authority shall establish an economic assistance fund from a portion of the funds of the Authority which exceeds those necessary to cover the administrative expenses of the Authority. The amount set aside for this purpose shall be determined by the Council from time to time, upon the recommendation of the Finance Committee. Only funds from payments received from contractors, including the Enterprise, and voluntary contributions shall be used for the establishment of the economic assistance fund;

   (b) Developing land-based producer States whose economies have been determined to be seriously affected by the production of minerals from the deep seabed shall be assisted from the economic assistance fund of the Authority;

(c) The Authority shall provide assistance from the fund to affected developing land-based producer States, where appropriate, in cooperation with existing global or regional development institutions which have the infrastructure and expertise to carry out such assistance programmes;

(d) The extent and period of such assistance shall be determined on a case-by-case basis. In doing so, due consideration shall be given to the nature and magnitude of the problems encountered by affected developing land-based producer States.

2. Article 151, paragraph 10, of the Convention shall be implemented by means of measures of economic assistance referred to in paragraph 1. Article 160, paragraph 2 (1), article 162, paragraph 2 (n), article 164, paragraph 2 (d), article 171, subparagraph (f), and article 173, paragraph 2 (c), of the Convention shall be interpreted accordingly.

SECTION 8. FINANCIAL TERMS OF CONTRACTS

1. The following principles shall provide the basis for establishing rules, regulations and procedures for financial terms of contracts:

(a) The system of payments to the Authority shall be fair both to the contractor and to the Authority and shall provide adequate means of determining compliance by the contractor with such system;

(b) The rates of payments under the system shall be within the range of those prevailing in respect of land-based mining of the same or similar minerals in order to avoid giving deep seabed miners an artificial competitive advantage or imposing on them a competitive disadvantage;

(c) The system should not be complicated and should not impose major administrative costs on the Authority or on a contractor. Consideration should be given to the adoption of a royalty system or a combination of a royalty and profit-sharing system. If alternative systems are decided upon, the contractor has the right to choose the system applicable to its contract. Any subsequent change in choice between alternative systems, however, shall be made by agreement between the Authority and the contractor;

(d) An annual fixed fee shall be payable from the date of commencement of commercial production. This fee may be credited against other payments due under the system adopted in accordance with subparagraph (c). The amount of the fee shall be established by the Council;

(e) The system of payments may be revised periodically in the light of changing circumstances. Any changes shall be applied in a non-discriminatory manner. Such changes may apply to existing contracts only at the election of the contractor. Any subsequent change in choice between alternative systems shall be made by agreement between the Authority and the contractor;

(f) Disputes concerning the interpretation or application of the rules and regulations based on these principles shall be subject to the dispute settlement procedures set out in the Convention.

2. The provisions of Annex III, article 13, paragraphs 3 to 10, of the Convention shall not apply.

3. With regard to the implementation of Annex III, article 13, paragraph 2, of the Convention, the fee for processing applications for approval of a plan of work limited to one phase, either the exploration phase or the exploitation phase, shall be US$ 250,000.

SECTION 9. THE FINANCE COMMITTEE

1. There is hereby established a Finance Committee. The Committee shall be composed of 15 members with appropriate qualifications relevant to financial matters. States Parties shall nominate candidates of the highest standards of competence and integrity.

2. No two members of the Finance Committee shall be nationals of the same State Party.

3. Members of the Finance Committee shall be elected by the Assembly and due account shall be taken of the need for equitable geographical distribution and the representation of special interests. Each group of States referred to in section 3, paragraph 15 (a), (b), (c) and (d), of this Annex shall be represented on the Committee by at least one member. Until the Authority has sufficient funds other than assessed contributions to meet its administrative expenses, the membership of the Committee shall include representatives of the five largest financial contributors to the administrative budget of the Authority. Thereafter, the election of one member from each group shall be on the basis of nomination by the members of the respective group, without prejudice to the possibility of further members being elected from each group.

4. Members of the Finance Committee shall hold office for a term of five years. They shall be eligible for re-election for a further term.

5. In the event of the death, incapacity or resignation of a member of the

Finance Committee prior to the expiration of the term of office, the Assembly shall elect for the remainder of the term a member from the same geographical region or group of States.

6. Members of the Finance Committee shall have no financial interest in any activity relating to matters upon which the Committee has the responsibility to make recommendations. They shall not disclose, even after the termination of their functions, any confidential information coming to their knowledge by reason of their duties for the Authority.

7. Decisions by the Assembly and the Council on the following issues shall take into account recommendations of the Finance Committee:

(a) Draft financial rules, regulations and procedures of the organs of the Authority and the financial management and internal financial administration of the Authority;

(b) Assessment of contributions of members to the administrative budget of the Authority in accordance with article 160, paragraph 2 (e), of the Convention;

(c) All relevant financial matters, including the proposed annual budget prepared by the Secretary-General of the Authority in accordance with article 172 of the Convention and the financial aspects of the implementation of the programmes of work of the Secretariat;

(d) The administrative budget;

(e) Financial obligations of States Parties arising from the implementation of this Agreement and Part XI as well as the administrative and budgetary implications of proposals and recommendations involving expenditure from the funds of the Authority;

(f) Rules, regulations and procedures on the equitable sharing of financial and other economic benefits derived from activities in the Area and the decisions to be made thereon.

8. Decisions in the Finance Committee on questions of procedure shall be taken by a majority of members present and voting. Decisions on questions of substance shall be taken by consensus.

9. The requirement of article 162, paragraph 2 (y), of the Convention to establish a subsidiary organ to deal with financial matters shall be deemed to have been fulfilled by the establishment of the Finance Committee in accordance with this section.

REPORT OF THE SIXTH MEETING OF THE PARTIES TO THE MONTREAL PROTOCOL ON SUBSTANCES THAT DEPLETE THE OZONE LAYER

D. DECISIONS

84. The Sixth Meeting of the Parties to the Montreal Protocol on Substances that Deplete the Ozone Layer decided:

Decision VI/1. Ratification, approval or accession to the Vienna Convention for the Protection of the Ozone Layer, the Montreal Protocol on Substances that Deplete the Ozone Layer and the Amendments to the Montreal Protocol

1. To note with satisfaction the large number of countries that have ratified the Vienna Convention for the Protection of the Ozone Layer, the Montreal Protocol on Substances that Deplete the Ozone Layer and the Amendments to the Montreal Protocol;

2. To urge all States that have not yet done so to ratify, approve or accede to the Vienna Convention, the Montreal Protocol and the Amendments to the Montreal Protocol;

Decision VI/2. Implementation of Article 7 and 9 of the Protocol

1. To note with satisfaction the implementation of the provisions of the Protocol by the Parties which have so far reported data and information under Articles 7 and 9 of the Protocol;

2. To note that the timely reporting of data and any other required information is a legal obligation for each Party and to request all Parties to comply with the provisions of Articles 7 and 9 of the Protocol;

Decision VI/3. Implementation Committee

To confirm the positions of Burkina Faso, Chile, Jordan, the Netherlands and the Russian Federation as members of the Implementation Committee for one further year, and to select Austria, Bulgaria, Peru, Philippines and the United Republic of Tanzania as members of the Committee for a two-year-period;

Decision VI/4. Application of trade measures under Article 4 to non-Parties to the London Amendment to the Protocol

1. To note the information reported by Poland and Turkey pursuant to decision V/3 (Application of trade measures under Article 4 to non-Parties to the London Amendment) of the Fifth Meeting of the Parties and to note that these two countries have thereby submitted data demonstrating that in 1993 they were in full compliance with Articles 2, 2A–2E and 4 of the Montreal Protocol and have submitted supporting data to that effect as specified in Article 7 of the Protocol;

2. To request those countries to submit data on their compliance with the above Articles of the Protocol by 31 March 1995 in order to establish their continued eligibility under Article 4, paragraph 8, to treatment as Parties during the year 1995–1996;

3. To welcome the fact that both countries intend to ratify or accede to the London Amendment in 1995;

Decision VI/5. Status of certain Parties *vis-à-vis* Article 5 of the Protocol

To adopt the following principles regarding treatment of classified and reclassified developing country Parties:

(a) The Secretariat should continue to classify, in absence of complete data, developing countries temporarily as operating or not operating under Article 5 based on the information available to the Secretariat, subject to the conditions that:

  (i) The Secretariat encourages these Parties to approach the Executive Committee and the Implementation Committee for assistance in establishing accurate data;

  (ii) A country may only be classified temporarily as operating under Article 5 for a period of two years applicable from the time of adoption of the present decision. After this period, Article 5 status can no longer be extended without data reporting as required by the Protocol, unless the country has sought the assistance of the Executive Committee and the Implementation Committee. In this case, the extension period shall not exceed two years;

  (iii) A developing country temporarily classified as operating under Article 5 would lose the status if it does not report base-year data as required by the Protocol within one year of the approval of its country programme and its institutional strengthening by the Executive Committee, unless otherwise decided by a Meeting of the Parties;

(b) The Executive Committee will consider projects from Parties temporarily classified as operating under Article 5. The projects approved when such temporary classification is operative will continue to be funded even if the countries subsequently are reclassified as not operating under Article 5 on receipt of data. However, no project will be sanctioned during a period during which the country is classified as not operating under Article 5;

(c) Parties may be allowed to correct the data submitted by them in the interest of accuracy for a given year but no change of classification will be permitted for that year pertaining to which the data has been corrected. Any such corrections should be accompanied by an explanatory note to facilitate the work of the Implementation Committee;

(d) Regarding developing-country Parties which are initially classified as not operating under Article 5 and then reclassified, any outstanding contribution to the Multilateral Fund will be disregarded, only for the years in which they are reclassified as operating under Article 5. Any Party reclassified as operating under Article 5 will be allowed to utilize the remainder of the ten-year grace period;

(e) Any developing-country Party initially classified as non-Article 5 but reclassified subsequently as operating under Article 5 shall not be requested to contribute to the Multilateral Fund. Such Parties are urged not to request financial assistance for national programmes from the Multilateral Fund but may seek other assistance under Article 10 of the Montreal Protocol. This will not apply if the initial classification of the Party as non-Article 5, made in the absence of complete data, is subsequently proved to be wrong on the basis of complete data;

Decision VI/6. Reviews under paragraph 8 of Article 5 of the Protocol and under section II, paragraph 4, of decision IV/18 of the Fourth Meeting of the Parties to the Montreal Protocol

1. To take note of the ongoing reviews under paragraph 8 of Article 5 of the Montreal Protocol and under section II, paragraph 4, of decision IV/18 of the Fourth Meeting of the Parties to the Montreal Protocol;

2. (a) To approve the loan of US$ 450,000 from the Multilateral Fund to the Secretariat as a one-time measure to facilitate the review of the Financial Mechanism;
   (b) To repay the loan to the Multilateral Fund through necessary additional contributions to the Trust Fund for the Montreal Protocol as proposed in the revised budgets for 1994 and 1995;

3. To request the Open-ended Working Group to consider the report of the review undertaken under decision IV/18 and to make recommendations, as appropriate, to the Seventh Meeting of the Parties;

Decision VI/7. Executive Committee of the Multilateral Fund for the Implementation of the Montreal Protocol

1. To endorse the selection of Australia, Austria, Denmark, Japan, Poland, United Kingdom, United States of America as members of the Executive Committee representing Parties not operating under paragraph 1 of Article 5 of the Protocol, and the selection of Algeria, Argentina, China, Colombia, Iran (Islamic Republic of), Cameroon, Thailand as members representing Parties operating under paragraph 1 of Article 5, for one year;

2. To endorse the selection of Mr. John Whitelaw of Australia to act as Chair and of Algeria to act as Vice-Chair of the Executive Committee for one year;

Decision VI/8. Essential use nominations for halons for 1995

That, for the year 1995 no level of production or consumption is necessary to satisfy essential uses of halons in Parties not operating under paragraph 1 of Article 5 of the Protocol, since there are technically and economically feasible alternatives and substitutes for most applications, and since halons are available in sufficient quantity and quality from existing stocks of banked and recycled halons;

Decision VI/9. Essential use nominations for controlled substances other than halons for 1996 and beyond

1. To note with appreciation the work done by the Technology and Economic Assessment Panel and its Technical Options Committees pursuant to decision IV/25 of the Fourth Meeting of the Parties;

2. That, for 1996 and 1997 for Parties not operating under paragraph 1 of Article 5 of the Protocol, levels of production or consumption necessary to satisfy essential uses of chlorofluorocarbons and 1,1,1-trichloroethane for: (i) metered dose inhalers (MDIs) for the treatment of asthma, chronic obstructive pulmonary disease (COPD), and for the delivery of leuprolide to the lungs and (ii) the Space Shuttle, are authorized as specified in annex I to the report of the Sixth Meeting of the Parties, subject to annual review of quantities;

3. That for 1996 and 1997, for Parties not operating under paragraph 1 of Article 5 of the Protocol, production or consumption necessary to satisfy essential uses of ozone-depleting substances for laboratory and analyt-

ical uses are authorized as specified in annex II to the report of the Sixth Meeting of the Parties;

4. That Parties shall endeavour to minimize use and emissions by all practical steps. in the case of metered dose inhalers, these steps include education of physicians and patients about other treatment options and good-faith efforts to eliminate or recapture emissions from filling and testing, consistent with national laws and regulations;

Decision VI/10. Use of controlled substances as process agents

Taking into account:

That some Parties may have interpreted use of controlled substances in some applications where they are used as process agents as feedstock application;

That other Parties have interpreted similar applications as use and thereby subject to phase-out;

That the Technology and Economic Assessment Panel has been unable to recommend exemption, under the essential use criteria, to Parties submitting applications of such uses nominated in 1994; and

The pressing requirement for elaboration of the issue and the need for appropriate action by all Parties;

1. To request the Technology and Economic Assessment Panel:
   (a) To identify uses of controlled substances as chemical process agents;
   (b) To estimate emissions of controlled substances when used as chemical process agents and the ultimate fate of such emissions and to evaluate emissions associated with the different control technologies and other process conditions under which chemical process agents are used;
   (c) To evaluate alternative process agents or technologies or products available to replace controlled substances in such uses; and
   (d) To submit its findings to the Open-ended Working Group of the Parties to the Montreal Protocol not later than March 1995, and to request the Open-ended Working Group to formulate recommendations, if any, for the consideration of the Parties at their Seventh Meeting;

2. That Parties, for an interim period of 1996 only, treat chemical process agents in a manner similar to feedstock, as recommended by the

Technology and Economic Assessment Panel, and take a final decision on such treatment at their Seventh Meeting;

Decision VI/11. Clarification of "quarantine" and "pre-shipment" applications for control of methyl bromide

1. Recognizing the need for non-Article 5 Parties to have, before 1 January 1995, common definitions of "quarantine" and "pre-shipment" applications for methyl bromide, for purposes of implementing Article 2H of the Montreal Protocol, and that non-Article 5 Parties have agreed on the following:

(a) Quarantine applications, with respect to methyl bromide, are applications to prevent the introduction, establishment and/or spread of quarantine pests (including diseases), or to ensure their official control, where:

(i) Official control is that performed by, or authorized by a national plant, animal or environmental protection, or health authority;

(ii) Quarantine pests are pests of potential importance to the areas endangered thereby and not yet present there, or present but not widely distributed and being officially controlled;

(b) Pre-shipment applications are those treatments applied directly preceding and in relation to export, to meet the phytosanitary or sanitary requirements of the importing country or existing phytosanitary or sanitary requirements of the exporting country;

(c) In applying these definitions, non-Article 5 countries are urged to refrain from use of methyl bromide and to use non-ozone-depleting technologies wherever possible. Where methyl bromide is used, Parties are urged to minimize emissions and use of methyl bromide through containment and recovery and recycling methodologies to the extent possible;

2. Acknowledging that Article 5 Parties have agreed to identify the following:

(a) That definitions relating to pre-shipment applications affect Article 5 countries and that new non-tariff barriers to trade should be avoided;

(b) That the Article 5 countries still need to have more consultations and further approaches to the quarantine and pre-shipment application definitions related to methyl bromide;

(c) That the Food and Agriculture Organization of the United Nations should play a fundamental role in the establishment of common definitions concerning quarantine and pre-shipment applications related to methyl bromide use;

(d) That it is anticipated that the use of methyl bromide by Article 5 countries may increase in the forthcoming years;

(e) That adequate resources from the Multilateral Fund for the Implementation of the Montreal Protocol and other sources are needed to facilitate the transfer of non-ozone-depleting technologies for quarantine and pre-shipment applications related to methyl bromide to the Article 5 countries;

3. Further recognizing that containment, recovery and recycling methodologies relating to methyl bromide should be given a wider application among all Parties;

4. To request the open-ended working group of the Parties at its eleventh and twelfth meetings

(a) To further study the most suitable definition for "quarantine" and "pre-shipment" applications relating to methyl bromide use, taking into consideration:

(i) The Methyl Bromide Technical Options Committee report;

(ii) The Methyl Bromide Scientific Assessment Report;

(iii) The FAO guidelines on Pests Risk Analysis; and

(iv) The development of lists of injurious pests;

(b) To consider jointly the definitions issues along with the methyl bromide issues contained in decision VI/13;

(c) To provide the necessary elements to be included for a decision of the Seventh Meeting of the Parties to the Montreal Protocol on all the above issues;

Decision VI/12. List of products containing controlled substances in Annex B of the Protocol

1. To note the conclusions of the Technology and Economic Assessment Panel and the recommendation of the Open-ended Working Group of the Parties on elaborating a list of products containing controlled substances in Annex B of the Protocol;

2. To agree that, in view of the tightening of the phase-out schedule for Annex B substances from 1 January 2000 to 1 January 1996 ratification of the Protocol by an overwhelming majority of countries, the elaboration of the list called for in Article 4, paragraph 3 *bis*, of the Montreal Protocol would be of little practical consequence and the work entailed in drawing up and adopting such a list would be disproportionate to the benefits, if any, to the ozone layer;

3. To decide not to elaborate the list specified in Article 4, paragraph 3 *bis*, of the Montreal Protocol;

Decision VI/13. Assessment Panels

To request the Panels, as an inclusion in their ongoing work, to evaluate, without prejudice to Article 5 of the Montreal Protocol, the technical and economic feasibility, and the environmental, scientific, and economic implications for non-Article 5 countries, as well as Article 5 countries, bearing in mind Article 5, paragraph 1 *bis*, of the Copenhagen Amendment, of:

(a) The alternatives to hydrochlorofluorocarbons in so doing, the Technology and Economic Assessment Panel is requested to consider the ozone-depleting substance substitution potential of not-in-kind alternatives, in-kind alternatives, and alternative technologies. In assessing this matter, the Technology and Economic Assessment Panel should consider how available alternatives compare with hydrochlorofluorocarbons with respect to such factors as energy efficiency, total global warming impact, potential flammability, and toxicity, and the potential impacts on the effective use and phase-out of chlorofluorocarbons and halons; in time for consideration by the Open-ended Working Group at its eleventh meeting;

(b) Alternatives to methyl bromide, in time for consideration by the Open-ended Working Group at its eleventh meeting;

In considering these matters, the Scientific Assessment Panel shall consider, if possible, atmospheric chlorine and bromine loadings and their impact on ozone depletion. The Technology and Economic Assessment Panel and Scientific Assessment Panel evaluations shall be solely for the purpose of discussions by the Parties and shall in no way be construed as recommendations for action.

Decision VI/14 A. Provision of information on the supply of controlled substances to Parties operating under Paragraph 1 of Article 5 of the Montreal Protocol

That, in order to facilitate implementation of the Protocol's provision concerning the supply of controlled substances to meet the basis domestic needs of Parties operating under Article 5, paragraph 1, of the Montreal Protocol, a Party may opt to use either decision V/25 or the following:

(a) Each Party operating under paragraph 1 of Article 5 of the Protocol, that requires controlled substances referred to in Articles 2A and 2E* from another Party is requested to furnish, with effect from 1 January 1995, to the Government of the supplying Party within 60 days of such imports a letter specifying the quantity of the substances imported and

* Editors' Note: This language was corrected to "2A to 2E:" see Doc. UNEP/Oz.L/Pro.6/7/Corr.1, 17 October 1994.

stating that the substances are to be used for the purposes of meeting its basic domestic needs. The Parties concerned will work out an internal mechanism so that enterprises in importing and exporting countries can trade directly in controlled substances;

(b) Each Party supplying the controlled substances is requested to provide annually to the Secretariat a summary of the letters received from Parties operating under paragraph 1 of Article 5 of the Protocol and to indicate therein whether each such Party receiving the substances had affirmed that such imports are to meet its basic domestic needs. It is expected that such supplies will be consistent with the provisions of the Protocol;

Decision VI/14 B. "Basic domestic needs"

To request the Open-ended Working Group to make recommendations to the Seventh Meeting of the Parties concerning the following issues:

(a) The need for clarification, amendment and/or further definition and of provisions regarding "basic domestic needs" in Articles 2 and 5 of the Montreal Protocol and under decision 1/12C of the First Meeting of the Parties;

(b) What appropriate measures, such as reports under Article 7, should be taken for implementation of provisions related to "basic domestic needs" in Articles 2 and 5 of the Protocol;

Decision VI/15. Co-Chairs of the Open-ended Working Group of the Parties to the Montreal Protocol

To endorse the selection of Mr. John Carstensen of Denmark and Mr. N.R. Krishnan of India as Co-Chairs of the Open-ended Working Group of the Parties to the Montreal Protocol for 1995;

Decision VI/16. Juridical personality, privileges and immunities of the Multilateral Fund

Recalling decision IV/18 of the Fourth Meeting of the Parties, which established the Financial Mechanism, including the Multilateral Fund for the Implementation of the Montreal Protocol, provided for in Article 10 of the Montreal Protocol, as amended in London on 29 June 1990,

To clarify the nature and legal status of the Fund as a body under international law as follows:

(a) *Juridical personality*: The Multilateral Fund shall enjoy such legal capacity as is necessary for the exercise of its functions and the protection of its interests, in particular the capacity to enter into contracts, to acquire and dispose of movable and immovable property and to institute legal proceedings in defence of its interests;

(b) *Privileges and immunities*:

(i) The Fund shall, in accordance with arrangements to be determined with the Government of Canada, enjoy in the territory of the host country, such privileges and immunities as are necessary for the fulfilment of its purposes;

(ii) The officials of the Fund Secretariat shall similarly enjoy such privileges and immunities as are necessary for the independent exercise of their functions in connection with the Multilateral Fund;

Decision VI/17. Budgets and financial matters

1. To take note of the financial report on the Trust Fund for the Montreal Protocol for 1993;

2. To urge all Parties to pay their outstanding contributions promptly and also to pay their future contributions promptly and in full, in accordance with the formula for contributions as set out in annex III to the report of the Sixth Meeting of the Parties;

3. To approve the revised budgets for the Trust Fund for the Montreal Protocol of US$ 3,048,735 for 1994 and of US$ 3,699,050 for 1995 and to adopt the proposed budget of US$ 2,818,215 for 1996, as set out in annex IV to the report of the Sixth Meeting of the Parties;

Decision VI/18. Modification of the indicative list of categories of incremental costs under the Montreal Protocol

To request the Open-ended Working Group to examine the proposal to amend the indicative list of categories of incremental costs under the Montreal Protocol, as proposed by India and Malaysia and any other related specific proposals brought by the Parties to the eleventh meeting of the Open-ended Working Group;

Decision VI/19. Trade in previously used ozone-depleting substances

1. To reaffirm the Parties' intent embodied in decision IV/24;

2. To restate that only used controlled substances may be excluded from

the calculated level of consumption of countries importing or exporting such substances;

3. To note further that, as required by decision IV/24, such exclusions from a Party's calculated level of consumption is [*sic*] made contingent on reporting of such imports and exports to the Secretariat and Parties should make their best efforts to report this information in a timely manner;

4. To request all Parties with reclamation facilities to submit to the Secretariat prior to the Seventh Meeting of the Parties and on an annual basis thereafter a list of the reclamation facilities and their capacities available in their countries;

5. To request all Parties that export previously used substances to take, where appropriate, steps to ensure that such substances are labelled correctly and are of the nature claimed and to report any related activities through the Secretariat to the seventh meeting of the Parties;

6. To request such exporting Parties to make best efforts to require their companies to include in documentation accompanying such exports, the name of the source firm of the used controlled substance and whether it was recovered, recycled or reclaimed and any further information available to allow or verification of the nature of the substance;

7. To request the Ozone Secretariat, drawing on the experience of the Technology and Economic Assessment Panel and the Parties, to study and report on trade in used/recycled/reclaimed ozone-depleting substances, taking particular account of Parties' experience in the control of such trade and the concerns and interests of all Parties that have facilities for the production of ozone-depleting substances, in time for the issues to be considered by the Open-ended Working Group at its twelfth meeting;

VI/20. Seventh Meeting of the Parties to the Montreal Protocol

1. To reaffirm decision V/28 of the Fifth Meeting of the Parties, by which the Parties expressed their gratitude to the Government of Austria for its generous offer to host the Seventh Meeting of the Parties to the Montreal Protocol in Vienna in 1995, to mark the tenth anniversary of the Vienna Convention for the Protection of the Ozone Layer;

2. To convene the Seventh Meeting of the Parties to the Montreal Protocol in Vienna from 28 November to 7 December 1995.

CIRCULAR COMMUNICATION TO COMMISSIONERS, CONTRACTING GOVERNMENTS AND MEMBERS OF THE SCIENTIFIC COMMITTEE

CHAIRMAN'S REPORT OF THE 46TH ANNUAL MEETING

12. WHALE SANCTUARY IN THE SOUTHERN OCEAN

12.1 Report of Intersessional Working Group
The Report of the intersessional Working Group on a Sanctuary in the Southern Ocean held on Norfolk Island, South Pacific, in February 1994 was presented to the Technical Committee by the Chairman of the Working Group, Dr. C.-G. Ducret (Switzerland). The Working Group recommended by consensus to the Commission the 15 recommendations shown in Appendix 8.

- Recommendations 1, 10 and 13 relate to the Antarctic Treaty system and other intergovernmental arrangements;
- Recommendations 3 and 7 were directed to the Scientific Committee;
- Recommendations 5, 6 and 14 proposed specific actions by the IWC;
- Recommendations 2, 8 and 12 related to legal questions;
- Recommendations 4, 9, 11 and 15 concerned the establishment of a sanctuary itself.

The Working Group proposed that the Commission should take note of its Report and further endorse the 15 recommendations, which was agreed by the Technical Committee and accepted by the Commission.

Japan asked the Chairman of the Scientific Committee if the Committee studied the specific questions raised at the Working Group. The Chairman of the Scientific Committee responded that there was no substantial discussion on the matter but there was little to gain in the context of the conservation performance of the RMP by modifying the procedure to take further account of environmental change. Also, the Scientific Committee believes that the RMP adequately considers the question of under-reporting of catches.

12.2 Proposal by France, Australia, Brazil, Ireland, Monaco, Netherlands, New Zealand, Spain, UK and USA
The Chairman of the Technical Committee identified three choices arising out of Recommendation 9 for the geographical boundaries of a sanctuary in the Southern Ocean contained in documents submitted by France and 9 co-sponsors, Japan and 5 co-sponsors, and Chile and 3 co-sponsors, and he invited comments from members on these proposals.

Following this exchange of views from all the members present, the Chairman concluded that this had been a valuable exercise which emphasised the range of opinions for the northern boundary set at 40°S through a series of other options. It was clear that there was room for further discussions which might lead to a compromise which could achieve a consensus in the Commission. Some delegations believed that no decision should be taken until the Scientific Committee had been asked to examine and report back on the scientific aspects of and give management advice on a Southern Ocean sanctuary, while others believed that there was no need to delay taking a decision since the time has now come for such action.

Japan, after hearing the Chairman's summary, called for a vote on the following proposal:

> "That the Technical Committee recommends the Commission to instruct the Scientific Committee to give management advice on the specific questions in the Norfolk Island Working Group report prior to taking any full and final decisions on a Southern Ocean sanctuary."

This was seconded by Norway although secondment was not required in the Technical Committee.

Prior to voting, Australia, seconded by France, proposed an amendment to replace the word "management" to "scientific", and to delete all the text from "prior to . . .".

This amendment was adopted with 22 votes in favour, 6 against and with 4 abstentions.

Japan stressed its strong commitment to the work on the RMP/RMS and introduced an amendment, seconded by Norway, which would have the effect of setting the northern boundary along the Antarctic Convergence except in the Indian Ocean where it would join that sanctuary at 55°S, and exempt minke whales from the prohibition on commercial whaling when the RMS is adopted for that species.

Grenada stated its position as one in which principles and science take precedence over political expediency. It believed culling would occur in a sanctuary and noted the views of Margaret Thatcher, President Clinton and Vice President Gore that science must be the basis and guiding principle at all times. Elephants in Zimbabwe and crocodiles in Zambia are too numerous because CITES regulations have stopped them being taken. Similar things are happening with seals and we may finish up with a sea of whales and no fish, with a consequential impact not on the developed, industrialised world but on developing countries. It supported the Japanese amendment but, if that failed, would abstain on the main proposal.

Japan questioned if the Commission could make a decision on the sanctuary proposal or amendment when the Scientific Committee had not seen either, but the Chairman stated that the Commission has the power to make decisions on management or conservation.

France identified that the Japanese amendment meant that whales not presently hunted will not be hunted in the future and the whales now hunted will be hunted in the future. All the positions are well known and it was time to take decisions.

The People's Republic of China spoke of its principles towards wildlife resources—protection, propagation and utilisation, and reserved its position on establishing the sanctuary until the Japanese amendment had been examined by the Scientific Committee.

Ireland pointed out that the original French proposal was considered by the Scientific Committee, a Working Group had discussed it, and the present proposal is a subset of that.

The Japanese amendment was then put to the vote and defeated with 6 in favour, 23 against and 2 abstentions.

Before the vote on the substantive Mexico, France and Chile proposal, with support from 17 other governments, Norway stated that it would not take part. This proposal was to amend the Schedule by designating existing paragraph 7 as sub-paragraph 7(a), and adding the following sub-paragraph:

> (b) In accordance with Article V(1)(c) of the Convention, commercial whaling, whether by pelagic operations or from land stations, is prohibited in a region designated as the Southern Ocean Sanctuary. This Sanctuary comprises the waters of the Southern Hemisphere southwards of the following line: starting from 40 degrees S, 50 degrees W; thence due east to 20 degrees E; thence due south to 55 degrees S; thence due east to 130 degrees E; thence due north to 40 degrees S; thence due east to 130 degrees W; thence due south to 60 degrees S; thence due east to 50 degrees W; thence due north to the point of beginning. This prohibition applies irrespective of the conservation status of baleen and toothed whale stocks in this Sanctuary, as may from time to time be determined by the Commission. However, this prohibition shall be reviewed ten years after its initial adoption and at succeeding ten year intervals, and could be revised at such times by the Commission. Nothing in this sub-paragraph is intended to prejudice the special legal and political status of Antarctica.

There were 23 votes in favour, 1 against and 6 abstentions, and so the amendment to the Schedule was approved by the necessary three-quarters majority.

Following the vote, Norway explained that it believed the action was not in accordance with the Convention, since there had been so scientific consultation. Japan repeated its view that these resources should not be denied for future human generations. Denmark saw no break in this action with its view of sustainable utilisation, while Chile expressed its satisfaction even though it would have preferred the CCAMLR northern boundary. Mexico emphasised the large responsibility now taken on by the Commission.

Japan's original proposal was thus not put to the vote.

Following an adjournment, the amended substantive motion was put to the vote and adopted with 22 votes in favour, 1 against and 9 abstentions.

Thus, the Technical Committee recommended the Commission to instruct the Scientific Committee to give scientific advice on the specific questions in the Norfolk Island Working Group report, which the Chairman of the Technical Committee interpreted to be Recommendation 7(a)–(e).

The Technical Committee therefore forwarded these conclusions together with the one proposal and two proposed amendments in the documents submitted by France, Japan, Chile and their co-sponsors.

In the Commission, Japan spoke of the need for such proposals to be based on scientific advice, and its concern over the amount of fish consumed by whales that could provide human nourishment. Japanese research had contributed much to our knowledge and it took pride in the development of the RMP. It saw no reason to hurry to adopt such a proposal as no commercial whaling can ever be conducted in the area until completion of the RMS.

Spain believed that the severe depletion of whale stocks in the past has made it imperative to consciously protect them now. This is a minimum precautionary approach. Responsible resource management through the RMP and RMS should not be rushed, and adoption of a Southern Ocean sanctuary is a clear example of responsibility.

St Vincent and The Grenadines emphasised the need for scientific advice to be presented before establishing a sanctuary, not to justify it afterwards. It believed the proposal would contravene Article V, and noted that the Chairman of the European Parliament's Intergroup on Conservation and Development wrote that the IWC should base all management decisions on advice from its Scientific Committee, and its basic task is to regulate whaling. It contrasted the need to justify aboriginal quotas yet the sanctuary is not put to any such test; and the haste over the sanctuary while the RMS needs so much more work. The majority countries should not impose their attitude to whales on people from other cultures.

Venezuela, although unable to exercise its voting rights, spoke of its belief in the self-determination of nations. Cetaceans in its territorial waters are protected under national legislation, but it respected other countries with whaling as a cultural tradition. Most countries would consider a global whale sanctuary so long as those few remaining nations engaged in domestic whaling can secure a regulated catch, and the question was can we share the planet's natural sustainable resources in peace and goodwill?

Argentina recalled that it has supported the sanctuary initiative from the beginning. It favoured a compromise on the northern boundary to enlarge the basis of support, which has a sound scientific basis and is in line with the precautionary principle.

Australia commented that it has also supported the concept of a sanctuary since it first came before the Commission in 1992. There has been consideration and discussion, and there has been advice from the Scientific Committee and other bodies. It was pleased to see emerging a proposal which seems to have secured a wide measure of agreement.

12.3 Action arising

Mexico introduced a compromise proposal on behalf of itself, France and Chile, supported by Antigua and Barbuda, Argentina, Australia, Austria, Brazil, Finland, Germany, Ireland, Monaco, Netherlands, New Zealand, Russian Federation, South Africa, Spain, Sweden, UK and USA. This was based on political will and scientific foundations for the protection of the whales. France, in seconding this proposal, withdrew its own original proposal. It thanked Chile for its helpful amendment in earlier discussions, and emphasised the strong scientific base of the latest formulation.

Dominica considered that the proposal was bypassing a science, and recalled the reasons for the resignation of the former Chairman of the Scientific Committee. It was not satisfied that there were enough data to justify the northern boundary and questioned the need of the Scientific Committee. It characterised the proposal as a triumph of chicanery over science, and Dominica's principles would not be compromised.

APPENDIX 21

AMENDMENTS TO THE SCHEDULE

At its 46th Annual Meeting held in Puerto Vallarta, Mexico, 23–27 May 1994, the International Whaling Commission adopted the following amendments to the Schedule (changes in **bold** type):

1. *Designate existing paragraph 7 as sub-paragraph 7(a), and add the following sub-paragraph:*

(b) In accordance with Article V(1)(c) of the Convention, commercial whaling, whether by pelagic operations or from land stations, is prohibited in a region designated as the Southern Ocean Sanctuary. This Sanctuary comprises the waters of the Southern Hemisphere southwards of the following

line: starting from 40 degrees S, 50 degrees W; thence due east to 20 degrees E; thence due south to 55 degrees S; thence due east to 130 degrees E; thence due north to 40 degrees S; thence due east to 130 degrees W; thence due south to 60 degrees S; thence due east to 50 degrees W; thence due north to the point of beginning. This prohibition applies irrespective of the conservation status of baleen and toothed whale stocks in this Sanctuary, as may from time to time be determined by the Commission. However, this prohibition shall be reviewed ten years after its initial adoption and at succeeding ten year intervals, and could be revised at such times by the Commission. Nothing in this sub-paragraph is intended to prejudice the special legal and political status of Antarctica.

Index

Appendix II: The Dispositions of Convicted Murderers in Canada From 1946 to 1967.*

Convicted Murderers, 1946 to 1967

Murder has always carried a mandatory death penalty in Canada. However, the definition of capital murder in the law, and the rights of appeal upon conviction of capital murder have been changed periodically over the last thirty years. Whatever these changes, the final review by the Governor in Council, essentially the Cabinet, has remained unchanged. After all other appeals have been exhausted, and usually shortly before the death sentence is to be carried out, the Cabinet considers all aspects of the case and decides whether or not to interfere with the sentence being carried out. If the Cabinet decides to exercise the so-called, Royal Prerogative of Mercy, then the appropriate formality of commuting the sentence is invoked.[1] The analysis which follows is based on data summarized from the trial records of 378 convicted murders in Canada between 1946 and 1967. The summaries and coding decisions were made by staff members in the offices of the Remissions Branch, Department of Justice and later in the Solicitor General's office.

Those convicted of capital murder represent only a small proportion of those charged. During the period examined, 1946 to 1967, about half of those charged were not convicted, another 10% were held as insane and the remainder, about 40%, were convicted by the trial court.[2] It is these 378 cases that will be studied here. Between 1946 and 1967, 29.1% of them were successfully appealed in the Provincial Court of Appeals or the Supreme Court of Canada.[3] The remainder reached the Cabinet for final review. Over this period the Cabinet commuted 56.3% and allowed 43.7% of the death sentences to stand. These figures do not reflect the progressive movement to defacto abolition which has characterised the policies of the various Cabinets.

There has been a steep decline in the proportion of convicted people who were permitted to be executed over the last forty years by Cabinets of each major party. In the 1930's, 75% of those con-

* I am indebted to Lorne Butchart of Carleton University for assistance in preparing this appendix.

victed were put to death. This was the highest proportion since the mid 1800's in Canada. In the 1940's, 66% died. In the 1950's this proportion declined to 50%. In the early 1960's, only 13% were executed after which Canada has had *de facto* abolition. Several characteristics are analysed for any effect they might have on the final outcome of each case.

Motive and final disposition

These cases were classified on the motive or situation of the murder. Seventeen categories of motives were abstracted from the transcripts and are presented in Table One. However, there are only four motives which have enough cases to make analysis useful. These are shown at the top of Table One under the heading "Major" and account for 68.8% of all capital convictions. While 29.1% of all cases are successfully appealed, Table One shows that when revenge or a quarrel is the motive, a much higher proportion of cases, 37.3% and 51.6% respectively, are successfully appealed. When these cases do receive Cabinet consideration the death sentence is infrequently applied. Overall 31.0% of those convicted are executed. Of those who kill in revenge only 16.4% were executed and for those who killed in a quarrel, only 19.4% died.

The other two types of major motive murders, murder during a robbery and murder during a sex assault, tend to have the opposite pattern. Relatively few of these cases are successfully appealed. Those who committed murder during a robbery are the largest single group of capital convicts (34.7%). They are somewhat more likely to be executed (35.9%) than the overall proportion (31.0%). Sex murderers comprise only 8.2% of the capital offender population but they are executed at a much higher rate (58.1%) than other offenders. Only those few who kill law officers while trying to escape, (less than 3% of the convicted murderers) are more likely to hang. Those who killed while escaping arrest or custody were almost all hanged (66.7% and 100% respectively). There appears to be fairly wide variation in the patterns of success in appeal when motive is taken into account. Also the motive of a murder seems to make a substantial difference in whether or not the Cabinet commutes the death penalty.

Ethnicity of offender and final disposition

Table Two shows the disposition of capital cases when the ethnicity of the offender is taken into account. Originally 33 separate ethnici-

Table One
Final Disposition of Convicted Murderers by Motive: Canada 1946-1967

Motive	Execute	Commute	Other	Total
(*Major*)				
Robbery	35.9(47)	42.0(55)	22.1(29)	34.7(131)
Revenge	16.4(11)	46.3(31)	37.3(25)	17.7(67)
Quarrel	19.4(6)	29.0(9)	51.6(16)	8.2(31)
Sex Assault	58.1(18)	32.3(10)	9.7(3)	8.2(31)
(*Minor*)				
Motiveless	25.0(7)	39.3(11)	35.7(10)	7.4(28)
Intoxication	16.7(2)	33.3(4)	50.0(6)	3.2(12)
Escape Arrest	66.7(6)	33.3(3)	0.0(0)	2.4(9)
Jealousy	37.5(3)	25.0(2)	37.5(3)	2.1(8)
Remove Marriage Obstacle	33.3(2)	50.0(3)	16.7(1)	1.6(6)
Gain	0.0	66.6(2)	33.3(1)	.8(3)
Insurance	100.0(3)	0.0	0.0	.8(3)
Passion	0.0	100.0(2)	0.0	.5(2)
Brawl	0.0	100.0(1)	0.0	.3(1)
Inheritance	100.0(1)	0.0	0.0	.3(1)
Illegal Operation	0.0	0.0	100.0(1)	.3(1)
Escape Custody	100.0(1)	0.0	0.0	.3(1)
Escape Discovery	0.0	0.0	100.0(1)	.3(1)
Other motives	32.1(9)	57.1(16)	10.7(3)	7.4(28)
No Information	7.1(1)	14.3(2)	78.6(11)	3.7(14)
TOTAL	31.0(117)	39.9(151)	29.1(110)	100.0(378)

ties were designated but only the eight which have the largest numbers are included in this analysis. These eight include 84.3% of those under death sentence in the study period. The remainder are included in the "other" category of Table Two.

Those designated English Canadian (Canadian born, English speaking) total 49.2% of all convicted murderers. However, they were underrepresented among those executed and over represented among those commuted. Only 27.4% of the English Canadians were executed, against the overall rate of 31.0%. And 49.9% were commuted as against the overall rate of 39.9%. The opposite pattern occurs in the disposition of cases of French Canadian murderers. Executions occur for 46.0% and commutations for 26.0% for this ethnic group which comprises 13.2% of the convicted murderers.

Table Two
Final Disposition of Convicted Murderers by Ethnicity: Canada 1946-1967

Ethnicity (largest groups)	Execute	Commute	Other	Total
English Canadian	27.4(51)	49.5(92)	23.1(43	49.2(186)
French Canadian	46.0(23)	26.0(13)	28.0(14)	13.2(50)
Indian	26.1(6)	30.4(7)	43.5(10)	6.1(23)
Ukrainian	31.8(7)	40.9(9)	27.3(6)	5.8(22)
English	27.3(3)	27.3(3)	45.5(5)	2.9(11)
Scottish	20.0(2)	20.0(2)	60.0(6)	2.6(10)
Black	55.6(5)	11.1(1)	33.3(3)	2.4(9)
German	62.5(5)	12.5(1)	25.0(2)	2.1(8)
All Others	29.4(15)	43.1(22)	27.5(14)	13.5(51)
No Information	0.0(0)	12.5(1)	87.5(7)	2.5(8)
TOTAL	31.0(117)	39.9(151)	29.1(110)	100.0(378)

The next largest group is Canadian Indian. Many cases with Indian offenders are successful on appeal (43.5%) and as a consequence, only a small proportion are commuted or executed, 26.1% and 30.4% respectively. The remaining groups are very small but Germans and Blacks appear to be executed more frequently than those of English or Scottish background. Ethnicity makes a difference in the disposition of murder cases. English speaking majority groups seem to enjoy lower execution rates than minority and non-English groups.

Motive, Ethnicity and final disposition

It is important to disentangle the relationship between ethnicity and motive since both are related to disposition of capital cases. Since ethnic groups may not be evenly distributed amongst the various types of motives for murder, what appears to be dispositional differences related to ethnicity may be primarily due to differences in motives.

Table Three compares the rates of final disposition of capital

Table Three
Final Disposition of Convicted Murderers by Selected Ethnicity and Selected Motives: Canada 1946-1967

Ethnicity	Execute	Commute	Other	Total
(Robbery)				
English Canadian	31.3(25	51.2(41)	17.5(14)	61.1(80)
French Canadian	50.0(8)	31.3(5)	18.8(3)	12.2(16)
Indian	0.0(0)	66.7(2)	33.3(1)	2.3(3)
Ukrainian	66.7(2)	33.3(1)	0.0(0)	2.3(3)
English	33.3(1)	33.3(1)	33.3(1)	2.3(3)
Scottish	33.3(1)	0.0(0)	66.7(2)	2.3(3)
Black	57.1(4)	0.0(0)	42.8(3)	5.3(7)
German	0.0(0)	0.0(0)	0.0(0)	0.0(0)
Others	37.5(6)	31.3(5)	31.3(5)	12.2(16)
TOTAL	35.9(47)	42.0(55)	22.1(29)	100.0(131)
(Sex Assault)				
English Canadian	54.2(13)	37.5(9)	8.3(2)	77.4(24)
French Canadian	0.0(0)	0.0(0)	100.0(1)	3.2(1)
Indian	100.0(3)	0.0(0)	0.0(0)	9.7(3)
Ukrainian	0.0(0)	0.0(0)	0.0(0)	0.0(0)
English	100.0(1)	0.0(0)	0.0(0)	3.2(1)
Scottish	0.0(0)	100.0(1)	0.0(0)	3.2(1)
Black	0.0(0)	0.0(0)	0.0(0)	0.0(0)
German	0.0(0)	0.0(0)	0.0(0)	0.0(0)
Other	100.0(1)	0.0(0)	3.2(1)	0.0(0)
TOTAL	58.1(18)	32.3(10)	9.7(3)	100.0(31)
(Revenge)				
English Canadian	6.9(2)	69.0(20)	24.1(7)	43.3(29)
French Canadian	60.0(3)	20.0(1)	20.0(1)	7.5(5)
Indian	0.0(0)	16.7(1)	83.3(5)	9.0(6)
Ukrainian	20.0(1)	60.0(3)	20.0(1)	7.5(5)
English	0.0(0)	0.0(0)	100.0(3)	4.5(3)
Scottish	0.0(0)	50.0(1)	50.0(1)	3.0(2)
Black	100.0(1)	0.0(0)	0.0(0)	1.5(1)
German	50.0(1)	0.0(0)	50.0(1)	3.0(2)
Other	21.4(3)	35.7(5)	42.9(6)	20.9(14)
TOTAL	16.4(11	46.3(31)	37.3(25)	100.0(67)

Table Three (Continued)
Final Disposition of Convicted Murderers by Selected Ethnicity and Selected Motives: Canada 1946-1967

Ethnicity	Execute	Commute	Other	Total
		(Quarrel)		
English Canadian	20.0(2)	10.0(1)	70.0(7)	32.3(10)
French Canadian	28.6(2)	42.9(3)	28.6(2)	22.6(7)
Indian	0.0(0)	50.0(1)	50.0(1)	6.5(2)
Ukrainian	14.3(1)	42.9(3)	42.9(3)	22.6(7)
English	0.0(0)	0.0(0)	0.0(0)	0.0(0)
Scottish	0.0(0)	0.0(0)	0.0(0)	0.0(0)
Black	0.0(0)	0.0(0)	0.0(0)	0.0(0)
German	0.0(0)	0.0(0)	0.0(0)	0.0(0)
Other	20.0(1)	20.0(1)	60.0(3)	16.1(5)
TOTAL	19.4(6)	29.0(9)	51.6(16)	100.0(31)

cases for the eight major ethnic groups within the four major motive types of murder. The simultaneous classification of these data on three variables further reduces the size of each cell in the table and diminishes the confidence possible in the analysis. Although there are differences in the execution rates for each type of murder the pattern of ethnic variation *within* each type is preserved.

English Canadians are less likely to be executed than French Canadians for the same kind of murder. Compared to their proportions in all murder types, English Canadians are over represented in robbery and sex murders. French Canadians are under represented in robbery and almost absent in sex murders. The opposite patterns holds for revenge and quarrel murders, with the French Canadians generally over represented and English Canadians under represented in these types. For each type of murder the French Canadian offender is consistently more likely to be executed than the overall rate and the English Canadian offender is less likely to die. There are indications in Table Three which point to the overall pattern of ethnic differences in executions being preserved in each of the major murder types. The English and Scottish offender is executed less often than the Black offender.

Canadian Indians are under represented in robbery murders, and none were executed. However, all Indians who were convicted of a sex murder were executed. Indians are over represented in the revenge murder type. In this type, 37.3% of all cases are disposed of on appeal. Indians had 83.3% of their cases reduced on appeal. None were executed for revenge murders. For the larger groups, at least, differential dispositions due to ethnicity are independent of differential dispositions due to motive.

Occupation of offender and final disposition

Occupation is one of the conventional indicators of social status. Table Four displays the relationship between the occupation of the offender and the disposition of the case. Most of the convicted murderers are in the lower occupational levels. Unskilled labourers comprised 38.4% which is the largest group. Another 2.1% were listed as unemployed and 19.6% had no information on their occupation. On the other extreme, only 4.2% were managers or professionals and another 5.3% were both types of white collar workers. So the population of convicted offenders appears to be distributed towards the lower end of the stratification range in Canada.

Table Four
Final Disposition of Convicted Murderers by Occupation: Canada 1946-1967

Occupation	Execute	Commute	Other	Total
Unemployed	37.5(3)	62.5(5)	0.0(0)	2.1(8)
Labourer	31.0(45)	37.9(55)	31.0(45)	38.4(145)
Skilled Worker	34.9(37	33.0(35)	32.1(34)	28.0(106)
White Collar and Sales	33.3(5)	46.7(7)	20.0(3)	4.0(15)
Lower White Collar	40.0(2)	20.0(1)	40.0(2)	1.3(5)
Manager and Professional	37.5(6)	37.5(6)	25.0(4)	4.2(16)
Housewife	25.0(2)	25.0(2)	50.0(4)	2.1(8)
Police and Prison Guard	0.0	0.0	100.0(1)	0.3(1)
No Information	23.0(17)	54.1(40)	23.0(17)	19.6(74)
TOTAL	31.0(117)	39.9(151)	29.4(110)	100.0(378)

Occupation does not seem to have much effect on the outcome of a capital conviction. There is very little difference between the largest groups, labourers and skilled workers in their chances of execution. Amongst the smaller groups the range from 25% to housewives to 40% for lower white collar workers is very small by comparison to the ranges in these proportions found for different ethnic groups and motives in the previous tables. While social class clearly affects life chances in society, it does not appear to affect death chances amongst convicted murders.

Age and Marital status and final disposition

Very few young capital offenders were executed. None of the 27 convicted felons under 19 years was executed. Amongst the older group, some reduction in execution rates occurred. Only 12% of the 15 murderers over 55 years of age were hanged. From age 20 to age 55 there were few differences in the execution rates between those who were married or single.

The disposition of capital cases in Canada between 1946 and 1967 is effected by the motive and ethnicity of the offender, but not by the offender's occupation, age or marital status.

Footnotes

[1] Thomas M. Sheehan, "Administrative Review and Capital Punishment: The Canadian Concept," *Thomas Sheehan American Journal of Correction, Vol. 27, No. 1 (Jan./Feb., 1965).*

[2] See Ezzat Fattah, *A study of the Deterrent Effect of Capital Punishment with special Reference to the Canadian Situation* (Ottawa: Information Canada, 1973), p. 182.

[3] Although speculative, it seems reasonable to assume that successful appeals are, at least in part, a result of legal flaws in the original conviction. Of the major motive murders in Table One, it would seem the trial courts are producing capital convictions which are flawed for revenge murders and particularly for murders resulting from quarrels. For robbery murders and particularly fox sex murders the convictions tend to be sustained. Table Two shows that Indians have greater success in the appeal courts than do other ethnic groups. This may also reflect unfavourably on the quality of the original convictions for this group.

Name and Subject Index*

*This index doesn't duplicate information which can be located through the table of contents and the extensive list of table titles.